MILITARY AIRCRAFT MARKINGS 2023

MILITARY AIRCRAFT MARKINGS 2023
Stuart R Schofield

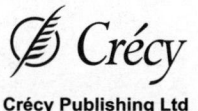

Crécy Publishing Ltd

This 44th edition published by Crécy Publishing Ltd 2023

ISBN 9781800352704

Printed in Malta by Melita

Crecy Publishing Ltd
1a Ringway Trading Est
Shadowmoss Rd
Manchester
M22 5LH
Tel +44 (0)161 499 0024
www.crecy.co.uk

Photo Credits in this edition of Military
Aircraft Markings are:
HJC: Howard Curtis
SRS: Stuart Schofield

Front cover:
Boeing P-8 Poseidon MRA1 ZP808, seen
at Newcastle Airport in September 2022.
©NCLairpics/Air Team Images

Rear cover:
Hawk HW-354 of the Finnish Air Force
seen at RAF Fairford, RIAT 2022.
©*HJC*

Middle: Avro 504K E3273 seen here at
its home base Old Warden airfield. ©*HJC*

Bottom: Hawk T.1 XX219 belongs to the
Red Arrows Aerobatic Team, and is seen
here at Bournemouth airport. ©*HJC*

CONTENTS

This 44th annual edition of *Military Aircraft Markings*, follows the pattern of previous years and lists in alphabetical and numerical order the aircraft that carry United Kingdom military registrations, and which are normally based, or might be seen, in the UK. It also includes airworthy and current RAF/RN/Army aircraft that are based permanently or temporarily overseas. Aircraft used as targets on MOD ranges to which access is restricted, and UK military aircraft that have been permanently grounded overseas and unlikely to return to Britain have generally been omitted.

Aircraft in UK military service which carry civil registrations are listed, as are historic aircraft wearing overseas markings which are based in the UK or likely to be seen in the UK. All aircraft carrying Irish military markings are listed in a separate section. Similarly, aircraft belonging to the armed forces or governments of foreign countries are listed, including American military aircraft based in the UK and Europe.

In the main, the registrations listed are those markings presently displayed on the aircraft. Where an aircraft carries a false registration, this is quoted in *italic type* and very often these registrations are carried by replicas, which are denoted by <R> after the type. The manufacturer and aircraft type are given, together with recent alternative, previous, secondary or civil identity (shown in round brackets). The operating unit and its based location, along with any known unit and code markings[in square brackets] are given as accurately as possible. Where aircraft carry special or commemorative markings, a $ indicates this. To help identification of RN bases and landing platforms on ships, a list of tail-letter codes with their appropriate name, helicopter code number, ship pennant number and type of vessel, is included, as is a helicopter code number/ship's tail-letter code grid cross-reference.

Up-to-date code changes, for example when aircraft move between units, might not be as printed here because of subsequent events, but code lists are regularly updated and uploaded to the 'Military Aircraft Markings' web site, www.militaryaircraftmarkings.co.uk, from which monthly UK updates can also be accessed. Airframes which will not appear in the next edition because of sale, accident, etc., have their fates, where known, shown in italic type in the *locations* column.

2022 saw the easing of Covid-19 restrictions and "the new normal" as it became known. Unfortunately, the expected Russian invasion of Ukraine alluded to in the introduction of the 43rd edition of this book did indeed occur, and almost a year down the line shows no signs of abating. Increasingly heavier weaponry is being offered by the Western allies, although so far (and with good reason) these allies have fallen short of offering cutting-edge aviation assets, in order to avoid additional escalation with Russia. The Ukraine military section in the World Air Arms areas of this book has been omitted, as it is simply impossible to tell what the current state of the air arm really is.

The UK armed forces have remained fairly static in 2022, with a handful of additional F-35B's delivered to Marham, and some of the early Typhoons being scrapped as they are no longer required. The remainder of the frontline Typhoon fleet remains in a state of constant flux, as airframes are rotated between the 2 active bases and the maintenance flights in order to balance airframe hours. Sadly unit markings, and certainly individual aircraft codes, are becoming less and less evident in many cases. Hawk T.1 operations for both the Air Force and Navy were wound down in 2022, with just the Red Arrows operating the type, having moved to their new base at Waddington following the closure of Scampton (the end of yet another era!). The AAC AH-64E fleet is growing in size as they get to grip with operations, as the -D model fleet also nears the end of its life, with most airframes already at the factory in the USA for conversion. The Royal Navy Merlin HC.4 upgrade programme was recently completed, with the final 2 examples going into post-modification depth maintenance at Culdrose before they will be released back to the squadrons.

European Air Forces continued in the same vein as 2022, with F-35s continuing to replace F-16s with Norway and the Netherlands, whilst Italy is also slowly building up it's F-35 fleet with both the Air Force and the Navy. Germany has finally committed to F-35s to replace the aging Tornado IDS in the NATO "nuclear sharing" strike role, having initially opted for the F/A-18E/F, until finally accepting that the prospect of implementing the B-61 on the Super Hornet was unlikely to happen.

The USAF removed the last of its F-15C/D fleet from the UK, as F-35A deliveries to Lakenheath continued apace. Lakenheath is now starting to stand up the second squadron of these jets as the future of the 2 main US bases in Suffolk appears assured once more, after a period of political uncertainty for the last few years. Finally, stateside US forces are slowly retiring more of their KC-10A and KC-135R fleets as more KC-46As come on stream, with legacy C-130Hs also finding their way to Davis-Monthan as additional C-130Js join the fleet.

ACKNOWLEDGEMENTS

The compiler wishes to thank the many people who have taken the trouble to send comments, additions, deletions and other useful information since the publication of the previous edition of Military Aircraft Markings, either directly or through logs online. In particular, the following individuals: John Alexander, Robert Belcher, Mike Bursell, Ian Carroll, Pete Carter, Howard J Curtis, Patrick Dirksen, Matt Ellis, Graham Gaff, Anthony Hutchings, Nige Howarth, Martin Kaye, Paul van der Linden, "MADFOX", Tom McGhee, David Moore, Tim Newman, Dave Oliver, Andy Patsalides, Ben Sadler, Tony Szulc, Mike Tighe, and any others I may have missed (for which, apologies in advance!)

This 2023 edition has also relied upon the printed publications and/or associated internet web-sites as follows: Air-Britain Information Exchange (AB-IX), Airfields Google Group, 'Air Forces Monthly' magazine, CAA G-INFO Web Site, Coningsby Aviation Site, Delta Reflex, Fighter Control, Humberside Air Review, Joe Baugher's Home Page, Mildenhall and Lakenheath Movements Group (SMAS), Mildenhall-Lakenheath blog, Brian Pickering/'Military Aviation Review', Mil Spotters' Forum, NAMAR Group, Planebase NG, RAF Shawbury Group, Lloyd P Robinson/Aviation Heritage UK, 'Scramble' magazine, Tom McGhee/UK Serials Resource Centre and Mark Ray/Wolverhampton Aviation Group.

Information shown is believed to be correct on 31 January 2023.

On a personal note, I would like to thank Howard Curtis for his unwavering support over the last 6 months. When he announced that the 43rd edition of "MAM" would be his last, I contacted him to see if there was a succession plan. This led me to conversations with the publishers, which started to gain some traction, culminating with an agreement from my side to take the project on in the early autumn of 2022. Through all of this, Howard has guided me in the right direction as I began to understand the enormity of the task I had taken on, whilst also holding down a full-time job! Now that the project is complete, I look at what I have achieved with a sense of great pride, and I hope that this will be reflected in the content of the new edition of the book. I recall my first "MAM", when Peter March was still compiling it, in 1987, and always remember the excitement of looking through a new copy for the first time. I hope the next generation still feels the same way as the 15-year-old me did!

Finally, thanks must go to Sam, my wife, who, more than ever, has found herself to be a "spotting widow" over the last 3 months. Every bit of my spare time has been dedicated to the book, and so what little family time we are normally able to share has been more or less non-existent. I trust that she knows that ignored definitely does not mean unloved, and I want to thank her for her unwavering support throughout the time I have spent working on the book.

Stuart R Schofield, Cheshire, 31 January 2023

Note: The publisher will be pleased to receive comments, corrections and further information for inclusion in subsequent editions of *Military Aircraft Markings*. Please send your information to Military Aircraft Markings, Crécy Publishing Ltd, 1a Ringway trading Estate, Shadowmoss Road, Manchester M22 5LH.

$	Aircraft in special markings
AAC	Army Air Corps
AACS	Airborne Air Control Squadron
AC	Air Cadets
ACCGS	Air Cadets Central Gliding School
ACS	Air Control Squadron
ACW	Air Control Wing
ADF	Air Defence Force
ADSU	Apache Depth Support Unit
AEF	Air Experience Flight
AESS	Air Engineering & Survival School
AEW	Airborne Early Warning
AFB	Air Force Base
AFD	Air Fleet Department
AFRC	Air Force Reserve Command
AG	Airlift Group
AGA	Academia General del Aire (General Air Academy)
AGS	Air Ground Surveillance
AK	Alaska
AL	Alabama
AMD-BA	Avions Marcel Dassault-Breguet Aviation
AMG	Aircraft Maintenance Group
AM&SU	Aircraft Maintenance & Storage Unit
AMRO	Aircraft Maintenance and Repair Organisation
AMW	Air Mobility Wing
ANG	Air National Guard
AR	Arkansas
ARS	Air Refueling Squadron
ARW	Air Refueling Wing
AS	Airlift Squadron/Air Squadron
ATC	Air Training Corps
ATCC	Air Traffic Control Centre
AVDEF	Aviation Defence Service
Avn	Aviation
AW	AgustaWestland/Airlift Wing/Armstrong Whitworth Aircraft
AWC	Air Warfare Centre
BAC	British Aircraft Corporation
BAe	British Aerospace
BAPC	British Aviation Preservation Council (now known as Aviation Heritage UK)
BATUK	British Army Training Unit Kenya
BATUS	British Army Training Unit Suffield
BBMF	Battle of Britain Memorial Flight
BDRF	Battle Damage Repair Flight
BDRT	Battle Damage Repair Training
Be	Beech
Bf	Bayerische Flugzeugwerke
BG	Bomber Group
BGA	British Gliding & Soaring Association
bk	black (squadron colours and markings)
bl	blue (squadron colours and markings)
Blt	Bojová letka (attack squadron)
BP	Boulton & Paul/Boulton Paul
br	brown (squadron colours and markings)
BS	Bomber Squadron
BUPERS SDC	Bureau of Personnel Sea Duty Component
BUTEC	British Underwater Test & Evaluation Centre
B-V	Boeing-Vertol
BW	Bomber Wing
CA	California
CAARP	Co-operative des Ateliers Air de la Région Parisienne
CAC	Commonwealth Aircraft Corporation
CACG	Command and Control Group
CAE	Centro Addastramento Equipaggi (Crew Training Centre)
CASA	Construcciones Aeronautics SA
CATS	Cassidian Aviation Training Services
CC	County Council
CC Air	Competence Centre Air
CCF	Combined Cadet Force/Canadian Car & Foundry Company
CEAM	Centre d'Expertise Aérienne Militaire (Centre of Military Air Expertise)

CEMAST	Centre of Excellence in Engineering & Manufacturing Advanced Skills Training
CEPA	Centre d'Expérimentation Pratique de l'Aéronautique Navale
CFAMI	Centre de Formation Aérienne Militaire Initiale de Salon
CFIA	Centre de Formation Interarmées NH.90
CFS	Central Flying School
CIEH	Centre d'Instruction des Equipages d'Hélicoptères
CHFMU	Commando Helicopter Force Maintenance Unit
CinC	Commander in Chief
CinCLANT	Commander in Chief Atlantic
CLV	Centrum Leteckeho Vycviku (Air Training Centre)
CMU	Central Maintenance Unit
Co	Company
CO	Colorado
COMALAT	Commandement de l'Aviation Légère de l'Armée de Terre
Comp	Composite with
CSP	Capability Sustainment Programme
CT	Connecticut
CV	Chance-Vought
D-BA	Daimler-Benz Aerospace
D-BD	Dassault-Breguet Dornier
D&G	Dumfries and Galloway
DCTT	Defence College of Technical Training
DE	Delaware
DE&S	Defence Equipment and Support
DEFTS	Defence Elementary Flying Training School
DEODS	Defence Explosives Ordnance Disposal School
Det	Detachment
D/F HFAZT	Deutsch/Französisches Heeresfligerausbildungszentrum Tiger
DGA	Délégation Générale de l'Armement
DH	de Havilland
DHC	de Havilland Canada
DMS	Defence Movements School
DS&TL	Defence Science & Technology Laboratory
DSAE	Defence School of Aeronautical Engineering
DSEME	Defence School of Electro-Mechanical Engineering
DSG	Defence Support Group
DSMarE	Defence School of Marine Engineering
Dvlt	Dopravná vrtuľníková letka (Helicopter Transport Squadron)
EA	Escadron Aérien (Air Squadron)
EAAT	Escadrille Avions de l'Armée de Terre
EAC	Ecole de l'Aviation de Chasse (Fighter Aviation School)
EALAT	Ecole de l'Aviation Légère de l'Armée de Terre
EAP	European Aircraft Project
EAT	Ecole de l'Aviation de Transport (Transport Aviation School)
EC	Escadre de Chasse (Fighter Wing)
E-CATS	EADS Cognac Aviation Training Services
ECG	Electronic Combat Group
ECM	Electronic Counter Measures
ECS	Electronic Countermeasures Squadron
EdC	Escadron de Convoyage
EDCA	Escadron de Détection et de Control Aéroportée (Airborne Detection & Control Sqn)
EE	English Electric/Escadrille Electronique
EEA	Escadron Electronique Aéroporté
EFA	Ecole Franco Allemande
EFATT	Escadron Franco-Allemande de Transport Tactique
EFTS	Elementary Flying Training School
EH	Escadron d'Helicoptères (Helicopter Squadron)
EHADT	Escadrille Helicoptères de l'Armée de Terre
EHI	European Helicopter Industries
EKW	Eidgenössisches Konstruktionswerkstätte
el	Eskadra Lotnicza (Air Sqn)
EL	Escadre de Liaison (Liaison Wing)
elt	Eskadra Lotnictwa Taktycznego (Tactical Air Squadron)
eltr	Eskadra Lotnictwa Transportowego (Air Transport Squadron)
EMA	East Midlands Airport
EMB	Ecoles Militaires de Bourges
EMVO	Elementaire Militaire Vlieg Opleiding (Elementary Flying Training)
EoN	Elliot's of Newbury
EPNER	Ecole du Personnel Navigant d'Essais et de Reception

ER	Escadre de Reconnaissance (Reconnaissance Wing)
ERV	Escadron de Ravitaillement en Vol (Aerial Refuelling Squadron)
ERVTS	Escadron de Ravitaillement en Vol et de Transport Stratégique (Air Refuelling and Strategic Transport Squadron]
ES	Escadrille de Servitude
ESAM	Ecole Supérieur d'Application du Matériel
Esc	Escuadron (Squadron)
ESHE	Ecole de Spécialisation sur Hélicoptères Embarqués (School of Specialisation on Embarked Helicopters)
Esk	Eskadrile/Eskadrille (Squadron)
Esq	Esquadra (Squadron)
ET	Escadre de Transport (Transport Wing)
ETED	Escadron de Transformation des Equipages Mirage 2000D
ETO	Escadron de Transition Operationnelle (Operational Transition Squadron)
ETPS	Empire Test Pilots' School
ETR	Escadron de Transformation Rafale
ETS	Engineering Training School/Escadron de Transport Stratégique
ETTL	Escadre de Transport Tactique et Logistique (Tactical and Logistics Transport Wing)
EVAA	Ecole de Voltige de l'Armée de l'Air (French Air Force Aerobatics School)
FAA	Fleet Air Arm (UK)/Federal Aviation Administration (USA)
FACO	Final Assembly & Check Out
FASGW	Future Anti-Surface Guided Weapon
FBS	Flugbereitschaftstaffel (Flight Readiness Squadron)
FBW	Fly-by-wire
FC	Forskokcentralen (Flight Centre)
FE	Further Education
FETC	Fire and Emergency Training Centre
ff	Front fuselage
FG	Fighter Group
FH	Fairchild-Hiller
FI	Falkland Islands
FJWOEU	Fast Jet & Weapons Operational Evaluation Unit
FL	Florida
FLO	Forsvarets Logistikk Organisasjon (Defence Logistics Organisation)
FISt	Fliegerstaffel (Flight Squadron)
Flt	Flight
FMA	Fabrica Militar de Aviones
FMV	Forsvarets Materielwerk (Defence Material Works)
FS	Fighter Squadron
FTS	Flying Training School
FTW	Flying Training Wing
Fw	Focke Wulf
FW	Fighter Wing/FlugWerk/Foster Wickner
FY	Fiscal Year
GA	Georgia
GAF	Government Aircraft Factory
GAL	General Aircraft Ltd
GAM	Groupe Aerien Mixte (Composite Air Group)
GAM/STAT	Groupement Aéromobile/Section Technique de l'Armée de Terre
GASU	Garda Air Support Unit
gd	gold (squadron colours and markings)
GD	General Dynamics
GEA	Gruppo Efficienza Aeromobili (Italian AF)/Gruppo Esplorazione Aeromarittima (GdiF)
GEM	Grupo de Escuelas de Matacán (Matacán Group of Schools)
GI	Ground Instruction/Groupement d'Instruction (Instructional Group)
GMS	Glider Maintenance Section
gn	green (squadron colours and markings)
GRD	Gruppe fur Rustunggdienste (Group for Service Preparation)
GT	Grupo de Transporte (Transport Wing)
GTT	Grupo de Transporte de Tropos (Troop Carrier Wing)
gy	grey (squadron colours and markings)
H&HS	Headquarters & Headquarters Squadron
HAF	Historic Aircraft Flight
HAPS	High Altitude Pseudo-Satellite
HavLLv	Hävittäjälentolaivue
HC	Helicopter Combat Support Squadron
HekoP	Helikopteripataljoona (Helicopter Battalion)
HF	Historic Flying Ltd
HI	Hawaii

HK	Helikopterikomppannia (Helicopter Company)
Hkp.Bat	Helikopter Bataljon (Helicopter Battalion)
HMA	Helicopter Maritime Attack
HMS	Her Majesty's Ship
HP	Handley-Page
HQ	Headquarters
HS	Hawker Siddeley
HSG	Hubschraubergeschwader (Helicopter Squadron)
IA	Iowa
IAF	Israeli Air Force
IAP	International Airport
IFTS	International Flying Training School
IL	Illinois
IlmaStk	IlmataiStelukeskus
IN	Indiana
IntHubschr-	Internationales Hubschrauberausbildungszentrum
AusbZ	(International Helicopter Training Centre)
IOW	Isle Of Wight
IWM	Imperial War Museums
JADTEU	Joint Air Delivery Test and Evaluation Unit
JARTS	Joint Aircraft Recovery & Transportation Sqn
JFACTSU	Joint Forward Air Control Training & Standards Unit
JHC	Joint Helicopter Command
JMRC	Joint Multinational Readiness Centre
KHR	Kampfhubschrauberregiment (Combat Helicopter Regiment)
Kridlo	Wing
KS	Kansas
LA	Louisiana
lbvr	letka Bitevnich Vrtulníkú (Attack Helicopter Squadron)
Letka	Squadron
LTDB	Lufttransportdienst des Bundes (Federal Air Transport Services)
LTG	Lufttransportgeschwader (Air Transport Wing)
lTHSSta	leichte Transporthubschrauberstaffel
LTO	Letalska Transportni Oddelek (Air Transport Department)
LtSt	Lufttransport Staffel
LTV	Ling-Temco-Vought
LVG	Luftwaffen Versorgungs Geschwader (Air Force Maintenance Wing)/Luft Verkehrs Gesellschaft
LZO	Letecky Zku ební Odbor (Aviation Test Department)
m	multi-coloured (squadron colours and markings)
MA	Massachusetts
MADG	Marshall Aerospace & Defence Group
MAPK	Mira Anachestisis Pantos Kerou (All Weather Interception Sqn)
MBB	Messerschmitt Bolkow-Blohm
MCAS	Marine Corps Air Station
McD	McDonnell Douglas
MD	Maryland
MDMF	Merlin Depth Maintenance Facility
Med	Medical
MFG	Marine Flieger Geschwader (Naval Air Wing)
MFSU	Merlin Depth Forward Support Unit
MH	Max Holste
MI	Maritime Interdiction/Michigan
MIB	Military Intelligence Battalion
MiG	Mikoyan — Gurevich
MMU	(European) Multinational Multi-Role Tanker Transport Unit
MN	Minnesota
MO	Missouri
Mod	Modified
MOD	Ministry of Defence
MPSU	Multi-Platform Support Unit
MR	Maritime Reconnaissance
MRH	Multi-role Helikopters
M&RU	Marketing & Recruitment Unit
MS	Mississippi/Morane-Saulnier
MT	Montana
MTHR	Mittlerer Transporthubschrauber Regiment (Medium Transport Helicopter Regiment)
MTM	Mira Taktikis Metaforon (Tactical Transport Sqn)
NA	North American

NACDS	Naval Air Command Driving School
NAEW&CF	NATO Airborne Early Warning & Control Force
NAF	Naval Air Facility
NAS	Naval Air Squadron (UK)/Naval Air Station (US)
NATO	North Atlantic Treaty Organisation
NAWC	Naval Air Warfare Center
NAWC-AD	Naval Air Warfare Center Aircraft Division
NBC	Nuclear, Biological and Chemical
ND	North Dakota
NDMA	Norwegian Defence Material Agency
NE	North-East/Nebraska
NFH	NATO Frigate Helicopter
NH	New Hampshire
NI	Northern Ireland
NJ	New Jersey
NM	New Mexico
NV	Nevada
NY	New York
NYARC	North Yorks Aircraft Restoration Centre
OEU	Operational Evaluation Unit
OFMC	Old Flying Machine Company
OGMA	Oficinas Gerais de Material Aeronautico
OH	Ohio
OK	Oklahoma
or	orange (squadron colours and markings)
OSAC	Operational Support Airlift Command
OSBL	Oddelek Sholskih Bojni Letal (Training & Combat School)
OT&E	Operational Test & Evaluation
P2MF	Puma 2 Maintenance Flight
PA	Pennsylvania
PAS	Presidential Airlift Squadron
PAT	Priority Air Transport Detachment
PBN	Pilatus Britten-Norman
PDSH	Puma Depth Support Hub
PLM	Pulk Lotnictwa Mysliwskiego (Fighter Regiment)
pr	purple (squadron colours and markings)
PR	Puerto Rico
r	red (squadron colours and markings)
R	Replica
RAeS	Royal Aeronautical Society
RAF	Royal Aircraft Factory/Royal Air Force
RAFC	Royal Air Force College
RAFM	Royal Air Force Museum
RAFGSA	Royal Air Force Gliding and Soaring Association
RE	Royal Engineers
Regt	Regiment
REME	Royal Electrical & Mechanical Engineers
rf	Rear fuselage
RFA	Royal Fleet Auxiliary
RHC	Régiment d'Helicoptères de Combat (Combat Helicopter Regiment)
RHFS	Régiment d'Helicoptères des Forces Spéciales (Special Forces Helicopter Regiment)
RI	Rhode Island
RJAF	Royal Jordanian Air Force
RM	Royal Marines
RMB	Royal Marines Base
RN	Royal Navy
RNAS	Royal Naval Air Station
RNGSA	Royal Navy Gliding and Soaring Association
RPAS	Remotely Piloted Air System
RQS	Rescue Squadron
R-R	Rolls-Royce
RS	Reid & Sigrist/Reconnaissance Squadron
RSV	Reparto Sperimentale Volo (Experimental Flight School)
RTP	Reduction To Produce
RW	Reconnaissance Wing
SA	Scottish Aviation
SAAB	Svenska Aeroplan Aktieboleg
SAAE	School of Army Aeronautical Engineering
SAC	Strategic Airlift Capability

SAL	Scottish Aviation Limited
SAR	Search and Rescue
Saro	Saunders-Roe
SARTU	Search and Rescue Training Unit
SC	South Carolina
SCW	Strategic Communications Wing
SD	South Dakota
SEPECAT	Société Européenne de Production de l'avion Ecole de Combat et d'Appui Tactique
SES	Science and Engineering Services
SFB	Space Force Base
SFDO	School of Flight Deck Operations
SHAPE	Supreme Headquarters Allied Powers Europe
si	silver (squadron colours and markings)
SKAMG	Sea King Aircraft Maintenance Group
Skv	Skvadron (Squadron)
SLK	Stíhacie Letecké Kridlo (Fighter Air Wing)
slt	stíhací letka (Fighter Squadron)
SLV	School Licht Vliegwezen (Flying School)
Sm	Smaldeel (Squadron)
SNCAN	Société Nationale de Constructions Aéronautiques du Nord
SOG	Special Operations Group
SOS	Special Operations Squadron
SoTT	School of Technical Training
SOW	Special Operations Wing
SPAD	Société Pour les Appareils Deperdussin
SPP	Strojirny Prvni Petilesky
Sqn	Squadron
Sz.D.REB	'Szentgyörgyi Deszö' Harcászati Repülö Bázis
TA	Territorial Army
TAP	Transporten Avio Polk (Air Transport Regiment)
TASF(N)	Tornado Aircraft Servicing Flight (North)
TAZLS	Technische Ausbildungs Zentrum Luftwaffe Süd (TAubZLwSüd, Technical Training Centre South)
TES	Test and Evaluation Squadron
TFC	The Fighter Collection
TGp	Test Groep
TH	Transporthelikopter
TIARA	Tornado Integrated Avionics Research Aircraft
tl	taktická letka (Tactical Squadron)
TLG	Taktisches Luftwaffegeschwader (Air Force Tactical Squadron)
TMU	Typhoon Maintenance Unit
TN	Tennessee
Tr AB	Transport Aviation Brigade
TS	Test Squadron
ts	transportnia speciálni letka (special transport squadron)
TsAGI	Tsentral'ny Aerogidrodinamicheski Instut (Central Aero & Hydrodynamics Institute)
TSF	Tucano Servicing Flight
TsLw	Technische Schule der Luftwaffe (Luftwaffe Technical School)
TST	Tornado Support Team
TTH	Tactical Transport Helicopter
TukiLLv	Tukilentolaivue
TW	Test Wing
TX	Texas
UAS	University Air Squadron
UAV	Unmanned Air Vehicle
Überwg	Überwachungsgeschwader
UK	United Kingdom
US	United States
USAF	United States Air Force
USAFE	United States Air Forces in Europe
USAREUR	US Army Europe
USCGS	US Coast Guard Station
USEUCOM	United States European Command
USMC	United States Marine Corps
USN	United States Navy
USNWTSPM	United States Navy Test Pilots School
USW	University of South Wales
UT	Utah
VA	Virginia

VAAC	Vectored thrust Advanced Aircraft flight Control
VADOR	Vecteur Aéroporté de Désignation, d'Observation et de Reconnaissance (airborne designation, observation and reconnaissance vector)
VFW	Vereinigte Flugtechnische Werke
VGS	Volunteer Gliding Squadron
vlt	výcviková letka (training squadron)
VMGR	Marine Aerial Refuelling/Transport Squadron
VMGRT	Marine Aerial Refuelling/Transport Training Squadron
VQ	Fleet Air Reconnaissance Squadron
VR	Fleet Logistic Support Squadron
vrl	vrtulníková letka (helicopter squadron)
VS	Vickers-Supermarine
w	white (squadron colours and markings)
WA	Washington
WCM	Wildcat Contractor Maintenance
Wg	Wing
WHL	Westland Helicopters Ltd
WI	Wisconsin
WLT	Weapons Loading Training
WMF	Wildcat Maintenance Facility
WR-ALC	Warner Robins Air Logistics Complex
WRS	Weather Reconnaissance Squadron
WS	Westland
WSK	Wytwornia Sprzetu Kominikacyjnego
WST	Wildcat Support Team
WTD	Wehrtechnische Dienstelle (Technical Support Unit)
WV	West Virginia
WW2	World War II
WY	Wyoming
WZM	Wildcat Zonal Maintenance
y	yellow (squadron colours and markings)
zDL	základna Dopravního Letectva (Air Transport Base)
zL	základna Letectva (Air Force Base)
zSL	základna Speciálního Letectva (Training Air Base)
zTL	základna Taktického Letectva (Tactical Air Base)
zVrL	základna Vrtulníkového Letectva (Helicopter Air Base)

A Guide to the Location of Operational Military Bases in the UK

This section is to assist the reader to locate the places in the United Kingdom where operational military aircraft (including helicopters and gliders) are based.

The alphabetical order listing gives each location in relation to its county and to its nearest classified road(s) (*by* means adjoining; *of* means close to), together with its approximate direction and mileage from the centre of a nearby major town or city. Some civil airports are included where active military units are also based, but **excluded** are MoD sites with non-operational aircraft (e.g. *gate guardians*), the bases of privately-owned civil aircraft that wear military markings and museums. For GPS users, Latitude and Longitude are also listed.

User	Base name	County/Region	Location [Lat./long.]	Distance/direction from (town)
Army	Abingdon	Oxfordshire	W by B4017, W of A34	5m SSW of Oxford [N51°41'16" W001°18'58"]
Army	Aldergrove/Belfast Airport	Co Antrim	W by A26	13m W of Belfast [N54°39'27" W006°12'578"]
RAF	Barkston Heath	Lincolnshire	W by B6404, S of A153	5m NNE of Grantham [N52°57'46" W000°33'38"]
RAF	Benson	Oxfordshire	E by A423	1m NE of Wallingford [N51°36'55" W001°05'45"]
QinetiQ/ RAF	Boscombe Down	Wiltshire	S by A303, W of A338	6m N of Salisbury [N51°09'12" W001°45'04"]
RAF	Brize Norton	Oxfordshire	W of A4095	5m SW of Witney [N51°45'00" W001°35'01"]

User	Base name	County/Region	Location [Lat./long.]	Distance/direction from (town)
Marshall	Cambridge Airport/ Teversham	Cambridgeshire	S by A1303	2m E of Cambridge [N52°12'18" E000°10'30"]
RAF	Coningsby	Lincolnshire	S of A153, W by B1192	10m NW of Boston [N53°05'35" W000°10'00"]
DCAE	Cosford	Shropshire	W of A41, N of A464	9m WNW of Wolverhampton [N52°38'25" W002°18'20"]
RAF	Cranwell	Lincolnshire	N of A17, S by B1429	5m WNW of Sleaford [N53°01'49" W000°29'00"]
RN	Culdrose	Cornwall	E by A3083	1m SE of Helston [N50°05'08" W005°15'17"]
USAF	Fairford	Gloucestershire	S of A417	9m ESE of Cirencester [N51°41'01" W001°47'24"]
Standard-Aero	Fleetlands	Hampshire	E by A32	2m SE of Fareham [N50°50'06" W001°10'07"]
RAF	Halton	Buckinghamshire	N of A4011, S of B4544	4m ESE of Aylesbury [N51°47'28" W000°44'11"]
RAF	Kenley	Greater London	W of A22	1m W of Warlingham [N51°18'20" W000°05'37"]
RAF	Kirknewton	Lothian	E by B7031, N by A70	8m SW of Edinburgh [N55°52'32" W003°24'04"]
USAF	Lakenheath	Suffolk	W by A1065	8m W of Thetford [N52°24'33" E000°33'40"]
RAF	Leeming	North Yorkshire	E by A1	5m SW of Northallerton [N54°17'33" W001°32'07"]
Army	Leuchars	Fife	E of A919	7m SE of Dundee [N56°22'28" W002°51'50"]
RAF	Lossiemouth	Moray	W of B9135, S of B9040	4m N of Elgin [N57°42'22" W003°20'20"]
RAF	Marham	Norfolk	N by A1122	6m W of Swaffham [N52°38'54" E000°33'02"]
Army	Middle Wallop	Hampshire	S by A343	6m SW of Andover [N51°08'35" W001°34'14"]
USAF	Mildenhall	Suffolk	S by A1101	9m NNE of Newmarket [N52°21'42" E000°29'12"]
RAF	Northolt	Greater London	N by A40	3m E of M40 jn 1 [N51°33'11" W000°25'06"]
RAF	Odiham	Hampshire	E of A32	2m S of M3 jn 5 [N51°14'03" W000°56'34"]
RN	Predannack	Cornwall	W by A3083	7m S of Helston [N50°00'07" W005°13'54"]
RAF	Scampton	Lincolnshire	W by A15	6m N of Lincoln [N53°18'28" W000°33'04"]
RAF	Shawbury	Shropshire	W of B5063	7m NNE of Shrewsbury [N52°47'53" W002°40'05"]
RAF	Syerston	Nottinghamshire	W by A46	5m SW of Newark [N53°01'22" W000°54'47"]
RAF	Ternhill	Shropshire	SW by A41	3m SW of Market Drayton [N52°52'24" W002°31'54"]
RAF/Army	Topcliffe	North Yorkshire	E of A167, W of A168	3m SW of Thirsk [N54°12'20" W001°22'55"]
RAF	Valley	Gwynedd	S of A5 on Anglesey	5m SE of Holyhead [N53°14'53" W004°32'06"]
RAF	Waddington	Lincolnshire	E by A607, W by A15	5m S of Lincoln [N53°09'58" W000°31'26"]
Army	Wattisham	Suffolk	N of B1078	5m SSW of Stowmarket [N52°07'38" E000°57'21"]
RAF	Woodvale	Merseyside	W by A565	5m SSW of Southport [N53°34'56" W003°03'24"]
RAF	Wittering	Cambridgeshire	W by A1, N of A47	3m S of Stamford [N52°36'52" W000°27'01"]
RN	Yeovilton	Somerset	S by B3151, S of A303	5m N of Yeovil [N51°00'30" W002°38'43"]

The Committee of Imperial Defence through its Air Committee introduced a standardised system of numbering aircraft in November 1912. The Air Department of the Admiralty was allocated the first batch 1-200 and used these to cover aircraft already in use and those on order. The Army was issued with the next block from 201-800, which included the number 304 which was given to the Cody Biplane now preserved in the Science Museum. By the outbreak of World War I, the Royal Navy was on its second batch of registrations 801-1600 and this system continued with alternating allocations between the Army and Navy until 1916 when number 10000, a Royal Flying Corps BE2C, was reached.

It was decided not to continue with five-digit numbers but instead to start again from 1, prefixing RFC aircraft with the letter A and RNAS aircraft with the prefix N. The RFC allocations commenced with A1 an FE2D and before the end of the year had reached A9999 an Armstrong Whitworth FK8. The next group commenced with B1 and continued in logical sequence through the C, D, E and F prefixes. G was used on a limited basis to identify captured German aircraft, while H was the last block of wartime-ordered aircraft. To avoid confusion I was not used, so the new post-war machines were allocated registrations in the J range. A further minor change was made in the numbering system in August 1929 when it was decided to maintain four numerals after the prefix letter, thus omitting numbers 1 to 999. The new K series therefore commenced at K1000, which was allocated to an AW Atlas.

The Naval N prefix was not used in such a logical way. Blocks of numbers were allocated for specific types of aircraft such as seaplanes or flying boats. By the late 1920s the sequence had largely been used up and a new series using the prefix S was commenced. In 1930 separate naval allocations were stopped and subsequent registrations were issued in the 'military' range which had by this time reached the K series. A further change in the pattern of allocations came in the L range. Commencing with L7272 numbers were issued in blocks with smaller blocks of registrations between not used; these were known as 'broken blocks'. As M had already been used as a suffix for Maintenance Command instructional airframes it was not used as a prefix. Although N had previously been used for naval aircraft it was used again for registrations allocated from 1937.

With the build-up to World War II, the rate of allocations quickly accelerated, and the prefix R was being used when war was declared. The letters O and Q were not allotted, nor was S, which had been used up to S1865 for naval aircraft before integration into the RAF series. By 1940 the registration Z9999 had been reached, as part of a broken block, with the letters U and Y not used to avoid confusion.

The option to recommence registration allocation at A1000 was not taken up; instead, it was decided to use an alphabetical two-letter prefix with three numerals running from 100 to 999. Thus, AA100 was allocated to a Blenheim IV and this two-letter, three-numeral registration system which started in 1940 continues today. The letters C, I, O, Q, U and Y were, with the exception of NC, not used. For various reasons the following letter combinations were not issued: DA, DB, DH, EA, GA to GZ, HA, HT, JE, JH, JJ, KR to KT, MR, NW, NZ, SA to SK, SV, TN, TR and VE. The first post-war registrations issued were in the VP range while the end of the WZs had been reached by the Korean War.

In January 1952 a civil servant at the then Air Ministry penned a memo to his superiors alerting them to the fact that a new military aircraft registration system would soon have to be devised. With allocations accelerating to accommodate a NATO response to the Korean War and a perceived Soviet threat building, he estimated that the end of the ZZs would quickly be reached. However, more than six decades later the allocations are only in the ZKs and at the present rate are unlikely to reach ZZ999 until the end of this century!

Military aircraft registrations are allocated by MOD Head Office and Corporate Services, where the Military Aircraft Register is maintained by the Military Aviation Authority. It should be pointed out that strictly the register places a space before the last three digits of the registration and, contrary to popular opinion, refers to them as 'registrations', not serials.

A change in policy in 2003 resulted in the use of the first 99 digits in the ZK sequence (ZK001 to ZK099), following on from ZJ999. The first of these, ZK001 to ZK004, were allocated to AgustaWestland Merlins. There is also a growing trend for 'out-of-sequence' registration numbers to be issued. At first this was to a manufacturer's prototype or development aircraft. However, following the Boeing C-17 Globemasters leased and subsequently purchased from Boeing (ZZ171-ZZ178), more allocations have been noted.

Since 2002 there has also been a new official policy concerning the use of military registration numbers on some types of UAV. 'Where a UAV is of modular construction the nationality and registration mark shall be applied to the fuselage of the vehicle or on the assembly forming the main part of the fuselage. To prevent the high usage of numbers for target drones which are eventually destroyed, a single registration mark (prefix) should be issued relating to the UAV type. The agency or service operating the target drone will be responsible for the identification of each individual UAV covered by that registration mark by adding a suffix.' This has resulted in the use of the same registration on a number of UAVs (or RPASs as they are now referred to) and drones with numbers following it - hence the appearance of ZZ420/001 etc. on Banshee drones. Aircraft using this system are denoted in the text by an asterisk (*).

A serial in *italics* denotes that it is not the genuine marking for that airframe.

Serial	Type (code/other identity)	Owner/operator, location or fate	Notes
168	Sopwith Tabloid Scout <R> (G-BFDE)	RAF Museum Reserve Collection, Stafford, Staffs	
304	Cody Biplane (BAPC.62)	Science Museum, South Kensington, London	
471	RAF BE2a <R> (BAPC.321)	Montrose Air Station Heritage Centre, Angus, Scotland	
687	RAF BE2c <R> (G-AWYI/*471*)	Privately owned, Sywell, Northants (wreck)	
687	RAF BE2b <R> (BAPC.181)	RAF Museum, Hendon, Gtr London	
1264	Bristol Scout C <R> (G-FDHB)	Privately owned, Old Warden, Beds	
2345	Vickers FB5 Gunbus <R> (G-ATVP)	RAF Museum, Hendon, Gtr London	
2699	RAF BE2c	IWM Duxford, Cambs	
2783	RAF BE2b <R> (BAPC.332)	Boscombe Down Aviation Collection, Old Sarum, Wilts	
3066	Caudron GIII (G-AETA/9203M)	RAF Museum, Hendon, Gtr London	
5191	Morane-Saulnier Type N <R> (BAPC.472)	North-East Land, Sea & Air Museums, Usworth, T&W	
5964	DH2 <R> (BAPC.112)	Privately owned, Wickenby, Lincs	
5964	DH2 <R> (G-BFVH)	RAF Scampton Heritage Centre, Lincs	
8359	Short 184 <ff>	FAA Museum, RNAS Yeovilton, Somerset	
9828	Avro 504K <R> (*H1968*/BAPC.42)	Yorkshire Air Museum, Elvington, N. Yorks	
9917	Sopwith Pup (G-EBKY/*N5180*)	The Shuttleworth Collection, Old Warden, Beds	
9970	RAF BE2c <R> (*6232*/BAPC.41)	Yorkshire Air Museum, Elvington, N. Yorks	
A126	Nieuport 11 <R> (G-CILI)	Privately owned, Sywell, Northants	
A301	Morane BB (frame)	RAF Museum Reserve Collection, Stafford, Staffs	
A653	Sopwith Pup <R> (*A7317*/BAPC.179)	Privately owned, Stow Maries, Essex	
A1452	Vickers FB5 Gunbus <R> (BAPC.234)	Spitfire Spares, Taunton, Somerset	
A1742	Bristol Scout D <R> (BAPC.38)	Aerospace Bristol, Filton, Glos	
A2943	RAF BE2e-1 <R> (G-CJZO)	WW1 Aviation Heritage Trust, Stow Maries, Essex	
A3930	RAF RE8 <R> (ZK-TVC)	RAF Museum, Hendon, Gtr London	
A4850	RAF SE5a <R> (BAPC.176)	Bygone Times Antique Warehouse, Eccleston, Lancs	
A6526	RAF FE2b <R> (BAPC.400)	RAF Museum, Hendon, Gtr London	
A6906	Sherwood Ranger ST (G-CLNZ) [5]	Privately owned, Dudleston Heath, Shropshire	
A7288	Bristol F2b Fighter <R> (BAPC.386)	Aerospace Bristol, Filton, Glos	
A8226	Sopwith 1½ Strutter <R> (G-BIDW)	RAF Museum, Cosford, Shropshire	
A8274	Sopwith 1½ Strutter <R> (BAPC.413)	WW1 Aviation Heritage Trust, Stow Maries, Essex	
A8936	Currie Wot (*C3009*/G-BFWD)	Privately owned, Duxford, Cambs	
B595	RAF SE5a <R> (G-BUOD) [W]	Privately owned, Defford, Worcs	
B619	Sopwith 1½ Strutter <R> (BAPC.468)	RAF Manston History Museum, Kent	
B1162	Bristol F2b Fighter (D8096/G-AEPH) [F]	The Shuttleworth Collection, Old Warden, Beds	
B1474	Henry Farman F.20 <R>	WW1 Aviation Heritage Trust, Stow Maries, Essex	
B5539	Sopwith F.1 Camel <R>	Privately owned, Booker, Bucks	
B6401	Sopwith F.1 Camel <R> (G-AWYY/*C1701*)	FAA Museum, stored Cobham Hall, RNAS Yeovilton, Somerset	
B7270	Sopwith F.1 Camel <R> (G-BFCZ)	Brooklands Museum, Weybridge, Surrey	
B7320	Sopwith F.1 Camel <R> (*D3419*/*B5577*/BAPC.59) [P]	Montrose Air Station Heritage Centre, Angus, Scotland	
C1096	Memorial Flight SE5a <R> (G-ERFC) [3]	Privately owned, Old Warden, Beds	
C1904	RAF SE5a <R> (G-PFAP) [Z]	Privately owned, Castle Bytham, Lincs	
C3009	Currie Wot (G-BFWD) [B]	*Repainted as A8936, April 2022*	
C3011	Phoenix Currie Super Wot (G-SWOT) [S]	Privately owned, Otherton, Staffs	
C3988	Sopwith 5F.1 Dolphin (BAPC.353) (comp D5329)	RAF Museum, Hendon, Gtr London	
C4451	Avro 504J <R> (BAPC.210)	Solent Sky, Southampton, Hants	
C4918	Bristol M1C <R> (G-BWJM)	The Shuttleworth Collection, Old Warden, Beds	
C4994	Bristol M1C <R> (G-BLWM)	RAF Museum, Cosford, Shropshire	
C5430	RAF SE5a <R> (G-CCXG) [V]	Privately owned, Wrexham, Clwyd	
C8996	RAF SE5a (G-ECAE/*A2-25*)	Privately owned, Audley End, Essex	
C9533	RAF SE5a <R> (G-BUWE) [M]	Privately owned, Spanhoe, Northants	
D276	RAF SE5a <R> (BAPC.208) [A]	Prince's Mead Shopping Centre, Farnborough, Hants	
D1851	Sopwith F.1 Camel <R> (G-BZSC) [X]	The Shuttleworth Collection, Old Warden, Beds	

Notes	Serial	Type (code/other identity)	Owner/operator, location or fate
	D3540	RAF SE5a <R> (N125QB) [K]	WW1 Aviation Heritage Trust, Stow Maries, Essex
	D5649	Airco DH9	IWM Duxford, Cambs
	D6447	Sopwith F.1 Camel <R> (BAPC.385)	Privately owned, Knutsford, Cheshire
	D7560	Avro 504K	Science Museum, South Kensington, London
	D8118	Sopwith F.1 Camel <R> (BAPC.567) [T]	Privately owned, Chalford, Glos
	E449	Avro 504K (G-EBJE/9205M)	RAF Museum, Hendon, Gtr London
	E2466	Bristol F2b Fighter (BAPC.165) [I]	RAF Museum, Hendon, Gtr London
	E2581	Bristol F2b Fighter [13]	IWM Duxford, Cambs
	E2977	Avro 504K (G-EBHB)	Privately owned, Duxford, Cambs
	E3273	Avro 504K (H5199/BK892/	The Shuttleworth Collection, Old Warden, Beds
		G-ACNB/G-ADEV/3118M)	
	E6655	Sopwith 7F.1 Snipe <R> (BAPC.348) [B]	RAF Museum, Hendon, Gtr London
	E8894	Airco DH9 (G-CDLI)	Aero Vintage, Duxford, Cambs
	F141	RAF SE5a <R> (G-SEVA) [G]	Privately owned, Boscombe Down, Wilts
	F235	RAF SE5a <R> (G-BMDB) [B]	Privately owned, Stow Maries, Essex
	F904	RAF SE5a (G-EBIA)	The Shuttleworth Collection, Old Warden, Beds
	F904	RAF SE5a <R>	South Yorkshire Aircraft Museum, Doncaster, S. Yorks
	F938	RAF SE5a (G-EBIC/9208M)	RAF Museum, Hendon, Gtr London
	F943	RAF SE5a <R> (G-BIHF) [S]	Privately owned, White Waltham, Berks
	F943	RAF SE5a <R> (G-BKDT) [S]	Yorkshire Air Museum, Elvington, N. Yorks
	F1010	Airco DH9A [C]	RAF Museum, Hendon, Gtr London
	F2211	Sopwith 1½ Strutter <R>	Privately owned, East Fortune, Scotland
	F3556	RAF RE8	IWM Duxford, Cambs
	F5447	RAF SE5a <R> (G-BKER) [N]	Privately owned, Bridge of Weir, Scotland
	F5459	RAF SE5a <R> (G-INNY) [Y]	Privately owned, Sywell, Northants
	F5475	RAF SE5a <R> (BAPC.250)	Brooklands Museum, Weybridge, Surrey
	F6314	Sopwith F.1 Camel (9206M) [B]	RAF Museum, Hendon, Gtr London
	F8010	RAF SE5a <R> (G-BDWJ) [Z]	Privately owned, Langport, Somerset
	F8614	Vickers FB27A Vimy IV <R> (G-AWAU)	RAF Museum Reserve Collection, Stafford, Staffs
	J7326	DH53 Humming Bird (G-EBQP)	*Currently not known*
	J7904	Gloster Gamecock (BAPC.259) <R>	Jet Age Museum, Gloucestershire Airport, Glos
	J8067	Westland Pterodactyl 1a	Science Museum, South Kensington, London
	J9941	Hawker Hart 2 (G-ABMR)	RAF Museum, Hendon, Gtr London
	K1786	Hawker Tomtit (G-AFTA)	The Shuttleworth Collection, Old Warden, Beds
	K1928	Hawker Fury I	Cambs Fighter & Bomber Society, Little Gransden
	K2048	Isaacs Fury II (G-BZNW)	Privately owned, Ledbury, Herefordshire
	K2050	Isaacs Fury II (G-ASCM)	Privately owned, Hinton-in-the-Hedges, Northants
	K2059	Isaacs Fury II (G-PFAR)	Privately owned, Netherthorpe, Derbys
	K2060	Isaacs Fury II (G-BKZM)	Privately owned stored, Limetree, Ireland
	K2065	Isaacs Fury II (G-AYJY/K2046)	Privately owned, Cranwell, Lincs
	K2075	Isaacs Fury II (G-BEER)	Privately owned, Combrook, Warks
	K2227	Bristol 105 Bulldog IIA (G-ABBB)	RAF Museum, Hendon, Gtr London
	K2567	DH82A Tiger Moth (DE306/G-MOTH/7035M)	Privately owned, Audley End, Cambs
	K2572	DH82A Tiger Moth (NM129/G-AOZH)	Privately owned, Frensham, Surrey
	K2585	DH82A Tiger Moth II (T6818/G-ANKT)	The Shuttleworth Collection, Old Warden, Beds
	K2587	DH82A Tiger Moth <R> (G-BJAP)	Privately owned, Shobdon, Herefordshire
	K3241	Avro 621 Tutor (K3215/G-AHSA)	The Shuttleworth Collection, Old Warden, Beds
	K3660	Isaacs Fury II (K5673/G-BZAS)	Privately owned, Middlezoy, Somerset
	K3661	Hawker Nimrod II (G-BURZ) [562]	Historic Aircraft Collection Ltd, Duxford, Cambs
	K3731	Isaacs Fury I (G-RODI)	Privately owned, RAF Waddington, Lincs
	K4232	Avro 671 Rota I (SE-AZB)	RAF Museum, Hendon, Gtr London
	K4259	DH82A Tiger Moth (G-ANMO) [71]	Privately owned, Headcorn, Kent
	K4556	Boulton & Paul Overstrand <R> (BAPC.358)	Norfolk & Suffolk Avn Museum, Flixton, Suffolk
		[F-101]	
	K4972	Hawker Hart Trainer IIA (1764M)	RAF Museum, Cosford, Shropshire
	K5054	Supermarine Spitfire <R> (EN398/BAPC.190)	*Currently not known*
	K5054	Supermarine Spitfire <R> (BAPC.214)	Tangmere Military Aviation Museum, W. Sussex
	K5054	Supermarine Spitfire <R> (G-BRDV)	Kent Battle of Britain Museum, Hawkinge, Kent

Serial	Type (code/other identity)	Owner/operator, location or fate	Notes
K5054	Supermarine Spitfire <R> (BAPC.297)	Kent Battle of Britain Museum, Hawkinge, Kent	
K5054	Supermarine Spitfire <R>	Southampton Airport, Hants, on display	
K5409	Hawker Hind	*Currently not known*	
K5414	Hawker Hind (G-AENP/BAPC.78) [XV]	The Shuttleworth Collection, Old Warden, Beds	
K5462	Hawker Hind	*Currently not known*	
K5554	Hawker Hind	*Currently not known*	
K5600	Hawker Audax I (G-BVVI/2015M)	Aero Vintage, Westfield, E. Sussex	
K5671	Isaacs Fury I (G-EMHF)	Privately owned, Prestwick, Scotland	
K5673	Hawker Fury I <R> (BAPC.249)	Brooklands Museum, Weybridge, Surrey	
K5674	Hawker Fury I (G-CBZP)	Historic Aircraft Collection Ltd, Duxford, Cambs	
K5682	Isaacs Fury II (S1579/G-BBVO) [6]	Privately owned, Felthorpe, Norfolk (wreck)	
K6035	Westland Wallace II (2361M)	RAF Museum Reserve Collection, Stafford, Staffs	
K6618	Hawker Hind	*Currently not known*	
K6833	Hawker Hind	*Currently not known*	
K7271	Hawker Fury II <R> (BAPC.148)	Shropshire Wartime Aircraft Recovery Grp Mus, Sleap	
K7271	Isaacs Fury II <R> (G-CCKV)	Privately owned, Middlezoy, Somerset	
K7985	Gloster Gladiator I (L8032/G-AMRK)	The Shuttleworth Collection, Old Warden, Beds	
K8042	Gloster Gladiator II (8372M)	RAF Museum, Cosford, Shropshire	
K8203	Hawker Demon I (G-BTVE/2292M)	Demon Displays, Old Warden, Beds	
K8303	Isaacs Fury II (G-BWWN) [D]	Privately owned, Turweston, Bucks	
K9926	VS300 Spitfire I <R> (BAPC.217) [JH-C]	Privately owned, Newquay, Cornwall	
K9942	VS300 Spitfire I (8383M) [SD-D]	RAF Museum, Cosford, Shropshire	
K9998	VS300 Spitfire I (BAPC.431) <R> [QJ-K]	RAF Biggin Hill, Kent, on display	
L1019	VS300 Spitfire I <R> (BAPC.308) [LO-S]	Morayvia, Kinloss, Scotland	
L1035	VS300 Spitfire I <R> (BAPC.500) [SH-D]	Battle of Britain Bunker, Uxbridge, Middlesex	
L1067	VS300 Spitfire I <R> (BAPC.227) [XT-D]	Edinburgh Airport, Scotland, on display	
L1592	Hawker Hurricane I [KW-Z]	Science Museum, South Kensington, London	
L1639	Hawker Hurricane I (BAPC.362)	Cambridge Fighter & Bomber Society, Little Gransden	
L1679	Hawker Hurricane I <R> (BAPC.241) [JX-G]	Tangmere Military Aviation Museum, W. Sussex	
L1684	Hawker Hurricane I <R> (BAPC.219)	RAF Northolt, Gtr London, on display	
L2005	Hawker Hurricane I	Hawker Restorations, Elmsett, Suffolk	
L2301	VS Walrus I (G-AIZG)	FAA Museum, RNAS Yeovilton, Somerset	
L2940	Blackburn Skua I	FAA Museum, RNAS Yeovilton, Somerset	
L5343	Fairey Battle I	RAF Museum, Hendon, Gtr London	
L6739	Bristol 149 Bolingbroke IVT (G-BPIV/*R3821*) [YP-Q]	Blenheim(Duxford) Ltd, Duxford, Cambs	
L6906	Miles M14A Magister I (G-AKKY/T9841/BAPC.44)	Museum of Berkshire Aviation, Woodley, Berks	
L7005	Boulton Paul P82 Defiant I <R> [PS-B]	Kent Battle of Britain Museum, Hawkinge, Kent	
L7181	Hawker Hind (G-CBLK)	Aero Vintage, Duxford, Cambs	
L7191	Hawker Hind	*Currently not known*	
L7775	Vickers Wellington B Ic <ff>	Lincolnshire Avn Heritage Centre, E Kirkby, Lincs	
L8756	Bristol 149 Bolingbroke IVT (RCAF 10001) [XD-E]	RAF Museum, Cosford, Shropshire	
N248	Supermarine S6A (*S1596*)	Solent Sky, Southampton, Hants	
N500	Sopwith LC-1T Triplane <R> (G-PENY/G-BWRA)	Privately owned, White Waltham, Berks	
N540	Port Victoria PV8 Eastchurch Kitten <R>	Yorkshire Air Museum, Elvington, N. Yorks	
N546	Wight Quadruplane 1 <R> (BAPC.164)	Solent Sky, Southampton, Hants	
N594	Nieuport 11 Scout <R> (G-CLPN) [3982]	Privately owned, Damyns Hall, Gtr London	
N1671	Boulton Paul P82 Defiant I (8370M) [EW-D]	RAF Museum, Cosford, Shropshire	
N1854	Fairey Fulmar II (G-AIBE)	FAA Museum, RNAS Yeovilton, Somerset	
N2078	Sopwith Baby (8214/8215/BAPC.442)	FAA Museum, RNAS Yeovilton, Somerset	
N2532	Hawker Hurricane I <R> (BAPC.272) [GZ-H]	Kent Battle of Britain Museum, Hawkinge, Kent	
N2980	Vickers Wellington Ia [R]	Brooklands Museum, Weybridge, Surrey	
N3200	VS300 Spitfire IA (G-CFGJ) [QV]	The Aircraft Restoration Co, Duxford, Cambs	
N3289	VS300 Spitfire I <R> (BAPC.65) [DW-K]	Kent Battle of Britain Museum, Hawkinge, Kent	
N3232	VS300 Spitfire Ia	Restoration, unknown location, UK	
N3290	VS300 Spitfire I <R> [AI-H]	Privately owned, St Mawgan, Cornwall	
N3310	VS361 Spitfire IX <R> (BAPC.393) [AI-A]	Privately owned, Abingdon, Oxon	
N3378	Boulton Paul P82 Defiant I (wreck)	RAF Museum, Cosford, Shropshire	
N3549	DH82A Tiger Moth II (PG645/N3549)	Privately owned, Gamston, Notts	
N3788	Miles M14A Magister I (V1075/G-AKPF)	Privately owned, Old Warden, Beds	

Notes	Serial	Type (code/other identity)	Owner/operator, location or fate
	N4389	Fairey Albacore (N4172) [4M]	FAA Museum, stored Cobham Hall, RNAS Yeovilton, Somerset
	N4877	Avro 652A Anson I (G-AMDA) [MK-V]	IWM Duxford, Cambs
	N5137	DH82A Tiger Moth (N6638/G-BNDW)	Caernarfon Air World, Wales
	N5177	Sopwith 1½ Strutter <R> (BAPC.452)	Privately owned, stored Merstham, Surrey
	N5182	Sopwith Pup <R> (G-APUP/9213M)	RAF Museum, Cosford, Shropshire
	N5195	Sopwith Pup (G-ABOX)	Army Flying Museum, Middle Wallop, Hants
	N5199	Sopwith Pup <R> (G-BZND)	Privately owned, Yarcombe, Devon
	N5459	Sopwith Triplane <R> (BAPC.111)	FAA Museum, stored Cobham Hall, RNAS Yeovilton, Somerset
	N5518	Gloster Sea Gladiator (N5579)	FAA Museum, stored Cobham Hall, RNAS Yeovilton, Somerset
	N5628	Gloster Gladiator II	RAF Museum, Cosford, Shropshire
	N5719	Gloster Gladiator II (G-CBHO)	Privately owned, Dursley, Glos
	N5903	Gloster Gladiator II (N2276/G-GLAD)	The Fighter Collection, Duxford, Cambs
	N5912	Sopwith Triplane (8385M)	RAF Museum, Hendon, Gtr London
	N5914	Gloster Gladiator II (frame)	Jet Age Museum, Gloucestershire Airport, Glos
	N6161	Sopwith Pup (G-ELRT)	Privately owned, Turweston, Bucks
	N6290	Sopwith Pup <R> (G-BOCK)	The Shuttleworth Collection, Old Warden, Beds
	N6377	Sopwith F.1 Camel <R> (G-BPOB/B2458)	Privately owned, Turweston, Bucks
	N6452	Sopwith Pup <R> (G-BIAU)	FAA Museum, RNAS Yeovilton, Somerset
	N6466	DH82A Tiger Moth (G-ANKZ)	Privately owned, Compton Abbas, Dorset
	N6473	DH82A Tiger Moth (F-GTBO)	Privately owned, Orbigny, France
	N6537	DH82A Tiger Moth (G-AOHY)	Privately owned, Wickenby, Lincs
	N6635	DH82A Tiger Moth (comp G-APAO & G-APAP) [25]	IWM Duxford, Cambs
	N6720	DH82A Tiger Moth (G-BYTN/7014M) [VX]	Privately owned, stored Darley Moor, Derbyshire
	N6797	DH82A Tiger Moth (G-ANEH)	Privately owned, Swyncombe, Oxon
	N6812	Sopwith 2F.1 Camel	IWM London, Lambeth, Gtr London
	N6847	DH82A Tiger Moth (G-APAL)	Privately owned, Langham, Rutland
	N6965	DH82A Tiger Moth (G-AJTW) [FL-J]	Privately owned, Tibenham, Norfolk
	N7033	Noorduyn AT-16 Harvard IIb (FX442)	Kent Battle of Britain Museum, Hawkinge, Kent
	N9181	DH82A Tiger Moth (composite) [5]	Kent Battle of Britain Museum, Hawkinge, Kent
	N9191	DH82A Tiger Moth (G-ALND)	Privately owned, Durley, Hants
	N9192	DH82A Tiger Moth (PG742/G-DHZF) [RCO-N]	Privately owned, Sywell, Northants
	N9328	DH82A Tiger Moth (G-ALWS) [69]	Privately owned, Yeovilton, Somerset
	N9372	DH82A Tiger Moth (G-ANHK)	Privately owned, Sturgate, Lincs
	N9389	DH82A Tiger Moth (G-ANJA)	Privately owned, stored Seething, Norfolk
	N9503	DH82A Tiger Moth II (G-ANFP) [39]	Privately owned, Podhořany, Czech Republic
	N9899	Supermarine Southampton I (fuselage)	RAF Museum, Hendon, Gtr London
	P1344	HP52 Hampden I (9175M) [PL-K]	Michael Beetham Conservation Centre, RAFM Cosford, Shropshire
	P2617	Hawker Hurricane I (8373M) [AF-F]	RAF Museum, Hendon, Gtr London
	P2725	Hawker Hurricane I (wreck)	IWM London, Lambeth, Gtr London
	P2725	Hawker Hurricane I <R> (BAPC.68) [TM-B]	Privately owned, Delabole, Cornwall
	P2725	Hawker Hurricane I <R> (Z3427/BAPC.205) [TM-B]	RAF Museum, Hendon, Gtr London
	P2793	Hawker Hurricane I <R> (BAPC.236) [SD-M]	Eden Camp Theme Park, stored Malton, N. Yorks
	P2793	Hawker Hurricane I <R> (BAPC.399) [SD-M]	Eden Camp Theme Park, Malton, N. Yorks
	P2902	Hawker Hurricane I (G-ROBT) [DX-R]	Privately owned, Duxford, Cambs
	P2921	Hawker Hurricane I <R> (BAPC.273) [GZ-L]	Kent Battle of Britain Museum, Hawkinge, Kent
	P2921	Hawker Hurricane I <R> (BAPC.477) [GZ-L]	RAF Biggin Hill, Kent, on display
	P2921	Hawker Sea Hurricane X (AE977/G-CHTK) [GZ-L]	Privately owned, Biggin Hill, Kent
	P2970	Hawker Hurricane I <R> (BAPC.291) [US-X]	Battle of Britain Memorial, Capel le Ferne, Kent
	P3059	Hawker Hurricane I <R> (BAPC.64) [SD-N]	Kent Battle of Britain Museum, Hawkinge, Kent
	P3175	Hawker Hurricane I (wreck)	RAF Museum Reserve Collection, Stafford, Staffs
	P3179	Hawker Hurricane I <ff>	Tangmere Military Aviation Museum, W. Sussex
	P3208	Hawker Hurricane I <R> (BAPC.63/L1592) [SD-T]	Kent Battle of Britain Museum, Hawkinge, Kent
	P3351	Hawker Hurricane IIa (DR393/L-AZXR) [K]	Privately owned, Cannes, France
	P3395	Hawker Hurricane IV (KX829)[JX-B]	Thinktank, Birmingham, Warks
	P3554	Hawker Hurricane I (composite)	The Air Defence Collection, Salisbury, Wilts
	P3679	Hawker Hurricane I <R> (BAPC.278) [GZ-K]	Kent Battle of Britain Museum, Hawkinge, Kent
	P3708	Hawker Hurricane I	Norfolk & Suffolk Avn Museum, Flixton, Suffolk (rebuild)

Serial	Type (code/other identity)	Owner/operator, location or fate	Notes
P3717	Hawker Hurricane I (composite) (DR348/G-HITT) [SW-P]	Privately owned, Old Warden, Beds	
P3873	Hawker Hurricane I <R> (BAPC.265) [YO-H]	Yorkshire Air Museum, Elvington, N. Yorks	
P3873	Hawker Hurricane I <R> (BAPC.499) [YO-H]	Battle of Britain Bunker, Uxbridge, Middlesex	
P3901	Hawker Hurricane I <R> (BAPC.475) [RF-E]	Battle of Britain Bunker, Uxbridge, Middlesex	
P4139	Fairey Swordfish II (HS618) [5H]	FAA Museum, RNAS Yeovilton, Somerset	
P6382	Miles M14A Hawk Trainer 3 (G-AJRS) [C]	The Shuttleworth Collection, Old Warden, Beds	
P7308	VS300 Spitfire IA (AR213/R9632/G-AIST) [XR-D]	Privately owned, Duxford, Cambs	
P7350	VS329 Spitfire IIa (G-AWIJ) [KL-B]	RAF BBMF, Coningsby, Lincs	
P7370	VS329 Spitfire II <R> (BAPC.410) [ZP-A]	Battle of Britain Experience, Canterbury, Kent	
P7540	VS329 Spitfire IIa (DU-W)	Dumfries & Galloway Avn Mus, Scotland	
P7666	VS329 Spitfire II <R> (BAPC.335) [EB-Z]	RAF High Wycombe, Bucks, on display	
P7819	VS329 Spitfire IIa (G-TCHZ)	Privately owned, Exeter, Devon	
P7823	VS329 Spitfire IIa <R> (BAPC.369) [TM-F]	Ulster Aviation Society, Long Kesh, NI	
P7913	VS329 Spitfire IIa	Privately owned, Biggin Hill, Kent (wreck)	
P7966	VS329 Spitfire II <R> [D-B]	Manx Aviation & Military Museum, Ronaldsway, IOM	
P8088	VS329 Spitfire IIa (G-CGRM) [NK-K]	Privately owned, Knutsford, Cheshire	
P8140	VS329 Spitfire II <R> (N3317/BAPC.71) [BO-U]	Kent Battle of Britain Museum, Hawkinge, Kent	
P8208	VS329 Spitfire IIb (G-RRFF)	Privately owned, Dursley, Glos	
P8331	VS329 Spitfire IIb (G-KOSC) [RF-M]	Privately owned, Glos	
P8448	VS329 Spitfire II <R> (BAPC.225) [UM-D]	RAF Cranwell, Lincs, on display	
P9337	VS300 Spitfire Ia (G-IADX)	Privately owned, Oxford, Oxon	
P9372	VS300 Spitfire I (G-CLIH)(PH-CAM reserved)	Privately owned, Biggin Hill, Kent	
P9373	VS300 Spitfire Ia (G-CFGN)	Privately owned, Duxford, Cambs (rebuild)	
P9398	Supermarine Aircraft Spitfire 26 (G-CEPL) [KL-B]	Privately owned, Rochester, Kent	
P9398	VS300 Spitfire I <R> (N3313/BAPC.69) [KL-B]	Kent Battle of Britain Museum, Hawkinge, Kent	
P9451	VS300 Spitfire I <ff>	Privately owned, Hooton Park, Cheshire	
P9444	VS300 Spitfire Ia (RN-D)	Science Museum, South Kensington, London	
P9637	Supermarine Aircraft Spitfire 26 (G-RORB) [GR-B]	Privately owned, Perth, Scotland	
R1914	Miles M14A Magister (G-AHUJ)	Privately owned, Gloucestershire Airport, Glos	
R4118	Hawker Hurricane I (G-HUPW) [UP-W]	Privately owned, North Moreton, Oxon	
R4175	Hawker Hurricane XIIa (P3700/G-HURI) [RF-R]	Historic Aircraft Collection, Duxford, Cambs	
R4229	Hawker Hurricane I <R> (BAPC.334) [GN-J]	Alexandra Park, Windsor, Berks	
R4922	DH82A Tiger Moth II (G-APAO)	Privately owned, Duxford, Cambs	
R4959	DH82A Tiger Moth II (G-ARAZ) [59]	Privately owned, Duxford, Cambs	
R5136	DH82A Tiger Moth II (G-APAP)	Privately owned, Darley Moor, Derbyshire	
R5172	DH82A Tiger Moth II (G-AOIS) [FIJE]	Privately owned, Sywell, Northants	
R5246	DH82A Tiger Moth II (G-AMIV) [40]	Privately owned, Podhořany, Czech Republic	
R5868	Avro 683 Lancaster I (7325M) [PO-S]	RAF Museum, Hendon, Gtr London	
R5868	Avro 683 Lancaster I <R> (BAPC.471) [PO-S] <ff>	Avro Heritage Museum, Woodford, Cheshire	
R6599	VS300 Spitfire I <R> (BAPC.539) [DW-J]	Romney Marsh Wartime Collection, Kent	
R6690	VS300 Spitfire I <R> (BAPC.254) [PR-A]	Yorkshire Air Museum, Elvington, N. Yorks	
R6775	VS300 Spitfire I <R> (BAPC.299) [YT-J]	Battle of Britain Memorial, Capel le Ferne, Kent	
R6800	Supermarine Aircraft Spitfire 26B (G-CLHJ) [LZ-N]	Privately owned, Enstone, Oxon	
R6904	VS300 Spitfire I <R> [BT-K]	Privately owned, Cornwall	
R6915	VS300 Spitfire I	IWM London, Lambeth, Gtr London	
R9125	Westland Lysander III (8377M)[JR-M]	RAF Museum, Hendon, Gtr London	
R9612	VS300 Spitfire I <R> (G-CGUK)[KL-A]	Privately owned, Duxford, Cambs	
S1287	Fairey Flycatcher <R> (G-BEYB) [5]	FAA Museum, stored Cobham Hall, RNAS Yeovilton, Somerset	
S1581	Hawker Nimrod I (G-BWWK) [573]	The Fighter Collection, Duxford, Cambs	
S1595	Supermarine S6B [1]	Science Museum, South Kensington, London	
S1615	Isaacs Fury II (G-BMEU)	Privately owned, Tatenhill, Staffs	
T5298	Bristol 156 Beaufighter I (4552M) <ff>	Midland Air Museum, Coventry, Warks	
T5424	DH82A Tiger Moth II (G-AJOA)	Privately owned, Swindon, Wilts	
T5854	DH82A Tiger Moth II (G-ANKK)	Privately owned, Baxterley, Warks	
T5879	DH82A Tiger Moth II (G-AXBW) [RUC-W]	Privately owned, Frensham, Surrey (damaged)	
T6296	DH82A Tiger Moth II (8387M)	RAF Museum, Cosford, Shropshire	
T6830	DH82A Tiger Moth (G-ANJI)	Privately owned, Insch, Scotland	

BRITISH MILITARY AIRCRAFT MARKINGS

Notes	Serial	Type (code/other identity)	Owner/operator, location or fate
	T6953	DH82A Tiger Moth II (G-ANNI)	Privately owned, Solent Airport, Hants
	T6991	DH82A Tiger Moth II (DE694/HB-UPY)	Privately owned, Fasno, Italy
	T7109	DH82A Tiger Moth II (G-AOIM)	Privately owned, Bicester, Oxon
	T7230	DH82A Tiger Moth II (G-AFVE)	Privately owned, Mazowiecke, Poland
	T7281	DH82A Tiger Moth II (G-ARTL)	Privately owned, Egton, nr Whitby, N. Yorks
	T7290	DH82A Tiger Moth II (G-ANNK) [14]	Privately owned, Podington, Beds
	T7793	DH82A Tiger Moth II (G-ANKV)	Privately owned, Wickenby, Lincs
	T7794	DH82A Tiger Moth II (G-ASPV)	Privately owned, Bagby, N. Yorks
	T7842	DH82A Tiger Moth II (G-AMTF)	Privately owned, Westfield, Surrey
	T7909	DH82A Tiger Moth II (G-ANON)	Privately owned, Sherburn-in-Elmet, N. Yorks
	T7997	DH82A Tiger Moth II (NL750/G-AHUF)	Privately owned, Henstridge, Somerset
	T8191	DH82A Tiger Moth II (G-BWMK)	Privately owned, Henstridge, Somerset
	T9707	Miles M14A Magister I (G-AKKR/8378M/T9708)	RAF Museum, Cosford, Shropshire
	T9738	Miles M14A Magister I (G-AKAT)	Privately owned, Breighton, E. Yorks
	V3388	Airspeed AS10 Oxford I (G-AHTW)	IWM Duxford, Cambs
	V6028	Bristol 149 Bolingbroke IVT (G-MKIV) [GB-D] <rf>	The Aircraft Restoration Co, stored Duxford, Cambs
	V6555	Hawker Hurricane I (BAPC.411/P3144) <R> [DT-A]	Battle of Britain Experience, Canterbury, Kent
	V6748	Hawker Hurricane XII (RCAF 5481/G-ORGI) [PO]	Privately owned, Sywell, Northants
	V6799	Hawker Hurricane I <R> (BAPC.72/V7767) [SD-X]	Jet Age Museum, Gloucestershire Airport, Glos
	V7313	Hawker Hurricane I <R> (BAPC.346) [US-F]	Privately owned, North Weald, Essex, on display
	V7350	Hawker Hurricane I <ff>	Romney Marsh Wartime Collection, Kent
	V7467	Hawker Hurricane I <R> (P2954/BAPC.267) [LE-D]	IWM Duxford, Cambs
	V7467	Hawker Hurricane I <R> (BAPC.288) [LE-D]	Wonderland Pleasure Park, Farnsfield, Notts
	V7467	Hawker Hurricane I <R> (BAPC.378) [LE-D]	RAF High Wycombe, Bucks, on display
	V7497	Hawker Hurricane I (G-HRLI) [SD-X]	Privately owned, Duxford, Cambs (damaged)
	V7752	Hawker Hurricane I <R> (V7467/BAPC.223) [ZJ-L]	Hangar 42 Visitors Centre, Blackpool, Lancs
	V9312	Westland Lysander IIIa (G-CCOM) [LX-E]	The Aircraft Restoration Co, Duxford, Cambs
	V9367	Westland Lysander IIIa (G-AZWT) [MA-B]	The Shuttleworth Collection, Old Warden, Beds
	V9673	Westland Lysander IIIa (V9300/G-LIZY) [MA-J]	IWM Duxford, Cambs
	V9723	Westland Lysander IIIa (V9546/OO-SOT) [MA-D]	SABENA Old Timers, Brussels, Belgium (under repair)
	V9875	Westland Lysander IIIa <R> (BAPC.371) [MA-J]	Tangmere Military Aviation Museum, W. Sussex
	W1048	HP59 Halifax II (8465M) [TL-S]	RAF Museum, Hendon, Gtr London
	W2068	Avro 652A Anson I (9261M/VH-ASM) [68]	RAF Museum, Hendon, Gtr London
	W3442	VS361 Spitfire IX <R> (PL256/BAPC.325) [FY-D]	Privately owned, Blackpool, Lancs
	W3644	VS349 Spitfire V <R> (BAPC.323) [QV-J]	Privately owned, Lake Fairhaven, Lancs
	W3850	VS349 Spitfire V <R> (BAPC.304) [PR-A]	Privately owned, Knutsford, Cheshire
	W4041	Gloster E28/39	Science Museum, South Kensington, London
	W4041	Gloster E28/39 <R> (BAPC.331)	Jet Age Museum, Gloucestershire Airport, Glos
	W4050	DH98 Mosquito [P]	de Havilland Aircraft Museum, London Colney
	W5856	Fairey Swordfish I (G-BMGC) [4A]	Fly Navy Heritage Trust, Yeovilton, Somerset
	W9385	DH87B Hornet Moth (G-ADND) [YG-L,3]	Privately owned, Oaksey Park, Wiltshire
	X4009	VS300 Spitfire I (G-EMET)	*Sold to Australia, 2021*
	X4253	VS300 Spitfire I <R> (BAPC.326) [FY-N]	Hangar 42 Visitors Centre, Blackpool, Lancs
	X4276	VS300 Spitfire I (G-CDGU)	Privately owned, Biggin Hill, Kent
	X4474	VS300 Spitfire I <R> (X4178/BAPC.394) [QV-I]	IWM Duxford, Cambs
	X4590	VS300 Spitfire I (8384M) [PR-F]	RAF Museum, Hendon, Gtr London
	X4650	VS300 Spitfire I (R9612/G-CGUK) [KL-A]	Privately owned, Duxford, Cambs
	X4683	Jurca MJ10 Spitfire (G-MUTS) [EB-N]	Privately owned, Fishburn, Co. Durham
	X4859	VS300 Spitfire I <R> (BAPC.319) [PQ-N]	Grangemouth Spitfire Memorial Trust, Scotland
	X9407	Percival P.16A Q6 (G-AFFD)	Privately owned, Seething, Norfolk (on rebuild)
	X9556	VS Walrus I (W2718/G-RNLI) [S]	The Aircraft Restoration Co, Duxford, Cambs
	Z1206	Vickers Wellington IV (fuselage)	Privately owned, Kenilworth, Warks
	Z2033	Fairey Firefly I (G-ASTL) [275/N]	FAA Museum, stored Cobham Hall, RNAS Yeovilton
	Z2315	Hawker Hurricane IIa [JU-E]	IWM Duxford, Cambs
	Z2389	Hawker Hurricane IIa [XR-J]	Brooklands Museum, Weybridge, Surrey
	Z5207	Hawker Hurricane IIb (G-BYDL)	Privately owned, Aalen, Germany (on rebuild)
	Z7015	Hawker Sea Hurricane Ib (G-BKTH) [7-L]	The Shuttleworth Collection, Old Warden, Beds
	Z7197	Percival P30 Proctor III (G-AKZN/8380M)	RAF Museum Reserve Collection, Stafford, Staffs

Serial	Type (code/other identity)	Owner/operator, location or fate	Notes
Z7258	DH89A Dragon Rapide (NR786/G-AHGD)	Privately owned, Membury, Wilts (wreck)	
AA810	VS353 Spitfire F IV (G-PRID)	Kennet Aviation, Old Warden, Beds	
AA937	VS349 Spitfire Vb <R> [AF-O]	IWM, Duxford, Cambs	
AB196	Supermarine Aircraft Spitfire 26 (G-CCGH)	Privately owned, Hawarden, Flintshire, Wales	
AB910	VS349 Spitfire Vb (G-AISU) [SH-F]	RAF BBMF, Coningsby, Lincs	
AD189	VS349 Spitfire Vb (G-CHVJ)	Privately owned, Raglan, Scotland	
AD370	Jurca MJ10 Spitfire (G-CHBW) [PJ-C]	Privately owned, Perranporth, Cornwall	
AD540	VS349 Spitfire Vb (wreck)	Privately owned, on rebuild Twyford, Bucks	
AE436	HP52 Hampden I [PL-J] (parts)	Lincolnshire Avn Heritage Centre, E Kirkby, Lincs	
AG244	Hawker Hurricane XII (RCAF 5487/G-CBOE)	Privately owned, Aalen, Germany	
AJ841	CCF T-6J Texan (MM53795/G-BJST/KF729)	Privately owned, Duxford, Cambs	
AL246	Grumman Martlet I	FAA Museum, RNAS Yeovilton, Somerset	
AP506	Cierva C30A (G-ACWM) (wreck)	The Helicopter Museum, Weston-super-Mare, Somerset	
AP507	Cierva C30A (G-ACWP) [KX-P]	Science Museum, South Kensington, London	
AR501	VS349 Spitfire LF Vc (G-AWII/AR4474) [DU-E]	The Shuttleworth Collection, Old Warden, Beds	
AV511	EHI-101 Merlin <R> [511]	SFDO, RNAS Culdrose, Cornwall	
AW101	AgustaWestland AW101 Mk.510 (G-17-510)	AgustaWestland, Yeovil, Somerset	
AX733	Grumman FM-2 Wildcat (G-KINL) [K]	Privately owned, Duxford, Cambs	
BA377	VS361 Spitfire F IX <R> (EN398/BAPC.377) [UF-J]	Privately owned, Belper, Derbyshire	
BB803	DH82A Tiger Moth (G-ADWJ) [75]	Privately owned, Henstridge, Somerset	
BB807	DH82A Tiger Moth (G-ADWO)	Solent Sky, Southampton, Hants	
BD713	Hawker Hurricane IIb	Currently not known	
BE505	Hawker Hurricane IIb(mod) (RCAF 5403/G-HHII) [XP-L]	Privately owned, Duxford, Cambs	
BH238	Hawker Hurricane IIb	Privately owned, Rochester, Kent (rebuild)	
BK897	BA Swallow II (G-AFGD)	Privately owned, Shobdon, Herefordshire	
BL614	VS349 Spitfire Vb (4354M) [ZD-F]	RAF Museum, Hendon, Gtr London	
BL655	VS349 Spitfire Vb (wreck)	Lincolnshire Avn Heritage Centre, East Kirkby, Lincs	
BL688	VS349 Spitfire LF Vb (G-LFVE)	Privately owned, Launceston, Cornwall (rebuild)	
BL735	Supermarine Aircraft Spitfire 26 (G-HABT) [BT-A]	Privately owned, Hohenems, Austria	
BL924	VS349 Spitfire Vb <R> (BAPC.242) [AZ-G]	North-East Land, Sea & Air Museums, Usworth, T&W	
BL927	Supermarine Aircraft Spitfire 26 (G-CGWI) [JH-I]	Privately owned, Perth, Scotland	
BM361	VS349 Spitfire Vb <R> (BAPC.269) [XR-C]	RAF Lakenheath, Suffolk, on display	
BM481	VS349 Spitfire Vb <R> (BAPC.301) [YO-T] (also wears PK651/RAO-T)	Thornaby Aerodrome Memorial, N. Yorks	
BM539	VS349 Spitfire LF Vb (G-SSVB)	Privately owned, Hastings, E. Sussex	
BM597	VS349 Spitfire LF Vb (G-MKVB/5718M) [RF-M]	Historic Aircraft Collection, Duxford	
BN230	Hawker Hurricane IIc (LF751/5466M) [FT-A]	RAF Manston, Kent, Memorial Pavilion	
BN230	Hawker Hurricane I <R> (BAPC.218) [FT-A]	RAF Bentley Priory, Gtr London, on display	
BP926	VS353 Spitfire PR IV (G-PRIV)	Privately owned, Newport Pagnell, Bucks	
BR954	VS353 Spitfire PR IV <R> (N3194/BAPC.220) [JP-A]	Merlin ERD, Perth, Scotland	
BS239	VS361 Spitfire IX <R> (BAPC.222) [5R-E]	Battle of Britain Bunker, Uxbridge, Middlesex	
BS410	VS509 Spitfire T9 (G-TCHI) [PK-A]	Privately owned, Sandown, IOW (2-seat conversion)	
BS435	VS361 Spitfire IX <R> (BAPC.324) [FY-F]	Hangar 42 Visitors Centre, Blackpool, Lancs	
BS548	VS361 Spitfire IX	Rebuild, Duxford, Cambs	
BW853	Hawker Hurricane XIIa (G-BRKE) (fuselage)	Currently not known	
DD931	Bristol 152 Beaufort VIII (9131M/BAPC.436) [L]	RAF Museum, Hendon, Gtr London	
DE208	DH82A Tiger Moth II (G-AGYU)	Privately owned, Treswell, Notts	
DE470	DH82A Tiger Moth II (G-ANMY) [16]	Privately owned, Garford, Oxon (rebuild)	
DE623	DH82A Tiger Moth II (G-ANFI)	Privately owned, Cardiff, Wales	
DE673	DH82A Tiger Moth II (G-ADNZ/6948M)	Privately owned, Tibenham, Norfolk	
DE971	DH82A Tiger Moth II (G-OOSY)	Privately owned, Bicester, Oxon	
DE974	DH82A Tiger Moth II (G-ANZZ)	Privately owned, Clacton/Duxford	
DE992	DH82A Tiger Moth II (G-AXXV)	Privately owned, White Waltham, Berks (damaged)	
DF112	DH82A Tiger Moth II (G-ANRM)	Privately owned, Clacton, Essex (on rebuild)	
DF128	DH82A Tiger Moth II (G-AOJJ) [RCO-U]	Privately owned, White Waltham, Berks	
DF198	DH82A Tiger Moth II (G-BBRB)	Privately owned, stored West Wickham, Kent	
DG202	Gloster F9/40 (5758M)	RAF Museum, stored Cosford, Shropshire	
DG590	Miles M2H Hawk Major (G-ADMW/8379M)	Montrose Air Station Heritage Centre, Scotland	

23

Notes	Serial	Type (code/other identity)	Owner/operator, location or fate
	DP872	Fairey Barracuda II <ff>	FAA Museum, stored Cobham Hall, RNAS Yeovilton, Somerset
	DP872	Fairey Barracuda II <rf>	FAA Museum, RNAS Yeovilton, Somerset
	DV372	Avro 683 Lancaster I <ff>	IWM London, Lambeth, Gtr London
	DZ313	DH98 Mosquito B IV <R>	Privately owned, Little Rissington, Glos
	EB518	Airspeed AS10 Oxford V	Hangar 42 Visitors Centre, Blackpool, Lancs
	EE416	Gloster Meteor F3 <ff>	Martin Baker Aircraft, Chalgrove, Oxon (fire section)
	EE425	Gloster Meteor F3 <ff>	Jet Age Museum, Gloucestershire Airport, Glos
	EE531	Gloster Meteor F4 (7090M)	Midland Air Museum, Coventry, Warks
	EE549	Gloster Meteor F4 (7008M) [A]	Tangmere Military Aviation Museum, W. Sussex
	EE602	VS349 Spitfire LF Vc (G-IBSY) [DV-V]	Privately owned, Biggin Hill, Kent
	EF545	VS349 Spitfire LF Vc (G-CDGY)	Biggin Hill Heritage Hangar, Kent (restoration)
	EJ922	Hawker Typhoon Ib <ff>	Privately owned, Uckfield, E Sussex
	EM720	DH82A Tiger Moth II (G-AXAN)	Privately owned, Cambridge, Cambs
	EM726	DH82A Tiger Moth II (G-ANDE) [FY]	Privately owned, Sywell, Northants
	EM840	DH82A Tiger Moth II (G-ANBY)	Privately owned, Hooton Park, Cheshire
	EM973	DH82A Tiger Moth II (T6774/G-ALNA) [OY]	Privately owned, Eggington, Derbyshire
	EN130	Supermarine Aircraft Spitfire 26B (G-ENAA) [FN-A]	Privately owned, Enstone, Oxon
	EN179	VS361 Spitfire F IX (G-TCHO)	Privately owned, Exeter, Devon
	EN223	VS366 Spitfire F XII (G-GXII)	Privately owned,
	EN224	VS366 Spitfire F XII (G-FXII)	Privately owned, Sywell, Northants
	EN398	VS361 Spitfire F IX <R> (BAPC.541) [JE-J]	RAF Coningsby, Lincs, on display
	EN398	VS361 Spitfire F IX <R> (BAPC.552) [JE-J]	AMSS, Pyle, Bridgend, Wales
	EN398	VS361 Spitfire F IX <R> (BAPC.555) [JE-J]	Spitfire Spares, Taunton, Somerset
	EN398	VS361 Spitfire F IX <R> (BAPC.580) [JE-J]	Secret Spitfires Memorial, Salisbury, Wilts
	EN570	VS361 Spitfire F IX (G-CISP/LN-AOA)	Privately owned, Biggin Hill, Kent
	EN961	Isaacs Spitfire <R> (G-CGIK) [SD-X]	Privately owned, Stoulton, Worcs
	EP120	VS349 Spitfire LF Vb (G-LFVB/5377M/8070M) [AE-A]	The Fighter Collection, Duxford, Cambs
	EP121	VS349 Spitfire LF Vb <R> (BAPC.320) [LO-D]	Montrose Air Station Heritage Centre, Scotland
	EV771	Fairchild UC-61 Argus <R> (BAPC.294)	Thorpe Camp Preservation Group, Lincs
	EX490	NA T-6H Texan (F-AZQK/G-CLCJ) [78]	Privately owned, Enstone, Oxon
	EX976	NA AT-6D Harvard III (FAP 1657)	FAA Museum, RNAS Yeovilton, Somerset
	FE511	Noorduyn AT-16 Harvard IIb (G-CIUW)	Privately owned, White Waltham, Berks
	FE695	Noorduyn AT-16 Harvard IIb (G-BTXI) [94]	Privately owned, Bicester, Oxon
	FE788	CCF Harvard IV (MM54137/G-CTKL)	Privately owned, Biggin Hill, Kent
	FE905	Noorduyn AT-16 Harvard IIb (LN-BNM)	RAF Museum, Hendon, Gtr London
	FJ801	Boeing-Stearman PT-27 Kaydet (N62842/BAPC.375)	Norfolk & Suffolk Avn Museum, Flixton, Suffolk
	FK338	Fairchild 24W-41 Argus I (G-AJOZ)	Yorkshire Air Museum, Elvington, N. Yorks
	FL586	Douglas C-47B Dakota (N99346) [4U-D] (fuselage) (fitted with nose of F-GEFU)	WWII Remembrance Museum, Handcross, W Sussex
	FR886	Piper L-4J Grasshopper (G-BDMS)	Privately owned, Melksham, Wilts
	FS628	Fairchild Argus 2 (43-14601/G-AIZE)	RAF Museum, Cosford, Shropshire
	FS728	Noorduyn AT-16 Harvard IIb (D-FRCP)	Privately owned, Gelnhausen, Germany
	FT118	Noorduyn AT-16 Harvard IIb (G-BZHL) [TM-13]	Privately owned, Hibaldstow, Lincs
	FT323	NA AT-6D Harvard III (FAP 1513/G-CCOY)	Privately owned, France
	FT391	Noorduyn AT-16 Harvard IIb (G-AZBN)	Privately owned, Blackpool, Lancs
	FX322	Noorduyn AT-16 Harvard IIb <ff>	Privately owned, Doncaster, S. Yorks
	FX760	Curtiss P-40N Kittyhawk IV (A29-556/9150M) [GA-?]	RAF Museum, Hendon, Gtr London
	FZ626	Douglas Dakota III (KN566/G-AMPO) [YS-DH]	RAF Brize Norton, Oxon, for display
	GZ100	AgustaWestland AW109SP Grand New (G-ZIOO)	RAF No 32(The Royal) Sqn, Northolt, Gtr London
	HB612	Fairchild Argus II (G-AJSN)	Ulster Aviation Society, Long Kesh, NI
	HB737	Fairchild Argus III (G-BCBH)	Privately owned, Spanhoe, Northants
	HB751	Fairchild Argus III (G-BCBL)	Privately owned, Breighton, E. Yorks
	HG691	DH89A Dragon Rapide (G-AIYR)	Privately owned, Clacton/Duxford
	HH268	GAL48 Hotspur II (HH379/BAPC.261) [H]	Army Flying Museum, Middle Wallop, Hants
	HJ711	DH98 Mosquito NF II (BAPC.434) [VI-C]	Lincolnshire Avn Heritage Centre, E Kirkby, Lincs

Serial	Type (code/other identity)	Owner/operator, location or fate	Notes
HM580	Cierva C-30A (G-ACUU) [KX-K]	IWM Duxford, Cambs	
HS503	Fairey Swordfish IV (BAPC.108)	RAF Museum Reserve Collection, Stafford, Staffs	
HS554	Fairey Swordfish III (G-RNMZ)	Privately owned, White Waltham, Berks	
IR206	Eurofighter Typhoon <R> (BAPC.360) [IR]	RAF M&RU, Bottesford, Leics	
IR808	B-V Chinook <R> (BAPC.361)	RAF M&RU, Bottesford, Leics	
JG241	Supermarine Aircraft Spitfire 26B (G-SMSP) [ZX-J]	Privately owned, Blackbushe, Hants	
JG668	VS502 Spitfire T8 (A58-441/G-CFGA)	Privately owned, Haverfordwest, Wales	
JG891	VS349 Spitfire F Vc (N5TF/G-LFVC) [T-B]	Privately owned, Duxford, Cambs	
JN768	Hawker Tempest V (4887M/G-TMPV)	Privately owned, Sywell, Northants	
JP843	Hawker Typhoon Ib [Y]	Privately owned, Shrewsbury, Shropshire	
JR505	Hawker Typhoon Ib <ff>	Currently not known	
JV482	Grumman Wildcat V	Ulster Aviation Society, Long Kesh, NI	
JV579	Grumman FM-2 Wildcat (N4845V/G-RUMW) [F]	The Fighter Collection, Duxford, Cambs	
KB889	Avro 683 Lancaster B X (G-LANC) [NA-I]	IWM Duxford, Cambs	
KB976	Avro 683 Lancaster B X [LQ] <ff>	Privately owned, Newquay, Cornwall	
KD345	Goodyear FG-1D Corsair (88297/G-FGID) [130-A]	The Fighter Collection, Duxford, Cambs	
KD431	CV Corsair IV [E2-M]	FAA Museum, RNAS Yeovilton, Somerset	
KE209	Grumman Hellcat II	FAA Museum, RNAS Yeovilton, Somerset	
KE418	Hawker Tempest <rf>	Currently not known	
KF183	Noorduyn AT-16 Harvard IIb (G-CORS) [3]	Privately owned, East Midlands, Leics	
KF388	Noorduyn AT-16 Harvard IIb (composite)	Bournemouth Aviation Museum, Dorset	
KF402	NA T-6G Texan (49-3072/G-TEXN) [HT-Y]	Boultbee Flight Academy, Goodwood, W. Sussex	
KF532	Noorduyn AT-16 Harvard IIb <ff>	Sywell Aviation Museum, Northants	
KF650	Noorduyn AT-16 Harvard IIb <ff>	Sywell Aviation Museum, Northants	
KF741	Noorduyn AT-16 Harvard IIb <ff>	Privately owned, Kenilworth, Warks	
KG374	Douglas Dakota IV (KP208) [YS-DM]	Merville Barracks, Colchester, Essex, on display	
KG651	Douglas Dakota III (G-AMHJ)	Metheringham Airfield Visitor Centre, Lincs	
KJ351	Airspeed AS58 Horsa II (TL659/BAPC.80) [23]	Army Flying Museum, Middle Wallop, Hants	
KJ994	Douglas Dakota III (F-AZTE)	Dakota et Cie, La Ferté Alais, France	
KK116	Douglas Dakota IV (G-AMPY)	Sold to USA, May 2022	
KK527	Fairchild 24R Argus III (44-83184/G-RGUS)	Privately owned, Fowlmere, Cambs	
KK995	Sikorsky Hoverfly I (KL110) [E]	RAF Museum, Hendon, Gtr London	
KL216	Republic P-47D Thunderbolt (45-49295/9212M) [RS-L]	RAF Museum, Hendon, Gtr London	
KN353	Douglas Dakota IV (G-AMYJ)	Yorkshire Air Museum, Elvington, N. Yorks	
KN645	Douglas Dakota IV (KG374/8355M)	RAF Museum, Cosford, Shropshire	
KN751	Consolidated Liberator C VI (IAF HE807) [F]	RAF Museum, Hendon, Gtr London	
KP220	Douglas Dakota IV (G-ANAF)	Privately owned, Lydd, Kent	
KZ191	Hawker Hurricane IV (frame only)	Privately owned, East Garston, Bucks	
KZ321	Hawker Hurricane IV (G-HURY/OO-HUR)	Crashed Cheb, Czech Republic, August 2022	
LA198	VS356 Spitfire F21 (7118M) [RAI-G]	Kelvingrove Art Gallery & Museum, Glasgow, Scotland	
LA226	VS356 Spitfire F21 (7119M)	RAF Museum Reserve Collection, Stafford, Staffs	
LA255	VS356 Spitfire F21 (6490M) [JX-U]	RAF Lossiemouth, Moray, Scotland, preserved	
LA543	VS474 Seafire F46 <ff>	The Air Defence Collection, Salisbury, Wilts	
LA546	VS474 Seafire F46 (G-CFZJ)	Privately owned, Colchester, Essex	
LA564	VS474 Seafire F46 (G-FRSX)	Kennet Aviation, stored Old Warden, Beds	
LB264	Taylorcraft Plus D (G-AIXA)	RAF Museum, Hendon, Gtr London	
LB286	Taylorcraft Plus D (EI-AMF)	Privately owned, Spanhoe Lodge, Northants	
LB294	Taylorcraft Plus D (G-AHWJ)	Saywell Heritage Centre, Worthing, W. Sussex	
LB312	Taylorcraft Plus D (HH982/G-AHXE)	Historic Army Aircraft Flight, Middle Wallop, Hants	
LB314	Taylorcraft Plus D (OY-DSZ)	South Yorkshire Aircraft Museum, Doncaster, S. Yorks	
LB323	Taylorcraft Plus D (G-AHSD)	Sold to Netherlands, Nov 2022	
LB352	Taylorcraft Plus D (G-AHCR)	Privately owned, Middlezoy, Somerset	
LB367	Taylorcraft Plus D (G-AHGZ)	Privately owned, Parkend, Glos	
LB369	Taylorcraft Plus D (G-AHHY)	Privately owned, Enstone, Oxon	
LB375	Taylorcraft Plus D (G-AHGW)	Privately owned, Spanhoe, Northants	
LF363	Hawker Hurricane IIc [RF-J]	RAF BBMF, Biggin Hill, Kent (servicing)	
LF738	Hawker Hurricane IIc (5405M) [UH-A]	RAF Museum, Cosford, Shropshire	

Notes	Serial	Type (code/other identity)	Owner/operator, location or fate
	LF789	DH82 Queen Bee (K3584/BAPC.186) [R2-K]	de Havilland Aircraft Museum, London Colney
	LF858	DH82 Queen Bee (G-BLUZ)	Privately owned, Old Warden, Beds
LH291	Airspeed AS51 Horsa I <R> (BAPC.279)	To Overloon Museum, The Netherlands
	LS326	Fairey Swordfish II (G-AJVH) [L2]	Fly Navy Heritage Trust, Yeovilton, Somerset
LV907	HP59 Halifax III (HR792/BAPC.449) [NP-F]	Yorkshire Air Museum, Elvington, N. Yorks
		(marked NP763 [H7-N] on port side)	
	LZ551	DH100 Vampire	FAA Museum, RNAS Yeovilton, Somerset
	LZ766	Percival P34 Proctor III (G-ALCK)	IWM Duxford, Cambs
	LZ842	VS361 Spitfire F IX (G-CGZU) [EF-F]	Privately owned, Biggin Hill, Kent
	LZ844	VS349 Spitfire F Vc [UP-X]	Currently not known
	MA764	VS361 Spitfire LF IXe (G-MCDB)	Privately owned, Biggin Hill, Kent
	MB293	VS358 Seafire IIc (G-CFGI)	The Aircraft Restoration Co, Duxford, Cambs
	MF628	Vickers Wellington T10 (9210M)	Michael Beetham Conservation Centre, RAFM Cosford, Shropshire
MH314	VS361 Spitfire IX <R> (EN526/BAPC.221) [SZ-G]	RAF Northolt, Gtr London, on display
	MH415	VS361 Spitfire LF IXb (G-AVDJ) [ZD-E]	Privately owned, Sywell, Northants
MH415	VS361 Spitfire IX <R> (MJ751/BAPC.209) [DU-V]	Sold to USA
	MH434	VS361 Spitfire LF IXb (G-ASJV) [ZD-B]	The Old Flying Machine Company, Duxford, Cambs
MH526	Supermarine Aircraft Spitfire 26 (G-CJWW) [LO-D]	Privately owned, Wethersfield, Essex
	MJ444	VS361 Spitfire HF IX (G-LEGD) (fuselage)	Privately owned, Sandown, IOW
	MJ627	VS509 Spitfire T9 (G-BMSB) [9G-Q]	Privately owned, Biggin Hill, Kent
	MJ772	VS509 Spitfire T9 (G-AVAV/PH-KDH) [GW-A]	Privately owned, Eindhoven, The Netherlands
MJ832	VS361 Spitfire IX <R> (L1096/BAPC.229) [DN-Y]	RAF Digby, Lincs, on display
	MK356	VS361 Spitfire LF IXe (5690M) [QJ-3]	RAF BBMF, Coningsby, Lincs
MK356	VS361 Spitfire LF IXc <R> [2I-V]	Kent Battle of Britain Museum, Hawkinge, Kent
MK356	VS361 Spitfire LF IXc <R> (BAPC.298)	Boscombe Down, Wilts (stored)
MK392	VS361 Spitfire LF IXc <R> (EN398/BAPC.184) [JE-J]	Boultbee Flight Academy, Goodwood, W. Sussex
MK805	VS361 Spitfire IX (BAPC.426) <R> [SH-B]	Simply Spitfires, Oulton Broad, Suffolk
	MK912	VS361 Spitfire LF IXc (G-BRRA) [SH-L]	Privately owned, stored Biggin Hill, Kent
ML135	VS361 Spitfire IX <R> (BAPC.513)	Essex Memorial Spitfire Monument, ON, Canada
	ML295	VS361 Spitfire LF IXb (G-CLXB) [DB-M]	Privately owned, Biggin Hill, Kent
	ML407	VS509 Spitfire T9 (G-LFIX) [OU-V]	Privately owned, Sywell, Northants
	ML411	VS361 Spitfire LF IXe (G-CBNU)	Privately owned, Ashford, Kent
	ML427	VS361 Spitfire IX (6457M) [HK-A]	Thinktank, Birmingham, Warks
	ML796	Short S25 Sunderland V [NS-F]	IWM Duxford, Cambs
	ML824	Short S25 Sunderland V [NS-Z]	RAF Museum, Hendon, Gtr London
	MN235	Hawker Typhoon Ib [I8-T]	RAF Museum, Hendon, Gtr London
	MP425	Airspeed AS10 Oxford I (G-AITB) [G]	RAF Museum, Hendon, Gtr London
	MS902	Miles M25 Martinet TT1 (TF-SHC)	Museum of Berkshire Aviation, Woodley, Berks
	MS968	Auster AOP5 (G-ALYG)	Privately owned, Old Sarum, Wilts
	MT166	Auster AOP5 (G-BICD)	Privately owned, South Scarle, Notts
MT182	Auster J/1 Autocrat (G-AJDY)	Privately owned, Spanhoe, Northants
	MT197	Auster IV (G-ANHS)	Privately owned, Spanhoe, Northants
	MT438	Auster III (G-AREI)	Privately owned, Eggesford, Devon
	MT818	VS502 Spitfire T8 (G-AIDN)	Privately owned, Biggin Hill, Kent
MT928	VS359 Spitfire HF VIIIc (G-BKMI/MV154/AR654) [ZX-M]	Privately owned, Duxford, Cambs
MV268	VS379 Spitfire FR XIVe (MV293/G-SPIT) [JE-J]	Privately owned, Duxford, Cambs
	MW401	Hawker Tempest II (IAF HA604/G-PEST)	Privately owned, Sywell, Northants
	MW810	Hawker Tempest II (IAF HA591) <ff>	Privately owned, Bentwaters, Suffolk
NF314	GEC Phoenix (BAPC.408)	Army, Larkhill, Wilts, on display
	NF370	Fairey Swordfish III [NH-L]	IWM Duxford, Cambs
	NF389	Fairey Swordfish III	RN, Yeovilton, Somerset
	NH238	VS361 Spitfire LF IXe (G-MKIX) [D-A]	Privately owned, stored Greenham Common, Berks
	NH341	VS509 Spitfire T9 (G-CICK) [DB-E]	Privately owned, Headcorn, Kent
	NJ633	Auster 5D (G-AKXP)	Privately owned, Old Sarum, Wilts
	NJ673	Auster 5D (G-AOCR)	Privately owned, Wisbech, Cambs
	NJ689	Auster AOP5 (G-ALXZ)	Privately owned, Breighton, E. Yorks
	NJ695	Auster AOP5 (G-AJXV)	Privately owned, Boarhunt, Hants

Serial	Type (code/other identity)	Owner/operator, location or fate	Notes
NJ703	Auster AOP5 (TJ207/G-AKPI) [P]	Privately owned, Wickenby, Lincs	
NJ719	Auster AOP5 (TW385/G-ANFU)	Thorpe Camp Preservation Group, Lincs	
NJ728	Auster AOP5 (G-AIKE)	Privately owned, Sandown, IOW	
NJ889	Auster AOP3 (G-AHLK)	Privately owned, Ledbury, Herefordshire	
NL750	DH82A Tiger Moth II (T7997/G-AOBH)	Privately owned, Henstridge, Somerset	
NL846	DH82A Tiger Moth I (F-BGEQ)	Brooklands Museum, Weybridge, Surrey (stored)	
NL985	DH82A Tiger Moth I (G-BWIK/7015M)	Privately owned, Oaksey Park, Wilts	
NM138	DH82A Tiger Moth I (G-ANEW) [41]	Privately owned, Henstridge, Somerset	
NM181	DH82A Tiger Moth I (G-AZGZ)	Privately owned, Rush Green, Gtr London	
NP294	Percival P31 Proctor IV [TB-M]	Lincolnshire Avn Heritage Centre, E Kirkby, Lincs	
NV778	Hawker Tempest TT5 (8386M)	RAF Museum, Hendon, Gtr London	
NS710	DH98 Mosquito TT35 (TJ118) <ff>	Victoria and Albert Museum, Knightsbridge, London	
NX534	Auster III (G-BUDL)	Privately owned, Spanhoe, Northants	
NX611	Avro 683 Lancaster B VII (G-ASXX/8375M) [DX-F,LE-H]	Lincolnshire Avn Heritage Centre, E Kirkby, Lincs	
PA474	Avro 683 Lancaster B I [AR-L,VN-T]	RAF BBMF, Coningsby, Lincs	
PD130	Avro 683 Lancaster B I <R> (fuselage) (BAPC.482)	Boscombe Down Aviation Collection, Old Sarum, Wilts	
PD685	Slingsby T7 Cadet TX1 (BAPC.355)	Tettenhall Transport Heritage Centre, W. Midlands	
PF179	HS Gnat T1 (XR541/8602M)	Privately owned, North Weald, Essex	
PG657	DH82A Tiger Moth II (G-AGPK)	Privately owned, Clacton/Duxford	
PG712	DH82A Tiger Moth II (PH-CSL) [2]	Privately owned, Hilversum, The Netherlands	
PK519	VS356 Spitfire F22 [G-SPXX]	Privately owned, Newport Pagnell, Bucks	
PK624	VS356 Spitfire F22 (8072M)	The Fighter Collection, Duxford, Cambs	
PK664	VS356 Spitfire F22 (7759M) [V6-B]	Kennet Aviation, Sandown, IOW	
PK683	VS356 Spitfire F24 (7150M)	Solent Sky, Southampton, Hants	
PK724	VS356 Spitfire F24 (7288M)	RAF Museum, Hendon, Gtr London	
PL258	VS361 Spitfire IX (G-NSFS)	Norwegian Spitfire Foundation, Duxford (restoration)	
PL279	VS361 Spitfire IX <R> (N3317/BAPC.268) [ZF-Z] (marked MK464 [Y2-Y] on port side)	Privately owned, Newquay, Cornwall (stored)	
PL788	Supermarine Aircraft Spitfire 26 (G-CIEN)	Privately owned, Perth, Scotland	
PL793	Supermarine Aircraft Spitfire 26 (G-CIXM)	Privately owned, Popham, Hants	
PL904	VS365 Spitfire PR XI <R> (EN343/BAPC.226)	RAF Benson, Oxon, on display	
PL965	VS365 Spitfire PR XI (G-MKXI) [R]	Hangar 11 Collection, North Weald, Essex	
PL983	VS365 Spitfire PR XI (G-PRXI)	The Aircraft Restoration Co, Duxford, Cambs	
PM631	VS390 Spitfire PR XIX	RAF BBMF, Coningsby, Lincs	
PM651	VS390 Spitfire PR XIX (7758M) [X]	Michael Beetham Conservation Centre, RAFM Cosford	
PN323	HP Halifax VII <ff>	IWM Duxford, Cambs	
PP566	Fairey Firefly I <rf>	Privately owned, Newton Abbott, Devon	
PP972	VS358 Seafire LF IIIc (G-BUAR) [11-5/N]	Privately owned, Stonesfield, Oxon	
PR005	General Atomics Protector RG1	RAF	
PR478	Supermarine Aircraft Spitfire 26 [S]	Privately owned, Dunkeswell, Devon	
PR533	Hawker Tempest II (MW763/IAF HA586/G-TEMT) [5R-V]	Anglia Aircraft Restorations Ltd, Sywell, Northants	
PR536	Hawker Tempest II (IAF HA457)[OQ-H]	Michael Beetham Conservation Centre, RAFM Cosford, Shropshire	
PS004	Airbus Zephyr 8B	For MOD	
PS853	VS390 Spitfire PR XIX (G-RRGN) [C]	Rolls-Royce, East Midlands, Leics	
PS890	VS390 Spitfire PR XIX (F-AZJS) [UM-E]	Privately owned, Dijon, France	
PS915	VS390 Spitfire PR XIX (7548M/7711M)	RAF BBMF, Coningsby, Lincs	
PT462	VS509 Spitfire T9 (G-CTIX/N462JC) [SW-A]	Privately owned, Caernarfon/Duxford	
PT462	VS361 Spitfire IX <R> (BAPC.318) [SW-A]	Privately owned, Moffat, Scotland	
PV144	VS361 Spitfire IX <R> (BAPC.581) [4D-A]	Privately owned, Carlisle, Cumbria	
PV202	VS509 Spitfire T9 (H-98/W3632/G-CCCA) [5R-H]	Historic Flying Ltd, Duxford, Cambs	
PV303	Supermarine Aircraft Spitfire 26 (G-CCJL) [ON-B]	Privately owned, Enstone, Oxon	
PZ460	BBC Mosquito (F-PMOZ) [NE-K]	Crashed and written off, 2015	
PZ865	Hawker Hurricane IIc (G-AMAU) [ZY-V]	RAF BBMF, Coningsby, Lincs	
RA848	Slingsby T7 Cadet TX1 <ff>	Privately owned, Hooton Park, Cheshire	
RA854	Slingsby T7 Cadet TX1	Yorkshire Air Museum, Elvington, N. Yorks	
RA897	Slingsby T7 Cadet TX1	Newark Air Museum, Winthorpe, Notts	
RA905	Slingsby T7 Cadet TX1 (BGA1143) [BQE]	Trenchard Museum, RAF Halton, Bucks	

Notes	Serial	Type (code/other identity)	Owner/operator, location or fate
	RB142	Supermarine Aircraft Spitfire 26 (G-CEFC) [DW-B]	Privately owned, Popham, Hants
	RB159	VS379 Spitfire F XIV <R> [DW-D]	Privately owned, Delabole, Cornwall
	RB396	Hawker Typhoon IB (G-TIFY) [XP-W] (fuselage)	Hawker Typhoon Preservation Group, Duxford
	RD220	Bristol 156 Beaufighter TF X	National Museum of Flight, stored E Fortune, Scotland
	RD253	Bristol 156 Beaufighter TF X (7931M)	RAF Museum, Hendon, Gtr London
	RF398	Avro 694 Lincoln B II (8376M) [398]	RAF Museum, Cosford, Shropshire
	RG333	Miles M38 Messenger IIA (G-AIEK)	Privately owned, Louth, Lincs
	RG904	VS Spitfire <R> (BAPC.333) [BT-K]	RAF Museum, Cosford, Shropshire
	RG907	Miles M25 Martinet <f> (BAPC.514)	Tettenhall Transport Heritage Centre, W. Midlands
	RH746	Bristol 164 Brigand TF1 (fuselage)	RAF Museum, stored Cosford, Shropshire
	RK838	VS349 Spitfire Vb <R> (BAPC.230/AB550) [GE-P]	Eden Camp Theme Park, Malton, N. Yorks
	RK855	Supermarine Aircraft Spitfire 26 (G-PIXY) [FT-C]	Privately owned, Henstridge, Somerset
	RK858	VS361 Spitfire IX (G-CGJE)	The Aircraft Restoration Co, Duxford, Cambs
	RK912	VS361 Spitfire LF IX (G-CLCS)	Privately owned, Duxford, Cambs
	RL962	DH89A Dominie II (G-AHED)	South Yorkshire Aircraft Museum, Doncaster, S. Yorks
	RM169	Percival P31 Proctor IV (G-ANVY) [4-47]	Privately owned, Kelvedon, Essex
	RM221	Percival P31 Proctor IV (G-ANXR)	Privately owned, Headcorn, Kent
	RM689	VS379 Spitfire F XIV (G-ALGT)	Rolls-Royce, stored East Midlands Airport, Leics
	RM694	VS379 Spitfire F XIV (G-DBKL/6640M)	Privately owned, Biggin Hill, Kent
	RM927	VS379 Spitfire F XIV (G-JNMA/G-SXIV) [X]	W Air Collection, Sywell, Northants
	RN201	VS379 Spitfire F XIVe (G-BSKP)	Privately owned, Duxford, Cambs
	RN203	VS379 Spitfire F XIV (G-CLCT)	Privately owned, Duxford, Cambs
	RN218	Isaacs Spitfire <R> (G-BBJI) [N]	Privately owned, Builth Wells, Powys, Wales
	RP001*	AeroVironment RQ-20 Puma AE Micro UAV	Royal Navy
	RP002*	AeroVironment RQ-12 Wasp AE Micro UAV	Royal Navy
	RP003*	AeroVironment Shrike Mk1 Micro UAV	MOD
	RR232	VS361 Spitfire HF IXc (PV181/G-BRSF)	Privately owned, Goodwood, W. Sussex
	RT486	Auster 5 (G-AJGJ)	RAF Manston History Museum, Kent
	RT520	Auster 5 (G-ALYB)	Thorpe Camp Visitor Centre, Tattershall Thorpe, Lincs
	RT578	Auster AOP5 (G-ALNV)	Privately owned, Dumfries area, Scotland (frame)
	RT610	Auster 5A-160 (G-AKWS)	Privately owned, Shobdon, Herefordshire (restoration)
	RW386	VS361 Spitfire LF XVIe (LN-BSP/6944M) [NG-D]	Privately owned, Angelholm, Sweden
	RW388	VS361 Spitfire LF XVIe (6946M) [U4-U]	Potteries Museum & Art Gallery, Hanley, Staffs
	RX168	VS358 Seafire L IIIc (IAC 157/G-BWEM)	Privately owned, stored Duxford, Cambs
	SL611	VS361 Spitfire LF XVIe (G-SAEA)	Supermarine Aero Engineering, Stoke-on-Trent, Staffs
	SL674	VS361 Spitfire LF IX (8392M) [RAS-H]	RAF Museum Reserve Collection, Stafford, Staffs
	SL721	VS361 Spitfire LF XVIe (OO-XVI) [AU-J]	Privately owned, Brasschaat, Belgium
	SM520	VS509 Spitfire T9 (H-99/G-ILDA) [KJ-I]	Boultbee Flight Academy, Goodwood, W. Sussex
	SM639	VS361 Spitfire LF IXe (G-CKYM)	Privately owned, Godalming, Surrey
	SN280	Hawker Tempest V <f>	South Yorkshire Aircraft Museum, Doncaster, S. Yorks
	SR462	VS377 Seafire F XV (UB415/G-TGVP)	Privately owned, stored Old Warden, Beds
	SR661	Hawker Fury ISS (G-CBEL)	Privately owned, Sywell, Northants
	SX137	VS384 Seafire F XVII	FAA Museum, RNAS Yeovilton, Somerset
	SX300	VS384 Seafire F XVII (G-RIPH)	Kennet Aviation, stored Old Warden, Beds
	SX336	VS384 Seafire F XVII (G-KASX) [105/VL]	Fly Navy Heritage Trust Ltd, Yeovilton, Somerset
	TA122	DH98 Mosquito FB VI [UP-G]	de Havilland Aircraft Museum, London Colney
	TA634	DH98 Mosquito TT35 (G-AWJV) [8K-K]	de Havilland Aircraft Museum, London Colney
	TA639	DH98 Mosquito TT35 (7806M) [AZ-E]	RAF Museum, Cosford, Shropshire
	TA719	DH98 Mosquito TT35 (G-ASKC) [56]	IWM Duxford, Cambs
	TA805	VS361 Spitfire HF IX (G-PMNF) [FX-M]	Privately owned, Biggin Hill, Kent
	TB288	VS361 Spitfire LF IX <R> (MH486/46/BAPC.206) [HT-H]	RAF Museum, Hendon, Gtr London
	TB382	VS361 Spitfire LF XVIe (X4277/MK673)	Airframe Assemblies, Sandown, IOW
	TB675	VS361 Spitfire LF XVIe (RW393/7293M) [4D-V]	RAF Museum, Hendon, Gtr London
	TB752	VS361 Spitfire LF XVIe (8086M) [KH-Z]	RAF Manston, Kent, Memorial Pavilion
	TB885	VS361 Spitfire LF XVIe (G-CKUE/PH-FVE) [3W-V]	Privately owned, Gilze-Rijen, The Netherlands
	TD248	VS361 Spitfire LF XVIe (G-OXVI/7246M) [CR-S]	Spitfire Ltd, Humberside, Lincs
	TD248	VS361 Spitfire LF XVIe (BAPC.368) [8Q-T] (fuselage)	Norfolk & Suffolk Avn Museum, Flixton, Suffolk
	TD314	VS361 Spitfire LF IX (G-CGYJ) [FX-P]	Privately owned, Duxford, Cambs

Serial	Type (code/other identity)	Owner/operator, location or fate	Notes
TE184	VS361 Spitfire LF XVIe (G-MXVI/6850M) [9N-B]	Privately owned, Biggin Hill/Bremgarten, Germany	
TE311	VS361 Spitfire LF XVIe (MK178/7241M) [SZ-G]	RAF BBMF, Biggin Hill, Kent (servicing)	
TE356	VS361 Spitfire LF XVIe (N356TE) [DD-E]	Privately owned, stored Biggin Hill, Kent	
TE462	VS361 Spitfire LF XVIe (7243M)	National Museum of Flight, E Fortune, Scotland	
TE517	VS361 Spitfire LF IXe (G-RYIX) [HL-K]	Privately owned, Biggin Hill, Kent	
TE566	VS509 Spitfire T9 (VH-IXT)	Privately owned, Enstone, Oxon (rebuild)	
TG263	Saro SR A1 (G-12-1)	Solent Sky, Southampton, Hants	
TG511	HP67 Hastings T5 (8554M) [511]	RAF Museum, Cosford, Shropshire	
TG517	HP67 Hastings T5 [517]	Newark Air Museum, Winthorpe, Notts	
TG528	HP67 Hastings C1A [528,T]	IWM Duxford, Cambs	
TJ138	DH98 Mosquito B35 (7607M) [VO-L]	RAF Museum, Hendon, Gtr London	
TJ320	Auster AOP5 (G-ANHW, derelict fuselage)	Privately owned, Walsall area, W. Midlands	
TJ343	Auster AOP5 (G-AJXC)	Privately owned, White Waltham, Berks	
TJ518	Auster J/1 Autocrat (G-AJIH)	Privately owned, Gloucester, Glos	
TJ534	Auster AOP5 (G-AKSY)	Privately owned, West Tisted, Hants	
TJ569	Auster AOP5 (G-AKOW)	Army Flying Museum, Middle Wallop, Hants	
TJ652	Auster AOP5 (TJ565/G-AMVD)	Privately owned, Hardwick, Norfolk	
TJ672	Auster 5D (G-ANIJ) [TS-D]	Privately owned, Netheravon, Wilts	
TK718	GAL59 Hamilcar I (fuselage)	The Tank Museum, Bovington, Dorset	
TK777	GAL59 Hamilcar I (fuselage)	Army Flying Museum, Middle Wallop, Hants	
TP280	VS394 Spitfire FR XVIIIe (D-FSPT) [VS-Z]	Hangar 10 Collection, Heringsdorf, Germany	
TP298	VS394 Spitfire FR XVIII (UM-T]	Airframe Assemblies, Sandown, IOW	
TS291	Slingsby T7 Cadet TX1 (BGA852)	Royal Scottish Mus'm of Flight, stored Granton	
TS798	Avro 685 York C1 (G-AGNV/*MW100*)	RAF Museum, Cosford, Shropshire	
TW439	Auster AOP5 (G-ANRP)	Privately owned, Breighton, E. Yorks	
TW462	Auster AOP5 (G-AOCP, frame)	Privately owned, Dumfries area, Scotland	
TW467	Auster AOP5 (G-ANIE)	Privately owned, Hardwick, Suffolk	
TW477	Auster AOP5 (OY-EFI)	Privately owned, Ringsted, Denmark	
TW501	Auster AOP5 (G-ALBJ)	Privately owned, Dunkeswell, Devon	
TW511	Auster AOP5 (G-APAF)	Privately owned, Chiseldon, Wilts	
TW519	Auster AOP5 (G-ANHX) [ROA-V]	Privately owned, Middlezoy, Somerset	
TW536	Auster AOP6 (G-BNGE/7704M)	Privately owned, Popham, Hants	
TW641	Beagle A61 Terrier 2 (G-ATDN)	Privately owned, Biggin Hill, Kent	
TX176	Avro XIX Anson Series 2 (G-AHKX)	BAE Systems, Old Warden, Beds	
TX213	Avro 652A Anson C19 (G-AWRS)	North-East Land, Sea & Air Museums, Usworth, T&W	
TX214	Avro 652A Anson C19 (7817M)	RAF Museum, Cosford, Shropshire	
TX226	Avro 652A Anson C19 (7865M)	Montrose Air Station Heritage Centre, Scotland	
TX235	Avro 652A Anson C19 (frame)	Avro Heritage Museum, Woodford, Cheshire	
TX310	DH89A Dragon Rapide 6 (G-AIDL)	Privately owned, Clacton/Duxford	
TZ164	Isaacs Spitfire (G-ISAC) [01-A]	Privately owned, Hampstead Norreys, Berks	
VF301	DH100 Vampire F1 (7060M) [RAL-G]	Midland Air Museum, Coventry, Warks	
VF512	Auster 6A (G-ARRX) [PF-M]	Privately owned, Popham, Hants	
VF516	Beagle A61 Terrier 2 (G-ASMZ)	Privately owned, Fowlmere, Cambs	
VF519	Auster AOP6 (G-ASYN)	Privately owned, stored Doncaster area, S. Yorks	
VF526	Auster 6A (G-ARXU) [T]	Privately owned, Strubby , Lincs	
VF530	Auster 6A (G-ARGI) (frame)	South Yorkshire Aircraft Museum, stored Doncaster	
VF557	Auster 6A (G-ARHM) [H]	Privately owned, Headcorn, Kent	
VF581	Beagle A61 Terrier 1 (G-ARSL) [G]	National Museum of Scotland, Edinburgh	
VF631	Auster AOP.(G-ASDK)	Privately owned, Hibaldstow, Lincs	
VF635	Auster AOP6 (G-ARGB)	Privately owned, Hooton Park, Merseyside	
VH127	Fairey Firefly TT4 [200/R]	FAA Museum, stored Cobham Hall, RNAS Yeovilton, Somerset	
VL348	Avro 652A Anson C19 (G-AVVO)	Newark Air Museum, Winthorpe, Notts	
VL349	Avro 652A Anson C19 (N5054/G-AWSA) [V7-Q]	Norfolk & Suffolk Avn Museum, Flixton, Suffolk	
VM325	Avro 652A Anson C19	Privately owned, Carew Cheriton, Pembrokeshire, Wales	
VM360	Avro 652A Anson C19 (G-APHV)	National Museum of Flight, E Fortune, Scotland	
VM657	Slingsby T8 Tutor TX2 (IGA-6)	Privately owned, stored Ashbourne, Eire	
VM684	Slingsby T8 Tutor TX2 (BGA791)	Privately owned, Knutsford, Cheshire	
VM687	Slingsby T8 Tutor (BGA794)	Privately owned, Saltby, Leics	
VN485	VS356 Spitfire F24 (7326M)	IWM Duxford, Cambs	

Notes	Serial	Type (code/other identity)	Owner/operator, location or fate
	VN799	EE Canberra T4 (WJ874/G-CDSX)	Cornwall Aviation Heritage Centre, Newquay
	VP293	Avro 696 Shackleton T4 [X] <ff>	Shackleton Preservation Trust, Coventry, Warks
	VP519	Avro 652A Anson C19 (G-AVVR) <ff>	South Yorkshire Aircraft Museum, Doncaster, S. Yorks
	VP952	DH104 Devon C2 (8820M)	RAF Museum, Cosford, Shropshire
	VP955	DH104 Devon C2 (G-DVON)	Privately owned, stored Wigan, Gtr. Manchester
	VP957	DH104 Devon C2 (8822M) <ff>	No 1137 Sqn ATC, Long Kesh, NI
	VP959	DH104 Devon C2 (N959VP)	Privately owned, stored Compton Verney, Warks
	VP967	DH104 Devon C2 (G-KOOL)	Yorkshire Air Museum, Elvington, N. Yorks
	VP975	DH104 Devon C2 [M]	Science Museum, stored Wroughton, Wilts
	VP981	DH104 Devon C2 (G-DHDV)	Aero Legends, Headcorn/Duxford
	VR137	Westland Wyvern TF1	FAA Museum, stored Cobham Hall, RNAS Yeovilton
	VR192	Percival P40 Prentice T1 (G-APIT)	Romney Marsh Wartime Collection, Kent
	VR249	Percival P40 Prentice T1 (G-APIY) [FA-EL]	Newark Air Museum, Winthorpe, Notts
	VR259	Percival P40 Prentice T1 (G-APJB) [M]	Privately owned, Postling, Kent
	VR930	Hawker Sea Fury FB11 (G-CLNJ/8382M) [110/Q]	Fly Navy Heritage Trust, Yeovilton, Somerset
	VS356	Percival P40 Prentice T1 (G-AOLU)	Privately owned, Fordoun, Aberdeenshire, Scotland
	VS562	Avro 652A Anson T21 (8012M) <ff>	Shannon Aviation Museum, Eire
	VS610	Percival P40 Prentice T1 (G-AOKL)[K-L]	Privately owned, Fordoun, Aberdeenshire
	VS618	Percival P40 Prentice T1 (G-AOLK)	RAF Museum Reserve Collection, Stafford, Staffs
	VS623	Percival P40 Prentice T1 (G-AOKZ)[KQ-F]	Midland Air Museum, Coventry, Warks
	VT812	DH100 Vampire F3 (7200M) [N]	RAF Museum, Hendon, Gtr London
	VT935	Boulton Paul P111A (VT769)	Midland Air Museum, Coventry, Warks
	VT987	Auster AOP6 (G-BKXP)	Privately owned, Thruxton, Hants
	VV106	Supermarine 510 (7175M)	FAA Museum, stored Cobham Hall, RNAS Yeovilton
	VV217	DH100 Vampire FB5 (7323M)	de Havilland Aircraft Museum, stored London Colney
	VV400	EoN Olympia 2 (BGA1697) [97]	Privately owned, Aston Down, Glos
	VV401	EoN Olympia 2 (BGA1125) [99]	Privately owned, Ringmer, E. Sussex
	VV901	Avro 652A Anson T21	Yorkshire Air Museum, Elvington, N. Yorks
	VW453	Gloster Meteor T7 (8703M)	Jet Age Museum, Gloucestershire Airport, Glos
	VW957	DH103 Sea Hornet NF21 <rf>	Privately owned, Chelmsford, Essex
	VW993	Beagle A61 Terrier 2 (G-ASCD)	Yorkshire Air Museum, Elvington, N. Yorks
	VX113	Auster AOP6 (G-ARNO) [36]	Privately owned, St. Athan, Wales (dismantled)
	VX185	EE Canberra B(I)8 (7631M) <ff>	National Museum of Flight, E. Fortune, Scotland
	VX250	DH103 Sea Hornet NF21 [48] <rf>	de Havilland Aircraft Museum, London Colney
	VX272	Hawker P.1052 (7174M)	FAA Museum, stored RNAS Yeovilton, Somerset
	VX275	Slingsby T21B Sedbergh TX1 (BGA572/8884M)	The Helicopter Museum, Weston-Super-Mare, Somerset
	VX281	Hawker Sea Fury T20S (G-BCOW) [120/VL]	The Fighter Collection, Duxford, Cambs (wreck)
	VX573	Vickers Valetta C2 (8389M)	RAF Museum, stored Cosford, Shropshire
	VX580	Vickers Valetta C2 [580]	Norfolk & Suffolk Avn Museum, Flixton, Suffolk
	VX595	WS51 Dragonfly HR1	FAA Museum, RNAS Yeovilton, Somerset
	VX653	Hawker Sea Fury FB11 (G-BUCM)	The Fighter Collection, Duxford, Cambs
	VX665	Hawker Sea Fury FB11 <rf>	RN Historic Flight, at BAE Systems Brough, E. Yorks
	VX926	Auster T7 (G-ASKJ)	Privately owned, Gamlingay, Cambs
	VX927	Auster T7 (G-ASYG)	Privately owned, Dubová, Slovakia
	VZ193	DH100 Vampire FB5 <ff>	Privately owned, Warrington, Cheshire
	VZ440	Gloster Meteor F8 (WA984) [X]	Yorkshire Air Museum, Elvington, N. Yorks
	VZ477	Gloster Meteor F8 (7741M) <ff>	Midland Air Museum, Coventry, Warks
	VZ568	Gloster Meteor F8 [C](7261M) <ff>	RAF Halton, Bucks
	VZ608	Gloster Meteor FR9	Newark Air Museum, Winthorpe, Notts
	VZ634	Gloster Meteor T7 (8657M)	Newark Air Museum, Winthorpe, Notts
	VZ638	Gloster Meteor T7 (G-JETM) [HF]	Gatwick Aviation Museum, Charlwood, Surrey
	VZ728	RS4 Desford Trainer (G-AGOS)	Newark Air Museum, Winthorpe, Notts
	WA123	DH100 Vampire FB6 (J-1196/VZ305/LN-DHY) [R-A]	Norwegian AF Historical Sqn, Rygge, Norway
	WA346	DH100 Vampire FB5	RAF Museum, stored Cosford, Shropshire
	WA473	VS Attacker F1 [102/J]	FAA Museum, RNAS Yeovilton, Somerset
	WA576	Bristol 171 Sycamore 3 (G-ALSS/7900M)	Dumfries & Galloway Avn Mus, Dumfries, Scotland
	WA577	Bristol 171 Sycamore 3 (G-ALST/7718M)	Boscombe Down Aviation Collection, Old Sarum, Wilts
	WA630	Gloster Meteor T7 [69] <ff>	Robertsbridge Aviation Society, Newhaven
	WA634	Gloster Meteor T7/8	Long Kesh Museum, Co. Antrim, NI
	WA638	Gloster Meteor T7(mod) (G-JWMA)	Martin-Baker Aircraft, Chalgrove, Oxon
	WA662	Gloster Meteor T7	South Yorkshire Aircraft Museum, Doncaster, S. Yorks

Serial	Type (code/other identity)	Owner/operator, location or fate	Notes
WB188	Hawker Hunter F3 (7154M)	Tangmere Military Aviation Museum, W. Sussex	
WB188	Hawker Hunter GA11 (XF300/G-BZPC)	Privately owned, Kent	
WB440	Fairey Firefly AS6 <ff>	Privately owned, Newton Abbott, Devon	
WB491	Avro 706 Ashton 2 (TS897/G-AJJW) <ff>	Newark Air Museum, Winthorpe	
WB549	DHC1 Chipmunk 22A (G-BAPB)	Privately owned, Audley End, Cambs	
WB555	DHC1 Chipmunk 22 (G-CLKX)	Privately owned, Henstridge, Kent	
WB560	DHC1 Chipmunk T10 (comp WG403) <ff>	Privately owned, Norwich, Norfolk	
WB565	DHC1 Chipmunk 22 (G-PVET) [X]	Privately owned, Rendcomb, Glos	
WB569	DHC1 Chipmunk 22 (G-BYSJ)	Privately owned, Turweston, Bucks	
WB571	DHC1 Chipmunk 22 (D-EOSF) [34]	Privately owned, Porta Westfalica, Germany	
WB584	DHC1 Chipmunk T10 (comp WG303/7706M)	Solway Aviation Museum, Carlisle, Cumbria	
WB585	DHC1 Chipmunk 22 (G-AOSY) [28]	Privately owned, Audley End, Essex	
WB588	DHC1 Chipmunk 22 (G-AOTD) [D]	Privately owned, Henstridge, Somerset	
WB615	DHC1 Chipmunk 22 (G-BXIA) [E]	Privately owned, Blackpool, Lancs	
WB624	DHC1 Chipmunk T10	Newark Air Museum, Winthorpe, Notts	
WB626	DHC1 Chipmunk T10 [19] <ff>	Trenchard Museum, RAF Halton, Bucks	
WB627	DHC1 Chipmunk T10 (9248M) (fuselage) [N]	Dulwich College CCF, Gtr London	
WB652	DHC1 Chipmunk 22 (G-CHPY) [V]	Privately owned, stored Cricklade, Wilts	
WB654	DHC1 Chipmunk 22 (G-BXGO) [U]	Privately owned, Finmere, Oxon	
WB657	DHC1 Chipmunk T10 (G-CNVH) [908]	Naval Aviation Ltd, Yeovilton, Somerset	
WB670	DHC1 Chipmunk T10 (comp WG303/8361M)	Privately owned, stored Carlisle, Cumbria	
WB671	DHC1 Chipmunk 22 (G-BWTG) [910]	Privately owned, Teuge, The Netherlands	
WB685	DHC1 Chipmunk T10 (comp WP969/G-ATHC)	North-East Land, Sea & Air Museums, stored Usworth, T&W	
WB697	DHC1 Chipmunk 22 (G-BXCT) [95]	Privately owned, Antwerp, Belgium	
WB702	DHC1 Chipmunk 22A (G-AOFE)	Privately owned, Goodwood, W. Sussex	
WB703	DHC1 Chipmunk 22A (G-ARMC)	Privately owned, Booker, Bucks	
WB711	DHC1 Chipmunk 22 (G-APPM)	Privately owned, Jersey, CI	
WB726	DHC1 Chipmunk 22A (G-AOSK) [E]	Privately owned, Turweston, Bucks	
WB733	DHC1 Chipmunk T10 (comp WG422)	South Yorkshire Aircraft Museum, Doncaster, S. Yorks	
WB763	DHC1 Chipmunk 22 (G-BBMR) [K]	Privately owned, Turweston, Bucks	
WB922	Slingsby T21B Sedbergh TX1 (BGA4366)	Privately owned, Nympsfield, Glos	
WB924	Slingsby T21B Sedbergh TX1 (BGA3901)	Privately owned, Bicester, Oxon	
WB944	Slingsby T21B Sedbergh TX1 (BGA3160)	Privately owned, Bicester, Oxon	
WB945	Slingsby T21B Sedbergh TX1 (BGA1254) [BUW]	Privately owned, stored RAF Halton, Bucks	
WB971	Slingsby T21B Sedbergh TX1 (BGA3324)	Privately owned, Eaglescott, Devon	
WB975	Slingsby T21B Sedbergh TX1 (BGA3288) [FJB]	Privately owned, Atkar, Hungary	
WB980	Slingsby T21B Sedbergh TX1 (BGA3290)	Privately owned, Husbands Bosworth, Leics	
WB981	Slingsby T21B Sedbergh TX1 (BGA3238)	Privately owned, Eaglescott, Devon	
WD286	DHC1 Chipmunk 22 (G-BBND)	Privately owned, Old Warden, Beds	
WD292	DHC1 Chipmunk 22 (G-BCRX)	Privately owned, White Waltham, Berks	
WD293	DHC1 Chipmunk T10 (7645M) <ff>	Privately owned, Evesham, Worcs	
WD310	DHC1 Chipmunk 22 (G-BWUN) [B]	Privately owned, Jersey, CI	
WD319	DHC1 Chipmunk 22 (F-AYDC)	Privately owned, Vannes-Meucon, France	
WD321	DHC1 Chipmunk 22 (G-BDCC)	Boscombe Down Aviation Collection, Old Sarum, Wilts	
WD325	DHC1 Chipmunk T10 (G-CLWK) [N]	Historic Army Aircraft Flight, Middle Wallop, Hants	
WD331	DHC1 Chipmunk 22 (G-BXDH)	Privately owned, Farnborough, Hants	
WD355	DHC1 Chipmunk T10 (WD335/G-CBAJ)	Privately owned, Eastleigh, Hants	
WD363	DHC1 Chipmunk 22 (G-BCIH) [5]	Privately owned, Netheravon, Wilts	
WD370	DHC1 Chipmunk T10 <ff>	No 225 Sqn ATC, Brighton, W. Sussex	
WD373	DHC1 Chipmunk 22 (G-BXDI) [12]	Privately owned, Turweston, Bucks	
WD377	DHC1 Chipmunk T10 <ff>	Wings Museum, Balcombe, W Sussex	
WD386	DHC1 Chipmunk T10 (comp WD377)	Ulster Aviation Soc, stored Upper Ballinderry, NI	
WD388	DHC1 Chipmunk 22 (D-EPAK) [68]	Privately owned, Prague/Kbely, Czech Republic	
WD390	DHC1 Chipmunk 22 (G-BWNK) [68]	Privately owned, Compton Abbas, Dorset	
WD413	Avro 652A Anson T21 (7881M/G-VROE)	Privately owned, Sleap, Shropshire	
WD615	Gloster Meteor TT20 (WD646/8189M) [R]	RAF Manston History Museum, Kent	
WD686	Gloster Meteor NF11	RAF Defford Museum, Croome Park, Worcs	
WD790	Gloster Meteor NF11 (8743M) <ff>	Boscombe Down Aviation Collection, Old Sarum, Wilts	
WD889	Fairey Firefly AS5 (comp VT809)	Privately owned, Newton Abbot, Devon	
WD935	EE Canberra B2 (8440M) <ff>	South Yorkshire Aircraft Museum, Doncaster, S. Yorks	
WD954	EE Canberra B2 <ff>	Privately owned, St. Columb Major, Cornwall	

Notes	Serial	Type (code/other identity)	Owner/operator, location or fate
	WD956	EE Canberra B2 <ff>	RAF Defford Museum, Croome Park, Worcs
	WE113	EE Canberra B2 <ff>	Privately owned, Tangmere, W. Sussex
	WE122	EE Canberra TT18 [845] <ff>	Blyth Valley Aviation Collection, Walpole, Suffolk
	WE139	EE Canberra PR3 (8369M)	RAF Museum, Hendon, Gtr London
	WE168	EE Canberra PR3 (8049M) <ff>	Norfolk & Suffolk Avn Museum, Flixton, Suffolk
	WE173	EE Canberra PR3 (8740M) <ff>	Robertsbridge Aviation Society, Mayfield, E. Sussex
	WE188	EE Canberra T4	Solway Aviation Society, Carlisle, Cumbria
	WE191	EE Canberra T4 (Indian AF Q497) <ff>	Stoneykirk Aviation Museum, D&G, Scotland
	WE192	EE Canberra T4 <ff>	Blyth Valley Aviation Collection, Walpole, Suffolk
	WE275	DH112 Venom FB50 (J-1601/G-VIDI)	BAE Systems Hawarden, Fire Section, Flintshire, Wales
	WE536	Auster T7 (G-ARTM)	Privately owned, Hooton Park, Merseyside
	WE558	Auster T7 (frame)	East Midlands Airport Aeropark, Leics
	WE569	Auster T7 (G-ASAJ)	Privately owned, Defford, Bucks
	WE570	Auster T7 (G-ASBU)	Privately owned, Stonehaven, Scotland
	WE591	Auster T7 (F-AZTJ)	Privately owned, Hassfurt, Germany
	WE600	Auster T7 Antarctic (7602M)	Midland Air Museum, Coventry, Warks
	WE724	Hawker Sea Fury FB11 (VX653/G-BUCM) [062]	The Fighter Collection, Duxford, Cambs
	WE982	Slingsby T30B Prefect TX1 (8781M)	RAF Museum, stored Cosford, Shropshire
	WE987	Slingsby T30B Prefect TX1 (BGA2517)	South Yorkshire Aircraft Museum, Doncaster, S. Yorks
	WE990	Slingsby T30B Prefect TX1 (BGA2583)	Privately owned, Tibenham, Norfolk
	WE992	Slingsby T30B Prefect TX1 (BGA2692)	Privately owned, stored Nympsfield, Glos
	WF118	Percival P57 Sea Prince T1 (G-DACA) [569/CU]	Privately owned, St Athan, Wales
	WF122	Percival P57 Sea Prince T1 [575/CU]	Ulster Aviation Society, Long Kesh, NI
	WF128	Percival P57 Sea Prince T1 (8611M)	Norfolk & Suffolk Avn Museum, Flixton, Suffolk
	WF145	Hawker Sea Hawk F1 <ff>	Privately owned, Newton Abbot, Devon
	WF219	Hawker Sea Hawk F1 <rf>	FAA Museum, stored Cobham Hall, RNAS Yeovilton, Somerset
	WF225	Hawker Sea Hawk F1 [CU]	RNAS Culdrose, Cornwall, at main gate
	WF259	Hawker Sea Hawk F2 [171/A]	National Museum of Flight, E Fortune, Scotland
	WF369	Vickers Varsity T1 [F]	Newark Air Museum, Winthorpe, Notts
	WF372	Vickers Varsity T1	Brooklands Museum, Weybridge, Surrey
	WF408	Vickers Varsity T1 (8395M) <ff>	Privately owned, Ashford, Kent
	WF643	Gloster Meteor F8 [F]	Norfolk & Suffolk Avn Museum, Flixton, Suffolk
	WF784	Gloster Meteor T7 (7895M)	South Wales Aviation Museum, St Athan, Wales
	WF825	Gloster Meteor T7 (8359M) [X]	Montrose Air Station Heritage Centre, Scotland
	WF911	EE Canberra B2 [CO] <ff>	Ulster Aviation Society, Long Kesh, NI
	WF922	EE Canberra PR3	Midland Air Museum, Coventry, Warks
	WG303	DHC1 Chipmunk T10 (8208M) <ff> [83]	Privately owned, Hooton Park, Cheshire
	WG308	DHC1 Chipmunk 22 (G-BYHL) [8]	Privately owned, Averham, Notts
	WG316	DHC1 Chipmunk 22 (G-BCAH) [22]	Privately owned, Gamston, Notts
	WG319	DHC1 Chipmunk T10 <ff>	Privately owned, Blandford Forum, Dorset
	WG321	DHC1 Chipmunk 22 (G-DHCC)	Privately owned, Wevelgem, Belgium
	WG322	DHC1 Chipmunk 22A (G-ARMF) [H]	Privately owned, Spanhoe, Northants
	WG348	DHC1 Chipmunk 22 (G-BBMV)	Boultbee Flight Academy, Goodwood, W. Sussex
	WG350	DHC1 Chipmunk 22 (G-BPAL)	Privately owned, Portimao, Portugal
	WG362	DHC1 Chipmunk T10 (8437M/8630M/*WX643*) <ff>	No 2523 Sqn ATC, Linton, Cambs
	WG407	DHC1 Chipmunk 22 (G-BWMX) [67]	Privately owned, Fen End Farm, Cambs
	WG418	DHC1 Chipmunk T10 (8209M/G-ATDY) <ff>	No 1940 Sqn ATC, Levenshulme, Gtr Manchester
	WG419	DHC1 Chipmunk T10 (8206M) <ff>	Sywell Aviation Museum, Northants
	WG422	DHC1 Chipmunk 22 (8394M/G-BFAX) [16]	Privately owned, Egginton, Derbys
	WG432	DHC1 Chipmunk T10 [L]	Army Flying Museum, Middle Wallop, Hants
	WG458	DHC1 Chipmunk 22 (N458BG/G-CLLI) [2]	Privately owned, Eshott, Northumberland
	WG465	DHC1 Chipmunk 22 (G-BCEY)	Privately owned, Kidlington, Oxon
	WG471	DHC1 Chipmunk T10 (8210M) <ff>	Privately owned, Yateley, Hants
	WG472	DHC1 Chipmunk 22A (G-AOTY)	Privately owned, Bryngwyn Bach, Clwyd, Wales
	WG477	DHC1 Chipmunk T10 (8362M/G-ATDP) <ff>	RAF Scampton Heritage Centre, Lincs
	WG479	DHC1 Chipmunk 22 (F-AZLO/G-CMFC) [F]	Privately owned, Eshott, Northumberland
	WG486	DHC1 Chipmunk T10 [E]	RAF BBMF, Coningsby, Lincs
	WG498	Slingsby T21B Sedbergh TX1 (BGA3245)	Privately owned, Aston Down, Glos

Serial	Type (code/other identity)	Owner/operator, location or fate	Notes
WG511	Avro 696 Shackleton T4 (fuselage)	Flambards Village Theme Park, Helston, Cornwall	
WG599	Hawker Sea Fury FB11 (G-SEAF) [161/R]	The Fighter Collection, Reno, Nevada, USA	
WG655	Hawker Sea Fury T20 (G-INVN) [910/GN]	Privately owned, Duxford, Cambs (damaged)	
WG719	WS51 Dragonfly HR5 (G-BRMA)	The Helicopter Museum, Weston-super-Mare, Somerset	
WG724	WS51 Dragonfly HR5 [932/LM]	North-East Land, Sea & Air Museums, Usworth, T&W	
WG751	WS51 Dragonfly HR5 [710/GJ]	World Naval Base, Chatham, Kent	
WG760	EE P1A (7755M)	RAF Museum, Cosford, Shropshire	
WG763	EE P1A (7816M)	Boscombe Down Aviation Collection, Old Sarum, Wilts	
WG768	Short SB5 (8005M)	RAF Museum, Cosford, Shropshire	
WG774	BAC 221	Science Museum, at FAA Museum, RNAS Yeovilton, Somerset	
WG777	Fairey FD2 (7986M)	RAF Museum, Cosford, Shropshire	
WG789	EE Canberra B2/6 <ff>	Norfolk & Suffolk Avn Museum, Flixton, Suffolk	
WH132	Gloster Meteor T7 (7906M) [J]	Privately owned, Hooton Park, Cheshire	
WH166	Gloster Meteor T7 (8052M) [A]	Privately owned, Birlingham, Worcs	
WH291	Gloster Meteor F8	Privately owned, Liverpool Airport, Merseyside	
WH301	Gloster Meteor F8 (7930M) [T]	RAF Museum, Hendon, Gtr London	
WH364	Gloster Meteor F8 (8169M)	Jet Age Museum, Gloucestershire Airport, Glos	
WH453	Gloster Meteor F8	Bentwaters Cold War Air Museum, Suffolk	
WH646	EE Canberra T17A <ff>	Midland Air Museum, Coventry, Warks	
WH657	EE Canberra B2 <ff>	Romney Marsh Wartime Collection , Kent	
WH725	EE Canberra B2	IWM Duxford, Cambs	
WH734	EE Canberra B2(mod) <ff>	Privately owned, Pershore, Worcs	
WH739	EE Canberra B2 <ff>	No 2475 Sqn ATC, Ammanford, Dyfed, Wales	
WH740	EE Canberra T17 (8762M) [K]	East Midlands Airport Aeropark, Leics	
WH775	EE Canberra PR7 (8128M/8868M) <ff>	Privately owned, Welshpool, Wales	
WH779	EE Canberra PR7 <ff>	South Yorkshire Aircraft Museum, Doncaster, S. Yorks	
WH779	EE Canberra PR7 [BP] <rf>	RAF AM&SU, stored Shawbury, Shropshire	
WH792	EE Canberra PR7 (WH791/8165M/8176M/8187M)	Newark Air Museum, Winthorpe, Notts	
WH798	EE Canberra PR7 (8130M) <ff>	Suffolk Aviation Heritage Centre, Foxhall Heath	
WH840	EE Canberra T4 (8350M)	Privately owned, Flixton, Suffolk	
WH846	EE Canberra T4	Yorkshire Air Museum, Elvington, N. Yorks	
WH850	EE Canberra T4 <ff>	RAF Marham Aviation Heritage Centre, Norfolk	
WH863	EE Canberra T17 (8693M) <ff>	Newark Air Museum, Winthorpe, Notts	
WH876	EE Canberra B2(mod) <ff>	Boscombe Down Aviation Collection, Old Sarum, Wilts	
WH887	EE Canberra TT18 [847] <ff>	Sywell Aviation Museum, Northants	
WH903	EE Canberra B2 <ff>	Yorkshire Air Museum, Elvington, N. Yorks	
WH904	EE Canberra T19	Newark Air Museum, Winthorpe, Notts	
WH953	EE Canberra B6(mod) <ff>	Blyth Valley Aviation Collection, Walpole, Suffolk	
WH957	EE Canberra E15 (8869M) <ff>	Lincolnshire Avn Heritage Centre, East Kirkby, Lincs	
WH960	EE Canberra B15 (8344M) <ff>	Rolls-Royce Heritage Trust, Derby, Derbyshire	
WH964	EE Canberra E15 (8870M) <ff>	Privately owned, Lewes, E. Sussex	
WH984	EE Canberra B15 (8101M) <ff>	City of Norwich Aviation Museum, Norfolk	
WH991	WS51 Dragonfly HR3	Yorkshire Helicopter Preservation Group, Elvington, N. Yorks	
WJ231	Hawker Sea Fury FB11 (*WE726*) [115/O]	FAA Museum, RNAS Yeovilton, Somerset	
WJ306	Slingsby T21B Sedbergh TX1 (BGA3240)	*To BGA3240*	
WJ306	Slingsby T21B Sedbergh TX1 (WB957/BGA2720)	Privately owned, Parham Park, W. Sussex	
WJ358	Auster AOP6 (G-ARYD)	Army Flying Museum, Middle Wallop, Hants	
WJ368	Auster AOP6 (G-ASZX)	Privately owned, Eggesford, Devon	
WJ404	Auster AOP6 (G-ASOI)	Privately owned, Bidford-on-Avon, Warks	
WJ476	Vickers Valetta T3 <ff>	South Yorkshire Aircraft Museum, Doncaster, S. Yorks	
WJ565	EE Canberra T17 (8871M) <ff>	South Yorkshire Aircraft Museum, Doncaster, S. Yorks	
WJ567	EE Canberra B2 <ff>	Privately owned, Houghton, Cambs	
WJ576	EE Canberra T17 <ff>	Tettenhall Transport Heritage Centre, W. Midlands	
WJ633	EE Canberra T17 <ff>	City of Norwich Aviation Museum, Norfolk	
WJ639	EE Canberra TT18 [39]	North-East Land, Sea & Air Museums, Usworth, T&W	
WJ677	EE Canberra B2 <ff>	Privately owned, Redruth, Cornwall	
WJ721	EE Canberra TT18 [21] <ff>	Moravvia, Kinloss, Scotland	
WJ731	EE Canberra B2T [BK] <ff>	Privately owned, Golders Green, Gtr London	

Notes	Serial	Type (code/other identity)	Owner/operator, location or fate
	WJ775	EE Canberra B6 (8581M) <ff>	Privately owned, stored Farnborough, Hants
	WJ865	EE Canberra T4 <ff>	Boscombe Down Aviation Collection, Old Sarum, Wilts
	WJ880	EE Canberra T4 (8491M) <ff>	Dumfries & Galloway Avn Mus, Dumfries, Scotland
	WJ903	Vickers Varsity T1 <ff>	South Yorkshire Aircraft Museum, Doncaster, S. Yorks
	WJ945	Vickers Varsity T1 (G-BEDV)	Cornwall Aviation Heritage Centre, Newquay, Cornwall
	WJ975	EE Canberra T19 <ff>	South Yorkshire Aircraft Museum, Doncaster, S. Yorks
	WJ992	EE Canberra T4 <ff>	Privately owned, St Athan, Wales
	WK001	Thales Watchkeeper 450 RPAS (4X-USC)	Army 47 Regt Royal Artillery, Larkhill, Wilts
	WK002	Thales Watchkeeper 450 RPAS (4X-USD)	Army 47 Regt Royal Artillery, Larkhill, Wilts
	WK003	Thales Watchkeeper 450 RPAS	Army 47 Regt Royal Artillery, Larkhill, Wilts
	WK004	Thales Watchkeeper 450 RPAS	Army 47 Regt Royal Artillery, Larkhill, Wilts
	WK005	Thales Watchkeeper 450 RPAS	Army 47 Regt Royal Artillery, Larkhill, Wilts
	WK007	Thales Watchkeeper 450 RPAS	Army 47 Regt Royal Artillery, Larkhill, Wilts
	WK008	Thales Watchkeeper 450 RPAS	Army 47 Regt Royal Artillery, Larkhill, Wilts
	WK009	Thales Watchkeeper 450 RPAS	Army 47 Regt Royal Artillery, Larkhill, Wilts
	WK010	Thales Watchkeeper 450 RPAS	Army 47 Regt Royal Artillery, Larkhill, Wilts
	WK011	Thales Watchkeeper 450 RPAS	Army 47 Regt Royal Artillery, Larkhill, Wilts
	WK012	Thales Watchkeeper 450 RPAS	Army 47 Regt Royal Artillery, Larkhill, Wilts
	WK013	Thales Watchkeeper 450 RPAS	Army 47 Regt Royal Artillery, Larkhill, Wilts
	WK014	Thales Watchkeeper 450 RPAS	Army 47 Regt Royal Artillery, Larkhill, Wilts
	WK015	Thales Watchkeeper 450 RPAS	Army 47 Regt Royal Artillery, Larkhill, Wilts
	WK016	Thales Watchkeeper 450 RPAS	Army 47 Regt Royal Artillery, Larkhill, Wilts
	WK017	Thales Watchkeeper 450 RPAS	Army 47 Regt Royal Artillery, Larkhill, Wilts
	WK018	Thales Watchkeeper 450 RPAS	Army 47 Regt Royal Artillery, Larkhill, Wilts
	WK019	Thales Watchkeeper 450 RPAS	Army 47 Regt Royal Artillery, Larkhill, Wilts
	WK020	Thales Watchkeeper 450 RPAS	Army 47 Regt Royal Artillery, Larkhill, Wilts
	WK021	Thales Watchkeeper 450 RPAS	Army 47 Regt Royal Artillery, Larkhill, Wilts
	WK022	Thales Watchkeeper 450 RPAS	Army 47 Regt Royal Artillery, Larkhill, Wilts
	WK023	Thales Watchkeeper 450 RPAS	Army 47 Regt Royal Artillery, Larkhill, Wilts
	WK024	Thales Watchkeeper 450 RPAS	Army 47 Regt Royal Artillery, Larkhill, Wilts
	WK025	Thales Watchkeeper 450 RPAS	Army 47 Regt Royal Artillery, Larkhill, Wilts
	WK026	Thales Watchkeeper 450 RPAS	Army 47 Regt Royal Artillery, Larkhill, Wilts
	WK027	Thales Watchkeeper 450 RPAS	Army 47 Regt Royal Artillery, Larkhill, Wilts
	WK028	Thales Watchkeeper 450 RPAS	Army 47 Regt Royal Artillery, Larkhill, Wilts
	WK029	Thales Watchkeeper 450 RPAS	Army 47 Regt Royal Artillery, Larkhill, Wilts
	WK030	Thales Watchkeeper 450 RPAS	Army 47 Regt Royal Artillery, Larkhill, Wilts
	WK032	Thales Watchkeeper 450 RPAS	Army 47 Regt Royal Artillery, Larkhill, Wilts
	WK033	Thales Watchkeeper 450 RPAS	Army 47 Regt Royal Artillery, Larkhill, Wilts
	WK034	Thales Watchkeeper 450 RPAS	Army 47 Regt Royal Artillery, Larkhill, Wilts
	WK035	Thales Watchkeeper 450 RPAS	Army 47 Regt Royal Artillery, Larkhill, Wilts
	WK036	Thales Watchkeeper 450 RPAS	Army 47 Regt Royal Artillery, Larkhill, Wilts
	WK037	Thales Watchkeeper 450 RPAS	Army 47 Regt Royal Artillery, Larkhill, Wilts
	WK038	Thales Watchkeeper 450 RPAS	Army 47 Regt Royal Artillery, Larkhill, Wilts
	WK039	Thales Watchkeeper 450 RPAS	Army 47 Regt Royal Artillery, Larkhill, Wilts
	WK040	Thales Watchkeeper 450 RPAS	Army 47 Regt Royal Artillery, Larkhill, Wilts
	WK041	Thales Watchkeeper 450 RPAS	Army 47 Regt Royal Artillery, Larkhill, Wilts
	WK044	Thales Watchkeeper 450 RPAS	Army 47 Regt Royal Artillery, Larkhill, Wilts
	WK045	Thales Watchkeeper 450 RPAS	Army 47 Regt Royal Artillery, Larkhill, Wilts
	WK046	Thales Watchkeeper 450 RPAS	Army 47 Regt Royal Artillery, Larkhill, Wilts
	WK047	Thales Watchkeeper 450 RPAS	Army 47 Regt Royal Artillery, Larkhill, Wilts
	WK048	Thales Watchkeeper 450 RPAS	Army 47 Regt Royal Artillery, Larkhill, Wilts
	WK049	Thales Watchkeeper 450 RPAS	Army 47 Regt Royal Artillery, Larkhill, Wilts
	WK051	Thales Watchkeeper 450 RPAS	Army 47 Regt Royal Artillery, Larkhill, Wilts
	WK052	Thales Watchkeeper 450 RPAS	Army 47 Regt Royal Artillery, Larkhill, Wilts
	WK053	Thales Watchkeeper 450 RPAS	Army 47 Regt Royal Artillery, Larkhill, Wilts
	WK054	Thales Watchkeeper 450 RPAS	Army 47 Regt Royal Artillery, Larkhill, Wilts
	WK060	Thales Watchkeeper 450 RPAS	MOD/Thales, Aberporth, Wales
	WK102	EE Canberra T17 (8780M) <ff>	Privately owned, Welshpool, Wales
	WK118	EE Canberra TT18 [CQ] <ff>	Avro Heritage Museum, Woodford, Cheshire
	WK122	EE Canberra TT18 <ff>	Lakes Lightnings, Spark Bridge, Cumbria
	WK124	EE Canberra B6 (9093M) (composite)	Privately owned, Gilberdyke, E. Yorks

Serial	Type (code/other identity)	Owner/operator, location or fate	Notes
WK124	EE Canberra TT18 (9093M) [CR] (fuselage)	Cornwall Aviation Heritage Centre, stored Newquay	
WK126	EE Canberra TT18 (N2138J) [843]	Jet Age Museum, stored Gloucestershire Airport, Glos	
WK127	EE Canberra TT18 (8985M) <ff>	Wings Museum, stored Balcombe, W. Sussex	
WK128	EE Canberra B2 <ff>	South Wales Aviation Museum, St Athan, Wales	
WK146	EE Canberra B2 <ff>	Gatwick Aviation Museum, Charlwood, Surrey	
WK163	EE Canberra B2/6 (G-BVWC/G-CTTS)	Vulcan To The Sky Trust, Doncaster Sheffield Airport, S. Yorks	
WK198	VS Swift F4 (7428M) (fuselage)	Brooklands Museum, Weybridge, Surrey	
WK275	VS Swift F4	Privately owned, Cumbria	
WK277	VS Swift FR5 (7719M) [N]	Newark Air Museum, Winthorpe, Notts	
WK281	VS Swift FR5 (7712M) [S]	Tangmere Military Aviation Museum, W. Sussex	
WK393	DH112 Venom FB1 <ff>	Privately owned, Lavendon, Bucks	
WK512	DHC1 Chipmunk 22 (G-BXIM) [A]	Privately owned, RAF Halton, Bucks	
WK514	DHC1 Chipmunk 22 (G-BBMO)	Privately owned, Wellesbourne Mountford, Warks	
WK517	DHC1 Chipmunk 22 (G-ULAS)	Privately owned, Compton Abbas, Dorset	
WK518	DHC1 Chipmunk T10 [D]	RAF BBMF, Coningsby, Lincs	
WK522	DHC1 Chipmunk 22 (G-BCOU)	Privately owned, Duxford, Cambs	
WK558	DHC1 Chipmunk 22A (G-ARMG) [DH]	Privately owned, Shenington, Oxon	
WK562	DHC1 Chipmunk 22 (F-AZUR) [91]	Privately owned, La Baule, France	
WK570	DHC1 Chipmunk T10 (8211M) <ff>	No 424 Sqn ATC, Solent Sky, Southampton, Hants	
WK576	DHC1 Chipmunk T10 (8357M) <ff>	Tettenhall Transport Heritage Centre, W. Midlands	
WK577	DHC1 Chipmunk 22 (G-BCYM)	Privately owned, Oaksey Park, Wilts	
WK584	DHC1 Chipmunk T10 (7556M) <ff>	No 511 Sqn ATC, Ramsey, Cambs	
WK585	DHC1 Chipmunk 22 (9265M/G-BZGA)	Privately owned, Compton Abbas, Dorset	
WK586	DHC1 Chipmunk 22 (G-BXGX) [V]	Privately owned, Shoreham, W. Sussex	
WK590	DHC1 Chipmunk 22 (G-BWVZ) [69]	Privately owned, Grimbergen, Belgium	
WK608	DHC1 Chipmunk T10 (G-CLNI) [906,Y]	Fly Navy Heritage Trust, Yeovilton, Somerset	
WK609	DHC1 Chipmunk 22 (G-BXDN) [93]	Privately owned, Booker, Bucks	
WK611	DHC1 Chipmunk 22 (G-ARWB)	Privately owned, Thruxton, Hants	
WK620	DHC1 Chipmunk T10 [T] (fuselage)	Privately owned, Hawarden, Flintshire, Wales	
WK622	DHC1 Chipmunk 22 (G-BCZH)	Privately owned, Wickenby, Lincs	
WK624	DHC1 Chipmunk 22A (G-BWHI)	Privately owned, Blackpool, Lancs	
WK626	DHC1 Chipmunk T10 (8213M) <ff> .	South Yorkshire Aircraft Museum, Doncaster, S. York	
WK628	DHC1 Chipmunk 22 (G-BBMW)	Privately owned, Goodwood, W. Sussex	
WK630	DHC1 Chipmunk 22 (G-BXDG)	Privately owned, Felthorpe, Norfolk	
WK633	DHC1 Chipmunk 22 (G-BXEC) [A]	Privately owned, Duxford, Cambs	
WK634	DHC1 Chipmunk T10 (G-CIGE) [902]	Privately owned, Dunkeswell, Devon	
WK635	DHC1 Chipmunk 22 (G-HFRH)	Privately owned, St. Athan, Wales	
WK638	DHC1 Chipmunk 22 (G-BWJZ) (fuselage)	Privately owned, Finningley, N. Yorks	
WK640	DHC1 Chipmunk 22A (G-BWUV) [C]	Yorkshire Air Museum, Elvington, N. Yorks (wreck)	
WK640	OGMA/DHC1 Chipmunk T20 (G-CERD)	Privately owned, St Athan, Wales	
WK642	DHC1 Chipmunk 22 (EI-AFZ) [94]	Privately owned, Kilrush, Eire	
WK654	Gloster Meteor F8 (8092M)	City of Norwich Aviation Museum, Norfolk	
WK800	Gloster Meteor D16 [Z]	Boscombe Down Aviation Collection, Old Sarum, Wilts	
WK864	Gloster Meteor F8 (WL168/7750M) [C]	Yorkshire Air Museum, Elvington, N. Yorks	
WK935	Gloster Meteor Prone Pilot (7869M)	RAF Museum, Cosford, Shropshire	
WK991	Gloster Meteor F8 (7825M)	IWM Duxford, Cambs	
WL131	Gloster Meteor F8 (7751M) <ff>	South Yorkshire Aircraft Museum, Doncaster, S. Yorks	
WL181	Gloster Meteor F8 [X]	North-East Land, Sea & Air Museums, Usworth, T&W	
WL332	Gloster Meteor T7 [888]	Privately owned, Newquay, Cornwall	
WL349	Gloster Meteor T7	Jet Age Museum, at Newquay, Cornwall	
WL375	Gloster Meteor T7(mod)	Dumfries & Galloway Avn Mus, Dumfries, Scotland	
WL405	Gloster Meteor T7 <ff>	South Wales Aviation Museum, St Athan, Wales	
WL419	Gloster Meteor T7(mod) (G-JSMA)	Martin-Baker Aircraft, Chalgrove, Oxon	
WL505	DH100 Vampire FB9 (7705M/G-FBIX)	Privately owned, Mendlesham, Suffolk	
WL626	Vickers Varsity T1 (G-BHDD) [P]	East Midlands Airport Aeropark, Leics	
WL627	Vickers Varsity T1 (8488M) [D] <ff>	Privately owned, Preston, E. Yorkshire	
WL679	Vickers Varsity T1 (9155M)	RAF Museum, Cosford, Shropshire	
WL732	BP P108 Sea Balliol T21	RAF Museum, Cosford, Shropshire	
WL795	Avro 696 Shackleton MR2C (8753M) [T]	Privately owned, Newquay, Cornwall	

Notes	Serial	Type (code/other identity)	Owner/operator, location or fate
	WL798	Avro 696 Shackleton MR2C (8114M) <ff>	Privately owned, Elgin, Scotland
	WM145	AW Meteor NF11 <ff>	Morayvia, Kinloss, Scotland
	WM167	AW Meteor NF11 (G-LOSM)	Preserved Bruntingthorpe, Leics
	WM224	AW Meteor TT20 (WM311/8177M) [X]	East Midlands Airport Aeropark, Leics
	WM267	AW Meteor NF11 <ff>	City of Norwich Aviation Museum, Norfolk
	WM292	AW Meteor TT20 [841]	FAA Museum, stored Cobham Hall, RNAS Yeovilton, Somerset
	WM366	AW Meteor NF13 (4X-FNA) (comp VZ462)	Jet Age Museum, Gloucestershire Airport, Glos
	WM367	AW Meteor NF13 <ff>	East Midlands Airport Aeropark, Leics
	WM571	DH112 Sea Venom FAW21 [VL]	Solent Sky, stored Romsey, Hants
	WM729	DH113 Vampire NF10 <ff>	de Havilland Aircraft Mus'm, stored London Colney
	WM913	Hawker Sea Hawk FB5 (8162M) [456/J]	Newark Air Museum, Winthorpe, Notts
	WM961	Hawker Sea Hawk FB5 [J]	Caernarfon Air World, Wales
	WM969	Hawker Sea Hawk FB5 [10/Z]	IWM Duxford, Cambs
	WN105	Hawker Sea Hawk FB3 (WF299/8164M)	Privately owned, Birlingham, Worcs
	WN108	Hawker Sea Hawk FB5 [033]	Ulster Aviation Society, Long Kesh, NI
	WN149	BP P108 Balliol T2 [AT]	Cornwall Aviation Heritage Centre, Newquay, Cornwall
	WN411	Fairey Gannet AS1 (fuselage)	Privately owned, Sholing, Hants
	WN493	WS51 Dragonfly HR5	FAA Museum, RNAS Yeovilton, Somerset
	WN499	WS51 Dragonfly HR5	South Yorkshire Aircraft Museum, stored Doncaster
	WN516	BP P108 Balliol T2 <ff>	Tettenhall Transport Heritage Centre, W. Midlands
	WN534	BP P108 Balliol T2 <ff>	Tettenhall Transport Heritage Centre, W. Midlands
	WN890	Hawker Hunter F2 <ff>	Boscombe Down Aviation Collection, Old Sarum, Wilts
	WN904	Hawker Hunter F2 (7544M) [Q] (wears WN921 [S] on starboard side)	Sywell Aviation Museum, Northants
	WN907	Hawker Hunter F2 (7416M) <ff>	Robertsbridge Aviation Society, E. Sussex
	WN957	Hawker Hunter F5 <ff>	Morayvia, Kinloss, Scotland
	WP185	Hawker Hunter F5 (7583M)	Privately owned, Great Dunmow, Essex
	WP190	Hawker Hunter F5 (7582M/8473M/WP180) [K]	Tangmere Military Aviation Museum, W. Sussex
	WP255	DH113 Vampire NF10 <ff>	South Yorkshire Aircraft Museum, stored Doncaster, S. Yorks
	WP266	EoN AP.5 Primary (BAPC.423)	Privately owned, Fishburn, Co. Durham
	WP269	EoN Eton TX1 (BGA3214)	Privately owned, Little Rissington, Glos
	WP270	EoN Eton TX1 (8598M)	Gliding Heritage Centre, Lasham, Hants
	WP308	Percival P57 Sea Prince T1 (G-GACA) [572/CU]	Gatwick Aviation Museum, Charlwood, Surrey
	WP313	Percival P57 Sea Prince T1 [568/CU]	FAA Museum, stored Cobham Hall, RNAS Yeovilton, Somerset
	WP314	Percival P57 Sea Prince T1 (8634M) [573/CU]	Privately owned, Carlisle Airport, Cumbria
	WP321	Percival P57 Sea Prince T1 (G-BRFC) [750/CU]	South Wales Aviation Museum, St Athan, Wales
	WP495	WS51 Dragonfly HR5 (G-AJOV) [915/LM]	Morayvia, Kinloss, Scotland
	WP772	DHC1 Chipmunk T10 (WK518) [4]	RAF Manston History Museum, Kent
	WP784	DHC1 Chipmunk T10 (comp WZ870) [RCY-E]	East Midlands Airport Aeropark, Leics
	WP788	DHC1 Chipmunk 22A (G-BCHL)	Privately owned, Sleap, Shropshire
	WP790	DHC1 Chipmunk T10 (G-BBNC) [T]	de Havilland Aircraft Museum, London Colney
	WP795	DHC1 Chipmunk 22 (G-BVZZ) [901]	Privately owned, Netheravon, Wilts
	WP800	DHC1 Chipmunk 22 (G-BCXN) [2]	Privately owned, White Waltham, Berks
	WP803	DHC1 Chipmunk 22 (G-HAPY) [G]	Privately owned, Booker, Bucks
	WP805	DHC1 Chipmunk 22 (G-MAJR) [D]	Privately owned, Solent Airport, Hants
	WP809	DHC1 Chipmunk 22A (G-BVTX) [78]	Privately owned, Leicester, Leics
	WP811	DHC1 Chipmunk 22 (G-BCKN)	Privately owned, Blackpool, Lancs
	WP835	DHC1 Chipmunk 22 (D-ERTY) [N]	Privately owned, Rinteln, Germany
	WP840	DHC1 Chipmunk 22 (F-AZQM) [9]	Privately owned, Reims, France
	WP844	DHC1 Chipmunk 22 (G-BWOX) [85]	Privately owned, Adriers, France
	WP848	DHC1 Chipmunk 22 (8342M/G-BFAW)	Privately owned, Old Buckenham, Norfolk
	WP859	DHC1 Chipmunk 22 (G-BXCP) (wreck)	Privately owned, Cam, Glos
	WP860	DHC1 Chipmunk 22 (G-BXDA) [6]	Privately owned, Eshott, Northumberland
	WP863	DHC1 Chipmunk T10 (8360M/G-ATJI) <ff>	No 2385 Sqn ATC, Melksham, Wilts
	WP869	DHC1 Chipmunk T10 (8215M) (G-CLXD)	Privately owned, White Waltham, Berks
	WP870	DHC1 Chipmunk 22 (G-BCOI) [12]	Privately owned, Rayne Hall Farm, Essex

Serial	Type (code/other identity)	Owner/operator, location or fate	Notes
WP872	DHC1 Chipmunk 22 (N198DD/G-IGES)	Privately owned, Audley End, Cambs	
WP896	DHC1 Chipmunk 22 (G-BWVY) [M]	Privately owned, RAF Halton, Bucks	
WP901	DHC1 Chipmunk 22 (G-BWNT/OO-...) [B]	Privately owned, Seppe, The Netherlands	
WP903	DHC1 Chipmunk 22 (G-BCGC)	Privately owned, Old Warden, Beds	
WP912	DHC1 Chipmunk T10 (8467M)	RAF Museum, Cosford, Shropshire	
WP921	DHC1 Chipmunk T10 (G-ATJJ) <ff>	Privately owned, Brooklands, Surrey	
WP925	DHC1 Chipmunk 22 (G-BXHA) [C]	Privately owned, Biggin Hill, Kent	
WP927	DHC1 Chipmunk T10 (8216M/G-ATJK) <ff>	Privately owned, Wyton, Cams	
WP928	DHC1 Chipmunk 22 (G-BXGM) [D]	Privately owned, Dunkeswell, Devon	
WP929	DHC1 Chipmunk 22 (G-BXCV) [F]	Privately owned, Duxford, Cambs	
WP930	DHC1 Chipmunk 22 (G-BXHF) [J]	Privately owned, Goodwood, W. Sussex	
WP962	DHC1 Chipmunk T10 (9287M) [C]	RAF Museum, Hendon, Gtr London	
WP964	DHC1 Chipmunk T20 (G-HDAE)	Privately owned, Wellesbourne Mountford, Warks	
WP971	DHC1 Chipmunk 22 (G-ATHD)	Privately owned, Turweston, Bucks	
WP973	DHC1 Chipmunk 22 (G-BCPU)	Privately owned, White Waltham, Berks	
WP977	DHC1 Chipmunk 22 (G-BHRD) <ff>	Privately owned, South Molton, Devon	
WP983	DHC1 Chipmunk 22 (G-BXNN) [B]	Privately owned, Eggesford, Devon	
WP984	DHC1 Chipmunk 22 (G-BWTO) [H]	Privately owned, Little Gransden, Cambs	
WR360	DH112 Venom FB50 (J-1626/G-DHSS) <ff>	Privately owned, Maddenstown, Co Kildare, Eire	
WR410	DH112 Venom FB50 (J-1539/G-DHUU)	Shannon Aviation Museum, Eire	
WR470	DH112 Venom FB50 (J-1542/G-DHVM)	*Currently not known (ex-Bruntingthorpe)*	
WR539	DH112 Venom FB4 (8399M) <ff>	Privately owned, Cantley, Norfolk	
WR960	Avro 696 Shackleton AEW2 (8772M)	Avro Heritage Museum, Woodford, Cheshire	
WR963	Avro 696 Shackleton AEW2 (G-SKTN) [B-M]	Shackleton Preservation Trust, Coventry, Warks	
WR971	Avro 696 Shackleton MR3/3 (8119M) [Q] (fuse)	Fenland & W Norfolk Aviation Museum (closed), Wisbech, Norfolk	
WR974	Avro 696 Shackleton MR3/3 (8117M) [K]	South Wales Aviation Museum, St Athan, Wales	
WR977	Avro 696 Shackleton MR3/3 (8186M) [B]	Newark Air Museum, Winthorpe, Notts	
WR982	Avro 696 Shackleton MR3/3 (8106M) [J]	Gatwick Aviation Museum, Charlwood, Surrey	
WS103	Gloster Meteor T7 [709]	FAA Museum, stored Cobham Hall, RNAS Yeovilton, Somerset	
WS692	Gloster Meteor NF12 (7605M) [C]	Newark Air Museum, Winthorpe, Notts	
WS726	Gloster Meteor NF14 (7960M) [H]	Under restoration, Billericay, Essex	
WS739	Gloster Meteor NF14 (7961M)	Newark Air Museum, Winthorpe, Notts	
WS760	Gloster Meteor NF14 (7964M)	East Midlands Airport Aeropark, Leics, stored	
WS776	Gloster Meteor NF14 (7716M) [K]	Bournemouth Aviation Museum, Dorset	
WS788	Gloster Meteor NF14 (7967M) [Z]	Yorkshire Air Museum, Elvington, N. Yorks	
WS792	Gloster Meteor NF14 (7965M) [K]	Brighouse Bay Caravan Park, Borgue, D&G, Scotland	
WS807	Gloster Meteor NF14 (7973M) [N]	Jet Age Museum, Gloucestershire Airport, Glos	
WS832	Gloster Meteor NF14 [W]	Solway Aviation Society, Carlisle, Cumbria	
WS838	Gloster Meteor NF14 [D]	Midland Air Museum, Coventry, Warks	
WS840	Gloster Meteor NF14 (7969M) [N] <rf>	Privately owned, Upper Ballinderry, NI	
WS843	Gloster Meteor NF14 (7937M) [J]	RAF Museum, Cosford, Shropshire	
WT001	Boeing E-7A Wedgetail AEW1 (N946BC)	MOD/STS Aviation Services, Birmingham, W. Midlands (conversion)	
WT002	Boeing E-7A Wedgetail AEW1 (N947BC)	MOD/STS Aviation Services, Birmingham, W. Midlands (conversion)	
WT003	Boeing E-7A Wedgetail AEW1 (N576JK)	MOD/STS Aviation Services, Birmingham, W. Midlands (conversion)	
.....	Boeing Wedgetail AEW1	MOD (on order)	
.....	Boeing Wedgetail AEW1	MOD (on order)	
WT121	Douglas Skyraider AEW1 (WT983) [415/CU]	FAA Museum, stored Cobham Hall, RNAS Yeovilton, Somerset	
WT205	EE Canberra B15 <ff>	RAF Manston History Museum, Kent	
WT309	EE Canberra B(I)6 <ff>	Farnborough Air Sciences Trust, Farnborough, Hants	
WT319	EE Canberra B(I)6 <ff>	South Yorkshire Aircraft Museum, Doncaster, S. Yorks	
WT333	EE Canberra B6(mod) (G-BVXC)	Preserved Bruntingthorpe, Leics	
WT339	EE Canberra B(I)8 (8198M)	RAF Barkston Heath Fire Section, Lincs	
WT482	EE Canberra T4 <ff>	Privately owned, Marske by the Sea, Co. Durham	

Notes	Serial	Type (code/other identity)	Owner/operator, location or fate
	WT486	EE Canberra T4 (8102M) <ff>	Privately owned, Westbury, Wilts
	WT507	EE Canberra PR7 (8131M/8548M) [44] <ff>	No 384 Sqn ATC, Mansfield, Notts
	WT520	EE Canberra PR7 (8094M/8184M) <ff>	Privately owned, Hooton Park, Cheshire
	WT525	EE Canberra T22 [855] <ff>	Cornwall Aviation Heritage Centre, Newquay, Cornwall
	WT532	EE Canberra PR7 (8728M/8890M) <ff>	Bournemouth Aviation Museum, Dorset
	WT534	EE Canberra PR7 (8549M) [43] <ff>	Privately owned, Wisbech, Cambs
	WT536	EE Canberra PR7 (8063M) <ff>	South Yorkshire Aircraft Museum, Doncaster, S. Yorks
	WT555	Hawker Hunter F1 (7499M)	Vanguard Haulage, North Weald, Essex (restoration)
	WT569	Hawker Hunter F1 (7491M)	Morayvia, Kinloss, Scotland
	WT612	Hawker Hunter F1 (7496M)	RAF Henlow, Beds, on display
	WT619	Hawker Hunter F1 (7525M)	Montrose Air Station Heritage Centre, Scotland
	WT648	Hawker Hunter F1 (7530M) <ff>	Boscombe Down Aviation Collection, Old Sarum, Wilts
	WT651	Hawker Hunter F1 (7532M) [C]	Newark Air Museum, Winthorpe, Notts
	WT660	Hawker Hunter F1 (7421M) [C]	Privately owned, West Raynham, Norfolk
	WT680	Hawker Hunter F1 (7533M) [J]	Privately owned, Holbeach, Lincs
	WT684	Hawker Hunter F1 (7422M) <ff>	Privately owned, Lavendon, Bucks
	WT694	Hawker Hunter F1 (7510M)	Caernarfon Air World, Wales
	WT711	Hawker Hunter GA11 [833/DD]	Lakes Lightnings, Spark Bridge, Cumbria
	WT722	Hawker Hunter T8C (G-BWGN) [873]	Cornwall Aviation Heritage Centre, Newquay
	WT723	Hawker Hunter PR11 (XG194/G-PRII) [692/LM]	Privately owned, Tyseley, Birmingham, W. Midlands
	WT741	Hawker Hunter GA11 [791] <ff>	Privately owned, South Yorks Air Mus'm, Doncaster
	WT744	Hawker Hunter GA11 [868/VL]	Privately owned, Braunton, Devon
	WT746	Hawker Hunter F4 (XF506/7770M) [A]	Dumfries & Galloway Avn Mus, Dumfries, Scotland
	WT799	Hawker Hunter T8C [879]	Blue Lagoon Diving Centre, Womersley, N. Yorks
	WT804	Hawker Hunter GA11 [831/DD]	Privately owned, Todenham, Glos
	WT806	Hawker Hunter GA11	Preserved Bruntingthorpe, Leics
	WT859	Supermarine 544 <ff>	Boscombe Down Aviation Collection, Old Sarum, Wilts
	WT867	Slingsby T31B Cadet TX3	Privately owned, Eaglescott, Devon
	WT874	Slingsby T31B Cadet TX3 (BGA1255)	Privately owned, Bicester, Oxon
	WT877	Slingsby T31B Cadet TX3	Tettenhall Transport Heritage Centre, W. Midlands
	WT900	Slingsby T31B Cadet TX3 (BGA3272) [FHK]	Privately owned, Saltby, Leics
	WT905	Slingsby T31B Cadet TX3	Privately owned, Keevil, Wilts
	WT908	Slingsby T31B Cadet TX3 (BGA3487)	Privately owned, Dunstable, Beds
	WT910	Slingsby T31B Cadet TX3 (BGA3953)	Privately owned, Llandegla, Denbighshire, Wales
	WT914	Slingsby T31B Cadet TX3 (BGA3194) (fuselage)	East Midlands Airport Aeropark, Leics
	WT933	Bristol 171 Sycamore 3 (G-ALSW/7709M)	Newark Air Museum, Winthorpe, Notts
	WV106	Douglas Skyraider AEW1 [427/C]	FAA Museum, stored Cobham Hall, RNAS Yeovilton, Somerset
	WV198	Sikorsky S55 Whirlwind HAR21 (G-BJWY) [K]	Solway Aviation Society, Carlisle, Cumbria
	WV256	Hawker Hunter GA11 (WB188/G-BZPB)	Cornwall Aviation Heritage Centre, Newquay
	WV314	Hawker Hunter F51 (G-9-445/E-424) [B]	South Yorkshire Aircraft Museum, Doncaster, S. Yorks
	WV322	Hawker Hunter T8C (G-BZSE/9096M) [22/VL]	Privately owned, North Weald, Essex
	WV332	Hawker Hunter F4 (7673M)	Tangmere Military Aircraft Museum, W. Sussex
	WV381	Hawker Hunter GA11 [732] <ff>	Hovercraft Museum, Solent Airport, Hants
	WV382	Hawker Hunter GA11 [830/VL]	East Midlands Airport Aeropark, Leics
	WV383	Hawker Hunter T7	Farnborough Air Sciences Trust, Farnborough, Hants
	WV396	Hawker Hunter T8C (9249M)	Tacla Taid Museum, Newborough, Anglesey, Wales
	WV493	Percival P56 Provost T1 (G-BDYG/7696M) [29]	National Museum of Flight, stored E. Fortune
	WV499	Percival P56 Provost T1 (G-BZRF/7698M) [P-G]	Privately owned, Middlezoy, Somerset
	WV514	Percival P56 Provost T51 (G-BLIW/177) [N-C]	Privately owned, Shoreham, W. Sussex
	WV562	Percival P56 Provost T1 (XF688/7606M) [P-C]	RAF Museum, Cosford, Shropshire
	WV605	Percival P56 Provost T1 [T-B]	Norfolk & Suffolk Avn Museum, Flixton, Suffolk
	WV606	Percival P56 Provost T1 (7622M)[P-B]	Newark Air Museum, Winthorpe, Notts
	WV679	Percival P56 Provost T1 (7615M) [O-J]	Wellesbourne Wartime Museum, Warks
	WV705	Percival P66 Pembroke C1 <ff>	Privately owned, Awbridge, Hants
	WV740	Percival P66 Pembroke C1 (G-BNPH)	Privately owned, St Athan, Wales
	WV746	Percival P66 Pembroke C1 (8938M)	RAF Museum, Cosford, Shropshire
	WV781	Bristol 171 Sycamore HR12 (G-ALTD/7839M) <ff>	Caernarfon Air World, Wales
	WV783	Bristol 171 Sycamore HR12 (G-ALSP/7841M)	RAF Museum, Hendon, Gtr London
	WV787	EE Canberra B2/8 (8799M)	Newark Air Museum, Winthorpe, Notts
	WV795	Hawker Sea Hawk FGA6 (8151M)	Privately owned, Dunsfold, Surrey

Serial	Type (code/other identity)	Owner/operator, location or fate	Notes
WV797	Hawker Sea Hawk FGA6 (8155M) [491/J]	Midland Air Museum, Coventry, Warks	
WV798	Hawker Sea Hawk FGA6 [147/E]	Cornwall Aviation Heritage Centre, Newquay, Cornwall	
WV838	Hawker Sea Hawk FGA4 [182] <ff>	Norfolk & Suffolk Avn Museum, Flixton, Suffolk	
WV856	Hawker Sea Hawk FGA6 [163]	FAA Museum, RNAS Yeovilton, Somerset	
WV903	Hawker Sea Hawk FGA6 (8153M) [128] <ff>	Stoneykirk Aviation Museum, D&G, Scotland	
WV908	Hawker Sea Hawk FGA6 (8154M/G-CMFB) [188/A]	Fly Navy Heritage Trust, stored Shawbury, Shropshire	
WV910	Hawker Sea Hawk FGA6 <ff>	Boscombe Down Aviation Collection, Old Sarum, Wilts	
WV911	Hawker Sea Hawk FGA4 [115/C]	RNAS Yeovilton, Fire Section, Somerset	
WW138	DH112 Sea Venom FAW22 [227/Z]	FAA Museum, RNAS Yeovilton, Somerset	
WW145	DH112 Sea Venom FAW22 [680/LM]	National Museum of Flight, E. Fortune, Scotland	
WW217	DH112 Sea Venom FAW22 [351]	Newark Air Museum, Winthorpe, Notts	
WW388	Percival P56 Provost T1 (7616M) [O-F]	Privately owned, Middlezoy, Somerset	
WW442	Percival P56 Provost T1 (7618M) [N]	East Midlands Airport Aeropark, Leics	
WW444	Percival P56 Provost T1 [D]	Privately owned, Brownhills, Staffs	
WW447	Percival P56 Provost T1 [F]	Privately owned, Shoreham, W. Sussex (stored)	
WW450	Percival P56 Provost T1 (*WW421*/G-BZRE/7689M)	Bournemouth Aviation Museum, Dorset	
WW453	Percival P56 Provost T1 (G-TMKI) [W-S]	Privately owned, Middlezoy, Somerset	
WW654	Hawker Hunter GA11 [834/DD]	Privately owned, Ford, W. Sussex	
WW664	Hawker Hunter F4 <ff>	Privately owned, Norfolk	
WX788	DH112 Venom NF3 <ff>	South Yorkshire Aircraft Museum, stored Doncaster, S. Yorks	
WX853	DH112 Venom NF3 (7443M)	de Havilland Aircraft Mus'm, stored London Colney	
WX905	DH112 Venom NF3 (7458M)	Newark Air Museum, Winthorpe, Notts	
WZ425	DH115 Vampire T11	Privately owned, Birlingham, Worcs	
WZ450	DH115 Vampire T11 <ff>	Cornwall Aviation Heritage Centre, Newquay, Cornwall	
WZ507	DH115 Vampire T11 (G-VTII) [74]	Privately owned, North Weald, Essex	
WZ515	DH115 Vampire T11 [60]	Solway Aviation Society, Carlisle, Cumbria	
WZ518	DH115 Vampire T11 [B]	North-East Land, Sea & Air Museums, Usworth, Notts	
WZ549	DH115 Vampire T11 (8118M) [F]	Ulster Aviation Society, Long Kesh, NI	
WZ553	DH115 Vampire T11 (G-DHYY) <ff>	Privately owned, Stockton, Warks	
WZ557	DH115 Vampire T11	Morayvia, Kinloss, Scotland	
WZ572	DH115 Vampire T11 (8124M) [65] <ff>	Privately owned, Sholing, Hants	
WZ581	DH115 Vampire T11 <ff>	The Vampire Collection, Hemel Hempstead, Herts	
WZ584	Gloster Meteor T7 (WL345, comp with WL360) [54]	Privately owned, Middlezoy, Somerset	
WZ589	DH115 Vampire T11 [19]	Privately owned, Wigmore, Kent	
WZ590	DH115 Vampire T11 [49]	IWM Duxford, Cambs	
WZ662	Auster AOP9 (G-BKVK)	Privately owned, Liverpool, Merseyside	
WZ679	Auster AOP9 (7863M/*XP248*/G-CIUX)	Privately owned, Whittlesford, Cambs	
WZ706	Auster AOP9 (7851M/G-BURR)	Privately owned, Darley Moor, Derbys	
WZ711	Auster AOP9/Beagle E3 (G-AVHT)	Privately owned, Messingham, Lincs	
WZ721	Auster AOP9	Army Flying Museum, Middle Wallop, Hants	
WZ724	Auster AOP9 (7432M) (frame)	Army Flying Museum, Middle Wallop, Hants	
WZ736	Avro 707A (7868M)	Boscombe Down Aviation Collection, Old Sarum, Wilts	
WZ744	Avro 707C (7932M)	RAF Museum, stored Cosford, Shropshire	
WZ753	Slingsby T38 Grasshopper TX1	Boscombe Down Aviation Collection, Old Sarum, Wilts	
WZ755	Slingsby T38 Grasshopper TX1 (BGA3481)	Tettenhall Transport Heritage Centre, W. Midlands	
WZ757	Slingsby T38 Grasshopper TX1 (comp XK820)	Privately owned, Saltby, Lincs	
WZ767	Slingsby T38 Grasshopper TX1	North-East Land, Sea & Air Museums, Usworth, Notts	
WZ772	Slingsby T38 Grasshopper TX1	Trenchard Museum, RAF Halton, Bucks	
WZ773	Slingsby T38 Grasshopper TX1	Edinburgh Academy, Scotland	
WZ784	Slingsby T38 Grasshopper TX1	Privately owned, stored Felixstowe, Kent	
WZ791	Slingsby T38 Grasshopper TX1 (8944M)	RAF Museum, Hendon, Gtr London	
WZ792	Slingsby T38 Grasshopper TX1 (comp WZ784 & WZ824)	Solway Aviation Society, Carlisle, Cumbria	
WZ793	Slingsby T38 Grasshopper TX1	Privately owned, Rufforth, N. Yorks	
WZ796	Slingsby T38 Grasshopper TX1	Privately owned, stored Aston Down, Glos	
WZ797	Slingsby T38 Grasshopper TX1 (BGA3359)	Privately owned, stored Shipdham, Norfolk	
WZ798	Slingsby T38 Grasshopper TX1	Privately owned, Eaglescott, Devon	
WZ818	Slingsby T38 Grasshopper TX1 (BGA4361)	Privately owned, Nympsfield, Glos	

Notes	Serial	Type (code/other identity)	Owner/operator, location or fate
	WZ819	Slingsby T38 Grasshopper TX1 (BGA3498) [FSV]	Privately owned, Halton, Bucks
	WZ820	Slingsby T38 Grasshopper TX1 <ff>	Sywell Aviation Museum, Northants, stored
	WZ822	Slingsby T38 Grasshopper TX1	South Yorkshire Aircraft Museum, stored Doncaster
	WZ824	Slingsby T38 Grasshopper TX1	Privately owned, Bridge of Weir, Scotland
	WZ826	Vickers Valiant B(K)1 (XD826/7872M) <ff>	Privately owned, Rayleigh, Essex
	WZ828	Slingsby T38 Grasshopper TX1 (BGA4421)	Privately owned, Little Rissington, Glos
	WZ831	Slingsby T38 Grasshopper TX1	Privately owned, stored Aston Down, Glos
	WZ846	DHC1 Chipmunk 22 (G-BCSC/8439M)	No 2427 Sqn ATC, Biggin Hill, Kent
	WZ847	DHC1 Chipmunk 22 (G-CPMK) [F]	Privately owned, Sleap, Shropshire
	WZ869	DHC1 Chipmunk T10 (8019M) <ff> [6]	South Wales Aviation Museum, stored St Athan
	WZ872	DHC1 Chipmunk 22 (G-BZGB) [E]	Privately owned, Spanhoe, Northants
	WZ876	DHC1 Chipmunk 22 (G-BBWN) <ff>	Tangmere Military Aviation Museum, W. Sussex
	WZ879	DHC1 Chipmunk 22 (G-BWUT) [X]	Privately owned, Audley End, Cambs
	WZ882	DHC1 Chipmunk 22 (G-BXGP) [K]	Privately owned, Popham, Hants
	XA109	DH115 Sea Vampire T22	Montrose Air Station Heritage Centre, Scotland
	XA127	DH115 Sea Vampire T22 <ff>	FAA Museum, RNAS Yeovilton, Somerset
	XA129	DH115 Sea Vampire T22	FAA Museum, stored Cobham Hall, RNAS Yeovilton, Somerset
	XA225	Slingsby T38 Grasshopper TX1	Gliding Heritage Centre, Lasham, Hants
	XA226	Slingsby T38 Grasshopper TX1	Norfolk & Suffolk Avn Museum, Flixton, Suffolk
	XA228	Slingsby T38 Grasshopper TX1	National Museum of Flight, East Fortune, Scotland
	XA230	Slingsby T38 Grasshopper TX1 (BGA4098)	Privately owned, Saltby, Leics
	XA231	Slingsby T38 Grasshopper TX1 (8888M)	RAF Manston History Museum, Kent
	XA240	Slingsby T38 Grasshopper TX1 (BGA4556)	Privately owned, Portmoak, Perth & Kinross, Scotland
	XA241	Slingsby T38 Grasshopper TX1	Shuttleworth Collection, stored Old Warden, Beds
	XA243	Slingsby T38 Grasshopper TX1 (8886M)	Privately owned, Gransden Lodge, Cambs
	XA244	Slingsby T38 Grasshopper TX1	Privately owned, Brent Tor, Devon
	XA282	Slingsby T31B Cadet TX3	Caernarfon Air World, Gwynedd, Wales
	XA290	Slingsby T31B Cadet TX3	Privately owned, Portmoak, Perth & Kinross, Scotland
	XA293	Slingsby T31B Cadet TX3 <ff>	Privately owned, Hooton Park, Cheshire
	XA295	Slingsby T31B Cadet TX3 (BGA3336)	Privately owned, Eaglescott, Devon
	XA302	Slingsby T31B Cadet TX3 (BGA3786)	RAF Museum, Hendon, Gtr London
	XA310	Slingsby T31B Cadet TX3 (BGA4963)	Privately owned, Nympsfield, Glos
	XA312	Slingsby Cadet TX3 (VM791/8876M)	RAF Manston History Museum, Kent
	XA459	Fairey Gannet ECM6 [E]	Solway Aviation Society, Carlisle, Cumbria
	XA460	Fairey Gannet ECM6 [768/BY]	Ulster Aviation Society, Long Kesh, NI
	XA466	Fairey Gannet COD4 [777/LM]	FAA Museum, RNAS Yeovilton, Somerset
	XA508	Fairey Gannet T2 [627/GN]	FAA Museum, at Midland Air Museum, Coventry,Warks
	XA564	Gloster Javelin FAW1 (7464M)	RAF Museum, Cosford, Shropshire
	XA634	Gloster Javelin FAW4 (7641M)	Jet Age Museum, stored Gloucestershire Airport, Glos
	XA699	Gloster Javelin FAW5 (7809M)	Midland Air Museum, Coventry, Warks
	XA847	EE P1B (8371M)	Privately owned, Stowmarket, Suffolk
	XA862	WS55 Whirlwind HAR1 (G-AMJT) [704] <ff>	South Yorkshire Aircraft Museum, Doncaster, S. Yorks
	XA864	WS55 Whirlwind HAR1	FAA Museum, stored Cobham Hall, RNAS Yeovilton, Somerset
	XA870	WS55 Whirlwind HAR1 [911]	South Yorkshire Aircraft Museum, Doncaster, S. Yorks
	XA880	DH104 Devon C2 (G-BVXR) <ff>	Privately owned, Elstree Studios, Herts
	XA893	Avro 698 Vulcan B1 (8591M) <ff>	RAF Museum, stored Cosford, Shropshire
	XA903	Avro 698 Vulcan B1 <ff>	Stoneykirk Aviation Museum, D&G, Scotland
	XA917	HP80 Victor B1 (7827M) <ff>	Privately owned, Cupar, Fife, Scotland
	XB259	Blackburn B101 Beverley C1 (G-AOAI)	Condor Aviation, Duffield, N. Yorks
	XB261	Blackburn B101 Beverley C1 <ff>	Newark Air Museum, Winthorpe, Notts
	XB446	Grumman TBM-3 Avenger ECM6B	FAA Museum, Yeovilton, Somerset
	XB480	Hiller HT1 [537]	FAA Museum, stored Cobham Hall, RNAS Yeovilton, Somerset
	XB812	Canadair CL-13 Sabre F4 (9227M) [U]	RAF Museum, Cosford, Shropshire
	XD145	Saro SR53	RAF Museum, Cosford, Shropshire
	XD163	WS55 Whirlwind HAR10 (8645M) [X]	The Helicopter Museum, Weston-super-Mare, Somerset
	XD165	WS55 Whirlwind HAR10 (8673M)	Caernarfon Airfield Fire Section, Wales

Serial	Type (code/other identity)	Owner/operator, location or fate	Notes
XD215	VS Scimitar F1 <ff>	Privately owned, Cheltenham, Glos	
XD235	VS Scimitar F1 [148] <ff>	Privately owned, Lavendon, Bucks	
XD317	VS Scimitar F1 [112/R]	FAA Museum, RNAS Yeovilton, Somerset	
XD332	VS Scimitar F1 [194/C]	Solent Sky, stored Romsey, Hants	
XD375	DH115 Vampire T11 (7887M)	Privately owned, Elland, W. Yorks	
XD377	DH115 Vampire T11 (8203M) <ff>	Privately owned, Gilberdyke, E. Yorks	
XD382	DH115 Vampire T11 (comp XD534) [41]	East Midlands Airport Aeropark, Leics	
XD425	DH115 Vampire T11 <ff>	Morayvia, Kinloss, Scotland	
XD434	DH115 Vampire T11 [25]	City of Norwich Aviation Museum, Norfolk	
XD445	DH115 Vampire T11 [51]	Privately owned, Wickenby, Lincs	
XD447	DH115 Vampire T11 [50]	East Midlands Airport Aeropark, Leics	
XD452	DH115 Vampire T11 (7990M) [66] <ff>	Privately owned, Dursley, Glos	
XD506	DH115 Vampire T11 (7983M)	Suffolk Aviation Heritage Centre, Foxhall Heath	
XD515	DH115 Vampire T11 (7998M/XM515)	RAF Museum, stored Cosford, Shropshire	
XD525	DH115 Vampire T11 (7882M) <ff>	Privately owned, Templepatrick, NI	
XD542	DH115 Vampire T11 (7604M) [N]	Privately owned, Patrington, E. Yorks	
XD547	DH115 Vampire T11 (composite) [Z]	Privately owned, Cantley, Norfolk	
XD593	DH115 Vampire T11	Newark Air Museum, Winthorpe, Notts	
XD595	DH115 Vampire T11 <ff>	Privately owned, Kirton in Lindsey, Lincs	
XD596	DH115 Vampire T11 (7939M)	Solent Sky, stored Timsbury, Hants	
XD599	DH115 Vampire T11 [A] <ff>	Sywell Aviation Museum, Northants	
XD616	DH115 Vampire T11 [56]	Suffolk Aviation Heritage Centre, Foxhall Heath	
XD624	DH115 Vampire T11	Privately owned, Hooton Park, Cheshire	
XD626	DH115 Vampire T11 [Q]	Midland Air Museum, stored Coventry, Warks	
XD674	Hunting Jet Provost T1 (7570M)	RAF Museum, Cosford, Shropshire	
XD693	Hunting Jet Provost T1 (XM129/G-AOBU) [Z-Q]	Kennet Aviation, North Weald, Essex	
XD816	Vickers Valiant B(K)1 <ff>	Brooklands Museum, Weybridge, Surrey	
XD818	Vickers Valiant B(K)1 (7894M)	RAF Museum, Cosford, Shropshire	
XD826	Vickers Valiant B(K)1 <ff>	Privately owned, Duxford, Cambs	
XD857	Vickers Valiant B(K)1 <ff>	RAF Marham Aviation Heritage Centre, Norfolk	
XD875	Vickers Valiant B(K)1 <ff>	Morayvia, Kinloss, Scotland	
XE317	Bristol 171 Sycamore HR14 (G-AMWO)	South Yorkshire Aircraft Museum, Doncaster, S. Yorks	
XE339	Hawker Sea Hawk FGA6 (8156M) [149] <ff>	Privately owned, Glos	
XE339	Hawker Sea Hawk FGA6 (8156M) [E] <rf>	Privately owned, Hooton Park, Cheshire	
XE340	Hawker Sea Hawk FGA6 [131/Z]	FAA Museum, stored Cobham Hall, RNAS Yeovilton, Somerset	
XE364	Hawker Sea Hawk FGA6 (XE489/G-JETH) (comp WM983) [485/J]	Gatwick Aviation Museum, Charlwood, Surrey	
XE368	Hawker Sea Hawk FGA6 [200/J]	Privately owned, Market Harborough, Leics	
XE521	Fairey Rotodyne Y (parts)	The Helicopter Museum, Weston-super-Mare, Somerset	
XE584	Hawker Hunter FGA9 <ff>	Privately owned, Hooton Park, Cheshire	
XE597	Hawker Hunter FGA9 (8874M) <ff>	Privately owned, Bromsgrove, Worcs	
XE620	Hawker Hunter F6A (XE606/8841M) [B]	North-East Land, Sea & Air Museums, Usworth, T&W	
XE624	Hawker Hunter FGA9 (8875M) [G]	Privately owned, Wickenby, Lincs	
XE627	Hawker Hunter F6A [T]	IWM Duxford, Cambs	
XE643	Hawker Hunter FGA9 (8586M) <ff>	No 1137 Sqn ATC, Long Kesh, NI	
XE664	Hawker Hunter F4 <ff>	Jet Age Museum, Gloucestershire Airport, Glos	
XE665	Hawker Hunter T8C (G-BWGM)	Privately owned, stored Cotswold Airport, Glos	
XE668	Hawker Hunter GA11 [832/DD]	Hamburger Hill Paintball, Marksbury, Somerset	
XE670	Hawker Hunter F4 (7762M/8585M) <ff>	RAF Museum, Cosford, Shropshire	
XE683	Hawker Hunter F51 (RDAF E-409) [G]	City of Norwich Aviation Museum, Norfolk	
XE685	Hawker Hunter GA11 (G-GAII) [861/VL]	Hawker Hunter Aviation, stored Scampton, Lincs	
XE688	Hawker Hunter T72 (XE704/PP-XHH)	Hawker Hunter Aviation, Leeming, N. Yorks	
XE689	Hawker Hunter GA11 (G-BWGK) <ff>	Privately owned, stored Bristol, Glos	
XE707	Hawker Hunter GA11 (N707XE) [865]	Bentwaters Cold War Museum, Suffolk	
XE761	Slingsby T8 Cadet TX1 (BGA804) [BAA]	Privately owned, Little Rissington, Glos	
XE762	Slingsby T8 Cadet TX2 (VM594)	Gliding Heritage Centre, Lasham, Hants	
XE786	Slingsby T31B Cadet TX3 (BGA4033)	Privately owned, Arbroath, Scotland	
XE793	Slingsby T31B Cadet TX3 (8666M)	Privately owned, Tamworth, Staffs	
XE797	Slingsby T31B Cadet TX3	South Yorkshire Aviation Museum, Doncaster, S. Yorks	
XE799	Slingsby T31B Cadet TX3 (8943M) [R]	Privately owned, stored Riseley, Berks	

Notes	Serial	Type (code/other identity)	Owner/operator, location or fate
	XE802	Slingsby T31B Cadet TX3 (BGA5283)	Privately owned, stored Eaglescott, Devon
	XE852	DH115 Vampire T11 [58]	No 2247 Sqn ATC, Hawarden, Flintshire, Wales
	XE855	DH115 Vampire T11 <ff>	Midland Air Museum, stored Coventry, Warks (wreck)
	XE856	DH115 Vampire T11 (G-DUSK) [V]	Bournemouth Aviation Museum, Dorset
	XE874	DH115 Vampire T11 (8582M)	Paintball Commando, Birkin, N. Yorks
	XE897	DH115 Vampire T11 (XD403)	Privately owned, Errol, Tayside, Scotland
	XE921	DH115 Vampire T11 [VR] <ff>	Stoneykirk Aviation Museum, D&G, Scotland
	XE935	DH115 Vampire T11	South Yorkshire Aircraft Museum, Doncaster, S. Yorks
	XE946	DH115 Vampire T11 (7473M) <ff>	RAF Cranwell Aviation Heritage Centre, Lincs
	XE956	DH115 Vampire T11 (G-OBLN)	South Wales Aviation Museum, St Athan, Wales
	XE979	DH115 Vampire T11 [54] <ff>	Privately owned, Cantley, Norfolk
	XE979	DH115 Vampire T11 (fuselage)	Privately owned, Birlingham, Worcs
	XE982	DH115 Vampire T11 (7564M) (fuselage)	Privately owned, Port Talbot, Wales
	XE985	DH115 Vampire T11 (*WZ476*)	Privately owned, New Inn, Torfaen, Wales
	XF113	VS Swift F7 [19] <ff>	Boscombe Down Aviation Collection, Old Sarum, Wilts
	XF114	VS Swift F7 (G-SWIF)	Solent Sky, Southampton, Hants
	XF321	Hawker Hunter T7 <ff>	Preserved Weeze Museum, Germany
	XF321	Hawker Hunter T7 <rf>	*Scrapped*
	XF368	Hawker Hunter F51 (RDAF E-412/*XF314*)	Brooklands Museum, Weybridge, Surrey
	XF375	Hawker Hunter F6A (8736M/G-BUEZ) [6]	Boscombe Down Aviation Collection, Old Sarum, Wilts
	XF382	Hawker Hunter F6A [15]	Midland Air Museum, Coventry, Warks
	XF383	Hawker Hunter F6 (8706M) <ff>	Gloster Aviation Club, Gloucester, Glos
	XF418	Hawker Hunter F51 (RDAF E-430)	Gatwick Aviation Museum, Charlwood, Surrey
	XF509	Hawker Hunter F6 (8708M)	RAF Manston History Museum, Kent
	XF522	Hawker Hunter F6 <ff>	Trenchard Museum, RAF Halton, Bucks
	XF526	Hawker Hunter F6 (8679M) [78/E]	Privately owned, Birlingham, Worcs
	XF527	Hawker Hunter F6 (8680M)	RAF Halton, Bucks, on display
	XF545	Percival P56 Provost T1 (7957M) [O-K]	Privately owned, France
	XF597	Percival P56 Provost T1 (G-BKFW) [AH]	Privately owned, Audley End, Essex
	XF603	Percival P56 Provost T1 (G-KAPW)	Shuttleworth Collection, Old Warden, Beds
	XF690	Percival P56 Provost T1 (8041M/G-MOOS)	Kennet Aviation, Yeovilton, Somerset (stored)
	XF708	Avro 716 Shackleton MR3/3 [C]	IWM Duxford, Cambs
	XF785	Bristol 173 (7648M/G-ALBN)	Aerospace Bristol, Filton, Glos
	XF836	Percival P56 Provost T1 (8043M/G-AWRY) [JG]	Privately owned, Middlezoy, Somerset
	XF840	Percival P56 Provost T1 <ff>	Tangmere Military Aviation Museum, W. Sussex
	XF926	Bristol 188 (8368M)	RAF Museum, Cosford, Shropshire
	XF940	Hawker Hunter F4 <ff>	Privately owned, Bournemouth, Dorset
	XF994	Hawker Hunter T8C (G-CGHU) [873/VL]	Hawker Hunter Aviation, stored Scampton, Lincs
	XF995	Hawker Hunter T8B (G-BZSF/9237M) [K]	RAF Scampton Heritage Centre, Lincs
	XG154	Hawker Hunter FGA9 (8863M)	RAF Museum, Hendon, Gtr London
	XG160	Hawker Hunter F6A (8831M/G-BWAF) [U]	Bournemouth Aviation Museum, Dorset
	XG164	Hawker Hunter F6 (8681M)	Davidstow Airfield & Cornwall At War Museum, Davidstow Moor, Cornwall
	XG168	Hawker Hunter F6A (XG172/8832M) [10]	City of Norwich Aviation Museum, Norfolk
	XG190	Hawker Hunter F51 (RDAF E-425) [C]	Solway Aviation Society, Carlisle, Cumbria
	XG193	Hawker Hunter FGA9 (XG297) (comp with WT741) <ff>	South Yorkshire Aircraft Museum, Doncaster, S. Yorks
	XG194	Hawker Hunter FGA9 (8839M)	Wattisham Station Heritage Museum, Suffolk
	XG195	Hawker Hunter FGA9 <ff>	Privately owned, Lewes, E. Sussex
	XG196	Hawker Hunter F6A (8702M) [31]	Privately owned, Bentwaters, Suffolk
	XG209	Hawker Hunter F6 (8709M) <ff>	Privately owned, Kingston-on-Thames, Gtr London
	XG210	Hawker Hunter F6	Privately owned, Beck Row, Suffolk
	XG225	Hawker Hunter F6A (8713M)	DSAE Cosford, Shropshire, at main gate
	XG226	Hawker Hunter F6A (8800M) <ff>	RAF Manston History Museum, Kent
	XG226	Hawker Hunter F6 (BAPC.548) (comp ET-222 & PH-NLM)	East Midlands Airport Aeropark, Leics
	XG254	Hawker Hunter FGA9 (8881M) [A]	Norfolk & Suffolk Avn Museum, Flixton, Suffolk
	XG274	Hawker Hunter F6 (8710M) [71]	Suffolk Aviation Heritage Centre, Foxhall Heath
	XG290	Hawker Hunter F6 (8711M) <ff>	Boscombe Down Aviation Collection, Old Sarum, Wilts

Serial	Type (code/other identity)	Owner/operator, location or fate	Notes
XG297	Hawker Hunter FGA9 [Y] <ff>	South Yorkshire Aircraft Museum, Doncaster, S. Yorks	
XG325	EE Lightning F1 <ff>	Privately owned, Norfolk	
XG329	EE Lightning F1 (8050M)	Privately owned, Flixton, Suffolk	
XG331	EE Lightning F1 <ff>	Privately owned, Glos	
XG337	EE Lightning F1 (8056M) [M]	RAF Museum, Cosford, Shropshire	
XG452	Bristol 192 Belvedere HC1 (7997M/G-BRMB)	The Helicopter Museum, Weston-super-Mare, Somerset	
XG454	Bristol 192 Belvedere HC1 (8366M)	The Helicopter Museum, Weston-super-Mare, Somerset	
XG462	Bristol 192 Belvedere HC1 <ff>	The Helicopter Museum, Weston-super-Mare, Somerset	
XG474	Bristol 192 Belvedere HC1 (8367M) [O]	RAF Museum, Hendon, Gtr London	
XG502	Bristol 171 Sycamore HR14	Army Flying Museum, Middle Wallop, Hants	
XG518	Bristol 171 Sycamore HR14 (8009M) [S-E]	Norfolk & Suffolk Avn Museum, Flixton, Suffolk	
XG523	Bristol 171 Sycamore HR14 <ff> [V]	Norfolk & Suffolk Avn Museum, Flixton, Suffolk	
XG545	Bristol 171 Sycamore HR52 (OE-XSY)	Flying Bulls, Salzburg, Austria	
XG574	WS55 Whirlwind HAR3 [752/PO]	FAA Museum, stored Cobham Hall, RNAS Yeovilton, Somerset	
XG588	WS55 Whirlwind HAR3 (G-BAMH/VR-BEP)	East Midlands Airport Aeropark, Leics	
XG592	WS55 Whirlwind HAS7 [54]	Task Force Adventure Park, Cowbridge, S. Glam, Wales	
XG594	WS55 Whirlwind HAS7 [517]	FAA Museum, stored Cobham Hall, RNAS Yeovilton, Somerset	
XG596	WS55 Whirlwind HAS7 [66]	The Helicopter Museum, stored Weston-super-Mare, Somerset	
XG629	DH112 Sea Venom FAW22 [668]	Privately owned, Stone, Staffs	
XG680	DH112 Sea Venom FAW22 [438]	North-East Land, Sea & Air Museums, Usworth, T&W	
XG692	DH112 Sea Venom FAW22 [668/LM]	Privately owned, Stockport, Cheshire	
XG730	DH112 Sea Venom FAW22	de Havilland Aircraft Museum, London Colney, Herts	
XG736	DH112 Sea Venom FAW22	Privately owned, East Midlands, Leics	
XG737	DH112 Sea Venom FAW22 [220/Z]	East Midlands Airport Aeropark, Leics	
XG743	DH115 Sea Vampire T22 [798/BY]	Historic Aviation Centre, Fishburn, Co. Durham	
XG775	DH115 Sea Vampire T22 <ff>	Privately owned, Fishburn, Co. Durham	
XG797	Fairey Gannet ECM6 [277]	IWM Duxford, Cambs	
XG831	Fairey Gannet ECM6 [396]	Davidstow Airfield & Cornwall At War Museum, Davidstow Moor, Cornwall	
XG882	Fairey Gannet T5 (8754M) [771/LM]	Privately owned, Errol, Tayside, Scotland	
XG883	Fairey Gannet T5 [773/BY]	FAA Museum, at Museum of Berkshire Aviation, Woodley, Berks	
XG900	Short SC1	Science Museum, South Kensington, London	
XG905	Short SC1	Ulster Folk & Transport Mus, Holywood, Co. Down, NI	
XH131	EE Canberra PR9	Ulster Aviation Society, Long Kesh, NI	
XH134	EE Canberra PR9 (G-OMHD)	Privately owned, stored Cotswold Airport, Glos	
XH135	EE Canberra PR9 <ff>	Preserved, West Raynham, Norfolk	
XH136	EE Canberra PR9 (8782M) [W] <ff>	Romney Marsh Wartime Collection, Kent	
XH165	EE Canberra PR9 <ff>	Blyth Valley Aviation Collection, Walpole, Suffolk	
XH169	EE Canberra PR9	RAF Marham, Norfolk, on display	
XH170	EE Canberra PR9 (8739M)	RAF Wyton, Cambs, on display	
XH171	EE Canberra PR9 (8746M) [U]	RAF Museum, Cosford, Shropshire	
XH174	EE Canberra PR9 <ff>	Privately owned, Devon	
XH175	EE Canberra PR9 <ff>	Privately owned, Bewdley, Worcs	
XH177	EE Canberra PR9 <ff>	Newark Air Museum, Winthorpe, Notts	
XH278	DH115 Vampire T11 (8595M/7866M) [42]	Yorkshire Air Museum, Elvington, N. Yorks	
XH312	DH115 Vampire T11	Outpost Paintball, Higher Kinnerton, Cheshire	
XH313	DH115 Vampire T11 (G-BZRD) [E]	Tangmere Military Aviation Museum, W. Sussex	
XH318	DH115 Vampire T11 (7761M) [64]	Privately owned, Sholing, Hants	
XH328	DH115 Vampire T11 <ff>	Privately owned, Cantley, Norfolk	
XH330	DH115 Vampire T11 [73]	Privately owned, Milton Keynes, Bucks	
XH537	Avro 698 Vulcan B2MRR (8749M) <ff>	Bournemouth Aviation Museum, Dorset	
XH558	Avro 698 Vulcan B2 (G-VLCN)	Vulcan To The Sky Trust, Doncaster Sheffield Airport, S. Yorks	
XH560	Avro 698 Vulcan K2 <ff>	Privately owned, Neatishead, Norfolk	
XH563	Avro 698 Vulcan B2MRR <ff>	Morayvia, Kinloss, Scotland	
XH584	EE Canberra T4 (G-27-374) <ff>	South Yorkshire Aircraft Museum, Doncaster, S. Yorks	
XH592	HP80 Victor B1A (8429M) <ff>	Midland Air Museum, Coventry, Warks	

Notes	Serial	Type (code/other identity)	Owner/operator, location or fate
	XH648	HP80 Victor K1A	IWM Duxford, Cambs
	XH669	HP80 Victor K2 (9092M) <ff>	Privately owned, Duxford, Cambs
	XH670	HP80 Victor SR2 <ff>	South Wales Aviation Museum, St Athan, Wales
	XH672	HP80 Victor K2 (9242M)	RAF Museum, Cosford, Shropshire
	XH767	Gloster Javelin FAW9 (7955M) [L]	Yorkshire Air Museum, Elvington, N. Yorks
	XH783	Gloster Javelin FAW7 (7798M) <ff>	Privately owned, Catford, Gtr London
	XH837	Gloster Javelin FAW7 (8032M) <ff>	Caernarfon Air World, Gwynedd, Wales
	XH892	Gloster Javelin FAW9R (7982M) [J]	Norfolk & Suffolk Avn Museum, Flixton, Suffolk
	XH897	Gloster Javelin FAW9	IWM Duxford, Cambs
	XH903	Gloster Javelin FAW9 (7938M) [G]	Jet Age Museum, Gloucestershire Airport, Glos
	XH992	Gloster Javelin FAW8 (7829M) [P]	Newark Air Museum, Winthorpe, Notts
	XJ314	RR Thrust Measuring Rig	Science Museum, South Kensington, London
	XJ380	Bristol 171 Sycamore HR14 (8628M)	Morayvia, Kinloss, Scotland
	XJ389	Fairey Jet Gyrodyne (XD759/G-AJJP)	Museum of Berkshire Aviation, Woodley, Berks
	XJ398	WS55 Whirlwind HAR10 (XD768/G-BDBZ)	South Yorkshire Aircraft Museum, Doncaster, S. Yorks
	XJ407	WS55 Whirlwind HAR10 (N7013H)	Privately owned, North Somercotes, Lincs
	XJ476	DH110 Sea Vixen FAW1 <ff>	Boscombe Down Aviation Collection, Old Sarum, Wilts
	XJ481	DH110 Sea Vixen FAW1 [VL]	FAA Museum, stored Cobham Hall, RNAS Yeovilton, Somerset
	XJ482	DH110 Sea Vixen FAW1 [713/VL]	Norfolk & Suffolk Avn Museum, Flixton, Suffolk
	XJ488	DH110 Sea Vixen FAW1 <ff>	Robertsbridge Aviation Society, Mayfield, E. Sussex
	XJ494	DH110 Sea Vixen FAW2 [121/E]	Preserved Bruntingthorpe, Leics
	XJ560	DH110 Sea Vixen FAW2 (8142M) [302]	Newark Air Museum, Winthorpe, Notts
	XJ565	DH110 Sea Vixen FAW2 [127/E]	de Havilland Aircraft Museum, London Colney, Herts
	XJ571	DH110 Sea Vixen FAW2 (8140M) [242]	Solent Sky, Southampton, Hants
	XJ575	DH110 Sea Vixen FAW2 <ff> [SAH-13]	Wellesbourne Wartime Museum, Warks
	XJ579	DH110 Sea Vixen FAW2 <ff>	Midland Air Museum, stored Coventry, Warks
	XJ580	DH110 Sea Vixen FAW2 [131/E]	Tangmere Military Aviation Museum, W. Sussex
	XJ714	Hawker Hunter FR10 (comp XG226)	East Midlands Airport Aeropark, Leics
	XJ723	WS55 Whirlwind HAR10	Morayvia, Kinloss, Scotland
	XJ726	WS55 Whirlwind HAR10	Caernarfon Air World, Gwynedd, Wales
	XJ727	WS55 Whirlwind HAR10 (8661M)	Combat Pilot Park, Thetford, Suffolk
	XJ729	WS55 Whirlwind HAR10 (8732M/G-BVGE)	Privately owned, Chard, Somerset
	XJ758	WS55 Whirlwind HAR10 (8464M) <ff>	Privately owned, Welshpool, Powys, Wales
	XJ772	DH115 Vampire T11 [H]	de Havilland Aircraft Museum, London Colney, Herts
	XJ823	Avro 698 Vulcan B2A	Solway Aviation Society, Carlisle, Cumbria
	XJ824	Avro 698 Vulcan B2A	IWM Duxford, Cambs
	XJ917	Bristol 171 Sycamore HR14 [H-S]	North-East Land, Sea & Air Museums, Usworth, T&W
	XJ918	Bristol 171 Sycamore HR14 (8190M)	Long Kesh Museum, Co. Antrim, NI
	XK416	Auster AOP9 (7855M/G-AYUA)	Privately owned, Widmerpool, Notts
	XK417	Auster AOP9 (G-AVXY)	Privately owned, Messingham, Lincs
	XK418	Auster AOP9 (7976M)	No 1894 Sqn ATC, Swaffham, Norfolk
	XK421	Auster AOP9 (8365M) (comp XP286) (frame)	South Yorkshire Aircraft Museum, stored Doncaster
	XK488	Blackburn NA39 Buccaneer S1	FAA Museum, stored Cobham Hall, RNAS Yeovilton, Somerset
	XK526	Blackburn NA39 Buccaneer S2 (8648M)	RAF Honington, Suffolk, at main gate
	XK527	Blackburn NA39 Buccaneer S2D (8818M) <ff>	Privately owned, North Wales
	XK532	Blackburn NA39 Buccaneer S1 (8867M) [632/LM]	Privately owned, Inverness, Scotland
	XK533	Blackburn NA39 Buccaneer S1 <ff>	Stoneykirk Aviation Museum, D&G, Scotland
	XK590	DH115 Vampire T11 [V]	Wellesbourne Wartime Museum, Warks
	XK623	DH115 Vampire T11 (G-VAMP) [56]	Caernarfon Air World, Gwynedd, Wales
	XK624	DH115 Vampire T11 [32]	Norfolk & Suffolk Avn Museum, Flixton, Suffolk
	XK625	DH115 Vampire T11 [14]	Romney Marsh Wartime Collection, Kent
	XK627	DH115 Vampire T11 <ff>	Davidstow Airfield & Cornwall At War Museum, Davidstow Moor, Cornwall
	XK632	DH115 Vampire T11 <ff>	Privately owned, Wickenby, Lincs
	XK637	DH115 Vampire T11 [56]	Top Gun Flight Simulation Centre, Stalybridge, Gtr Mcr
	XK695	DH106 Comet C2(RC) (G-AMXH/9164M) <ff>	de Havilland Aircraft Museum, London Colney, Herts
	XK699	DH106 Comet C2 (7971M) <ff>	Boscombe Down Aviation Collection, Old Sarum, Wilts
	XK724	Folland Gnat F1 (7715M)	Midland Air Museum, Coventry, Warks

Serial	Type (code/other identity)	Owner/operator, location or fate	Notes
XK740	Folland Gnat F1 (8396M)	Solent Sky, Southampton, Hants	
XK776	ML Utility 1	Army Flying Museum, Middle Wallop, Hants	
XK789	Slingsby T38 Grasshopper TX1	Midland Air Museum, Coventry, Warks	
XK790	Slingsby T38 Grasshopper TX1	Privately owned, stored Husbands Bosworth, Leics	
XK819	Slingsby T38 Grasshopper TX1	Privately owned, stored Rufforth, N. Yorks	
XK820	Slingsby T38 Grasshopper TX1 (comp WZ754/WZ778)	Privately owned, Bridge of Weir, Renfrew, Scotland	
XK885	Percival P66 Pembroke C1 (8452M/N46EA)	Cornwall Aviation Heritage Centre, Newquay, Cornwall	
XK895	DH104 Sea Devon C20 (G-SDEV) [19/CU]	South Wales Aviation Museum, St Athan, Wales	
XK907	WS55 Whirlwind HAS7	Midland Air Museum, stored Coventry, Warks	
XK911	WS55 Whirlwind HAS7(mod)	Privately owned, Glastonbury, Somerset	
XK936	WS55 Whirlwind HAS7 [62]	IWM Duxford, Cambs	
XK940	WS55 Whirlwind HAS7 (G-AYXT) [911]	The Helicopter Museum, Weston-super-Mare, Somerset	
XK970	WS55 Whirlwind HAR10 (8789M)	Army, Bramley, Hants (for disposal)	
XL149	Blackburn B101 Beverley C1 (7988M) <ff>	South Yorkshire Aircraft Museum, Doncaster, S. Yorks	
XL160	HP80 Victor K2 (8910M) <ff>	RAF Marham Aviation Heritage Centre, Norfolk	
XL164	HP80 Victor K2 (9215M) <ff>	Bournemouth Aviation Museum, Dorset	
XL190	HP80 Victor K2 (9216M) <ff>	RAF Manston History Museum, Kent	
XL231	HP80 Victor K2	Yorkshire Air Museum, Elvington, N. Yorks	
XL318	Avro 698 Vulcan B2 (8733M)	RAF Museum, Hendon, Gtr London	
XL319	Avro 698 Vulcan B2	North-East Land, Sea & Air Museums, Usworth, T&W	
XL360	Avro 698 Vulcan B2A	Midland Air Museum, Coventry, Warks	
XL388	Avro 698 Vulcan B2 <ff>	South Yorkshire Aircraft Museum, Doncaster, S. Yorks	
XL426	Avro 698 Vulcan B2 (G-VJET)	Vulcan Restoration Trust, Southend, Essex	
XL445	Avro 698 Vulcan K2 (8811M) <ff>	RAF Scampton Heritage Centre, Lincs	
XL449	Fairey Gannet AEW3 <ff>	Privately owned, Steventon, Oxon	
XL472	Fairey Gannet AEW3 [044/R]	South Wales Aviation Museum, stored St Athan, Wales	
XL497	Fairey Gannet AEW3 [041/R]	Dumfries & Galloway Avn Mus, Dumfries, Scotland	
XL500	Fairey Gannet AEW3 (G-KAEW) [CU]	South Wales Aviation Museum, St Athan, Wales	
XL502	Fairey Gannet AEW3 (8610M/G-BMYP)	Yorkshire Air Museum, Elvington, N. Yorks	
XL503	Fairey Gannet AEW3 [070/E]	FAA Museum, stored Cobham Hall, RNAS Yeovilton	
XL563	Hawker Hunter T7 (9218M)	Farnborough Air Sciences Trust, Farnborough, Hants	
XL564	Hawker Hunter T7 <ff>	City of Norwich Aviation Museum, Norfolk	
XL565	Hawker Hunter T7 (parts of WT745) [Y]	Preserved Bruntingthorpe, Leics	
XL568	Hawker Hunter T7A (9224M) [X]	RAF Museum, Cosford, Shropshire	
XL569	Hawker Hunter T7 (8833M)	East Midlands Airport Aeropark, Leics	
XL571	Hawker Hunter T7 (8834M/XL572/G-HNTR) [V]	Yorkshire Air Museum, Elvington, N. Yorks	
XL573	Hawker Hunter T7 (G-BVGH)	South Wales Aviation Museum, St Athan, Wales	
XL580	Hawker Hunter T8M [723]	FAA Museum, stored Cobham Hall, RNAS Yeovilton, Somerset	
XL586	Hawker Hunter T7 (comp XL578)	Action Park, Wickford, Essex	
XL587	Hawker Hunter T7 (8807M/G-HPUX)	Hawker Hunter Aviation, stored Scampton, Lincs	
XL591	Hawker Hunter T7	Gatwick Aviation Museum, Charlwood, Surrey	
XL592	Hawker Hunter T7 (8836M) [Y]	Maidenhead Heritage Centre, Berks	
XL609	Hawker Hunter T7 <ff>	Lakes Lightnings, Spark Bridge, Cumbria	
XL621	Hawker Hunter T7 (G-BNCX)	Privately owned, Dunsfold, Surrey	
XL623	Hawker Hunter T7 (8770M)	Privately owned, Dunsfold, Surrey	
XL629	EE Lightning T4	MOD/QinetiQ Boscombe Down, Wilts, at main gate	
XL714	DH82A Tiger Moth II (T6099/G-AOGR)	Privately owned, Boughton, Lincs	
XL736	Saro Skeeter AOP12	The Helicopter Museum, stored, Weston-super-Mare, Somerset	
XL738	Saro Skeeter AOP12 (XM565/7861M)	Privately owned, Storwood, E. Yorks	
XL739	Saro Skeeter AOP12	Norfolk Tank Museum, Forncett St Peter, Norfolk	
XL762	Saro Skeeter AOP12 (8017M)	National Museum of Flight, stored E Fortune, Scotland	
XL763	Saro Skeeter AOP12	Privately owned, Storwood, E. Yorks	
XL764	Saro Skeeter AOP12 (7940M) [J]	Newark Air Museum, Winthorpe, Notts	
XL765	Saro Skeeter AOP12	Privately owned, Sandown, IOW	
XL770	Saro Skeeter AOP12 (8046M)	Solent Sky, Southampton, Hants	
XL809	Saro Skeeter AOP12 (G-BLIX)	Privately owned, Wilden, Beds	
XL811	Saro Skeeter AOP12	The Helicopter Museum, Weston-super-Mare, Somerset	
XL812	Saro Skeeter AOP12 (G-SARO)	Historic Army Aircraft Flight, stored Middle Wallop, Hants	

45

Notes	Serial	Type (code/other identity)	Owner/operator, location or fate
	XL813	Saro Skeeter AOP12	Army Flying Museum, Middle Wallop, Hants
	XL814	Saro Skeeter AOP12	Army Flying Museum, stored Middle Wallop, Hants
	XL824	Bristol 171 Sycamore HR14 (8021M)	Aerospace Bristol, Filton, Glos
	XL829	Bristol 171 Sycamore HR14	The Helicopter Museum, Weston-super-Mare, Somerset
	XL840	WS55 Whirlwind HAS7	Privately owned, Bawtry, S. Yorks
	XL853	WS55 Whirlwind HAS7 [PO]	FAA Museum, stored Cobham Hall, RNAS Yeovilton, Somerset
	XL875	WS55 Whirlwind HAR9	Privately owned, Scotland
	XL929	Percival P66 Pembroke C1 (G-BNPU)	South Wales Aviation Museum, stored St Athan
	XL954	Percival P66 Pembroke C1 (9042M/N4234C/G-BXES)	Privately owned, St. Athan, Glamorgan, Wales
	XL993	SAL Twin Pioneer CC2 (8388M)	RAF Museum, Cosford, Shropshire
	XM135	BAC Lightning F1 [B]	IWM Duxford, Cambs
	XM144	BAC Lightning F1 (8417M) <ff>	Shannon Aviation Museum, Eire (stored)
	XM169	BAC Lightning F1A (8422M) <ff>	Morayvia, Kinloss, Scotland
	XM172	BAC Lightning F1A (8427M)	Lakes Lightnings, Spark Bridge, Cumbria
	XM173	BAC Lightning F1A (8414M) [A]	Privately owned, Malmesbury, Glos
	XM191	BAC Lightning F1A (7854M/8590M) <ff>	Privately owned, Thorpe Wood, N Yorks
	XM192	BAC Lightning F1A (8413M) [K]	Thorpe Camp Visitor Centre, Tattershall Thorpe, Lincs
	XM223	DH104 Devon C2 (G-BWWC) [J]	Privately owned, stored Compton Verney, Warks
	XM279	EE Canberra B(I)8 <ff>	Norfolk & Suffolk Avn Museum, Flixton, Suffolk
	XM300	WS58 Wessex HAS1	Privately owned, Nantgarw, Rhondda, Wales
	XM328	WS58 Wessex HAS3 [653/PO]	The Helicopter Museum, Weston-super-Mare, Somerset
	XM330	WS58 Wessex HAS1	The Helicopter Museum, Weston-super-Mare, Somerset
	XM350	Hunting Jet Provost T3A (9036M)	South Yorkshire Aircraft Museum, Doncaster, S. Yorks
	XM351	Hunting Jet Provost T3 (8078M) [Y]	RAF Museum, Cosford, Shropshire
	XM355	Hunting Jet Provost T3 (8229M)	Newcastle Aviation Academy, Tyne and Wear
	XM358	Hunting Jet Provost T3A (8987M) [53]	Privately owned, Newbridge, Powys, Wales
	XM362	Hunting Jet Provost T3 (8230M)	DSAE No 1 SoTT, Cosford, Shropshire
	XM365	Hunting Jet Provost T3 (G-BXBH)	Preserved Bruntingthorpe, Leics
	XM373	Hunting Jet Provost T3 (7726M) [2] <ff>	Yorkshire Air Museum, Elvington, N. Yorks
	XM383	Hunting Jet Provost T3A [90]	Newark Air Museum, Winthorpe, Notts
	XM402	Hunting Jet Provost T3 (8055AM) [18]	Fenland & W Norfolk Aviation Museum, Wisbech, Norfolk
	XM404	Hunting Jet Provost T3 (8055BM) <ff>	Bournemouth Aviation Museum, Dorset
	XM409	Hunting Jet Provost T3 (8082M) <ff>	Air Scouts, Guernsey Airport
	XM410	Hunting Jet Provost T3 (8054AM) [B]	Privately owned, Gillingham, Kent
	XM411	Hunting Jet Provost T3 (8434M) <ff>	South Yorkshire Aircraft Museum, Doncaster, S. Yorks
	XM412	Hunting Jet Provost T3A (9011M) [41]	Privately owned, Balado Bridge, Scotland
	XM414	Hunting Jet Provost T3A (8996M) [101]	Ulster Aviation Society, Long Kesh, NI
	XM417	Hunting Jet Provost T3 (8054BM) [D] <ff>	Privately owned, Bracknell, Berks
	XM419	Hunting Jet Provost T3A (8990M) [102]	Newcastle Aviation Academy, Tyne and Wear
	XM424	Hunting Jet Provost T3 (G-BWDS)	Privately owned, Dunkeswell, Devon
	XM425	Hunting Jet Provost T3A (8995M) [88]	Privately owned, Longton, Staffs
	XM463	Hunting Jet Provost T3A [38] (fuselage)	RAF Museum, Hendon, Gtr London
	XM468	Hunting Jet Provost T3 (8081M) <ff>	Privately owned, Balcombe, W. Sussex
	XM473	Hunting Jet Provost T3A (8974M/G-TINY)	Privately owned, Wethersfield, Essex
	XM474	Hunting Jet Provost T3 (8121M) <ff>	No 247 Sqn ATC, Ashton-under-Lyne, Gtr Manchester
	XM479	Hunting Jet Provost T3A (G-BVEZ) [U]	Privately owned, Leeds East, N. Yorks
	XM480	Hunting Jet Provost T3 (8080M)	4x4 Car Centre, Chesterfield, Derbyshire
	XM496	Bristol 253 Britannia C1 (EL-WXA) [496]	Britannia Preservation Society, Cotswold Airport, Glos
	XM497	Bristol 175 Britannia 312F (G-AOVF) [497]	RAF Museum, Cosford, Shropshire
	XM529	Saro Skeeter AOP12 (7979M/G-BDNS)	Privately owned, Handforth, Cheshire
	XM553	Saro Skeeter AOP12 (G-AWSV)	Yorkshire Air Museum, Elvington, N. Yorks
	XM555	Saro Skeeter AOP12 (8027M)	North-East Land, Sea & Air Museums, Usworth, T&W
	XM557	Saro Skeeter AOP12 <ff>	The Helicopter Museum, stored Weston-super-Mare, Somerset
	XM564	Saro Skeeter AOP12	The Tank Museum, stored Bovington, Dorset
	XM569	Avro 698 Vulcan B2 <ff>	Jet Age Museum, Gloucestershire Airport, Glos
	XM575	Avro 698 Vulcan B2A (G-BLMC)	East Midlands Airport Aeropark, Leics
	XM594	Avro 698 Vulcan B2	Newark Air Museum, Winthorpe, Notts

Serial	Type (code/other identity)	Owner/operator, location or fate	Notes
XM597	Avro 698 Vulcan B2	National Museum of Flight, E Fortune, Scotland	
XM598	Avro 698 Vulcan B2 (8778M)	RAF Museum, Cosford, Shropshire	
XM602	Avro 698 Vulcan B2 (8771M) <ff>	Avro Heritage Museum, Woodford, Cheshire	
XM603	Avro 698 Vulcan B2	Avro Heritage Museum, Woodford, Cheshire	
XM607	Avro 698 Vulcan B2 (8779M)	RAF Waddington, Lincs, on display	
XM612	Avro 698 Vulcan B2	City of Norwich Aviation Museum, Norfolk	
XM651	Saro Skeeter AOP12 (XM561/7980M)	South Yorkshire Aircraft Museum, Doncaster, S. Yorks	
XM652	Avro 698 Vulcan B2 <ff>	Privately owned, Welshpool, Powys, Wales	
XM655	Avro 698 Vulcan B2 (G-VULC)	Privately owned, Wellesbourne Mountford, Warks	
XM685	WS55 Whirlwind HAS7 (G-AYZJ) [513/PO]	Newark Air Museum, Winthorpe, Notts	
XM692	HS Gnat T1 <ff>	Privately owned, Dunkeswell, Devon	
XM693	HS Gnat T1 (7891M)	GE Aviation Hamble, Hants, on display	
XM697	HS Gnat T1 (G-NAAT)	Privately owned, Blantyre, S Lanarkshire, Scotland	
XM708	HS Gnat T1 (8573M)	Privately owned, Lytham St Annes, Lancs	
XM715	HP80 Victor K2	Preserved Bruntingthorpe, Leics	
XM717	HP80 Victor K2 <ff>	RAF Museum, Hendon, Gtr London	
XM819	Lancashire EP9 Prospector (G-APXW)	Army Flying Museum, stored Middle Wallop, Hants	
XM833	WS58 Wessex HAS3	South Wales Aviation Museum, stored St Athan, Wales	
XN137	Hunting Jet Provost T3 <ff>	Privately owned, Little Addington, Northants	
XN149	Slingsby T21B (BGA1085/9G-ABD)	Boscombe Down Aviation Collection, Old Sarum, Wilts	
XN156	Slingsby T21B Sedbergh TX1 (BGA3250)	Privately owned, Portmoak, Perth & Kinross, Scotland	
XN157	Slingsby T21B Sedbergh TX1 (BGA3255)	Privately owned, Long Mynd, Shropshire	
XN185	Slingsby T21B Sedbergh TX1 (8942M/BGA4077)	Privately owned, Scampton, Lincs	
XN186	Slingsby T21B Sedbergh TX1 (BGA3905) [HFG]	Privately owned, Wattisham, Suffolk	
XN238	Slingsby T31B Cadet TX3 <ff>	Privately owned, Barnstaple, Devon	
XN239	Slingsby T31B Cadet TX3 (8889M) [G]	IWM Duxford, Cambs (for disposal)	
XN246	Slingsby T31B Cadet TX3	Privately owned, stored Riseley, Berks	
XN258	WS55 Whirlwind HAR9 [589/CU]	North-East Land, Sea & Air Museums, Usworth, T&W	
XN304	WS55 Whirlwind HAS7 [WW/B]	Norfolk & Suffolk Avn Museum, Flixton, Suffolk	
XN332	Saro P531 (G-APNV) [759]	FAA Museum, stored Cobham Hall, RNAS Yeovilton, Somerset	
XN334	Saro P531	FAA Museum, stored Cobham Hall, RNAS Yeovilton, Somerset	
XN344	Saro Skeeter AOP12 (8018M)	Science Museum, South Kensington, London	
XN345	Saro Skeeter AOP12 <ff>	The Helicopter Museum, stored Weston-super-Mare, Somerset	
XN351	Saro Skeeter AOP12 (G-BKSC)	Morayvia, Kinloss, Scotland	
XN385	WS55 Whirlwind HAS7	Battlezone Paintball, Yarm, N. Yorks	
XN386	WS55 Whirlwind HAR9 [435/ED]	South Yorkshire Aircraft Museum, Doncaster, S. Yorks	
XN412	Auster AOP9	Auster 9 Group, Melton Mowbray, Leics	
XN437	Auster AOP9 (G-AXWA)	Privately owned, Rush Green, Gtr London	
XN441	Auster AOP9 (G-BGKT)	Privately owned, Week St Mary, Cornwall	
XN458	Hunting Jet Provost T3 (8234M/XN594) [19]	Historic Aviation Centre, Fishburn, Co. Durham	
XN459	Hunting Jet Provost T3A (G-BWOT) [59]	Privately owned, Hawarden, Flintshire, Wales	
XN462	Hunting Jet Provost T3A [17]	FAA Museum, stored Cobham Hall, RNAS Yeovilton, Somerset	
XN466	Hunting Jet Provost T3A [29] <ff>	No 247 Sqn ATC, Ashton-under-Lyne, Gtr Manchester	
XN492	Hunting Jet Provost T3 (8079M) <ff>	East Midlands Airport Aeropark, Leics	
XN494	Hunting Jet Provost T3A (9012M) [43]	Cornwall Aviation Heritage Centre, Newquay, Cornwall	
XN495	Hunting Jet Provost T3A (8786M) <ff>	Wings Museum, stored Balcombe, W Sussex	
XN500	Hunting Jet Provost T3A	Norfolk & Suffolk Avn Museum, Flixton, Suffolk	
XN503	Hunting Jet Provost T3 <ff>	North-East Land, Sea & Air Museums, Usworth, T&W	
XN511	Hunting Jet Provost T3 [12] <ff>	South Yorkshire Aircraft Museum, Doncaster, S. Yorks	
XN549	Hunting Jet Provost T3 (8235M) <ff>	Privately owned, Chester, Cheshire	
XN551	Hunting Jet Provost T3A (8984M)	Privately owned, Felton Common, Bristol	
XN554	Hunting Jet Provost T3 (8436M) [K]	Privately owned, Abbotts Ripton, Cambs	
XN573	Hunting Jet Provost T3 [E] <ff>	Newark Air Museum, Winthorpe, Notts	
XN579	Hunting Jet Provost T3A (9137M) [14]	Gunsmoke Paintball, Colchester, Essex	
XN582	Hunting Jet Provost T3A (8957M)	Yorkshire Air Museum, Elvington, N. Yorks	
XN584	Hunting Jet Provost T3A (9014M) [E]	South Wales Aviation Museum, St Athan, Wales	
XN586	Hunting Jet Provost T3A (9039M) [91]	Jurby Transport Museum, Isle of Man	

Notes	Serial	Type (code/other identity)	Owner/operator, location or fate
	XN589	Hunting Jet Provost T3A (9143M) [46]	Yorkshire Air Museum, Elvington, N. Yorks
	XN597	Hunting Jet Provost T3 (7984M) <ff>	Privately owned, Kent
	XN607	Hunting Jet Provost T3 <ff>	Morayvia, Kinloss, Scotland
	XN623	Hunting Jet Provost T3 (XN632/8352M)	Privately owned, Birlingham, Worcs
	XN629	Hunting Jet Provost T3A (G-BVEG/G-KNOT) [49]	Suffolk Aviation Heritage Centre, Foxhall Heath
	XN634	Hunting Jet Provost T3A <ff>	Lakes Lightnings, Spark Bridge, Cumbria
	XN637	Hunting Jet Provost T3 (G-BKOU) [03]	Privately owned, North Weald, Essex
	XN647	DH110 Sea Vixen FAW2 <ff>	Privately owned, Steventon, Oxon
	XN650	DH110 Sea Vixen FAW2 [456] <ff>	Privately owned, Norfolk
	XN651	DH110 Sea Vixen FAW2 <ff>	Privately owned, Lavendon, Bucks
	XN685	DH110 Sea Vixen FAW2 (8173M) [703/VL]	Midland Air Museum, Coventry, Warks
	XN696	DH110 Sea Vixen FAW2 [751] <ff>	North-East Land, Sea & Air Museums, Usworth, T&W
	XN714	Hunting H126	RAF Museum, Cosford, Shropshire
	XN726	EE Lightning F2A (8545M) <ff>	Boscombe Down Aviation Collection, Old Sarum, Wilts
	XN728	EE Lightning F2A (8546M) <ff>	Privately owned, Binbrook, Lincs
	XN776	EE Lightning F2A (8535M) [C]	National Museum of Flight, E Fortune, Scotland
	XN795	EE Lightning F2A <ff>	Privately owned, stored Neatishead, Norfolk
	XN819	AW660 Argosy C1 (8205M) <ff>	Newark Air Museum, Winthorpe, Notts
	XN923	HS Buccaneer S1 [13]	Gatwick Aviation Museum, Charlwood, Surrey
	XN928	HS Buccaneer S1 (8179M) <ff>	Privately owned, Gravesend, Kent
	XN957	HS Buccaneer S1 [630/LM]	FAA Museum, RNAS Yeovilton, Somerset
	XN964	HS Buccaneer S1 [630/LM]	Newark Air Museum, Winthorpe, Notts
	XN967	HS Buccaneer S1 [233] <ff>	City of Norwich Aviation Museum, Norfolk
	XN972	HS Buccaneer S1 (8183M/XN962) <ff>	RAF Museum, Cosford, Shropshire
	XN974	HS Buccaneer S2A	Yorkshire Air Museum, Elvington, N. Yorks
	XN981	HS Buccaneer S2B (fuselage)	Privately owned, Errol, Tayside, Scotland
	XN983	HS Buccaneer S2B <ff>	Fenland & W Norfolk Aviation Museum (closed), Wisbech, Norfolk
	XP110	WS58 Wessex HAS1 [55/FL]	DSAE RNAESS, *HMS Sultan,* Gosport, Hants
	XP142	WS58 Wessex HAS3	FAA Museum, RNAS Yeovilton, Somerset
	XP142	WS58 Wessex HAS3 (A2636/XP110)	DSAE RNAESS, *HMS Sultan,* Gosport
	XP150	WS58 Wessex HAS3 [LS]	South Wales Aviation Museum, stored St Athan, Wales
	XP165	WS Scout AH1	The Helicopter Museum, Weston-super-Mare, Somerset
	XP190	WS Scout AH1	South Yorkshire Aircraft Museum, Doncaster, S. Yorks
	XP191	WS Scout AH1	Privately owned, Prenton, Merseyside
	XP226	Fairey Gannet AEW3	Newark Air Museum, Winthorpe, Notts
	XP241	Auster AOP9 (G-CEHR)	Privately owned, Spanhoe, Northants
	XP242	Auster AOP9 (G-BUCI)	Privately owned, Messingham, Lincs
	XP244	Auster AOP9 (7864M/M7922)	Privately owned, Deddington, Oxon
	XP254	Auster AOP11 (G-ASCC)	Privately owned, Whittlesford, Cambs
	XP279	Auster AOP9 (G-BWKK)	Privately owned, stored Winchester, Hants
	XP280	Auster AOP9	Privately owned, stored Leics
	XP281	Auster AOP9	IWM, stored Duxford, Cambs
	XP282	Auster AOP9 (G-BGTC)	Privately owned, North Reston, Lincs
	XP286	Auster AOP9	*Used in the rebuild of Auster AOP9 XK421*
	XP299	WS55 Whirlwind HAR10 (8726M)	RAF Museum, Hendon, Gtr London
	XP328	WS55 Whirlwind HAR10 (G-BKHC)	Privately owned, North Somercotes, Lincs (wreck)
	XP329	WS55 Whirlwind HAR10 (8791M) [V]	Privately owned, North Somercotes, Lincs (wreck)
	XP330	WS55 Whirlwind HAR10	CAA Fire School, Teesside International Airport, Co. Durham
	XP344	WS55 Whirlwind HAR10 (8764M) [H723]	RAF North Luffenham Training Area, Rutland
	XP345	WS55 Whirlwind HAR10 (8792M) [UN]	Yorkshire Helicopter Preservation Group, Doncaster, S. Yorks
	XP346	WS55 Whirlwind HAR10 (8793M)	Privately owned, Honeybourne, Worcs
	XP350	WS55 Whirlwind HAR10	Privately owned, Bassetts Pole, Staffs
	XP351	WS55 Whirlwind HAR10 (8672M) [Z]	*Currently not known (scrapped?)*
	XP355	WS55 Whirlwind HAR10 (8463M/G-BEBC)	City of Norwich Aviation Museum, Norfolk
	XP360	WS55 Whirlwind HAR10 [V]	Privately owned, Bicton, nr Leominster, Herefordshire
	XP398	WS55 Whirlwind HAR10 (8794M)	*Currently not known (scrapped?)*
	XP404	WS55 Whirlwind HAR10 (8682M)	The Helicopter Museum, stored Weston-super-Mare, Somerset

Serial	Type (code/other identity)	Owner/operator, location or fate	Notes
XP411	AW660 Argosy C1 (8442M) [C]	RAF Museum, Cosford, Shropshire	
XP454	Slingsby T38 Grasshopper TX1	Privately owned, Sywell, Northants	
XP459	Slingsby T38 Grasshopper TX1	Privately owned, Wattisham, Suffolk	
XP463	Slingsby T38 Grasshopper TX1 (frame)	Privately owned, Rufforth, N. Yorks	
XP463	Slingsby T38 Grasshopper TX1 (BGA4372)	Privately owned, Lasham, Hants	
XP488	Slingsby T38 Grasshopper TX1	Privately owned, stored Rufforth, N. Yorks	
XP490	Slingsby T38 Grasshopper TX1 (BGA4552)	Privately owned, stored Watton, Norfolk	
XP492	Slingsby T38 Grasshopper TX1 (BGA3480)	Currently not known	
XP493	Slingsby T38 Grasshopper TX1	Privately owned, stored Aston Down, Glos	
XP494	Slingsby T38 Grasshopper TX1	Privately owned, stored Tettenhall, W. Midlands	
XP505	HS Gnat T1	Science Museum, stored Wroughton, Wilts	
XP513	HS Gnat T1 (N513X)	Privately owned, North Weald, Essex	
XP516	HS Gnat T1 (8580M) [16]	Farnborough Air Sciences Trust, Farnborough, Hants	
XP540	HS Gnat T1 (8608M) [62]	Currently not known (ex-Bruntingthorpe, Leics)	
XP542	HS Gnat T1 (8575M)	No 424 Sqn ATC, Southampton, Hants	
XP556	Hunting Jet Provost T4 (9027M) [B]	RAF Cranwell Aviation Heritage Centre, Lincs	
XP557	Hunting Jet Provost T4 (8494M) [72]	Dumfries & Galloway Avn Mus, Dumfries, Scotland	
XP558	Hunting Jet Provost T4 (8627M) <ff>	Stoneykirk Aviation Museum, D&G, Scotland	
XP558	Hunting Jet Provost T4 (8627M)[20] <rf>	Privately owned, Sproughton, Suffolk	
XP568	Hunting Jet Provost T4	East Midlands Airport Aeropark, Leics	
XP573	Hunting Jet Provost T4 (8236M) [19]	Jersey Airport Fire Section, CI	
XP585	Hunting Jet Provost T4 (8407M) [24]	Glyndwr University, Wrexham, Wales	
XP627	Hunting Jet Provost T4	North-East Land, Sea & Air Museums, Usworth, T&W	
XP629	Hunting Jet Provost T4 (9026M) [P]	Privately owned, Hemswell, Lincs	
XP640	Hunting Jet Provost T4 (8501M) [M]	Yorkshire Air Museum, Elvington, N. Yorks	
XP642	Hunting Jet Provost T4 <ff>	Cornwall Aviation Heritage Centre, Newquay, Cornwall	
XP672	Hunting Jet Provost T4 (8458M/G-RAFI) [03]	South Wales Aviation Museum, St Athan, Wales	
XP677	Hunting Jet Provost T4 (8587M) <ff>	Privately owned, Bolton, Lancs	
XP680	Hunting Jet Provost T4 (8460M)	FETC, Moreton-in-Marsh, Glos	
XP686	Hunting Jet Provost T4 (8401M/8502M) [G]	Gunsmoke Paintball, Colchester, Essex	
XP701	BAC Lightning F3 (8924M) <ff>	Robertsbridge Aviation Society, Mayfield, E. Sussex	
XP703	BAC Lightning F3 <ff>	Cold War Jets Collection, Bruntingthorpe, Leics	
XP706	BAC Lightning F3 (8925M)	South Yorkshire Aircraft Museum, Doncaster, S. Yorks	
XP743	BAC Lightning F3 <ff>	Norfolk & Suffolk Avn Museum, Flixton, Suffolk	
XP745	BAC Lightning F3 (8453M) [H]	Vanguard Self Storage, Bristol, Glos	
XP757	BAC Lightning F3 <ff>	Privately owned, Boston, Lincs	
XP765	BAC Lightning F6 (XS897) [A]	Lakes Lightnings, RAF Coningsby, Lincs	
XP820	DHC2 Beaver AL1 (G-CICP)	Historic Army Aircraft Flight, Middle Wallop, Hants	
XP821	DHC2 Beaver AL1 [MCO]	Army Flying Museum, Middle Wallop, Hants	
XP822	DHC2 Beaver AL1	Army Flying Museum, Middle Wallop, Hants	
XP831	Hawker P.1127 (8406M)	Science Museum, South Kensington, London	
XP841	Handley-Page HP115	FAA Museum, RNAS Yeovilton, Somerset	
XP847	WS Scout AH1	Army Flying Museum, Middle Wallop, Hants	
XP848	WS Scout AH1	Farnborough Air Sciences Trust, Farnborough, Hants	
XP849	WS Scout AH1 (XP895)	Museum of Berkshire Aviation, Woodley, Berks	
XP853	WS Scout AH1	Privately owned, Sutton, Surrey	
XP854	WS Scout AH1 (7898M/TAD 043)	Mayhem Paintball, Abridge, Essex	
XP855	WS Scout AH1	Privately owned, Arncott, Oxon	
XP883	WS Scout AH1	Privately owned, Wymeswold, Leics	
XP883	WS Scout AH1 (XW281/G-BYNZ) [T]	Privately owned, Dungannon, NI	
XP884	WS Scout AH1 (G-WDST)	Privately owned, North Weald, Essex	
XP885	WS Scout AH1	AAC Wattisham, Suffolk, instructional use	
XP886	WS Scout AH1	The Helicopter Museum, stored Weston-super-Mare, Somerset	
XP888	WS Scout AH1	Privately owned, Doncaster, S. Yorks	
XP890	WS Scout AH1 [G] (fuselage)	Privately owned, Ipswich, Suffolk	
XP899	WS Scout AH1	Boscombe Down Aviation Collection, Old Sarum, Wilts	
XP900	WS Scout AH1	AAC Wattisham, Suffolk, instructional use	
XP902	WS Scout AH1 <ff>	South Yorkshire Aircraft Museum, Doncaster, S. Yorks	
XP905	WS Scout AH1	South Yorkshire Aircraft Museum, stored Doncaster, S. Yorks	
XP907	WS Scout AH1 (G-SROE)	Privately owned, Wattisham, Suffolk	
XP910	WS Scout AH1	Army Flying Museum, Middle Wallop, Hants	

Notes	Serial	Type (code/other identity)	Owner/operator, location or fate
	XP924	DH110 Sea Vixen D3 (G-CVIX) [134/E]	Naval Aviation Ltd, Yeovilton, Somerset
	XP925	DH110 Sea Vixen FAW2 [752] <ff>	Stoneykirk Aviation Museum, D&G, Scotland
	XP980	Hawker P.1127	FAA Museum, RNAS Yeovilton, Somerset
	XP984	Hawker P.1127	Brooklands Museum, Weybridge, Surrey
	XR220	BAC TSR2 (7933M)	RAF Museum, Cosford, Shropshire
	XR222	BAC TSR2	IWM Duxford, Cambs
	XR232	Sud Alouette AH2 (F-WEIP)	Army Flying Museum, Middle Wallop, Hants
	XR239	Auster AOP9	Privately owned, Deddington, Oxon
	XR240	Auster AOP9 (G-BDFH)	Privately owned, Eggesford, Devon
	XR241	Auster AOP9 (G-AXRR)	Privately owned, Eggesford, Devon
	XR244	Auster AOP9 (G-CICR)	Historic Army Aircraft Flight, Middle Wallop, Hants
	XR246	Auster AOP9 (7862M/G-AZBU)	Privately owned, Gaddesby, Leics
	XR267	Auster AOP9 (G-BJXR)	Privately owned, Tatenhill, Staffs
	XR271	Auster AOP9	Privately owned, stored Wroughton, Wilts
	XR346	Northrop Shelduck D1 (comp XW578)	Bournemouth Aviation Museum, Dorset
	XR371	SC5 Belfast C1	RAF Museum, Cosford, Shropshire
	XR447	Northrop Shelduck D1 (wreck)	Morayvia, Kinloss, Scotland
	XR453	WS55 Whirlwind HAR10 (8873M) [A]	RAF Odiham, Hants, on gate
	XR485	WS55 Whirlwind HAR10 [Q]	Norfolk & Suffolk Avn Museum, Flixton, Suffolk
	XR486	WS55 Whirlwind HCC12 (8727M/G-RWWW)	The Helicopter Museum, Weston-super-Mare, Somerset
	XR498	WS58 Wessex HC2 (9342M)	DSAE Cosford, Shropshire, on display
	XR502	WS58 Wessex HC2 (G-CCUP/N486KA) [Z]	Privately owned, Stonegate, E Sussex
	XR506	WS58 Wessex HC2 (9343M) [V]	Privately owned, Corley Moor, Warks
	XR516	WS58 Wessex HC2 (9319M) [V]	RAF Shawbury, Shropshire, on display
	XR517	WS58 Wessex HC2 [N]	Ulster Aviation Society, Long Kesh, NI
	XR523	WS58 Wessex HC2 [M]	MOD Pembrey Sands Air Weapons Range, GI use
	XR525	WS58 Wessex HC2 [G]	RAF Museum, Cosford, Shropshire
	XR526	WS58 Wessex HC2 (8147M)	The Helicopter Museum, stored Weston-super-Mare, Somerset
	XR528	WS58 Wessex HC2	Morayvia, Kinloss, Scotland
	XR529	WS58 Wessex HC2 (9268M) [E]	Crumlin Road Gaol Experience, Belfast, NI
	XR534	HS Gnat T1 (8578M) [65]	Newark Air Museum, Winthorpe, Notts
	XR537	HS Gnat T1 (8642M/G-NATY)	Privately owned, North Weald, Essex
	XR538	HS Gnat T1 (8621M/G-RORI) [01]	Heritage Aircraft Trust, North Weald, Essex
	XR540	HS Gnat T1 (XP502/8576M) [2]	Privately owned, Cotswold Airport, Glos
	XR571	HS Gnat T1 (8493M)	Privately owned, Leyburn, N. Yorks (for sale)
	XR574	HS Gnat T1 (8631M) [72]	Trenchard Museum, RAF Halton, Bucks
	XR595	WS Scout AH1 (G-BWHU) [M]	Privately owned, Southam, Warks
	XR601	WS Scout AH1	Privately owned,
	XR627	WS Scout AH1 [X]	Privately owned, Storwood, E. Yorks
	XR628	WS Scout AH1	Privately owned, Ipswich, Suffolk
	XR629	WS Scout AH1 (fuselage)	Privately owned, Ipswich, Suffolk
	XR635	WS Scout AH1	Midland Air Museum, Coventry, Warks
	XR650	Hunting Jet Provost T4 (8459M) [28]	Boscombe Down Aviation Collection, Old Sarum, Wilts
	XR654	Hunting Jet Provost T4 <ff>	Privately owned, Chester, Cheshire
	XR658	Hunting Jet Provost T4 (8192M)	RAF Manston History Museum, Kent
	XR662	Hunting Jet Provost T4 (8410M) [25]	Privately owned, Gilberdyke, E Yorks
	XR673	Hunting Jet Provost T4 (G-BXLO/9032M) [L]	Privately owned, Gamston, Notts (at N. Weald)
	XR681	Hunting Jet Provost T4 (8588M) <ff>	Robertsbridge Aviation Society, Mayfield, E, Sussex
	XR700	Hunting Jet Provost T4 (8589M) <ff>	No 1137 Sqn ATC, Long Kesh, NI
	XR713	BAC Lightning F3 (8935M) [C]	Preserved Bruntingthorpe, Leics
		(wears *XR718* on starboard side)	
	XR718	BAC Lightning F6 (8932M)	Privately owned, Over Dinsdale, N Yorks
	XR724	BAC Lightning F6 (G-BTSY)	The Lightning Association, Binbrook, Lincs
	XR725	BAC Lightning F6 [BA]	Privately owned, Binbrook, Lincs
	XR726	BAC Lightning F6 <ff>	Privately owned, Harrogate, N. Yorks
	XR728	BAC Lightning F6 [JS]	Cold War Jets Collection, Bruntingthorpe, Leics
	XR747	BAC Lightning F6 <ff>	No 20 Sqn ATC, Bideford, Devon
	XR749	BAC Lightning F3 (8934M) [DA]	Privately owned, Peterhead, Scotland
	XR751	BAC Lightning F3 <ff>	Privately owned, Thorpe Wood, N Yorks
	XR753	BAC Lightning F6 (8969M) [XI]	RAF Coningsby, Lincs, on display

Serial	Type (code/other identity)	Owner/operator, location or fate	Notes
XR753	BAC Lightning F53 (ZF578) [A]	Tangmere Military Aviation Museum, W. Sussex	
XR754	BAC Lightning F6 (8972M) <ff>	Privately owned, Upwood, Cambs	
XR755	BAC Lightning F6 [BN]	Privately owned, Callington, Cornwall	
XR757	BAC Lightning F6 <ff>	Newark Air Museum, Winthorpe, Notts	
XR759	BAC Lightning F6 <ff>	Privately owned, North Weald, Essex	
XR770	BAC Lightning F6 [AA]	RAF Manston History Museum, Kent	
XR771	BAC Lightning F6 [BF]	Midland Air Museum, Coventry, Warks	
XR808	BAC VC10 C1K [R] $	RAF Museum, Cosford, Shropshire	
XR810	BAC VC10 C1K <ff>	Privately owned, Crondall, Hants	
XR898	Northrop Shelduck D (XT005/BAPC.365)	Medway Aircraft Preservation Society, Rochester, Kent	
XR944	Wallis WA116 (G-ATTB)	Privately owned, Old Buckenham, Norfolk	
XR977	HS Gnat T1 (8640M)	RAF Museum, Hendon, Gtr London	
XR992	HS Gnat T1 (8624M/XS102/G-MOUR)	Heritage Aircraft Trust, North Weald, Essex	
XR993	HS Gnat T1 (8620M/XP534/G-BVPP)	South Wales Aviation Museum, St Athan, Wales	
XS100	HS Gnat T1 (8561M) <ff>	Privately owned, stored Wimbledon, Gtr London	
XS100	HS Gnat T1 (8561M) <rf>	Privately owned, North Weald, Essex	
XS104	HS Gnat T1 (8604M/G-FRCE)	Privately owned, North Weald, Essex	
XS149	WS58 Wessex HAS3 [661/GL]	The Helicopter Museum, stored Weston-super-Mare	
XS176	Hunting Jet Provost T4 (8514M) <ff>	Morayvia, Kinloss, Scotland	
XS177	Hunting Jet Provost T4 (9044M) [N]	Privately owned, Westbury, Wilts	
XS179	Hunting Jet Provost T4 (8237M) [20]	Secret Nuclear Bunker, Hack Green, Cheshire	
XS180	Hunting Jet Provost T4 (8238M/8338M) [21]	MOD JARTS, Boscombe Down, Wilts	
XS181	Hunting Jet Provost T4 (9033M) <ff>	Lakes Lightnings, Spark Bridge, Cumbria	
XS183	Hunting Jet Provost T4 <ff>	Privately owned, Plymouth, Devon	
XS186	Hunting Jet Provost T4 (8408M) [M]	Privately owned, Fishlake, S. Yorks	
XS209	Hunting Jet Provost T4 (8409M)	Solway Aviation Society, Carlisle, Cumbria	
XS216	Hunting Jet Provost T4 <ff>	South Yorkshire Aircraft Museum, Doncaster, S. Yorks	
XS218	Hunting Jet Provost T4 (8508M) <ff>	No 447 Sqn ATC, Henley-on-Thames, Berks	
XS228	Hunting Jet Provost T52 (104)	Privately owned, St. Athan, Glamorgan, Wales	
XS231	BAC Jet Provost T5 (G-ATAJ)	Boscombe Down Aviation Collection, Old Sarum, Wilts	
XS235	DH106 Comet 4C (G-CPDA)	Currently not known (ex-Bruntingthorpe, Leics)	
XS238	Auster AOP9 (TAD 200)	Newark Air Museum, Winthorpe, Notts	
XS416	BAC Lightning T5	Privately owned, Binbrook, Lincs	
XS417	BAC Lightning T5 [DZ]	Newark Air Museum, Winthorpe, Notts	
XS420	BAC Lightning T5	Privately owned, FAST, Farnborough, Hants	
XS421	BAC Lightning T5 <ff>	Privately owned, stored Neatishead, Norfolk	
XS456	BAC Lightning T5 [DX]	Skegness Water Leisure Park, Lincs	
XS457	BAC Lightning T5 <ff>	Privately owned, Binbrook, Lincs	
XS458	BAC Lightning T5 [T]	T5 Projects, Cranfield, Beds	
XS459	BAC Lightning T5 [AW]	Privately owned, Binbrook, Lincs	
XS481	WS58 Wessex HU5 [VY]	South Yorkshire Aircraft Museum, Doncaster, S. Yorks	
XS482	WS58 Wessex HU5	RAF Manston History Museum, Kent	
XS486	WS58 Wessex HU5 (9272M) [524/CU,F]	The Helicopter Museum, stored Weston-super-Mare, Somerset	
XS488	WS58 Wessex HU5 (9056M) [F]	Submerged, Cromhall Diving Centre, Glos	
XS489	WS58 Wessex HU5 [R]	Privately owned, Westerham, Kent	
XS493	WS58 Wessex HU5	StandardAero, stored Fleetlands, Hants	
XS507	WS58 Wessex HU5	South Wales Aviation Museum, St Athan, Wales	
XS508	WS58 Wessex HU5	FAA Museum, RNAS Yeovilton, Somerset	
XS510	WS58 Wessex HU5 [626/PO]	Morayvia, stored Spey Bay, Moray, Scotland	
XS511	WS58 Wessex HU5 [M]	Tangmere Military Aircraft Museum, W. Sussex	
XS513	WS58 Wessex HU5	RNAS Yeovilton Fire Section, Somerset	
XS515	WS58 Wessex HU5 [N]	Army, Keogh Barracks, Aldershot, instructional use	
XS516	WS58 Wessex HU5 [Q]	Privately owned, Redruth, Cornwall	
XS522	WS58 Wessex HU5 [ZL]	Blackball Paintball, Truro, Cornwall	
XS527	WS Wasp HAS1	FAA Museum, stored Cobham Hall, RNAS Yeovilton, Somerset	
XS529	WS Wasp HAS1	Privately owned, Redruth, Cornwall	
XS539	WS Wasp HAS1 [435]	StandardAero, Fleetlands, Hants on display	
XS567	WS Wasp HAS1 [434/E]	IWM Duxford, Cambs	
XS568	WS Wasp HAS1 (A2715) [441]	DSAE, stored HMS Sultan, Gosport, Hants	

Notes	Serial	Type (code/other identity)	Owner/operator, location or fate
	XS574	Northrop Shelduck D1 <R>	FAA Museum, stored Cobham Hall, RNAS Yeovilton, Somerset
	XS576	DH110 Sea Vixen FAW2 [125/E]	IWM Duxford, Cambs
	XS587	DH110 Sea Vixen FAW(TT)2 (8828M/G-VIXN)	Gatwick Aviation Museum, Charlwood, Surrey
	XS590	DH110 Sea Vixen FAW2 [131/E]	FAA Museum, RNAS Yeovilton, Somerset
	XS639	HS Andover E3A (9241M)	RAF Museum, Cosford, Shropshire
	XS641	HS Andover C1PR (9198M) (fuselage)	Privately owned, Sandbach, Cheshire
	XS643	HS Andover E3A (9278M) <ff>	Privately owned, Bramcote, Notts
	XS646	HS Andover C1(mod) (fuselage)	MOD JARTS, Boscombe Down, Wilts
	XS651	Slingsby T45 Swallow TX1 (BGA1211) [BYB]	Privately owned, Lasham, Hants
	XS652	Slingsby T45 Swallow TX1 (BGA1107)	Privately owned, Chipping, Lancs
	XS674	WS58 Wessex HC2 [R]	Privately owned, Biggin Hill, Kent
	XS694	HS Kestrel FGA1 (64-18268)	Wings Museum, stored Balcombe, W. Sussex
	XS695	HS Kestrel FGA1 [5]	RAF Museum, Cosford, Shropshire
	XS709	HS125 Dominie T1 [M]	RAF Museum, Cosford, Shropshire
	XS710	HS125 Dominie T1 (9259M) [O]	RAF Cranwell Fire Section, Lincs
	XS713	HS125 Dominie T1 [C]	Morayvia, Kinloss, Scotland
	XS726	HS125 Dominie T1 (9273M) [T]	Newark Air Museum, Winthorpe, Notts
	XS727	HS125 Dominie T1 [D]	RAF Cranwell, Lincs, on display
	XS731	HS125 Dominie T1 (N19XY) (fuselage)	Privately owned, Marlborough, Wilts
	XS734	HS125 Dominie T1 (9260M) [N]	Privately owned,
	XS735	HS125 Dominie T1 (9264M) [R]	South Yorkshire Aircraft Museum, Doncaster, S. Yorks
	XS736	HS125 Dominie T1 [S]	MOD Winterbourne Gunner, Wilts
	XS743	Beagle B206Z	Boscombe Down Aviation Collection, Old Sarum, Wilts
	XS790	HS748 Andover CC2 <ff>	Boscombe Down Aviation Collection, Old Sarum, Wilts
	XS859	Slingsby T45 Swallow TX1 (BGA1136) [859]	Privately owned, stored Felthorpe, Norfolk
	XS863	WS58 Wessex HAS1 [304/R]	IWM Duxford, Cambs
	XS865	WS58 Wessex HAS1 (A2694)	Privately owned, Ballygowan, NI
	XS885	WS58 Wessex HAS1 [512/DD]	Delta Force Paintball, Burnley, Lancs
	XS886	WS58 Wessex HAS1 [527/CU]	Privately owned, Ditchling, E. Sussex
	XS887	WS58 Wessex HAS1 [403/FI]	Thorpe Camp Visitor Centre, Tattershall Thorpe, Lincs
	XS898	BAC Lightning F6 <ff>	Privately owned, Lavendon, Bucks
	XS899	BAC Lightning F6 <ff>	Privately owned, Binbrook, Lincs
	XS903	BAC Lightning F6 [BA]	Yorkshire Air Museum, Elvington, N. Yorks
	XS904	BAC Lightning F6 [BQ]	Cold War Jets Collection, Bruntingthorpe, Leics
	XS919	BAC Lightning F6	Privately owned, Wiltshire
	XS921	BAC Lightning F6 <R> (BAPC.357) [BA]	BAE Systems, Samlesbury, Lancs, on display
	XS922	BAC Lightning F6 (8973M) <ff>	Lakes Lightnings, Spark Bridge, Cumbria
	XS923	BAC Lightning F6 <ff>	Privately owned, Welshpool, Powys, Wales
	XS925	BAC Lightning F6 (8961M) [BA]	RAF Museum, Hendon, Gtr London
	XS928	BAC Lightning F6 [AD]	BAE Systems Warton, Lancs, on display
	XS932	BAC Lightning F6 <ff>	Privately owned, Walcott, Lincs
	XS933	BAC Lightning F6 <ff>	Privately owned, Farnham, Surrey
	XS933	BAC Lightning F53 (ZF594) [BE]	North-East Land, Sea & Air Museums, Usworth, T&W
	XS935	BAC Lightning F53 (53-672/204/ZF580/XR768) [AK]	Cornwall Aviation Heritage Centre, Newquay, Cornwall
	XS936	BAC Lightning F6	Castle Motors, Liskeard, Cornwall
	XT108	Agusta-Bell 47G-3 Sioux AH1 [U]	Army Flying Museum, Middle Wallop, Hants
	XT123	WS Sioux AH1 (XT827) [D]	AAC Middle Wallop, Hants, at main gate
	XT131	Agusta-Bell 47G-3 Sioux AH1 (G-CICN) [B]	Historic Army Aircraft Flight, Middle Wallop, Hants
	XT140	Agusta-Bell 47G-3 Sioux AH1	Privately owned, Malmesbury, Wilts
	XT147	Agusta-Bell 47G-3 Sioux AH1 (frame only)	Privately owned, Hooton Park, Cheshire
	XT148	Agusta-Bell 47G-3 Sioux AH1	Privately owned, Hooton Park, Cheshire
	XT150	Agusta-Bell 47G-3 Sioux AH1 (7883M) [R]	South Yorkshire Aircraft Museum, stored Doncaster, S. Yorks
	XT151	WS Sioux AH1	Army Flying Museum, stored Middle Wallop, Hants
	XT176	WS Sioux AH1 [U]	FAA Museum, stored Cobham Hall, RNAS Yeovilton, Somerset
	XT190	WS Sioux AH1	The Helicopter Museum, Weston-super-Mare, Somerset
	XT200	WS Sioux AH1 [F]	Newark Air Museum, Winthorpe, Notts
	XT208	WS Sioux AH1 (wreck)	Privately owned, Fivemiletown, Co Tyrone, NI
	XT236	WS Sioux AH1 (frame only)	Privately owned, Hooton Park, Merseyside

Serial	Type (code/other identity)	Owner/operator, location or fate	Notes
XT242	WS Sioux AH1 (comp XW179) [12]	South Yorkshire Aircraft Museum, Doncaster, S. Yorks	
XT257	WS58 Wessex HAS3 (8719M)	Bournemouth Aviation Museum, Dorset	
XT277	HS Buccaneer S2A (8853M) <ff>	Privately owned, Welshpool, Powys, Wales	
XT280	HS Buccaneer S2A <ff>	Dumfries & Galloway Avn Mus, Dumfries, Scotland	
XT284	HS Buccaneer S2A (8855M) <ff>	Privately owned, Felixstowe, Suffolk	
XT288	HS Buccaneer S2B (9134M)	National Museum of Flight, E Fortune, Scotland	
XT420	WS Wasp HAS1 (G-CBUI) [422]	Fly Navy Heritage Trust, RNAS Yeovilton, Somerset	
XT427	WS Wasp HAS1 [606]	FAA Museum, stored Cobham Hall, RNAS Yeovilton, Somerset	
XT431	WS Wasp HAS1 (comp XS463) [462]	Bournemouth Aviation Museum, Dorset	
XT434	WS Wasp HAS1 (G-CGGK) [455]	Westland Wasp Historic Flt, Chard, Somerset	
XT435	WS Wasp HAS1 (NZ3907/G-RIMM) [426/AR]	Privately owned, North Weald, Essex	
XT437	WS Wasp HAS1 [423]	Boscombe Down Aviation Collection, Old Sarum, Wilts	
XT439	WS Wasp HAS1 [605]	Privately owned, Hemel Hempstead, Herts	
XT443	WS Wasp HAS1 [422/AU]	The Helicopter Museum, Weston-super-Mare, Somerset	
XT453	WS58 Wessex HU5 (A2756) [B/PO]	DSAE, stored HMS Sultan, Gosport, Hants	
XT455	WS58 Wessex HU5 (A2654) [U]	Mayhem Paintball, Abridge, Essex	
XT456	WS58 Wessex HU5 (8941M) [XZ]	Belfast Airport Fire Section, NI	
XT466	WS58 Wessex HU5 (A2617/8921M) [528/CU]	Morayvia, Kinloss, Scotland	
XT467	WS58 Wessex HU5 (8922M) [BF]	Gunsmoke Paintball, Wickford, Essex	
XT469	WS58 Wessex HU5 (8920M)	Privately owned, Clatterford, Isle of Wight	
XT472	WS58 Wessex HU5 [XC]	The Helicopter Museum, stored Weston-super-Mare, Somerset	
XT480	WS58 Wessex HU5 [468/RG]	Rednal Paintball, Shropshire	
XT482	WS58 Wessex HU5 [ZM/VL]	FAA Museum, RNAS Yeovilton, Somerset	
XT486	WS58 Wessex HU5 (8919M)	Dumfries & Galloway Avn Mus, Dumfries, Scotland	
XT493	SARO SR.N6 Winchester	Hovercraft Museum, Solent Airport, Hants	
XT550	WS Sioux AH1 [D]	Currently not known	
XT575	Vickers Viscount 837 <ff>	Brooklands Museum, Weybridge, Surrey	
XT581	Northrop Shelduck D1	IWM Duxford, Cambs	
XT581	Northrop Shelduck D1 (BAPC.501)	Muckleburgh Collection, Weybourne, Norfolk	
XT583	Northrop Shelduck D1	Privately owned, stored Netheravon, Wilts	
XT596	McD F-4K Phantom FG1	FAA Museum, RNAS Yeovilton, Somerset	
XT597	McD F-4K Phantom FG1	Privately owned, Cotswold Airport, Glos	
XT601	WS58 Wessex HC2 (9277M) (composite)	RAF Odiham, Hants, BDRT	
XT604	WS58 Wessex HC2	East Midlands Airport Aeropark, Leics	
XT617	WS Scout AH1	Wattisham Station Heritage Museum, Suffolk	
XT621	WS Scout AH1	Privately owned, Colsterworth, Lincs	
XT623	WS Scout AH1	DSAE SAAE, Lyneham, Wilts	
XT626	WS Scout AH1 (G-CIBW) [Q]	Army Historic Aircraft Flt, Middle Wallop, Hants	
XT630	WS Scout AH1 (G-BXRL) [X]	Privately owned, Rough Close, Staffs	
XT631	WS Scout AH1 [D]	Privately owned, Ipswich, Suffolk	
XT633	WS Scout AH1	Bridgwater & Taunton College, Bridgwater, GI use	
XT638	WS Scout AH1 [N]	AAC Middle Wallop, Hants, at main gate	
XT640	WS Scout AH1	Privately owned, South Clifton, Notts	
XT643	WS Scout AH1	Army, Thorpe Camp, East Wretham, Norfolk (wreck)	
XT653	Slingsby T45 Swallow TX1 (BGA3469)	Privately owned, Keevil, Wilts	
XT672	WS58 Wessex HC2 [WE]	RAF Stafford, Staffs, on display	
XT681	WS58 Wessex HC2 (9279M) [U] <ff>	Privately owned, stored Oxon	
XT761	WS58 Wessex HU5 (G-WSEX)	Privately owned, Chard, Somerset	
XT762	WS58 Wessex HU5	Hamburger Hill Paintball, Marksbury, Somerset	
XT765	WS58 Wessex HU5 [J]	FAA Museum, stored Cobham Hall, RNAS Yeovilton, Somerset	
XT765	WS58 Wessex HU5 (XT458/A2768) [P/VL]	RNAS Yeovilton, Somerset, on display	
XT769	WS58 Wessex HU5 [823]	FAA Museum, RNAS Yeovilton, Somerset	
XT771	WS58 Wessex HU5 [620/PO]	Privately owned, stored Chard, Somerset	
XT773	WS58 Wessex HU5 (9123M)	Morayvia, stored Spey Bay, Moray, Scotland	
XT778	WS Wasp HAS1 [430]	FAA Museum, stored Cobham Hall, RNAS Yeovilton, Somerset	
XT780	WS Wasp HAS1 [636]	Westland Wasp Historic Flt, Everleigh, Wilts	
XT787	WS Wasp HAS1 (NZ3905/G-KAXT)	Westland Wasp Historic Flt, Everleigh, Wilts	
XT788	WS Wasp HAS1 (G-BMIR) [474]	Privately owned, Storwood, E. Yorks	

BRITISH MILITARY AIRCRAFT MARKINGS

Notes	Serial	Type (code/other identity)	Owner/operator, location or fate
	XT793	WS Wasp HAS1 (G-BZPP) <ff>	South Yorkshire Aircraft Museum, Doncaster, S. Yorks
	XT863	McD F-4K Phantom FG1 <ff>	Privately owned, Northwood, IOW
	XT864	McD F-4K Phantom FG1 (8998M/XT684) [007/R]	Ulster Aviation Society, Long Kesh, NI
	XT891	McD F-4M Phantom FGR2 (9136M)	RAF Coningsby, Lincs, at main gate
	XT895	McD F-4M Phantom FGR2 <ff> (8171M)	Privately owned, Newburgh, Lancs
	XT903	McD F-4M Phantom FGR2 <ff>	RAF Museum, stored Cosford, Shropshire
	XT905	McD F-4M Phantom FGR2 (9286M) [P]	Privately owned, Cotswold Airport, Glos
	XT907	McD F-4M Phantom FGR2 (9151M) [W]	Privately owned, Bentwaters, Suffolk
	XT914	McD F-4M Phantom FGR2 (9269M) [Z]	Wattisham Station Heritage Museum, Suffolk
	XV104	BAC VC10 C1K <ff>	South Wales Aviation Museum, stored St Athan, Wales
	XV106	BAC VC10 C1K <ff>	Avro Heritage Museum, Woodford, Cheshire
	XV108	BAC VC10 C1K <ff>	East Midlands Airport Aeropark, Leics
	XV109	BAC VC10 C1K <ff>	South Wales Aviation Museum, stored St Athan, Wales
	XV118	WS Scout AH1 (9141M) <ff>	Kennet Aviation, North Weald, Essex
	XV122	WS Scout AH1 [D]	Defence Academy of the UK, Shrivenham, Oxon
	XV123	WS Scout AH1 [V]	Vanguard Self Storage, Greenford, Gtr London
	XV124	WS Scout AH1 [W]	Privately owned, Godstone, Surrey
	XV126	WS Scout AH1 (G-SCTA) [50K]	Privately owned, Whepstead, Suffolk
	XV127	WS Scout AH1	Army Flying Museum, Middle Wallop, Hants
	XV130	WS Scout AH1 (G-BWJW) [R]	Privately owned, North Weald, Essex
	XV136	WS Scout AH1 [X]	Ulster Aviation Society, Long Kesh, NI
	XV137	WS Scout AH1 (G-CRUM)	Privately owned, Chiseldon, Wilts
	XV138	WS Scout AH1 (G-SASM) [S]	Privately owned, North Weald, Essex
	XV139	WS Scout AH1 (comp XP886)	South Yorkshire Aircraft Museum, Doncaster, S. Yorks
	XV141	WS Scout AH1	REME Museum, Lyneham, Wilts
	XV148	HS Nimrod MR1(mod) <ff>	Cornwall Aviation Heritage Centre, Newquay, Cornwall
	XV161	HS Buccaneer S2B (9117M) <ff>	Currently not known
	XV165	HS Buccaneer S2B <ff>	Privately owned, Ashford, Kent
	XV168	HS Buccaneer S2B [AF]	Yorkshire Air Museum, Elvington, N. Yorks
	XV201	Lockheed C-130K Hercules C1K <ff>	Marshall Aerospace, Cambridge, Cambs
	XV202	Lockheed C-130K Hercules C3 [202]	RAF Museum, Cosford, Shropshire
	XV208	Lockheed C-130K Hercules W2 <ff>	Marshall Aerospace, Stored Cambridge, Cambs
	XV226	HS Nimrod MR2 $	Preserved Bruntingthorpe, Leics
	XV229	HS Nimrod MR2 [29] <ff>	RAF Manston History Museum, Kent
	XV231	HS Nimrod MR2 [31]	Aviation Viewing Park, Manchester, Gtr Manchester
	XV232	HS Nimrod MR2 [32]	Privately owned, Coventry, Warks
	XV235	HS Nimrod MR2 [35] <ff>	Avro Heritage Museum, Woodford, Cheshire
	XV240	HS Nimrod MR2 [40] <ff>	Morayvia, Kinloss, Scotland
	XV241	HS Nimrod MR2 [41] <ff>	National Museum of Flight, E Fortune, Scotland
	XV244	HS Nimrod MR2 [44]	Morayvia, Kinloss Barracks, Scotland
	XV249	HS Nimrod R1 $	RAF Museum, Cosford, Shropshire
	XV250	HS Nimrod MR2 [50]	Yorkshire Air Museum, Elvington, N. Yorks
	XV252	HS Nimrod MR2 [52] <ff>	Privately owned, Cullen, Moray, Scotland
	XV254	HS Nimrod MR2 [54] <ff>	South Wales Aviation Museum, St Athan, Wales
	XV255	HS Nimrod MR2 [55]	City of Norwich Aviation Museum, Norfolk
	XV259	BAe Nimrod AEW3 <ff>	Privately owned, Wales
	XV268	DHC2 Beaver AL1 (G-BVER)	Privately owned, Cumbernauld, Scotland
	XV277	HS P.1127(RAF)	National Museum of Flight, E Fortune, Scotland
	XV279	HS P.1127(RAF) (8566M)	Harrier Heritage Centre, RAF Wittering, Cambs
	XV280	HS P.1127(RAF) <ff>	South Yorkshire Aviation Museum, Doncaster, S. Yorks
	XV281	HS P.1127(RAF) (BAPC 484)	South Yorkshire Aviation Museum, Doncaster ,S. Yorks
	XV304	Lockheed C-130K Hercules C3A	RAF JADTEU, Brize Norton, Oxon, instructional use
	XV328	BAC Lightning T5 <ff>	Cold War Jets Collection, Bruntingthorpe, Leics
	XV333	HS Buccaneer S2B [234/H]	FAA Museum, RNAS Yeovilton, Somerset
	XV344	HS Buccaneer S2C	QinetiQ Farnborough, Hants, on display
	XV350	HS Buccaneer S2B	East Midlands Airport Aeropark, Leics
	XV352	HS Buccaneer S2B <ff>	RAF Manston History Museum, Kent
	XV359	HS Buccaneer S2B [035/R]	Privately owned, Topsham, Devon
	XV361	HS Buccaneer S2B	Ulster Aviation Society, Long Kesh, NI
	XV370	Sikorsky SH-3D (A2682) [260]	DSAE RNAESS, HMS Sultan, Gosport, Hants
	XV371	WS61 Sea King HAS1(DB) [61/DD]	Privately owned, Glastonbury, Somerset

Serial	Type (code/other identity)	Owner/operator, location or fate	Notes
XV372	WS61 Sea King HAS1	MOD Pembrey Sands Air Weapons Range, Wales, GI use	
XV383	Northrop MQM-57A/3 (fuselage)	Privately owned, Wimborne, Dorset	
XV401	McD F-4M Phantom FGR2 [I]	Privately owned, Bentwaters, Suffolk	
XV402	McD F-4M Phantom FGR2 <ff>	Privately owned, Kent	
XV406	McD F-4M Phantom FGR2 (9098M) [D]	Solway Aviation Society, Carlisle, Cumbria	
XV408	McD F-4M Phantom FGR2 (9165M) [L]	Tangmere Military Aviation Museum, W. Sussex	
XV415	McD F-4M Phantom FGR2 (9163M) [E]	RAF Boulmer, Northumberland, on display	
XV419	McD F-4M Phantom FGR2 <ff>	Privately owned, Wales	
XV424	McD F-4M Phantom FGR2 (9152M) [I]	RAF Museum, Hendon, Gtr London	
XV426	McD F-4M Phantom FGR2 <ff>	City of Norwich Aviation Museum, Norfolk	
XV460	McD F-4M Phantom FGR2 <ff>	Privately owned, Bentwaters, Suffolk	
XV474	McD F-4M Phantom FGR2 [T]	The Old Flying Machine Company, Duxford, Cambs	
XV490	McD F-4M Phantom FGR2 [R] <ff>	Newark Air Museum, Winthorpe, Notts	
XV497	McD F-4M Phantom FGR2 (9295M) [D]	Norfolk & Suffolk Avn Museum, Flixton, Suffolk	
XV499	McD F-4M Phantom FGR2 <ff>	South Wales Aviation Museum, St Athan, Wales	
XV581	McD F-4K Phantom FG1 (9070M) <ff>	Staffordshire Wing ATC Aerospace & Technology Centre	
XV582	McD F-4K Phantom FG1 (9066M) [M]	South Wales Aviation Museum, St Athan, Wales	
XV586	McD F-4K Phantom FG1 (9067M) [010-R]	Morayvia, Kinloss, Scotland	
XV591	McD F-4K Phantom FG1 [013] <ff>	RAF Museum, Cosford, Shropshire	
XV631	WS Wasp HAS1 (fuselage)	Farnborough Air Sciences Trust, stored Farnborough, Hants	
XV642	WS61 Sea King HAS2A (A2614) [259]	DSAE RNAESS, HMS Sultan, Gosport, Hants	
XV643	WS61 Sea King HAS6 [262]	DSAE, stored HMS Sultan, Gosport, Hants	
XV647	WS61 Sea King HU5 [28/GJ]	Privately owned, Chard, Somerset	
XV648	WS61 Sea King HU5	Privately owned, Acharacle, Argyll, Scotland	
XV649	WS61 Sea King ASaC7 [180]	DSAE, stored HMS Sultan, Gosport, Hants	
XV651	WS61 Sea King HU5	Holmside Park, Edmondsley, Co. Durham	
XV653	WS61 Sea King HAS6 (9326M) [63/CU]	DSAE, stored HMS Sultan, Gosport, Hants	
XV654	WS61 Sea King HAS6 [705/DD] (wreck)	RN, Predannack Fire School, Cornwall	
XV655	WS61 Sea King HAS6 [270/N]	DSAE RNAESS, HMS Sultan, Gosport, Hants	
XV656	WS61 Sea King ASaC7 [185]	HeliOperations Ltd, stored Somerton, Somerset	
XV657	WS61 Sea King HAS5 (ZA135) [32/DD]	RN, Predannack Fire School, Cornwall	
XV659	WS61 Sea King HAS6 (9324M) [62/CU]	DSAE, stored HMS Sultan, Gosport, Hants	
XV660	WS61 Sea King HAS6 [269/N]	DSAE RNAESS, HMS Sultan, Gosport, Hants	
XV661	WS61 Sea King HU5 [26]	Currently not known	
XV663	WS61 Sea King HAS6 [18]	FAA Museum, RNAS Yeovilton, Somerset	
XV664	WS61 Sea King ASaC7 [190]	HeliOperations Ltd, stored Somerton, Somerset	
XV665	WS61 Sea King HAS6 [507/CU]	DSAE RNAESS, HMS Sultan, Gosport, Hants	
XV666	WS61 Sea King HU5	Transferred to Ukraine, December 2022	
XV670	WS61 Sea King HU5 [17]	HeliOperations Ltd, stored Somerton, Somerset	
XV671	WS61 Sea King ASaC7 [183/CU]	HeliOperations Ltd, stored Somerton, Somerset	
XV672	WS61 Sea King ASaC7 [187]	DSAE, stored HMS Sultan, Gosport, Hants	
XV673	WS61 Sea King HU5 [827/CU]	RNAS Culdrose, Cornwall, on display	
XV674	WS61 Sea King HAS6	Privately owned, Horsham, W. Sussex	
XV675	WS61 Sea King HAS6 [701/PW]	DSAE RNAESS, HMS Sultan, Gosport, Hants	
XV676	WS61 Sea King HC6 [ZE]	DSAE RNAESS, HMS Sultan, Gosport, Hants	
XV677	WS61 Sea King HAS6 [269]	South Yorkshire Aircraft Museum, Doncaster, S. Yorks	
XV696	WS61 Sea King HAS6 [267/L]	SFDO, RNAS Culdrose, Cornwall	
XV697	WS61 Sea King ASaC7 [181/CU]	HeliOperations Ltd, stored Somerton, Somerset	
XV699	WS61 Sea King HU5 [823]	DSAE RNAESS, HMS Sultan, Gosport, Hants	
XV700	WS61 Sea King HC6 [ZC]	RAF St Mawgan, , Cornwall, instructional use	
XV701	WS61 Sea King HAS6 [268/N,64]	DSAE RNAESS, HMS Sultan, Gosport, Hants	
XV703	WS61 Sea King HC6 [ZD]	DSAE RNAESS, stored HMS Sultan, Gosport, Hants	
XV705	WS61 Sea King HU5 [29]	Privately owned, Stockie Muir, Stirling, Scotland	
XV706	WS61 Sea King HAS6 (9344M) [017/L]	DSAE RNAESS, HMS Sultan, Gosport, Hants	
XV707	WS61 Sea King ASaC7 [184]	DSAE RNAESS, stored HMS Sultan, Gosport, Hants	
XV708	WS61 Sea King HAS6 [501/CU]	DSAE RNAESS, HMS Sultan, Gosport, Hants	
XV711	WS61 Sea King HAS6 [15/CW]	DSAE, stored HMS Sultan, Gosport, Hants	
XV712	WS61 Sea King HAS6 [66]	IWM Duxford, Cambs	
XV713	WS61 Sea King HAS6 (A2646) [018/L]	DSAE RNAESS, HMS Sultan, Gosport, Hants	
XV714	WS61 Sea King ASaC7 [188]	HeliOperations Ltd, stored Somerton, Somerset	

Notes	Serial	Type (code/other identity)	Owner/operator, location or fate
	XV720	WS58 Wessex HC2 (A2701)	Privately owned, Culham, Oxon
	XV722	WS58 Wessex HC2 (8805M) [WH]	Privately owned, Badgers Mount, Kent
	XV724	WS58 Wessex HC2	DSAE RNAESS, HMS Sultan, Gosport, Hants
	XV725	WS58 Wessex HC2 [C]	Morayvia, stored Spey Bay, Moray, Scotland
	XV726	WS58 Wessex HC2 [J]	Privately owned, Biggin Hill, Kent
	XV728	WS58 Wessex HC2 [A]	Newark Air Museum, Winthorpe, Notts
	XV731	WS58 Wessex HC2 [Y]	Privately owned, Badgers Mount, Kent
	XV732	WS58 Wessex HCC4	RAF Museum, Hendon, Gtr London
	XV733	WS58 Wessex HCC4	The Helicopter Museum, Weston-super-Mare, Somerset
	XV741	HS Harrier GR3 (A2608)	Brooklands Museum, Weybridge, Surrey
	XV744	HS Harrier GR3 (9167M) [3K]	Tangmere Military Aviation Museum, W. Sussex
	XV748	HS Harrier GR3 [B]	Yorkshire Air Museum, Elvington, N. Yorks
	XV751	HS Harrier GR3 [AU]	Gatwick Aviation Museum, Charlwood, Surrey
	XV752	HS Harrier GR3 (9075M) [B]	South Yorkshire Aircraft Museum, Doncaster, S. Yorks
	XV753	HS Harrier GR3 (9078M)	Cornwall Aviation Heritage Centre, Newquay, Cornwall
	XV759	HS Harrier GR3 [O] <ff>	Privately owned, Hitchin, Herts
	XV760	HS Harrier GR3 <ff>	Solent Sky, Southampton, Hants
	XV779	HS Harrier GR3 (8931M) <ff>	Privately owned, Thorpe Wood, N. Yorks
	XV779	HS Harrier GR3	Harrier Heritage Centre, RAF Wittering, Cambs
	XV783	HS Harrier GR3 [N]	Privately owned, Corley Moor, Warks
	XV784	HS Harrier GR3 (8909M) <ff>	Boscombe Down Aviation Collection, Old Sarum, Wilts
	XV786	HS Harrier GR3 [123] <ff>	RNAS Culdrose Fire Section, Cornwall
	XV786	HS Harrier GR3 [S] <rf>	RN, Predannack Fire School, Cornwall
	XV798	HS Harrier GR1(mod) (BAPC 450)	Rolls Royce Heritage Trust, Hucknall, Derbyshire
	XV806	HS Harrier GR3 <ff>	Privately owned, Doncaster, S. Yorks
	XV808	HS Harrier GR3 (9076M/A2687) [08/DD]	Privately owned, Chetton, Shropshire
	XV810	HS Harrier GR3 (9038M)	Privately owned, Walcott, Lincs
	XV814	DH106 Comet 4 (G-APDF) <ff>	Privately owned, Chipping Campden, Glos
	XV864	HS Buccaneer S2B (9234M)	RAF Manston History Museum, Kent
	XV865	HS Buccaneer S2B (9226M)	IWM Duxford, Cambs
	XV867	HS Buccaneer S2B <ff>	Morayvia, Kinloss, Scotland
	XW175	HS Harrier T4(VAAC)	Privately owned, Thorpe Wood, N Yorks
	XW198	WS Puma HC1	RAF AM&SU, stored Shawbury, Shropshire
	XW199	WS Puma HC2 [A]	RAF No 28 Sqn/No 33 Sqn/No 230 Sqn, Benson, Oxon
	XW202	WS Puma HC1	Army, Stensall Barracks, York
	XW204	WS Puma HC2 [B]	RAF, stored Benson, Oxon
	XW208	WS Puma HC1	Newark Air Museum, Winthorpe, Notts
	XW209	WS Puma HC2	RAF, stored Benson, Oxon
	XW210	WS Puma HC1 (comp XW215)	RAF AM&SU, stored Shawbury, Shropshire
	XW212	WS Puma HC2 [D]	RAF No 1563 Flt, Seria, Brunei
	XW213	WS Puma HC2 [E]	RAF No 28 Sqn/No 33 Sqn/No 230 Sqn, Benson, Oxon
	XW214	WS Puma HC2 [F]	RAF No 1563 Flt, Seria, Brunei
	XW216	WS Puma HC2 (F-ZWDD) [G]	RAF No 28 Sqn/No 33 Sqn/No 230 Sqn, Benson, Oxon
	XW217	WS Puma HC2 [H]	RAF, stored Benson, Oxon
	XW219	WS Puma HC2	RAF, stored Benson, Oxon
	XW220	WS Puma HC2 [K]	RAF No 28 Sqn/No 33 Sqn/No 230 Sqn, Benson, Oxon
	XW222	WS Puma HC1	Ulster Aviation Society, Long Kesh, NI
	XW223	WS Puma HC1	RAF AM&SU, stored Shawbury, Shropshire
	XW224	WS Puma HC2 $	RAF No 28 Sqn/No 33 Sqn/No 230 Sqn, Benson, Oxon
	XW225	WS Puma HC1	Army, Beckingham Training Camp, Lincs
	XW226	WS Puma HC1	RAF AM&SU, stored Shawbury, Shropshire
	XW231	WS Puma HC2 [N]	RAF No 28 Sqn/No 33 Sqn/No 230 Sqn, Benson, Oxon
	XW232	WS Puma HC2 (F-ZWDE) [P]	RAF No 84 Sqn, Akrotiri, Cyprus
	XW235	WS Puma HC2 (F-ZWBI) [Q]	RAF No 28 Sqn/No 33 Sqn/No 230 Sqn, Benson, Oxon
	XW236	WS Puma HC1	RAF Brize Norton Fire Dump
	XW237	WS Puma HC2 [R]	RAF No 84 Sqn, Akrotiri, Cyprus
	XW241	Sud SA330E Puma	Farnborough Air Sciences Trust, Farnborough, Hants
	XW264	HS Harrier T2 <ff>	Jet Age Museum, Gloucestershire Airport, Glos
	XW265	HS Harrier T4A (9258M) <ff>	No 2345 Sqn ATC, RAF Leuchars, Scotland
	XW267	HS Harrier T4 (9263M)	Privately owned, Bentwaters, Suffolk
	XW268	HS Harrier T4N	City of Norwich Aviation Museum, Norfolk

Serial	Type (code/other identity)	Owner/operator, location or fate	Notes
XW269	HS Harrier T4 [TB]	Caernarfon Air World, Gwynedd, Wales	
XW270	HS Harrier T4 [T]	Coventry University, Warks, instructional use	
XW276	Aérospatiale SA341 Gazelle (F-ZWRI)	Newark Air Museum, Winthorpe, Notts	
XW283	WS Scout AH1 (G-CIMX) [U]	Privately owned, Badwell Green, Suffolk	
XW289	BAC Jet Provost T5A (G-BVXT/G-JPVA) [73]	RAF St Athan, Wales, on display	
XW290	BAC Jet Provost T5A (9199M) [41,MA]	*Currently not known (ex-Bruntingthorpe, Leics)*	
XW293	BAC Jet Provost T5 (G-BWCS) [Z]	Privately owned, Bournemouth, Dorset	
XW299	BAC Jet Provost T5A (G-CLJW/9146M) [60,MB]	Privately owned, Hawarden, Flintshire, Wales (for export to Australia)	
XW303	BAC Jet Provost T5A (9119M) [127]	RAF Halton, Bucks	
XW304	BAC Jet Provost T5 (9172M) [MD]	Privately owned, Eye, Suffolk	
XW309	BAC Jet Provost T5 (9179M) [V,ME]	Hartlepool College of Further Education, Co. Durham	
XW311	BAC Jet Provost T5 (9180M) [W,MF]	Privately owned, North Weald, Essex	
XW315	BAC Jet Provost T5A <ff>	Privately owned, Preston, Lancs	
XW320	BAC Jet Provost T5A (9015M) [71]	Privately owned, St Athan, Wales	
XW321	BAC Jet Provost T5A (9154M) [62,MH]	Privately owned, Bentwaters, Suffolk	
XW323	BAC Jet Provost T5A (9166M) [86]	RAF Museum, Hendon, Gtr London	
XW324	BAC Jet Provost T5 (G-BWSG) [U]	Privately owned, North Weald, Essex (dismantled)	
XW325	BAC Jet Provost T5B (G-BWGF) [E]	Privately owned, St. Athan, Wales	
XW327	BAC Jet Provost T5A (9130M) [62]	RAF Museum, Cosford, Shropshire (stored)	
XW330	BAC Jet Provost T5A (9195M) [82,MJ]	Privately owned, Knutsford, Cheshire	
XW333	BAC Jet Provost T5A (G-BVTC)	Global Aviation, Humberside, Lincs	
XW353	BAC Jet Provost T5A (9090M) [3]	RAF Cranwell, Lincs, on display	
XW358	BAC Jet Provost T5A (9181M) [59,MK] (fuselage)	Privately owned, Berkshire	
XW360	BAC Jet Provost T5A (9153M) [61,ML]	Privately owned, Thorpe Wood, N. Yorks	
XW363	BAC Jet Provost T5A [36]	Dumfries & Galloway Avn Mus, stored Dumfries, Scotland	
XW364	BAC Jet Provost T5A (9188M) [35,MN]	RAF Halton, Bucks, Gl use	
XW370	BAC Jet Provost T5A (9196M) [72,MP]	Privately owned,	
XW375	BAC Jet Provost T5A (9149M) [52]	Privately owned, Inverness, Scotland	
XW404	BAC Jet Provost T5A (9049M) [77]	Hartlepool College of Further Education, Co. Durham	
XW405	BAC Jet Provost T5A (9187M)	Hartlepool College of Further Education, Co. Durham	
XW409	BAC Jet Provost T5A (9047M)	Privately owned, Hawarden, Flintshire, Wales	
XW410	BAC Jet Provost T5A (9125M) [80] <ff>	Privately owned, Conington, Cambs	
XW418	BAC Jet Provost T5A (9173M) [MT]	Privately owned, Bentwaters, Suffolk	
XW419	BAC Jet Provost T5A (9120M) [125]	Privately owned, Tore, Highland, Scotland	
XW420	BAC Jet Provost T5A (9194M) [83,MU]	South Wales Aviation Museum, St Athan, Wales	
XW422	BAC Jet Provost T5A (G-BWEB) [3]	Privately owned, Cotswold Airport, Glos	
XW423	BAC Jet Provost T5A (G-BWUW) [14]	Deeside College, Connah's Quay, Flintshire, Wales	
XW430	BAC Jet Provost T5A (9176M) [77,MW]	Privately owned, Arncott, Oxon	
XW432	BAC Jet Provost T5A (9127M) [76,MX]	Privately owned, Thame, Bucks	
XW433	BAC Jet Provost T5A (G-JPRO)	Privately owned, Inverness Airport, Scotland	
XW434	BAC Jet Provost T5A (9091M) [78,MY]	Halfpenny Green Airport, Staffs, on display	
XW436	BAC Jet Provost T5A (9148M) [68]	Privately owned, St Athan, Wales	
XW530	HS Buccaneer S2B [530]	Privately owned, Cupar, Fife, Scotland	
XW541	HS Buccaneer S2B (8858M) <ff>	Privately owned, Lavendon, Bucks	
XW544	HS Buccaneer S2B (8857M) [O]	The Buccaneer Aviation Group, Cotswold Airport, Glos	
XW547	HS Buccaneer S2B (9095M/9169M) [R]	RAF Museum, Hendon, Gtr London	
XW550	HS Buccaneer S2B <ff>	The Buccaneer Aviation Group, Cotswold Airport, Glos	
XW560	SEPECAT Jaguar S <ff>	Boscombe Down Aviation Collection, Old Sarum, Wilts	
XW563	SEPECAT Jaguar S (XX822/8563M)	County Hall, Norwich, Norfolk, on display	
XW566	SEPECAT Jaguar B	Farnborough Air Sciences Trust, Farnborough, Hants	
XW612	WS Scout AH1 (G-KAXW)	Privately owned, Southam, Warks	
XW613	WS Scout AH1 (G-BXRS)	*Sold to the USA, January 2023*	
XW616	WS Scout AH1	*Currently not known*	
XW630	HS Harrier GR3	RNAS Yeovilton, Somerset, Fire Section	
XW635	Beagle D5/180 (G-AWSW)	Privately owned, Spanhoe, Northants	
XW664	HS Nimrod R1	East Midlands Airport Aeropark, Leics	
XW666	HS Nimrod R1 <ff>	South Yorkshire Aircraft Museum, Doncaster, S. Yorks	
XW763	HS Harrier GR3 (9002M/9041M) <ff>	Privately owned, Wigston, Leics	
XW768	HS Harrier GR3 (9072M) [N]	Spadeadam Ranges, Cumbria	
XW784	Mitchell-Procter Kittiwake I (G-BBRN) [VL]	Privately owned, RNAS Yeovilton, Somerset	

Notes	Serial	Type (code/other identity)	Owner/operator, location or fate
	XW795	WS Scout AH1	Privately owned, Fivemiletown, Co Tyrone, NI
	XW796	WS Scout AH1 (wreck)	Privately owned, Sutton, Surrey
	XW838	WS Lynx (TAD009)	RAF Cranwell, Lincs, GI use
	XW839	WS Lynx	The Helicopter Museum, Weston-super-Mare, Somerset
	XW844	WS Gazelle AH1	StandardAero Fleetlands, Hants, preserved
	XW846	WS Gazelle AH1	AAC No 665 Sqn/5 Regt, Aldergrove, NI
	XW847	WS Gazelle AH1	AAC No 7 Regiment Conversion Flt, Middle Wallop, Hants
	XW848	WS Gazelle AH1 [D]	Privately owned, Stapleford Tawney, Essex
	XW849	WS Gazelle AH1	Privately owned, East Hanney, Oxon
	XW851	WS Gazelle AH1 (G-CIEY)	Privately owned, Deighton, N. Yorks
	XW852	WS Gazelle HCC4 (9331M)	DSAE No 1 SoTT, Cosford, Shropshire
	XW855	WS Gazelle HCC4	RAF Museum, Hendon, Gtr London
	XW858	WS Gazelle HT3 (G-ONNE) [C]	Privately owned, Steeple Bumstead, Cambs
	XW860	WS Gazelle HT2 (TAD 021)	RAF Honington, Suffolk, G.I.
	XW864	WS Gazelle HT2 [54/CU]	FAA Museum, stored Cobham Hall, RNAS Yeovilton
	XW865	WS Gazelle AH1	MOD/StandardAero, stored Fleetlands, Hants
	XW870	WS Gazelle HT3 (9299M) [F]	Privately owned, Selby, N. Yorks
	XW888	WS Gazelle AH1 (TAD 017)	Privately owned, East Hanney, Oxon
	XW889	WS Gazelle AH1 (TAD 018)	DSAE No 1 SoTT, Cosford, Shropshire
	XW890	WS Gazelle HT2	RNAS Yeovilton, Somerset, on display
	XW892	WS Gazelle AH1 (G-CGJX/9292M)	Privately owned, Peasemore, Berks
	XW899	WS Gazelle AH1 (G-CLSA) [Z]	Privately owned, stored Deighton, N. Yorks
	XW900	WS Gazelle AH1 (TAD 900)	Army, Bramley, Hants
	XW906	WS Gazelle HT3 (G-CMFK) [J]	The Gazelle Squadron Display Team, Garford, Oxon
	XW908	WS Gazelle AH1 [A]	QinetiQ, Boscombe Down, Wilts (spares use)
	XW909	WS Gazelle AH1 (G-HSDL)	Privately owned, Hapton, Lancs
	XW912	WS Gazelle AH1 (TAD 019)	MOD JARTS, Boscombe Down, Wilts
	XW913	WS Gazelle AH1	Privately owned, Stapleford Tawney, Essex
	XW917	HS Harrier GR3 (8975M)	NATS Air Traffic Control Centre, Swanwick, Hants
	XW922	HS Harrier GR3 (8885M)	Privately owned, Selby, N. Yorks
	XW923	HS Harrier GR3 (8724M) <ff>	Harrier Heritage Centre, RAF Wittering, Cambs
	XW924	HS Harrier GR3 (9073M) [G]	RAF Coningsby, Lincs, preserved
	XW927	HS Harrier T4 <ff>	Privately owned, Doncaster, S. Yorks
	XW934	HS Harrier T4 [Y]	Farnborough Air Sciences Trust, Farnborough, Hants
	XW994	Northrop Chukar D1	FAA Museum, stored Cobham Hall, RNAS Yeovilton, Somerset
	XW999	Northrop Chukar D1	Davidstow Airfield & Cornwall At War Museum, Davidstow Moor, Cornwall
	XX108	SEPECAT Jaguar GR1(mod)	IWM Duxford, Cambs
	XX109	SEPECAT Jaguar GR1 (8918M) [GH]	City of Norwich Aviation Museum, Norfolk
	XX110	SEPECAT Jaguar GR1 (8955M) [EP]	RAF Cosford, Shropshire, on display
	XX110	SEPECAT Jaguar GR1 <R> (BAPC 169)	DSAE No 1 SoTT, Cosford, Shropshire
	XX112	SEPECAT Jaguar GR3A [EA]	DSAE No 1 SoTT, Cosford, Shropshire
	XX116	SEPECAT Jaguar GR3A [EO]	Privately owned, Selby, N. Yorks
	XX117	SEPECAT Jaguar GR3A [ES]	DSAE No 1 SoTT, Cosford, Shropshire
	XX119	SEPECAT Jaguar GR3A (8898M) [AI]$	DSAE No 1 SoTT, Cosford, Shropshire
	XX121	SEPECAT Jaguar GR1 [EQ]	Privately owned, Selby, N. Yorks
	XX139	SEPECAT Jaguar T1 $	Privately owned, Sproughton, Suffolk
	XX140	SEPECAT Jaguar T2 (9008M) <ff>	Privately owned, Stockbury, Kent
	XX141	SEPECAT Jaguar T2A (9297M) [T]	DSAE No 1 SoTT, Cosford, Shropshire
	XX144	SEPECAT Jaguar T2A [U]	Privately owned, Sproughton, Suffolk
	XX145	SEPECAT Jaguar T2A	DSAE No 1 SoTT, Cosford, Shropshire
	XX146	SEPECAT Jaguar T4 [GT]	Solway Aviation Museum, Carlisle, Cumbria
	XX153	WS Lynx AH1 (9320M)	Army Flying Museum, Middle Wallop, Hants
	XX154	HS Hawk T1 $	Boscombe Down Aviation Collection, Old Sarum, Wilts
	XX156	HS Hawk T1 [156]	RAF Valley, Gwynedd, Wales, on display
	XX157	HS Hawk T1A [157]	RAMCO, Skegness, Lincs (for disposal)
	XX158	HS Hawk T1A [158]	RAF AM&SU, stored Shawbury, Shropshire
	XX159	HS Hawk T1A [159]	RAF AM&SU, stored Shawbury, Shropshire
	XX160	HS Hawk T1 [160]	RAF AM&SU, stored Shawbury, Shropshire

Serial	Type (code/other identity)	Owner/operator, location or fate	Notes
XX161	HS Hawk T1 [161]	RAF Valley, Gwynedd, Wales, G.I.	
XX162	HS Hawk T1 $	RAF AM&SU, stored Shawbury, Shropshire	
XX165	HS Hawk T1 [165] <rf>	MOD JARTS, Boscombe Down, Wilts	
XX167	HS Hawk T1 [167]	RAF AM&SU, stored Shawbury, Shropshire	
XX168	HS Hawk T1 [168]	DSAE No 1 SoTT, Cosford, Shropshire	
XX169	HS Hawk T1W [169]	RAF AM&SU, stored Shawbury, Shropshire	
XX170	HS Hawk T1 [CH]	RAF AM&SU, stored Shawbury, Shropshire	
XX171	HS Hawk T1 [171]	RAF AM&SU, stored Shawbury, Shropshire	
XX172	HS Hawk T1 [172] (fuselage)	QinetiQ Boscombe Down, Wilts, GI use	
XX173	HS Hawk T1 (fuselage)	MOD JARTS, Boscombe Down, Wilts	
XX174	HS Hawk T1 [174]	RAF AM&SU, stored Shawbury, Shropshire	
XX175	HS Hawk T1 [175]	Privately owned, Thorpe Wood, N. Yorks	
XX176	HS Hawk T1W [176]	RAF AM&SU, stored Shawbury, Shropshire	
XX177	HS Hawk T1	RAF *Red Arrows*, Waddington, Lincs	
XX178	HS Hawk T1W [178]	DSAE No 1 SoTT, Cosford, Shropshire	
XX181	HS Hawk T1 [181]	DSAE No 1 SoTT, Cosford, Shropshire	
XX184	HS Hawk T1 [CQ]	Sheffield University, S. Yorks, GI use	
XX185	HS Hawk T1 [185]	DSAE No 1 SoTT, Cosford, Shropshire	
XX187	HS Hawk T1A [CO]	RAF AM&SU, stored Shawbury, Shropshire	
XX188	HS Hawk T1A	RAF AMRO, Valley, Gwynedd, Wales	
XX190	HS Hawk T1A [CN]	RAF AM&SU, stored Shawbury, Shropshire	
XX191	HS Hawk T1A [CC]	RAF AM&SU, stored Shawbury, Shropshire	
XX194	HS Hawk T1A [CP]	RAF AM&SU, stored Shawbury, Shropshire	
XX195	HS Hawk T1W [195]	RAF AM&SU, stored Shawbury, Shropshire	
XX198	HS Hawk T1A [CH]	RAF AM&SU, stored Shawbury, Shropshire	
XX199	HS Hawk T1A [199]	RAF AMRO, Valley, Gwynedd, Wales, RTP	
XX200	HS Hawk T1A [CO]	RAF AMRO, Valley, Gwynedd, Wales, RTP	
XX201	HS Hawk T1A [CQ]	RAF AM&SU, stored Shawbury, Shropshire	
XX202	HS Hawk T1A	RAF *Red Arrows*, Waddington, Lincs	
XX203	HS Hawk T1A [CF]	RAF AM&SU, stored Shawbury, Shropshire	
XX205	HS Hawk T1A [CK]	RAF AM&SU, stored Shawbury, Shropshire	
XX217	HS Hawk T1A [217]	RAF AM&SU, stored Shawbury, Shropshire	
XX218	HS Hawk T1A [218]	DSAE No 1 SoTT, Cosford, Shropshire	
XX219	HS Hawk T1A	RAF *Red Arrows*, Waddington, Lincs	
XX220	HS Hawk T1A [220]	RAF AMRO, Valley, Gwynedd, Wales, RTP	
XX221	HS Hawk T1A [CO] $	RAF AMRO, Valley, Gwynedd, Wales	
XX222	HS Hawk T1A [CI]	RAF AM&SU, stored Shawbury, Shropshire	
XX224	HS Hawk T1 [224]	DSAE No 1 SoTT, Cosford, Shropshire	
XX225	HS Hawk T1 [322]	RAF AM&SU, stored Shawbury, Shropshire	
XX226	HS Hawk T1 [226]	Privately owned, Thorpe Wood, N. Yorks	
XX227	HS Hawk T1 <R> (XX226/BAPC 152)	RAF Scampton Heritage Centre, Lincs	
XX227	HS Hawk T1A	DSAE No 1 SoTT, Cosford, Shropshire	
XX228	HS Hawk T1 [CG]	RAF AM&SU, stored Shawbury, Shropshire	
XX230	HS Hawk T1A [CM]	RAF AM&SU, stored Shawbury, Shropshire	
XX231	HS Hawk T1W [213]	RAF AM&SU, stored Shawbury, Shropshire	
XX232	HS Hawk T1	RAF *Red Arrows*, Waddington, Lincs	
XX234	HS Hawk T1 [234]	RAF AM&SU, stored Shawbury, Shropshire	
XX235	HS Hawk T1 [235]	DSAE No 1 SoTT, Cosford, Shropshire	
XX236	HS Hawk T1W [236]	DSAE No 1 SoTT, Cosford, Shropshire	
XX238	HS Hawk T1 [238]	DSAE No 1 SoTT, Cosford, Shropshire	
XX239	HS Hawk T1W	RAF *Red Arrows*, Waddington, Lincs	
XX240	HS Hawk T1 [840/CU]	MOD, Cornwall Aviation Heritage Centre, Newquay, Cornwall	
XX242	HS Hawk T1	RAF AMRO, Valley, Gwynedd, Wales	
XX244	HS Hawk T1	DSAE No 1 SoTT, Cosford, Shropshire	
XX245	HS Hawk T1	RAF *Red Arrows*, Waddington, Lincs	
XX246	HS Hawk T1A [CA]	RAF AMRO, Valley, Gwynedd, Wales, RTP	
XX247	HS Hawk T1A [247]	RAF Woodvale, Merseyside, at main gate	
XX248	HS Hawk T1A [CJ]	RAF AM&SU, stored Shawbury, Shropshire	
XX250	HS Hawk T1W [250]	RAF AM&SU, stored Shawbury, Shropshire	
XX253	HS Hawk T1A	RAF Leeming, N. Yorks, stored	
XX254	HS Hawk T1A <R>	Privately owned, Marlow, Bucks	

Notes	Serial	Type (code/other identity)	Owner/operator, location or fate
	XX255	HS Hawk T1A [CB]	RAF AM&SU, stored Shawbury, Shropshire
	XX256	HS Hawk T1A [846/CU]	RAF AM&SU, stored Shawbury, Shropshire
	XX258	HS Hawk T1A [CE]	RAF AMRO, Valley, Gwynedd, Wales, stored
	XX260	HS Hawk T1A	RAF AM&SU, stored Shawbury, Shropshire
	XX261	HS Hawk T1A [CJ]	RAF AM&SU, stored Shawbury, Shropshire
	XX263	HS Hawk T1A	South Wales Aviation Museum, St Athan
	XX264	HS Hawk T1A $	RAF AM&SU, stored Shawbury, Shropshire
	XX265	HS Hawk T1A [CP]	RAF AM&SU, stored Shawbury, Shropshire
	XX266	HS Hawk T1A	RAF Waddington, Lincs, stored
	XX278	HS Hawk T1A	RAF *Red Arrows*, Waddington, Lincs (repairs)
	XX280	HS Hawk T1A [280]	RN, Culdrose, Cornwall (wfu)
	XX281	HS Hawk T1A	RAF AM&SU, stored Shawbury, Shropshire
	XX283	HS Hawk T1W [283]	DSAE No 1 SoTT, Cosford, Shropshire
	XX284	HS Hawk T1A [CN]	RAF AM&SU, stored Shawbury, Shropshire
	XX285	HS Hawk T1A [CK]	RAF AM&SU, stored Shawbury, Shropshire
	XX286	HS Hawk T1A [286]	RAF AM&SU, stored Shawbury, Shropshire
	XX287	HS Hawk T1A [287]	RAF AM&SU, stored Shawbury, Shropshire
	XX289	HS Hawk T1A [CO]	RAF AM&SU, stored Shawbury, Shropshire
	XX290	HS Hawk T1W	Privately owned, Thorpe Wood, N Yorks
	XX294	HS Hawk T1	RAF AM&SU, stored Shawbury, Shropshire
	XX295	HS Hawk T1	RAF *Red Arrows*, Waddington, Lincs
	XX296	HS Hawk T1 [296]	RAF AM&SU, stored Shawbury, Shropshire
	XX299	HS Hawk T1W [299]	RAF AM&SU, stored Shawbury, Shropshire
	XX301	HS Hawk T1A $	RAF AM&SU, stored Shawbury, Shropshire
	XX303	HS Hawk T1A [CR]	RAF AM&SU, stored Shawbury, Shropshire
	XX306	HS Hawk T1A	RAF Scampton, Lincs, on display
	XX307	HS Hawk T1 [307]	RAF AM&SU, stored Shawbury, Shropshire
	XX308	HS Hawk T1	National Museum of Flight, E Fortune, Scotland
	XX308	HS Hawk T1 <R> (*XX263*/BAPC 171)	RAF M&RU, Bottesford, Leics
	XX309	HS Hawk T1	RAF AM&SU, stored Shawbury, Shropshire
	XX310	HS Hawk T1	RAF AMRO, Valley, Gwynedd, Wales
	XX311	HS Hawk T1	RAF AMRO, Valley, Gwynedd, Wales
	XX313	HS Hawk T1W [313]	RAF AM&SU, stored Shawbury, Shropshire
	XX314	HS Hawk T1W [314]	RAF AM&SU, stored Shawbury, Shropshire
	XX315	HS Hawk T1A [315]	RAF AM&SU, stored Shawbury, Shropshire
	XX316	HS Hawk T1A [849/CU]	RAF AMRO, Valley, Gwynedd, Wales, RTP
	XX317	HS Hawk T1A [849/CU]	RAF, preserved Leeming, N. Yorks
	XX318	HS Hawk T1A [CG]	RAF AM&SU, stored Shawbury, Shropshire
	XX319	HS Hawk T1A	RAF AMRO, Valley, Gwynedd, Wales
	XX320	HS Hawk T1A <ff>	Privately owned, Plymouth, Devon
	XX321	HS Hawk T1A [CI]	RAF AMRO, Valley, Gwynedd, Wales, RTP
	XX322	HS Hawk T1A	RAF *Red Arrows*, Waddington, Lincs
	XX323	HS Hawk T1A	RAF *Red Arrows*, Waddington, Lincs
	XX324	HS Hawk T1A [324]	RAF AM&SU, stored Shawbury, Shropshire
	XX325	HS Hawk T1	RAF *Red Arrows*, Waddington, Lincs
	XX327	HS Hawk T1	RAF AM&SU, stored Shawbury, Shropshire
	XX329	HS Hawk T1A [844/CU]	MOD JARTS, Boscombe Down, Wilts
	XX330	HS Hawk T1A [330]	RAF AM&SU, stored Shawbury, Shropshire
	XX331	HS Hawk T1A [331]	RAF AM&SU, stored Shawbury, Shropshire
	XX332	HS Hawk T1A [CD]	RAMCO, Skegness, Lincs (for disposal)
	XX335	HS Hawk T1A [335]	DSAE No 1 SoTT, Cosford, Shropshire
	XX337	HS Hawk T1A [CM]	RAF AM&SU, stored Shawbury, Shropshire
	XX338	HS Hawk T1W	RAF AM&SU, stored Shawbury, Shropshire
	XX339	HS Hawk T1A [CL]	RAF AM&SU, stored Shawbury, Shropshire
	XX341	HS Hawk T1 ASTRA	Privately owned, Thorpe Wood, N. Yorks
	XX342	HS Hawk T1 (G-HAWC) [2]	Privately owned, St Athan, Wales
	XX343	HS Hawk T1 [3] (fuselage)	Boscombe Down Aviation Collection, Old Sarum, Wilts
	XX345	HS Hawk T1A [CB]	RAF AM&SU, stored Shawbury, Shropshire
	XX346	HS Hawk T1A [CP]	MOD JARTS, Boscombe Down, Wilts
	XX348	HS Hawk T1A [CQ]	RAF AM&SU, stored Shawbury, Shropshire
	XX349	HS Hawk T1W <ff>	RAF Scampton Fire Section, Lincs (for sale)
	XX350	HS Hawk T1A [D] $	RAF AM&SU, stored Shawbury, Shropshire

Serial	Type (code/other identity)	Owner/operator, location or fate	Notes
XX351	HS Hawk T1A	RAF No 71(IR) Sqn, Wittering, Cambs, GI use	
XX352	HS Hawk T1A <rf>	QinetiQ Farnborough, Hants, on display	
XX372	WS Gazelle AH1 <ff>	Privately owned,	
XX375	WS Gazelle AH1	Privately owned,	
XX378	WS Gazelle AH1 <ff>	Privately owned, East Hanney, Oxon (stored)	
XX379	WS Gazelle AH1 [Y]	MOD Boscombe Down, Wilts, GI use	
XX380	WS Gazelle AH1 [A]	AAC Wattisham, Suffolk, on display	
XX381	WS Gazelle AH1	Privately owned, Welbeck, Notts	
XX386	WS Gazelle AH1 (G-KEMH)	Privately owned, Redhill, Surrey	
XX387	WS Gazelle AH1 (TAD 014)	Privately owned, stored Cranfield, Beds	
XX392	WS Gazelle AH1	Army, Wattisham, Suffolk, preserved	
XX394	WS Gazelle AH1 [X]	Privately owned, Stapleford Tawney, Essex	
XX396	WS Gazelle HT3 (8718M) [N]	Privately owned, Arncott, Oxon	
XX398	WS Gazelle AH1	Privately owned, Stapleford Tawney, Essex	
XX405	WS Gazelle AH1	AAC No 665 Sqn/5 Regt, Aldergrove, NI	
XX406	WS Gazelle HT3 (G-CBSH) [P]	Privately owned, Peasemore, Berks	
XX411	WS Gazelle AH1 [X]	South Yorkshire Aircraft Museum, Doncaster, S. Yorks	
XX412	WS Gazelle AH1 [B]	DSAE No 1 SoTT, Cosford, Shropshire	
XX414	WS Gazelle AH1 [V]	Privately owned, Biggin Hill, Kent	
XX418	WS Gazelle AH1 <ff>	Privately owned, Andover area, Hants	
XX431	WS Gazelle HT2 (9300M) [43/CU]	Travelling exhibit, HMS Sultan, Gosport, Hants	
XX433	WS Gazelle AH1 <ff>	Privately owned, Andover area, Hants	
XX435	WS Gazelle AH1 (fuselage)	QinetiQ, Boscombe Down, Wilts (spares use)	
XX436	WS Gazelle HT2 (G-ZZLE) [39/CU]	Privately owned, East Hanney, Oxon	
XX437	WS Gazelle AH1	Privately owned, Stapleford Tawney, Essex (sold to South Africa)	
XX438	WS Gazelle AH1 [F]	Privately owned, Stapleford Tawney, Essex (stored)	
XX442	WS Gazelle AH1 <ff>	Privately owned, East Hanney, Oxon (stored)	
XX443	WS Gazelle AH1 [Y]	Army, Aldergrove, NI, on display	
XX444	WS Gazelle AH1	Army, Wattisham, Suffolk (restoration)	
XX447	WS Gazelle AH1 [D1]	Privately owned, Colsterworth, Lincs	
XX449	WS Gazelle AH1 (G-CMME)	Privately owned, Deighton, N. Yorks	
XX450	WS Gazelle AH1 [D]	Privately owned, Peasemore, Berks	
XX452	WS Gazelle AH1 (wreck)	AAC Middle Wallop Fire Section, Hants	
XX453	WS Gazelle AH1 (G-CMMF)	Privately owned, Deighton, N. Yorks	
XX453	WS Gazelle AH1 (XZ331/G-CLXM) [D]	Privately owned, Peasemore, Berks (restoration)	
XX454	WS Gazelle AH1 (TAD 023)	DSAE SAAE, Lyneham, Wilts	
XX455	WS Gazelle AH1 (G-GRAK)	Privately owned, Stapleford Tawney, Essex	
XX457	WS Gazelle AH1 (TAD 001)	East Midlands Airport Aeropark, Leics	
XX460	WS Gazelle AH1 (G-CMMB)	Privately owned, Deighton, N. Yorks	
XX462	WS Gazelle AH1 [W]	Privately owned, Stapleford Tawney, Essex (stored)	
XX466	HS Hunter T66B/T7 (830) <ff>	Privately owned, Glos	
XX467	HS Hunter T66B/T7 (XL605/G-TVII) [86]	Newark Air Museum, Winthorpe, Notts	
XX477	HP137 Jetstream T1 (G-AXXS/8462M) <ff>	Solway Aviation Society, Carlisle, Cumbria	
XX478	HP137 Jetstream T2 (G-AXXT) [564/CU]	Solihull College, Woodlands Campus, W. Mids	
XX483	SA Jetstream T2 (562) <ff>	Dumfries & Galloway Avn Mus, Dumfries, Scotland	
XX487	SA Jetstream T2 (568/CU]	Int'l Centre for Aerospace Training, Cardiff Airport	
XX491	SA Jetstream T1 [K]	Northbrook College, Shoreham, W. Sussex, G.I.	
XX492	SA Jetstream T1 [A]	Newark Air Museum, Winthorpe, Notts	
XX494	SA Jetstream T1 [B]	East Midlands Airport Aeropark, Leics	
XX495	SA Jetstream T1 [C]	South Yorkshire Aircraft Museum, Doncaster, S. Yorks	
XX496	SA Jetstream T1 [D]	RAF Museum, Cosford, Shropshire	
XX499	SA Jetstream T1 [G]	Privately owned, Wainfleet, Lincs	
XX510	WS Lynx HAS2 [69/DD]	SFDO, RNAS Culdrose, Cornwall	
XX513	SA Bulldog T1 (G-KKKK) [10]	Privately owned, Breighton, E. Yorks	
XX515	SA Bulldog T1 (G-CBBC) [4]	Privately owned, Blackbushe, Hants	
XX518	SA Bulldog T1 (G-UDOG) [S]	Privately owned, Ursel, Belgium	
XX520	SA Bulldog T1 (9288M) [A]	No 172 Sqn ATC, Haywards Heath, W. Sussex	
XX521	SA Bulldog T1 (G-CBEH) [H]	Privately owned, North Moreton, Oxon	
XX522	SA Bulldog T1 (G-DAWG) [06]	Privately owned, Blackpool, Lancs	
XX524	SA Bulldog T1 (G-DDOG) [04]	Privately owned, Malaga, Spain	
XX528	SA Bulldog T1 (G-BZON) [D]	Privately owned, Earls Colne, Essex	

Notes	Serial	Type (code/other identity)	Owner/operator, location or fate
	XX530	SA Bulldog T1 (XX637/9197M) [F]	Ulster Aviation Society, Long Kesh, NI
	XX534	SA Bulldog T1 (G-EDAV) [B]	Privately owned, Tollerton, Notts
	XX537	SA Bulldog T1 (G-CBCB) [C]	Privately owned, RAF Halton, Bucks
	XX538	SA Bulldog T1 (G-TDOG) [O]	Privately owned, Shobdon, Herefordshire
	XX539	SA Bulldog T1	Privately owned, Ashbourne, Derbyshire
	XX546	SA Bulldog T1 (G-WINI) [03]	Privately owned, Conington, Cambs
	XX549	SA Bulldog T1 (G-CBID) [6]	Privately owned, White Waltham, Berks
	XX550	SA Bulldog T1 (G-CBBL) [Z]	Privately owned, Abbeyshrule, Eire
	XX551	SA Bulldog T1 (G-BZDP) [E]	Privately owned, Boscombe Down, Wilts
	XX554	SA Bulldog T1 (G-BZMD) [09]	Privately owned, stored Thruxton, Hants
	XX555	SA Bulldog T1 (F-AZKJ)	Privately owned, St Rambert d'Albon, France
	XX557	SA Bulldog T1	*Currently not known* (ex-Fort Paull, E. Yorks)
	XX561	SA Bulldog T1 (G-BZEP) [7]	Privately owned, Eggesford, Devon
	XX611	SA Bulldog T1 (G-CBDK) [7]	Privately owned, Cotswold Airport, Glos
	XX612	SA Bulldog T1 (G-BZXC) [A,03]	Ayr College, Scotland, instructional use
	XX614	SA Bulldog T1 (G-GGRR) [1]	Privately owned, Cotswold Airport, Glos
	XX619	SA Bulldog T1 (G-CBBW) [T]	Privately owned, Coventry, Warks
	XX621	SA Bulldog T1 (G-CBEF) [H]	Privately owned, Little Gransden, Cambs
	XX622	SA Bulldog T1 (G-CBGX) [B]	Privately owned, Dunsfold, Surrey (off-site)
	XX624	SA Bulldog T1 (G-KDOG) [E]	Privately owned, Redhill, Surrey
	XX625	SA Bulldog T1 (XX543/G-UWAS) [45]	Privately owned, Tibenham, Norfolk
	XX626	SA Bulldog T1 (G-CDVV/9290M) [W,02]	Privately owned, Sleap, Shropshire
	XX628	SA Bulldog T1 (G-CBFU) [9]	Privately owned, Alkham, Kent
	XX629	SA Bulldog T1 (G-BZXZ)	Privately owned, Turweston, Bucks
	XX630	SA Bulldog T1 (G-SIJW) [5]	Privately owned, Audley End, Essex
	XX631	SA Bulldog T1 (G-BZXS) [W]	Privately owned, stored Sligo, Eire
	XX634	SA Bulldog T1 [T]	Newark Air Museum, Winthorpe, Notts
	XX636	SA Bulldog T1 (G-CBFP) [Y]	Privately owned, Empingham, Rutland
	XX638	SA Bulldog T1 (G-DOGG)	Privately owned, Popham, Hants
	XX639	SA Bulldog T1 (F-AZTF) [D]	Privately owned, La Baule, France
	XX654	SA Bulldog T1 [3]	RAF Museum, Cosford, Shropshire
	XX655	SA Bulldog T1 (9294M) [V] <ff>	Privately owned, Bramcote, Warks
	XX656	SA Bulldog T1 [C]	Privately owned, Derbyshire
	XX658	SA Bulldog T1 (G-SMAT) [07]	Privately owned, Duxford, Cambs
	XX659	SA Bulldog T1 [E]	Privately owned, Ashbourne, Derbyshire
	XX664	SA Bulldog T1 (F-AZTV) [04]	Privately owned, Pontoise, France
	XX665	SA Bulldog T1 (9289M) [V]	Privately owned, Evesham, Worcs
	XX667	SA Bulldog T1 (G-BZFN) [16]	Privately owned, Ronaldsway, IoM
	XX668	SA Bulldog T1 (G-CBAN) [1]	Privately owned, RNAS Yeovilton, Somerset
	XX669	SA Bulldog T1 (8997M) [B]	South Yorkshire Aircraft Museum, Doncaster, S. Yorks
	XX687	SA Bulldog T1 [F]	Int'l Centre for Aerospace Training, Cardiff Airport
	XX692	SA Bulldog T1 (G-BZMH) [I]	Privately owned, Wellesbourne Mountford, Warks
	XX693	SA Bulldog T1 (G-BZML) [07]	Privately owned, Elmsett, Suffolk
	XX694	SA Bulldog T1 (G-CBBS) [E]	Privately owned, Turweston, Bucks
	XX695	SA Bulldog T1 (G-CBBT)	Privately owned, Perth, Scotland
	XX698	SA Bulldog T1 (G-BZME) [9]	Privately owned, Sleap, Shropshire
	XX699	SA Bulldog T1 (G-IDID)	Privately owned, Blackbushe, Hants
	XX700	SA Bulldog T1 (G-CBEK) [17]	Privately owned, Thruxton, Hants
	XX702	SA Bulldog T1 (G-CBCR) [π]	Privately owned, Goodwood, W. Sussex
	XX704	SA122 Bulldog (G-BCUV/G-112)	Privately owned, Bournemouth, Dorset
	XX705	SA Bulldog T1 [5]	Privately owned, Thorpe Wood, N. Yorks
	XX707	SA Bulldog T1 (G-CBDS) [4]	Privately owned, stored Caernarfon, Wales
	XX720	SEPECAT Jaguar GR3A [FL]	Privately owned, Stockbury, Kent
	XX722	SEPECAT Jaguar GR1 (9252M) <ff>	*Currently not known*
	XX723	SEPECAT Jaguar GR3A [EU]	DSAE No 1 SoTT, Cosford, Shropshire
	XX724	SEPECAT Jaguar GR3A [C]	DSAE No 1 SoTT, Cosford, Shropshire
	XX725	SEPECAT Jaguar GR3A [KC-F,T]	DSAE No 1 SoTT, Cosford, Shropshire
	XX726	SEPECAT Jaguar GR1 (8947M) [EB]	DSAE No 1 SoTT, Cosford, Shropshire
	XX727	SEPECAT Jaguar GR1 (8951M) [ER]	DSAE No 1 SoTT, Cosford, Shropshire
	XX729	SEPECAT Jaguar GR3A [EL]	DSAE No 1 SoTT, Cosford, Shropshire
	XX734	SEPECAT Jaguar GR1 (8816M)	Boscombe Down Aviation Collection, Old Sarum, Wilts
	XX736	SEPECAT Jaguar GR1 (9110M) <ff>	South Yorkshire Aircraft Museum, Doncaster, S. Yorks

Serial	Type (code/other identity)	Owner/operator, location or fate	Notes
XX738	SEPECAT Jaguar GR3A [ED]	DSAE No 1 SoTT, Cosford, Shropshire	
XX739	SEPECAT Jaguar GR1 (8902M) [I]	Delta Force Paintball, Birmingham, W. Mids	
XX741	SEPECAT Jaguar GR1A [EJ]	Bentwaters Cold War Museum, Suffolk	
XX743	SEPECAT Jaguar GR1 (8949M) [EG]	Morayvia, Kinloss, Scotland	
XX744	SEPECAT Jaguar GR1 (9251M)	Mayhem Paintball, Abridge, Essex	
XX745	SEPECAT Jaguar GR1A <ff>	No 1350 Sqn ATC, Fareham, Hants	
XX746	SEPECAT Jaguar GR1 (8895M) [S]	DSAE No 1 SoTT, Cosford, Shropshire	
XX748	SEPECAT Jaguar GR3A [L]	DSAE No 1 SoTT, Cosford, Shropshire	
XX751	SEPECAT Jaguar GR1 (8937M) [10]	Iron Curtain Museum, Alton, Hants	
XX752	SEPECAT Jaguar GR3A [EK]	DSAE No 1 SoTT, Cosford, Shropshire	
XX753	SEPECAT Jaguar GR1 (9087M) <ff>	Newark Air Museum, Winthorpe, Notts	
XX756	SEPECAT Jaguar GR1 (8899M) [W]	DSAE No 1 SoTT, Cosford, Shropshire	
XX761	SEPECAT Jaguar GR1 (8600M) <ff>	Boscombe Down Aviation Collection, Old Sarum, Wilts	
XX763	SEPECAT Jaguar GR1 (9009M) [24]	Bournemouth Aviation Museum, Dorset	
XX764	SEPECAT Jaguar GR1 (9010M)	Privately owned, Enstone, Oxon	
XX765	SEPECAT Jaguar ACT	RAF Museum, Cosford, Shropshire	
XX766	SEPECAT Jaguar GR3A [EF]	DSAE No 1 SoTT, Cosford, Shropshire	
XX767	SEPECAT Jaguar GR3A [Z]	DSAE No 1 SoTT, Cosford, Shropshire	
XX818	SEPECAT Jaguar GR1 (8945M) [DE]	Fire Service training facility, RAF Waddington, Lincs	
XX819	SEPECAT Jaguar GR1 (8923M) [CE]	DSAE No 1 SoTT, Cosford, Shropshire	
XX821	SEPECAT Jaguar GR1 (8896M) [P]	DSAE No 1 SoTT, Cosford, Shropshire	
XX824	SEPECAT Jaguar GR1 (9019M) [AD]	RAF Museum, Hendon, Gtr London	
XX825	SEPECAT Jaguar GR1 (9020M) [BN]	DSAE No 1 SoTT, Cosford, Shropshire	
XX826	SEPECAT Jaguar GR1 (9021M) [34] <ff>	Shannon Aviation Museum, Eire (stored)	
XX829	SEPECAT Jaguar T2A [GZ]	Newark Air Museum, Winthorpe, Notts	
XX830	SEPECAT Jaguar T2 <ff>	City of Norwich Aviation Museum, Norfolk	
XX833	SEPECAT Jaguar T2B	DSAE No 1 SoTT, Cosford, Shropshire	
XX835	SEPECAT Jaguar T4 [P]	DSAE No 1 SoTT, Cosford, Shropshire	
XX836	SEPECAT Jaguar T2A [X]	Privately owned, Sproughton, Suffolk	
XX837	SEPECAT Jaguar T2 (8978M) [Z]	DSAE No 1 SoTT, Cosford, Shropshire	
XX838	SEPECAT Jaguar T4 [FZ]	Privately owned, Bentwaters, Suffolk	
XX840	SEPECAT Jaguar T4 [T]	DSAE No 1 SoTT, Cosford, Shropshire	
XX841	SEPECAT Jaguar T4 (VH-UXB) [EW]	Privately owned, North Weald, Essex	
XX842	SEPECAT Jaguar T2A [FX]	Privately owned, Bentwaters, Suffolk	
XX845	SEPECAT Jaguar T4 [EV]	South Wales Aviation Museum, St Athan, Wales	
XX847	SEPECAT Jaguar T4 [EZ]	DSAE No 1 SoTT, Cosford, Shropshire	
XX885	HS Buccaneer S2B (9225M/G-HHAA)	Hawker Hunter Aviation, Scampton, Lincs	
XX888	HS Buccaneer S2B <ff>	South Yorkshire Aircraft Museum, Doncaster, S. Yorks	
XX889	HS Buccaneer S2B [T]	Privately owned, Cosford, Shropshire	
XX892	HS Buccaneer S2B <ff>	Privately owned, Lincs	
XX894	HS Buccaneer S2B [020/R]	The Buccaneer Aviation Group, Cotswold Airport, Glos	
XX895	HS Buccaneer S2B <ff>	Thorpe Camp Visitor Centre, Tattershall Thorpe, Lincs	
XX897	HS Buccaneer S2B(mod)	Shannon Aviation Museum, Eire	
XX899	HS Buccaneer S2B <ff>	Newark Air Museum, Winthorpe, Notts	
XX900	HS Buccaneer S2B [900]	Privately owned, Tatenhill, Staffs	
XX901	HS Buccaneer S2B [N]	Yorkshire Air Museum, Elvington, N. Yorks	
XX910	WS Lynx HAS2	The Helicopter Museum, Weston-super-Mare, Somerset	
XX919	BAC 1-11/402AP (PI-C1121) <ff>	Boscombe Down Aviation Collection, Old Sarum, Wilts	
XX946	Panavia Tornado (P02) (8883M) [WT]	RAF Museum, stored Cosford, Shropshire	
XX956	SEPECAT Jaguar GR1 (8950M) [BE]	Morayvia, stored Spey Bay, Moray, Scotland	
XX959	SEPECAT Jaguar GR1 (8953M) [CJ]	DSAE No 1 SoTT, Cosford, Shropshire	
XX962	SEPECAT Jaguar GR1B (9257M) <ff>	RAF Coningsby, Lincs	
XX965	SEPECAT Jaguar GR1A (9254M) [C]	DSAE No 1 SoTT, Cosford, Shropshire	
XX967	SEPECAT Jaguar GR1 (9006M) [AC]	DSAE No 1 SoTT, Cosford, Shropshire	
XX968	SEPECAT Jaguar GR1 (9007M) [AJ]	DSAE No 1 SoTT, Cosford, Shropshire	
XX969	SEPECAT Jaguar GR1 (8897M) [01]	DSAE No 1 SoTT, Cosford, Shropshire	
XX970	SEPECAT Jaguar GR3A [EH]	DSAE No 1 SoTT, Cosford, Shropshire	
XX975	SEPECAT Jaguar GR1 (8905M) [07]	DSAE No 1 SoTT, Cosford, Shropshire	
XX976	SEPECAT Jaguar GR1 (8906M) [BD]	DSAE No 1 SoTT, Cosford, Shropshire	
XX977	SEPECAT Jaguar GR1 (9132M) [DL,05] <rf>	Privately owned, Sproughton, Suffolk	
XX979	SEPECAT Jaguar GR1A (9306M) <ff>	RAF Air Defence Radar Museum, Neatishead, Norfolk	

Notes	Serial	Type (code/other identity)	Owner/operator, location or fate
	XZ103	SEPECAT Jaguar GR3A [EF]	DSAE No 1 SoTT, Cosford, Shropshire
	XZ104	SEPECAT Jaguar GR3A [FM]	DSAE No 1 SoTT, Cosford, Shropshire
	XZ106	SEPECAT Jaguar GR3A [FR]	RAF Manston History Museum, Kent
	XZ107	SEPECAT Jaguar GR3A [FH]	Privately owned, Selby, N. Yorks
	XZ109	SEPECAT Jaguar GR3A [EN]	DSAE No 1 SoTT, Cosford, Shropshire
	XZ112	SEPECAT Jaguar GR3A [GW]	DSAE No 1 SoTT, Cosford, Shropshire
	XZ113	SEPECAT Jaguar GR3 [A,30]	Morayvia, Kinloss, Scotland
	XZ114	SEPECAT Jaguar GR3 [EO]	DSAE No 1 SoTT, Cosford, Shropshire
	XZ115	SEPECAT Jaguar GR3 [ER]	DSAE No 1 SoTT, Cosford, Shropshire
	XZ117	SEPECAT Jaguar GR3 [ES]	DSAE No 1 SoTT, Cosford, Shropshire
	XZ119	SEPECAT Jaguar GR1A (9266M) [FG]	National Museum of Flight, E Fortune, Scotland
	XZ131	HS Harrier GR3 (9174M) <ff>	Privately owned, Wolverhampton, W. Mids
	XZ132	HS Harrier GR3 (9168M) [C]	Privately owned, Gloucestershire Airport, Glos
	XZ133	HS Harrier GR3 [10]	IWM Duxford, Cambs
	XZ138	HS Harrier GR3 (9040M) <ff>	RAF Scampton Heritage Centre, Lincs
	XZ146	HS Harrier T4 (9281M) [S]	Harrier Heritage Centre, RAF Wittering, Cambs
	XZ166	WS Lynx HAS2 <ff>	Farnborough Air Sciences Trust, stored Farnborough
	XZ170	WS Lynx AH9	DSEME SAAE, Lyneham, Wilts
	XZ171	WS Lynx AH7	Army, Salisbury Plain, Wilts (derelict)
	XZ172	WS Lynx AH7	DSEME SAAE, Lyneham, Wilts
	XZ173	WS Lynx AH7 [6] <ff>	Privately owned, Weeton, Lancs
	XZ174	WS Lynx AH7 <ff>	Defence School of Policing, Gosport, Hants, G.I.
	XZ175	WS Lynx AH7	Privately owned, Wickford, Essex
	XZ177	Aérospatiale SA341G Gazelle (G-SFTA/*XZ345*) [T]	North-East Land, Sea & Air Museums, Usworth, T&W
	XZ177	WS Lynx AH7	Delta Force Paintball, Kegworth, Leics
	XZ178	WS Lynx AH7 <ff>	Bilsthorpe Paintball Park, Notts
	XZ179	WS Lynx AH7 (G-NCKS) [W]	Privately owned, North Weald, Essex
	XZ180	WS Lynx AH7 [C]	DSEME SAAE, Lyneham, Wilts
	XZ181	WS Lynx AH1	AAC Middle Wallop Fire Section, Hants
	XZ184	WS Lynx AH7 [B]	AAC Middle Wallop, Hants, at main gate
	XZ187	WS Lynx AH7	FETC, Moreton-in-Marsh, Glos
	XZ188	WS Lynx AH7	Privately owned, North Weald, Essex
	XZ190	WS Lynx AH7 <ff>	Army, Longmoor Camp, Hants, GI use
	XZ191	WS Lynx AH7 [R]	DSEME SAAE, Lyneham, Wilts
	XZ192	WS Lynx AH7 [H]	AAC, stored St Athan, Wales
	XZ193	WS Lynx AH7 [4] <ff>	Kidderminster Paintball, Worcs
	XZ194	WS Lynx AH7 [V]	IWM Duxford, Cambs
	XZ195	WS Lynx AH7 <ff>	Privately owned, Mildenhall, Suffolk
	XZ196	WS Lynx AH7	Privately owned, Burwell, Cambs
	XZ203	WS Lynx AH7 [F]	Army, Salisbury Plain, Wilts (derelict)
	XZ205	WS Lynx AH7 [239-UA]	Divers Wood Paintball, Crawley, W. Sussex
	XZ207	WS Lynx AH7 <rf>	FETC, Moreton-in-Marsh, Glos
	XZ208	WS Lynx AH7	Privately owned, *location unknown*
	XZ211	WS Lynx AH7	Bawtry Paintball Park, S. Yorks
	XZ212	WS Lynx AH7 [X]	AAC Middle Wallop Fire Section, Hants
	XZ213	WS Lynx AH1 (TAD 213)	Privately owned, Telford, Shropshire
	XZ214	WS Lynx AH7 <ff>	DSEME SAAE, Lyneham, Wilts
	XZ216	WS Lynx AH7 <ff>	Spadeadam Ranges, Cumbria
	XZ217	WS Lynx AH7	Paintball Park, Guildford, Surrey
	XZ218	WS Lynx AH7	Privately owned, Raigmore Estate, Inverness, Scotland
	XZ219	WS Lynx AH7 <ff>	Army, Bramley, Hants
	XZ220	WS Lynx AH7 [H]	Privately owned, stored Chard, Somerset
	XZ222	WS Lynx AH7	DSEME SAAE, Lyneham, Wilts
	XZ228	WS Lynx HAS3GMS [313]	FAA Museum, RNAS Yeovilton, Somerset (stored outside)
	XZ230	WS Lynx HAS3GMS	RNAS Yeovilton, Somerset, GI (Wildcat ground trainer)
	XZ232	WS Lynx HAS3GMS	Falck Nutec UK, Aberdeen, Scotland, GI use
	XZ233	WS Lynx HAS3S [696] $	Yorkshire Air Museum, Elvington, N. Yorks
	XZ234	WS Lynx HAS3S [630]	Privately owned, Sproughton, Suffolk
	XZ235	WS Lynx HAS3S(ICE) [630]	Wild Park Derbyshire, Brailsford, Derbys
	XZ236	WS Lynx HMA8 [LST-1]	Privately owned, Woodmancote, W. Sussex
	XZ237	WS Lynx HAS3S [631]	Wild Park Derbyshire, Brailsford, Derbys
	XZ246	WS Lynx HAS3S(ICE) [434/EE]	South Yorkshire Aircraft Museum, Doncaster, S. Yorks

Serial	Type (code/other identity)	Owner/operator, location or fate	Notes
XZ248	WS Lynx HAS3S	SFDO, RNAS Culdrose, Cornwall	
XZ250	WS Lynx HAS3S [426/PO] $	RN, Portland, Dorset, on display	
XZ252	WS Lynx HAS3S	Privately owned, Hixon, Staffs	
XZ254	WS Lynx HAS3S	Privately owned, Hixon, Staffs	
XZ255	WS Lynx HMA8SRU [454/DF]	DSEME SAAE, Lyneham, Wilts	
XZ257	WS Lynx HAS3S	RNAS Yeovilton, Somerset, GI (Wildcat ground trainer)	
XZ290	WS Gazelle AH1	AAC No 665 Sqn/5 Regt, Aldergrove, NI	
XZ292	WS Gazelle AH1	Privately owned, Stapleford Tawney, Essex	
XZ294	WS Gazelle AH1 (G-CMLO) [X]	Privately owned, Deighton, N. Yorks	
XZ295	WS Gazelle AH1 (G-CLXR)	Privately owned, Peasemore, Berks	
XZ298	WS Gazelle AH1 <ff>	AAC Middle Wallop, Hants, GI use	
XZ300	WS Gazelle AH1	Army, Bramley, Hants	
XZ303	WS Gazelle AH1	Privately owned, Peasemore, Berks	
XZ304	WS Gazelle AH1	Privately owned, Stapleford Tawney, Essex	
XZ305	WS Gazelle AH1 (TAD 020)	DSAE No 1 SoTT, Cosford, Shropshire	
XZ308	WS Gazelle AH1	QinetiQ, Boscombe Down, Wilts (spares use)	
XZ311	WS Gazelle AH1 <ff>	Privately owned, East Hanney, Oxon (stored)	
XZ312	WS Gazelle AH1	RAF Henlow, Beds, instructional use	
XZ313	WS Gazelle AH1	Privately owned, Deighton, N. Yorks	
XZ314	WS Gazelle AH1 [A]	Privately owned, Stapleford Tawney, Essex (stored)	
XZ316	WS Gazelle AH1 [B]	Privately owned, stored Deighton, N. Yorks	
XZ318	WS Gazelle AH1 (fuselage)	Warped Outdoor Activities, Tong, Shropshire	
XZ320	WS Gazelle AH1	AAC No 665 Sqn/5 Regt, Aldergrove, NI	
XZ321	WS Gazelle AH1 (G-CDNS) [D]	Gazelle Squadron Display Team, Babcary, Somerset (restoration)	
XZ322	WS Gazelle AH1 (G-CMBB/9283M) [N]	Privately owned, Deighton, N. Yorks	
XZ323	WS Gazelle AH1 (G-CLXP) [J]	Privately owned, Peasemore, Berks	
XZ324	WS Gazelle AH1	Privately owned, Stapleford Tawney, Essex	
XZ325	WS Gazelle AH1	Privately owned, N. Yorks area	
XZ326	WS Gazelle AH1	AAC No 665 Sqn/5 Regt, Aldergrove, NI	
XZ327	WS Gazelle AH1	AAC Middle Wallop, Hants (recruiting aid)	
XZ328	WS Gazelle AH1 [C]	Privately owned, Deighton, N. Yorks	
XZ329	WS Gazelle AH1 (G-BZYD) [J]	Privately owned, Lewes, E. Sussex	
XZ330	WS Gazelle AH1	*Currently not known*	
XZ332	WS Gazelle AH1	DSAE SAAE, Lyneham, Wilts	
XZ333	WS Gazelle AH1	DSAE SAAE, Lyneham, Wilts	
XZ334	WS Gazelle AH1	AAC 7 Regiment Conversion Flt, Middle Wallop, Hants	
XZ335	WS Gazelle AH1 <ff>	Boscombe Down Aviation Collection, Old Sarum, Wilts	
XZ337	WS Gazelle AH1 [Z]	Privately owned, Freiston, Lincs	
XZ340	WS Gazelle AH1	MOD/StandardAero, stored Fleetlands, Hants	
XZ341	WS Gazelle AH1 (G-CMMA)	Privately owned, Deighton, N. Yorks	
XZ342	WS Gazelle AH1	*Currently not known*	
XZ343	WS Gazelle AH1	Privately owned, Deighton, N. Yorks	
XZ344	WS Gazelle AH1 [Y]	Privately owned, Stapleford Tawney, Essex (stored)	
XZ345	WS Gazelle AH1 [M]	DSAE SAAE, Lyneham, Wilts	
XZ346	WS Gazelle AH1	AAC Middle Wallop, Hants, at main gate	
XZ356	SEPECAT Jaguar GR3A [FU]	Privately owned, Welshpool, Wales	
XZ358	SEPECAT Jaguar GR1A (9262M) [L]	DSAE No 1 SoTT, Cosford, Shropshire	
XZ360	SEPECAT Jaguar GR3 [FN]	Teesside Airport Fire Section, Co. Durham	
XZ363	SEPECAT Jaguar GR1A <R> (XX824/BAPC 151) [A]	RAF M&RU, Bottesford, Leics	
XZ364	SEPECAT Jaguar GR3A <ff>	Privately owned, Thorpe Wood, N. Yorks	
XZ366	SEPECAT Jaguar GR3A [FC]	Privately owned, Bentwaters, Suffolk	
XZ367	SEPECAT Jaguar GR3 [EE]	DSAE No 1 SoTT, Cosford, Shropshire	
XZ368	SEPECAT Jaguar GR1 (8900M) [E]	DSAE No 1 SoTT, Cosford, Shropshire	
XZ369	SEPECAT Jaguar GR3A [EU]	East Midlands Airport Aeropark, Leics	
XZ370	SEPECAT Jaguar GR1 (9004M) [JB]	DSAE No 1 SoTT, Cosford, Shropshire	
XZ371	SEPECAT Jaguar GR1 (8907M) [AP]	DSAE No 1 SoTT, Cosford, Shropshire	
XZ372	SEPECAT Jaguar GR3 [FV]	Aberdeen Airport Fire Section, Scotland	
XZ374	SEPECAT Jaguar GR1 (9005M) [JC]	DSAE, stored Cosford, Shropshire	
XZ375	SEPECAT Jaguar GR1A (9255M) <ff>	City of Norwich Aviation Museum, Norfolk	
XZ377	SEPECAT Jaguar GR3A [P]	DSAE No 1 SoTT, Cosford, Shropshire	
XZ378	SEPECAT Jaguar GR1A [EP]	Privately owned, Topsham, Devon	

Notes	Serial	Type (code/other identity)	Owner/operator, location or fate
	XZ382	SEPECAT Jaguar GR1 (8908M)	*Currently not known (ex-Bruntingthorpe, Leics)*
	XZ383	SEPECAT Jaguar GR1 (8901M) [AF]	DSAE No 1 SoTT, Cosford, Shropshire
	XZ384	SEPECAT Jaguar GR1 (8954M) [BC]	DSAE No 1 SoTT, Cosford, Shropshire
	XZ385	SEPECAT Jaguar GR3A [FT] <ff>	Privately owned, Biddulph, Staffs
	XZ389	SEPECAT Jaguar GR1 (8946M) [BL]	DSAE No 1 SoTT, Cosford, Shropshire
	XZ390	SEPECAT Jaguar GR1 (9003M) [DM]	DSAE No 1 SoTT, Cosford, Shropshire
	XZ391	SEPECAT Jaguar GR3A [ET]	DSAE No 1 SoTT, Cosford, Shropshire
	XZ392	SEPECAT Jaguar GR3A [EM]	DSAE No 1 SoTT, Cosford, Shropshire
	XZ394	SEPECAT Jaguar GR3	Privately owned, Tattersett, Norfolk
	XZ398	SEPECAT Jaguar GR3A [EQ]	DSAE No 1 SoTT, Cosford, Shropshire
	XZ399	SEPECAT Jaguar GR3A [EJ]	DSAE No 1 SoTT, Cosford, Shropshire
	XZ400	SEPECAT Jaguar GR3A [FQ]	Privately owned, Selby, N. Yorks
	XZ431	HS Buccaneer S2B (9233M) <ff>	South Yorkshire Aircraft Museum, Doncaster, S. Yorks
	XZ440	BAe Sea Harrier FA2 [40/DD]	SFDO, RNAS Culdrose, Cornwall
	XZ455	BAe Sea Harrier FA2 [001] (wreck)	Privately owned, Thorpe Wood, N. Yorks
	XZ457	BAe Sea Harrier FA2 [104/VL]	Boscombe Down Aviation Collection, Old Sarum, Wilts
	XZ459	BAe Sea Harrier FA2 [25]	Tangmere Military Aviation Museum, W. Sussex
	XZ493	BAe Sea Harrier FRS1 (comp XV760) [001/N]	FAA Museum, RNAS Yeovilton, Somerset
	XZ493	BAe Sea Harrier FRS1 <ff>	RNAS Yeovilton, Somerset, Fire Section
	XZ494	BAe Sea Harrier FA2 [128]	Privately owned, Wedmore, Somerset
	XZ497	BAe Sea Harrier FA2 [126]	Privately owned, Charlwood, Surrey
	XZ499	BAe Sea Harrier FA2 [003]	FAA Museum, stored Cobham Hall, RNAS Yeovilton, Somerset
	XZ550	Slingsby T61F Venture T2 (G-BTDA)	Privately owned, Easterton, Moray, Scotland
	XZ559	Slingsby T61F Venture T2 (G-BUEK)	Privately owned, Shipdam, Norfolk
	XZ570	WS61 Sea King HAS5(mod)	RN, Predannack Fire School, Cornwall
	XZ574	WS61 Sea King HAS6	FAA Museum, stored Cobham Hall, RNAS Yeovilton, Somerset
	XZ575	WS61 Sea King HU5	Privately owned, Charlwood, Surrey
	XZ576	WS61 Sea King HAS6	DSAE RNAESS, *HMS Sultan*, Gosport, Hants
	XZ579	WS61 Sea King HAS6 [707/PW]	DSAE RNAESS, *HMS Sultan*, Gosport, Hants (Stored)
	XZ580	WS61 Sea King HC6 [ZB]	DSAE RNAESS, *HMS Sultan*, Gosport, Hants
	XZ581	WS61 Sea King HAS6 [69/CU]	DSAE RNAESS, *HMS Sultan*, Gosport, Hants
	XZ585	WS61 Sea King HAR3 [A]	RAF Museum, Hendon, Gtr London
	XZ586	WS61 Sea King HAR3 [B]	HeliOperations Ltd, stored Somerton, Somerset
	XZ587	WS61 Sea King HAR3 [C]	RAF St Mawgan, Cornwall, at main gate
	XZ588	WS61 Sea King HAR3 (G-SEAK) [D]	Privately owned, Chard, Somerset
	XZ589	WS61 Sea King HAR3 [E] $	Privately owned, Scalby, N. Yorks
	XZ590	WS61 Sea King HAR3 [F]	HeliOperations Ltd, stored Somerton, Somerset
	XZ592	WS61 Sea King HAR3 [H]	Morayvia, Kinloss, Scotland
	XZ594	WS61 Sea King HAR3	HeliOperations Ltd, stored Somerton, Somerset
	XZ595	WS61 Sea King HAR3 [K]	Privately owned, Charlwood, Surrey
	XZ596	WS61 Sea King HAR3 [L]	HeliOperations Ltd, stored Somerton, Somerset
	XZ597	WS61 Sea King HAR3 (G-SKNG) [M]	Privately owned, Chard, Somerset
	XZ605	WS Lynx AH7 [L]	AAC Wattisham, Suffolk, Station Heritage Museum
	XZ606	WS Lynx AH7 [O]	Delta Force Paintball, Billericay, Essex
	XZ607	WS Lynx AH7 <ff>	MOD, Cornwall Aviation Heritage Centre, Newquay, Cornwall
	XZ607	WS Lynx AH7 (comp XZ215)	Spadeadam Ranges, Cumbria
	XZ608	WS Lynx AH7 (fuselage)	Army, Bury St Edmunds, Suffolk, GI use
	XZ608	WS Lynx AH7 (comp XZ680) [N]	Privately owned, East Grinstead, W. Sussex
	XZ609	WS Lynx AH7	Army, Bury St Edmunds, Suffolk, GI use
	XZ611	WS Lynx AH7 <ff>	Bilsthorpe Paintball Park, Notts
	XZ612	WS Lynx AH7	Delta Force Paintball, Bovingdon, Herts
	XZ613	WS Lynx AH7 [F]	Privately owned, Billericay, Essex
	XZ615	WS Lynx AH7 (XZ209) <ff>	MOD JARTS, Boscombe Down, Wilts
	XZ616	WS Lynx AH7 (G-LNKX)	Privately owned, Chard, Somerset
	XZ617	WS Lynx AH7 <ff>	DSEME SAAE, Lyneham, Wilts
	XZ630	Panavia Tornado (P12) (8976M)	RAF Halton, Bucks, on display
	XZ631	Panavia Tornado (P15)	Yorkshire Air Museum, Elvington, N. Yorks
	XZ642	WS Lynx AH7	DSEME SAAE, Lyneham, Wilts
	XZ643	WS Lynx AH7 [C]	Culham Paintball, Oxon

Serial	Type (code/other identity)	Owner/operator, location or fate	Notes
XZ645	WS Lynx AH7	Delta Force Paintball, Romsey, Hants	
XZ646	WS Lynx AH7 (XZ649)	Bristol University, Glos, instructional use	
XZ647	WS Lynx AH7 <ff>	Aberdeen Airport Fire Section, Scotland	
XZ651	WS Lynx AH7 [O]	Army, Pirbright, Surrey, GI use	
XZ652	WS Lynx AH7	IFTC, Teesside International Airport, Co. Durham	
XZ653	WS Lynx AH7	DSEME SAAE, Lyneham, Wilts	
XZ654	WS Lynx AH7	Shannon Aviation Museum, Eire (stored)	
XZ655	WS Lynx AH7 [A/3] <ff>	Privately owned, Werrington, Peterborough, Cambs	
XZ661	WS Lynx AH7 [V]	Army, Bramley, Hants	
XZ664	WS Lynx AH7	R6 Warfighters Paintball, Barby, Warks	
XZ665	WS Lynx AH7	R6 Warfighters Paintball, Barby, Warks	
XZ666	WS Lynx AH7	DSEME SAAE, Lyneham, Wilts	
XZ668	WS Lynx AH7 [UN] <ff>	Privately owned, stored Cranfield, Beds	
XZ670	WS Lynx AH7 [A]	RNAS Yeovilton, Somerset, on display	
XZ671	WS Lynx AH7 <ff>	Leonardo MW, Yeovil, Somerset, instructional use	
XZ672	WS Lynx AH7 <ff>	AAC Middle Wallop, Hants, Fire Section	
XZ673	WS Lynx AH7 [5]	Privately owned, Weeton, Lancs	
XZ674	WS Lynx AH7 [T]	RNAS Yeovilton, Somerset, Fire Section	
XZ675	WS Lynx AH7 [H]	Army Flying Museum, Middle Wallop, Hants	
XZ676	WS Lynx AH7 [N]	Privately owned, Weeton, Lancs	
XZ677	WS Lynx AH7 <ff>	Army, Longmoor Camp, Hants, GI use	
XZ678	WS Lynx AH7 (G-NCKY)	Privately owned, Peasemore, Berks	
XZ679	WS Lynx AH7 [W]	DSEME SAAE, Lyneham, Wilts	
XZ680	WS Lynx AH7 (XZ648)	Privately owned, Mabe Burnthouse, Cornwall	
XZ689	WS Lynx HMA8SRU [314]	Privately owned, Woodmancote, W. Sussex	
XZ690	WS Lynx HMA8SRU [640]	Delta Force Paintball, West Glasgow, Scotland	
XZ691	WS Lynx HMA8SRU [310]	FAA Museum, stored Cobham Hall, RNAS Yeovilton, Somerset	
XZ692	WS Lynx HMA8SRU [764/SN] $	DSAE HMS Sultan, Gosport, Hants, on display	
XZ693	WS Lynx HAS3S [311]	Wild Park Derbyshire, Brailsford, Derbys	
XZ694	WS Lynx HAS3GMS [434]	Privately owned, South Clifton, Notts	
XZ697	WS Lynx HMA8SRU [313]	MOD/StandardAero, preserved Fleetlands, Hants	
XZ698	WS Lynx HMA8SRU (ZD258) [365]	Privately owned, Blackpool, Lancs	
XZ699	WS Lynx HAS2	FAA Museum, RNAS Yeovilton, Somerset	
XZ719	WS Lynx HMA8SRU [64]	RNAS Yeovilton, Somerset, Fire Section	
XZ720	WS Lynx HAS3GMS [410/GC]	FAA Museum, RNAS Yeovilton, Somerset	
XZ721	WS Lynx HAS3GMS [322]	East Midlands Airport Aeropark, Leics	
XZ723	WS Lynx HMA8SRU [672]	Delta Force Paintball, Thornbury, Glos	
XZ725	WS Lynx HMA8SRU [415/MM]	DSAE RNAESS, HMS Sultan, Gosport, Hants	
XZ726	WS Lynx HMA8SRU [316]	School of Maritime Survival, HMS Raleigh, Plymouth	
XZ727	WS Lynx HAS3S	Battersea Park, London	
XZ728	WS Lynx HMA8 [326/AW]	RNAS Yeovilton, Somerset, on display	
XZ729	WS Lynx HMA8SRU [425/DT]	DSAE RNAESS, HMS Sultan, Gosport, Hants	
XZ731	WS Lynx HMA8SRU [311/VL]	DSEME SAAE, Lyneham, Wilts	
XZ732	WS Lynx HMA8SRU [315/VL]	DSEME SAAE, Lyneham, Wilts	
XZ735	WS Lynx HAS3GMS [305,404]	Privately owned, Sproughton, Suffolk	
XZ736	WS Lynx HMA8SRU [815]	RN Yeovilton, Somerset, GI use	
XZ791	Northrop Shelduck D1	Davidstow Airfield & Cornwall at War Museum, Davidstow Moor, Cornwall	
XZ795	Northrop Shelduck D1	Army Flying Museum, Middle Wallop, Hants	
XZ920	WS61 Sea King HU5	Transferred to Ukraine, November 2022	
XZ921	WS61 Sea King HAS6 [269/N]	Holmside Park, Edmondsley, Co. Durham	
XZ922	WS61 Sea King HC6 [ZA]	DSAE RNAESS, HMS Sultan, Gosport, Hants	
XZ930	WS Gazelle HT3 (A2713) [SN]	DSAE, HMS Sultan, Gosport, Hants, on display	
XZ932	WS Gazelle HT3 (G-CBJZ) [S]	Privately owned, Hamburg, Germany	
XZ933	WS Gazelle HT3 (XZ936/G-CGJZ)	Privately owned, Peasemore, Berks (restoration)	
XZ934	WS Gazelle HT3 (G-CBSI)	Privately owned, Redhill, Surrey	
XZ935	WS Gazelle HCC4 (9332M)	Privately owned, Peasemore, Berks	
XZ936	WS Gazelle HT3 (G-CLHO) [6]	Privately owned, Peasemore, Berks	
XZ939	WS Gazelle HT3 (G-CLGO)	Privately owned, East Hanney, Oxon	
XZ941	WS Gazelle HT3 (9301M) [B]	DSAE No 1 SoTT, Cosford, Shropshire	
XZ964	BAe Harrier GR3 [D]	Royal Engineers Museum, Chatham, Kent	

Notes	Serial	Type (code/other identity)	Owner/operator, location or fate
	XZ966	BAe Harrier GR3 (9221M) [G]	Spadeadam Ranges, Cumbria
	XZ968	BAe Harrier GR3 (9222M) [3G]	Muckleborough Collection, Weybourne, Norfolk
	XZ969	BAe Harrier GR3 [69/DD]	RN, Predannack Fire School, Cornwall
	XZ971	BAe Harrier GR3 (9219M) [G]	HQ DSDA, Donnington, Shropshire, on display
	XZ987	BAe Harrier GR3 (9185M) [C]	RAF Stafford, Staffs, at main gate
	XZ990	BAe Harrier GR3 <ff>	*Currently not known*
	XZ990	BAe Harrier GR3 <rf>	RAF Wittering, Cambs, derelict
	XZ991	BAe Harrier GR3 (9162M)	DSAE Cosford, Shropshire, on display
	XZ993	BAe Harrier GR3 (9240M) <ff>	Privately owned, Upwood, Cambs
	XZ995	BAe Harrier GR3 (9220M/G-CBGK) [3G]	Privately owned, Dolly's Grove, Co Dublin, Eire
	XZ997	BAe Harrier GR3 (9122M) [V]	RAF Museum, stored Cosford, Shropshire
	ZA101	BAe Hawk 100 (G-HAWK)	Brooklands Museum, Weybridge, Surrey
	ZA105	WS61 Sea King HAR3 [Q]	HeliOperations Ltd, stored Somerton, Somerset
	ZA110	BAe Jetstream T2 (F-BTMI) [563/CU]	Aberdeen Airport Fire Section, Scotland
	ZA111	BAe Jetstream T2 (9Q-CTC) [565/CU]	RN, Predannack Fire School, Cornwall
	ZA126	WS61 Sea King ASaC7 [91]	HeliOperations Ltd, stored Somerton, Somerset
	ZA127	WS61 Sea King HAS6 [509/CU]	Privately owned, Thornhill, Stirlingshire, Scotland
	ZA128	WS61 Sea King HAS6 [010]	DSAE, stored *HMS Sultan*, Gosport, Hants
	ZA130	WS61 Sea King HU5 [19]	Privately owned, Charlwood, Surrey
	ZA131	WS61 Sea King HAS6 [271/N]	DSAE RNAESS, *HMS Sultan*, Gosport, Hants
	ZA133	WS61 Sea King HAS6 [831/CU]	DSAE RNAESS, *HMS Sultan*, Gosport, Hants
	ZA134	WS61 Sea King HU5 [25]	HeliOperations Ltd, Portland, Dorset
	ZA135	WS61 Sea King HAS6 [705/CU]	Privately owned, Woodperry, Oxon
	ZA136	WS61 Sea King HAS6 [018]	Mayhem Paintball, Abridge, Essex
	ZA137	WS61 Sea King HU5 [20]	HeliOperations Ltd, stored Somerton, Hants
	ZA147	BAe VC10 K3 (5H-MMT/N147ZA) <ff>	*Currently not known (ex-Bruntingthorpe, Leics)*
	ZA148	BAe VC10 K3 (5Y-ADA/N148ZA) [G]	Privately owned, Newquay, Cornwall
	ZA150	BAe VC10 K3 (5H-MOG/N150ZA) [J]	Privately owned, Dunsfold, Surrey
	ZA166	WS61 Sea King HU5	*Transferred to Ukraine, February 2022*
	ZA167	WS61 Sea King HU5 [22/CU]	*Currently not known*
	ZA168	WS61 Sea King HAS6 [830/CU]	DSAE RNAESS, *HMS Sultan*, Gosport, Hants
	ZA169	WS61 Sea King HAS6 [515/CW]	DSAE, stored *HMS Sultan*, Gosport, Hants
	ZA170	WS61 Sea King HAS5	*Currently not known*
	ZA175	BAe Sea Harrier FA2	Norfolk & Suffolk Avn Museum, Flixton, Suffolk
	ZA176	BAe Sea Harrier FA2 [126/R]	Newark Air Museum, Winthorpe, Notts
	ZA180	Diamond Twin Star DA42MPP (G-DOSB)	Privately owned, Bournemouth, Dorset
	ZA195	BAe Sea Harrier FA2 [710]	South Wales Aviation Museum, St Athan, Wales
	ZA209	Short MATS-B	Army Flying Museum, stored Middle Wallop, Hants
	ZA220	Short MATS-B (ZA242)	Boscombe Down Aviation Collection, Old Sarum, Wilts
	ZA250	BAe Harrier T52 (G-VTOL)	Brooklands Museum, Weybridge, Surrey
	ZA267	Panavia Tornado ADV (9284M) [FA]	Privately owned, RAF Syerston, Notts
	ZA291	WS61 Sea King HC4 [N]	Holmside Park, Edmondsley, Co. Durham
	ZA298	WS61 Sea King HC4 (G-BJNM) [U/Y]	FAA Museum, RNAS Yeovilton, Somerset
	ZA312	WS61 Sea King HC4 [E]	Privately owned, Charlwood, Surrey
	ZA313	WS61 Sea King HC4 [M]	Holmside Park, Edmondsley, Co. Durham
	ZA314	WS61 Sea King HC4 (G-CMDO) [WT]	Privately owned, Chard, Somerset
	ZA319	Panavia Tornado GR1 (9315M)	Boscombe Down Aviation Collection, Old Sarum, Wilts
	ZA320	Panavia Tornado GR1 (9314M) [CA]	RAF Cosford, Shropshire, on display
	ZA323	Panavia Tornado GR1 [TAZ]	DSAE RNAESS, *HMS Sultan*, Gosport, Hants
	ZA325	Panavia Tornado GR1 <ff>	RAF Manston History Museum, Kent
	ZA325	Panavia Tornado GR1 [TAX] <rf>	RAF AM&SU, stored Shawbury, Shropshire
	ZA326	Panavia Tornado GR1P	South Wales Aviation Museum, St Athan, Wales
	ZA327	Panavia Tornado GR1 <ff>	Lakes Lightnings, Spark Bridge, Cumbria
	ZA328	Panavia Tornado GR1	BAE Systems, stored Salmesbury, Lancs
	ZA353	Panavia Tornado GR1 [B-53]	Privately owned, Topsham, Devon
	ZA354	Panavia Tornado GR1	Yorkshire Air Museum, Elvington, N. Yorks
	ZA355	Panavia Tornado GR1 (9310M) [EA]	Privately owned, White Waltham, Berks
	ZA356	Panavia Tornado GR1 <ff>	DSAE No 1 SoTT, Cosford, Shropshire
	ZA357	Panavia Tornado GR1 [TTV]	Privately owned, RAF Syerston, Notts
	ZA359	Panavia Tornado GR1	Privately owned, Thorpe Wood, N. Yorks
	ZA360	Panavia Tornado GR1 (9318M) <ff>	*Currently not known*

Serial	Type (code/other identity)	Owner/operator, location or fate	Notes
ZA362	Panavia Tornado GR1	Privately owned, New York, Lincs	
ZA398	Panavia Tornado GR4A [087]	MOD, Cornwall Aviation Heritage Centre, Newquay, Cornwall	
ZA399	Panavia Tornado GR1 (9316M) [AJ-C]	Privately owned, Knutsford, Cheshire	
ZA407	Panavia Tornado GR1 (9336M) [AJ-N]	RAF Marham, Norfolk, fire section	
ZA447	Panavia Tornado GR4 [019]	DSAE No 1 SoTT, Cosford, Shropshire	
ZA450	Panavia Tornado GR1 (9317M) [TH]	DSAE No 1 SoTT, Cosford, Shropshire	
ZA452	Panavia Tornado GR4 [021]	Midland Air Museum, Coventry, Warks	
ZA457	Panavia Tornado GR1 [AJ-J]	RAF Museum, Hendon, Gtr London	
ZA459	Panavia Tornado GR4 [025]	DSAE No 1 SoTT, Cosford, Shropshire	
ZA463	Panavia Tornado GR4 [046]	RAF Lossiemouth, Moray, Scotland, on display	
ZA465	Panavia Tornado GR1 [FF]	IWM Duxford, Cambs	
ZA469	Panavia Tornado GR4 [029]	IWM Duxford, Cambs	
ZA475	Panavia Tornado GR1 (9311M) [AJ-G]	RAF Lossiemouth, Moray, Scotland, main gate	
ZA549	Panavia Tornado GR4 [041]	BAE Systems Aircraft Maintenance Academy, Humberside, Lincs	
ZA553	Panavia Tornado GR4 [045]	RAF Honington, Suffolk, GI use	
ZA556	Panavia Tornado GR4 [047]	Defence Academy of the UK, Shrivenham, Oxon	
ZA556	Panavia Tornado GR1 <R> (ZA368/BAPC.155) [Z]	RAF M&RU, Bottesford, Leics	
ZA560	Panavia Tornado GR4 [EB-Q]	MOD JARTS, Boscombe Down, Wilts	
ZA585	Panavia Tornado GR4 [054]	DSAE No 1 SoTT, Cosford, Shropshire	
ZA587	Panavia Tornado GR4 [055]	RAF Honington, Suffolk, GI use	
ZA607	Panavia Tornado GR4 [EB-X]	MoD Sealand, Flintshire, Wales, on display	
ZA612	Panavia Tornado GR4 [074]	South Wales Aviation Museum, St Athan, Wales	
ZA613	Panavia Tornado GR4 [075]	RAF Honington, Suffolk, GI use	
ZA614	Panavia Tornado GR4 $	RAF Marham, Norfolk, at main gate	
ZA630	Slingsby T61F Venture T2 (G-BUGL)	Privately owned, Tibenham, Norfolk	
ZA634	Slingsby T61F Venture T2 (G-BUHA) [C]	Privately owned, Saltby, Leics	
ZA652	Slingsby T61F Venture T2 (G-BUDC)	Privately owned, Enstone, Oxon	
ZA656	Slingsby T61F Venture T2 (G-BTWC)	Privately owned, Nympsfield, Glos	
ZA665	Slingsby T61F Venture T2 (G-BVKK)	Privately owned, Saltby, Leics	
ZA670	B-V Chinook HC6A (N37010)	MOD/Boeing/QinetiQ, Boscombe Down (conversion)	
ZA671	B-V Chinook HC6A (N37011)	RAF No 28 Sqn, Benson, Oxon	
ZA674	B-V Chinook HC6A (N37019)	RAF No 28 Sqn, Benson, Oxon	
ZA675	B-V Chinook HC6A (N37020)	RAF CMF, Odiham, Hants	
ZA677	B-V Chinook HC6A (N37022)	RAF No 27 Sqn, Odiham, Hants	
ZA678	B-V Chinook HC1 (N37023/9229M) [EZ] (wreck)	RAF Odiham, Hants, BDRT	
ZA679	B-V Chinook HC6A (N37025)	Boeing, Middle Wallop, Hants (rework)	
ZA680	B-V Chinook HC6A (N37026)	RAF No 18 Sqn, Odiham, Hants	
ZA681	B-V Chinook HC6A (N37027)	RAF, Odiham (withdrawn from use)	
ZA682	B-V Chinook HC6A (N37029)	RAF No 18 Sqn, Odiham, Hants	
ZA683	B-V Chinook HC6A (N37030)	RAF No 18 Sqn, Odiham, Hants	
ZA684	B-V Chinook HC6A (N37031)	RAF No 27 Sqn, Odiham, Hants	
ZA704	B-V Chinook HC6A (N37033)	RAF No 28 Sqn, Benson, Oxon	
ZA705	B-V Chinook HC6A (N37035)	RAF CMF, Odiham, Hants	
ZA707	B-V Chinook HC6A (N37040)	RAF CMF, Odiham, Hants	
ZA708	B-V Chinook HC6A (N37042)	RAF No 18 Sqn, Odiham, Hants	
ZA710	B-V Chinook HC6A (N37044)	RAF No 28 Sqn, Benson, Oxon	
ZA711	B-V Chinook HC6A (N37046)	RAF CMF, Odiham, Hants	
ZA712	B-V Chinook HC6A (N37047)	RAF No 28 Sqn, Benson, Oxon	
ZA713	B-V Chinook HC6A (N37048)	RAF No 7 Sqn, Odiham, Hants	
ZA714	B-V Chinook HC6A (N37051)	RAF No 18 Sqn, Odiham, Hants	
ZA717	B-V Chinook HC1 (N37056/9238M) (wreck)	Newark Air Museum, Winthorpe, Notts	
ZA718	B-V Chinook HC6A (N37058) [BN]	RAF Museum, Cosford, Shropshire	
ZA718	WS Lynx AH7 (XZ183) <ff>	MOD JARTS, Boscombe Down, Wilts	
ZA720	B-V Chinook HC6A (N37060)	RAF No 27 Sqn, Odiham, Hants	
ZA726	WS Gazelle AH1 [F1]	Privately owned, Stapleford Tawney, Essex	
ZA726	WS Gazelle AH1 (XW851/G-CIEY)	Privately owned, Escrick, N Yorks	
ZA729	WS Gazelle AH1	AAC Wattisham, Suffolk, BDRT	
ZA730	WS Gazelle AH1 (G-FUKM) <ff>	Privately owned, Andover area, Hants	
ZA731	WS Gazelle AH1	MOD/StandardAero, stored Fleetlands, Hants	
ZA731	WS Gazelle AH1 (comp XZ313)	Privately owned, Deighton, N. Yorks	

Notes	Serial	Type (code/other identity)	Owner/operator, location or fate
	ZA735	WS Gazelle AH1	DSAE SAAE, Lyneham, Wilts
	ZA736	WS Gazelle AH1	MOD/StandardAero, stored Fleetlands, Hants
	ZA737	WS Gazelle AH1	Army Flying Museum, Middle Wallop, Hants
	ZA766	WS Gazelle AH1	AAC No 665 Sqn/5 Regt, Aldergrove, NI
	ZA769	WS Gazelle AH1 [K]	DSAE SAAE, Lyneham, Wilts
	ZA772	WS Gazelle AH1	MOD/StandardAero, Fleetlands, Hants
	ZA773	WS Gazelle AH1 [F]	AAC AM&SU, stored Shawbury, Shropshire
	ZA775	WS Gazelle AH1	AAC No 665 Sqn/5 Regt, Aldergrove, NI
	ZA776	WS Gazelle AH1 [F]	Privately owned, Stapleford Tawney, Essex (stored)
	ZA804	WS Gazelle HT3	Privately owned, Solstice Park, Amesbury, Wilts
	ZA935	WS Puma HC2 [S]	RAF No 1563 Flt, Seria, Brunei
	ZA936	WS Puma HC2 [T]	RAF, stored Benson, Oxon .
	ZA937	WS Puma HC1	RAF Benson, Oxon, on display
	ZA939	WS Puma HC2 [U]	RAF No 84 Sqn, Akrotiri, Cyprus
	ZA940	WS Puma HC2 (F-ZWBZ) [V]	RAF No 28 Sqn/No 33 Sqn/No 230 Sqn, Benson, Oxon
	ZA947	Douglas Dakota C3	RAF BBMF, Coningsby, Lincs (overhaul Duxford)
	ZB131	BAE Systems Hawk Mk.167	RAF Joint Hawk Training Sqn/No 11 Sqn QEAF, Leeming, N. Yorks
	ZB132	BAE Systems Hawk Mk.167	RAF Joint Hawk Training Sqn/No 11 Sqn QEAF, Leeming, N. Yorks
	ZB133	BAE Systems Hawk Mk.167	RAF Joint Hawk Training Sqn/No 11 Sqn QEAF, Leeming, N. Yorks
	ZB134	BAE Systems Hawk Mk.167	RAF Joint Hawk Training Sqn/No 11 Sqn QEAF, Leeming, N. Yorks
	ZB135	BAE Systems Hawk Mk.167	RAF Joint Hawk Training Sqn/No 11 Sqn QEAF, Leeming, N. Yorks
	ZB136	BAE Systems Hawk Mk.167	RAF Joint Hawk Training Sqn/No 11 Sqn QEAF, Leeming, N. Yorks
	ZB137	BAE Systems Hawk Mk.167	RAF Joint Hawk Training Sqn/No 11 Sqn QEAF, Leeming, N. Yorks
	ZB138	BAE Systems Hawk Mk.167	RAF Joint Hawk Training Sqn/No 11 Sqn QEAF, Leeming, N. Yorks
	ZB139	BAE Systems Hawk Mk.167	RAF Joint Hawk Training Sqn/No 11 Sqn QEAF, Leeming, N. Yorks
	ZB500	WS Lynx 800 (G-LYNX/ZA500)	The Helicopter Museum, Weston-super-Mare, Somerset
	ZB506	WS61 Sea King Mk 4X	Privately owned, White Waltham, Berks (dismantled)
	ZB507	WS61 Sea King HC4 [F]	Currently not known
	ZB601	BAe Harrier T4 (fuselage)	Privately owned, Thorpe Wood, N. Yorks (stored)
	ZB603	BAe Harrier T8 [T03/DD]	SFDO, RNAS Culdrose, Cornwall
	ZB604	BAe Harrier T8 [722]	FAA Museum, stored Cobham Hall, RNAS Yeovilton
	ZB615	SEPECAT Jaguar T2A	DSAE No 1 SoTT, Cosford, Shropshire
	ZB625	WS Gazelle HT3 (G-TSTR)	Privately owned, Babcary, Somerset (to Australia)
	ZB627	WS Gazelle HT3 (G-CBSK) [A]	Privately owned, East Hanney, Oxon
	ZB646	WS Gazelle HT2 (G-CBGZ) [59/CU]	Privately owned, Knebworth, Herts
	ZB647	WS Gazelle HT2 (G-CBSF) [40]	Privately owned, Babcary, Somerset (restoration)
	ZB665	WS Gazelle AH1	MOD/StandardAero, Fleetlands, Somerset
	ZB668	WS Gazelle AH1 (TAD 015)	DSAE SAAE, Lyneham, Wilts
	ZB669	WS Gazelle AH1	AAC No 665 Sqn/5 Regt, Aldergrove, NI
	ZB670	WS Gazelle AH1	TA Centre, Taunton, Somerset, on display
	ZB671	WS Gazelle AH1	AAC 7 Regiment Conversion Flt, Middle Wallop, Hants
	ZB672	WS Gazelle AH1	Army Training Regiment, Winchester, Hants
	ZB674	WS Gazelle AH1	AAC No 665 Sqn/5 Regt, Aldergrove, NI
	ZB677	WS Gazelle AH1 (G-CMKP)	Privately owned, Deighton, N. Yorks
	ZB678	WS Gazelle AH1	MOD/StandardAero, Fleetlands, Hants
	ZB679	WS Gazelle AH1	AAC 7 Regiment Conversion Flt, Middle Wallop, Hants
	ZB683	WS Gazelle AH1 (G-CMKS)	Privately owned, Deighton, N. Yorks
	ZB684	WS Gazelle AH1	RAF JADTEU, Brize Norton, Oxon, instructional use
	ZB686	WS Gazelle AH1 <ff>	The Helicopter Museum, Weston-super-Mare, Somerset
	ZB689	WS Gazelle AH1 (G-CMKT)	Privately owned, Hungary
	ZB690	WS Gazelle AH1	AAC No 665 Sqn/5 Regt, Aldergrove, NI

Serial	Type (code/other identity)	Owner/operator, location or fate	Notes
ZB691	WS Gazelle AH1 [S]	AAC 7 Regiment Conversion Flt, Middle Wallop, Hants	
ZB692	WS Gazelle AH1 [Y]	Privately owned, Deighton, North Yorks	
ZB693	WS Gazelle AH1	AAC No 665 Sqn/5 Regt, Aldergrove, NI	
ZD230	BAC Super VC10 K4 (G-ASGA) <ff>	Privately owned, Crondall, Hants	
ZD240	BAC Super VC10 K4 (G-ASGL) <ff>	Privately owned, Crondall, Hants	
ZD242	BAC Super VC10 K4 (G-ASGP) <ff>	JARTS, Boscombe Down, Wilts	
ZD249	WS Lynx HMA8SRU (XZ698) (comp ZD249) [316]	Delta Force Paintball, Edinburgh, Scotland	
ZD249	WS Lynx HAS3S [635] <ff>	Privately owned, Sproughton, Suffolk	
ZD250	WS Lynx HAS3S [636]	RAF Henlow, Beds, instructional use	
ZD252	WS Lynx HMA8SRU (G-NCKZ) [312/VL]	Privately owned, North Weald, Essex	
ZD254	WS Lynx HAS3S [305/GJ]	DSAE AESS, HMS Sultan, Gosport, Hants	
ZD255	WS Lynx HAS3GMS [635]	Bawtry Paintball Park, S Yorks	
ZD257	WS Lynx HMA8SRU [302/VL]	Privately owned, Woodmancote, W. Sussex	
ZD259	WS Lynx HMA8SRU [474/RM]	DSEME DCTT, Lyneham, Wilts	
ZD260	WS Lynx HMA8SRU [313/VL]	DSEME DCTT, Lyneham, Wilts	
ZD261	WS Lynx HMA8SRU [314]	DSEME DCTT, Lyneham, Wilts	
ZD262	WS Lynx HMA8SRU [316]	DSEME SAAE, Lyneham, Wilts	
ZD263	WS Lynx HAS3S [632]	Bawtry Paintball Park, S. Yorks	
ZD264	WS Lynx HAS3GMS [407] (fuselage)	Air Defence Collection, Wilts	
ZD265	WS Lynx HMA8SRU [302]	AAC Middle Wallop, Hants, dumped	
ZD266	WS Lynx HMA8SRU [673]	Privately owned, North Weald, Essex	
ZD267	WS Lynx HMA8 (comp XZ672) [LST-2]	RN, stored St Athan, Wales	
ZD268	WS Lynx HMA8SRU [366/YB]	DSEME SAAE, Lyneham, Wilts	
ZD274	WS Lynx AH7 [M]	Privately owned, Sproughton, Suffolk	
ZD276	WS Lynx AH7	Mayhem Paintball, Abridge, Essex	
ZD278	WS Lynx AH7 [F]	Delta Force, Liverpool, Merseyside	
ZD280	WS Lynx AH7	Farnborough Air Sciences Trust, Farnborough, Hants	
ZD281	WS Lynx AH7 [K]	Privately owned, Willenhall, Staffs	
ZD283	WS Lynx AH7 <ff>	Privately owned, Stoke-on-Trent, Staffs	
ZD283	WS Lynx AH7 (ZE379)	Privately owned, Sproughton, Suffolk	
ZD284	WS Lynx AH7 [K]	Privately owned, Corley Moor, Warks	
ZD285	WS Lynx AH7	MOD JARTS, Boscombe Down, Wilts	
ZD318	BAe Harrier GR7A	Harrier Heritage Centre, RAF Wittering, Cambs	
ZD433	BAe Harrier GR9A [45A]	FAA Museum, RNAS Yeovilton, Somerset	
ZD461	BAe Harrier GR9A [51A]	IWM London, Lambeth, Gtr London	
ZD462	BAe Harrier GR7 (9302M) [52]	Privately owned, Malmesbury, Glos	
ZD465	BAe Harrier GR9 [55]	DSAE RNAESS, HMS Sultan, Gosport, Hants	
ZD469	BAe Harrier GR7A [59A]	RAF Wittering, Cambs, on display	
ZD476	WS61 Sea King HC4 [WZ]	Privately owned, Charlwood, Surrey	
ZD477	WS61 Sea King HC4 [E]	East Midlands Airport Aeropark, Leics	
ZD478	WS61 Sea King HC4 [J]	Privately owned, Hixon, Staffs	
ZD479	WS61 Sea King HC4 [WQ]	DSAE RNAESS, HMS Sultan, Gosport, Hants	
ZD480	WS61 Sea King HC4 [J]	StandardAero, Fleetlands, Hants, on display	
ZD559	WS Lynx AH5X	QinetiQ Apprentice Training School, Boscombe Down, Wilts	
ZD560	WS Lynx AH7	Leonardo MW, Yeovil, Somerset, on display	
ZD565	WS Lynx HMA8SRU [404/IR]	Delta Force Paintball, Cardiff, Wales	
ZD566	WS Lynx HMA8SRU [305]	Privately owned, Sproughton, Suffolk	
ZD574	B-V Chinook HC6A (N37077)	RAF CMF, Odiham, Hants	
ZD575	B-V Chinook HC6A (N37078)	RAF No 28 Sqn, Benson, Oxon	
ZD578	BAe Sea Harrier FA2 [000,122]	RNAS Yeovilton, Somerset, at main gate	
ZD579	BAe Sea Harrier FA2 [79/DD]	SFDO, RNAS Culdrose, Cornwall	
ZD581	BAe Sea Harrier FA2 [124]	RN, Predannack Fire School, Cornwall	
ZD582	BAe Sea Harrier FA2 [002/N]	North-East Land, Sea & Air Museums, Usworth, T&W	
ZD607	BAe Sea Harrier FA2	DSDA, Arncott, Oxon, preserved	
ZD610	BAe Sea Harrier FA2 [714,002/N]	Aerospace Bristol, Filton, Glos	
ZD611	BAe Sea Harrier FA2 [001]	RN, Portsmouth Dockyard, Hants, preserved	
ZD612	BAe Sea Harrier FA2 [724]	Privately owned, Topsham, Devon	
ZD613	BAe Sea Harrier FA2 [122/R]	Privately owned, Thorpe Wood, N. Yorks	
ZD614	BAe Sea Harrier FA2 <ff>	Privately owned, Walcott, Lincs	
ZD620	BAe 125 CC3	Bournemouth Aviation Museum, Dorset	

Notes	Serial	Type (code/other identity)	Owner/operator, location or fate
	ZD621	BAe 125 CC3	RAF Northolt, Gtr London, on display
	ZD625	WS61 Sea King HC4 [P]	Holmside Park, Edmondsley, Co. Durham
	ZD627	WS61 Sea King HC4 <ff>	South Wales Aviation Museum, stored St Athan, Wales
	ZD630	WS61 Sea King HAS6 [012/L]	*Currently not known*
	ZD631	WS61 Sea King HAS6 [66] (fuselage)	Privately owned, St Agnes, Cornwall
	ZD634	WS61 Sea King HAS6 [503]	SFDO, RNAS Culdrose, Cornwall
	ZD636	WS61 Sea King ASaC7 [182/CU]	DSAE, stored *HMS Sultan*, Gosport, Hants
	ZD637	WS61 Sea King ASaC7 [700/PW]	DSAE RNAESS, *HMS Sultan*, Gosport, Hants
	ZD667	BAe Harrier GR3 (9201M) [U]	Bentwaters Cold War Museum, Suffolk
	ZD703	BAe 125 CC3	Privately owned, Shepton Mallet, Somerset
	ZD704	BAe 125 CC3	MOD, Cornwall Aviation Heritage Centre, Newquay, Cornwall
	ZD710	Panavia Tornado GR1 <ff>	Privately owned, Lincs
	ZD711	Panavia Tornado GR4 [079]	RAF Honington, Suffolk, GI use
	ZD715	Panavia Tornado GR4 [083]	RAF Cosford, Shropshire, GI use
	ZD744	Panavia Tornado GR4 [092]	Preserved Montrose Museum, Angus, Scotland
	ZD793	Panavia Tornado GR4 [101]	DSAE No 1 SoTT, Cosford, Shropshire
	ZD849	Panavia Tornado GR4 [110]	DSAE No 1 SoTT, Cosford, Shropshire
	ZD899	Panavia Tornado F2	Privately owned, Thorpe Wood, N. Yorks
	ZD902	Panavia Tornado F2A(TIARA)	Privately owned, Church Fenton, N. Yorks
	ZD932	Panavia Tornado F2 (comp ZE255) (9308M) (fuselage)	Privately owned, Thorpe Wood, N. Yorks
	ZD936	Panavia Tornado F2 (comp ZE251) <ff>	Boscombe Down Aviation Collection, Old Sarum, Wilts
	ZD938	Panavia Tornado F2 (comp ZE295) <ff>	South Yorkshire Aircraft Museum, Doncaster, S. Yorks
	ZD939	Panavia Tornado F2 (comp ZE292) <ff>	DSAE No 1 SoTT, Cosford, Shropshire, G.I.
	ZD948	Lockheed TriStar KC1 (G-BFCA/N304CS) <ff>	*Currently not known (ex-Bruntingthorpe, Leics)*
	ZD980	B-V Chinook HC6A (N37082)	MOD/Boeing/QinetiQ, Boscombe Down, Wilts (conversion)
	ZD981	B-V Chinook HC6A (N37083)	RAF No 27 Sqn, Odiham, Hants
	ZD982	B-V Chinook HC6A (N37085)	RAF CMF, Odiham, Hants
	ZD983	B-V Chinook HC6A (N37086)	RAF No 7 Sqn, Odiham, Hants
	ZD984	B-V Chinook HC6A (N37088) $	RAF No 27 Sqn, Odiham, Hants
	ZD990	BAe Harrier T8 (G-RNTB) [T90/DD]	Privately owned, St Athan, Wales
	ZD992	BAe Harrier T8 [724]	Privately owned, Knutsford, Cheshire
	ZE165	Panavia Tornado F3 [GE]	Fire Service College, Moreton-in-Marsh, Glos
	ZE168	Panavia Tornado F3 <ff>	Privately owned, Thorpe Wood, N. Yorks
	ZE204	Panavia Tornado F3 [FC]	North-East Land, Sea & Air Museums, Usworth, T&W
	ZE340	Panavia Tornado F3 (ZE758/9298M) [GO]	DSAE No 1 SoTT, Cosford, Shropshire
	ZE352	McD F-4J(UK) Phantom (9086M) <ff>	Privately owned, Newburgh, Lancs
	ZE360	McD F-4J(UK) Phantom (9059M) [O]	Privately owned, Manston, Kent
	ZE368	WS61 Sea King HAR3 [R]	Holmside Park, stored Edmondsley, Co. Durham
	ZE369	WS61 Sea King HAR3 [S]	Privately owned, Scalby, N. Yorks
	ZE370	WS61 Sea King HAR3 [T]	Privately owned, Scalby, N .Yorks
	ZE375	WS Lynx AH9A	Privately owned, Bentwaters, Suffolk
	ZE376	WS Lynx AH9A	Sheffield University, S. Yorks, GI use
	ZE378	WS Lynx AH7	RAF Cranwell, Lincs, GI use
	ZE380	WS Lynx AH9A	Army, Pirbright, Surrey, GI use
	ZE381	WS Lynx AH7 [X]	DSEME SAAE, Lyneham, Wilts
	ZE395	BAe 125 CC3	Privately owned, Dunsfold, Surrey
	ZE410	Agusta A109A (AE-334)	Army Flying Museum, Middle Wallop, Hants
	ZE412	Agusta A109A	Army, Credenhill, Herefordshire, on display
	ZE413	Agusta A109A	Perth Technical College, Scotland
	ZE418	WS61 Sea King ASaC7 [186]	DSAE, stored *HMS Sultan*, Gosport, Hants
	ZE420	WS61 Sea King ASaC7 [189]	DSAE RNAESS, *HMS Sultan*, Gosport, Hants
	ZE422	WS61 Sea King ASaC7 [192]	HeliOperations Ltd, stored Somerton, Somerset
	ZE425	WS61 Sea King HC4 [WR]	Holmside Park, Edmondsley, Co. Durham
	ZE426	WS61 Sea King HC4 [WX]	DSAE RNAESS, *HMS Sultan*, Gosport, Hants
	ZE428	WS61 Sea King HC4 [H]	Holmside Park, Edmondsley, Co. Durham (damaged)
	ZE432	BAC 1-11/479FU (DQ-FBV) <ff>	Bournemouth Aviation Museum, Dorset
	ZE449	SA330L Puma HC1 (9017M/PA-12)	Army, Whittington Barracks, Lichfield, on display
	ZE477	WS Lynx 3	The Helicopter Museum, Weston-super-Mare, Somerset
	ZE495	Grob G103 Viking T1 (BGA3000) [VA]	RAF No 661 VGS, Kirknewton, W. Lothian, Scotland

Serial	Type (code/other identity)	Owner/operator, location or fate	Notes
ZE496	Grob G103 Viking T1 (BGA3001) [VB]	RAF/Serco GMS, stored Syerston, Notts (dismantled)	
ZE498	Grob G103 Viking T1 (BGA3003) [VC]	RAF, stored Little Rissington, Glos	
ZE499	Grob G103 Viking T1 (BGA3004) [VD]	RAF CGS/No 644 VGS, Syerston, Notts	
ZE500	Grob G103 Viking T1 (BGA3005) <ff>	Privately owned, Gransden Lodge	
ZE502	Grob G103 Viking T1 (BGA3007) [VF]	RAF/Serco GMS, stored Syerston (dismantled)	
ZE503	Grob G103 Viking T1 (BGA3008) [VG]	RAF, stored Little Rissington, Glos	
ZE504	Grob G103 Viking T1 (BGA3009) [VH]	RAF/Serco GMS, Syerston, Notts	
ZE520	Grob G103 Viking T1 (BGA3010) [VJ]	RAF/Serco GMS, stored Syerston, Notts (dismantled)	
ZE521	Grob G103 Viking T1 (BGA3011) [VK]	RAF No 622 VGS, Upavon, Wilts	
ZE522	Grob G103 Viking T1 (BGA3012) [VL]	RAF No 645 VGS, Topcliffe, N. Yorks	
ZE524	Grob G103 Viking T1 (BGA3014) [VM]	RAF, stored Little Rissington, Glos	
ZE526	Grob G103 Viking T1 (BGA3016) [VN]	RAF/Serco GMS, stored Syerston, Notts (dismantled)	
ZE527	Grob G103 Viking T1 (BGA3017) [VP]	RAF CGS/No 644 VGS, Syerston, Notts	
ZE528	Grob G103 Viking T1 (BGA3018) [VQ]	RAF No 661 VGS, Kirknewton, W. Lothian, Scotland	
ZE529	Grob G103 Viking T1 (BGA3019) (comp ZE655) [VR]	RAF No 645 VGS, Topcliffe, N. Yorks	
ZE530	Grob G103 Viking T1 (BGA3020) [VS]	RAF, stored Little Rissington, Glos	
ZE531	Grob G103 Viking T1 (BGA3021) [VT]	RAF, stored Little Rissington, Glos	
ZE532	Grob G103 Viking T1 (BGA3022) [VU]	RAF No 615 VGS, Kenley, Surrey	
ZE533	Grob G103 Viking T1 (BGA3023) [VV]	RAF, stored Little Rissington, Glos	
ZE550	Grob G103 Viking T1 (BGA3025) [VX] (fuselage)	RAF Syerston, Notts, GI use	
ZE551	Grob G103 Viking T1 (BGA3026) [VY]	RAF No 622 VGS, Upavon, Wilts	
ZE552	Grob G103 Viking T1 (BGA3027) [VZ]	RAF, stored Little Rissington, Glos	
ZE553	Grob G103 Viking T1 (BGA3028) [WA]	RAF CGS/No 644 VGS, Syerston, Notts	
ZE554	Grob G103 Viking T1 (BGA3029) [WB]	RAF, stored Little Rissington, Glos	
ZE555	Grob G103 Viking T1 (BGA3030) [WC]	RAF ACCGS/No 644 VGS, Syerston, Notts	
ZE556	Grob G103 Viking T1 (BGA3031) <ff>	No 308 Sqn ATC, Colchester, Essex	
ZE557	Grob G103 Viking T1 (BGA3032) [WE]	RAF/Serco GMS, stored Syerston, Notts (dismantled)	
ZE558	Grob G103 Viking T1 (BGA3033) [WF]	RAF, stored Little Rissington, Glos	
ZE559	Grob G103 Viking T1 (BGA3034) [WG]	RAF/Serco GMS, stored Syerston, Notts (dismantled)	
ZE560	Grob G103 Viking T1 (BGA3035) [WH]	RAF CGS/No 644 VGS, Syerston, Notts	
ZE561	Grob G103 Viking T1 (BGA3036) [WJ]	RAF/Southern Sailplanes, Membury, Wilts	
ZE562	Grob G103 Viking T1 (BGA3037) [WK]	RAF, stored Little Rissington, Glos	
ZE563	Grob G103 Viking T1 (BGA3038) [WL]	RAF, stored Little Rissington, Glos	
ZE564	Grob G103 Viking T1 (BGA3039) [WN]	RAF No 661 VGS, Kirknewton, W. Lothian, Scotland	
ZE584	Grob G103 Viking T1 (BGA3040) [WP]	RAF No 621 VGS/No 637 VGS, Little Rissington, Glos	
ZE585	Grob G103 Viking T1 (BGA3041) [WQ]	RAF/Serco GMS, Syerston, Notts	
ZE586	Grob G103 Viking T1 (BGA3042) [WR]	RAF No 622 VGS, Upavon, Wilts	
ZE587	Grob G103 Viking T1 (BGA3043) [WS]	RAF/Serco GMS, Syerston, Notts (dismantled)	
ZE590	Grob G103 Viking T1 (BGA3046) [WT]	RAF CGS/No 644 VGS, Syerston, Notts	
ZE591	Grob G103 Viking T1 (BGA3047) [WU]	RAF, stored Little Rissington, Glos	
ZE592	Grob G103 Viking T1 (BGA3048) <ff>	RAF, Upavon, Wilts, GI use	
ZE593	Grob G103 Viking T1 (BGA3049) [WW]	RAF, stored Little Rissington, Glos	
ZE594	Grob G103 Viking T1 (BGA3050) [WX]	RAF No 615 VGS, Kenley, Surrey	
ZE595	Grob G103 Viking T1 (BGA3051) [WY]	RAF/Serco GMS, stored Syerston, Notts (dismantled)	
ZE600	Grob G103 Viking T1 (BGA3052) [WZ]	RAF No 621 VGS/No 637 VGS, Little Rissington, Glos	
ZE601	Grob G103 Viking T1 (BGA3053) [XA]	RAF CGS/No 644 VGS, Syerston, Notts	
ZE602	Grob G103 Viking T1 (BGA3054) [XB]	RAF No 645 VGS, Topcliffe, N. Yorks	
ZE603	Grob G103 Viking T1 (BGA3055) [XC]	RAF, stored Little Rissington, Glos	
ZE604	Grob G103 Viking T1 (BGA3056) [XD]	RAF, stored Little Rissington, Glos	
ZE605	Grob G103 Viking T1 (BGA3057) [XE]	RAF No 615 VGS, Kenley, Surrey	
ZE606	Grob G103 Viking T1 (BGA3058) [XF]	RAF/Serco GMS, Syerston, Notts (dismantled)	
ZE607	Grob G103 Viking T1 (BGA3059) [XG]	RAF, stored Little Rissington, Glos	
ZE608	Grob G103 Viking T1 (BGA3060) [XH]	RAF CGS/No 644 VGS, Syerston, Notts	
ZE609	Grob G103 Viking T1 (BGA3061) [XJ]	RAF No 622 VGS, Upavon, Wilts	
ZE610	Grob G103 Viking T1 (BGA3062) [XK]	RAF, stored Little Rissington, Glos	
ZE611	Grob G103 Viking T1 (BGA3063) [XL]	RAF, stored Little Rissington, Glos	
ZE613	Grob G103 Viking T1 (BGA3065) [XM]	RAF/Serco GMS, stored Syerston, Notts (dismantled)	
ZE614	Grob G103 Viking T1 (BGA3066) [XN]	RAF/Serco GMS, stored Syerston, Notts (dismantled)	
ZE625	Grob G103 Viking T1 (BGA3067) [XP]	RAF No 661 VGS, Kirknewton, W. Lothian, Scotland	
ZE626	Grob G103 Viking T1 (BGA3068) [XQ]	RAF No 645 VGS, Topcliffe, N. Yorks	
ZE627	Grob G103 Viking T1 (BGA3069) [XR]	RAF, stored Little Rissington, Glos	
ZE628	Grob G103 Viking T1 (BGA3070) [XS]	RAF CGS/No 644 VGS, Syerston, Notts	

Notes	Serial	Type (code/other identity)	Owner/operator, location or fate
	ZE629	Grob G103 Viking T1 (BGA3071) [XT]	RAF CGS/No 644 VGS, Syerston, Notts
	ZE630	Grob G103 Viking T1 (BGA3072) [XU]	RAF CGS/No 644 VGS, Syerston, Notts
	ZE631	Grob G103 Viking T1 (BGA3073) [XV]	RAF/Serco GMS, stored Syerston, Notts (dismantled)
	ZE632	Grob G103 Viking T1 (BGA3074) [XW]	RAF No 621 VGS/No 637 VGS, Little Rissington, Glos
	ZE633	Grob G103 Viking T1 (BGA3075) [XX]	RAF CGS/No 644 VGS, Syerston, Notts
	ZE636	Grob G103 Viking T1 (BGA3078) [XZ]	RAF CGS/No 644 VGS, Syerston, Notts
	ZE637	Grob G103 Viking T1 (BGA3079) [YA]	RAF/Serco GMS, Syerston, Notts
	ZE650	Grob G103 Viking T1 (BGA3080) [YB]	RAF No 621 VGS/No 637 VGS, Little Rissington, Glos
	ZE651	Grob G103 Viking T1 (BGA3081) [YC]	RAF/Serco GMS, stored Syerston, Notts (dismantled)
	ZE652	Grob G103 Viking T1 (BGA3082) [YD]	RAF/Serco GMS, Syerston, Notts
	ZE653	Grob G103 Viking T1 (BGA3083) [YE]	RAF/Serco GMS, stored Syerston, Notts (dismantled)
	ZE656	Grob G103 Viking T1 (BGA3086) [YH]	RAF, stored Little Rissington, Glos
	ZE657	Grob G103 Viking T1 (BGA3087) [YJ]	RAF, stored Little Rissington, Glos
	ZE658	Grob G103 Viking T1 (BGA3088) [YK]	RAF/Serco GMS, Syerston, Notts
	ZE677	Grob G103 Viking T1 (BGA3090) [YM]	RAF, stored Little Rissington, Glos
	ZE678	Grob G103 Viking T1 (BGA3091) [YN]	RAF ACCGS/No 644 VGS, Syerston, Notts
	ZE679	Grob G103 Viking T1 (BGA3092) [YP]	RAF, stored Little Rissington, Glos
	ZE680	Grob G103 Viking T1 (BGA3093) [YQ]	RAF No 645 VGS, Topcliffe, N. Yorks
	ZE681	Grob G103 Viking T1 (BGA3094) <ff>	Privately owned, Frampton Cotterell, Glos, GI use
	ZE682	Grob G103 Viking T1 (BGA3095) [YS]	RAF CGS/No 644 VGS, Syerston, Notts
	ZE683	Grob G103 Viking T1 (BGA3096) [YT]	RAF, stored Little Rissington, Glos
	ZE684	Grob G103 Viking T1 (BGA3097) [YU]	RAF, stored Little Rissington, Glos
	ZE685	Grob G103 Viking T1 (BGA3098) [YV]	RAF No 626 VGS, Predannack, Cornwall
	ZE686	Grob G103 Viking T1 (BGA3099) <ff>	Privately owned, Stow Maries, Essex
	ZE690	BAe Sea Harrier FA2 [90/DD]	SFDO, RNAS Culdrose, Cornwall
	ZE691	BAe Sea Harrier FA2 [710]	Classic Autos, Winsford, Cheshire
	ZE692	BAe Sea Harrier FA2 [92/DD]	RN, stored Culdrose, Cornwall
	ZE694	BAe Sea Harrier FA2 [004/N]	Midland Air Museum, Coventry, Warks
	ZE697	BAe Sea Harrier FA2 [006]	Privately owned, Walcott, Norfolk
	ZE698	BAe Sea Harrier FA2 [123]	Privately owned, Charlwood, Surrey
	ZE700	BAe 146 CC2 (G-6-021)	South Wales Aviation Museum, St Athan, Wales
	ZE701	BAe 146 CC2 (G-6-029/G-CMEU)	Duxford Aviation Society, Duxford, Cambs
	ZE704	Lockheed TriStar C2 (N508PA/N507CS)	Scrapped at Bruntingthorpe, Leics, April 2022
	ZE705	Lockheed TriStar C2 (N509PA/N703CS)	Scrapped at Bruntingthorpe, Leics, April 2022
	ZE707	BAe 146 C3 (OO-TAZ)	Privately owned, Cranfield Airport, Beds
	ZE708	BAe 146 C3 (OO-TAY)	Privately owned, Cranfield Airport, Beds
	ZE760	Panavia Tornado F3 (MM7206) [AP]	RAF Coningsby, Lincs, on display
	ZE788	Panavia Tornado F3 <ff>	Privately owned, Ruthin, Clwyd, Wales
	ZE887	Panavia Tornado F3 [GF] $	RAF Museum, Hendon, Gtr London
	ZE934	Panavia Tornado F3 [TA]	National Museum of Flight, E. Fortune, Scotland
	ZE936	Panavia Tornado F3 <ff>	RAF Air Defence Radar Museum, Neatishead, Norfolk
	ZE965	Panavia Tornado F3 <ff>	Privately owned, Thorpe Wood, N. Yorks
	ZE966	Panavia Tornado F3 [VT]	Tornado Heritage Centre, Hawarden, Flintshire, Wales
	ZE967	Panavia Tornado F3 [UT]	RAF Leuchars, Scotland, at main gate
	ZF115	WS61 Sea King HC4 [R,WV]	DSAE, stored HMS Sultan, Gosport, Hants
	ZF116	WS61 Sea King HC4 [WP]	Privately owned, White Waltham, Berks
	ZF118	WS61 Sea King HC4 [O]	DSAE RNAESS, HMS Sultan, Gosport, Hants
	ZF119	WS61 Sea King HC4 [WY]	DSAE RNAESS, HMS Sultan, Gosport, Hants
	ZF121	WS61 Sea King HC4 [T]	Holmside Park, Edmondsley, Co. Durham
	ZF122	WS61 Sea King HC4 [V]	Privately owned, stored Chard, Somerset
	ZF135	Shorts Tucano T1 [135]	RAF, stored Linton-on-Ouse, N. Yorks (for disposal)
	ZF137	Shorts Tucano T1 [137]	Sold to USA – Noted Germany November 2022
	ZF139	Shorts Tucano T1 [139]	RAF, stored Linton-on-Ouse, N. Yorks (for disposal)
	ZF140	Shorts Tucano T1 [140] $	RAF, stored Linton-on-Ouse, N. Yorks (for disposal)
	ZF142	Shorts Tucano T1 [142]	RAF, stored Linton-on-Ouse, N. Yorks (for disposal)
	ZF143	Shorts Tucano T1 [143]	RAF, stored Linton-on-Ouse, N. Yorks (for disposal)
	ZF144	Shorts Tucano T1 [144]	RAF, stored Linton-on-Ouse, N. Yorks (for disposal)
	ZF145	Shorts Tucano T1 [145]	RAF, stored Linton-on-Ouse, N. Yorks (for disposal)
	ZF160	Shorts Tucano T1 [160]	Unknown (ex Bentwaters, Suffolk)
	ZF163	Shorts Tucano T1 [163]	RAF AM&SU, stored Shawbury, Shropshire

Serial	Type (code/other identity)	Owner/operator, location or fate	Notes
ZF166	Shorts Tucano T1 [166]	*Unknown (ex AM&SU, Shawbury, Shropshire)*	
ZF167	Shorts Tucano T1 (fuselage)	Ulster Aviation Society, Long Kesh, NI	
ZF169	Shorts Tucano T1 [169]	*Sold to USA – Noted Germany November 2022*	
ZF170	Shorts Tucano T1 [MP-A]	*Sold to USA – Noted Germany November 2022*	
ZF171	Shorts Tucano T1 [171]	*Sold to USA – Noted Germany November 2022*	
ZF172	Shorts Tucano T1 [172]	*Sold to USA – Noted Germany November 2022*	
ZF202	Shorts Tucano T1 [202]	RAF Syerston, Notts, on display	
ZF204	Shorts Tucano T1 [204]	RAF, stored Linton-on-Ouse, N. Yorks (for disposal)	
ZF205	Shorts Tucano T1 [205]	*Sold to USA – Noted Germany November 2022*	
ZF210	Shorts Tucano T1 [210]	RAF, stored Linton-on-Ouse, N. Yorks (for disposal)	
ZF211	Shorts Tucano T1 [211]	*Unknown (ex AM&SU, Shawbury, Shropshire)*	
ZF239	Shorts Tucano T1 [239]	*Sold to USA – Noted Germany November 2022*	
ZF240	Shorts Tucano T1 [240]	RAF, stored Linton-on-Ouse, N. Yorks (for disposal)	
ZF243	Shorts Tucano T1 [243]	RAF, stored Linton-on-Ouse, N. Yorks (for disposal)	
ZF244	Shorts Tucano T1 [244]	RAF, stored Linton-on-Ouse, N. Yorks (for disposal)	
ZF263	Shorts Tucano T1 [263]	RAF AM&SU, stored Shawbury, Shropshire	
ZF264	Shorts Tucano T1 [264]	RAF, stored Linton-on-Ouse, N. Yorks (for disposal)	
ZF268	Shorts Tucano T1 [268]	RAF AM&SU, stored Shawbury, Shropshire	
ZF269	Shorts Tucano T1 [269]	RAF, stored Linton-on-Ouse, N. Yorks (for disposal)	
ZF286	Shorts Tucano T1 [286]	RAF AM&SU, stored Shawbury, Shropshire	
ZF287	Shorts Tucano T1 [287]	RAF, stored Linton-on-Ouse, N. Yorks (for disposal)	
ZF288	Shorts Tucano T1 [288]	RAF AM&SU, stored Shawbury, Shropshire	
ZF289	Shorts Tucano T1 [289]	*RAF, scrapped Linton-on-Ouse, N. Yorks, 2019*	
ZF290	Shorts Tucano T1 [290] $	RAF, stored Linton-on-Ouse, N. Yorks (for disposal)	
ZF291	Shorts Tucano T1 [291]	RAF, stored Linton-on-Ouse, N. Yorks (for disposal)	
ZF292	Shorts Tucano T1 [292]	*Sold to USA – Noted Germany November 2022*	
ZF293	Shorts Tucano T1 [293] $	RAF, stored Linton-on-Ouse, N. Yorks (for disposal)	
ZF294	Shorts Tucano T1 [294]	*Sold to USA – Noted Germany November 2022*	
ZF295	Shorts Tucano T1 [295] $	Bombardier, Belfast, NI	
ZF315	Shorts Tucano T1 [315]	RAF AM&SU, stored Shawbury, Shropshire	
ZF317	Shorts Tucano T1 [317]	*Sold to USA – Noted Germany November 2022*	
ZF318	Shorts Tucano T1 [318] $	RAF AM&SU, stored Shawbury, Shropshire	
ZF319	Shorts Tucano T1 [319]	*Sold to USA – Noted Germany November 2022*	
ZF338	Shorts Tucano T1 [338]	RAF, stored Linton-on-Ouse, N. Yorks (for disposal)	
ZF341	Shorts Tucano T1 [341]	*Sold to USA – Noted Germany November 2022*	
ZF342	Shorts Tucano T1 [342]	RAF, stored Linton-on-Ouse, N. Yorks (for disposal)	
ZF343	Shorts Tucano T1 [343]	RAF, stored Linton-on-Ouse, N. Yorks (for disposal)	
ZF347	Shorts Tucano T1 [347]	RAF, stored Linton-on-Ouse, N. Yorks (for disposal)	
ZF348	Shorts Tucano T1 [348]	RAF, stored Linton-on-Ouse, N. Yorks (for disposal)	
ZF350	Shorts Tucano T1 [350]	RAF AM&SU, stored Shawbury, Shropshire	
ZF355	WS Lynx HAS3S(ICE) (XZ238) [633]	Privately owned, White Waltham, Berks	
ZF372	Shorts Tucano T1 [372]	RAF AM&SU, stored Shawbury, Shropshire	
ZF374	Shorts Tucano T1 [374]	RAF, stored Linton-on-Ouse, N. Yorks (for disposal)	
ZF376	Shorts Tucano T1 [376]	RAF AM&SU, stored Shawbury, Shropshire	
ZF377	Shorts Tucano T1 [377]	RAF, stored Linton-on-Ouse, N. Yorks (for disposal)	
ZF378	Shorts Tucano T1 [RN-S] $	RAF, stored Linton-on-Ouse, N. Yorks (for disposal)	
ZF379	Shorts Tucano T1 [379]	RAF, stored Linton-on-Ouse, N. Yorks (for disposal)	
ZF380	Shorts Tucano T1 [380]	*Unknown (ex AM&SU, Shawbury, Shropshire)*	
ZF405	Shorts Tucano T1 [405]	RAF AM&SU, stored Shawbury, Shropshire	
ZF406	Shorts Tucano T1 [406]	RAF, stored Linton-on-Ouse, N. Yorks (for disposal)	
ZF407	Shorts Tucano T1 [407]	RAF, stored Linton-on-Ouse, N. Yorks (for disposal)	
ZF408	Shorts Tucano T1 [408]	RAF AM&SU, stored Shawbury, Shropshire	
ZF412	Shorts Tucano T1 [412]	*Unknown (ex Bentwaters, Suffolk)*	
ZF414	Shorts Tucano T1 [414]	RAF AM&SU, stored Shawbury, Shropshire	
ZF416	Shorts Tucano T1 [416]	RAF AM&SU, stored Shawbury, Shropshire	
ZF417	Shorts Tucano T1 [417]	RAF, stored Linton-on-Ouse, N. Yorks (for disposal)	
ZF418	Shorts Tucano T1 [418]	RAF AM&SU, stored Shawbury, Shropshire	
ZF446	Shorts Tucano T1 [446]	RAF AM&SU, stored Shawbury, Shropshire	
ZF448	Shorts Tucano T1 [448] $	RAF, stored Linton-on-Ouse, N. Yorks (for disposal)	
ZF449	Shorts Tucano T1 [449]	RAF AM&SU, stored Shawbury, Shropshire	
ZF485	Shorts Tucano T1 (G-BULU) [485]	RAF, stored Linton-on-Ouse, N. Yorks (for disposal)	
ZF486	Shorts Tucano T1 [486]	RAF AM&SU, stored Shawbury, Shropshire	

Notes	Serial	Type (code/other identity)	Owner/operator, location or fate
	ZF487	Shorts Tucano T1 [487]	RAF AM&SU, stored Shawbury, Shropshire
	ZF488	Shorts Tucano T1 [488]	RAF AM&SU, stored Shawbury, Shropshire
	ZF489	Shorts Tucano T1 [489]	RAF, stored Linton-on-Ouse, N. Yorks (for disposal)
	ZF490	Shorts Tucano T1 [490]	RAF AM&SU, stored Shawbury, Shropshire
	ZF491	Shorts Tucano T1 [491]	*Sold to USA – Noted Germany November 2022*
	ZF492	Shorts Tucano T1 [492]	RAF AM&SU, stored Shawbury, Shropshire
	ZF512	Shorts Tucano T1 [512]	RAF, stored Linton-on-Ouse, N. Yorks (for disposal)
	ZF513	Shorts Tucano T1 [513]	RAF AM&SU, stored Shawbury, Shropshire
	ZF515	Shorts Tucano T1 [515]	RAF, stored Linton-on-Ouse, N. Yorks (for disposal)
	ZF534	BAe EAP	RAF Museum, Cosford, Shropshire
	ZF537	WS Lynx AH9A	*Unknown location*
	ZF538	WS Lynx AH9A	*Unknown location*
	ZF539	WS Lynx AH9A	Privately owned, Kessingland, Suffolk
	ZF557	WS Lynx HMA8SRU [426/PD]	Privately owned, Woodmancote, W. Sussex
	ZF558	WS Lynx HMA8SRU [336/WK]	Privately owned, Woodmancote, W. Sussex
	ZF560	WS Lynx HMA8SRU [456]	Privately owned, Woodmancote, W. Sussex
	ZF562	WS Lynx HMA8SRU [353/MB]	Privately owned, Woodmancote, W. Sussex
	ZF563	WS Lynx HMA8SRU [312/VL]	Privately owned, Woodmancote, W. Sussex
	ZF581	BAC Lightning F53 (53-675/206)	Bentwaters Cold War Museum, Suffolk
	ZF582	BAC Lightning F53 (53-676/210/207) <ff>	Bournemouth Aviation Museum, Dorset
	ZF583	BAC Lightning F53 (53-681/306/210)	Solway Aviation Society, Carlisle, Cumbria
	ZF584	BAC Lightning F53 (53-682/307/211)	Dumfries & Galloway Avn Mus, Dumfries, Scotland
	ZF587	BAC Lightning F53 (53-691/215) <ff>	Lashenden Air Warfare Museum, Headcorn, Kent
	ZF587	BAC Lightning F53 (53-691/215) <rf>	Privately owned, Stowmarket, Suffolk
	ZF588	BAC Lightning F53 (53-693/216) [L]	East Midlands Airport Aeropark, Leics
	ZF589	BAC Lightning F53 (53-700/218) <ff>	Privately owned,
	ZF590	BAC Lightning F53 (53-679/206/1302/220) <ff>	*Current status unknown (ex-Bruntingthorpe)*
	ZF595	BAC Lightning T55 (55-714/212/1317/231) <ff>	Privately owned, North Weald, Essex
	ZF595	BAC Lightning T55 (55-714/212/1317/231) <rf>	Privately owned, Binbrook, Lincs
	ZF596	BAC Lightning T55 (55-715/305/205/220/233) <ff>	Lakes Lightnings, Spark Bridge, Cumbria
	ZF622	Piper PA-31 Navajo Chieftain 350 (N3548Y)	MOD JARTS, Boscombe Down, Wilts
	ZF641	EHI-101 [PP1]	SFDO, RNAS Culdrose, Cornwall
	ZF649	EHI-101 Merlin (A2714) [PP5]	DSAE RNAESS, *HMS Sultan*, Gosport, Hants
	ZG347	Northrop Chukar D2	Davidstow Airfield & Cornwall At War Museum, Davidstow Moor, Cornwall
	ZG477	BAe Harrier GR9 $	RAF Museum, Hendon, Gtr London
	ZG478	BAe Harrier GR9 (fuselage)	Privately owned, Sproughton, Suffolk
	ZG509	BAe Harrier GR7 [80]	Privately owned, Petersfield, Hants
	ZG631	Northrop Chukar D2	Farnborough Air Sciences Trust, Farnborough, Hants
	ZG751	Panavia Tornado F3 (fuselage)	MOD JARTS, Boscombe Down, Wilts
	ZG752	Panavia Tornado GR4 $	RAF Honington, Suffolk, GI use
	ZG771	Panavia Tornado GR4 $	Ulster Aviation Society, Long Kesh, NI
	ZG773	Panavia Tornado GR4	Fire Service College, Moreton-in-Marsh, Glos
	ZG816	WS61 Sea King HAS6 [014/L]	*Believed scrapped, HMS Sultan*, Gosport, Hants
	ZG817	WS61 Sea King HAS6 [702/PW]	DSAE RNAESS, *HMS Sultan*, Gosport, Hants
	ZG818	WS61 Sea King HAS6 [707/PW]	*Believed scrapped, HMS Sultan*, Gosport, Hants
	ZG819	WS61 Sea King HAS6 [265/N]	DSAE RNAESS, *HMS Sultan*, Gosport, Hants
	ZG822	WS61 Sea King HC4 [WS]	South Wales Aviation Museum, St Athan, Wales
	ZG875	WS61 Sea King HAS6 [013] <ff>	Privately owned, Market Drayton, Shropshire
	ZG884	WS Lynx AH9A	Privately owned, Bentwaters, Suffolk
	ZG885	WS Lynx AH9A	Privately owned, Sproughton, Suffolk
	ZG886	WS Lynx AH9A	Privately owned, Bentwaters, Suffolk
	ZG887	WS Lynx AH9A	Privately owned, Sproughton, Suffolk
	ZG888	WS Lynx AH9A	Privately owned, Sproughton, Suffolk
	ZG889	WS Lynx AH9A	Privately owned, White Waltham, Berks
	ZG914	WS Lynx AH9A	Privately owned, Wainfleet, Lincs
	ZG915	WS Lynx AH9A	RN, Predannack Fire School, Cornwall
	ZG916	WS Lynx AH9A	Privately owned, Sproughton, Suffolk
	ZG917	WS Lynx AH9A $	AAC Middle Wallop, Hants, on display
	ZG918	WS Lynx AH9A	AAC Middle Wallop, Hants, G.I.
	ZG919	WS Lynx AH9A	RN, Predannack Fire School, Cornwall

Serial	Type (code/other identity)	Owner/operator, location or fate	Notes
ZG920	WS Lynx AH9A	AAC, DSTL Porton Down, Wilts, G.I.	
ZG921	WS Lynx AH9A	National Army Museum, Chelsea, London	
ZG923	WS Lynx AH9A	Army Bury St Edmunds, Suffolk, GI use	
ZG969	Pilatus PC-9 (HB-HQE)	BAE Systems, Warton, Lancs, GI use	
ZG993	PBN 2T Islander AL1 (G-BOMD)	Army Flying Museum, Middle Wallop, Hants	
ZG995	PBN 2T Defender R2 (G-SURV) [5]	Britten-Norman, stored Solent Airport, Hants	
ZG996	PBN 2T Defender R2 (G-BWPR) [6]	Britten-Norman, stored Solent Airport, Hants	
ZG997	PBN 2T Defender R2 (G-BWPV) [7]	Britten-Norman, stored Solent Airport, Hants	
ZG998	PBN 2T Defender R2 (G-BWPX) [8]	Britten-Norman, stored Solent Airport, Hants	
ZH001	PBN 2T Defender R2 (G-CEIO) [1]	Britten-Norman, stored Solent Airport, Hants	
ZH002	PBN 2T Defender R2 (G-CEIP) [2]	Britten-Norman, stored Solent Airport, Hants	
ZH003	PBN 2T Defender R2 (G-CEIR) [3]	Britten-Norman, stored Solent Airport, Hants	
ZH004	PBN 2T Defender T3 (G-BWPO) [4]	Britten-Norman, stored Solent Airport, Hants	
ZH005	PBN 2T Defender R2 (G-CGVB) [05]	Britten-Norman, stored Solent Airport, Hants	
ZH101	Boeing E-3D Sentry AEW1 [01]	RAF, stored Waddington, Lincs (for Chile)	
ZH102	Boeing E-3D Sentry AEW1 [02]	RAF, stored Waddington, Lincs (for Chile)	
ZH103	Boeing E-3D Sentry AEW1 [03]	*Sold to FACh, July 2022*	
ZH105	Boeing E-3D Sentry AEW1 [05]	RAF, stored Waddington, Lincs	
ZH106	Boeing E-3D Sentry AEW1 [06]	*Sold to FACh, July 2022*	
ZH107	Boeing E-3D Sentry AEW1 [07] $	RAF, stored Waddington, Lincs	
ZH139	BAe Harrier GR7 <R> (BAPC.191/ZD472)	*Currently not known*	
ZH185	Grob G109B Vigilant T1 [TX]	RAF/Serco, stored Syerston, Notts	
ZH200	BAe Hawk 200	Loughborough University, Leics, G.I.	
ZH257	B-V CH-47C Chinook (9217M) (fuselage)	RAF Odiham, Hants, BDRT	
ZH552	Panavia Tornado F3	RAF Leeming, N. Yorks, at main gate	
ZH553	Panavia Tornado F3 [RT]	MOD, Cornwall Aviation Heritage Centre, Newquay, Cornwall	
ZH580	Westland Super Lynx Mk.95A (FAP 19201)	Leonardo MW, Yeovil, Somerset (upgrade)	
ZH581	Westland Super Lynx Mk.95A (FAP 19202)	Leonardo MW, Yeovil, Somerset (upgrade)	
ZH582	Westland Super Lynx Mk.95A (FAP 19203)	Leonardo MW, Yeovil, Somerset (upgrade)	
ZH584	Westland Super Lynx Mk.95A (FAP 19205)	Leonardo MW, Yeovil, Somerset (upgrade)	
ZH588	Eurofighter Typhoon (DA2)	RAF Museum, Hendon, Gtr London	
ZH590	Eurofighter Typhoon (DA4)	IWM Duxford, Cambs	
ZH655	BAe Harrier T10 <ff>	Privately owned, Worksop, Notts	
ZH658	BAe Harrier T10 (fuselage)	Privately owned, Sproughton, Suffolk	
ZH763	BAC 1-11/539GL (G-BGKE)	Cornwall Aviation Heritage Centre, Newquay, Cornwall	
ZH775	B-V Chinook HC6A (N7424J)	RAF CMF, Odiham, Hants	
ZH776	B-V Chinook HC6A (N7424L)	RAF CMF, Odiham, Hants	
ZH777	B-V Chinook HC6A (N7424M)	RAF No 27 Sqn, Odiham, Hants	
ZH796	BAe Sea Harrier FA2 [001/L]	DSAE No 1 SoTT, stored Cosford, Shropshire	
ZH797	BAe Sea Harrier FA2 [97/DD]	SFDO, RNAS Culdrose, Cornwall	
ZH798	BAe Sea Harrier FA2 [002/L]	Privately owned, Church Fenton, N. Yorks	
ZH800	BAe Sea Harrier FA2 (ZH801) [123]	RNAS Yeovilton, Somerset, stored	
ZH801	BAe Sea Harrier FA2 (ZH800) [001]	RNAS Yeovilton, Somerset, stored	
ZH802	BAe Sea Harrier FA2 [02/DD]	SFDO, RNAS Culdrose, Cornwall	
ZH803	BAe Sea Harrier FA2 (G-RNFA) [03/DD]	Privately owned, St Athan, Wales	
ZH804	BAe Sea Harrier FA2 [003/L]	Privately owned, Thorpe Wood, N. Yorks	
ZH806	BAe Sea Harrier FA2 [007]	Privately owned, Bentwaters, Suffolk	
ZH807	BAe Sea Harrier FA2 <ff>	Privately owned, Thorpe Wood, N. Yorks	
ZH811	BAe Sea Harrier FA2 [002/L]	Privately owned, Chippenham Lodge, Suffolk	
ZH812	BAe Sea Harrier FA2 [005/L]	Privately owned, Bentwaters, Suffolk	
ZH813	BAe Sea Harrier FA2 [13/DD]	SFDO, RNAS Culdrose, Cornwall	
ZH814	Bell 212HP AH1 (G-BGMH)	*Sold as G-BGMH, 2022*	
ZH815	Bell 212HP AH1 (G-BGCZ)	*Sold to Canada, November 2022*	
ZH816	Bell 212HP AH1 (G-BGMG)	*Sold to Canada, November 2022*	
ZH821	EHI-101 Merlin HM1	Morayvia, Kinloss, Scotland	
ZH822	EHI-101 Merlin HM1	MOD/Leonardo MW, stored Yeovil, Somerset	
ZH824	EHI-101 Merlin HM2 [83]	RN No 820 NAS, Culdrose, Cornwall	
ZH825	EHI-101 Merlin HM1 [583]	MOD/Leonardo MW, stored Yeovil, Somerset	
ZH826	EHI-101 Merlin HM2 [CU]	RN No 814 NAS, Culdrose, Cornwall	
ZH827	EHI-101 Merlin HM2	RN No 820 NAS, Culdrose, Cornwall	

Notes	Serial	Type (code/other identity)	Owner/operator, location or fate
	ZH828	EHI-101 Merlin HM2	RN No 820 NAS, Culdrose, Cornwall
	ZH829	EHI-101 Merlin HM2 (Crowsnest)	MOD/Leonardo MW, Yeovil, Somerset
	ZH830	EHI-101 Merlin HM1 [88]	DSAE, stored HMS Sultan, Gosport, Hants
	ZH831	EHI-101 Merlin HM2 (Crowsnest)	MOD/Leonardo MW, Yeovil, Somerset
	ZH832	EHI-101 Merlin HM2	RN MDMF, Culdrose, Cornwall
	ZH833	EHI-101 Merlin HM2 (Crowsnest) [82]	MOD/QinetiQ, Boscombe Down, Wilts
	ZH834	EHI-101 Merlin HM2	RN MDMF, Culdrose, Cornwall
	ZH835	EHI-101 Merlin HM2 (Crowsnest)	RN No 820 NAS, Culdrose, Cornwall
	ZH836	EHI-101 Merlin HM2 [80]	RN No 824 NAS, Culdrose, Cornwall
	ZH837	EHI-101 Merlin HM2 [84]	RN No 824 NAS, Culdrose, Cornwall
	ZH838	EHI-101 Merlin HM1 [70]	DSAE, stored HMS Sultan, Gosport, Hants
	ZH839	EHI-101 Merlin HM2	RN No 814 NAS, Culdrose, Cornwall
	ZH840	EHI-101 Merlin HM2 [88]	RN MDMF, Culdrose, Cornwall
	ZH841	EHI-101 Merlin HM2	RN MDMF, Culdrose, Cornwall
	ZH842	EHI-101 Merlin HM2	RN MDMF, Culdrose, Cornwall
	ZH843	EHI-101 Merlin HM2 (Crowsnest)	RN No 820 NAS, Culdrose, Cornwall
	ZH845	EHI-101 Merlin HM2	RN No 820 NAS, Culdrose, Cornwal
	ZH846	EHI-101 Merlin HM2 (Crowsnest)	RN No 820 NAS, Culdrose, Cornwall
	ZH847	EHI-101 Merlin HM2	RN No 814 NAS, Culdrose, Cornwall
	ZH848	EHI-101 Merlin HM1	DSAE, stored HMS Sultan, Gosport, Hants
	ZH849	EHI-101 Merlin HM1 [67]	DSAE, stored HMS Sultan, Gosport, Hants
	ZH850	EHI-101 Merlin HM2	RN MDMF, Culdrose, Cornwall
	ZH851	EHI-101 Merlin HM2	RN No 824 NAS, Culdrose, Cornwall
	ZH852	EHI-101 Merlin HM1(mod)	DSAE, stored HMS Sultan, Gosport, Hants
	ZH853	EHI-101 Merlin HM2	RN MDMF, Culdrose, Cornwall, Cornwall
	ZH854	EHI-101 Merlin HM2	RN No 820 NAS, Culdrose, Cornwall
	ZH855	EHI-101 Merlin HM1 [68]	DSAE, stored HMS Sultan, Gosport, Hants
	ZH856	EHI-101 Merlin HM2 (Crowsnest)	RN No 820 NAS, Culdrose, Cornwall
	ZH857	EHI-101 Merlin HM2	RN MDMF, Culdrose, Cornwall, Cornwall
	ZH858	EHI-101 Merlin HM1 [17]	DSAE RNAESS, HMS Sultan, Gosport, Hants
	ZH860	EHI-101 Merlin HM2	RN No 814 NAS, Culdrose, Cornwall
	ZH861	EHI-101 Merlin HM2 (Crowsnest)	RN No 824 NAS, Culdrose, Cornwall
	ZH862	EHI-101 Merlin HM2	RN MDMF, Culdrose, Cornwall, Cornwall
	ZH863	EHI-101 Merlin HM1 [80]	DSAE, stored HMS Sultan, Gosport, Hants
	ZH864	EHI-101 Merlin HM2 (Crowsnest)	RN No 820 NAS, Culdrose, Cornwall
	ZH865	Lockheed C-130J-30 Hercules C4 (N130JA) [865]	RAF No 24 Sqn/No 47 Sqn, Brize Norton, Oxon
	ZH866	Lockheed C-130J-30 Hercules C4 (N130JE) [866]	RAF No 24 Sqn/No 47 Sqn, Brize Norton, Oxon
	ZH867	Lockheed C-130J-30 Hercules C4 (N130JJ) [867]	RAF No 24 Sqn/No 47 Sqn, Brize Norton, Oxon
	ZH868	Lockheed C-130J-30 Hercules C4 (N130JN) [868]	RAF No 24 Sqn/No 47 Sqn, Brize Norton, Oxon
	ZH869	Lockheed C-130J-30 Hercules C4 (N130JV) [869]	RAF No 24 Sqn/No 47 Sqn, Brize Norton, Oxon
	ZH870	Lockheed C-130J-30 Hercules C4 (N78235) [870]	RAF No 24 Sqn/No 47 Sqn, Brize Norton, Oxon
	ZH871	Lockheed C-130J-30 Hercules C4 (N73238) [871]	RAF No 24 Sqn/No 47 Sqn, Brize Norton, Oxon
	ZH872	Lockheed C-130J-30 Hercules C4 (N4249Y) [872]	MOD/MADG, Cambridge, Cambs
	ZH874	Lockheed C-130J-30 Hercules C4 (N41030) [874]	MOD/MADG, Cambridge, Cambs
	ZH875	Lockheed C-130J-30 Hercules C4 (N4099R) [875]	MOD/MADG, stored Cambridge, Cambs
	ZH877	Lockheed C-130J-30 Hercules C4 (N4081M) [877]	MOD/MADG, stored Cambridge, Cambs
	ZH878	Lockheed C-130J-30 Hercules C4 (N73232) [878]	MOD/MADG, stored Cambridge, Cambs
	ZH879	Lockheed C-130J-30 Hercules C4 (N4080M) [879]	RAF No 24 Sqn/No 47 Sqn, Brize Norton, Oxon
	ZH883	Lockheed C-130J Hercules C5 (N4242N) [883] $	MADG, Cambridge, for Bangladesh AF as 99-5481
	ZH888	Lockheed C-130J Hercules C5 (N4187) [888]	MOD/MADG, Cambridge, Cambs
	ZH889	Lockheed C-130J Hercules C5 (N4099R) [889]	MOD/MADG, Cambridge, Cambs
	ZH891	B-V Chinook HC6A (N20075)	RAF, Odiham, Hants (withdrawn from use)
	ZH892	B-V Chinook HC6A (N2019V)	RAF No 18 Sqn, Odiham, Hants (Op Peleda, Estonia)
	ZH893	B-V Chinook HC6A (N2025L)	RAF No 28 Sqn, Benson, Oxon
	ZH894	B-V Chinook HC6A (N2026E)	RAF No 18 Sqn, Odiham, Hants
	ZH895	B-V Chinook HC6A (N2034K)	RAF, Odiham, Hants (withdrawn from use)
	ZH896	B-V Chinook HC6A (N2038G)	RAF No 18 Sqn, Odiham, Hants
	ZH897	B-V Chinook HC5 (N2045G)	RAF No 27 Sqn, Odiham, Hants
	ZH898	B-V Chinook HC5 (N2057Q)	MoD/Boeing, Middle Wallop, Hants
	ZH899	B-V Chinook HC5 (N2057R)	RAF No 27 Sqn, Odiham, Hants
	ZH900	B-V Chinook HC5 (N2060H)	RAF No 18 Sqn, Odiham, Hants
	ZH901	B-V Chinook HC5 (N2060M)	RAF No 18 Sqn, Odiham, Hants (Op Peleda, Estonia)

Serial	Type (code/other identity)	Owner/operator, location or fate	Notes
ZH902	B-V Chinook HC5 (N2064W)	RAF No 18 Sqn, Odiham, Hants (Op Peleda, Estonia)	
ZH903	B-V Chinook HC5 (N20671)	RAF CMF, Odiham, Hants	
ZH904	B-V Chinook HC5 (N2083K)	MOD/StandardAero, Fleetlands, Hants	
ZH961	Westland Super Lynx Mk21A (Brazilian Navy N-4010)	Leonardo MW, Yeovil, Somerset (upgrade)	
ZJ100	BAe Hawk 102D	BAE Systems, Brough, E. Yorks, G.I.	
ZJ117	EHI-101 Merlin HC3 [A]	DSAE RNAESS, *HMS Sultan*, Gosport, Hants	
ZJ118	EHI-101 Merlin HC4 [B]	RN No 845 NAS, Yeovilton, Somerset	
ZJ119	EHI-101 Merlin HC4 [C]	RN No 846 NAS, Yeovilton, Somerset	
ZJ120	EHI-101 Merlin HC4 [D]	RN No 845 NAS, Yeovilton, Somerset	
ZJ121	EHI-101 Merlin HC4 [E]	RN No 845 NAS, Yeovilton, Somerset	
ZJ122	EHI-101 Merlin HC4 [F]	RN No 845 NAS, Yeovilton, Somerset	
ZJ123	EHI-101 Merlin HC4 [G]	RN No 845 NAS, Yeovilton, Somerset	
ZJ124	EHI-101 Merlin HC4 [H]	RN No 845 NAS, Yeovilton, Somerset	
ZJ125	EHI-101 Merlin HC4 [J]	RN No 845 NAS, Yeovilton, Somerset	
ZJ126	EHI-101 Merlin HC4 [K]	RN No 846 NAS, Yeovilton, Somerset	
ZJ127	EHI-101 Merlin HC4 [L]	RN No 845 NAS, Yeovilton, Somerset	
ZJ128	EHI-101 Merlin HC4 [M]	RN No 845 NAS, Yeovilton, Somerset	
ZJ129	EHI-101 Merlin HC4 [N]	RN No 845 NAS, Yeovilton, Somerset	
ZJ130	EHI-101 Merlin HC4 [O]	MOD/Leonardo MW, Yeovil, Somerset (depth maint.)	
ZJ131	EHI-101 Merlin HC4 [P]	RN No 845 NAS, Yeovilton, Somerset	
ZJ132	EHI-101 Merlin HC4 [Q]	MOD/Leonardo MW, Yeovil, Somerset (depth maint.)	
ZJ133	EHI-101 Merlin HC3 [R]	RAF Brize Norton, Oxon, GI use	
ZJ134	EHI-101 Merlin HC4 [S]	RN No 846 NAS, Yeovilton, Somerset	
ZJ135	EHI-101 Merlin HC4 [T]	RN No 846 NAS, Yeovilton, Somerset	
ZJ136	EHI-101 Merlin HC4 [U]	RN No 845 NAS, Yeovilton, Somerset	
ZJ137	EHI-101 Merlin HC4 [W]	RN No 846 NAS, Yeovilton, Somerset	
ZJ138	EHI-101 Merlin HC3 <ff>	Privately owned, Spey Bay, Moray, Scotland	
ZJ164	AS365N-2 Dauphin 2 (G-BTLC)	RN/Bond Helicopters, Newquay, Cornwall	
ZJ165	AS365N-2 Dauphin 2 (G-NTOO)	RN/Bond Helicopters, Newquay, Cornwall	
ZJ171	WAH-64 Apache AH1 (N3266T)	AAC, stored Wattisham, Suffolk	
ZJ177	WAH-64 Apache AH1	RN No 1710 NAS, Portsmouth, Hants	
ZJ182	WAH-64 Apache AH1	*To Huntsville, USA for CSP, July 2022*	
ZJ188	WAH-64 Apache AH1	*To Huntsville, USA for CSP, July 2022*	
ZJ189	WAH-64 Apache AH1	AAC No 656 Sqn/No 4 Regt, Wattisham, Suffolk	
ZJ191	WAH-64 Apache AH1	AAC No 656 Sqn/No 4 Regt, Wattisham, Suffolk	
ZJ192	WAH-64 Apache AH1	AAC No 656 Sqn/No 4 Regt, Wattisham, Suffolk	
ZJ197	WAH-64 Apache AH1	AAC No 664 Sqn/No 4 Regt, Wattisham, Suffolk	
ZJ199	WAH-64 Apache AH1	*To Huntsville, USA for CSP, July 2022*	
ZJ208	WAH-64 Apache AH1	AAC No 656 Sqn/No 4 Regt, Wattisham, Suffolk	
ZJ209	WAH-64 Apache AH1	*To Huntsville, USA for CSP, July 2022*	
ZJ210	WAH-64 Apache AH1	AAC No 664 Sqn/No 4 Regt, Wattisham, Suffolk	
ZJ211	WAH-64 Apache AH1	AAC No 656 Sqn/No 4 Regt, Wattisham, Suffolk	
ZJ213	WAH-64 Apache AH1	AAC No 656 Sqn/No 4 Regt, Wattisham, Suffolk	
ZJ215	WAH-64 Apache AH1	AAC No 664 Sqn/No 4 Regt, Wattisham, Suffolk	
ZJ220	WAH-64 Apache AH1	AAC No 664 Sqn/No 4 Regt, Wattisham, Suffolk	
ZJ221	WAH-64 Apache AH1	AAC No 656 Sqn/No 4 Regt, Wattisham, Suffolk	
ZJ223	WAH-64 Apache AH1	AAC No 656 Sqn/No 4 Regt, Wattisham, Suffolk	
ZJ224	WAH-64 Apache AH1	AAC No 656 Sqn/No 4 Regt, Wattisham, Suffolk	
ZJ226	WAH-64 Apache AH1	AAC No 664 Sqn/No 4 Regt, Wattisham, Suffolk	
ZJ369	GEC Phoenix RPAS	Defence Academy of the UK, Shrivenham, Oxon	
ZJ385	GEC Phoenix RPAS	Muckleburgh Collection, Weybourne, Norfolk	
ZJ449	GEC Phoenix RPAS	REME Museum, Lyneham, Wilts	
ZJ452	GEC Phoenix RPAS	Science Museum, stored Wroughton, Wilts	
ZJ469	GEC Phoenix RPAS	Army, Larkhill, Wilts, on display	
ZJ477	GEC Phoenix RPAS	Boscombe Down Aviation Collection, Old Sarum, Wilts	
ZJ481	Northrop MQM-74C Chukar D2	RNAS Culdrose, Cornwall, preserved	
ZJ493	GAF Jindivik 104AL (A92-814)	RAF Museum Reserve Collection, Stafford, Staffs	
ZJ496	GAF Jindivik 104AL (A92-901)	Farnborough Air Sciences Trust, Farnborough, Hants	
ZJ515	BAE Systems Nimrod MRA4 (XV258) <ff>	Cranfield University, Beds, instructional use	
ZJ620	AgustaWestland Merlin Simulator	RN No 824 NAS, Culdrose, Cornwall	

Notes	Serial	Type (code/other identity)	Owner/operator, location or fate
	ZJ621	AgustaWestland Merlin Simulator	RN No 824 NAS, Culdrose, Cornwall
	ZJ622	AgustaWestland Merlin Simulator	RN No 824 NAS, Culdrose, Cornwall
	ZJ623	AgustaWestland Merlin Simulator	RN No 824 NAS, Culdrose, Cornwall
	ZJ624	AgustaWestland Merlin Simulator	RN No 824 NAS, Culdrose, Cornwall
	ZJ625	AgustaWestland Merlin Simulator	RN No 824 NAS, Culdrose, Cornwall
	ZJ626	AgustaWestland Merlin Simulator	RN No 824 NAS, Culdrose, Cornwall
	ZJ690	Bombardier Sentinel R1 (C-GJRG)	RAF, stored Waddington as N690BD (for US Army)
	ZJ691	Bombardier Sentinel R1 (C-FZVM)	*To USA, 2022 as N691BD (for US Army)*
	ZJ692	Bombardier Sentinel R1 (C-FZWW)	RAF, stored Waddington as N692BD (for US Army)
	ZJ693	Bombardier Sentinel R1 (C-FZXC)	*To USA, 2022 as N693BD (for US Army)*
	ZJ694	Bombardier Sentinel R1 (C-FZYL)	*To USA, 2022 as N694BD (for US Army)*
	ZJ699	Eurofighter Typhoon (PT001)	MOD/BAE Systems, Warton, Lancs
	ZJ700	Eurofighter Typhoon (PS002)	MOD/BAE Systems, Warton, Lancs
	ZJ703	Bell 412EP Griffin HAR2 (G-CBST) [Spades,3]	RAF No 84 Sqn, Akrotiri, Cyprus
	ZJ704	Bell 412EP Griffin HAR2 (G-CBWT) [Clubs,4]	RAF No 84 Sqn, Akrotiri, Cyprus
	ZJ705	Bell 412EP Griffin HAR2 (G-CBXL) [Hearts,5]	RAF No 84 Sqn, Akrotiri, Cyprus
	ZJ748	Meteor Mirach 100/5	Boscombe Down Aviation Collection, Old Sarum, Wilts
	ZJ765	Meteor Mirach 100/5	QinetiQ Apprentice Training School, Boscombe Down, Wilts
	ZJ780	AS365N-3 Dauphin AH1 (G-CEXT)	AAC No 658 Sqn, Credenhill, Herefordshire
	ZJ781	AS365N-3 Dauphin AH1 (G-CEXU)	AAC No 658 Sqn, Credenhill, Herefordshire
	ZJ782	AS365N-3 Dauphin AH1 (G-CEXV)	AAC No 658 Sqn, Credenhill, Herefordshire
	ZJ783	AS365N-3 Dauphin AH1 (G-CEXW)	AAC No 658 Sqn, Credenhill, Herefordshire
	ZJ785	AS365N-3 Dauphin AH1 (G-CFFW)	AAC No 658 Sqn, Credenhill, Herefordshire
	ZJ787	AS365N-3 Dauphin AH1 (G-CHNJ)	AAC No 658 Sqn, Credenhill, Herefordshire
	ZJ800	Eurofighter Typhoon T3 [BC]	BAE Systems Aircraft Maintenance Academy, Humberside, Lincs
	ZJ801	Eurofighter Typhoon T3 [BJ]	BAE Systems, Warton, Lancs (stress testing)
	ZJ807	Eurofighter Typhoon T3 (fuselage)	MOD JARTS, Boscombe Down, Wilts
	ZJ810	Eurofighter Typhoon T3 (fuselage)	RAF No 71(IR) Sqn, Wittering, Cambs, GI use
	ZJ910	Eurofighter Typhoon FGR4 [DO]	RAF AM&SU, stored Shawbury, Shropshire
	ZJ911	Eurofighter Typhoon FGR4 [QO-Z]	RAF AM&SU, stored Shawbury, Shropshire
	ZJ912	Eurofighter Typhoon FGR4 [912]	RAF AM&SU, stored Shawbury, Shropshire
	ZJ913	Eurofighter Typhoon FGR4 [913]	RAF No 29 Sqn, Coningsby, Lincs
	ZJ914	Eurofighter Typhoon FGR4 $	RAF No 29 Sqn, Coningsby, Lincs
	ZJ915	Eurofighter Typhoon FGR4 [F]	RAF No 1435 Flt, Mount Pleasant, FI
	ZJ916	Eurofighter Typhoon FGR4 [916]	RAF No 29 Sqn, Coningsby, Lincs
	ZJ917	Eurofighter Typhoon FGR4 [917,WS-R]	RAF No 29 Sqn, Coningsby, Lincs
	ZJ918	Eurofighter Typhoon FGR4	RAF AM&SU, stored Shawbury, Shropshire
	ZJ919	Eurofighter Typhoon FGR4 [919,WS-L]	RAF No 9 Sqn, Lossiemouth, Moray, Scotland
	ZJ920	Eurofighter Typhoon FGR4 [920]	RAF TMF, Coningsby, Lincs
	ZJ921	Eurofighter Typhoon FGR4 [921]	RAF TEF, Lossiemouth, Moray, Scotland
	ZJ922	Eurofighter Typhoon FGR4 [QO-C]	MOD/BAE Systems, Warton, Lancs
	ZJ923	Eurofighter Typhoon FGR4 [923,WS-T]	RAF No 9 Sqn, Lossiemouth, Moray, Scotland
	ZJ924	Eurofighter Typhoon FGR4 [924,WS-J]	RAF No 9 Sqn, Lossiemouth, Moray, Scotland
	ZJ925	Eurofighter Typhoon FGR4 [DXI] $	RAF AM&SU, stored Shawbury, Shropshire
	ZJ926	Eurofighter Typhoon FGR4 [H]	RAF No 1435 Flt, Mount Pleasant, FI
	ZJ927	Eurofighter Typhoon FGR4 [927]	RAF AM&SU, stored Shawbury, Shropshire
	ZJ928	Eurofighter Typhoon FGR4 [928,WS-Y]	RAF No 9 Sqn, Lossiemouth, Moray, Scotland
	ZJ929	Eurofighter Typhoon FGR4 [929]	RAF No 11 Sqn, Coningsby, Lincs
	ZJ930	Eurofighter Typhoon FGR4 [930]	RAF AM&SU, stored Shawbury, Shropshire
	ZJ931	Eurofighter Typhoon FGR4 [931]	RAF No 2 Sqn, Lossiemouth, Moray, Scotland
	ZJ932	Eurofighter Typhoon FGR4 [DB]	RAF AM&SU, stored Shawbury, Shropshire
	ZJ933	Eurofighter Typhoon FGR4 [C]	RAF No 1435 Flt, Mount Pleasant, FI
	ZJ934	Eurofighter Typhoon FGR4 [934]	RAF AM&SU, stored Shawbury, Shropshire
	ZJ935	Eurofighter Typhoon FGR4 [935,WS-G]	RAF No 9 Sqn, Lossiemouth, Moray, Scotland
	ZJ936	Eurofighter Typhoon FGR4 [QO-C]	RAF AM&SU, stored Shawbury, Shropshire
	ZJ937	Eurofighter Typhoon FGR4 [937]	RAF No 29 Sqn, Coningsby, Lincs
	ZJ938	Eurofighter Typhoon FGR4	MOD/BAE Systems, Warton, Lancs
	ZJ939	Eurofighter Typhoon FGR4 [939,WS-U]	RAF No 9 Sqn, Lossiemouth, Moray, Scotland
	ZJ940	Eurofighter Typhoon FGR4 [DJ666]	RAF, stored Coningsby, Lincs
	ZJ941	Eurofighter Typhoon FGR4 [D]	RAF No 1435 Flt, Mount Pleasant, FI

Serial	Type (code/other identity)	Owner/operator, location or fate	Notes
ZJ942	Eurofighter Typhoon FGR4 [942]	RAF No 29 Sqn, Coningsby, Lincs	
ZJ944	Eurofighter Typhoon FGR4	RAF TMF, Coningsby, Lincs (stored, pending repair)	
ZJ945	Eurofighter Typhoon FGR4	RAF TMF, stored Coningsby, Lincs	
ZJ946	Eurofighter Typhoon FGR4 [946]	RAF No 3 Sqn, Coningsby, Lincs	
ZJ947	Eurofighter Typhoon FGR4 [947]	RAF No 2 Sqn, Lossiemouth, Moray, Scotland	
ZJ948	Eurofighter Typhoon FGR4	RAF TMF, stored Coningsby, Lincs	
ZJ949	Eurofighter Typhoon FGR4 [949]	RAF No 3 Sqn, Coningsby, Lincs	
ZJ950	Eurofighter Typhoon FGR4 [950]	RAF TMF, Coningsby, Lincs	
ZJ951	BAE Systems Advanced Hawk 120D	MOD/BAE Systems, Warton, Lancs (wfu)	
ZJ954	SA330H Puma HC2 (SAAF 144) [W]	RAF No 28 Sqn/No 33 Sqn/No 230 Sqn, Benson, Oxon	
ZJ955	SA330H Puma HC2 (SAAF 148) [X]	RAF, stored Benson, Oxon	
ZJ956	SA330H Puma HC2 (SAAF 172/F-ZWCC) [Y]	RAF No 28 Sqn/No 33 Sqn/No 230 Sqn, Benson, Oxon	
ZJ957	SA330H Puma HC2 (SAAF 169) [Z]	RAF No 28 Sqn/No 33 Sqn/No 230 Sqn, Benson, Oxon	
ZJ963	Grob G109B Vigilant T1 (D-KMSN) [SL]	RAF, stored Syerston, Notts	
ZJ969	Bell 212HP AH1 (G-BGLJ) [K]	*Sold to Canada, November 2022*	
ZJ990	EHI-101 Merlin HC4A (M-501) [AA]	RN No 846 NAS, Yeovilton, Somerset	
ZJ992	EHI-101 Merlin HC4A (M-503) [AB]	RN No 846 NAS, Yeovilton, Somerset	
ZJ994	EHI-101 Merlin HC4A (M-505) [AC]	RN No 846 NAS, Yeovilton, Somerset	
ZJ995	EHI-101 Merlin HC4A (M-506) [AD]	RN MDFM, Culdrose, Cornwall	
ZJ998	EHI-101 Merlin HC4A (M-509) [AE]	RN No 846 NAS, Yeovilton, Somerset	
ZK001	EHI-101 Merlin HC4A (M-511) [AF]	RN No 846 NAS, Yeovilton, Somerset	
ZK010	BAE Systems Hawk T2 [FN]	RAF No 4 FTS/25 Sqn, Valley, Wales	
ZK011	BAE Systems Hawk T2 [B]	RAF No 4 FTS/4 Sqn, Valley, Wales	
ZK012	BAE Systems Hawk T2 [C]	RAF No 4 FTS/4 Sqn, Valley, Wales	
ZK013	BAE Systems Hawk T2 [D]	RAF No 4 FTS/4 Sqn, Valley, Wales	
ZK014	BAE Systems Hawk T2 [E]	RAF No 4 FTS/4 Sqn, Valley, Wales	
ZK015	BAE Systems Hawk T2 [F]	RAF No 4 FTS/4 Sqn, Valley, Wales	
ZK016	BAE Systems Hawk T2 [G]	RAF No 4 FTS/4 Sqn, Valley, Wales	
ZK017	BAE Systems Hawk T2 [H]	RAF No 4 FTS/4 Sqn, Valley, Wales	
ZK018	BAE Systems Hawk T2 [I]	RAF No 4 FTS/4 Sqn, Valley, Wales	
ZK019	BAE Systems Hawk T2 [J]	RAF No 4 FTS/4 Sqn, Valley, Wales	
ZK020	BAE Systems Hawk T2 [K] $	RAF No 4 FTS/4 Sqn, Valley, Wales	
ZK021	BAE Systems Hawk T2 [L]	RAF No 4 FTS/4 Sqn, Valley, Wales	
ZK022	BAE Systems Hawk T2 [M]	RAF No 4 FTS/4 Sqn, Valley, Wales	
ZK023	BAE Systems Hawk T2 [N]	RAF No 4 FTS/4 Sqn, Valley, Wales	
ZK024	BAE Systems Hawk T2 [O]	RAF No 4 FTS/4 Sqn, Valley, Wales	
ZK025	BAE Systems Hawk T2 [FA]	RAF No 4 FTS/25 Sqn, Valley, Wales	
ZK026	BAE Systems Hawk T2 [FB]	RAF No 4 FTS/25 Sqn, Valley, Wales	
ZK027	BAE Systems Hawk T2 [FC]	RAF No 4 FTS/25 Sqn, Valley, Wales	
ZK028	BAE Systems Hawk T2 [FD]	RAF No 4 FTS/25 Sqn, Valley, Wales	
ZK029	BAE Systems Hawk T2 [FE]	RAF No 4 FTS/25 Sqn, Valley, Wales	
ZK030	BAE Systems Hawk T2 [FF]	RAF No 4 FTS/25 Sqn, Valley, Wales	
ZK031	BAE Systems Hawk T2 [FG]	RAF No 4 FTS/25 Sqn, Valley, Wales	
ZK032	BAE Systems Hawk T2 [FH]	RAF No 4 FTS/25 Sqn, Valley, Wales	
ZK033	BAE Systems Hawk T2 [FI]	RAF No 4 FTS/25 Sqn, Valley, Wales	
ZK034	BAE Systems Hawk T2 [FJ]	RAF No 4 FTS/25 Sqn, Valley, Wales	
ZK035	BAE Systems Hawk T2 [FK]	RAF No 4 FTS/25 Sqn, Valley, Wales	
ZK036	BAE Systems Hawk T2 [FL]	RAF No 4 FTS/25 Sqn, Valley, Wales	
ZK037	BAE Systems Hawk T2 [FM]	RAF No 4 FTS/25 Sqn, Valley, Wales	
ZK067	Bell 212HP AH3 (G-BFER) [B]	*Sold 2022 as G-BFER*	
ZK114	M2370 RPAS	QinetiQ	
ZK150*	Lockheed Martin Desert Hawk 3 RPAS	Army 47 Regt Royal Artillery, Thorney Island, W. Sussex	
ZK150	Lockheed Martin Desert Hawk 3 RPAS (ZK150/617)	Imperial War Museum, Lambeth, London	
ZK155*	Honeywell T-Hawk RPAS	Army 32 Regt Royal Artillery, Larkhill, Wilts	
ZK210	BAE Systems Mantis RPAS	MOD/BAE Systems, Warton, Lancs	
ZK300	Eurofighter Typhoon FGR4 [300]	RAF No 11 Sqn, Coningsby, Lincs	
ZK301	Eurofighter Typhoon FGR4 [301]	RAF TEF, Lossiemouth, Moray, Scotland	
ZK302	Eurofighter Typhoon FGR4 [302]	RAF No 9 Sqn, Lossiemouth, Moray, Scotland	
ZK303	Eurofighter Typhoon T3 [AX]	MOD/BAE Systems, Warton, Lancs	
ZK304	Eurofighter Typhoon FGR4 [304]	RAF TEF, Lossiemouth, Moray, Scotland	
ZK305	Eurofighter Typhoon FGR4 [305]	RAF No 6 Sqn, Coningsby, Lincs	

Notes	Serial	Type (code/other identity)	Owner/operator, location or fate
	ZK306	Eurofighter Typhoon FGR4 [306]	RAF No 11 Sqn, Coningsby, Lincs
	ZK307	Eurofighter Typhoon FGR4 [307]	RAF, Operation Shader, Akrotiri, Cyprus
	ZK308	Eurofighter Typhoon FGR4 [308]	RAF No 9 Sqn, Lossiemouth, Moray, Scotland
	ZK309	Eurofighter Typhoon FGR4 [309]	RAF No 29 Sqn, Coningsby, Lincs
	ZK310	Eurofighter Typhoon FGR4 [310]	RAF No 12 Sqn, Coningsby, Lincs
	ZK311	Eurofighter Typhoon FGR4 [311]	RAF No 12 Sqn, Coningsby, Lincs
	ZK312	Eurofighter Typhoon FGR4 [312]	RAF No 6 Sqn, Lossiemouth, Moray, Scotland
	ZK313	Eurofighter Typhoon FGR4 [313]	RAF No 6 Sqn, Lossiemouth, Moray, Scotland
	ZK314	Eurofighter Typhoon FGR4 [314]	RAF No 9 Sqn, Lossiemouth, Moray, Scotland
	ZK315	Eurofighter Typhoon FGR4 [315]	RAF TMF, Coningsby, Lincs
	ZK316	Eurofighter Typhoon FGR4 [316]	RAF TMF, Coningsby, Lincs
	ZK317	Eurofighter Typhoon FGR4 [317]	RAF No 2 Sqn, Lossiemouth, Moray, Scotland
	ZK318	Eurofighter Typhoon FGR4 [318]	RAF No 29 Sqn, Coningsby, Lincs
	ZK319	Eurofighter Typhoon FGR4 [319]	RAF No 3 Sqn, Coningsby, Lincs
	ZK320	Eurofighter Typhoon FGR4 [320]	RAF No 9 Sqn, Lossiemouth, Moray, Scotland
	ZK321	Eurofighter Typhoon FGR4 [321]	RAF No 29 Sqn, Coningsby, Lincs
	ZK322	Eurofighter Typhoon FGR4 [322]	RAF, Operation Shader, Akrotiri, Cyprus
	ZK323	Eurofighter Typhoon FGR4 [323]	RAF TMF, Coningsby, Lincs
	ZK324	Eurofighter Typhoon FGR4 [324]	RAF No 11 Sqn, Coningsby
	ZK325	Eurofighter Typhoon FGR4 [325]	RAF No 3 Sqn, Coningsby, Lincs
	ZK326	Eurofighter Typhoon FGR4 [FB]	RAF, stored Coningsby, Lincs
	ZK327	Eurofighter Typhoon FGR4 [327]	RAF TMF, Coningsby, Lincs
	ZK328	Eurofighter Typhoon FGR4 [328]	RAF, Operation Shader, Akrotiri, Cyprus
	ZK329	Eurofighter Typhoon FGR4 [329]	RAF No 29 Sqn, Coningsby, Lincs
	ZK330	Eurofighter Typhoon FGR4 [330]	RAF TEF, Lossiemouth, Moray, Scotland
	ZK331	Eurofighter Typhoon FGR4 [331]	RAF No 12 Sqn, Coningsby, Lincs
	ZK332	Eurofighter Typhoon FGR4 [332]	RAF No 3 Sqn, Coningsby, Lincs
	ZK333	Eurofighter Typhoon FGR4 [333]	RAF No 2 Sqn, Lossiemouth, Moray, Scotland
	ZK334	Eurofighter Typhoon FGR4 [334]	RAF TMF, Coningsby, Lincs
	ZK335	Eurofighter Typhoon FGR4 [335]	RAF AWC/FJWOEU/No 41 Sqn, Coningsby, Lincs
	ZK336	Eurofighter Typhoon FGR4 [336]	RAF No 6 Sqn, Coningsby, Lincs
	ZK337	Eurofighter Typhoon FGR4 [337]	RAF TEF, Lossiemouth, Moray, Scotland
	ZK338	Eurofighter Typhoon FGR4 [338]	RAF, Operation Shader, Akrotiri, Cyprus
	ZK339	Eurofighter Typhoon FGR4 [339]	RAF AWC/FJWOEU/No 41 Sqn, Coningsby, Lincs
	ZK340	Eurofighter Typhoon FGR4 [340]	RAF No 12 Sqn, Coningsby, Lincs
	ZK341	Eurofighter Typhoon FGR4 [341]	RAF No 12 Sqn, Coningsby, Lincs
	ZK342	Eurofighter Typhoon FGR4 [342]	RAF No 29 Sqn, Coningsby, Lincs
	ZK343	Eurofighter Typhoon FGR4 [343]	RAF, Operation Shader, Akrotiri, Cyprus
	ZK344	Eurofighter Typhoon FGR4 [344]	RAF TMF, Coningsby, Lincs
	ZK345	Eurofighter Typhoon FGR4 [345]	RAF No 2 Sqn, Lossiemouth, Moray, Scotland
	ZK346	Eurofighter Typhoon FGR4 [346]	RAF, Operation Shader, Akrotiri, Cyprus
	ZK347	Eurofighter Typhoon FGR4 [347]	RAF No 3 Sqn, Coningsby, Lincs
	ZK348	Eurofighter Typhoon FGR4 [348]	RAF TMF, Coningsby, Lincs
	ZK349	Eurofighter Typhoon FGR4 [349]	RAF, Operation Shader, Akrotiri, Cyprus
	ZK350	Eurofighter Typhoon FGR4 [350]	RAF No 3 Sqn, Coningsby, Lincs
	ZK351	Eurofighter Typhoon FGR4 [351]	RAF No 11 Sqn, Coningsby, Lincs
	ZK352	Eurofighter Typhoon FGR4 [352]	RAF No 3 Sqn, Coningsby, Lincs
	ZK353	Eurofighter Typhoon FGR4 [353]	RAF, Operation Shader, Akrotiri, Cyprus
	ZK354	Eurofighter Typhoon FGR4 [354]	RAF TMF, Coningsby, Lincs
	ZK355	Eurofighter Typhoon FGR4	MOD/BAE Systems, Warton, Lancs
	ZK356	Eurofighter Typhoon FGR4	MOD/BAE Systems, Warton, Lancs
	ZK357	Eurofighter Typhoon FGR4 [357]	RAF No 3 Sqn, Coningsby, Lincs
	ZK358	Eurofighter Typhoon FGR4 [358]	RAF No 11 Sqn, Coningsby, Lincs
	ZK359	Eurofighter Typhoon FGR4 [359]	RAF No 2 Sqn, Lossiemouth, Moray, Scotland
	ZK360	Eurofighter Typhoon FGR4 [360]	RAF No 11 Sqn, Coningsby, Lincs
	ZK361	Eurofighter Typhoon FGR4 [361]	RAF No 9 Sqn, Lossiemouth, Moray, Scotland
	ZK362	Eurofighter Typhoon FGR4 [362]	RAF No 6 Sqn, Coningsby, Lincs
	ZK363	Eurofighter Typhoon FGR4 [363]	RAF, Operation Shader, Akrotiri, Cyprus
	ZK364	Eurofighter Typhoon FGR4 [364]	RAF No 11 Sqn, Coningsby, Lincs
	ZK365	Eurofighter Typhoon FGR4 [365]	RAF TMF, Coningsby, Lincs
	ZK366	Eurofighter Typhoon FGR4 [366]	RAF No 12 Sqn, Coningsby, Lincs
	ZK367	Eurofighter Typhoon FGR4 [367]	RAF AWC/FJWOEU/No 41 Sqn, Coningsby, Lincs

Serial	Type (code/other identity)	Owner/operator, location or fate	Notes
ZK368	Eurofighter Typhoon FGR4 [368]	RAF No 29 Sqn, Coningsby, Lincs	
ZK369	Eurofighter Typhoon FGR4 [369]	RAF No 3 Sqn, Coningsby, Lincs	
ZK370	Eurofighter Typhoon FGR4	RAF TMF, Coningsby, Lincs	
ZK371	Eurofighter Typhoon FGR4 [371]	RAF No 11 Sqn, Coningsby, Lincs	
ZK372	Eurofighter Typhoon FGR4 [372]	RAF TMF, Coningsby, Lincs	
ZK373	Eurofighter Typhoon FGR4 [373]	RAF No 12 Sqn, Coningsby, Lincs	
ZK374	Eurofighter Typhoon FGR4 [374]	RAF TMF, Coningsby, Lincs	
ZK375	Eurofighter Typhoon FGR4 [375]	RAF AWC/FJWOEU/No 41 Sqn, Coningsby, Lincs	
ZK376	Eurofighter Typhoon FGR4 [376]	RAF No 6 Sqn, Lossiemouth, Moray, Scotland	
ZK377	Eurofighter Typhoon FGR4 [377]	RAF No 3 Sqn, Coningsby, Lincs	
ZK378	Eurofighter Typhoon FGR4 [378]	RAF No 6 Sqn, Coningsby, Lincs	
ZK379	Eurofighter Typhoon T3 [379]	RAF AWC/FJWOEU/No 41 Sqn, Coningsby, Lincs	
ZK380	Eurofighter Typhoon T3 [380]	RAF No 29 Sqn, Coningsby, Lincs	
ZK381	Eurofighter Typhoon T3 [381]	RAF TMF, Coningsby, Lincs	
ZK382	Eurofighter Typhoon T3 [382]	RAF No 29 Sqn, Coningsby, Lincs	
ZK383	Eurofighter Typhoon T3 [383]	RAF No 12 Sqn, Coningsby, Lincs	
ZK424	Eurofighter Typhoon FGR4 [424]	RAF No 29 Sqn, Coningsby, Lincs	
ZK425	Eurofighter Typhoon FGR4 [425]	RAF No 2 Sqn, Lossiemouth, Moray, Scotland	
ZK426	Eurofighter Typhoon FGR4 [426]	RAF, Operation Shader, Akrotiri, Cyprus	
ZK427	Eurofighter Typhoon FGR4 [427]	RAF No 2 Sqn, Lossiemouth, Moray, Scotland	
ZK428	Eurofighter Typhoon FGR4 [428]	RAF No 29 Sqn, Coningsby, Lincs	
ZK429	Eurofighter Typhoon FGR4 [429]	RAF No 6 Sqn, Lossiemouth, Moray, Scotland	
ZK430	Eurofighter Typhoon FGR4 [430]	RAF, Operation Shader, Akrotiri, Cyprus	
ZK431	Eurofighter Typhoon FGR4 [431]	RAF No 3 Sqn, Coningsby, Lincs	
ZK432	Eurofighter Typhoon FGR4 [432]	RAF No 29 Sqn, Coningsby, Lincs	
ZK433	Eurofighter Typhoon FGR4 [433]	RAF AWC/FJWOEU/No 41 Sqn, Coningsby, Lincs	
ZK434	Eurofighter Typhoon FGR4 [434]	RAF No 11 Sqn, Coningsby, Lincs	
ZK435	Eurofighter Typhoon FGR4 [435]	RAF No 11 Sqn, Coningsby, Lincs	
ZK436	Eurofighter Typhoon FGR4 [436]	RAF No 29 Sqn, Coningsby, Lincs	
ZK437	Eurofighter Typhoon FGR4 [437]	RAF No 3 Sqn, Coningsby, Lincs	
ZK438	Eurofighter Typhoon FGR4 [438]	RAF No 6 Sqn, Lossiemouth, Moray, Scotland	
ZK439	Eurofighter Typhoon FGR4 [439]	RAF No 6 Sqn, Lossiemouth, Moray, Scotland	
ZK531	BAe Hawk T53 (LL-5306)	Humberside Airport, Lincs, on display	
ZK532	BAe Hawk T53 (LL-5315)	MOD/BAE Systems, Samlesbury, Lancs, GI use	
ZK533	BAe Hawk T53 (LL-5317)	MOD/BAE Systems, Samlesbury, Lancs, GI use	
ZK535	BAe Hawk T53 (LL-5320)	BAE Systems Aircraft Maintenance Academy, Humberside, Lincs	
ZK550	Boeing Chinook HC6 (N701UK)	RAF No 7 Sqn, Odiham, Hants	
ZK551	Boeing Chinook HC6 (N702UK)	RAF No 7 Sqn, Odiham, Hants	
ZK552	Boeing Chinook HC6 (N703UK)	RAF, Operation Shader, Akrotiri, Cyprus	
ZK553	Boeing Chinook HC6 (N700UK)	RAF No 7 Sqn, Odiham, Hants	
ZK554	Boeing Chinook HC6 (N705UK)	RAF No 7 Sqn, Odiham, Hants	
ZK555	Boeing Chinook HC6 (N706UK)	RAF No 7 Sqn, Odiham, Hants	
ZK556	Boeing Chinook HC6 (N707UK)	RAF, Operation Shader, Akrotiri, Cyprus	
ZK557	Boeing Chinook HC6 (N708UK)	RAF, Operation Shader, Akrotiri, Cyprus	
ZK558	Boeing Chinook HC6 (N709UK)	MOD/StandardAero, Fleetlands, Hants	
ZK559	Boeing Chinook HC6 (N710UK)	RAF No 7 Sqn, Odiham, Hants	
ZK560	Boeing Chinook HC6 (N711UK)	RAF No 7 Sqn, Odiham, Hants	
ZK561	Boeing Chinook HC6 (N712UK)	RAF No 7 Sqn, Odiham, Hants	
ZK562	Boeing Chinook HC6 (N713UK)	RAF No 7 Sqn, Odiham, Hants	
ZK563	Boeing Chinook HC6 (N714UK)	RAF CMF, Odiham, Hants	
ZM135	Lockheed Martin F-35B Lightning II (168315) [001]	RAF No 17 Sqn, Edwards AFB, California	
ZM136	Lockheed Martin F-35B Lightning II (168316) [002]	RAF No 17 Sqn, Edwards AFB, California	
ZM137	Lockheed Martin F-35B Lightning II (168737) [003]	RAF No 207 Sqn, Marham, Norfolk	
ZM138	Lockheed Martin F-35B Lightning II (169170) [004]	RAF No 17 Sqn, Edwards AFB, California	
ZM139	Lockheed Martin F-35B Lightning II (169298) [005]	MCAS Cherry Point, SC (maintenance)	
ZM140	Lockheed Martin F-35B Lightning II (169299) [006]	RAF No 207 Sqn, Marham, Norfolk	
ZM141	Lockheed Martin F-35B Lightning II (169300) [007]	MCAS Cherry Point, SC (maintenance)	
ZM142	Lockheed Martin F-35B Lightning II (169301) [008]	RAF No 207 Sqn, Marham, Norfolk	
ZM143	Lockheed Martin F-35B Lightning II (169417) [009]	RAF No 207 Sqn, Marham, Norfolk	
ZM144	Lockheed Martin F-35B Lightning II (169418) [010]	RAF No 207 Sqn, Marham, Norfolk	

Notes	Serial	Type (code/other identity)	Owner/operator, location or fate
	ZM145	Lockheed Martin F-35B Lightning II (169419) [011]	RAF No 207 Sqn, Marham, Norfolk
	ZM146	Lockheed Martin F-35B Lightning II (169420) [012]	RAF No 617 Sqn, Marham, Norfolk
	ZM147	Lockheed Martin F-35B Lightning II (169421) [013]	RAF No 617 Sqn, Marham, Norfolk
	ZM148	Lockheed Martin F-35B Lightning II (169422) [014]	RAF No 617 Sqn, Marham, Norfolk
	ZM149	Lockheed Martin F-35B Lightning II (169596) [015]	RAF No 207 Sqn, Marham, Norfolk
	ZM150	Lockheed Martin F-35B Lightning II (169597) [016]	RAF No 617 Sqn, Marham, Norfolk
	ZM151	Lockheed Martin F-35B Lightning II (169598) [017]	RAF No 617 Sqn, Marham, Norfolk
	ZM152	Lockheed Martin F-35B Lightning II (169629) [018]	RAF Marham, Norfolk (wreckage)
	ZM153	Lockheed Martin F-35B Lightning II (169698) [019]	RAF No 207 Sqn, Marham, Norfolk
	ZM154	Lockheed Martin F-35B Lightning II (169699) [020]	RAF No 617 Sqn, Marham, Norfolk
	ZM155	Lockheed Martin F-35B Lightning II (169700) [021]	RAF No 617 Sqn, Marham, Norfolk
	ZM156	Lockheed Martin F-35B Lightning II (169928) [022]	RAF No 617 Sqn, Marham, Norfolk
	ZM157	Lockheed Martin F-35B Lightning II (169929) [023]	RAF No 207 Sqn, Marham, Norfolk
	ZM158	Lockheed Martin F-35B Lightning II (169930) [024]	RAF No 207 Sqn, Marham, Norfolk
	ZM159	Lockheed Martin F-35B Lightning II (169931) [025]	RAF No 617 Sqn, Marham, Norfolk
	ZM160	Lockheed Martin F-35B Lightning II (169932) [026]	RAF No 617 Sqn, Marham, Norfolk
	ZM161	Lockheed Martin F-35B Lightning II (169933) [027]	RAF No 617 Sqn, Marham, Norfolk
	ZM162	Lockheed Martin F-35B Lightning II [028]	RAF M&FF, Marham, Norfolk
	ZM163	Lockheed Martin F-35B Lightning II [029]	RAF M&FF, Marham, Norfolk
	ZM164	Lockheed Martin F-35B Lightning II [030]	RAF M&FF, Marham, Norfolk
	ZM165	Lockheed Martin F-35B Lightning II	Reservation for RAF/RN
	ZM166	Lockheed Martin F-35B Lightning II	Reservation for RAF/RN
	ZM167	Lockheed Martin F-35B Lightning II	Reservation for RAF/RN
	ZM168	Lockheed Martin F-35B Lightning II	Reservation for RAF/RN
	ZM169	Lockheed Martin F-35B Lightning II	Reservation for RAF/RN
	ZM170	Lockheed Martin F-35B Lightning II	Reservation for RAF/RN
	ZM171	Lockheed Martin F-35B Lightning II	Reservation for RAF/RN
	ZM172	Lockheed Martin F-35B Lightning II	Reservation for RAF/RN
	ZM173	Lockheed Martin F-35B Lightning II	Reservation for RAF/RN
	ZM174	Lockheed Martin F-35B Lightning II	Reservation for RAF/RN
	ZM175	Lockheed Martin F-35B Lightning II	Reservation for RAF/RN
	ZM176	Lockheed Martin F-35B Lightning II	Reservation for RAF/RN
	ZM177	Lockheed Martin F-35B Lightning II	Reservation for RAF/RN
	ZM178	Lockheed Martin F-35B Lightning II	Reservation for RAF/RN
	ZM179	Lockheed Martin F-35B Lightning II	Reservation for RAF/RN
	ZM180	Lockheed Martin F-35B Lightning II	Reservation for RAF/RN
	ZM181	Lockheed Martin F-35B Lightning II	Reservation for RAF/RN
	ZM182	Lockheed Martin F-35B Lightning II	Reservation for RAF/RN
	ZM183	Lockheed Martin F-35 Lightning II	Reservation for RAF/RN
	ZM184	Lockheed Martin F-35 Lightning II	Reservation for RAF/RN
	ZM185	Lockheed Martin F-35 Lightning II	Reservation for RAF/RN
	ZM186	Lockheed Martin F-35 Lightning II	Reservation for RAF/RN
	ZM187	Lockheed Martin F-35 Lightning II	Reservation for RAF/RN
	ZM188	Lockheed Martin F-35 Lightning II	Reservation for RAF/RN
	ZM189	Lockheed Martin F-35 Lightning II	Reservation for RAF/RN
	ZM190	Lockheed Martin F-35 Lightning II	Reservation for RAF/RN
	ZM191	Lockheed Martin F-35 Lightning II	Reservation for RAF/RN
	ZM192	Lockheed Martin F-35 Lightning II	Reservation for RAF/RN
	ZM193	Lockheed Martin F-35 Lightning II	Reservation for RAF/RN
	ZM194	Lockheed Martin F-35 Lightning II	Reservation for RAF/RN
	ZM195	Lockheed Martin F-35 Lightning II	Reservation for RAF/RN
	ZM196	Lockheed Martin F-35 Lightning II	Reservation for RAF/RN
	ZM197	Lockheed Martin F-35 Lightning II	Reservation for RAF/RN
	ZM198	Lockheed Martin F-35 Lightning II	Reservation for RAF/RN
	ZM199	Lockheed Martin F-35 Lightning II	Reservation for RAF/RN
	ZM200	Lockheed Martin F-35 Lightning II	Reservation for RAF/RN
	ZM300	Grob G120TP-A Prefect T1 (D-ETPJ/G-MFTS) [00]	RAF No 3 FTS, Cranwell/Barkston Heath, Lincs
	ZM301	Grob G120TP-A Prefect T1 (D-EGUX/G-MEFT) [01]	RAF No 3 FTS, Cranwell/Barkston Heath, Lincs
	ZM302	Grob G120TP-A Prefect T1 (D-ETPT/G-CJYB) [02]	RAF No 3 FTS, Cranwell/Barkston Heath, Lincs
	ZM303	Grob G120TP-A Prefect T1 (G-CJYG) [03]	RAF No 3 FTS, Cranwell/Barkston Heath, Lincs
	ZM304	Grob G120TP-A Prefect T1 (G-CJYH) [04]	RAF No 3 FTS, Cranwell/Barkston Heath, Lincs
	ZM305	Grob G120TP-A Prefect T1 (G-CJZR) [05]	RAF No 3 FTS, Cranwell/Barkston Heath, Lincs

Serial	Type (code/other identity)	Owner/operator, location or fate	Notes
ZM306	Grob G120TP-A Prefect T1 (G-CJZJ) [06]	RAF No 3 FTS, Cranwell/Barkston Heath, Lincs	
ZM307	Grob G120TP-A Prefect T1 (G-CJZI) [07]	RAF No 3 FTS, Cranwell/Barkston Heath, Lincs	
ZM308	Grob G120TP-A Prefect T1 (G-CJZF) [08]	RAF No 3 FTS, Cranwell/Barkston Heath, Lincs	
ZM309	Grob G120TP-A Prefect T1 (G-CKCO) [09]	RAF No 3 FTS, Cranwell/Barkston Heath, Lincs	
ZM310	Grob G120TP-A Prefect T1 (G-CKCS) [10]	RAF No 3 FTS, Cranwell/Barkston Heath, Lincs	
ZM311	Grob G120TP-A Prefect T1 (G-CKIA) [11]	RAF No 3 FTS, Cranwell/Barkston Heath, Lincs	
ZM312	Grob G120TP-A Prefect T1 (G-CKIB) [12]	RAF No 3 FTS, Cranwell/Barkston Heath, Lincs	
ZM313	Grob G120TP-A Prefect T1 (G-CKIC) [13]	RAF No 3 FTS, Cranwell/Barkston Heath, Lincs	
ZM314	Grob G120TP-A Prefect T1 (G-CKID) [14]	RAF No 3 FTS, Cranwell/Barkston Heath, Lincs	
ZM315	Grob G120TP-A Prefect T1 (G-CKIV) [15]	RAF No 3 FTS, Cranwell/Barkston Heath, Lincs	
ZM316	Grob G120TP-A Prefect T1 (G-CKIW) [16]	RAF No 3 FTS, Cranwell/Barkston Heath, Lincs	
ZM317	Grob G120TP-A Prefect T1 (G-CKLJ) [17]	RAF No 3 FTS, Cranwell/Barkston Heath, Lincs	
ZM318	Grob G120TP-A Prefect T1 (G-CKLO) [18]	RAF No 3 FTS, Cranwell/Barkston Heath, Lincs	
ZM319	Grob G120TP-A Prefect T1 (G-CKRY) [19]	RAF No 3 FTS, Cranwell/Barkston Heath, Lincs	
ZM320	Grob G120TP-A Prefect T1 (G-CKRP) [20]	RAF No 3 FTS, Cranwell/Barkston Heath, Lincs	
ZM321	Grob G120TP-A Prefect T1 (G-CKSJ) [21]	RAF No 3 FTS, Cranwell/Barkston Heath, Lincs	
ZM322	Grob G120TP-A Prefect T1 (G-CKSI) [22]	RAF No 3 FTS, Cranwell/Barkston Heath, Lincs	
ZM323	Beechcraft T-6C Texan T1 (N2824B/G-TBFT) [323]	Affinity/RAF No 4 FTS/No 72 Sqn, Valley, Wales	
ZM324	Beechcraft T-6C Texan T1 (N2826B/G-CKGO) [324]	Affinity/RAF No 4 FTS/No 72 Sqn, Valley, Wales	
ZM325	Beechcraft T-6C Texan T1 (N2843B/G-CKGP) [325]	Affinity/RAF No 4 FTS/No 72 Sqn, Valley, Wales	
ZM326	Beechcraft T-6C Texan T1 (N2770B/G-CKGW) [326]	Affinity/RAF No 4 FTS/No 72 Sqn, Valley, Wales	
ZM327	Beechcraft T-6C Texan T1 (N2856B/G-CKVL) [327]	Affinity/RAF No 4 FTS/No 72 Sqn, Valley, Wales	
ZM328	Beechcraft T-6C Texan T1 (N2857B/G-CKVN) [328]	Affinity/RAF No 4 FTS/No 72 Sqn, Valley, Wales	
ZM329	Beechcraft T-6C Texan T1 (N2858B/G-CKVO) [329]	Affinity/RAF No 4 FTS/No 72 Sqn, Valley, Wales	
ZM330	Beechcraft T-6C Texan T1 (N2859B/G-CKVR) [330]	Affinity/RAF No 4 FTS/No 72 Sqn, Valley, Wales	
ZM331	Beechcraft T-6C Texan T1 (N2860B/G-CKVS) [331]	Affinity/RAF No 4 FTS/No 72 Sqn, Valley, Wales	
ZM332	Beechcraft T-6C Texan T1 (N2872B/G-CKVU) [332]	Affinity/RAF No 4 FTS/No 72 Sqn, Valley, Wales	
ZM333	Embraer EMB-500 Phenom T1 (PR-PHK/G-MEPT)	Affinity/RAF No 3 FTS/No 45 Sqn, Cranwell, Lincs	
ZM334	Embraer EMB-500 Phenom T1 (PR-ING/G-MEPS)	Affinity/RAF No 3 FTS/No 45 Sqn, Cranwell, Lincs	
ZM335	Embraer EMB-500 Phenom T1 (PR-LTE/G-CJXH)	Affinity/RAF No 3 FTS/No 45 Sqn, Cranwell, Lincs	
ZM336	Embraer EMB-500 Phenom T1 (PR-LTF/G-CKCU)	Affinity/RAF No 3 FTS/No 45 Sqn, Cranwell, Lincs	
ZM337	Embraer EMB-500 Phenom T1 (PR-LTJ/G-CKEF)	Affinity/RAF No 3 FTS/No 45 Sqn, Cranwell, Lincs	
ZM340	Beechcraft T-6C Texan T1 (N2786B/G-CLTZ) [340]	Affinity/RAF No 4 FTS/No 72 Sqn, Valley, Wales	
ZM341	Beechcraft T-6C Texan T1 (N2789B/G-CLUC) [341]	Affinity/RAF No 4 FTS/No 72 Sqn, Valley, Wales	
ZM342	Beechcraft T-6C Texan T1 (N2790B/G-CLUF) [342]	Affinity/RAF No 4 FTS/No 72 Sqn, Valley, Wales	
ZM343	Beechcraft T-6C Texan T1 (N2811B/G-CLUA) [343]	Affinity/RAF No 4 FTS/No 72 Sqn, Valley, Wales	
ZM398	Airbus A400M Atlas Full Flight Simulator	RAF Brize Norton, Oxon	
ZM399	Airbus A400M Atlas Full Flight Simulator	RAF Brize Norton, Oxon	
ZM400	Airbus A400M Atlas C1 (A4M015/EC-405)	MOD/Airbus Defence & Space, Sevilla/Morón, Spain	
ZM401	Airbus A400M Atlas C1 (A4M016/EC-406)	RAF No 24/No 30/No 70 Sqn, Brize Norton, Oxon	
ZM402	Airbus A400M Atlas C1 (A4M017/EC-407)	RAF No 24/No 30/No 70 Sqn, Brize Norton, Oxon	
ZM403	Airbus A400M Atlas C1 (A4M020)	MOD/Airbus Defence & Space, Getafe, Spain (upgrade)	
ZM404	Airbus A400M Atlas C1 (A4M021/EC-401)	RAF No 24/No 30/No 70 Sqn, Brize Norton, Oxon	
ZM405	Airbus A400M Atlas C1 (A4M024)	RAF No 24/No 30/No 70 Sqn, Brize Norton, Oxon	
ZM406	Airbus A400M Atlas C1 (A4M025/EC-405)	RAF No 24/No 30/No 70 Sqn, Brize Norton, Oxon	
ZM407	Airbus A400M Atlas C1 (A4M026)	RAF No 24/No 30/No 70 Sqn, Brize Norton, Oxon	
ZM408	Airbus A400M Atlas C1 (A4M027)	RAF, stored Brize Norton, Oxon	
ZM409	Airbus A400M Atlas C1 (A4M034)	RAF No 24/No 30/No 70 Sqn, Brize Norton, Oxon	
ZM410	Airbus A400M Atlas C1 (A4M038)	RAF, stored Brize Norton, Oxon	
ZM411	Airbus A400M Atlas C1 (A4M039)	RAF No 24/No 30/No 70 Sqn, Brize Norton, Oxon	
ZM412	Airbus A400M Atlas C1 (A4M042)	RAF No 24/No 30/No 70 Sqn, Brize Norton, Oxon	
ZM413	Airbus A400M Atlas C1 (A4M045)	RAF No 24/No 30/No 70 Sqn, Brize Norton, Oxon	
ZM414	Airbus A400M Atlas C1 (A4M047)	RAF No 24/No 30/No 70 Sqn, Brize Norton, Oxon	
ZM415	Airbus A400M Atlas C1 (A4M052)	RAF No 24/No 30/No 70 Sqn, Brize Norton, Oxon	
ZM416	Airbus A400M Atlas C1 (A4M058)	MOD/Airbus Defence & Space, Getafe, Spain (upgrade)	
ZM417	Airbus A400M Atlas C1 (A4M060)	MOD/Airbus Defence & Space, Getafe, Spain (upgrade)	
ZM418	Airbus A400M Atlas C1 (A4M063)	RAF No 24/No 30/No 70 Sqn, Brize Norton, Oxon	
ZM419	Airbus A400M Atlas C1 (A4M077)	RAF No 24/No 30/No 70 Sqn, Brize Norton, Oxon	
ZM420	Airbus A400M Atlas C1 (A4M056/EC-400)	RAF No 24/No 30/No 70 Sqn, Brize Norton, Oxon	
ZM421	Airbus A400M Atlas C1 (A4M129)	Airbus Defence & Space, Seville, Spain, for RAF	
ZM496	Airbus H145 Jupiter HT1 (D-HADR/G-CLKI) [96]	RAF No 1 FTS, Shawbury, Shropshire	
ZM497	Airbus H145 Jupiter HT1 (G-CLKO) [97]	RAF No 202 Sqn, Valley, Wales	

Notes	Serial	Type (code/other identity)	Owner/operator, location or fate
	ZM498	Airbus H145 Jupiter HT1 (G-CLKP) [98]	RAF No 1 FTS, Shawbury, Shropshire
	ZM499	Airbus H145 Jupiter HT1 (D-HADI/G-CLKS) [99]	RAF No 202 Sqn, Valley, Wales
	ZM500	Airbus H145 Jupiter HT1 (D-HADT/G-CJIV) [00]	RAF No 1 FTS, Shawbury, Shropshire
	ZM501	Airbus H145 Jupiter HT1 (D-HADM/G-CJIZ/G-CKGE) [01]	RAF No 1 FTS, Shawbury, Shropshire
	ZM502	Airbus H145 Jupiter HT1 (D-HADQ/G-CJRW) [02]	RAF No 1 FTS, Shawbury, Shropshire
	ZM503	Airbus H145 Jupiter HT1	Reservation for MOD
	ZM504	Airbus H135 Juno HT1 (D-HECZ/G-CJJG) [04]	RAF No 1 FTS, Shawbury, Shropshire
	ZM505	Airbus H135 Juno HT1 (D-HECV/G-CJIW) [05]	RAF No 1 FTS, Shawbury, Shropshire
	ZM506	Airbus H135 Juno HT1 (D-HECW/G-CJIY) [06]	RAF No 1 FTS, Shawbury, Shropshire
	ZM507	Airbus H135 Juno HT1 (D-HECX/G-CJRP) [07]	RAF No 1 FTS, Shawbury, Shropshire
	ZM508	Airbus H135 Juno HT1 (D-HECD/G-CJRY) [08]	RAF No 1 FTS, Shawbury, Shropshire
	ZM509	Airbus H135 Juno HT1 (D-HECB/G-CJTZ) [09]	RAF No 1 FTS, Shawbury, Shropshire
	ZM510	Airbus H135 Juno HT1 (D-HECG/G-CJUA) [10]	RAF No 1 FTS, Shawbury, Shropshire
	ZM511	Airbus H135 Juno HT1 (D-HECJ/G-CJUC) [11]	RAF No 1 FTS, Shawbury, Shropshire
	ZM512	Airbus H135 Juno HT1 (D-HECQ/G-CJXS) [12]	RAF No 1 FTS, Shawbury, Shropshire
	ZM513	Airbus H135 Juno HT1 (D-HECP/G-CJXU) [13]	RAF No 1 FTS, Shawbury, Shropshire
	ZM514	Airbus H135 Juno HT1 (D-HECV/G-CJXV) [14]	RAF No 1 FTS, Shawbury, Shropshire
	ZM515	Airbus H135 Juno HT1 (D-HECT/G-CJSO) [15]	RAF No 1 FTS, Shawbury, Shropshire
	ZM516	Airbus H135 Juno HT1 (D-HECY/G-CJZS) [16]	RAF No 1 FTS, Shawbury, Shropshire
	ZM517	Airbus H135 Juno HT1 (D-HECL/G-CJZT) [17]	RAF No 1 FTS, Shawbury, Shropshire
	ZM518	Airbus H135 Juno HT1 (D-HCBA/G-CKEO) [18]	RAF No 1 FTS, Shawbury, Shropshire
	ZM519	Airbus H135 Juno HT1 (D-HCBC/G-CKEU) [19]	RAF No 1 FTS, Shawbury, Shropshire
	ZM520	Airbus H135 Juno HT1 (D-HCBD/G-CKEW) [20]	RAF No 1 FTS, Shawbury, Shropshire
	ZM521	Airbus H135 Juno HT1 (D-HECJ/G-CKIK) [21]	RAF No 1 FTS, Shawbury, Shropshire
	ZM522	Airbus H135 Juno HT1 (D-HCBB/G-CKIM) [22]	RAF No 1 FTS, Shawbury, Shropshire
	ZM523	Airbus H135 Juno HT1 (D-HECJ/G-CKJW) [23]	RAF No 1 FTS, Shawbury, Shropshire
	ZM524	Airbus H135 Juno HT1 (D-HECK/G-CKJU) [24]	RAF No 1 FTS, Shawbury, Shropshire
	ZM525	Airbus H135 Juno HT1 (D-HECQ/G-CKJX) [25]	RAF No 1 FTS, Shawbury, Shropshire
	ZM526	Airbus H135 Juno HT1 (D-HECU/G-CKOC) [26]	RAF No 1 FTS, Shawbury, Shropshire
	ZM527	Airbus H135 Juno HT1 (D-HECX/G-CKOB) [27]	RAF No 1 FTS, Shawbury, Shropshire
	ZM528	Airbus H135 Juno HT1 (D-HECF/G-CKOA) [28] $	RAF No 1 FTS, Shawbury, Shropshire
	ZM529	Airbus H135 Juno HT1 (D-HECW/G-CKPT) [29]	RAF No 1 FTS, Shawbury, Shropshire
	ZM530	Airbus H135 Juno HT1 (D-HECD/G-CKRA) [30]	RAF No 1 FTS, Shawbury, Shropshire
	ZM531	Airbus H135 Juno HT1 (D-HECA/G-CKSB) [31]	RAF No 1 FTS, Shawbury, Shropshire
	ZM532	Airbus H135 Juno HT1 (D-HECY/G-CKSA) [32]	RAF No 1 FTS, Shawbury, Shropshire
	ZM700	Boeing Apache AH-64E	AAC No 663 Sqn/No 3 Regiment, Wattisham, Suffolk
	ZM701	Boeing Apache AH-64E	AAC No 673 Sqn/No 7 Regiment, Middle Wallop, Hants
	ZM702	Boeing Apache AH-64E	AAC No 673 Sqn/No 7 Regiment, Middle Wallop, Hants
	ZM703	Boeing Apache AH-64E	AAC No 663 Sqn/No 3 Regiment, Wattisham, Suffolk
	ZM704	Boeing Apache AH-64E	AAC No 662 Sqn/No 3 Regiment, Wattisham, Suffolk
	ZM705	Boeing Apache AH-64E	AAC No 663 Sqn/No 3 Regiment, Wattisham, Suffolk
	ZM706	Boeing Apache AH-64E	AAC No 662 Sqn/No 3 Regiment, Wattisham, Suffolk
	ZM707	Boeing Apache AH-64E	AAC No 662 Sqn/No 3 Regiment, Wattisham, Suffolk
	ZM708	Boeing Apache AH-64E	AAC No 673 Sqn/No 7 Regiment, Middle Wallop, Hants
	ZM709	Boeing Apache AH-64E	AAC No 663 Sqn/No 3 Regiment, Wattisham, Suffolk
	ZM710	Boeing Apache AH-64E	AAC No 663 Sqn/No 3 Regiment, Wattisham, Suffolk
	ZM711	Boeing Apache AH-64E	AAC No 662 Sqn/No 3 Regiment, Wattisham, Suffolk
	ZM712	Boeing Apache AH-64E	AAC No 662 Sqn/No 3 Regiment, Wattisham, Suffolk
	ZM713	Boeing Apache AH-64E	AAC No 662 Sqn/No 3 Regiment, Wattisham, Suffolk
	ZM714	Boeing Apache AH-64E	AAC No 673 Sqn/No 7 Regiment, Middle Wallop, Hants
	ZM715	Boeing Apache AH-64E	AAC No 673 Sqn/No 7 Regiment, Middle Wallop, Hants
	ZM716	Boeing Apache AH-64E	AAC No 673 Sqn/No 7 Regiment, Middle Wallop, Hants
	ZM717	Boeing Apache AH-64E	AAC No 673 Sqn/No 7 Regiment, Middle Wallop, Hants
	ZM718	Boeing Apache AH-64E	AAC No 673 Sqn/No 7 Regiment, Middle Wallop, Hants
	ZM719	Boeing Apache AH-64E	AAC No 663 Sqn/No 3 Regiment, Wattisham, Suffolk
	ZM720	Boeing Apache AH-64E	AAC No 7 AAB REME, Wattisham, Suffolk
	ZM721	Boeing Apache AH-64E	AAC No 673 Sqn/No 7 Regiment, Middle Wallop, Hants
	ZM722	Boeing Apache AH-64E	AAC No 673 Sqn/No 7 Regiment, Middle Wallop, Hants
	ZM723	Boeing Apache AH-64E	AAC No 7 AAB REME, Wattisham, Suffolk
	ZM724	Boeing Apache AH-64E	AAC No 7 AAB REME, Wattisham, Suffolk

Serial	Type (code/other identity)	Owner/operator, location or fate	Notes
ZM725	Boeing Apache AH-64E	AAC No 7 AAB REME, Wattisham, Suffolk	
ZM726	Boeing Apache AH-64E	AAC No 7 AAB REME, Wattisham, Suffolk	
ZM727	Boeing Apache AH-64E	AAC No 7 AAB REME, Wattisham, Suffolk	
ZM728	Boeing Apache AH-64E	For AAC	
ZM729	Boeing Apache AH-64E	For AAC	
ZM730	Boeing Apache AH-64E	For AAC	
ZM731	Boeing Apache AH-64E	For AAC	
ZM732	Boeing Apache AH-64E	For AAC	
ZM733	Boeing Apache AH-64E	For AAC	
ZM734	Boeing Apache AH-64E	For AAC	
ZM735	Boeing Apache AH-64E	For AAC	
ZM736	Boeing Apache AH-64E	For AAC	
ZM737	Boeing Apache AH-64E	For AAC	
ZM738	Boeing Apache AH-64E	For AAC	
ZM739	Boeing Apache AH-64E	For AAC	
ZM740	Boeing Apache AH-64E	For AAC	
ZM741	Boeing Apache AH-64E	For AAC	
ZM742	Boeing Apache AH-64E	For AAC	
ZM743	Boeing Apache AH-64E	For AAC	
ZM744	Boeing Apache AH-64E	For AAC	
ZM745	Boeing Apache AH-64E	For AAC	
ZM746	Boeing Apache AH-64E	For AAC	
ZM747	Boeing Apache AH-64E	For AAC	
ZM748	Boeing Apache AH-64E	For AAC	
ZM749	Boeing Apache AH-64E	For AAC	
ZP801	Boeing P-8A Poseidon MRA1 (169573/N456DS) [01]	RAF No 54 Sqn/No 120 Sqn/No 201 Sqn, Lossiemouth	
ZP802	Boeing P-8A Poseidon MRA1 (169574/N469DS) [02]	RAF No 54 Sqn/No 120 Sqn/No 201 Sqn, Lossiemouth	
ZP803	Boeing P-8A Poseidon MRA1 (169575/N481DS) [03]	RAF No 54 Sqn/No 120 Sqn/No 201 Sqn, Lossiemouth	
ZP804	Boeing P-8A Poseidon MRA1 (169576/N482DS) [04]	RAF No 54 Sqn/No 120 Sqn/No 201 Sqn, Lossiemouth	
ZP805	Boeing P-8A Poseidon MRA1 (169577/N534DS) [05]	RAF No 54 Sqn/No 120 Sqn/No 201 Sqn, Lossiemouth	
ZP806	Boeing P-8A Poseidon MRA1 (169578/N634DS) [06]	RAF No 54 Sqn/No 120 Sqn/No 201 Sqn, Lossiemouth	
ZP807	Boeing P-8A Poseidon MRA1 (169579/N665DS) [07]	RAF No 54 Sqn/No 120 Sqn/No 201 Sqn, Lossiemouth	
ZP808	Boeing P-8A Poseidon MRA1 (169580/N667DS) [08]	RAF No 54 Sqn/No 120 Sqn/No 201 Sqn, Lossiemouth	
ZP809	Boeing P-8A Poseidon MRA1 (169581/N673DS) [09]	RAF No 54 Sqn/No 120 Sqn/No 201 Sqn, Lossiemouth	
ZP810	Boeing P-8A Poseidon MRA1	Reservation for RAF	
ZP811	Boeing P-8A Poseidon MRA1	Reservation for RAF	
ZP812	Boeing P-8A Poseidon MRA1	Reservation for RAF	
ZP813	Boeing P-8A Poseidon MRA1	Reservation for RAF	
ZP814	Boeing P-8A Poseidon MRA1	Reservation for RAF	
ZP815	Boeing P-8A Poseidon MRA1	Reservation for RAF	
ZR285	AgustaWestland AW101 Mk.614	Leonardo MW, for Poland as 6201	
ZR286	AgustaWestland AW101 Mk.614	Leonardo MW, for Poland as 6202	
ZR287	AgustaWestland AW101 Mk.614	Leonardo MW, for Poland as 6203	
ZR288	AgustaWestland AW101 Mk.614	Leonardo MW, for Poland as 6204	
ZR334	AgustaWestland AW101 Mk.640 (RSAF HMH-1)	Leonardo MW, stored Yeovil, Somerset	
ZR335	AgustaWestland AW101 Mk.640 (RSAF HMH-2)	Leonardo MW, stored Yeovil, Somerset	
ZR342	AgustaWestland AW101 Mk.641 (ZW-4305)	Leonardo MW, stored Yeovil, Somerset	
ZR346	AgustaWestland AW101 Mk.641 (ZW-4309)	Leonardo MW, stored Yeovil, Somerset	
ZR347	AgustaWestland AW101 Mk.641 (ZW-4310)	Leonardo MW, stored Yeovil, for Azerbaijan?	
ZR348	AgustaWestland AW101 Mk.641 (ZW-4311)	Leonardo MW, stored Yeovil, for Azerbaijan?	
ZR349	AgustaWestland AW101 Mk.641 (ZW-4312)	Leonardo MW, stored Yeovil, for Azerbaijan?	
ZR501	Eurofighter Typhoon T (MT001)	*To Qatar as QA400, 2 November 2022*	
ZR502	Eurofighter Typhoon T (MT002)	*To Qatar as QA401, 15 November 2022*	
ZR503	Eurofighter Typhoon T (MT003)	*BAe Systems, for Qatar as QA402*	
ZR504	Eurofighter Typhoon T (MT004)	*BAe Systems, for Qatar as QA403*	
ZR505	Eurofighter Typhoon (MS001)	*To Qatar as QA404, 25 August 2022*	
ZR506	Eurofighter Typhoon (MS002)	*To Qatar as QA405, 25 August 2022*	
ZR507	Eurofighter Typhoon (MS003)	*To Qatar as QA406, 30 August 2022*	
ZR508	Eurofighter Typhoon (MS004)	*To Qatar as QA407, 30 August 2022*	
ZR509	Eurofighter Typhoon (MS005)	*To Qatar as QA408, 2 November 2022*	

Notes	Serial	Type (code/other identity)	Owner/operator, location or fate
	ZR510	Eurofighter Typhoon (MS006)	*To Qatar as QA409, 15 November 2022*
	ZR511	Eurofighter Typhoon (MS007)	BAe Systems, for Qatar as QA410
	ZR512	Eurofighter Typhoon (MS008)	BAe Systems, for Qatar as QA411
	ZR513	Eurofighter Typhoon (MS009)	BAe Systems, for Qatar
	ZR514	Eurofighter Typhoon	BAe Systems, for Qatar
	ZR515	Eurofighter Typhoon	BAe Systems, for Qatar
	ZR516	Eurofighter Typhoon	BAe Systems, for Qatar
	ZR517	Eurofighter Typhoon	BAe Systems, for Qatar
	ZR518	Eurofighter Typhoon	BAe Systems, for Qatar
	ZR519	Eurofighter Typhoon	BAe Systems, for Qatar
	ZR520	Eurofighter Typhoon	BAe Systems, for Qatar
	ZR521	Eurofighter Typhoon	BAe Systems, for Qatar
	ZR522	Eurofighter Typhoon	BAe Systems, for Qatar
	ZR523	Eurofighter Typhoon	BAe Systems, for Qatar
	ZR524	Eurofighter Typhoon	BAe Systems, for Qatar
	ZS782	WS WG25 Sharpeye (BAPC.451)	The Helicopter Museum, Weston-super-Mare, Somerset
	ZT800	WS Super Lynx Mk 300	Yeovil College, Somerset, instructional use
	ZZ100	AgustaWestland AW101 Mk.612 (0262)	Leonardo MW, Yeovil, for Norway as 0262
	ZZ102	AgustaWestland AW101 Mk.612 (0265)	To Norway as 0265, 01 February 2023
	ZZ114	AgustaWestland AW101 Mk.612	*To Norway as 0283, 25 November 2022*
	ZZ115	AgustaWestland AW101 Mk.612	Leonardo MW, Yeovil, for Norway as 0284
	ZZ171	Boeing C-17A Globemaster III (00-201/N171UK) $	RAF No 99 Sqn, Brize Norton, Oxon
	ZZ172	Boeing C-17A Globemaster III (00-202/N172UK)	RAF No 99 Sqn, Brize Norton, Oxon
	ZZ173	Boeing C-17A Globemaster III (00-203/N173UK)	RAF No 99 Sqn, Brize Norton, Oxon
	ZZ174	Boeing C-17A Globemaster III (00-204/N174UK)	RAF No 99 Sqn, Brize Norton, Oxon
	ZZ175	Boeing C-17A Globemaster III (06-0205/N9500Z)	RAF No 99 Sqn, Brize Norton, Oxon
	ZZ176	Boeing C-17A Globemaster III (08-0206/N9500B)	RAF No 99 Sqn, Brize Norton, Oxon
	ZZ177	Boeing C-17A Globemaster III (09-8207/N9500B)	RAF No 99 Sqn, Brize Norton, Oxon
	ZZ178	Boeing C-17A Globemaster III (12-0208/N9500N)	RAF No 99 Sqn, Brize Norton, Oxon
	ZZ190	Hawker Hunter F58 (J-4066/G-HHAE)	Hawker Hunter Aviation, Leeming, N. Yorks
	ZZ191	Hawker Hunter F58 (J-4058/G-HHAD)	Hawker Hunter Aviation, Leeming, N. Yorks
	ZZ194	Hawker Hunter F58 (J-4021/G-HHAC)	Hawker Hunter Aviation, Leeming, N. Yorks (stored?)
	ZZ202	General Atomics Reaper RPAS (07-0117)	RAF No 13 Sqn/No 39 Sqn, Creech AFB, NV, USA
	ZZ203	General Atomics Reaper RPAS (08-0113)	RAF No 13 Sqn/No 39 Sqn, Creech AFB, NV, USA
	ZZ204	General Atomics Reaper RPAS (10-0157)	RAF No 13 Sqn/No 39 Sqn, Creech AFB, NV, USA
	ZZ205	General Atomics Reaper RPAS (10-0157)	RAF, Creech AFB, Nevada, USA (damaged)
	ZZ206	General Atomics Reaper RPAS (12-0707)	RAF No 13 Sqn/No 39 Sqn, Creech AFB, Nevada, USA
	ZZ207	General Atomics Reaper RPAS (12-0708)	RAF No 13 Sqn/No 39 Sqn, Creech AFB, Nevada, USA
	ZZ208	General Atomics Reaper RPAS (12-0709)	RAF No 13 Sqn/No 39 Sqn, Creech AFB, Nevada, USA
	ZZ209	General Atomics Reaper RPAS (12-0710)	RAF No 13 Sqn/No 39 Sqn, Creech AFB, Nevada, USA
	ZZ210	General Atomics Reaper RPAS (12-0711)	RAF No 13 Sqn/No 39 Sqn, Creech AFB, Nevada, USA
	ZZ211	General Atomics Reaper RPAS	RAF No 13 Sqn/No 39 Sqn, Creech AFB, Nevada, USA
	ZZ212	General Atomics Reaper RPAS	RAF No 13 Sqn/No 39 Sqn, Creech AFB, Nevada, USA
	ZZ213	General Atomics Reaper RPAS	RAF No 13 Sqn/No 39 Sqn, Creech AFB, Nevada, USA
	ZZ250	BAE Systems Taranis RPAS	BAE Systems, Warton, Lancs
	ZZ251	BAE Systems HERTI RPAS	BAE Systems, Warton, Lancs
	ZZ252	BAE Systems HERTI RPAS	BAE Systems, Woomera, Australia
	ZZ253	BAE Systems HERTI RPAS	BAE Systems, Woomera, Australia
	ZZ254	BAE Systems HERTI RPAS	BAE Systems, Woomera, Australia
	ZZ330	Airbus A330 Voyager KC2 (MRTT017/EC-337/G-VYGA)	RAF No 10 Sqn/No 101 Sqn, Brize Norton, Oxon
	ZZ331	Airbus A330 Voyager KC2 (MRTT018/EC-331/G-VYGB)	RAF No 10 Sqn/No 101 Sqn, Brize Norton, Oxon
	ZZ332	Airbus A330 Voyager KC3 (MRTT019/EC-330/G-VYGC)	RAF No 10 Sqn/No 101 Sqn, Brize Norton, Oxon
	ZZ333	Airbus A330 Voyager KC3 (MRTT020/EC-337/G-VYGD)	RAF No 10 Sqn/No 101 Sqn, Brize Norton, Oxon
	ZZ334	Airbus A330 Voyager KC3 (MRTT016/EC-335/G-VYGE)	RAF No 1312 Flt, Mount Pleasant, Falkland Islands

Serial	Type (code/other identity)	Owner/operator, location or fate	Notes
ZZ335	Airbus A330 Voyager KC3 (MRTT021/EC-338/G-VYGF)	RAF No 10 Sqn/No 101 Sqn, Brize Norton, Oxon	
ZZ336	Airbus A330 Voyager KC3 (MRTT022/EC-333/G-VYGG) $	RAF No 10 Sqn/No 101 Sqn, Brize Norton, Oxon	
ZZ337	Airbus A330 Voyager KC3 (MRTT023/EC-336/G-VYGH)	RAF No 10 Sqn/No 101 Sqn, Brize Norton, Oxon	
ZZ338	Airbus A330 Voyager KC3 (MRTT024/EC-331/G-VYGI)	RAF No 10 Sqn/No 101 Sqn, Brize Norton, Oxon	
ZZ339	Airbus A330-243 (MRTT025/EC-333/G-VYGJ)	Airtanker Ltd, Brize Norton [flies as G-VYGJ]	
ZZ340	Airbus A330-243 (MRTT026/EC-330/G-VYGK)	Airtanker Ltd, Brize Norton [flies as G-VYGK]	
ZZ341	Airbus A330-243 (MRTT027/EC-336/G-VYGL)	Airtanker Ltd, Brize Norton [flies as G-VYGL]	
ZZ342	Airbus A330-243 (MRTT028/EC-332/G-VYGM)	Airtanker Ltd, Brize Norton [flies as G-VYGM]	
ZZ343	Airbus A330 Voyager KC2 (MRTT029/EC-331/G-VYGN)	RAF No 10 Sqn/No 101 Sqn, Brize Norton, Oxon	
ZZ375	AgustaWestland AW159 Wildcat HMA2	RN No 825 NAS, Yeovilton, Somerset	
ZZ376	AgustaWestland AW159 Wildcat HMA2	RN No 815 NAS, Yeovilton, Somerset	
ZZ377	AgustaWestland AW159 Wildcat HMA2	RN No 825 NAS, Yeovilton, Somerset	
ZZ378	AgustaWestland AW159 Wildcat HMA2	MOD/Leonardo MW, Yeovil, Somerset (FASGW trials)	
ZZ379	AgustaWestland AW159 Wildcat HMA2	RN No 825 NAS, Yeovilton, Somerset	
ZZ380	AgustaWestland AW159 Wildcat HMA2	RN No 847 NAS, Yeovilton, Somerset	
ZZ381	AgustaWestland AW159 Wildcat HMA2	RN No 825 NAS, Yeovilton, Somerset	
ZZ382	AgustaWestland AW159 Wildcat AH1	AAC WCM (652 Sqn), Yeovilton, Somerset	
ZZ383	AgustaWestland AW159 Wildcat AH1	RN No 847 NAS, Yeovilton, Somerset	
ZZ384	AgustaWestland AW159 Wildcat AH1	AAC No 1 Regiment, Yeovilton, Somerset	
ZZ385	AgustaWestland AW159 Wildcat AH1	AAC No 1 Regiment, Yeovilton, Somerset	
ZZ386	AgustaWestland AW159 Wildcat AH1	MOD/Leonardo MW, Yeovil. Somerset	
ZZ387	AgustaWestland AW159 Wildcat AH1	RN No 847 NAS, Yeovilton, Somerset	
ZZ388	AgustaWestland AW159 Wildcat AH1	AAC WST/WZM, Yeovilton, Somerset	
ZZ389	AgustaWestland AW159 Wildcat AH1	AAC No 1 Regiment, Yeovilton, Somerset	
ZZ390	AgustaWestland AW159 Wildcat AH1	AAC No 1 Regiment, Yeovilton, Somerset	
ZZ391	AgustaWestland AW159 Wildcat AH1	AAC WST/WZM, Yeovilton, Somerset	
ZZ392	AgustaWestland AW159 Wildcat AH1	AAC No 1 Regiment, Yeovilton, Somerset	
ZZ393	AgustaWestland AW159 Wildcat AH1	AAC WCM (652 Sqn), Yeovilton, Somerset	
ZZ394	AgustaWestland AW159 Wildcat AH1	RN No 847 NAS, Yeovilton, Somerset	
ZZ395	AgustaWestland AW159 Wildcat AH1	AAC No 1 Regiment, Yeovilton, Somerset	
ZZ396	AgustaWestland AW159 Wildcat HMA2	RN No 815 NAS, Yeovilton, Somerset	
ZZ397	AgustaWestland AW159 Wildcat HMA2	RN No 815 NAS, Yeovilton, Somerset	
ZZ398	AgustaWestland AW159 Wildcat AH1	AAC WCM (652 Sqn), Yeovilton, Somerset	
ZZ399	AgustaWestland AW159 Wildcat AH1	RN No 847 NAS, Yeovilton, Somerset	
ZZ400	AgustaWestland AW159 Wildcat (TI01)	RNAS Yeovilton, Somerset, GI use	
ZZ401	AgustaWestland AW159 Wildcat (TI02)	RNAS Yeovilton, Somerset, GI use	
ZZ402	AgustaWestland AW159 Wildcat (TI03)	DSAE RNAESS, HMS Sultan, Gosport, Hants	
ZZ403	AgustaWestland AW159 Wildcat AH1	AAC WST/WZM, Yeovilton, Somerset	
ZZ404	AgustaWestland AW159 Wildcat AH1	RN No 825 NAS, Yeovilton, Somerset	
ZZ405	AgustaWestland AW159 Wildcat AH1	AAC 661 Sqn/No 1 Regiment, Yeovilton, Somerset	
ZZ406	AgustaWestland AW159 Wildcat AH1	RN No 847 NAS, Yeovilton, Somerset	
ZZ407	AgustaWestland AW159 Wildcat AH1	AAC WST/WZM, Yeovilton, Somerset	
ZZ408	AgustaWestland AW159 Wildcat AH1	AAC No 1 Regiment, Yeovilton, Somerset	
ZZ409	AgustaWestland AW159 Wildcat AH1	AAC WCM (652 Sqn), Yeovilton, Somerset	
ZZ410	AgustaWestland AW159 Wildcat AH1	AAC WCM (652 Sqn), Yeovilton, Somerset	
ZZ413	AgustaWestland AW159 Wildcat HMA2	RN No 815 NAS, Yeovilton, Somerset	
ZZ414	AgustaWestland AW159 Wildcat HMA2	RN No 815 NAS, Yeovilton, Somerset	
ZZ415	AgustaWestland AW159 Wildcat HMA2	MOD/Leonardo MW, Yeovil, Somerset (FASGW trials)	
ZZ416	Hawker Beechcraft Shadow R1+ (G-JENC)	RAF No 14 Sqn/No 54 Sqn, Waddington, Lincs	
ZZ417	Hawker Beechcraft Shadow R1+ (G-NICY)	RAF No 14 Sqn/No 54 Sqn, Waddington, Lincs	
ZZ418	Hawker Beechcraft Shadow R2 (G-JIMG)	MOD/Raytheon, Hawarden, Flintshire, Wales (upgrade)	
ZZ419	Hawker Beechcraft Shadow R1+ (G-OTCS)	RAF No 14 Sqn/No 54 Sqn, Waddington, Lincs	
ZZ500	Hawker Beechcraft Avenger T1 (G-MFTA)	RN No 750 NAS, Culdrose, Cornwall	
ZZ501	Hawker Beechcraft Avenger T1 (G-MFTB)	RN No 750 NAS, Culdrose, Cornwall	
ZZ502	Hawker Beechcraft Avenger T1 (G-MFTC)	RN No 750 NAS, Culdrose, Cornwall	
ZZ503	Hawker Beechcraft Avenger T1 (G-MFTD)	RN No 750 NAS, Culdrose, Cornwall	
ZZ504	Hawker Beechcraft Shadow R1+ (G-CGUM)	RAF No 14 Sqn/No 54 Sqn, Waddington, Lincs	

Notes	Serial	Type (code/other identity)	Owner/operator, location or fate
	ZZ505	Hawker Beechcraft Shadow R2 (G-DAYP)	MOD/Raytheon, Hawarden, Flintshire, Wales (upgrade)
	ZZ506	Hawker Beechcraft Shadow R2 (G-GMAD)	MOD/Raytheon, Hawarden, Flintshire, Wales (upgrade)
	ZZ507	Hawker Beechcraft Shadow R1+ (G-LBSB)	RAF No 14 Sqn/No 54 Sqn, Waddington, Lincs
	ZZ510	AgustaWestland AW159 Wildcat AH1	AAC WCM (652 Sqn), Yeovilton, Somerset
	ZZ511	AgustaWestland AW159 Wildcat AH1	MOD/Leonardo MW, Yeovil, Somerset
	ZZ512	AgustaWestland AW159 Wildcat AH1	AAC No 1 Regiment, Yeovilton, Somerset
	ZZ513	AgustaWestland AW159 Wildcat HMA2	MOD/Leonardo MW, Yeovil, Somerset (FASGW trials)
	ZZ514	AgustaWestland AW159 Wildcat HMA2	RN No 825 NAS, Yeovilton, Somerset
	ZZ515	AgustaWestland AW159 Wildcat HMA2	RN No 815 NAS, Yeovilton, Somerset
	ZZ516	AgustaWestland AW159 Wildcat HMA2	RN No 825 NAS, Yeovilton, Somerset
	ZZ517	AgustaWestland AW159 Wildcat HMA2	RN No 825 NAS, Yeovilton, Somerset
	ZZ518	AgustaWestland AW159 Wildcat HMA2	RN No 825 NAS, Yeovilton, Somerset
	ZZ519	AgustaWestland AW159 Wildcat HMA2	RN No 815 NAS, Yeovilton, Somerset
	ZZ520	AgustaWestland AW159 Wildcat AH1	AAC No 1 Regiment, Yeovilton, Somerset
	ZZ521	AgustaWestland AW159 Wildcat AH1	AAC WCM (652 Sqn), Yeovilton, Somerset
	ZZ522	AgustaWestland AW159 Wildcat HMA2	AAC WST/WZM, Yeovilton, Somerset
	ZZ523	AgustaWestland AW159 Wildcat AH1	AAC No 1 Regiment, Yeovilton, Somerset
	ZZ524	AgustaWestland AW159 Wildcat AH1	AAC No 1 Regiment, Yeovilton, Somerset
	ZZ525	AgustaWestland AW159 Wildcat AH1	AAC No 1 Regiment, Yeovilton, Somerset
	ZZ526	AgustaWestland AW159 Wildcat AH1	AAC WST/WZM, Yeovilton, Somerset
	ZZ527	AgustaWestland AW159 Wildcat AH1	AAC WCM (652 Sqn), Yeovilton, Somerset
	ZZ528	AgustaWestland AW159 Wildcat HMA2	RN No 825 NAS, Yeovilton, Somerset
	ZZ529	AgustaWestland AW159 Wildcat HMA2	RN No 815 NAS, Yeovilton, Somerset
	ZZ530	AgustaWestland AW159 Wildcat HMA2	AAC WST/WZM, Yeovilton, Somerset
	ZZ531	AgustaWestland AW159 Wildcat HMA2	RN No 815 NAS, Yeovilton, Somerset
	ZZ532	AgustaWestland AW159 Wildcat HMA2	MOD/Leonardo MW, Yeovil, Somerset
	ZZ533	AgustaWestland AW159 Wildcat HMA2	RN No 815 NAS, Yeovilton, Somerset
	ZZ534	AgustaWestland AW159 Wildcat HMA2	RN No 815 NAS, Yeovilton, Somerset
	ZZ535	AgustaWestland AW159 Wildcat HMA2	RN No 815 NAS, Yeovilton, Somerset
	ZZ664	Boeing RC-135W (64-14833)	RAF No 51 Sqn, Waddington, Lincs
	ZZ665	Boeing RC-135W (64-14838)	RAF No 51 Sqn, Waddington, Lincs
	ZZ666	Boeing RC-135W (64-14838)	RAF No 51 Sqn, Waddington, Lincs
	Z....	General Atomics Protector RG1 RPAS	MOD (on order for No 13 Sqn, RAF)
	Z....	General Atomics Protector RG1 RPAS	MOD (on order for No 13 Sqn, RAF)
	Z....	General Atomics Protector RG1 RPAS	MOD (on order for No 13 Sqn, RAF)
	Z....	General Atomics Protector RG1 RPAS	MOD (on order for No 13 Sqn, RAF)
	Z....	General Atomics Protector RG1 RPAS	MOD (on order for No 13 Sqn, RAF)
	Z....	General Atomics Protector RG1 RPAS	MOD (on order for No 13 Sqn, RAF)
	Z....	General Atomics Protector RG1 RPAS	MOD (on order for No 13 Sqn, RAF)
	Z....	General Atomics Protector RG1 RPAS	MOD (on order for No 13 Sqn, RAF)
	Z....	General Atomics Protector RG1 RPAS	MOD (on order for No 13 Sqn, RAF)
	Z....	General Atomics Protector RG1 RPAS	MOD (on order for No 13 Sqn, RAF)
	Z....	General Atomics Protector RG1 RPAS	MOD (on order for No 13 Sqn, RAF)
	Z....	General Atomics Protector RG1 RPAS	MOD (on order for No 13 Sqn, RAF)
	Z....	General Atomics Protector RG1 RPAS	MOD (on order for No 13 Sqn, RAF)
	Z....	General Atomics Protector RG1 RPAS	MOD (on order for No 13 Sqn, RAF)
	Z....	General Atomics Protector RG1 RPAS	MOD (on order for No 13 Sqn, RAF)
	Z....	General Atomics Protector RG1 RPAS	MOD (on order for No 13 Sqn, RAF)
	.....	Airbus H135 Juno HT1 (D-HCBG/G-CMIR)	MOD, stored Shawbury, Shropshire (canx AAC order)
	.....	Airbus H135 Juno HT1 (D-HCBH/G-CMIS)	MOD, stored Shawbury, Shropshire (canx AAC order)
	.....	Airbus H135 Juno HT1 (D-HCBM/G-CMIT)	MOD, stored Shawbury, Shropshire (canx AAC order)
	.....	Airbus H135 Juno HT1 (D-HCBJ/G-CMIU)	MOD, stored Kidlington, Oxon (canx AAC order)
	.....	Airbus H135 Juno HT1 (D-HCBE/G-CMIV)	MOD, stored Kidlington, Oxon (canx AAC order)

Serial	Type (code/other identity)	Owner/operator, location or fate	Notes
G-BYUB	Grob G.115E Tutor T1	Babcock/Cambridge UAS/East Midlands Universities AS/ University of London AS/No 115 Sqn, Wittering, Cambs	
G-BYUC	Grob G.115E Tutor T1	Babcock/Cambridge UAS/East Midlands Universities AS/ University of London AS/No 115 Sqn, Wittering, Cambs	
G-BYUD	Grob G.115E Tutor T1	Babcock/Yorkshire Universities AS, Leeming, N. Yorks	
G-BYUE	Grob G.115E Tutor T1	Babcock/Cambridge UAS/East Midlands Universities AS/ University of London AS/No 115 Sqn, Wittering, Cambs	
G-BYUF	Grob G.115E Tutor T1	Babcock/Oxford UAS, Benson, Oxon	
G-BYUH	Grob G.115E Tutor T1	Babcock/Bristol UAS/Southampton UAS, Boscombe Down, Wilts	
G-BYUI	Grob G.115E Tutor T1	Babcock, stored Boscombe Down, Wilts	
G-BYUJ	Grob G.115E Tutor T1	Babcock/Universities of Glasgow & Strathclyde AS, Glasgow, Scotland	
G-BYUK	Grob G.115E Tutor T1	Babcock/Bristol UAS/Southampton UAS, Boscombe Down, Wilts	
G-BYUL	Grob G.115E Tutor T1	Babcock/Liverpool UAS/Manchester and Salford Universities AS, Woodvale, Merseyside	
G-BYUM	Grob G.115E Tutor T1	Babcock/Southern Sailplanes, Membury, Wilts (maint.)	
G-BYUN	Grob G.115E Tutor T1	Babcock/No 3 FTS/No 16 Sqn, Cranwell, Lincs	
G-BYUO	Grob G.115E Tutor T1	Babcock/No 3 FTS/No 16 Sqn, Cranwell, Lincs	
G-BYUR	Grob G.115E Tutor T1	Babcock/East of Scotland UAS, Leuchars, Scotland	
G-BYUS	Grob G.115E Tutor T1	Babcock/East of Scotland UAS, Leuchars, Scotland	
G-BYUU	Grob G.115E Tutor T1	Babcock/Cambridge UAS/East Midlands Universities AS/ University of London AS/No 115 Sqn, Wittering, Cambs	
G-BYUV	Grob G.115E Tutor T1	Babcock/Bristol UAS/Southampton UAS, Boscombe Down, Wilts	
G-BYUW	Grob G.115E Tutor T1	Babcock/No 3 FTS/No 16 Sqn, Cranwell, Lincs	
G-BYUX	Grob G.115E Tutor T1	Babcock/No 3 FTS/No 16 Sqn, Cranwell, Lincs	
G-BYUY	Grob G.115E Tutor T1	Babcock/Cambridge UAS/East Midlands Universities AS/ University of London AS/No 115 Sqn, Wittering, Cambs	
G-BYUZ	Grob G.115E Tutor T1	Babcock/No 3 FTS/No 16 Sqn, Cranwell, Lincs	
G-BYVA	Grob G.115E Tutor T1	Babcock/Bristol UAS/Southampton UAS, Boscombe Down, Wilts	
G-BYVB	Grob G.115E Tutor T1	Babcock/University of Wales AS, St Athan, Wales	
G-BYVC	Grob G.115E Tutor T1	Babcock/Yorkshire Universities AS, Leeming, N. Yorks	
G-BYVD	Grob G.115E Tutor T1	Babcock/Southern Sailplanes, Membury, Wilts (maint.)	
G-BYVE	Grob G.115E Tutor T1	Babcock/Cambridge UAS/East Midlands Universities AS/ University of London AS/No 115 Sqn, Wittering, Cambs	
G-BYVF	Grob G.115E Tutor T1	Babcock/RN No 727 NAS, Yeovilton, Somerset	
G-BYVG	Grob G.115E Tutor T1	Babcock/Southern Sailplanes, Membury, Wilts (maint.)	
G-BYVH	Grob G.115E Tutor T1	Babcock/RN No 727 NAS, Yeovilton, Somerset	
G-BYVI	Grob G.115E Tutor T1	Babcock/Liverpool UAS/Manchester and Salford Universities AS, Woodvale, Merseyside	
G-BYVK	Grob G.115E Tutor T1	Babcock/RN No 727 NAS, Yeovilton, Somerset	
G-BYVL	Grob G.115E Tutor T1	Babcock/University of Birmingham AS, Cosford, Shropshire	
G-BYVM	Grob G.115E Tutor T1	Babcock/Cambridge UAS/East Midlands Universities AS/ University of London AS/No 115 Sqn, Wittering, Cambs	
G-BYVO	Grob G.115E Tutor T1	Babcock/Liverpool UAS/Manchester and Salford Universities AS, Woodvale, Merseyside	
G-BYVP	Grob G.115E Tutor T1	Babcock/Liverpool UAS/Manchester and Salford Universities AS, Woodvale, Merseyside	
G-BYVR	Grob G.115E Tutor T1	Babcock/Universities of Glasgow & Strathclyde AS, Glasgow, Scotland	
G-BYVU	Grob G.115E Tutor T1	Babcock/Army Flying Grading, Middle Wallop, Hants	
G-BYVW	Grob G.115E Tutor T1	Babcock/University of Birmingham AS, Cosford, Shropshire	
G-BYVY	Grob G.115E Tutor T1	Babcock/Southern Sailplanes, Membury, Wilts (maint.)	
G-BYVZ	Grob G.115E Tutor T1	Babcock/Army Flying Grading, Middle Wallop, Hants	
G-BYWA	Grob G.115E Tutor T1	Babcock/Yorkshire Universities AS, Leeming, N. Yorks	
G-BYWB	Grob G.115E Tutor T1	Babcock/Bristol UAS/Southampton UAS, Boscombe Down, Wilts	
G-BYWD	Grob G.115E Tutor T1	Babcock/University of Birmingham AS, Cosford, Shropshire	
G-BYWF	Grob G.115E Tutor T1	Babcock/Bristol UAS/Southampton UAS, Boscombe Down, Wilts	
G-BYWG	Grob G.115E Tutor T1	Babcock/University of Birmingham AS, Cosford, Shropshire	

Aircraft in UK Military Service with Civil Registrations

Notes	Serial	Type (code/other identity)	Owner/operator, location or fate
	G-BYWH	Grob G.115E Tutor T1	Babcock/Cambridge UAS/East Midlands Universities AS/ University of London AS/No 115 Sqn, Wittering, Cambs
	G-BYWI	Grob G.115E Tutor T1	Babcock/Northern Ireland Universities AS, Aldergrove, NI
	G-BYWK	Grob G.115E Tutor T1	Babcock/University of Wales AS, St Athan, Wales
	G-BYWL	Grob G.115E Tutor T1	Babcock/Bristol UAS/Southampton UAS, Boscombe Down
	G-BYWM	Grob G.115E Tutor T1	Babcock/RN No 727 NAS, Yeovilton, Somerset
	G-BYWO	Grob G.115E Tutor T1	Babcock/Cambridge UAS/East Midlands Universities AS/ University of London AS/No 115 Sqn, Wittering, Cambs
	G-BYWR	Grob G.115E Tutor T1	Babcock/University of Birmingham AS, Cosford, Shropshire
	G-BYWS	Grob G.115E Tutor T1	Babcock/Northern Ireland Universities AS, Aldergrove, NI
	G-BYWU	Grob G.115E Tutor T1	Babcock/University of Birmingham AS, Cosford, Shropshire
	G-BYWV	Grob G.115E Tutor T1	Babcock/Cambridge UAS/East Midlands Universities AS/ University of London AS/No 115 Sqn, Wittering, Cambs
	G-BYWW	Grob G.115E Tutor T1	Babcock/Bristol UAS/Southampton UAS, Boscombe Down, Wilts
	G-BYWX	Grob G.115E Tutor T1	Babcock/Bristol UAS/Southampton UAS, Boscombe Down, Wilts
	G-BYWY	Grob G.115E Tutor T1	Babcock/University of Birmingham AS, Cosford, Shropshire
	G-BYWZ	Grob G.115E Tutor T1	Babcock/Southern Sailplanes, Membury, Wilts (maint.)
	G-BYXA	Grob G.115E Tutor T1	Babcock/Northern Ireland Universities AS, Aldergrove, NI
	G-BYXC	Grob G.115E Tutor T1	Babcock/No 3 FTS/No 16 Sqn, Cranwell, Lincs
	G-BYXD	Grob G.115E Tutor T1	Babcock, stored Boscombe Down, Wilts
	G-BYXE	Grob G.115E Tutor T1	Babcock/No 3 FTS/No 16 Sqn, Cranwell, Lincs
	G-BYXF	Grob G.115E Tutor T1	Babcock/Southern Sailplanes, Membury, Wilts (maint.)
	G-BYXG	Grob G.115E Tutor T1	Babcock/Bristol UAS/Southampton UAS, Boscombe Down, Wilts
	G-BYXH	Grob G.115E Tutor T1	Babcock/Cambridge UAS/East Midlands Universities AS/ University of London AS/No 115 Sqn, Wittering, Cambs
	G-BYXI	Grob G.115E Tutor T1	Babcock/Army Flying Grading, Middle Wallop, Hants
	G-BYXJ	Grob G.115E Tutor T1	Babcock/Yorkshire Universities AS, Leeming, N. Yorks
	G-BYXK	Grob G.115E Tutor T1	Babcock/RN No 727 NAS, Yeovilton, Somerset
	G-BYXL	Grob G.115E Tutor T1	Babcock/University of Wales AS, St Athan, Wales
	G-BYXM	Grob G.115E Tutor T1	Babcock/Cambridge UAS/East Midlands Universities AS/ University of London AS/No 115 Sqn, Wittering, Cambs
	G-BYXO	Grob G.115E Tutor T1	Babcock/Liverpool UAS/Manchester and Salford Universities AS, Woodvale, Merseyside
	G-BYXP	Grob G.115E Tutor T1	Babcock/Universities of Glasgow & Strathclyde AS, Glasgow, Scotland
	G-BYXS	Grob G.115E Tutor T1	Babcock/RN No 727 NAS, Yeovilton, Somerset
	G-BYXT	Grob G.115E Tutor T1	Babcock/Yorkshire Universities AS, Leeming, N. Yorks
	G-BYXX	Grob G.115E Tutor T1	Babcock/East of Scotland UAS, Leuchars, Scotland
	G-BYXZ	Grob G.115E Tutor T1	Babcock/Cambridge UAS/East Midlands Universities AS/ University of London AS/No 115 Sqn, Wittering, Cambs
	G-BYYA	Grob G.115E Tutor T1	Babcock/Northumbrian Universities AS, Leeming, N. Yorks
	G-BYYB	Grob G.115E Tutor T1	Babcock/Liverpool UAS/Manchester and Salford Universities AS, Woodvale, Merseyside
	G-CGKD	Grob G.115E Tutor T1EA	Babcock/Cambridge UAS/East Midlands Universities AS/ University of London AS/No 115 Sqn, Wittering, Cambs
	G-CGKE	Grob G.115E Tutor T1EA	Babcock/Oxford UAS, Benson, Oxon
	G-CGKG	Grob G.115E Tutor T1EA	Babcock/Oxford UAS, Benson, Oxon
	G-CGKH	Grob G.115E Tutor T1EA	Babcock/Oxford UAS, Benson, Oxon
	G-CGKK	Grob G.115E Tutor T1	Babcock/Oxford UAS, Benson, Oxon
	G-CGKL	Grob G.115E Tutor T1	Babcock/Bristol UAS/Southampton UAS, Boscombe Down, Wilts
	G-CGKN	Grob G.115E Tutor T1EA	Babcock/Oxford UAS, Benson, Oxon
	G-CGKP	Grob G.115E Tutor T1EA	Babcock/Oxford UAS, Benson, Oxon
	G-CGKR	Grob G.115E Tutor T1EA	Babcock/Southern Sailplanes, Membury, Wilts (maint.)
	G-CGKS	Grob G.115E Tutor T1EA	Babcock/Oxford UAS, Benson, Oxon
	G-CGKU	Grob G.115E Tutor T1EA	Babcock/Oxford UAS, Benson, Oxon
	G-CGKW	Grob G.115E Tutor T1EA	Babcock/Army Flying Grading, Middle Wallop, Hants
	G-DAYP	Hawker Beechcraft Super King Air 350C	MOD/Raytheon, Hawarden, Flintshire, Wales (for conversion to Shadow R2 ZZ505)

Serial	Type (code/other identity)	Owner/operator, location or fate	Notes
G-DKNA	Aero L-159E ALCA (6034)	Draken International, Teesside International Airport, Co. Durham	
G-DKNB	Aero L-159E ALCA (6019/N264EM)	Draken International, Teesside International Airport, Co. Durham	
G-DKNC	Aero L-159E ALCA (6020/N265EM)	Draken International, Teesside International Airport, Co. Durham	
G-DKND	Aero L-159E ALCA (6039/N267EM)	Draken International, Teesside International Airport, Co. Durham	
G-DKNE	Aero L-159E ALCA (6029/N269EM)	Draken International, Teesside International Airport, Co. Durham	
G-DKNF	Aero L-159E ALCA (6030/N259EM)	Draken International, Teesside International Airport, Co. Durham	
G-DRAK	Canadair Challenger 604 (N420AJ)	Draken International, Bournemouth, Hants	
G-ETPA	Pilatus PC-21 (HB-HYX)	QinetiQ/ETPS, MOD Boscombe Down, Wilts	
G-ETPB	Pilatus PC-21 (HB-HYY)	QinetiQ/ETPS, MOD Boscombe Down, Wilts	
G-ETPC	Grob G.120TP-A (D-ETQI)	QinetiQ/ETPS, MOD Boscombe Down, Wilts	
G-ETPD	Grob G.120TP-A (D-ETIQ)	QinetiQ/ETPS, MOD Boscombe Down, Wilts	
G-ETPE	Airbus Helicopters H.125	QinetiQ/ETPS, MOD Boscombe Down, Wilts	
G-ETPF	Airbus Helicopters H.125	QinetiQ/ETPS, MOD Boscombe Down, Wilts	
G-ETPG	Airbus Helicopters H.125	QinetiQ/ETPS, MOD Boscombe Down, Wilts	
G-ETPH	Airbus Helicopters H.125	QinetiQ/ETPS, MOD Boscombe Down, Wilts	
G-ETPI	Agusta A109E Power Elite (G-CFVB/QQ100)	QinetiQ/ETPS, MOD Boscombe Down, Wilts	
G-ETPJ	Agusta A109E Power Elite (G-ESLH/ZE416)	QinetiQ/ETPS, MOD Boscombe Down, Wilts	
G-ETPK	BAe RJ.70ER (G-BVRJ/QQ102)	QinetiQ/ETPS, MOD Boscombe Down, Wilts	
G-ETPL	BAe RJ.100 (G-BZAY/QQ101)	QinetiQ/ETPS, MOD Boscombe Down, Wilts	
G-ETPM	Diamond DA.42M-NG Twin Star (G-LTPA/QQ103)	QinetiQ/ETPS, MOD Boscombe Down, Wilts	
G-ETPN	Agusta A109S Grand (N519CG)	QinetiQ/ETPS, MOD Boscombe Down, Wilts	
G-ETPO	Agusta A109S Grand (XA-ANU)	QinetiQ/ETPS, MOD Boscombe Down, Wilts	
G-ETPP	AgustaWestland AW139 (B-725D)	QinetiQ/ETPS, MOD Boscombe Down, Wilts	
G-FFRA	Dassault Falcon 20DC (N902FR)	Draken International, Teesside International Airport	
G-FRAD	Dassault Falcon 20E (9M-BDK)	Draken International, Bournemouth, Hants	
G-FRAF	Dassault Falcon 20E (N911FR)	Draken International, Bournemouth, Hants	
G-FRAH	Dassault Falcon 20DC (N900FR)	Draken International, Bournemouth, Hants	
G-FRAI	Dassault Falcon 20E (N901FR)	Draken International, Bournemouth, Hants	
G-FRAJ	Dassault Falcon 20E (N903FR)	Draken International, Teesside International Airport	
G-FRAK	Dassault Falcon 20DC (N905FR)	Draken International, Bournemouth, Hants	
G-FRAL	Dassault Falcon 20DC (N904FR)	Draken International, Bournemouth, Hants	
G-FRAP	Dassault Falcon 20DC (N908FR)	Draken International, Teesside International Airport	
G-FRAR	Dassault Falcon 20DC (N909FR)	Draken International, Bournemouth, Hants	
G-FRAS	Dassault Falcon 20C (117501)	Draken International, Bournemouth, Hants	
G-FRAT	Dassault Falcon 20C (117502)	Draken International, Bournemouth, Hants	
G-FRAU	Dassault Falcon 20C (117504)	Draken International, Teesside International Airport	
G-FRAW	Dassault Falcon 20ECM (117507)	Draken International, Teesside International Airport	
G-FRSB	Dassault Falcon 20F (N459SB)	Draken International, Bournemouth, Hants	
G-GBNI	Airbus A.321-251NX	Titan Airways/UK Government, Stansted, Essex	
G-RNGS	Airbus Helicopters H.145	QinetiQ/BUTEC, Kyle of Lochalsh, Scotland	
G-XATW	Airbus A.321-251NX	Titan Airways/UK Government, Stansted, Essex	
G-ZABH	Dassault Envoy IV CC.1 (Falcon 900LX) (F-WWVF)	MOD/Centreline, No 32(The Royal) Sqn, RAF Northolt, Gtr London	
G-ZAHS	Dassault Envoy IV CC.1 (Falcon 900LX) (F-WWVE)	MOD/Centreline, No 32(The Royal) Sqn, RAF Northolt, Gtr London	

1764M/K4972	7473M/XE946	7829M/XH992	8018M/XN344
2015M/K5600	7491M/WT569	7839M/WV781	8019M/WZ869
2292M/K8203	7496M/WT612	7841M/WV783	8021M/XL824
2361M/K6035	7499M/WT555	7851M/WZ706	8027M/XM555
3118M/H5199/(BK892)	7510M/WT694	7854M/XM191	8032M/XH837
3858M/X7688	7525M/WT619	7855M/XK416	8034M/*XL554*/ (XL703)
4354M/BL614	7530M/WT648	7859M/XP283	8041M/XF690
4552M/T5298	7532M/WT651	7861M/*XL738*/(XM565)	8043M/XF836
4887M/JN768	7533M/WT680	7862M/XR246	8046M/XL770
5377M/EP120	7544M/WN904	7863M/*XP248*	8049M/WE168
5405M/LF738	7548M/PS915	7864M/XP244	8050M/XG329
5466M/*BN230*/(LF751)	7556M/WK584	7865M/TX226	8052M/WH166
5690M/MK356	7564M/XE982	7866M/XH278	8054AM/XM410
5718M/BM597	7570M/XD674	7868M/WZ736	8054BM/XM417
5758M/DG202	7582M/WP190	7869M/WK935	8055AM/XM402
6457M/ML427	7583M/WP185	7872M/*WZ826*/(XD826)	8055BM/XM404
6490M/LA255	7602M/WE600	7881M/WD413	8056M/XG337
6640M/RM694	7605M/WS692	7882M/XD525	8057M/XR243
6850M/TE184	7606M/*XF688*/ (WV562)	7883M/XT150	8063M/WT536
6946M/RW388	7607M/TJ138	7887M/XD375	8070M/EP120
6948M/DE673	7615M/WV679	7891M/XM693	8072M/PK624
6960M/MT847	7616M/WW388	7894M/XD818	8073M/TB252
7008M/EE549	7618M/WW442	7895M/WF784	8075M/RW382
7014M/N6720	7622M/WV606	7898M/XP854	8078M/XM351
7015M/NL985	7631M/VX185	7900M/WA576	8080M/XM480
7035M/*K2567*/(DE306)	7641M/XA634	7906M/WH132	8081M/XM468
7060M/VF301	7645M/WD293	7917M/WA591	8082M/XM409
7090M/EE531	7648M/XF785	7930M/WH301	8086M/TB752
7118M/LA198	7673M/WV332	7931M/RD253	8092M/WK654
7119M/LA226	7689M/WW450	7932M/WZ744	8094M/WT520
7150M/PK683	7696M/WV493	7933M/XR220	8097M/XN492
7154M/WB188	7698M/WV499	7937M/WS843	8101M/WH984
7174M/VX272	7704M/TW536	7938M/XH903	8102M/WT486
7175M/VV106	7705M/WL505	7939M/XD596	8106M/WR982
7200M/VT812	7706M/WB584	7940M/XL764	8114M/WL798
7241M/TE311/*(MK178)*	7709M/WT933	7955M/XH767	8117M/WR974
7243M/TE462	7711M/PS915	7957M/XF545	8118M/WZ549
7245M/RW382	7712M/WK281	7960M/WS726	8119M/WR971
7246M/TD248	7715M/XK724	7961M/WS739	8121M/XM474
7256M/TB752	7716M/WS776	7964M/WS760	8124M/WZ572
7257M/TB252	7718M/WA577	7965M/WS792	8128M/WH775
7261M/VZ568	7719M/WK277	7967M/WS788	8130M/WH798
7279M/TB752	7726M/XM373	7969M/WS840	8131M/WT507
7281M/TB252	7741M/VZ477	7971M/XK699	8140M/XJ571
7288M/PK724	7750M/*WK864*/(WL168)	7973M/WS807	8142M/XJ560
7293M/*TB675*/(RW393)	7751M/WL131	7979M/XM529	8147M/XR526
7323M/VV217	7755M/WG760	7980M/XM561	8151M/WV795
7325M/R5868	7759M/PK664	7982M/XH892	8153M/WV903
7326M/VN485	7761M/XH318	7983M/XD506	8154M/WV908
7362M/475081/(VP546)	7762M/XE670	7984M/XN597	8155M/WV797
7416M/WN907	7764M/XH318	7986M/WG777	8156M/XE339
7421M/WT660	7770M/*XF506*/(WT746)	7988M/XL149	8158M/XE369
7422M/WT684	7793M/XG523	7990M/XD452	8162M/WM913
7428M/WK198	7798M/XH783	7997M/XG452	8164M/*WN105*/(WF299)
7432M/WZ724	7806M/TA639	7998M/*XM515*/(XD515)	8165M/WH791
7438M/*18671*/(WP905)	7809M/XA699	8005M/WG768	8169M/WH364
7443M/WX853	7816M/WG763	8009M/XG518	8171M/XT895
7458M/WX905	7817M/TX214	8010M/XG547	8173M/XN685
7464M/XA564	7825M/WK991	8012M/VS562	8176M/WH791
7470M/XA553	7827M/XA917	8017M/XL762	8177M/WM224

8179M/XN928	8392M/SL674	8535M/XN776	8706M/XF383
8183M/*XN972*/(XN962)	8394M/WG422	8538M/XN781	8708M/XF509
8184M/WT520	8395M/WF408	8545M/XN726	8709M/XG209
8186M/WR977	8396M/XK740	8546M/XN728	8710M/XG274
8187M/WH791	8399M/WR539	8548M/WT507	8711M/XG290
8189M/*WD615* (WD646)	8401M/XP686	8549M/WT534	8713M/XG225
8190M/XJ918	8406M/XP831	8554M/TG511	8718M/XX396
8192M/XR658	8407M/XP585	8561M/XS100	8719M/XT257
8198M/WT339	8408M/XS186	8563M/*XX822*/(XW563)	8721M/XP354
8203M/XD377	8409M/XS209	8565M/*349*/(E-408)	8724M/XW923
8205M/XN819	8410M/XR662	8566M/XV279	8726M/XP299
8206M/WG419	8413M/XM192	8573M/XM708	8727M/XR486
8208M/WG303	8414M/XM173	8575M/XP542	8728M/WT532
8209M/WG418	8417M/XM144	8576M/XP502	8729M/WJ815
8210M/WG471	8422M/XM169	8578M/XR534	8732M/XJ729
8211M/WK570	8427M/XM172	8581M/WJ775	8733M/XL318
8213M/WK626	8429M/XH592	8582M/XE874	8736M/XF375
8215M/WP869	8434M/XM411	8583M/BAPC 94	8739M/XH170
8216M/WP927	8436M/XN554	8585M/XE670	8740M/WE173
8218M/WB645	8437M/WG362	8586M/XE643	8741M/XW329
8229M/XM355	8439M/WZ846	8587M/XP677	8743M/WD790
8230M/XM362	8440M/WD935	8588M/XR681	8746M/XH171
8234M/XN458	8442M/XP411	8589M/XR700	8749M/XH537
8235M/XN549	8452M/XK885	8590M/XM191	8751M/XT255
8236M/XP573	8453M/XP745	8591M/XA813	8753M/WL795
8237M/XS179	8458M/XP672	8595M/XH278	8762M/WH740
*8238*M/XS180	8459M/XR650	8598M/WP270	8764M/XP344
8338M/XS180	8460M/XP680	8600M/XX761	8768M/A-522
8342M/WP848	8462M/XX477	8602M/*PF179*/(XR541)	8769M/A-528
8344M/WH960	8463M/XP355	8604M/XS104	8770M/XL623
8350M/WH840	8464M/XJ758	8606M/XP530	8771M/XM602
8352M/XN632	8465M/W1048	8608M/XP540	8772M/WR960
8355M/KN645	8466M/L-866	8610M/XL502	8778M/XM598
8357M/WK576	8467M/WP912	8611M/WF128	8779M/XM607
8359M/WF825	8468M/MM5701/(BT474)	8620M/XP534	8780M/WK102
8361M/WB670	8469M/100503	8621M/XR538	8781M/WE982
8362M/WG477	8470M/584219	8624M/*XR991*/(XS102)	8782M/XH136
8364M/WG464	8471M/701152	8627M/XP558	8785M/XS642
8365M/XK421	8472M/120227/(VN679)	8628M/XJ380	8786M/XN495
8366M/XG454	8473M/WP190	8630M/WG362	8789M/XK970
8367M/XG474	8474M/494083	8631M/XR574	8791M/XP329
8368M/XF926	8475M/360043/(PJ876)	8633M/3W-17/MK732	8792M/XP345
8369M/WE139	8476M/24	8634M/WP314	8793M/XP346
8370M/N1671	8477M/4101/(DG200)	8640M/XR977	8794M/XP398
8371M/XA847	8478M/10639	8642M/XR537	8796M/XK943
8372M/K8042	8479M/730301	8645M/XD163	8799M/WV787
8373M/P2617	8481M/191614	8648M/XK526	8800M/XG226
8375M/NX611	8482M/112372/(VK893)	8653M/XS120	8805M/XV722
8376M/RF398	8483M/420430	8656M/XP405	8807M/XL587
8377M/R9125	8484M/5439	8657M/VZ634	8810M/XJ825
8378M/*T9707*	8485M/997	8661M/XJ727	8816M/XX734
8379M/DG590	8486M/BAPC 99	8666M/XE793	8818M/XK527
8380M/Z7197	8487M/J-1172	8672M/XP351	8820M/VP952
8382M/VR930	8488M/WL627	8673M/XD165	8822M/VP957
8383M/K9942	8491M/WJ880	8676M/XL577	8828M/XS587
8384M/X4590	8493M/XR571	8679M/XF526	8830M/*N-294*/(XF515)
8385M/N5912	8494M/XP557	8680M/XR527	8831M/XG160
8386M/NV778	8501M/XP640	8681M/XG164	8832M/*XG168*/(XG172)
8387M/T6296	8502M/XP686	8682M/XP404	8833M/XL569
8388M/XL993	8508M/XS218	8693M/WH863	8834M/XL572
8389M/VX573	8509M/XT141	8702M/XG196	8836M/XL592
8390M/SL542	8514M/XS176	8703M/VW453	8838M/*34037*/(429356)

8839M/XG194	8950M/XX956	9076M/XV808	9198M/XS641
8841M/XE606	8951M/XX727	9078M/XV753	9199M/XW290
8853M/XT277	8953M/XX959	9080M/ZE350	9201M/ZD667
8855M/XT284	8954M/XZ384	9086M/ZE352	9203M/*3066*
8857M/XW544	8955M/XX110	9087M/XX753	9205M/*E449*
8858M/XW541	8957M/XN582	9090M/XW353	9206M/F6314
8863M/XG154	8961M/XS925	9091M/XW434	9207M/8417/18
8867M/XK532	8967M/XV263	9092M/XH669	9208M/F938
8868M/WH775	8969M/XR753	9093M/WK124	9210M/MF628
8869M/WH957	8972M/XR754	9095M/XW547	9211M/733682
8870M/WH964	8973M/XS922	9096M/WV322	9212M/*KL216*/(45-49295)
8871M/WJ565	8974M/XM473	9098M/XV406	9213M/N5182
8873M/XR453	8975M/XW917	9110M/XX736	9215M/XL164
8874M/XE597	8976M/XZ630	9111M/XW421	9216M/XL190
8875M/XE624	8978M/XX837	9117M/XV161	9217M/ZH257
8876M/XA312	8984M/XN551	9119M/XW303	9218M/XL563
8880M/XF435	8985M/WK127	9120M/XW419	9219M/XZ971
8881M/XG254	8986M/XV261	9122M/XZ997	9222M/XZ968
8883M/XX946	8987M/XM358	9123M/XT773	9224M/XL568
8884M/VX275	8990M/XM419	9125M/XW410	9225M/XX885
8885M/XW922	8995M/XM425	9127M/XW432	9226M/XV865
8886M/XA243	8996M/XM414	9130M/XW327	9227M/XB812
8888M/XA231	8997M/XX669	9131M/*DD931*	9229M/ZA678
8889M/XN239	8998M/XT864	9132M/XX977	9233M/XZ431
8890M/WT532	9002M/XW763	9133M/*413573*	9234M/XV864
8895M/XX746	9003M/XZ390	9134M/XT288	9236M/WV318
8896M/XX821	9004M/XZ370	9136M/XT891	9237M/XF445
8897M/XX969	9005M/XZ374	9137M/XN579	9238M/ZA717
8898M/XX119	9006M/XX967	9140M/XZ287	9239M/7198/18
8899M/XX756	9007M/XX968	9141M/XV118	9241M/XS639
8900M/XZ368	9008M/XX140	9143M/XN589	9242M/XH672
8901M/XZ383	9009M/XX763	9146M/XW299	9248M/WB627
8902M/XX739	9010M/XX764	9148M/XW436	9249M/WV396
8903M/XX747	9011M/XM412	9149M/XW375	9251M/XX744
8905M/XX975	9012M/XN494	9150M/*FX760*	9252M/XX722
8906M/XX976	9014M/XN584	9151M/XT907	9254M/XX965
8907M/XZ371	9015M/XW320	9152M/XV424	9255M/XZ375
8908M/XZ382	9017M/ZE449	9153M/XW360	9257M/XX962
8909M/XV784	9019M/XX824	9154M/XW321	9258M/XW265
8910M/XL160	9020M/XX825	9155M/WL679	9259M/XS710
8918M/XX109	9021M/XX826	9162M/XZ991	9260M/XS734
8919M/XT486	9026M/XP629	9163M/XV415	9261M/*W2068*
8920M/XT469	9027M/XP556	9166M/XW323	9262M/XZ358
8921M/XT466	9032M/XR673	9167M/XV744	9263M/XW267
8922M/XT467	9033M/XS181	9168M/XZ132	9264M/XS735
8923M/XX819	9036M/XM350	9169M/XW547	9265M/WK585
8924M/XP701	9038M/XV810	9170M/XZ994	9266M/XZ119
8925M/XP706	9039M/XN586	9172M/XW304	9267M/XW269
8931M/XV779	9040M/XZ138	9173M/XW418	9268M/XR529
8932M/XR718	9041M/XW763	9174M/XZ131	9269M/XT914
8934M/XR749	9042M/XL954	9175M/P1344	9270M/XZ145
8935M/XR713	9044M/XS177	9176M/XW430	9272M/XS486
8937M/XX751	9047M/XW409	9179M/XW309	9273M/XS726
8938M/WV746	9048M/XM403	9180M/XW311	9275M/XS729
8941M/XT456	9049M/XW404	9181M/XW358	9277M/XT601
8942M/XN185	9052M/WJ717	9185M/XZ987	9278M/XS643
8943M/XE799	9059M/ZE360	9187M/XW405	9279M/XT681
8944M/WZ791	9066M/XV582	9188M/XW364	9281M/XZ146
8945M/XX818	9067M/XV586	9194M/XW420	9283M/XZ322
8946M/XZ389	9070M/XV581	9195M/XW330	9284M/ZA267
8947M/XX726	9073M/XW924	9196M/XW370	9285M/XR806
8949M/XX743	9075M/XV752	9197M/*XX530*/(XX637)	9286M/XT905

9287M/WP962	9301M/XZ941	9318M/ZA360	9331M/XW852
9288M/XX520	9302M/ZD462	9319M/XR516	9332M/XZ935
9289M/XX665	9303M/XV709	9320M/XX153	9336M/ZA407
9290M/XX626	9306M/XX979	9321M/XZ367	9337M/ZA774
9292M/XW892	9308M/ZD932	9322M/ZB686	9338M/ZA325
9293M/XX830	9310M/ZA355	9323M/XV643	9339M/ZA323
9294M/XX655	9311M/ZA475	9324M/XV659	9340M/XX745
9295M/XV497	9314M/ZA320	9326M/XV653	9341M/ZA357
9298M/ZE340	9315M/ZA319	9328M/ZD607	9342M/XR498
9299M/XW870	9316M/ZA399	9329M/ZD578	9343M/XR506
9300M/XX431	9317M/ZA450	9330M/ZB684	9344M/XV706

Early prototype Tornado XX946 was used for many years as a trials aircraft, and is now one of two examples of the type that can be found with the Yorkshire Air Museum at Elvington. *SRS*

Deck Letters	Vessel Name and Pennant No.	Vessel Type and Unit
AB	HMS *Albion* (L14)	Assault
AS	RFA *Argus* (A135)	Aviation Training ship
AY	HMS *Argyll* (F231)	Type 23
BK	HMS *Bulwark* (L15)	Assault
CB	RFA *Cardigan Bay* (L3009)	Landing ship
CU	RNAS Culdrose (HMS *Seahawk*)	
DA	HMS *Daring* (D32)	Type 45
DF	HMS *Defender* (D36)	Type 45
DM	HMS *Diamond* (D34)	Type 45
DN	HMS *Dragon* (D35)	Type 45
DT	HMS *Dauntless* (D33)	Type 45
DU	HMS *Duncan* (D37)	Type 45
FA	RFA *Fort Austin* (A386)	Support ship
FE	RFA *Fort Rosalie* (A385)	Support ship
FH	HMS *Forth* (P222)	Offshore Patrol Vessel
FV	RFA *Fort Victoria* (A387)	Auxiliary Oiler
IR	HMS *Iron Duke* (F234)	Type 23
KT	HMS *Kent* (F78)	Type 23
LA	HMS *Lancaster* (F229)	Type 23
MB	RFA *Mounts Bay* (L3008)	Landing ship
MM	HMS *Monmouth* (F235)	Type 23
MR	HMS *Montrose* (F236)	Type 23
MY	HMS *Medway* (P223)	Offshore Patrol Vessel
NL	HMS *Northumberland* (F238)	Type 23
P	HMS *Prince of Wales* (R09)	Aircraft carrier
Q	HMS *Queen Elizabeth* (R08)	Aircraft carrier
PD	HMS *Portland* (F79)	Type 23
RM	HMS *Richmond* (F239)	Type 23
SB	HMS *St Albans* (F83)	Type 23
SM	HMS *Somerset* (F82)	Type 23
SU	HMS *Sutherland* (F81)	Type 23
TF	RFA *Tideforce* (A136)	Fleet tanker
TR	RFA *Tiderace* (A137)	Fleet tanker
TS	RFA *Tidespring* (A138)	Fleet tanker
TU	RFA *Tidesurge* (A139)	Fleet tanker
VL	RNAS Yeovilton (HMS *Heron*)	
WK	RFA *Wave Knight* (A389)	Fleet tanker
WM	HMS *Westminster* (F237)	Type 23
WR	RFA *Wave Ruler* (A390)	Fleet tanker
YB	RFA *Lyme Bay* (L3007)	Landing ship
-	HMS *Protector* (A173)	Ice patrol
-	HMS *Spey* (P234)	Offshore Patrol Vessel
-	HMS *Tamar* (P233)	Offshore Patrol Vessel
-	HMS *Trent* (P224)	Offshore Patrol Vessel

RN CODE – SQUADRON – BASE – AIRCRAFT CROSS-CHECK

Deck/Base Code Numbers	Letters	Unit	Location	Aircraft Type(s)
010 — 015	CU	820 NAS	Culdrose	Merlin HM2
264 — 274	CU	814 NAS	Culdrose	Merlin HM2
580 — 588	CU	824 NAS	Culdrose	Merlin HM2

Note that only the 'last two' digits of the Code are generally worn and indeed increasingly few helicopters now carry codes.

This table gives brief details of the markings worn by aircraft of RAF squadrons. While this may help to identify the operator of a particular machine, it may not always give the true picture. For example, from time to time aircraft are loaned to other units while others wear squadron marks but are actually operated on a pool basis. Squadron badges are usually located on the front fuselage.

Squadron	Type(s) operated	Base(s)	Distinguishing marks & other comments
No 1(F) Sqn	Typhoon FGR4	RAF Lossiemouth	Badge (on tail): A red 1 with yellow wings on a white background, flanked in red. Roundel is flanked by two white chevrons, edged in red.
No 2(AC) Sqn/ II(AC) Sqn	Typhoon FGR4	RAF Lossiemouth	Badge: A wake knot on a white circular background flanked on either side by black and white triangles. Tail fin has a black stripe with white triangles and the badge repeated on it.
No 3(F) Sqn	Typhoon FGR4	RAF Coningsby	Badge: A blue cockatrice on a white circular background flanked by two green bars edged with yellow. Tail fin as a green stripe edged with yellow.
No 4 Sqn/ IV Sqn	Hawk T2	RAF Valley	Badge (on nose): A yellow lightning flash on a red background with IV superimposed. Aircraft carry a yellow lightning flash on a red and black background on the tail and this is repeated in bars either side of the roundel on the fuselage. Part of No 4 FTS.
No 6 Sqn	Typhoon FGR4	RAF Lossiemouth	Badge (on tail): A red, winged can opener on a blue shield, edged in red. The roundel is flanked by a red zigzag on a blue background.
No 7 Sqn	Chinook HC6/HC6A	RAF Odiham	Badge (on tail): A blue badge containing the seven stars of Ursa Major ('The Plough') in yellow.
No 8 Sqn	Sentry AEW1	RAF Waddington	Badge (on tail): A grey, sheathed, Arabian dagger. Aircraft pooled with No 54 Sqn. [To convert to the E-7 Wedgetail when the Sentry retires.]
No 9 Sqn/ IX Sqn	Typhoon FGR4	RAF Lossiemouth	Badge: A green bat on a black circular background, flanked by yellow and green horizontal stripes. The green bat also appears on the tail, edged in yellow.
No 10 Sqn	Voyager KC2/KC3	RAF Brize Norton	No markings worn.
No 11 Sqn	Typhoon FGR4	RAF Coningsby	Badge (on tail): Two eagles in flight on a white shield. The roundel is flanked by yellow and black triangles.
No 12 Sqn	Typhoon T3/FGR4	RAF Coningsby	Badge (on tail): A fox's head over a Union Flag and Qatari flag. Either side of the roundel are stripes of black, white and green.
No 13 Sqn	Reaper/Protector RG1 (from 2023)	RAF Waddington	No markings worn.
No 14 Sqn	Shadow R1/R1+/R2	RAF Waddington	No markings worn.
No 16 Sqn	Tutor T1	RAF Cranwell	No markings carried. Part of No 1 EFTS.
No 17 Test & Evaluation Sqn	Lightning II	Edwards AFB, USA	No markings worn

Squadron	Type(s) operated	Base(s)	Distinguishing marks & other comments
No 18(B) Sqn	Chinook HC4/ HC5/HC6/HC6A	RAF Odiham	Badge (on tail): A red winged horse on a black circle. Aircraft pooled with No 27 Sqn.
No 22 Sqn	All helicopter types	RAF Benson	No markings worn (aircraft borrowed from other units as needed)
No 24 Sqn/ XXIV Sqn	Hercules C4/ Atlas C1	RAF Brize Norton	No squadron markings carried. Aircraft pooled with No 30 Sqn, No 47 Sqn and No 70 Sqn.
No 25 Sqn/ XXV Sqn	Hawk T2	RAF Valley	Badge (on tail): A hawk on a gauntlet. Aircraft have XXV on the tail and silver and grey bars either side of the roundel on the fuselage. Part of No 4 FTS. Aircraft are coded F*.
No 27 Sqn	Chinook HC4/ HC5/HC6	RAF Odiham	Badge (on tail): A dark green elephant on a green circle, flanked by green and dark green stripes. Aircraft pooled with No 18 Sqn.
No 28 Sqn	Chinook HC4/ Puma HC2	RAF Benson	Badge: A winged horse above two white crosses on a red shield.
No 29 Sqn	Typhoon T3/FGR4	RAF Coningsby	Badge (on tail): An eagle in flight, preying on a buzzard, with three red Xs across the top. The roundel is flanked by two white bars outlined by a red line, each containing three red Xs.
No 30 Sqn	Atlas C1	RAF Brize Norton	No squadron markings carried. Aircraft pooled with No 24 Sqn and No 47 Sqn.
No 32(The Royal) Sqn	Agusta 109SP	RAF Northolt	No squadron markings carried but aircraft carry a distinctive livery with a red stripe, edged in blue along the middle of the fuselage and a red tail.
No 33 Sqn	Puma HC2	RAF Benson	Badge: A stag's head.
No 39 Sqn	Predator/ Reaper	Nellis AFB/ Creech AFB	No markings worn.
No 41 Test & Evaluation Sqn [FJWOEU]	Typhoon T3/FGR4	RAF Coningsby	Badge: A red, double armed cross on the tail with a gold crown above. White and red horizontal bars flanking the roundel on the fuselage. Aircraft are coded EB-*.
No 45 Sqn	Phenom T1	RAF Cranwell	The Phenoms carry a black stripe on the tail superimposed with red diamonds. Part of No 3 FTS.
No 47 Sqn	Hercules C4	RAF Brize Norton	No squadron markings usually carried. Aircraft pooled with No 24 Sqn and No 30 Sqn.
No 51 Sqn	RC-135W	RAF Waddington	Badge (on tail): A red goose in flight.
No 54 Sqn [ISTAR OCU]	Poseidon MRA1/ Shadow R1	RAF Waddington	Based aircraft as required.
No 56 Sqn [ISTAR Test & Evaluation Sqn]	Shadow R1	RAF Waddington	Based aircraft as required.
No 57 Sqn	Prefect T1	RAF Barkston Heath/ RAF Cranwell	No markings carried. Part of No 1 EFTS.

Squadron	Type(s) operated	Base(s)	Distinguishing marks & other comments
No 70 Sqn Fixed Wing Air Mobility OCU/LXX Sqn	Atlas C1	RAF Brize Norton	No squadron markings usually carried. Aircraft pooled with No 24 Sqn.
No 72 Sqn	Texan T1	RAF Valley	Badge: A black swift in flight on a red disk, flanked with blue bars edged with red. Part of No 4 FTS.
No 84 Sqn	Griffin HAR2	RAF Akrotiri	Badge (on tail): A scorpion on a playing card symbol (diamonds, clubs etc.). Aircraft carry a vertical light blue stripe through the roundel on the fuselage.
No 99 Sqn	Globemaster III	RAF Brize Norton	Badge (on tail): A black puma leaping.
No 101 Sqn	Voyager KC2/KC3	RAF Brize Norton	No markings worn.
No 115 Sqn	Tutor T1	Wittering	No markings carried. Part of the CFS.
No 120 Sqn	Poseidon MRA1	Lossiemouth	No markings worn.
No 201 Sqn	Poseidon MRA1	Lossiemouth	No markings worn.
No 202 Sqn	Jupiter HT1	RAF Valley	Badge: A mallard alighting on a white circle.
No 206 Sqn [HAT&ES]	Hercules C4/C5	RAF Brize Norton/ Boscombe Down	No squadron markings usually carried.
No 207 Sqn	Lightning II	RAF Marham	No markings worn
No 216 Sqn	(no aircraft assigned yet)	RAF Waddington	No markings worn
No 230 Sqn	Puma HC2	RAF Benson	Badge: A tiger in front of a palm tree on a black pentagon.
No 617 Sqn	Lightning II	RAF Marham	No markings worn
No 1310 Flt	Chinook HC4	Mount Pleasant, FI	No markings worn
No 1312 Flt	Voyager KC2/KC3	Mount Pleasant, FI	No markings worn
No 1435 Flt	Typhoon FGR4	Mount Pleasant, FI	Badge (on tail): A red Maltese cross on a white circle, flanked by red and white horizontal bars.

As from 7 September 2015 all UAS flights and AEFs are commanded and managed by No 6 FTS RAF. Some UAS aircraft carry squadron badges and markings, usually on the tail. Squadron crests all consist of a white circle surrounded by a blue circle, topped with a red crown and having a yellow scroll beneath. Each differs by the motto on the scroll, the UAS name running around the blue circle & by the contents at the centre and it is the latter which are described below.

* All AEFs come under the administration of local UASs and these are listed here.

UAS	Base	Marks
Bristol UAS/ No 3 AEF	Boscombe Down	A sailing ship on water.
Cambridge UAS/ No 5 AEF	Wittering	A heraldic lion in front of a red badge. Aircraft pooled with University of London AS.
East Midlands Universities AS/ No 7 AEF	Wittering	A yellow quiver, full of arrows.
East of Scotland UAS/ No 12 AEF	RAF Leuchars	An open book in front of a white diagonal cross edged in blue.
Liverpool UAS	RAF Woodvale	A bird atop an open book, holding a branch in its beak. Aircraft pooled with Manchester and Salford Universities AS
Manchester and Salford Universities AS/ No 10 AEF	RAF Woodvale Aircraft pooled with Liverpool UAS	A bird of prey with a green snake in its beak.
Northern Ireland Universities AS/ No 14 AEF	JHC FS Aldergrove	(Currently not known)
Northumbrian Universities AS/ No 11 AEF	RAF Leeming	A white cross on a blue background.
Oxford UAS/ No 6 AEF	RAF Benson	An open book in front of crossed swords.
Southampton UAS/ No 2 AEF	Boscombe Down	A red stag in front of a stone pillar.
Universities of Glasgow and Strathclyde AS/ No 4 AEF	Glasgow	A bird of prey in flight, holding a branch in its beak, in front of an upright sword.
University of Birmingham AS/ No 8 AEF	DCAE Cosford	A blue griffon with two heads.
University of London AS	Wittering	A globe superimposed over an open book. Aircraft pooled with Cambridge UAS.
University of Wales AS/ No 1 AEF	MOD St Athan	A red Welsh dragon in front of an open book, clasping a sword. Some aircraft have the dragon in front of white and green squares.
Yorkshire Universities AS/ No 9 AEF	RAF Leeming	An open book in front of a Yorkshire rose with leaves..

This table gives brief details of the markings worn by aircraft of FAA squadrons. Squadron badges, when worn, are usually located on the front fuselage. All FAA squadron badges comprise a crown atop a circle edged in gold braid and so the badge details below list only what appears in the circular part.

Squadron	Type(s) operated	Base(s)	Distinguishing marks & other comments
No 700X NAS	RQ-12 Wasp/ RQ-20 Puma/Scan Eagle RM1	RNAS Culdrose	Badge: No markings carried.
No 727 NAS	Tutor T1	RNAS Yeovilton	Badge: The head of Britannia wearing a gold helmet on a background of blue and white waves.
No 744 NAS	Chinook HC6A/ Merlin (Crowsnest)	MOD Boscombe Down	Badge: No details
No 750 NAS	Avenger T1	RNAS Culdrose	Badge: A Greek runner bearing a torch & sword on a background of blue and white waves.
No 814 NAS	Merlin HM2	RNAS Culdrose	Badge: A winged tiger mask on a background of dark blue and white waves.
No 815 NAS	Wildcat HMA2	RNAS Yeovilton	Badge: A winged, gold harpoon on a background of blue and white waves.
No 820 NAS	Merlin HM2	RNAS Culdrose	Badge: A flying fish on a background of blue and white waves.
No 824 NAS	Merlin HM2	RNAS Culdrose	Badge: A heron on a background of blue and white waves.
No 825 NAS	Wildcat HMA2	RNAS Yeovilton	Badge: An eagle over a Maltese cross.
No 845 NAS	Merlin HC4	RNAS Yeovilton	Badge: A dragonfly on a background of blue and white waves.
No 846 NAS	Merlin HC4/HC4A	RNAS Yeovilton	Badge: A swordsman riding a winged horse whilst attacking a serpent on a background of blue and white waves.
No 847 NAS	Wildcat AH1	RNAS Yeovilton	Badge (not currently worn): A gold sea lion on a blue background. Aircraft wear ARMY titles.

This section is aimed at giving a quick reference to the units and types that operate from mainland UK military bases.

Joint Helicopter Command Flying Station (JHCFS) Aldergrove, County Antrim [13m W of Belfast]
Northern Ireland Universities AS/No 14 AEF RAF, operating the Tutor T1.

RAF Barkston Heath, Lincolnshire [5m NNE of Grantham]
No 57 Sqn RAF, operating the Prefect T1 (also at RAF Cranwell)

RAF Benson, Oxfordshire [1m NE of Wallingford]
No 28 Sqn RAF, operating the Chinook HC4 and Puma HC2.
No 33 Sqn RAF, operating the Puma HC2.
No 230 Sqn, operating the Puma HC2.
Oxford UAS/No 6 AEF RAF, operating the Tutor T1EA.

Boscombe Down, Wiltshire [6m N of Salisbury]
Bristol UAS/No 3 AEF RAF, operating the Tutor T1.
Southampton UAS/No 2 AEF RAF, operating the tutor T1.

RAF Brize Norton, Oxfordshire [5m SW of Witney]
No 10 Sqn RAF, operating the Voyager KC2/KC3.
No 24 Sqn RAF, operating the Hercules C4 and the Atlas C1.
No 30 Sqn RAF, operating the Atlas C1.
No 47 Sqn RAF, operating the Hercules C4.
No 70 Sqn RAF, operating the Atlas C1.
No 99 Sqn RAF, operating the Globemaster III.
No 101 Sqn RAF, operating the Voyager KC2/KC3.

RAF Coningsby, Lincolnshire [10m NW of Boston]
No 3(F) Sqn operating the Typhoon FGR4.
No 11 Sqn RAF, operating the Typhoon FGR4.
No 12 Sqn RAF/Qatar Emiri Air Force, operating the Typhoon T3 and FGR4.
No 29 Sqn RAF, operating the Typhoon T3 and FGR4.
No 41 (Test and Evaluation) Sqn RAF, operating the Typhoon T3 and FGR4.
The Battle of Britain Memorial Flight (BBMF) RAF, operating the Chipmunk, Dakota, Hurricane & Spitfire.

DCAE Cosford, Shropshire [9m WNW of Wolverhampton]
University of Birmingham AS/No 8 AEF RAF, operating the Tutor T1.

RAF Cranwell, Lincolnshire [5m WNW of Sleaford]
No 16 Sqn RAF, operating the Tutor T1.
No 45 Sqn RAF, operating the Phenom T1.
No 57 Sqn RAF, operating the Prefect T1 (also at RAF Barkston Heath).

RNAS Culdrose (HMS Seahawk), Cornwall [1m SE of Helston]
No 700X NAS RN, operating the RQ-12 Wasp, RQ-20 Puma and Scan Eagle RM1.
No 736 NAS RN, operating the Hawk T1 and T1A (until March 2022).
No 750 NAS RN, operating the Avenger T1.
No 814 NAS RN, operating the Merlin HM2.
No 820 NAS RN, operating the Merlin HM2.
No 824 NAS RN, operating the Merlin HM2.

RAF Kenley, Greater London [1m W of Warlingham]
No 615 VGS RAF, operating the Viking T1.

RAF Kirknewton, Lothian [8m SW of Edinburgh]
No 661 VGS RAF, operating the Viking T1.

RAF Leeming, North Yorkshire [5m SW of Northallerton]
Joint RAF/Qatar Emiri Air Force Hawk Training Sqn, operating the Hawk Mk.167.
Northumbrian Universities AS/No 11 AEF RAF, operating the Tutor T1.
Yorkshire Universities AS/No 9 AEF, RAF, flying the Tutor T1.

Leuchars Station, Fife [7m SE of Dundee]
East of Scotland UAS/No 12 AEF RAF, flying the Tutor T1.

RAF Lakenheath, Suffolk [8m W of Thetford]
492nd Fighter Sqn USAF, operating the F-15E Strike Eagle.
493rd Fighter Sqn USAF, working up on the F-35A Lightning II
494th Fighter Sqn USAF, operating the F-15E Strike Eagle.
495th Fighter Sqn USAF, operating the F-35A Lightning II.

RAF Little Rissington, Gloucestershire [5 miles S of Stow-on-the-Wold]
No 621 VGS RAF, operating the Viking T1.
No 637 VGS RAF, operating the Viking T1.

RAF Lossiemouth, Moray [4m N of Elgin]
No 1(F) Sqn RAF, operating the Typhoon FGR4.
No 2(AC) Sqn RAF, operating the Typhoon FGR4.
No 6 Sqn RAF, operating the Typhoon FGR4.
No 9 Sqn RAF, operating the Typhoon FGR4.
No 120 Sqn RAF, operating the Poseidon MRA1.
No 201 Sqn RAF, operating the Poseidon MRA1.

RAF Marham, Norfolk [6m W of Swaffham]
No 207 Sqn RAF/RN, operating the Lightning II.
No 617 Sqn RAF, operating the Lightning II.

AAC Middle Wallop, Hampshire [6m SW of Andover]
Army Flying Grading (AFG) AAC, operating the Tutor T1.

RAF Mildenhall, Suffolk [9m NNE of Newmarket]
7th Special Operations Sqn, operating the CV-22B Osprey.
67th Special Operations Sqn, operating the MC-130J Commando II.
351st Air Refuelling Sqn, operating the KC-135R and KC-135T Stratotanker.

RAF Northolt, Greater London [3m E of M40 junction 1]
No 32 (The Royal) Sqn RAF, operating the Agusta 109SP.

RAF Odiham, Hampshire [2m S of junction 5 of the M3]
No 7 Sqn RAF, operating the Chinook HC6 and HC6A.
No 18(B) Sqn RAF, operating the Chinook HC4, HC5, HC6 and HC6A.

No 27 Sqn RAF, operating the Chinook HC4, HC5 and HC6.

RN Predannack, Cornwall [7m S of Helston]
No 626 VGS RAF, operating the Viking T1.

RAF Scampton, Lincolnshire [6m N of Lincoln]
The Red Arrows, operating the Hawk T1 and T1A.

RAF Shawbury, Shropshire [7m NNE of Shrewsbury]
No 1 FTS RAF, operating the Juno HT1 and Jupiter HT1.

RAF Syerston, Nottinghamshire [5m SW of Newark]
ACCGS/No 644 VGS RAF, operating the Viking T1.

RAF Topcliffe (Alanbrooke Barracks), North Yorkshire [3m SW of Thirsk]
No 645 VGS RAF, operating the Viking T1.

RAF Upavon, Wiltshire [13m N of Salisbury]
No 622 VGS RAF, operating the Viking T1.

RAF Valley, Gwynedd [5m SE of Holyhead]
No 4 Sqn RAF, operating the Hawk T2.
No 25 Sqn RAF, operating the Hawk T2.
No 72 Sqn RAF, operating the Texan T1.
No 202 Sqn RAF, operating the Jupiter HT1.

RAF Waddington, Lincolnshire [5m S of Lincoln]
No 13 Sqn RAF, operating the Reaper.
No 14 Sqn RAF, operating the Shadow.
No 51 Sqn RAF, operating the RC-135W.
No 54 Sqn RAF, operating the Shadow.
No 56 Sqn RAF, operating the Shadow.

Wattisham Airfield, Suffolk [5m SSW of Stowmarket]
653 Sqn/3 Regiment AAC, operating the Apache.
656 Sqn/4 Regiment AAC, operating the Apache.
662 Sqn/3 Regiment AAC, operating the Apache.
663 Sqn/3 Regiment AAC, operating the Apache.
664 Sqn/4 Regiment AAC, operating the Apache.

RAF Wittering, Cambridgeshire [3m S of Stamford]
No 115 Sqn RAF, operating the Tutor T1.
Cambridge UAS/No 5 AEF RAF, operating the Tutor T1.
East Midlands Universities AS/No 7 AEF RAF, operating the Tutor T1.
University of London AS RAF, operating the Tutor T1.

RAF Woodvale, Merseyside [5m SSW of Southport]
Liverpool UAS RAF, operating the Tutor T1.
Manchester & Salford Universities AS/No 10 AEF RAF, operating the Tutor T1.

RNAS Yeovilton (HMS Heron), Somerset [5m N of Yeovil]
652 Sqn AAC/WCM, operating the Wildcat AH1.
659 Sqn/1 Regiment AAC, operating the Wildcat AH1.
661 Sqn/1 Regiment AAC, operating the Wildcat AH1.
No 727 NAS RN, operating the Tutor T1.
No 815 NAS RN, operating the Wildcat HMA2.
No 825 NAS RN, operating the Wildcat HMA2.
No 845 NAS RN, operating the Merlin HC4.
No 846 NAS RN, operating the Merlin HC4 and HC4A.
No 847 NAS RN, operating the Wildcat AH1 for the Royal Marines.

Additionally, although not strictly military bases, the following are listed, for completion:
Glasgow Airport, Renfrewshire [10m W of Glasgow]
Universities of Glasgow & Strathclyde AS/No 4 AEF RAF, operating the Tutor T1EA.

MOD St. Athan, Vale of Glamorgan [8m W of Barry]
University of Wales AS/No 1 AEF RAF, operating the Tutor T1.

Seen here at its home base at RAF Coningsby, AB910 is a Spitfire Mk.V, and is a part of the impressive fleet owned by the Battle of Britain Memorial Flight that are based here. *HJC*

This section lists the codes worn by some UK military aircraft and, alongside, the serial of the aircraft currently wearing this code. It should be pointed out that in some cases more than one aircraft wears the same code but the aircraft listed is the one believed to be in service with the unit concerned at the time of going to press. This list will be updated regularly and those with Internet access can download the latest version via the 'Military Aircraft Markings' Web Site, www.militaryaircraftmarkings.co.uk and the Military Aircraft Markings Group, MilitaryAircraftMarkings@Groups.io.

Code	Serial	Code	Serial	Code	Serial	Code	Serial
ROYAL AIR FORCE		**Lockheed Martin F-35B**		**WS Puma HC2**		**ROYAL NAVY**	
BAE Hawk T2		**Lightning II**		A	XW199	**EHI-101 Merlin**	
B	ZK011	001	ZM135	B	XW204	A	ZJ117
C	ZK012	002	ZM136	E	XW213	B	ZJ118
D	ZK013	003	ZM137	F	XW214	C	ZJ119
E	ZK014	004	ZM138	G	XW216	D	ZJ120
F	ZK015	005	ZM139	H	XW217	E	ZJ121
G	ZK016	006	ZM140	K	XW220	F	ZJ122
H	ZK017	007	ZM141	N	XW231	G	ZJ123
I	ZK018	008	ZM142	P	XW232	H	ZJ124
J	ZK019	009	ZM143	Q	XW235	J	ZJ125
K	ZK020	010	ZM144	R	XW237	K	ZJ126
L	ZK021	011	ZM145	S	ZA935	L	ZJ127
M	ZK022	012	ZM146	T	ZA936	M	ZJ128
N	ZK023	013	ZM147	U	ZA939	N	ZJ129
O	ZK024	014	ZM148	V	ZA940	O	ZJ130
FA	ZK025	015	ZM149	W	ZJ954	P	ZJ131
FB	ZK026	016	ZM150	X	ZJ955	Q	ZJ132
FC	ZK027	017	ZM151	Y	ZJ956	R	ZJ133
FD	ZK028	019	ZM153	Z	ZJ957	S	ZJ134
FE	ZK029	020	ZM154			T	ZJ135
FF	ZK030	021	ZM155			U	ZJ136
FG	ZK031	022	ZM156			W	ZJ137
FH	ZK032	023	ZM157			X	ZJ138
FI	ZK033	024	ZM158			AA	ZJ990
FJ	ZK034	025	ZM159			AB	ZJ992
FK	ZK035	026	ZM160			AC	ZJ994
FL	ZK036	027	ZM161			AD	ZJ995
FM	ZK037					AE	ZJ998
FN	ZK010					AF	ZK001
Eurofighter Typhoon							
C	ZJ933						
D	ZJ941						
F	ZJ915						
H	ZJ926						
AX	ZK303						
WS-G	ZJ935						
WS-J	ZJ924						
WS-L	ZJ919						
WS-T	ZJ923						
WS-U	ZJ939						
WS-Y	ZJ928						

Some *historic, classic and warbird* aircraft carry the markings of overseas air arms and can be seen in the UK, mainly preserved in museums and collections or taking part in air shows.

Serial	Type (code/other identity)	Owner/operator, location or fate	Notes
AFGHANISTAN			
--	Hawker Afghan Hind (K4672/BAPC.82)	RAF Museum Reserve Collection, Stafford, Staffs	
ARGENTINA			
0729	Beech T-34C Turbo Mentor	FAA Museum, stored Cobham Hall, RNAS Yeovilton, Somerset	
0767	Aermacchi MB339AA	South Yorkshire Aircraft Museum, Doncaster, S. Yorks	
A-515	FMA IA58 Pucará (ZD485)	RAF Museum, stored Cosford, Shropshire	
A-522	FMA IA58 Pucará (8768M)	FAA Museum, at North-East Land, Sea & Air Museums, Usworth, T&W	
A-528	FMA IA58 Pucará (8769M)	Norfolk & Suffolk Avn Museum, Flixton, Suffolk	
A-533	FMA IA58 Pucará (ZD486) <ff>	Privately owned, Chelmsford, Essex	
A-549	FMA IA58 Pucará (ZD487)	IWM Duxford, Cambs	
AE-331	Agusta A109A (ZE411)	FAA Museum, stored Cobham Hall, RNAS Yeovilton, Somerset	
AE-406	Bell UH-1H Iroquois (998-8888) [Z]	South Yorkshire Aircraft Museum, Doncaster, S. Yorks	
AE-409	Bell UH-1H Iroquois [656]	Army Flying Museum, Middle Wallop, Hants	
AE-422	Bell UH-1H Iroquois	FAA Museum, stored Cobham Hall, RNAS Yeovilton, Somerset	
AUSTRALIA			
369	Hawker Fury ISS (F-AZXL) [D]	Privately owned, Cannes, France	
A2-4	Supermarine Seagull V (VH-ALB)	RAF Museum Reserve Collection, Stafford, Staffs	
A11-301	Auster J/5G (G-ARKG) [931-NW]	Privately owned, Langham, Rutland	
A16-199	Lockheed Hudson IIIA (G-BEOX) [SF-R]	RAF Museum, Hendon, Gtr London	
A17-48	DH82A Tiger Moth (G-BPHR)	Privately owned, Wanborough, Wilts	
A17-376	DH82A Tiger Moth (G-ANJI)	*Repainted as T6830*	
A19-144	Bristol 156 Beaufighter XIc (JM135/A8-324)	The Fighter Collection, Duxford, Cambs	
A23-005	Pilatus PC-9A	Privately owned, St Athan, Wales	
A23-013	Pilatus PC-9A (G-SBST)	Privately owned, St Athan, Wales	
A23-033	Pilatus PC-9A (G-CMJO)	Privately owned, St Athan, Wales	
A23-051	Pilatus PC-9A	Privately owned, St Athan, Wales	
A58-606	VS509 Spitfire T9 (TE308/G-AWGB) [ZP-W]	Privately owned, Biggin Hill, Kent	
A92-255	GAF Jindivik 102	Privately owned, Thorpe Wood, N Yorks	
A92-466	GAF Jindivik 103A (BAPC.485)	Boscombe Down Aviation Collection, Old Sarum, Wilts	
A92-708	GAF Jindivik 103BL	Newark Air Museum, Winthorpe, Notts	
A92-908	GAF Jindivik 104AL (ZJ503)	Privately owned, Llanbedr, Wales	
N16-114	WS61 Sea King Mk.50A [05]	Privately owned, Horsham, W. Sussex	
N16-125	WS61 Sea King Mk.50A [10]	Privately owned, Horsham, W. Sussex	
N16-238	WS61 Sea King Mk.50A [20]	Privately owned, Horsham, W. Sussex	
N16-239	WS61 Sea King Mk.50A [21]	Privately owned, Horsham, W. Sussex	
N16-918	WS61 Sea King Mk.50B (XZ918) [22]	Privately owned, Horsham, W. Sussex	
WH589	Hawker Fury ISS (F-AZXJ) [115-NW]	Privately owned, Dijon, France	
AUSTRIA			
3F-SX	SAAB S91D Safir (G-EKTP) [04]	Privately owned, Breighton, E. Yorks	
BELGIUM			
A-41	SA318C Alouette II	The Helicopter Museum, Weston-super-Mare, Somerset	
A-79	SA318C Alouette II (2-LOUD)	Privately owned, Thelwall, Cheshire	
FT-36	Lockheed T-33A Shooting Star	Dumfries & Galloway Avn Mus, Dumfries, Scotland	
H-02	Agusta A109HO (N504TS)	Privately owned, Cotswold Airport, Glos	
H-50	Noorduyn AT-16 Harvard IIb (OO-DAF)	Privately owned, Brasschaat, Belgium	
IF-68	Hawker Hunter F6 <ff>	Privately owned, Kings Lynn, Norfolk	

Notes	Serial	Type (code/other identity)	Owner/operator, location or fate
	L-44	Piper L-18C Super Cub (OO-SPQ)	Royal Aéro Para Club de Spa, Belgium
	L-47	Piper L-18C Super Cub (OO-SPG)	Aeroclub Brasschaat VZW, Brasschaat, Belgium
	OL-L49	Piper L-18C Super Cub (L-156/OO-LGB)	Aeroclub Brasschaat VZW, Brasschaat, Belgium
	RS-02	Westland Sea King Mk.48 (OO-SEE/G-BDNI)	Privately owned, Chard, Somerset
	RS-04	Westland Sea King Mk.48 (OO-KNG/G-BDNK)	Privately owned, Chard, Somerset
	V-4	SNCAN Stampe SV-4B (OO-EIR)	Antwerp Stampe Centre, Antwerp-Deurne, Belgium
	V-18	SNCAN Stampe SV-4B (OO-GWD)	Antwerp Stampe Centre, Antwerp-Deurne, Belgium
	V-29	SNCAN Stampe SV-4B (OO-GWB)	Antwerp Stampe Centre, Antwerp-Deurne, Belgium
	V-66	SNCAN Stampe SV-4C (OO-GWA)	Antwerp Stampe Centre, Antwerp-Deurne, Belgium
	BOLIVIA		
	FAB-108	BAe RJ.70	Privately owned, Southend, Essex
	BRAZIL		
	0931	Cessna T-37C (N3127M)	Wastelands Salvage, Eire
	BURKINA FASO		
	BF8431	SIAI-Marchetti SF.260 (G-NRRA) [31]	Privately owned, Lydd, Kent
	CANADA		
	622	Piasecki HUP-3 Retriever (51-16622/N6699D)	The Helicopter Museum, Weston-super-Mare, Somerset
	920	VS Stranraer (CF-BXO) [Q-N]	RAF Museum, Hendon, Gtr London
	3091	NA81 Harvard II (3019/G-CPPM)	Privately owned, stored Enstone, Oxon
	3349	NA64 Yale (G-BYNF)	Privately owned, Duxford, Cambs
	5084	DH82C Tiger Moth (G-FCTK)	Privately owned, Hailsham, E. Sussex
	9041	Bristol 149 Bolingbroke IV <ff>	Manx Aviation Museum, Ronaldsway, IOM
	9048	Bristol 149 Bolingbroke IV	Aerospace Bristol, Filton, Glos
	9893	Bristol 149 Bolingbroke IVT <ff> (BAPC.603)	Kent Battle of Britain Museum, Hawkinge, Kent
	9893	Bristol 149 Bolingbroke IVT <rf>	IWM, stored Duxford, Cambs
	9940	Bristol 149 Bolingbroke IVT	National Museum of Flight, E Fortune, Scotland
	15252	Fairchild PT-19A Cornell (comp 15195)	RAF Museum Reserve Collection, Stafford, Staffs
	16693	Auster J/1N Alpha (G-BLPG) [693]	Privately owned, Norfolk (dismantled)
	17447	McD F-101F Voodoo (56-0312)	Midland Air Museum, Coventry, Warks
	18072	DHC1B-2-S5 Chipmunk (G-FCTY)	Privately owned, Audley End, Cambs
	18393	Avro Canada CF-100 Canuck 4B (G-BCYK)	IWM Duxford, Cambs
	18671	DHC1 Chipmunk 22 (WP905/7438M/G-BNZC) [671]	The Shuttleworth Collection, Old Warden, Beds
	20249	Noorduyn AT-16 Harvard IIb (PH-KLU) [XS-249]	Privately owned, Texel, The Netherlands
	21417	Canadair CT-133 Silver Star	Yorkshire Air Museum, Elvington, N. Yorks
	23140	Canadair CL-13A Sabre 5 [AX] <rf>	Midland Air Museum, Coventry, Warks
	23380	Canadair CL-13B Sabre 6 <rf>	Privately owned, Haverigg, Cumbria
	FE992	Noorduyn AT-16 Harvard IIb (G-BDAM) [ER-992]	Privately owned, Duxford, Cambs
	FJ662	Fairchild PT-26 Cornell (G-CRNL) [662]	Privately owned, Wickenby, Lincs
	KN448	Douglas Dakota IV <ff>	Science Museum, South Kensington, London
	CHILE		
	H-255	Aérospatiale SA330H Puma	Ultimate Activity, Faygate, W. Sussex
	CHINA		
	68 r	Nanchang CJ-6A Chujiao (2751219/G-BVVG)	Privately owned, stored Strubby, Lincs
	61367	Nanchang CJ-6A Chujiao (4532009/G-CGHB) [37]	Privately owned, Redhill, Surrey
	CZECH REPUBLIC		
	3677	Letov S-103 (MiG-15bisSB) (613677)	National Museum of Flight, E Fortune, Scotland
	3794	Letov S-102 (MiG-15) (623794) (starboard side only, painted in Polish marks as 1972 on port side)	Norfolk & Suffolk Avn Museum, Flixton, Suffolk

Serial	Type (code/other identity)	Owner/operator, location or fate	Notes
9147	Mil Mi-4	The Helicopter Museum, Weston-super-Mare, Somerset	
DENMARK			
A-011	SAAB A-35XD Draken	Privately owned, Hindley Green, Gtr Manchester	
AR-107	SAAB S-35XD Draken	Newark Air Museum, Winthorpe, Notts	
E-196	SABCA (GD) F-16A MLU Fighting Falcon <ff>	Martin-Baker, Chalgrove, Oxon	
E-419	Hawker Hunter F51 (G-9-441)	North-East Land, Sea & Air Museums, Usworth, T&W	
E-420	Hawker Hunter F51 (G-9-442) <ff>	Privately owned, Walton-on-Thames, Surrey	
E-421	Hawker Hunter F51 (G-9-443)	Brooklands Museum, Weybridge, Surrey	
ET-272	Hawker Hunter T53 <ff>	Norfolk & Suffolk Avn Museum, Flixton, Suffolk	
ET-626	SABCA (GD) F-16B MLU Fighting Falcon <ff>	Martin-Baker, Chalgrove, Oxon	
L-866	Consolidated PBY-6A Catalina (8466M)	RAF Museum, Cosford, Shropshire	
P-129	DHC-1 Chipmunk 22 (OY-ATO)	Privately owned, Tonder, Denmark	
P-139	DHC-1 Chipmunk 22 (OY-AVF)	Privately owned, Ringsted, Denmark	
R-756	Lockheed F-104G Starfighter	Midland Air Museum, Coventry, Warks	
S-881	Sikorsky S-55C	The Helicopter Museum, stored Weston-super-Mare, Somerset	
S-882	Sikorsky S-55C	Skirmish Paintball, Portishead, Somerset	
S-886	Sikorsky S-55C	Hamburger Hill Paintball, Marksbury, Somerset	
S-887	Sikorsky S-55C	The Helicopter Museum, stored Weston-super-Mare, Somerset	
EGYPT			
764	Mikoyan MiG-21SPS <ff>	Privately owned, Northampton, Northants	
771	WS61 Sea King Mk.47 (WA.826)	DSTO Shoeburyness, Essex, GI use	
773	WS61 Sea King Mk.47 (WA.823)	RNAS Yeovilton Fire Section, Somerset	
776	WS61 Sea King Mk.47 (WA.825) <ff>	Mayhem Paintball, Aybridge, Essex	
5634	Mikoyan MiG-21UM (0446) <ff>	Lakes Lightnings, Spark Bridge, Cumbria	
7735	Sukhoi Su-7 <ff>	Lakes Lightnings, Spark Bridge, Cumbria	
FINLAND			
GA-43	Gloster Gamecock II (G-CGYF)	Privately owned, Dursley, Glos	
GN-101	Folland Gnat F1 (XK741)	Midland Air Museum, Coventry, Warks	
SZ-12	Focke-Wulf Fw44J Stieglitz (D-EXWO)	Privately owned, Bienenfarm, Germany	
VI-3	Valtion Viima 2 (OO-EBL)	To Finland as OH-VIG	
FRANCE			
1/4513	Spad XIII <R> (G-BFYO/S3398) [1]	American Air Museum, Duxford, Cambs	
5	MH1521C Broussard (C-GRBL/G-CLLK) [30-QA]	Privately owned, Oaksey Park, Glos	
7	Nord NC854 (G-NORD)	Privately owned, English Bicknor, Glos	
28	Fouga CM175 Zéphyr [F-AZPF]	Association Zéphyr 28, Nîmes, France	
32	Morane-Saulnier MS760 Paris (F-AZLT)	Armor Aéro Passion, Morlaix, France	
37	Nord 3400 (G-ZARA) [MAB]	Privately owned, stored Swaffham, Norfolk	
45	Dassault Mirage IVP [BR]	Yorkshire Air Museum, Elvington, N. Yorks	
54	SNCAN NC856A Norvigie (G-CGWR) [AOM]	Privately owned, Spanhoe, Northants	
59	Breguet Br1050 Alizé (F-AZYI)	Alizé Marine, Nîmes/Garons, France	
67	SNCAN 1101 Noralpha (F-GMCY) [CY]	Privately owned, la Ferté-Alais, France	
70	Dassault Mystère IVA [8-NV]	Midland Air Museum, Coventry, Warks	
78	Nord 3202B-1 (G-BIZK)	Privately owned, Swaffham, Norfolk	
79	Dassault Mystère IVA [2-EG]	Norfolk & Suffolk Avn Museum, Flixton, Suffolk	
82	Curtiss H75-C1 Hawk (G-CCVH) [X-881]	The Fighter Collection, Duxford, Cambs	
82	NA T-28D Fennec (F-AZKG)	Privately owned, Strasbourg, France	
83	Dassault Mystère IVA [8-MS]	Newark Air Museum, Winthorpe, Notts	
83	Morane-Saulnier MS733 Alcyon (F-AZKS)	Privately owned, Montlucon, France	
85	Dassault Mystère IVA [8-MV]	Preserved Bruntingthorpe, Leics	
104	MH1521M Broussard (F-GHFG) [307-FG]	Privately owned, Montceau-les-Mines, France	
105	Nord N2501F Noratlas (F-AZVM) [62-SI]	Le Noratlas de Provence, Marseille, France	
106	MH1521M Broussard (F-GKJT) [33-JT]	Privately owned, Montceau-les-Mines, France	
108	MH1521M Broussard (F-BNEX) [50S9]	Privately owned, Bantheville, France	
108	SO1221 Djinn (FR108) [CDL]	The Helicopter Museum, Weston-super-Mare, Somerset	

Notes	Serial	Type (code/other identity)	Owner/operator, location or fate
	121	Dassault Mystère IVA [8-MY]	City of Norwich Aviation Museum, Norfolk
	128	Morane-Saulnier MS733 Alcyon (F-BMMY)	Privately owned, St Cyr, France
	143	Morane-Saulnier MS733 Alcyon (G-MSAL)	Privately owned, Spanhoe, Northants
	154	MH1521M Broussard (G-TNUP) [315-SM]	Privately owned, Postling, Kent
	156	SNCAN Stampe SV-4B (G-NIFE)	Privately owned, Headcorn, Kent
	158	Dassault MD312 Flamant (F-AZGE) [12-XA]	Privately owned, Albert, France
	160	Dassault MD312 Flamant (F-AZDR) [V]	Privately owned, Alençon, France
	189	Dassault MD312 Flamant (F-AZVG) [G]	Ailes Anciennes de Corbas, Lyon, France
	208	MH1521C1 Broussard (G-YYYY) [IR]	Privately owned, Eggesford, Devon
	226	Dassault MD312 Flamant (F-AZES) [319-CG]	Privately owned, Montbeliard, France
	237	Dassault MD312 Flamant (F-AZFE) [319-DM]	Privately owned, Alençon, France
	255	MH1521M Broussard (G-CIGH) [5-ML]	Privately owned, Breighton, E. Yorks
	260	Dassault MD311 Flamant (F-AZKT) [316-KT]	Privately owned, Albert, France
	261	MH1521M Broussard (F-GIBN) [30-QA]	Privately owned, Walldürn, Germany
	276	Dassault MD311 Flamant (F-AZER) [OA-N]	Privately owned, Alençon, France
	290	Dewoitine D27 (F-AZJD)	Les Casques de Cuir, La Ferté-Alais, France
	316	MH1521M Broussard (F-GGKR) [315-SN]	Privately owned, Lognes, France
	318	Dassault Mystère IVA [8-NY]	Dumfries & Galloway Avn Mus, Dumfries, Scotland
	319	Dassault Mystère IVA [8-ND]	Rebel Air Museum, Andrewsfield, Essex
	354	Morane-Saulnier MS315E-D2 (G-BZNK)	Privately owned, Wickenby, Lincs (restoration)
	538	Dassault Mirage IIIE [3-QH]	Yorkshire Air Museum, Elvington, N. Yorks
	569	Fouga CM170R Magister [F-AZZP]	Privately owned, Le Havre, France
	1101	SNCAN Stampe SV-4B (G-HJSS)	Privately owned, Redhill, Surrey
	1139	SNCAN Stampe SV-4B (G-AYCK)	Privately owned, Dinton – Manor Farm, Wilts
	3615	Aérospatiale SA.342M Gazelle (HA-HSG)	Privately owned, Breighton, E. Yorks
	24541	Cessna L-19E Bird Dog (G-JDOG) [BMG]	Privately owned, Cotswold Airport, Glos
	24545	Cessna L-19E Bird Dog (F-AZTA) [BYA]	Privately owned, Chavenay, France
	42157	NA F-100D Super Sabre [11-ER]	North-East Land, Sea & Air Museums, Usworth, T&W
	54439	Lockheed T-33A Shooting Star (55-4439) [WI]	South Wales Aviation Museum, St Athan, Wales
	125716	Douglas AD-4N Skyraider (F-AZFN) [22-DG]	Privately owned, Melun, France
	18-1391	Piper L-18C Super Cub (51-15391/G-BHOM) [AN-R]	Privately owned, Shobdon, Herefordshire
	18-5395	Piper L-18C Super Cub (52-2436/G-CUBJ) [CDG]	Privately owned, Old Warden, Beds
	C850	Salmson 2A2 <R>	Barton Aviation Heritage Centre, Barton, Gtr Manchester
	FR41	Piasecki H-21C (56-2025)	The Helicopter Museum, Weston-super-Mare, Somerset
	FR150	SO1221 Djinn	Privately owned, Sproughton, Suffolk
	MS824	Morane-Saulnier Type N <R> (G-AWBU)	Privately owned, Turweston, Bucks
	N856	SNCAN NC856 (G-CDWE)	Privately owned, Wickenby, Lincs
	N1977	Nieuport Scout 17/23 <R> (*N1723*/G-BWMJ) [8]	Privately owned, Old Warden, Beds
	XC	Piper L-4J Grasshopper (44-80513/G-BSYO)	Privately owned, Postling, Kent
	GERMANY		
	-	Fieseler Fi103R-IV (V-1) (BAPC.91)	Lashenden Air Warfare Museum, Headcorn, Kent
	-	Fieseler Fi103R-IV (V-1) (BAPC.327)	National Military Museum, Soesterberg, Neth.
	-	Fokker Dr1 Dreidekker <R> (BAPC.88) [102/17]	FAA Museum, stored Cobham Hall, RNAS Yeovilton, Somerset
	-	Messerschmitt Bf109 <R> [<-]	Battle of Britain Experience, Canterbury, Kent
	<+-	Messerschmitt Bf109 <R> (BAPC.66) [6]	Kent Battle of Britain Museum, Hawkinge, Kent
	I+1	Messerschmitt Bf109 <R> (6357/BAPC.74) [6]	Kent Battle of Britain Museum, Hawkinge, Kent
	White 1	Hispano HA 1.112M1L Buchón (C.4K-111/G-HISP)	Privately owned, Sywell, Northants
	White 1	Focke-Wulf Fw190 <R> (G-WULF)	Privately owned, Tatenhill, Staffs
	3	SNCAN 1101 Noralpha (G-BAYV) (fuselage)	Privately owned, Bentwaters, Suffolk
	Yellow 3	Hispano HA 1.112M1L Buchón (C.4K-40/D-FDME)	Messerschmitt Stiftung, Manching, Germany
	Red 7	Hispano HA 1.112M1L Buchón (C.4K-75/D-FWME)	Messerschmitt Stiftung, Manching, Germany
	Yellow 7	Hispano HA 1.112M1L Buchón (C.4K-99/G-AWHM)	Privately owned, Sywell, Northants
	White 9	Hispano HA 1.112M1L Buchón (C.4K-105/G-AWHH)	Privately owned, Sywell, Northants
	Yellow 10	Hispano HA 1.112M1L Buchón (C.4K-102/G-AWHK)	Historic Flying Ltd, Duxford, Cambs
	Red 11	Hispano HA 1.112K1L Buchón (C.4K-112/G-AWHC)	Privately owned, Sywell, Northants
	White 14	Messerschmitt Bf109 <R> (BAPC.67)	Kent Battle of Britain Museum, Hawkinge, Kent

Serial	Type (code/other identity)	Owner/operator, location or fate	Notes
Yellow 27	Hispano HA 1.112K1L Buchón (D-FMGZ)	Air Fighter Academy, Heringsdorf, Germany	
33/15	Fokker EIII <R> (G-CHAW)	Privately owned, Membury, Wilts	
87	Heinkel He111 <R> <ff>	Privately owned, East Kirkby, Lincs	
105/15	Fokker EIII <R> (G-UDET)	Privately owned, Horsham, W. Sussex	
152/17	Fokker Dr1 Dreidekker <R> (F-AZPQ)	Les Casques de Cuir, la Ferté-Alais, France	
152/17	Fokker Dr1 Dreidekker <R> (G-BVGZ)	Privately owned, Breighton, E. Yorks	
157/18	Fokker D.VIII <R> (BAPC.239)	Norfolk & Suffolk Air Museum, Flixton, Suffolk	
210/16	Fokker EIII (BAPC.56)	Science Museum, South Kensington, London	
403/17	Fokker Dr1 Dreidekker <R> (G-CDXR)	Privately owned, Popham, Hants	
416/15	Fokker EIII <R> (G-GSAL)	Privately owned, Aston Down, Glos	
422/15	Fokker EIII <R> (G-AVJO)	Privately owned, Turweston, Bucks	
422/15	Fokker EIII <R> (G-FOKR)	Privately owned, Eshott, Northumberland	
425/17	Fokker Dr1 Dreidekker <R> (BAPC.133)	Kent Battle of Britain Museum, Hawkinge, Kent	
425/17	Fokker Dr1 Dreidekker <R> (G-DREI)	Privately owned, Felthorpe, Norfolk	
477/17	Fokker Dr1 Dreidekker <R> (G-FOKK)	Privately owned, Sywell, Northants	
556/17	Fokker Dr1 Dreidekker <R> (G-CFHY)	Privately owned, Tibenham, Norfolk	
626/8	Fokker DVII <R> (N6268)	Privately owned, Booker, Bucks	
764	Mikoyan MiG-21SPS <ff>	Privately owned, Norfolk	
959	Mikoyan MiG-21SPS	Midland Air Museum, Coventry	
1160	Dornier Do17Z-2	Michael Beetham Conservation Centre, Cosford, Shropshire	
1190	Messerschmitt Bf109E-3 [White 4]	IWM Duxford, Cambs	
1801/18	Bowers Fly Baby 1A (G-BNPV)	Privately owned, Chessington, Gtr London	
1803/18	Bowers Fly Baby 1A (G-BUYU)	Privately owned, Chessington, Gtr London	
1983	Messerschmitt Bf109E-3 (G-EMIL)	Privately owned, Colchester, Essex	
3579	Messerschmitt Bf109E-7 (G-CIPB) [White 14]	Privately owned, Biggin Hill, Kent	
4101	Messerschmitt Bf109E-3 (DG200/8477M) [Black 12]	RAF Museum, Hendon, Gtr London	
4477	CASA 1.131E Jungmann (G-RETA) [GD+EG]	The Shuttleworth Collection, Old Warden, Beds	
7198/18	LVG CVI (G-AANJ/9239M)	Michael Beetham Conservation Centre, Cosford, Shropshire	
8417/18	Fokker DVII (9207M)	RAF Museum, Hendon, Gtr London	
10639	Messerschmitt Bf109G-2/Trop (8478M/G-USTV) [Black 6]	RAF Museum, Cosford, Shropshire	
12802	Antonov An-2T (D-FOFM)	Historische Flugzeuge, Grossenhain, Germany	
13605	Messerschmitt Bf109G-2(G-JIMP) [Yellow 12]	Privately owned, Knutsford, Cheshire	
15919	Messerschmitt Bf109G <R> (BAPC.240) [Green 1]	Yorkshire Air Museum, Elvington, N. Yorks	
100143	Focke-Achgelis Fa330A-1 Bachstelze	IWM Duxford, Cambs	
100502	Focke-Achgelis Fa330A-1 Bachstelze	Privately owned, Millom, Cumbria	
100503	Focke-Achgelis Fa330A-1 Bachstelze (8469M)	RAF Museum, Cosford, Shropshire	
100509	Focke-Achgelis Fa330A-1 Bachstelze	Science Museum, stored Wroughton, Wilts	
100545	Focke-Achgelis Fa330A-1 Bachstelze	FAA Museum, RNAS Yeovilton, Somerset	
100549	Focke-Achgelis Fa330A-1 Bachstelze	Lashenden Air Warfare Museum, Headcorn, Kent	
112372	Messerschmitt Me262A-2a (VK893/8482M) [Yellow 4]	RAF Museum, Cosford, Shropshire	
120227	Heinkel He162A-2 Salamander (VN679/8472M) [Red 2]	RAF Museum, Hendon, Gtr London	
120235	Heinkel He162A-1 Salamander (AM.68) [Yellow 6]	IWM Duxford, Cambs	
191316	Messerschmitt Me163B Komet [Yellow 6]	Science Museum, South Kensington, London	
191454	Messerschmitt Me163B Komet <R> (BAPC.271)	The Shuttleworth Collection, Old Warden, Beds	
191461	Messerschmitt Me163B Komet (191614/8481M) [Yellow 14]	RAF Museum, Hendon, Gtr London	
191659	Messerschmitt Me163B Komet (8480M) [Yellow 15]	National Museum of Flight, E Fortune, Scotland	
280020	Flettner Fl282/B-V20 Kolibri (frame only)	Midland Air Museum, Coventry, Warks	
360043	Junkers Ju88R-1 (PJ876/8475M) [D5+EV]	RAF Museum, Cosford, Shropshire	
420430	Messerschmitt Me410A-1/U2 (AM.72/8483M)[3U+CC]	Michael Beetham Conservation Centre, Cosford, Shropshire	
475081	Fieseler Fi156C-7 Storch (VP546/AM.101/7362M) [GM+AK]	RAF Museum, Cosford, Shropshire	
494083	Junkers Ju87D-3 (8474M) [RI+JK]	RAF Museum, Hendon, Gtr London	
584219	Focke-Wulf Fw190F-8/U1 (AM.29/8470M) [Black 38]	RAF Museum, Hendon, Gtr London	
701152	Heinkel He111H-23 (8471M) [NT+SL]	RAF Museum, Hendon, Gtr London	
730301	Messerschmitt Bf110G-4 (AM.34/8479M) [D5+RL]	RAF Museum, Hendon, Gtr London	
733682	Focke-Wulf Fw190A-8/R7 (AM.75/9211M)	RAF Museum, Cosford, Shropshire	
980554	Flug Werk FW190A-8/N (D-FWMW) [1+V]	Meier Motors, Bremgarten, Germany	
2+1	Focke-Wulf Fw190 <R> (G-SYFW) [7334]	Privately owned, Halfpenny Green, Staffs	
20+45	Mikoyan MiG-23BN	Privately owned, Danbury, Essex	

Notes	Serial	Type (code/other identity)	Owner/operator, location or fate
	22+35	Lockheed F-104G Starfighter	*Current status unknown (ex-Bruntingthorpe, Leics)*
	28+08	Aero L-39ZO Albatros (142/28+04)	Pinewood Studios, Bucks
	2E+RA	Fieseler Fi-156C-3 Storch (F-AZRA)	Amicale J-B Salis, la Ferté-Alais, France
	4+1	Focke-Wulf Fw190 <R> (G-BSLX)	Privately owned, Norwich, Norfolk
	6G+ED	Slepcev Storch (G-BZOB) [5447]	Privately owned, Breighton, E. Yorks
	37+86	McD F-4F Phantom II <ff>	*Current status unknown (ex-Bruntingthorpe, Leics)*
	37+89	McD F-4F Phantom II	Hawker Hunter Aviation Ltd, Scampton, Lincs (spares)
	58+89	Dornier Do28D-2 Skyservant (D-ICDY)	Privately owned, Uetersen, Germany
	72+59	Dornier UH-1D Iroquois (comp 73+01)	Privately owned, Dunsfold, Surrey
	80+55	MBB Bo.105M	Lufthansa Resource Technical Training, Cotswold Airport, Glos
	80+77	MBB Bo.105M	Lufthansa Resource Technical Training, Cotswold Airport, Glos
	81+00	MBB Bo.105M (D-HZYR)	The Helicopter Museum, Weston-super-Mare, Somerset
	96+26	Mil Mi-24D (421)	The Helicopter Museum, Weston-super-Mare, Somerset
	98+14	Sukhoi Su-22M-4	Hawker Hunter Aviation Ltd, stored Scampton, Lincs
	99+18	NA OV-10B Bronco (G-ONAA)	Bronco Demo Team, Wevelgem, Belgium
	99+26	NA OV-10B Bronco (G-BZGL)	Bronco Demo Team, Wevelgem, Belgium
	AZ+JU	CASA 3.52L (F-AZJU)	Amicale J-B Salis, la Ferté-Alais, France
	BB+103	Canadair CL-13B Sabre 6 (1730/JB+114)	*Current status unknown (ex-Bruntingthorpe, Leics)*
	BF+070	CCF T-6J Texan (G-CHYN)	Privately owned, Dunkeswell, Devon
	BG+KM	Nord 1002 Pingouin (G-ASTG)	Privately owned, Haddon, Cambs
	BU+CC	CASA 1.131E Jungmann (G-BUCC)	Privately owned, Deanland, E. Sussex
	CX+HI	CASA 1.131E Jungmann (E.3B-379/G-CDJU)	Privately owned, Sleap, Shropshire
	D2263	Albatros DVA-1 <R> (ZK-ALB/G-WAHT)	Privately owned, Stow Maries, Essex
	D7343/17	Albatros DVA <R> (ZK-TVD)	RAF Museum, Hendon, Gtr London
	DG+BE	CASA 1.131E Jungmann (E.3B-350/G-BHPL)	Privately owned, Henstridge, Somerset
	DM+BK	Morane-Saulnier MS505 (G-BPHZ)	Historic Aircraft Collection, Duxford
	E37/15	Fokker EIII <R> (G-CGJF)	Privately owned, Whepstead, Suffolk
	ES+BH	Messerschmitt Bf108B-2 (D-ESBH)	Messerschmitt Stiftung, Manching, Germany
	F8+CA	Nord 1002 (G-ETME)	Privately owned, White Waltham, Berks
	FI+S	Morane-Saulnier MS505 (G-BIRW)	National Museum of Flight, stored E Fortune
	FM+BB	Messerschmitt Bf109G-6 (D-FMBB)	Messerschmitt Stiftung, Manching, Germany
	KG+GB	CASA 1.131E Jungmann (G-BHSL)	Privately owned, Old Warden, Beds
	LG+01	CASA 1.133L Jungmeister (ES.1-16/G-CIJV)	Privately owned, Sleap, Shropshire
	LG+03	Bücker Bü133C Jungmeister (G-AEZX)	Privately owned, Milden, Suffolk
	NJ+C11	Nord 1002 (G-ATBG)	Privately owned, Duxford, Cambs
	NM+AA	CASA 1.131E Jungmann 1000 (G-BZJV)	Privately owned, Sleap, Shropshire
	NQ+NR	Klemm Kl35D (D-EQXD)	Quax Flieger, Paderborn, Germany
	NV+KG	Focke-Wulf Fw44J Stieglitz (D-ENAY)	Quax Flieger, Paderborn, Germany
	S4-A07	CASA 1.131E Jungmann (G-BWHP)	Privately owned, Yarcombe, Devon
	TP+WX	Heliopolis Gomhouria Mk 6 (G-TPWX)	Privately owned, Swanborough, E. Sussex
	GHANA		
	G360	PBN 2T Islander (G-BRSR)	Privately owned, stored Badgers Mount, Leics
	G361	PBN 2T Islander (G-BRPB)	Privately owned, Biggin Hill, Kent
	G363	PBN 2T Islander (G-BRSV)	Privately owned, Cumbernauld, Scotland
	GREECE		
	26541	Republic F-84F Thunderflash (52-6541) [541]	North-East Land, Sea & Air Museums, Usworth, T&W
	HONG KONG		
	HKG-5	SA128 Bulldog (G-BULL)	Privately owned, Cotswold Airport, Glos
	HKG-6	SA128 Bulldog (G-BPCL)	Privately owned, North Weald, Essex
	HKG-11	Slingsby T.67M Firefly 200 (G-LDGU)	Privately owned, Oxford, Oxon
	HKG-13	Slingsby T.67M Firefly 200 (G-BXKW)	Privately owned, St Ghislain, Belgium

Serial	Type (code/other identity)	Owner/operator, location or fate	Notes
HUNGARY			
125	Aero L-39ZO Albatros (831125/G-JMGP)	Stored, St. Athan, Wales	
335	Mil Mi-24D (3532461715415) (Red 03)	Privately owned, Dunsfold, Surrey	
501	Mikoyan MiG-21PF	IWM Duxford, Cambs	
503	Mikoyan MiG-21SMT (G-BRAM)	RAF Museum, Cosford, Shropshire	
INDIA			
E296	Hindustan Gnat F1 (G-SLYR)	Privately owned, North Weald, Essex	
HA561	Hawker Tempest II (MW743)	Privately owned, stored Wickenby, Lincs	
HS683	VS394 Spitfire FR XVIIIe (TZ219)	Privately owned, Sywell, Northants	
INDONESIA			
LL-5313	BAe Hawk T53	BAE Systems, Brough, E. Yorks, on display	
IRAQ			
-	Mil Mi-24D (Iraqi 3137)	Spadeadam Ranges, Cumbria	
249	Hawker Fury ISS (OO-ISS)	Privately owned, Brasschaat, Belgium	
333	DH115 Vampire T55 <ff>	South Yorkshire Aircraft Museum, stored Doncaster, S. Yorks	
349	Hawker Hunter F51 (E-408/G-9-436/*WT720*/8565M)	Centreprise International, Chineham, Hants	
ISRAEL			
353	Beech A36 Bonanza (N336EU)	*To the USA, 2022 as N336EU*	
360	Beech A36 Bonanza (N436EU)	*To the USA, 2022 as N436EU*	
ITALY			
MM5701	Fiat CR42 (BT474/8468M) [13-95]	RAF Museum, Hendon, Gtr London	
MM6976	Fiat CR42 (2542/G-CBLS) [85-16]	The Fighter Collection, Duxford, Cambs	
MM53211	Fiat G46-1B (MM52799) [ZI-4]	Privately owned, Shipdham, Norfolk	
MM53692	CCF T-6G Texan	RAeS Medway Branch, Rochester, Kent	
MM53774	Fiat G59-4B (I-MRSV) [181]	Privately owned, Parma, Italy	
MM54099	NA T-6G Texan (G-BRBC) [RR-56]	Privately owned, Chigwell, Essex	
MM54532	SIAI-Marchetti SF.260AM (G-ITAF) [70-42]	Privately owned, Leicester, Leics	
MM80927	Agusta-Bell AB206A-1 JetRanger [CC-49]	The Helicopter Museum, Weston-super-Mare, Somerset	
MM81205	Agusta A109A-2 SEM [GF-128]	The Helicopter Museum, Weston-super-Mare, Somerset	
MM81220	Agusta A109A-2 SEM	Air Service Training, Perth, Scotland	
MM81335	Agusta A109A-2 SEM	Air Service Training, Perth, Scotland	
MM51-15302	Piper L-18C Super Cub (G-BJTP) [E.I.51]	Privately owned, Sleap, Shropshire	
MM52-2392	Piper L-21B Super Cub (G-HELN) [E.I.69]	Privately owned, White Waltham, Berks	
MM54-2372	Piper L-21B Super Cub (I-EIXM) [EI-184]	Privately owned, Foxhall Heath, Suffolk	
PS-45	Agusta A109A (MM80745)	Privately owned, stored Hixon, Staffs	
PS-48	Agusta A109A (MM80748)	Privately owned, stored Hixon, Staffs	
PS-49	Agusta A109A (MM80749)	Privately owned, stored Hixon, Staffs	
PS-59	Agusta A109A (MM80759)	Privately owned, stored Hixon, Staffs	
PS-64	Agusta A109A (MM81646)	Privately owned, stored Hixon, Staffs	
JAPAN			
-	Kawasaki Ki100-1B (16336/8476M/BAPC.83) [24]	RAF Museum, Hendon, Gtr London	
-	Mitsubishi A6M5-52 Zero (196) [BI-05] <ff>	IWM Duxford, Cambs	
-	Yokosuka MXY 7 Ohka II (BAPC.159)	IWM Lambeth, London	
997	Yokosuka MXY 7 Ohka II (8485M/BAPC.98)	*To transfer to Pima Air and Space Museum, AZ*	
3443	NA T-6 Texan Zero (F-AZRO)	Privately owned, St Rambert d'Albon, France	
5439	Mitsubishi Ki46-III (8484M/BAPC.84)	RAF Museum, Hendon, Gtr London	
15-1585	Yokosuka MXY 7 Ohka II (BAPC.58)	Science Museum, stored Cobham Hall, RNAS Yeovilton, Somerset	
I-13	Yokosuka MXY 7 Ohka II (8486M/BAPC.99)	RAF Museum, Hendon, Gtr London	
Y2-176	Mitsubishi A6M3-2 Zero (3685) [76]	IWM London, Lambeth, London	
KENYA			
115	Dornier Do28D-2 Skyservant (D-IAAI)	Privately owned, stored Hibaldstow, Lincs	
117	Dornier Do28D-2 Skyservant (D-ISCO)	Privately owned, stored Hibaldstow, Lincs	

Notes	Serial	Type (code/other identity)	Owner/operator, location or fate
	MALAYSIA		
	M25-04	SA102 Bulldog (FM1224) (fuselage)	South Wales Aviation Museum, stored St Athan, Wales
	MALTA		
	AS0022	SA Bulldog T1 (XX709/G-CLJC)	Privately owned, Oxon
	AS0023	SA Bulldog T1 (XX714/G-CLJD)	Privately owned, Oxon
	MYANMAR		
	UB441	VS361 Spitfire IX (ML119/G-SDNI)	Privately owned, Biggin Hill, Kent
	THE NETHERLANDS		
	174	Fokker S-11 Instructor (E-31/G-BEPV) [K]	Privately owned, Spanhoe, Northants
	179	Fokker S-11 Instructor (PH-ACG) [K]	Privately owned, Lelystad, The Netherlands
	197	Fokker S-11 Instructor (PH-GRY) [197-K]	KLu Historic Flt, Gilze-Rijen, The Netherlands
	204	Lockheed SP-2H Neptune [V]	RAF Museum, Cosford, Shropshire
	272	Westland SH-14D Lynx	Privately owned, Woodmancote, W. Sussex
	A-57	DH82A Tiger Moth (PH-TYG)	KLu Historic Flt, Gilze-Rijen, The Netherlands
	B-64	Noorduyn AT-16 Harvard IIb (PH-LSK)	KLu Historic Flt, Gilze-Rijen, The Netherlands
	B-71	Noorduyn AT-16 Harvard IIb (PH-MLM)	KLu Historic Flt, Gilze-Rijen, The Netherlands
	B-118	Noorduyn AT-16 Harvard IIb (PH-IIB)	KLu Historic Flt, Gilze-Rijen, The Netherlands
	B-182	Noorduyn AT-16 Harvard IIb (PH-TBR)	KLu Historic Flt, Gilze-Rijen, The Netherlands
	E-14	Fokker S-11 Instructor (PH-AFS)	Privately owned, Lelystad, The Netherlands
	E-15	Fokker S-11 Instructor (G-BIYU)	Privately owned, Breighton, E. Yorks
	E-20	Fokker S-11 Instructor (PH-GRB)	Privately owned, Gilze-Rijen, The Netherlands
	E-27	Fokker S-11 Instructor (PH-HOL)	Privately owned, Lelystad, The Netherlands
	E-29	Fokker S-11 Instructor (PH-HOI)	Privately owned, Lelystad, The Netherlands
	E-32	Fokker S-11 Instructor (PH-HOl)	Privately owned, Gilze-Rijen, The Netherlands
	E-39	Fokker S-11 Instructor (PH-HOG)	Privately owned, Lelystad, The Netherlands
	G-29	Beech D18S (PH-KHV)	KLu Historic Flt, Gilze-Rijen, The Netherlands
	MK732	VS361 Spitfire LF IXc (8633M/PH-OUQ) [3W-17]	KLu Historic Flt, Gilze-Rijen, The Netherlands
	N-202	Hawker Hunter F6 [10] <ff>	Privately owned, Stockport, Cheshire
	N-250	Hawker Hunter F6 (G-9-185) <ff>	IWM Duxford, Cambs
	N-302	Hawker Hunter T7 (ET-273/G-9-431) <ff>	South Yorkshire Aircraft Museum, Doncaster, S. Yorks
	N-315	Hawker Hunter T7 (comp XM121)	Privately owned, Netherley, Aberdeenshire
	N-321	Hawker Hunter T8C (XF357/G-BWGL)	Privately owned, St Athan, Wales
	N5-149	NA B-25J Mitchell (44-29507/HD346/PH-XXV) [232511]	KLu Historic Flt, Gilze-Rijen, The Netherlands
	R-18	Auster III (PH-NGK)	KLu Historic Flt, Gilze-Rijen, The Netherlands
	R-45	Piper L-18C Super Cub (52-2452/G-AXLZ)	Privately owned, Shoreham, W. Sussex (stored)
	R-55	Piper L-18C Super Cub (52-2466/G-BLMI)	Privately owned, Antwerp-Deurne, Belgium
	R-109	Piper L-21B Super Cub (54-2337/PH-GAZ)	KLu Historic Flt, Gilze-Rijen, The Netherlands
	R-122	Piper L-21B Super Cub (54-2412/PH-PPW)	KLu Historic Flt, Gilze-Rijen, The Netherlands
	R-124	Piper L-21B Super Cub (54-2414/PH-APA)	Privately owned, Eindhoven, The Netherlands
	R-137	Piper L-21B Super Cub (54-2427/PH-PSC)	Privately owned, Gilze-Rijen, The Netherlands
	R-151	Piper L-21B Super Cub (54-2441/G-BIYR)	Privately owned, Yarcombe, Devon
	R-156	Piper L-21B Super Cub (54-2446/G-ROVE)	Privately owned, Damyn's Hall, Gtr London
	R-167	Piper L-21B Super Cub (54-2457/G-LION)	Privately owned, Druid, Denbighshire, Wales
	R-170	Piper L-21B Super Cub (52-6222/PH-ENJ)	Privately owned, Seppe, The Netherlands
	R-177	Piper L-21B Super Cub (54-2467/PH-KNR)	KLu Historic Flt, Gilze-Rijen, The Netherlands
	R-181	Piper L-21B Super Cub (54-2471/PH-GAU)	Privately owned, Gilze-Rijen, The Netherlands
	R-184	Piper L-21A Super Cub (54-2474/G-PCUB)	Privately owned, stored Paddock Wood, Kent
	R-213	Piper L-21A Super Cub (51-15682/PH-RED)	Privately owned, Seppe, The Netherlands
	R-345	Piper L-4J Grasshopper (PH-UCS)	Privately owned, Hilversum, The Netherlands
	S-9	DHC2 L-20A Beaver (55-4585/PH-DHC)	KLu Historic Flt, Gilze-Rijen, The Netherlands
	NETHERLANDS EAST INDIES		
	S11	Ryan STM-2 (S-40/N7779)	Privately owned, Old Warden, Beds
	NEW ZEALAND		
	NZ3909	WS Wasp HAS1 (XT782/G-CMBE)	Privately owned, Thruxton, Hants
	NZ5911	Bristol 170 Freighter 31M (ZK-EPG)	Aerospace Bristol, stored Filton, Glos
	NZ6300	BAC Strikemaster Mk.80 (G-RNAF)	Privately owned, Hawarden, Flintshire, Wales

Serial	Type (code/other identity)	Owner/operator, location or fate	Notes
NORTH KOREA			
-	WSK Lim-2 (MiG-15) (01420/G-BMZF)	FAA Museum, RNAS Yeovilton, Somerset	
NORTH VIETNAM			
1211	WSK Lim-5 (MiG-17F) (G-MIGG)	Privately owned, North Weald, Essex	
NORWAY			
145	DH82A Tiger Moth II (DE248/LN-BDM)	Privately owned, Kjeller, Norway	
163	Fairchild PT-19A Cornell (42-83641/LN-BIF)	Privately owned, Kjeller, Norway	
171	DH82A Tiger Moth II (T6168/LN-KAY)	Privately owned, Kjeller, Norway	
599	Canadair CT-133AUP Silver Star Mk.3 (133599/LN-DPS)	Norwegian AF Historical Sqn, Ørland, Norway	
848	Piper L-18C Super Cub (LN-ACL) [FA-N]	Privately owned, Kjeller, Norway	
56321	SAAB S91B Safir (G-BKPY)	Newark Air Museum, Winthorpe, Notts	
PX-M	DH115 Vampire T55 (U-1230/*WZ447*/LN-DHZ)	Norwegian AF Historical Sqn, Rygge, Norway	
OMAN			
417	BAC Strikemaster Mk.80A (G-RSAF)	Privately owned, Hawarden, Flintshire, Wales	
425	BAC Strikemaster Mk.82A (G-SOAF)	Privately owned, Hawarden, Flintshire, Wales	
801	Hawker Hunter T66B <rf>	Privately owned, Hawarden, Flintshire, Wales	
853	Hawker Hunter FR10 (XF426)	RAF Museum, stored Cosford, Shropshire	
XL554	SAL Pioneer CC1 (XL703/8034M)	RAF Museum, stored Cosford, Shropshire	
POLAND			
05	WSK SM-2 (Mi-2) (S2-03006)	The Helicopter Museum, Weston-super-Mare, Somerset	
309	WSK SBLim-2A (MiG-15UTI) <ff>	Scottish Mus'm of Flight, stored Granton	
458	Mikoyan MiG-23ML (04 red/024003607)	Newark Air Museum, Winthorpe, Notts	
1018	WSK-PZL Mielec TS-11 Iskra (1H-1018/G-ISKA)	*Current status unknown (ex-Bruntingthorpe, Leics)*	
1120	WSK Lim-2 (MiG-15bis)	RAF Museum, Cosford, Shropshire	
1706	WSK-PZL Mielec TS-11 Iskra (1H-0408)	Midland Air Museum, Coventry, Warks	
1708	WSK-PZL Mielec TS-11 Iskra bis DF (3H-1625/G-BXVZ) [4]	RAF Manston History Museum, Kent	
1972	Letov S-102 (MiG-15) (623794) (port side only, painted in Czech marks as 3794 on starboard side)	Norfolk & Suffolk Avn Museum, Flixton, Suffolk	
7811	Mikoyan MiG-21MF (96N7811)	Privately owned, Alton, Hants	
PORTUGAL			
1350	OGMA/DHC1 Chipmunk T20 (G-CGAO)	Privately owned, Duxford, Cambs	
1365	OGMA/DHC1 Chipmunk T20 (G-DHPM)	Privately owned, Sleap, Shropshire	
1367	OGMA/DHC1 Chipmunk T20 (G-UANO)	Privately owned, Breighton, E. Yorks	
1372	OGMA/DHC1 Chipmunk T20 (HB-TUM)	Privately owned, Switzerland	
1373	OGMA/DHC1 Chipmunk T20 (G-CBJG)	Privately owned, Winwick, Cambs	
1375	OGMA/DHC1 Chipmunk T20 (F-AZJV)	Privately owned, Valenciennes, France	
1377	DHC1 Chipmunk 22 (WK520/G-BARS)	Privately owned, Yeovilton, Somerset	
1741	CCF T-6J Texan (G-HRVD)	Privately owned, Perigeux, France	
1747	CCF T-6J Texan (*20385*/G-BGPB)	Privately owned, Gloucestershire Airport, Glos	
3303	MH1521M Broussard (G-CBGL)	Privately owned, stored Postling, Kent	
QATAR			
QA10	Hawker Hunter FGA78	Yorkshire Air Museum, Elvington, N. Yorks	
QA12	Hawker Hunter FGA78 <ff>	Privately owned, New Inn, Torfaen, Wales	
QP30	WS Lynx Mk.28 (G-BFDV/TAD013/ZZ003)	FETC, Moreton-in-Marsh, Glos	
QP31	WS Lynx Mk.28 (ZZ004)	Newark Air Museum, Winthorpe, Notts	
QP32	WS Lynx Mk.28 (TD 016/ZZ005) [A]	DSAE SAAE, Lyneham, Wilts, on display	
ROMANIA			
29	LET L-29 Delfin	Privately owned, Skirpenbeck, E. Yorks	
42	LET L-29 Delfin <ff>	Privately owned,	
42	LET L-29 Delfin <rf>	Privately owned,	
47	LET L-29 Delfin <ff>	Top Gun Flight Simulator Centre, Stalybridge, Gtr Manchester	
53	LET L-29 Delfin [66654]	*Current status unknown (ex-Bruntingthorpe, Leics)*	

Notes	Serial	Type (code/other identity)	Owner/operator, location or fate
		RUSSIA (& FORMER SOVIET UNION)	
	-	Mil Mi-24D (3532464505029)	Midland Air Museum, Coventry, Warks
00 w		Yakovlev Yak-3M (0470202/G-OLEG)	Privately owned, Sywell, Northants
1 w		SPP Yak C-11 (171314/G-BZMY)	Privately owned, Alscot Park, Warks
01 y		Yakovlev Yak-52 (9311709/G-YKSZ)	Privately owned, White Waltham, Berks
03 bl		Yakovlev Yak-55M (910103/RA-01274)	Privately owned, Halfpenny Green, Staffs
03 w		Yakovlev Yak-18A (1160403/G-CEIB)	Privately owned, Breighton, E. Yorks
5 w		Yakovlev Yak-3UA (0470204/D-FYGJ)	Privately owned, Bremgarten, Germany
06 y		Yakovlev Yak-9UM (HB-RYA)	To the USA as N16YK
6 w		Yakovlev Yak-3UA (127612/F-AZOS)	Privately owned, Melun, France
07 r		Mil Mi-8P (10618)	The Helicopter Museum, Weston-super-Mare, Somerset
07 y		WSK SM-1 (Mi-1) (Polish AF 2007)	The Helicopter Museum, Weston-super-Mare, Somerset
07 y		Yakovlev Yak-18M (G-BMJY)	Privately owned, Membury, Bucks
9 w		SPP Yak C-11 (1701139/G-OYAK)	Privately owned, Little Gransden, Cambs
10 r		Yakovlev Yak-52 (877610/G-YAKE)	Privately owned, Henstridge, Somerset
14 r		WSK-PZL An-2R (HA-MKE)	Morayvia, Kinloss, Scotland
15 w		SPP Yak C-11 (170103/D-FYAK)	Classic Aviation Company, Hannover, Germany
17 w		Bell P-63C Kingcobra (44-4315)	Wings Museum, Balcombe, W. Sussex
18 r		LET L-29 Delfin (591771/YL-PAF)	Privately owned, Hawarden, Flintshire, Wales
18 r		WSK SBLim-2 (MiG-15UTI) (1A01004/N104CJ)	Norwegian AF Historical Sqn, Rygge, Norway
18 r		Yakovlev Yak-50 (801810/G-BTZB)	Privately owned, Henstridge, Somerset
20 r		Yakovlev Yak-50 (812003/G-YAAK)	Privately owned, Henstridge, Somerset
20 w		Lavochkin La-11	The Fighter Collection, stored Duxford, Cambs
21 w		Yakovlev Yak-3UA (0470203/G-CDBJ)	Privately owned, Folkestone, Kent
21 w		Yakovlev Yak-9UM (0470403/D-FENK)	Privately owned, Magdeburg, Germany
23 y		Bell P-39Q Airacobra (44-2911)	Privately owned, Sussex
23 r		Mikoyan MiG-27D (83712515040)	Privately owned, Hawarden, Flintshire, Wales
26 bl		Yakovlev Yak-52 (9111306/G-BVXK)	Privately owned, White Waltham, Berks
27 w		Yakovlev Yak-3UTI-PW (9/04623/F-AZIM)	Privately owned, North Weald, Essex
27 r		Yakovlev Yak-52 (9111307/G-YAKX)	Privately owned, Popham, Hants
27 w		Yakovlev Yak-3UTI-PW <R> (F-AZIM)	Privately owned, Blackbushe, Hants
28 w		Polikarpov Po-2 (0094/G-BSSY)	The Shuttleworth Collection, Old Warden, Beds
33 r		Yakovlev Yak-50 (853206/G-YAKZ)	Privately owned, Henstridge, Somerset
33 w		Yakovlev Yak-52 (899915/G-YAKH)	Privately owned, White Waltham, Berks
35 r		Sukhoi Su-17M-3 (25102)	Privately owned, Hawarden, Flintshire, Wales
36 w		LET/Yak C-11 (171101/G-KYAK)	Privately owned, North Weald, Essex
36 r		Yakovlev Yak-52 (9111604/G-IUII)	Privately owned, St Athan, Wales
43 bl		Yakovlev Yak-52 (877601/G-BWSV)	Privately owned, North Weald, Essex
48 w		Yakovlev Yak-3UPW <R> (F-AZZK)	Privately owned, Lelystad, The Netherlands
49 r		Yakovlev Yak-50 (822305/G-YAKU)	Privately owned, Henstridge, Somerset
50 gy		Yakovlev Yak-52 (9111415/G-CBRW)	Privately owned, Duxford, Cambs
50 y		Yakovlev Yak-50 (801804/G-EYAK)	Privately owned, Leicester, Leics
51 r		LET L-29S Delfin (491273/YL-PAC)	Privately owned, Breighton, E. Yorks
52 bk		Yakovlev Yak-52 (877409/G-FLSH)	Privately owned, St Athan, Wales
52 w		Yakovlev Yak-52 (9612001/G-CCJK)	Privately owned, White Waltham, Berks
52 y		Yakovlev Yak-52 (878202/G-BWVR)	Privately owned, Eshott, Northumberland
54 r		Sukhoi Su-17M (69004)	Privately owned, Hawarden, Flintshire, Wales
61 r		Yakovlev Yak-50 (842710/G-YAKM)	Privately owned, Henstridge, Somerset
66 r		Yakovlev Yak-52 (855905/G-YAKN)	Privately owned, Henstridge, Somerset
71 r		Mikoyan MiG-27K (61912507006)	Newark Air Museum, Winthorpe, Notts
74 w		Yakovlev Yak-52 (877404/G-OUGH) [JA-74, IV-62]	Privately owned, Swansea, Wales
86 w		Yakovlev Yak-52 (867212/G-YAKC)	Privately owned, Henstridge, Somerset
100 bl		Yakovlev Yak-52 (866904/G-YAKI)	Privately owned, Popham, Hants
526 bk		Mikoyan MiG-29 (2960725887) <ff>	South Wales Aviation Museum, St Athan, Wales
1342		Yakovlev Yak-1 (G-BTZD)	Privately owned, Westfield, E. Sussex
1870710		Ilyushin Il-2 (G-BZVW)	Privately owned, Wickenby, Lincs
1878576		Ilyushin Il-2 (G-BZVX)	Privately owned, Wickenby, Lincs
PT879		VS361 Spitfire F IX (G-PTIX)	Privately owned, North Weald, Essex
(RK858)		VS361 Spitfire LF IX (G-CGJE)	The Fighter Collection, Duxford, Cambs

Serial	Type (code/other identity)	Owner/operator, location or fate	Notes
SAUDI ARABIA			
1115	BAC Strikemaster Mk.80A	Global Aviation, Humberside, Lincs	
1129	BAC Strikemaster Mk.80A	Humberside Airport, Lincs, on display	
1133	BAC Strikemaster Mk.80A (G-BESY)	IWM Duxford, Cambs	
53-671	BAC Lightning F53 (203/ZF579)	Gatwick Aviation Museum, Charlwood, Surrey	
53-686	BAC Lightning F53 (G-AWON/201/1305/223/ZF592)	City of Norwich Aviation Museum, Norfolk	
55-713	BAC Lightning T55 (206/1316/235/ZF598) [C]	Midland Air Museum, Coventry, Warks	
SINGAPORE			
311	BAC Strikemaster Mk.84 (G-MXPH)	Privately owned, stored Hawarden, Flintshire, Wales	
323	BAC Strikemaster Mk.81 (N21419)	Privately owned, stored Hawarden, Flintshire, Wales	
SOUTH AFRICA			
91	Westland Wasp HAS1 (pod)	Privately owned, Oaksey Park, Wilts	
92	Westland Wasp HAS1 (G-BYCX)	Privately owned, Dunchurch, Warks	
6130	Lockheed Ventura II (AJ469)	RAF Museum, stored Cosford, Shropshire	
7429	NA AT-6D Harvard III (D-FASS)	Privately owned, Aachen, Germany	
SOUTH ARABIA			
104	BAC Jet Provost T52A (G-PROV)	Privately owned, North Weald, Essex	
SOUTH VIETNAM			
24550	Cessna L-19E Bird Dog (G-PDOG) [GP]	Privately owned, Old Warden, Beds	
112471	Cessna L-19G Bird Dog (51-12471/VH-FXY) [DF]	Privately owned, Lydd, Kent	
SPAIN			
A1+DA	CASA 2.111B (He111H-16) (B.2I-103)	Kent Battle of Britain Museum, Hawkinge, Kent	
C.4K-30	Hispano HA 1.112M1L Buchón [471-26]	Privately owned, Sywell, Northants	
E.3B-143	CASA 1.131E Jungmann (G-JUNG)	Privately owned, Breighton, E. Yorks	
E.3B-153	CASA 1.131E Jungmann (G-BPTS) [781-75]	Privately owned, Egginton, Derbyshire	
E.3B-494	CASA 1.131E Jungmann (G-CDLC) [81-47]	Privately owned, Chiseldon, Wilts	
E.3B-521	CASA 1.131E Jungmann [781-3]	RAF Museum Reserve Collection, Stafford, Staffs	
E.3B-599	CASA 1.131E Jungmann (G-CGTX) [791-31]	Privately owned, Archerfield, Lothian, Scotland	
E.18-2	Piper PA-31P Navajo 425 [42-71]	High Harthay Outdoor Pursuits, Huntingdon, Cambs	
ES.1-31	CASA 1.133C Jungmeister (G-RPAX) [35-23]	Privately owned, Breighton, E. Yorks	
T.2B-272	CASA C.352L (G-AFAP)	Kent Battle of Britain Museum, Hawkinge, Kent	
SRI LANKA			
CT130	Nanchang CJ-6A Chujiao (3151215/G-CJSA)	Privately owned, White Waltham, Berks	
CT180	Nanchang CJ-6A Chujiao (2632016/G-BXZB)	Privately owned, White Waltham, Berks	
SWEDEN			
-	Thulin A/Bleriot XI (SE-XMC)	Privately owned, Loberod, Sweden	
087	CFM 01 Tummelisa <R> (SE-XIL)	Privately owned, Loberod, Sweden	
5033	Klemm Kl35D (SE-BPT) [78]	Privately owned, Barkaby, Sweden	
5060	Klemm Kl35D (SE-BPU) [174]	Privately owned, Barkaby, Sweden	
05108	DH60 Moth	Privately owned, Langham, Norfolk	
17239	SAAB B 17A (SE-BYH) [7-J]	Flygvapenmuseum, Linköping, Sweden	
29640	SAAB J 29F [20-08]	Midland Air Museum, Coventry, Warks	
29670	SAAB J 29F (SE-DXB) [10-R]	Swedish Air Force Historic Flt, Såtenäs, Sweden	
32028	SAAB 32A Lansen (G-BMSG) <ff>	Privately owned, Willenhall, Staffs	
32542	SAAB J 32B Lansen (SE-RMD) [23]	Swedish Air Force Historic Flt, Såtenäs, Sweden	
35075	SAAB J 35A Draken [40]	Dumfries & Galloway Aviation Museum, Scotland	
35515	SAAB J 35F Draken [49]	Airborne Systems, Llangeinor, Wales	
35556	SAAB J 35J Draken (SE-DXR) [56]	Swedish Air Force Historic Flt, Såtenäs, Sweden	
35810	SAAB Sk 35C Draken (SE-DXP) [79]	Swedish Air Force Historic Flt, Såtenäs, Sweden	
37098	SAAB AJSF 37 Viggen (SE-DXN) [52]	Swedish Air Force Historic Flt, Såtenäs, Sweden	
37809	SAAB Sk 37E Viggen (SE-DXO) [61]	Swedish Air Force Historic Flt, Såtenäs, Sweden	
37918	SAAB AJSH 37 Viggen [57]	Newark Air Museum, Winthorpe, Notts	

Notes	Serial	Type (code/other identity)	Owner/operator, location or fate
	50042	SAAB S91B Safir (G-CLSP) [72]	Privately owned, Eshott, Northumberland
	60140	SAAB Sk 60E (SE-DXG) [140-5]	Swedish Air Force Historic Flt, Såtenäs, Sweden
	91130	SAAB S91A Safir (SE-BNN) [10-30]	Privately owned, Barkaby, Sweden
	103003	Cessna 550 Citation 2 (SE-RMI) [003]	Swedish Air Force Historic Flt, Trollhattan, Sweden
	SWITZERLAND		
	A-10	CASA 1.131E Jungmann (G-BECW)	Privately owned, Postling, Kent
	A-35	Bücker Bü131B Jungmann (G-CLKV)	Privately owned, Henstridge, Somerset
	A-44	CASA 1.131E Jungmann 2000 (G-CIUE)	Privately owned, Breighton, E. Yorks
	A-57	CASA 1.131E Jungmann (G-BECT)	Privately owned, Goodwood, W. Sussex
	A-125	Pilatus P2-05 (G-BLKZ) (fuselage)	Privately owned, Newquay, Cornwall
	A-806	Pilatus P3-03 (G-BTLL)	Privately owned, Guist, Norfolk
	A-815	Pilatus P3-03 (HB-RCQ)	Privately owned, Locarno, Switzerland
	A-818	Pilatus P3-03 (HB-RCH)	Privately owned, Ambri, Switzerland
	A-829	Pilatus P3-03 (HB-RCJ)	Privately owned, Altenrhein, Switzerland
	A-873	Pilatus P3-03 (OO-RDS)	Privately owned, Brustem, Belgium
	C-509	EKW C-3605 (HB-RDH)	46 Aviation, Sion, Switzerland
	C-552	EKW C-3605 (G-DORN)	Privately owned, Little Gransden, Cambs
	C-558	EKW C-3605 (G-CCYZ)	Privately owned, Wickenby, Lincs
	J-143	F+W D-3801 (MS406) (HB-RCF)	Privately owned, Bex, Switzerland
	J-1008	DH100 Vampire FB6	de Havilland Aircraft Museum, London Colney
	J-1169	DH100 Vampire FB6	Privately owned, Henley-on-Thames, Oxon
	J-1172	DH100 Vampire FB6 (8487M)	RAF Museum Reserve Collection, Stafford, Staffs
	J-1573	DH112 Venom FB50 (G-VICI) <ff>	Privately owned, Tetbury, Glos
	J-1605	DH112 Venom FB50 (G-BLID)	Gatwick Aviation Museum, Charlwood, Surrey
	J-1632	DH112 Venom FB50 (G-VNOM) <ff>	Privately owned, Lavendon, Bucks
	J-1649	DH112 Venom FB50 <ff>	Cornwall Aviation Heritage Centre, Newquay, Cornwall
	J-1704	DH112 Venom FB54	RAF Museum, stored Cosford, Shropshire
	J-1790	DH112 Venom FB54 (G-BLKA/*WR410*)	Historic Aviation Centre, Fishburn, Co. Durham
	J-4015	Hawker Hunter F58 (J-4040/HB-RVS)	Privately owned, St Stephan, Switzerland
	J-4086	Hawker Hunter F58 (HB-RVU)	*Sold as N348AX, 2022*
	J-4110	Hawker Hunter F58A (XF318/G-CJWL)	Hawker Hunter Aviation Ltd, stored Leeming, N. Yorks
	J-4201	Hawker Hunter T68 (HB-RVR)	Amici dell'Hunter, Sion, Switzerland
	N-322	Hawker Hunter T68 (J-4205/G-EHLW)	Privately owned, St. Athan, Wales
	J-4206	Hawker Hunter T68 (HB-RVV)	Fliegermuseum Altenrhein, Switzerland
	U-80	Bücker Bü133D Jungmeister (G-BUKK)	Privately owned, Coventry, Warks
	U-95	Bücker Bü133C Jungmeister (G-BVGP)	Privately owned, Turweston, Bucks
	U-99	Bücker Bü133C Jungmeister (G-AXMT)	Privately owned, Breighton, E. Yorks
	U-1215	DH115 Vampire T11 (XE998)	Solent Sky, Southampton, Hants
	V-54	SE3130 Alouette II (2-BVSD)	Privately owned, Glos
	UNITED ARAB EMIRATES		
	005	Piper PA.44	Privately owned, Shoreham, W. Sussex (stored)
	DU-103	Bell 206B JetRanger II	Privately owned, Coney Park, Leeds, W. Yorks
	USA		
	-	Noorduyn AT-16 Harvard IIB (KLu B-168)	American Air Museum, Duxford, Cambs
	07	Boeing-Stearman PT-17 Kaydet (N62658)	Privately owned,
	14	Boeing-Stearman A75N-1 Kaydet (3486/G-ISDN)	Privately owned, Oaksey Park, Wilts
	18	Agusta-Bell AB204B (MM80279/*MM80270*)	MAG36-UK, Manston, Kent
	23	Fairchild PT-23 (N49272) [23]	Privately owned, Sleap, Shropshire
	26	Boeing-Stearman A75N-1 Kaydet (G-BAVO)	Privately owned, Enstone, Oxon
	27	Boeing-Stearman N2S-3 Kaydet (4304/G-CJYK)	Privately owned, Dublin, Eire
	28	Boeing-Stearman PT-27 Kaydet (42-15666/G-CKSR)	Privately owned, RAF Woodvale, Merseyside
	31	Boeing-Stearman A75N-1 Kaydet (42-16338/G-KAYD)	Privately owned, Sherburn in Elmet, N. Yorks
	37-002	Douglas AD-4NA Skyraider (F-AZHK) [TC]	Privately owned, Avignon, France
	43	Boeing-Stearman PT-13D Kaydet (42-17152/G-CIPE)	Privately owned, Gloucester, Glos
	43	Noorduyn AT-16 Harvard IIB (43-13064/G-AZSC) [SC]	Privately owned, Goodwood, W. Sussex
	44	Boeing-Stearman D75N-1 Kaydet (42-15852/G-LIIZ)	Privately owned, Breighton, E. Yorks

Serial	Type (code/other identity)	Owner/operator, location or fate	Notes
72	NA SNJ-5 Texan (42-85897/431917/G-DHHF) [JF]	DH Heritage Flights Ltd, Compton Abbas, Dorset	
85	WAR P-47 Thunderbolt <R> (G-BTBI)	Privately owned, Perth, Scotland	
104	Boeing-Stearman PT-13D Kaydet (42-16931/N4712V) [W]	Privately owned, Hardwick, Norfolk	
107	Boeing-Stearman PT-17 Kaydet (42-16107/N62658)	Privately owned,	
112	Boeing-Stearman PT-13D Kaydet (42-17397/G-BSWC)	Privately owned, Gloucester, Glos	
131	Boeing-Stearman PT-17 Kaydet (38254/N74677)	Privately owned, Enstone, Oxon	
164	Boeing-Stearman PT-13B Kaydet (41-0823/N60320)	Privately owned, Fenland, Cambs	
286	Boeing-Stearman N2S-4 Kaydet (55749/N10053)	Privately owned, Breighton, E. Yorks	
317	Boeing-Stearman PT-18 Kaydet (41-61042/G-CIJN)	Privately owned, Goodwood, W. Sussex	
349	Boeing-Stearman N2S-2 Kaydet (3572/N2JS) [1349]	Privately owned, Old Warden, Beds	
371	Boeing-Stearman PT-17 Kaydet (41-0927/G-CKXY)	Privately owned, Old Warden, Beds	
379	Boeing-Stearman PT-13D Kaydet (42-14865/G-ILLE)	Privately owned, Hohenems, Austria	
399	Boeing-Stearman N2S-5 Kaydet (38495/N67193)	Privately owned, Gelnhausen, Germany	
405	Boeing-Stearman PT-17 Kaydet (40-1885/F-AZSN)	Privately owned, Saint Rambert, France	
441	Boeing-Stearman N2S-4 Kaydet (30010/G-BTFG)	Privately owned, Postling, Kent	
443	Boeing-Stearman E75 Kaydet (N43YP) [6018]	Privately owned, East Hanney, Oxon	
466	Boeing-Stearman PT-13A Kaydet (37-0089/G-PTBA)	Privately owned, Gloucestershire Airport, Glos	
540	Piper L-4H Grasshopper (43-29877/G-BCNX)	Privately owned, Monewden, Suffolk	
560	Bell UH-1H Iroquois (73-22077/G-HUEY)	Privately owned, North Weald, Essex	
578	Boeing-Stearman N2S-5 Kaydet (N1364V)	Privately owned, North Weald, Essex	
582	Boeing-Stearman PT-17 Kaydet (42-16663/4826/G-CJIN)	Privately owned, Breighton, E. Yorks	
586	Boeing-Stearman N2S-3 Kaydet (07874/N74650)	Privately owned, Seppe, The Netherlands	
628	Beech D17S (44-67761/N18V)	Privately owned, stored East Garston, Bucks	
669	Boeing-Stearman A75N-1 Kaydet (37869/G-CCXA)	Privately owned, Old Buckenham, Norfolk	
671	Boeing-Stearman PT-13D Kaydet (61181/G-CGPY)	Privately owned, Dunkeswell, Devon	
699	Boeing-Stearman N2S-3 Kaydet (38233/G-CCXB)	Privately owned, Goodwood, W. Sussex	
716	Boeing-Stearman PT-13D Kaydet (42-17553/N1731B)	Privately owned, Oaksey Park, Wilts	
718	Boeing-Stearman PT-13D Kaydet (42-17555/N5345N)	Privately owned, Tibenham, Norfolk	
744	Boeing-Stearman A75N-1 Kaydet (42-16532/OO-USN)	Privately owned, Wevelgem, Belgium	
805	Boeing-Stearman PT-17 Kaydet (42-17642/N3922B)	Privately owned, Tibenham, Norfolk	
854	Ryan PT-22 Recruit (41-20854/G-BTBH)	Privately owned, Turweston, Bucks	
855	Ryan PT-22 Recruit (41-15510/N56421)	Privately owned, Sleap, Shropshire	
897	Aeronca 11AC Chief (G-BJEV) [E]	Privately owned, English Bicknor, Glos	
985	Boeing-Stearman PT-13D Kaydet (42-16930/OO-OPS)	Noted derelict, Ak-Chin, AZ, USA, 2021	
1102	Boeing-Stearman N2S-5 Kaydet (43449/G-AZLE) [102]	DH Heritage Flights Ltd, Compton Abbas, Dorset	
2610	Boeing-Stearman A75 Kaydet (4280/G-FRDM) [408]	Privately owned, Bicester, Oxon	
3397	Boeing-Stearman N2S-3 Kaydet (G-OBEE) [174]	Privately owned, Inverness, Scotland	
3583	Piper L-4B Grasshopper (43-0583/G-FINT) [44-D]	Privately owned, Eggesford, Devon	
3681	Piper L-4J Grasshopper (44-80248/G-AXGP)	Privately owned, Bentwaters, Suffolk	*
3914	Piper L-4B Grasshopper (43-0914/G-BHZU)	Privately owned, Fishburn, Co. Durham	
4406	Naval Aircraft Factory N3N-3 (G-ONAF) [12]	Privately owned, Sandown, IOW	
4445	Naval Aircraft Factory N3N-3 (G-CFXT) [228]	Privately owned, Wickenby, Lincs (restoration)	
4826	Boeing-Stearman PT-17 Kaydet (42-16663/G-CJIN) [582]	Privately owned, Breighton, E. Yorks	
6136	Boeing-Stearman A75N-1 Kaydet(42-16136/G-BRUJ) [205]	Privately owned, Dubová, Slovakia	
6771	Republic F-84F Thunderstreak (BAF FU-6)	Bentwaters Cold War Museum, Suffolk	
7797	Aeronca L-16A Grasshopper (47-0797/G-BFAF)	Privately owned, Finmere, Oxon	
8242	NA F-86A Sabre (48-0242) [FU-242]	Midland Air Museum, Coventry, Warks	
01532	Northrop F-5E Tiger II <R> (BAPC.336)	RAF Alconbury, Cambs, on display	
02538	Fairchild PT-19B (N33870)	Privately owned, Mendlesham, Suffolk	
07539	Boeing-Stearman N2S-3 Kaydet (N63590) [143]	Privately owned, North Weald, Essex	
14286	Lockheed T-33A Shooting Star (51-4286)	Noted Warner-Robins, GA, USA	
O-14419	Lockheed T-33A Shooting Star (51-4419)	Midland Air Museum, Coventry, Warks	
O-14781	Cessna L-19A Bird Dog (51-4781/G-VNAM)	Privately owned, Membury, Wilts	
14863	NA AT-6D Harvard III (41-33908/G-BGOR)	Repainted as 133908	
15372	Piper L-18C Super Cub (51-15372/N123SA) [372-A]	Privately owned, Crowfield, Suffolk	
15979	Hughes OH-6A Cayuse (69-15979)	RAF Mildenhall, Suffolk, instructional use	
15990	Bell AH-1F Hueycobra (70-15990)	Army Flying Museum, Middle Wallop, Hants	
16037	Piper J-3C-65 Cub (G-BSFD)	Privately owned, Sleap, Shropshire	

Notes	Serial	Type (code/other identity)	Owner/operator, location or fate
	16171	NA F-86D Sabre (51-6171)	North-East Land, Sea & Air Museums, Usworth, T&W
	16445	Bell AH-1F Hueycobra (69-16445)	Defence Academy of the UK, Shrivenham, Oxon
	16506	Hughes OH-6A Cayuse (67-16506)	The Helicopter Museum, Weston-super-Mare, Somerset
	16544	NA AT-6A Texan (41-16544/N13FY) [FY]	Privately owned, Hilversum, The Netherlands
	16579	Bell UH-1H Iroquois (66-16579)	The Helicopter Museum, Weston-super-Mare, Somerset
	16718	Lockheed T-33A Shooting Star (51-6718) [TR-999]	City of Norwich Aviation Museum, Norfolk
	O-16957	Cessna L-19A Bird Dog (N51-16957/N5308G)	Privately owned, Sleap, Shropshire
	17692	NA T-28S Fennec (51-7692/G-TROY) [TL-692]	Privately owned, Sywell, Northants
	17962	Lockheed SR-71A Blackbird (61-7962)	American Air Museum, Duxford, Cambs
	18263	Boeing-Stearman PT-17 Kaydet (41-8263/N38940) [822]	Privately owned, Tibenham, Norfolk
	19252	Lockheed T-33A Shooting Star (51-9252)	Bentwaters Cold War Museum, Suffolk
	21300	Cessna O-2A Super Skymaster (67-21300/N590D)	Privately owned, Lelystad, The Netherlands
	21509	Bell UH-1H Iroquois (72-21509/G-UHIH)	Privately owned, Wesham, Lancs
	21605	Bell UH-1H Iroquois (72-21605)	American Air Museum, Duxford, Cambs
	23648	Breda-Nardi NH-500MC (MM81000)	Privately owned, Bristol, Glos
	24538	Kaman HH-43F Huskie (62-4535)	Midland Air Museum, Coventry, Warks
	24568	Cessna L-19E Bird Dog (LN-WNO)	Army Aviation Norway, Kjeller, Norway
	24582	Cessna L-19E Bird Dog (G-VDOG)	Privately owned, Dundee, Scotland
	26359	Piper L-21B Super Cub (54-2619/G-BNXM) [32]	Privately owned, White Waltham, Berks
	30274	Piper AE-1 Cub Cruiser (F-AZTY)	Privately owned, Nangis, France
	30861	NA TB-25J Mitchell (44-30861/N9089Z)	Privately owned, Balcombe, W. Sussex
	31145	Piper L-4B Grasshopper (43-1145/G-BBLH) [26-G]	Privately owned, Biggin Hill, Kent
	31430	Piper L-4B Grasshopper (43-1430/G-BHVV)	Privately owned, Perranporth, Cornwall
	31952	Aeronca O-58B Defender (G-BRPR)	Privately owned, Solent Airport, Hants
	34037	NA TB-25N Mitchell (44-29366/N9115Z/8838M)	Privately owned, East Kirkby, Lincs
	34064	NA B-25J Mitchell (44-31171/N7614C) [8U]	American Air Museum, Duxford, Cambs
	36922	Titan T-51 Mustang (G-CMPC) [WD-Y]	Privately owned, Benwick, Cambs
	37414	McD F-4C Phantom II (63-7414)	Midland Air Museum, stored Coventry
	39624	Wag Aero Sport Trainer (EI-GMH) [39-D]	Privately owned, Abbeyshrule, Eire
	41386	Thomas-Morse S4 Scout <R> (G-MJTD)	Privately owned, Lutterworth, Leics
	42165	NA F-100D Super Sabre (54-2165) [VM]	IWM, stored Duxford, Cambs
	42196	NA F-100D Super Sabre (54-2196)	Norfolk & Suffolk Avn Museum, Flixton, Suffolk
	43517	Boeing-Stearman N2S-5 Kaydet (G-NZSS) [227]	Privately owned, Woodchurch, Kent
	46214	Grumman TBM-3E Avenger (69327/CF-KCG) [X-3]	American Air Museum, Duxford
	51970	NA AT-6D Texan (41-33888/D-FURI) [V-970]	Privately owned, Aalen, Germany
	53319	Grumman TBM-3E Avenger (HB-RDG) [19]	Privately owned, Bitburg, Germany
	54433	Lockheed T-33A Shooting Star (55-4433) [TR-433]	Norfolk & Suffolk Avn Museum, Flixton, Suffolk
*	54884	Piper L-4J Grasshopper (45-4884/N61787) [57-D]	Privately owned, Sywell, Northants
	55771	Boeing-Stearman N2S-4 Kaydet (N68427) [427]	Privately owned, Dunkeswell, Devon (damaged)
	56498	Douglas C-54Q Skymaster (N44914)	Privately owned, stored North Weald, Essex
	60344	Ryan Navion (N4956C)	Privately owned, Earls Colne, Essex
	60689	Boeing B-52D Stratofortress (56-0689)	American Air Museum, Duxford
	O-63008	NA F-100D Super Sabre (54-2223) [LT]	Newark Air Museum, Winthorpe, Notts
	63319	NA F-100D Super Sabre (54-2269) [FW-319]	RAF Lakenheath, Suffolk, on display
	66692	Lockheed U-2CT (56-6692)	American Air Museum, Duxford, Cambs
	70270	McD F-101B Voodoo (57-270) (fuselage)	Midland Air Museum, stored Coventry, Warks
	80105	Replica SE5a <R> (PH-WWI/G-CCBN) [19]	Privately owned, White Waltham, Berks
	82062	DHC U-6A Beaver (58-2062)	Midland Air Museum, Coventry, Warks
	82127	Cessna 310 (G-APNJ)	Newark Air Museum, Winthorpe, Notts
	85061	NA SNJ-5 Texan (G-OSNJ) [7F]	Privately owned, Kidlington, Oxon
	86690	Grumman FM-2 Wildcat (G-KINL) [F-2]	Privately owned, Duxford, Cambs
	96995	CV F4U-4 Corsair (OE-EAS) [RB-37]	Flying Bulls, Salzburg, Austria
	111836	NA AT-6C Harvard IIa (41-33262/G-TSIX) [JZ-6]	Privately owned, Earls Colne, Oxon
	111989	Cessna L-19A Bird Dog (51-11989/N33600)	Army Flying Museum, Middle Wallop, Hants
	114700	NA T-6G Texan (51-14700/G-TOMC)	Privately owned, Sibbertoft, Northants
	115042	NA T-6G Texan (51-15042/G-BGHU) [TA-042]	Privately owned, Postling, Kent
	115227	NA T-6G Texan (51-15227/G-BKRA)	Privately owned, Shoreham, W. Sussex
	115302	Piper L-18C Super Cub (51-15302/G-BJTP) [TP]	Privately owned, Sleap, Shropshire
	115373	Piper L-18C Super Cub (51-15373/G-AYPM) [A-373]	Privately owned, Popham, Hants
	115684	Piper L-21A Super Cub (51-15684/G-BKVM) [849-DC]	Privately owned, Dunkeswell, Devon

Serial	Type (code/other identity)	Owner/operator, location or fate	Notes
117415	Canadair CT-133 Silver Star (G-BYOY) [TR-415]	RAF Manston History Museum, Kent	
117529	Lockheed T-33A Shooting Star (17473) [TR-529]	Midland Air Museum, Coventry, Warks	
121714	Grumman F8F-2P Bearcat (G-RUMM) [201-B]	The Fighter Collection, Duxford, Cambs	
123716	CV F4U-5NL Corsair (124541/D-FCOR) [19-WF]	Meier Motors, Bremgarten, Germany	
124143	Douglas AD-4NA Skyraider (F-AZDP) [205-RM]	Amicale J-B Salis, la Ferté-Alais, France	
124485	Boeing B-17G Flying Fortress (44-85784/G-BEDF)[DF-A]	B-17 Preservation Ltd, Duxford, Cambs	
124724	CV F4U-5NL Corsair (F-AZEG) [22-NP]	Les Casques de Cuir, la Ferté-Alais, France	
126922	Douglas AD-4NA Skyraider (G-RADR) [503-H]	Kennet Aviation, North Weald, Essex	
133908	NA AT-6D Texan (41-33908/EX935/G-BGOR)	Privately owned, Sywell, Shropshire	
134076	NA AT-6D Texan (41-34671/F-AZSC) [TA076]	Privately owned, Yvetot, France	
138266	NA T-28B Trojan (HB-RCT) [266-CT]	Jet Alpine Fighter, Sion, Switzerland	
138343	NA T-28B Trojan (F-AYSL) [212]	Privately owned, Nangis-Les-Loges, France	
140547	NA T-28C Trojan (F-AZHN) [IF-28]	Privately owned, Toussus le Noble, France	
140566	NA T-28C Trojan (N556EB) [252]	Privately owned, la Ferté-Alais, France	
146289	NA T-28C Trojan (N99153) [2W]	Norfolk & Suffolk Avn Museum, Flixton, Suffolk	
150225	WS58 Wessex 60 (G-AWOX) [123]	Privately owned, Lulsgate, Glos	
155454	NA OV-10B Bronco (158300/99+24/F-AZKM) [26]	Privately owned, Montelimar, France	
155529	McD F-4J(UK) Phantom II (ZE359) [AJ-114]	American Air Museum, Duxford, Cambs	
155848	McD F-4S Phantom II [WT-11]	National Museum of Flight, E Fortune, Scotland	
159233	HS AV-8A Harrier [CG-33]	IWM North, Salford Quays, Gtr Manchester	
162068	McD AV-8B Harrier II (fuselage)	Harrier Heritage Centre, RAF Wittering, Cambs	
162071	McD AV-8B Harrier II (fuselage)	Rolls-Royce, Filton, Glos	
162074	McD AV-8B Harrier II <ff>	Privately owned, Redditch, Worcs	
162730	McD AV-8B Harrier II <ff>	Privately owned, Liverpool, Merseyside	
162737	McD AV-8B Harrier II (fuselage) [38]	RAF, Wittering, Cambs	
162958	McD AV-8B Harrier II <ff>	QinetiQ, Farnborough, Hants	
162964	McD AV-8B Harrier II <ff>	Harrier Heritage Centre, RAF Wittering, Cambs	
162964	McD AV-8B Harrier II <rf>	Privately owned, Charlwood, Surrey	
163205	McD AV-8B Harrier II (fuselage)	Privately owned, Thorpe Wood, N. Yorks	
163423	McD AV-8B Harrier II <ff>	QinetiQ, Boscombe Down, Wilts	
163423	McD AV-8B Harrier II	Privately owned, Leeds Castle, Kent	
210766	Douglas C-47B Skytrain (composite) (K-1) [4U]	Wings Museum, Balcombe, W. Sussex	
217786	Boeing-Stearman PT-17 Kaydet (41-8169/CF-EQS) [25]	American Air Museum, Duxford, Cambs	
224319	Douglas C-47B Skytrain (44-77047/G-AMSN) <ff>	Privately owned, Sussex	
226413	Republic P-47D Thunderbolt (45-49192/N47DD) [UN-Z]	American Air Museum, Duxford, Cambs	
234539	Fairchild PT-19B Cornell (42-34539/N50429) [63]	Flying Bulls, Salzburg, Austria	
236657	Piper L-4A Grasshopper (42-36657/G-BGSJ) [72-D]	Privately owned, Langport, Somerset	
237123	Waco CG-4A Hadrian <R> (fuselage)	Yorkshire Air Museum, Elvington, N. Yorks	
238133	Boeing B-17G Flying Fortress (44-83735/F-BDRS) [C]	American Air Museum, Duxford, Cambs	
238410	Piper L-4A Grasshopper (42-38410/G-BHPK) [44-A]	Privately owned, Tibenham, Norfolk	
241079	Waco CG-4A Hadrian <R> (BAPC.370)	RAF Museum, stored Cosford, Shropshire	
243809	Waco CG-4A Hadrian (BAPC.185)	Army Flying Museum, Middle Wallop, Hants	
252983	Schweizer TG-3A (42-52983/N66630)	IWM Duxford, Cambs, stored	
285068	NA AT-6D Texan (42-85068/G-KAMY)	Privately owned, Old Warden, Beds	
298177	Stinson L-5A Sentinel (42-98177/N6438C) [8-R]	Privately owned, Tibenham, Norfolk	
313048	NA AT-6D Texan (44-81506/OO-JOY)	Privately owned, Wevelgem, Belgium	
314887	Fairchild Argus III (43-14887/G-AJPI)	Privately owned, Eelde, The Netherlands	
315509	Douglas C-47A Skytrain (43-15509/G-BHUB) [W7-S]	American Air Museum, Duxford, Cambs	
315536	Douglas C-47A Skytrain (43-15536/G-BGCG)	Skysport Engineering Ltd, Hatch, Hants	
319764	Waco CG-4A Hadrian (237123/BAPC.157) (fuselage)	Yorkshire Air Museum, Elvington, N. Yorks	
329282	Piper J-3C-65 Cub (N46779)	Privately owned, Abbots Bromley, Staffs	
329405	Piper L-4H Grasshopper (43-29405/G-BCOB) [23-A]	Privately owned, Bicester, Oxon	
329417	Piper L-4A Grasshopper (42-38400/G-BDHK)	Privately owned, English Bicknor, Glos	
329471	Piper L-4H Grasshopper (43-29471/G-BGXA) [44-F]	Privately owned, Martley, Worcs	
329594	Piper L-4H Grasshopper (43-29594/G-BROR)	Privately owned, East Winch, Norfolk	
329601	Piper L-4H Grasshopper (43-29601/G-AXHR) [44-D]	Privately owned, Nayland, Suffolk	
329707	Piper L-4H Grasshopper (43-29707/G-BFBY) [44-S]	Privately owned, Old Buckenham, Norfolk	
329854	Piper L-4H Grasshopper (43-29854/G-BMKC) [44-R]	Privately owned, Biggin Hill, Kent	
329934	Piper L-4H Grasshopper (43-29934/G-BCPH) [72-B]	Privately owned, Garford, Oxon	
330238	Piper L-4H Grasshopper (43-30238/G-LIVH) [24-A]	Privately owned, Yarcombe, Devon	
330244	Piper L-4H Grasshopper (43-30244/G-CGIY) [46-C]	Privately owned, Church Fenton, N. Yorks	
330314	Piper L-4H Grasshopper (43-30314/G-BAET)	Privately owned, Winwick, Cambs	
330372	Piper L-4H Grasshopper (43-30372/G-AISX)	Privately owned, Booker, Bucks	

Notes	Serial	Type (code/other identity)	Owner/operator, location or fate
	330426	Piper L-4J Grasshopper (45-4884/N61787) [53-K]	Privately owned, Podington, Beds
	330485	Piper L-4H Grasshopper (43-30485/G-AJES) [44-C]	Privately owned, Shifnal, Shropshire
	379994	Piper J-3L-65 Cub (G-BPUR) [52-J]	Privately owned, Popham, Hants
	411622	NA P-51D Mustang (44-74427/F-AZSB) [G4-C]	Flying Bulls, Salzburg, Austria
	411631	NA P-51D Mustang (44-73979/472218) [MX-V]	American Air Museum, Duxford, Cambs
	413317	NA P-51D Mustang (44-74409/N51RT) [VF-B]	RAF Museum, Hendon, Gtr London
	413357	NA P-51D Mustang <R> [B7-R]	Privately owned, Byfleet, Surrey
	413410	NA P-51D Mustang <R> (BAPC.255)	Bottisham Airfield Museum, Cambs
	413573	NA P-51D Mustang (44-73415/9133M/N6526D) [B6-V]	RAF Museum, stored Cosford, Shropshire
	413578	NA P-51D Mustang (44-74923/PH-JAT) [C5-W]	Privately owned, Lelystad, The Netherlands
	413779	NA P-51D Mustang (44-73877/G-CMDK) [WD-C]	Privately owned, East Midlands Airport, Leics
	413926	Stewart S-51 Mustang (G-CGOI) [E2-S]	Privately owned, Benwick, Cambs
	414251	NA TF-51D Mustang (44-84847/G-TFSI) [WZ-I]	Privately owned, Sywell, Northants
	414419	NA P-51D Mustang (45-11518/G-MSTG/G-CLNV) [LH-F]	Privately owned, Dunmow, Essex
	414673	Bonsall Replica Mustang (G-BDWM) [LH-I]	Privately owned, Netherthorpe, Derbyshire
	414907	Titan T-51 Mustang (G-DHYS) [CY-S]	Privately owned, Pershore, Worcs
	433915	Consolidated PBV-1A Canso A (RCAF 11005/G-PBYA)	Privately owned, Duxford, Cambs
	434602	Douglas A-26B Invader (44-34602/LN-IVA) [B]	Nordic Warbirds, Västerås, Sweden
	436021	Piper J-3C-65 Cub (G-BWEZ)	Privately owned, Archerfield, Lothian
	436784	Beech G18S (N45CF)	Privately owned, Bressaucourt, Switzerland
	441968	Titan T-51 Mustang (G-FION) [VF-E]	Privately owned, Netherthorpe, Derbyshire
	442268	Noorduyn AT-16 Harvard IIb (KF568/LN-TEX) [TA-268]	Privately owned, Kjeller, Norway
	454467	Piper L-4J Grasshopper (45-4467/G-BILI) [44-J]	Privately owned, Bicester, Oxon
	454471	Piper L-4J Grasshopper (45-4471/G-AKTH)	Privately owned, Goodwood, W. Sussex
	454537	Piper L-4J Grasshopper (45-4537/G-BFDL) [04-J]	Privately owned, Shempston Farm, Lossiemouth
	454630	Piper L-4J Grasshopper (45-4446/G-BDOL) [LI-7]	Privately owned, Bidford-on-Avon, Warks
	461748	Boeing B-29A Superfortress (44-61748/G-BHDK) [Y]	American Air Museum, Duxford, Cambs
	463209	NA P-51D Mustang <R> (BAPC.255) [WZ-S]	To Bottisham Airfield Museum, Cambs as 413410
	464005	NA P-51D Mustang (44-64005/N51CK) [E9-Z]	Privately owned, Sywell, Northants
	472216	NA P-51D Mustang (44-72216/G-BIXL) [HO-M]	Privately owned, Goodwood, W. Sussex
	472218	Titan T-51 Mustang (G-MUZY) [WZ-I]	Privately owned, Tibenham, Norfolk
	472773	NA P-51D Mustang (44-72773/D-FPSI) [QP-M]	Meier Motors, Bremgarten, Germany
	472922	NA TF-51D Mustang (44-72922/OO-RYL) [L2-W]	Privately owned, Brasschaat, Belgium
	472927	NA P-51D Mustang (44-74453/NL51ZW) [WZ-W]	Privately owned, Bremgarten, Germany
	473871	NA TF-51D Mustang (44-73871/D-FTSI) [SX-B]	To USA as N551TF
	474008	Jurca MJ77 Gnatsum (G-PSIR) [VF-R]	Privately owned, Fishburn, Co. Durham
	474425	NA P-51D Mustang (44-74425/PH-PSI) [OC-G]	Privately owned, Lelystad, The Netherlands
	479712	Piper L-4H Grasshopper (44-79826/G-AHIP) [8-R]	Privately owned, Coleford, Glos
	479744	Piper L-4H Grasshopper (44-79744/G-BGPD) [49-M]	Privately owned, Marsh, Bucks
	479766	Piper L-4H Grasshopper (44-79766/G-BKHG) [63-D]	Privately owned, Duxford, Cambs
	479781	Piper L-4H Grasshopper (44-79781/G-AISS)	Privately owned, Insch, Scotland (restoration)
	479878	Piper L-4H Grasshopper (44-79878/G-BEUI) [MF-D]	Privately owned, Roche, Cornwall
	479897	Piper L-4H Grasshopper (44-79897/G-BOXJ) [JD]	Privately owned, Rochester, Kent
	480015	Piper L-4H Grasshopper (44-80015/G-AKIB) [44-M]	Privately owned, Perranporth, Cornwall
	480133	Piper L-4J Grasshopper (44-80133/G-BDCD) [44-B]	Privately owned, Slinfold, W. Sussex
	480173	Piper L-4J Grasshopper (44-80609/G-RRSR) [57-H]	Privately owned, Shotteswell, Warks
	480321	Piper L-4J Grasshopper (44-80321/G-FRAN) [44-H]	Privately owned, Rayne, Essex
	480480	Piper L-4J Grasshopper (44-80480/G-BECN) [44-E]	Privately owned, Audley End, Cambs
	480636	Piper L-4J Grasshopper (44-80636/G-AXHP) [58-A]	Privately owned, Great Ponton, Lincs
	480723	Piper L-4J Grasshopper (44-80723/G-BFZB) [E5-J]	Privately owned, Duxford, Cambs
	480752	Piper L-4J Grasshopper (44-80752/G-BCXJ) [39-E]	Privately owned, Melksham, Wilts
	480762	Piper L-4J Grasshopper (44-80762/EI-BBV)	Privately owned, Ballyboy, Eire
	481273	CCF T-6J Harvard IV (20306/G-CJWE) [NG]	Privately owned, Leicester, Leics
	483868	Boeing B-17G Flying Fortress (44-83868/N5237V) [A-N]	RAF Museum, Hendon, Gtr London
	484786	NA F-6D Mustang (44-84786/N15BS) [5M-K]	Privately owned, Duxford, Cambs (damaged)
	493209	NA T-6G Texan (49-3209/G-DDMV/41)	Privately owned, Headcorn, Kent
	542454	Piper L-21B Super Cub (54-2454/G-KUBY)	Privately owned, Duxford, Cambs
	549192	Republic P-47D Thunderbolt (45-49192/G-THUN) [F4-J]	Privately owned, Duxford/Sywell
	779465	Hiller UH-12C (N5315V)	Privately owned, Lower Upham, Hants
	2106638	Titan T-51 Mustang (G-CIFD) [E9-R]	Privately owned, Shobdon, Herefordshire
	2100882	Douglas C-47A Skytrain (42-100882/N473DC) [3X-P]	Privately owned, Lydd, Kent
	2100884	Douglas C-47A Skytrain (42-100884/N147DC) [S6-A]	Privately owned, Dunsfold, Surrey

Serial	Type (code/other identity)	Owner/operator, location or fate	Notes
2105915	Curtiss P-40N Kittyhawk (42-105915/F-AZKU)	France's Flying Warbirds, Melun, France	
03-08003	B-V CH-47F Chinook [DT]	RAF Odiham, Hants, at main gate	
03-33119	General Atomics MQ-1B Predator [CH]	RAF Museum, Hendon, Gtr London	
03-33120	General Atomics MQ-1B Predator [CH]	American Air Museum, Duxford, Cambs	
3-1923	Aeronca O-58B Defender (43-1923/G-BRHP)	Privately owned, Chiseldon, Wilts	
18-2001	Piper L-18C Super Cub (52-2401/G-BIZV)	Privately owned, Wicklow, Ireland	
22-296	Eberhardt SE5E Replica (G-BLXT)	Privately owned	
37-002	Douglas AD-4NA Skyraider (127002/F-AZHK) [TC]	Privately owned, Avignon, France	
39-139	Beech YC-43 Traveler (N295BS)	Duke of Brabant AF, Eindhoven, The Netherlands	
39-0285	Curtiss P-40B Warhawk	The Fighter Collection, Duxford, Cambs (wreck)	
39-0287	Curtiss P-40B Warhawk	The Fighter Collection, Duxford, Cambs (wreck)	
40-2538	Fairchild PT-19A Cornell (N33870)	Privately owned, Mendlesham, Suffolk	
41-8689	Boeing-Stearman PT-17D Kaydet (G-BIXN) (frame)	Privately owned, Rendcomb, Glos	
41-13357	Curtiss P-40C Warhawk (G-CIIO) [160,10AB]	The Fighter Collection, Duxford, Cambs	
41-19393	Douglas A-20C Havoc (wreck)	Wings Museum, Balcombe, W. Sussex	
41-33275	NA AT-6C Texan (G-BICE) [CE]	Privately owned, Great Oakley, Essex	
41-35253	Martin B-26C Marauder <rf>	Boxted Airfield Museum, Essex	
42-12417	Noorduyn AT-16 Harvard IIb (KLu. B-163)	Newark Air Museum, Winthorpe, Notts	
42-35870	Taylorcraft DCO-65 (G-BWLJ) [129]	Privately owned, Nayland, Suffolk	
42-38384	Piper L-4A Grasshopper (G-BHVV)	Privately owned, Old Warden, Beds	
42-66841	Lockheed P-38H Lightning [153]	Privately owned, Bentwaters, Suffolk	
42-46703	Stinson AT-19 Reliant (FK877/N69745)	Privately owned, RNAS Yeovilton, Somerset	
42-58678	Taylorcraft DF-65 (G-BRIY) [IY]	Privately owned, Carlisle, Cumbria	
42-66841	Lockheed P-38H Lightning [153]	Privately owned, stored Sywell, Northants	
42-78044	Aeronca 11AC Chief (G-BRXL)	Privately owned, Andrewsfield, Essex	
42-84555	NA AT-6D Harvard III (FAP.1662/G-ELMH) [EP-H]	Privately owned, Hardwick, Norfolk	
42-93510	Douglas C-47A Skytrain [CM] <ff>	Privately owned, Welford Park, Berks	
43-9628	Douglas A-20G Havoc <ff>	Privately owned, Hinckley, Leics	
43-11137	Bell P-63C Kingcobra (wreck)	Wings Museum, Balcombe, W. Sussex	
43-21664	Douglas A-20G Havoc (wreck)	Wings Museum, Balcombe, W. Sussex	
43-35943	Beech 3N (G-BKRN) [943]	Privately owned, Oakham, Leics	
43-36140	NA B-25J Mitchell <ff>	Wings Museum, Balcombe, W. Sussex	
44-4368	Bell P-63C Kingcobra	Wings Museum, Balcombe, W. Sussex	
44-14574	NA P-51D Mustang (fuselage)	East Essex Aviation Museum, Clacton, Essex	
44-30861	NA TB-25J Mitchell (N9089Z)	Wings Museum, Balcombe, W. Sussex	
44-42914	Douglas DC-4 (N31356) <ff>	Privately owned, Burtonwood, Cheshire	
44-51228	Consolidated B-24M Liberator [EC-493]	American Air Museum, Duxford, Cambs	
44-63684	Titan T-51 Mustang (G-CKVJ)	Privately owned, Rochester, Kent	
44-79609	Piper L-4H Grasshopper (G-BHXY) [PR]	Privately owned, Bealbury, Cornwall	
44-79649	Piper L-4H Grasshopper (G-AIIH)	Privately owned, Stonesfield, Oxon	
44-80594	Piper L-4J Grasshopper (G-BEDJ)	Privately owned, Stow Maries, Essex	
44-80647	Piper L-4J Grasshopper (D-EGAF)	Privately owned, Donauwörth, Germany	
51-7655	NA T-28A Fennec (ZU-FWH)	Privately owned, Sywell, Northants	
51-9036	Lockheed T-33A Shooting Star	Newark Air Museum, Winthorpe, Notts	
51-15319	Piper L-18C Super Cub (G-FUZZ) [A-319]	Privately owned, Elvington, N. Yorks	
51-1555	Piper L-18C Super Cub (G-OSPS) [A-555]	Privately owned, East Winch, Norfolk	
54-005	NA F-100D Super Sabre (54-2163) [HA]	Dumfries & Galloway Avn Mus, Dumfries, Scotland	
54-174	NA F-100D Super Sabre (54-2174) [SM]	Midland Air Museum, Coventry, Warks	
54-2445	Piper L-21B Super Cub (G-OTAN) [A-445]	Privately owned, Hawarden, Flintshire, Wales	
54-2447	Piper L-21B Super Cub (G-SCUB)	Privately owned, Anwick, Lincs	
55-138354	NA T-28B Trojan (138354/N1328B) [TL-354]	Privately owned, Zwartberg, Belgium	
63-699	McD F-4C Phantom II (63-7699) [CG]	Midland Air Museum, Coventry, Warks	
64-0553	Lockheed WC-130E Hercules <ff>	RAF Museum, Hendon, Gtr London	
64-17657	Douglas B-26K Counter Invader (N99218) <ff>	Wings Museum, Balcombe, W. Sussex	
65-777	McD F-4C Phantom II (63-7419) [SA]	RAF Lakenheath, Suffolk, on display	
66-374	Helio H.295 Super Courier (G-BAGT) [EO]	Privately owned, Spanhoe, Northants	
67-120	GD F-111E Aardvark (67-0120) [UH]	American Air Museum, Duxford, Cambs	
68-0060	GD F-111E Aardvark <ff>	Dumfries & Galloway Avn Mus, Dumfries, Scotland	
68-8284	Sikorsky MH-53M Pave Low IV	RAF Museum, Cosford, Shropshire	
70-0389	GD F-111E Aardvark (68-0011) [LN]	RAF Lakenheath, Suffolk, on display	

Notes	Serial	Type (code/other identity)	Owner/operator, location or fate
	72-1447	GD F-111F Aardvark <ff>	American Air Museum, Duxford, Cambs
	74-0177	GD F-111F Aardvark [FN]	RAF Museum, Cosford, Shropshire
	76-020	McD F-15A Eagle (76-0020) [BT]	American Air Museum, Duxford, Cambs
	76-124	McD F-15B Eagle (76-0124) [LN]	RAF Lakenheath, Suffolk, instructional use
	77-259	Fairchild A-10A Thunderbolt (77-0259) [AR]	American Air Museum, Duxford, Cambs
	80-219	Fairchild GA-10A Thunderbolt (80-0219) [WR]	Bentwaters Cold War Museum, Suffolk
	82-23762	B-V CH-47D Chinook <ff>	RAF Benson, Oxon, instructional use
	83-24104	B-V CH-47D Chinook [BN] <ff>	RAF Museum, Hendon, Gtr London
	84-0001	McD F-15C Eagle [LN] *bk/y*	RAF Lakenheath, Suffolk, GI use
86-180	McD F-15A Eagle (74-0131) [LN]	RAF Lakenheath, Suffolk, on display
	(starboard side only, painted as 86-169 on port side)		
	86-01677	B-V CH-47D Chinook	RAF, stored Odiham, Hants
	89-00159	B-V CH-47D Chinook	RAF, stored Odiham, Hants
108-1601	Stinson 108-1 Voyager (G-CFGE) [H]	Privately owned, Spanhoe, Northants
146-11042	Wolf W-11 Boredom Fighter (G-BMZX) [7]	Privately owned, Popham, Hants
146-11083	Wolf W-11 Boredom Fighter (G-BNAI) [5]	Privately owned, Haverfordwest, Wales
A3-3	NA P-51D Mustang (44-72035/G-SIJJ)	Hangar 11 Collection, North Weald, Essex
S666	Noorduyn AT-16 Harvard IIb (KF435) [BS]	Maidenhead Heritage Centre, Berks
X-17	Curtiss P-40F Warhawk (41-19841/G-CGZP)	The Fighter Collection, Duxford, Cambs
CY-G	Titan T-51 Mustang (G-TSIM)	Privately owned, Shobdon, Herefordshire
PA50	Curtiss P-36C Hawk (38-0210/G-CIXJ)	The Fighter Collection, Duxford, Cambs
(RW382)	VS361 Spitfire LF XVIe (G-PBIX) [WZ-RR]	Privately owned, Biggin Hill, Kent

YUGOSLAVIA

Notes	Serial	Type (code/other identity)	Owner/operator, location or fate
	30140	Soko P-2 Kraguj (G-RADA) [140]	Privately owned, Fishburn, Co. Durham
	30146	Soko P-2 Kraguj (G-BSXD) [146]	Privately owned, Eshott, Northumberland
	30149	Soko P-2 Kraguj (G-SOKO) [149]	Privately owned, Fenland, Cambs
	51109	Utva-66 (G-CLJX)	Privately owned, Eshott, Northumberland

Kaydet marked only as "14", also registested G-ISDN, is seen here at Compton Abbas airfield in an authentic colour scheme for this wartime type. *HJC*

Serial	Type (code/other identity)	Owner/operator, location or fate	Notes
C7	Avro 631 Cadet (EI-AGO)	IAC Museum, Baldonnel	
34	Miles M14A Magister I (N5392)	National Museum of Ireland, Dublin	
141	Avro 652A Anson C19	IAC Museum, Baldonnel	
164	DHC1 Chipmunk T20	IAC Museum, Baldonnel	
168	DHC1 Chipmunk T20 (EI-HFA)	Irish Historic Flight, Ballyboy	
169	DHC1 Chipmunk 22 (WD305/EI-HFB)	Irish Historic Flight, Ballyboy	
170	DHC1 Chipmunk 22 (WP857/EI-HFC)	Irish Historic Flight, Ballyboy	
172	DHC1 Chipmunk T20	IAC Museum, Baldonnel	
173	DHC1 Chipmunk T20	South-East Aviation Enthusiasts, Dromod	
176	DH104 Dove 4 (VP-YKF)	South-East Aviation Enthusiasts, Waterford	
183	Percival P56 Provost T51	IAC Museum, Baldonnel	
184	Percival P56 Provost T51	South-East Aviation Enthusiasts, Dromod	
187	DH115 Vampire T55	South-East Aviation Enthusiasts, Dromod	
191	DH115 Vampire T55	IAC Museum, Baldonnel	
192	DH115 Vampire T55 <ff>	South-East Aviation Enthusiasts, Dromod	
195	Sud SA316 Alouette III (F-WJDH)	IAC Museum, stored Baldonnel	
198	DH115 Vampire T11 (XE977)	National Museum of Ireland, Dublin	
199	DHC1 Chipmunk T20	IAC Museum, Baldonnel	
202	Sud SA316 Alouette III	Ulster Aviation Society, Long Kesh	
203	Reims-Cessna FR172H	Ulster Aviation Society, Long Kesh	
205	Reims-Cessna FR172H	IAC Baldonnel (wfu)	
206	Reims-Cessna FR172H	IAC Museum, Baldonnel	
208	Reims-Cessna FR172H	IAC Baldonnel (wfu)	
210	Reims-Cessna FR172H	Shannon Aviation Museum	
215	Fouga CM170R Super Magister	IAC Baldonnel, GI use	
216	Fouga CM170R Super Magister	Shannon Aviation Museum	
218	Fouga CM170R Super Magister	Ulster Aviation Society, Long Kesh	
219	Fouga CM170R Super Magister	IAC Museum, Baldonnel	
220	Fouga CM170R Super Magister	Cork University, instructional use	
221	Fouga CM170R Super Magister [79/3-KE]	IAC Museum, stored Baldonnel	
231	SIAI SF-260WE Warrior	IAC Museum, Baldonnel	
252	Airtech CN.235 MPA Persuader	IAC No 101 Sqn/1 Operations Wing, Baldonnel	
253	Airtech CN.235 MPA Persuader	IAC No 101 Sqn/1 Operations Wing, Baldonnel	
254	PBN-2T Defender 4000 (G-BWPN)	IAC, stored Baldonnel	
256	Eurocopter EC135T-1 (G-BZRM)	IAC GASU (No 106 Sqn)/1 Operations Wing, Baldonnel	
258	Gates Learjet 45 (N5009T)	IAC No 102 Sqn/1 Operations Wing, Baldonnel	
260	Pilatus PC-9M (HB-HQS)	IAC Flying Training School, Baldonnel	
261	Pilatus PC-9M (HB-HQT)	IAC Flying Training School, Baldonnel	
262	Pilatus PC-9M (HB-HQU)	IAC Flying Training School, Baldonnel	
263	Pilatus PC-9M (HB-HQV)	IAC Flying Training School, Baldonnel	
264	Pilatus PC-9M (HB-HQW)	IAC Flying Training School, Baldonnel	
266	Pilatus PC-9M (HB-HQY)	IAC Flying Training School, Baldonnel	
267	Pilatus PC-9M (HB-HQZ)	IAC Flying Training School, Baldonnel	
269	Pilatus PC-9M (HB-HXI)	IAC Flying Training School, Baldonnel	
270	Eurocopter EC135P-2 (D-HECF)	IAC No 302 Sqn/3 Operations Wing, Baldonnel	
271	Eurocopter EC135P-2 (D-HECB)	IAC No 302 Sqn/3 Operations Wing, Baldonnel	
272	Eurocopter EC135T-2 (G-CECT)	IAC GASU (No 106 Sqn)/1 Operations Wing, Baldonnel	
274	AgustaWestland AW139	IAC No 301 Sqn/3 Operations Wing, Baldonnel	
275	AgustaWestland AW139	IAC No 301 Sqn/3 Operations Wing, Baldonnel	
276	AgustaWestland AW139	IAC No 301 Sqn/3 Operations Wing, Baldonnel	
277	AgustaWestland AW139	IAC No 301 Sqn/3 Operations Wing, Baldonnel	
278	AgustaWestland AW139	IAC No 301 Sqn/3 Operations Wing, Baldonnel	
279	AgustaWestland AW139	IAC No 301 Sqn/3 Operations Wing, Baldonnel	
280	Pilatus PC.XII/47E (HB-FXT) $	IAC No 102 Sqn/1 Operations Wing, Baldonnel	
281	Pilatus PC.XII/47E Spectre (N280NG)	IAC No 104 Sqn/1 Operations Wing, Baldonnel	
282	Pilatus PC.XII/47E Spectre (N281NG)	IAC No 104 Sqn/1 Operations Wing, Baldonnel	
283	Pilatus PC.XII/47E Spectre (N282NG)	IAC No 104 Sqn/1 Operations Wing, Baldonnel	
2..	CASA C-295W	IAC (on order)	
2..	CASA C-295W	IAC (on order)	
2..	CASA C-295M	IAC (on order)	

Notes	Serial	Type (code/other identity)	Owner/operator, location or fate

Aircraft included in this section include those likely to be seen visiting UK civil and military airfields on transport flights, exchange visits, exercises and for air shows. It is not a comprehensive list of *all* aircraft operated by the air arms concerned.

ALBANIA

	TC-ANA	Airbus A.319CJ-115X	Albanian Government, Tirana

ALGERIA

Ministry of Defence

	7T-VPC	Grumman G.1159C Gulfstream IVSP (1418)	Ministry of Defence, Boufarik
	7T-VPG	Gulfstream Aerospace Gulfstream V (617)	Ministry of Defence, Boufarik
	7T-VPM	Grumman G.1159C Gulfstream IVSP (1421)	Ministry of Defence, Boufarik
	7T-VPP	Airbus A.340-541	Ministry of Defence, Boufarik
	7T-VPR	Grumman G.1159C Gulfstream IVSP (1288)	Ministry of Defence, Boufarik
	7T-VPS	Grumman G.1159C Gulfstream IVSP (1291)	Ministry of Defence, Boufarik

Force Aérienne Algérienne (FAA)/Al Quwwat al Jawwiya al Jaza'eriya

	7T-WHA	Lockheed C-130H-30 Hercules (4997)	FAA 2 ETTL, Boufarik *(damaged 2010)*
	7T-WHB	Lockheed C-130H-30 Hercules (5224)	FAA 2 ETTL, Boufarik
	7T-WHD	Lockheed C-130H-30 Hercules (4987)	FAA 2 ETTL, Boufarik
	7T-WHE	Lockheed C-130H Hercules (4935)	FAA 2 ETTL, Boufarik
	7T-WHF	Lockheed C-130H Hercules (4934)	FAA 2 ETTL, Boufarik
	7T-WHI	Lockheed C-130H Hercules (4930)	FAA 2 ETTL, Boufarik
	7T-WHJ	Lockheed C-130H Hercules (4928)	FAA 2 ETTL, Boufarik
	7T-WHL	Lockheed C-130H-30 Hercules (4989)	FAA 2 ETTL, Boufarik
	7T-WHN	Lockheed C-130H-30 Hercules (4894)	FAA 2 ETTL, Boufarik
	7T-WHO	Lockheed C-130H-30 Hercules (4897)	FAA 2 ETTL, Boufarik
	7T-WHP	Lockheed C-130H-30 Hercules (4921)	FAA 2 ETTL, Boufarik
	7T-WHR	Lockheed C-130H Hercules (4924)	FAA 2 ETTL, Boufarik
	7T-WHS	Lockheed C-130H Hercules (4912)	FAA 2 ETTL, Boufarik
	7T-WHY	Lockheed C-130H Hercules (4913)	FAA 2 ETTL, Boufarik
	7T-WHZ	Lockheed C-130H Hercules (4914)	FAA 2 ETTL, Boufarik
	7T-WIA	Ilyushin Il-76MD	FAA 347 ETS, Boufarik
	7T-WIB	Ilyushin Il-76MD	FAA 347 ETS, Boufarik
	7T-WIC	Ilyushin Il-76MD	FAA 347 ETS, Boufarik
	7T-WID	Ilyushin Il-76TD	FAA 347 ETS, Boufarik
	7T-WIE	Ilyushin Il-76TD	FAA 347 ETS, Boufarik
	7T-WIF	Ilyushin Il-76	FAA 347 ETS, Boufarik
	7T-WIG	Ilyushin Il-76TD	FAA 347 ETS, Boufarik
	7T-WIL	Ilyushin Il-78	FAA 357 ERV, Boufarik
	7T-WIM	Ilyushin Il-76TD	FAA 347 ETS, Boufarik
	7T-WIN	Ilyushin Il-78	FAA 357 ERV, Boufarik
	7T-WIP	Ilyushin Il-76TD	FAA 347 ETS, Boufarik
	7T-WIQ	Ilyushin Il-78	FAA 357 ERV, Boufarik
	7T-WIR	Ilyushin Il-76TD	FAA 347 ETS, Boufarik
	7T-WIS	Ilyushin Il-78	FAA 357 ERV, Boufarik
	7T-WIT	Ilyushin Il-76TD	FAA 347 ETS, Boufarik
	7T-WIU	Ilyushin Il-76TD	FAA 347 ETS, Boufarik
	7T-WJA	Lockheed LM.100J Super Hercules (5818)	FAA 2 ETTL, Boufarik
	7T-WJB	Lockheed LM.100J Super Hercules (5824)	FAA, on order
	7T-WJC	Lockheed LM.100J Super Hercules (5952/N5104Q)	FAA, on order
	7T-WJD	Lockheed LM.100J Super Hercules (5954/N5104S)	FAA, on order

ANGOLA

	D2-ANG	Bombardier Global Express XRS	Angola Government, Luanda
	D2-ANH	Bombardier Global Express	Angola Government, Luanda

ARMENIA

	701	Airbus A.319CJ-132	Armenian Government, Yerevan

AUSTRALIA

Royal Australian Air Force (RAAF)

	A9-657	Lockheed EAP-3C Orion	RAAF 10 Sqn/42 Wing, Edinburgh, South Australia

Serial	Type (code/other identity)	Owner/operator, location or fate	Notes
A9-660	Lockheed EAP-3C Orion	RAAF 10 Sqn/42 Wing, Edinburgh, South Australia	
A30-001	Boeing E-7A Wedgetail (737-7ES)	RAAF 2 Sqn/41 Wing, Canberra, ACT	
A30-002	Boeing E-7A Wedgetail (737-7ES)	RAAF 2 Sqn/41 Wing, Canberra, ACT	
A30-003	Boeing E-7A Wedgetail (737-7ES)	RAAF 2 Sqn/41 Wing, Canberra, ACT	
A30-004	Boeing E-7A Wedgetail (737-7ES)	RAAF 2 Sqn/41 Wing, Canberra, ACT	
A30-005	Boeing E-7A Wedgetail (737-7ES)	RAAF 2 Sqn/41 Wing, Canberra, ACT	
A30-006	Boeing E-7A Wedgetail (737-7ES)	RAAF 2 Sqn/41 Wing, Canberra, ACT	
A36-001	Boeing 737-7DT	RAAF 34 Sqn/84 Wing, Canberra, ACT	
A36-002	Boeing 737-7DF	RAAF 34 Sqn/84 Wing, Canberra, ACT	
A39-001	Airbus KC-30A (A.330-203 MRTT) (MRTT001)	RAAF 33 Sqn/84 Wing, Amberley, Queensland	
A39-002	Airbus KC-30A (A.330-203 MRTT) (MRTT002)	RAAF 33 Sqn/84 Wing, Amberley, Queensland	
A39-003	Airbus KC-30A (A.330-203 MRTT) (MRTT003)	RAAF 33 Sqn/84 Wing, Amberley, Queensland	
A39-004	Airbus KC-30A (A.330-203 MRTT) (MRTT004)	RAAF 33 Sqn/84 Wing, Amberley, Queensland	
A39-005	Airbus KC-30A (A.330-203 MRTT) (MRTT005)	RAAF 33 Sqn/84 Wing, Amberley, Queensland	
A39-006	Airbus KC-30A (A.330-203 MRTT) (VH-EBH) (MRTT039)	RAAF 33 Sqn/84 Wing, Amberley, Queensland	
A39-007	Airbus KC-30A (A.330-203 MRTT) (VH-EBI) (MRTT040)	RAAF 33 Sqn/84 Wing, Amberley, Queensland	
A41-206	Boeing C-17A Globemaster III (06-0206)	RAAF 36 Sqn/86 Wing, Amberley, Queensland	
A41-207	Boeing C-17A Globemaster III (06-0207)	RAAF 36 Sqn/86 Wing, Amberley, Queensland	
A41-208	Boeing C-17A Globemaster III (06-0208)	RAAF 36 Sqn/86 Wing, Amberley, Queensland	
A41-209	Boeing C-17A Globemaster III (06-0209)	RAAF 36 Sqn/86 Wing, Amberley, Queensland	
A41-210	Boeing C-17A Globemaster III (11-0210)	RAAF 36 Sqn/86 Wing, Amberley, Queensland	
A41-211	Boeing C-17A Globemaster III (12-0211)	RAAF 36 Sqn/86 Wing, Amberley, Queensland	
A41-212	Boeing C-17A Globemaster III (14-0001)	RAAF 36 Sqn/86 Wing, Amberley, Queensland	
A41-213	Boeing C-17A Globemaster III (14-0002)	RAAF 36 Sqn/86 Wing, Amberley, Queensland	
A47-001	Boeing P-8A Poseidon (N940DS)	RAAF 11 Sqn/92 Wing, Edinburgh, South Australia	
A47-002	Boeing P-8A Poseidon (N956DS)	RAAF 11 Sqn/92 Wing, Edinburgh, South Australia	
A47-003	Boeing P-8A Poseidon (N959DS)	RAAF 11 Sqn/92 Wing, Edinburgh, South Australia	
A47-004	Boeing P-8A Poseidon (N974DS)	RAAF 11 Sqn/92 Wing, Edinburgh, South Australia	
A47-005	Boeing P-8A Poseidon (N832DS)	RAAF 11 Sqn/92 Wing, Edinburgh, South Australia	
A47-006	Boeing P-8A Poseidon (N849DS)	RAAF 11 Sqn/92 Wing, Edinburgh, South Australia	
A47-007	Boeing P-8A Poseidon (N862DS)	RAAF 11 Sqn/92 Wing, Edinburgh, South Australia	
A47-008	Boeing P-8A Poseidon (N872DS)	RAAF 11 Sqn/92 Wing, Edinburgh, South Australia	
A47-009	Boeing P-8A Poseidon (N391DS)	RAAF 11 Sqn/92 Wing, Edinburgh, South Australia	
A47-010	Boeing P-8A Poseidon (N397DS)	RAAF 11 Sqn/92 Wing, Edinburgh, South Australia	
A47-011	Boeing P-8A Poseidon (N398DS)	RAAF 11 Sqn/92 Wing, Edinburgh, South Australia	
A47-012	Boeing P-8A Poseidon (N468DS) $	RAAF 11 Sqn/92 Wing, Edinburgh, South Australia	
A47-013	Boeing P-8A Poseidon	RAAF (on order)	
A47-014	Boeing P-8A Poseidon	RAAF (on order)	
A47-015	Boeing P-8A Poseidon	RAAF (on order)	
A56-001	Dassault Falcon 7X (F-WWHE)	RAAF 34 Sqn/84 Wing, Canberra, ACT	
A56-002	Dassault Falcon 7X (F-WWHF)	RAAF 34 Sqn/84 Wing, Canberra, ACT	
A56-003	Dassault Falcon 7X (F-WWHK)	RAAF 34 Sqn/84 Wing, Canberra, ACT	
A97-440	Lockheed C-130J-30 Hercules II	RAAF 37 Sqn/86 Wing, Richmond, NSW	
A97-441	Lockheed C-130J-30 Hercules II	RAAF 37 Sqn/86 Wing, Richmond, NSW	
A97-442	Lockheed C-130J-30 Hercules II	RAAF 37 Sqn/86 Wing, Richmond, NSW	
A97-447	Lockheed C-130J-30 Hercules II	RAAF 37 Sqn/86 Wing, Richmond, NSW	
A97-448	Lockheed C-130J-30 Hercules II	RAAF 37 Sqn/86 Wing, Richmond, NSW	
A97-449	Lockheed C-130J-30 Hercules II	RAAF 37 Sqn/86 Wing, Richmond, NSW	
A97-450	Lockheed C-130J-30 Hercules II	RAAF 37 Sqn/86 Wing, Richmond, NSW	

Notes	Serial	Type (code/other identity)	Owner/operator, location or fate
	A97-464	Lockheed C-130J-30 Hercules II	RAAF 37 Sqn/86 Wing, Richmond, NSW
	A97-465	Lockheed C-130J-30 Hercules II	RAAF 37 Sqn/86 Wing, Richmond, NSW
	A97-466	Lockheed C-130J-30 Hercules II	RAAF 37 Sqn/86 Wing, Richmond, NSW
	A97-467	Lockheed C-130J-30 Hercules II	RAAF 37 Sqn/86 Wing, Richmond, NSW
	A97-468	Lockheed C-130J-30 Hercules II	RAAF 37 Sqn/86 Wing, Richmond, NSW
	A..-...	Gulfstream Aerospace MC-55A Peregrine (N542GD)	RAAF (on order)
	A..-...	Gulfstream Aerospace MC-55A Peregrine (N540GA)	RAAF (on order)
	AUSTRIA		
	Öesterreichische Luftstreitkräfte (OL)		
	3C-OA	Bell OH-58B Kiowa	OL Mehrzweckhubschrauberstaffel, Tulln
	3C-OB	Bell OH-58B Kiowa	OL Mehrzweckhubschrauberstaffel, Tulln
	3C-OC	Bell OH-58B Kiowa	OL Mehrzweckhubschrauberstaffel, Tulln
	3C-OD	Bell OH-58B Kiowa	OL Mehrzweckhubschrauberstaffel, Tulln
	3C-OE	Bell OH-58B Kiowa	OL Mehrzweckhubschrauberstaffel, Tulln
	3C-OH	Bell OH-58B Kiowa $	OL Mehrzweckhubschrauberstaffel, Tulln
	3C-OI	Bell OH-58B Kiowa	OL Mehrzweckhubschrauberstaffel, Tulln
	3C-OJ	Bell OH-58B Kiowa	OL Mehrzweckhubschrauberstaffel, Tulln
	3C-OK	Bell OH-58B Kiowa $	OL Mehrzweckhubschrauberstaffel, Tulln
	3C-OL	Bell OH-58B Kiowa	OL Mehrzweckhubschrauberstaffel, Tulln
	3G-EB	Pilatus PC-6B/B2-H2 Turbo Porter	OL leichte Lufttransportstaffel, Tulln
	3G-ED	Pilatus PC-6B/B2-H2 Turbo Porter	OL leichte Lufttransportstaffel, Tulln
	3G-EE	Pilatus PC-6B/B2-H2 Turbo Porter	OL leichte Lufttransportstaffel, Tulln
	3G-EF	Pilatus PC-6B/B2-H2 Turbo Porter	OL leichte Lufttransportstaffel, Tulln
	3G-EG	Pilatus PC-6B/B2-H2 Turbo Porter	OL leichte Lufttransportstaffel, Tulln
	3G-EH	Pilatus PC-6B/B2-H2 Turbo Porter	OL leichte Lufttransportstaffel, Tulln
	3G-EL	Pilatus PC-6B/B2-H2 Turbo Porter	OL leichte Lufttransportstaffel, Tulln
	3G-EN	Pilatus PC-6B/B2-H4 Turbo Porter $	OL leichte Lufttransportstaffel, Tulln
	3H-FA	Pilatus PC-7 Turbo Trainer	OL Lehrabteilung Fläche, Zeltweg
	3H-FB	Pilatus PC-7 Turbo Trainer	OL Lehrabteilung Fläche, Zeltweg
	3H-FC	Pilatus PC-7 Turbo Trainer $	OL Lehrabteilung Fläche, Zeltweg
	3H-FD	Pilatus PC-7 Turbo Trainer	OL Lehrabteilung Fläche, Zeltweg
	3H-FE	Pilatus PC-7 Turbo Trainer	OL Lehrabteilung Fläche, Zeltweg
	3H-FF	Pilatus PC-7 Turbo Trainer	OL Lehrabteilung Fläche, Zeltweg
	3H-FG	Pilatus PC-7 Turbo Trainer $	OL Lehrabteilung Fläche, Zeltweg
	3H-FH	Pilatus PC-7 Turbo Trainer	OL Lehrabteilung Fläche, Zeltweg
	3H-FJ	Pilatus PC-7 Turbo Trainer	OL Lehrabteilung Fläche, Zeltweg
	3H-FK	Pilatus PC-7 Turbo Trainer	OL Lehrabteilung Fläche, Zeltweg
	3H-FL	Pilatus PC-7 Turbo Trainer	OL Lehrabteilung Fläche, Zeltweg
	3H-FM	Pilatus PC-7 Turbo Trainer	OL Lehrabteilung Fläche, Zeltweg
	3H-FO	Pilatus PC-7 Turbo Trainer	OL Lehrabteilung Fläche, Zeltweg
	5D-HB	Agusta-Bell AB.212	OL 1 Staffel/2 Staffel ITHSSta, Linz
	5D-HC	Agusta-Bell AB.212	OL 1 Staffel/2 Staffel ITHSSta, Linz
	5D-HD	Agusta-Bell AB.212	OL 1 Staffel/2 Staffel ITHSSta, Linz
	5D-HF	Agusta-Bell AB.212	OL 1 Staffel/2 Staffel ITHSSta, Linz
	5D-HG	Agusta-Bell AB.212	OL 1 Staffel/2 Staffel ITHSSta, Linz
	5D-HH	Agusta-Bell AB.212	OL 1 Staffel/2 Staffel ITHSSta, Linz
	5D-HI	Agusta-Bell AB.212	OL 1 Staffel/2 Staffel ITHSSta, Linz
	5D-HJ	Agusta-Bell AB.212	OL 1 Staffel/2 Staffel ITHSSta, Linz
	5D-HK	Agusta-Bell AB.212	OL 1 Staffel/2 Staffel ITHSSta, Linz
	5D-HL	Agusta-Bell AB.212	OL 1 Staffel/2 Staffel ITHSSta, Linz
	5D-HN	Agusta-Bell AB.212	OL 1 Staffel/2 Staffel ITHSSta, Linz
	5D-HO	Agusta-Bell AB.212	OL 1 Staffel/2 Staffel ITHSSta, Linz
	5D-HP	Agusta-Bell AB.212	OL 1 Staffel/2 Staffel ITHSSta, Linz
	5D-HQ	Agusta-Bell AB.212	OL 1 Staffel/2 Staffel ITHSSta, Linz
	5D-HR	Agusta-Bell AB.212	OL 1 Staffel/2 Staffel ITHSSta, Linz
	5D-HS	Agusta-Bell AB.212	OL 1 Staffel/2 Staffel ITHSSta, Linz
	5D-HT	Agusta-Bell AB.212	OL 1 Staffel/2 Staffel ITHSSta, Linz
	5D-HU	Agusta-Bell AB.212	OL 1 Staffel/2 Staffel ITHSSta, Linz
	5D-HV	Agusta-Bell AB.212	OL 1 Staffel/2 Staffel ITHSSta, Linz
	5D-HW	Agusta-Bell AB.212	OL 1 Staffel/2 Staffel ITHSSta, Linz
	5D-HX	Agusta-Bell AB.212	OL 1 Staffel/2 Staffel ITHSSta, Linz

Serial	Type (code/other identity)	Owner/operator, location or fate	Notes
5D-HY	Bell 212	OL 1 Staffel/2 Staffel ITHSSta, Linz	
5D-HZ	Agusta-Bell AB.212 $	OL 1 Staffel/2 Staffel ITHSSta, Linz	
5M-IB	Leonardo AW169B	OL	
..-..	Leonardo AW169B	OL (on order)	
..-..	Leonardo AW169B	OL (on order)	
..-..	Leonardo AW169B	OL (on order)	
..-..	Leonardo AW169B	OL (on order)	
..-..	Leonardo AW169B	OL (on order)	
6M-BA	Sikorsky S-70A	OL mittlere Transporthubschrauberstaffel, Tulln	
6M-BB	Sikorsky S-70A	OL mittlere Transporthubschrauberstaffel, Tulln	
6M-BC	Sikorsky S-70A	OL mittlere Transporthubschrauberstaffel, Tulln	
6M-BD	Sikorsky S-70A	OL mittlere Transporthubschrauberstaffel, Tulln	
6M-BE	Sikorsky S-70A	OL mittlere Transporthubschrauberstaffel, Tulln	
6M-BF	Sikorsky S-70A	OL mittlere Transporthubschrauberstaffel, Tulln	
6M-BG	Sikorsky S-70A	OL mittlere Transporthubschrauberstaffel, Tulln	
6M-BH	Sikorsky S-70A	OL mittlere Transporthubschrauberstaffel, Tulln	
6M-BI	Sikorsky S-70A	OL mittlere Transporthubschrauberstaffel, Tulln	
7L-WA	Eurofighter EF.2000	OL 1 Staffel/2 Staffel Überwg, Zeltweg	
7L-WB	Eurofighter EF.2000 $	OL 1 Staffel/2 Staffel Überwg, Zeltweg	
7L-WC	Eurofighter EF.2000 $	OL 1 Staffel/2 Staffel Überwg, Zeltweg	
7L-WD	Eurofighter EF.2000	OL 1 Staffel/2 Staffel Überwg, Zeltweg	
7L-WE	Eurofighter EF.2000	OL 1 Staffel/2 Staffel Überwg, Zeltweg	
7L-WF	Eurofighter EF.2000	OL 1 Staffel/2 Staffel Überwg, Zeltweg	
7L-WG	Eurofighter EF.2000	OL 1 Staffel/2 Staffel Überwg, Zeltweg	
7L-WH	Eurofighter EF.2000	OL 1 Staffel/2 Staffel Überwg, Zeltweg	
7L-WI	Eurofighter EF.2000	OL 1 Staffel/2 Staffel Überwg, Zeltweg	
7L-WJ	Eurofighter EF.2000	OL 1 Staffel/2 Staffel Überwg, Zeltweg	
7L-WK	Eurofighter EF.2000	OL 1 Staffel/2 Staffel Überwg, Zeltweg	
7L-WL	Eurofighter EF.2000	OL 1 Staffel/2 Staffel Überwg, Zeltweg	
7L-WM	Eurofighter EF.2000	OL 1 Staffel/2 Staffel Überwg, Zeltweg	
7L-WN	Eurofighter EF.2000	OL 1 Staffel/2 Staffel Überwg, Zeltweg	
7L-WO	Eurofighter EF.2000	OL 1 Staffel/2 Staffel Überwg, Zeltweg	
8T-CA	Lockheed C-130K Hercules (XV181)	OL Lufttransportstaffel, Linz	
8T-CB	Lockheed C-130K Hercules (XV291)	OL Lufttransportstaffel, Linz	
8T-CC	Lockheed C-130K Hercules (XV292)	OL Lufttransportstaffel, Linz	
..-..	Sikorsky UH-60L Black Hawk	OL, on order	
..-..	Sikorsky UH-60L Black Hawk	OL, on order	
..-..	Sikorsky UH-60L Black Hawk	OL, on order	

AZERBAIJAN

4K-AI01	Boeing 767-32LER	Azerbaijan Government, Baku	
4K-AI001	Boeing 777-200LR	Azerbaijan Government, Baku	
4K-AI06	Gulfstream Aerospace G.550	Azerbaijan Government, Baku	
4K-AI07	Airbus ACJ320-214X	Azerbaijan Government, Baku	
4K-AI08	Airbus ACJ340-642X	Azerbaijan Government, Baku	
4K-AI88	Gulfstream Aerospace G.650	Azerbaijan Government, Baku	
4K-8888	Airbus A.319-115LR	Azerbaijan Government, Baku	

BAHRAIN

A9C-AWL	BAE RJ.100	Royal Bahraini Air Force	
A9C-BAH	Gulfstream Aerospace G.650	Bahrain Royal Flight	
A9C-BDF	BAE RJ.85	Royal Bahraini Air Force	
A9C-BG	Grumman G.1159 Gulfstream IITT	Bahrain Royal Flight, stored Bahrain	
A9C-BHR	Gulfstream Aerospace G.600	Bahrain Royal Flight	
A9C-BRF	BAE RJ.70ER (M-STRY)	Bahrain Royal Flight	
A9C-BRN	Gulfstream Aerospace G.550	Bahrain Royal Flight	
A9C-HAK	Boeing 747-4F6	Bahrain Royal Flight	
A9C-HMH	Boeing 767-4FSER	Bahrain Royal Flight	
A9C-HMK	Boeing 747-4P8	Bahrain Royal Flight	
A9C-HWR	BAE RJ.85	Royal Bahraini Air Force	
A9C-ISA	Boeing 737-86J	Bahrain Royal Flight	
A9C-KAS	BAE RJ.100 (SE-DSZ)	Royal Bahraini Air Force	

Notes	Serial	Type (code/other identity)	Owner/operator, location or fate
	A9C-SLM	Gulfstream Aerospace G.550	Bahrain Royal Flight

BELGIUM

Force Aérienne Belge (FAB)/Belgische Luchtmacht: Composante Aérienne Belge/Belgische Luchtcomponent

Notes	Serial	Type (code/other identity)	Owner/operator, location or fate
	CT-01	Airbus Military A.400M	FAB/Luxembourg Armed Forces 20 Smaldeel (15 Wg), Brussels/Melsbroek
	CT-02	Airbus Military A.400M	FAB 20 Smaldeel (15 Wg), Brussels/Melsbroek
	CT-03	Airbus Military A.400M	FAB 20 Smaldeel (15 Wg), Brussels/Melsbroek
	CT-04	Airbus Military A.400M	FAB 20 Smaldeel (15 Wg), Brussels/Melsbroek
	CT-05	Airbus Military A.400M	FAB 20 Smaldeel (15 Wg), Brussels/Melsbroek
	CT-06	Airbus Military A.400M	FAB 20 Smaldeel (15 Wg), Brussels/Melsbroek
	CT-07	Airbus Military A.400M	FAB 20 Smaldeel (15 Wg), Brussels/Melsbroek
	CT-08	Airbus Military A.400M	FAB/NATO (on order)
	FA-56	SABCA (GD) F-16A MLU Fighting Falcon	FAB 1 Sm/350 Sm (2 Wg), Florennes
	FA-57	SABCA (GD) F-16A MLU Fighting Falcon $	FAB 1 Sm/350 Sm (2 Wg), Florennes
	FA-67	SABCA (GD) F-16A MLU Fighting Falcon	FAB 1 Sm/350 Sm (2 Wg), Florennes
	FA-68	SABCA (GD) F-16A MLU Fighting Falcon $	FAB 1 Sm/350 Sm (2 Wg), Florennes
	FA-69	SABCA (GD) F-16A MLU Fighting Falcon	FAB 31 Sm/349 Sm/OCU (10 Wg), Kleine-Brogel
	FA-70	SABCA (GD) F-16A MLU Fighting Falcon	FAB 1 Sm/350 Sm (2 Wg), Florennes
	FA-71	SABCA (GD) F-16A MLU Fighting Falcon	FAB 1 Sm/350 Sm (2 Wg), Florennes
	FA-72	SABCA (GD) F-16A MLU Fighting Falcon	FAB 1 Sm/350 Sm (2 Wg), Florennes
	FA-77	SABCA (GD) F-16A MLU Fighting Falcon $	FAB 31 Sm/349 Sm/OCU (10 Wg), Kleine-Brogel
	FA-81	SABCA (GD) F-16A MLU Fighting Falcon	FAB 1 Sm/350 Sm (2 Wg), Florennes
	FA-82	SABCA (GD) F-16A MLU Fighting Falcon	FAB 31 Sm/349 Sm/OCU (10 Wg), Kleine-Brogel
	FA-83	SABCA (GD) F-16A MLU Fighting Falcon	FAB 1 Sm/350 Sm (2 Wg), Florennes
	FA-84	SABCA (GD) F-16A MLU Fighting Falcon $	FAB 1 Sm/350 Sm (2 Wg), Florennes
	FA-86	SABCA (GD) F-16A MLU Fighting Falcon $	FAB 1 Sm/350 Sm (2 Wg), Florennes
	FA-87	SABCA (GD) F-16A MLU Fighting Falcon $	FAB 31 Sm/349 Sm/OCU (10 Wg), Kleine-Brogel
	FA-89	SABCA (GD) F-16A MLU Fighting Falcon	FAB 31 Sm/349 Sm/OCU (10 Wg), Kleine-Brogel
	FA-91	SABCA (GD) F-16A MLU Fighting Falcon	FAB 1 Sm/350 Sm (2 Wg), Florennes
	FA-92	SABCA (GD) F-16A MLU Fighting Falcon	FAB 1 Sm/350 Sm (2 Wg), Florennes
	FA-94	SABCA (GD) F-16A MLU Fighting Falcon	FAB 31 Sm/349 Sm/OCU (10 Wg), Kleine-Brogel
	FA-95	SABCA (GD) F-16A MLU Fighting Falcon	FAB 31 Sm/349 Sm/OCU (10 Wg), Kleine-Brogel
	FA-97	SABCA (GD) F-16A MLU Fighting Falcon $	FAB 31 Sm/349 Sm/OCU (10 Wg), Kleine-Brogel
	FA-98	SABCA (GD) F-16A MLU Fighting Falcon $	FAB 1 Sm/350 Sm (2 Wg), Florennes
	FA-101	SABCA (GD) F-16A MLU Fighting Falcon $	FAB 1 Sm/350 Sm (2 Wg), Florennes
	FA-102	SABCA (GD) F-16A MLU Fighting Falcon	FAB 31 Sm/349 Sm/OCU (10 Wg), Kleine-Brogel
	FA-103	SABCA (GD) F-16A MLU Fighting Falcon	FAB 31 Sm/349 Sm/OCU (10 Wg), Kleine-Brogel
	FA-104	SABCA (GD) F-16A MLU Fighting Falcon	FAB 31 Sm/349 Sm/OCU (10 Wg), Kleine-Brogel
	FA-106	SABCA (GD) F-16A MLU Fighting Falcon	FAB 31 Sm/349 Sm/OCU (10 Wg), Kleine-Brogel
	FA-107	SABCA (GD) F-16A MLU Fighting Falcon	FAB 31 Sm/349 Sm/OCU (10 Wg), Kleine-Brogel
	FA-109	SABCA (GD) F-16A MLU Fighting Falcon	FAB 1 Sm/350 Sm (2 Wg), Florennes
	FA-110	SABCA (GD) F-16A MLU Fighting Falcon	FAB 31 Sm/349 Sm/OCU (10 Wg), Kleine-Brogel
	FA-114	SABCA (GD) F-16A MLU Fighting Falcon	FAB 31 Sm/349 Sm/OCU (10 Wg), Kleine-Brogel
	FA-116	SABCA (GD) F-16A MLU Fighting Falcon $	FAB 31 Sm/349 Sm/OCU (10 Wg), Kleine-Brogel
	FA-117	SABCA (GD) F-16A MLU Fighting Falcon	FAB 1 Sm/350 Sm (2 Wg), Florennes
	FA-118	SABCA (GD) F-16A MLU Fighting Falcon	FAB 1 Sm/350 Sm (2 Wg), Florennes
	FA-119	SABCA (GD) F-16A MLU Fighting Falcon	FAB 31 Sm/349 Sm/OCU (10 Wg), Kleine-Brogel
	FA-121	SABCA (GD) F-16A MLU Fighting Falcon	FAB 1 Sm/350 Sm (2 Wg), Florennes
	FA-123	SABCA (GD) F-16A MLU Fighting Falcon	FAB 31 Sm/349 Sm/OCU (10 Wg), Kleine-Brogel
	FA-124	SABCA (GD) F-16A MLU Fighting Falcon [GE-S] $	FAB 31 Sm/349 Sm/OCU (10 Wg), Kleine-Brogel
	FA-126	SABCA (GD) F-16A MLU Fighting Falcon	FAB 31 Sm/349 Sm/OCU (10 Wg), Kleine-Brogel
	FA-127	SABCA (GD) F-16A MLU Fighting Falcon	FAB 31 Sm/349 Sm/OCU (10 Wg), Kleine-Brogel
	FA-129	SABCA (GD) F-16A MLU Fighting Falcon	FAB 1 Sm/350 Sm (2 Wg), Florennes
	FA-131	SABCA (GD) F-16A MLU Fighting Falcon	FAB 31 Sm/349 Sm/OCU (10 Wg), Kleine-Brogel
	FA-132	SABCA (GD) F-16A MLU Fighting Falcon $	FAB 1 Sm/350 Sm (2 Wg), Florennes
	FA-133	SABCA (GD) F-16A MLU Fighting Falcon	FAB 1 Sm/350 Sm (2 Wg), Florennes
	FA-134	SABCA (GD) F-16A MLU Fighting Falcon	FAB 31 Sm/349 Sm/OCU (10 Wg), Kleine-Brogel
	FA-135	SABCA (GD) F-16A MLU Fighting Falcon $	FAB 1 Sm/350 Sm (2 Wg), Florennes
	FA-136	SABCA (GD) F-16A MLU Fighting Falcon	FAB 31 Sm/349 Sm/OCU (10 Wg), Kleine-Brogel
	FB-12	SABCA (GD) F-16B MLU Fighting Falcon	FAB, *Kleine-Brogel, G.I.*
	FB-14	SABCA (GD) F-16B MLU Fighting Falcon	FAB 1 Sm/350 Sm (2 Wg), Florennes

Serial	Type (code/other identity)	Owner/operator, location or fate	Notes
FB-15	SABCA (GD) F-16B MLU Fighting Falcon	FAB 31 Sm/349 Sm/OCU (10 Wg), Kleine-Brogel	
FB-17	SABCA (GD) F-16B MLU Fighting Falcon	FAB 31 Sm/349 Sm/OCU (10 Wg), Kleine-Brogel	
FB-20	SABCA (GD) F-16B MLU Fighting Falcon	FAB 31 Sm/349 Sm/OCU (10 Wg), Kleine-Brogel	
FB-21	SABCA (GD) F-16B MLU Fighting Falcon	FAB 31 Sm/349 Sm/OCU (10 Wg), Kleine-Brogel	
FB-22	SABCA (GD) F-16B MLU Fighting Falcon	FAB 1 Sm/350 Sm (2 Wg), Florennes	
FB-23	SABCA (GD) F-16B MLU Fighting Falcon	FAB 31 Sm/349 Sm/OCU (10 Wg), Kleine-Brogel	
FB-24	SABCA (GD) F-16B MLU Fighting Falcon $	FAB 31 Sm/349 Sm/OCU (10 Wg), Kleine-Brogel	
G-01	Cessna 182Q Skylane	FAB Federal Police, Brussels/Melsbroek	
G-04	Cessna 182R Skylane	FAB Federal Police, Brussels/Melsbroek	
G-10	MDH MD.902 Explorer	FAB Federal Police, Brussels/Melsbroek	
G-11	MDH MD.902 Explorer	FAB Federal Police, Brussels/Melsbroek	
G-12	MDH MD.902 Explorer	FAB Federal Police, Brussels/Melsbroek	
G-14	MDH MD.520N	FAB Federal Police, Brussels/Melsbroek	
G-15	MDH MD.520N	FAB Federal Police, Brussels/Melsbroek	
G-16	MDH MD.902 Explorer	FAB Federal Police, Brussels/Melsbroek	
G-17	MDH MD.902 Explorer	FAB Federal Police, Brussels/Melsbroek	
H-20	Agusta A109HA	FAB, stored Beauvechain	
H-21	Agusta A109HA	FAB 17 Smaldeel MRH (1 Wg), Beauvechain	
H-24	Agusta A109HA $	FAB 17 Smaldeel MRH (1 Wg), Beauvechain	
H-26	Agusta A109HA	FAB 17 Smaldeel MRH (1 Wg), Beauvechain	
H-27	Agusta A109HA	FAB 17 Smaldeel MRH (1 Wg), Beauvechain	
H-28	Agusta A109HA	FAB 17 Smaldeel MRH (1 Wg), Beauvechain	
H-29	Agusta A109HA $	FAB 17 Smaldeel MRH (1 Wg), Beauvechain	
H-30	Agusta A109HA	FAB, dumped Liege-Bierset	
H-31	Agusta A109HA	FAB 17 Smaldeel MRH (1 Wg), Beauvechain	
H-33	Agusta A109HA	FAB, stored Beauvechain	
H-35	Agusta A109HA	FAB 17 Smaldeel MRH (1 Wg), Beauvechain	
H-36	Agusta A109HA	FAB, stored Beauvechain	
H-38	Agusta A109HA	FAB 17 Smaldeel MRH (1 Wg), Beauvechain	
H-40	Agusta A109HA	FAB, stored Beauvechain	
H-41	Agusta A109HA	FAB, stored Beauvechain	
H-42	Agusta A109HA	FAB SLV (1 Wg), Beauvechain	
H-44	Agusta A109HA	FAB, stored Beauvechain	
H-45	Agusta A109HA	FAB, stored Beauvechain	
H-46	Agusta A109HA $	FAB 17 Smaldeel MRH (1 Wg), Beauvechain	
LB-01	Piper L-21B Super Cub	FAB Air Cadets, Florennes/Goetsenhoven/Zoersel	
LB-02	Piper L-21B Super Cub	FAB Air Cadets, Florennes/Goetsenhoven/Zoersel	
LB-03	Piper L-21B Super Cub	FAB Air Cadets, Florennes/Goetsenhoven/Zoersel	
LB-05	Piper L-21B Super Cub	FAB Air Cadets, Florennes/Goetsenhoven/Zoersel	
LB-06	Piper L-21B Super Cub	FAB Air Cadets, Florennes/Goetsenhoven/Zoersel	
RN-01	NH Industries NH.90-NFH	FAB 40 Smaldeel (1 Wg), Koksijde	
RN-02	NH Industries NH.90-NFH	FAB 40 Smaldeel (1 Wg), Koksijde	
RN-03	NH Industries NH.90-NFH	FAB 40 Smaldeel (1 Wg), Koksijde	
RN-04	NH Industries NH.90-NFH	FAB 40 Smaldeel (1 Wg), Koksijde	
RN-05	NH Industries NH.90-TTH	FAB 18 Smaldeel MRH (1 Wg), Beauvechain	
RN-06	NH Industries NH.90-TTH	FAB 18 Smaldeel MRH (1 Wg), Beauvechain	
RN-07	NH Industries NH.90-TTH	FAB 18 Smaldeel MRH (1 Wg), Beauvechain	
RN-08	NH Industries NH.90-TTH	FAB 18 Smaldeel MRH (1 Wg), Beauvechain	
ST-02	SIAI Marchetti SF260M+	FAB 5 Smaldeel/9 Smaldeel, CC Air, Beauvechain	
ST-03	SIAI Marchetti SF260M+	FAB 5 Smaldeel/9 Smaldeel, CC Air, Beauvechain	
ST-04	SIAI Marchetti SF260M+	FAB 5 Smaldeel/9 Smaldeel, CC Air, Beauvechain	
ST-06	SIAI Marchetti SF260M+	FAB *Red Devils*, CC Air, Beauvechain	
ST-12	SIAI Marchetti SF260M+	FAB 5 Smaldeel/9 Smaldeel, CC Air, Beauvechain	
ST-15	SIAI Marchetti SF260M+	FAB *Red Devils*, CC Air, Beauvechain	
ST-16	SIAI Marchetti SF260M+	FAB *Red Devils*, CC Air, Beauvechain	
ST-17	SIAI Marchetti SF260M+	FAB 5 Smaldeel/9 Smaldeel, CC Air, Beauvechain	
ST-18	SIAI Marchetti SF260M+	FAB *Red Devils*, CC Air, Beauvechain	

Notes	Serial	Type (code/other identity)	Owner/operator, location or fate
	ST-22	SIAI Marchetti SF260M+ $	FAB *Red Devils*, CC Air, Beauvechain
	ST-23	SIAI Marchetti SF260M+	FAB *Red Devils*, CC Air, Beauvechain
	ST-24	SIAI Marchetti SF260M+	FAB 5 Smaldeel/9 Smaldeel, CC Air, Beauvechain
	ST-25	SIAI Marchetti SF260M+	FAB *Red Devils*, CC Air, Beauvechain
	ST-26	SIAI Marchetti SF260M+	FAB 5 Smaldeel/9 Smaldeel, CC Air, Beauvechain
	ST-30	SIAI Marchetti SF260M+ $	FAB 5 Smaldeel/9 Smaldeel, CC Air, Beauvechain
	ST-31	SIAI Marchetti SF260M+	FAB *Red Devils*, CC Air, Beauvechain
	ST-32	SIAI Marchetti SF260M+	FAB 5 Smaldeel/9 Smaldeel, CC Air, Beauvechain
	ST-34	SIAI Marchetti SF260M+	FAB *Red Devils*, CC Air, Beauvechain
	ST-35	SIAI Marchetti SF260M+	FAB *Red Devils*, CC Air, Beauvechain
	ST-36	SIAI Marchetti SF260M+	FAB *Red Devils*, CC Air, Beauvechain
	ST-40	SIAI Marchetti SF260D	FAB 5 Smaldeel/9 Smaldeel, CC Air, Beauvechain
	ST-41	SIAI Marchetti SF260D	FAB 5 Smaldeel/9 Smaldeel, CC Air, Beauvechain
	ST-42	SIAI Marchetti SF260D	FAB 5 Smaldeel/9 Smaldeel, CC Air, Beauvechain
	ST-43	SIAI Marchetti SF260D	FAB 5 Smaldeel/9 Smaldeel, CC Air, Beauvechain
	ST-44	SIAI Marchetti SF260D	FAB 5 Smaldeel/9 Smaldeel, CC Air, Beauvechain
	ST-45	SIAI Marchetti SF260D	FAB 5 Smaldeel/9 Smaldeel, CC Air, Beauvechain
	ST-46	SIAI Marchetti SF260D	FAB 5 Smaldeel/9 Smaldeel, CC Air, Beauvechain
	ST-47	SIAI Marchetti SF260D	FAB 5 Smaldeel/9 Smaldeel, CC Air, Beauvechain
	ST-48	SIAI Marchetti SF260D	FAB 5 Smaldeel/9 Smaldeel, CC Air, Beauvechain
	OO-FAE	Dassault Falcon 7X	FAB 21 Smaldeel (15 Wg), Brussels/Melsbroek
	OO-LUM	Dassault Falcon 7X	FAB 21 Smaldeel (15 Wg), Brussels/Melsbroek

BOLIVIA
Fuerza Aérea Boliviana

	FAB-001	Dassault Falcon 900X EASy	FAB Escuadron de Ejecutivos, La Paz

BOTSWANA
Botswana Defence Force (BDF)

	OK1	Bombardier Global Express	BDF VIP Sqn, Sir Seretse Kharma IAP, Gaborone
	OM-1	Lockheed C-130B Hercules	BDF Z10 Sqn, Thebephatshwa
	OM-2	Lockheed C-130B Hercules	BDF Z10 Sqn, Thebephatshwa
	OM-3	Lockheed C-130B Hercules	BDF Z10 Sqn, Thebephatshwa

BRAZIL
Força Aérea Brasileira (FAB)

	2101	Airbus A.319-133CJ (VC-1A)	FAB 1° GT Especial, 1° Esq, Brasilia
	2461	Lockheed KC-130M Hercules	FAB 1° GT, 1° Esq, Galeão
	2462	Lockheed KC-130H Hercules	FAB 1° GT, 1° Esq, Galeão
	2466	Lockheed C-130M Hercules	FAB 1° GT, 1° Esq, Galeão (w.f.u. November 2022)
	2467	Lockheed C-130M Hercules	FAB 1° GT, 1° Esq, Galeão
	2471	Lockheed C-130H Hercules	FAB 1° GT, 1° Esq, Galeão
	2472	Lockheed C-130H Hercules	FAB 1° GT, 1° Esq, Galeão
	2473	Lockheed C-130M Hercules	FAB 1° GT, 1° Esq, Galeão
	2474	Lockheed C-130M Hercules	FAB 1° GT, 1° Esq, Galeão (w.f.u. November 2022)
	2475	Lockheed C-130H Hercules	FAB 1° GT, 1° Esq, Galeão

Serial	Type (code/other identity)	Owner/operator, location or fate	Notes
2476	Lockheed C-130M Hercules	FAB 1º GTT, 1º Esq, Afonsos	
2477	Lockheed C-130H Hercules	FAB 1º GT, 1º Esq, Galeão	
2479	Lockheed C-130M Hercules	FAB 1º GT, 1º Esq, Galeão	
		(w.f.u. November 2022)	
2550	Embraer VC-99A Legacy	FAB 2º GT Especial, 1º Esq, Brasilia	
2560	Embraer VC-99C Legacy	FAB 2º GT Especial, 1º Esq, Brasilia	
2561	Embraer VC-99C Legacy	FAB 2º GT Especial, 1º Esq, Brasilia	
2580	Embraer VC-99B Legacy	FAB 2º GT Especial, 1º Esq, Brasilia	
2581	Embraer VC-99B Legacy	FAB 2º GT Especial, 1º Esq, Brasilia	
2582	Embraer VC-99B Legacy	FAB 2º GT Especial, 1º Esq, Brasilia	
2583	Embraer VC-99B Legacy	FAB 2º GT Especial, 1º Esq, Brasilia	
2584	Embraer VC-99B Legacy	FAB 2º GT Especial, 1º Esq, Brasilia	
2585	Embraer VC-99B Legacy	FAB 2º GT Especial, 1º Esq, Brasilia	
2586	Embraer VC-99B Legacy	FAB 2º GT Especial, 1º Esq, Brasilia	
2590	Embraer EMB.190-190IGW (VC-2)	FAB 1º GT Especial, 1º Esq, Brasilia	
2591	Embraer EMB.190-190IGW (VC-2)	FAB 1º GT Especial, 1º Esq, Brasilia	
2853	Embraer KC-390 Millennium	FAB 1º GTT, 2º Esq, Galeão	
2854	Embraer KC-390 Millennium	FAB 1º GTT, 2º Esq, Galeão	
2855	Embraer KC-390 Millennium	FAB 1º GTT, 2º Esq, Galeão	
2856	Embraer KC-390 Millennium	FAB 1º GTT, 2º Esq, Galeão	
2857	Embraer KC-390 Millennium	FAB 1º GTT, 2º Esq, Galeão	
2901	Airbus A.330-200	FAB 2º GT, 2º Esq, Galeão (KC-30M conversion)	
2902	Airbus A.330-200	FAB 2º GT, 2º Esq, Galeão (KC-30M conversion)	
6700	Embraer E-99M Guardião	FAB 2º Esq, 6º GAv, Anapolis	
6701	Embraer E-99M Guardião	FAB 2º Esq, 6º GAv, Anapolis	
6702	Embraer E-99M Guardião	FAB 2º Esq, 6º GAv, Anapolis	
6703	Embraer E-99M	FAB 2º Esq, 6º GAv, Anapolis	
6704	Embraer E-99	FAB 2º Esq, 6º GAv, Anapolis	
6750	Embraer R-99	FAB 2º Esq, 6º GAv, Anapolis	
6751	Embraer R-99	FAB 2º Esq, 6º GAv, Anapolis	
6752	Embraer R-99	FAB 2º Esq, 6º GAv, Anapolis	

BRUNEI

Serial	Type	Owner/operator	Notes
V8-BKH	Boeing 747-8LQ	Brunei Government, Bandar Seri Bergawan	
V8-MHB	Boeing 767-27GER	Brunei Government, Bandar Seri Bergawan	
V8-OAS	Boeing 787-8 (N508BJ)	Brunei Government, Bandar Seri Bergawan	

BULGARIA
Bulgarsky Voenno-Vazdushni Sily (BVVS)

Serial	Type	Owner/operator	Notes
020	Pilatus PC.XII/45	BVVS 16.TrAB, Sofia/Vrazhdebna (damaged)	
055	Antonov An-30	BVVS 16.TrAB, Sofia/Vrazhdebna	
071	Aeritalia C-27J Spartan	BVVS 16.TrAB, Sofia/Vrazhdebna	
072	Aeritalia C-27J Spartan	BVVS 16.TrAB, Sofia/Vrazhdebna	
073	Aeritalia C-27J Spartan	BVVS 16.TrAB, Sofia/Vrazhdebna	

Bulgarian Government

Serial	Type	Owner/operator	Notes
LZ-AOB	Airbus A.319-112	Bulgarian Government/BH Air, Sofia/Vrazhdebna	
LZ-OOI	Dassault Falcon 2000	Bulgarian Government, Sofia/Vrazhdebna	

BURKINA FASO

Serial	Type	Owner/operator	Notes
XT-BFA	Boeing 727-282	Government of Burkina Faso, Ouagadougou	

CAMEROON

Serial	Type	Owner/operator	Notes
TJ-AAW	Grumman G.1159A Gulfstream III	Government of Cameroon, Yaounde	

CANADA
Royal Canadian Air Force (RCAF)

Serial	Type	Owner/operator	Notes
15001	Airbus CC-150 Polaris (A.310-304) [991]	RCAF 437 Sqn (8 Wing), Trenton	
15002	Airbus CC-150 Polaris (A.310-304F) [992]	RCAF 437 Sqn (8 Wing), Trenton	
15003	Airbus CC-150 Polaris (A.310-304F) [993] $	RCAF 437 Sqn (8 Wing), Trenton	
15004	Airbus CC-150 Polaris (A.310-304F) [994]	RCAF 437 Sqn (8 Wing), Trenton	
15005	Airbus CC-150 Polaris (A.310-304F) [995]	RCAF 437 Sqn (8 Wing), Trenton	
130332	Lockheed CC-130H(SAR) Hercules	RCAF 413 Sqn (14 Wing), Greenwood	

Notes	Serial	Type (code/other identity)	Owner/operator, location or fate
	130333	Lockheed CC-130H(SAR) Hercules	RCAF 413 Sqn (14 Wing), Greenwood
	130334	Lockheed CC-130H(SAR) Hercules	RCAF 413 Sqn (14 Wing), Greenwood
	130335	Lockheed CC-130H Hercules	RCAF 426 Sqn (8 Wing), Trenton
	130336	Lockheed CC-130H Hercules	RCAF 426 Sqn (8 Wing), Trenton
	130337	Lockheed CC-130H Hercules	RCAF 426 Sqn (8 Wing), Trenton
	130338	Lockheed CC-130H(T) Hercules	RCAF 435 Sqn (17 Wing), Winnipeg
	130339	Lockheed CC-130H(T) Hercules	RCAF 435 Sqn (17 Wing), Winnipeg
	130340	Lockheed CC-130H(T) Hercules	RCAF 435 Sqn (17 Wing), Winnipeg
	130341	Lockheed CC-130H(T) Hercules	RCAF 435 Sqn (17 Wing), Winnipeg
	130343	Lockheed CC-130H-30 Hercules	RCAF 426 Sqn (8 Wing), Trenton
	130344	Lockheed CC-130H-30 Hercules	RCAF 426 Sqn (8 Wing), Trenton
	130601	Lockheed CC-130J Hercules II	RCAF 436 Sqn (8 Wing), Trenton
	130602	Lockheed CC-130J Hercules II	RCAF 436 Sqn (8 Wing), Trenton
	130603	Lockheed CC-130J Hercules II	RCAF 436 Sqn (8 Wing), Trenton
	130604	Lockheed CC-130J Hercules II	RCAF 436 Sqn (8 Wing), Trenton
	130605	Lockheed CC-130J Hercules II	RCAF 436 Sqn (8 Wing), Trenton
	130606	Lockheed CC-130J Hercules II	RCAF 436 Sqn (8 Wing), Trenton
	130607	Lockheed CC-130J Hercules II	RCAF 436 Sqn (8 Wing), Trenton
	130608	Lockheed CC-130J Hercules II	RCAF 436 Sqn (8 Wing), Trenton
	130609	Lockheed CC-130J Hercules II	RCAF 436 Sqn (8 Wing), Trenton
	130610	Lockheed CC-130J Hercules II	RCAF 436 Sqn (8 Wing), Trenton
	130611	Lockheed CC-130J Hercules II	RCAF 436 Sqn (8 Wing), Trenton
	130612	Lockheed CC-130J Hercules II	RCAF 436 Sqn (8 Wing), Trenton
	130613	Lockheed CC-130J Hercules II	RCAF 436 Sqn (8 Wing), Trenton
	130614	Lockheed CC-130J Hercules II $	RCAF 436 Sqn (8 Wing), Trenton
	130615	Lockheed CC-130J Hercules II	RCAF 436 Sqn (8 Wing), Trenton
	130616	Lockheed CC-130J Hercules II	RCAF 436 Sqn (8 Wing), Trenton
	130617	Lockheed CC-130J Hercules II	RCAF 436 Sqn (8 Wing), Trenton
	140101	Lockheed CP-140M Aurora	RCAF 404 Sqn/405 Sqn (14 Wing), Greenwood
	140103	Lockheed CP-140M Aurora	RCAF 404 Sqn/405 Sqn (14 Wing), Greenwood
	140104	Lockheed CP-140M Aurora	RCAF 404 Sqn/405 Sqn (14 Wing), Greenwood
	140105	Lockheed CP-140M Aurora	RCAF 407 Sqn (19 Wing), Comox
	140106	Lockheed CP-140 Aurora	RCAF 407 Sqn (19 Wing), Comox
	140108	Lockheed CP-140M Aurora	RCAF 404 Sqn/405 Sqn (14 Wing), Greenwood
	140110	Lockheed CP-140M Aurora	RCAF 407 Sqn (19 Wing), Comox
	140111	Lockheed CP-140M Aurora	RCAF 404 Sqn/405 Sqn (14 Wing), Greenwood
	140112	Lockheed CP-140M Aurora	RCAF 404 Sqn/405 Sqn (14 Wing), Greenwood
	140113	Lockheed CP-140 Aurora	RCAF 404 Sqn/405 Sqn (14 Wing), Greenwood
	140114	Lockheed CP-140M Aurora	RCAF 407 Sqn (19 Wing), Comox
	140115	Lockheed CP-140M Aurora	RCAF 404 Sqn/405 Sqn (14 Wing), Greenwood
	140116	Lockheed CP-140M Aurora	RCAF 407 Sqn (19 Wing), Comox
	140117	Lockheed CP-140M Aurora	RCAF 407 Sqn (19 Wing), Comox
	140118	Lockheed CP-140M Aurora	RCAF 404 Sqn/405 Sqn (14 Wing), Greenwood
	142803	De Havilland Canada CT-142	RCAF 402 Sqn (17 Wing), Winnipeg
	142804	De Havilland Canada CT-142	RCAF 402 Sqn (17 Wing), Winnipeg
	142805	De Havilland Canada CT-142	RCAF 402 Sqn (17 Wing), Winnipeg
	142806	De Havilland Canada CT-142	RCAF 402 Sqn (17 Wing), Winnipeg
	144617	Canadair CC-144C Challenger (C-GKGR)	RCAF 412 Sqn (8 Wing), Ottawa
	144618	Canadair CC-144C Challenger (C-GKGS)	RCAF 412 Sqn (8 Wing), Ottawa
	144619	Canadair CC-144D Challenger (C-GRIS)	RCAF 412 Sqn (8 Wing), Ottawa
	144620	Canadair CC-144D Challenger (C-FAMN)	RCAF 412 Sqn (8 Wing), Ottawa
	177701	Boeing CC-177 Globemaster III (07-7701/N9500B)	RCAF 429 Sqn (8 Wing), Trenton
	177702	Boeing CC-177 Globemaster III (07-7702/N9500H)	RCAF 429 Sqn (8 Wing), Trenton
	177703	Boeing CC-177 Globemaster III (07-7703/N9500N)	RCAF 429 Sqn (8 Wing), Trenton
	177704	Boeing CC-177 Globemaster III (07-7704/N9500R) $	RCAF 429 Sqn (8 Wing), Trenton
	177705	Boeing CC-177 Globemaster III (14-0004/N273ZD)	RCAF 429 Sqn (8 Wing), Trenton
	CHAD		
	TT-ABD	Boeing 737-74Q	Chad Government, N'djamena

Serial	Type (code/other identity)	Owner/operator, location or fate	Notes

CHILE
Fuerza Aérea de Chile (FACh)

Serial	Type (code/other identity)	Owner/operator, location or fate	Notes
20	Game Composites GB1 GameBird (N259GC)	FACh *Los Halcones*, Santiago	
21	Game Composites GB1 GameBird (N963GC)	FACh *Los Halcones*, Santiago	
22	Game Composites GB1 GameBird (N898GC)	FACh *Los Halcones*, Santiago	
....	Game Composites GB1 GameBird (N146GC)	FACh *Los Halcones*, Santiago	
....	Game Composites GB1 GameBird (N174GC)	FACh *Los Halcones*, Santiago	
....	Game Composites GB1 GameBird (N219GC)	FACh *Los Halcones*, Santiago	
....	Game Composites GB1 GameBird (N228GC)	FACh *Los Halcones*, Santiago	
145	Extra EA-300L [5]	FACh *Los Halcones*, Santiago	
146	Extra EA-300L [4]	FACh *Los Halcones*, Santiago	
147	Extra EA-300L [2]	FACh *Los Halcones*, Santiago	
904	Boeing 707-358C Phalcon AEW	FACh, Grupo de Aviación 10, Santiago	
911	Grumman G.1159C Gulfstream IV	FACh, Grupo de Aviación 10, Santiago	
912	Grumman G.1159C Gulfstream IV	FACh, Grupo de Aviación 10, Santiago	
913	Grumman G.1159C Gulfstream IV-SP	FACh, Grupo de Aviación 10, Santiago	
914	Grumman G.1159C Gulfstream IV-SP	FACh, Grupo de Aviación 10, Santiago	
921	Boeing 737-58N	FACh, Grupo de Aviación 10, Santiago	
922	Boeing 737-330	FACh, Grupo de Aviación 10, Santiago	
982	Boeing KC-135E Stratotanker	FACh, Grupo de Aviación 10, Santiago	
983	Boeing KC-135E Stratotanker	FACh, Grupo de Aviación 10, Santiago	
985	Boeing 767-3Y0ER	FACh, Grupo de Aviación 10, Santiago	
991	Lockheed C-130R Hercules	FACh, Grupo de Aviación 10, Santiago	
992	Lockheed C-130R Hercules	FACh, Grupo de Aviación 10, Santiago	
993	Lockheed C-130H Hercules	FACh, Grupo de Aviación 10, Santiago	
994	Lockheed C-130H Hercules	FACh, Grupo de Aviación 10, Santiago	
995	Lockheed C-130H Hercules	FACh, Grupo de Aviación 10, Santiago	
996	Lockheed C-130H Hercules	FACh, Grupo de Aviación 10, Santiago	
999	Lockheed KC-130R Hercules	FACh, Grupo de Aviación 10, Santiago	
1304	Extra EA-300L [3]	FACh *Los Halcones*, Santiago	
1325	Extra EA-300L [1]	FACh *Los Halcones*, Santiago	

COLOMBIA
Fuerza Aérea Colombiana (FAC)

Serial	Type (code/other identity)	Owner/operator, location or fate	Notes
FAC-0001	Boeing 737-74V	FAC Escuadrón de Transporte Especial, Bogotà	
FAC-1202	Boeing 767-2J6ER	FAC Escuadrón de Transporte 811, Bogota	
FAC-1219	Boeing 737-732	FAC Escuadrón de Transporte 811, Bogota	
FAC-1220	Boeing 737-732	FAC Escuadrón de Transporte 811, Bogota	

CROATIA
Hrvatske Zračne Snage (HZS)

Serial	Type (code/other identity)	Owner/operator, location or fate	Notes
054	Pilatus PC-9M	HZS 392.Eskadrila Aviona/93.Krilo, Zadar	
055	Pilatus PC-9M	HZS 392.Eskadrila Aviona/93.Krilo, Zadar	
056	Pilatus PC-9M	HZS 392.Eskadrila Aviona/93.Krilo, Zadar	
057	Pilatus PC-9M	HZS 392.Eskadrila Aviona/93.Krilo, Zadar	
059	Pilatus PC-9M $	HZS 392.Eskadrila Aviona/93.Krilo, Zadar	
061	Pilatus PC-9M	HZS 392.Eskadrila Aviona/93.Krilo, Zadar	
062	Pilatus PC-9M	HZS 392.Eskadrila Aviona/93.Krilo, Zadar	
063	Pilatus PC-9M	HZS 392.Eskadrila Aviona/93.Krilo, Zadar	
064	Pilatus PC-9M	HZS 392.Eskadrila Aviona/93.Krilo, Zadar	
066	Pilatus PC-9M	HZS 392.Eskadrila Aviona/93.Krilo, Zadar	
067	Pilatus PC-9M	HZS 392.Eskadrila Aviona/93.Krilo, Zadar	
068	Pilatus PC-9M	HZS 392.Eskadrila Aviona/93.Krilo, Zadar	
069	Pilatus PC-9M	HZS 392.Eskadrila Aviona/93.Krilo, Zadar	
070	Pilatus PC-9M	HZS 392.Eskadrila Aviona/93.Krilo, Zadar	
...	Dassault Rafale C	HZS, on order	
...	Dassault Rafale C	HZS, on order	
...	Dassault Rafale C	HZS, on order	
...	Dassault Rafale C	HZS, on order	
...	Dassault Rafale C	HZS, on order	
...	Dassault Rafale C	HZS, on order	
...	Dassault Rafale C	HZS, on order	

Notes	Serial	Type (code/other identity)	Owner/operator, location or fate
	...	Dassault Rafale C	HZS, on order
	...	Dassault Rafale C	HZS, on order
	...	Dassault Rafale C	HZS, on order
	...	Dassault Rafale C	HZS, on order
	...	Dassault Rafale C	HZS, on order
	Croatian Government		
	9A-CRO	Canadair CL.601 Challenger	Croatian Government, Zagreb
	CYPRUS		
	Cyprus Government		
	CAF-001	Embraer ERJ.135BJ Legacy	Cyprus Government, Paphos
	CZECH REPUBLIC		
	Vzdušné Síly Armády (Czech Air Force)		
	0113	Aero L-39C Albatros	Czech AF CLV, Pardubice
	0115	Aero L-39C Albatros	Czech AF CLV, Pardubice
	0441	Aero L-39C Albatros	Czech AF CLV, Pardubice
	0444	Aero L-39C Albatros	Czech AF CLV, Pardubice
	0445	Aero L-39C Albatros	Czech AF CLV, Pardubice
	0448	Aero L-39C Albatros	Czech AF CLV, Pardubice
	0452	CASA C-295M	Czech AF 242.tsl/24.zDL, Praha/Kbely
	0453	CASA C-295M	Czech AF 242.tsl/24.zDL, Praha/Kbely
	0454	CASA C-295M	Czech AF 242.tsl/24.zDL, Praha/Kbely
	0455	CASA C-295M	Czech AF 242.tsl/24.zDL, Praha/Kbely
	0457	Mil Mi-17V-11	Czech AF CLV, Pardubice
	0475	Aero L-39NG Albatros (7001)	Aero, Vodochody
	0476	Aero L-39NG Albatros (7004)	Aero, Vodochody
	0481	CASA C-295W	Czech AF 242.tsl/24.zDL, Praha/Kbely
	0482	CASA C-295W	Czech AF 242.tsl/24.zDL, Praha/Kbely
	0731	LET L-410UVP-E Turbolet	Czech AF CLV, Pardubice
	0825	Mil Mi-17	Czech AF CLV, Pardubice
	0828	Mil Mi-17	Czech AF CLV, Pardubice
	0832	Mil Mi-17	Czech AF CLV, Pardubice
	0834	Mil Mi-17	Czech AF 243.vrl/24.zDL, Praha/Kbely
	0835	Mil Mi-17	Czech AF CLV, Pardubice
	0836	Mil Mi-17	Czech AF CLV, Pardubice
	0837	Mil Mi-17	Czech AF CLV, Pardubice
	0839	Mil Mi-17	Czech AF 243.vrl/24.zDL, Praha/Kbely
	0848	Mil Mi-17	Czech AF 243.vrl/24.zDL, Praha/Kbely
	0849	Mil Mi-17	Czech AF 243.vrl/24.zDL, Praha/Kbely
	0850	Mil Mi-17	Czech AF 243.vrl/24.zDL, Praha/Kbely
	0928	LET L-410UVP-T Turbolet	Czech AF CLV, Pardubice
	0981	Mil Mi-24V2	Czech AF 221.lbvr/22.zL, Náměšt
	1525	LET L-410FG Turbolet	Czech AF 242.tsl/24.zDL, Praha/Kbely
	1526	LET L-410FG Turbolet	Czech AF 242.tsl/24.zDL, Praha/Kbely
	2312	LET L-410UVP-E Turbolet	Czech AF 242.tsl/24.zDL, Praha/Kbely
	2601	LET L-410UVP-E Turbolet	Czech AF 242.tsl/24.zDL, Praha/Kbely
	2602	LET L-410UVP-E Turbolet	Czech AF 242.tsl/24.zDL, Praha/Kbely
	2626	Aero L-39NG Albatros	Aero, stored Vodochody
	2710	LET L-410UVP-E Turbolet	Czech AF 242.tsl/24.zDL, Praha/Kbely
	2801	Airbus A.319CJ-115X	Czech AF 241.dlt/24.zDL, Praha/Kbely
	3085	Airbus A.319CJ-115X	Czech AF 241.dlt/24.zDL, Praha/Kbely
	3362	Mil Mi-35	*To Ukraine, July 2022*
	3365	Mil Mi-35	Czech AF 221.lbvr/22.zL, Náměšt
	3366	Mil Mi-35 $	Czech AF 221.lbvr/22.zL, Náměšt
	3367	Mil Mi-35	Czech AF 221.lbvr/22.zL, Náměšt
	3368	Mil Mi-35	Czech AF 221.lbvr/22.zL, Náměšt
	3369	Mil Mi-35 $	Czech AF 221.lbvr/22.zL, Náměšt
	3370	Mil Mi-35 $	Czech AF 221.lbvr/22.zL, Náměšt
	3371	Mil Mi-35	Czech AF 221.lbvr/22.zL, Náměšt
	5105	Canadair CL.601-3A Challenger	Czech AF 241.dlt/24.zDL, Praha/Kbely
	6028	Aero L-159T-2 ALCA	Czech AF 213.vlt/21.zTL, Čáslav

Serial	Type (code/other identity)	Owner/operator, location or fate	Notes
6031	Aero L-159T-2 ALCA	Czech AF 213.vlt/21.zTL, Cáslav	
6038	Aero L-159T-2 ALCA	Czech AF 213.vlt/21.zTL, Cáslav	
6046	Aero L-159T-1 ALCA	Czech AF 213.vlt/21.zTL, Cáslav	
6047	Aero L-159T-1 ALCA	Czech AF 213.vlt/21.zTL, Cáslav	
6048	Aero L-159A ALCA	Czech AF 212.tl/21.zTL, Cáslav	
6050	Aero L-159A ALCA	Czech AF 212.tl/21.zTL, Cáslav	
6051	Aero L-159A ALCA	Czech AF 212.tl/21.zTL, Cáslav	
6052	Aero L-159A ALCA	Czech AF 212.tl/21.zTL, Cáslav	
6053	Aero L-159A ALCA	Czech AF 212.tl/21.zTL, Cáslav	
6054	Aero L-159A ALCA	Czech AF 212.tl/21.zTL, Cáslav	
6057	Aero L-159A ALCA	Czech AF 212.tl/21.zTL, Cáslav	
6058	Aero L-159A ALCA	Czech AF 212.tl/21.zTL, Cáslav	
6059	Aero L-159A ALCA	Czech AF 212.tl/21.zTL, Cáslav	
6060	Aero L-159A ALCA	Czech AF 212.tl/21.zTL, Cáslav	
6062	Aero L-159A ALCA	Czech AF 212.tl/21.zTL, Cáslav	
6063	Aero L-159A ALCA	Czech AF 212.tl/21.zTL, Cáslav	
6064	Aero L-159A ALCA	Czech AF 212.tl/21.zTL, Cáslav	
6066	Aero L-159A ALCA	Czech AF 212.tl/21.zTL, Cáslav	
6067	Aero L-159T-1 ALCA	Czech AF 213.vlt/21.zTL, Cáslav	
6070	Aero L-159A ALCA $	Czech AF 212.tl/21.zTL, Cáslav	
6073	Aero L-159T-2X ALCA	Aero, stored Vodochody	
6077	Aero L-159T-1 ALCA	Czech AF 213.vlt/21.zTL, Cáslav	
6078	Aero L-159T-1 ALCA	Czech AF 213.vlt/21.zTL, Cáslav	
7353	Mil Mi-24V $	Czech AF 221.lbvr/22.zL, Náměšt (damaged)	
7354	Mil Mi-24V	Czech AF 221.lbvr/22.zL, Náměšt	
7355	Mil Mi-24V	Czech AF 221.lbvr/22.zL, Náměšt	
7356	Mil Mi-24V	Czech AF 221.lbvr/22.zL, Náměšt	
7357	Mil Mi-24V	Czech AF 221.lbvr/22.zL, Náměšt	
7360	Mil Mi-24V	Czech AF 221.lbvr/22.zL, Náměšt	
9234	SAAB JAS 39C Gripen	Czech AF 211.tl/21.zTL, Cáslav	
9235	SAAB JAS 39C Gripen	Czech AF 211.tl/21.zTL, Cáslav	
9236	SAAB JAS 39C Gripen	Czech AF 211.tl/21.zTL, Cáslav	
9237	SAAB JAS 39C Gripen	Czech AF 211.tl/21.zTL, Cáslav	
9238	SAAB JAS 39C Gripen	Czech AF 211.tl/21.zTL, Cáslav	
9239	SAAB JAS 39C Gripen	Czech AF 211.tl/21.zTL, Cáslav	
9240	SAAB JAS 39C Gripen	Czech AF 211.tl/21.zTL, Cáslav	
9241	SAAB JAS 39C Gripen	Czech AF 211.tl/21.zTL, Cáslav	
9242	SAAB JAS 39C Gripen	Czech AF 211.tl/21.zTL, Cáslav	
9243	SAAB JAS 39C Gripen	Czech AF 211.tl/21.zTL, Cáslav	
9244	SAAB JAS 39C Gripen	Czech AF 211.tl/21.zTL, Cáslav	
9245	SAAB JAS 39C Gripen	Czech AF 211.tl/21.zTL, Cáslav	
9767	Mil Mi-171Sh	Czech AF 221.lbvr & 222.vrlt/22.zVrL, Náměšt	
9781	Mil Mi-171Sh	Czech AF 221.lbvr & 222.vrlt/22.zVrL, Náměšt	
9799	Mil Mi-171Sh	Czech AF 221.lbvr & 222.vrlt/22.zVrL, Náměšt	
9806	Mil Mi-171Sh	Czech AF 221.lbvr & 222.vrlt/22.zVrL, Náměšt	
9813	Mil Mi-171Sh	Czech AF 221.lbvr & 222.vrlt/22.zVrL, Náměšt	
9819	SAAB JAS 39D Gripen $	Czech AF 211.tl/21.zTL, Cáslav	
9820	SAAB JAS 39D Gripen	Czech AF 211.tl/21.zTL, Cáslav	
9825	Mil Mi-171Sh	Czech AF 221.lbvr & 222.vrlt/22.zVrL, Náměšt	
9837	Mil Mi-171Sh	Czech AF 221.lbvr & 222.vrlt/22.zVrL, Náměšt	
9844	Mil Mi-171Sh	Czech AF 221.lbvr & 222.vrlt/22.zVrL, Náměšt	
9868	Mil Mi-171Sh	Czech AF 221.lbvr & 222.vrlt/22.zVrL, Náměšt	
9873	Mil Mi-171Sh	Czech AF 221.lbvr & 222.vrlt/22.zVrL, Náměšt	
9887	Mil Mi-171Sh	Czech AF 221.lbvr & 222.vrlt/22.zVrL, Náměšt	
9892	Mil Mi-171Sh	Czech AF 221.lbvr & 222.vrlt/22.zVrL, Náměšt	
9904	Mil Mi-171Sh	Czech AF 221.lbvr & 222.vrlt/22.zVrL, Náměšt	
9915	Mil Mi-171Sh	Czech AF 221.lbvr & 222.vrlt/22.zVrL, Náměšt	
9926	Mil Mi-171Sh	Czech AF 221.lbvr & 222.vrlt/22.zVrL, Náměšt	
....	Bombardier Global 5000	Czech AF (on order)	
....	Bombardier Global 5000	Czech AF (on order)	

Notes	Serial	Type (code/other identity)	Owner/operator, location or fate

DENMARK

Kongelige Danske Flyvevåben (KDF)

	Serial	Type (code/other identity)	Owner/operator, location or fate
	B-536	Lockheed C-130J-30 Hercules II	KDF Eskadrille 721, Aalborg
	B-537	Lockheed C-130J-30 Hercules II	KDF Eskadrille 721, Aalborg
	B-538	Lockheed C-130J-30 Hercules II	KDF Eskadrille 721, Aalborg
	B-583	Lockheed C-130J-30 Hercules II	KDF Eskadrille 721, Aalborg
	C-080	Canadair CL.604 Challenger	KDF Eskadrille 721, Aalborg
	C-168	Canadair CL.604 Challenger	KDF Eskadrille 721, Aalborg
	C-172	Canadair CL.604 Challenger	KDF Eskadrille 721, Aalborg
	C-215	Canadair CL.604 Challenger	KDF Eskadrille 721, Aalborg
	E-004	SABCA (GD) F-16A MLU Fighting Falcon	KDF Eskadrille 727, Skrydstrup
	E-005	SABCA (GD) F-16A MLU Fighting Falcon	KDF Eskadrille 727, Skrydstrup
	E-006	SABCA (GD) F-16A MLU Fighting Falcon	KDF Eskadrille 730, Skrydstrup
	E-007	SABCA (GD) F-16A MLU Fighting Falcon	KDF Eskadrille 727, Skrydstrup
	E-008	SABCA (GD) F-16A MLU Fighting Falcon $	KDF Eskadrille 727, Skrydstrup
	E-011	GD F-16A MLU Fighting Falcon	KDF Eskadrille 727, Skrydstrup
	E-016	SABCA (GD) F-16A MLU Fighting Falcon	KDF Eskadrille 727, Skrydstrup
	E-017	SABCA (GD) F-16A MLU Fighting Falcon	KDF Eskadrille 727, Skrydstrup
	E-018	SABCA (GD) F-16A MLU Fighting Falcon	KDF Eskadrille 730, Skrydstrup
	E-024	GD F-16A MLU Fighting Falcon	KDF Eskadrille 730, Skrydstrup
	E-074	GD F-16A MLU Fighting Falcon	KDF Eskadrille 730, Skrydstrup
	E-075	GD F-16A MLU Fighting Falcon	KDF Eskadrille 727, Skrydstrup
	E-107	GD F-16A MLU Fighting Falcon	KDF Eskadrille 730, Skrydstrup
	E-189	SABCA (GD) F-16A MLU Fighting Falcon	KDF Eskadrille 730, Skrydstrup
	E-190	SABCA (GD) F-16A MLU Fighting Falcon	KDF Eskadrille 730, Skrydstrup
	E-191	SABCA (GD) F-16A MLU Fighting Falcon $	KDF Eskadrille 727, Skrydstrup
	E-194	SABCA (GD) F-16A MLU Fighting Falcon	KDF Eskadrille 730, Skrydstrup
	E-596	SABCA (GD) F-16A MLU Fighting Falcon	KDF Eskadrille 730, Skrydstrup
	E-597	SABCA (GD) F-16A MLU Fighting Falcon	KDF Eskadrille 730, Skrydstrup
	E-598	SABCA (GD) F-16A MLU Fighting Falcon	KDF Eskadrille 730, Skrydstrup
	E-599	SABCA (GD) F-16A MLU Fighting Falcon	KDF Eskadrille 727, Skrydstrup
	E-600	SABCA (GD) F-16A MLU Fighting Falcon	KDF Eskadrille 730, Skrydstrup
	E-601	SABCA (GD) F-16A MLU Fighting Falcon $	KDF Eskadrille 727, Skrydstrup
	E-602	SABCA (GD) F-16A MLU Fighting Falcon	KDF Eskadrille 730, Skrydstrup
	E-603	SABCA (GD) F-16A MLU Fighting Falcon	KDF Eskadrille 730, Skrydstrup
	E-604	SABCA (GD) F-16A MLU Fighting Falcon	KDF Eskadrille 730, Skrydstrup
	E-605	SABCA (GD) F-16A MLU Fighting Falcon	KDF Eskadrille 730, Skrydstrup
	E-606	SABCA (GD) F-16A MLU Fighting Falcon	KDF Eskadrille 730, Skrydstrup
	E-607	SABCA (GD) F-16A MLU Fighting Falcon $	KDF Eskadrille 727, Skrydstrup
	E-608	SABCA (GD) F-16A MLU Fighting Falcon	KDF Eskadrille 727, Skrydstrup
	E-609	SABCA (GD) F-16A MLU Fighting Falcon	KDF Eskadrille 727, Skrydstrup
	E-610	SABCA (GD) F-16A MLU Fighting Falcon	KDF Eskadrille 730, Skrydstrup
	E-611	SABCA (GD) F-16A MLU Fighting Falcon	KDF Eskadrille 727, Skrydstrup
	ET-022	Fokker (GD) F-16B MLU Fighting Falcon	KDF Eskadrille 730, Skrydstrup
	ET-197	Fokker (GD) F-16B MLU Fighting Falcon	KDF Eskadrille 727, Skrydstrup
	ET-198	Fokker (GD) F-16B MLU Fighting Falcon	KDF Eskadrille 727, Skrydstrup
	ET-199	Fokker (GD) F-16B MLU Fighting Falcon	KDF Eskadrille 730, Skrydstrup
	ET-207	SABCA (GD) F-16B MLU Fighting Falcon	KDF Eskadrille 727, Skrydstrup
	ET-208	SABCA (GD) F-16B MLU Fighting Falcon	KDF Eskadrille 730, Skrydstrup
	ET-612	SABCA (GD) F-16B MLU Fighting Falcon	KDF Eskadrille 727, Skrydstrup
	ET-613	SABCA (GD) F-16B MLU Fighting Falcon	KDF Eskadrille 727, Skrydstrup
	ET-614	SABCA (GD) F-16B MLU Fighting Falcon	KDF Eskadrille 727, Skrydstrup
	ET-615	SABCA (GD) F-16B MLU Fighting Falcon	KDF Eskadrille 727, Skrydstrup
	L-001	Lockheed Martin F-35A Lightning II	KDF 308th FS/56th FW, Luke AFB, AZ, USA
	L-002	Lockheed Martin F-35A Lightning II	KDF 308th FS/56th FW, Luke AFB, AZ, USA
	L-003	Lockheed Martin F-35A Lightning II	KDF 308th FS/56th FW, Luke AFB, AZ, USA
	L-004	Lockheed Martin F-35A Lightning II	KDF 308th FS/56th FW, Luke AFB, AZ, USA
	L-005	Lockheed Martin F-35A Lightning II	KDF 308th FS/56th FW, Luke AFB, AZ, USA
	L-006	Lockheed Martin F-35A Lightning II	KDF 308th FS/56th FW, Luke AFB, AZ, USA
	L-007	Lockheed Martin F-35A Lightning II	KDF (on order)
	L-008	Lockheed Martin F-35A Lightning II	KDF (on order)
	L-009	Lockheed Martin F-35A Lightning II	KDF (on order)

Serial	Type (code/other identity)	Owner/operator, location or fate	Notes
L-010	Lockheed Martin F-35A Lightning II	KDF (on order)	
L-011	Lockheed Martin F-35A Lightning II	KDF (on order)	
L-012	Lockheed Martin F-35A Lightning II	KDF (on order)	
L-013	Lockheed Martin F-35A Lightning II	KDF (on order)	
L-014	Lockheed Martin F-35A Lightning II	KDF (on order)	
L-015	Lockheed Martin F-35A Lightning II	KDF (on order)	
L-016	Lockheed Martin F-35A Lightning II	KDF (on order)	
L-017	Lockheed Martin F-35A Lightning II	KDF (on order)	
L-018	Lockheed Martin F-35A Lightning II	KDF (on order)	
L-019	Lockheed Martin F-35A Lightning II	KDF (on order)	
L-020	Lockheed Martin F-35A Lightning II	KDF (on order)	
L-021	Lockheed Martin F-35A Lightning II	KDF (on order)	
L-022	Lockheed Martin F-35A Lightning II	KDF (on order)	
L-023	Lockheed Martin F-35A Lightning II	KDF (on order)	
L-024	Lockheed Martin F-35A Lightning II	KDF (on order)	
L-025	Lockheed Martin F-35A Lightning II	KDF (on order)	
L-026	Lockheed Martin F-35A Lightning II	KDF (on order)	
L-027	Lockheed Martin F-35A Lightning II	KDF (on order)	
M-502	AgustaWestland EH.101 Mk.512 (ZJ991)	KDF Eskadrille 722, Karup	
M-504	AgustaWestland EH.101 Mk.512 (ZJ993)	KDF Eskadrille 722, Karup	
M-507	AgustaWestland EH.101 Mk.512 (ZJ996)	KDF Eskadrille 722, Karup	
M-508	AgustaWestland EH.101 Mk.512 (ZJ997)	KDF Eskadrille 722, Karup	
M-510	AgustaWestland EH.101 Mk.512 (ZJ999)	KDF Eskadrille 722, Karup	
M-512	AgustaWestland EH.101 Mk.512 (ZK002)	KDF Eskadrille 722, Karup	
M-513	AgustaWestland EH.101 Mk.512 (ZK003)	KDF Eskadrille 722, Karup	
M-514	AgustaWestland EH.101 Mk.512 (ZK004)	KDF Eskadrille 722, Karup	
M-515	AgustaWestland EH.101 Mk.512 (ZK160)	KDF Eskadrille 722, Karup	
M-516	AgustaWestland EH.101 Mk.512 (ZK161)	KDF Eskadrille 722, Karup	
M-517	AgustaWestland EH.101 Mk.512 (ZK162)	KDF Eskadrille 722, Karup	
M-518	AgustaWestland EH.101 Mk.512 (ZK163)	KDF Eskadrille 722, Karup	
M-519	AgustaWestland EH.101 Mk.512 (ZK164)	KDF Eskadrille 722, Karup	
M-520	AgustaWestland EH.101 Mk.512 (ZK165)	KDF Eskadrille 722, Karup	
N-971	Sikorsky MH-60R Sea Hawk	KDF Eskadrille 723, Karup	
N-972	Sikorsky MH-60R Sea Hawk	KDF Eskadrille 723, Karup	
N-973	Sikorsky MH-60R Sea Hawk	KDF Eskadrille 723, Karup	
N-974	Sikorsky MH-60R Sea Hawk	KDF Eskadrille 723, Karup	
N-975	Sikorsky MH-60R Sea Hawk	KDF Eskadrille 723, Karup	
N-976	Sikorsky MH-60R Sea Hawk	KDF Eskadrille 723, Karup	
N-977	Sikorsky MH-60R Sea Hawk	KDF Eskadrille 723, Karup	
N-978	Sikorsky MH-60R Sea Hawk	KDF Eskadrille 723, Karup	
N-979	Sikorsky MH-60R Sea Hawk	KDF Eskadrille 723, Karup	
P-234	Aérospatiale AS.550C-2 Fennec	KDF Eskadrille 724, Karup	
P-254	Aérospatiale AS.550C-2 Fennec	KDF Eskadrille 724, Karup	
P-275	Aérospatiale AS.550C-2 Fennec	KDF Eskadrille 724, Karup	
P-276	Aérospatiale AS.550C-2 Fennec	KDF Eskadrille 724, Karup	
P-287	Aérospatiale AS.550C-2 Fennec	KDF Eskadrille 724, Karup	
P-288	Aérospatiale AS.550C-2 Fennec	KDF Eskadrille 724, Karup	
P-319	Aérospatiale AS.550C-2 Fennec	KDF Eskadrille 724, Karup	
P-320	Aérospatiale AS.550C-2 Fennec	KDF Eskadrille 724, Karup	
P-339	Aérospatiale AS.550C-2 Fennec	KDF Eskadrille 724, Karup	
P-352	Aérospatiale AS.550C-2 Fennec	KDF Eskadrille 724, Karup	
P-369	Aérospatiale AS.550C-2 Fennec	KDF Eskadrille 724, Karup	
T-401	SAAB T-17 Supporter	KDF Flyveskolen, Karup	
T-402	SAAB T-17 Supporter	KDF Flyveskolen, Karup	
T-403	SAAB T-17 Supporter	KDF Flyveskolen, Karup	
T-404	SAAB T-17 Supporter	KDF Flyveskolen, Karup	
T-405	SAAB T-17 Supporter	KDF Skrydstrup Station Flight	
T-407	SAAB T-17 Supporter	KDF Eskadrille 721, Aalborg	
T-409	SAAB T-17 Supporter	KDF Flyveskolen, Karup	
T-410	SAAB T-17 Supporter	KDF Flyveskolen, Karup	
T-411	SAAB T-17 Supporter	KDF, *Baby Blue Display Team, Skrydstrup*	
T-412	SAAB T-17 Supporter	KDF Flyveskolen, Karup	

Notes	Serial	Type (code/other identity)	Owner/operator, location or fate
	T-413	SAAB T-17 Supporter	KDF, *Baby Blue Display Team, Skrydstrup*
	T-414	SAAB T-17 Supporter	KDF Eskadrille 721, Aalborg
	T-415	SAAB T-17 Supporter $	KDF, *Baby Blue Display Team, Skrydstrup*
	T-417	SAAB T-17 Supporter	KDF Flyveskolen, Karup
	T-418	SAAB T-17 Supporter	KDF Skrydstrup Station Flight
	T-419	SAAB T-17 Supporter	KDF Flyveskolen, Karup
	T-420	SAAB T-17 Supporter	KDF Skrydstrup Station Flight
	T-421	SAAB T-17 Supporter	KDF, *Baby Blue Display Team, Skrydstrup*
	T-423	SAAB T-17 Supporter	KDF, *Baby Blue Display Team, Skrydstrup*
	T-425	SAAB T-17 Supporter	KDF Flyveskolen, Karup
	T-426	SAAB T-17 Supporter	KDF, *Baby Blue Display Team, Skrydstrup*
	T-427	SAAB T-17 Supporter	KDF Flyveskolen, Karup
	T-428	SAAB T-17 Supporter	KDF, *Baby Blue Display Team, Skrydstrup*
	T-429	SAAB T-17 Supporter	KDF Flyveskolen, Karup
	T-430	SAAB T-17 Supporter	KDF Flyveskolen, Karup
	T-431	SAAB T-17 Supporter	KDF Flyveskolen, Karup
	T-432	SAAB T-17 Supporter	KDF Flyveskolen, Karup

ECUADOR
Fuerza Aérea Ecuatoriana (FAE)

	FAE-051	Embraer ERJ.135 Legacy 600	FAE Escuadrón de Transporte 1114, Quito
	FAE-052	Dassault Falcon 7X	FAE Escuadrón de Transporte 1114, Quito

EGYPT
Al Quwwat al-Jawwiya il Misriya (Egyptian Air Force)

	1331	Ilyushin Il-76MF (SU-BTX)	Egyptian AF 16 Sqn, Cairo West
	1332	Ilyushin Il-76MF (SU-BTY)	Egyptian AF 16 Sqn, Cairo West
	1271	Lockheed C-130H Hercules (SU-BAB)	Egyptian AF 16 Sqn, Cairo West
	1273	Lockheed C-130H Hercules (SU-BAD)	Egyptian AF 16 Sqn, Cairo West
	1274	Lockheed C-130H Hercules (SU-BAE)	Egyptian AF 16 Sqn, Cairo West
	1275	Lockheed C-130H Hercules (SU-BAF)	Egyptian AF 16 Sqn, Cairo West
	1277	Lockheed C-130H Hercules (SU-BAI)	Egyptian AF 16 Sqn, Cairo West
	1278	Lockheed C-130H Hercules (SU-BAJ)	Egyptian AF 16 Sqn, Cairo West
	1279	Lockheed C-130H Hercules (SU-BAK)	Egyptian AF 16 Sqn, Cairo West
	1280	Lockheed C-130H Hercules (SU-BAL)	Egyptian AF 16 Sqn, Cairo West
	1281	Lockheed C-130H Hercules (SU-BAM)	Egyptian AF 16 Sqn, Cairo West
	1282	Lockheed C-130H Hercules (SU-BAN)	Egyptian AF 16 Sqn, Cairo West
	1283	Lockheed C-130H Hercules (SU-BAP)	Egyptian AF 16 Sqn, Cairo West
	1284	Lockheed C-130H Hercules (SU-BAQ)	Egyptian AF 16 Sqn, Cairo West
	1285	Lockheed C-130H Hercules (SU-BAR)	Egyptian AF 16 Sqn, Cairo West
	1286	Lockheed C-130H Hercules (SU-BAS)	Egyptian AF 16 Sqn, Cairo West
	1287	Lockheed C-130H Hercules (SU-BAT)	Egyptian AF 16 Sqn, Cairo West
	1288	Lockheed C-130H Hercules (SU-BAU)	Egyptian AF 16 Sqn, Cairo West
	1289	Lockheed C-130H Hercules (SU-BAV)	Egyptian AF 16 Sqn, Cairo West
	1290	Lockheed C-130H Hercules (SU-BEW)	Egyptian AF 16 Sqn, Cairo West
	1291	Lockheed C-130H Hercules (SU-BEX)	Egyptian AF 16 Sqn, Cairo West
	1292	Lockheed C-130H Hercules (SU-BEY)	Egyptian AF 16 Sqn, Cairo West
	1293	Lockheed C-130H-30 Hercules (SU-BKS)	Egyptian AF 16 Sqn, Cairo West
	1294	Lockheed C-130H-30 Hercules (SU-BKT)	Egyptian AF 16 Sqn, Cairo West
	1295	Lockheed C-130H-30 Hercules (SU-BKU)	Egyptian AF 16 Sqn, Cairo West
	1296	Lockheed C-130H Hercules (SU-BPJ)	Egyptian AF 16 Sqn, Cairo West
	1297	Lockheed C-130H Hercules (SU-BPK)	Egyptian AF 16 Sqn, Cairo West
	1298	Lockheed C-130H Hercules (SU-BPL)	Egyptian AF 16 Sqn, Cairo West
	....	Lockheed C-130J Hercules II	Egyptian AF (on order)
	....	Lockheed C-130J Hercules II	Egyptian AF (on order)

Egyptian Government

	SU-BGV	Grumman G.1159A Gulfstream III	Egyptian AF/Government, Cairo
	SU-BNC	Grumman G.1159C Gulfstream IV	Egyptian AF/Government, Cairo
	SU-BND	Grumman G.1159C Gulfstream IV	Egyptian AF/Government, Cairo
	SU-BNO	Grumman G.1159C Gulfstream IV-SP	Egyptian AF/Government, Cairo
	SU-BNP	Grumman G.1159C Gulfstream IV-SP	Egyptian AF/Government, Cairo
	SU-BPE	Gulfstream Aerospace G.400	Egyptian AF/Government, Cairo

Serial	Type (code/other identity)	Owner/operator, location or fate	Notes
SU-BPF	Gulfstream Aerospace G.400	Egyptian AF/Government, Cairo	
SU-BRF	Cessna 680 Citation Sovereign	Egyptian Government, Cairo	
SU-BRG	Cessna 680 Citation Sovereign	Egyptian Government, Cairo	
SU-BTT	Dassault Falcon 7X (F-WWHP)	Egyptian AF/Government, Cairo	
SU-BTU	Dassault Falcon 7X (F-WWUR)	Egyptian AF/Government, Cairo	
SU-BTV	Dassault Falcon 7X (F-WWUQ)	Egyptian AF/Government, Cairo	
SU-BTW	Dassault Falcon 8X (F-WWVL)	Egyptian AF/Government, Cairo	
SU-EGY	Boeing 747-830	Egyptian Government, Cairo (stored Hamburg)	
SU-GGG	Airbus A.340-211	Egyptian Government, Cairo	

ESTONIA
Estonian Air Force

40 y	WSK-PZL An-2T	Estonian AF 1.Eskadrill/Lennugrupp, Ämari	
41 y	Antonov An-2	Estonian AF 1.Eskadrill/Lennugrupp, Ämari	
43 bk	PZL-Mielec M28-05 Skytruck (09-0320)	Estonian AF 1.Eskadrill/Lennugrupp, Ämari	
44 bk	PZL-Mielec M28-05 Skytruck (09-0317)	Estonian AF 1.Eskadrill/Lennugrupp, Ämari	

ESWATINI

3DC-SDF	Airbus A.340-213X	Government of Eswatini, Manzini/Sikhupe	

FINLAND
Suomen Ilmavoimat (Finnish Air Force) & Suomen Maavoimat (Finnish Army)

CC-1	CASA C-295M	Ilmavoimat TukiLLv, Tampere/Pirkkala	
CC-2	CASA C-295M	Ilmavoimat TukiLLv, Tampere/Pirkkala	
CC-3	CASA C-295M	Ilmavoimat TukiLLv, Tampere/Pirkkala	
HN-401	McDonnell Douglas F-18C Hornet	Ilmavoimat HävLLv 11, Roveniemi	
HN-402	McDonnell Douglas F-18C Hornet	Ilmavoimat HävLLv 11, Roveniemi	
HN-403	McDonnell Douglas F-18C Hornet	Ilmavoimat HävLLv 31, Kuopio/Rissala	
HN-404	McDonnell Douglas F-18C Hornet	Ilmavoimat HävLLv 11, Roveniemi	
HN-405	McDonnell Douglas F-18C Hornet	Ilmavoimat HävLLv 31, Kuopio/Rissala	
HN-406	McDonnell Douglas F-18C Hornet	Ilmavoimat HävLLv 11, Roveniemi	
HN-407	McDonnell Douglas F-18C Hornet	Ilmavoimat HävLLv 31, Kuopio/Rissala	
HN-408	McDonnell Douglas F-18C Hornet	Ilmavoimat HävLLv 31, Kuopio/Rissala	
HN-409	McDonnell Douglas F-18C Hornet	Ilmavoimat HävLLv 11, Roveniemi	
HN-410	McDonnell Douglas F-18C Hornet	Ilmavoimat HävLLv 31, Kuopio/Rissala	
HN-411	McDonnell Douglas F-18C Hornet	Ilmavoimat HävLLv 31, Kuopio/Rissala	
HN-412	McDonnell Douglas F-18C Hornet	Ilmavoimat HävLLv 11, Roveniemi	
HN-414	McDonnell Douglas F-18C Hornet	Ilmavoimat HävLLv 31, Kuopio/Rissala	
HN-415	McDonnell Douglas F-18C Hornet	Ilmavoimat HävLLv 31, Kuopio/Rissala	
HN-416	McDonnell Douglas F-18C Hornet	Ilmavoimat HävLLv 11, Roveniemi	
HN-417	McDonnell Douglas F-18C Hornet	Ilmavoimat HävLLv 31, Kuopio/Rissala	
HN-418	McDonnell Douglas F-18C Hornet	Ilmavoimat HävLLv 11, Roveniemi	
HN-419	McDonnell Douglas F-18C Hornet	Ilmavoimat HävLLv 11, Roveniemi	
HN-420	McDonnell Douglas F-18C Hornet	Ilmavoimat HävLLv 31, Kuopio/Rissala	
HN-421	McDonnell Douglas F-18C Hornet	Ilmavoimat HävLLv 31, Kuopio/Rissala	
HN-422	McDonnell Douglas F-18C Hornet	Ilmavoimat HävLLv 11, Roveniemi	
HN-423	McDonnell Douglas F-18C Hornet	Ilmavoimat HävLLv 31, Kuopio/Rissala	
HN-424	McDonnell Douglas F-18C Hornet	Ilmavoimat HävLLv 31, Kuopio/Rissala	
HN-425	McDonnell Douglas F-18C Hornet	Ilmavoimat HävLLv 31, Kuopio/Rissala	
HN-426	McDonnell Douglas F-18C Hornet	Ilmavoimat HävLLv 31, Kuopio/Rissala	
HN-427	McDonnell Douglas F-18C Hornet	Ilmavoimat HävLLv 11, Roveniemi	
HN-428	McDonnell Douglas F-18C Hornet	Ilmavoimat HävLLv 11, Roveniemi	
HN-429	McDonnell Douglas F-18C Hornet	Ilmavoimat HävLLv 11, Roveniemi	
HN-431	McDonnell Douglas F-18C Hornet	Ilmavoimat HävLLv 31, Kuopio/Rissala	
HN-432	McDonnell Douglas F-18C Hornet	Ilmavoimat HävLLv 31, Kuopio/Rissala	
HN-433	McDonnell Douglas F-18C Hornet	Ilmavoimat HävLLv 31, Kuopio/Rissala	
HN-434	McDonnell Douglas F-18C Hornet	Ilmavoimat HävLLv 11, Roveniemi	
HN-435	McDonnell Douglas F-18C Hornet	Ilmavoimat HävLLv 31, Kuopio/Rissala	
HN-436	McDonnell Douglas F-18C Hornet	Ilmavoimat HävLLv 31, Kuopio/Rissala	
HN-437	McDonnell Douglas F-18C Hornet	Ilmavoimat HävLLv 31, Kuopio/Rissala	
HN-438	McDonnell Douglas F-18C Hornet	Ilmavoimat HävLLv 31, Kuopio/Rissala	
HN-439	McDonnell Douglas F-18C Hornet	Ilmavoimat HävLLv 31, Kuopio/Rissala	

Notes	Serial	Type (code/other identity)	Owner/operator, location or fate
	HN-440	McDonnell Douglas F-18C Hornet	Ilmavoimat HävLLv 11, Roveniemi
	HN-441	McDonnell Douglas F-18C Hornet	Ilmavoimat HävLLv 11, Roveniemi
	HN-442	McDonnell Douglas F-18C Hornet	Ilmavoimat HävLLv 11, Roveniemi
	HN-443	McDonnell Douglas F-18C Hornet	Ilmavoimat HävLLv 31, Kuopio/Rissala
	HN-444	McDonnell Douglas F-18C Hornet	Ilmavoimat HävLLv 11, Roveniemi
	HN-445	McDonnell Douglas F-18C Hornet	Ilmavoimat HävLLv 11, Roveniemi
	HN-446	McDonnell Douglas F-18C Hornet	Ilmavoimat HävLLv 11, Roveniemi
	HN-447	McDonnell Douglas F-18C Hornet	Ilmavoimat HävLLv 11, Roveniemi
	HN-448	McDonnell Douglas F-18C Hornet	Ilmavoimat HävLLv 31, Kuopio/Rissala
	HN-449	McDonnell Douglas F-18C Hornet	Ilmavoimat HävLLv 11, Roveniemi
	HN-450	McDonnell Douglas F-18C Hornet	Ilmavoimat HävLLv 11, Roveniemi
	HN-451	McDonnell Douglas F-18C Hornet	Ilmavoimat HävLLv 31, Kuopio/Rissala
	HN-452	McDonnell Douglas F-18C Hornet	Ilmavoimat HävLLv 11, Roveniemi
	HN-453	McDonnell Douglas F-18C Hornet	Ilmavoimat HävLLv 31, Kuopio/Rissala
	HN-454	McDonnell Douglas F-18C Hornet	Ilmavoimat HävLLv 31, Kuopio/Rissala
	HN-455	McDonnell Douglas F-18C Hornet	Ilmavoimat HävLLv 31, Kuopio/Rissala
	HN-456	McDonnell Douglas F-18C Hornet	Ilmavoimat HävLLv 31, Kuopio/Rissala
	HN-457	McDonnell Douglas F-18C Hornet $	Ilmavoimat HävLLv 11, Roveniemi
	HN-461	McDonnell Douglas F-18D Hornet	Ilmavoimat HävLLv 31, Kuopio/Rissala
	HN-462	McDonnell Douglas F-18D Hornet	Ilmavoimat HävLLv 31, Kuopio/Rissala
	HN-463	McDonnell Douglas F-18D Hornet	Ilmavoimat HävLLv 11, Roveniemi
	HN-464	McDonnell Douglas F-18D Hornet	Ilmavoimat HävLLv 11, Roveniemi
	HN-465	McDonnell Douglas F-18D Hornet	Ilmavoimat HävLLv 11, Roveniemi
	HN-466	McDonnell Douglas F-18D Hornet	Ilmavoimat HävLLv 31, Kuopio/Rissala
	HN-467	McDonnell Douglas F-18D Hornet	Ilmavoimat HävLLv 31, Kuopio/Rissala
	HW-307	BAe Hawk 51	Ilmavoimat HävLLv 41, Jyväskylä/Tikkakoski
	HW-320	BAe Hawk 51	Ilmavoimat HävLLv 41, Jyväskylä/Tikkakoski
	HW-321	BAe Hawk 51	Ilmavoimat HävLLv 41, Jyväskylä/Tikkakoski
	HW-327	BAe Hawk 51	Ilmavoimat HävLLv 41, Jyväskylä/Tikkakoski
	HW-330	BAe Hawk 51	Ilmavoimat, stored Halli (for upgrade)
	HW-334	BAe Hawk 51	Ilmavoimat HävLLv 41, Jyväskylä/Tikkakoski
	HW-336	BAe Hawk 51	*Withdrawn from use. To Tampere college*
	HW-338	BAe Hawk 51	Ilmavoimat HävLLv 41, Jyväskylä/Tikkakoski
	HW-339	BAe Hawk 51	Ilmavoimat HävLLv 41, Jyväskylä/Tikkakoski
	HW-340	BAe Hawk 51 $	Ilmavoimat HävLLv 41, Jyväskylä/Tikkakoski
	HW-341	BAe Hawk 51	Ilmavoimat HävLLv 41, Jyväskylä/Tikkakoski
	HW-343	BAe Hawk 51	Ilmavoimat HävLLv 41, Jyväskylä/Tikkakoski
	HW-344	BAe Hawk 51	Ilmavoimat HävLLv 41, Jyväskylä/Tikkakoski
	HW-345	BAe Hawk 51	Ilmavoimat HävLLv 41, Jyväskylä/Tikkakoski
	HW-348	BAe Hawk 51	Ilmavoimat HävLLv 41, Jyväskylä/Tikkakoski
	HW-349	BAe Hawk 51	Ilmavoimat HävLLv 41, Jyväskylä/Tikkakoski
	HW-350	BAe Hawk 51	Ilmavoimat HävLLv 41, Jyväskylä/Tikkakoski
	HW-351	BAe Hawk 51A	Ilmavoimat HävLLv 41, Jyväskylä/Tikkakoski
	HW-352	BAe Hawk 51A [4]	Ilmavoimat HävLLv 41, Jyväskylä/Tikkakoski
	HW-353	BAe Hawk 51A $	Ilmavoimat HävLLv 41, Jyväskylä/Tikkakoski
	HW-354	BAe Hawk 51A [3]	Ilmavoimat HävLLv 41, Jyväskylä/Tikkakoski
	HW-355	BAe Hawk 51A	Ilmavoimat HävLLv 41, Jyväskylä/Tikkakoski
	HW-356	BAe Hawk 51A	Ilmavoimat HävLLv 41, Jyväskylä/Tikkakoski
	HW-357	BAe Hawk 51A [2]	Ilmavoimat HävLLv 41, Jyväskylä/Tikkakoski
	HW-360	BAe Hawk 66	Ilmavoimat HävLLv 41, Jyväskylä/Tikkakoski
	HW-361	BAe Hawk 66	Ilmavoimat HävLLv 41, Jyväskylä/Tikkakoski
	HW-362	BAe Hawk 66	Ilmavoimat HävLLv 41, Jyväskylä/Tikkakoski
	HW-363	BAe Hawk 66	Ilmavoimat HävLLv 41, Jyväskylä/Tikkakoski
	HW-364	BAe Hawk 66	Ilmavoimat HävLLv 41, Jyväskylä/Tikkakoski
	HW-365	BAe Hawk 66	Ilmavoimat HävLLv 41, Jyväskylä/Tikkakoski
	HW-366	BAe Hawk 66	Ilmavoimat HävLLv 41, Jyväskylä/Tikkakoski
	HW-367	BAe Hawk 66	Ilmavoimat HävLLv 41, Jyväskylä/Tikkakoski
	HW-368	BAe Hawk 66	Ilmavoimat HävLLv 41, Jyväskylä/Tikkakoski
	HW-370	BAe Hawk 66	Ilmavoimat HävLLv 41, Jyväskylä/Tikkakoski
	HW-371	BAe Hawk 66	Ilmavoimat HävLLv 41, Jyväskylä/Tikkakoski
	HW-373	BAe Hawk 66	Ilmavoimat HävLLv 41, Jyväskylä/Tikkakoski
	HW-374	BAe Hawk 66	Ilmavoimat HävLLv 41, Jyväskylä/Tikkakoski

A1742, a Bristol scout replica, seen here as part of the collection at Bristol Filton. The replica was originally built by engineering apprentices at RAF Weeton in 1962, and appeared at the Royal Tournament at London Olympia that year. *HJC*

N3788 is a Miles M14 Magister, a basic trainer designed and built just prior to the outbreak of World War II. This immaculate example is seen taking part in one of the regular air days to be held with the Shuttleworth Collection at Old Warden airfield. *HJC*

N6466, An Tiger Moth based at Compton Abbas airfield in Dorset and seen here in an eye-catching yellow scheme. *HJC*

EX490 is a T-6 Texan, also seen here at the hilltop Dorset airfield of Compton Abbas. *HJC*

Sea Hurricane Z7015 is one of only 2 airworthy examples currently in the UK, this one based with the Shuttleworth Collection at Old Warden, whilst the other lives at Biggin Hill, an iconic wartime airfield! *HJC*

Anson C.19 TX216 was built at the Avro factory at Woodford, no more than 5 or 6 miles from where I write this, and is seen here at Old Warden as a part of the Shuttleworth Collection. *HJC*

Canberra T.4 VN799 is a part of the impressive collection owned by the Cornwall Aviation Heritage Centre at the former RAF St. Mawgan. Recently this venture looked to be on rocky ground as the local authority looked to re-purpose the land, but now they have been given a reprieve and will continue their great work. *HJC*

Chipmunk T.10 WK608 was a former Royal Navy aircraft, so when taken out of service it was fitting that she continued to serve with the Navy's' Historic Flight, based here at Yeovilton. *HJC*

XT420 is one of a number of airworthy Scouts that can be seen on the UK airshow circuit. This example is based at RNAS Yeovilton, but is seen here at Henstridge. *HJC*

One of a number of new-generation Hawk Mk. 132s belonging to the joint RAF/Qatari squadron, based at RAF Leeming, to train Qatari pilots that will ultimately fly their newly-acquired Typhoons. *HJC*

ZJ135 is one of a number of former RAF Merlins that were handed over to the Navy at Yeovilton and re-purposed, getting modified to HC.4 standard to replace the old Sea King 'junglies'. *HJC*

Typhoon FGR.4 ZK324 is currently assigned to 3 squadron at RAF Coningsby, but is seen here still wearing 1 squadron marks, something that is quite common with so much movement of airframes within the fleet. *HJC*

The RAF'S 5th generation great hope, seen here is F-35B Lightning ZM157 of 617 squadron, demonstrating the ability to hover in front of the crowd at RIAT 2022. Anyone who has seen such a demonstration will recall how loud it is! *HJC*

The Navy modernised its frigate helicopter fleet several years ago, removing the old Lynxes from service and replacing them with the new-build Wildcat. ZZ397 is seen here at RNAS Yeovilton, just up the road from her birthplace at Leonardo's airfield at Yeovil. *HJC*

Grob Tutor G-BYXH painted in an experimental yellow colour scheme, as a part of a test to see which colour is the easiest to see. When a similar thing was done with the Hawk T.1 fleet many years ago, the surprising answer was that black is the easiest to see. *HJC*

Another Grob Tutor, this time G-BYXS in the "standard" white scheme, seen here at RNAS Yeovilton. *HJC*

QinetiQ/ETPS have recently invested in a modern fleet, operated from their base at Boscombe Down. AW.139 G-ETPP is seen here at a Fairford RIAT. *HJC*

The only aircraft on the UK historic register from the Netherlands East Indies, this Ryan STM-2 is marked as S-11 and is also registered N7779, and is seen here at its home base of Old Warden, as a part of the Shuttleworth Collection. *HJC*

As far as warbirds go, this former Swedish Air Force SK-37E Viggen, serialled 378/09, takes some beating! Seen here at RIAT 2022, the Viggen was part of a contingent of historic Swedish aircraft operated by their Historic Flight. *HJC*

If you want a big, beefy, impressive warbird, you'd probably want a P-47 Thunderbolt. "Nellie B" is former 45-49192, also registered G-THUN, which splits its time between Sywell and Duxford. *HJC*

The Irish Air Corps operate a total of 8 PC-9Ms from their base at Baldonnel, just outside Dublin, including the latest one seen here, serial 269, which replaced an earlier example lost in a crash. *HJC*

Austria took a number of Typhoons on strength early in the development programme, including a number that were diverted from the German order whilst still on the production line. *HJC*

Still soldiering on, Danish Saab Supporter serialled T-415 was seen as part of the displays at RIAT 2022 at RAF Fairford. *HJC*

The Finnish Air Force Hawks are used to equip the "Midnight Hawks" display team. HW-354 is part of the team and is seen here at RAF Fairford whilst displaying at RIAT 2022. *HJC*

The French Air Force has recently upgraded its training fleet, now utilising a couple of dozen brand-new PC-21s out of Cognac Air Base, former base for the long-serving TB-30 Epsilon fleet. 07 was one of 3 examples that attended Fairford for RIAT 2022. *HJC*

One operator that seems to be having more luck with its NH-90s than some customers is the German Army. TTH model 79+09 is seen here at RAF Fairford during RIAT 2022. *HJC*

An export customer for the Gripen is Hungary, who bought a small fleet of these smart-looking fighters. Number 31 is seen here on the runway at RIAT 2022 at RAF Fairford. *HJC*

The only European-based US Air Force CV-22B Osprey fleet is based at RAF Mildenhall in the UK. Here we see 10-0053 at RAF Fairford for RIAT 2022. *HJC*

The USAF also have a fleet of MC-130J special Operations aircraft based at Mildenhall. Here we see 14-5805 at its home base. *HJC*

A stalwart of the Suffolk aviation scene for 60-odd years, there's still life left in the KC-135R/T fleet yet! Here we see Mildenhall-based 58-0125 at home. *HJC*

A Lakenheath-based Strike Eagle, specially-marked F-15E 93-0364 operating from its home base. *HJC*

Highly-capable, with communications suites that are mostly classified, the E-4B fleet of 4 aircraft exists to operate as an airborne command post in times of national emergency. Often dubbed the 'Doomsday Plane' for this reason, there will always be one deployed wherever the President travels overseas. Unusually, the USAF sent 73-1676 to RIAT 2022. *HJC*

Serial	Type (code/other identity)	Owner/operator, location or fate	Notes
HW-375	BAe Hawk 66	Ilmavoimat HävLLv 41, Jyväskylä/Tikkakoski	
HW-376	BAe Hawk 66	Ilmavoimat HävLLv 41, Jyväskylä/Tikkakoski	
HW-377	BAe Hawk 66	Ilmavoimat HävLLv 41, Jyväskylä/Tikkakoski	
LJ-1	Gates Learjet 35A	Ilmavoimat TukiLLv (Det.), Kuopio/Rissala	
LJ-2	Gates Learjet 35A	Ilmavoimat TukiLLv, Tampere/Pirkkala	
LJ-3	Gates Learjet 35A	Ilmavoimat TukiLLv, Tampere/Pirkkala	
NH-201	NH Industries NH.90-TTH (F-ZWTF)	Eurocopter, Marseille (trials)	
NH-202	NH Industries NH.90-TTH	Maavoimat 1.HK/HekoP, Utti	
NH-203	NH Industries NH.90-TTH	Maavoimat 1.HK/HekoP, Utti	
NH-204	NH Industries NH.90-TTH	Maavoimat 1.HK/HekoP, Utti	
NH-205	NH Industries NH.90-TTH	Maavoimat 1.HK/HekoP, Utti	
NH-206	NH Industries NH.90-TTH	Maavoimat 1.HK/HekoP, Utti	
NH-207	NH Industries NH.90-TTH	Maavoimat 1.HK/HekoP, Utti	
NH-208	NH Industries NH.90-TTH	Maavoimat 1.HK/HekoP, Utti	
NH-209	NH Industries NH.90-TTH	Maavoimat 1.HK/HekoP, Utti	
NH-210	NH Industries NH.90-TTH	Maavoimat 1.HK/HekoP, Utti	
NH-211	NH Industries NH.90-TTH	Maavoimat 1.HK/HekoP, Utti	
NH-212	NH Industries NH.90-TTH	Maavoimat 1.HK/HekoP, Utti	
NH-213	NH Industries NH.90-TTH	Maavoimat 1.HK/HekoP, Utti	
NH-214	NH Industries NH.90-TTH	Maavoimat 1.HK/HekoP, Utti	
NH-215	NH Industries NH.90-TTH	Maavoimat 1.HK/HekoP, Utti	
NH-216	NH Industries NH.90-TTH	Maavoimat 1.HK/HekoP, Utti	
NH-217	NH Industries NH.90-TTH	Maavoimat 1.HK/HekoP, Utti	
NH-218	NH Industries NH.90-TTH	Maavoimat 1.HK/HekoP, Utti	
NH-219	NH Industries NH.90-TTH	Maavoimat 1.HK/HekoP, Utti	
NH-220	NH Industries NH.90-TTH	Maavoimat 1.HK/HekoP, Utti	
NH-221	NH Industries NH.90-TTH	Maavoimat 1.HK/HekoP, Utti	
PI-01	Pilatus PC-12/47E	Ilmavoimat TukiLLv, Tampere/Pirkkala	
PI-02	Pilatus PC-12/47E	Ilmavoimat TukiLLv, Tampere/Pirkkala	
PI-03	Pilatus PC-12/47E	Ilmavoimat TukiLLv, Tampere/Pirkkala	
PI-04	Pilatus PC-12/47E	Ilmavoimat TukiLLv, Tampere/Pirkkala	
PI-05	Pilatus PC-12/47E	Ilmavoimat TukiLLv, Tampere/Pirkkala	
PI-06	Pilatus PC-12/47E	Ilmavoimat TukiLLv, Tampere/Pirkkala	

FRANCE

NB: Due to the way in which French military aircraft serials are issued, this section is sorted by type. Each Armée de l'Air aircraft has its own, fixed registration, in the form F-xxxx, but in general these are only worn on transports, tankers and a handful of other aircraft.

Armée de l'Air et de l'Espace (AA)

240	Airbus A.330-223 (F-RARF)	AA ET 00.060, Evreux	
1608	Airbus A.330-243 [F-UJCS]	AA ET 02.031 *Esterel*, Paris/Charles de Gaulle	
1657	Airbus A.330-243 [F-UJCT]	AA ET 02.031 *Esterel*, Paris/Charles de Gaulle	
2022	Airbus A.330-243 [F-UJCU]	AA ET 02.031 *Esterel*, Paris/Charles de Gaulle	
041	Airbus A.330-243 MRTT Phénix (MRTT041) [F-UJCG]	AA ERVTS 01.031 *Bretagne*, Istres	
042	Airbus A.330-243 MRTT Phénix (MRTT042) [F-UJCH]	AA ERVTS 01.031 *Bretagne*, Istres	
043	Airbus A.330-243 MRTT Phénix (MRTT043) [F-UJCI]	AA ERVTS 01.031 *Bretagne*, Istres	
044	Airbus A.330-243 MRTT Phénix (MRTT044) [F-UJCJ]	AA ERVTS 02.031 *Esterel*, Istres	
045	Airbus A.330-243 MRTT Phénix (MRTT045) [F-UJCK]	AA ERVTS 01.031 *Bretagne*, Istres	
046	Airbus A.330-243 MRTT Phénix (MRTT046) [F-UJCL]	AA ERVTS 02.031 *Esterel*, Istres	
047	Airbus A.330-243 MRTT Phénix (MRTT047) [F-UJCM]	AA ETP 03.031 *Bretagne*, Istres	
048	Airbus A.330-243 MRTT Phénix (MRTT048)[F-UJCN]	AA ERVTS 02.031 *Esterel*, Istres	
049	Airbus A.330-243 MRTT Phénix (MRTT049)[F-UJCO]	AA ERVTS 02.031 *Esterel*, Istres	
...	Airbus A.330-243 MRTT Phénix (MRTT067) [F-UJCP]	AA ERVTS 01.031 *Bretagne*, Istres (on order)	
...	Airbus A.330-243 MRTT Phénix [F-UJCQ]	AA ERVTS 01.031 *Bretagne*, Istres (on order)	
...	Airbus A.330-243 MRTT Phénix [F-UJCR]	AA ERVTS 01.031 *Bretagne*, Istres (on order)	
...	Airbus A.330-243 MRTT Phénix	AA ERVTS 01.031 *Bretagne*, Istres (on order)	
...	Airbus A.330-243 MRTT Phénix	AA ERVTS 01.031 *Bretagne*, Istres (on order)	
...	Airbus A.330-243 MRTT Phénix	AA ERVTS 01.031 *Bretagne*, Istres (on order)	
0007	Airbus Military A.400M [F-RBAA] $	AA ET 01.061 *Touraine*, Orléans	
0008	Airbus Military A.400M [F-RBAB]	AA ET 01.061 *Touraine*, Orléans	
0010	Airbus Military A.400M [F-RBAC]	AA ET 01.061 *Touraine*, Orléans	
0011	Airbus Military A.400M [F-RBAD]	AA ET 01.061 *Touraine*, Orléans	

145

Notes	Serial	Type (code/other identity)	Owner/operator, location or fate
	0012	Airbus Military A.400M [F-RBAE]	AA ET 01.061 *Touraine*, Orléans
	0014	Airbus Military A.400M [F-RBAF]	AA ET 01.061 *Touraine*, Orléans
	0019	Airbus Military A.400M [F-RBAG]	AA ET 01.061 *Touraine*, Orléans
	0031	Airbus Military A.400M [F-RBAH]	AA ET 01.061 *Touraine*, Orléans
	0033	Airbus Military A.400M [F-RBAI]	AA ET 01.061 *Touraine*, Orléans
	0037	Airbus Military A.400M [F-RBAJ]	AA ET 01.061 *Touraine*, Orléans
	0053	Airbus Military A.400M [F-RBAK]	AA ET 01.061 *Touraine*, Orléans
	0062	Airbus Military A.400M [F-RBAL] $	AA ET 01.061 *Touraine*, Orléans
	0065	Airbus Military A.400M [F-RBAM]	AA ET 01.061 *Touraine*, Orléans
	0073	Airbus Military A.400M [F-RBAN]	AA ET 01.061 *Touraine*, Orléans
	0075	Airbus Military A.400M [F-RBAT]	AA ET 01.061 *Touraine*, Orléans
	0089	Airbus Military A.400M [F-RBAO]	AA ET 01.061 *Touraine*, Orléans
	0095	Airbus Military A.400M [F-RBAP]	AA ET 01.061 *Touraine*, Orléans
	0102	Airbus Military A.400M [F-RBAQ]	AA ET 01.061 *Touraine*, Orléans
	0110	Airbus Military A.400M [F-RBAR] $	AA ET 04.061 *Bearn*, Orléans
	0122	Airbus Military A.400M [F-RBAS]	AA ET 01.061 *Touraine*, Orléans
	0127	Airbus Military A.400M [F-RBAU]	AA ET 01.061 Touraine, Orléans
	0130	Airbus Military A.400M [F-RBAV]	AA (on order)
	0132	Airbus Military A.400M [F-RB..]	AA (on order)
	0137	Airbus Military A.400M [F-RB..]	AA (on order)
	0146	Airbus Military A.400M [F-RB..]	AA (on order)
	0153	Airbus Military A.400M [F-RB..]	AA (on order)
	0154	Airbus Military A.400M [F-RB..]	AA (on order)
	...	Airbus Military A.400M [F-RB..]	AA (on order)
	...	Airbus Military A.400M [F-RB..]	AA (on order)
	...	Airbus Military A.400M [F-RB..]	AA (on order)
	...	Airbus Military A.400M [F-RB..]	AA (on order)
	045	Airtech CN-235M-200 [64-IB]	AA ET 01.062 *Vercours*, Evreux
	065	Airtech CN-235M-200 [52-IC]	AA ET 00.052 *La Tontouta*, Nouméa
	066	Airtech CN-235M-200 [62-ID]	AA ET 01.062 *Vercours*, Evreux
	071	Airtech CN-235M-200 [62-IE]	AA ET 01.062 *Vercours*, Evreux
	072	Airtech CN-235M-200 [64-IF]	AA ET 01.062 *Vercours*, Evreux
	105	Airtech CN-235M-200 [82-IG]	AA ET 00.082 *La Tontouta*, Nouméa
	107	Airtech CN-235M-200 [82-IH]	AA ET 00.082 *La Tontouta*, Nouméa
	111	Airtech CN-235M-200 [64-II] $	AA ET 03.062 *Ventoux*, Evreux
	114	Airtech CN-235M-200 [62-IJ]	AA ET 01.062 *Vercours*, Evreux
	123	Airtech CN-235M-200 [64-IM]	AA ET 01.062 *Vercours*, Evreux
	128	Airtech CN-235M-200 [64-IK]	AA ET 01.062 *Vercours*, Evreux
	129	Airtech CN-235M-200 [68-IL]	AA ET 00.068 *Antilles*, Fort-de-France
	137	Airtech CN-235M-200 [68-IN]	AA ET 00.068 *Antilles*, Fort-de-France
	141	Airtech CN-235M-200 [62-IO]	AA ET 01.062 *Vercours*, Evreux
	152	Airtech CN-235M-200 [64-IP]	AA ET 01.062 *Vercours*, Evreux
	156	Airtech CN-235M-200 [64-IQ]	AA ET 01.062 *Vercours*, Evreux
	158	Airtech CN-235M-200 [62-IR]	AA ET 01.062 *Vercours*, Evreux
	160	Airtech CN-235M-200 [64-IS]	AA ET 01.062 *Vercours*, Evreux
	165	Airtech CN-235M-200 [64-IT]	AA ET 01.062 *Vercours*, Evreux
	193	Airtech CN-235M-300 [64-HA]	AA ET 03.062 *Ventoux*, Evreux
	194	Airtech CN-235M-300 [64-HB]	AA ET 03.062 *Ventoux*, Evreux
	195	Airtech CN-235M-300 [64-HC]	AA ET 03.062 *Ventoux*, Evreux
	196	Airtech CN-235M-300 [62-HD]	AA ET 03.062 *Ventoux*, Evreux
	197	Airtech CN-235M-300 [64-HE]	AA ET 03.062 *Ventoux*, Evreux
	198	Airtech CN-235M-300 [62-HF]	AA ET 03.062 *Ventoux*, Evreux
	199	Airtech CN-235M-300 [62-HG]	AA ET 03.062 *Ventoux*, Evreux
	200	Airtech CN-235M-300 [62-HH]	AA ET 03.062 *Ventoux*, Evreux
	479	Beechcraft King Air 350 VADOR (F-GYEE)	AA (on order)
	1018	Beechcraft King Air 350 VADOR (F-WTAO) [F-RACG]	AA EEA 01.054 *Dunkerque*, Evreux
	1030	Beechcraft King Air 350 VADOR (F-WTAP) [F-RACH]	AA EEA 01.054 *Dunkerque*, Evreux
	470	Boeing C-135FR Stratotanker [31-CA]	AA ERV 04.031 *Sologne*, Istres
	525	Boeing KC-135RG Stratotanker [31-CN]	AA ERV 04.031 *Sologne*, Istres
	574	Boeing KC-135RG Stratotanker [31-CP]	AA ERV 04.031 *Sologne*, Istres
	735	Boeing C-135FR Stratotanker [31-CG]	*Withdrawn from use at Nîmes, 2022*
	737	Boeing C-135FR Stratotanker [31-CI]	AA ERV 04.031 *Sologne*, Istres

Serial	Type (code/other identity)	Owner/operator, location or fate	Notes
738	Boeing C-135FR Stratotanker [31-CJ]	*Withdrawn from use at Nîmes, 2022*	
739	Boeing C-135FR Stratotanker [31-CK]	AA ERV 04.031 *Sologne*, Istres	
740	Boeing C-135FR Stratotanker [31-CL]	AA ERV 04.031 *Sologne*, Istres	
201	Boeing E-3F Sentry [36-CA]	AA EDCA 00.036, Avord	
202	Boeing E-3F Sentry [36-CB]	AA EDCA 00.036, Avord	
203	Boeing E-3F Sentry [36-CC]	AA EDCA 00.036, Avord	
204	Boeing E-3F Sentry [36-CD] $	AA EDCA 00.036, Avord	
377	CASA 212-300 Aviocar [F-ZAEA]	AA DGA EV, Cazaux & Istres	
378	CASA 212-300 Aviocar [MP]	AA, *stored Istres*	
386	CASA 212-300 Aviocar [MQ]	AA, *stored Istres*	
E4	D-BD Alpha Jet E	AA DGA EV, Cazaux & Istres	
E8	D-BD Alpha Jet E	AA DGA EV, Cazaux & Istres	
E11	D-BD Alpha Jet E [8-UB]	AA EE 03.008 *Côte d'Or*, Cazaux	
E12	D-BD Alpha Jet E	AA DGA EV, Cazaux & Istres	
E13	D-BD Alpha Jet E [8-MM]	AA, stored Ambérieu-en-Bugey	
E20	D-BD Alpha Jet E [F-TEMS,2]	AA *Patrouille de France*, Salon de Provence	
E22	D-BD Alpha Jet E [8-LS] $	AA EE 03.008 *Côte d'Or*, Cazaux	
E25	D-BD Alpha Jet E [8-TJ]	AA EE 03.008 *Côte d'Or*, Cazaux	
E29	D-BD Alpha Jet E [102-NB]	AA	
E32	D-BD Alpha Jet E [102-FI]	AA	
E33	D-BD Alpha Jet E [8-FJ]	AA EE 03.008 *Côte d'Or*, Cazaux	
E35	D-BD Alpha Jet E [F-TEMA,6]	AA *Patrouille de France*, Salon de Provence	
E38	D-BD Alpha Jet E [8-LH]	AA	
E42	D-BD Alpha Jet E [8-TA]	AA EE 03.008 *Côte d'Or*, Cazaux	
E44	D-BD Alpha Jet E [F-UHRE]	AA *Patrouille de France*, Salon de Provence	
E45	D-BD Alpha Jet E [F-TETF]	AA *Patrouille de France*, Salon de Provence	
E46	D-BD Alpha Jet E [8-RF]	AA	
E48	D-BD Alpha Jet E [F-TEMH]	AA *Patrouille de France*, Salon de Provence	
E53	D-BD Alpha Jet E [102-LI]	AA	
E60	D-BD Alpha Jet E	AA EPNER, Istres	
E67	D-BD Alpha Jet E [705-TB]	AA	
E68	D-BD Alpha Jet E [8-MO]	AA EE 03.008 *Côte d'Or*, Cazaux	
E73	D-BD Alpha Jet E [F-TENE,0]	AA *Patrouille de France*, Salon de Provence	
E79	D-BD Alpha Jet E [8-NA]	AA	
E80	D-BD Alpha Jet E	AA DGA EV, Cazaux & Istres	
E81	D-BD Alpha Jet E [F-UGFO,9]	AA *Patrouille de France*, Salon de Provence	
E82	D-BD Alpha Jet E [8-LW]	AA EE 03.008 *Côte d'Or*, Cazaux	
E83	D-BD Alpha Jet E [8-TZ]	AA EE 03.008 *Côte d'Or*, Cazaux	
E85	D-BD Alpha Jet E [F-UGFF]	*Withdrawn from use, 2022*	
E87	D-BD Alpha Jet E [F-TELC,8]	AA *Patrouille de France*, Salon de Provence	
E88	D-BD Alpha Jet E [8-LL]	AA EE 03.008 *Côte d'Or*, Cazaux	
E90	D-BD Alpha Jet E [8-TH]	AA EE 03.008 *Côte d'Or*, Cazaux	
E93	D-BD Alpha Jet E [8-TX]	AA EE 03.008 *Côte d'Or*, Cazaux	
E94	D-BD Alpha Jet E [705-RH]	AA	
E98	D-BD Alpha Jet E [F-TEMF]	AA *Patrouille de France*, Salon de Provence	
E100	D-BD Alpha Jet E $	AA EPNER, Istres	
E101	D-BD Alpha Jet E	AA	
E102	D-BD Alpha Jet E [8-LM]	AA EE 03.008 *Côte d'Or*, Cazaux	
E105	D-BD Alpha Jet E [F-UGFM,7]	AA *Patrouille de France*, Salon de Provence	
E107	D-BD Alpha Jet E [8-UD]	AA EE 03.008 *Côte d'Or*, Cazaux	
E108	D-BD Alpha Jet E [8-AF]	AA EE 03.008 *Côte d'Or*, Cazaux	
E109	D-BD Alpha Jet E [8-AG]	AA EE 03.008 *Côte d'Or*, Cazaux	
E112	D-BD Alpha Jet E [705-AO]	AA	
E113	D-BD Alpha Jet E [F-TETD]	AA *Patrouille de France*, Salon de Provence	
E114	D-BD Alpha Jet E [705-RR] $	AA	
E115	D-BD Alpha Jet E [8-MR]	AA	
E116	D-BD Alpha Jet E [8-FN]	AA	
E117	D-BD Alpha Jet E [8-RI]	AA EE 03.008 *Côte d'Or*, Cazaux	
E118	D-BD Alpha Jet E [8-LN]	AA	
E119	D-BD Alpha Jet E [F-UGFE,3]	AA *Patrouille de France*, Salon de Provence	
E123	D-BD Alpha Jet E [8-RM]	AA EE 03.008 *Côte d'Or*, Cazaux	
E124	D-BD Alpha Jet E [8-RN]	AA	

Notes	Serial	Type (code/other identity)	Owner/operator, location or fate
	E127	D-BD Alpha Jet E [F-UGFK]	AA *Patrouille de France*, Salon de Provence
	E128	D-BD Alpha Jet E [8-TM]	AA
	E129	D-BD Alpha Jet E [F-TELP,5]	AA *Patrouille de France*, Salon de Provence
	E130	D-BD Alpha Jet E [8-RP]	AA EE 03.008 *Côte d'Or*, Cazaux
	E131	D-BD Alpha Jet E [8-RO]	AA
	E135	D-BD Alpha Jet E [8-RX]	AA, stored Ambérieu-en-Bugey
	E138	D-BD Alpha Jet E [8-RQ]	AA EE 03.008 *Côte d'Or*, Cazaux
	E139	D-BD Alpha Jet E [F-UGFC]	AA *Patrouille de France*, Salon de Provence
	E141	D-BD Alpha Jet E [8-NF]	AA EE 03.008 *Côte d'Or*, Cazaux
	E142	D-BD Alpha Jet E [8-LO]	AA
	E144	D-BD Alpha Jet E [8-AK]	AA
	E147	D-BD Alpha Jet E [8-LT]	AA
	E148	D-BD Alpha Jet E [8-LU]	AA
	E149	D-BD Alpha Jet E [8-RS]	AA EE 03.008 *Côte d'Or*, Cazaux
	E151	D-BD Alpha Jet E [8-FD]	AA EE 03.008 *Côte d'Or*, Cazaux
	E152	D-BD Alpha Jet E [F-UHRT]	AA *Patrouille de France*, Salon de Provence
	E153	D-BD Alpha Jet E	AA
	E154	D-BD Alpha Jet E [8-AL]	AA
	E157	D-BD Alpha Jet E [8-UC]	AA
	E158	D-BD Alpha Jet E	AA
	E160	D-BD Alpha Jet E [8-UH]	AA
	E162	D-BD Alpha Jet E [8-RJ]	AA EE 03.008 *Côte d'Or*, Cazaux
	E163	D-BD Alpha Jet E [705-RB]	AA
	E164	D-BD Alpha Jet E [8-RV]	AA EE 03.008 *Côte d'Or*, Cazaux
	E165	D-BD Alpha Jet E [8-RE]	AA EE 03.008 *Côte d'Or*, Cazaux
	E166	D-BD Alpha Jet E [705-RW]	AA
	E168	D-BD Alpha Jet E [8-FP]	AA EE 03.008 *Côte d'Or*, Cazaux
	E169	D-BD Alpha Jet E [F-UHRX]	AA *Patrouille de France*, Salon de Provence
	E170	D-BD Alpha Jet E [705-RY]	AA
	E171	D-BD Alpha Jet E [705-RZ]	AA *Patrouille de France*, Salon de Provence
	E173	D-BD Alpha Jet E [8-MA]	AA
	E176	D-BD Alpha Jet E [8-MB]	AA EE 03.008 *Côte d'Or*, Cazaux
	1372	Daher TBM 940 [F-ZCEV,EV]	AA DGA EV, Cazaux & Istres
	1376	Daher TBM 940 [F-ZDGA,GA]	AA DGA EV, Cazaux & Istres
	1381	Daher TBM 940 [F-ZCER,ER]	AA DGA EV, Cazaux & Istres
	1382	Daher TBM 940 [F-ZCPN,PN]	AA DGA EV, Cazaux & Istres
	68	Dassault Falcon 7X (F-RAFA)	AA ET 00.060, Villacoublay
	86	Dassault Falcon 7X (F-RAFB)	AA ET 00.060, Villacoublay
	79	Dassault Falcon 20C [CT]	*Scrapped Cazaux*
	104	Dassault Falcon 20C [CW]	AA DGA EV, stored Cazaux
	138	Dassault Falcon 20C [CR]	*Scrapped Cazaux*
	288	Dassault Falcon 20E [CV]	AA DGA EV, stored Istres
	342	Dassault Falcon 20F [CU]	AA DGA EV, stored Cazaux
	375	Dassault Falcon 20F [CZ]	*Scrapped Cazaux*
	2	Dassault Falcon 900 (F-RAFP)	AA, stored Orange
	4	Dassault Falcon 900 (F-RAFQ)	AA ET 00.060, Villacoublay
	231	Dassault Falcon 2000LX (F-RAFC)	AA ET 00.060, Villacoublay
	237	Dassault Falcon 2000LX (F-RAFD)	AA ET 00.060, Villacoublay
	501	Dassault Mirage 2000B (BX1)	AA DGA EV, Cazaux & Istres
	523	Dassault Mirage 2000B [3-KJ]	AA EC 02.003 *Champagne*, Nancy
	524	Dassault Mirage 2000B [115-OA]	AA EC 02.005 *Ile de France*, Orange
	525	Dassault Mirage 2000B [3-AM]	AA EC 02.003 *Champagne*, Nancy
	527	Dassault Mirage 2000B [115-OR]	AA EC 02.005 *Ile de France*, Orange
	528	Dassault Mirage 2000B [3-KS]	AA EC 02.003 *Champagne*, Nancy
	529	Dassault Mirage 2000B [115-OC]	AA EC 02.005 *Ile de France*, Orange
	530	Dassault Mirage 2000B [3-OL]	AA EC 02.003 *Champagne*, Nancy
	01	Dassault Mirage 2000-5F	AA DGA EV, Istres
	2	Dassault Mirage 2000C	AA, stored Cazaux
	38	Dassault Mirage 2000-5F [2-EI]	AA GC 01.002 *Cigognes*, Luxeuil
	40	Dassault Mirage 2000-5F [2-EX]	AA GC 01.002 *Cigognes*, Luxeuil
	41	Dassault Mirage 2000-5F [2-FZ]	AA GC 01.002 *Cigognes*, Luxeuil
	42	Dassault Mirage 2000-5F [2-EY]	AA GC 01.002 *Cigognes*, Luxeuil

Serial	Type (code/other identity)	Owner/operator, location or fate	Notes
43	Dassault Mirage 2000-5F [2-EJ]	*Written off 3rd November 2022*	
44	Dassault Mirage 2000-5F [2-EQ]	AA GC 01.002 *Cigognes*, Luxeuil	
45	Dassault Mirage 2000-5F [2-EF]	AA GC 01.002 *Cigognes*, Luxeuil	
46	Dassault Mirage 2000-5F [2-EN]	AA GC 01.002 *Cigognes*, Luxeuil	
47	Dassault Mirage 2000-5F [2-EP]	AA GC 01.002 *Cigognes*, Luxeuil	
48	Dassault Mirage 2000-5F [188-EW]	AA EC 03.011 *Corse*, Djibouti	
49	Dassault Mirage 2000-5F [2-EA]	AA GC 01.002 *Cigognes*, Luxeuil	
51	Dassault Mirage 2000-5F	AA DGA EV, Istres	
52	Dassault Mirage 2000-5F [2-EH]	AA, stored Luxeuil	
54	Dassault Mirage 2000-5F [188-EZ]	AA EC 03.011 *Corse*, Djibouti	
55	Dassault Mirage 2000-5F [2-EU]	AA GC 01.002 *Cigognes*, Luxeuil	
56	Dassault Mirage 2000-5F [2-EG]	AA GC 01.002 *Cigognes*, Luxeuil	
57	Dassault Mirage 2000-5F [188-ET]	AA EC 03.011 *Corse*, Djibouti	
58	Dassault Mirage 2000-5F [188-EL]	AA EC 03.011 *Corse*, Djibouti	
59	Dassault Mirage 2000-5F [2-EV]	AA GC 01.002 *Cigognes*, Luxeuil	
61	Dassault Mirage 2000-5F [2-ME]	AA GC 01.002 *Cigognes*, Luxeuil	
62	Dassault Mirage 2000-5F [188-ED]	AA EC 03.011 *Corse*, Djibouti	
63	Dassault Mirage 2000-5F [2-EM]	AA GC 01.002 *Cigognes*, Luxeuil	
64	Dassault Mirage 2000C	AA, stored Cazaux	
65	Dassault Mirage 2000-5F [2-MG]	AA GC 01.002 *Cigognes*, Luxeuil	
66	Dassault Mirage 2000-5F [2-EO]	AA GC 01.002 *Cigognes*, Luxeuil	
67	Dassault Mirage 2000-5F [2-MH]	AA GC 01.002 *Cigognes*, Luxeuil	
71	Dassault Mirage 2000-5F [188-EE]	AA EC 03.011 *Corse*, Djibouti	
74	Dassault Mirage 2000-5F [188-MK]	AA EC 03.011 *Corse*, Djibouti	
77	Dassault Mirage 2000-5F [2-AX]	AA GC 01.002 *Cigognes*, Luxeuil	
78	Dassault Mirage 2000-5F [2-EC]	AA GC 01.002 *Cigognes*, Luxeuil	
83	Dassault Mirage 2000C [115-YC]	*AA, Orange for G.I.*	
105	Dassault Mirage 2000C [115-LJ]	*AA, stored Istres*	
107	Dassault Mirage 2000C [115-YD]	*AA, stored Istres*	
108	Dassault Mirage 2000C [115-LC]	*AA, stored Istres*	
109	Dassault Mirage 2000C [115-YH]	*AA, stored Istres*	
113	Dassault Mirage 2000C [115-YO]	*AA, stored Istres*	
118	Dassault Mirage 2000C [115-YG]	*AA, stored Istres*	
120	Dassault Mirage 2000C [115-KC] $	*AA, stored Istres*	
121	Dassault Mirage 2000C [115-KN]	AA GC 01.002 *Cigognes*, Luxeuil	
122	Dassault Mirage 2000C [115-YE]	AA GC 01.002 *Cigognes*, Luxeuil	
123	Dassault Mirage 2000C [115-KD]	AA GC 01.002 *Cigognes*, Luxeuil	
124	Dassault Mirage 2000C [115-YT]	AA GC 01.002 *Cigognes*, Luxeuil	
601	Dassault Mirage 2000D [3-JG]	AA EC 01.003 *Navarre*, Nancy	
602	Dassault Mirage 2000D [3-XJ]	AA EC 02.003 *Champagne*, Nancy	
603	Dassault Mirage 2000D [3-XL]	AA EC 03.003 *Ardennes*, Nancy	
604	Dassault Mirage 2000D [3-IP]	AA EC 03.003 *Ardennes*, Nancy	
605	Dassault Mirage 2000D [133-LF]	AA EC 02.003 *Champagne*, Nancy	
606	Dassault Mirage 2000D [3-JC]	AA EC 02.003 *Champagne*, Nancy	
607	Dassault Mirage 2000D	AA DGA EV, Istres	
609	Dassault Mirage 2000D [3-IF]	AA EC 01.003 *Navarre*, Nancy	
610	Dassault Mirage 2000D [133-XX]	AA EC 03.003 *Ardennes*, Nancy	
611	Dassault Mirage 2000D [3-JP]	AA EC 02.003 *Champagne*, Nancy	
613	Dassault Mirage 2000D [3-MO]	AA EC 01.003 *Navarre*, Nancy	
614	Dassault Mirage 2000D [3-JU]	AA EC 02.003 *Champagne*, Nancy	
615	Dassault Mirage 2000D [3-JY]	AA EC 02.003 *Champagne*, Nancy	
616	Dassault Mirage 2000D	AA, stored Ambérieu-en-Bugey	
617	Dassault Mirage 2000D [3-IS]	AA EC 01.003 *Navarre*, Nancy	
618	Dassault Mirage 2000D [3-XC] $	AA EC 03.003 *Ardennes*, Nancy	
620	Dassault Mirage 2000D [3-IU] $	AA EC 01.003 *Navarre*, Nancy	
622	Dassault Mirage 2000D [3-IL]	AA EC 01.003 *Navarre*, Nancy	
624	Dassault Mirage 2000D [3-IT] $	AA EC 01.003 *Navarre*, Nancy	
625	Dassault Mirage 2000D [3-XG]	AA EC 03.003 *Ardennes*, Nancy	
626	Dassault Mirage 2000D [3-IC]	AA EC 01.003 *Navarre*, Nancy	
627	Dassault Mirage 2000D [3-JO]	AA EC 02.003 *Champagne*, Nancy	
628	Dassault Mirage 2000D [3-JL] $	AA EC 02.003 *Champagne*, Nancy	
629	Dassault Mirage 2000D [3-XO]	AA EC 03.003 *Ardennes*, Nancy	

Notes	Serial	Type (code/other identity)	Owner/operator, location or fate
	630	Dassault Mirage 2000D [3-XD] $	AA EC 03.003 *Ardennes*, Nancy
	631	Dassault Mirage 2000D [3-IH]	AA EC 01.003 *Navarre*, Nancy
	632	Dassault Mirage 2000D [3-XE]	AA EC 01.003 *Navarre*, Nancy
	634	Dassault Mirage 2000D [133-JE]	*Believed scrapped? (Ex-Chateaudun)*
	635	Dassault Mirage 2000D [3-AS]	AA EC 03.003 *Navarre*, Nancy
	636	Dassault Mirage 2000D [3-JV]	AA EC 02.003 *Champagne*, Nancy
	637	Dassault Mirage 2000D [30-XQ]	AA CEAM/ECE 01.030 *Côte d'Argent*, Mont-de-Marsan
	638	Dassault Mirage 2000D [3-IJ]	AA EC 03.003 *Ardennes*, Nancy
	639	Dassault Mirage 2000D MLU [3-JJ]	AA EC 02.003 *Champagne*, Nancy
	640	Dassault Mirage 2000D [3-IN]	AA EC 01.003 *Navarre*, Nancy
	641	Dassault Mirage 2000D [3-JW]	AA EC 02.003 *Champagne*, Nancy
	642	Dassault Mirage 2000D [3-IE]	AA EC 01.003 *Navarre*, Nancy
	643	Dassault Mirage 2000D [3-JD]	AA EC 03.003 *Champagne*, Nancy
	644	Dassault Mirage 2000D $	AA DGA EV, Istres
	645	Dassault Mirage 2000D [3-XP]	AA EC 03.003 *Ardennes*, Nancy
	646	Dassault Mirage 2000D [3-MQ]	AA EC 01.003 *Navarre*, Nancy
	647	Dassault Mirage 2000D [3-IO]	AA EC 01.003 *Navarre*, Nancy
	648	Dassault Mirage 2000D [3-XT] $	AA EC 03.003 *Ardennes*, Nancy
	649	Dassault Mirage 2000D [3-XY]	AA EC 03.003 *Ardennes*, Nancy
	650	Dassault Mirage 2000D [3-IA]	AA EC 01.003 *Navarre*, Nancy
	652	Dassault Mirage 2000D [3-XN]	AA EC 03.003 *Ardennes*, Nancy
	653	Dassault Mirage 2000D [3-AU]	AA EC 02.003 *Champagne*, Nancy
	654	Dassault Mirage 2000D [3-ID]	AA EC 01.003 *Navarre*, Nancy
	655	Dassault Mirage 2000D [3-LH]	AA EC 01.003 *Navarre*, Nancy
	657	Dassault Mirage 2000D [3-JM]	AA EC 02.003 *Champagne*, Nancy
	658	Dassault Mirage 2000D [3-JN]	AA EC 02.003 *Champagne*, Nancy
	659	Dassault Mirage 2000D [3-XR]	AA EC 01.003 *Navarre*, Nancy
	660	Dassault Mirage 2000D [3-JF]	AA EC 02.003 *Champagne*, Nancy
	661	Dassault Mirage 2000D [3-XI]	AA EC 03.003 *Ardennes*, Nancy
	662	Dassault Mirage 2000D [3-XA]	AA EC 01.003 *Navarre*, Nancy
	664	Dassault Mirage 2000D [133-IW]	AA EC 01.003 *Navarre*, Nancy
	666	Dassault Mirage 2000D [3-IQ]	AA EC 02.003 *Champagne*, Nancy
	668	Dassault Mirage 2000D [3-IG]	AA EC 01.003 *Navarre*, Nancy
	670	Dassault Mirage 2000D [3-XF]	AA EC 03.003 *Ardennes*, Nancy
	671	Dassault Mirage 2000D [3-XK]	AA EC 03.003 *Ardennes*, Nancy
	672	Dassault Mirage 2000D [3-XV]	AA EC 03.003 *Ardennes*, Nancy
	673	Dassault Mirage 2000D	AA DGA EV, Istres
	674	Dassault Mirage 2000D [3-IR]	AA EC 02.003 *Champagne*, Nancy
	675	Dassault Mirage 2000D [3-JI] $	AA EC 01.003 *Navarre*, Nancy
	676	Dassault Mirage 2000D $	AA DGA EV, Istres
	677	Dassault Mirage 2000D [3-JT]	AA EC 02.003 *Champagne*, Nancy
	678	Dassault Mirage 2000D [30-JB]	AA CEAM/ECE 01.030 *Côte d'Argent*, Mont-de-Marsan
	679	Dassault Mirage 2000D [3-JX]	AA EC 02.003 *Navarre*, Nancy
	680	Dassault Mirage 2000D [3-XM]	AA EC 03.003 *Ardennes*, Nancy
	681	Dassault Mirage 2000D [3-AG]	AA EC 01.003 *Navarre*, Nancy
	682	Dassault Mirage 2000D [3-JR]	AA EC 02.003 *Champagne*, Nancy
	683	Dassault Mirage 2000D [3-IV]	AA EC 01.003 *Navarre*, Nancy
	685	Dassault Mirage 2000D [3-XZ]	AA EC 01.003 *Navarre*, Nancy
	686	Dassault Mirage 2000D [3-JH]	AA EC 02.003 *Champagne*, Nancy
	D02	Dassault Mirage 2000D	*AA DGA EV, preserved Istres*
	301	Dassault Rafale B	AA DGA EV, Istres
	302	Dassault Rafale B	AA DGA EV, Istres
	303	Dassault Rafale B [4-EA]	AA ETR 03.004 *Aquitaine*, St Dizier
	304	Dassault Rafale B [30-EB]	AA CEAM/ECE 01.030 *Côte d'Argent*, Mont-de-Marsan
	307	Dassault Rafale B [4-IA]	AA EC 02.004 *La Fayette*, St Dizier
	308	Dassault Rafale B [4-HA]	AA EC 01.004 *Gascogne*, St Dizier
	309	Dassault Rafale B [30-HB]	AA CEAM/ECE 03.030 *Lorraine*, Mont-de-Marsan
	310	Dassault Rafale B [4-HC]	AA EC 01.004 *Gascogne*, St Dizier

Serial	Type (code/other identity)	Owner/operator, location or fate	Notes
311	Dassault Rafale B [4-HD]	AA EC 01.004 *Gascogne*, St Dizier	
312	Dassault Rafale B [4-HF]	AA EC 01.004 *Gascogne*, St Dizier	
313	Dassault Rafale B [4-HI]	AA ETR 03.004 *Aquitaine*, St Dizier	
314	Dassault Rafale B [4-HP]	AA EC 01.004 *Gascogne*, St Dizier	
315	Dassault Rafale B [4-HK]	AA EC 01.004 *Gascogne*, St Dizier	
317	Dassault Rafale B [4-HO]	AA ETR 03.004 *Aquitaine*, St Dizier	
318	Dassault Rafale B [4-HM]	AA EC 02.004 *La Fayette*, St Dizier	
319	Dassault Rafale B [4-HN]	AA EC 01.004 *Gascogne*, St Dizier	
320	Dassault Rafale B [4-HV]	AA EC 01.004 *Gascogne*, St Dizier	
321	Dassault Rafale B [4-HQ]	AA EC 02.004 *La Fayette*, St Dizier	
322	Dassault Rafale B [4-HU]	AA EC 01.004 *Gascogne*, St Dizier	
323	Dassault Rafale B [4-HT]	AA EC 01.004 *Gascogne*, St Dizier	
324	Dassault Rafale B [30-HW]	AA EC 03.030 *Lorraine*, St Dizier	
325	Dassault Rafale B [4-HX]	AA ETR 03.004 *Aquitaine*, St Dizier	
326	Dassault Rafale B [4-HY]	AA EC 01.004 *Gascogne*, St Dizier	
327	Dassault Rafale B [4-HZ]	AA EC 01.004 *Gascogne*, St Dizier	
328	Dassault Rafale B [4-IC]	AA EC 01.004 *Gascogne*, St Dizier	
329	Dassault Rafale B [30-ID]	AA CEAM/ECE 01.030 *Côte d'Argent*, Mont-de-Marsan	
330	Dassault Rafale B [4-IE]	AA EC 01.004 *Gascogne*, St Dizier	
331	Dassault Rafale B [4-IF]	AA EC 01.004 *Gascogne*, St Dizier	
332	Dassault Rafale B [4-IG]	AA EC 02.004 *La Fayette*, St Dizier	
333	Dassault Rafale B [4-IH]	AA ETR 03.004 *Aquitaine*, St Dizier	
334	Dassault Rafale B [4-II]	AA EC 02.004 *La Fayette*, St Dizier	
335	Dassault Rafale B [4-IJ]	AA EC 01.004 *Gascogne*, St Dizier	
336	Dassault Rafale B [4-IK] $	AA EC 02.004 *La Fayette*, St Dizier	
337	Dassault Rafale B [4-IL]	AA EC 01.004 *Gascogne*, St Dizier	
338	Dassault Rafale B [4-IO]	AA EC 02.004 *La Fayette*, St Dizier	
339	Dassault Rafale B [4-FF]	AA ETR 03.004 *Aquitaine*, St Dizier	
340	Dassault Rafale B [4-FG]	AA EC 01.004 *Gascogne*, St Dizier	
341	Dassault Rafale B [4-FH]	AA EC 01.004 *Gascogne*, St Dizier	
342	Dassault Rafale B [4-FI]	AA EC 01.004 *Gascogne*, St Dizier	
343	Dassault Rafale B [4-FJ]	AA EC 02.004 *La Fayette*, St Dizier	
344	Dassault Rafale B [4-FK]	AA EC 01.004 *Gascogne*, St Dizier	
345	Dassault Rafale B [4-FL]	AA EC 02.004 *La Fayette*, St Dizier	
346	Dassault Rafale B [4-FM]	AA ETR 03.004 *Aquitaine*, St Dizier	
347	Dassault Rafale B [4-FN]	AA EC 01.004 *Gascogne*, St Dizier	
348	Dassault Rafale B	AA DGA EV, Istres	
349	Dassault Rafale B [4-FP] $	AA ETR 03.004 *Aquitaine*, St Dizier	
350	Dassault Rafale B [4-FQ]	AA ETR 03.004 *Aquitaine*, St Dizier	
351	Dassault Rafale B [4-FR]	AA EC 02.004 *La Fayette*, St Dizier	
352	Dassault Rafale B [4-FS]	AA EC 02.004 *La Fayette*, St Dizier	
353	Dassault Rafale B [4-FT]	AA EC 02.004 *La Fayette*, St Dizier	
354	Dassault Rafale B [4-FU]	AA EC 01.004 *Gascogne*, St Dizier	
355	Dassault Rafale B [4-FV]	AA EC 01.004 *Gascogne*, St Dizier	
356	Dassault Rafale B [4-FW]	AA ETR 03.004 *Aquitaine*, St Dizier	
357	Dassault Rafale B [4-FX]	AA EC 02.004 *La Fayette*, St Dizier	
358	Dassault Rafale B [4-FY]	AA EC 02.004 *La Fayette*, St Dizier	
359	Dassault Rafale B	AA	
360	Dassault Rafale B	AA (on order)	
361	Dassault Rafale B	AA (on order)	
362	Dassault Rafale B	AA (on order)	
363	Dassault Rafale B	AA (on order)	
101	Dassault Rafale C	AA DGA EV, Istres	
102	Dassault Rafale C [30-EF]	AA EC 02.030 *Normandie-Niémen*, Mont-de-Marsan	
104	Dassault Rafale C [30-HH]	AA EC 03.030 *Lorraine*, St Dizier	
105	Dassault Rafale C [30-HE]	AA EC 02.030 *Normandie-Niémen*, Mont-de-Marsan	
106	Dassault Rafale C [30-HG]	AA EC 03.030 *Lorraine*, St Dizier	
107	Dassault Rafale C [113-HJ] $	AA (To Greece?)	
108	Dassault Rafale C [30-HS]	AA EC 03.030 *Lorraine*, St Dizier	

Notes	Serial	Type (code/other identity)	Owner/operator, location or fate
	109	Dassault Rafale C [30-IM]	AA EC 03.030 *Lorraine*, St Dizier
	110	Dassault Rafale C [30-IN]	AA EC 03.030 *Lorraine*, St Dizier (damaged)
	111	Dassault Rafale C [30-IP]	*Sold to Greece as 414, 2023*
	113	Dassault Rafale C [30-IR]	AA EC 02.030 *Normandie-Niémen*, Mont-de-Marsan
	114	Dassault Rafale C [30-IS]	AA (To Greece?)
	115	Dassault Rafale C [30-IT]	AA EC 03.030 *Lorraine*, St Dizier
	116	Dassault Rafale C [30-IU]	AA EC 02.030 *Normandie-Niémen*, Mont-de-Marsan
	117	Dassault Rafale C [30-IV]	AA EC 02.030 *Normandie-Niémen*, Mont-de-Marsan
	119	Dassault Rafale C [30-IX]	AA EC 03.030 *Lorraine*, St Dizier
	120	Dassault Rafale C [30-IY] $	*Sold to Greece, 2023*
	121	Dassault Rafale C [30-IZ]	AA EC 03.030 *Lorraine*, St Dizier
	122	Dassault Rafale C [30-GA]	AA EC 03.030 *Lorraine*, St Dizier (damaged)
	124	Dassault Rafale C [30-GC]	AA EC 02.030 *Normandie-Niémen*, Mont-de-Marsan
	125	Dassault Rafale C [30-GD] $	AA EC 02.030 *Normandie-Niémen*, Mont-de-Marsan
	126	Dassault Rafale C [30-GE]	AA EC 02.030 *Normandie-Niémen*, Mont-de-Marsan
	127	Dassault Rafale C [30-GF]	AA EC 02.030 *Normandie-Niémen*, Mont-de-Marsan
	128	Dassault Rafale C [30-GG]	*Sold to Greece, 2023*
	129	Dassault Rafale C [30-GH]	AA EC 02.030 *Normandie-Niémen*, Mont-de-Marsan
	130	Dassault Rafale C [30-GI]	AA EC 02.030 *Normandie-Niémen*, Mont-de-Marsan
	131	Dassault Rafale C [30-GJ]	AA EC 03.030 *Lorraine*, St Dizier
	132	Dassault Rafale C [7-GK] $	AA EC 01.007 *Provence*, Al Dhafra, UAE
	133	Dassault Rafale C [30-GL]	AA EC 02.030 *Normandie-Niémen*, Mont-de-Marsan
	134	Dassault Rafale C [30-GM]	*Sold to Greece, 2023*
	135	Dassault Rafale C [30-GN] $	AA EC 03.030 *Lorraine*, St Dizier
	136	Dassault Rafale C [4-GO]	AA ETR 03.004 *Aquitaine*, St Dizier
	137	Dassault Rafale C [7-GP]	*Sold to Greece, 2023*
	138	Dassault Rafale C [7-GQ]	AA EC 01.007 *Provence*, Al Dhafra, UAE
	139	Dassault Rafale C [4-GR] $	AA ETR 03.004 *Aquitaine*, St Dizier
	140	Dassault Rafale C [4-GS]	AA ETR 03.004 *Aquitaine*, St Dizier
	141	Dassault Rafale C [7-GT] $	AA EC 01.007 *Provence*, Al Dhafra, UAE
	142	Dassault Rafale C [30-GU] $	AA EC 03.030 *Lorraine*, St Dizier
	143	Dassault Rafale C [30-GV]	*Sold to Greece as 415, 2023*
	144	Dassault Rafale C [30-GW]	AA EC 03.030 *Lorraine*, St Dizier
	145	Dassault Rafale C [30-GX]	AA EC 03.030 *Lorraine*, St Dizier
	146	Dassault Rafale C [30-GY]	AA EC 03.030 *Lorraine*, St Dizier
	147	Dassault Rafale C [4-GZ]	AA ETR 03.004 *Aquitaine*, St Dizier
	148	Dassault Rafale C [7-VA]	AA EC 01.007 *Provence*, Al Dhafra, UAE
	149	Dassault Rafale C	AA (on order)
	150	Dassault Rafale C	AA (on order)
	151	Dassault Rafale C	AA (on order)
	152	Dassault Rafale C	AA (on order)
	153	Dassault Rafale C	AA (on order)
	154	Dassault Rafale C	AA (on order)
	155	Dassault Rafale C	AA (on order)
	156	Dassault Rafale C	AA (on order)
	157	Dassault Rafale C	AA (on order)
	158	Dassault Rafale C	AA (on order)
	159	Dassault Rafale C	AA (on order)
	160	Dassault Rafale C	AA (on order)
	161	Dassault Rafale C	AA (on order)
	162	Dassault Rafale C	AA (on order)
	163	Dassault Rafale C	AA (on order)

Serial	Type (code/other identity)	Owner/operator, location or fate	Notes
164	Dassault Rafale C	AA (on order)	
165	Dassault Rafale C	AA (on order)	
166	Dassault Rafale C	AA (on order)	
167	Dassault Rafale C	AA (on order)	
168	Dassault Rafale C	AA (on order)	
169	Dassault Rafale C	AA (on order)	
292	DHC-6 Twin Otter 200 [F-RACC]	AA GAM 00.056 *Vaucluse*, Evreux	
298	DHC-6 Twin Otter 200 [F-RACD]	AA GAM 00.056 *Vaucluse*, Evreux	
300	DHC-6 Twin Otter 200 [F-RACE]	AA GAM 00.056 *Vaucluse*, Evreux	
730	DHC-6 Twin Otter 300 [F-RACA]	AA ET 03.061 *Poitou*, Orléans	
745	DHC-6 Twin Otter 300 [CV]	AA ET 03.061 *Poitou*, Orléans	
054	Embraer EMB.121AA Xingu [YX]	AA, stored Avord	
064	Embraer EMB.121AA Xingu [YY]	AA EAT 00.319 *Capitaine Dartigues*, Avord	
066	Embraer EMB.121AN Xingu [ZA]	AA EAT 00.319 *Capitaine Dartigues*, Avord	
072	Embraer EMB.121AA Xingu [YA]	AA EAT 00.319 *Capitaine Dartigues*, Avord	
075	Embraer EMB.121AA Xingu [YC]	AA, stored Avord	
078	Embraer EMB.121AA Xingu [YE]	AA EAT 00.319 *Capitaine Dartigues*, Avord	
082	Embraer EMB.121AA Xingu [YG]	AA EAT 00.319 *Capitaine Dartigues*, Avord	
083	Embraer EMB.121AN Xingu [ZE]	AA EAT 00.319 *Capitaine Dartigues*, Avord	
084	Embraer EMB.121AA Xingu [YH]	AA EAT 00.319 *Capitaine Dartigues*, Avord	
086	Embraer EMB.121AA Xingu [YI]	AA EAT 00.319 *Capitaine Dartigues*, Avord	
089	Embraer EMB.121AA Xingu [YJ]	AA EAT 00.319 *Capitaine Dartigues*, Avord	
090	Embraer EMB.121AN Xingu [ZF]	AA EAT 00.319 *Capitaine Dartigues*, Avord	
091	Embraer EMB.121AA Xingu [YK]	AA, stored Avord	
092	Embraer EMB.121AA Xingu [YL]	AA EAT 00.319 *Capitaine Dartigues*, Avord	
096	Embraer EMB.121AA Xingu [YN]	AA, stored Avord	
098	Embraer EMB.121AA Xingu [YO]	AA EAT 00.319 *Capitaine Dartigues*, Avord	
099	Embraer EMB.121AA Xingu [YP]	AA EAT 00.319 *Capitaine Dartigues*, Avord	
102	Embraer EMB.121AA Xingu [YS]	AA, stored Avord	
103	Embraer EMB.121AA Xingu [YT]	AA EAT 00.319 *Capitaine Dartigues*, Avord	
105	Embraer EMB.121AA Xingu [YU]	AA EAT 00.319 *Capitaine Dartigues*, Avord	
107	Embraer EMB.121AA Xingu [YV]	AA EAT 00.319 *Capitaine Dartigues*, Avord	
108	Embraer EMB.121AA Xingu [YW]	AA EAT 00.319 *Capitaine Dartigues*, Avord	
2233	Eurocopter AS.332L-1 Super Puma [FY]	AA EH 03.067 *Parisis*, Villacoublay	
2235	Eurocopter AS.332L-1 Super Puma [FZ]	AA EH 03.067 *Parisis*, Villacoublay	
2377	Eurocopter AS.332L-1 Super Puma [FU]	AA EH 03.067 *Parisis*, Villacoublay	
2461	Eurocopter EC.725AP Caracal [SA]	AA EH 01.067 *Pyrénées*, Cazaux	
2549	Eurocopter EC.725AP Caracal [SB]	AA EH 01.067 *Pyrénées*, Cazaux	
2552	Eurocopter EC.725AP Caracal [SE]	AA EH 01.067 *Pyrénées*, Cazaux	
2619	Eurocopter EC.725AP Caracal [SC]	AA EH 01.067 *Pyrénées*, Cazaux	
2626	Eurocopter EC.725AP Caracal [SD]	AA EH 01.067 *Pyrénées*, Cazaux	
2741	Eurocopter EC.225LP Caracal [SY]	AA GAM 00.056 *Vaucluse*, Evreux	
2752	Eurocopter EC.225LP Caracal [SZ]	AA GAM 00.056 *Vaucluse*, Evreux	
2770	Eurocopter EC.725R-2 Caracal [SG]	AA EH 01.067 *Pyrénées*, Cazaux	
2772	Eurocopter EC.725R-2 Caracal [SH]	AA EH 01.067 *Pyrénées*, Cazaux	
2778	Eurocopter EC.725R-2 Caracal [SI]	AA EH 01.067 *Pyrénées*, Cazaux	
2789	Eurocopter EC.725R-2 Caracal [SJ]	AA EH 01.067 *Pyrénées*, Cazaux	
2802	Eurocopter EC.725R-2 Caracal [SK]	AA EH 01.067 *Pyrénées*, Cazaux	
2897	Eurocopter EC.225LP Super Puma 2+ [F-ZAJB]	AA DGA EV, Istres	
2932	Eurocopter EC.225LP Super Puma 2+ [F-ZAJC]	AA DGA EV, Istres	
5361	Eurocopter AS.555AN Fennec [UT]	AA EH 05.067 *Alpilles*, Orange	
5382	Eurocopter AS.555AN Fennec [UV]	AA EH 05.067 *Alpilles*, Orange (at Marseille)	
5386	Eurocopter AS.555AN Fennec [UX]	AA EH 05.067 *Alpilles*, Orange	
5387	Eurocopter AS.555AN Fennec [UY]	AA EH 05.067 *Alpilles*, Orange	
5390	Eurocopter AS.555AN Fennec [UZ]	AA EH 03.067 *Parisis*, Villacoublay	
5391	Eurocopter AS.555AN Fennec [VA]	AA EH 05.067 *Alpilles*, Orange	
5392	Eurocopter AS.555AN Fennec [VB]	AA EH 05.067 *Alpilles*, Orange	
5393	Eurocopter AS.555AN Fennec [VC]	AA EH 05.067 *Alpilles*, Orange	
5396	Eurocopter AS.555AN Fennec [VD]	AA EH 05.067 *Alpilles*, Orange	
5397	Eurocopter AS.555AN Fennec [VE]	AA EH 05.067 *Alpilles*, Orange	
5398	Eurocopter AS.555AN Fennec [VF]	AA EH 05.067 *Alpilles*, Orange	
5399	Eurocopter AS.555AN Fennec [VG] $	AA	

Notes	Serial	Type (code/other identity)	Owner/operator, location or fate
	5400	Eurocopter AS.555AN Fennec [VH]	AA EH 05.067 *Alpilles*, Orange
	5412	Eurocopter AS.555AN Fennec [VI]	AA EH 05.067 *Alpilles*, Orange
	5427	Eurocopter AS.555AN Fennec [VJ]	AA EH 03.067 *Parisis*, Villacoublay
	5430	Eurocopter AS.555AN Fennec [VL]	AA EH 03.067 *Parisis*, Villacoublay
	5431	Eurocopter AS.555AN Fennec [VM] $	AA EH 05.067 *Alpilles*, Orange
	5441	Eurocopter AS.555AN Fennec [VO]	AA EH 03.067 *Parisis*, Villacoublay
	5444	Eurocopter AS.555AN Fennec [VP]	AA EH 03.067 *Parisis*, Villacoublay
	5445	Eurocopter AS.555AN Fennec [VQ] $	AA EH 05.067 *Alpilles*, Orange
	5448	Eurocopter AS.555AN Fennec [VR]	AA EH 05.067 *Alpilles*, Orange
	5452	Eurocopter AS.555AN Fennec [VS]	AA EH 05.067 *Alpilles*, Orange
	5455	Eurocopter AS.555AN Fennec [VT]	AA EH 03.067 *Parisis*, Villacoublay
	5457	Eurocopter AS.555AN Fennec [VU]	AA ET 00.068 *Antilles-Guyane*, Cayenne
	5458	Eurocopter AS.555AN Fennec [VV]	AA EH 05.067 *Alpilles*, Orange
	5466	Eurocopter AS.555AN Fennec [VW]	AA ET 00.068 *Antilles-Guyane*, Cayenne
	5468	Eurocopter AS.555AN Fennec [VX]	AA EH 03.067 *Parisis*, Villacoublay
	5490	Eurocopter AS.555AN Fennec [VY]	AA EH 05.067 *Alpilles*, Orange
	5506	Eurocopter AS.555AN Fennec [WA]	AA EH 05.067 *Alpilles*, Orange
	5509	Eurocopter AS.555AN Fennec [WB]	AA EH 05.067 *Alpilles*, Orange
	5511	Eurocopter AS.555AN Fennec [WC] $	AA EH 03.067 *Parisis*, Villacoublay
	5516	Eurocopter AS.555AN Fennec [WD]	AA EH 03.067 *Parisis*, Villacoublay
	5520	Eurocopter AS.555AN Fennec [WE]	AA EH 03.067 *Parisis*, Villacoublay
	5523	Eurocopter AS.555AN Fennec [WF]	AA EH 05.067 *Alpilles*, Orange
	5526	Eurocopter AS.555AN Fennec [WG]	AA EH 03.067 *Parisis*, Villacoublay
	5530	Eurocopter AS.555AN Fennec [WH]	AA EH 05.067 *Alpilles*, Orange
	5532	Eurocopter AS.555AN Fennec [WI]	AA EH 05.067 *Alpilles*, Orange
	5534	Eurocopter AS.555AN Fennec [WJ]	AA EH 05.067 *Alpilles*, Orange
	5536	Eurocopter AS.555AN Fennec [WK]	AA EH 03.067 *Parisis*, Villacoublay
	5559	Eurocopter AS.555AN Fennec [WL]	AA EH 05.067 *Alpilles*, Orange
	04	Extra EA-330SC [F-TGCI]	AA EVAA, Salon de Provence
	05	Extra EA-330SC [F-TGCJ]	AA EVAA, Salon de Provence
	290	Fokker 100 [F-ZAFT]	AA DGA EV, Bordeaux
	400	Fokker 100	AA DGA EV, Istres (on order) (stored Dinard)
	4588	Lockheed C-130H Hercules [61-PM] $	AA ET 03.061 *Poitou*, Evreux
	4589	Lockheed C-130H Hercules [61-PN]	AA ET 03.061 *Poitou*, Evreux
	5114	Lockheed C-130H Hercules [61-PA]	AA ET 03.061 *Poitou*, Evreux
	5116	Lockheed C-130H Hercules [61-PB]	AA ET 03.061 *Poitou*, Evreux
	5119	Lockheed C-130H Hercules [61-PC]	AA ET 03.061 *Poitou*, Evreux
	5140	Lockheed C-130H Hercules [61-PD]	AA ET 03.061 *Poitou*, Evreux
	5142	Lockheed C-130H-30 Hercules [61-PE]	AA ET 03.061 *Poitou*, Evreux
	5144	Lockheed C-130H-30 Hercules [61-PF] $	AA ET 03.061 *Poitou*, Evreux
	5150	Lockheed C-130H-30 Hercules [61-PG]	AA ET 03.061 *Poitou*, Evreux
	5151	Lockheed C-130H-30 Hercules [61-PH]	AA ET 03.061 *Poitou*, Evreux
	5152	Lockheed C-130H-30 Hercules [61-PI]	AA ET 03.061 *Poitou*, Evreux
	5153	Lockheed C-130H-30 Hercules [61-PJ]	AA ET 03.061 *Poitou*, Evreux
	5226	Lockheed C-130H-30 Hercules [61-PK]	AA ET 03.061 *Poitou*, Evreux
	5227	Lockheed C-130H-30 Hercules [61-PL]	AA ET 03.061 *Poitou*, Evreux
	5836	Lockheed C-130J Hercules II [61-PO]	AA ET 02.061 *Franche-Comté*, Orléans
	5847	Lockheed C-130J Hercules II [61-PP]	AA ET 02.061 *Franche-Comté*, Orléans
	5874	Lockheed KC-130J Hercules II [61-PQ]	AA ET 02.061 *Franche-Comté*, Orléans
	5890	Lockheed KC-130J Hercules II [61-PR]	AA ET 02.061 *Franche-Comté*, Orléans
	01	Pilatus PC-21 (HB-HVA) [709-FC]	AA EAC 00.315, Cognac
	02	Pilatus PC-21 (HB-HVB) [709-FD]	AA EAC 00.315, Cognac
	03	Pilatus PC-21 (HB-HVC/F-ZXAC) [709-FE]	AA EAC 00.315, Cognac
	04	Pilatus PC-21 (HB-HVD) [709-FF]	AA EAC 00.315, Cognac
	05	Pilatus PC-21 (HB-HVE) [709-FG]	AA EAC 00.315, Cognac
	06	Pilatus PC-21 (HB-HVF) [709-FH]	AA EAC 00.315, Cognac
	07	Pilatus PC-21 (HB-HVG) [709-FI]	AA EAC 00.315, Cognac
	08	Pilatus PC-21 (HB-HVH) [709-FJ]	AA EAC 00.315, Cognac
	09	Pilatus PC-21 (HB-HVI) [709-FK]	AA EAC 00.315, Cognac
	10	Pilatus PC-21 (HB-HVJ) [709-FL]	AA EAC 00.315, Cognac
	11	Pilatus PC-21 (HB-HVK) [709-FM]	AA EAC 00.315, Cognac
	12	Pilatus PC-21 (HB-HVL) [709-FN]	AA EAC 00.315, Cognac

Serial	Type (code/other identity)	Owner/operator, location or fate	Notes
13	Pilatus PC-21 (HB-HVM) [709-FO]	AA EAC 00.315, Cognac	
14	Pilatus PC-21 (HB-HVN) [709-FP]	AA EAC 00.315, Cognac	
15	Pilatus PC-21 (HB-HVO) [709-FQ]	AA EAC 00.315, Cognac	
16	Pilatus PC-21 (HB-HVP) [709-FR]	AA EAC 00.315, Cognac	
17	Pilatus PC-21 (HB-HVQ) [709-FS]	AA EAC 00.315, Cognac	
18	Pilatus PC-21 (HB-HXA) [709-GA]	AA EAC 00.315, Cognac	
19	Pilatus PC-21 (HB-HXB) [709-GB]	AA EAC 00.315, Cognac	
20	Pilatus PC-21 (HB-HXC) [709-GC]	AA EAC 00.315, Cognac	
21	Pilatus PC-21 (HB-HXD) [709-GD]	AA EAC 00.315, Cognac	
22	Pilatus PC-21 (HB-HXE) [709-GE]	AA EAC 00.315, Cognac	
23	Pilatus PC-21 (HB-HXF) [709-GF]	AA EAC 00.315, Cognac	
24	Pilatus PC-21 (HB-HXG) [709-GG]	AA EAC 00.315, Cognac	
25	Pilatus PC-21 (HB-HXH) [709-GH]	AA EAC 00.315, Cognac	
26	Pilatus PC-21 (HB-HXI) [709-GI]	AA (on order)	
27	Pilatus PC-21	AA (on order)	
28	Pilatus PC-21	AA (on order)	
29	Pilatus PC-21	AA (on order)	
30	Pilatus PC-21	AA (on order)	
33	SOCATA TBM 700A [XA]	AA ET 00.043 *Médoc*, Bordeaux	
35	SOCATA TBM 700A [BW]	AA DGA EV, Cazaux & Istres	
77	SOCATA TBM 700A [XD]	AA ET 00.043 *Médoc*, Bordeaux	
78	SOCATA TBM 700A [XE]	AA CEAM, Mont-de-Marsan	
80	SOCATA TBM 700A [ABY]	*Transferred to ALAT, 2022*	
93	SOCATA TBM 700A [XL]	AA ET 00.041 *Verdun*, Villacoublay	
94	SOCATA TBM 700A [XG]	AA ET 00.041 *Verdun*, Villacoublay	
95	SOCATA TBM 700A [XH]	AA CEAM, Mont-de-Marsan	
103	SOCATA TBM 700A [XI]	AA ET 00.041 *Verdun*, Villacoublay	
104	SOCATA TBM 700A [XJ]	AA ET 00.043 *Médoc*, Bordeaux	
105	SOCATA TBM 700A [XK] $	AA ET 00.043 *Médoc*, Bordeaux	
110	SOCATA TBM 700A [XP]	AA ET 00.041 *Verdun*, Villacoublay	
111	SOCATA TBM 700A [XM]	AA ET 00.041 *Verdun*, Villacoublay	
115	SOCATA TBM 700A [ABQ]	*Transferred to ALAT, 2022*	
117	SOCATA TBM 700A [XN]	AA ET 00.043 *Médoc*, Bordeaux	
125	SOCATA TBM 700A [XO]	AA ET 00.043 *Médoc*, Bordeaux	
131	SOCATA TBM 700A [XQ]	AA ET 00.041 *Verdun*, Villacoublay	
146	SOCATA TBM 700A [XR]	AA ET 00.041 *Verdun*, Villacoublay	
147	SOCATA TBM 700A [XS]	AA ET 00.041 *Verdun*, Villacoublay	
R202	Transall C-160R [64-GB]	*Preserved Vannes-Meucon, 2022*	
R203	Transall C-160R [64-GC] $	*CANOPEE Museum, Chateaudun*	
R204	Transall C-160R [64-GD] $	*Stored Toulouse-Francazal*	
R206	Transall C-160R [64-GF]	*Stored Evreux*	
R212	Transall C-160R [64-GL] $	*Preserved Toulouse, 2022*	
F216	Transall C-160NG GABRIEL [GT]	*Stored le Bourget, 2022*	
F221	Transall C-160NG GABRIEL [GS] $	*Preserved Chateaudun, 2022*	
R225	Transall C-160R [64-GY]	*Withdrawn from use, Evreux, 2022*	
R226	Transall C-160R [64-GZ]	*Stored Toulouse-Francazal*	

Aéronautique Navale/Marine (AN)

Serial	Type (code/other identity)	Owner/operator, location or fate	Notes
008	Airbus Helicopters H.160B (F-WWOA)	AN 32 Flottille, Lanvéoc/Poulmic	
...	Airbus Helicopters H.160B	AN, Lanvéoc/Poulmic (on order)	
...	Airbus Helicopters H.160B	AN, Lanvéoc/Poulmic (on order)	
...	Airbus Helicopters H.160B	AN, Lanvéoc/Poulmic (on order)	
...	Airbus Helicopters H.160B	AN, Lanvéoc/Poulmic (on order)	
...	Airbus Helicopters H.160B	AN, Lanvéoc/Poulmic (on order)	
3	Dassault-Breguet Atlantique 2	AN 23 Flottille, Lorient/Lann Bihoué	
4	Dassault-Breguet Atlantique 2	AN 23 Flottille, Lorient/Lann Bihoué	
5	Dassault-Breguet Atlantique 2	AN 21 Flottille, Lorient/Lann Bihoué	
9	Dassault-Breguet Atlantique 2	AN 23 Flottille, Lorient/Lann Bihoué	
11	Dassault-Breguet Atlantique 2	AN 21 Flottille, Lorient/Lann Bihoué	
12	Dassault-Breguet Atlantique 2	AN 21 Flottille, Lorient/Lann Bihoué	
13	Dassault-Breguet Atlantique 2	AN 21 Flottille, Lorient/Lann Bihoué	
15	Dassault-Breguet Atlantique 2	AN 21 Flottille, Lorient/Lann Bihoué	

Notes	Serial	Type (code/other identity)	Owner/operator, location or fate
	16	Dassault-Breguet Atlantique 2	AN 23 Flottille, Lorient/Lann Bihoué
	17	Dassault-Breguet Atlantique 2 $	AN 21 Flottille, Lorient/Lann Bihoué
	18	Dassault-Breguet Atlantique 2	AN 21 Flottille, Lorient/Lann Bihoué
	19	Dassault-Breguet Atlantique 2	AN 23 Flottille, Lorient/Lann Bihoué
	20	Dassault-Breguet Atlantique 2	AN 23 Flottille, Lorient/Lann Bihoué
	21	Dassault-Breguet Atlantique 2	AN 21 Flottille, Lorient/Lann Bihoué
	22	Dassault-Breguet Atlantique 2	AN 21 Flottille, Lorient/Lann Bihoué
	23	Dassault-Breguet Atlantique 2	AN 21 Flottille, Lorient/Lann Bihoué
	24	Dassault-Breguet Atlantique 2	AN 21 Flottille, Lorient/Lann Bihoué
	25	Dassault-Breguet Atlantique 2	AN CEPA, Istres
	26	Dassault-Breguet Atlantique 2	AN 21 Flottille, Lorient/Lann Bihoué
	27	Dassault-Breguet Atlantique 2	AN 21 Flottille, Lorient/Lann Bihoué
	28	Dassault-Breguet Atlantique 2	AN 23 Flottille, Lorient/Lann Bihoué
	32	Dassault Falcon 10(MER)	AN 57 Escadrille, Landivisiau
	101	Dassault Falcon 10(MER)	AN 57 Escadrille, Landivisiau
	129	Dassault Falcon 10(MER)	AN 57 Escadrille, Landivisiau
	133	Dassault Falcon 10(MER)	AN 57 Escadrille, Landivisiau
	143	Dassault Falcon 10(MER)	AN 57 Escadrille, Landivisiau
	185	Dassault Falcon 10(MER) $	AN 57 Escadrille, Landivisiau
	48	Dassault Falcon 20G Guardian	AN 25 Flottille, Papeete & Tontouta
	65	Dassault Falcon 20G Guardian	AN 25 Flottille, Papeete & Tontouta
	72	Dassault Falcon 20G Guardian	AN 25 Flottille, Papeete & Tontouta
	77	Dassault Falcon 20G Guardian	AN 25 Flottille, Papeete & Tontouta
	80	Dassault Falcon 20G Guardian	AN 25 Flottille, Papeete & Tontouta
	5	Dassault Falcon 50MS SURMAR	AN 24 Flottille, Lorient/Lann Bihoué
	7	Dassault Falcon 50MI SURMAR	AN 24 Flottille, Lorient/Lann Bihoué
	27	Dassault Falcon 50MS SURMAR (F-ZWMM)	AN 24 Flottille, Lorient/Lann Bihoué
	30	Dassault Falcon 50MI SURMAR	AN 24 Flottille, Lorient/Lann Bihoué
	34	Dassault Falcon 50MS SURMAR (F-ZWMT)	AN 24 Flottille, Lorient/Lann Bihoué
	36	Dassault Falcon 50MI SURMAR	AN 24 Flottille, Lorient/Lann Bihoué
	78	Dassault Falcon 50MS SURMAR (F-ZWMO)	AN 24 Flottille, Lorient/Lann Bihoué
	132	Dassault Falcon 50MI SURMAR	AN 24 Flottille, Lorient/Lann Bihoué
	1	Dassault Rafale M	AN DGA EV, Istres
	2	Dassault Rafale M	AN 17 Flottille, Landivisiau
	3	Dassault Rafale M	AN ETR 03.004 *Aquitaine*, St Dizier
	5	Dassault Rafale M	AN 12 Flottille, Landivisiau
	6	Dassault Rafale M	AN 12 Flottille, Landivisiau
	7	Dassault Rafale M	AN 11 Flottille, Landivisiau
	8	Dassault Rafale M	AN ETR 03.004 *Aquitaine*, St Dizier
	9	Dassault Rafale M	AN 12 Flottille, Landivisiau
	10	Dassault Rafale M $	AN 11 Flottille, Landivisiau
	11	Dassault Rafale M $	AN 11 Flottille, Landivisiau
	12	Dassault Rafale M	AN ETR 03.004 *Aquitaine*, St Dizier
	13	Dassault Rafale M	AN 11 Flottille, Landivisiau
	14	Dassault Rafale M	AN 11 Flottille, Landivisiau
	15	Dassault Rafale M	AN 12 Flottille, Landivisiau
	16	Dassault Rafale M	AN 12 Flottille, Landivisiau
	17	Dassault Rafale M	AN 12 Flottille, Landivisiau
	19	Dassault Rafale M	AN 11 Flottille, Landivisiau
	20	Dassault Rafale M	AN 17 Flottille, Landivisiau
	21	Dassault Rafale M	AN 12 Flottille, Landivisiau
	23	Dassault Rafale M	AN 12 Flottille, Landivisiau
	26	Dassault Rafale M	AN 12 Flottille, Landivisiau
	27	Dassault Rafale M $	AN ETR 03.004 *Aquitaine*, St Dizier
	28	Dassault Rafale M	AN ETR 03.004 *Aquitaine*, St Dizier
	29	Dassault Rafale M	AN 12 Flottille, Landivisiau
	30	Dassault Rafale M	AN CEPA/10 Escadrille, Landivisiau
	31	Dassault Rafale M	AN 11 Flottille, Landivisiau
	32	Dassault Rafale M $	AN 12 Flottille, Landivisiau
	33	Dassault Rafale M	AN ETR 03.004 *Aquitaine*, St Dizier
	34	Dassault Rafale M	AN 11 Flottille, Landivisiau
	35	Dassault Rafale M $	AN 12 Flottille, Landivisiau

Serial	Type (code/other identity)	Owner/operator, location or fate	Notes
36	Dassault Rafale M $	AN 11 Flottille, Landivisiau	
37	Dassault Rafale M $	AN 11 Flottille, Landivisiau	
38	Dassault Rafale M	AN 12 Flottille, Landivisiau	
39	Dassault Rafale M	AN 11 Flottille, Landivisiau	
40	Dassault Rafale M	AN ETR 03.004 *Aquitaine*, St Dizier	
41	Dassault Rafale M	AN 12 Flottille, Landivisiau	
42	Dassault Rafale M	AN 11 Flottille, Landivisiau	
43	Dassault Rafale M	AN 11 Flottille, Landivisiau	
44	Dassault Rafale M	AN 11 Flottille, Landivisiau	
45	Dassault Rafale M	AN 11 Flottille, Landivisiau	
46	Dassault Rafale M	AN 11 Flottille, Landivisiau	
47	Dassault Rafale M	AN (on order)	
48	Dassault Rafale M	AN (on order)	
49	Dassault Rafale M	AN (on order)	
50	Dassault Rafale M	AN (on order)	
M02	Dassault Rafale M	AN DGA EV, Istres	
65	Embraer EMB.121AN Xingu	AN 28 Flottille, Hyères	
67	Embraer EMB.121AN Xingu	AN 28 Flottille, Hyères	
68	Embraer EMB.121AN Xingu	AN 28 Flottille, Hyères	
69	Embraer EMB.121AN Xingu	AN 28 Flottille, Hyères	
71	Embraer EMB.121AN Xingu	AN 28 Flottille, Hyères	
74	Embraer EMB.121AN Xingu	AN 28 Flottille, Hyères	
77	Embraer EMB.121AN Xingu	AN 28 Flottille, Hyères	
81	Embraer EMB.121AN Xingu	AN 28 Flottille, Hyères	
85	Embraer EMB.121AN Xingu	AN 28 Flottille, Hyères	
87	Embraer EMB.121AN Xingu	AN 28 Flottille, Hyères	
17	Eurocopter AS.365N Dauphin	AN 35 Flottille, Hyères	
19	Eurocopter AS.365N Dauphin	AN 35 Flottille, Hyères	
24	Eurocopter AS.365N Dauphin	AN 35 Flottille, Hyères	
57	Eurocopter AS.365N Dauphin	AN 35 Flottille, Hyères	
81	Eurocopter AS.365N Dauphin	AN 35 Flottille, Hyères	
91	Eurocopter AS.365N Dauphin $	AN 35 Flottille, Hyères	
157	Eurocopter AS.365N Dauphin	AN 35 Flottille, Hyères	
313	Eurocopter SA.365F-1 Dauphin II	AN 35 Flottille, Hyères	
318	Eurocopter SA.365F-1 Dauphin II	AN 35 Flottille, Hyères	
322	Eurocopter SA.365F-1 Dauphin II	AN 35 Flottille, Hyères	
355	Eurocopter AS.565MA Panther	AN 36 Flottille, Hyères	
362	Eurocopter AS.565MA Panther	AN 36 Flottille, Hyères	
403	Eurocopter AS.565MA Panther	AN 36 Flottille, Hyères	
436	Eurocopter AS.565MA Panther	AN 36 Flottille, Hyères	
452	Eurocopter AS.565MA Panther	AN 36 Flottille, Hyères	
453	Eurocopter AS.565MA Panther	AN 36 Flottille, Hyères	
466	Eurocopter AS.565MA Panther	AN 36 Flottille, Hyères	
482	Eurocopter AS.565MA Panther	AN 36 Flottille, Hyères	
486	Eurocopter AS.565MA Panther	AN 36 Flottille, Hyères	
488	Eurocopter AS.565MA Panther	AN 36 Flottille, Hyères	
503	Eurocopter AS.565MA Panther	AN 36 Flottille, Hyères	
505	Eurocopter AS.565MA Panther	AN 36 Flottille, Hyères	
506	Eurocopter AS.565MA Panther	AN 36 Flottille, Hyères	
507	Eurocopter AS.565MA Panther	AN 36 Flottille, Hyères	
511	Eurocopter AS.565MA Panther	AN 36 Flottille, Hyères	
519	Eurocopter AS.565MA Panther	AN 36 Flottille, Hyères	
522	Eurocopter AS.565MA Panther	AN 36 Flottille, Hyères	
524	Eurocopter AS.565MA Panther	AN 36 Flottille, Hyères	
001	Eurocopter AS.365N-3 Dauphin (F-HURX)	AN 34 Flottille, Lanvéoc/Poulmic	
705	Eurocopter AS.365N-3 Dauphin (F-GNYH)	AN 34 Flottille, Lanvéoc/Poulmic	
710	Eurocopter AS.365N-3 Dauphin (F-GTCH)	AN 34 Flottille, Lanvéoc/Poulmic	
724	Eurocopter AS.365N-3 Dauphin (F-GVGV)	AN 34 Flottille, Lanvéoc/Poulmic	
726	Eurocopter AS.365N-3 Dauphin (F-HUZS)	AN (on order)	
745	Eurocopter AS.365N-3 Dauphin (F-HUDT)	AN 35 Flottille, Tahiti	
751	Eurocopter AS.365N-3 Dauphin (F-HABF)	AN (on order)	
756	Eurocopter AS.365N-3 Dauphin (F-GLTB)	AN (on order)	

Notes	Serial	Type (code/other identity)	Owner/operator, location or fate
	772	Eurocopter AS.365N-3 Dauphin (F-XHUK)	AN (on order)
	810	Eurocopter AS.365N-3 Dauphin (F-GZAD)	AN (on order)
	879	Eurocopter AS.365N-3 Dauphin (F-HUAJ)	AN (on order)
	...	Eurocopter AS.365N-3 Dauphin	AN (on order)
	...	Eurocopter AS.365N-3 Dauphin	AN (on order)
	6872	Eurocopter AS.365N-3 Dauphin	AN 35 Flottille, Tahiti
	6928	Eurocopter AS.365N-3 Dauphin	AN 35 Flottille, Tahiti
	1	NH Industries NH.90-NFH Caïman (F-ZWTO)	AN 33 Flottille, Lanvéoc/Poulmic
	2	NH Industries NH.90-NFH Caïman	AN CEPA/10 Escadrille, Hyères
	3	NH Industries NH.90-NFH Caïman	AN 33 Flottille, Lanvéoc/Poulmic
	4	NH Industries NH.90-NFH Caïman	AN 33 Flottille, Lanvéoc/Poulmic
	5	NH Industries NH.90-NFH Caïman	AN 33 Flottille, Lanvéoc/Poulmic
	6	NH Industries NH.90-NFH Caïman	AN 33 Flottille, Lanvéoc/Poulmic
	7	NH Industries NH.90-NFH Caïman	AN 33 Flottille, Lanvéoc/Poulmic
	8	NH Industries NH.90-NFH Caïman	AN 33 Flottille, Lanvéoc/Poulmic
	9	NH Industries NH.90-NFH Caïman	AN 31 Flottille, Hyères
	10	NH Industries NH.90-NFH Caïman	AN 33 Flottille, Lanvéoc/Poulmic
	11	NH Industries NH.90-NFH Caïman	AN 33 Flottille, Lanvéoc/Poulmic
	12	NH Industries NH.90-NFH Caïman	AN 33 Flottille, Lanvéoc/Poulmic
	13	NH Industries NH.90-NFH Caïman	AN 31 Flottille, Hyères
	14	NH Industries NH.90-NFH Caïman	AN 33 Flottille, Lanvéoc/Poulmic
	15	NH Industries NH.90-NFH Caïman	AN CEPA/10 Escadrille, Hyères
	16	NH Industries NH.90-NFH Caïman	AN 31 Flottille, Hyères
	17	NH Industries NH.90-NFH Caïman	AN 31 Flottille, Hyères
	18	NH Industries NH.90-NFH Caïman	AN 31 Flottille, Hyères
	19	NH Industries NH.90-NFH Caïman	AN
	20	NH Industries NH.90-NFH Caïman	AN 33 Flottille, Lanvéoc/Poulmic
	21	NH Industries NH.90-NFH Caïman	AN 31 Flottille, Hyères
	22	NH Industries NH.90-NFH Caïman	AN 31 Flottille, Hyères
	23	NH Industries NH.90-NFH Caïman	AN 33 Flottille, Lanvéoc/Poulmic
	24	NH Industries NH.90-NFH Caïman	AN (on order)
	25	NH Industries NH.90-NFH Caïman	AN (on order)
	26	NH Industries NH.90-NFH Caïman	AN (on order)
	27	NH Industries NH.90-NFH Caïman	AN 33 Flottille, Lanvéoc/Poulmic
	1	Northrop Grumman E-2C Hawkeye (165455)	AN 4 Flottille, Lorient/Lann Bihoué
	2	Northrop Grumman E-2C Hawkeye (165456)	AN 4 Flottille, Lorient/Lann Bihoué
	3	Northrop Grumman E-2C Hawkeye (166417)	AN 4 Flottille, Lorient/Lann Bihoué
	100	Sud Aviation SA.319B Alouette III	AN
	106	Sud Aviation SA.319B Alouette III	*To Rochefort – St. Agnant, for G.I.*
	161	Sud Aviation SA.319B Alouette III	*Withdrawn from use, 2022*
	262	Sud Aviation SA.319B Alouette III	*Withdrawn from use*
	268	Sud Aviation SA.319B Alouette III	*Withdrawn from use*
	302	Sud Aviation SA.319B Alouette III	*Withdrawn from use*
	303	Sud Aviation SA.319B Alouette III	*Withdrawn from use*
	997	Sud Aviation SA.319B Alouette III	*Withdrawn from use, 2022*
	Aviation Legére de l'Armée de Terre (ALAT)		
	1006	Aérospatiale SA.330Ba Puma [DAA]	ALAT 5 RHC, Pau
	1036	Aérospatiale SA.330Ba Puma [DAC]	ALAT 3 RHC, Etain
	1037	Aérospatiale SA.330Ba Puma [DAD]	ALAT EALAT, Le Luc
	1049	Aérospatiale SA.330Ba Puma [DAE]	ALAT
	1055	Aérospatiale SA.330Ba Puma [DAF]	ALAT GIH, Cazaux
	1069	Aérospatiale SA.330Ba Puma [DAG]	ALAT 3 RHC, Etain
	1071	Aérospatiale SA.330Ba Puma [DCE]	ALAT EALAT, Le Luc
	1073	Aérospatiale SA.330Ba Puma [DCF]	ALAT EALAT, Le Luc
	1078	Aérospatiale SA.330Ba Puma [DAH]	ALAT 3 RHC, Etain
	1092	Aérospatiale SA.330Ba Puma [DAI]	ALAT
	1100	Aérospatiale SA.330Ba Puma [DAJ]	ALAT 3 RHC, Etain
	1102	Aérospatiale SA.330Ba Puma [DAK]	ALAT 3 RHC, Etain
	1107	Aérospatiale SA.330Ba Puma [DAL]	ALAT 3 RHC, Etain
	1109	Aérospatiale SA.330Ba Puma [DAM]	ALAT EALAT, Le Luc
	1128	Aérospatiale SA.330Ba Puma [DAN]	ALAT 3 RHC, Etain
	1143	Aérospatiale SA.330Ba Puma [DAO]	ALAT EALAT, Le Luc

Serial	Type (code/other identity)	Owner/operator, location or fate	Notes
1149	Aérospatiale SA.330Ba Puma [DAP]	ALAT 3 RHC, Etain	
1156	Aérospatiale SA.330Ba Puma [DAQ]	ALAT 3 RHC, Etain	
1173	Aérospatiale SA.330Ba Puma [DAR]	ALAT 3 RHC, Etain	
1176	Aérospatiale SA.330Ba Puma [DAS]	ALAT 3 RHC, Etain	
1198	Aérospatiale SA.330Ba Puma [DDD]	ALAT	
1211	Aérospatiale SA.330Ba Puma [DAW]	ALAT 3 RHC, Etain	
1214	Aérospatiale SA.330Ba Puma [DAX]	ALAT 3 RHC, Etain	
1217	Aérospatiale SA.330Ba Puma [DAY]	ALAT 3 RHC, Etain	
1219	Aérospatiale SA.330Ba Puma [DAZ]	ALAT 3 RHC, Etain	
1222	Aérospatiale SA.330Ba Puma [DDG]	*Withdrawn from use at Montauban*	
1231	Aérospatiale SA.330Ba Puma [DDK]	ALAT 3 RHC, Etain	
1232	Aérospatiale SA.330Ba Puma [DBA]	ALAT	
1236	Aérospatiale SA.330Ba Puma [DDM]	ALAT EALAT, Le Luc	
1243	Aérospatiale SA.330Ba Puma [DBB]	ALAT 3 RHC, Etain	
1252	Aérospatiale SA.330Ba Puma [DDP]	ALAT EALAT, Le Luc	
1269	Aérospatiale SA.330Ba Puma [DDT]	ALAT 3 RHC, Etain	
1417	Aérospatiale SA.330Ba Puma [DBF]	ALAT 3 RHC, Etain	
1438	Aérospatiale SA.330Ba Puma [DBG]	ALAT	
1447	Aérospatiale SA.330Ba Puma [DDW]	ALAT 3 RHC, Etain	
1451	Aérospatiale SA.330Ba Puma [DBH]	ALAT	
1507	Aérospatiale SA.330Ba Puma [DBI]	ALAT EALAT, Le Luc	
1510	Aérospatiale SA.330Ba Puma [DBJ]	ALAT 3 RHC, Etain	
1512	Aérospatiale SA.330Ba Puma [DBK]	ALAT 3 RHC, Etain	
1519	Aérospatiale SA.330Ba Puma [DBL]	ALAT 3 RHC, Etain	
1617	Aérospatiale SA.330Ba Puma [DBM]	ALAT	
1632	Aérospatiale SA.330Ba Puma [DBN]	ALAT	
1634	Aérospatiale SA.330Ba Puma [DBO]	ALAT 3 RHC, Etain	
1654	Aérospatiale SA.330Ba Puma [DBP]	ALAT 3 RHC, Etain	
1662	Aérospatiale SA.330Ba Puma [DDX]	ALAT EALAT, Le Luc (damaged)	
1663	Aérospatiale SA.330Ba Puma [DBQ]	ALAT 3 RHC, Etain	
5682	Aérospatiale SA.330Ba Puma [DBR]	ALAT 3 RHC, Etain	
3459	Aérospatiale SA.342M-1 Gazelle [GAA]	ALAT 1 RHC, Phalsbourg	
3511	Aérospatiale SA.342M Gazelle [GJC]	ALAT EALAT, Le Luc	
3512	Aérospatiale SA.342M-1 Gazelle [GAC]	ALAT 1 RHC, Phalsbourg	
3530	Aérospatiale SA.342M-1 Gazelle [GAD]	ALAT 4 RHFS, Pau	
3567	Aérospatiale SA.342M Gazelle [GMA]	ALAT 4 RHFS, Pau	
3617	Aérospatiale SA.342M Gazelle [GND]	ALAT GAM/STAT, Valence	
3664	Aérospatiale SA.342M-1 Gazelle [GAF]	ALAT 5 RHC, Pau	
3848	Aérospatiale SA.342M-1 Gazelle [GAG]	ALAT 5 RHC, Pau	
3849	Aérospatiale SA.342M-1 Gazelle [GAH]	ALAT 5 RHC, Pau	
3850	Aérospatiale SA.342M-1 Gazelle [GAI]	ALAT 1 RHC, Phalsbourg	
3856	Aérospatiale SA.342M-1 Gazelle [GAJ]	ALAT 3 RHC, Etain	
3857	Aérospatiale SA.342M Gazelle [GJK]	ALAT, stored Marseille	
3859	Aérospatiale SA.342M-1 Gazelle [GAK]	ALAT 5 RHC, Pau	
3862	Aérospatiale SA.342M-1 Gazelle [GAL] $	ALAT 3 RHC, Etain	
3863	Aérospatiale SA.342M-1 Gazelle [GAM]	ALAT 3 RHC, Etain	
3865	Aérospatiale SA.342M-1 Gazelle [GAN]	ALAT EALAT, Le Luc	
3868	Aérospatiale SA.342M-1 Gazelle [GAO]	ALAT EALAT, Le Luc	
3911	Aérospatiale SA.342M-1 Gazelle [GAP]	ALAT 1 RHC, Phalsbourg	
3921	Aérospatiale SA.342M-1 Gazelle [GAQ]	ALAT EALAT, Le Luc	
3938	Aérospatiale SA.342M-1 Gazelle [GAR]	ALAT EALAT, Le Luc	
3947	Aérospatiale SA.342M-1 Gazelle [GAS]	ALAT 3 RHC, Etain	
3948	Aérospatiale SA.342M-1 Gazelle [GAT]	ALAT 1 RHC, Phalsbourg	
3957	Aérospatiale SA.342M-1 Gazelle [GAU]	ALAT 5 RHC, Pau	
3964	Aérospatiale SA.342M-1 Gazelle [GAV]	ALAT 3 RHC, Etain	
3996	Aérospatiale SA.342M-1 Gazelle [GAW]	ALAT 5 RHC, Pau	
4018	Aérospatiale SA.342M-1 Gazelle [GAX]	ALAT 4 RHFS, Pau	
4022	Aérospatiale SA.342M Gazelle [GJQ]	ALAT, stored Marseille	
4026	Aérospatiale SA.342M-1 Gazelle [GBA]	ALAT 1 RHC, Phalsbourg	
4034	Aérospatiale SA.342M-1 Gazelle [GBB]	ALAT 1 RHC, Phalsbourg	
4039	Aérospatiale SA.342M-1 Gazelle [GBC]	ALAT 3 RHC, Etain	
4042	Aérospatiale SA.342M Gazelle [GMB]	ALAT EALAT, Le Luc	

Notes	Serial	Type (code/other identity)	Owner/operator, location or fate
	4053	Aérospatiale SA.342M-1 Gazelle [GBE]	ALAT 3 RHC, Etain
	4059	Aérospatiale SA.342M-1 Gazelle [GBF]	ALAT 1 RHC, Phalsbourg
	4061	Aérospatiale SA.342M-1 Gazelle [GBG]	ALAT GAM/STAT, Valence
	4066	Aérospatiale SA.342M-1 Gazelle [GBH]	ALAT 3 RHC, Etain
	4071	Aérospatiale SA.342M Gazelle [GNS]	ALAT, stored Montauban
	4072	Aérospatiale SA.342M-1 Gazelle [GBI]	ALAT 3 RHC, Etain
	4079	Aérospatiale SA.342M-1 Gazelle [GMC]	ALAT EALAT, Le Luc
	4083	Aérospatiale SA.342M Gazelle [GNT]	ALAT, stored Marseille
	4084	Aérospatiale SA.342M-1 Gazelle [GBJ] $	ALAT 3 RHC, Etain
	4095	Aérospatiale SA.342M-1 Gazelle [GBL]	ALAT
	4109	Aérospatiale SA.342M-1 Gazelle [GBN]	ALAT
	4114	Aérospatiale SA.342M-1 Gazelle [GBO]	ALAT
	4115	Aérospatiale SA.342M-1 Gazelle [GBP]	ALAT
	4118	Aérospatiale SA.342M Gazelle [GNV]	ALAT, stored Marseille
	4119	Aérospatiale SA.342M-1 Gazelle [GBQ]	ALAT 1 RHC, Phalsbourg
	4120	Aérospatiale SA.342M-1 Gazelle [GBR]	ALAT EALAT, Le Luc
	4124	Aérospatiale SA.342M-1 Gazelle [GBS]	ALAT 1 RHC, Phalsbourg
	4136	Aérospatiale SA.342M-1 Gazelle [GBT]	ALAT
	4140	Aérospatiale SA.342M-1 Gazelle [GBU]	ALAT 5 RHC, Pau
	4141	Aérospatiale SA.342M-1 Gazelle [GBV]	ALAT
	4142	Aérospatiale SA.342M-1 Gazelle [GBW]	ALAT 5 RHC, Pau
	4144	Aérospatiale SA.342M-1 Gazelle [GBX]	ALAT 3 RHC, Etain
	4145	Aérospatiale SA.342M-1 Gazelle [GBY] $	ALAT 3 RHC, Etain
	4160	Aérospatiale SA.342M-1 Gazelle [GCC]	ALAT 3 RHC, Etain
	4161	Aérospatiale SA.342M-1 Gazelle [GCD]	ALAT 5 RHC, Pau
	4162	Aérospatiale SA.342M-1 Gazelle [GCE]	ALAT
	4164	Aérospatiale SA.342M-1 Gazelle [GCF]	ALAT
	4168	Aérospatiale SA.342M-1 Gazelle [GCG]	ALAT 5 RHC, Pau
	4175	Aérospatiale SA.342M-1 Gazelle [GCI]	ALAT 1 RHC, Phalsbourg
	4179	Aérospatiale SA.342M-1 Gazelle [GCJ]	ALAT 3 RHC, Etain
	4180	Aérospatiale SA.342M-1 Gazelle [GCK]	ALAT
	4181	Aérospatiale SA.342M-1 Gazelle [GCL]	ALAT 3 RHC, Etain
	4186	Aérospatiale SA.342M-1 Gazelle [GCM]	ALAT 3 RHC, Etain
	4189	Aérospatiale SA.342M-1 Gazelle [GCN]	ALAT
	4191	Aérospatiale SA.342M-1 Gazelle [GCO]	ALAT
	4195	Aérospatiale SA.342M-1 Gazelle [GCP]	ALAT 3 RHC, Etain
	4198	Aérospatiale SA.342M-1 Gazelle [GCQ]	ALAT 3 RHC, Etain
	4205	Aérospatiale SA.342Ma Gazelle [GEA]	ALAT 1 RHC, Phalsbourg
	4206	Aérospatiale SA.342Ma Gazelle [GEB]	ALAT
	4207	Aérospatiale SA.342Ma Gazelle [GEC]	ALAT 3 RHC, Etain
	4208	Aérospatiale SA.342Ma Gazelle [GED]	ALAT GAM/STAT, Valence
	4210	Aérospatiale SA.342Ma Gazelle [GEF]	ALAT
	4211	Aérospatiale SA.342Ma Gazelle [GEG]	ALAT
	4214	Aérospatiale SA.342Ma Gazelle [GEI]	ALAT EALAT, Le Luc
	4215	Aérospatiale SA.342Ma Gazelle [GEJ]	ALAT 4 RHFS, Pau
	4216	Aérospatiale SA.342Ma Gazelle [GEK]	ALAT 1 RHC, Phalsbourg
	4217	Aérospatiale SA.342Ma Gazelle [GEL]	ALAT
	4218	Aérospatiale SA.342Ma Gazelle [GEM]	ALAT
	4219	Aérospatiale SA.342Ma Gazelle [GEN]	ALAT 4 RHFS, Pau
	4220	Aérospatiale SA.342Ma Gazelle [GEO]	ALAT 3 RHC, Etain
	4221	Aérospatiale SA.342Ma Gazelle [GEP]	ALAT 3 RHC, Etain
	4222	Aérospatiale SA.342Ma Gazelle [GEQ]	ALAT EALAT, Le Luc
	4223	Aérospatiale SA.342Ma Gazelle [GER]	ALAT GAM/STAT, Valence
	4224	Aérospatiale SA.342Ma Gazelle [GES]	ALAT
	4225	Aérospatiale SA.342Ma Gazelle [GET]	ALAT 4 RHFS, Pau
	4226	Aérospatiale SA.342Ma Gazelle [GEU]	ALAT GAM/STAT, Valence
	4227	Aérospatiale SA.342Ma Gazelle [GEV]	ALAT 1 RHC, Phalsbourg
	4228	Aérospatiale SA.342Ma Gazelle [GEW]	ALAT 1 RHC, Phalsbourg
	4229	Aérospatiale SA.342Ma Gazelle [GEX]	ALAT 3 RHC, Etain
	4230	Aérospatiale SA.342Ma Gazelle [GEY]	ALAT GAM/STAT, Valence
	4232	Aérospatiale SA.342Ma Gazelle [GFA]	ALAT
	4233	Aérospatiale SA.342Ma Gazelle [GFB]	ALAT

Serial	Type (code/other identity)	Owner/operator, location or fate	Notes
2252	Aérospatiale AS.532UL Cougar [CGA]	ALAT GAM/STAT, Valence	
2266	Aérospatiale AS.532UL Cougar [CGB]	ALAT 5 RHC, Pau	
2267	Aérospatiale AS.532UL Cougar [CGC]	ALAT 4 RHFS, Pau	
2271	Aérospatiale AS.532UL Cougar [CGD]	ALAT	
2273	Aérospatiale AS.532UL Cougar [CGF]	ALAT	
2282	Aérospatiale AS.532UL Cougar [CGG]	ALAT	
2285	Aérospatiale AS.532UL Cougar [CGH]	ALAT	
2290	Aérospatiale AS.532UL Cougar [CGI]	ALAT 4 RHFS, Pau	
2293	Aérospatiale AS.532UL Cougar [CGJ]	ALAT 1 RHC, Phalsbourg	
2299	Aérospatiale AS.532UL Cougar [CGK]	ALAT 4 RHFS, Pau	
2300	Aérospatiale AS.532UL Cougar [CGL]	ALAT	
2301	Aérospatiale AS.532UL Cougar [CGM]	ALAT	
2303	Aérospatiale AS.532UL Cougar [CGN]	ALAT	
2316	Aérospatiale AS.532UL Cougar [CGO]	ALAT 1 RHC, Phalsbourg	
2323	Aérospatiale AS.532UL Cougar [CGQ]	ALAT 4 RHFS, Pau	
2324	Aérospatiale AS.532UL Cougar [CGR]	ALAT 4 RHFS, Pau	
2325	Aérospatiale AS.532UL Cougar [CGS]	ALAT	
2327	Aérospatiale AS.532UL Cougar [CGT]	ALAT	
2331	Aérospatiale AS.532UL Cougar [CGU]	ALAT	
2342	Aérospatiale AS.532UL Cougar [CHA]	ALAT 5 RHC, Pau	
2369	Aérospatiale AS.532UL Cougar [CHB]	ALAT	
2375	Aérospatiale AS.532UL Cougar [CHC]	ALAT 5 RHC, Pau	
2443	Aérospatiale AS.532UL Cougar [CGW]	ALAT 1 RHC, Phalsbourg	
2446	Aérospatiale AS.532UL Cougar [CGX]	ALAT 5 RHC, Pau	
2001	Eurocopter EC.665 Tigre HAP [BHH]	ALAT 5 RHC, Pau	
2002	Eurocopter EC.665 Tigre HAP [BHI]	ALAT 5 RHC, Pau	
2003	Eurocopter EC.665 Tigre HAP (F-ZWRM) [BHJ]	ALAT 5 RHC, Pau	
2004	Eurocopter EC.665 Tigre HAD [BHK]	Airbus Helicopters, Marseille (conversion)	
2006	Eurocopter EC.665 Tigre HAD [BHL]	Airbus Helicopters, Marseille (conversion)	
2009	Eurocopter EC.665 Tigre HAD [BHB]	Airbus Helicopters, Marseille (conversion)	
2010	Eurocopter EC.665 Tigre HAD [BHA]	ALAT 5 RHC, Pau	
2011	Eurocopter EC.665 Tigre HAD [BHM]	Airbus Helicopters, Marseille (conversion)	
2012	Eurocopter EC.665 Tigre HAP [BHT]	ALAT 5 RHC, Pau	
2013	Eurocopter EC.665 Tigre HAP [BHC]	ALAT 5 RHC, Pau	
2015	Eurocopter EC.665 Tigre HAD (F-ZKBO) [BHD]	ALAT 5 RHC, Pau	
2016	Eurocopter EC.665 Tigre HAD [BIA]	Airbus Helicopters, Marseille (conversion)	
2018	Eurocopter EC.665 Tigre HAP [BHE]	ALAT 5 RHC, Pau	
2019	Eurocopter EC.665 Tigre HAD [BHF]	Airbus Helicopters, Marseille (conversion)	
2021	Eurocopter EC.665 Tigre HAP [BHN]	ALAT 5 RHC, Pau	
2022	Eurocopter EC.665 Tigre HAP [BHG]	ALAT 5 RHC, Pau	
2023	Eurocopter EC.665 Tigre HAD [BHP]	Airbus Helicopters, Marseille (conversion)	
2024	Eurocopter EC.665 Tigre HAD [BHO]	Airbus Helicopters, Marseille (conversion)	
2025	Eurocopter EC.665 Tigre HAD [BHQ]	ALAT 5 RHC, Pau	
2026	Eurocopter EC.665 Tigre HAD (F-ZKBA) [BHR]	Airbus Helicopters, Marseille (conversion)	
2027	Eurocopter EC.665 Tigre HAD [BHS]	Airbus Helicopters, Marseille (conversion)	
2029	Eurocopter EC.665 Tigre HAD [BHV]	ALAT EFA, Le Luc	
2030	Eurocopter EC.665 Tigre HAP [BHW]	ALAT 4 RHFS, Pau	
2031	Eurocopter EC.665 Tigre HAP [BHX]	ALAT 4 RHFS, Pau	
2033	Eurocopter EC.665 Tigre HAD [BHZ]	ALAT EFA, Le Luc	
2034	Eurocopter EC.665 Tigre HAP [BIB]	ALAT 4 RHFS, Pau	
2035	Eurocopter EC.665 Tigre HAD [BIC]	Airbus Helicopters, Marseille (conversion)	
2037	Eurocopter EC.665 Tigre HAP [BIE]	ALAT 5 RHC, Pau	
2038	Eurocopter EC.665 Tigre HAD [BIF]	ALAT 1 RHC, Phalsbourg	
2039	Eurocopter EC.665 Tigre HAD [BIG]	Airbus Helicopters, Marseille (conversion)	
2040	Eurocopter EC.665 Tigre HAD [BIH]	ALAT 4 RHFS, Pau	
2041	Eurocopter EC.665 Tigre HAP [BII]	ALAT 4 RHFS, Pau	
2042	Eurocopter EC.665 Tigre HAD [BIJ]	Airbus Helicopters, Marseille (conversion)	
2043	Eurocopter EC.665 Tigre HAP [BIK]	ALAT 4 RHFS, Pau	
2044	Eurocopter EC.665 Tigre HAD [BIL]	Airbus Helicopters, Marseille (conversion)	
2045	Eurocopter EC.665 Tigre HAP [BIM]	ALAT 4 RHFS, Pau	
2046	Eurocopter EC.665 Tigre HAD [BIN]	Airbus Helicopters, Marseille (conversion)	
2047	Eurocopter EC.665 Tigre HAP [BIO]	ALAT (on order)	

Notes	Serial	Type (code/other identity)	Owner/operator, location or fate
	6001	Eurocopter EC.665 Tigre HAD [BJA]	ALAT EFA, Le Luc
	6002	Eurocopter EC.665 Tigre HAD [BJB]	ALAT 5 RHC, Pau
	6003	Eurocopter EC.665 Tigre HAD [BJC]	ALAT EFA, Le Luc
	6004	Eurocopter EC.665 Tigre HAD [BJD]	ALAT 4 RHFS, Pau
	6005	Eurocopter EC.665 Tigre HAD [BJE]	ALAT 5 RHC, Pau
	6006	Eurocopter EC.665 Tigre HAD [BJF]	ALAT 1 RHC, Phalsbourg
	6007	Eurocopter EC.665 Tigre HAD [BJG]	ALAT EFA, Le Luc
	6008	Eurocopter EC.665 Tigre HAD [BJH]	ALAT 1 RHC, Phalsbourg
	6009	Eurocopter EC.665 Tigre HAD [BJI]	ALAT EFA, Le Luc
	6010	Eurocopter EC.665 Tigre HAD [BJJ]	ALAT 4 RHFS, Pau
	6011	Eurocopter EC.665 Tigre HAD [BJK]	ALAT 1 RHC, Phalsbourg
	6012	Eurocopter EC.665 Tigre HAD [BJL]	ALAT 1 RHC, Phalsbourg
	6013	Eurocopter EC.665 Tigre HAD [BJM]	ALAT EFA, Le Luc
	6014	Eurocopter EC.665 Tigre HAD [BJN]	ALAT EFA, Le Luc
	6015	Eurocopter EC.665 Tigre HAD [BJO]	ALAT 1 RHC, Phalsbourg
	6016	Eurocopter EC.665 Tigre HAD [BJP]	ALAT GAM/STAT, Valence
	6018	Eurocopter EC.665 Tigre HAD [BJR]	ALAT 1 RHC, Phalsbourg
	6019	Eurocopter EC.665 Tigre HAD [BJS]	ALAT 1 RHC, Phalsbourg
	6020	Eurocopter EC.665 Tigre HAD [BJT]	ALAT 1 RHC, Phalsbourg
	6021	Eurocopter EC.665 Tigre HAD [BJU]	ALAT 4 RHFS, Pau
	6022	Eurocopter EC.665 Tigre HAD (F-ZWDM) [BJV]	Airbus Helicopters, Marseille
	6023	Eurocopter EC.665 Tigre HAD [BJW]	ALAT EFA, Le Luc
	6024	Eurocopter EC.665 Tigre HAD [BJX]	ALAT 1 RHC, Phalsbourg
	6025	Eurocopter EC.665 Tigre HAD [BJY]	ALAT 1 RHC, Phalsbourg
	6026	Eurocopter EC.665 Tigre HAD [BJZ]	Airbus Helicopters, Marseille
	6027	Eurocopter EC.665 Tigre HAD [BKA]	Airbus Helicopters, Marseille
	6028	Eurocopter EC.665 Tigre HAD [BKB]	ALAT 1 RHC, Phalsbourg
	6029	Eurocopter EC.665 Tigre HAD [BKC]	ALAT 1 RHC, Phalsbourg
	6030	Eurocopter EC.665 Tigre HAD [BKD]	ALAT 5 RHC, Pau
	6031	Eurocopter EC.665 Tigre HAD [BKE]	ALAT 5 RHC, Pau
	2611	Eurocopter EC.725AP Caracal [CAA]	ALAT 4 RHFS, Pau
	2628	Eurocopter EC.725AP Caracal [CAB]	ALAT, *Airbus Helicopters, Marseille, Oct 2022*
	2630	Eurocopter EC.725AP Caracal [CAC]	ALAT 4 RHFS, Pau
	2631	Eurocopter EC.725AP Caracal [CAD]	ALAT 4 RHFS, Pau
	2633	Eurocopter EC.725AP Caracal [CAE]	ALAT 4 RHFS, Pau
	2638	Eurocopter EC.725AP Caracal [CAF]	ALAT
	2640	Eurocopter EC.725AP Caracal [CAG]	ALAT
	2642	Eurocopter EC.725AP Caracal [CAH]	ALAT
	1239	NH Industries NH.90-TTH Caïman [EAA]	ALAT CFIA NH.90, Le Luc
	1256	NH Industries NH.90-TTH Caïman [EAB]	ALAT
	1271	NH Industries NH.90-TTH Caïman [EAC]	ALAT CFIA NH.90, Le Luc
	1273	NH Industries NH.90-TTH Caïman [EAD]	ALAT 1 RHC, Phalsbourg
	1290	NH Industries NH.90-TTH Caïman [EAE]	ALAT, *Airbus Helicopters, Marseille, Nov 2021*
	1291	NH Industries NH.90-TTH Caïman [EAF]	ALAT 1 RHC, Phalsbourg
	1292	NH Industries NH.90-TTH Caïman [EAG]	ALAT 1 RHC, Phalsbourg
	1293	NH Industries NH.90-TTH Caïman [EAH]	ALAT CFIA NH.90, Le Luc
	1294	NH Industries NH.90-TTH Caïman [EAI]	ALAT 1 RHC, Phalsbourg
	1295	NH Industries NH.90-TTH Caïman [EAJ]	ALAT
	1306	NH Industries NH.90-TTH Caïman [EAK]	ALAT
	1307	NH Industries NH.90-TTH Caïman [EAL]	ALAT 1 RHC, Phalsbourg
	1308	NH Industries NH.90-TTH Caïman [EAM]	ALAT
	1309	NH Industries NH.90-TTH Caïman [EAN]	ALAT
	1310	NH Industries NH.90-TTH Caïman [EAO]	ALAT 1 RHC, Phalsbourg
	1311	NH Industries NH.90-TTH Caïman [EAP]	ALAT 1 RHC, Phalsbourg
	1312	NH Industries NH.90-TTH Caïman [EAQ]	ALAT 1 RHC, Phalsbourg
	1313	NH Industries NH.90-TTH Caïman [EAR]	ALAT 1 RHC, Phalsbourg
	1332	NH Industries NH.90-TTH Caïman [EAS]	ALAT 1 RHC, Phalsbourg (damaged)
	1333	NH Industries NH.90-TTH Caïman [EAT]	ALAT
	1334	NH Industries NH.90-TTH Caïman [EAU]	ALAT 1 RHC, Phalsbourg
	1335	NH Industries NH.90-TTH Caïman [EAV]	ALAT 1 RHC, Phalsbourg
	1336	NH Industries NH.90-TTH Caïman [EAW]	ALAT
	1337	NH Industries NH.90-TTH Caïman [EAX]	ALAT 1 RHC, Phalsbourg

Serial	Type (code/other identity)	Owner/operator, location or fate	Notes
1338	NH Industries NH.90-TTH Caïman [EAY]	ALAT 1 RHC, Phalsbourg	
1386	NH Industries NH.90-TTH Caïman [EAZ]	ALAT	
1387	NH Industries NH.90-TTH Caïman [EBC]	ALAT 1 RHC, Phalsbourg	
1390	NH Industries NH.90-TTH Caïman [EBA]	ALAT 1 RHC, Phalsbourg	
1391	NH Industries NH.90-TTH Caïman [EBB]	ALAT 1 RHC, Phalsbourg	
1392	NH Industries NH.90-TTH Caïman [EBD]	ALAT 1 RHC, Phalsbourg	
1401	NH Industries NH.90-TTH Caïman [EBE]	ALAT 5 RHC, Pau	
1402	NH Industries NH.90-TTH Caïman [EBF]	ALAT 1 RHC, Phalsbourg	
1403	NH Industries NH.90-TTH Caïman [EBG]	ALAT	
1404	NH Industries NH.90-TTH Caïman [EBH]	ALAT 1 RHC, Phalsbourg	
1405	NH Industries NH.90-TTH Caïman [EBI]	ALAT 5 RHC, Pau	
1427	NH Industries NH.90-TTH Caïman [EBK]	ALAT 5 RHC, Pau	
1428	NH Industries NH.90-TTH Caïman [EBL]	ALAT 5 RHC, Pau	
1429	NH Industries NH.90-TTH Caïman [EBM]	ALAT 5 RHC, Pau	
1430	NH Industries NH.90-TTH Caïman [EBO]	ALAT	
1431	NH Industries NH.90-TTH Caïman [EBP]	ALAT 1 RHC, Phalsbourg	
1432	NH Industries NH.90-TTH Caïman [EBJ]	ALAT 5 RHC, Pau	
1433	NH Industries NH.90-TTH Caïman [EBN]	ALAT 5 RHC, Pau	
1441	NH Industries NH.90-TTH Caïman [EBR]	ALAT (on order)	
1442	NH Industries NH.90-TTH Caïman [EBQ]	ALAT (on order)	
1443	NH Industries NH.90-TTH Caïman [EBS]	ALAT 5 RHC, Pau	
1454	NH Industries NH.90-TTH Caïman [EBT]	ALAT 5 RHC, Pau	
1455	NH Industries NH.90-TTH Caïman [EBU]	ALAT 1 RHC, Phalsbourg	
1456	NH Industries NH.90-TTH Caïman (F-ZKCE) [EBV]	ALAT (on order)	
1457	NH Industries NH.90-TTH Caïman [EBW]	ALAT 5 RHC, Pau	
1458	NH Industries NH.90-TTH Caïman [EBX]	ALAT (on order)	
1479	NH Industries NH.90-TTH Caïman (F-ZKBT) [EBY]	ALAT (on order)	
1480	NH Industries NH.90-TTH Caïman (F-ZWBW) [EBZ]	ALAT (on order)	
1481	NH Industries NH.90-TTH Caïman (F-ZKCG) [ECA]	ALAT (on order)	
1482	NH Industries NH.90-TTH Caïman (F-ZKBC) [ECB]	ALAT (on order)	
1483	NH Industries NH.90-TTH Caïman (F-ZKBV) [ECC]	ALAT (on order)	
1484	NH Industries NH.90-TTH Caïman (F-ZKBB) [ECD]	ALAT (on order)	
1496	NH Industries NH.90-TTH Caïman [ECF]	ALAT (on order)	
887	Pilatus PC-6B/B2-H4 Turbo Porter [MCA]	ALAT 1 GSALAT, Montauban	
888	Pilatus PC-6B/B2-H4 Turbo Porter [MCB]	ALAT 1 GSALAT, Montauban	
889	Pilatus PC-6B/B2-H4 Turbo Porter [MCC]	ALAT 1 GSALAT, Montauban	
890	Pilatus PC-6B/B2-H4 Turbo Porter [MCD]	ALAT 1 GSALAT, Montauban	
891	Pilatus PC-6B/B2-H4 Turbo Porter [MCE]	ALAT 1 GSALAT, Montauban	
80	SOCATA TBM 700A [ABY]	ALAT EAAT, Rennes	
99	SOCATA TBM 700A [ABO]	ALAT EAAT, Rennes	
100	SOCATA TBM 700A [ABP]	ALAT EAAT, Rennes	
115	SOCATA TBM 700A [ABQ]	ALAT EAAT, Rennes	
136	SOCATA TBM 700A [ABR]	ALAT EAAT, Rennes	
139	SOCATA TBM 700A [ABS]	ALAT EAAT, Rennes	
156	SOCATA TBM 700B [ABT]	ALAT EAAT, Rennes	
159	SOCATA TBM 700B [ABU]	ALAT EAAT, Rennes	
160	SOCATA TBM 700B [ABV]	ALAT EAAT, Rennes	

French Government

Note: The main base and maintenance centre for the Sécurité Civile fleet is Nimes, with helicopters placed on "détachements saisonniers" across France through the summer months

JBA	Eurocopter EC.145C-1 (9008)	Gendarmerie	
JBC	Eurocopter EC.145C-1 (9018)	Gendarmerie	
JBD	Eurocopter EC.145C-1 (9019)	Gendarmerie	
JBE	Eurocopter EC.145C-1 (9025)	Gendarmerie	
JBF	Eurocopter EC.145C-2 (9035)	Gendarmerie	
JBG	Eurocopter EC.145C-2 (9036)	Gendarmerie	
JBH	Eurocopter EC.145C-2 (9037)	Gendarmerie	
JBI	Eurocopter EC.145C-2 (9127)	Gendarmerie	
JBJ	Eurocopter EC.145C-2 (9140)	Gendarmerie	
JBK	Eurocopter EC.145C-2 (9162)	Gendarmerie	
JBM	Eurocopter EC.145C-2 (9113)	Gendarmerie	
JBO	Eurocopter EC.145C-2 (9124)	Gendarmerie	

Notes	Serial	Type (code/other identity)	Owner/operator, location or fate
	JBR	Eurocopter EC.145C-2 (9169)	Gendarmerie
	JBT	Eurocopter EC.145C-2 (9173)	Gendarmerie
	JBU	Eurocopter EC.145C-2 (9700)	Gendarmerie
	JCA	*Aérospatiale AS.350BA Ecureuil (1028)*	*Instructional airframe, Rochefort-Soubise*
	JCB	Aérospatiale AS.350BA Ecureuil (1574)	Gendarmerie
	JCD	Aérospatiale AS.350BA Ecureuil (1576)	Gendarmerie
	JCE	Aérospatiale AS.350B-2 Ecureuil (1812)	Gendarmerie
	JCF	Aérospatiale AS.350B-2 Ecureuil (1691)	Gendarmerie
	JCI	Aérospatiale AS.350B-2 Ecureuil (2222)	Gendarmerie
	JCK	Aérospatiale AS.350BA Ecureuil (1953)	Gendarmerie
	JCM	Aérospatiale AS.350BA Ecureuil (1952)	Gendarmerie
	JCN	Aérospatiale AS.350BA Ecureuil (2044)	Gendarmerie
	JCO	Aérospatiale AS.350BA Ecureuil (1917)	Gendarmerie
	JCP	Aérospatiale AS.350BA Ecureuil (2045)	Gendarmerie
	JCQ	Aérospatiale AS.350BA Ecureuil (2057)	Gendarmerie
	JCR	Aérospatiale AS.350BA Ecureuil (2088)	Gendarmerie
	JCS	Aérospatiale AS.350B-2 Ecureuil (1575)	Gendarmerie
	JCT	Aérospatiale AS.350BA Ecureuil (2104)	Gendarmerie
	JCU	Aérospatiale AS.350BA Ecureuil (2117)	Gendarmerie
	JCV	Aérospatiale AS.350BA Ecureuil (2118)	Gendarmerie
	JCW	Aérospatiale AS.350BA Ecureuil (2218)	Gendarmerie
	JCX	Aérospatiale AS.350BA Ecureuil (2219)	Gendarmerie
	JCY	Aérospatiale AS.350BA Ecureuil (2221)	Gendarmerie
	JCZ	Aérospatiale AS.350BA Ecureuil (1467) $	Gendarmerie
	JDA	Eurocopter EC.135T-2 (0642)	Gendarmerie
	JDB	Eurocopter EC.135T-2 (0654)	Gendarmerie
	JDC	Eurocopter EC.135T-2 (0717)	Gendarmerie
	JDD	Eurocopter EC.135T-2 (0727)	Gendarmerie
	JDE	Eurocopter EC.135T-2 (0747)	Gendarmerie
	JDF	Eurocopter EC.135T-2 (0757)	Gendarmerie
	JDG	Eurocopter EC.135T-2 (0772)	Gendarmerie
	JDH	Eurocopter EC.135T-2 (0787)	Gendarmerie
	JDI	Eurocopter EC.135T-2 (0797)	Gendarmerie
	JDJ	Eurocopter EC.135T-2 (0806)	Gendarmerie
	JDK	Eurocopter EC.135T-2 (0857)	Gendarmerie
	JDL	Eurocopter EC.135T-2 (0867)	Gendarmerie
	JDM	Eurocopter EC.135T-2 (1055)	Gendarmerie
	JDN	Eurocopter EC.135T-2 (1058)	Gendarmerie
	JDO	Eurocopter EC.135T-2 (1086)	Gendarmerie
	JED	Aérospatiale AS.350B-2 Ecureuil (2096)	Gendarmerie
	JEE	Aérospatiale AS.350B-2 Ecureuil (2423)	Gendarmerie
	JEF	Aérospatiale AS.350B-2 Ecureuil (2225)	Gendarmerie
	F-ZBAD	Aérospatiale AS.355F-2 Twin Ecureuil	Douanes Françaises
	F-ZBCE	Cessna F.406 Caravan II (0042)	*Withdrawn from use*
	F-ZBCG	Cessna F.406 Caravan II (0066)	*Withdrawn from use, Bordeaux*
	F-ZBEF	Aérospatiale AS.355F-1 Twin Ecureuil	Douanes Françaises
	F-ZBEG	Canadair CL-415 [39]	Sécurité Civile, Nîmes/Garons
	F-ZBEK	Aérospatiale AS.355F-1 Twin Ecureuil	Douanes Françaises
	F-ZBEL	Aérospatiale AS.355F-1 Twin Ecureuil	Douanes Françaises
	F-ZBEU	Canadair CL-415 [42]	Sécurité Civile, Nîmes/Garons
	F-ZBFJ	Beech Super King Air B200 [98]	Sécurité Civile, Nîmes/Garons
	F-ZBFK	Beech Super King Air B200 [96]	Sécurité Civile, Nîmes/Garons
	F-ZBFN	Canadair CL-415 [33]	Sécurité Civile, Nîmes/Garons
	F-ZBFP	Canadair CL-415 [31]	Sécurité Civile, Nîmes/Garons
	F-ZBFS	Canadair CL-415 [32] $	Sécurité Civile, Nîmes/Garons
	F-ZBFV	Canadair CL-415 [37]	Sécurité Civile, Nîmes/Garons
	F-ZBFW	Canadair CL-415 [38]	Sécurité Civile, Nîmes/Garons
	F-ZBFX	Canadair CL-415 [34]	Sécurité Civile, Nîmes/Garons
	F-ZBFY	Canadair CL-415 [35]	Sécurité Civile, Nîmes/Garons
	F-ZBGA	Cessna F.406 Caravan II (0086)	*Withdrawn from use*
	F-ZBGD	Cessna F.406 Caravan II (0090)	*Withdrawn from use*
	F-ZBGF	Eurocopter EC.135T-2	Douanes Françaises

Serial	Type (code/other identity)	Owner/operator, location or fate	Notes
F-ZBGG	Eurocopter EC.135T-2	Douanes Françaises	
F-ZBGH	Eurocopter EC.135T-2	Douanes Françaises	
F-ZBGI	Eurocopter EC.135T-2	Douanes Françaises	
F-ZBGJ	Eurocopter EC.135T-2	Douanes Françaises	
F-ZBGK	Hawker Beechcraft King Air B350ER (FL-682)	Douanes Françaises	
F-ZBGL	Hawker Beechcraft King Air B350ER (FL-746)	Douanes Françaises	
F-ZBGM	Hawker Beechcraft King Air B350ER (FL-752)	Douanes Françaises	
F-ZBGN	Hawker Beechcraft King Air B350ER (FL-781)	Douanes Françaises	
F-ZBGO	Hawker Beechcraft King Air B350ER (FL-800)	Douanes Françaises	
F-ZBGP	Hawker Beechcraft King Air B350ER (FL-802)	Douanes Françaises	
F-ZBGQ	Hawker Beechcraft King Air B350ER (FL-777)	Douanes Françaises	
F-ZBGR	Hawker Beechcraft King Air B350ER	Douanes Francaises (on order)	
F-ZBMB	Beech Super King Air B200 [97]	Sécurité Civile, Nîmes/Garons	
F-ZBMC	De Havilland Canada DHC-8-Q401MR [73]	Sécurité Civile, Nîmes/Garons	
F-ZBMD	De Havilland Canada DHC-8-Q401MR [74]	Sécurité Civile, Nîmes/Garons	
F-ZBME	Canadair CL-415 [44]	Sécurité Civile, Nîmes/Garons	
F-ZBMF	Canadair CL-415 [45]	Sécurité Civile, Nîmes/Garons	
F-ZBMG	Canadair CL-415 [48]	Sécurité Civile, Nîmes/Garons	
F-ZBMH	De Havilland Canada DHC-8-Q402MR [75]	Sécurité Civile, Nîmes/Garons	
F-ZBMI	De Havilland Canada DHC-8-Q402MR [76]	Sécurité Civile, Nîmes/Garons	
F-ZBMJ	De Havilland Canada DHC-8-Q402MR [77]	Sécurité Civile, Nîmes/Garons	
F-ZBMK	De Havilland Canada DHC-8-Q402MR [78]	Sécurité Civile, Nîmes/Garons	
F-ZBML	De Havilland Canada DHC-8-Q402MR [79]	Sécurité Civile, Nîmes/Garons	
F-ZBMM	De Havilland Canada DHC-8-Q402MR (C-GUKH) [80]	Sécurité Civile (on order)	
F-ZBPA	Eurocopter EC.145C-1	Sécurité Civile	
F-ZBPD	Eurocopter EC.145C-1	Sécurité Civile	
F-ZBPF	Eurocopter EC.145C-1	Sécurité Civile	
F-ZBPG	Eurocopter EC.145C-1	Sécurité Civile	
F-ZBPH	Eurocopter EC.145C-1	Sécurité Civile	
F-ZBPI	Eurocopter EC.145C-1	Sécurité Civile	
F-ZBPJ	Eurocopter EC.145C-1	Sécurité Civile	
F-ZBPK	Eurocopter EC.145C-1	Sécurité Civile	
F-ZBPL	Eurocopter EC.145C-1	Sécurité Civile	
F-ZBPM	Eurocopter EC.145C-1	Sécurité Civile	
F-ZBPN	Eurocopter EC.145C-1	Sécurité Civile	
F-ZBPO	Eurocopter EC.145C-1	Sécurité Civile	
F-ZBPP	Eurocopter EC.145C-2	Sécurité Civile	
F-ZBPQ	Eurocopter EC.145C-2	Sécurité Civile	
F-ZBPS	Eurocopter EC.145C-2	Sécurité Civile	
F-ZBPT	Eurocopter EC.145C-2	Sécurité Civile	
F-ZBPU	Eurocopter EC.145C-2	Sécurité Civile	
F-ZBPV	Eurocopter EC.145C-2	Sécurité Civile	
F-ZBPW	Eurocopter EC.145C-2	Sécurité Civile	
F-ZBPX	Eurocopter EC.145C-2	Sécurité Civile	
F-ZBPY	Eurocopter EC.145C-2	Sécurité Civile	
F-ZBPZ	Eurocopter EC.145C-2	Sécurité Civile	
F-ZBQA	Eurocopter EC.145C-2	Sécurité Civile	
F-ZBQB	Eurocopter EC.145C-2	Sécurité Civile	
F-ZBQC	Eurocopter EC.145C-2	Sécurité Civile	
F-ZBQD	Eurocopter EC.145C-2	Sécurité Civile	
F-ZBQE	Eurocopter EC.145C-2	Sécurité Civile	
F-ZBQF	Eurocopter EC.145C-2	Sécurité Civile	
F-ZBQH	Eurocopter EC.145C-2	Sécurité Civile	
F-ZBQI	Eurocopter EC.145C-2	Sécurité Civile	
F-ZBQJ	Eurocopter EC.145C-2	Sécurité Civile	
F-ZBQK	Eurocopter EC.145C-2	Sécurité Civile	
F-ZBQL	Eurocopter EC.145C-2	Sécurité Civile	
F-ZBQM	Airbus H.145	Sécurité Civile	
F-ZBQN	Airbus H.145	Sécurité Civile	
F-ZBQO	Airbus H.145	Sécurité Civile	
F-ZBQP	Airbus H.145	Sécurité Civile	

Notes	Serial	Type (code/other identity)	Owner/operator, location or fate
	Civil operated aircraft in military use		
	F-GJDB	Dassault Falcon 20C	AVDEF, Nîmes/Garons
	F-GKCI	Cirrus SR.22	CATS/CFAMI 05.312, Salon de Provence
	F-GPAA	Dassault Falcon 20ECM	AVDEF, Nîmes/Garons
	F-GPAD	Dassault Falcon 20E	AVDEF, Nîmes/Garons
	F-GUKA	Grob G120A-F	CATS/EAC 00.315, Cognac
	F-GUKB	Grob G120A-F	CATS/EAC 00.315, Cognac
	F-GUKC	Grob G120A-F	CATS/EAC 00.315, Cognac
	F-GUKD	Grob G120A-F	CATS/EAC 00.315, Cognac
	F-GUKE	Grob G120A-F	CATS/EAC 00.315, Cognac
	F-GUKF	Grob G120A-F	CATS/EAC 00.315, Cognac
	F-GUKG	Grob G120A-F	CATS/EAC 00.315, Cognac
	F-GUKH	Grob G120A-F	CATS/EAC 00.315, Cognac
	F-GUKI	Grob G120A-F	CATS/EAC 00.315, Cognac
	F-GUKJ	Grob G120A-F	CATS/EAC 00.315, Cognac
	F-GUKK	Grob G120A-F	CATS/EAC 00.315, Cognac
	F-GUKL	Grob G120A-F	CATS/EAC 00.315, Cognac
	F-GUKM	Grob G120A-F	CATS/EAC 00.315, Cognac
	F-GUKN	Grob G120A-F	CATS/EAC 00.315, Cognac
	F-GUKO	Grob G120A-F	CATS/EAC 00.315, Cognac
	F-GUKP	Grob G120A-F	CATS/EAC 00.315, Cognac
	F-GUKR	Grob G120A-F	CATS/EAC 00.315, Cognac
	F-GUKS	Grob G120A-F	CATS/EAC 00.315, Cognac
	F-HAVD	BAE Jetstream 41	AVDEF, Nîmes/Garons
	F-HAVF	BAE Jetstream 41	AVDEF, Nîmes/Garons
	F-HDHN	Eurocopter AS.365N-3 Dauphin	AN 34 Flottille/ESHE, Lanvéoc/Poulmic
	F-HGHN	Eurocopter AS.365N-3 Dauphin	AN 34 Flottille/ESHE, Lanvéoc/Poulmic
	F-HGDU	Cirrus SR.20	CATS/CFAMI 05.312, Salon de Provence
	F-HKCA	Cirrus SR.22	CATS/CFAMI 05.312, Salon de Provence
	F-HKCB	Cirrus SR.20	CATS/CFAMI 05.312, Salon de Provence
	F-HKCC	Cirrus SR.22	CATS/CFAMI 05.312, Salon de Provence
	F-HKCD	Cirrus SR.20	CATS/CFAMI 05.312, Salon de Provence
	F-HKCE	Cirrus SR.20	CATS/CFAMI 05.312, Salon de Provence
	F-HKCF	Cirrus SR.22	CATS/CFAMI 05.312, Salon de Provence
	F-HKCG	Cirrus SR.20	CATS/CFAMI 05.312, Salon de Provence
	F-HKCH	Cirrus SR.20	CATS/CFAMI 05.312, Salon de Provence
	F-HKCI	Cirrus SR.22	CATS/CFAMI 05.312, Salon de Provence
	F-HKCJ	Cirrus SR.20	CATS/CFAMI 05.312, Salon de Provence
	F-HKCK	Cirrus SR.20	CATS/CFAMI 05.312, Salon de Provence
	F-HKCL	Cirrus SR.22	CATS/CFAMI 05.312, Salon de Provence
	F-HKCN	Cirrus SR.20	CATS/CFAMI 05.312, Salon de Provence
	F-HKCO	Cirrus SR.22	CATS/CFAMI 05.312, Salon de Provence
	F-HKCP	Cirrus SR.20	CATS/CFAMI 05.312, Salon de Provence
	F-HKCQ	Cirrus SR.20	CATS/CFAMI 05.312, Salon de Provence
	F-HKCT	Cirrus SR.20	CATS/CFAMI 05.312, Salon de Provence
	F-HKCU	Cirrus SR.20	CATS/CFAMI 05.312, Salon de Provence
	F-HKCV	Cirrus SR.20	CATS/CFAMI 05.312, Salon de Provence
	F-HKCX	Cirrus SR.20	CATS/CFAMI 05.312, Salon de Provence
	F-HKCY	Cirrus SR.22	CATS/CFAMI 05.312, Salon de Provence
	F-HKCZ	Cirrus SR.22	CATS/CFAMI 05.312, Salon de Provence
	F-HNHN	Eurocopter AS.365N-3 Dauphin	AN 34 Flottille/ESHE, Lanvéoc/Poulmic
	F-HOHN	Eurocopter AS.365N-3 Dauphin	AN 34 Flottille/ESHE, Lanvéoc/Poulmic
	F-HYHN	Eurocopter AS.365N-3 Dauphin	AN 34 Flottille/ESHE, Lanvéoc/Poulmic
	GABON		
	TR-KGM	Gulfstream Aerospace G.650ER	Gabonese Government, Libreville
	TR-KPR	Boeing 777-236	Gabonese Government, stored Basel
	TR-KSP	Grumman G.1159C Gulfstream IVSP	Gabonese Government, Libreville

GERMANY

Please note that German serials do not officially include the '+' part in them but aircraft wearing German markings are often painted with a cross in the middle, which is why it is included here.

TLG 33, normally based at Buchel, has moved to Norvenich until 2026 whilst Buchel is upgraded to receive the recently-ordered F-35, and as a result the base for TLG 33 is shown here as Norvenich. In a similar vein, TLG 71 moved from Wittmund to Laage in January 2022 while major work is undertaken at the former base. This move will last for up to three years and consequently the base for TLG 71 is shown as Laage in this edition.

Luftwaffe, Marineflieger & Heeresfliegertruppe (Heer)

Serial	Type (code/other identity)	Owner/operator, location or fate	Notes
10+01	Airbus A350-941 (F-WZGL)	Luftwaffe 1/FBS, Köln-Bonn	
10+02	Airbus A350-941 (F-WZHF/D-AKAY)	Luftwaffe (on order)	
10+03	Airbus A350-941 (D-AGAF)	Luftwaffe 1/FBS, Köln-Bonn	
14+02	Bombardier Global 5000	Luftwaffe 3/FBS, Köln-Bonn	
14+03	Bombardier Global 5000	Luftwaffe 3/FBS, Köln-Bonn	
14+04	Bombardier Global 5000	Luftwaffe 3/FBS, Köln-Bonn	
14+05	Bombardier Global 6000 (C-GDRL)	Luftwaffe 3/FBS, Köln-Bonn	
14+06	Bombardier Global 6000 (C-GEVP)	Luftwaffe 3/FBS, Köln-Bonn	
14+07	Bombardier Global 6000 (C-GEVX)	Luftwaffe 3/FBS, Köln-Bonn	
14+08	Bombardier Global 6000 (D-AEND)	Luftwaffe (on order)	
15+01	Airbus A.319CJ-115X	Luftwaffe 3/FBS, Köln-Bonn	
15+02	Airbus A.319CJ-115X	Luftwaffe 3/FBS, Köln-Bonn	
15+03	Airbus A.319CJ-133X (98+11)	Luftwaffe 3/FBS, Köln-Bonn	
15+04	Airbus A.321-231 (D-AISE/98+10)	Luftwaffe 3/FBS, Köln-Bonn	
15+10	Airbus A.321-251NX (D-AVXU)	Luftwaffe 3/FBS, Köln-Bonn	
15+11	Airbus A.321-251NX (D-AYAA)	Luftwaffe 3/FBS, Köln-Bonn	
16+01	Airbus A.340-313X	Luftwaffe 3/FBS, Köln-Bonn	
16+02	Airbus A.340-313X	Luftwaffe 3/FBS, Köln-Bonn	
30+01	Eurofighter EF.2000GT	Luftwaffe TLG 73 *Steinhoff*, Laage	
30+02	Eurofighter EF.2000GT	Luftwaffe TLG 73 *Steinhoff*, Laage	
30+03	Eurofighter EF.2000GT	Luftwaffe TLG 74 *Molders*, Neuburg/Donau	
30+04	Eurofighter EF.2000GT	*Instructional airframe, Jever*	
30+05	Eurofighter EF.2000GT	Luftwaffe TLG 31 *Boelcke*, Nörvenich	
30+06	Eurofighter EF.2000GS	Luftwaffe TLG 71 *Richthofen*, Laage	
30+07	Eurofighter EF.2000GS	Luftwaffe TLG 71 *Richthofen*, Laage	
30+09	Eurofighter EF.2000GS	Luftwaffe TAubZLwSüd, Kaufbeuren	
30+10	Eurofighter EF.2000GT	Luftwaffe TLG 73 *Steinhoff*, Laage	
30+11	Eurofighter EF.2000GS	Luftwaffe TLG 71 *Richthofen*, Laage	
30+12	Eurofighter EF.2000GS	Luftwaffe TLG 71 *Richthofen*, Laage	
30+14	Eurofighter EF.2000GT	Luftwaffe TLG 31 *Boelcke*, Nörvenich	
30+15	Eurofighter EF.2000GS	Luftwaffe TLG 74 *Molders*, Neuburg/Donau	
30+17	Eurofighter EF.2000GT	Luftwaffe TLG 73 *Steinhoff*, Laage	
30+20	Eurofighter EF.2000GT	Luftwaffe TLG 73 *Steinhoff*, Laage	
30+22	Eurofighter EF.2000GS	Luftwaffe TLG 74 *Molders*, Neuburg/Donau	
30+23	Eurofighter EF.2000GS	Luftwaffe TLG 31 *Boelcke*, Nörvenich	
30+24	Eurofighter EF.2000GT	Luftwaffe TLG 73 *Steinhoff*, Laage	
30+28	Eurofighter EF.2000GS	Luftwaffe TLG 71 *Richthofen*, Laage	
30+29	Eurofighter EF.2000GS	Luftwaffe TLG 71 *Richthofen*, Laage	
30+30	Eurofighter EF.2000GS	Luftwaffe TLG 71 *Richthofen*, Laage	
30+31	Eurofighter EF.2000GT	Luftwaffe TLG 31 *Boelcke*, Nörvenich	
30+32	Eurofighter EF.2000GS	Luftwaffe TLG 71 *Richthofen*, Laage	
30+33	Eurofighter EF.2000GS	Luftwaffe TLG 71 *Richthofen*, Laage	
30+35	Eurofighter EF.2000GT	Luftwaffe TLG 73 *Steinhoff*, Laage	
30+38	Eurofighter EF.2000GT	Luftwaffe TLG 73 *Steinhoff*, Laage	
30+40	Eurofighter EF.2000GS	Luftwaffe TLG 31 *Boelcke*, Nörvenich	
30+42	Eurofighter EF.2000GT	Luftwaffe TLG 73 *Steinhoff*, Laage	
30+45	Eurofighter EF.2000GS	Luftwaffe TLG 74 *Molders*, Neuburg/Donau	
30+46	Eurofighter EF.2000GS	Luftwaffe TLG 73 *Steinhoff*, Laage	
30+47	Eurofighter EF.2000GS	Luftwaffe TLG 73 *Steinhoff*, Laage	
30+49	Eurofighter EF.2000GS	Luftwaffe TLG 73 *Steinhoff*, Laage	
30+50	Eurofighter EF.2000GS	Luftwaffe TLG 73 *Steinhoff*, Laage	
30+51	Eurofighter EF.2000GS	Luftwaffe TLG 73 *Steinhoff*, Laage	
30+52	Eurofighter EF.2000GS	Luftwaffe TLG 31 *Boelcke*, Nörvenich	
30+53	Eurofighter EF.2000GS	Luftwaffe TLG 74 *Molders*, Neuburg/Donau	

Notes	Serial	Type (code/other identity)	Owner/operator, location or fate
	30+54	Eurofighter EF.2000GT	Luftwaffe TLG 31 *Boelcke*, Nörvenich
	30+56	Eurofighter EF.2000GS	Luftwaffe TLG 74 *Molders*, Neuburg/Donau
	30+57	Eurofighter EF.2000GS	Luftwaffe TLG 71 *Richthofen*, Laage
	30+58	Eurofighter EF.2000GS	Luftwaffe TLG 71 *Richthofen*, Laage
	30+59	Eurofighter EF.2000GT	Luftwaffe TLG 73 *Steinhoff*, Laage
	30+60	Eurofighter EF.2000GS	Luftwaffe TLG 73 *Steinhoff*, Laage
	30+61	Eurofighter EF.2000GS	Luftwaffe TLG 73 *Steinhoff*, Laage
	30+62	Eurofighter EF.2000GS	Luftwaffe TLG 74 *Molders*, Neuburg/Donau
	30+63	Eurofighter EF.2000GS	Luftwaffe TLG 74 *Molders*, Neuburg/Donau
	30+64	Eurofighter EF.2000GS	Luftwaffe TLG 73 *Steinhoff*, Laage
	30+65	Eurofighter EF.2000GS	Luftwaffe TLG 73 *Steinhoff*, Laage
	30+66	Eurofighter EF.2000GS	Luftwaffe TLG 74 *Molders*, Neuburg/Donau
	30+67	Eurofighter EF.2000GT	Luftwaffe TLG 71 *Richthofen*, Laage
	30+68	Eurofighter EF.2000GS $	Luftwaffe TLG 74 *Molders*, Neuburg/Donau
	30+69	Eurofighter EF.2000GS	Luftwaffe TLG 74 *Molders*, Neuburg/Donau
	30+70	Eurofighter EF.2000GS	Luftwaffe TLG 74 *Molders*, Neuburg/Donau
	30+71	Eurofighter EF.2000GT	Luftwaffe TLG 71 *Richthofen*, Laage
	30+72	Eurofighter EF.2000GS	Luftwaffe TLG 74 *Molders*, Neuburg/Donau
	30+73	Eurofighter EF.2000GS $	Luftwaffe TLG 73 *Steinhoff*, Laage
	30+74	Eurofighter EF.2000GS	Luftwaffe TLG 74 *Molders*, Neuburg/Donau
	30+75	Eurofighter EF.2000GS $	Luftwaffe TLG 74 *Molders*, Neuburg/Donau
	30+76	Eurofighter EF.2000GS	Luftwaffe TLG 74 *Molders*, Neuburg/Donau
	30+77	Eurofighter EF.2000GT	Luftwaffe TLG 73 *Steinhoff*, Laage
	30+78	Eurofighter EF.2000GS	Luftwaffe TLG 71 *Richthofen*, Laage
	30+79	Eurofighter EF.2000GS	Luftwaffe TLG 73 *Steinhoff*, Laage
	30+80	Eurofighter EF.2000GS	Luftwaffe TLG 74 *Molders*, Neuburg/Donau
	30+81	Eurofighter EF.2000GS	Luftwaffe TLG 74 *Molders*, Neuburg/Donau
	30+82	Eurofighter EF.2000GS	Luftwaffe TLG 71 *Richthofen*, Laage
	30+83	Eurofighter EF.2000GS	Luftwaffe TLG 71 *Richthofen*, Laage
	30+84	Eurofighter EF.2000GT	Luftwaffe TLG 73 *Steinhoff*, Laage
	30+85	Eurofighter EF.2000GS	Luftwaffe TLG 71 *Richthofen*, Laage
	30+86	Eurofighter EF.2000GS	Luftwaffe TLG 71 *Richthofen*, Laage
	30+87	Eurofighter EF.2000GS $	Luftwaffe TLG 71 *Richthofen*, Laage
	30+88	Eurofighter EF.2000GS	Luftwaffe TLG 74 *Molders*, Neuburg/Donau
	30+89	Eurofighter EF.2000GS	Luftwaffe TLG 71 *Richthofen*, Laage
	30+90	Eurofighter EF.2000GS $	Luftwaffe TLG 71 *Richthofen*, Laage
	30+91	Eurofighter EF.2000GS	Luftwaffe TLG 31 *Boelcke*, Nörvenich
	30+92	Eurofighter EF.2000GS	Luftwaffe TLG 71 *Richthofen*, Laage
	30+93	Eurofighter EF.2000GS	Luftwaffe TLG 74 *Molders*, Neuburg/Donau
	30+94	Eurofighter EF.2000GS	Luftwaffe TLG 74 *Molders*, Neuburg/Donau
	30+95	Eurofighter EF.2000GT	Luftwaffe TLG 74 *Molders*, Neuburg/Donau
	30+96	Eurofighter EF.2000GS $	Luftwaffe TLG 31 *Boelcke*, Nörvenich
	30+97	Eurofighter EF.2000GS	Luftwaffe TLG 31 *Boelcke*, Nörvenich
	30+98	Eurofighter EF.2000GS	Luftwaffe TLG 71 *Richthofen*, Laage
	30+99	Eurofighter EF.2000GT	Luftwaffe TLG 71 *Richthofen*, Laage
	31+00	Eurofighter EF.2000GS	Luftwaffe TLG 74 *Molders*, Neuburg/Donau
	31+01	Eurofighter EF.2000GS $	Luftwaffe TLG 74 *Molders*, Neuburg/Donau
	31+02	Eurofighter EF.2000GS	Luftwaffe TLG 74 *Molders*, Neuburg/Donau
	31+03	Eurofighter EF.2000GT	Airbus Defence & Space, Manching
	31+04	Eurofighter EF.2000GS	Luftwaffe TLG 73 *Steinhoff*, Laage
	31+05	Eurofighter EF.2000GS	Luftwaffe TLG 31 *Boelcke*, Nörvenich
	31+06	Eurofighter EF.2000GS	Luftwaffe TLG 71 *Richthofen*, Laage
	31+07	Eurofighter EF.2000GS	Luftwaffe TLG 71 *Richthofen*, Laage
	31+08	Eurofighter EF.2000GS	Luftwaffe TLG 71 *Richthofen*, Laage
	31+09	Eurofighter EF.2000GS	Luftwaffe TLG 74 *Molders*, Neuburg/Donau
	31+10	Eurofighter EF.2000GS	Luftwaffe TAubZLwSüd, Kaufbeuren
	31+11	Eurofighter EF.2000GS	Luftwaffe TLG 74 *Molders*, Neuburg/Donau
	31+12	Eurofighter EF.2000GS	Luftwaffe TLG 71 *Richthofen*, Laage
	31+13	Eurofighter EF.2000GT	Luftwaffe TLG 74 *Molders*, Neuburg/Donau
	31+14	Eurofighter EF.2000GS	Airbus Defence & Space, stored Manching
	31+15	Eurofighter EF.2000GS	Airbus Defence & Space, Manching
	31+16	Eurofighter EF.2000GS	Luftwaffe TLG 31 *Boelcke*, Nörvenich

Serial	Type (code/other identity)	Owner/operator, location or fate	Notes
31+17	Eurofighter EF.2000GS	Luftwaffe TLG 73 *Steinhoff*, Laage	
31+18	Eurofighter EF.2000GS $	Luftwaffe TLG 73 *Steinhoff*, Laage	
31+19	Eurofighter EF.2000GS	Luftwaffe TLG 74 *Molders*, Neuburg/Donau	
31+20	Eurofighter EF.2000GS	Luftwaffe TLG 31 *Boelcke*, Nörvenich	
31+21	Eurofighter EF.2000GS	Luftwaffe TLG 73 *Steinhoff*, Laage	
31+22	Eurofighter EF.2000GS	Luftwaffe TLG 74 *Molders*, Neuburg/Donau	
31+24	Eurofighter EF.2000GT	Luftwaffe TLG 73 *Steinhoff*, Laage	
31+25	Eurofighter EF.2000GT	Luftwaffe TLG 74 *Molders*, Neuburg/Donau	
31+26	Eurofighter EF.2000GT	Luftwaffe TLG 73 *Steinhoff*, Laage	
31+27	Eurofighter EF.2000GT	Luftwaffe TLG 31 *Boelcke*, Nörvenich	
31+28	Eurofighter EF.2000GT	Luftwaffe TLG 74 *Molders*, Neuburg/Donau	
31+29	Eurofighter EF.2000GS	Luftwaffe TLG 31 *Boelcke*, Nörvenich	
31+30	Eurofighter EF.2000GS	Luftwaffe TLG 73 *Steinhoff*, Laage	
31+31	Eurofighter EF.2000GS $	Luftwaffe TLG 31 *Boelcke*, Nörvenich	
31+32	Eurofighter EF.2000GS $	Luftwaffe TLG 31 *Boelcke*, Nörvenich	
31+33	Eurofighter EF.2000GS	Luftwaffe TLG 31 *Boelcke*, Nörvenich	
31+34	Eurofighter EF.2000GS	Luftwaffe TLG 31 *Boelcke*, Nörvenich	
31+35	Eurofighter EF.2000GS	Luftwaffe TLG 74 *Molders*, Neuburg/Donau	
31+36	Eurofighter EF.2000GS	Luftwaffe TLG 74 *Molders*, Neuburg/Donau	
31+37	Eurofighter EF.2000GS	Luftwaffe TLG 31 *Boelcke*, Nörvenich	
31+38	Eurofighter EF.2000GS	Luftwaffe TLG 31 *Boelcke*, Nörvenich	
31+39	Eurofighter EF.2000GS	Luftwaffe TLG 73 *Steinhoff*, Laage	
31+40	Eurofighter EF.2000GS	Luftwaffe TLG 31 *Boelcke*, Nörvenich	
31+41	Eurofighter EF.2000GS	Luftwaffe TLG 31 *Boelcke*, Nörvenich	
31+42	Eurofighter EF.2000GS	Luftwaffe TLG 31 *Boelcke*, Nörvenich	
31+43	Eurofighter EF.2000GS	Luftwaffe TLG 31 *Boelcke*, Nörvenich	
31+44	Eurofighter EF.2000GS	Luftwaffe TLG 71 *Richthofen*, Laage	
31+45	Eurofighter EF.2000GS	Luftwaffe TLG 71 *Richthofen*, Laage	
31+46	Eurofighter EF.2000GS	Luftwaffe TLG 31 *Boelcke*, Nörvenich	
31+47	Eurofighter EF.2000GS	Luftwaffe TLG 31 *Boelcke*, Nörvenich	
31+48	Eurofighter EF.2000GS	Luftwaffe TLG 31 *Boelcke*, Nörvenich	
31+49	Eurofighter EF.2000GS $	Luftwaffe TLG 31 *Boelcke*, Nörvenich	
31+50	Eurofighter EF.2000GS	Luftwaffe TLG 74 *Molders*, Neuburg/Donau	
31+51	Eurofighter EF.2000GS	Luftwaffe TLG 31 *Boelcke*, Nörvenich	
31+52	Eurofighter EF.2000GS	Luftwaffe TLG 31 *Boelcke*, Nörvenich	
31+53	Eurofighter EF.2000GS	Luftwaffe TLG 31 *Boelcke*, Nörvenich	
43+07	Panavia Tornado IDS(T)	Luftwaffe TLG 51 *Immelmann*, Schleswig/Jagel	
43+10	Panavia Tornado IDS(T)	Luftwaffe TLG 33, Nörvenich	
43+25	Panavia Tornado IDS $	Luftwaffe TLG 51 *Immelmann*, Schleswig/Jagel	
43+29	Panavia Tornado IDS(T)	Luftwaffe TLG 51 *Immelmann*, Schleswig/Jagel	
43+38	Panavia Tornado IDS	Luftwaffe TLG 33, Nörvenich	
43+42	Panavia Tornado IDS(T)	Luftwaffe TLG 33, Nörvenich	
43+45	Panavia Tornado IDS(T)	Luftwaffe TLG 51 *Immelmann*, Schleswig/Jagel	
43+46	Panavia Tornado IDS	Luftwaffe TLG 33, Nörvenich	
43+48	Panavia Tornado IDS	Luftwaffe TLG 33, Nörvenich	
43+50	Panavia Tornado IDS	Luftwaffe TLG 33, Nörvenich	
43+52	Panavia Tornado IDS	*Scrapped*	
43+54	Panavia Tornado IDS	Luftwaffe TAubZLwSüd, Kaufbeuren	
43+59	Panavia Tornado IDS	Luftwaffe TLG 51 *Immelmann*, Schleswig/Jagel	
43+92	Panavia Tornado IDS(T)	Luftwaffe TLG 33, Nörvenich	
43+97	Panavia Tornado IDS(T)	Luftwaffe TLG 51 *Immelmann*, Schleswig/Jagel	
43+98	Panavia Tornado IDS	Luftwaffe TLG 33, Nörvenich	
44+06	Panavia Tornado IDS	Luftwaffe TLG 33, Nörvenich	
44+16	Panavia Tornado IDS(T)	Luftwaffe TLG 33, Nörvenich	
44+17	Panavia Tornado IDS	*Ground instructional airframe, EADS Manching*	
44+21	Panavia Tornado IDS	Luftwaffe TLG 51 *Immelmann*, Schleswig/Jagel	
44+23	Panavia Tornado IDS	Luftwaffe TLG 33, Nörvenich	
44+29	Panavia Tornado IDS	Luftwaffe TLG 33, Nörvenich	
44+30	Panavia Tornado IDS	Luftwaffe TLG 51 *Immelmann*, Schleswig/Jagel	
44+33	Panavia Tornado IDS	Luftwaffe TLG 33, Nörvenich	
44+34	Panavia Tornado IDS	Luftwaffe TLG 33, Nörvenich	
44+58	Panavia Tornado IDS	Luftwaffe TLG 33, Nörvenich	

Notes	Serial	Type (code/other identity)	Owner/operator, location or fate
	44+61	Panavia Tornado IDS $	Luftwaffe TLG 33, Nörvenich
	44+64	Panavia Tornado IDS	Luftwaffe TLG 33, Nörvenich
	44+65	Panavia Tornado IDS	Luftwaffe TLG 51 *Immelmann*, Schleswig/Jagel
	44+69	Panavia Tornado IDS	Luftwaffe TLG 51 *Immelmann*, Schleswig/Jagel
	44+70	Panavia Tornado IDS	Luftwaffe TLG 33, Nörvenich
	44+72	Panavia Tornado IDS(T)	Luftwaffe TLG 33, Nörvenich
	44+73	Panavia Tornado IDS(T)	Luftwaffe TLG 33, Nörvenich
	44+75	Panavia Tornado IDS(T)	Luftwaffe TLG 51 *Immelmann*, Schleswig/Jagel
	44+78	Panavia Tornado IDS	Luftwaffe TLG 33, Nörvenich
	44+79	Panavia Tornado IDS	Luftwaffe TLG 33, Nörvenich
	44+90	Panavia Tornado IDS	Luftwaffe TLG 33, Nörvenich
	45+00	Panavia Tornado IDS	Luftwaffe TLG 33, Nörvenich
	45+09	Panavia Tornado IDS	Luftwaffe TLG 33, Nörvenich
	45+13	Panavia Tornado IDS(T)	Luftwaffe TLG 51 *Immelmann*, Schleswig/Jagel
	45+14	Panavia Tornado IDS(T)	Luftwaffe TLG 51 *Immelmann*, Schleswig/Jagel
	45+16	Panavia Tornado IDS(T)	Luftwaffe TLG 51 *Immelmann*, Schleswig/Jagel
	45+19	Panavia Tornado IDS	Luftwaffe TLG 33, Nörvenich
	45+20	Panavia Tornado IDS	Luftwaffe TLG 33, Nörvenich
	45+23	Panavia Tornado IDS	Luftwaffe TLG 33, Nörvenich
	45+28	Panavia Tornado IDS	Luftwaffe TLG 33, Nörvenich
	45+35	Panavia Tornado IDS	Luftwaffe TLG 33, Nörvenich
	45+39	Panavia Tornado IDS	Luftwaffe TLG 51 *Immelmann*, Schleswig/Jagel
	45+50	Panavia Tornado IDS	Luftwaffe TLG 51 *Immelmann*, Schleswig/Jagel
	45+53	Panavia Tornado IDS	Luftwaffe TAubZLwSüd, Kaufbeuren
	45+57	Panavia Tornado IDS	Luftwaffe TLG 33, Nörvenich
	45+59	Panavia Tornado IDS	Luftwaffe TLG 51 *Immelmann*, Schleswig/Jagel
	45+61	Panavia Tornado IDS(T)	Luftwaffe TLG 51 *Immelmann*, Schleswig/Jagel
	45+64	Panavia Tornado IDS	Luftwaffe TLG 33, Nörvenich
	45+66	Panavia Tornado IDS	Luftwaffe TLG 33, Nörvenich
	45+67	Panavia Tornado IDS	Luftwaffe TLG 33, Nörvenich
	45+68	Panavia Tornado IDS	Luftwaffe TLG 33, Nörvenich
	45+69	Panavia Tornado IDS	Luftwaffe TLG 33, Nörvenich
	45+70	Panavia Tornado IDS(T)	Luftwaffe TLG 51 *Immelmann*, Schleswig/Jagel
	45+71	Panavia Tornado IDS	Luftwaffe TLG 33, Nörvenich
	45+74	Panavia Tornado IDS	Luftwaffe TAubZLwSüd, Kaufbeuren
	45+76	Panavia Tornado IDS	Luftwaffe TLG 33, Nörvenich
	45+77	Panavia Tornado IDS(T)	Luftwaffe TLG 51 *Immelmann*, Schleswig/Jagel
	45+84	Panavia Tornado IDS	*Withdrawn from use, Büchel*
	45+85	Panavia Tornado IDS	Luftwaffe TLG 33, Nörvenich
	45+88	Panavia Tornado IDS	Luftwaffe TLG 33, Nörvenich
	45+90	Panavia Tornado IDS	*Scrapped*
	45+92	Panavia Tornado IDS	Luftwaffe TLG 33, Nörvenich
	45+93	Panavia Tornado IDS	*Ground instructional airframe, Büchel*
	45+94	Panavia Tornado IDS	Luftwaffe TLG 33, Nörvenich
	46+02	Panavia Tornado IDS	Luftwaffe TLG 33, Nörvenich
	46+05	Panavia Tornado IDS(T)	Luftwaffe TLG 51 *Immelmann*, Schleswig/Jagel
	46+07	Panavia Tornado IDS(T)	Luftwaffe TLG 33, Nörvenich
	46+10	Panavia Tornado IDS	Luftwaffe TLG 33, Nörvenich
	46+11	Panavia Tornado IDS	Luftwaffe TLG 33, Nörvenich
	46+15	Panavia Tornado IDS	Luftwaffe TLG 33, Nörvenich
	46+18	Panavia Tornado IDS	Luftwaffe TLG 33, Nörvenich
	46+20	Panavia Tornado IDS	Withdrawn from use, Schleswig/Jagel
	46+21	Panavia Tornado IDS	Luftwaffe TLG 33, Nörvenich
	46+22	Panavia Tornado IDS	Luftwaffe TLG 33, Nörvenich
	46+23	Panavia Tornado ECR $	Luftwaffe TLG 51 *Immelmann*, Schleswig/Jagel
	46+24	Panavia Tornado ECR	Luftwaffe TLG 51 *Immelmann*, Schleswig/Jagel
	46+25	Panavia Tornado ECR	Luftwaffe TLG 51 *Immelmann*, Schleswig/Jagel
	46+28	Panavia Tornado ECR $	Luftwaffe TLG 51 *Immelmann*, Schleswig/Jagel
	46+32	Panavia Tornado ECR	Luftwaffe TLG 51 *Immelmann*, Schleswig/Jagel
	46+35	Panavia Tornado ECR	Luftwaffe TLG 51 *Immelmann*, Schleswig/Jagel
	46+36	Panavia Tornado ECR	Luftwaffe TLG 51 *Immelmann*, Schleswig/Jagel
	46+38	Panavia Tornado ECR	Luftwaffe TLG 51 *Immelmann*, Schleswig/Jagel

Serial	Type (code/other identity)	Owner/operator, location or fate	Notes
46+39	Panavia Tornado ECR	Luftwaffe TAubZLwSüd, Kaufbeuren	
46+40	Panavia Tornado ECR	Luftwaffe TLG 51 *Immelmann*, Schleswig/Jagel	
46+44	Panavia Tornado ECR	Luftwaffe TLG 51 *Immelmann*, Schleswig/Jagel	
46+45	Panavia Tornado ECR	Luftwaffe TLG 51 *Immelmann*, Schleswig/Jagel	
46+46	Panavia Tornado ECR	Luftwaffe TLG 51 *Immelmann*, Schleswig/Jagel	
46+48	Panavia Tornado ECR	Luftwaffe TLG 51 *Immelmann*, Schleswig/Jagel	
46+49	Panavia Tornado ECR	Luftwaffe TLG 51 *Immelmann*, Schleswig/Jagel	
46+50	Panavia Tornado ECR	Luftwaffe TLG 51 *Immelmann*, Schleswig/Jagel	
46+51	Panavia Tornado ECR	Luftwaffe TLG 51 *Immelmann*, Schleswig/Jagel	
46+52	Panavia Tornado ECR	Luftwaffe TLG 51 *Immelmann*, Schleswig/Jagel	
46+54	Panavia Tornado ECR $	Luftwaffe TLG 51 *Immelmann*, Schleswig/Jagel	
46+55	Panavia Tornado ECR	Luftwaffe TLG 51 *Immelmann*, Schleswig/Jagel	
46+56	Panavia Tornado ECR	Luftwaffe TLG 51 *Immelmann*, Schleswig/Jagel	
46+57	Panavia Tornado ECR $	Luftwaffe TLG 51 *Immelmann*, Schleswig/Jagel	
54+01	Airbus Military A.400M	Luftwaffe LTG 62, Wunstorf	
54+02	Airbus Military A.400M	Luftwaffe LTG 62, Wunstorf	
54+03	Airbus Military A.400M $	Luftwaffe LTG 62, Wunstorf	
54+04	Airbus Military A.400M	Luftwaffe LTG 62, Wunstorf	
54+05	Airbus Military A.400M	Luftwaffe LTG 62, Wunstorf	
54+06	Airbus Military A.400M	Luftwaffe LTG 62, Wunstorf	
54+07	Airbus Military A.400M	Luftwaffe LTG 62, Wunstorf	
54+08	Airbus Military A.400M	Luftwaffe LTG 62, Wunstorf	
54+09	Airbus Military A.400M	Luftwaffe LTG 62, Wunstorf	
54+10	Airbus Military A.400M	Luftwaffe LTG 62, Wunstorf	
54+11	Airbus Military A.400M	Luftwaffe LTG 62, Wunstorf	
54+12	Airbus Military A.400M	Luftwaffe LTG 62, Wunstorf	
54+13	Airbus Military A.400M	Luftwaffe LTG 62, Wunstorf	
54+14	Airbus Military A.400M	Luftwaffe LTG 62, Wunstorf	
54+15	Airbus Military A.400M	Luftwaffe LTG 62, Wunstorf	
54+16	Airbus Military A.400M	Luftwaffe LTG 62, Wunstorf	
54+17	Airbus Military A.400M	Luftwaffe LTG 62, Wunstorf	
54+18	Airbus Military A.400M	Luftwaffe LTG 62, Wunstorf	
54+19	Airbus Military A.400M	Luftwaffe LTG 62, Wunstorf	
54+20	Airbus Military A.400M	Luftwaffe LTG 62, Wunstorf	
54+21	Airbus Military A.400M	Luftwaffe LTG 62, Wunstorf	
54+22	Airbus Military A.400M	Luftwaffe LTG 62, Wunstorf	
54+23	Airbus Military A.400M	Luftwaffe LTG 62, Wunstorf	
54+24	Airbus Military A.400M	Luftwaffe LTG 62, Wunstorf	
54+25	Airbus Military A.400M	Luftwaffe LTG 62, Wunstorf	
54+26	Airbus Military A.400M	Luftwaffe LTG 62, Wunstorf	
54+27	Airbus Military A.400M	Luftwaffe LTG 62, Wunstorf	
54+28	Airbus Military A.400M	Luftwaffe LTG 62, Wunstorf	
54+29	Airbus Military A.400M	Luftwaffe LTG 62, Wunstorf	
54+30	Airbus Military A.400M	Luftwaffe LTG 62, Wunstorf	
54+31	Airbus Military A.400M	Luftwaffe LTG 62, Wunstorf	
54+32	Airbus Military A.400M	Luftwaffe LTG 62, Wunstorf	
54+33	Airbus Military A.400M	Luftwaffe LTG 62, Wunstorf	
54+34	Airbus Military A.400M	Luftwaffe LTG 62, Wunstorf	
54+35	Airbus Military A.400M	Airbus Military, Sevilla/Morón	
54+36	Airbus Military A.400M	Luftwaffe LTG 62, Wunstorf	
54+37	Airbus Military A.400M	Luftwaffe LTG 62, Wunstorf	
54+38	Airbus Military A.400M	Luftwaffe LTG 62, Wunstorf	
54+39	Airbus Military A.400M	Luftwaffe LTG 62, Wunstorf	
54+40	Airbus Military A.400M	Luftwaffe LTG 62, Wunstorf	
54+41	Airbus Military A.400M	Luftwaffe LTG 62, Wunstorf	
54+42	Airbus Military A.400M	Luftwaffe (on order)	
54+43	Airbus Military A.400M	Luftwaffe (on order)	
54+44	Airbus Military A.400M	Luftwaffe (on order)	
54+45	Airbus Military A.400M	Luftwaffe (on order)	
54+46	Airbus Military A.400M	Luftwaffe (on order)	
54+47	Airbus Military A.400M	Luftwaffe (on order)	
54+48	Airbus Military A.400M	Luftwaffe (on order)	

Notes	Serial	Type (code/other identity)	Owner/operator, location or fate
	54+49	Airbus Military A.400M	Luftwaffe (on order)
	54+50	Airbus Military A.400M	Luftwaffe (on order)
	54+51	Airbus Military A.400M	Luftwaffe (on order)
	54+52	Airbus Military A.400M	Luftwaffe (on order)
	54+53	Airbus Military A.400M	Luftwaffe (on order)
	57+04	Dornier Do.228LM	Marineflieger MFG 3, Nordholz
	57+05	Dornier Do.228NG	Marineflieger MFG 3, Nordholz
	55+01	Lockheed C-130J Hercules II	Luftwaffe EFATT, Evreux
	55+02	Lockheed C-130J Hercules II	Luftwaffe EFATT, Evreux
	55+03	Lockheed C-130J Hercules II	Luftwaffe EFATT, Evreux
	55+04	Lockheed KC-130J Hercules II	Luftwaffe (on order)
	55+05	Lockheed KC-130J Hercules II	Luftwaffe (on order)
	55+06	Lockheed KC-130J Hercules II	Luftwaffe (on order)
	60+03	Lockheed P-3C CUP Orion	Marineflieger MFG 3, Nordholz
	60+04	Lockheed P-3C CUP Orion	Marineflieger MFG 3, Nordholz
	60+05	Lockheed P-3C CUP Orion $	Marineflieger, stored Nordholz
	60+06	Lockheed P-3C CUP Orion	Marineflieger, stored Nordholz
	60+07	Lockheed P-3C CUP Orion	Marineflieger, stored Nordholz
	60+08	Lockheed P-3C CUP Orion	Marineflieger MFG 3, Nordholz
	6.+01	Boeing P-8A Poseidon	Marineflieger (on order)
	6.+02	Boeing P-8A Poseidon	Marineflieger (on order)
	6.+03	Boeing P-8A Poseidon	Marineflieger (on order)
	6.+04	Boeing P-8A Poseidon	Marineflieger (on order)
	6.+05	Boeing P-8A Poseidon	Marineflieger (on order)
	6.+06	Boeing P-8A Poseidon	Marineflieger (on order)
	6.+07	Boeing P-8A Poseidon	Marineflieger (on order)
	6.+08	Boeing P-8A Poseidon	Marineflieger (on order)
	74+01	Eurocopter EC.665 Tiger UHT	Heer KHR 36, Fritzlar
	74+02	Eurocopter EC.665 Tiger UHT	Spares use, Fritzlar
	74+03	Eurocopter EC.665 Tiger UHT	Luftwaffe TsLw 3, Fassberg
	74+04	Eurocopter EC.665 Tiger UHT	Airbus Helicopters, Donauwörth (upgrade)
	74+05	Eurocopter EC.665 Tiger UHT	Heer IntHubschrAusbZ, Le Luc, France
	74+06	Eurocopter EC.665 Tiger UHT	Ground instructional airframe, Fritzlar
	74+07	Eurocopter EC.665 Tiger UHT	Luftwaffe TsLw 3, Fassberg
	74+08	Eurocopter EC.665 Tiger UHT	Luftwaffe TsLw 3, Fassberg
	74+09	Eurocopter EC.665 Tiger UHT	Ground instructional airframe, Fritzlar
	74+10	Eurocopter EC.665 Tiger UHT	Luftwaffe TsLw 3, Fassberg
	74+11	Eurocopter EC.665 Tiger UHT	Heer IntHubschrAusbZ, Le Luc, France
	74+13	Eurocopter EC.665 Tiger UHT	Luftwaffe TsLw 3, Fassberg
	74+14	Eurocopter EC.665 Tiger UHT	Luftwaffe TsLw 3, Fassberg
	74+15	Eurocopter EC.665 Tiger UHT	Heer IntHubschrAusbZ, Le Luc, France
	74+16	Eurocopter EC.665 Tiger UHT	Heer KHR 36, Fritzlar
	74+17	Eurocopter EC.665 Tiger UHT	Heer KHR 36, Fritzlar
	74+18	Eurocopter EC.665 Tiger UHT	Heer KHR 36, Fritzlar
	74+19	Eurocopter EC.665 Tiger UHT	Heer KHR 36, Fritzlar
	74+20	Eurocopter EC.665 Tiger UHT	Heer KHR 36, Fritzlar
	74+21	Eurocopter EC.665 Tiger UHT	Heer KHR 36, Fritzlar
	74+22	Eurocopter EC.665 Tiger UHT	Heer KHR 36, Fritzlar
	74+23	Eurocopter EC.665 Tiger UHT	Luftwaffe WTD 61, Ingolstadt
	74+24	Eurocopter EC.665 Tiger UHT	Heer KHR 36, Fritzlar
	74+25	Eurocopter EC.665 Tiger UHT	Heer KHR 36, Fritzlar
	74+26	Eurocopter EC.665 Tiger UHT	Heer KHR 36, Fritzlar
	74+28	Eurocopter EC.665 Tiger UHT	Heer KHR 36, Fritzlar
	74+29	Eurocopter EC.665 Tiger UHT	Heer KHR 36, Fritzlar
	74+30	Eurocopter EC.665 Tiger UHT	Heer KHR 36, Fritzlar
	74+31	Eurocopter EC.665 Tiger UHT	Heer KHR 36, Fritzlar
	74+32	Eurocopter EC.665 Tiger UHT	Heer KHR 36, Fritzlar
	74+34	Eurocopter EC.665 Tiger UHT	Heer KHR 36, Fritzlar
	74+35	Eurocopter EC.665 Tiger UHT	Heer KHR 36, Fritzlar
	74+36	Eurocopter EC.665 Tiger UHT	Heer KHR 36, Fritzlar
	74+37	Eurocopter EC.665 Tiger UHT	Heer IntHubschrAusbZ, Le Luc, France
	74+38	Eurocopter EC.665 Tiger UHT	Heer D/F HFAZT, Le Luc, France

Serial	Type (code/other identity)	Owner/operator, location or fate	Notes
74+39	Eurocopter EC.665 Tiger UHT	Heer	
74+40	Eurocopter EC.665 Tiger UHT	Heer KHR 36, Fritzlar	
74+41	Eurocopter EC.665 Tiger UHT	Heer D/F HFAZT, Le Luc, France	
74+42	Eurocopter EC.665 Tiger UHT	Heer KHR 36, Fritzlar	
74+43	Eurocopter EC.665 Tiger UHT	Heer KHR 36, Fritzlar	
74+44	Eurocopter EC.665 Tiger UHT	Heer	
74+45	Eurocopter EC.665 Tiger UHT	Heer KHR 36, Fritzlar	
74+46	Eurocopter EC.665 Tiger UHT	Heer KHR 36, Fritzlar	
74+47	Eurocopter EC.665 Tiger UHT	Luftwaffe WTD 61, Ingolstadt	
74+48	Eurocopter EC.665 Tiger UHT	Heer KHR 26, Roth	
74+50	Eurocopter EC.665 Tiger UHT	Heer KHR 36, Fritzlar	
74+51	Eurocopter EC.665 Tiger UHT	Heer IntHubschrAusbZ, Le Luc, France	
74+52	Eurocopter EC.665 Tiger UHT	Heer KHR 36, Fritzlar	
74+53	Eurocopter EC.665 Tiger UHT	Heer KHR 36, Fritzlar	
74+54	Eurocopter EC.665 Tiger UHT	Heer KHR 36, Fritzlar	
74+55	Eurocopter EC.665 Tiger UHT	Heer D/F HFAZT, Le Luc, France	
74+56	Eurocopter EC.665 Tiger UHT	Heer KHR 36, Fritzlar	
74+57	Eurocopter EC.665 Tiger UHT	Heer KHR 36, Fritzlar	
74+58	Eurocopter EC.665 Tiger UHT	Heer KHR 36, Fritzlar	
74+59	Eurocopter EC.665 Tiger UHT	Heer	
74+60	Eurocopter EC.665 Tiger UHT	Heer KHR 36, Fritzlar	
74+61	Eurocopter EC.665 Tiger UHT	Heer KHR 36, Fritzlar	
74+62	Eurocopter EC.665 Tiger UHT	Heer KHR 36, Fritzlar	
74+63	Eurocopter EC.665 Tiger UHT	Heer KHR 36, Fritzlar	
74+64	Eurocopter EC.665 Tiger UHT $	Heer IntHubschrAusbZ, Le Luc, France	
74+65	Eurocopter EC.665 Tiger UHT	Heer (on order)	
74+66	Eurocopter EC.665 Tiger UHT	Heer KHR 36, Fritzlar	
74+67	Eurocopter EC.665 Tiger UHT	Heer KHR 36, Fritzlar	
74+68	Eurocopter EC.665 Tiger UHT	Airbus Helicopters, Donauwörth	
74+69	Eurocopter EC.665 Tiger UHT	Heer	
74+70	Eurocopter EC.665 Tiger UHT	Heer KHR 36, Fritzlar	
76+01	Airbus Helicopters H.145M	Luftwaffe HSG 64, Laupheim	
76+02	Airbus Helicopters H.145M	Luftwaffe HSG 64, Laupheim	
76+03	Airbus Helicopters H.145M	Luftwaffe HSG 64, Laupheim	
76+04	Airbus Helicopters H.145M	Luftwaffe HSG 64, Laupheim	
76+05	Airbus Helicopters H.145M	Luftwaffe HSG 64, Laupheim	
76+06	Airbus Helicopters H.145M	Luftwaffe HSG 64, Laupheim	
76+07	Airbus Helicopters H.145M	Luftwaffe HSG 64, Laupheim	
76+08	Airbus Helicopters H.145M	Luftwaffe HSG 64, Laupheim	
76+09	Airbus Helicopters H.145M	Luftwaffe HSG 64, Laupheim	
76+10	Airbus Helicopters H.145M	Luftwaffe HSG 64, Laupheim	
76+11	Airbus Helicopters H.145M	Luftwaffe HSG 64, Laupheim	
76+12	Airbus Helicopters H.145M	Luftwaffe HSG 64, Laupheim	
76+13	Airbus Helicopters H.145M	Luftwaffe HSG 64, Laupheim	
76+14	Airbus Helicopters H.145M	Luftwaffe HSG 64, Laupheim	
76+15	Airbus Helicopters H.145M	Luftwaffe HSG 64, Laupheim	
78+01	NH Industries NH.90-TTH (98+91)	Heer IntHubschrAusbZ, Bückeburg	
78+02	NH Industries NH.90-TTH (98+92)	Heer IntHubschrAusbZ, Bückeburg	
78+03	NH Industries NH.90-TTH (98+93)	Heer IntHubschrAusbZ, Bückeburg	
78+04	NH Industries NH.90-TTH (98+94)	Luftwaffe TsLw 3, Fassberg	
78+05	NH Industries NH.90-TTH	Luftwaffe TsLw 3, Fassberg	
78+06	NH Industries NH.90-TTH	Heer IntHubschrAusbZ, Bückeburg	
78+07	NH Industries NH.90-TTH	Heer IntHubschrAusbZ, Bückeburg	
78+08	NH Industries NH.90-TTH	Heer IntHubschrAusbZ, Bückeburg	
78+09	NH Industries NH.90-TTH (98+92)	Heer THR 30, Niederstetten	
78+10	NH Industries NH.90-TTH (98+94)	Heer THR 10, Fassberg	
78+11	NH Industries NH.90-TTH (98+95)	Heer THR 30, Niederstetten	
78+12	NH Industries NH.90-TTH (98+96)	Heer THR 30, Niederstetten	
78+13	NH Industries NH.90-TTH (98+97)	Heer THR 10, Fassberg	
78+14	NH Industries NH.90-TTH	Heer THR 30, Niederstetten	
78+15	NH Industries NH.90-TTH	Heer THR 10, Fassberg	
78+16	NH Industries NH.90-TTH	Heer THR 30, Niederstetten	

Notes	Serial	Type (code/other identity)	Owner/operator, location or fate
	78+17	NH Industries NH.90-TTH	Heer THR 10, Fassberg
	78+18	NH Industries NH.90-TTH	Heer THR 10, Fassberg
	78+19	NH Industries NH.90-TTH (98+49)	Heer THR 10, Fassberg
	78+20	NH Industries NH.90-TTH (98+52)	Heer THR 10, Fassberg
	78+21	NH Industries NH.90-TTH (98+56)	Heer THR 10, Fassberg
	78+22	NH Industries NH.90-TTH (98+57)	Heer IntHubschrAusbZ, Bückeburg
	78+23	NH Industries NH.90-TTH	Heer THR 10, Fassberg
	78+24	NH Industries NH.90-TTH	Heer THR 10, Fassberg
	78+25	NH Industries NH.90-TTH	Luftwaffe TsLw 3, Fassberg
	78+26	NH Industries NH.90-TTH	Heer THR 10, Fassberg
	78+27	NH Industries NH.90-TTH	Heer THR 10, Fassberg
	78+28	NH Industries NH.90-TTH	Heer THR 10, Fassberg
	78+29	NH Industries NH.90-TTH	Heer THR 10, Fassberg
	78+30	NH Industries NH.90-TTH	Heer IntHubschrAusbZ, Bückeburg
	78+31	NH Industries NH.90-TTH	Heer THR 10, Fassberg
	78+32	NH Industries NH.90-TTH	Heer IntHubschrAusbZ, Bückeburg
	78+33	NH Industries NH.90-TTH	Heer THR 10, Fassberg
	78+34	NH Industries NH.90-TTH	Heer THR 10, Fassberg
	78+35	NH Industries NH.90-TTH	Heer THR 10, Fassberg
	78+36	NH Industries NH.90-TTH	Heer THR 30, Niederstetten
	78+37	NH Industries NH.90-TTH	Heer THR 30, Niederstetten
	78+38	NH Industries NH.90-TTH	Heer THR 10, Fassberg
	78+39	NH Industries NH.90-TTH	Heer THR 30, Niederstetten
	78+40	NH Industries NH.90-TTH	Heer THR 30, Niederstetten
	79+01	NH Industries NH.90-TTH (98+91)	Heer THR 10, Fassberg
	79+02	NH Industries NH.90-TTH (79+09)	Heer THR 30, Niederstetten
	79+03	NH Industries NH.90-TTH (79+10)	Heer THR 10, Fassberg
	79+04	NH Industries NH.90-TTH (79+11)	Heer THR 10, Fassberg
	79+05	NH Industries NH.90-TTH (79+12)	Heer THR 10, Fassberg
	79+06	NH Industries NH.90-TTH (79+13)	Heer THR 10, Fassberg
	79+07	NH Industries NH.90-TTH	Heer THR 10, Fassberg
	79+08	NH Industries NH.90-TTH (98+50)	Luftwaffe TsLw 3, Fassberg
	79+09	NH Industries NH.90-TTH	Heer THR 10, Fassberg
	79+10	NH Industries NH.90-TTH	Heer THR 10, Fassberg
	79+11	NH Industries NH.90-TTH	Heer THR 30, Niederstetten
	79+12	NH Industries NH.90-TTH	Heer THR 30, Niederstetten
	79+13	NH Industries NH.90-TTH	Heer THR 30, Niederstetten
	79+14	NH Industries NH.90-TTH	Heer THR 30, Niederstetten
	79+15	NH Industries NH.90-TTH	Heer THR 30, Niederstetten
	79+16	NH Industries NH.90-TTH	Heer THR 30, Niederstetten
	79+17	NH Industries NH.90-TTH	Heer THR 10, Fassberg
	79+18	NH Industries NH.90-TTH	Heer THR 10, Fassberg
	79+19	NH Industries NH.90-TTH	Heer IntHubschrAusbZ, Bückeburg
	79+20	NH Industries NH.90-TTH	Heer IntHubschrAusbZ, Bückeburg
	79+21	NH Industries NH.90-TTH	Heer THR 30, Niederstetten
	79+22	NH Industries NH.90-TTH	Heer IntHubschrAusbZ, Bückeburg
	79+23	NH Industries NH.90-TTH	Heer THR 30, Niederstetten
	79+24	NH Industries NH.90-TTH (79+02/98+93)	Heer THR 10, Fassberg
	79+25	NH Industries NH.90-TTH (79+03/98+97)	Heer IntHubschrAusbZ, Bückeburg
	79+26	NH Industries NH.90-TTH (79+04/98+99)	Heer THR 10, Fassberg
	79+27	NH Industries NH.90-TTH (79+05)	Heer THR 30, Niederstetten
	79+28	NH Industries NH.90-TTH (79+06)	Heer IntHubschrAusbZ, Bückeburg
	79+29	NH Industries NH.90-TTH (79+07)	Heer IntHubschrAusbZ, Bückeburg
	79+30	NH Industries NH.90-TTH (79+08)	Heer IntHubschrAusbZ, Bückeburg
	79+31	NH Industries NH.90-TTH	Heer THR 30, Niederstetten
	79+32	NH Industries NH.90-TTH	Heer THR 30, Niederstetten
	79+33	NH Industries NH.90-TTH	Heer THR 30, Niederstetten
	79+34	NH Industries NH.90-TTH	Heer THR 10, Fassberg
	79+35	NH Industries NH.90-TTH	Airbus Helicopters, Donauwörth
	79+36	NH Industries NH.90-TTH	Heer IntHubschrAusbZ, Bückeburg
	79+37	NH Industries NH.90-TTH	Heer THR 10, Fassberg
	79+38	NH Industries NH.90-TTH	Heer THR 10, Fassberg

Serial	Type (code/other identity)	Owner/operator, location or fate	Notes
79+39	NH Industries NH.90-TTH	Heer IntHubschrAusbZ, Bückeburg	
79+40	NH Industries NH.90-TTH	Heer IntHubschrAusbZ, Bückeburg	
79+41	NH Industries NH.90-TTH	Heer IntHubschrAusbZ, Bückeburg	
79+42	NH Industries NH.90-TTH	Heer IntHubschrAusbZ, Bückeburg	
79+43	NH Industries NH.90-TTH	Heer (on order)	
79+44	NH Industries NH.90-TTH	Heer (on order)	
79+45	NH Industries NH.90-TTH	Heer (on order)	
79+46	NH Industries NH.90-TTH	Heer (on order)	
79+47	NH Industries NH.90-TTH	Heer (on order)	
79+48	NH Industries NH.90-TTH	Heer (on order)	
79+49	NH Industries NH.90-TTH	Heer (on order)	
79+50	NH Industries NH.90-TTH	Heer (on order)	
79+51	NH Industries NH.90-NFH Sea Lion (98+51)	Marineflieger MFG 5, Nordholz	
79+52	NH Industries NH.90-NFH Sea Lion (98+56)	Marineflieger MFG 5, Nordholz	
79+53	NH Industries NH.90-NFH Sea Lion (98+40)	Marineflieger MFG 5, Nordholz	
79+54	NH Industries NH.90-NFH Sea Lion (98+41)	Marineflieger MFG 5, Nordholz	
79+55	NH Industries NH.90-NFH Sea Lion (98+50)	Marineflieger MFG 5, Nordholz	
79+56	NH Industries NH.90-NFH Sea Lion	Marineflieger MFG 5, Nordholz	
79+57	NH Industries NH.90-NFH Sea Lion	Marineflieger MFG 5, Nordholz	
79+58	NH Industries NH.90-NFH Sea Lion	Marineflieger MFG 5, Nordholz	
79+59	NH Industries NH.90-NFH Sea Lion	Marineflieger MFG 5, Nordholz	
79+60	NH Industries NH.90-NFH Sea Lion	Marineflieger MFG 5, Nordholz	
79+61	NH Industries NH.90-NFH Sea Lion	Marineflieger MFG 5, Nordholz	
79+62	NH Industries NH.90-NFH Sea Lion	Marineflieger MFG 5, Nordholz	
79+63	NH Industries NH.90-NFH Sea Lion	Marineflieger MFG 5, Nordholz	
79+64	NH Industries NH.90-NFH Sea Lion	Marineflieger (on order)	
79+65	NH Industries NH.90-NFH Sea Lion	Marineflieger (on order)	
79+66	NH Industries NH.90-NFH Sea Lion	Marineflieger (on order)	
79+67	NH Industries NH.90-NFH Sea Lion	Marineflieger (on order)	
79+68	NH Industries NH.90-NFH Sea Lion	Marineflieger (on order)	
82+01	Eurocopter AS.532U-2 Cougar	Luftwaffe 3/FBS, Berlin-Tegel	
82+02	Eurocopter AS.532U-2 Cougar	Luftwaffe 3/FBS, Berlin-Tegel	
82+03	Eurocopter AS.532U-2 Cougar	Luftwaffe 3/FBS, Berlin-Tegel	
82+51	Eurocopter EC.135P-1	Heer IntHubschrAusbZ, Bückeburg	
82+52	Eurocopter EC.135P-1	Heer IntHubschrAusbZ, Bückeburg	
82+53	Eurocopter EC.135P-1	Heer IntHubschrAusbZ, Bückeburg	
82+54	Eurocopter EC.135P-1	Heer IntHubschrAusbZ, Bückeburg	
82+55	Eurocopter EC.135P-1	Heer IntHubschrAusbZ, Bückeburg	
82+56	Eurocopter EC.135P-1	Heer IntHubschrAusbZ, Bückeburg	
82+57	Eurocopter EC.135P-1	Heer IntHubschrAusbZ, Bückeburg	
82+59	Eurocopter EC.135P-1	Heer IntHubschrAusbZ, Bückeburg	
82+60	Eurocopter EC.135P-1	Heer IntHubschrAusbZ, Bückeburg	
82+61	Eurocopter EC.135P-1	Heer IntHubschrAusbZ, Bückeburg	
82+63	Eurocopter EC.135P-1	Heer IntHubschrAusbZ, Bückeburg	
82+64	Eurocopter EC.135P-1	Heer IntHubschrAusbZ, Bückeburg	
82+65	Eurocopter EC.135P-1	Heer IntHubschrAusbZ, Bückeburg	
83+02	Westland Sea Lynx Mk88A	Marineflieger MFG 5, Nordholz	
83+03	Westland Sea Lynx Mk88A	Marineflieger MFG 5, Nordholz	
83+04	Westland Sea Lynx Mk88A	Marineflieger MFG 5, Nordholz	
83+05	Westland Sea Lynx Mk88A	Marineflieger MFG 5, Nordholz	
83+06	Westland Sea Lynx Mk88A	Marineflieger MFG 5, Nordholz	
83+07	Westland Sea Lynx Mk88A	Marineflieger MFG 5, Nordholz	
83+09	Westland Sea Lynx Mk88A	Marineflieger MFG 5, Nordholz	
83+10	Westland Sea Lynx Mk88A	Marineflieger MFG 5, Nordholz	
83+11	Westland Sea Lynx Mk88A	Marineflieger MFG 5, Nordholz	
83+12	Westland Sea Lynx Mk88A	Marineflieger MFG 5, Nordholz	
83+13	Westland Sea Lynx Mk88A	Marineflieger MFG 5, Nordholz	
83+15	Westland Sea Lynx Mk88A	Marineflieger MFG 5, Nordholz	
83+17	Westland Sea Lynx Mk88A	Marineflieger MFG 5, Nordholz	
83+18	Westland Sea Lynx Mk88A	Marineflieger MFG 5, Nordholz	
83+19	Westland Sea Lynx Mk88A	Marineflieger MFG 5, Nordholz	
83+20	Westland Sea Lynx Mk88A	Marineflieger MFG 5, Nordholz	

Notes	Serial	Type (code/other identity)	Owner/operator, location or fate
	83+21	Westland Sea Lynx Mk88A	Marineflieger MFG 5, Nordholz
	83+22	Westland Sea Lynx Mk88A	Marineflieger MFG 5, Nordholz
	83+23	Westland Sea Lynx Mk88A	Marineflieger MFG 5, Nordholz
	83+24	Westland Sea Lynx Mk88A	Marineflieger MFG 5, Nordholz
	83+25	Westland Sea Lynx Mk88A	Marineflieger MFG 5, Nordholz
	84+05	Sikorsky/VFW CH-53G	Luftwaffe HSG 64, Laupheim
	84+09	Sikorsky/VFW CH-53G	Luftwaffe TsLw 3, Fassberg
	84+13	Sikorsky/VFW CH-53GA	Luftwaffe HSG 64, Laupheim
	84+14	Sikorsky/VFW CH-53GE	Luftwaffe HSG 64, Laupheim
	84+15	Sikorsky/VFW CH-53GS	Luftwaffe HSG 64, Laupheim
	84+18	Sikorsky/VFW CH-53G	Luftwaffe HSG 64, Laupheim
	84+19	Sikorsky/VFW CH-53G	Luftwaffe TsLw 3, Fassberg
	84+24	Sikorsky/VFW CH-53GA	Luftwaffe HSG 64, Laupheim
	84+25	Sikorsky/VFW CH-53GS	Luftwaffe HSG 64, Laupheim
	84+26	Sikorsky/VFW CH-53GE	Luftwaffe WTD 61, Ingolstadt
	84+27	Sikorsky/VFW CH-53G	Luftwaffe
	84+28	Sikorsky/VFW CH-53GA	Luftwaffe HSG 64, Laupheim
	84+29	Sikorsky/VFW CH-53G	Luftwaffe HSG 64, Laupheim
	84+30	Sikorsky/VFW CH-53GS	Luftwaffe HSG 64, Laupheim
	84+31	Sikorsky/VFW CH-53GA	Luftwaffe HSG 64, Laupheim
	84+32	Sikorsky/VFW CH-53G	Luftwaffe HSG 64, Laupheim
	84+33	Sikorsky/VFW CH-53GA	Luftwaffe HSG 64, Laupheim
	84+34	Sikorsky/VFW CH-53G	Luftwaffe HSG 64, Laupheim
	84+35	Sikorsky/VFW CH-53GA	Luftwaffe HSG 64, Laupheim
	84+37	Sikorsky/VFW CH-53GA	Luftwaffe HSG 64, Laupheim
	84+38	Sikorsky/VFW CH-53G	Luftwaffe HSG 64, Laupheim
	84+39	Sikorsky/VFW CH-53GA	Luftwaffe HSG 64, Laupheim
	84+40	Sikorsky/VFW CH-53G	Luftwaffe HSG 64, Laupheim
	84+42	Sikorsky/VFW CH-53GS	Luftwaffe HSG 64, Laupheim
	84+43	Sikorsky/VFW CH-53GS	Luftwaffe HSG 64, Laupheim
	84+44	Sikorsky/VFW CH-53G	Luftwaffe HSG 64, Laupheim
	84+45	Sikorsky/VFW CH-53GS	Luftwaffe HSG 64, Laupheim
	84+46	Sikorsky/VFW CH-53G	Luftwaffe HSG 64, Laupheim
	84+47	Sikorsky/VFW CH-53GA	Luftwaffe HSG 64, Laupheim
	84+48	Sikorsky/VFW CH-53G	Luftwaffe HSG 64, Laupheim
	84+49	Sikorsky/VFW CH-53GA	Luftwaffe HSG 64, Laupheim
	84+50	Sikorsky/VFW CH-53GA	Luftwaffe HSG 64, Laupheim
	84+51	Sikorsky/VFW CH-53GS	Luftwaffe HSG 64, Laupheim
	84+52	Sikorsky/VFW CH-53GS	Luftwaffe HSG 64, Laupheim
	84+53	Sikorsky/VFW CH-53GE	Luftwaffe HSG 64, Laupheim
	84+54	Sikorsky/VFW CH-53G	Luftwaffe HSG 64, Laupheim
	84+55	Sikorsky/VFW CH-53G	Airbus Helicopters, Donauwörth
	84+57	Sikorsky/VFW CH-53G	Luftwaffe HSG 64, Laupheim
	84+58	Sikorsky/VFW CH-53G	Luftwaffe HSG 64, Laupheim
	84+59	Sikorsky/VFW CH-53GS	Luftwaffe HSG 64, Laupheim
	84+62	Sikorsky/VFW CH-53GS	Luftwaffe HSG 64, Laupheim
	84+63	Sikorsky/VFW CH-53GA	Luftwaffe HSG 64, Laupheim
	84+64	Sikorsky/VFW CH-53GS	Luftwaffe HSG 64, Laupheim
	84+65	Sikorsky/VFW CH-53GA	Luftwaffe HSG 64, Laupheim
	84+66	Sikorsky/VFW CH-53GS	Luftwaffe HSG 64, Laupheim
	84+67	Sikorsky/VFW CH-53GS	Luftwaffe HSG 64, Laupheim
	84+68	Sikorsky/VFW CH-53GS	Luftwaffe HSG 64, Laupheim
	84+70	Sikorsky/VFW CH-53GA	Luftwaffe TsLw 3, Fassberg
	84+71	Sikorsky/VFW CH-53G	Luftwaffe HSG 64, Laupheim
	84+72	Sikorsky/VFW CH-53G	Luftwaffe HSG 64, Laupheim
	84+73	Sikorsky/VFW CH-53GS	Luftwaffe HSG 64, Laupheim
	84+74	Sikorsky/VFW CH-53G	Luftwaffe HSG 64, Laupheim
	84+75	Sikorsky/VFW CH-53G	Luftwaffe HSG 64, Laupheim
	84+76	Sikorsky/VFW CH-53G	Luftwaffe HSG 64, Laupheim
	84+78	Sikorsky/VFW CH-53GS	Luftwaffe TsLw 3, Fassberg
	84+79	Sikorsky/VFW CH-53GS	Luftwaffe HSG 64, Laupheim
	84+80	Sikorsky/VFW CH-53G	Luftwaffe HSG 64, Laupheim

Serial	Type (code/other identity)	Owner/operator, location or fate	Notes
84+82	Sikorsky/VFW CH-53GE	Luftwaffe HSG 64, Laupheim	
84+83	Sikorsky/VFW CH-53G	Luftwaffe TsLw 3, Fassberg	
84+85	Sikorsky/VFW CH-53GS	Luftwaffe HSG 64, Laupheim	
84+86	Sikorsky/VFW CH-53GA	Luftwaffe HSG 64, Laupheim	
84+87	Sikorsky/VFW CH-53GS	Luftwaffe HSG 64, Laupheim	
84+88	Sikorsky/VFW CH-53G	Luftwaffe HSG 64, Laupheim	
84+89	Sikorsky/VFW CH-53GA	Luftwaffe HSG 64, Laupheim	
84+90	Sikorsky/VFW CH-53G	Luftwaffe HSG 64, Laupheim	
84+91	Sikorsky/VFW CH-53GS	Luftwaffe HSG 64, Laupheim	
84+92	Sikorsky/VFW CH-53GS	Luftwaffe HSG 64, Laupheim	
84+94	Sikorsky/VFW CH-53G	Luftwaffe WTD 61, Ingolstadt	
84+96	Sikorsky/VFW CH-53GE	Luftwaffe WTD 61, Ingolstadt	
84+97	Sikorsky/VFW CH-53GA	Luftwaffe HSG 64, Laupheim	
84+98	Sikorsky/VFW CH-53GS	Luftwaffe HSG 64, Laupheim	
84+99	Sikorsky/VFW CH-53GA	Luftwaffe HSG 64, Laupheim	
85+00	Sikorsky/VFW CH-53GS	Luftwaffe HSG 64, Laupheim	
85+01	Sikorsky/VFW CH-53GS	Luftwaffe HSG 64, Laupheim	
85+02	Sikorsky/VFW CH-53G	Luftwaffe HSG 64, Laupheim	
85+03	Sikorsky/VFW CH-53GA	Luftwaffe HSG 64, Laupheim	
85+04	Sikorsky/VFW CH-53GA	Luftwaffe HSG 64, Laupheim	
85+05	Sikorsky/VFW CH-53GS	Luftwaffe HSG 64, Laupheim	
85+06	Sikorsky/VFW CH-53GA	Luftwaffe HSG 64, Laupheim	
85+07	Sikorsky/VFW CH-53GS	Luftwaffe HSG 64, Laupheim	
85+08	Sikorsky/VFW CH-53GS	Luftwaffe HSG 64, Laupheim	
85+10	Sikorsky/VFW CH-53GS	Luftwaffe HSG 64, Laupheim	
85+12	Sikorsky/VFW CH-53GS	Luftwaffe HSG 64, Laupheim	
89+50	Westland Sea King Mk.41	Marineflieger MFG 5, Nordholz	
89+51	Westland Sea King Mk.41	Marineflieger MFG 5, Nordholz	
89+52	Westland Sea King Mk.41	*Instructional airframe, Nordholz*	
89+53	Westland Sea King Mk.41	Marineflieger MFG 5, Nordholz	
89+54	Westland Sea King Mk.41	Marineflieger MFG 5, Nordholz	
89+55	Westland Sea King Mk.41 $	Marineflieger MFG 5, Nordholz	
89+56	Westland Sea King Mk.41	Marineflieger MFG 5, Nordholz	
89+57	Westland Sea King Mk.41	Marineflieger MFG 5, Nordholz	
89+58	Westland Sea King Mk.41 $	Marineflieger MFG 5, Nordholz	
89+60	Westland Sea King Mk.41	Marineflieger MFG 5, Nordholz	
89+61	Westland Sea King Mk.41	Marineflieger MFG 5, Nordholz	
89+62	Westland Sea King Mk.41	*Dumped Nordholz, 2022*	
89+63	Westland Sea King Mk.41	Marineflieger MFG 5, Nordholz	
89+64	Westland Sea King Mk.41 $	Marineflieger MFG 5, Nordholz	
89+65	Westland Sea King Mk.41	Marineflieger MFG 5, Nordholz	
89+66	Westland Sea King Mk.41	Marineflieger MFG 5, Nordholz	
89+68	Westland Sea King Mk.41	Marineflieger MFG 5, Nordholz	
89+69	Westland Sea King Mk.41	Marineflieger MFG 5, Nordholz	
89+70	Westland Sea King Mk.41	Marineflieger MFG 5, Nordholz	
89+71	Westland Sea King Mk.41	Marineflieger MFG 5, Nordholz	
98+03	Eurofighter EF.2000(T) (IPA3)	Luftwaffe WTD 61, Ingolstadt	
98+07	Eurofighter EF.2000 (IPA7) $	Luftwaffe WTD 61, Ingolstadt	
98+08	Eurofighter EF.2000GT (IPA8)	Airbus Defence & Space, Manching	
98+16	Eurocopter EC.665 Tiger UHT	Luftwaffe TsLw 3, Fassberg	
98+18	Eurocopter EC.665 Tiger UHT (74+04)	Airbus Helicopters, Donauwörth	
98+49	Eurocopter EC.665 Tiger UHT (74+49)	Airbus Helicopters, Donauwörth	
98+51	NH Industries NH.90-NFH Sea Lion	Airbus Helicopters, Donauwörth	
98+59	Panavia Tornado IDS(T) (43+21) $	Luftwaffe WTD 61, Ingolstadt	
98+60	Panavia Tornado IDS (43+89)	Luftwaffe WTD 61, Ingolstadt	
98+77	Panavia Tornado IDS (45+29) $	Luftwaffe WTD 61, Ingolstadt	
98+79	Panavia Tornado ECR (45+75) $	Luftwaffe WTD 61, Ingolstadt	
98+90	NH Industries NH.90-TTH	Airbus Helicopters, Donauwörth	
Civil operated aircraft in military use			
D-HCDL	Eurocopter EC.135P-2+	Marineflieger MFG 5, Nordholz	
D-HDDL	Eurocopter EC.135P-2+	Marineflieger MFG 5, Nordholz	
D-HTMG	Eurocopter EC.135P-2+	Marineflieger MFG 5, Nordholz	

Notes	Serial	Type (code/other identity)	Owner/operator, location or fate
	GHANA		
	9G-EXE	Dassault Falcon 900EASy	Ghana Air Force VIP Flight, Accra
	GREECE		
	Ellinikí Polemikí Aeroporía/Hellenic Air Force (HAF)		
	001	Lockheed Martin F-16C-52 Fighting Falcon	HAF 335 Mira/116 PM, Áraxos
	002	Lockheed Martin F-16C-52 Fighting Falcon	HAF 336 Mira/116 PM, Áraxos
	003	Lockheed Martin F-16C-52 Fighting Falcon	HAF 335 Mira/116 PM, Áraxos
	004	Lockheed Martin F-16C-52 Fighting Falcon	HAF 336 Mira/116 PM, Áraxos
	005	Lockheed Martin F-16V Fighting Falcon	HAF/Hellenic Aerospace Industry, Fort Worth, USA
	006	Lockheed Martin F-16V Fighting Falcon	HAF 336 Mira/116 PM, Áraxos
	007	Lockheed Martin F-16C-52 Fighting Falcon	HAF 335 Mira/116 PM, Áraxos
	008	Lockheed Martin F-16C-52 Fighting Falcon	HAF 336 Mira/116 PM, Áraxos
	009	Lockheed Martin F-16C-52 Fighting Falcon	HAF 335 Mira/116 PM, Áraxos
	010	Lockheed Martin F-16C-52 Fighting Falcon	HAF 336 Mira/116 PM, Áraxos
	011	Lockheed Martin F-16C-52 Fighting Falcon	HAF 335 Mira/116 PM, Áraxos
	012	Lockheed Martin F-16C-52 Fighting Falcon	HAF 336 Mira/116 PM, Áraxos
	013	Lockheed Martin F-16C-52 Fighting Falcon	HAF 335 Mira/116 PM, Áraxos
	014	Lockheed Martin F-16C-52 Fighting Falcon	HAF 336 Mira/116 PM, Áraxos
	015	Lockheed Martin F-16C-52 Fighting Falcon	HAF 335 Mira/116 PM, Áraxos
	016	Lockheed Martin F-16C-52 Fighting Falcon	HAF 336 Mira/116 PM, Áraxos
	017	Lockheed Martin F-16C-52 Fighting Falcon	HAF 335 Mira/116 PM, Áraxos
	018	Lockheed Martin F-16C-52 Fighting Falcon	HAF 336 Mira/116 PM, Áraxos
	019	Lockheed Martin F-16C-52 Fighting Falcon	HAF 335 Mira/116 PM, Áraxos
	020	Lockheed Martin F-16C-52 Fighting Falcon	HAF 336 Mira/116 PM, Áraxos
	021	Lockheed Martin F-16D-52 Fighting Falcon	HAF 335 Mira/116 PM, Áraxos
	022	Lockheed Martin F-16D-52 Fighting Falcon	HAF 335 Mira/116 PM, Áraxos
	023	Lockheed Martin F-16D-52 Fighting Falcon $	HAF 335 Mira/116 PM, Áraxos
	024	Lockheed Martin F-16D-52 Fighting Falcon	HAF 336 Mira/116 PM, Áraxos
	025	Lockheed Martin F-16D-52 Fighting Falcon	HAF 335 Mira/116 PM, Áraxos
	026	Lockheed Martin F-16D-52 Fighting Falcon	HAF 336 Mira/116 PM, Áraxos
	027	Lockheed Martin F-16D-52 Fighting Falcon	HAF 335 Mira/116 PM, Áraxos
	028	Lockheed Martin F-16D-52 Fighting Falcon	HAF 336 Mira/116 PM, Áraxos
	029	Lockheed Martin F-16D-52 Fighting Falcon	HAF 335 Mira/116 PM, Áraxos
	030	Lockheed Martin F-16D-52 Fighting Falcon	HAF 336 Mira/116 PM, Áraxos
	045	Lockheed Martin F-16C-50 Fighting Falcon	HAF 347 Mira/111 PM, Nea Ankhialos
	046	Lockheed Martin F-16C-50 Fighting Falcon	HAF 341 Mira/111 PM, Nea Ankhialos
	047	Lockheed Martin F-16C-50 Fighting Falcon	HAF 347 Mira/111 PM, Nea Ankhialos
	048	Lockheed Martin F-16C-50 Fighting Falcon	HAF 341 Mira/111 PM, Nea Ankhialos
	049	Lockheed Martin F-16C-50 Fighting Falcon	HAF 347 Mira/111 PM, Nea Ankhialos
	050	Lockheed Martin F-16C-50 Fighting Falcon	HAF 341 Mira/111 PM, Nea Ankhialos
	051	Lockheed Martin F-16C-50 Fighting Falcon	HAF 347 Mira/111 PM, Nea Ankhialos
	052	Lockheed Martin F-16C-50 Fighting Falcon	HAF 341 Mira/111 PM, Nea Ankhialos
	053	Lockheed Martin F-16C-50 Fighting Falcon	HAF 347 Mira/111 PM, Nea Ankhialos
	054	Lockheed Martin F-16C-50 Fighting Falcon	HAF 341 Mira/111 PM, Nea Ankhialos
	055	Lockheed Martin F-16C-50 Fighting Falcon	HAF 347 Mira/111 PM, Nea Ankhialos
	056	Lockheed Martin F-16C-50 Fighting Falcon	HAF 341 Mira/111 PM, Nea Ankhialos
	057	Lockheed Martin F-16C-50 Fighting Falcon	HAF 347 Mira/111 PM, Nea Ankhialos
	058	Lockheed Martin F-16C-50 Fighting Falcon	HAF 341 Mira/111 PM, Nea Ankhialos
	060	Lockheed Martin F-16C-50 Fighting Falcon	HAF 347 Mira/111 PM, Nea Ankhialos
	061	Lockheed Martin F-16C-50 Fighting Falcon	HAF 347 Mira/111 PM, Nea Ankhialos
	062	Lockheed Martin F-16C-50 Fighting Falcon $	HAF 341 Mira/111 PM, Nea Ankhialos
	063	Lockheed Martin F-16C-50 Fighting Falcon	HAF 347 Mira/111 PM, Nea Ankhialos
	064	Lockheed Martin F-16C-50 Fighting Falcon	HAF 341 Mira/111 PM, Nea Ankhialos
	065	Lockheed Martin F-16C-50 Fighting Falcon	HAF 347 Mira/111 PM, Nea Ankhialos
	066	Lockheed Martin F-16C-50 Fighting Falcon	HAF 341 Mira/111 PM, Nea Ankhialos
	067	Lockheed Martin F-16C-50 Fighting Falcon	HAF 347 Mira/111 PM, Nea Ankhialos
	068	Lockheed Martin F-16C-50 Fighting Falcon	HAF 341 Mira/111 PM, Nea Ankhialos
	069	Lockheed Martin F-16C-50 Fighting Falcon	HAF 347 Mira/111 PM, Nea Ankhialos
	070	Lockheed Martin F-16C-50 Fighting Falcon	HAF 341 Mira/111 PM, Nea Ankhialos
	071	Lockheed Martin F-16C-50 Fighting Falcon	HAF 347 Mira/111 PM, Nea Ankhialos

Serial	Type (code/other identity)	Owner/operator, location or fate	Notes
072	Lockheed Martin F-16C-50 Fighting Falcon	HAF 341 Mira/111 PM, Nea Ankhialos	
073	Lockheed Martin F-16C-50 Fighting Falcon	HAF 347 Mira/111 PM, Nea Ankhialos	
074	Lockheed Martin F-16C-50 Fighting Falcon	HAF 341 Mira/111 PM, Nea Ankhialos	
075	Lockheed Martin F-16C-50 Fighting Falcon	HAF 347 Mira/111 PM, Nea Ankhialos	
076	Lockheed Martin F-16C-50 Fighting Falcon $	HAF 341 Mira/111 PM, Nea Ankhialos	
077	Lockheed Martin F-16D-50 Fighting Falcon	HAF 341 Mira/111 PM, Nea Ankhialos	
078	Lockheed Martin F-16D-50 Fighting Falcon	HAF 347 Mira/111 PM, Nea Ankhialos	
079	Lockheed Martin F-16D-50 Fighting Falcon	HAF 347 Mira/111 PM, Nea Ankhialos	
080	Lockheed Martin F-16D-50 Fighting Falcon	HAF 341 Mira/111 PM, Nea Ankhialos	
081	Lockheed Martin F-16D-50 Fighting Falcon	HAF 347 Mira/111 PM, Nea Ankhialos	
082	Lockheed Martin F-16D-50 Fighting Falcon	HAF 341 Mira/111 PM, Nea Ankhialos	
083	Lockheed Martin F-16D-50 Fighting Falcon	HAF 347 Mira/111 PM, Nea Ankhialos	
110	Lockheed Martin F-16C-30 Fighting Falcon	HAF 330 Mira/111 PM, Nea Ankhialos	
111	Lockheed Martin F-16C-30 Fighting Falcon	HAF 330 Mira/111 PM, Nea Ankhialos	
112	Lockheed Martin F-16C-30 Fighting Falcon	HAF 330 Mira/111 PM, Nea Ankhialos	
113	Lockheed Martin F-16C-30 Fighting Falcon	HAF 330 Mira/111 PM, Nea Ankhialos	
114	Lockheed Martin F-16C-30 Fighting Falcon	HAF 330 Mira/111 PM, Nea Ankhialos	
115	Lockheed Martin F-16C-30 Fighting Falcon	HAF 330 Mira/111 PM, Nea Ankhialos	
116	Lockheed Martin F-16C-30 Fighting Falcon	HAF 330 Mira/111 PM, Nea Ankhialos	
117	Lockheed Martin F-16C-30 Fighting Falcon	HAF 330 Mira/111 PM, Nea Ankhialos	
118	Lockheed Martin F-16C-30 Fighting Falcon	HAF 330 Mira/111 PM, Nea Ankhialos	
119	Lockheed Martin F-16C-30 Fighting Falcon	HAF 330 Mira/111 PM, Nea Ankhialos	
120	Lockheed Martin F-16C-30 Fighting Falcon	HAF 330 Mira/111 PM, Nea Ankhialos	
121	Lockheed Martin F-16C-30 Fighting Falcon	HAF 341 Mira/111 PM, Nea Ankhialos	
122	Lockheed Martin F-16C-30 Fighting Falcon	HAF 330 Mira/111 PM, Nea Ankhialos	
124	Lockheed Martin F-16C-30 Fighting Falcon	HAF 330 Mira/111 PM, Nea Ankhialos	
125	Lockheed Martin F-16C-30 Fighting Falcon	HAF 330 Mira/111 PM, Nea Ankhialos	
126	Lockheed Martin F-16C-30 Fighting Falcon	HAF 330 Mira/111 PM, Nea Ankhialos	
127	Lockheed Martin F-16C-30 Fighting Falcon	HAF 330 Mira/111 PM, Nea Ankhialos	
128	Lockheed Martin F-16C-30 Fighting Falcon	HAF 330 Mira/111 PM, Nea Ankhialos	
129	Lockheed Martin F-16C-30 Fighting Falcon	HAF 330 Mira/111 PM, Nea Ankhialos	
130	Lockheed Martin F-16C-30 Fighting Falcon	HAF 330 Mira/111 PM, Nea Ankhialos	
132	Lockheed Martin F-16C-30 Fighting Falcon	HAF 330 Mira/111 PM, Nea Ankhialos	
133	Lockheed Martin F-16C-30 Fighting Falcon	HAF 330 Mira/111 PM, Nea Ankhialos	
134	Lockheed Martin F-16C-30 Fighting Falcon	HAF 330 Mira/111 PM, Nea Ankhialos	
136	Lockheed Martin F-16C-30 Fighting Falcon	HAF 330 Mira/111 PM, Nea Ankhialos	
138	Lockheed Martin F-16C-30 Fighting Falcon	HAF 330 Mira/111 PM, Nea Ankhialos	
139	Lockheed Martin F-16C-30 Fighting Falcon	HAF 330 Mira/111 PM, Nea Ankhialos	
140	Lockheed Martin F-16C-30 Fighting Falcon	HAF 330 Mira/111 PM, Nea Ankhialos	
141	Lockheed Martin F-16C-30 Fighting Falcon	HAF 330 Mira/111 PM, Nea Ankhialos	
143	Lockheed Martin F-16C-30 Fighting Falcon	HAF 330 Mira/111 PM, Nea Ankhialos	
144	Lockheed Martin F-16D-30 Fighting Falcon	HAF 330 Mira/111 PM, Nea Ankhialos	
145	Lockheed Martin F-16D-30 Fighting Falcon	HAF 330 Mira/111 PM, Nea Ankhialos	
148	Lockheed Martin F-16D-30 Fighting Falcon	HAF 330 Mira/111 PM, Nea Ankhialos	
149	Lockheed Martin F-16D-30 Fighting Falcon	HAF 330 Mira/111 PM, Nea Ankhialos	
201	Dassault Mirage 2000-BG	HAF, stored Tanagra	
202	Dassault Mirage 2000-BG	HAF, stored Tanagra	
210	Dassault Mirage 2000-EG	HAF, stored Tanagra	
212	Dassault Mirage 2000-EG	HAF, stored Tanagra	
213	Dassault Mirage 2000-EG	HAF, stored Tanagra	
215	Dassault Mirage 2000-EG	HAF, stored Tanagra	
216	Dassault Mirage 2000-EG	HAF, stored Tanagra	
217	Dassault Mirage 2000-EG	HAF 332 MAPK/114 PM, Tanagra	
218	Dassault Mirage 2000-EG	HAF, stored Tanagra	
219	Dassault Mirage 2000-EG	HAF, stored Tanagra	
220	Dassault Mirage 2000-EG	HAF, stored Tanagra	
221	Dassault Mirage 2000-EG	HAF 332 MAPK/114 PM, Tanagra	
226	Dassault Mirage 2000-EG	HAF 332 MAPK/114 PM, Tanagra	
231	Dassault Mirage 2000-EG	HAF, stored Tanagra	
232	Dassault Mirage 2000-EG	HAF 332 MAPK/114 PM, Tanagra	
233	Dassault Mirage 2000-EG	HAF, stored Tanagra	
237	Dassault Mirage 2000-EG	HAF 332 MAPK/114 PM, Tanagra	

Notes	Serial	Type (code/other identity)	Owner/operator, location or fate
	242	Dassault Mirage 2000-EG	HAF, stored Tanagra
	273	Dassault Falcon 7X (F-HHED)	HAF 352 MMYP/112 PM, Elefsis
	...	Dassault Rafale EG	HAF 332 MAPK/114 PM, Tanagra (on order)
	...	Dassault Rafale EG	HAF 332 MAPK/114 PM, Tanagra (on order)
	...	Dassault Rafale EG	HAF 332 MAPK/114 PM, Tanagra (on order)
	...	Dassault Rafale EG	HAF 332 MAPK/114 PM, Tanagra (on order)
	...	Dassault Rafale EG	HAF 332 MAPK/114 PM, Tanagra (on order)
	...	Dassault Rafale EG	HAF 332 MAPK/114 PM, Tanagra (on order)
	...	Dassault Rafale EG	HAF 332 MAPK/114 PM, Tanagra (on order)
	...	Dassault Rafale EG	HAF 332 MAPK/114 PM, Tanagra (on order)
	...	Dassault Rafale EG	HAF 332 MAPK/114 PM, Tanagra (on order)
	...	Dassault Rafale EG	HAF 332 MAPK/114 PM, Tanagra (on order)
	...	Dassault Rafale EG	HAF 332 MAPK/114 PM, Tanagra (on order)
	...	Dassault Rafale EG	HAF 332 MAPK/114 PM, Tanagra (on order)
	...	Dassault Rafale EG	HAF 332 MAPK/114 PM, Tanagra (on order)
	...	Dassault Rafale EG	HAF 332 MAPK/114 PM, Tanagra (on order)
	374	Embraer ERJ.145H AEW&C	HAF 380 Mira/112 PM, Elefsis
	401	Dassault Rafale DG (305)	HAF 332 MAPK/114 PM, Tanagra
	402	Dassault Rafale DG (306)	HAF 332 MAPK/114 PM, Tanagra
	...	Dassault Rafale DG	HAF 332 MAPK/114 PM, Tanagra (on order)
	...	Dassault Rafale DG	HAF 332 MAPK/114 PM, Tanagra (on order)
	410	Dassault Rafale EG (103)	HAF 332 MAPK/114 PM, Tanagra
	411	Dassault Rafale EG (118)	HAF 332 MAPK/114 PM, Tanagra
	412	Dassault Rafale EG (123)	HAF 332 MAPK/114 PM, Tanagra
	413	Dassault Rafale EG (112)	HAF 332 MAPK/114 PM, Tanagra
	414	Dassault Rafale EG	HAF 332 MAPK/114 PM, Tanagra (on order)
	415	Dassault Rafale EG	HAF 332 MAPK/114 PM, Tanagra (on order)
	416	Dassault Rafale EG	HAF 332 MAPK/114 PM, Tanagra (on order)
	417	Dassault Rafale EG	HAF 332 MAPK/114 PM, Tanagra (on order)
	418	Dassault Rafale EG	HAF 332 MAPK/114 PM, Tanagra (on order)
	419	Dassault Rafale EG	HAF 332 MAPK/114 PM, Tanagra (on order)
	451	Dassault Rafale EG	HAF 332 MAPK/114 PM, Tanagra
	452	Dassault Rafale EG	HAF 332 MAPK/114 PM, Tanagra
	453	Dassault Rafale EG	HAF 332 MAPK/114 PM, Tanagra
	500	Lockheed Martin F-16C-52 Fighting Falcon	HAF 343 Mira/115 PM, Souda
	501	Lockheed Martin F-16C-52 Fighting Falcon	HAF 337 Mira/110 PM, Larissa
	502	Lockheed Martin F-16C-52 Fighting Falcon	HAF 337 Mira/110 PM, Larissa
	503	Lockheed Martin F-16C-52 Fighting Falcon	HAF 343 Mira/115 PM, Souda
	504	Lockheed Martin F-16C-52 Fighting Falcon	HAF 343 Mira/115 PM, Souda
	505	Dassault Mirage 2000-5BG	HAF 331 MAPK/114 PM, Tanagra
	505	Lockheed Martin F-16V Fighting Falcon $	HAF 343 Mira/115 PM, Souda
	506	Dassault Mirage 2000-5BG	HAF 331 MAPK/114 PM, Tanagra
	506	Lockheed Martin F-16C-52 Fighting Falcon	HAF 340 Mira/115 PM, Souda
	507	Dassault Mirage 2000-5BG	HAF 331 MAPK/114 PM, Tanagra
	507	Lockheed Martin F-16C-52 Fighting Falcon	HAF 337 Mira/110 PM, Larissa
	508	Dassault Mirage 2000-5BG	HAF 331 MAPK/114 PM, Tanagra
	508	Lockheed Martin F-16C-52 Fighting Falcon	HAF 337 Mira/110 PM, Larissa
	509	Dassault Mirage 2000-5BG	HAF 331 MAPK/114 PM, Tanagra
	509	Lockheed Martin F-16C-52 Fighting Falcon	HAF 343 Mira/115 PM, Souda
	510	Lockheed Martin F-16C-52 Fighting Falcon	HAF 343 Mira/115 PM, Souda
	511	Dassault Mirage 2000-5EG	HAF 331 MAPK/114 PM, Tanagra
	511	Lockheed Martin F-16C-52 Fighting Falcon	HAF 343 Mira/115 PM, Souda
	514	Dassault Mirage 2000-5EG	HAF 331 MAPK/114 PM, Tanagra
	515	Lockheed Martin F-16C-52 Fighting Falcon	HAF 337 Mira/110 PM, Larissa
	517	Lockheed Martin F-16C-52 Fighting Falcon	HAF 337 Mira/110 PM, Larissa
	518	Lockheed Martin F-16C-52 Fighting Falcon	HAF 340 Mira/115 PM, Souda
	519	Lockheed Martin F-16C-52 Fighting Falcon	HAF 340 Mira/115 PM, Souda
	520	Lockheed Martin F-16C-52 Fighting Falcon	HAF 340 Mira/115 PM, Souda
	521	Lockheed Martin F-16C-52 Fighting Falcon	HAF 340 Mira/115 PM, Souda
	523	Lockheed Martin F-16C-52 Fighting Falcon $	HAF 340 Mira/115 PM, Souda
	524	Lockheed Martin F-16C-52 Fighting Falcon	HAF 337 Mira/110 PM, Larissa
	525	Lockheed Martin F-16C-52 Fighting Falcon	HAF 343 Mira/115 PM, Souda

Serial	Type (code/other identity)	Owner/operator, location or fate	Notes
526	Lockheed Martin F-16C-52 Fighting Falcon	HAF 343 Mira/115 PM, Souda	
527	Dassault Mirage 2000-5EG	HAF 331 MAPK/114 PM, Tanagra	
527	Lockheed Martin F-16C-52 Fighting Falcon	HAF 343 Mira/115 PM, Souda	
528	Lockheed Martin F-16C-52 Fighting Falcon	HAF 337 Mira/110 PM, Larissa	
529	Lockheed Martin F-16C-52 Fighting Falcon	HAF 343 Mira/115 PM, Souda	
530	Dassault Mirage 2000-5EG	HAF 331 MAPK/114 PM, Tanagra	
530	Lockheed Martin F-16C-52 Fighting Falcon	HAF 337 Mira/110 PM, Larissa	
531	Lockheed Martin F-16C-52 Fighting Falcon $	HAF 337 Mira/110 PM, Larissa	
532	Lockheed Martin F-16C-52 Fighting Falcon	HAF 337 Mira/110 PM, Larissa	
533	Lockheed Martin F-16C-52 Fighting Falcon	HAF 340 Mira/115 PM, Souda	
534	Dassault Mirage 2000-5EG	HAF 331 MAPK/114 PM, Tanagra	
534	Lockheed Martin F-16C-52 Fighting Falcon	HAF 340 Mira/115 PM, Souda	
535	Dassault Mirage 2000-5EG	HAF 331 MAPK/114 PM, Tanagra	
535	Lockheed Martin F-16C-52 Fighting Falcon	HAF 340 Mira/115 PM, Souda	
536	Dassault Mirage 2000-5EG	HAF 331 MAPK/114 PM, Tanagra	
536	Lockheed Martin F-16C-52 Fighting Falcon	HAF 340 Mira/115 PM, Souda	
537	Lockheed Martin F-16C-52 Fighting Falcon	HAF 340 Mira/115 PM, Souda	
538	Lockheed Martin F-16C-52 Fighting Falcon	HAF 340 Mira/115 PM, Souda	
539	Lockheed Martin F-16C-52 Fighting Falcon	HAF 337 Mira/110 PM, Larissa	
540	Dassault Mirage 2000-5BG	HAF 331 MAPK/114 PM, Tanagra	
543	Dassault Mirage 2000-5BG	HAF 331 MAPK/114 PM, Tanagra	
545	Dassault Mirage 2000-5BG	HAF 331 MAPK/114 PM, Tanagra	
547	Dassault Mirage 2000-5BG	HAF 331 MAPK/114 PM, Tanagra	
548	Dassault Mirage 2000-5BG	HAF 331 MAPK/114 PM, Tanagra	
549	Dassault Mirage 2000-5BG	HAF 331 MAPK/114 PM, Tanagra	
550	Dassault Mirage 2000-5BG	HAF 331 MAPK/114 PM, Tanagra	
551	Dassault Mirage 2000-5BG $	HAF 331 MAPK/114 PM, Tanagra	
552	Dassault Mirage 2000-5BG	HAF 331 MAPK/114 PM, Tanagra	
553	Dassault Mirage 2000-5BG	HAF 331 MAPK/114 PM, Tanagra	
554	Dassault Mirage 2000-5BG	HAF 331 MAPK/114 PM, Tanagra	
555	Dassault Mirage 2000-5BG	HAF 331 MAPK/114 PM, Tanagra	
600	Lockheed Martin F-16D-52 Fighting Falcon	HAF 337 Mira/110 PM, Larissa	
601	Lockheed Martin F-16D-52 Fighting Falcon	HAF 340 Mira/115 PM, Souda	
602	Lockheed Martin F-16D-52 Fighting Falcon	HAF 340 Mira/115 PM, Souda	
603	Lockheed Martin F-16D-52 Fighting Falcon	HAF 340 Mira/115 PM, Souda	
605	Lockheed Martin F-16D-52 Fighting Falcon	HAF 340 Mira/115 PM, Souda	
606	Lockheed Martin F-16D-52 Fighting Falcon	HAF 337 Mira/110 PM, Larissa	
607	Lockheed Martin F-16D-52 Fighting Falcon	HAF 343 Mira/115 PM, Souda	
608	Lockheed Martin F-16D-52 Fighting Falcon	HAF 340 Mira/115 PM, Souda	
609	Lockheed Martin F-16D-52 Fighting Falcon	HAF 337 Mira/110 PM, Larissa	
610	Lockheed Martin F-16D-52 Fighting Falcon	HAF 340 Mira/115 PM, Souda	
611	Lockheed Martin F-16D-52 Fighting Falcon	HAF 337 Mira/110 PM, Larissa	
612	Lockheed Martin F-16D-52 Fighting Falcon	HAF 337 Mira/110 PM, Larissa	
613	Lockheed Martin F-16D-52 Fighting Falcon	HAF 343 Mira/115 PM, Souda	
615	Lockheed Martin F-16D-52 Fighting Falcon	HAF 343 Mira/115 PM, Souda	
616	Lockheed Martin F-16D-52 Fighting Falcon	HAF 343 Mira/115 PM, Souda	
617	Lockheed Martin F-16D-52 Fighting Falcon	HAF 343 Mira/115 PM, Souda	
618	Lockheed Martin F-16D-52 Fighting Falcon	HAF 343 Mira/115 PM, Souda	
619	Lockheed Martin F-16D-52 Fighting Falcon $	HAF 337 Mira/110 PM, Larissa	
671	Embraer ERJ.145H AEW&C	HAF 380 Mira/112 PM, Elefsís	
678	Gulfstream Aerospace Gulfstream V	HAF 352 MMYP/112 PM, Elefsís	
729	Embraer ERJ.145H AEW&C	HAF 380 Mira/112 PM, Elefsís	
741	Lockheed C-130H Hercules (ECM)	HAF 356 MTM/112 PM, Elefsís	
742	Lockheed C-130H Hercules	HAF 356 MTM/112 PM, Elefsís	
743	Lockheed C-130H Hercules	HAF, stored Tanagra	
744	Lockheed C-130H Hercules	HAF, stored Tanagra	
745	Lockheed C-130H Hercules $	HAF, stored Tanagra	
746	Lockheed C-130H Hercules	HAF, stored Tanagra	
747	Lockheed C-130H Hercules (ECM)	HAF 356 MTM/112 PM, Elefsís	
749	Lockheed C-130H Hercules	HAF 356 MTM/112 PM, Elefsís	
751	Lockheed C-130H Hercules	HAF 356 MTM/112 PM, Elefsís	
752	Lockheed C-130H Hercules $	HAF 356 MTM/112 PM, Elefsís	

Notes	Serial	Type (code/other identity)	Owner/operator, location or fate
	757	Embraer ERJ.145H AEW&C	HAF 380 Mira/112 PM, Elefsís
	4117	Aeritalia C-27J Spartan	HAF 354 Mira, Elefsís
	4118	Aeritalia C-27J Spartan	HAF 354 Mira, Elefsís
	4120	Aeritalia C-27J Spartan	HAF 354 Mira, Elefsís
	4121	Aeritalia C-27J Spartan	HAF 354 Mira, Elefsís
	4122	Aeritalia C-27J Spartan	HAF 354 Mira, Elefsís
	4123	Aeritalia C-27J Spartan	HAF 354 Mira, Elefsís
	4124	Aeritalia C-27J Spartan	HAF 354 Mira, Elefsís
	4125	Aeritalia C-27J Spartan	HAF 354 Mira, Elefsís
	135L-484	Embraer ERJ.135BJ Legacy	*To Cyprus as CAF-001*
	145-209	Embraer ERJ.135LR	HAF 352 MMYP/112 PM, Elefsís

HONDURAS
Fuerza Aérea Hondureña (FAH)/Honduran Air Force

	FAH-001	Embraer ERJ.135BJ Legacy 600	FAH, Tegucigalpa

HUNGARY
Magyar Légierö/Hungarian Air Force

	01	Boeing C-17A Globemaster III (08-0001)	NATO SAC, Heavy Airlift Wing, Pápa
	02	Boeing C-17A Globemaster III (08-0002)	NATO SAC, Heavy Airlift Wing, Pápa
	03	Boeing C-17A Globemaster III (08-0003)	NATO SAC, Heavy Airlift Wing, Pápa
	30	SAAB JAS 39C Gripen	Hungarian AF 59 Sz.D.REB, Kecskemét
	31	SAAB JAS 39C Gripen	Hungarian AF 59 Sz.D.REB, Kecskemét
	32	SAAB JAS 39C Gripen	Hungarian AF 59 Sz.D.REB, Kecskemét
	33	SAAB JAS 39C Gripen	Hungarian AF 59 Sz.D.REB, Kecskemét
	34	SAAB JAS 39C Gripen	Hungarian AF 59 Sz.D.REB, Kecskemét
	35	SAAB JAS 39C Gripen	Hungarian AF 59 Sz.D.REB, Kecskemét
	36	SAAB JAS 39C Gripen	Hungarian AF 59 Sz.D.REB, Kecskemét
	37	SAAB JAS 39C Gripen	Hungarian AF 59 Sz.D.REB, Kecskemét
	38	SAAB JAS 39C Gripen	Hungarian AF 59 Sz.D.REB, Kecskemét
	39	SAAB JAS 39C Gripen	Hungarian AF 59 Sz.D.REB, Kecskemét
	40	SAAB JAS 39C Gripen	Hungarian AF 59 Sz.D.REB, Kecskemét
	41	SAAB JAS 39C Gripen	Hungarian AF 59 Sz.D.REB, Kecskemét
	43	SAAB JAS 39D Gripen	Hungarian AF 59 Sz.D.REB, Kecskemét
	44	SAAB JAS 39D Gripen (39842)	Hungarian AF 59 Sz.D.REB, Kecskemét
	604	Airbus A.319-112 (9H-AGM)	Hungarian AF 59 Sz.D.REB, Kecskemét
	605	Airbus A.319-112 (9H-AGN)	Hungarian AF 59 Sz.D.REB, Kecskemét
	606	Dassault Falcon 7X (9H-AGO)	Hungarian AF 59 Sz.D.REB, Kecskemét
	607	Dassault Falcon 7X (HA-LKX)	Hungarian AF 59 Sz.D.REB, Kecskemét

INDIA
Bharatiya Vayu Sena/Indian Air Force (IAF)

	CB-8001	Boeing C-17A Globemaster III (11-0101)	IAF 81 Sqn, Hindon AB
	CB-8002	Boeing C-17A Globemaster III (11-0102)	IAF 81 Sqn, Hindon AB
	CB-8003	Boeing C-17A Globemaster III (11-0103)	IAF 81 Sqn, Hindon AB
	CB-8004	Boeing C-17A Globemaster III (11-0104)	IAF 81 Sqn, Hindon AB
	CB-8005	Boeing C-17A Globemaster III (11-0105)	IAF 81 Sqn, Hindon AB
	CB-8006	Boeing C-17A Globemaster III (11-0106)	IAF 81 Sqn, Hindon AB
	CB-8007	Boeing C-17A Globemaster III (11-0107)	IAF 81 Sqn, Hindon AB
	CB-8008	Boeing C-17A Globemaster III (11-0108)	IAF 81 Sqn, Hindon AB
	CB-8009	Boeing C-17A Globemaster III (11-0109)	IAF 81 Sqn, Hindon AB
	CB-8010	Boeing C-17A Globemaster III (11-0110)	IAF 81 Sqn, Hindon AB
	CB-8011	Boeing C-17A Globemaster III (14-0003)	IAF 81 Sqn, Hindon AB
	KC-3801	Lockheed C-130J-30 Hercules II	IAF 77 Sqn, Hindon AB
	KC-3802	Lockheed C-130J-30 Hercules II	IAF 77 Sqn, Hindon AB
	KC-3804	Lockheed C-130J-30 Hercules II	IAF 77 Sqn, Hindon AB
	KC-3805	Lockheed C-130J-30 Hercules II	IAF 77 Sqn, Hindon AB
	KC-3806	Lockheed C-130J-30 Hercules II	IAF 77 Sqn, Hindon AB
	KC-3807	Lockheed C-130J-30 Hercules II	IAF 87 Sqn, Arjan Singh AB
	KC-3808	Lockheed C-130J-30 Hercules II	IAF 87 Sqn, Arjan Singh AB
	KC-3809	Lockheed C-130J-30 Hercules II	IAF 87 Sqn, Arjan Singh AB
	KC-3810	Lockheed C-130J-30 Hercules II	IAF 87 Sqn, Arjan Singh AB

Serial	Type (code/other identity)	Owner/operator, location or fate	Notes
KC-3811	Lockheed C-130J-30 Hercules II	IAF 87 Sqn, Arjan Singh AB	
KC-3812	Lockheed C-130J-30 Hercules II	IAF 87 Sqn, Arjan Singh AB	
KC-3813	Lockheed C-130J-30 Hercules II	IAF 77 Sqn, Hindon AB	
Indian Government			
K-7066	Boeing 777-337ER (VT-ALV)	Indian Government, New Delhi	
K-7067	Boeing 777-337ER (VT-ALW)	Indian Government, New Delhi	
INDONESIA			
Indonesian Government			
A-001	Boeing 737-8U3	Government of Indonesia, Jakarta	
IRAQ			
Iraqi Government			
YI-ASF	Boeing 737-81Z	Government of Iraq, Baghdad	
ISRAEL			
Heyl ha'Avir/Israeli Air Force			
102	Lockheed C-130HI Karnaf	Israeli AF 131 Sqn, Nevatim	
250	Boeing KC-707 Re'em	Israeli AF 120 Sqn, Nevatim	
260	Boeing KC-707 Re'em	Israeli AF 120 Sqn, Nevatim	
264	Boeing KC-707 Re'em	Israeli AF 120 Sqn, Nevatim	
272	Boeing KC-707 Re'em	Israeli AF 120 Sqn, Nevatim	
275	Boeing KC-707 Re'em	Israeli AF 120 Sqn, Nevatim	
290	Boeing KC-707 Re'em	Israeli AF 120 Sqn, Nevatim	
295	Boeing KC-707 Re'em	Israeli AF 120 Sqn, Nevatim	
420	Lockheed KC-130HI Karnaf	Israeli AF 131 Sqn, Nevatim	
427	Lockheed C-130HI Karnaf	Israeli AF 131 Sqn, Nevatim	
428	Lockheed C-130HI Karnaf	Israeli AF 131 Sqn, Nevatim	
435	Lockheed C-130HI Karnaf	Israeli AF 131 Sqn, Nevatim	
436	Lockheed KC-130HI Karnaf	Israeli AF 131 Sqn, Nevatim	
522	Lockheed KC-130HI Karnaf	Israeli AF 131 Sqn, Nevatim	
545	Lockheed KC-130HI Karnaf	Israeli AF 131 Sqn, Nevatim	
661	Lockheed C-130J-30 Shimshon	Israeli AF 103 Sqn, Nevatim	
662	Lockheed C-130J-30 Shimshon	Israeli AF 103 Sqn, Nevatim	
663	Lockheed C-130J-30 Shimshon	Israeli AF 103 Sqn, Nevatim	
664	Lockheed C-130J-30 Shimshon	(on order)	
665	Lockheed C-130J-30 Shimshon	Israeli AF 103 Sqn, Nevatim	
667	Lockheed C-130J-30 Shimshon	Israeli AF 103 Sqn, Nevatim	
668	Lockheed C-130J-30 Shimshon	Israeli AF 103 Sqn, Nevatim	
669	Lockheed C-130J-30 Shimshon	Israeli AF 103 Sqn, Nevatim	
...	Boeing KC-46A Pegasus	Israeli AF (on order)	
...	Boeing KC-46A Pegasus	Israeli AF (on order)	
...	Boeing KC-46A Pegasus	Israeli AF (on order)	
...	Boeing KC-46A Pegasus	Israeli AF (on order)	
...	Boeing KC-46A Pegasus	Israeli AF (on order)	
...	Boeing KC-46A Pegasus	Israeli AF (on order)	
...	Boeing KC-46A Pegasus	Israeli AF (on order)	
...	Boeing KC-46A Pegasus	Israeli AF (on order)	
Israeli Government			
4X-ISR	Boeing 767-338ER	Israeli AF/State of Israel, stored Nevatim	
ITALY:			
Aeronautica Militare Italiana (AMI), Aviazione dell'Esercito, Guardia di Finanza (GdiF) &			
Marina Militare Italiana (MMI)			
MMX614	Eurofighter TF-2000A Typhoon	Alenia, Torino/Caselle	
CPX622	Aermacchi M-346FA	Leonardo, Venegono	
CPX624	Aermacchi T-345A	Leonardo, Venegono	
CPX625	Aermacchi M-346LFFA	Leonardo, Venegono	
MM7004	Panavia A-200C Tornado (IDS (MLU)) [6-55]	AMI GEA 6° Stormo, Ghedi	
MM7006	Panavia A-200C Tornado (IDS (MLU)) [6-31] $	AMI GEA 6° Stormo, Ghedi	
MM7007	Panavia A-200A Tornado (IDS) [6-01] $	AMI GEA 6° Stormo, Ghedi	
MM7008	Panavia A-200C Tornado (IDS (MLU)) [50-53]	AMI GEA 6° Stormo, Ghedi	

Notes	Serial	Type (code/other identity)	Owner/operator, location or fate
	MM7013	Panavia A-200C Tornado (IDS (MLU)) [6-75]	AMI GEA 6° Stormo, Ghedi
	MM7014	Panavia A-200C Tornado (IDS (MLU)) [6-13]	AMI GEA 6° Stormo, Ghedi
	MM7015	Panavia A-200C Tornado (IDS (MLU)) [6-32]	AMI GEA 6° Stormo, Ghedi
	MM7019	Panavia EA-200B Tornado (ECR) [6-02]	AMI GEA 6° Stormo, Ghedi
	MM7020	Panavia EA-200D Tornado (ECR (MLU)) [6-77]	AMI GEA 6° Stormo, Ghedi
	MM7021	Panavia EA-200B Tornado (ECR) [6-20]	AMI GEA 6° Stormo, Ghedi
	MM7023	Panavia A-200A Tornado (IDS) [6-63]	AMI GEA 6° Stormo, Ghedi
	MM7024	Panavia A-200C Tornado (IDS (MLU)) [6-50]	AMI GEA 6° Stormo, Ghedi
	MM7025	Panavia A-200A Tornado (IDS) [6-05]	AMI GEA 6° Stormo, Ghedi
	MM7026	Panavia A-200C Tornado (IDS (MLU)) [6-35]	AMI GEA 6° Stormo, Ghedi
	MM7029	Panavia A-200A Tornado (IDS) [6-22]	AMI GEA 6° Stormo, Ghedi
	MM7030	Panavia EA-200D Tornado (ECR (MLU)) [6-73]	AMI GEA 6° Stormo, Ghedi
	MM7034	Panavia EA-200B Tornado (ECR) [50-50]	AMI, stored Gioia del Colle
	MM7035	Panavia A-200C Tornado (IDS (MLU)) [6-27]	AMI GEA 6° Stormo, Ghedi
	MM7036	Panavia EA-200D Tornado (ECR MLU) [6-06]	AMI GEA 6° Stormo, Ghedi
	MM7038	Panavia A-200C Tornado (IDS (MLU)) [6-37]	AMI GEA 6° Stormo, Ghedi
	MM7039	Panavia EA-200D Tornado (IDS (MLU)) [6-33]	AMI GEA 6° Stormo, Ghedi
	MM7040	Panavia A-200C Tornado (IDS (MLU)) [6-21]	AMI GEA 6° Stormo, Ghedi
	MM7043	Panavia A-200A Tornado (IDS) [6-25]	AMI GEA 6° Stormo, Ghedi
	MM7044	Panavia A-200C Tornado (IDS (MLU)) [6-76]	AMI GEA 6° Stormo, Ghedi
	MM7047	Panavia EA-200D Tornado (ECR (MLU)) [6-61]	AMI GEA 6° Stormo, Ghedi
	MM7051	Panavia EA-200D Tornado (ECR (MLU)) [6-72]	AMI GEA 6° Stormo, Ghedi
	MM7052	Panavia EA-200D Tornado (ECR (MLU)) [6-64]	AMI GEA 6° Stormo, Ghedi
	MM7053	Panavia EA-200D Tornado (ECR (MLU)) [6-101]	AMI GEA 6° Stormo, Ghedi
	MM7054	Panavia EA-200D Tornado (ECR (MLU)) [6-100] $	AMI GEA 6° Stormo, Ghedi
	MM7055	Panavia EA-200D Tornado (ECR (MLU)) [6-65]	AMI GEA 6° Stormo, Ghedi
	MM7056	Panavia A-200A Tornado (IDS)	AMI GEA 6° Stormo, Ghedi
	MM7057	Panavia A-200C Tornado (IDS (MLU)) [6-04]	AMI GEA 6° Stormo, Ghedi
	MM7058	Panavia A-200C Tornado (IDS (MLU)) [6-11]	AMI GEA 6° Stormo, Ghedi
	MM7059	Panavia EA-200D Tornado (ECR (MLU)) [6-66]	AMI GEA 6° Stormo, Ghedi
	MM7062	Panavia EA-200D Tornado (ECR (MLU)) [6-74]	AMI GEA 6° Stormo, Ghedi
	MM7063	Panavia A-200C Tornado (IDS (MLU)) [6-26]	AMI GEA 6° Stormo, Ghedi .
	MM7064	Panavia A-200C Tornado (IDS (MLU)) [6-24]	AMI GEA 6° Stormo, Ghedi
	MM7066	Panavia EA-200D Tornado (ECR (MLU)) [6-43]	AMI GEA 6° Stormo, Ghedi
	MM7067	Panavia EA-200D Tornado (ECR (MLU)) [6-41]	AMI GEA 6° Stormo, Ghedi
	MM7068	Panavia EA-200D Tornado (ECR (MLU)) [6-67]	AMI GEA 6° Stormo, Ghedi
	MM7070	Panavia EA-200D Tornado (ECR (MLU)) [6-71]	AMI GEA 6° Stormo, Ghedi
	MM7071	Panavia A-200C Tornado (IDS (MLU)) [6-12]	AMI GEA 6° Stormo, Ghedi
	MM7072	Panavia A-200C Tornado (IDS (MLU)) [6-30]	AMI GEA 6° Stormo, Ghedi
	MM7073	Panavia EA-200D Tornado (ECR (MLU)) [6-34]	AMI GEA 6° Stormo, Ghedi
	MM7075	Panavia A-200C Tornado (IDS (MLU)) [6-07]	AMI GEA 6° Stormo, Ghedi
	CSX7079	Panavia EA-200D Tornado (ECR (MLU)) [RS-01]	AMI RSV, Pratica di Mare
	MM7081	Panavia EA-200D Tornado (ECR (MLU)) [6-57]	AMI GEA 6° Stormo, Ghedi
	MM7082	Panavia EA-200D Tornado (ECR (MLU)) [6-62]	AMI GEA 6° Stormo, Ghedi
	MM7084	Panavia EA-200D Tornado (ECR (MLU)) [6-03]	AMI GEA 6° Stormo, Ghedi
	CMX7085	Panavia A-200A Tornado (IDS) [36-50]	Alenia, Torino/Caselle
	MM7086	Panavia A-200A Tornado (IDS) [6-60]	AMI GEA 6° Stormo, Ghedi
	MM7088	Panavia A-200A Tornado (IDS) [6-10]	AMI GEA 6° Stormo, Ghedi
	MM7114	Aeritalia-EMB A-11B Ghibli (AMX-ACOL) [51-27] $	AMI GEA 51° Stormo, Istrana
	MM7126	Aeritalia-EMB A-11B Ghibli (AMX-ACOL) [51-61]	AMI, stored Istrana
	MM7129	Aeritalia-EMB A-11B Ghibli (AMX-ACOL) [32-15]	AMI, stored Amendola
	MM7149	Aeritalia-EMB A-11B Ghibli (AMX-ACOL) [51-26]	AMI GEA 51° Stormo, Istrana
	MM7160	Aeritalia-EMB A-11B Ghibli (AMX-ACOL) [32-10]	AMI, stored Amendola
	MM7161	Aeritalia-EMB A-11B Ghibli (AMX-ACOL) [51-31]	AMI, stored Istrana
	MM7162	Aeritalia-EMB A-11B Ghibli (AMX-ACOL) [51-33]	AMI GEA 51° Stormo, Istrana
	MM7163	Aeritalia-EMB A-11B Ghibli (AMX-ACOL) [51-72]	AMI GEA 51° Stormo, Istrana
	MM7164	Aeritalia-EMB A-11B Ghibli (AMX-ACOL) [51-40]	*Preserved at Viterbo, 2022*
	MM7165	Aeritalia-EMB A-11B Ghibli (AMX-ACOL) [32-16]	AMI, stored Amendola
	MM7166	Aeritalia-EMB A-11B Ghibli (AMX-ACOL) [51-32]	AMI, stored Istrana
	MM7167	Aeritalia-EMB A-11B Ghibli (AMX-ACOL) [51-56]	AMI, stored Istrana
	MM7168	Aeritalia-EMB A-11B Ghibli (AMX-ACOL) [51-55]	AMI, stored Grazzanise
	MM7169	Aeritalia-EMB A-11B Ghibli (AMX-ACOL) [51-66]	AMI GEA 51° Stormo, Istrana

Serial	Type (code/other identity)	Owner/operator, location or fate	Notes
MM7170	Aeritalia-EMB A-11B Ghibli (AMX-ACOL) [51-30]	AMI GEA 51° Stormo, Istrana	
MM7171	Aeritalia-EMB A-11B Ghibli (AMX-ACOL) [51-52]	AMI GEA 51° Stormo, Istrana	
MM7172	Aeritalia-EMB A-11B Ghibli (AMX-ACOL) [51-67]	AMI, stored Istrana	
MM7174	Aeritalia-EMB A-11B Ghibli (AMX-ACOL) [51-60]	AMI GEA 51° Stormo, Istrana	
MM7175	Aeritalia-EMB A-11B Ghibli (AMX-ACOL) [51-45]	AMI, stored Istrana	
MM7176	Aeritalia-EMB A-11B Ghibli (AMX-ACOL) [51-47]	AMI GEA 51° Stormo, Istrana	
MM7177	Aeritalia-EMB A-11B Ghibli (AMX-ACOL) [51-42]	AMI, stored Istrana	
MM7178	Aeritalia-EMB A-11B Ghibli (AMX-ACOL) [51-43]	*Preserved at Istrana, 2022*	
MM7180	Aeritalia-EMB A-11B Ghibli (AMX-ACOL) [51-53] $	AMI GEA 51° Stormo, Istrana	
MM7182	Aeritalia-EMB A-11B Ghibli (AMX-ACOL) [51-62]	AMI GEA 51° Stormo, Istrana	
MM7183	Aeritalia-EMB A-11B Ghibli (AMX-ACOL) [51-41]	AMI GEA 51° Stormo, Istrana	
MM7184	Aeritalia-EMB A-11B Ghibli (AMX-ACOL) [51-65]	AMI GEA 51° Stormo, Istrana	
MM7185	Aeritalia-EMB A-11B Ghibli (AMX-ACOL) [51-36]	AMI, stored Istrana	
MM7186	Aeritalia-EMB A-11B Ghibli (AMX-ACOL) [51-50]	AMI GEA 51° Stormo, Istrana	
MM7189	Aeritalia-EMB A-11B Ghibli (AMX-ACOL) [51-71]	AMI GEA 51° Stormo, Istrana	
MM7190	Aeritalia-EMB A-11B Ghibli (AMX-ACOL) [51-57]	AMI GEA 51° Stormo, Istrana	
MM7191	Aeritalia-EMB A-11B Ghibli (AMX-ACOL) [51-34]	AMI, stored Istrana	
MM7192	Aeritalia-EMB A-11B Ghibli (AMX-ACOL) [51-70]	AMI GEA 51° Stormo, Istrana	
MM7194	Aeritalia-EMB A-11B Ghibli (AMX-ACOL) $	AMI GEA 51° Stormo, Istrana	
MM7196	Aeritalia-EMB A-11B Ghibli (AMX-ACOL) [51-35]	AMI GEA 51° Stormo, Istrana	
MM7197	Aeritalia-EMB A-11B Ghibli (AMX-ACOL) [51-46]	AMI GEA 51° Stormo, Istrana	
MM7198	Aeritalia-EMB A-11B Ghibli (AMX-ACOL) [51-44] $	AMI, stored Istrana	
MM7199	McDonnell Douglas AV-8B Harrier II+ [1-03]	MMI Gruppo Aerei Imbarcarti, Taranto/Grottaglie	
MM7200	McDonnell Douglas AV-8B Harrier II+ [1-04] $	MMI Gruppo Aerei Imbarcarti, Taranto/Grottaglie	
MM7201	McDonnell Douglas AV-8B Harrier II+ [1-05]	MMI Gruppo Aerei Imbarcarti, Taranto/Grottaglie	
MM7213	McDonnell Douglas AV-8B Harrier II+ [1-07]	MMI Gruppo Aerei Imbarcarti, Taranto/Grottaglie	
MM7214	McDonnell Douglas AV-8B Harrier II+ [1-08]	MMI Gruppo Aerei Imbarcarti, Taranto/Grottaglie	
MM7215	McDonnell Douglas AV-8B Harrier II+ [1-09]	MMI Gruppo Aerei Imbarcarti, Taranto/Grottaglie	
MM7217	McDonnell Douglas AV-8B Harrier II+ [1-11]	MMI Gruppo Aerei Imbarcarti, Taranto/Grottaglie	
MM7218	McDonnell Douglas AV-8B Harrier II+ [1-12]	MMI Gruppo Aerei Imbarcarti, Taranto/Grottaglie	
MM7219	McDonnell Douglas AV-8B Harrier II+ [1-13] $	MMI Gruppo Aerei Imbarcarti, Taranto/Grottaglie	
MM7220	McDonnell Douglas AV-8B Harrier II+ [1-14]	MMI Gruppo Aerei Imbarcarti, Taranto/Grottaglie	
MM7222	McDonnell Douglas AV-8B Harrier II+ [1-16]	MMI Gruppo Aerei Imbarcarti, Taranto/Grottaglie	
MM7223	McDonnell Douglas AV-8B Harrier II+ [1-18] $	MMI Gruppo Aerei Imbarcarti, Taranto/Grottaglie	
MM7224	McDonnell Douglas AV-8B Harrier II+ [1-19] $	MMI Gruppo Aerei Imbarcarti, Taranto/Grottaglie	
MM7235	Eurofighter F-2000A Typhoon [4-13]	AMI 904° GEA, Grosseto	
MM7270	Eurofighter F-2000A Typhoon	AMI 904° GEA, Grosseto	
MM7271	Eurofighter F-2000A Typhoon [4-15]	AMI 904° GEA, Grosseto	
MM7272	Eurofighter F-2000A Typhoon [4-18]	AMI	
MM7273	Eurofighter F-2000A Typhoon [4-10]	AMI 904° GEA, Grosseto	
MM7274	Eurofighter F-2000A Typhoon [4-4]	AMI 904° GEA, Grosseto	
MM7275	Eurofighter F-2000A Typhoon [4-19]	AMI 904° GEA, Grosseto	
MM7276	Eurofighter F-2000A Typhoon [36-05]	AMI 936° GEA, Gioia del Colle	
MM7277	Eurofighter F-2000A Typhoon [36-14]	AMI 936° GEA, Gioia del Colle	
MM7279	Eurofighter F-2000A Typhoon [36-07]	AMI	
MM7280	Eurofighter F-2000A Typhoon [36-30]	AMI 936° GEA, Gioia del Colle	
MM7281	Eurofighter F-2000A Typhoon [36-03]	AMI 936° GEA, Gioia del Colle	
MM7282	Eurofighter F-2000A Typhoon [4-8]	AMI 904° GEA, Grosseto	
MM7284	Eurofighter F-2000A Typhoon [36-15]	AMI 936° GEA, Gioia del Colle	
MM7285	Eurofighter F-2000A Typhoon	AMI 904° GEA, Grosseto	
MM7286	Eurofighter F-2000A Typhoon [4-1]	AMI 904° GEA, Grosseto	
MM7287	Eurofighter F-2000A Typhoon [4-3]	AMI 904° GEA, Grosseto	
MM7288	Eurofighter F-2000A Typhoon [36-42]	AMI 936° GEA, Gioia del Colle	
MM7289	Eurofighter F-2000A Typhoon [4-5]	AMI 904° GEA, Grosseto	
MM7290	Eurofighter F-2000A Typhoon [51-05]	AMI 132° Gruppo/51° Stormo, Istrana	
MM7291	Eurofighter F-2000A Typhoon [4-11]	AMI 904° GEA, Grosseto	
MM7292	Eurofighter F-2000A Typhoon [37-21] $	AMI 18° Gruppo/37° Stormo, Trapani/Birgi	
MM7293	Eurofighter F-2000A Typhoon [37-22]	AMI 18° Gruppo/37° Stormo, Trapani/Birgi	
MM7294	Eurofighter F-2000A Typhoon [4-52]	AMI 904° GEA, Grosseto	
MM7295	Eurofighter F-2000A Typhoon [51-15]	AMI 132° Gruppo/51° Stormo, Istrana	
MM7296	Eurofighter F-2000A Typhoon [36-22]	AMI 936° GEA, Gioia del Colle	
MM7297	Eurofighter F-2000A Typhoon [36-23] $	AMI 936° GEA, Gioia del Colle	

Notes	Serial	Type (code/other identity)	Owner/operator, location or fate
	MM7298	Eurofighter F-2000A Typhoon [51-01]	AMI 132º Gruppo/51º Stormo, Istrana
	MM7299	Eurofighter F-2000A Typhoon [4-41]	AMI 904º GEA, Grosseto
	MM7300	Eurofighter F-2000A Typhoon [4-44]	AMI 904º GEA, Grosseto
	MM7301	Eurofighter F-2000A Typhoon	AMI
	MM7302	Eurofighter F-2000A Typhoon [36-10]	AMI 936º GEA, Gioia del Colle
	MM7303	Eurofighter F-2000A Typhoon [4-2]	AMI 904º GEA, Grosseto
	MM7304	Eurofighter F-2000A Typhoon [37-04]	AMI 18º Gruppo/37º Stormo, Trapani/Birgi
	CSX7305	Eurofighter F-2000A Typhoon	AMI RSV, Pratica di Mare
	MM7306	Eurofighter F-2000A Typhoon [4-50]	AMI 132º Gruppo/51º Stormo, Istrana
	MM7307	Eurofighter F-2000A Typhoon [51-11]	*Crashed near Trapani, 13th December 2022*
	MM7308	Eurofighter F-2000A Typhoon [36-31]	AMI 936º GEA, Gioia del Colle
	MM7309	Eurofighter F-2000A Typhoon [37-03]	AMI 18º Gruppo/37º Stormo, Trapani/Birgi
	MM7310	Eurofighter F-2000A Typhoon [36-32]	AMI 936º GEA, Gioia del Colle
	MM7311	Eurofighter F-2000A Typhoon [51-14]	AMI 132º Gruppo/51º Stormo, Istrana
	MM7312	Eurofighter F-2000A Typhoon [36-34]	AMI 936º GEA, Gioia del Colle
	MM7313	Eurofighter F-2000A Typhoon [37-05]	AMI 18º Gruppo/37º Stormo, Trapani/Birgi
	MM7314	Eurofighter F-2000A Typhoon [36-33]	AMI 936º GEA, Gioia del Colle
	MM7315	Eurofighter F-2000A Typhoon [36-46]	AMI 936º GEA, Gioia del Colle
	MM7316	Eurofighter F-2000A Typhoon [4-42]	AMI 904o GEA, Grosseto (51o Stormo, marks)
	MM7317	Eurofighter F-2000A Typhoon [4-43]	AMI 904º GEA, Grosseto
	MM7318	Eurofighter F-2000A Typhoon [37-35]	AMI 18º Gruppo/37º Stormo, Trapani/Birgi
	MM7319	Eurofighter F-2000A Typhoon [51-04]	AMI 132º Gruppo/51º Stormo, Istrana
	MM7320	Eurofighter F-2000A Typhoon [51-02]	AMI 132º Gruppo/51º Stormo, Istrana
	MM7321	Eurofighter F-2000A Typhoon [36-43]	AMI 936º GEA, Gioia del Colle
	MM7322	Eurofighter F-2000A Typhoon [36-40] $	AMI 936º GEA, Gioia del Colle
	MM7323	Eurofighter F-2000A Typhoon [37-23]	AMI 18º Gruppo/37º Stormo, Trapani/Birgi
	MM7324	Eurofighter F-2000A Typhoon [36-41] $	AMI 936º GEA, Gioia del Colle
	MM7325	Eurofighter F-2000A Typhoon [36-44]	AMI 936º GEA, Gioia del Colle
	MM7326	Eurofighter F-2000A Typhoon [4-46] $	AMI 904º GEA, Grosseto
	MM7327	Eurofighter F-2000A Typhoon [37-27]	AMI 18º Gruppo/37º Stormo, Trapani/Birgi
	MM7328	Eurofighter F-2000A Typhoon [4-57]	AMI 904º GEA, Grosseto
	MM7329	Eurofighter F-2000A Typhoon [4-58]	AMI 904º GEA, Grosseto
	MM7330	Eurofighter F-2000A Typhoon [4-56]	AMI 904º GEA, Grosseto
	MM7331	Eurofighter F-2000A Typhoon [37-47]	AMI 18º Gruppo/37º Stormo, Trapani/Birgi
	MM7332	Lockheed Martin F-35A Lightning II [32-01]	AMI 62nd FS/56th FW, Luke AFB, AZ, USA
	MM7333	Lockheed Martin F-35A Lightning II [32-02]	AMI 62nd FS/56th FW, Luke AFB, AZ, USA
	MM7334	Lockheed Martin F-35A Lightning II [32-03]	AMI 13º Gruppo/32º Stormo, Amendola
	MM7335	Lockheed Martin F-35A Lightning II [32-04]	AMI 62nd FS/56th FW, Luke AFB, AZ, USA
	MM7336	Lockheed Martin F-35A Lightning II [32-05] $	AMI 13º Gruppo/32º Stormo, Amendola
	MM7337	Lockheed Martin F-35A Lightning II [32-13] $	AMI 13º Gruppo/32º Stormo, Amendola
	MM7338	Eurofighter F-2000A Typhoon [4-60]	AMI 904º GEA, Grosseto
	MM7339	Eurofighter F-2000A Typhoon [51-12]	AMI 132º Gruppo/51º Stormo, Istrana
	MM7340	Eurofighter F-2000A Typhoon [4-64]	AMI 904º GEA, Grosseto
	MM7341	Eurofighter F-2000A Typhoon [4-67] $	AMI 904º GEA, Grosseto
	MM7342	Eurofighter F-2000A Typhoon [4-68]	AMI 904º GEA, Grosseto
	MM7343	Eurofighter F-2000A Typhoon [36-50]	AMI 936º GEA, Gioia del Colle
	MM7344	Eurofighter F-2000A Typhoon [4-62]	AMI 904º GEA, Grosseto
	MM7345	Eurofighter F-2000A Typhoon [37-45]	AMI 18º Gruppo/37º Stormo, Trapani/Birgi
	MM7346	Eurofighter F-2000A Typhoon [37-37]	AMI 18º Gruppo/37º Stormo, Trapani/Birgi
	MM7347	Eurofighter F-2000A Typhoon [36-53]	AMI 936º GEA, Gioia del Colle
	MM7348	Eurofighter F-2000A Typhoon [37-24]	AMI 18º Gruppo/37º Stormo, Trapani/Birgi
	MM7349	Eurofighter F-2000A Typhoon [36-54] $	AMI 936º GEA, Gioia del Colle
	MM7350	Eurofighter F-2000A Typhoon [RS-22]	AMI RSV, Pratica di Mare
	MM7351	Eurofighter F-2000A Typhoon [4-9]	AMI 904º GEA, Grosseto
	MM7352	Eurofighter F-2000A Typhoon [36-55]	AMI 936º GEA, Gioia del Colle
	MM7353	Eurofighter F-2000A Typhoon [4-61]	AMI 904º GEA, Grosseto
	MM7354	Eurofighter F-2000A Typhoon [37-54]	AMI 18º Gruppo/37º Stormo, Trapani/Birgi
	MM7355	Eurofighter F-2000A Typhoon [4-66]	AMI 904º GEA, Grosseto
	MM7356	Eurofighter F-2000A Typhoon [51-06]	AMI 132º Gruppo/51º Stormo, Istrana
	MM7357	Lockheed Martin F-35A Lightning II [32-07] $	AMI 13º Gruppo/32º Stormo, Amendola
	MM7358	Lockheed Martin F-35A Lightning II [32-08]	AMI 13º Gruppo/32º Stormo, Amendola
	MM7359	Lockheed Martin F-35A Lightning II [32-09]	AMI 13º Gruppo/32º Stormo, Amendola

Serial	Type (code/other identity)	Owner/operator, location or fate	Notes
MM7360	Lockheed Martin F-35A Lightning II [32-10]	AMI 13° Gruppo/32° Stormo, Amendola	
MM7361	Lockheed Martin F-35A Lightning II [32-11]	AMI 13° Gruppo/32° Stormo, Amendola	
MM7362	Lockheed Martin F-35A Lightning II [32-12]	AMI 13° Gruppo/32° Stormo, Amendola	
MM7363	Lockheed Martin F-35A Lightning II [32-06]	AMI 13° Gruppo/32° Stormo, Amendola	
MM7364	Lockheed Martin F-35A Lightning II [32-15]	AMI 13° Gruppo/32° Stormo, Amendola	
MM7365	Lockheed Martin F-35A Lightning II [32-16]	AMI 13° Gruppo/32° Stormo, Amendola	
MM7366	Lockheed Martin F-35A Lightning II [6-01]	AMI GEA 6° Stormo, Ghedi	
MM7451	Lockheed Martin F-35B Lightning II [4-01]	MMI Gruppo Aerei Imbarcarti, Amendola	
MM7452	Lockheed Martin F-35B Lightning II [4-02]	MMI Gruppo Aerei Imbarcarti, Amendola	
MM7453	Lockheed Martin F-35B Lightning II [32-14]	AMI 13° Gruppo/32° Stormo, Amendola	
MM7454	Lockheed Martin F-35B Lightning II [4-03]	MMI Gruppo Aerei Imbarcarti, Amendola	
MM7455	Lockheed Martin F-35B Lightning II [32-18]	AMI 13° Gruppo/32° Stormo, Amendola	
MM7456	Lockheed Martin F-35B Lightning II [4-04]	MMI Gruppo Aerei Imbarcarti, Amendola	
MM7...	Lockheed Martin F-35 Lightning II	AMI/MMI (on order)	
MM7...	Lockheed Martin F-35 Lightning II	AMI/MMI (on order)	
MM7...	Lockheed Martin F-35 Lightning II	AMI/MMI (on order)	
MM7...	Lockheed Martin F-35 Lightning II	AMI/MMI (on order)	
MM54456	Aermacchi T-339A (MB339A) [61-10]	AMI, stored Lecce	
MM54457	Aermacchi T-339A (MB339A(MLU)) [61-11]	AMI 214° Gruppo/61° Stormo, Lecce	
MM54458	Aermacchi T-339A (MB339A(MLU)) [61-121]	AMI 214° Gruppo/61° Stormo, Lecce	
MM54465	Aermacchi T-339A (MB339A(MLU)) [61-116]	AMI 214° Gruppo/61° Stormo, Lecce	
MM54468	Aermacchi T-339A (MB339A(MLU)) [61-241]	AMI 214° Gruppo/61° Stormo, Lecce	
MM54473	Aermacchi AT-339A (MB339PAN)	AMI *Frecce Tricolori* (313° Gruppo), Rivolto	
MM54477	Aermacchi AT-339A (MB339PAN)	AMI *Frecce Tricolori* (313° Gruppo), Rivolto	
MM54479	Aermacchi AT-339A (MB339PAN)	AMI, stored Lecce	
MM54480	Aermacchi AT-339A (MB339PAN)	AMI *Frecce Tricolori* (313° Gruppo), Rivolto	
MM54482	Aermacchi AT-339A (MB339PAN)	AMI *Frecce Tricolori* (313° Gruppo), Rivolto	
MM54487	Aermacchi AT-339A (MB339PAN)	AMI *Frecce Tricolori* (313° Gruppo), Rivolto	
MM54488	Aermacchi T-339A (MB339A(MLU)) [61-32]	AMI 214° Gruppo/61° Stormo, Lecce	
MM54492	Aermacchi T-339A (MB339A(MLU)) [61-36]	AMI 214° Gruppo/61° Stormo, Lecce	
MM54493	Aermacchi T-339A (MB339A(MLU)) [61-37]	AMI 214° Gruppo/61° Stormo, Lecce	
MM54496	Aermacchi T-339A (MB339A(MLU)) [61-42]	AMI 214° Gruppo/61° Stormo, Lecce	
MM54499	Aermacchi T-339A (MB339A(MLU)) [61-45]	AMI 214° Gruppo/61° Stormo, Lecce	
MM54500	Aermacchi AT-339A (MB339PAN)	AMI *Frecce Tricolori* (313° Gruppo), Rivolto	
MM54504	Aermacchi T-339A (MB339A(MLU)) [61-52]	AMI 214° Gruppo/61° Stormo, Lecce	
MM54505	Aermacchi AT-339A (MB339PAN)	AMI *Frecce Tricolori* (313° Gruppo), Rivolto	
MM54507	Aermacchi T-339A (MB339A(MLU)) [61-55]	AMI 214° Gruppo/61° Stormo, Lecce	
MM54509	Aermacchi T-339A (MB339A(MLU)) [61-57]	AMI 214° Gruppo/61° Stormo, Lecce	
MM54510	Aermacchi AT-339A (MB339PAN) [10]	AMI *Frecce Tricolori* (313° Gruppo), Rivolto	
MM54511	Aermacchi T-339A (MB339A(MLU)) [61-61]	AMI 214° Gruppo/61° Stormo, Lecce	
MM54512	Aermacchi T-339A (MB339A(MLU)) [61-62]	AMI 214° Gruppo/61° Stormo, Lecce	
MM54514	Aermacchi AT-339A (MB339PAN) [6]	AMI *Frecce Tricolori* (313° Gruppo), Rivolto	
MM54515	Aermacchi T-339A (MB339A(MLU)) [61-65]	AMI 214° Gruppo/61° Stormo, Lecce	
MM54516	Aermacchi T-339A (MB339A(MLU)) [61-66]	AMI 214° Gruppo/61° Stormo, Lecce	
MM54517	Aermacchi AT-339A (MB339PAN) [9]	AMI *Frecce Tricolori* (313° Gruppo), Rivolto	
MM54518	Aermacchi AT-339A (MB339PAN) [3]	AMI *Frecce Tricolori* (313° Gruppo), Rivolto	
MM54533	Aermacchi T-339A (MB339A(MLU)) [61-72]	AMI 214° Gruppo/61° Stormo, Lecce	
MM54534	Aermacchi AT-339A (MB339PAN) [4]	AMI *Frecce Tricolori* (313° Gruppo), Rivolto	
MM54535	Aermacchi T-339A (MB339A(MLU)) [61-74]	AMI 214° Gruppo/61° Stormo, Lecce	
MM54538	Aermacchi AT-339A (MB339PAN) [7]	AMI *Frecce Tricolori* (313° Gruppo), Rivolto	
MM54539	Aermacchi AT-339A (MB339PAN)	AMI *Frecce Tricolori* (313° Gruppo), Rivolto	
MM54548	Aermacchi T-339A (MB339A(MLU)) [61-106]	AMI 214° Gruppo/61° Stormo, Lecce	
MM54549	Aermacchi T-339A (MB339A(MLU)) [61-107]	AMI 214° Gruppo/61° Stormo, Lecce	
MM54551	Aermacchi AT-339A (MB339PAN) [9]	AMI *Frecce Tricolori* (313° Gruppo), Rivolto	
MM55002	Panavia TA-200A Tornado (IDS Trainer) [6-52] $	AMI GEA 6° Stormo, Ghedi	
MM55004	Panavia TA-200A Tornado (IDS Trainer) [6-53]	AMI, stored Ghedi	
MM55006	Panavia TA-200C Tornado (IDS Trainer (MLU)) [6-15]	AMI GEA 6° Stormo, Ghedi	
MM55007	Panavia TA-200A Tornado (IDS Trainer) [6-56]	AMI GEA 6° Stormo, Ghedi	
MM55008	Panavia TA-200A Tornado (IDS Trainer) [6-45]	AMI GEA 6° Stormo, Ghedi	
MM55009	Panavia TA-200A Tornado (IDS Trainer) [6-44] $	AMI GEA 6° Stormo, Ghedi	
MM55010	Panavia TA-200A Tornado (IDS Trainer) [6-42]	AMI GEA 6° Stormo, Ghedi	
MM55032	McDonnell Douglas TAV-8B Harrier II+ [1-01]	MMI Gruppo Aerei Imbarcarti, Taranto/Grottaglie	

Notes	Serial	Type (code/other identity)	Owner/operator, location or fate
	MM55033	McDonnell Douglas TAV-8B Harrier II+ [1-02]	MMI, stored Taranto/Grottaglie
	MM55034	Aeritalia-EMB TA-11B Ghibli (AMX-T-ACOL) [RS-20]	AMI RSV, Pratica di Mare
	MM55036	Aeritalia-EMB TA-11B Ghibli (AMX-T-ACOL) [32-51]	AMI, stored Amendola
	MM55037	Aeritalia-EMB TA-11B Ghibli (AMX-T-ACOL) [51-80]	AMI GEA 51° Stormo, Istrana
	MM55042	Aeritalia-EMB TA-11B Ghibli (AMX-T-ACOL) [32-56]	AMI, stored Amendola
	MM55043	Aeritalia-EMB TA-11B Ghibli (AMX-T-ACOL) [51-81]	AMI GEA 51° Stormo, Istrana
	MM55044	Aeritalia-EMB TA-11B Ghibli (AMX-T-ACOL) [51-82] $	AMI GEA 51° Stormo, Istrana
	MM55046	Aeritalia-EMB TA-11B Ghibli (AMX-T-ACOL) [32-60]	AMI, stored Amendola
	MM55047	Aeritalia-EMB TA-11B Ghibli (AMX-T-ACOL) [32-53]	AMI, stored Amendola
	MM55049	Aeritalia-EMB TA-11B Ghibli (AMX-T-ACOL) [51-83]	AMI GEA 51° Stormo, Istrana
	MM55051	Aeritalia-EMB TA-11B Ghibli (AMX-T-ACOL) [51-84]	AMI GEA 51° Stormo, Istrana
	MM55052	Aermacchi AT-339A (MB339PAN) [6]	AMI *Frecce Tricolori* (313° Gruppo), Rivolto
	MM55053	Aermacchi AT-339A (MB339PAN) [1]	AMI *Frecce Tricolori* (313° Gruppo), Rivolto
	MM55054	Aermacchi AT-339A (MB339PAN)	AMI *Frecce Tricolori* (313° Gruppo), Rivolto
	MM55055	Aermacchi AT-339A (MB339PAN)	AMI *Frecce Tricolori* (313° Gruppo), Rivolto
	MM55058	Aermacchi AT-339A (MB339PAN) [2]	AMI *Frecce Tricolori* (313° Gruppo), Rivolto
	MM55059	Aermacchi AT-339A (MB339PAN) [5]	AMI *Frecce Tricolori* (313° Gruppo), Rivolto
	MM55062	Aermacchi FT-339C (MB339CD) [61-126]	AMI 213° Gruppo/61° Stormo, Lecce
	MM55063	Aermacchi FT-339C (MB339CD) [61-127]	AMI 213° Gruppo/61° Stormo, Lecce
	MM55064	Aermacchi FT-339C (MB339CD) [61-130]	AMI 213° Gruppo/61° Stormo, Lecce
	MM55065	Aermacchi FT-339C (MB339CD) [61-131] $	AMI 213° Gruppo/61° Stormo, Lecce
	MM55066	Aermacchi FT-339C (MB339CD) [61-132]	AMI 632ª SC/32° Stormo, Amendola
	MM55067	Aermacchi FT-339C (MB339CD) [61-133]	AMI 213° Gruppo/61° Stormo, Lecce
	MM55068	Aermacchi FT-339C (MB339CD) [RS-33]	AMI RSV, Pratica di Mare
	MM55069	Aermacchi FT-339C (MB339CD) [61-135]	AMI 213° Gruppo/61° Stormo, Lecce
	MM55070	Aermacchi FT-339C (MB339CD) [61-136]	AMI 213° Gruppo/61° Stormo, Lecce
	MM55072	Aermacchi FT-339C (MB339CD) [61-140]	AMI 213° Gruppo/61° Stormo, Lecce
	MM55073	Aermacchi FT-339C (MB339CD) [61-141]	AMI 213° Gruppo/61° Stormo, Lecce
	MM55074	Aermacchi FT-339C (MB339CD) [36-06]	AMI 12° Gruppo/36° Stormo, Gioia del Colle
	MM55075	Aermacchi FT-339C (MB339CD) [61-143]	AMI 213° Gruppo/61° Stormo, Lecce
	MM55076	Aermacchi FT-339C (MB339CD)	Leonardo, Venegono
	MM55077	Aermacchi FT-339C (MB339CD) [61-145]	AMI 213° Gruppo/61° Stormo, Lecce
	MM55078	Aermacchi FT-339C (MB339CD) [61-146]	AMI 213° Gruppo/61° Stormo, Lecce
	MM55079	Aermacchi FT-339C (MB339CD) [61-147]	AMI 213° Gruppo/61° Stormo, Lecce
	MM55080	Aermacchi FT-339C (MB339CD) [61-150]	AMI 213° Gruppo/61° Stormo, Lecce
	MM55081	Aermacchi FT-339C (MB339CD) [61-151]	AMI 213° Gruppo/61° Stormo, Lecce
	MM55082	Aermacchi FT-339C (MB339CD) [61-152]	AMI 213° Gruppo/61° Stormo, Lecce
	MM55084	Aermacchi FT-339C (MB339CD) [61-154]	AMI 213° Gruppo/61° Stormo, Lecce
	MM55085	Aermacchi FT-339C (MB339CD) [61-155]	AMI 213° Gruppo/61° Stormo, Lecce
	MM55086	Aermacchi FT-339C (MB339CD) [61-156]	AMI 213° Gruppo/61° Stormo, Lecce
	MM55087	Aermacchi FT-339C (MB339CD) [61-157]	AMI 213° Gruppo/61° Stormo, Lecce
	MM55088	Aermacchi FT-339C (MB339CD) [61-160]	AMI 213° Gruppo/61° Stormo, Lecce
	MM55089	Aermacchi FT-339C (MB339CD) [32-161]	AMI 632ª SC/32° Stormo, Amendola
	MM55090	Aermacchi FT-339C (MB339CD) [61-162]	AMI 213° Gruppo/61° Stormo, Lecce
	MM55091	Aermacchi FT-339C (MB339CD) [RS-32]	AMI RSV, Pratica di Mare
	MM55092	Eurofighter TF-2000A Typhoon [4-25]	AMI 904° GEA, Grosseto
	MM55093	Eurofighter TF-2000A Typhoon [4-31]	AMI 904° GEA, Grosseto
	MM55094	Eurofighter TF-2000A Typhoon [36-60]	AMI 904° GEA, Grosseto
	MM55095	Eurofighter TF-2000A Typhoon [4-23]	AMI 904° GEA, Grosseto
	MM55096	Eurofighter TF-2000A Typhoon [4-30]	AMI 904° GEA, Grosseto
	MM55097	Eurofighter TF-2000A Typhoon [4-24]	AMI 904° GEA, Grosseto
	MM55128	Eurofighter TF-2000A Typhoon [36-64]	AMI 936° GEA, Gioia del Colle
	MM55129	Eurofighter TF-2000A Typhoon [4-32]	AMI 904° GEA, Grosseto
	MM55130	Eurofighter TF-2000A Typhoon [4-33]	AMI 904° GEA, Grosseto
	MM55131	Eurofighter TF-2000A Typhoon [4-34]	AMI 904° GEA, Grosseto
	MM55132	Eurofighter TF-2000A Typhoon [51-22]	AMI 132° Gruppo/51° Stormo, Istrana
	MM55133	Eurofighter TF-2000A Typhoon [37-33]	AMI 18° Gruppo/37° Stormo, Trapani/Birgi
	MM55144	Aermacchi T-346A Master [61-02]	AMI 212° Gruppo/61° Stormo, Lecce
	MM55145	Aermacchi T-346A Master [61-03]	AMI 212° Gruppo/61° Stormo, Lecce
	MM55152	Aermacchi T-346A Master [61-11]	AMI 212° Gruppo/61° Stormo, Lecce
	MM55153	Aermacchi T-346A Master [61-05]	AMI 212° Gruppo/61° Stormo, Lecce
	MM55154	Aermacchi T-346A Master [61-01]	AMI 212° Gruppo/61° Stormo, Lecce

Serial	Type (code/other identity)	Owner/operator, location or fate	Notes
MM55155	Aermacchi T-346A Master [61-04]	AMI 212º Gruppo/61º Stormo, Lecce	
MM55168	Eurofighter TF-2000A Typhoon [37-34]	AMI 18º Gruppo/37º Stormo, Trapani/Birgi	
CSX55169	Eurofighter TF-2000A Typhoon	Leonardo, Turin	
MM55213	Aermacchi T-346A Master [61-06]	AMI 212º Gruppo/61º Stormo, Lecce	
MM55214	Aermacchi T-346A Master [61-07]	AMI 212º Gruppo/61º Stormo, Lecce	
MM55215	Aermacchi T-346A Master [61-10] $	AMI 212º Gruppo/61º Stormo, Lecce	
MM55216	Aermacchi T-346A Master [61-12]	AMI 212º Gruppo/61º Stormo, Lecce	
MM55217	Aermacchi T-346A Master [61-13]	AMI 212º Gruppo/61º Stormo, Lecce	
MM55218	Aermacchi T-346A Master [61-14]	AMI 212º Gruppo/61º Stormo, Lecce	
MM55219	Aermacchi T-346A Master [61-20]	AMI 212º Gruppo/61º Stormo, Lecce	
MM55220	Aermacchi T-346A Master [61-16]	AMI 212º Gruppo/61º Stormo, Lecce	
MM55221	Aermacchi T-346A Master [61-15]	AMI 212º Gruppo/61º Stormo, Lecce	
MM55222	Aermacchi T-346A Master [61-21]	AMI 212º Gruppo/61º Stormo, Lecce	
MM55223	Aermacchi T-346A Master [61-22]	AMI 212º Gruppo/61º Stormo, Lecce	
MM55224	Aermacchi T-346A Master [61-23]	AMI 212º Gruppo/61º Stormo, Lecce	
MM55229	Aermacchi T-346A Master [61-24]	AMI IFTS, Lecce	
MM55230	Aermacchi T-346A Master [61-25]	AMI 212º Gruppo/61º Stormo, Lecce	
MM55231	Aermacchi T-346A Master [61-26]	AMI IFTS, Lecce	
MM55232	Aermacchi T-346A Master [61-27]	AMI IFTS, Lecce	
CSX55233	Aermacchi T-345A	Leonardo, Venegono	
MM55234	Aermacchi T-345A [61-202]	AMI 214º Gruppo/61º Stormo, Lecce	
MM55235	Aermacchi T-345A [61-203]	AMI 214º Gruppo/61º Stormo, Lecce	
MM55236	Aermacchi T-345A [61-204]	AMI 214º Gruppo/61º Stormo, Lecce	
MM55237	Aermacchi T-345A [61-205]	AMI 214º Gruppo/61º Stormo, Lecce	
MM55239	Aermacchi T-346B Master [61-30]	AMI 212º Gruppo/61º Stormo, Lecce	
MM55240	Aermacchi T-346B Master [61-31]	AMI 212º Gruppo/61º Stormo, Lecce	
MM55241	Aermacchi T-346B Master [61-32]	AMI 212º Gruppo/61º Stormo, Lecce	
MM55242	Aermacchi T-346B Master [61-33]	AMI 212º Gruppo/61º Stormo, Lecce	
CSX55249	Aermacchi T-345A [61-206]	AMI (on order)	
CSX55250	Aermacchi T-345A [61-207]	AMI (on order)	
MM552..	Aermacchi T-345A	AMI (on order)	
MM552..	Aermacchi T-345A	AMI (on order)	
MM552..	Aermacchi T-345A	AMI (on order)	
MM552..	Aermacchi T-345A	AMI (on order)	
MM62026	Dassault VC-50A (Falcon 50)	AMI 93º Gruppo/31º Stormo, Roma-Ciampino	
MM62029	Dassault VC-50A (Falcon 50)	AMI 93º Gruppo/31º Stormo, Roma-Ciampino	
CSX62127	Aeritalia MC-27J Pretorian	Alenia, Turin	
MM62156	Dornier UC-228 (Do.228-212) [E.I.101]	Esercito 28º Gruppo Squadroni, Viterbo	
MM62157	Dornier UC-228 (Do.228-212) [E.I.102]	Esercito 28º Gruppo Squadroni, Viterbo	
MM62158	Dornier UC-228 (Do.228-212) [E.I.103]	Esercito 28º Gruppo Squadroni, Viterbo	
MM62159	Piaggio VC-180A (P-180AM) Avanti	AMI RSV, Pratica di Mare	
MM62160	Piaggio EC-180A (P-180RM) Avanti	AMI 71º Gruppo/14º Stormo, Pratica di Mare	
MM62161	Piaggio VC-180A (P-180AM) Avanti	AMI RSV, Pratica di Mare	
MM62162	Piaggio EC-180A (P-180RM) Avanti	AMI 71º Gruppo/14º Stormo, Pratica di Mare	
MM62163	Piaggio EC-180A (P-180RM) Avanti	AMI 71º Gruppo/14º Stormo, Pratica di Mare	
CSX62164	Piaggio EC-180A (P-180RM) Avanti	Piaggio Aerospace, stored Genoa	
MM62165	Aérospatiale P-42A (ATR.42-400MP) [GF-13]	GdiF GEA, Pratica di Mare	
MM62166	Aérospatiale P-42A (ATR.42-400MP) [GF-14]	GdiF GEA, Pratica di Mare	
MM62167	Piaggio VC-180A (P-180AM) Avanti	Esercito 28º Gruppo Sqd Det, Roma/Ciampino	
MM62168	Piaggio VC-180A (P-180AM) Avanti	Esercito 28º Gruppo Sqd Det, Roma/Ciampino	
MM62169	Piaggio VC-180A (P-180AM) Avanti	Esercito 28º Gruppo Sqd Det, Roma/Ciampino	
MM62170	Aérospatiale P-42A (ATR.42-400MP) [10-01]	Guardia Costiera 3º Nucleo, Pescara	
MM62174	Airbus VC-319A (A.319CJ-115X)	AMI 306º Gruppo/31º Stormo, Roma-Ciampino	
MM62175	Lockheed C-130J Hercules II [46-40]	AMI, stored Pisa	
MM62177	Lockheed C-130J Hercules II [46-42]	AMI 46ª Brigata Aerea, Pisa	
MM62178	Lockheed C-130J Hercules II [46-43]	AMI 46ª Brigata Aerea, Pisa	
MM62179	Lockheed C-130J Hercules II [46-44]	AMI 46ª Brigata Aerea, Pisa	
MM62180	Lockheed C-130J Hercules II [46-45]	AMI 46ª Brigata Aerea, Pisa	
MM62181	Lockheed KC-130J Hercules II [46-46]	AMI 46ª Brigata Aerea, Pisa	
MM62182	Lockheed C-130J Hercules II [46-47]	AMI, stored Venice	
MM62183	Lockheed KC-130J Hercules II [46-48]	AMI, stored Venice	
MM62184	Lockheed KC-130J Hercules II [46-49]	AMI 46ª Brigata Aerea, Pisa	

Notes	Serial	Type (code/other identity)	Owner/operator, location or fate
	MM62185	Lockheed C-130J Hercules II [46-50]	AMI 46ª Brigata Aerea, Pisa
	MM62186	Lockheed C-130J Hercules II [46-51]	AMI 46ª Brigata Aerea, Pisa
	MM62187	Lockheed C-130J-30 Hercules II [46-53]	AMI 46ª Brigata Aerea, Pisa
	MM62188	Lockheed C-130J-30 Hercules II [46-54]	AMI, stored Pisa
	MM62189	Lockheed C-130J-30 Hercules II [46-55]	AMI 46ª Brigata Aerea, Pisa
	MM62190	Lockheed C-130J-30 Hercules II [46-56]	AMI 46ª Brigata Aerea, Pisa
	MM62191	Lockheed C-130J-30 Hercules II [46-57]	AMI 46ª Brigata Aerea, Pisa
	MM62192	Lockheed C-130J-30 Hercules II [46-58]	AMI, stored Pisa
	MM62193	Lockheed C-130J-30 Hercules II [46-59]	AMI 46ª Brigata Aerea, Pisa
	MM62194	Lockheed C-130J-30 Hercules II [46-60]	AMI 46ª Brigata Aerea, Pisa
	MM62195	Lockheed C-130J-30 Hercules II [46-61]	AMI 46ª Brigata Aerea, Pisa
	MM62196	Lockheed C-130J-30 Hercules II [46-62]	AMI 46ª Brigata Aerea, Pisa
	MM62199	Piaggio VC-180A (P-180AM) Avanti	AMI CAE Multicrew, Pratica di Mare
	MM62200	Piaggio VC-180A (P-180AM) Avanti	AMI 71º Gruppo/14º Stormo, Pratica di Mare
	MM62201	Piaggio VC-180A (P-180AM) Avanti	AMI CAE Multicrew, Pratica di Mare
	MM62202	Piaggio VC-180A (P-180AM) Avanti	AMI 71º Gruppo/14º Stormo, Pratica di Mare
	MM62203	Piaggio VC-180A (P-180AM) Avanti	AMI CAE Multicrew, Pratica di Mare
	MM62204	Piaggio VC-180A (P-180AM) Avanti	AMI 71º Gruppo/14º Stormo, Pratica di Mare
	MM62205	Piaggio VC-180A (P-180AM) Avanti	AMI CAE Multicrew, Pratica di Mare
	MM62206	Piaggio VC-180A (P-180AM) Avanti	AMI CAE Multicrew, Pratica di Mare
	MM62207	Piaggio VC-180A (P-180AM) Avanti	AMI CAE Multicrew, Pratica di Mare
	MM62208	Aérospatiale P-42B (ATR.42-500MP) [10-02]	Guardia Costiera 2º Nucleo, Catania
	MM62209	Airbus VC-319A (A.319CJ-115X)	AMI 306º Gruppo/31º Stormo, Roma-Ciampino
	MM62210	Dassault VC-900A (Falcon 900EX)	AMI 93º Gruppo/31º Stormo, Roma-Ciampino
	MM62211	Piaggio VC-180A (P-180AM) Avanti [9-02]	MMI 9ª Brigata Aerea, Pratica di Mare
	MM62212	Piaggio VC-180A (P-180AM) Avanti [9-01]	MMI 9ª Brigata Aerea, Pratica di Mare
	MM62213	Piaggio VC-180A (P-180AM) Avanti [9-03]	MMI 9ª Brigata Aerea, Pratica di Mare
	MM62214	Aeritalia C-27J Spartan [46-84]	AMI 46ª Brigata Aerea, Pisa
	MM62215	Aeritalia C-27J Spartan [46-80]	AMI RSV, Pratica di Mare
	MM62217	Aeritalia C-27J Spartan [46-81]	AMI 98º Gruppo/46ª Brigata Aerea, Pisa
	MM62218	Aeritalia C-27J Spartan [46-82]	AMI 98º Gruppo/46ª Brigata Aerea, Pisa
	CSX62219	Aeritalia C-27J Spartan [RS-50]	AMI RSV, Pratica di Mare
	MM62220	Aeritalia MC-27J Pretorian [46-83]	AMI 98º Gruppo/46ª Brigata Aerea, Pisa
	MM62221	Aeritalia EC-27J JEDI [46-85]	AMI 98º Gruppo/46ª Brigata Aerea, Pisa
	MM62222	Aeritalia C-27J Spartan [46-86]	AMI 98º Gruppo/46ª Brigata Aerea, Pisa
	MM62223	Aeritalia C-27J Spartan [46-88]	AMI 98º Gruppo/46ª Brigata Aerea, Pisa
	MM62224	Aeritalia EC-27J JEDI [46-89]	AMI 98º Gruppo/46ª Brigata Aerea, Pisa
	CSX62225	Aeritalia YEC-27J JEDI [46-90]	Leonardo, Turin
	MM62226	Boeing KC-767A (767-2EYER) [14-01] $	AMI 8º Gruppo/14º Stormo, Pratica di Mare
	MM62227	Boeing KC-767A (767-2EYER) [14-02]	AMI 8º Gruppo/14º Stormo, Pratica di Mare
	MM62228	Boeing KC-767A (767-2EYER) [14-03]	AMI 8º Gruppo/14º Stormo, Pratica di Mare
	MM62229	Boeing KC-767A (767-2EYER) [14-04]	AMI 8º Gruppo/14º Stormo, Pratica di Mare
	MM62230	Aérospatiale P-42B (ATR.42-500MP) [GF-15]	GdiF GEA, Pratica di Mare
	MM62243	Airbus VC-319A (A.319CJ-115X)	AMI 306º Gruppo/31º Stormo, Roma-Ciampino
	MM62244	Dassault VC-900B (Falcon 900EX EASy)	AMI 93º Gruppo/31º Stormo, Roma-Ciampino
	MM62245	Dassault VC-900B (Falcon 900EX EASy)	AMI 93º Gruppo/31º Stormo, Roma-Ciampino
	MM62248	Piaggio VC-180A (P-180AM) Avanti [GF-18]	GdiF GEA, Pratica di Mare
	MM62249	Piaggio VC-180B (P-180AM) Avanti II [GF-19]	GdiF GEA, Pratica di Mare
	MM62250	Aeritalia C-27J Spartan [46-91]	AMI 98º Gruppo/46ª Brigata Aerea, Pisa
	MM62251	Aérospatiale P-42B (ATR.42-500MP) [GF-16]	GdiF GEA, Pratica di Mare
	MM62270	Aérospatiale P-42B (ATR.42-500MP) [10-03]	Guardia Costiera 2º Nucleo, Catania
	MM62274	Piaggio VC-180B (P-180AM) Avanti II [12-01]	Guardia Costiera 2º Nucleo, Catania
	MM62279	Aérospatiale P-72A Argo (ATR.72-600MP) [41-01]	AMI 88º Gruppo/41º Stormo, Catania
	MM62280	Aérospatiale P-72A Argo (ATR.72-600MP) [41-02]	AMI 88º Gruppo/41º Stormo, Catania
	MM62281	Aérospatiale P-72A Argo (ATR.72-600MP) [41-04]	AMI 88º Gruppo/41º Stormo, Catania
	CSX62282	Aérospatiale P-72A Argo (ATR.72-600MP) [41-05]	(on order)
	MM62286	Piaggio VC-180B (P-180AM) Avanti II	AMI 93º Gruppo/31º Stormo, Roma-Ciampino
	MM62287	Piaggio VC-180B (P-180AM) Avanti II	AMI 93º Gruppo/31º Stormo, Roma-Ciampino
	MM62293	Gulfstream Aerospace E-550A (N849GA) [14-11]	AMI 71º Gruppo/14º Stormo, Pratica di Mare
	MM62298	Aérospatiale P-72A Argo (ATR.72-600MP) [41-03]	AMI 71º Gruppo/14º Stormo, Pratica di Mare
	MM62300	Beechcraft King Air 350ER	AMI 71º Gruppo/14º Stormo, Pratica di Mare
	MM62303	Gulfstream Aerospace E-550A (N554GA) [14-12]	AMI 71º Gruppo/14º Stormo, Pratica di Mare

Serial	Type (code/other identity)	Owner/operator, location or fate	Notes
MM62311	Aérospatiale P-72B (ATR.72-600MP) [GF-20]	GdiF GEA, Pratica di Mare	
MM62315	Aérospatiale P-72B (ATR.72-600MP) [GF-21]	GdiF GEA, Pratica di Mare	
MM62317	Beechcraft King Air 350ER	AMI 71° Gruppo/14° Stormo, Pratica di Mare	
MM62321	Aérospatiale P-72B (ATR.72-600MP) [GF-22]	GdiF GEA, Pratica di Mare	
MM62329	Gulfstream Aerospace E-550A (N581GA) [14-13]	AMI 71° Gruppo/14° Stormo, Pratica di Mare	
CSX62330	Aeritalia C-27J Spartan NG	Aeritalia, Turin (for Slovenian AF as L2-01)	
MM62..	Piaggio P-180 EVO Plus	AMI/MMI (on order)	
MM62..	Piaggio P-180 EVO Plus	AMI/MMI (on order)	
MM62..	Piaggio P-180 EVO Plus	AMI/MMI (on order)	
MM62..	Piaggio P-180 EVO Plus	AMI/MMI (on order)	
MM62..	Piaggio P-180 EVO Plus	AMI/MMI (on order)	
MM62..	Piaggio P-180 EVO Plus	AMI/MMI (on order)	
MM81480	AgustaWestland SH-101A (EH-101 Mk110 ASW) [2-01]	MMI 3° Grupelicot, Catania	
MM81481	AgustaWestland SH-101A (EH-101 Mk110 ASW) [2-02]	MMI 3° Grupelicot, Catania	
MM81482	AgustaWestland SH-101A (EH-101 Mk110 ASW) [2-03]	MMI 3° Grupelicot, Catania	
MM81483	AgustaWestland SH-101A (EH-101 Mk110 ASW) [2-04]	MMI 3° Grupelicot, Catania	
MM81484	AgustaWestland SH-101A (EH-101 Mk110 ASW) [2-05]	MMI 3° Grupelicot, Catania	
MM81485	AgustaWestland SH-101A (EH-101 Mk110 ASW) [2-06]	MMI 3° Grupelicot, Catania	
MM81486	AgustaWestland SH-101A (EH-101 Mk110 ASW) [2-07]	MMI 3° Grupelicot, Catania	
MM81488	AgustaWestland EH-101A (EH-101 Mk112 AEW) [2-09]	MMI 1° Grupelicot, La Spezia/Luni	
MM81489	AgustaWestland EH-101A (EH-101 Mk112 AEW) [2-10]	MMI 3° Grupelicot, Catania	
MM81490	AgustaWestland EH-101A (EH-101 Mk112 AEW) [2-11]	MMI 3° Grupelicot, Catania	
MM81491	AgustaWestland EH-101A (EH-101 Mk112 AEW) [2-12]	MMI 1° Grupelicot, La Spezia/Luni	
MM81492	AgustaWestland MH-101A (EH-101 Mk410 UTY) [2-13]	MMI 1° Grupelicot, La Spezia/Luni	
MM81493	AgustaWestland MH-101A (EH-101 Mk410 UTY) [2-14]	MMI 1° Grupelicot, La Spezia/Luni	
MM81494	AgustaWestland MH-101A (EH-101 Mk410 UTY) [2-15]	MMI 1° Grupelicot, La Spezia/Luni	
MM81495	AgustaWestland MH-101A (EH-101 Mk410 UTY) [2-16]	MMI 1° Grupelicot, La Spezia/Luni	
MM81623	NH Industries MH-90A (NH-90-MITT) [3-51]	MMI 5° Grupelicot, La Spezia/Luni	
MM81624	NH Industries MH-90A (NH-90-MITT) [3-52]	MMI 5° Grupelicot, La Spezia/Luni	
MM81625	NH Industries MH-90A (NH-90-MITT) [3-53]	MMI 5° Grupelicot, La Spezia/Luni	
MM81626	NH Industries MH-90A (NH-90-MITT) [3-54]	MMI 5° Grupelicot, La Spezia/Luni	
MM81627	NH Industries MH-90A (NH-90-MITT) [3-55]	MMI 4° Grupelicot, Taranto/Grottaglie	
MM81629	NH Industries MH-90A (NH-90-MITT) [3-57]	MMI 4° Grupelicot, Taranto/Grottaglie	
MM81630	NH Industries MH-90A (NH-90-MITT) [3-58]	MMI 4° Grupelicot, Taranto/Grottaglie	
MM81631	NH Industries MH-90A (NH-90-MITT) [3-59]	MMI 5° Grupelicot, La Spezia/Luni	
MM81632	NH Industries MH-90A (NH-90-MITT) [3-60]	MMI 5° Grupelicot, La Spezia/Luni	
MM81633	AgustaWestland MH-101A (EH-101 Mk413 ASH) [2-18]	MMI 1° Grupelicot, La Spezia/Luni	
MM81634	AgustaWestland MH-101A (EH-101 Mk413 ASH) [2-19]	MMI 1° Grupelicot, La Spezia/Luni	
MM81635	AgustaWestland MH-101A (EH-101 Mk413 ASH) [2-20]	MMI 1° Grupelicot, La Spezia/Luni	
MM81636	AgustaWestland MH-101A (EH-101 Mk413 ASH) [2-21]	MMI 1° Grupelicot, La Spezia/Luni	
MM81714	AgustaWestland PH-139D [GF-401]	GdiF GEA, Pratica di Mare	
MM81719	AgustaWestland SH-101A (EH-101 Mk110 ASW) [2-22]	MMI 3° Grupelicot, Catania	
MM81726	AgustaWestland SH-101A (EH-101 Mk110 ASW) [2-23]	MMI 1° Grupelicot, La Spezia/Luni	
MM81796	AgustaWestland HH-139A [15-40]	AMI 83° Gruppo CSAR/15° Stormo, Cervia	
MM81797	AgustaWestland HH-139A [15-41]	AMI 80°Centro CSAR/15° Stormo, Decimomannu	
MM81798	AgustaWestland HH-139A [15-42]	AMI 83° Gruppo CSAR/15° Stormo, Cervia	
MM81799	AgustaWestland HH-139A [15-43]	AMI 83° Gruppo CSAR/15° Stormo, Cervia	
MM81800	AgustaWestland HH-139A [15-44]	AMI 85° Centro CSAR/15° Stormo, Pratica di Mare	
MM81801	AgustaWestland HH-139A [15-45]	AMI 85° Centro CSAR/15° Stormo, Pratica di Mare	
MM81802	AgustaWestland HH-139A [15-46]	AMI 83° Gruppo CSAR/15° Stormo, Cervia	
MM81803	AgustaWestland HH-139A [15-47]	AMI 85° Centro CSAR/15° Stormo, Pratica di Mare	
MM81804	AgustaWestland HH-139A [15-48]	AMI 84° Centro CSAR/15° Stormo, Brindisi	
MM81805	AgustaWestland HH-139A [15-49]	AMI 82° Centro CSAR/15° Stormo, Trapani/Birgi	
MM81806	AgustaWestland VH-139A	AMI 93° Gruppo/31° Stormo, Roma-Ciampino	
MM81807	AgustaWestland VH-139A	AMI 93° Gruppo/31° Stormo, Roma-Ciampino	
MM81811	AgustaWestland UH-139A	AMI 208° Gruppo/72° Stormo, Frosinone	
MM81812	AgustaWestland UH-139A	AMI 208° Gruppo/72° Stormo, Frosinone	
MM81822	AgustaWestland HH-139A [15-50]	AMI 85° Centro CSAR/15° Stormo, Pratica di Mare	

Notes	Serial	Type (code/other identity)	Owner/operator, location or fate
	MM81823	AgustaWestland HH-139A [15-51]	AMI 81º Centro/15º Stormo, Cervia
	MM81824	AgustaWestland HH-139A [15-52]	AMI 85º Centro CSAR/15º Stormo, Pratica di Mare
	CSX81848	AgustaWestland AW149 [1-49]	Leonardo
	MM81864	AgustaWestland HH-101A Caesar (ZR352) [9-01]	AMI 21º Gruppo/9º Stormo, Grazzanise
	MM81865	AgustaWestland HH-101A Caesar (ZR353) [15-02]	AMI 23º Gruppo /15º Stormo, Cervia
	MM81866	AgustaWestland HH-101A Caesar (ZR354) [15-03]	AMI 85º Centro CSAR/15º Stormo, Pratica di Mare
	MM81867	AgustaWestland HH-101A Caesar (ZR355) [15-04]	AMI 23º Gruppo/15º Stormo, Cervia
	MM81868	AgustaWestland HH-101A Caesar (ZR356) [15-05]	AMI 81º Centro/15º Stormo, Cervia
	MM81869	AgustaWestland HH-101A Caesar (ZR357) [15-06]	AMI 81º Centro/15º Stormo, Cervia
	MM81870	AgustaWestland HH-101A Caesar (ZR358) [15-07]	AMI 81º Centro/15º Stormo, Cervia
	MM81871	AgustaWestland HH-101A Caesar (ZR359) [9-10]	AMI 21º Gruppo/9º Stormo, Grazzanise
	MM81872	AgustaWestland HH-101A Caesar (ZR360) [9-11]	AMI 21º Gruppo/9º Stormo, Grazzanise
	MM81873	AgustaWestland HH-101A Caesar (ZR361) [15-12]	AMI 21º Gruppo/9º Stormo, Grazzanise
	MM81874	AgustaWestland HH-101A Caesar (ZR362) [15-13]	AMI 21º Gruppo/9º Stormo, Grazzanise
	MM81875	AgustaWestland HH-101A Caesar (ZR363) [15-14]	AMI 23º Gruppo/15º Stormo, Cervia
	CSX81890	AgustaWestland AW149	Leonardo
	MM81985	AgustaWestland HH-139B [15-55]	AMI 85º Centro CSAR/15º Stormo, Pratica di Mare
	MM81986	AgustaWestland HH-139A [15-56]	AMI 81º Centro/15º Stormo, Cervia
	MM81989	AgustaWestland HH-139B [15-57]	AMI 85º Centro CSAR/15º Stormo, Pratica di Mare
	MM81990	AgustaWestland HH-139B [15-60]	AMI 85º Centro CSAR/15º Stormo, Pratica di Mare
	MM81991	AgustaWestland HH-139B [15-61]	AMI 82º Centro CSAR/15º Stormo, Trapani/Birgi
	MM82003	AgustaWestland HH-139B [15-62]	AMI 85º Centro CSAR/15º Stormo, Pratica di Mare
	MM82007	AgustaWestland HH-139B [15-63]	AMI 83º Gruppo CSAR/15º Stormo, Cervia
	MM82011	AgustaWestland HH-139B [15-64]	AMI 81º Centro/15º Stormo, Cervia
	MM82013	AgustaWestland HH-139B [15-65]	AMI 83º Gruppo CSAR/15º Stormo, Cervia
	CSX82017	AgustaWestland HH-139B [15-66]	AMI (on order)
	MM82018	AgustaWestland HH-139B [15-67]	AMI 83º Gruppo CSAR/15º Stormo, Cervia
	MM82023	AgustaWestland HH-139B [15-70]	AMI 85º Centro CSAR/15º Stormo, Pratica di Mare
	MM82026	AgustaWestland HH-139B [15-71] $	AMI 82º Centro CSAR/15º Stormo, Trapani/Birgi
	MM82028	AgustaWestland HH-139B [15-72]	AMI 85º Centro CSAR/15º Stormo, Pratica di Mare
	MM82029	AgustaWestland HH-139B [15-73]	AMI 85º Centro CSAR/15º Stormo, Pratica di Mare
	MM82030	AgustaWestland HH-139B [15-74]	AMI 85º Centro CSAR/15º Stormo, Pratica di Mare
	MM82038	AgustaWestland HH-139B [15-75]	AMI 83º Gruppo CSAR/15º Stormo, Cervia
	Italian Government		
	I-DIEM	Dassault Falcon 900LX	Italian Government/Soc. CAI, Roma/Ciampino
	I-GATC	Gulfstream Aerospace G.600	Italian Government/Soc. CAI, Roma/Ciampino
	I-NEMO	Dassault Falcon 900LX	Italian Government/Soc. CAI, Roma/Ciampino
	I-OUNI	Dassault Falcon 900EX (MM62171)	*Sold to the USA as N30HQ*
	I-TARH	Dassault Falcon 900EX (MM62172)	Italian Government/Soc. CAI, Roma/Ciampino
	IVORY COAST		
	TU-VAD	Grumman G.1159C Gulfstream IV	Ivory Coast Government, Abidjan
	TU-VAE	Gulfstream Aerospace G.550	Ivory Coast Government, Abidjan
	TU-VAG	Gulfstream Aerospace G.450 (T7-LIA)	Ivory Coast Government, Abidjan
	TU-VAI	Grumman G.1159C Gulfstream IV-SP	Ivory Coast Government, Abidjan
	TU-VAS	Airbus A.319CJ-133	Ivory Coast Government, Abidjan
	JAPAN		
	Japan Air Self Defence Force (JASDF)		
	07-3604	Boeing KC-767J	JASDF 404th Hikotai, Nagoya
	14-3611	Boeing KC-46A (N6018N)	JASDF 405th Hikotai, Yonago-Miho
	24-3612	Boeing KC-46A (N5512S)	JASDF 405th Hikotai, Yonago-Miho

Serial	Type (code/other identity)	Owner/operator, location or fate	Notes
.4-3613	Boeing KC-46A	JASDF (on order)	
.4-3614	Boeing KC-46A	JASDF (on order)	
.4-3615	Boeing KC-46A	JASDF (on order)	
.4-3616	Boeing KC-46A	JASDF (on order)	
80-1111	Boeing 777-3SB(ER) (N509BJ)	JASDF 701st Hikotai, Chitose	
80-1112	Boeing 777-3SB(ER) (N511BJ)	JASDF 701st Hikotai, Chitose	
87-3601	Boeing KC-767J	JASDF 404th Hikotai, Nagoya	
87-3602	Boeing KC-767J	JASDF 404th Hikotai, Nagoya	
97-3603	Boeing KC-767J	JASDF 404th Hikotai, Nagoya	

JORDAN
Al Quwwat al Jawwiya al Malakiya al Urduniya/Jordanian Air Force

344	Lockheed C-130H Hercules	Jordanian AF 3 Sqn, Amman/Marka	
345	Lockheed C-130H Hercules $	Jordanian AF 3 Sqn, Amman/Marka	
346	Lockheed C-130H Hercules	Jordanian AF 3 Sqn, Amman/Marka	
347	Lockheed C-130H Hercules $	Jordanian AF 3 Sqn, Amman/Marka	
357	Lockheed C-130H Hercules	Jordanian AF 3 Sqn, Amman/Marka	
358	Lockheed C-130H Hercules	Jordanian AF 3 Sqn, Amman/Marka	
359	Lockheed C-130H Hercules	Jordanian AF 3 Sqn, Amman/Marka	
RJF 01	Extra EA-330LX	Jordanian AF *Royal Jordanian Falcons*, Aqaba	
RJF 02	Extra EA-330LX	Jordanian AF *Royal Jordanian Falcons*, Aqaba	
RJF 03	Extra EA-330LX	Jordanian AF *Royal Jordanian Falcons*, Aqaba	
RJF 04	Extra EA-330LX	Jordanian AF *Royal Jordanian Falcons*, Aqaba	
RJF 05	Extra EA-330LX	Jordanian AF *Royal Jordanian Falcons*, Aqaba	

Jordanian Government

VQ-BNZ	Gulfstream Aerospace G.650ER	Jordanian Government, Amman/Queen Alia Int'l	

KAZAKHSTAN

01 r	CASA C-295M	Kazakhstan ADF 18th Air Transport Sqn, Almaty	
02 r	CASA C-295M	Kazakhstan ADF 18th Air Transport Sqn, Almaty	
03 r	CASA C-295M	Kazakhstan ADF 18th Air Transport Sqn, Almaty	
04 r	CASA C-295M	Kazakhstan ADF 18th Air Transport Sqn, Almaty	
05 r	CASA C-295M	Kazakhstan ADF 18th Air Transport Sqn, Almaty	
06 r	CASA C-295M	Kazakhstan ADF 18th Air Transport Sqn, Almaty	
07 r	Antonov An-72	Kazakhstan ADF 18th Air Transport Sqn, Almaty	
07 r	CASA C-295M	Kazakhstan ADF 18th Air Transport Sqn, Almaty	
08 r	Antonov An-72	Kazakhstan ADF 18th Air Transport Sqn, Almaty	
08 r	CASA C-295M	Kazakhstan ADF 18th Air Transport Sqn, Almaty	
65001	Embraer Legacy 650	Kazakhstan Border Guards, Almaty	
..	Airbus Military A.400M	Kazakhstan ADF (on order)	
..	Airbus Military A.400M	Kazakhstan ADF (on order)	
UP-A2001	Airbus A.320CJ-214X	Government of Kazakhstan, Almaty	
UP-A2101	Airbus A.321CJ-211SL	Government of Kazakhstan, Almaty	
UP-A3001	Airbus A.330-223	Government of Kazakhstan, Almaty	
UP-B5701	Boeing 757-2M6	Government of Kazakhstan, Almaty	
UP-T5401	Tupolev Tu-154M	Government of Kazakhstan, Almaty	

KENYA

KAF 308	Fokker 70ER	Kenyan Government, Nairobi	

KUWAIT
Al Quwwat al Jawwiya al Kuwaitiya/Kuwaiti Air Force

KAF 323	Lockheed L100-30 Hercules	Kuwaiti AF, stored Kuwait International	
KAF 324	Lockheed L100-30 Hercules	Kuwaiti AF, stored Kuwait International	
KAF 325	Lockheed L100-30 Hercules	Kuwaiti AF, stored Kuwait International	
KAF 326	Lockheed KC-130J Hercules II	Kuwaiti AF 41 Sqn, Kuwait International	
KAF 327	Lockheed KC-130J Hercules II	Kuwaiti AF 41 Sqn, Kuwait International	
KAF 328	Lockheed KC-130J Hercules II	Kuwaiti AF 41 Sqn, Kuwait International	
KAF 342	Boeing C-17A Globemaster III (13-0001)	Kuwaiti AF 41 Sqn, Kuwait International	
KAF 343	Boeing C-17A Globemaster III (13-0002)	Kuwaiti AF 41 Sqn, Kuwait International	

Kuwaiti Government

9K-AKD	Airbus A.320-212	Kuwaiti Government, Safat	

Notes	Serial	Type (code/other identity)	Owner/operator, location or fate
	9K-GAA	Boeing 747-8JK	Kuwaiti Government, Safat
	9K-GBA	Airbus A.340-542	Kuwaiti Government, Safat
	9K-GBB	Airbus A.340-542	Kuwaiti Government, Safat
	9K-GCC	Boeing 737-9BQER	Kuwaiti Government, Safat
	9K-GEA	Airbus A.319CJ-115X	Kuwaiti Government, Safat
	9K-GFA	Gulfstream Aerospace G.550	Kuwaiti Government, Safat
	9K-GGA	Gulfstream Aerospace G.650	Kuwaiti Government, Safat
	9K-GGB	Gulfstream Aerospace G.650	Kuwaiti Government, Safat
	9K-GGC	Gulfstream Aerospace G.650	Kuwaiti Government, Safat
	9K-GGD	Gulfstream Aerospace G.650	Kuwaiti Government, Safat
	LIBYA		
	5A-DCN	Dassault Falcon 900EX	Libyan Government, Tripoli
	5A-ONE	Airbus A.340-213	Libyan Government, Tripoli
	LITHUANIA		
	Karines Oro Pajegos (KOP)		
	01 bl	LET 410UVP Turbolet	KOP Transporto Esk, Siauliai/Zokniai
	012 bl	LET 410UVP Turbolet	KOP Transporto Esk, Siauliai/Zokniai
	06 bl	Aeritalia C-27J Spartan	KOP Transporto Esk, Siauliai/Zokniai
	07 bl	Aeritalia C-27J Spartan	KOP Transporto Esk, Siauliai/Zokniai
	08 bl	Aeritalia C-27J Spartan	KOP Transporto Esk, Siauliai/Zokniai
	21 bl	Mil Mi-8MTV-1	KOP Sraigtasparniu Esk, Siauliai/Zokniai
	23 bl	Mil Mi-8T	KOP Sraigtasparniu Esk, Siauliai/Zokniai
	25 bl	Mil Mi-8T (10 bl)	KOP Sraigtasparniu Esk, Siauliai/Zokniai
	26 bl	Mil Mi-8T (09 bl)	KOP Sraigtasparniu Esk, Siauliai/Zokniai
	28 bl	Mil Mi-8T	KOP Sraigtasparniu Esk, Siauliai/Zokniai
	LUXEMBOURG		
	Note: see also Belgium for A400M		
	NATO		
	LX-N90442	Boeing E-3A Sentry	NATO NAEW&CF, Geilenkirchen, Germany
	LX-N90443	Boeing E-3A Sentry	NATO NAEW&CF, Geilenkirchen, Germany
	LX-N90444	Boeing E-3A Sentry	NATO NAEW&CF, Geilenkirchen, Germany
	LX-N90445	Boeing E-3A Sentry	NATO NAEW&CF, Geilenkirchen, Germany
	LX-N90446	Boeing E-3A Sentry	NATO NAEW&CF, Geilenkirchen, Germany
	LX-N90447	Boeing E-3A Sentry	NATO NAEW&CF, Geilenkirchen, Germany
	LX-N90448	Boeing E-3A Sentry	NATO NAEW&CF, Geilenkirchen, Germany
	LX-N90450	Boeing E-3A Sentry $	NATO NAEW&CF, Geilenkirchen, Germany
	LX-N90451	Boeing E-3A Sentry	NATO NAEW&CF, Geilenkirchen, Germany
	LX-N90452	Boeing E-3A Sentry	NATO NAEW&CF, Geilenkirchen, Germany
	LX-N90453	Boeing E-3A Sentry	NATO NAEW&CF, Geilenkirchen, Germany
	LX-N90454	Boeing E-3A Sentry	NATO NAEW&CF, Geilenkirchen, Germany
	LX-N90456	Boeing E-3A Sentry	NATO NAEW&CF, Geilenkirchen, Germany
	LX-N90459	Boeing E-3A Sentry	NATO NAEW&CF, Geilenkirchen, Germany
	MACEDONIA		
	Z3-MKD	Bombardier Lear 60	Macedonian Government, Skopje
	MALAYSIA		
	Tentera Udara Diraja Malaysia/Royal Malaysian Air Force (RMAF)		
	M30-01	Lockheed C-130T Hercules	RMAF 20 Sqn, Subang
	M30-02	Lockheed C-130H Hercules	RMAF 20 Sqn, Subang
	M30-03	Lockheed C-130H Hercules	RMAF 14 Sqn, Labuan
	M30-04	Lockheed C-130H-30 Hercules	RMAF 20 Sqn, Subang
	M30-05	Lockheed C-130H-30 Hercules	RMAF 14 Sqn, Labuan
	M30-06	Lockheed C-130H-30 Hercules	RMAF 14 Sqn, Labuan
	M30-07	Lockheed C-130H(MP) Hercules	RMAF 20 Sqn, Subang
	M30-08	Lockheed C-130H(MP) Hercules	RMAF 20 Sqn, Subang
	M30-09	Lockheed C-130H(MP) Hercules	RMAF 20 Sqn, Subang
	M30-10	Lockheed C-130H-30 Hercules	RMAF 20 Sqn, Subang
	M30-11	Lockheed C-130H-30 Hercules	RMAF 20 Sqn, Subang

Serial	Type (code/other identity)	Owner/operator, location or fate	Notes
M30-12	Lockheed C-130H-30 Hercules	RMAF 20 Sqn, Subang	
M30-14	Lockheed C-130H-30 Hercules	RMAF 14 Sqn, Labuan	
M30-15	Lockheed C-130H-30 Hercules	RMAF 20 Sqn, Subang	
M30-16	Lockheed C-130H-30 Hercules	RMAF 20 Sqn, Subang	
M37-01	Dassault Falcon 900	RMAF 2 Sqn, Simpang	
M48-02	Bombardier BD.700-1A10 Global Express	RMAF 2 Sqn, Simpang	
M53–01	Boeing 737-7H6	*Sold as VP-BTV*	
M54-01	Airbus Military A.400M	RMAF 22 Sqn, Subang	
M54-02	Airbus Military A.400M	RMAF 22 Sqn, Subang	
M54-03	Airbus Military A.400M	RMAF 22 Sqn, Subang	
M54-04	Airbus Military A.400M	RMAF 22 Sqn, Subang	
9M-NAA	Airbus A.319CJ-115X	RMAF, Subang	
9M-NAB	Airbus A.320CJ-214	RMAF, Subang	

MALI
TZ-PRM	Boeing 737-7DW	Government of Mali, Bamako	

MALTA
Armed Forces of Malta

AS1428	AgustaWestland AW139	AFM Air Wing, 2nd Regiment, Luqa	
AS1429	AgustaWestland AW139	AFM Air Wing, 2nd Regiment, Luqa	
AS1630	AgustaWestland AW139	AFM Air Wing, 2nd Regiment, Luqa	

Maltese Government

9H-AFK	Bombardier Learjet 60	Government of Malta, Luqa	

MAURITANIA
Mauritanian Government

5T-ONE	Boeing 737-7BQ	Government of Mauritania, Nouakchott	

MEXICO
Armada de Mexico/Mexican Navy

ANX-1201	Gulfstream Aerospace G.550	Armada PRIESCAERTRANS, Mexico City	
ANX-1202	Gulfstream Aerospace G.450 (XC-LMF)	Armada Esc Aeronaval 031, Mexico City	

MOROCCO
Al Quwwat al Jawwiya al Malakiya Marakishiya/Force Aérienne Royaume Marocaine/Royal Moroccan Air Force (RMAF) & Moroccan Government

CN-ABP	CAP-232 (28) [6]	RMAF *Marche Verte*, Marrakech/Ménara	
CN-ABQ	CAP-232 (29) [7]	RMAF *Marche Verte*, Marrakech/Ménara	
CN-ABR	CAP-232 (31) [2]	RMAF *Marche Verte*, Marrakech/Ménara	
CN-ABS	CAP-232 (36) [3]	RMAF *Marche Verte*, Marrakech/Ménara	
CN-ABT	CAP-232 (37) [1]	RMAF *Marche Verte*, Marrakech/Ménara	
CN-ABU	CAP-232 (41) [5]	RMAF *Marche Verte*, Marrakech/Ménara	
CN-ABV	CAP-232 (42) [4]	RMAF *Marche Verte*, Marrakech/Ménara	
CN-ABW	CAP-232 (43) [8]	RMAF *Marche Verte*, Marrakech/Ménara	
CN-ABX	CAP-232 (44) [7]	RMAF *Marche Verte*, Marrakech/Ménara	
CN-AMA	Airtech CN.235M-100 (023)	RMAF Escadrille de Transport 3, Kenitra	
CN-AMB	Airtech CN.235M-100 (024)	RMAF Escadrille de Transport 3, Kenitra	
CN-AMC	Airtech CN.235M-100 (025)	RMAF Escadrille de Transport 3, Kenitra	
CN-AMD	Airtech CN.235M-100 (026)	RMAF Escadrille de Transport 3, Kenitra	
CN-AMG	Airtech CN.235M-100 (031)	RMAF Escadrille de Transport 3, Kenitra	
CN-AMN	Aeritalia C-27J Spartan	RMAF Escadrille de Transport 3, Kenitra	
CN-AMO	Aeritalia C-27J Spartan	RMAF Escadrille de Transport 3, Kenitra	
CN-AMP	Aeritalia C-27J Spartan	RMAF Escadrille de Transport 3, Kenitra	
CN-AMQ	Aeritalia C-27J Spartan	RMAF Escadrille de Transport 3, Kenitra	
CN-ANO	Dassault Falcon 50	RMAF VIP Flight, Rabat	
CN-ANU	Grumman G.1159A Gulfstream III	RMAF VIP Flight, Rabat	
CNA-NV	Cessna 560 Citation V	RMAF VIP Flight, Rabat	
CNA-NW	Cessna 560 Citation V	RMAF VIP Flight, Rabat	
CN-AOA	Lockheed C-130H Hercules (4535)	RMAF Escadrille de Transport 3, Kenitra	
CNA-OC	Lockheed C-130H Hercules (4551)	RMAF Escadrille de Transport 3, Kenitra	
CN-AOD	Lockheed C-130H Hercules (4575)	RMAF Escadrille de Transport 3, Kenitra	

Notes	Serial	Type (code/other identity)	Owner/operator, location or fate
	CN-AOE	Lockheed C-130H Hercules (4581)	RMAF Escadrille de Transport 3, Kenitra
	CN-AOF	Lockheed C-130H Hercules (4583)	RMAF, stored Perpignan, France
	CN-AOG	Lockheed C-130H Hercules (4713)	RMAF Escadrille de Transport 3, Kenitra
	CN-AOI	Lockheed C-130H Hercules (4733)	RMAF Escadrille de Transport 3, Kenitra
	CN-AOJ	Lockheed C-130H Hercules (4738)	RMAF Escadrille de Transport 3, Kenitra
	CN-AOK	Lockheed C-130H Hercules (4739)	RMAF Escadrille de Transport 3, Kenitra
	CN-AOL	Lockheed C-130H Hercules (4742)	RMAF Escadrille de Transport 3, Kenitra
	CN-AOM	Lockheed C-130H Hercules (4875)	RMAF Escadrille de Transport 3, Kenitra
	CN-AON	Lockheed C-130H Hercules (4876)	RMAF Escadrille de Transport 3, Kenitra
	CN-AOO	Lockheed EC-130H Hercules (4877)	RMAF Escadron Electronique, Kenitra
	CN-AOP	Lockheed C-130H Hercules (4888)	RMAF, stored Perpignan, France
	CN-AOR	Lockheed KC-130H Hercules (4907)	RMAF Escadrille de Transport 3, Kenitra
	CN-AOS	Lockheed KC-130H Hercules (4909)	RMAF Escadrille de Transport 3, Kenitra
	Moroccan Government		
	CN-MBH	Boeing 747-8Z5 (A6-PFA)	Government of Morocco, Rabat
	CN-MMH	Gulfstream Aerospace G.650 (CN-AMH)	Government of Morocco, Rabat
	CN-MMJ	Cessna 560XLS+ Citation Excel (CN-AMJ)	Government of Morocco, Rabat
	CN-MMK	Cessna 560XLS+ Citation Excel (CN-AMK)	Government of Morocco, Rabat
	CN-MMR	Gulfstream Aerospace G.550 (CN-AMR)	Government of Morocco, Rabat
	CN-MMT	Gulfstream Aerospace G.550 (CN-AMS)	Government of Morocco, Rabat
	CN-MMY	Cessna 560XLS+ Citation Excel (CN-AMY)	Government of Morocco, Rabat
	CN-MSM	BAE RJ100 (CNA-SM)	Government of Morocco, Rabat
	CN-MVI	Boeing 737-8KB	Government of Morocco, Rabat
	CN-RGA	Boeing 747-428	Government of Morocco, Rabat
	NAMIBIA		
	V5-GON	Dassault Falcon 7X	Government of Namibia, Eros
	V5-NAM	Dassault Falcon 900B	Government of Namibia, Eros
	NETHERLANDS		
	Koninklijke Luchtmacht (KLu)		
	D-472	Boeing-Vertol CH-47F Chinook	KLu 298 Sqn, Gilze-Rijen
	D-473	Boeing-Vertol CH-47F Chinook	KLu 298 Sqn, Gilze-Rijen
	D-474	Boeing-Vertol CH-47F Chinook	KLu 302 Sqn, Fort Hood, Texas, USA
	D-475	Boeing-Vertol CH-47F Chinook	KLu 302 Sqn, Fort Hood, Texas, USA
	D-476	Boeing-Vertol CH-47F Chinook	KLu 302 Sqn, Fort Hood, Texas, USA
	D-477	Boeing-Vertol CH-47F Chinook	KLu 302 Sqn, Fort Hood, Texas, USA
	D-478	Boeing-Vertol CH-47F Chinook	KLu 302 Sqn, Fort Hood, Texas, USA
	D-479	Boeing-Vertol CH-47F Chinook	KLu 298 Sqn, Gilze-Rijen
	D-480	Boeing-Vertol CH-47F Chinook	KLu 298 Sqn, Gilze-Rijen
	D-481	Boeing-Vertol CH-47F Chinook	KLu 298 Sqn, Gilze-Rijen
	D-482	Boeing-Vertol CH-47F Chinook	KLu 302 Sqn, Fort Hood, Texas, USA
	D-483	Boeing-Vertol CH-47F Chinook	KLu 298 Sqn, Gilze-Rijen
	D-484	Boeing-Vertol CH-47F Chinook	KLu 298 Sqn, Gilze-Rijen
	D-485	Boeing-Vertol CH-47F Chinook	KLu 298 Sqn, Gilze-Rijen
	D-601	Boeing-Vertol CH-47F Chinook	KLu 298 Sqn, Gilze-Rijen
	D-602	Boeing-Vertol CH-47F Chinook	KLu 298 Sqn, Gilze-Rijen
	D-603	Boeing-Vertol CH-47F Chinook	KLu (on order)
	D-604	Boeing-Vertol CH-47F Chinook	KLu (on order)
	D-605	Boeing-Vertol CH-47F Chinook	KLu (on order)
	D-606	Boeing-Vertol CH-47F Chinook	KLu (on order)
	D-890	Boeing-Vertol CH-47F Chinook	Boeing, Philadelphia, USA (for modifications)
	D-891	Boeing-Vertol CH-47F Chinook	Boeing, Philadelphia, USA (for modifications)
	D-892	Boeing-Vertol CH-47F Chinook	Boeing, Philadelphia, USA (for modifications)
	D-893	Boeing-Vertol CH-47F Chinook	Boeing, Philadelphia, USA (for modifications)
	D-894	Boeing-Vertol CH-47F Chinook	Boeing, Philadelphia, USA (for modifications)
	D-895	Boeing-Vertol CH-47F Chinook	Boeing, Philadelphia, USA (for modifications)
	F-001	Lockheed Martin F-35A Lightning II	KLu 308th FS/56th FW, Luke AFB, Arizona, USA
	F-002	Lockheed Martin F-35A Lightning II	KLu 308th FS/56th FW, Luke AFB, Arizona, USA
	F-003	Lockheed Martin F-35A Lightning II	KLu 308th FS/56th FW, Luke AFB, Arizona, USA
	F-004	Lockheed Martin F-35A Lightning II	KLu 308th FS/56th FW, Luke AFB, Arizona, USA
	F-005	Lockheed Martin F-35A Lightning II	KLu 308th FS/56th FW, Luke AFB, Arizona, USA

Serial	Type (code/other identity)	Owner/operator, location or fate	Notes
F-006	Lockheed Martin F-35A Lightning II	KLu 308th FS/56th FW, Luke AFB, Arizona, USA	
F-007	Lockheed Martin F-35A Lightning II	KLu 308th FS/56th FW, Luke AFB, Arizona, USA	
F-008	Lockheed Martin F-35A Lightning II	KLu 308th FS/56th FW, Luke AFB, Arizona, USA	
F-009	Lockheed Martin F-35A Lightning II	KLu 322 Sqn, Leeuwarden	
F-010	Lockheed Martin F-35A Lightning II	KLu 322 Sqn, Leeuwarden	
F-011	Lockheed Martin F-35A Lightning II	KLu 322 Sqn, Leeuwarden	
F-012	Lockheed Martin F-35A Lightning II	KLu 322 Sqn, Leeuwarden	
F-013	Lockheed Martin F-35A Lightning II	KLu 322 Sqn, Leeuwarden	
F-014	Lockheed Martin F-35A Lightning II	KLu 322 Sqn, Leeuwarden	
F-015	Lockheed Martin F-35A Lightning II	KLu 322 Sqn, Leeuwarden	
F-016	Lockheed Martin F-35A Lightning II	KLu 322 Sqn, Leeuwarden	
F-017	Lockheed Martin F-35A Lightning II	KLu 322 Sqn, Leeuwarden	
F-018	Lockheed Martin F-35A Lightning II	KLu 322 Sqn, Leeuwarden	
F-019	Lockheed Martin F-35A Lightning II	KLu 322 Sqn, Leeuwarden	
F-020	Lockheed Martin F-35A Lightning II	KLu 313 Sqn, Volkel (322 Sqn loan)	
F-021	Lockheed Martin F-35A Lightning II	KLu 322 Sqn, Leeuwarden	
F-022	Lockheed Martin F-35A Lightning II	KLu 322 Sqn, Leeuwarden	
F-023	Lockheed Martin F-35A Lightning II	KLu 313 Sqn, Volkel	
F-024	Lockheed Martin F-35A Lightning II	KLu 313 Sqn, Volkel	
F-025	Lockheed Martin F-35A Lightning II	KLu 313 Sqn, Volkel	
F-026	Lockheed Martin F-35A Lightning II	KLu 313 Sqn, Volkel (322 Sqn loan)	
F-027	Lockheed Martin F-35A Lightning II	KLu 313 Sqn, Volkel	
F-028	Lockheed Martin F-35A Lightning II	KLu 313 Sqn, Volkel	
F-029	Lockheed Martin F-35A Lightning II	KLu 313 Sqn, Volkel	
F-030	Lockheed Martin F-35A Lightning II	KLu 322 Sqn, Leeuwarden	
F-031	Lockheed Martin F-35A Lightning II	KLu 322 Sqn, Leeuwarden	
F-032	Lockheed Martin F-35A Lightning II	KLu 313 Sqn, Volkel	
F-033	Lockheed Martin F-35A Lightning II	KLu 313 Sqn, Volkel	
F-034	Lockheed Martin F-35A Lightning II	KLu (on order)	
F-035	Lockheed Martin F-35A Lightning II	KLu (on order)	
F-036	Lockheed Martin F-35A Lightning II	KLu (on order)	
F-037	Lockheed Martin F-35A Lightning II	KLu (on order)	
F-038	Lockheed Martin F-35A Lightning II	KLu (on order)	
F-039	Lockheed Martin F-35A Lightning II	KLu (on order)	
G-273	Lockheed C-130H-30 Hercules	KLu 336 Sqn, Eindhoven	
G-275	Lockheed C-130H-30 Hercules	KLu 336 Sqn, Eindhoven	
G-781	Lockheed C-130H Hercules $	KLu 336 Sqn, Eindhoven	
G-988	Lockheed C-130H Hercules	KLu 336 Sqn, Eindhoven	
J-003	Fokker (GD) F-16AM Fighting Falcon	KLu 312 Sqn, Volkel	
J-004	Fokker (GD) F-16AM Fighting Falcon [AZ]	*Sold to Bulgaria, 2022 (Rework SABCA, Charleroi)*	
J-005	Fokker (GD) F-16AM Fighting Falcon	KLu 312 Sqn, Volkel	
J-006	Fokker (GD) F-16AM Fighting Falcon	KLu 312 Sqn, Volkel	
J-008	Fokker (GD) F-16AM Fighting Falcon	KLu 312 Sqn, Volkel	
J-010	Fokker (GD) F-16AM Fighting Falcon [AZ] [148 FS]	*Sold to Bulgaria, 2022 (Rework SABCA, Charleroi)*	
J-011	Fokker (GD) F-16AM Fighting Falcon	KLu 312 Sqn, Volkel	
J-013	Fokker (GD) F-16AM Fighting Falcon	KLu 312 Sqn, Volkel	
J-014	Fokker (GD) F-16AM Fighting Falcon	KLu 312 Sqn, Volkel	
J-015	Fokker (GD) F-16AM Fighting Falcon [AZ]	KLu 312 Sqn, Volkel	
J-016	Fokker (GD) F-16AM Fighting Falcon	KLu 312 Sqn, Volkel	
J-017	Fokker (GD) F-16AM Fighting Falcon	KLu 312 Sqn, Volkel	
J-018	Fokker (GD) F-16AM Fighting Falcon [AZ]	*Sold to Bulgaria, 2022 (Rework SABCA, Charleroi)*	
J-019	Fokker (GD) F-16AM Fighting Falcon [AZ]	*Sold to Bulgaria, 2022 (Rework SABCA, Charleroi)*	
J-020	Fokker (GD) F-16AM Fighting Falcon	KLu 312 Sqn, Volkel	
J-021	Fokker (GD) F-16AM Fighting Falcon	*Withdrawn from use at Volkel, 2022*	
J-055	Fokker (GD) F-16AM Fighting Falcon	KLu 312 Sqn, Volkel	
J-060	Fokker (GD) F-16AM Fighting Falcon	KLu 312 Sqn, Volkel	
J-062	Fokker (GD) F-16AM Fighting Falcon	KLu 312 Sqn, Volkel	
J-063	Fokker (GD) F-16AM Fighting Falcon	*Withdrawn from use at Volkel, 2022*	

Notes	Serial	Type (code/other identity)	Owner/operator, location or fate
	J-064	Fokker (GD) F-16BM Fighting Falcon [AZ]	*Sold to Bulgaria, 2022 (Rework SABCA, Charleroi)*
	J-067	Fokker (GD) F-16BM Fighting Falcon [AZ]	*Sold to Bulgaria, 2022 (Rework SABCA, Charleroi)*
	J-136	Fokker (GD) F-16AM Fighting Falcon	KLu 312 Sqn, Volkel
	J-144	Fokker (GD) F-16AM Fighting Falcon	*Withdrawn from use at Volkel, 2022*
	J-146	Fokker (GD) F-16AM Fighting Falcon	KLu 312 Sqn, Volkel
	J-197	Fokker (GD) F-16AM Fighting Falcon $	KLu 312 Sqn, Volkel
	J-201	Fokker (GD) F-16AM Fighting Falcon	KLu 312 Sqn, Volkel
	J-202	Fokker (GD) F-16AM Fighting Falcon	KLu, stored Volkel
	J-209	Fokker (GD) F-16BM Fighting Falcon [AZ]	*Sold to Bulgaria, 2022 (Rework SABCA, Charleroi)*
	J-210	Fokker (GD) F-16BM Fighting Falcon [AZ]	*Sold to Bulgaria, 2022 (Rework SABCA, Charleroi)*
	J-366	Fokker (GD) F-16AM Fighting Falcon [AZ]	*Sold to Bulgaria, 2022 (Rework SABCA, Charleroi)*
	J-367	Fokker (GD) F-16AM Fighting Falcon	KLu 312 Sqn, Volkel
	J-368	Fokker (GD) F-16BM Fighting Falcon	*Sold to Bulgaria, 2022 (Rework SABCA, Charleroi)*
	J-369	Fokker (GD) F-16BM Fighting Falcon [AZ]	*Sold to Bulgaria, 2022 (Rework SABCA, Charleroi)*
	J-508	Fokker (GD) F-16AM Fighting Falcon	KLu 312 Sqn, Volkel
	J-509	Fokker (GD) F-16AM Fighting Falcon	*Withdrawn from use at Volkel, 2022*
	J-512	Fokker (GD) F-16AM Fighting Falcon	KLu 312 Sqn, Volkel
	J-514	Fokker (GD) F-16AM Fighting Falcon	KLu 312 Sqn, Volkel
	J-515	Fokker (GD) F-16AM Fighting Falcon	KLu 312 Sqn, Volkel
	J-516	Fokker (GD) F-16AM Fighting Falcon	KLu 312 Sqn, Volkel
	J-632	Fokker (GD) F-16AM Fighting Falcon	*Withdrawn from use at Volkel, 2022*
	J-641	Fokker (GD) F-16AM Fighting Falcon	KLu 312 Sqn, Volkel
	J-644	Fokker (GD) F-16AM Fighting Falcon	*Withdrawn from use at Volkel, 2022*
	J-646	Fokker (GD) F-16AM Fighting Falcon $	*Withdrawn from use at Volkel, 2022*
	J-879	Fokker (GD) F-16AM Fighting Falcon $	*Withdrawn from use at Volkel, 2022*
	J-882	Fokker (GD) F-16BM Fighting Falcon $	*Sold to Bulgaria, 2022 (Rework SABCA, Charleroi)*
	L-01	Pilatus PC-7 Turbo Trainer	KLu 131 EMVO Sqn, Woensdrecht
	L-02	Pilatus PC-7 Turbo Trainer $	KLu 131 EMVO Sqn, Woensdrecht
	L-03	Pilatus PC-7 Turbo Trainer	KLu 131 EMVO Sqn, Woensdrecht
	L-04	Pilatus PC-7 Turbo Trainer	KLu 131 EMVO Sqn, Woensdrecht
	L-05	Pilatus PC-7 Turbo Trainer	KLu 131 EMVO Sqn, Woensdrecht
	L-06	Pilatus PC-7 Turbo Trainer	KLu 131 EMVO Sqn, Woensdrecht
	L-07	Pilatus PC-7 Turbo Trainer	KLu 131 EMVO Sqn, Woensdrecht
	L-08	Pilatus PC-7 Turbo Trainer	KLu 131 EMVO Sqn, Woensdrecht
	L-09	Pilatus PC-7 Turbo Trainer	KLu 131 EMVO Sqn, Woensdrecht
	L-10	Pilatus PC-7 Turbo Trainer	KLu 131 EMVO Sqn, Woensdrecht
	L-11	Pilatus PC-7 Turbo Trainer	KLu 131 EMVO Sqn, Woensdrecht
	L-12	Pilatus PC-7 Turbo Trainer	KLu 131 EMVO Sqn, Woensdrecht
	L-13	Pilatus PC-7 Turbo Trainer $	KLu 131 EMVO Sqn, Woensdrecht
	N-088	NH Industries NH.90-NFH	KLu 860 Sqn, De Kooij
	N-102	NH Industries NH.90-NFH	KLu 860 Sqn, De Kooij
	N-110	NH Industries NH.90-NFH	KLu 860 Sqn, De Kooij
	N-164	NH Industries NH.90-NFH	KLu 860 Sqn, De Kooij
	N-175	NH Industries NH.90-NFH	KLu 860 Sqn, De Kooij
	N-195	NH Industries NH.90-NFH	KLu 860 Sqn, De Kooij
	N-227	NH Industries NH.90-NFH	KLu 860 Sqn, De Kooij
	N-228	NH Industries NH.90-NFH	KLu 860 Sqn, De Kooij
	N-233	NH Industries NH.90-NFH	KLu 860 Sqn, De Kooij
	N-234	NH Industries NH.90-NFH	KLu 860 Sqn, De Kooij
	N-258	NH Industries NH.90-NFH	KLu 860 Sqn, De Kooij
	N-277	NH Industries NH.90-NFH	KLu 860 Sqn, De Kooij
	N-316	NH Industries NH.90-NFH	KLu 860 Sqn, De Kooij
	N-317	NH Industries NH.90-NFH	KLu 860 Sqn, De Kooij
	N-318	NH Industries NH.90-NFH	KLu 860 Sqn, De Kooij

Serial	Type (code/other identity)	Owner/operator, location or fate	Notes
N-319	NH Industries NH.90-NFH	KLu 860 Sqn, De Kooij	
N-325	NH Industries NH.90-NFH	KLu 860 Sqn, De Kooij	
N-326	NH Industries NH.90-NFH	KLu 860 Sqn, De Kooij	
N-327	NH Industries NH.90-NFH	KLu 860 Sqn, De Kooij	
Q-01	MDH AH-64D Apache Longbow	KLu 301 Sqn, Gilze-Rijen	
Q-02	MDH AH-64D Apache Longbow	KLu 302 Sqn, Fort Hood, Texas, USA	
Q-03	MDH AH-64D Apache Longbow	Boeing, Mesa, Arizona, USA	
Q-04	MDH AH-64D Apache Longbow	Boeing, Mesa, Arizona, USA	
Q-05	MDH AH-64D Apache Longbow	Boeing, Mesa, Arizona, USA	
Q-06	MDH AH-64D Apache Longbow	KLu 302 Sqn, Fort Hood, Texas, USA	
Q-07	MDH AH-64D Apache Longbow	KLu 302 Sqn, Fort Hood, Texas, USA	
Q-08	MDH AH-64D Apache Longbow	KLu 301 Sqn, Gilze-Rijen	
Q-09	MDH AH-64D Apache Longbow	Boeing, Mesa, Arizona, USA	
Q-10	MDH AH-64D Apache Longbow	Boeing, Mesa, Arizona, USA	
Q-11	MDH AH-64D Apache Longbow	KLu 302 Sqn, Fort Hood, Texas, USA	
Q-12	MDH AH-64D Apache Longbow	KLu 302 Sqn, Fort Hood, Texas, USA	
Q-13	MDH AH-64D Apache Longbow	KLu 301 Sqn, Gilze-Rijen	
Q-14	MDH AH-64D Apache Longbow	KLu 301 Sqn, Gilze-Rijen	
Q-16	MDH AH-64D Apache Longbow	KLu 301 Sqn, Gilze-Rijen	
Q-17	MDH AH-64D Apache Longbow	KLu 301 Sqn, Gilze-Rijen	
Q-18	MDH AH-64D Apache Longbow	KLu 301 Sqn, Gilze-Rijen	
Q-19	MDH AH-64D Apache Longbow	KLu 301 Sqn, Gilze-Rijen	
Q-21	MDH AH-64D Apache Longbow	Boeing, Mesa, Arizona, USA	
Q-22	MDH AH-64D Apache Longbow	KLu 301 Sqn, Gilze-Rijen	
Q-23	MDH AH-64D Apache Longbow	KLu 301 Sqn, Gilze-Rijen	
Q-24	MDH AH-64D Apache Longbow	KLu 301 Sqn, Gilze-Rijen	
Q-25	MDH AH-64D Apache Longbow	Boeing, Mesa, Arizona, USA	
Q-26	MDH AH-64D Apache Longbow	KLu 301 Sqn, Gilze-Rijen	
Q-27	MDH AH-64D Apache Longbow	KLu 302 Sqn, Fort Hood, Texas, USA	
Q-28	MDH AH-64D Apache Longbow	KLu 302 Sqn, Fort Hood, Texas, USA	
Q-29	MDH AH-64D Apache Longbow	KLu 301 Sqn, Gilze-Rijen	
Q-30	MDH AH-64D Apache Longbow	KLu 301 Sqn, Gilze-Rijen	
S-419	Eurocopter AS.532U-2 Cougar	KLu 300 Sqn, Gilze-Rijen	
S-440	Eurocopter AS.532U-2 Cougar	KLu 300 Sqn, Gilze-Rijen	
S-441	Eurocopter AS.532U-2 Cougar	KLu 300 Sqn, Gilze-Rijen	
S-442	Eurocopter AS.532U-2 Cougar	KLu 300 Sqn, Gilze-Rijen	
S-444	Eurocopter AS.532U-2 Cougar	KLu 300 Sqn, Gilze-Rijen	
S-445	Eurocopter AS.532U-2 Cougar	KLu 300 Sqn, Gilze-Rijen	
S-447	Eurocopter AS.532U-2 Cougar	KLu 300 Sqn, Gilze-Rijen	
S-453	Eurocopter AS.532U-2 Cougar	KLu 300 Sqn, Gilze-Rijen	
S-454	Eurocopter AS.532U-2 Cougar	KLu 300 Sqn, Gilze-Rijen	
S-456	Eurocopter AS.532U-2 Cougar	KLu 300 Sqn, Gilze-Rijen	
S-458	Eurocopter AS.532U-2 Cougar	KLu 300 Sqn, Gilze-Rijen	
S-459	Eurocopter AS.532U-2 Cougar	KLu 300 Sqn, Gilze-Rijen	
T-054	Airbus A.330-243 MRTT (KC-30) (EC-340/MRTT054)	KLu/MMU, 334 Sqn, Eindhoven	
T-055	Airbus A.330-243 MRTT (KC-30) (EC-336/MRTT055)	KLu/MMU, 334 Sqn, Eindhoven	
T-056	Airbus A.330-243 MRTT (KC-30) (EC-331/MRTT056)	KLu/MMU, 334 Sqn, Eindhoven	
T-057	Airbus A.330-243 MRTT (KC-30) (EC-337/MRTT057)	KLu/MMU, 334 Sqn, Eindhoven	
T-058	Airbus A.330-243 MRTT (KC-30) (EC-335/MRTT058)	KLu/MMU, 334 Sqn, Eindhoven	
T-059	Airbus A.330-243 MRTT (KC-30) (EC-338/MRTT059)	KLu/MMU, 334 Sqn, Eindhoven	
T-060	Airbus A.330-243 MRTT (KC-30) (EC-340/MRTT060)	KLu/MMU, 334 Sqn, Eindhoven	
T-061	Airbus A.330-243 MRTT (KC-30) (MRTT061)	KLu/MMU (or order)	
T-...	Airbus A.330-243 MRTT (KC-30)	KLu/MMU (or order)	
V-11	Grumman G.1159C Gulfstream IV	KLu 334 Sqn, Eindhoven	
Kustwacht & Netherlands Government			
PH-CGC	Dornier Do.228-212	Kustwacht, Amsterdam/Schiphol	
PH-CG.	De Havilland Canada DHC-8-102 (C-FCGE)	Kustwacht (on order)	
PH-CG.	De Havilland Canada DHC-8-102 (C-GCFK)	Kustwacht (on order)	
PH-CGN	Dornier Do.228-212	Kustwacht, Amsterdam/Schiphol	
PH-GOV	Boeing 737-700(BBJ) (N513BJ)	Dutch Royal Flight, Amsterdam/Schiphol	

Notes	Serial	Type (code/other identity)	Owner/operator, location or fate
	NEW ZEALAND		
	Royal New Zealand Air Force (RNZAF)		
	NZ4201	Lockheed P-3K2 Orion	*Withdrawn from use, Woodbourne*
	NZ4202	Lockheed P-3K2 Orion	*Withdrawn from use, Woodbourne*
	NZ4203	Lockheed P-3K2 Orion	*Withdrawn from use, Woodbourne, September 2021*
	NZ4204	Lockheed P-3K2 Orion	Withdrawn from use, Woodbourne
	NZ4205	Lockheed P-3K2 Orion	*Withdrawn from use, Woodbourne*
	NZ4206	Lockheed P-3K2 Orion	Withdrawn from use, Woodbourne
	NZ7001	Lockheed C-130H(NZ) Hercules $	RNZAF 40 Sqn, Whenuapai
	NZ7002	Lockheed C-130H(NZ) Hercules	RNZAF 40 Sqn, Whenuapai
	NZ7003	Lockheed C-130H(NZ) Hercules	Withdrawn from use, Woodbourne
	NZ7004	Lockheed C-130H(NZ) Hercules	RNZAF 40 Sqn, Whenuapai
	NZ7005	Lockheed C-130H(NZ) Hercules	RNZAF 40 Sqn, Whenuapai
	NZ7571	Boeing 757-2K2	RNZAF 40 Sqn, Whenuapai
	NZ7572	Boeing 757-2K2	RNZAF 40 Sqn, Whenuapai
	NZ4801	Boeing P-8A Poseidon	RNZAF 5 Sqn, Ohakea
	NZ4802	Boeing P-8A Poseidon	RNZAF (on order)
	NZ4803	Boeing P-8A Poseidon	RNZAF (on order)
	NZ4804	Boeing P-8A Poseidon	RNZAF (on order)
	NIGER		
	5U-GRN	Boeing 737-75U	Government of Niger, Niamey
	NIGERIA		
	Nigerian Air Force (NAF)		
	NAF-913	Lockheed C-130H Hercules	NAF 301 HAG, Ikeja
	NAF-917	Lockheed C-130H-30 Hercules	NAF 301 HAG, Ikeja
	NAF-918	Lockheed C-130H-30 Hercules	NAF 301 HAG, Ikeja
	NAF-961	Dassault Falcon 900	NAF 307 HAG, Minna
	Nigerian Government		
	5N-FGS	Gulfstream Aerospace Gulfstream V	Federal Government of Nigeria, Abuja
	5N-FGT	Boeing 737-7N6 [001]	Federal Government of Nigeria, Abuja
	5N-FGU	Dassault Falcon 7X	Federal Government of Nigeria, Abuja
	5N-FGV	Dassault Falcon 7X	Federal Government of Nigeria, Abuja
	5N-FGW	Gulfstream Aerospace G.550	Federal Government of Nigeria, Abuja
	5N-FGZ	Bombardier CL-605	Federal Government of Nigeria, Abuja
	NORWAY		
	Luftforsvaret/Royal Norwegian Air Force (RNoAF)		
	013	NH Industries NH.90-NFH (CSX81691)	*Withdrawn from use, June 2022*
	027	NH Industries NH.90-NFH (CSX81752)	*Withdrawn from use, June 2022*
	041	Dassault Falcon 20 ECM	*Withdrawn from use, Gardermoen September 2022*
	049	NH Industries NH.90-NFH	*Withdrawn from use, June 2022*
	053	Dassault Falcon 20 ECM	*Preserved Bodo Museum*
	057	NH Industries NH.90-NFH	*Withdrawn from use, June 2022*
	058	NH Industries NH.90-NFH	*Withdrawn from use, June 2022*
	060	Westland Sea King Mk.43B	RNoAF, stored Bodø
	062	Westland Sea King Mk.43B	RNoAF 330 Skv Bodø/Banak/Ørland & Sola
	066	Westland Sea King Mk.43B	RNoAF, stored Rygge
	069	Westland Sea King Mk.43B	RNoAF, stored Rygge
	070	Westland Sea King Mk.43B	RNoAF 330 Skv Bodø/Banak/Ørland & Sola
	071	Westland Sea King Mk.43B	RNoAF, stored Bodø
	073	Westland Sea King Mk.43B	RNoAF 330 Skv Bodø/Banak/Ørland & Sola
	074	Westland Sea King Mk.43B	RNoAF 330 Skv Bodø/Banak/Ørland & Sola
	087	NH Industries NH.90-NFH (CSX81745)	*Withdrawn from use, June 2022*
	139	Bell 412HP	RNoAF 339 Skv, Bardufoss
	140	Bell 412HP	RNoAF 339 Skv, Bardufoss
	141	Bell 412HP	RNoAF 339 Skv, Bardufoss
	142	Bell 412HP	RNoAF 339 Skv, Bardufoss
	143	Bell 412HP	RNoAF 339 Skv, Bardufoss

Serial	Type (code/other identity)	Owner/operator, location or fate	Notes
144	Bell 412HP	RNoAF 339 Skv, Bardufoss	
145	Bell 412HP	RNoAF 339 Skv, Bardufoss	
146	Bell 412HP	RNoAF 339 Skv, Bardufoss	
147	Bell 412HP	RNoAF 339 Skv, Bardufoss	
148	Bell 412HP	RNoAF 339 Skv, Bardufoss	
149	Bell 412HP	RNoAF 339 Skv, Bardufoss	
161	Bell 412HP	RNoAF 339 Skv, Bardufoss	
162	Bell 412HP	RNoAF 339 Skv, Bardufoss	
163	Bell 412HP	RNoAF 339 Skv, Bardufoss	
164	Bell 412HP	RNoAF 339 Skv, Bardufoss	
165	Bell 412HP	RNoAF 339 Skv, Bardufoss	
166	Bell 412HP	RNoAF 339 Skv, Bardufoss	
167	Bell 412HP	RNoAF 339 Skv, Bardufoss	
171	NH Industries NH.90-NFH	*Withdrawn from use, June 2022*	
189	Westland Sea King Mk.43B	RNoAF 330 Skv Bodø/Banak/Ørland & Sola	
217	NH Industries NH.90-ASW (CSX81843)	*Withdrawn from use, June 2022*	
0262	AgustaWestland AW101 Mk.612 (ZZ100)	RNoAF (on order)	
0264	AgustaWestland AW101 Mk.612 (ZZ101)	RNoAF 330 SKV, Sola	
0265	AgustaWestland AW101 Mk.612 (ZZ102)	RNoAF (on order)	
0268	AgustaWestland AW101 Mk.612 (ZZ103)	RNoAF 330 SKV, Sola	
0270	AgustaWestland AW101 Mk.612 (ZZ104)	RNoAF 330 SKV, Sola	
0273	AgustaWestland AW101 Mk.612 (ZZ105)	RNoAF 330 SKV, Sola	
0275	AgustaWestland AW101 Mk.612 (ZZ106)	RNoAF 330 SKV, Sola	
0276	AgustaWestland AW101 Mk.612 (ZZ107)	RNoAF 330 SKV, Sola	
0277	AgustaWestland AW101 Mk.612 (ZZ108)	RNoAF 330 SKV, Sola	
0278	AgustaWestland AW101 Mk.612 (ZZ109)	RNoAF 330 SKV, Sola	
0279	AgustaWestland AW101 Mk.612 (ZZ110)	RNoAF 330 SKV, Sola	
0280	AgustaWestland AW101 Mk.612 (ZZ111)	RNoAF 330 SKV, Sola	
0281	AgustaWestland AW101 Mk.612 (ZZ112)	RNoAF 330 SKV, Sola	
0282	AgustaWestland AW101 Mk.612 (ZZ113)	RNoAF 330 SKV, Sola	
0283	AgustaWestland AW101 Mk.612 (ZZ114)	RNoAF 330 SKV, Sola	
0284	AgustaWestland AW101 Mk.612 (ZZ115)	RNoAF (on order)	
329	Westland Sea King Mk.43B (ZJ162)	RNoAF, stored Rygge	
352	NH Industries NH.90-ASW	*Withdrawn from use, June 2022*	
353	NH Industries NH.90-ASW	*Withdrawn from use, June 2022*	
354	NH Industries NH.90-ASW	*Withdrawn from use, June 2022*	
358	NH Industries NH.90-NFH	*Withdrawn from use, June 2022*	
1216	NH Industries NH.90-NFH (CSX81751)	*Withdrawn from use, June 2022*	
3296	Lockheed P-3C UIP Orion	RNoAF, stored Andøya	
3297	Lockheed P-3C UIP Orion	RNoAF 333 Skv, Andøya	
3298	Lockheed P-3C UIP Orion	RNoAF 333 Skv, Andøya	
3299	Lockheed P-3C UIP Orion	RNoAF 333 Skv, Andøya	
5087	Lockheed Martin F-35A Lightning II	RNoAF 62nd FS/56th FW, Luke AFB, AZ, USA	
5088	Lockheed Martin F-35A Lightning II	RNoAF 62nd FS/56th FW, Luke AFB, AZ, USA	
5110	Lockheed Martin F-35A Lightning II	RNoAF 62nd FS/56th FW, Luke AFB, AZ, USA	
5111	Lockheed Martin F-35A Lightning II	RNoAF 62nd FS/56th FW, Luke AFB, AZ, USA	
5145	Lockheed Martin F-35A Lightning II	RNoAF 62nd FS/56th FW, Luke AFB, AZ, USA	
5146	Lockheed Martin F-35A Lightning II $	RNoAF 62nd FS/56th FW, Luke AFB, AZ, USA	
5147	Lockheed Martin F-35A Lightning II	RNoAF 62nd FS/56th FW, Luke AFB, AZ, USA	
5148	Lockheed Martin F-35A Lightning II	RNoAF 332 Skv, Ørland	
5149	Lockheed Martin F-35A Lightning II	RNoAF 332 Skv, Ørland	
5150	Lockheed Martin F-35A Lightning II	RNoAF 332 Skv, Ørland	
5205	Lockheed Martin F-35A Lightning II	RNoAF 332 Skv, Ørland	
5206	Lockheed Martin F-35A Lightning II	RNoAF 332 Skv, Ørland	
5207	Lockheed Martin F-35A Lightning II	RNoAF 332 Skv, Ørland	
5208	Lockheed Martin F-35A Lightning II	RNoAF 332 Skv, Ørland	
5209	Lockheed Martin F-35A Lightning II	RNoAF 332 Skv, Ørland	
5210	Lockheed Martin F-35A Lightning II	RNoAF 332 Skv, Ørland	
5288	Lockheed Martin F-35A Lightning II	RNoAF 332 Skv, Ørland	
5289	Lockheed Martin F-35A Lightning II	RNoAF 332 Skv, Ørland	
5290	Lockheed Martin F-35A Lightning II	RNoAF 62nd FS/56th FW, Luke AFB, AZ, USA	
5291	Lockheed Martin F-35A Lightning II	RNoAF 62nd FS/56th FW, Luke AFB, AZ, USA	

Notes	Serial	Type (code/other identity)	Owner/operator, location or fate
	5292	Lockheed Martin F-35A Lightning II	RNoAF 62nd FS/56th FW, Luke AFB, AZ, USA
	5293	Lockheed Martin F-35A Lightning II	RNoAF 332 Skv, Ørland
	5384	Lockheed Martin F-35A Lightning II	RNoAF 332 Skv, Ørland
	5385	Lockheed Martin F-35A Lightning II	RNoAF 332 Skv, Ørland
	5386	Lockheed Martin F-35A Lightning II	RNoAF 332 Skv, Ørland
	5387	Lockheed Martin F-35A Lightning II	RNoAF 332 Skv, Ørland
	5388	Lockheed Martin F-35A Lightning II	RNoAF 332 Skv, Ørland
	5389	Lockheed Martin F-35A Lightning II	RNoAF 332 Skv, Ørland
	5501	Lockheed Martin F-35A Lightning II	RNoAF 332 Skv, Ørland
	5502	Lockheed Martin F-35A Lightning II	RNoAF 332 Skv, Ørland
	5503	Lockheed Martin F-35A Lightning II	RNoAF 332 Skv, Ørland
	5504	Lockheed Martin F-35A Lightning II	RNoAF 332 Skv, Ørland
	5505	Lockheed Martin F-35A Lightning II	RNoAF 332 Skv, Ørland
	5506	Lockheed Martin F-35A Lightning II	RNoAF 332 Skv, Ørland
	5564	Lockheed Martin F-35A Lightning II	RNoAF 332 Skv, Ørland
	5565	Lockheed Martin F-35A Lightning II	RNoAF 332 Skv, Ørland
	5566	Lockheed Martin F-35A Lightning II	RNoAF 332 Skv, Ørland
	5567	Lockheed Martin F-35A Lightning II	RNoAF (on order)
	5568	Lockheed Martin F-35A Lightning II	RNoAF (on order)
	5569	Lockheed Martin F-35A Lightning II	RNoAF (on order)
	....	Lockheed Martin F-35A Lightning II	RNoAF (on order)
	....	Lockheed Martin F-35A Lightning II	RNoAF (on order)
	....	Lockheed Martin F-35A Lightning II	RNoAF (on order)
	....	Lockheed Martin F-35A Lightning II	RNoAF (on order)
	....	Lockheed Martin F-35A Lightning II	RNoAF (on order)
	....	Lockheed Martin F-35A Lightning II	RNoAF (on order)
	5601	Lockheed C-130J-30 Hercules II	RNoAF 335 Skv, Gardermoen
	5607	Lockheed C-130J-30 Hercules II	RNoAF 335 Skv, Gardermoen
	5629	Lockheed C-130J-30 Hercules II	RNoAF 335 Skv, Gardermoen
	5699	Lockheed C-130J-30 Hercules II	RNoAF 335 Skv, Gardermoen
	9582	Boeing P-8A Poseidon (N682DS)	RNoAF 333 Skv, Evenes
	9583	Boeing P-8A Poseidon (N684DS)	RNoAF 333 Skv, Evenes
	9584	Boeing P-8A Poseidon (N685DS)	RNoAF 333 Skv, Evenes
	9585	Boeing P-8A Poseidon (N687DS)	RNoAF 333 Skv, Evenes
	9586	Boeing P-8A Poseidon (N688DS)	RNoAF 333 Skv, Evenes

OMAN

Royal Air Force of Oman (RAFO)

Notes	Serial	Type (code/other identity)	Owner/operator, location or fate
	501	Lockheed C-130H Hercules	RAFO 16 Sqn, Al Musana
	502	Lockheed C-130H Hercules	RAFO 16 Sqn, Al Musana
	503	Lockheed C-130H Hercules	RAFO 16 Sqn, Al Musana
	505	Lockheed C-130J Hercules II	RAFO 16 Sqn, Al Musana
	506	Lockheed C-130J Hercules II	RAFO 16 Sqn, Al Musana
	507	Lockheed C-130J-30 Hercules II	RAFO (on order)
	508	Lockheed C-130J-30 Hercules II	RAFO (on order)
	525	Lockheed C-130J-30 Hercules II	RAFO Royal Flt, Seeb
	554	Airbus A.320CJ-214X	RAFO 4 Sqn, Seeb
	555	Airbus A.320CJ-214X	RAFO 4 Sqn, Seeb
	556	Airbus A.320CJ-214X	RAFO 4 Sqn, Seeb
	557	Grumman G.1159C Gulfstream IV	RAFO 4 Sqn, Seeb
	558	Grumman G.1159C Gulfstream IV	RAFO 4 Sqn, Seeb
	901	CASA C-295M	RAFO 5 Sqn, Salalah
	902	CASA C-295M	RAFO 5 Sqn, Salalah
	903	CASA C-295M	RAFO 5 Sqn, Salalah
	904	CASA C-295M	RAFO 5 Sqn, Salalah
	905	CASA C-295M	RAFO (on order)
	906	CASA C-295M	RAFO (on order)
	907	CASA C-295M	RAFO (on order)
	908	CASA C-295M	RAFO (on order)
	909	CASA C-295M	RAFO (on order)
	910	CASA C-295MPA Persuader	RAFO 2 Sqn, Al Musana
	911	CASA C-295MPA Persuader	RAFO 2 Sqn, Al Musana

Serial	Type (code/other identity)	Owner/operator, location or fate	Notes
912	CASA C-295MPA Persuader	RAFO 2 Sqn, Al Musana	
913	CASA C-295MPA Persuader	RAFO 2 Sqn, Al Musana	
914	CASA C-295MPA Persuader	RAFO (on order)	
915	CASA C-295MPA Persuader	RAFO (on order)	
916	CASA C-295MPA Persuader	RAFO (on order)	
Omani Government			
A4O-AA	Airbus A.320-233	Government of Oman, Seeb	
A4O-AD	Gulfstream Aerospace G.550	Government of Oman, Seeb	
A4O-AE	Gulfstream Aerospace G.550	Government of Oman, Seeb	
A4O-AJ	Airbus A.319-115CJ	Government of Oman, Seeb	
A4O-SO	Boeing 747SP-27	Government of Oman, Seeb	
A4O-HMS	Boeing 747-8H0	Government of Oman, Seeb	
A4O-OMN	Boeing 747-430	Government of Oman, Seeb	
PAKISTAN			
Pakistan Air Force (PAF)/Pakistani Army			
4119	Lockheed C-130E Hercules [119]	PAF 21 Sqn, Karachi	
4144	Lockheed L.100 Hercules [144]	PAF 6 Sqn, Islamabad	
4148	Lockheed C-130E Hercules [148]	PAF 6 Sqn, Islamabad	
4153	Lockheed C-130E Hercules [153] $	PAF 21 Sqn, Karachi	
4159	Lockheed C-130E Hercules [159]	PAF 21 Sqn, Karachi	
4171	Lockheed C-130E Hercules [171]	PAF 6 Sqn, Islamabad	
4177	Lockheed C-130E Hercules [177]	PAF 6 Sqn, Islamabad	
4178	Lockheed C-130E Hercules [178]	PAF 21 Sqn, Karachi	
4189	Lockheed C-130E Hercules [189]	PAF 6 Sqn, Islamabad	
4270	Gulfstream Aerospace G.450	Pakistani Army, Rawalpindi	
4282	Lockheed C-130E Hercules [282]	PAF 6 Sqn, Islamabad	
J-754	Cessna 560 Citation VI	PAF 12 VIP Communications Sqn, Islamabad	
J-755	Gulfstream Aerospace G.1159C Gulfstream IV-SP	PAF 12 VIP Communications Sqn, Islamabad	
J-756	Gulfstream Aerospace G.450	PAF 12 VIP Communications Sqn, Islamabad	
J-758	Bombardier Global 6000	PAF 12 VIP Communications Sqn, Islamabad	
POLAND			
Sily Powietrzne (SP)/Polish Air Force & Lotnictwo Marynarki Wojennej (LMW)/Polish Navy			
0001	Gulfstream Aerospace G.550 (N547GA)	SP 1.BLTr, Warszawa	
0002	Gulfstream Aerospace G.550 (N554GD)	SP 1.BLTr, Warszawa	
011	CASA C-295M	SP 13.eltr/8.BLTr, Kraków/Balice	
012	CASA C-295M	SP 13.eltr/8.BLTr, Kraków/Balice	
013	CASA C-295M	SP 13.eltr/8.BLTr, Kraków/Balice	
014	CASA C-295M	SP 13.eltr/8.BLTr, Kraków/Balice	
015	CASA C-295M	SP 13.eltr/8.BLTr, Kraków/Balice	
15	Mikoyan MiG-29UBM	SP 41.elt/22.BLT, Malbork	
016	CASA C-295M	SP 13.eltr/8.BLTr, Kraków/Balice	
017	CASA C-295M	SP 13.eltr/8.BLTr, Kraków/Balice	
018	CASA C-295M	SP 13.eltr/8.BLTr, Kraków/Balice	
019	PZL 130TC-I Orlik	SP 2.OSzL/42.BLSz, Radom	
020	CASA C-295M	SP 13.eltr/8.BLTr, Kraków/Balice	
020	PZL 130TC-I Orlik	SP 2.OSzL/42.BLSz, Radom	
021	CASA C-295M	SP 13.eltr/8.BLTr, Kraków/Balice	
022	CASA C-295M	SP 13.eltr/8.BLTr, Kraków/Balice	
022	PZL 130TC-I Orlik	SP 2.OSzL/42.BLSz, Radom	
023	CASA C-295M	SP 13.eltr/8.BLTr, Kraków/Balice	
023	PZL 130TC-I Orlik	SP 2.OSzL/42.BLSz, Radom	
024	CASA C-295M	SP 13.eltr/8.BLTr, Kraków/Balice	
024	PZL 130TC-I Orlik	SP 2.OSzL/42.BLSz, Radom	
025	CASA C-295M	SP 13.eltr/8.BLTr, Kraków/Balice	
025	PZL 130TC-I Orlik	SP 2.OSzL/42.BLSz, Radom	
026	CASA C-295M	SP 13.eltr/8.BLTr, Kraków/Balice	
026	PZL 130TC-I Orlik	SP 2.OSzL/42.BLSz, Radom	
027	CASA C-295M	SP 13.eltr/8.BLTr, Kraków/Balice	
28	Mikoyan MiG-29UBM	SP 41.elt/22.BLT, Malbork	
029	PZL 130TC-II Orlik	SP 2.OSzL/42.BLSz, Radom	

Notes	Serial	Type (code/other identity)	Owner/operator, location or fate
	030	PZL 130TC-II Orlik	SP 2.OSzL/42.BLSz, Radom
	031	PZL 130TC-II Orlik	SP 2.OSzL/42.BLSz, Radom
	032	PZL 130TC-II Orlik	SP 2.OSzL/42.BLSz, Radom
	035	PZL 130TC-I Orlik	SP 2.OSzL/42.BLSz, Radom
	036	PZL 130TC-I Orlik	SP 2.OSzL/42.BLSz, Radom
	037	PZL 130TC-II Orlik	SP 2.OSzL/42.BLSz, Radom
	38	Mikoyan MiG-29M	SP 41.elt/22.BLT, Malbork
	038	PZL 130TC-II Orlik	SP 2.OSzL/42.BLSz, Radom
	040	PZL 130TC-II Orlik	SP 2.OSzL/42.BLSz, Radom
	041	PZL 130TC-II Orlik	SP 2.OSzL/42.BLSz, Radom
	42	Mikoyan MiG-29UBM	SP 41.elt/22.BLT, Malbork
	042	PZL 130TC-II Orlik	SP 2.OSzL/42.BLSz, Radom
	043	PZL 130TC-II Orlik	SP 2.OSzL/42.BLSz, Radom
	044	PZL 130TC-II Orlik	SP 2.OSzL/42.BLSz, Radom
	045	PZL 130TC-I Orlik	SP 2.OSzL/42.BLSz, Radom
	046	PZL 130TC-II Orlik	SP 2.OSzL/42.BLSz, Radom
	047	PZL 130TC-II Orlik	SP 2.OSzL/42.BLSz, Radom
	048	PZL 130TC-II Orlik	SP 2.OSzL/42.BLSz, Radom
	049	PZL 130TC-II Orlik	SP 2.OSzL/42.BLSz, Radom
	050	PZL 130TC-II Orlik	SP 2.OSzL/42.BLSz, Radom
	051	PZL 130TC-II Orlik	SP 2.OSzL/42.BLSz, Radom
	052	PZL 130TC-II Orlik	SP 2.OSzL/42.BLSz, Radom
	54	Mikoyan MiG-29M	SP 41.elt/22.BLT, Malbork
	56	Mikoyan MiG-29M	SP 41.elt/22.BLT, Malbork
	59	Mikoyan MiG-29M	SP 41.elt/22.BLT, Malbork
	65	Mikoyan MiG-29M	SP 41.elt/22.BLT, Malbork
	66	Mikoyan MiG-29M	SP 41.elt/22.BLT, Malbork
	70	Mikoyan MiG-29M	SP 41.elt/22.BLT, Malbork
	83	Mikoyan MiG-29M	SP 41.elt/22.BLT, Malbork
	89	Mikoyan MiG-29M	SP 41.elt/22.BLT, Malbork
	92	Mikoyan MiG-29M	SP 41.elt/22.BLT, Malbork
	105	Mikoyan MiG-29M	SP 41.elt/22.BLT, Malbork
	108	Mikoyan MiG-29M	SP 41.elt/22.BLT, Malbork
	0110	Boeing 737-800 (N893BA)	SP 1.BLTr, Warszawa
	111	Mikoyan MiG-29M	SP 41.elt/22.BLT, Malbork
	0111	Boeing 737-800 (F-WTBK)	SP 1.BLTr, Warszawa
	0112	Boeing 737-800 (N785BJ)	SP 1.BLTr, Warszawa
	114	Mikoyan MiG-29M	SP 41.elt/22.BLT, Malbork
	115	Mikoyan MiG-29M	SP 41.elt/22.BLT, Malbork
	0204	PZL M28B-TD Bryza	SP 1.OSzL/41.BLSz, Deblin
	0205	PZL M28B-TD Bryza	SP 1.OSzL/41.BLSz, Deblin
	0206	PZL M28B-TD Bryza	SP 14.eltr/33.BLTr, Powidz
	0207	PZL M28B-TD Bryza	SP 1.OSzL/41.BLSz, Deblin
	0208	PZL M28B-TD Bryza	SP 14.eltr/33.BLTr, Powidz
	0209	PZL M28B-TD Bryza	SP 1.OSzL/41.BLSz, Deblin
	0210	PZL M28B-TD Bryza	SP 1.OSzL/41.BLSz, Deblin
	0211	PZL M28B-TD Bryza	SP 1.OSzL/41.BLSz, Deblin
	0212	PZL M28B-TD Bryza	SP 1.OSzL/41.BLSz, Deblin
	0213	PZL M28B/PT Bryza	SP 13.eltr/8.BLTr, Kraków/Balice
	0214	PZL M28B/PT Bryza	SP 14.eltr/33.BLTr, Powidz
	0215	PZL M28B/PT Bryza	SP 14.eltr/33.BLTr, Powidz
	0216	PZL M28B/PT Bryza	SP 13.eltr/8.BLTr, Kraków/Balice
	0217	PZL M28B/PT Bryza	SP 13.eltr/8.BLTr, Kraków/Balice
	0218	PZL M28B/PT Bryza	SP 13.eltr/8.BLTr, Kraków/Balice
	0219	PZL M28B/PT Bryza	SP 13.eltr/8.BLTr, Kraków/Balice
	0220	PZL M28B/PT Bryza	SP 13.eltr/8.BLTr, Kraków/Balice
	0221	PZL M28B/PT Bryza	SP 13.eltr/8.BLTr, Kraków/Balice
	0222	PZL M28B/PT Bryza	SP 13.eltr/8.BLTr, Kraków/Balice
	0223	PZL M28B/PT Bryza	SP 13.eltr/8.BLTr, Kraków/Balice
	0224	PZL M28B/PT Bryza	SP 13.eltr/8.BLTr, Kraków/Balice
	0225	PZL M28B/PT Bryza	SP 13.eltr/8.BLTr, Kraków/Balice
	305	Sukhoi Su-22UM-3K $	SP 8.elt/21.BLT, Swidwin

Serial	Type (code/other identity)	Owner/operator, location or fate	Notes
308	Sukhoi Su-22UM-3K	SP 40.elt/21.BLT, Swidwin	
310	Sukhoi Su-22UM-3K	SP 40.elt/21.BLT, Swidwin	
0404	PZL M28B-1E Bryza	LMW 30.el/44.BLMW, Cewice/Siemirowice	
0405	PZL M28B-1E Bryza	LMW 30.el/44.BLMW, Cewice/Siemirowice	
508	Sukhoi Su-22UM-3K	SP 8.elt/21.BLT, Swidwin	
509	Sukhoi Su-22UM-3K	SP 40.elt/21.BLT, Swidwin	
707	Sukhoi Su-22UM-3K $	SP 8.elt/21.BLT, Swidwin	
0723	PZL M28B-TD Bryza	LMW 28.el/43.BLMW, Gdynia/Babie Doly	
0810	PZL M28B-1RM Bryza	LMW 30.el/44.BLMW, Cewice/Siemirowice	
1001	Mil Mi-14PL	LMW 29.el/44.BLMW, Darlowo	
1002	Mil Mi-14PL	LMW 29.el/44.BLMW, Darlowo	
1003	Mil Mi-14PL	LMW 29.el/44.BLMW, Darlowo	
1003	PZL M28B-TD Bryza	LMW 28.el/43.BLMW, Gydnia/Babie Doly	
1005	Mil Mi-14PL	LMW 29.el/44.BLMW, Darlowo	
1006	PZL M28B-1R Bryza	LMW 30.el/44.BLMW, Cewice/Siemirowice	
1007	Mil Mi-14PL	LMW 29.el/44.BLMW, Darlowo	
1008	Mil Mi-14PL	LMW 29.el/44.BLMW, Darlowo	
1008	PZL M28B-1R Bryza	LMW 30.el/44.BLMW, Cewice/Siemirowice	
1009	Mil Mi-14PL	LMW 29.el/44.BLMW, Darlowo	
1010	Mil Mi-14PL	LMW 29.el/44.BLMW, Darlowo	
1011	Mil Mi-14PL	LMW 29.el/44.BLMW, Darlowo	
1012	Mil Mi-14PL/R	LMW 29.el/44.BLMW, Darlowo	
1017	PZL M28B-1R Bryza $	LMW 30.el/44.BLMW, Cewice/Siemirowice	
1022	PZL M28B-1R Bryza	LMW 30.el/44.BLMW, Cewice/Siemirowice	
1114	PZL M28B-1R Bryza	LMW 30.el/44.BLMW, Cewice/Siemirowice	
1115	PZL M28B-1R Bryza	LMW 30.el/44.BLMW, Cewice/Siemirowice	
1116	PZL M28B-1R Bryza	LMW 30.el/44.BLMW, Cewice/Siemirowice	
1117	PZL M28B-1 Bryza	LMW 28.el/43.BLMW, Gydnia/Babie Doly	
1118	PZL M28B-1 Bryza	LMW 28.el/43.BLMW, Gydnia/Babie Doly	
1501	Lockheed C-130E Hercules	SP 14.eltr/33.BLTr, Powidz	
1502	Lockheed C-130E Hercules	SP 14.eltr/33.BLTr, Powidz	
1503	Lockheed C-130E Hercules	SP 14.eltr/33.BLTr, Powidz	
1504	Lockheed C-130E Hercules	SP 14.eltr/33.BLTr, Powidz	
1505	Lockheed C-130E Hercules $	SP 14.eltr/33.BLTr, Powidz	
....	Lockheed C-130H Hercules (85-0035)	SP, stored Bydgoszcz, (ex 309th AMARG)	
....	Lockheed C-130H Hercules	SP (on order, ex 309th AMARG)	
....	Lockheed C-130H Hercules	SP (on order, ex 309th AMARG)	
3201	Sukhoi Su-22M-4	SP 8.elt/21.BLT, Swidwin	
3304	Sukhoi Su-22M-4	SP 8.elt/21.BLT, Swidwin	
3612	Sukhoi Su-22M-4	SP 40.elt/21.BLT, Swidwin	
3713	Sukhoi Su-22M-4	SP 40.elt/21.BLT, Swidwin	
3715	Sukhoi Su-22M-4	SP 40.elt/21.BLT, Swidwin	
3816	Sukhoi Su-22M-4	SP 40.elt/21.BLT, Swidwin	
3817	Sukhoi Su-22M-4	SP 40.elt/21.BLT, Swidwin	
3819	Sukhoi Su-22M-4	SP 8.elt/21.BLT, Swidwin	
3920	Sukhoi Su-22M-4	SP 40.elt/21.BLT, Swidwin	
4040	Lockheed Martin F-16C-52 Fighting Falcon	SP 6.elt/31.BLT, Poznan/Krzesiny	
4041	Lockheed Martin F-16C-52 Fighting Falcon	SP 6.elt/31.BLT, Poznan/Krzesiny	
4042	Lockheed Martin F-16C-52 Fighting Falcon	SP 3.elt/31.BLT, Poznan/Krzesiny	
4043	Lockheed Martin F-16C-52 Fighting Falcon	SP 3.elt/31.BLT, Poznan/Krzesiny	
4044	Lockheed Martin F-16C-52 Fighting Falcon	SP 3.elt/31.BLT, Poznan/Krzesiny	
4045	Lockheed Martin F-16C-52 Fighting Falcon	SP 3.elt/31.BLT, Poznan/Krzesiny	
4046	Lockheed Martin F-16C-52 Fighting Falcon	SP 3.elt/31.BLT, Poznan/Krzesiny	
4047	Lockheed Martin F-16C-52 Fighting Falcon	SP 3.elt/31.BLT, Poznan/Krzesiny	
4048	Lockheed Martin F-16C-52 Fighting Falcon	SP 3.elt/31.BLT, Poznan/Krzesiny	
4049	Lockheed Martin F-16C-52 Fighting Falcon	SP 3.elt/31.BLT, Poznan/Krzesiny	
4050	Lockheed Martin F-16C-52 Fighting Falcon	SP 3.elt/31.BLT, Poznan/Krzesiny	
4051	Lockheed Martin F-16C-52 Fighting Falcon	SP 3.elt/31.BLT, Poznan/Krzesiny	
4052	Lockheed Martin F-16C-52 Fighting Falcon $	SP 6.elt/31.BLT, Poznan/Krzesiny	
4053	Lockheed Martin F-16C-52 Fighting Falcon	SP 6.elt/31.BLT, Poznan/Krzesiny	
4054	Lockheed Martin F-16C-52 Fighting Falcon	SP 6.elt/31.BLT, Poznan/Krzesiny	
4055	Lockheed Martin F-16C-52 Fighting Falcon $	SP 6.elt/31.BLT, Poznan/Krzesiny	

Notes	Serial	Type (code/other identity)	Owner/operator, location or fate
	4056	Lockheed Martin F-16C-52 Fighting Falcon	SP 6.elt/31.BLT, Poznan/Krzesiny
	4057	Lockheed Martin F-16C-52 Fighting Falcon	SP 6.elt/31.BLT, Poznan/Krzesiny
	4058	Lockheed Martin F-16C-52 Fighting Falcon $	SP 6.elt/31.BLT, Poznan/Krzesiny
	4059	Lockheed Martin F-16C-52 Fighting Falcon	SP 6.elt/31.BLT, Poznan/Krzesiny
	4060	Lockheed Martin F-16C-52 Fighting Falcon	SP 6.elt/31.BLT, Poznan/Krzesiny
	4061	Lockheed Martin F-16C-52 Fighting Falcon	SP 6.elt/31.BLT, Poznan/Krzesiny
	4062	Lockheed Martin F-16C-52 Fighting Falcon $	SP 6.elt/31.BLT, Poznan/Krzesiny
	4063	Lockheed Martin F-16C-52 Fighting Falcon	SP 10.elt/32.BLT, Lask
	4064	Lockheed Martin F-16C-52 Fighting Falcon	SP 10.elt/32.BLT, Lask
	4065	Lockheed Martin F-16C-52 Fighting Falcon	SP 10.elt/32.BLT, Lask
	4066	Lockheed Martin F-16C-52 Fighting Falcon	SP 10.elt/32.BLT, Lask
	4067	Lockheed Martin F-16C-52 Fighting Falcon	SP 10.elt/32.BLT, Lask
	4068	Lockheed Martin F-16C-52 Fighting Falcon	SP 10.elt/32.BLT, Lask
	4069	Lockheed Martin F-16C-52 Fighting Falcon	SP 10.elt/32.BLT, Lask
	4070	Lockheed Martin F-16C-52 Fighting Falcon	SP 10.elt/32.BLT, Lask
	4071	Lockheed Martin F-16C-52 Fighting Falcon	SP 10.elt/32.BLT, Lask
	4072	Lockheed Martin F-16C-52 Fighting Falcon	SP 10.elt/32.BLT, Lask
	4073	Lockheed Martin F-16C-52 Fighting Falcon	SP 10.elt/32.BLT, Lask
	4074	Lockheed Martin F-16C-52 Fighting Falcon	SP 10.elt/32.BLT, Lask
	4075	Lockheed Martin F-16C-52 Fighting Falcon	SP 10.elt/32.BLT, Lask
	4076	Lockheed Martin F-16D-52 Fighting Falcon	SP 3.elt/31.BLT, Poznan/Krzesiny
	4077	Lockheed Martin F-16D-52 Fighting Falcon	SP 3.elt/31.BLT, Poznan/Krzesiny
	4078	Lockheed Martin F-16D-52 Fighting Falcon	SP 3.elt/31.BLT, Poznan/Krzesiny
	4079	Lockheed Martin F-16D-52 Fighting Falcon	SP 3.elt/31.BLT, Poznan/Krzesiny
	4080	Lockheed Martin F-16D-52 Fighting Falcon	SP 3.elt/31.BLT, Poznan/Krzesiny
	4081	Lockheed Martin F-16D-52 Fighting Falcon	SP 3.elt/31.BLT, Poznan/Krzesiny
	4082	Lockheed Martin F-16D-52 Fighting Falcon $	SP 6.elt/31.BLT, Poznan/Krzesiny
	4083	Lockheed Martin F-16D-52 Fighting Falcon	SP 6.elt/31.BLT, Poznan/Krzesiny
	4084	Lockheed Martin F-16D-52 Fighting Falcon $	SP 6.elt/31.BLT, Poznan/Krzesiny
	4085	Lockheed Martin F-16D-52 Fighting Falcon	SP 10.elt/32.BLT, Lask
	4086	Lockheed Martin F-16D-52 Fighting Falcon	SP 10.elt/32.BLT, Lask
	4087	Lockheed Martin F-16D-52 Fighting Falcon	SP 10.elt/32.BLT, Lask
	4101	Mikoyan MiG-29A	SP 41.elt/22.BLT, Malbork
	4104	Mikoyan MiG-29A	SP 41.elt/22.BLT, Malbork
	4105	Mikoyan MiG-29UB	SP 41.elt/22.BLT, Malbork
	4110	Mikoyan MiG-29UB	SP 41.elt/22.BLT, Malbork
	4113	Mikoyan MiG-29A	SP 41.elt/22.BLT, Malbork
	4116	Mikoyan MiG-29A	SP 41.elt/22.BLT, Malbork
	4120	Mikoyan MiG-29A	SP 41.elt/22.BLT, Malbork
	4121	Mikoyan MiG-29A	SP 41.elt/22.BLT, Malbork
	4122	Mikoyan MiG-29A	SP 41.elt/22.BLT, Malbork
	4123	Mikoyan MiG-29UB	SP 41.elt/22.BLT, Malbork
	6201	AgustaWestland AW101 Mk.614 (ZR285)	LMW (on order)
	6202	AgustaWestland AW101 Mk.614 (ZR286)	LMW (on order)
	6203	AgustaWestland AW101 Mk.614 (ZR287)	LMW (on order)
	6204	AgustaWestland AW101 Mk.614 (ZR288)	LMW (on order)
	7701	Aermacchi M-346 Bielik (CSX55209)	SP 48.el/41.BLSz, Deblin
	7702	Aermacchi M-346 Bielik (CSX55210)	SP 48.el/41.BLSz, Deblin
	7703	Aermacchi M-346 Bielik (CSX55211)	SP 48.el/41.BLSz, Deblin
	7704	Aermacchi M-346 Bielik (CSX55212)	SP 48.el/41.BLSz, Deblin
	7705	Aermacchi M-346 Bielik (MT55225)	SP 48.el/41.BLSz, Deblin
	7706	Aermacchi M-346 Bielik (MT55226)	SP 48.el/41.BLSz, Deblin
	7707	Aermacchi M-346 Bielik (MT55227)	SP 48.el/41.BLSz, Deblin
	7708	Aermacchi M-346 Bielik (MT55228)	SP 48.el/41.BLSz, Deblin
	7709	Aermacchi M-346 Bielik (CSX55238)	SP 48.el/41.BLSz, Deblin
	7710	Aermacchi M-346 Bielik (CSX55245)	SP 48.el/41.BLSz, Deblin
	7711	Aermacchi M-346 Bielik (CSX55246)	SP 48.el/41.BLSz, Deblin
	7712	Aermacchi M-346 Bielik (CSX55247)	SP 48.el/41.BLSz, Deblin
	7713	Aermacchi M-346 Bielik (CSX55271)	SP 48.el/41.BLSz, Deblin
	7714	Aermacchi M-346 Bielik (CSX55272)	SP 48.el/41.BLSz, Deblin
	7715	Aermacchi M-346 Bielik (CSX55275)	SP 48.el/41.BLSz, Deblin
	7716	Aermacchi M-346 Bielik (CSX55276)	SP 48.el/41.BLSz, Deblin

Serial	Type (code/other identity)	Owner/operator, location or fate	Notes
8101	Sukhoi Su-22M-4	SP 40.elt/21.BLT, Swidnin	
8205	Sukhoi Su-22M-4	SP 40.elt/21.BLT, Swidnin	
8309	Sukhoi Su-22M-4	SP 40.elt/21.BLT, Swidnin	
Straz Graniczna (Polish Border Guard)			
SN-50YG	PZL M20 Mewa	Straz Graniczna, Gdansk/Rebiechowo	
SN-60YG	PZL M28-05 Skytruck	Straz Graniczna, Gdansk/Rebiechowo	
SN-61YG	LET L-410UVP-E Turbolet	Straz Graniczna, Gdansk/Rebiechowo	
SN-62YG	LET L-410UVP-E Turbolet	Straz Graniczna, Gdansk/Rebiechowo	
Polish Government			
SP-LIG	Embraer EMB.175-200LR	Polish Government, Warszawa	
SP-LIH	Embraer EMB.175-200LR	Polish Government, Warszawa	
PORTUGAL			
Força Aérea Portuguesa (FAP)/Marinha			
11401	Aérospatiale TB-30 Epsilon	FAP Esq 101, Beja	
11402	Aérospatiale TB-30 Epsilon $	FAP Esq 101, Beja	
11403	Aérospatiale TB-30 Epsilon	FAP Esq 101, Beja	
11404	Aérospatiale TB-30 Epsilon	FAP Esq 101, Beja	
11405	Aérospatiale TB-30 Epsilon $	FAP Esq 101, Beja	
11406	Aérospatiale TB-30 Epsilon	FAP Esq 101, Beja	
11407	Aérospatiale TB-30 Epsilon	FAP Esq 101, Beja	
11410	Aérospatiale TB-30 Epsilon $	FAP Esq 101, Beja	
11411	Aérospatiale TB-30 Epsilon	FAP Esq 101, Beja	
11413	Aérospatiale TB-30 Epsilon	FAP Esq 101, Beja	
11414	Aérospatiale TB-30 Epsilon	FAP Esq 101, Beja	
11415	Aérospatiale TB-30 Epsilon	FAP Esq 101, Beja	
11416	Aérospatiale TB-30 Epsilon $	FAP, stored Beja	
11417	Aérospatiale TB-30 Epsilon	FAP Esq 101, Beja	
11418	Aérospatiale TB-30 Epsilon	FAP Esq 101, Beja	
14807	Lockheed P-3C CUP+ Orion	FAP, stored Beja	
14808	Lockheed P-3C CUP+ Orion $	FAP Esq 601, Beja	
14809	Lockheed P-3C CUP+ Orion	FAP Esq 601, Beja	
14810	Lockheed P-3C CUP+ Orion	FAP Esq 601, Beja	
14811	Lockheed P-3C CUP+ Orion	FAP, stored Beja	
15101	Lockheed Martin F-16A MLU Fighting Falcon	FAP Esq 201/Esq 301, Monte Real	
15102	Lockheed Martin F-16A MLU Fighting Falcon	FAP Esq 201/Esq 301, Monte Real	
15103	Lockheed Martin F-16A MLU Fighting Falcon $	FAP Esq 201/Esq 301, Monte Real	
15104	Lockheed Martin F-16A MLU Fighting Falcon	FAP Esq 201/Esq 301, Monte Real	
15105	Lockheed Martin F-16A MLU Fighting Falcon $	FAP Esq 201/Esq 301, Monte Real	
15106	Lockheed Martin F-16A MLU Fighting Falcon $	FAP Esq 201/Esq 301, Monte Real	
15107	Lockheed Martin F-16A MLU Fighting Falcon	FAP Esq 201/Esq 301, Monte Real	
15108	Lockheed Martin F-16A MLU Fighting Falcon	FAP Esq 201/Esq 301, Monte Real	
15109	Lockheed Martin F-16A MLU Fighting Falcon	FAP Esq 201/Esq 301, Monte Real	
15110	Lockheed Martin F-16A MLU Fighting Falcon	FAP Esq 201/Esq 301, Monte Real	
15112	Lockheed Martin F-16A MLU Fighting Falcon	FAP Esq 201/Esq 301, Monte Real	
15113	Lockheed Martin F-16A MLU Fighting Falcon	FAP Esq 201/Esq 301, Monte Real	
15114	Lockheed Martin F-16A MLU Fighting Falcon	FAP Esq 201/Esq 301, Monte Real	
15115	Lockheed Martin F-16A MLU Fighting Falcon	FAP Esq 201/Esq 301, Monte Real	
15116	Lockheed Martin F-16A MLU Fighting Falcon $	FAP Esq 201/Esq 301, Monte Real	
15117	Lockheed Martin F-16A MLU Fighting Falcon	FAP Esq 201/Esq 301, Monte Real	
15118	Lockheed Martin F-16B MLU Fighting Falcon	FAP Esq 201/Esq 301, Monte Real	
15119	Lockheed Martin F-16B MLU Fighting Falcon	FAP Esq 201/ESQ 301, Monte Real	
15120	Lockheed Martin F-16B MLU Fighting Falcon	FAP Esq 201/Esq 301, Monte Real	
15131	Lockheed Martin F-16A MLU Fighting Falcon	FAP Esq 201/Esq 301, Monte Real	
15133	Lockheed Martin F-16A MLU Fighting Falcon	FAP Esq 201/Esq 301, Monte Real	
15136	Lockheed Martin F-16A MLU Fighting Falcon $	FAP Esq 201/Esq 301, Monte Real	
15142	Lockheed Martin F-16A MLU Fighting Falcon	FAP Esq 201/Esq 301, Monte Real	
15143	Lockheed Martin F-16A MLU Fighting Falcon	FAP Esq 201/Esq 301, Monte Real	
15144	Lockheed Martin F-16B MLU Fighting Falcon	FAP (on order)	
15145	Lockheed Martin F-16A MLU Fighting Falcon	FAP (on order)	
15146	Lockheed Martin F-16A MLU Fighting Falcon	FAP (on order)	
15147	Lockheed Martin F-16A MLU Fighting Falcon	FAP (on order)	

Notes	Serial	Type (code/other identity)	Owner/operator, location or fate
	16701	CASA C-295M	FAP Esq 502, Lisbon/Montijo & Lajes
	16702	CASA C-295M	FAP, stored Beja
	16703	CASA C-295M	FAP Esq 502, Lisbon/Montijo & Lajes
	16704	CASA C-295M	FAP Esq 502, Lisbon/Montijo & Lajes
	16705	CASA C-295M	FAP Esq 502, Lisbon/Montijo & Lajes
	16706	CASA C-295M	FAP Esq 502, Lisbon/Montijo & Lajes
	16707	CASA C-295M	FAP Esq 502, Lisbon/Montijo & Lajes
	16708	CASA C-295MPA	FAP Esq 502, Lisbon/Montijo & Lajes
	16709	CASA C-295MPA	FAP Esq 502, Lisbon/Montijo & Lajes
	16710	CASA C-295MPA	FAP Esq 502, Lisbon/Montijo & Lajes
	16711	CASA C-295MPA	FAP Esq 502, Lisbon/Montijo & Lajes
	16712	CASA C-295MPA	FAP Esq 502, Lisbon/Montijo & Lajes
	16801	Lockheed C-130H-30 Hercules	FAP Esq 501, Lisbon/Montijo
	16802	Lockheed C-130H-30 Hercules	FAP, stored Lisbon/Montijo
	16803	Lockheed C-130H Hercules	FAP Esq 501, Lisbon/Montijo
	16805	Lockheed C-130H Hercules	FAP Esq 501, Lisbon/Montijo
	16806	Lockheed C-130H-30 Hercules $	FAP Esq 501, Lisbon/Montijo
	17401	Dassault Falcon 50	FAP Esq 504, Lisbon/Montijo
	17402	Dassault Falcon 50	FAP Esq 504, Lisbon/Montijo
	17403	Dassault Falcon 50	FAP Esq 504, Lisbon/Montijo
	19201	Westland Super Lynx Mk.95A (ZH580)	Leonardo MW, Yeovil, UK (update)
	19202	Westland Super Lynx Mk.95A (ZH581)	Leonardo MW, Yeovil, UK (update)
	19203	Westland Super Lynx Mk.95A (ZH582)	Leonardo MW, Yeovil, UK (update)
	19204	Westland Super Lynx Mk.95A (ZH583)	Marina Esq de Helicopteros, Lisbon/Montijo
	19205	Westland Super Lynx Mk.95A (ZH584)	Marina Esq de Helicopteros, Lisbon/Montijo
	19601	EHI EH-101 Mk.514	FAP Esq 751, Lisbon/Montijo
	19602	EHI EH-101 Mk.514	FAP Esq 751, Lisbon/Montijo
	19603	EHI EH-101 Mk.514	FAP Esq 751, Lisbon/Montijo
	19604	EHI EH-101 Mk.514	FAP Esq 751, Lisbon/Montijo
	19605	EHI EH-101 Mk.514	FAP Esq 751, Lisbon/Montijo
	19606	EHI EH-101 Mk.514	FAP Esq 751, Lisbon/Montijo
	19607	EHI EH-101 Mk.515	FAP Esq 751, Lisbon/Montijo
	19608	EHI EH-101 Mk.515	FAP Esq 751, Lisbon/Montijo
	19609	EHI EH-101 Mk.516	FAP Esq 751, Lisbon/Montijo
	19610	EHI EH-101 Mk.516	FAP Esq 751, Lisbon/Montijo
	19611	EHI EH-101 Mk.516	FAP Esq 751, Lisbon/Montijo
	19612	EHI EH-101 Mk.516	FAP Lisbon/Montijo (damaged)
	26901	Embraer KC-390 (PT-ZDK)	FAP Esq 501, Lisbon/Montijo
	26902	Embraer KC-390	FAP (on order)
	26903	Embraer KC-390	FAP (on order)
	26904	Embraer KC-390	FAP (on order)
	26905	Embraer KC-390	FAP (on order)
	29701	AgustaWestland AW119	FAP Esq 552, Beja
	29702	AgustaWestland AW119	FAP Esq 552, Beja
	29703	AgustaWestland AW119	FAP Esq 552, Beja
	29704	AgustaWestland AW119	FAP Esq 552, Beja
	29705	AgustaWestland AW119	FAP Esq 552, Beja
		QATAR	
		Qatar Emiri Air Force (QEAF)	
	211	Lockheed C-130J-30 Hercules II (08-0211) [MAH]	QEAF 12 Transport Sqn, Al-Udeid
	212	Lockheed C-130J-30 Hercules II (08-0212) [MAI]	QEAF 12 Transport Sqn, Al-Udeid
	213	Lockheed C-130J-30 Hercules II (08-0213) [MAJ]	QEAF 12 Transport Sqn, Al-Udeid
	214	Lockheed C-130J-30 Hercules II (08-0214) [MAK]	QEAF 12 Transport Sqn, Al-Udeid
	MAA	Boeing C-17A Globemaster III (08-0201)	QEAF 12 Transport Sqn, Al-Udeid
	MAB	Boeing C-17A Globemaster III (08-0202)	QEAF 12 Transport Sqn, Al-Udeid
	MAC	Boeing C-17A Globemaster III (12-0203)	QEAF 12 Transport Sqn, Al-Udeid
	MAE	Boeing C-17A Globemaster III (12-0204)	QEAF 12 Transport Sqn, Al-Udeid
	MAM	Boeing C-17A Globemaster III (14-0005)	QEAF 12 Transport Sqn, Al-Udeid
	MAN	Boeing C-17A Globemaster III (14-0006)	QEAF 12 Transport Sqn, Al-Udeid
	MAO	Boeing C-17A Globemaster III (14-0009)	QEAF 12 Transport Sqn, Al-Udeid
	MAP	Boeing C-17A Globemaster III (14-0010)	QEAF 12 Transport Sqn, Al-Udeid

Serial	Type (code/other identity)	Owner/operator, location or fate	Notes
MAX	Dassault Falcon 2000LXS (F-WWJR)	QEAF, Doha	
QA397	Pilatus PC-24	QEAF, Doha	
QA...	Pilatus PC-24	QEAF (on order)	

Qatari Government

A7-AAG	Airbus A.320-232	Qatari Amiri Flight, Doha	
A7-AAH	Airbus A.340-313X	Qatari Amiri Flight, Doha	
A7-HBJ	Boeing 747-8KB	Qatari Amiri Flight, Doha	
A7-HHE	Boeing 747-8KB	Qatari Amiri Flight, Doha	
A7-HHF	Boeing 747-8Z5	Qatari Amiri Flight, Doha	
A7-HHH	Airbus A.340-541	Qatari Amiri Flight, Doha	
A7-HHJ	Airbus A.319CJ-133	Qatari Amiri Flight, Doha	
A7-HHK	Airbus A.340-211	Qatari Amiri Flight, Doha	
A7-HHM	Airbus A.330-203	Qatari Amiri Flight, Doha	
A7-HJJ	Airbus A.330-202	Qatari Amiri Flight, Doha	
A7-HSJ	Airbus A.320-232CJ	Qatari Amiri Flight, Doha	
A7-MBK	Airbus A.320-232CJ	Qatari Amiri Flight, Doha	
A7-MED	Airbus A.319CJ-133	Qatari Amiri Flight, Doha	
A7-MHH	Airbus A.319CJ-115	Qatari Amiri Flight, Doha	

ROMANIA
Fortele Aeriene Romania (FAR)

2701	Alenia C-27J Spartan	FAR Escadrilla 902, Bucharest/Otopeni	
2702	Alenia C-27J Spartan	FAR Escadrilla 902, Bucharest/Otopeni	
2703	Alenia C-27J Spartan	FAR Escadrilla 902, Bucharest/Otopeni	
2704	Alenia C-27J Spartan	FAR Escadrilla 902, Bucharest/Otopeni	
2705	Alenia C-27J Spartan	FAR Escadrilla 902, Bucharest/Otopeni	
2706	Alenia C-27J Spartan	FAR Escadrilla 902, Bucharest/Otopeni	
2707	Alenia C-27J Spartan	FAR Escadrilla 902, Bucharest/Otopeni	
5930	Lockheed C-130B Hercules	FAR Escadrilla 901, Bucharest/Otopeni	
6166	Lockheed C-130H Hercules	FAR, stored Bucharest/Otopeni	
6191	Lockheed C-130H Hercules	FAR Escadrilla 901, Bucharest/Otopeni	
7432	Lockheed C-130H Hercules (74-2132)	FAR Escadrilla 901, Bucharest/Otopeni	

RUSSIA
Voenno-Vozdushniye Sily Rossioki Federatsii (VVS) (Russian Air Force)/Russian Government

595 w	Sukhoi Su-27P(LL) (36911037511)	VVS, Gromov Research Institute, Zhukhovsky	
597 w	Sukhoi Su-30LL (79371010102)	VVS, Gromov Research Institute, Zhukhovsky	
598 w	Sukhoi Su-27P(LL) (36911037820)	VVS, Gromov Research Institute, Zhukhovsky	
RA-09007	Dassault Falcon 7X	Rossiya Special Flight Det, Moscow/Vnukovo	
RA-09090	Dassault Falcon 7X	Rossiya Special Flight Det, Moscow/Vnukovo	
RA-26226	Antonov An-30	VVS (Open Skies), Moscow/Kubinka	
RA-30078	Antonov An-30	VVS (Open Skies), Moscow/Kubinka	
RA-64057	Tupolev Tu-204-300	Rossiya Special Flight Det, Moscow/Vnukovo	
RA-64058	Tupolev Tu-204-300	Rossiya Special Flight Det, Moscow/Vnukovo	
RA-64059	Tupolev Tu-204-300	Rossiya Special Flight Det, Moscow/Vnukovo	
RA-64504	Tupolev Tu-214	Stored, Kazan Borisoglebskoe	
RA-64505	Tupolev Tu-214	Rossiya Special Flight Det, Moscow/Vnukovo	
RA-64506	Tupolev Tu-214	Rossiya Special Flight Det, Moscow/Vnukovo	
RA-64515	Tupolev Tu-214SR	Rossiya Special Flight Det, stored	
RA-64516	Tupolev Tu-214SR	Rossiya Special Flight Det, Moscow/Vnukovo	
RA-64517	Tupolev Tu-214PU	Rossiya Special Flight Det, Moscow/Vnukovo	
RA-64520	Tupolev Tu-214PU	Rossiya Special Flight Det, Moscow/Vnukovo	
RA-64521	Tupolev Tu-214	Rossiya Special Flight Det, Ulyanovsk	
RA-64522	Tupolev Tu-214SUS	Rossiya Special Flight Det, Moscow/Vnukovo	
RA-64524	Tupolev Tu-214SUS	Rossiya Special Flight Det, Moscow/Vnukovo	
RA-64526	Tupolev Tu-214SR	Rossiya Special Flight Det, Moscow/Vnukovo	
RA-64527	Tupolev Tu-214SR	Rossiya Special Flight Det, Moscow/Vnukovo	
RA-64528	Tupolev Tu-214SR	Rossiya Special Flight Det, Moscow/Vnukovo	
RA-64531	Tupolev Tu-214PU	Rossiya Special Flight Det, Moscow/Vnukovo	
RA-64532	Tupolev Tu-214PU	Rossiya Special Flight Det, Moscow/Vnukovo	
RA-64533	Tupolev Tu-214PU	Rossiya Special Flight Det, Moscow/Vnukovo	

Notes	Serial	Type (code/other identity)	Owner/operator, location or fate
	RA-65905	Tupolev Tu-134AK-3	Rossiya Special Flight Det, Moscow/Vnukovo
	RA-65911	Tupolev Tu-134AK-3	Rossiya Special Flight Det, Moscow/Vnukovo
	RA-73025	Airbus A.319-115CJ	Rossiya Special Flight Det, stored
	RA-73026	Airbus A.319-115CJ	Rossiya Special Flight Det, Moscow/Vnukovo
	RA-82010	Antonov An-124-100	VVS 224th Transport Regiment, Seshcha/Bryansk
	RA-82013	Antonov An-124-100	VVS 224th Transport Regiment, Seshcha/Bryansk
	RA-82014	Antonov An-124-100	VVS 224th Transport Regiment, Seshcha/Bryansk
	RA-82030	Antonov An-124-100	VVS 224th Transport Regiment, Seshcha/Bryansk
	RA-82035	Antonov An-124-100	VVS 224th Transport Regiment, Seshcha/Bryansk
	RA-82038	Antonov An-124-100	VVS 224th Transport Regiment, Seshcha/Bryansk
	RA-82039	Antonov An-124-100	VVS 224th Transport Regiment, Seshcha/Bryansk
	RA-85041	Tupolev Tu-154M	VVS 6991 AvB, Chalovskiy
	RA-85042	Tupolev Tu-154M	VVS 6991 AvB, Chalovskiy
	RA-85155	Tupolev Tu-154M	VVS 8 oae, Chalovskiy
	RA-96012	Ilyushin Il-96-300PU	Stored, Moscow/Vnukovo
	RA-96014	Ilyushin Il-96-300	Rossiya Special Flight Det, Moscow/Vnukovo
	RA-96016	Ilyushin Il-96-300PU	Rossiya Special Flight Det, Moscow/Vnukovo
	RA-96017	Ilyushin Il-96-300S	Rossiya Special Flight Det, Moscow/Vnukovo
	RA-96018	Ilyushin Il-96-300	Rossiya Special Flight Det, Moscow/Vnukovo
	RA-96019	Ilyushin Il-96-300PU	Rossiya Special Flight Det, Moscow/Vnukovo
	RA-96020	Ilyushin Il-96-300PU	Rossiya Special Flight Det, Moscow/Vnukovo
	RA-96021	Ilyushin Il-96-300PU	Rossiya Special Flight Det, Moscow/Vnukovo
	RA-96022	Ilyushin Il-96-300PU	Rossiya Special Flight Det, Moscow/Vnukovo
	RA-96023	Ilyushin Il-96-300PU	Rossiya Special Flight Det, Moscow/Vnukovo
	RA-96024	Ilyushin Il-96-300PU	Rossiya Special Flight Det (on order)
	RA-96025	Ilyushin Il-96-300PU	Rossiya Special Flight Det (on order)
	RA-96102	Ilyushin Il-96-400VPU	Rossiya Special Flight Det, Moscow/Vnukovo
	RA-96104	Ilyushin Il-96-400VPU	Rossiya Special Flight Det, Moscow/Vnukovo
	RF-36052	Antonov An-30B (87 bk)	VVS (Open Skies), Moscow/Kubinka
	RF-64519	Tupolev Tu-214ON	VVS (Open Skies), Moscow/Kubinka
	RF-82011	Antonov An-124-100	VVS 224th Transport Regiment, Seshcha/Bryansk
	RF-82032	Antonov An-124-100	VVS 224th Transport Regiment, Seshcha/Bryansk
	RF-82034	Antonov An-124-100	VVS 224th Transport Regiment, Seshcha/Bryansk
	RF-82041	Antonov An-124-100	VVS 224th Transport Regiment, Seshcha/Bryansk
	RF-85655	Tupolev Tu-154M-LK1	VVS (Open Skies), Moscow/Kubinka

SAUDI ARABIA

Al Quwwat al Jawwiya as Sa'udiya/Royal Saudi Air Force (RSAF) & Saudi Government

	111	Lockheed VC-130H Hercules	RSAF 1 Sqn, Riyadh
	112	Lockheed VC-130H Hercules	RSAF 1 Sqn, Riyadh
	464	Lockheed C-130H Hercules	RSAF 4 Sqn, Jeddah
	465	Lockheed C-130H Hercules	RSAF 4 Sqn, Jeddah
	466	Lockheed C-130H Hercules	RSAF 4 Sqn, Jeddah
	467	Lockheed C-130H Hercules	RSAF 4 Sqn, Jeddah
	468	Lockheed C-130H Hercules	RSAF 4 Sqn, Jeddah
	472	Lockheed C-130H Hercules	RSAF 4 Sqn, Jeddah
	473	Lockheed C-130H Hercules	RSAF 4 Sqn, Jeddah
	474	Lockheed C-130H Hercules	RSAF 4 Sqn, Jeddah
	475	Lockheed C-130H Hercules	RSAF 4 Sqn, Jeddah
	477	Lockheed C-130H Hercules	RSAF 4 Sqn, Jeddah
	478	Lockheed C-130H Hercules	RSAF 4 Sqn, Jeddah

Serial	Type (code/other identity)	Owner/operator, location or fate	Notes
482	Lockheed C-130H Hercules	RSAF 4 Sqn, Jeddah	
483	Lockheed C-130H Hercules	RSAF 4 Sqn, Jeddah	
484	Lockheed C-130H Hercules	RSAF 4 Sqn, Jeddah	
485	Lockheed C-130H Hercules	RSAF 4 Sqn, Jeddah	
486	Lockheed C-130H Hercules	RSAF 4 Sqn, Jeddah	
1601	Lockheed C-130H Hercules	RSAF 16 Sqn, Jeddah	
1602	Lockheed C-130H Hercules	RSAF 16 Sqn, Jeddah	
1604	Lockheed C-130H Hercules	RSAF 16 Sqn, Jeddah	
1605	Lockheed C-130H Hercules	RSAF 16 Sqn, Jeddah	
1615	Lockheed C-130H Hercules	RSAF 16 Sqn, Jeddah	
1622	Lockheed C-130H-30 Hercules	RSAF 16 Sqn, Jeddah	
1623	Lockheed C-130H Hercules	RSAF 16 Sqn, Jeddah	
1624	Lockheed C-130H Hercules	RSAF 16 Sqn, Jeddah	
1625	Lockheed C-130H Hercules	RSAF 16 Sqn, Jeddah	
1626	Lockheed C-130H Hercules	RSAF 16 Sqn, Jeddah	
1627	Lockheed C-130H Hercules	RSAF 16 Sqn, Jeddah	
1628	Lockheed C-130H Hercules	RSAF 16 Sqn, Jeddah	
1629	Lockheed C-130H Hercules	RSAF 16 Sqn, Jeddah	
1630	Lockheed C-130H-30 Hercules	RSAF 16 Sqn, Jeddah	
1631	Lockheed C-130H-30 Hercules	RSAF 16 Sqn, Jeddah	
1632	Lockheed C-130H Hercules	RSAF 16 Sqn, Jeddah	
1801	Boeing E-3A Sentry	RSAF 18 Sqn, Al Kharj	
1802	Boeing E-3A Sentry	RSAF 18 Sqn, Al Kharj	
1803	Boeing E-3A Sentry	RSAF 18 Sqn, Al Kharj	
1804	Boeing E-3A Sentry	RSAF 18 Sqn, Al Kharj	
1805	Boeing E-3A Sentry	RSAF 18 Sqn, Al Kharj	
1901	Boeing RE-3A (1817)	RSAF 19 Sqn, Al Kharj	
1902	Boeing RE-3B	RSAF 19 Sqn, Al Kharj	
2301	Boeing KE-3A Sentry (1811)	RSAF 23 Sqn, Al Kharj	
2302	Boeing KE-3A Sentry (1812)	RSAF 23 Sqn, Al Kharj	
2303	Boeing KE-3A Sentry (1813)	RSAF 23 Sqn, Al Kharj	
2304	Boeing KE-3A Sentry (1814)	RSAF 23 Sqn, Al Kharj	
2305	Boeing KE-3A Sentry (1815)	RSAF 23 Sqn, Al Kharj	
2306	Boeing KE-3A Sentry (1816)	RSAF 23 Sqn, Al Kharj	
2307	Boeing KE-3A Sentry (1818)	RSAF 23 Sqn, Al Kharj	
2401	Airbus A.330-203 MRTT	RSAF 24 Sqn, Al Kharj	
2402	Airbus A.330-203 MRTT $	RSAF 24 Sqn, Al Kharj	
2403	Airbus A.330-203 MRTT $	RSAF 24 Sqn, Al Kharj	
2404	Airbus A.330-203 MRTT	RSAF 24 Sqn, Al Kharj	
2405	Airbus A.330-203 MRTT $	RSAF 24 Sqn, Al Kharj	
2406	Airbus A.330-203 MRTT $	RSAF 24 Sqn, Al Kharj	
3201	Lockheed KC-130H Hercules	RSAF 32 Sqn, Al Kharj	
3202	Lockheed KC-130H Hercules	RSAF 32 Sqn, Al Kharj	
3203	Lockheed KC-130H Hercules	RSAF 32 Sqn, Al Kharj	
3204	Lockheed KC-130H Hercules	RSAF 32 Sqn, Al Kharj	
3205	Lockheed KC-130H Hercules	RSAF 32 Sqn, Al Kharj	
3206	Lockheed KC-130H Hercules	RSAF 32 Sqn, Al Kharj	
3207	Lockheed KC-130H Hercules	RSAF 32 Sqn, Al Kharj	
3208	Lockheed KC-130J Hercules II	RSAF 32 Sqn, Al Kharj	
3209	Lockheed KC-130J Hercules II	RSAF 32 Sqn, Al Kharj	
8805	BAe Hawk 65A	RSAF 88 Sqn, *Saudi Hawks*, Tabuk	
8806	BAe Hawk 65A	RSAF 88 Sqn, *Saudi Hawks*, Tabuk	
8807	BAe Hawk 65	RSAF 88 Sqn, *Saudi Hawks*, Tabuk	
8808	BAe Hawk 65	RSAF 88 Sqn, *Saudi Hawks*, Tabuk	
8810	BAe Hawk 65	RSAF 88 Sqn, *Saudi Hawks*, Tabuk	
8811	BAe Hawk 65A	RSAF 88 Sqn, *Saudi Hawks*, Tabuk	
8812	BAe Hawk 65A	RSAF 88 Sqn, *Saudi Hawks*, Tabuk	
8813	BAe Hawk 65	RSAF 88 Sqn, *Saudi Hawks*, Tabuk	
8814	BAe Hawk 65	RSAF 88 Sqn, *Saudi Hawks*, Tabuk	
8816	BAe Hawk 65A	RSAF 88 Sqn, *Saudi Hawks*, Tabuk	
8817	BAe Hawk 65A	RSAF 88 Sqn, *Saudi Hawks*, Tabuk	
8818	BAe Hawk 65A	RSAF 88 Sqn, *Saudi Hawks*, Tabuk	

Notes	Serial	Type (code/other identity)	Owner/operator, location or fate
	8819	BAe Hawk 65A	RSAF 88 Sqn, *Saudi Hawks*, Tabuk
	8820	BAe Hawk 65	RSAF 88 Sqn, *Saudi Hawks*, Tabuk
	8821	BAe Hawk 65	RSAF 88 Sqn, *Saudi Hawks*, Tabuk
	HZ-101	Boeing 737-7DP	RSAF 1 Sqn, Riyadh
	HZ-102	Boeing 737-8DP	RSAF 1 Sqn, Riyadh
	HZ-103	Grumman G.1159C Gulfstream IV	RSAF 1 Sqn, Riyadh
	HZ-104	Grumman G.1159C Gulfstream IV-SP (HZ-MS4)	RSAF 33 Sqn, Riyadh
	HZ-105	BAe 125-800A	*Preserved, Riyadh museum*
	HZ-109	BAe 125-800B	*Preserved, Riyadh museum*
	HZ-110	BAe 125-800B	*Preserved, Riyadh museum*
	HZ-117	Lockheed L.100-30 Hercules	RSAF 1 Sqn, Riyadh
	HZ-124	Airbus A.340-211	RSAF 1 Sqn, Riyadh
	HZ-128	Lockheed L.100-30 Hercules	RSAF 1 Sqn, Riyadh
	HZ-129	Lockheed L.100-30 Hercules	RSAF 1 Sqn, Riyadh
	HZ-130	BAe 125-800B	*Preserved, Riyadh museum*
	HZ-132	Lockheed L.100-30 Hercules	RSAF 1 Sqn, Riyadh
	HZ-133	Cessna 550 Citation II	RSAF 1 Sqn, Riyadh
	HZ-134	Cessna 550 Citation II	RSAF 1 Sqn, Riyadh
	HZ-135	Cessna 550 Citation II	RSAF 1 Sqn, Riyadh
	HZ-136	Cessna 550 Citation II	RSAF 1 Sqn, Riyadh
	HZ-AFN	Grumman G.1159A Gulfstream III	*Withdrawn from use, Jeddah*
	HZ-AFR	Grumman G.1159A Gulfstream III	*Withdrawn from use, Jeddah*
	HZ-AFT	Dassault Falcon 900	*Withdrawn from use, Jeddah*
	HZ-AFZ	Dassault Falcon 900	*Withdrawn from use, Jeddah*
	HZ-AS99	Airbus A.318-112CJ	Saudi Royal Flight, Jeddah
	HZ-HM1	Boeing 747-468	Saudi Royal Flight, Jeddah
	HZ-HMED	Boeing 757-23A	Saudi Royal Flight, Riyadh
	HZ-MS1A	Bombardier Lear 60	Saudi Armed Forces Medical Services, Riyadh
	HZ-MS1B	Bombardier Lear 60	Saudi Armed Forces Medical Services, Riyadh
	HZ-MS2	Lockheed C-130H Hercules	Saudi Armed Forces Medical Services, Riyadh
	HZ-MS4	Grumman G.1159C Gulfstream IV-SP	*To RSAF as HZ-104, 2021*
	HZ-MS4A	Gulfstream Aerospace G.450	Saudi Armed Forces Medical Services, Riyadh
	HZ-MS4B	Gulfstream Aerospace G.450	Saudi Armed Forces Medical Services, Riyadh
	HZ-MS4C	Gulfstream Aerospace G.450	Saudi Armed Forces Medical Services, Riyadh
	HZ-MS5A	Gulfstream Aerospace Gulfstream V	Saudi Armed Forces Medical Services, Riyadh
	HZ-MS5B	Gulfstream Aerospace Gulfstream V	Saudi Armed Forces Medical Services, Riyadh
	HZ-MS6	Lockheed L.100-30 Hercules	Saudi Armed Forces Medical Services, Riyadh
	HZ-MS7	Lockheed C-130H Hercules	Saudi Armed Forces Medical Services, Riyadh
	HZ-MS9	Lockheed L.100-30 Hercules	Saudi Armed Forces Medical Services, Riyadh

SENEGAL

	6V-ONE	Airbus A.319CJ-115X	Government of Senegal, Dakar
	6V-SEN	Airbus A.321-251NX	Government of Senegal, Dakar

SERBIA

	YU-BNA	Dassault Falcon 50	Government of Serbia, Belgrade
	YU-SRB	Embraer ERJ.135BJ Legacy 600	Government of Serbia, Belgrade

SINGAPORE
Republic of Singapore Air Force (RSAF)

	720	Lockheed KC-130B Hercules	RSAF 122 Sqn, Paya Labar
	721	Lockheed KC-130B Hercules	RSAF 122 Sqn, Paya Labar
	724	Lockheed KC-130B Hercules	RSAF 122 Sqn, Paya Labar
	725	Lockheed KC-130B Hercules	RSAF 122 Sqn, Paya Labar
	730	Lockheed C-130H Hercules	RSAF 122 Sqn, Paya Labar
	731	Lockheed KC-130H Hercules	RSAF 122 Sqn, Paya Labar
	732	Lockheed C-130H Hercules	RSAF 122 Sqn, Paya Labar
	733	Lockheed C-130H Hercules	RSAF 122 Sqn, Paya Labar
	734	Lockheed KC-130H Hercules	RSAF 122 Sqn, Paya Labar
	735	Lockheed C-130H Hercules	RSAF 122 Sqn, Paya Labar
	760	Airbus A.330-203 MRTT (EC-333/MRTT033)	RSAF 112 Sqn, Changi
	761	Airbus A.330-203 MRTT (EC-332/MRTT034) $	RSAF 112 Sqn, Changi

Serial	Type (code/other identity)	Owner/operator, location or fate	Notes
762	Airbus A.330-203 MRTT (EC-336/MRTT035)	RSAF 112 Sqn, Changi	
763	Airbus A.330-203 MRTT (EC-337/MRTT036)	RSAF 112 Sqn, Changi	
764	Airbus A.330-203 MRTT (EC-335/MRTT037)	RSAF 112 Sqn, Changi	
765	Airbus A.330-203 MRTT (EC-332/MRTT038)	RSAF 112 Sqn, Changi	

SLOVAKIA
Slovenské Vojenske Letectvo (SVL)

Serial	Type (code/other identity)	Owner/operator, location or fate	Notes
0619	Mikoyan MiG-29AS	*Withdrawn from use, Sliač*	
0807	Mil Mi-17	*Transferred to Ukraine, 2022*	
0808	Mil Mi-17	SVL 2.Dvlt/Vrtulnikové Letcecké Kridlo, Prešov	
0820	Mil Mi-17	SVL 2.Dvlt/Vrtulnikové Letcecké Kridlo, Prešov	
0821	Mil Mi-17	*Transferred to Ukraine, 2022*	
0823	Mil Mi-17M	SVL 2.Dvlt/Vrtulnikové Letcecké Kridlo, Prešov	
0824	Mil Mi-17	SVL, stored Prešov	
0826	Mil Mi-17	SVL 2.Dvlt/Vrtulnikové Letcecké Kridlo, Prešov	
0841	Mil Mi-17	SVL 2.Dvlt/Vrtulnikové Letcecké Kridlo, Prešov	
0844	Mil Mi-17	*Transferred to Ukraine, 2022*	
0845	Mil Mi-17	SVL 2.Dvlt/Vrtulnikové Letcecké Kridlo, Prešov	
0846	Mil Mi-17	SVL 2.Dvlt/Vrtulnikové Letcecké Kridlo, Prešov	
0847	Mil Mi-17	*Transferred to Ukraine, 2022*	
0921	Mikoyan MiG-29AS	*Withdrawn from use, Sliač*	
1133	LET L-410T Turbolet	SVL, stored Malacky	
1303	Mikoyan MiG-29UBS $	*Withdrawn from use, Sliač*	
1521	LET L-410FG Turbolet	SVL 1.Dopravná Letka/Dopravné Kridlo, Malacky	
1931	Aeritalia C-27J Spartan (CSX62302)	SVL 1.Dopravná Letka/Dopravné Kridlo, Malacky	
1962	Aeritalia C-27J Spartan (CSX62306)	SVL 1.Dopravná Letka/Dopravné Kridlo, Malacky	
2123	Mikoyan MiG-29AS	*Withdrawn from use, Sliač*	
2311	LET L-410UVP Turbolet	SVL 1.Dopravná Letka/Dopravné Kridlo, Malacky	
2421	LET L-410UVP Turbolet	SVL 1.Dopravná Letka/Dopravné Kridlo, Malacky	
2718	LET L-401UVP-E Turbolet	SVL 1.Dopravná Letka/Dopravné Kridlo, Malacky	
2721	LET L-401UVP-E Turbolet	SVL 1.Dopravná Letka/Dopravné Kridlo, Malacky	
2818	LET L-401UVP-20 Turbolet	SVL 1.Dopravná Letka/Dopravné Kridlo, Malacky	
2901	LET L-401UVP-20 Turbolet	SVL 1.Dopravná Letka/Dopravné Kridlo, Malacky	
3709	Mikoyan MiG-29AS	*Withdrawn from use, Sliač*	
3911	Mikoyan MiG-29AS	*Withdrawn from use, Sliač*	
4701	Aero L-39ZAM Albatros	SVL 2.vlt/Zmiešané Letecké Kridlo, Sliač	
4703	Aero L-39ZAM Albatros	SVL 2.vlt/Zmiešané Letecké Kridlo, Sliač	
4707	Aero L-39ZAM Albatros	SVL 2.vlt/Zmiešané Letecké Kridlo, Sliač	
5251	Aero L-39CM Albatros	SVL 2.vlt/Zmiešané Letecké Kridlo, Sliač	
5252	Aero L-39CM Albatros	SVL 2.vlt/Zmiešané Letecké Kridlo, Sliač	
5253	Aero L-39CM Albatros	SVL 2.vlt/Zmiešané Letecké Kridlo, Sliač	
5254	Aero L-39CM Albatros	SVL 2.vlt/Zmiešané Letecké Kridlo, Sliač	
5301	Aero L-39CM Albatros $	SVL 2.vlt/Zmiešané Letecké Kridlo, Sliač	
5302	Aero L-39CM Albatros	SVL 2.vlt/Zmiešané Letecké Kridlo, Sliač	
5304	Mikoyan MiG-29UBS $	*Withdrawn from use, Sliač*	
6124	Mikoyan MiG-29AS	*Withdrawn from use, Sliač*	
6627	Mikoyan MiG-29AS	*Withdrawn from use, Sliač*	
6728	Mikoyan MiG-29AS	*Withdrawn from use, Sliač*	
7445	Sikorsky UH-60M Black Hawk	SVL 1.vlt/Vrtulnikové Letecké Kridlo, Prešov	
7446	Sikorsky UH-60M Black Hawk	SVL 1.vlt/Vrtulnikové Letecké Kridlo, Prešov	
7447	Sikorsky UH-60M Black Hawk	SVL 1.vlt/Vrtulnikové Letecké Kridlo, Prešov	
7448	Sikorsky UH-60M Black Hawk	SVL 1.vlt/Vrtulnikové Letecké Kridlo, Prešov	
7449	Sikorsky UH-60M Black Hawk	SVL 1.vlt/Vrtulnikové Letecké Kridlo, Prešov	
7639	Sikorsky UH-60M Black Hawk	SVL 1.vlt/Vrtulnikové Letecké Kridlo, Prešov	
7640	Sikorsky UH-60M Black Hawk	SVL 1.vlt/Vrtulnikové Letecké Kridlo, Prešov	
7641	Sikorsky UH-60M Black Hawk	SVL 1.vlt/Vrtulnikové Letecké Kridlo, Prešov	
7642	Sikorsky UH-60M Black Hawk	SVL 1.vlt/Vrtulnikové Letecké Kridlo, Prešov	

Slovak Government

Serial	Type (code/other identity)	Owner/operator, location or fate	Notes
OM-BYA	Airbus A.319-115	Slovak Government, Bratislava/Ivanka	
OM-BYB	Fokker 100	Slovak Government, Bratislava/Ivanka	
OM-BYC	Fokker 100	Slovak Government, Bratislava/Ivanka	
OM-BYK	Airbus A.319-115XCJ	Slovak Government, Bratislava/Ivanka	

Notes	Serial	Type (code/other identity)	Owner/operator, location or fate
	SLOVENIA		
	Slovenska Vojska (SV)/Slovenian Armed Forces		
	L1-01	Dassault Falcon 2000EX	Government of Slovenia, Ljubljana
	L4-01	LET 410UVP-E Turbolet	SV 107.Letalska Baza, Cerklje ob Krki
	L9-61	Pilatus PC-9M	SV Letalska Šola, Cerklje ob Krki
	L9-62	Pilatus PC-9M	SV Letalska Šola, Cerklje ob Krki
	L9-63	Pilatus PC-9M	SV Letalska Šola, Cerklje ob Krki
	L9-64	Pilatus PC-9M	SV Letalska Šola, Cerklje ob Krki
	L9-65	Pilatus PC-9M	SV Letalska Šola, Cerklje ob Krki
	L9-66	Pilatus PC-9M	SV Letalska Šola, Cerklje ob Krki
	L9-67	Pilatus PC-9M	SV Letalska Šola, Cerklje ob Krki
	L9-68	Pilatus PC-9M	SV Letalska Šola, Cerklje ob Krki
	L9-69	Pilatus PC-9M	SV Letalska Šola, Cerklje ob Krki
	L.-01	Alenia C-27J Spartan	SV (on order)
	SOUTH AFRICA		
	Suid Afrikaanse Lugmag/South African Air Force (SAAF)		
	401	Lockheed C-130BZ Hercules	SAAF 28 Sqn, Waterkloof
	402	Lockheed C-130BZ Hercules	SAAF 28 Sqn, Waterkloof
	405	Lockheed C-130BZ Hercules $	SAAF 28 Sqn, Waterkloof
	406	Lockheed C-130BZ Hercules	SAAF 28 Sqn, Waterkloof
	409	Lockheed C-130BZ Hercules	SAAF 28 Sqn, Waterkloof
	ZS-NAN	Dassault Falcon 900	SAAF 21 Sqn, Waterkloof
	ZS-RSA	Boeing 737-7ED	SAAF 21 Sqn, Waterkloof
	SOUTH KOREA		
	Han Guk Gong Gun/Republic of Korea Air Force		
	18-001	Airbus KC-330 Cygnus (MRTT050)	RoKAF 261 Air Tanker Sqn/5 Tactical Air Transport Wing, Gimhae
	19-002	Airbus KC-330 Cygnus (MRTT051)	RoKAF 261 Air Tanker Sqn/5 Tactical Air Transport Wing, Gimhae
	19-003	Airbus KC-330 Cygnus (MRTT052)	RoKAF 261 Air Tanker Sqn/5 Tactical Air Transport Wing, Gimhae
	19-004	Airbus KC-330 Cygnus (MRTT053)	RoKAF 261 Air Tanker Sqn/5 Tactical Air Transport Wing, Gimhae
	22001	Boeing 747-8I (HL7643)	RoKAF 257 Special Flight Squadron, Seongmu
	SPAIN		
	Arma Aérea de l'Armada Española, Ejército del Aire (EdA)/Spanish Air Force & Guardia Civil		
	CE.15-01	McDonnell Douglas EF-18BM Hornet [15-70] $	EdA 151 Esc/152 Esc/153 Esc/Ala 15, Zaragoza
	CE.15-02	McDonnell Douglas EF-18BM Hornet [15-71]	EdA 151 Esc/152 Esc/153 Esc/Ala 15, Zaragoza
	CE.15-03	McDonnell Douglas EF-18BM Hornet [15-72]	EdA 151 Esc/152 Esc/153 Esc/Ala 15, Zaragoza
	CE.15-04	McDonnell Douglas EF-18BM Hornet [15-73]	EdA 151 Esc/152 Esc/153 Esc/Ala 15, Zaragoza
	CE.15-05	McDonnell Douglas EF-18BM Hornet [15-74]	EdA 151 Esc/152 Esc/153 Esc/Ala 15, Zaragoza
	CE.15-06	McDonnell Douglas EF-18BM Hornet [15-75]	EdA 151 Esc/152 Esc/153 Esc/Ala 15, Zaragoza
	CE.15-07	McDonnell Douglas EF-18BM Hornet [15-76]	EdA 151 Esc/152 Esc/153 Esc/Ala 15, Zaragoza
	CE.15-08	McDonnell Douglas EF-18BM Hornet [12-71]	EdA 121 Esc/122 Esc/Ala 12, Madrid/Torrejón
	CE.15-09	McDonnell Douglas EF-18BM Hornet [15-77]	EdA 151 Esc/152 Esc/153 Esc/Ala 15, Zaragoza
	CE.15-10	McDonnell Douglas EF-18BM Hornet [12-73]	EdA 121 Esc/122 Esc/Ala 12, Madrid/Torrejón
	CE.15-11	McDonnell Douglas EF-18BM Hornet [12-74]	EdA 121 Esc/122 Esc/Ala 12, Madrid/Torrejón
	CE.15-12	McDonnell Douglas EF-18BM Hornet [12-75]	EdA 121 Esc/122 Esc/Ala 12, Madrid/Torrejón
	C.15-13	McDonnell Douglas EF-18M Hornet [12-01]	EdA 121 Esc/122 Esc/Ala 12, Madrid/Torrejón
	C.15-14	McDonnell Douglas EF-18M Hornet [15-01] $	EdA 151 Esc/152 Esc/153 Esc/Ala 15, Zaragoza
	C.15-15	McDonnell Douglas EF-18M Hornet [15-02]	EdA 151 Esc/152 Esc/153 Esc/Ala 15, Zaragoza
	C.15-16	McDonnell Douglas EF-18M Hornet [15-03]	EdA 151 Esc/152 Esc/153 Esc/Ala 15, Zaragoza
	C.15-18	McDonnell Douglas EF-18M Hornet [15-05]	EdA 151 Esc/152 Esc/153 Esc/Ala 15, Zaragoza
	C.15-21	McDonnell Douglas EF-18M Hornet [15-08]	EdA 151 Esc/152 Esc/153 Esc/Ala 15, Zaragoza
	C.15-22	McDonnell Douglas EF-18M Hornet [15-09]	EdA 151 Esc/152 Esc/153 Esc/Ala 15, Zaragoza
	C.15-23	McDonnell Douglas EF-18M Hornet [15-10]	EdA 151 Esc/152 Esc/153 Esc/Ala 15, Zaragoza
	C.15-24	McDonnell Douglas EF-18M Hornet [15-11]	EdA 151 Esc/152 Esc/153 Esc/Ala 15, Zaragoza
	C.15-25	McDonnell Douglas EF-18M Hornet [15-12]	EdA 151 Esc/152 Esc/153 Esc/Ala 15, Zaragoza
	C.15-26	McDonnell Douglas EF-18M Hornet [15-13] $	EdA 151 Esc/152 Esc/153 Esc/Ala 15, Zaragoza

Serial	Type (code/other identity)	Owner/operator, location or fate	Notes
C.15-27	McDonnell Douglas EF-18M Hornet [15-14]	EdA 151 Esc/152 Esc/153 Esc/Ala 15, Zaragoza	
C.15-28	McDonnell Douglas EF-18M Hornet [15-15]	EdA 151 Esc/152 Esc/153 Esc/Ala 15, Zaragoza	
C.15-29	McDonnell Douglas EF-18M Hornet [15-16]	EdA 151 Esc/152 Esc/153 Esc/Ala 15, Zaragoza	
C.15-30	McDonnell Douglas EF-18M Hornet [15-17]	EdA 151 Esc/152 Esc/153 Esc/Ala 15, Zaragoza	
C.15-31	McDonnell Douglas EF-18M Hornet [15-18]	EdA 151 Esc/152 Esc/153 Esc/Ala 15, Zaragoza	
C.15-32	McDonnell Douglas EF-18M Hornet [15-19]	EdA 151 Esc/152 Esc/153 Esc/Ala 15, Zaragoza	
C.15-33	McDonnell Douglas EF-18M Hornet [15-20]	EdA 151 Esc/152 Esc/153 Esc/Ala 15, Zaragoza	
C.15-34	McDonnell Douglas EF-18M Hornet [12-50]	EdA 121 Esc/122 Esc/Ala 12, Madrid/Torrejón	
C.15-35	McDonnell Douglas EF-18M Hornet [15-22]	EdA 151 Esc/152 Esc/153 Esc/Ala 15, Zaragoza	
C.15-36	McDonnell Douglas EF-18M Hornet [15-23]	EdA 151 Esc/152 Esc/153 Esc/Ala 15, Zaragoza	
C.15-37	McDonnell Douglas EF-18M Hornet [15-24]	EdA 151 Esc/152 Esc/153 Esc/Ala 15, Zaragoza	
C.15-38	McDonnell Douglas EF-18M Hornet [15-25]	EdA 151 Esc/152 Esc/153 Esc/Ala 15, Zaragoza	
C.15-39	McDonnell Douglas EF-18M Hornet [15-26]	EdA 151 Esc/152 Esc/153 Esc/Ala 15, Zaragoza	
C.15-40	McDonnell Douglas EF-18M Hornet [15-27]	EdA 151 Esc/152 Esc/153 Esc/Ala 15, Zaragoza	
C.15-41	McDonnell Douglas EF-18M Hornet [15-28] $	EdA 151 Esc/152 Esc/153 Esc/Ala 15, Zaragoza	
C.15-43	McDonnell Douglas EF-18M Hornet [15-30]	EdA 151 Esc/152 Esc/153 Esc/Ala 15, Zaragoza	
C.15-44	McDonnell Douglas EF-18M Hornet [12-02]	EdA 121 Esc/122 Esc/Ala 12, Madrid/Torrejón	
C.15-45	McDonnell Douglas EF-18M Hornet [12-03]	EdA 121 Esc/122 Esc/Ala 12, Madrid/Torrejón	
C.15-46	McDonnell Douglas EF-18M Hornet [12-04]	EdA 121 Esc/122 Esc/Ala 12, Madrid/Torrejón	
C.15-47	McDonnell Douglas EF-18M Hornet [15-31]	EdA 151 Esc/152 Esc/153 Esc/Ala 15, Zaragoza	
C.15-48	McDonnell Douglas EF-18M Hornet [12-06]	EdA 121 Esc/122 Esc/Ala 12, Madrid/Torrejón	
C.15-49	McDonnell Douglas EF-18M Hornet [12-07]	EdA 121 Esc/122 Esc/Ala 12, Madrid/Torrejón	
C.15-50	McDonnell Douglas EF-18M Hornet [12-08]	EdA 121 Esc/122 Esc/Ala 12, Madrid/Torrejón	
C.15-51	McDonnell Douglas EF-18M Hornet [12-09]	EdA 121 Esc/122 Esc/Ala 12, Madrid/Torrejón	
C.15-53	McDonnell Douglas EF-18M Hornet [12-11]	EdA 121 Esc/122 Esc/Ala 12, Madrid/Torrejón	
C.15-54	McDonnell Douglas EF-18M Hornet [12-12]	EdA 121 Esc/122 Esc/Ala 12, Madrid/Torrejón	
C.15-55	McDonnell Douglas EF-18M Hornet [12-13]	EdA 121 Esc/122 Esc/Ala 12, Madrid/Torrejón	
C.15-56	McDonnell Douglas EF-18M Hornet [12-14]	EdA 121 Esc/122 Esc/Ala 12, Madrid/Torrejón	
C.15-57	McDonnell Douglas EF-18M Hornet [12-15]	EdA 121 Esc/122 Esc/Ala 12, Madrid/Torrejón	
C.15-59	McDonnell Douglas EF-18M Hornet [12-17]	EdA 121 Esc/122 Esc/Ala 12, Madrid/Torrejón	
C.15-60	McDonnell Douglas EF-18M Hornet [12-18]	EdA 121 Esc/122 Esc/Ala 12, Madrid/Torrejón	
C.15-61	McDonnell Douglas EF-18M Hornet [12-19]	EdA 121 Esc/122 Esc/Ala 12, Madrid/Torrejón	
C.15-62	McDonnell Douglas EF-18M Hornet [12-20]	EdA 121 Esc/122 Esc/Ala 12, Madrid/Torrejón	
C.15-64	McDonnell Douglas EF-18M Hornet [15-34]	EdA 151 Esc/152 Esc/153 Esc/Ala 15, Zaragoza	
C.15-65	McDonnell Douglas EF-18M Hornet [12-23]	EdA 121 Esc/122 Esc/Ala 12, Madrid/Torrejón	
C.15-66	McDonnell Douglas EF-18M Hornet [12-24]	EdA 121 Esc/122 Esc/Ala 12, Madrid/Torrejón	
C.15-67	McDonnell Douglas EF-18M Hornet [15-33]	EdA 151 Esc/152 Esc/153 Esc/Ala 15, Zaragoza	
C.15-68	McDonnell Douglas EF-18M Hornet [12-26]	EdA 121 Esc/122 Esc/Ala 12, Madrid/Torrejón	
C.15-69	McDonnell Douglas EF-18M Hornet [12-27]	EdA 121 Esc/122 Esc/Ala 12, Madrid/Torrejón	
C.15-70	McDonnell Douglas EF-18M Hornet [12-28]	EdA 121 Esc/122 Esc/Ala 12, Madrid/Torrejón	
C.15-72	McDonnell Douglas EF-18M Hornet [12-30]	EdA 121 Esc/122 Esc/Ala 12, Madrid/Torrejón	
C.15-73	McDonnell Douglas F/A-18A+ Hornet [46-01] $	EdA 462 Esc/Ala 46, Gando, Gran Canaria	
C.15-75	McDonnell Douglas F/A-18A+ Hornet [46-03]	EdA 462 Esc/Ala 46, Gando, Gran Canaria	
C.15-77	McDonnell Douglas F/A-18A+ Hornet [46-05]	EdA 462 Esc/Ala 46, Gando, Gran Canaria	
C.15-79	McDonnell Douglas F/A-18A+ Hornet [46-07]	EdA 462 Esc/Ala 46, Gando, Gran Canaria	
C.15-80	McDonnell Douglas F/A-18A+ Hornet [46-08]	EdA 462 Esc/Ala 46, Gando, Gran Canaria	
C.15-81	McDonnell Douglas F/A-18A+ Hornet [46-09]	EdA 462 Esc/Ala 46, Gando, Gran Canaria	
C.15-82	McDonnell Douglas F/A-18A+ Hornet [46-10]	EdA 462 Esc/Ala 46, Gando, Gran Canaria	
C.15-83	McDonnell Douglas F/A-18A+ Hornet [46-11]	EdA 462 Esc/Ala 46, Gando, Gran Canaria	
C.15-84	McDonnell Douglas F/A-18A+ Hornet [46-12]	EdA 462 Esc/Ala 46, Gando, Gran Canaria	
C.15-85	McDonnell Douglas F/A-18A+ Hornet [46-13]	EdA 462 Esc/Ala 46, Gando, Gran Canaria	
C.15-86	McDonnell Douglas F/A-18A+ Hornet [46-14]	EdA 462 Esc/Ala 46, Gando, Gran Canaria	
C.15-87	McDonnell Douglas F/A-18A+ Hornet [46-15]	EdA, stored Albacete	
C.15-88	McDonnell Douglas F/A-18A+ Hornet [46-16] $	EdA 462 Esc/Ala 46, Gando, Gran Canaria	
C.15-89	McDonnell Douglas F/A-18A+ Hornet [46-17]	EdA 462 Esc/Ala 46, Gando, Gran Canaria	
C.15-90	McDonnell Douglas F/A-18A+ Hornet [46-18]	EdA 462 Esc/Ala 46, Gando, Gran Canaria	
C.15-92	McDonnell Douglas F/A-18A+ Hornet [46-20]	EdA 462 Esc/Ala 46, Gando, Gran Canaria	
C.15-93	McDonnell Douglas F/A-18A+ Hornet [46-21]	EdA 462 Esc/Ala 46, Gando, Gran Canaria	
C.15-94	McDonnell Douglas F/A-18A+ Hornet [46-22]	EdA 462 Esc/Ala 46, Gando, Gran Canaria	
C.15-95	McDonnell Douglas F/A-18A+ Hornet [46-23]	EdA 462 Esc/Ala 46, Gando, Gran Canaria	
C.15-96	McDonnell Douglas F/A-18A+ Hornet [46-24]	EdA 462 Esc/Ala 46, Gando, Gran Canaria	
CE.16-01	Eurofighter EF.2000(T) Tifón [11-01]	EdA 111 Esc/113 Esc/Ala 11, Sevilla/Morón	

Notes	Serial	Type (code/other identity)	Owner/operator, location or fate
	CE.16-02	Eurofighter EF.2000(T) Tifón [11-02]	EdA 111 Esc/113 Esc/Ala 11, Sevilla/Morón
	CE.16-03	Eurofighter EF.2000(T) Tifón [11-72]	EdA 111 Esc/113 Esc/Ala 11, Sevilla/Morón
	CE.16-04	Eurofighter EF.2000(T) Tifón [11-04]	EdA 111 Esc/113 Esc/Ala 11, Sevilla/Morón
	CE.16-05	Eurofighter EF.2000(T) Tifón [11-05]	EdA 111 Esc/113 Esc/Ala 11, Sevilla/Morón
	CE.16-06	Eurofighter EF.2000(T) Tifón [11-75]	EdA 111 Esc/113 Esc/Ala 11, Sevilla/Morón
	CE.16-07	Eurofighter EF.2000(T) Tifón [11-07]	EdA 111 Esc/113 Esc/Ala 11, Sevilla/Morón
	CE.16-09	Eurofighter EF.2000(T) Tifón [11-09]	EdA 111 Esc/113 Esc/Ala 11, Sevilla/Morón
	CE.16-10	Eurofighter EF.2000(T) Tifón [11-10]	EdA 111 Esc/113 Esc/Ala 11, Sevilla/Morón
	CE.16-11	Eurofighter EF.2000(T) Tifón [14-11]	EdA 142 Esc/Ala 14, Albacete/Los Llanos
	CE.16-12	Eurofighter EF.2000(T) Tifón (10000) [14-12]	EdA 142 Esc/Ala 14, Albacete/Los Llanos
	CE.16-13	Eurofighter EF.2000(T) Tifón (10005) [11-13]	EdA 111 Esc/113 Esc/Ala 11, Sevilla/Morón
	CE.16-14	Eurofighter EF.2000(T) Tifón (10015) [11-14]	EdA 111 Esc/113 Esc/Ala 11, Sevilla/Morón
	C.16-20	Eurofighter EF.2000 Tifón [11-91]	Airbus Defence & Space, Getafe
	C.16-21	Eurofighter EF.2000 Tifón [11-21]	EdA 111 Esc/113 Esc/Ala 11, Sevilla/Morón
	C.16-22	Eurofighter EF.2000 Tifón [11-02]	EdA 111 Esc/113 Esc/Ala 11, Sevilla/Morón
	C.16-23	Eurofighter EF.2000 Tifón [11-23]	EdA 111 Esc/113 Esc/Ala 11, Sevilla/Morón
	C.16-24	Eurofighter EF.2000 Tifón [11-24]	EdA 111 Esc/113 Esc/Ala 11, Sevilla/Morón
	C.16-25	Eurofighter EF.2000 Tifón [11-25]	EdA 111 Esc/113 Esc/Ala 11, Sevilla/Morón
	C.16-26	Eurofighter EF.2000 Tifón [11-26]	EdA 111 Esc/113 Esc/Ala 11, Sevilla/Morón
	C.16-27	Eurofighter EF.2000 Tifón [11-27]	EdA 111 Esc/113 Esc/Ala 11, Sevilla/Morón
	C.16-28	Eurofighter EF.2000 Tifón [11-28]	EdA 111 Esc/113 Esc/Ala 11, Sevilla/Morón
	C.16-29	Eurofighter EF.2000 Tifón [11-29]	EdA 111 Esc/113 Esc/Ala 11, Sevilla/Morón
	C.16-30	Eurofighter EF.2000 Tifón [11-30]	EdA 111 Esc/113 Esc/Ala 11, Sevilla/Morón
	C.16-31	Eurofighter EF.2000 Tifón [14-01] $	EdA 142 Esc/Ala 14, Albacete/Los Llanos
	C.16-32	Eurofighter EF.2000 Tifón [11-32]	EdA 111 Esc/113 Esc/Ala 11, Sevilla/Morón
	C.16-33	Eurofighter EF.2000 Tifón [11-33]	EdA 111 Esc/113 Esc/Ala 11, Sevilla/Morón
	C.16-35	Eurofighter EF.2000 Tifón [11-35]	EdA 111 Esc/113 Esc/Ala 11, Sevilla/Morón
	C.16-36	Eurofighter EF.2000 Tifón [14-03]	EdA 142 Esc/Ala 14, Albacete/Los Llanos
	C.16-37	Eurofighter EF.2000 Tifón [14-37]	EdA 142 Esc/Ala 14, Albacete/Los Llanos
	C.16-38	Eurofighter EF.2000 Tifón [11-38]	EdA 111 Esc/113 Esc/Ala 11, Sevilla/Morón
	C.16-39	Eurofighter EF.2000 Tifón [14-39]	EdA 142 Esc/Ala 14, Albacete/Los Llanos
	C.16-40	Eurofighter EF.2000 Tifón [11-40]	EdA 111 Esc/113 Esc/Ala 11, Sevilla/Morón
	C.16-41	Eurofighter EF.2000 Tifón [11-41]	EdA 111 Esc/113 Esc/Ala 11, Sevilla/Morón
	C.16-42	Eurofighter EF.2000 Tifón [11-42]	EdA 111 Esc/113 Esc/Ala 11, Sevilla/Morón
	C.16-43	Eurofighter EF.2000 Tifón [11-43]	EdA 111 Esc/113 Esc/Ala 11, Sevilla/Morón
	C.16-44	Eurofighter EF.2000 Tifón [14-09]	EdA 142 Esc/Ala 14, Albacete/Los Llanos
	C.16-45	Eurofighter EF.2000 Tifón [14-45]	EdA 142 Esc/Ala 14, Albacete/Los Llanos
	C.16-46	Eurofighter EF.2000 Tifón [11-46]	EdA 111 Esc/113 Esc/Ala 11, Sevilla/Morón
	C.16-47	Eurofighter EF.2000 Tifón [14-47]	EdA 142 Esc/Ala 14, Albacete/Los Llanos
	C.16-48	Eurofighter EF.2000 Tifón [14-48]	EdA 142 Esc/Ala 14, Albacete/Los Llanos
	C.16-49	Eurofighter EF.2000 Tifón [14-49]	EdA 142 Esc/Ala 14, Albacete/Los Llanos
	C.16-50	Eurofighter EF.2000 Tifón [14-14]	EdA 142 Esc/Ala 14, Albacete/Los Llanos
	C.16-51	Eurofighter EF.2000 Tifón [11-51]	EdA 111 Esc/113 Esc/Ala 11, Sevilla/Morón
	C.16-52	Eurofighter EF.2000 Tifón (C.16-10001) [11-52]	EdA 111 Esc/113 Esc/Ala 11, Sevilla/Morón
	C.16-53	Eurofighter EF.2000 Tifón (C.16-10002) [11-53]	EdA 111 Esc/113 Esc/Ala 11, Sevilla/Morón
	C.16-54	Eurofighter EF.2000 Tifón (C.16-10003) [11-54]	EdA 111 Esc/113 Esc/Ala 11, Sevilla/Morón
	C.16-55	Eurofighter EF.2000 Tifón (C.16-10004) [11-55]	EdA 111 Esc/113 Esc/Ala 11, Sevilla/Morón
	C.16-56	Eurofighter EF.2000 Tifón (10007) [11-56]	EdA 111 Esc/113 Esc/Ala 11, Sevilla/Morón
	C.16-57	Eurofighter EF.2000 Tifón (10012) [11-57]	EdA 111 Esc/113 Esc/Ala 11, Sevilla/Morón
	C.16-58	Eurofighter EF.2000 Tifón (10019) [14-58]	EdA 142 Esc/Ala 14, Albacete/Los Llanos
	C.16-59	Eurofighter EF.2000 Tifón (10020) [14-59]	EdA 142 Esc/Ala 14, Albacete/Los Llanos
	C.16-60	Eurofighter EF.2000 Tifón (10040) [14-60]	EdA 142 Esc/Ala 14, Albacete/Los Llanos
	C.16-61	Eurofighter EF.2000 Tifón (10046) [14-61]	EdA 142 Esc/Ala 14, Albacete/Los Llanos
	C.16-62	Eurofighter EF.2000 Tifón (10047) [14-62]	EdA 142 Esc/Ala 14, Albacete/Los Llanos
	C.16-63	Eurofighter EF.2000 Tifón (10048) [11-63]	EdA 111 Esc/113 Esc/Ala 11, Sevilla/Morón
	C.16-64	Eurofighter EF.2000 Tifón (10053) [14-64]	EdA 142 Esc/Ala 14, Albacete/Los Llanos
	C.16-65	Eurofighter EF.2000 Tifón (10054) [14-65]	EdA 142 Esc/Ala 14, Albacete/Los Llanos
	C.16-66	Eurofighter EF.2000 Tifón (10064) [14-66]	EdA 142 Esc/Ala 14, Albacete/Los Llanos
	C.16-67	Eurofighter EF.2000 Tifón (10090) [14-67]	EdA 142 Esc/Ala 14, Albacete/Los Llanos
	C.16-68	Eurofighter EF.2000 Tifón (10091) [14-68]	EdA 142 Esc/Ala 14, Albacete/Los Llanos
	C.16-70	Eurofighter EF.2000 Tifón (10145) [14-28]	Airbus Defence & Space, Getafe
	C.16-71	Eurofighter EF.2000 Tifón (10146) [14-71]	EdA 142 Esc/Ala 14, Albacete/Los Llanos

Serial	Type (code/other identity)	Owner/operator, location or fate	Notes
C.16-72	Eurofighter EF.2000 Tifón (10147) [14-72]	EdA 142 Esc/Ala 14, Albacete/Los Llanos	
C.16-73	Eurofighter EF.2000 Tifón (10155) [14-31] $	EdA 142 Esc/Ala 14, Albacete/Los Llanos	
C.16-74	Eurofighter EF.2000 Tifón (10202) [14-74]	EdA 142 Esc/Ala 14, Albacete/Los Llanos	
C.16-75	Eurofighter EF.2000 Tifón (10205) [14-75]	EdA 142 Esc/Ala 14, Albacete/Los Llanos	
C.16-76	Eurofighter EF.2000 Tifón (10215) [14-34]	EdA 142 Esc/Ala 14, Albacete/Los Llanos	
C.16-77	Eurofighter EF.2000 Tifón (10234) [14-77]	EdA 142 Esc/Ala 14, Albacete/Los Llanos	
C.16-78	Eurofighter EF.2000 Tifón (10235) [14-78]	EdA 142 Esc/Ala 14, Albacete/Los Llanos	
D.4-01	Airtech CN.235M-100(MPA) (T.19B-12)	EdA 801 Esc/Ala 49, Palma/Son San Juan	
D.4-02	Airtech CN.235M-100(MPA) (T.19B-09) [37-02]	EdA 801 Esc/Ala 49, Palma/Son San Juan	
D.4-03	Airtech CN.235M-100(MPA) (T.19B-10) [37-03]	EdA 801 Esc/Ala 49, Palma/Son San Juan	
D.4-04	Airtech CN.235M-100(MPA) (T.19B-08)	EdA 802 Esc/Ala 46, Gran Canaria	
D.4-05	Airtech CN.235M-100(MPA) (T.19B-06)	EdA 801 Esc/Ala 49, Palma/Son San Juan	
D.4-06	Airtech CN.235M-100(MPA) (T.19B-05) [37-06]	EdA 801 Esc/Ala 49, Palma/Son San Juan	
D.4-07	Airtech CN.235M-100(MPA) (T.19B-15)	EdA 803 Esc/Ala 48, Madrid/Getafe	
D.4-08	Airtech CN.235M-100(MPA) (T.19B-14) [37-08]	EdA 802 Esc/Ala 46, Gran Canaria	
E.25-05	CASA 101EB Aviojet [79-05]	EdA 794 Esc/AGA, Murcia/San Javier	
E.25-06	CASA 101EB Aviojet [79-06]	EdA 794 Esc/AGA, Murcia/San Javier	
E.25-08	CASA 101EB Aviojet [79-08,2]	EdA Patrulla Aguila/AGA, Murcia/San Javier	
E.25-11	CASA 101EB Aviojet [79-11]	EdA 794 Esc/AGA, Murcia/San Javier	
E.25-12	CASA 101EB Aviojet [79-12]	EdA Patrulla Aguila/AGA, Murcia/San Javier	
E.25-13	CASA 101EB Aviojet [79-13,5]	EdA Patrulla Aguila/AGA, Murcia/San Javier	
E.25-14	CASA 101EB Aviojet [79-14]	Preserved, Los Alcazares	
E.25-15	CASA 101EB Aviojet [79-15]	EdA, stored Albacete	
E.25-17	CASA 101EB Aviojet [74-40]	EdA, stored Albacete	
E.25-18	CASA 101EB Aviojet [74-42] $	EdA, stored Albacete	
E.25-21	CASA 101EB Aviojet [79-21]	EdA 794 Esc/AGA, Murcia/San Javier	
E.25-24	CASA 101EB Aviojet [79-24]	EdA, stored Albacete	
E.25-25	CASA 101EB Aviojet [79-25]	EdA 794 Esc/AGA, Murcia/San Javier	
E.25-26	CASA 101EB Aviojet [79-26]	EdA 794 Esc/AGA, Murcia/San Javier	
E.25-27	CASA 101EB Aviojet [79-27,7]	EdA Patrulla Aguila/AGA, Murcia/San Javier	
E.25-28	CASA 101EB Aviojet [79-28]	EdA Patrulla Aguila/AGA, Murcia/San Javier	
E.25-31	CASA 101EB Aviojet [79-31,1]	EdA Patrulla Aguila/AGA, Murcia/San Javier	
E.25-33	CASA 101EB Aviojet [74-02]	GEM, Salamanca/Matacán	
E.25-34	CASA 101EB Aviojet [74-44]	EdA 794 Esc/AGA, Murcia/San Javier	
E.25-35	CASA 101EB Aviojet [54-20] $	EdA 541 Esc/CLAEX/Grupo 54, Madrid/Torrejón	
E.25-37	CASA 101EB Aviojet [79-37]	EdA, stored San Javier	
E.25-38	CASA 101EB Aviojet [79-38,2]	EdA Patrulla Aguila/AGA, Murcia/San Javier	
E.25-40	CASA 101EB Aviojet [794-40]	EdA, preserved Albacete	
E.25-43	CASA 101EB Aviojet [74-43]	EdA, stored Albacete	
E.25-44	CASA 101EB Aviojet [79-44]	EdA 794 Esc/AGA, Murcia/San Javier	
E.25-51	CASA 101EB Aviojet [74-07]	EdA 741 Esc/GEM, Salamanca/Matacán	
E.25-52	CASA 101EB Aviojet [794-52]	EdA 794 Esc, Murcia/San Javier	
E.25-53	CASA 101EB Aviojet [74-09]	EdA 794 Esc, Murcia/San Javier	
E.25-54	CASA 101EB Aviojet [79-35]	EdA GEM, Salamanca/Matacán	
E.25-55	CASA 101EB Aviojet [54-21]	EdA 541 Esc/CLAEX/Grupo 54, Madrid/Torrejón	
E.25-56	CASA 101EB Aviojet [74-11]	EdA 794 Esc/AGA, Murcia/San Javier	
E.25-57	CASA 101EB Aviojet [793-57]	EdA 794 Esc/AGA, Murcia/San Javier	
E.25-59	CASA 101EB Aviojet [74-13]	EdA 794 Esc/AGA, Murcia/San Javier	
E.25-61	CASA 101EB Aviojet [54-22]	EdA 794 Esc/AGA, Murcia/San Javier	
E.25-62	CASA 101EB Aviojet [79-17]	EdA 794 Esc/AGA, Murcia/San Javier	
E.25-63	CASA 101EB Aviojet [74-17]	EdA Patrulla Aguila/AGA, Murcia/San Javier	
E.25-66	CASA 101EB Aviojet [74-20]	EdA 794 Esc/AGA, Murcia/San Javier	
E.25-67	CASA 101EB Aviojet [74-21]	EdA GEM, Salamanca/Matacán	
E.25-68	CASA 101EB Aviojet [741-68]	EdA Patrulla Aguila/AGA, Murcia/San Javier	
E.25-69	CASA 101EB Aviojet [79-97,8]	EdA Patrulla Aguila/AGA, Murcia/San Javier	
E.25-71	CASA 101EB Aviojet [74-25]	EdA 794 Esc/AGA, Murcia/San Javier	
E.25-72	CASA 101EB Aviojet [74-26]	EdA GEM, Salamanca/Matacán	
E.25-73	CASA 101EB Aviojet [79-98]	EdA 794 Esc/AGA, Murcia/San Javier	
E.25-74	CASA 101EB Aviojet [74-28]	EdA GEM, Salamanca/Matacán	
E.25-76	CASA 101EB Aviojet [74-30]	EdA 794 Esc/AGA, Murcia/San Javier	
E.25-78	CASA 101EB Aviojet [79-02,5]	EdA Patrulla Aguila/AGA, Murcia/San Javier	
E.25-79	CASA 101EB Aviojet [79-39]	EdA 794 Esc/AGA, Murcia/San Javier	

Notes	Serial	Type (code/other identity)	Owner/operator, location or fate
	E.25-80	CASA 101EB Aviojet [79-03]	EdA 794 Esc/AGA, Murcia/San Javier
	E.25-81	CASA 101EB Aviojet [793-81]	EdA 794 Esc/AGA, Murcia/San Javier
	E.25-83	CASA 101EB Aviojet [74-35]	EdA, stored Albacete
	E.25-84	CASA 101EB Aviojet [79-04]	EdA 794 Esc/AGA, Murcia/San Javier
	E.25-86	CASA 101EB Aviojet [79-32]	EdA 794 Esc/AGA, Murcia/San Javier
	E.25-87	CASA 101EB Aviojet [79-29]	EdA, stored Albacete
	E.25-88	CASA 101EB Aviojet [74-39]	EdA, stored Albacete
	E.27-01	Pilatus PC-21 (10239) [792-01]	EdA 792 Esc/AGA, Murcia/San Javier
	E.27-02	Pilatus PC-21 (10240) [792-02]	EdA 792 Esc/AGA, Murcia/San Javier
	E.27-03	Pilatus PC-21 (10241) [792-03]	EdA 792 Esc/AGA, Murcia/San Javier
	E.27-04	Pilatus PC-21 (10242) [792-04]	EdA 792 Esc/AGA, Murcia/San Javier
	E.27-05	Pilatus PC-21 (10243) [792-05]	EdA 792 Esc/AGA, Murcia/San Javier
	E.27-06	Pilatus PC-21 (10244) [792-06]	EdA 792 Esc/AGA, Murcia/San Javier
	E.27-07	Pilatus PC-21 (10245) [792-07]	EdA 792 Esc/AGA, Murcia/San Javier
	E.27-08	Pilatus PC-21 (10246) [792-08]	EdA 792 Esc/AGA, Murcia/San Javier
	E.27-09	Pilatus PC-21 (10247) [792-09]	EdA 792 Esc/AGA, Murcia/San Javier
	E.27-10	Pilatus PC-21 (10248) [792-10]	EdA 792 Esc/AGA, Murcia/San Javier
	E.27-11	Pilatus PC-21 (10249) [792-11]	EdA 792 Esc/AGA, Murcia/San Javier
	E.27-12	Pilatus PC-21 (10250) [792-12]	EdA 792 Esc/AGA, Murcia/San Javier
	E.27-13	Pilatus PC-21 (10251) [792-13]	EdA 792 Esc/AGA, Murcia/San Javier
	E.27-14	Pilatus PC-21 (10252) [792-14]	EdA 792 Esc/AGA, Murcia/San Javier
	E.27-15	Pilatus PC-21 (10253) [792-15]	EdA 792 Esc/AGA, Murcia/San Javier
	E.27-16	Pilatus PC-21 (10254) [792-16]	EdA 792 Esc/AGA, Murcia/San Javier
	E.27-17	Pilatus PC-21 (10255) [792-17]	EdA 792 Esc/AGA, Murcia/San Javier
	E.27-18	Pilatus PC-21 (10256) [792-18]	EdA 792 Esc/AGA, Murcia/San Javier
	E.27-19	Pilatus PC-21 (10257) [792-19]	EdA 792 Esc/AGA, Murcia/San Javier
	E.27-20	Pilatus PC-21 (10258) [792-20]	EdA 792 Esc/AGA, Murcia/San Javier
	E.27-21	Pilatus PC-21 (10259) [792-21]	EdA 792 Esc/AGA, Murcia/San Javier
	E.27-22	Pilatus PC-21 (10260) [792-22]	EdA 792 Esc/AGA, Murcia/San Javier
	E.27-23	Pilatus PC-21 (10261) [792-23]	EdA 792 Esc/AGA, Murcia/San Javier
	E.27-24	Pilatus PC-21 (10262) [792-24]	EdA 792 Esc/AGA, Murcia/San Javier
	HS.23-01	Sikorsky SH-60B Seahawk [01-1001]	Armada 10 Esc, Rota
	HS.23-02	Sikorsky SH-60B Seahawk [01-1002]	Armada 10 Esc, Rota
	HS.23-03	Sikorsky SH-60B Seahawk [01-1003]	Armada 10 Esc, Rota
	HS.23-04	Sikorsky SH-60B Seahawk [01-1004]	Armada 10 Esc, Rota
	HS.23-05	Sikorsky SH-60B Seahawk [01-1005]	Armada 10 Esc, Rota
	HS.23-06	Sikorsky SH-60B Seahawk [01-1006]	Armada 10 Esc, Rota
	HS.23-07	Sikorsky SH-60B Seahawk [01-1007]	Armada 10 Esc, Rota
	HS.23-08	Sikorsky SH-60B Seahawk [01-1008]	Armada 10 Esc, Rota
	HS.23-09	Sikorsky SH-60B Seahawk [01-1009]	Armada 10 Esc, Rota
	HS.23-10	Sikorsky SH-60B Seahawk [01-1010]	Armada 10 Esc, Rota
	HS.23-11	Sikorsky SH-60B Seahawk [01-1011]	Armada 10 Esc, Rota
	HS.23-12	Sikorsky SH-60B Seahawk [01-1012]	Armada 10 Esc, Rota
	HT.23-13	Sikorsky SH-60F Seahawk (10013) [01-1014]	Armada 10 Esc, Rota
	HT.23-14	Sikorsky SH-60F Seahawk (10014) [01-1015]	Armada 10 Esc, Rota
	HT.23-15	Sikorsky SH-60F Seahawk (10267) [01-1016]	Armada 10 Esc, Rota
	HT.23-16	Sikorsky SH-60F Seahawk (10268) [01-1017]	Armada 10 Esc, Rota
	HT.23-17	Sikorsky SH-60F Seahawk [01-1018]	Armada 10 Esc, Rota
	HT.23-18	Sikorsky SH-60F Seahawk [01-1019]	Armada 10 Esc, Rota
	HE.25-1	Eurocopter EC.120B Colibri [78-20]	EdA *Patrulla Aspa*/Ala 78, Granada/Armilla
	HE.25-02	Eurocopter EC.120B Colibri [782-02]	EdA *Patrulla Aspa*/Ala 78, Granada/Armilla
	HE.25-03	Eurocopter EC.120B Colibri [782-03]	EdA *Patrulla Aspa*/Ala 78, Granada/Armilla
	HE.25-4	Eurocopter EC.120B Colibri [78-23]	EdA *Patrulla Aspa*/Ala 78, Granada/Armilla
	HE.25-6	Eurocopter EC.120B Colibri [78-25]	EdA 541 Esc/CLAEX/Grupo 54, Madrid/Torrejón
	HE.25-7	Eurocopter EC.120B Colibri [78-26]	EdA *Patrulla Aspa*/Ala 78, Granada/Armilla
	HE.25-8	Eurocopter EC.120B Colibri [78-27]	EdA *Patrulla Aspa*/Ala 78, Granada/Armilla
	HE.25-9	Eurocopter EC.120B Colibri [782-09]	EdA *Patrulla Aspa*/Ala 78, Granada/Armilla
	HE.25-10	Eurocopter EC.120B Colibri [78-29]	EdA 782 Esc/Ala 78, Granada/Armilla
	HE.25-11	Eurocopter EC.120B Colibri [782-11]	EdA 782 Esc/Ala 78, Granada/Armilla
	HE.25-12	Eurocopter EC.120B Colibri [78-31]	EdA *Patrulla Aspa*/Ala 78, Granada/Armilla
	HE.25-13	Eurocopter EC.120B Colibri [782-13]	EdA *Patrulla Aspa*/Ala 78, Granada/Armilla
	HE.25-14	Eurocopter EC.120B Colibri [782-14]	EdA *Patrulla Aspa*/Ala 78, Granada/Armilla

Serial	Type (code/other identity)	Owner/operator, location or fate	Notes
HE.25-15	Eurocopter EC.120B Colibri [78-34]	EdA *Patrulla Aspa*/Ala 78, Granada/Armilla	
P.3M-08	Lockheed P-3M Orion [22-31]	EdA, stored Sevilla/Morón	
P.3M-09	Lockheed P-3M Orion [22-32]	EdA, stored Sevilla/Morón	
P.3M-12	Lockheed P-3M Orion [22-35]	EdA, stored Sevilla/Morón	
TM.11-3	Dassault Falcon 20D [472-03]	*Withdrawn from use, Madrid/Torrejón*	
T.12B-13	CASA 212A Aviocar [72-13]	EdA 721 Esc, Murcia/Alcantarilla	
T.12B-49	CASA 212A Aviocar [72-49]	EdA 721 Esc, Murcia/Alcantarilla	
T.12B-62	CASA 212A Aviocar (D.3A-2) [72-62]	EdA 721 Esc, Murcia/Alcantarilla	
T.12B-63	CASA 212A Aviocar [72-63]	EdA 721 Esc, Murcia/Alcantarilla	
T.12B-65	CASA 212A Aviocar [72-11]	EdA 721 Esc, Murcia/Alcantarilla	
T.12B-66	CASA 212A Aviocar [72-66]	EdA 721 Esc, Murcia/Alcantarilla	
T.12B-67	CASA 212A Aviocar [72-12]	EdA 721 Esc, Murcia/Alcantarilla	
T.12B-69	CASA 212A Aviocar [72-69]	EdA 721 Esc, Murcia/Alcantarilla	
T.12B-70	CASA 212A Aviocar [72-70]	EdA 721 Esc, Murcia/Alcantarilla	
T.12B-71	CASA 212A Aviocar [72-71] $	EdA 721 Esc, Murcia/Alcantarilla	
T.12D-74	CASA 212-200 Aviocar [54-11]	EdA CLAEX/Grupo 54, Madrid/Torrejón	
T.12D-75	CASA 212-200 Aviocar [47-14]	EdA, stored Cuatro Vientos	
T.18-1	Dassault Falcon 900 [45-40]	EdA 451 Esc/Grupo 45, Madrid/Torrejón	
T.18-2	Dassault Falcon 900 [45-41]	EdA 451 Esc/Grupo 45, Madrid/Torrejón	
T.18-3	Dassault Falcon 900B [45-42]	EdA 451 Esc/Grupo 45, Madrid/Torrejón	
T.18-4	Dassault Falcon 900B [45-04]	EdA 451 Esc/Grupo 45, Madrid/Torrejón	
T.18-5	Dassault Falcon 900B [45-05]	EdA 451 Esc/Grupo 45, Madrid/Torrejón	
T.19A-01	Airtech CN.235M-10 [403-01]	EdA 403 Esc, Madrid/Getafe	
T.19A-02	Airtech CN.235M-10 [403-02]	EdA 403 Esc, Madrid/Getafe	
T.19B-07	Airtech CN.235M-100 [744-07]	EdA 744 Esc/GEM, Salamanca/Matacán	
T.19B-11	Airtech CN.235M-100 [744-11]	EdA 744 Esc/GEM, Salamanca/Matacán	
T.19B-13	Airtech CN.235M-100 [74-13]	EdA 744 Esc/GEM, Salamanca/Matacán	
T.19B-16	Airtech CN.235M-100 [744-16]	EdA 744 Esc/GEM, Salamanca/Matacán	
T.19B-17	Airtech CN.235M-100 [744-17]	EdA 744 Esc/GEM, Salamanca/Matacán	
T.19B-18	Airtech CN.235M-100 [74-18]	EdA 744 Esc/GEM, Salamanca/Matacán	
T.19B-19	Airtech CN.235M-100 [744-19]	EdA 744 Esc/GEM, Salamanca/Matacán	
T.19B-20	Airtech CN.235M-100 [744-20]	EdA 744 Esc/GEM, Salamanca/Matacán	
T.19B-21	Airtech CN.235M VIGMA [09-501]	Guardia Civil Servicio Aéreo, Gran Canaria	
T.19B-22	Airtech CN.235M VIGMA [09-502]	Guardia Civil Servicio Aéreo, Gran Canaria	
TR.20-01	Cessna 560 Citation VI [403-11]	EdA 403 Esc, Madrid/Getafe	
TR.20-02	Cessna 560 Citation VI [403-12]	EdA 403 Esc, Madrid/Getafe	
TR.20-03	Cessna 560 Citation VI [403-21]	EdA 403 Esc, Madrid/Getafe	
T.21-01	CASA C-295M [35-01]	EdA 353 Esc/Ala 35, Madrid/Getafe	
T.21-02	CASA C-295M [35-02] $	EdA 353 Esc/Ala 35, Madrid/Getafe	
T.21-03	CASA C-295M [35-03]	EdA 353 Esc/Ala 35, Madrid/Getafe	
T.21-04	CASA C-295M [35-42]	EdA 353 Esc/Ala 35, Madrid/Getafe	
T.21-05	CASA C-295M [35-05]	EdA 353 Esc/Ala 35, Madrid/Getafe	
T.21-06	CASA C-295M [35-06]	EdA 353 Esc/Ala 35, Madrid/Getafe	
T.21-07	CASA C-295M [35-07]	EdA 353 Esc/Ala 35, Madrid/Getafe	
T.21-08	CASA C-295M [35-08] $	EdA 353 Esc/Ala 35, Madrid/Getafe	
T.21-09	CASA C-295M [35-09]	EdA 353 Esc/Ala 35, Madrid/Getafe	
T.21-11	CASA C-295M [35-11]	EdA 353 Esc/Ala 35, Madrid/Getafe	
T.21-12	CASA C-295M [35-12]	EdA 353 Esc/Ala 35, Madrid/Getafe	
T.21-13	CASA C-295M [35-13]	EdA 353 Esc/Ala 35, Madrid/Getafe	
T.22-1	Airbus A.310-304 [45-50]	EdA 451 Esc/Grupo 45, Madrid/Torrejón	
T.22-2	Airbus A.310-304 [45-51]	EdA 451 Esc/Grupo 45, Madrid/Torrejón	
T.23-01	Airbus Military A.400M (10074) [31-21]	EdA 311 Esc/312 Esc/Ala 31, Zaragoza	
TK.23-02	Airbus Military A.400M (10075) [31-22]	EdA 311 Esc/312 Esc/Ala 31, Zaragoza	
TK.23-03	Airbus Military A.400M (10076) [31-23]	EdA 311 Esc/312 Esc/Ala 31, Zaragoza	
T.23-04	Airbus Military A.400M (10174) [31-24]	EdA 311 Esc/312 Esc/Ala 31, Zaragoza	
T.23-05	Airbus Military A.400M (10206) [31-25]	EdA 311 Esc/312 Esc/Ala 31, Zaragoza	
T.23-06	Airbus Military A.400M (10207) [31-26]	EdA 311 Esc/312 Esc/Ala 31, Zaragoza	
TK.23-07	Airbus Military A.400M (10208) [31-27]	EdA 311 Esc/312 Esc/Ala 31, Zaragoza	
T.23-08	Airbus Military A.400M (10217) [31-28]	EdA 311 Esc/312 Esc/Ala 31, Zaragoza	
TK.23-09	Airbus Military A.400M (10218) [31-29]	EdA 311 Esc/312 Esc/Ala 31, Zaragoza	
T.23-10	Airbus Military A.400M (10219) [31-30]	EdA 311 Esc/312 Esc/Ala 31, Zaragoza	
T.23-11	Airbus Military A.400M (10220) [31-31]	EdA 311 Esc/312 Esc/Ala 31, Zaragoza	

Notes	Serial	Type (code/other identity)	Owner/operator, location or fate
	T.23-12	Airbus Military A.400M (10221) [31-32]	EdA 311 Esc/312 Esc/Ala 31, Zaragoza
	T.23-13	Airbus Military A.400M (10222) [31-33]	EdA 311 Esc/312 Esc/Ala 31, Zaragoza
	TK.23-14	Airbus Military A.400M (10223) [31-34]	EdA (on order)
	T.24-1	Airbus A.330-202 (10273) [452-01]	EdA 451 Esc/Grupo 45, Madrid/Torrejón
	T.24-2	Airbus A.330-202 (10274) [452-02]	EdA 451 Esc/Grupo 45, Madrid/Torrejón
	T.24-3	Airbus A.330-202 (10275) [452-03]	EdA (on order)
	U.20-1	Cessna 550 Citation II [01-405]	Armada 4 Esc, Rota
	U.20-2	Cessna 550 Citation II [01-406]	Armada 4 Esc, Rota
	U.20-3	Cessna 550 Citation II [01-407]	Armada 4 Esc, Rota
	U.21-01	Cessna 650 Citation VII [01-408]	Armada 4 Esc, Rota
	VA.1B-24	McDonnell Douglas EAV-8B+ Matador [01-914]	Armada 9 Esc, Rota
	VA.1B-25	McDonnell Douglas EAV-8B+ Matador [01-915]	Armada, stored Rota
	VA.1B-26	McDonnell Douglas EAV-8B+ Matador [01-916]	Armada 9 Esc, Rota
	VA.1B-27	McDonnell Douglas EAV-8B+ Matador [01-917]	Armada 9 Esc, Rota
	VA.1B-28	McDonnell Douglas EAV-8B+ Matador [01-918]	Armada, stored Rota
	VA.1B-29	McDonnell Douglas EAV-8B+ Matador [01-919]	Armada 9 Esc, Rota
	VA.1B-30	McDonnell Douglas EAV-8B+ Matador [01-920]	Armada 9 Esc, Rota
	VA.1B-33	McDonnell Douglas TAV-8B Matador [01-922]	*Withdrawn from use, Rota*
	VA.1B-35	McDonnell Douglas EAV-8B+ Matador [01-923]	Armada 9 Esc, Rota
	VA.1B-36	McDonnell Douglas EAV-8B+ Matador [01-924]	Armada 9 Esc, Rota
	VA.1B-37	McDonnell Douglas EAV-8B+ Matador [01-925]	Armada 9 Esc, Rota
	VA.1B-38	McDonnell Douglas EAV-8B+ Matador [01-926]	Armada 9 Esc, Rota
	VA.1B-39	McDonnell Douglas EAV-8B+ Matador [01-927]	Armada 9 Esc, Rota
	VA.1B-40	McDonnell Douglas EAV-8B+ Matador [01-999]	Armada 9 Esc, Rota
	SUDAN		
	ST-PSA	Dassault Falcon 900B	Sudanese Government, Khartoum
	ST-PSR	Dassault Falcon 50	Sudanese Government, Khartoum

SWEDEN
Försvarsmakten/Swedish Armed Forces: Försvarsmaktens Helikopterflottilj (Hkpflj)/Armed Forces Helicopter Wing & Svenska Flygvapnet/Swedish Air Force

Notes	Serial	Type (code/other identity)	Owner/operator, location or fate
	35-075	Gates Learjet 35A (Tp.104) (SE-DHP)	Flygvapnet FMV, Linköping/Malmen
	35-195	Gates Learjet 35A (Tp.104) (SE-DHO)	Flygvapnet FMV, Linköping/Malmen
	39-6	SAAB JAS 39C Gripen [6]	SAAB, Linköping/Malmen
	39-7	SAAB JAS 39NG Gripen	SAAB, Linköping/Malmen
	39-8	SAAB JAS 39E Gripen	SAAB, Linköping/Malmen
	39-9	SAAB JAS 39E Gripen	SAAB, Linköping/Malmen
	39-10	SAAB JAS 39E Gripen	SAAB, Linköping/Malmen
	39208	SAAB JAS 39C Gripen [208]	Flygvapnet Flottiljer 17, Ronneby/Kallinge
	39209	SAAB JAS 39C Gripen [209]	Flygvapnet Flottiljer 7, Såtenäs
	39210	SAAB JAS 39C Gripen [210]	Flygvapnet Flottiljer 17, Ronneby/Kallinge
	39211	SAAB JAS 39C Gripen [211]	Flygvapnet Flottiljer 7, Såtenäs
	39212	SAAB JAS 39C Gripen [212]	Flygvapnet Flottiljer 21, Luleå/Kallax
	39213	SAAB JAS 39C Gripen [213]	Flygvapnet Flottiljer 7, Såtenäs
	39214	SAAB JAS 39C Gripen [214]	Flygvapnet Flottiljer 7, Såtenäs
	39215	SAAB JAS 39C Gripen [215]	Flygvapnet Flottiljer 7, Såtenäs
	39216	SAAB JAS 39C Gripen [216]	Flygvapnet Flottiljer 21, Luleå/Kallax
	39217	SAAB JAS 39C Gripen [217]	Flygvapnet Flottiljer 7, Såtenäs
	39218	SAAB JAS 39C Gripen [218]	Flygvapnet Flottiljer 21, Luleå/Kallax
	39219	SAAB JAS 39C Gripen [219]	Flygvapnet Flottiljer 21, Luleå/Kallax
	39220	SAAB JAS 39C Gripen [220]	Flygvapnet Flottiljer 7, Såtenäs
	39221	SAAB JAS 39C Gripen [221]	Flygvapnet Flottiljer 17, Ronneby/Kallinge
	39222	SAAB JAS 39C Gripen [222]	Flygvapnet Flottiljer 17, Ronneby/Kallinge
	39223	SAAB JAS 39C Gripen [223]	Flygvapnet Flottiljer 21, Luleå/Kallax
	39224	SAAB JAS 39C Gripen [224]	Flygvapnet Flottiljer 17, Ronneby/Kallinge
	39225	SAAB JAS 39C Gripen [225]	Flygvapnet Flottiljer 7, Såtenäs
	39226	SAAB JAS 39C Gripen [226]	Flygvapnet Flottiljer 7, Såtenäs
	39227	SAAB JAS 39C Gripen [227]	Flygvapnet Flottiljer 7, Såtenäs
	39228	SAAB JAS 39C Gripen [228]	Flygvapnet Flottiljer 17, Ronneby/Kallinge
	39229	SAAB JAS 39C Gripen [229]	Flygvapnet Flottiljer 21, Luleå/Kallax
	39230	SAAB JAS 39C Gripen [230]	Flygvapnet Flottiljer 17, Ronneby/Kallinge

Serial	Type (code/other identity)	Owner/operator, location or fate	Notes
39231	SAAB JAS 39C Gripen [231]	Flygvapnet Flottiljer 7, Såtenäs	
39232	SAAB JAS 39C Gripen [232]	Flygvapnet Flottiljer 21, Luleå/Kallax	
39233	SAAB JAS 39C Gripen [233]	Flygvapnet Flottiljer 17, Ronneby/Kallinge	
39246	SAAB JAS 39C Gripen [246]	Flygvapnet Flottiljer 17, Ronneby/Kallinge	
39247	SAAB JAS 39C Gripen [247]	Flygvapnet Flottiljer 17, Ronneby/Kallinge	
39248	SAAB JAS 39C Gripen [248]	Flygvapnet Flottiljer 21, Luleå/Kallax	
39249	SAAB JAS 39C Gripen [249]	Flygvapnet Flottiljer 21, Luleå/Kallax	
39250	SAAB JAS 39C Gripen [250]	Flygvapnet FC, Linköping/Malmen	
39251	SAAB JAS 39C Gripen [251]	Flygvapnet FC, Linköping/Malmen	
39253	SAAB JAS 39C Gripen [253]	Flygvapnet Flottiljer 7, Såtenäs	
39254	SAAB JAS 39C Gripen [254]	Flygvapnet Flottiljer 17, Ronneby/Kallinge	
39255	SAAB JAS 39C Gripen [255]	Flygvapnet Flottiljer 17, Ronneby/Kallinge	
39256	SAAB JAS 39C Gripen [256]	Flygvapnet Flottiljer 17, Ronneby/Kallinge	
39257	SAAB JAS 39C Gripen [257]	Flygvapnet Flottiljer 21, Luleå/Kallax	
39258	SAAB JAS 39C Gripen [258]	Flygvapnet Flottiljer 21, Luleå/Kallax	
39260	SAAB JAS 39C Gripen [260]	Flygvapnet Flottiljer 21, Luleå/Kallax	
39261	SAAB JAS 39C Gripen [261]	Flygvapnet Flottiljer 21, Luleå/Kallax	
39262	SAAB JAS 39C Gripen [262]	Flygvapnet Flottiljer 17, Ronneby/Kallinge	
39263	SAAB JAS 39C Gripen [263]	Flygvapnet Flottiljer 21, Luleå/Kallax	
39264	SAAB JAS 39C Gripen [264]	Flygvapnet Flottiljer 17, Ronneby/Kallinge	
39265	SAAB JAS 39C Gripen [265]	Flygvapnet Flottiljer 21, Luleå/Kallax	
39266	SAAB JAS 39C Gripen [266]	Flygvapnet Flottiljer 7, Såtenäs	
39267	SAAB JAS 39C Gripen [267]	Flygvapnet Flottiljer 21, Luleå/Kallax	
39268	SAAB JAS 39C Gripen [268]	Flygvapnet Flottiljer 7, Såtenäs	
39269	SAAB JAS 39C Gripen [269]	Flygvapnet Flottiljer 17, Ronneby/Kallinge	
39270	SAAB JAS 39C Gripen [270]	Flygvapnet Flottiljer 17, Ronneby/Kallinge	
39271	SAAB JAS 39C Gripen [271]	Flygvapnet Flottiljer 21, Luleå/Kallax	
39272	SAAB JAS 39C Gripen [272]	Flygvapnet Flottiljer 7, Såtenäs	
39273	SAAB JAS 39C Gripen [273]	Flygvapnet Flottiljer 17, Ronneby/Kallinge	
39274	SAAB JAS 39C Gripen [274]	Flygvapnet Flottiljer 21, Luleå/Kallax	
39275	SAAB JAS 39C Gripen [275]	Flygvapnet Flottiljer 7, Såtenäs	
39276	SAAB JAS 39C Gripen [276]	Flygvapnet Flottiljer 21, Luleå/Kallax	
39277	SAAB JAS 39C Gripen [277]	Flygvapnet Flottiljer 7, Såtenäs	
39278	SAAB JAS 39C Gripen [278]	Flygvapnet Flottiljer 17, Ronneby/Kallinge	
39279	SAAB JAS 39C Gripen [279]	Flygvapnet Flottiljer 21, Luleå/Kallax	
39280	SAAB JAS 39C Gripen [280]	Flygvapnet Flottiljer 21, Luleå/Kallax	
39281	SAAB JAS 39C Gripen [281]	Flygvapnet Flottiljer 17, Ronneby/Kallinge	
39282	SAAB JAS 39C Gripen [282]	Flygvapnet Flottiljer 7, Såtenäs	
39283	SAAB JAS 39C Gripen [283]	Flygvapnet Flottiljer 21, Luleå/Kallax	
39284	SAAB JAS 39C Gripen [284]	Flygvapnet Flottiljer 17, Ronneby/Kallinge	
39285	SAAB JAS 39C Gripen [285]	Flygvapnet Flottiljer 21, Luleå/Kallax	
39286	SAAB JAS 39C Gripen [286]	Flygvapnet Flottiljer 21, Luleå/Kallax	
39287	SAAB JAS 39C Gripen [287]	Flygvapnet Flottiljer 17, Ronneby/Kallinge	
39288	SAAB JAS 39C Gripen [288]	Flygvapnet Flottiljer 21, Luleå/Kallax	
39289	SAAB JAS 39C Gripen [289]	Flygvapnet Flottiljer 7, Såtenäs	
39290	SAAB JAS 39C Gripen [290]	Flygvapnet Flottiljer 21, Luleå/Kallax	
39291	SAAB JAS 39C Gripen [291]	Flygvapnet Flottiljer 7, Såtenäs	
39292	SAAB JAS 39C Gripen [292]	Flygvapnet Flottiljer 17, Ronneby/Kallinge	
39293	SAAB JAS 39C Gripen [293]	Flygvapnet Flottiljer 7, Såtenäs	
39294	SAAB JAS 39C Gripen [294]	Flygvapnet Flottiljer 17, Ronneby/Kallinge	
39815	SAAB JAS 39D Gripen [815]	Flygvapnet Flottiljer 7, Såtenäs	
39816	SAAB JAS 39D Gripen [816]	Flygvapnet Flottiljer 7, Såtenäs	
39817	SAAB JAS 39D Gripen [817]	Flygvapnet Flottiljer 21, Luleå/Kallax	
39821	SAAB JAS 39D Gripen [821]	Flygvapnet Flottiljer 7, Såtenäs	
39822	SAAB JAS 39D Gripen [822]	Flygvapnet Flottiljer 21, Luleå/Kallax	
39823	SAAB JAS 39D Gripen [823]	Flygvapnet Flottiljer 21, Luleå/Kallax	
39824	SAAB JAS 39D Gripen [824]	Flygvapnet Flottiljer 21, Luleå/Kallax	
39825	SAAB JAS 39D Gripen [825]	Flygvapnet Flottiljer 7, Såtenäs	
39826	SAAB JAS 39D Gripen [826]	Flygvapnet Flottiljer 17, Ronneby/Kallinge	
39827	SAAB JAS 39D Gripen [827]	Flygvapnet Flottiljer 7, Såtenäs	
39829	SAAB JAS 39D Gripen [829]	Flygvapnet Flottiljer 17, Ronneby/Kallinge	
39830	SAAB JAS 39D Gripen [830]	Flygvapnet Flottiljer 7, Såtenäs	

Notes	Serial	Type (code/other identity)	Owner/operator, location or fate
	39831	SAAB JAS 39D Gripen [831]	Flygvapnet Flottiljer 17, Ronneby/Kallinge
	39832	SAAB JAS 39D Gripen [832]	Flygvapnet Flottiljer 21, Luleå/Kallax
	39833	SAAB JAS 39D Gripen [833]	Flygvapnet Flottiljer 21, Luleå/Kallax
	39834	SAAB JAS 39D Gripen [834]	Flygvapnet Flottiljer 7, Såtenäs
	39835	SAAB JAS 39D Gripen [835]	Flygvapnet Flottiljer 7, Såtenäs
	39836	SAAB JAS 39D Gripen [836]	Flygvapnet Flottiljer 17, Ronneby/Kallinge
	39837	SAAB JAS 39D Gripen [837]	Flygvapnet Flottiljer 21, Luleå/Kallax
	39838	SAAB JAS 39D Gripen [838]	Flygvapnet Flottiljer 21, Luleå/Kallax
	39839	SAAB JAS 39D Gripen [839]	Flygvapnet Flottiljer 7, Såtenäs
	39840	SAAB JAS 39D Gripen [840]	Flygvapnet Flottiljer 21, Luleå/Kallax
	39841	SAAB JAS 39D Gripen [841]	Flygvapnet Flottiljer 7, Såtenäs
	396...	SAAB JAS 39E Gripen	SAAB, Linköping/Malmen
	396002	SAAB JAS 39E Gripen	SAAB, Linköping/Malmen
	396003	SAAB JAS 39E Gripen	SAAB, Linköping/Malmen
	396004	SAAB JAS 39E Gripen	Flygvapnet FMV, Linköping/Malmen
	396005	SAAB JAS 39E Gripen	Flygvapnet FMV, Linköping/Malmen
	396006	SAAB JAS 39E Gripen	Flygvapnet (on order)
	396007	SAAB JAS 39E Gripen	Flygvapnet (on order)
	396008	SAAB JAS 39E Gripen	Flygvapnet (on order)
	396009	SAAB JAS 39E Gripen	Flygvapnet (on order)
	396010	SAAB JAS 39E Gripen	Flygvapnet (on order)
	396011	SAAB JAS 39E Gripen	SAAB, Linköping/Malmen
	396012	SAAB JAS 39E Gripen	SAAB, Linköping/Malmen
	84001	Lockheed C-130H Hercules (Tp.84) [841]	Flygvapnet, preserved Linköping/Malmen
	84002	Lockheed C-130H Hercules (Tp.84) [842]	Flygvapnet TSFE, Såtenäs
	84003	Lockheed C-130H Hercules (Tp.84) [843]	Flygvapnet, instructional airframe, Såtenäs
	84004	Lockheed C-130H Hercules (Tp.84) [844]	Flygvapnet TSFE, Såtenäs
	84005	Lockheed C-130H Hercules (Tp.84) [845]	Flygvapnet TSFE, Såtenäs
	84006	Lockheed C-130H Hercules (Tp.84) [846]	Flygvapnet TSFE, Såtenäs
	84007	Lockheed C-130H Hercules (Tp.84) [847]	Flygvapnet TSFE, Såtenäs
	84008	Lockheed C-130H Hercules (Tp.84) [848]	Flygvapnet TSFE, Såtenäs
	86001	Rockwell Sabreliner-40 (Tp.86) [861]	Flygvapnet FC, Linköping/Malmen
	100001	SAAB SF.340 (OS.100) [001]	Flygvapnet TSFE, Linköping/Malmen
	100003	SAAB SF.340AEW&C (S.100D Argus) [003]	Flygvapnet TSFE, Linköping/Malmen
	100004	SAAB SF.340AEW&C (S.100D Argus) [004]	Flygvapnet TSFE, Linköping/Malmen
	100008	SAAB SF.340 (Tp.100C) [008]	Flygvapnet TSFE, Linköping/Malmen
	102002	Grumman G.1159C Gulfstream IV (S.102B Korpen)[022]	Flygvapnet TSFE, Linköping/Malmen
	102003	Grumman G.1159C Gulfstream IV (S.102B Korpen)[023]	Flygvapnet TSFE, Linköping/Malmen
	102004	Grumman G.1159C Gulfstream IV-SP (Tp.102C)	Flygvapnet TSFE, Linköping/Malmen
	102005	Gulfstream Aerospace G.550 (Tp.102D)	Flygvapnet TSFE, Linköping/Malmen
	142044	NH Industries NH.90-TTH (Hkp.14B) (141044) [44]	Hkpflj 3.HkpSkv, Ronneby/Kallinge
	142045	NH Industries NH.90-TTH (Hkp.14B) (141045) [45]	Hkpflj 1.HkpSkv, Luleå/Kallax
	144048	NH Industries NH.90-TTH (Hkp.14F) (141048) [48]	Hkpflj 1.HkpSkv, Luleå/Kallax
	144049	NH Industries NH.90-TTH (Hkp.14F) (141049) [49]	Hkpflj 1.HkpSkv, Luleå/Kallax
	144051	NH Industries NH.90-TTH (Hkp.14D) (141051) [51]	Hkpflj 1.HkpSkv, Luleå/Kallax
	144052	NH Industries NH.90-TTH (Hkp.14D) (141052) [52]	Hkpflj 1.HkpSkv, Luleå/Kallax
	145053	NH Industries NH.90-TTH (Hkp.14D) (144053) [53]	Hkpflj 1.HkpSkv, Luleå/Kallax
	145057	NH Industries NH.90-SAR (Hkp.14E) (142057) [57]	Hkpflj 3.HkpSkv, Ronneby/Kallinge
	145058	NH Industries NH.90-SAR (Hkp.14E) (141041) [58]	Hkpflj 3.HkpSkv, Ronneby/Kallinge
	145059	NH Industries NH.90-SAR (Hkp.14E) (142059) [59]	Hkpflj 3.HkpSkv, Ronneby/Kallinge
	146042	NH Industries NH.90-TTH (Hkp.14F) (142042) [42]	Airbus, Marignane, France
	146043	NH Industries NH.90-TTH (Hkp.14F) (141043) [43]	Airbus, Marignane, France
	146046	NH Industries NH.90-TTH (Hkp.14F) (145046) [46]	Hkpflj 1.HkpSkv, Luleå/Kallax
	146047	NH Industries NH.90-TTH (Hkp.14F) (145047) [47]	Hkpflj 1.HkpSkv, Luleå/Kallax
	146050	NH Industries NH.90-TTH (Hkp.14F) (145050) [50]	Hkpflj 1.HkpSkv, Luleå/Kallax
	146054	NH Industries NH.90-TTH (Hkp.14F) (144054) [54]	Hkpflj 1.HkpSkv, Luleå/Kallax
	146055	NH Industries NH.90-SAR (Hkp.14B) (142055) [55]	Hkpflj 3.HkpSkv, Ronneby/Kallinge
	146056	NH Industries NH.90-SAR (Hkp.14E) (145056) [56]	Hkpflj 3.HkpSkv, Ronneby/Kallinge
	146057	NH Industries NH.90-SAR (Hkp.14F) [57]	Hkpflj 3.HkpSkv, Ronneby/Kallinge
	146058	NH Industries NH.90-SAR (Hkp.14F) [58]	Hkpflj 3.HkpSkv, Ronneby/Kallinge
	146059	NH Industries NH.90-SAR (Hkp.14F) [59]	Hkpflj 3.HkpSkv, Ronneby/Kallinge
	151751	Agusta A109LUH Power (Hkp.15A) [21]	Hkpflj 2.HkpSkv, Linköping/Malmen

Serial	Type (code/other identity)	Owner/operator, location or fate	Notes
151752	Agusta A109LUH Power (Hkp.15A) [22]	Hkpflj 2.HkpSkv, Linköping/Malmen	
151753	Agusta A109LUH Power (Hkp.15A) [23]	Hkpflj 2.HkpSkv, Linköping/Malmen	
151754	Agusta A109LUH Power (Hkp.15A) [24]	Hkpflj 2.HkpSkv, Linköping/Malmen	
151755	Agusta A109LUH Power (Hkp.15A) [25]	Hkpflj 2.HkpSkv, Linköping/Malmen	
151756	Agusta A109LUH Power (Hkp.15A) [26]	Hkpflj 2.HkpSkv, Linköping/Malmen	
151757	Agusta A109LUH Power (Hkp.15A) [27]	Hkpflj 2.HkpSkv, Linköping/Malmen	
151758	Agusta A109LUH Power (Hkp.15A) [28]	Hkpflj 2.HkpSkv, Linköping/Malmen	
151759	Agusta A109LUH Power (Hkp.15A) [29]	Hkpflj 2.HkpSkv, Linköping/Malmen	
152760	Agusta A109LUH Power (Hkp.15B) [30]	Hkpflj 3.HkpSkv, Ronneby/Kallinge	
151761	Agusta A109LUH Power (Hkp.15A) [31]	Hkpflj 2.HkpSkv, Linköping/Malmen	
151762	Agusta A109LUH Power (Hkp.15A) [32]	Hkpflj 2.HkpSkv, Linköping/Malmen	
152763	Agusta A109LUH Power (Hkp.15B) [33]	Hkpflj 3.HkpSkv, Ronneby/Kallinge	
151764	Agusta A109LUH Power (Hkp.15A) [34]	Hkpflj 2.HkpSkv, Linköping/Malmen	
152765	Agusta A109LUH Power (Hkp.15B) [35]	Hkpflj 3.HkpSkv, Ronneby/Kallinge	
152766	Agusta A109LUH Power (Hkp.15B) [36]	Hkpflj 3.HkpSkv, Ronneby/Kallinge	
152767	Agusta A109LUH Power (Hkp.15B) [37]	Hkpflj 3.HkpSkv, Ronneby/Kallinge	
152768	Agusta A109LUH Power (Hkp.15B) [38]	Hkpflj 3.HkpSkv, Ronneby/Kallinge	
152769	Agusta A109LUH Power (Hkp.15B) [39]	Hkpflj 3.HkpSkv, Ronneby/Kallinge	
152770	Agusta A109LUH Power (Hkp.15B) [40]	Hkpflj 3.HkpSkv, Ronneby/Kallinge	
161226	Sikorsky UH-60M Black Hawk (Hkp.16A) [01]	Hkpflj 2.HkpSkv, Linköping/Malmen	
161227	Sikorsky UH-60M Black Hawk (Hkp.16A) [02]	Hkpflj 2.HkpSkv, Linköping/Malmen	
161228	Sikorsky UH-60M Black Hawk (Hkp.16A) [03]	Hkpflj 2.HkpSkv, Linköping/Malmen	
161229	Sikorsky UH-60M Black Hawk (Hkp.16A) [04]	Hkpflj 2.HkpSkv, Linköping/Malmen	
161230	Sikorsky UH-60M Black Hawk (Hkp.16A) [05]	Hkpflj 2.HkpSkv, Linköping/Malmen	
161231	Sikorsky UH-60M Black Hawk (Hkp.16A) [06]	Hkpflj 2.HkpSkv, Linköping/Malmen	
161232	Sikorsky UH-60M Black Hawk (Hkp.16A) [07]	Hkpflj 2.HkpSkv, Linköping/Malmen	
161233	Sikorsky UH-60M Black Hawk (Hkp.16A) [08]	Hkpflj 2.HkpSkv, Linköping/Malmen	
161234	Sikorsky UH-60M Black Hawk (Hkp.16A) [09]	Hkpflj 2.HkpSkv, Linköping/Malmen	
161235	Sikorsky UH-60M Black Hawk (Hkp.16A) [10]	Hkpflj 2.HkpSkv, Linköping/Malmen	
161236	Sikorsky UH-60M Black Hawk (Hkp.16A) [11]	Hkpflj 2.HkpSkv, Linköping/Malmen	
161237	Sikorsky UH-60M Black Hawk (Hkp.16A) [12]	Hkpflj 2.HkpSkv, Linköping/Malmen	
161238	Sikorsky UH-60M Black Hawk (Hkp.16A) [13]	Hkpflj 2.HkpSkv, Linköping/Malmen	
161239	Sikorsky UH-60M Black Hawk (Hkp.16A) [14]	Hkpflj 2.HkpSkv, Linköping/Malmen	
161240	Sikorsky UH-60M Black Hawk (Hkp.16A) [15]	Hkpflj 2.HkpSkv, Linköping/Malmen	

Kustbevakning/Swedish Coast Guard

SE-MAA	Bombardier DHC-8Q-311 [501]	Kustbevakning, Nykoping	
SE-MAB	Bombardier DHC-8Q-311 [502]	Kustbevakning, Nykoping	
SE-MAC	Bombardier DHC-8Q-311 [503]	Kustbevakning, Nykoping	

SWITZERLAND
Schweizer Luftwaffe/Swiss Air Force

(Most aircraft are pooled centrally. Some carry unit badges but these rarely indicate actual operators.)

A-101	Pilatus PC-21	Swiss AF Pilotenschule, Emmen	
A-102	Pilatus PC-21	Swiss AF Pilotenschule, Emmen	
A-103	Pilatus PC-21	Swiss AF Pilotenschule, Emmen	
A-104	Pilatus PC-21	Swiss AF Pilotenschule, Emmen	
A-105	Pilatus PC-21	Swiss AF Pilotenschule, Emmen	
A-106	Pilatus PC-21	Swiss AF Pilotenschule, Emmen	
A-107	Pilatus PC-21	Swiss AF Pilotenschule, Emmen	
A-108	Pilatus PC-21	Swiss AF Pilotenschule, Emmen	
A-912	Pilatus NCPC-7 Turbo Trainer	Swiss AF Instrumentenflugstaffel 14, Emmen	
A-913	Pilatus NCPC-7 Turbo Trainer	Swiss AF Instrumentenflugstaffel 14, Emmen	
A-914	Pilatus NCPC-7 Turbo Trainer	Swiss AF Instrumentenflugstaffel 14, Emmen	
A-915	Pilatus NCPC-7 Turbo Trainer	Swiss AF Instrumentenflugstaffel 14, Emmen	
A-916	Pilatus NCPC-7 Turbo Trainer	Swiss AF Instrumentenflugstaffel 14, Emmen	
A-917	Pilatus NCPC-7 Turbo Trainer	Swiss AF Instrumentenflugstaffel 14, Emmen	
A-918	Pilatus NCPC-7 Turbo Trainer	Swiss AF Instrumentenflugstaffel 14, Emmen	
A-919	Pilatus NCPC-7 Turbo Trainer	Swiss AF Instrumentenflugstaffel 14, Emmen	
A-922	Pilatus NCPC-7 Turbo Trainer	Swiss AF Instrumentenflugstaffel 14, Emmen	
A-923	Pilatus NCPC-7 Turbo Trainer	Swiss AF Instrumentenflugstaffel 14, Emmen	
A-924	Pilatus NCPC-7 Turbo Trainer	Swiss AF Instrumentenflugstaffel 14, Emmen	
A-925	Pilatus NCPC-7 Turbo Trainer	Swiss AF Instrumentenflugstaffel 14, Emmen	

Notes	Serial	Type (code/other identity)	Owner/operator, location or fate
	A-926	Pilatus NCPC-7 Turbo Trainer	Swiss AF Instrumentenflugstaffel 14, Emmen
	A-927	Pilatus NCPC-7 Turbo Trainer	Swiss AF Instrumentenflugstaffel 14, Emmen
	A-928	Pilatus NCPC-7 Turbo Trainer	Swiss AF Instrumentenflugstaffel 14, Emmen
	A-929	Pilatus NCPC-7 Turbo Trainer	Swiss AF Instrumentenflugstaffel 14, Emmen
	A-930	Pilatus NCPC-7 Turbo Trainer	Swiss AF Instrumentenflugstaffel 14, Emmen
	A-931	Pilatus NCPC-7 Turbo Trainer	Swiss AF Instrumentenflugstaffel 14, Emmen
	A-932	Pilatus NCPC-7 Turbo Trainer	Swiss AF Instrumentenflugstaffel 14, Emmen
	A-933	Pilatus NCPC-7 Turbo Trainer	Swiss AF Instrumentenflugstaffel 14, Emmen
	A-934	Pilatus NCPC-7 Turbo Trainer	Swiss AF Instrumentenflugstaffel 14, Emmen
	A-935	Pilatus NCPC-7 Turbo Trainer	Swiss AF Instrumentenflugstaffel 14, Emmen
	A-936	Pilatus NCPC-7 Turbo Trainer	Swiss AF Instrumentenflugstaffel 14, Emmen
	A-938	Pilatus NCPC-7 Turbo Trainer	Swiss AF Instrumentenflugstaffel 14, Emmen
	A-939	Pilatus NCPC-7 Turbo Trainer	Swiss AF Instrumentenflugstaffel 14, Emmen
	A-940	Pilatus NCPC-7 Turbo Trainer	Swiss AF Instrumentenflugstaffel 14, Emmen
	A-941	Pilatus NCPC-7 Turbo Trainer	Swiss AF Instrumentenflugstaffel 14, Emmen
	C-405	Pilatus PC-9	Preserved Fliegermuseum, Altenrhein
	C-407	Pilatus PC-9	Swiss AF, stored Lodrino
	C-408	Pilatus PC-9	Swiss AF, stored Lodrino
	C-409	Pilatus PC-9	Instructional airframe, Payerne
	C-411	Pilatus PC-9	Instructional airframe, Payerne
	C-412	Pilatus PC-9	Swiss AF, stored Lodrino
	J-3033	Northrop F-5E Tiger II $	Swiss AF, stored Meiringen
	J-3044	Northrop F-5E Tiger II	Swiss AF FlSt 6 & 19, Payerne
	J-3070	Northrop F-5E Tiger II	Swiss AF FlSt 6 & 19, Payerne
	J-3073	Northrop F-5E Tiger II $	Swiss AF, preserved Meiringen
	J-3077	Northrop F-5E Tiger II	Swiss AF FlSt 6 & 19, Payerne
	J-3080	Northrop F-5E Tiger II	Swiss AF Patrouille Suisse, Emmen
	J-3081	Northrop F-5E Tiger II	Swiss AF Patrouille Suisse, Emmen
	J-3082	Northrop F-5E Tiger II	Swiss AF Patrouille Suisse, Emmen
	J-3083	Northrop F-5E Tiger II	Swiss AF Patrouille Suisse, Emmen
	J-3084	Northrop F-5E Tiger II	Swiss AF Patrouille Suisse, Emmen
	J-3085	Northrop F-5E Tiger II	Swiss AF Patrouille Suisse, Emmen
	J-3087	Northrop F-5E Tiger II	Swiss AF Patrouille Suisse, Emmen
	J-3088	Northrop F-5E Tiger II	Swiss AF Patrouille Suisse, Emmen
	J-3090	Northrop F-5E Tiger II	Swiss AF Patrouille Suisse, Emmen
	J-3091	Northrop F-5E Tiger II	Swiss AF Patrouille Suisse, Emmen
	J-3093	Northrop F-5E Tiger II	Swiss AF FlSt 6 & 19, Payerne
	J-3094	Northrop F-5E Tiger II	Swiss AF FlSt 6 & 19, Payerne
	J-3095	Northrop F-5E Tiger II	Swiss AF FlSt 6 & 19, Payerne
	J-3097	Northrop F-5E Tiger II	Swiss AF FlSt 6 & 19, Payerne
	J-3201	Northrop F-5F Tiger II	Swiss AF FlSt 6 & 19, Payerne
	J-3203	Northrop F-5F Tiger II	Swiss AF FlSt 6 & 19, Payerne
	J-3210	Northrop F-5F Tiger II	Swiss AF FlSt 6 & 19, Payerne
	J-3211	Northrop F-5F Tiger II	Swiss AF FlSt 6 & 19, Payerne
	J-3212	Northrop F-5F Tiger II	Swiss AF FlSt 6 & 19, Payerne
	J-5001	McDonnell Douglas F/A-18C Hornet	Swiss AF FlSt 11, Meiringen/FlSt 17 & 18 Payerne
	J-5002	McDonnell Douglas F/A-18C Hornet	Swiss AF FlSt 11, Meiringen/FlSt 17 & 18 Payerne
	J-5003	McDonnell Douglas F/A-18C Hornet	Swiss AF FlSt 11, Meiringen/FlSt 17 & 18 Payerne
	J-5004	McDonnell Douglas F/A-18C Hornet	Swiss AF FlSt 11, Meiringen/FlSt 17 & 18 Payerne
	J-5005	McDonnell Douglas F/A-18C Hornet	Swiss AF FlSt 11, Meiringen/FlSt 17 & 18 Payerne
	J-5006	McDonnell Douglas F/A-18C Hornet	Swiss AF FlSt 11, Meiringen/FlSt 17 & 18 Payerne
	J-5007	McDonnell Douglas F/A-18C Hornet	Swiss AF FlSt 11, Meiringen/FlSt 17 & 18 Payerne
	J-5008	McDonnell Douglas F/A-18C Hornet	Swiss AF FlSt 11, Meiringen/FlSt 17 & 18 Payerne

Serial	Type (code/other identity)	Owner/operator, location or fate	Notes
J-5009	McDonnell Douglas F/A-18C Hornet	Swiss AF FlSt 11, Meiringen/FlSt 17 & 18 Payerne	
J-5010	McDonnell Douglas F/A-18C Hornet	Swiss AF FlSt 11, Meiringen/FlSt 17 & 18 Payerne	
J-5011	McDonnell Douglas F/A-18C Hornet $	Swiss AF FlSt 11, Meiringen/FlSt 17 & 18 Payerne	
J-5012	McDonnell Douglas F/A-18C Hornet	Swiss AF FlSt 11, Meiringen/FlSt 17 & 18 Payerne	
J-5013	McDonnell Douglas F/A-18C Hornet	Swiss AF FlSt 11, Meiringen/FlSt 17 & 18 Payerne	
J-5014	McDonnell Douglas F/A-18C Hornet	Swiss AF FlSt 11, Meiringen/FlSt 17 & 18 Payerne	
J-5015	McDonnell Douglas F/A-18C Hornet	Swiss AF FlSt 11, Meiringen/FlSt 17 & 18 Payerne	
J-5016	McDonnell Douglas F/A-18C Hornet	Swiss AF FlSt 11, Meiringen/FlSt 17 & 18 Payerne	
J-5017	McDonnell Douglas F/A-18C Hornet $	Swiss AF FlSt 11, Meiringen/FlSt 17 & 18 Payerne	
J-5018	McDonnell Douglas F/A-18C Hornet $	Swiss AF FlSt 11, Meiringen/FlSt 17 & 18 Payerne	
J-5019	McDonnell Douglas F/A-18C Hornet	Swiss AF FlSt 11, Meiringen/FlSt 17 & 18 Payerne	
J-5020	McDonnell Douglas F/A-18C Hornet	Swiss AF FlSt 11, Meiringen/FlSt 17 & 18 Payerne	
J-5021	McDonnell Douglas F/A-18C Hornet	Swiss AF FlSt 11, Meiringen/FlSt 17 & 18 Payerne	
J-5023	McDonnell Douglas F/A-18C Hornet	Swiss AF FlSt 11, Meiringen/FlSt 17 & 18 Payerne	
J-5024	McDonnell Douglas F/A-18C Hornet	Swiss AF FlSt 11, Meiringen/FlSt 17 & 18 Payerne	
J-5025	McDonnell Douglas F/A-18C Hornet	Swiss AF FlSt 11, Meiringen/FlSt 17 & 18 Payerne	
J-5026	McDonnell Douglas F/A-18C Hornet	Swiss AF FlSt 11, Meiringen/FlSt 17 & 18 Payerne	
J-5232	McDonnell Douglas F/A-18D Hornet	Swiss AF FlSt 11, Meiringen/FlSt 17 & 18 Payerne	
J-5233	McDonnell Douglas F/A-18D Hornet	Swiss AF FlSt 11, Meiringen/FlSt 17 & 18 Payerne	
J-5234	McDonnell Douglas F/A-18D Hornet	Swiss AF FlSt 11, Meiringen/FlSt 17 & 18 Payerne	
J-5236	McDonnell Douglas F/A-18D Hornet	Swiss AF FlSt 11, Meiringen/FlSt 17 & 18 Payerne	
J-5238	McDonnell Douglas F/A-18D Hornet	Swiss AF FlSt 11, Meiringen/FlSt 17 & 18 Payerne	
R-711	Aurora Flight Services Centaur OPA	Armasuisse, Emmen	
T-311	Aérospatiale AS.332M-1 Super Puma (TH 06)	Swiss AF LtSt 6 & 8, Alpnach/LtSt 3 & 4, Dübendorf/LtSt 1 & 5, Payerne	
T-312	Aérospatiale AS.332M-1 Super Puma (TH 06)	Swiss AF LtSt 6 & 8, Alpnach/LtSt 3 & 4, Dübendorf/LtSt 1 & 5, Payerne	
T-313	Aérospatiale AS.332M-1 Super Puma (TH 06)	Swiss AF LtSt 6 & 8, Alpnach/LtSt 3 & 4, Dübendorf/LtSt 1 & 5, Payerne	
T-314	Aérospatiale AS.332M-1 Super Puma (TH 06)	Swiss AF LtSt 6 & 8, Alpnach/LtSt 3 & 4, Dübendorf/LtSt 1 & 5, Payerne	
T-315	Aérospatiale AS.332M-1 Super Puma (TH 06)	Swiss AF LtSt 6 & 8, Alpnach/LtSt 3 & 4, Dübendorf/LtSt 1 & 5, Payerne	
T-316	Aérospatiale AS.332M-1 Super Puma (TH 06)	Swiss AF LtSt 6 & 8, Alpnach/LtSt 3 & 4, Dübendorf/LtSt 1 & 5, Payerne	
T-317	Aérospatiale AS.332M-1 Super Puma (TH 06)	Swiss AF LtSt 6 & 8, Alpnach/LtSt 3 & 4, Dübendorf/LtSt 1 & 5, Payerne	
T-318	Aérospatiale AS.332M-1 Super Puma (TH 06)	Swiss AF LtSt 6 & 8, Alpnach/LtSt 3 & 4, Dübendorf/LtSt 1 & 5, Payerne	

Notes	Serial	Type (code/other identity)	Owner/operator, location or fate
	T-319	Aérospatiale AS.332M-1 Super Puma (TH 06)	Swiss AF LtSt 6 & 8, Alpnach/ LtSt 3 & 4, Dübendorf/LtSt 1 & 5, Payerne
	T-320	Aérospatiale AS.332M-1 Super Puma (TH 06)	Swiss AF LtSt 6 & 8, Alpnach/ LtSt 3 & 4, Dübendorf/LtSt 1 & 5, Payerne
	T-321	Aérospatiale AS.332M-1 Super Puma (TH 06)	Swiss AF LtSt 6 & 8, Alpnach/ LtSt 3 & 4, Dübendorf/LtSt 1 & 5, Payerne
	T-322	Aérospatiale AS.332M-1 Super Puma (TH 06)	Swiss AF LtSt 6 & 8, Alpnach/ LtSt 3 & 4, Dübendorf/LtSt 1 & 5, Payerne
	T-323	Aérospatiale AS.332M-1 Super Puma (TH 06)	Swiss AF LtSt 6 & 8, Alpnach/ LtSt 3 & 4, Dübendorf/LtSt 1 & 5, Payerne
	T-324	Aérospatiale AS.332M-1 Super Puma (TH 06)	Swiss AF LtSt 6 & 8, Alpnach/ LtSt 3 & 4, Dübendorf/LtSt 1 & 5, Payerne
	T-325	Aérospatiale AS.332M-1 Super Puma (TH 06)	Swiss AF LtSt 6 & 8, Alpnach/ LtSt 3 & 4, Dübendorf/LtSt 1 & 5, Payerne
	T-331	Aérospatiale AS.532UL Super Puma (TH 98)	Swiss AF LtSt 6 & 8, Alpnach/ LtSt 3 & 4, Dübendorf/LtSt 1 & 5, Payerne
	T-332	Aérospatiale AS.532UL Super Puma (TH 98)	Swiss AF LtSt 6 & 8, Alpnach/ LtSt 3 & 4, Dübendorf/LtSt 1 & 5, Payerne
	T-333	Aérospatiale AS.532UL Super Puma (TH 98)	Swiss AF LtSt 6 & 8, Alpnach/ LtSt 3 & 4, Dübendorf/LtSt 1 & 5, Payerne
	T-334	Aérospatiale AS.532UL Super Puma (TH 98)	Swiss AF LtSt 6 & 8, Alpnach/ LtSt 3 & 4, Dübendorf/LtSt 1 & 5, Payerne
	T-335	Aérospatiale AS.532UL Super Puma (TH 98)	Swiss AF LtSt 6 & 8, Alpnach/ LtSt 3 & 4, Dübendorf/LtSt 1 & 5, Payerne
	T-336	Aérospatiale AS.532UL Super Puma (TH 98)	Swiss AF LtSt 6 & 8, Alpnach/ LtSt 3 & 4, Dübendorf/LtSt 1 & 5, Payerne
	T-337	Aérospatiale AS.532UL Super Puma (TH 98)	Swiss AF LtSt 6 & 8, Alpnach/ LtSt 3 & 4, Dübendorf/LtSt 1 & 5, Payerne
	T-339	Aérospatiale AS.532UL Super Puma (TH 98)	Swiss AF LtSt 6 & 8, Alpnach/ LtSt 3 & 4, Dübendorf/LtSt 1 & 5, Payerne
	T-340	Aérospatiale AS.532UL Super Puma (TH 98)	Swiss AF LtSt 6 & 8, Alpnach/ LtSt 3 & 4, Dübendorf/LtSt 1 & 5, Payerne
	T-342	Aérospatiale AS.532UL Super Puma (TH 98)	Swiss AF LtSt 6 & 8, Alpnach/ LtSt 3 & 4, Dübendorf/LtSt 1 & 5, Payerne
	T-351	Eurocopter EC.135P-2	Swiss AF LTDB, Dübendorf
	T-352	Eurocopter EC.135P-2	Swiss AF LTDB, Dübendorf
	T-353	Eurocopter EC.635P-2+	Swiss AF LtSt 6 & 8, Alpnach/ LtSt 3 & 4, Dübendorf/LtSt 1 & 5, Payerne
	T-354	Eurocopter EC.635P-2+	Swiss AF LtSt 6 & 8, Alpnach/ LtSt 3 & 4, Dübendorf/LtSt 1 & 5, Payerne
	T-355	Eurocopter EC.635P-2+	Swiss AF LtSt 6 & 8, Alpnach/ LtSt 3 & 4, Dübendorf/LtSt 1 & 5, Payerne
	T-356	Eurocopter EC.635P-2+	Swiss AF LtSt 6 & 8, Alpnach/ LtSt 3 & 4, Dübendorf/LtSt 1 & 5, Payerne
	T-357	Eurocopter EC.635P-2+	Swiss AF LtSt 6 & 8, Alpnach/ LtSt 3 & 4, Dübendorf/LtSt 1 & 5, Payerne
	T-358	Eurocopter EC.635P-2+	Swiss AF LtSt 6 & 8, Alpnach/ LtSt 3 & 4, Dübendorf/LtSt 1 & 5, Payerne
	T-359	Eurocopter EC.635P-2+	Swiss AF LtSt 6 & 8, Alpnach/ LtSt 3 & 4, Dübendorf/LtSt 1 & 5, Payerne
	T-360	Eurocopter EC.635P-2+	Swiss AF LtSt 6 & 8, Alpnach/ LtSt 3 & 4, Dübendorf/LtSt 1 & 5, Payerne
	T-361	Eurocopter EC.635P-2+	Swiss AF LtSt 6 & 8, Alpnach/ LtSt 3 & 4, Dübendorf/LtSt 1 & 5, Payerne
	T-362	Eurocopter EC.635P-2+	Swiss AF LtSt 6 & 8, Alpnach/ LtSt 3 & 4, Dübendorf/LtSt 1 & 5, Payerne
	T-363	Eurocopter EC.635P-2+	Swiss AF LtSt 6 & 8, Alpnach/ LtSt 3 & 4, Dübendorf/LtSt 1 & 5, Payerne
	T-364	Eurocopter EC.635P-2+	Swiss AF LtSt 6 & 8, Alpnach/ LtSt 3 & 4, Dübendorf/LtSt 1 & 5, Payerne
	T-365	Eurocopter EC.635P-2+	Swiss AF LtSt 6 & 8, Alpnach/ LtSt 3 & 4, Dübendorf/LtSt 1 & 5, Payerne

Serial	Type (code/other identity)	Owner/operator, location or fate	Notes
T-366	Eurocopter EC.635P-2+	Swiss AF LtSt 6 & 8, Alpnach/ LtSt 3 & 4, Dübendorf/LtSt 1 & 5, Payerne	
T-367	Eurocopter EC.635P-2+	Swiss AF LtSt 6 & 8, Alpnach/ LtSt 3 & 4, Dübendorf/LtSt 1 & 5, Payerne	
T-368	Eurocopter EC.635P-2+	Swiss AF LtSt 6 & 8, Alpnach/ LtSt 3 & 4, Dübendorf/LtSt 1 & 5, Payerne	
T-369	Eurocopter EC.635P-2+	Swiss AF LtSt 6 & 8, Alpnach/ LtSt 3 & 4, Dübendorf/LtSt 1 & 5, Payerne	
T-370	Eurocopter EC.635P-2+	Swiss AF LtSt 6 & 8, Alpnach/ LtSt 3 & 4, Dübendorf/LtSt 1 & 5, Payerne	
T-721	Beech King Air 350C	Swiss AF LTDB, Dübendorf	
T-751	Bombardier Challenger 604 (HB-JRB)	Swiss AF LTDB, Dübendorf	
T-752	Bombardier Challenger 604 (HB-JRC)	Swiss AF LTDB, Dübendorf	
T-784	Cessna 560XL Citation Excel	Swiss AF LTDB, Bern/Belp	
T-785	Dassault Falcon 900EX EASy II	Swiss AF LTDB, Bern/Belp	
T-786	Pilatus PC-24	*Sold as OE-GLB, December 2022*	
V-612	Pilatus PC-6B/B2-H2 Turbo Porter	Swiss AF LtSt 7, Emmen	
V-613	Pilatus PC-6B/B2-H2 Turbo Porter	Swiss AF LtSt 7, Emmen	
V-614	Pilatus PC-6B/B2-H2 Turbo Porter	Swiss AF LtSt 7, Emmen	
V-616	Pilatus PC-6B/B2-H2 Turbo Porter	Swiss AF LtSt 7, Emmen	
V-617	Pilatus PC-6B/B2-H2 Turbo Porter	Swiss AF LtSt 7, Emmen	
V-618	Pilatus PC-6B/B2-H2 Turbo Porter	Swiss AF LtSt 7, Emmen	
V-619	Pilatus PC-6B/B2-H2 Turbo Porter	Swiss AF LtSt 7, Emmen	
V-620	Pilatus PC-6B/B2-H2 Turbo Porter	Swiss AF LtSt 7, Emmen	
V-622	Pilatus PC-6B/B2-H2 Turbo Porter $	Swiss AF LtSt 7, Emmen	
V-623	Pilatus PC-6B/B2-H2 Turbo Porter	Swiss AF LtSt 7, Emmen	
V-631	Pilatus PC-6B/B2-H2 Turbo Porter	Swiss AF LtSt 7, Emmen	
V-632	Pilatus PC-6B/B2-H2 Turbo Porter	Swiss AF LtSt 7, Emmen	
V-633	Pilatus PC-6B/B2-H2 Turbo Porter	Swiss AF LtSt 7, Emmen	
V-634	Pilatus PC-6B/B2-H2 Turbo Porter	Swiss AF LtSt 7, Emmen	
V-635	Pilatus PC-6B/B2-H2 Turbo Porter	Swiss AF LtSt 7, Emmen	

Swiss Government

HB-FOG	Pilatus PC-12/45	Armasuisse, Emmen	

SYRIA

YK-ASC	Dassault Falcon 900	Government of Syria, Damascus	

TANZANIA

5H-ONE	Gulfstream Aerospace G.550	Tanzanian Government, Dar-es-Salaam	

THAILAND

60206	Sukhoi SSJ100-95LR Superjet [L18-1/59]	Royal Thai AF 602 Sqn/6 Wing, Bangkok/Don Muang	
60207	Sukhoi SSJ100-95LR Superjet [L18-2/60]	Royal Thai AF 602 Sqn/6 Wing, Bangkok/Don Muang	
60208	Sukhoi SSJ100-95LR Superjet [L18-3/61]	Royal Thai AF 602 Sqn/6 Wing, Bangkok/Don Muang	
HS-CMV	Boeing 737-4Z6 (L11Kh.MWK-01/38) [11-111, 90401]	Royal Thai AF 904 Sqn/6 Wing, Bangkok/Don Muang	
HS-HMK	Boeing 737-8Z6 (L11k.VPR-03/59) [99-904, 90410]	Royal Thai AF 904 Sqn/6 Wing, Bangkok/Don Muang	
HS-HRH	Boeing 737-448 (L11Kh.MWK-02/47) [99-999, 90409]	Royal Thai AF 904 Sqn/6 Wing, Bangkok/Don Muang	
HS-MVS	Boeing 737-8Z6 (L11Kh2-1/50) [99-904, 90411]	Royal Thai AF 904 Sqn/6 Wing, Bangkok/Don Muang	
HS-TYR	Airbus A.319CJ-133 (L15-1/47) [60202]	Royal Thai AF 602 Sqn/6 Wing, Bangkok/Don Muang	
HS-TYT	Airbus A.320CJ-214 (L15K-1/58) [60203]	Royal Thai AF 602 Sqn/6 Wing, Bangkok/Don Muang	
HS-TYV	Airbus A.340-541 (L19-1/59) [60204]	Royal Thai AF 602 Sqn/6 Wing, Bangkok/Don Muang	

Notes	Serial	Type (code/other identity)	Owner/operator, location or fate
	HS-TYW	Airbus A.320CJ-214X (L15K-2/63) [60205]	Royal Thai AF 602 Sqn/6 Wing, Bangkok/Don Muang

TUNISIA

Tunisian Air Force/Al Quwwat al-Jawwiya al-Jamahiriyah At'Tunisia & Tunisian Government

	Z21012	Lockheed C-130H Hercules (TS-MTB)	Tunisian AF 21 Sqn, Bizerte/Sidi Ahmed
	Z21014	Lockheed C-130H Hercules (TS-MTN)	Tunisian AF 21 Sqn, Bizerte/Sidi Ahmed
	Z21121	Lockheed C-130J-30 Hercules II (TS-MTK)	Tunisian AF 11 Sqn, Tunis
	Z21122	Lockheed C-130J-30 Hercules II (TS-MTL)	Tunisian AF 11 Sqn, Tunis
	TS-IOO	Boeing 737-7HJ	Government of Tunisia, Tunis

TURKEY

Türk Hava Kuvvetleri (THK)/Turkish Air Force & Turkish Government

	004	Cessna 650 Citation VII	THK 212 Filo/11 HUAÜK, Ankara/Etimesgut
	3004	Canadair NF-5A-2000 Freedom Fighter [3]	THK 134 Filo, *Turkish Stars*/3 AJEÜ, Konya
	3023	Canadair NF-5A-2000 Freedom Fighter [2]	THK 134 Filo, *Turkish Stars*/3 AJEÜ, Konya
	3025	Canadair NF-5A-2000 Freedom Fighter [5]	THK 134 Filo, *Turkish Stars*/3 AJEÜ, Konya
	3032	Canadair NF-5A-2000 Freedom Fighter [6]	THK 134 Filo, *Turkish Stars*/3 AJEÜ, Konya
	3036	Canadair NF-5A-2000 Freedom Fighter [36]	THK 134 Filo, *Turkish Stars*/3 AJEÜ, Konya
	3039	Canadair NF-5A-2000 Freedom Fighter [39]	THK 134 Filo, *Turkish Stars*/3 AJEÜ, Konya
	3046	Canadair NF-5A-2000 Freedom Fighter [5]	THK 134 Filo, *Turkish Stars*/3 AJEÜ, Konya
	3048	Canadair NF-5A-2000 Freedom Fighter [8]	THK 134 Filo, *Turkish Stars*/3 AJEÜ, Konya
	3049	Canadair NF-5A-2000 Freedom Fighter [6]	THK 134 Filo, *Turkish Stars*/3 AJEÜ, Konya
	3052	Canadair NF-5A-2000 Freedom Fighter [2]	THK 134 Filo, *Turkish Stars*/3 AJEÜ, Konya
	3072	Canadair NF-5A-2000 Freedom Fighter [2]	THK 134 Filo, *Turkish Stars*/3 AJEÜ, Konya
	4001	Canadair NF-5B-2000 Freedom Fighter [4]	THK 134 Filo, *Turkish Stars*/3 AJEÜ, Konya
	4005	Canadair NF-5B-2000 Freedom Fighter	THK 134 Filo, *Turkish Stars*/3 AJEÜ, Konya
	4009	Canadair NF-5B-2000 Freedom Fighter [4]	THK 134 Filo, *Turkish Stars*/3 AJEÜ, Konya
	4013	Canadair NF-5B-2000 Freedom Fighter [4]	THK 134 Filo, *Turkish Stars*/3 AJEÜ, Konya
	4020	Canadair NF-5B-2000 Freedom Fighter	THK 134 Filo, *Turkish Stars*/3 AJEÜ, Konya
	4021	Canadair NF-5B-2000 Freedom Fighter [1]	THK 134 Filo, *Turkish Stars*/3 AJEÜ, Konya
	4026	Canadair NF-5B-2000 Freedom Fighter [1]	THK 134 Filo, *Turkish Stars*/3 AJEÜ, Konya
	57-2609	Boeing KC-135R Stratotanker	THK 101 Filo/10 TÜK, Incirlik
	58-0110	Boeing KC-135R Stratotanker	THK 101 Filo/10 TÜK, Incirlik
	60-0325	Boeing KC-135R Stratotanker	THK 101 Filo/10 TÜK, Incirlik
	60-0326	Boeing KC-135R Stratotanker	THK 101 Filo/10 TÜK, Incirlik
	62-3539	Boeing KC-135R Stratotanker	THK 101 Filo/10 TÜK, Incirlik
	62-3563	Boeing KC-135R Stratotanker	THK 101 Filo/10 TÜK, Incirlik
	62-3567	Boeing KC-135R Stratotanker	THK 101 Filo/10 TÜK, Incirlik
	63-13186	Lockheed C-130E Hercules	THK 222 Filo/12 HUAÜ, Erkilet
	63-13187	Lockheed C-130E Hercules $	THK 222 Filo/12 HUAÜ, Erkilet
	63-13188	Lockheed C-130E Hercules	THK 222 Filo/12 HUAÜ, Erkilet
	63-13189	Lockheed C-130E Hercules $	THK 222 Filo/12 HUAÜ, Erkilet
	67-0455	Lockheed C-130E Hercules	THK 222 Filo/12 HUAÜ, Erkilet
	68-023	Transall C-160D	*Withdrawn from use, Erkilet*
	68-1606	Lockheed C-130E Hercules	THK 222 Filo/12 HUAÜ, Erkilet
	68-1608	Lockheed C-130E Hercules	THK 222 Filo/12 HUAÜ, Erkilet
	68-1609	Lockheed C-130E Hercules	THK 222 Filo/12 HUAÜ, Erkilet
	69-029	Transall C-160D	*Withdrawn from use, Erkilet*
	69-031	Transall C-160D	*Withdrawn from use, Erkilet*
	69-036	Transall C-160D	THK 221 Filo/12 HUAÜ, Erkilet
	70-01610	Lockheed C-130E Hercules	THK 222 Filo/12 HUAÜ, Erkilet
	70-1947	Lockheed C-130E Hercules	THK 222 Filo/12 HUAÜ, Erkilet
	71-01468	Lockheed C-130E Hercules	THK 222 Filo/12 HUAÜ, Erkilet
	73-0991	Lockheed C-130E Hercules $	THK 222 Filo/12 HUAÜ, Erkilet
	86-0066	TUSAS (GD) F-16C-30 Fighting Falcon	THK 113 Filo/1 AJÜ, Eskisehir
	86-0069	TUSAS (GD) F-16C-30 Fighting Falcon	THK 132 Filo/3 AJEÜ, Konya
	86-0070	TUSAS (GD) F-16C-30 Fighting Falcon	THK 132 Filo/3 AJEÜ, Konya
	86-0071	TUSAS (GD) F-16C-30 Fighting Falcon	THK 132 Filo/3 AJEÜ, Konya
	86-0072	TUSAS (GD) F-16C-30 Fighting Falcon	THK 132 Filo/3 AJEÜ, Konya
	86-0192	TUSAS (GD) F-16D-30 Fighting Falcon	THK 113 Filo/1 AJÜ, Eskisehir
	86-0193	TUSAS (GD) F-16D-30 Fighting Falcon	THK 132 Filo/3 AJEÜ, Konya

Serial	Type (code/other identity)	Owner/operator, location or fate	Notes
86-0194	TUSAS (GD) F-16D-30 Fighting Falcon	THK 132 Filo/3 AJEÜ, Konya	
86-0195	TUSAS (GD) F-16D-30 Fighting Falcon	THK 132 Filo/3 AJEÜ, Konya	
86-0196	TUSAS (GD) F-16D-30 Fighting Falcon	THK 132 Filo/3 AJEÜ, Konya	
87-0002	TUSAS (GD) F-16D-30 Fighting Falcon	THK 113 Filo/1 AJÜ, Eskisehir	
87-0003	TUSAS (GD) F-16D-30 Fighting Falcon	THK 401 Filo/1 AJÜ, Eskisehir	
87-0009	TUSAS (GD) F-16C-30 Fighting Falcon	THK 113 Filo/1 AJÜ, Eskisehir	
87-0010	TUSAS (GD) F-16C-30 Fighting Falcon	THK 132 Filo/3 AJEÜ, Konya	
87-0011	TUSAS (GD) F-16C-30 Fighting Falcon	THK 132 Filo/3 AJEÜ, Konya	
87-0013	TUSAS (GD) F-16C-30 Fighting Falcon	THK 132 Filo/3 AJEÜ, Konya	
87-0014	TUSAS (GD) F-16C-30 Fighting Falcon	THK 113 Filo/1 AJÜ, Eskisehir	
87-0015	TUSAS (GD) F-16C-30 Fighting Falcon	THK 113 Filo/1 AJÜ, Eskisehir	
87-0016	TUSAS (GD) F-16C-30 Fighting Falcon	THK 132 Filo/3 AJEÜ, Konya	
87-0018	TUSAS (GD) F-16C-30 Fighting Falcon	THK 152 Filo/10 TÜK, Incirlik	
87-0019	TUSAS (GD) F-16C-30 Fighting Falcon	THK 132 Filo/3 AJEÜ, Konya	
87-0020	TUSAS (GD) F-16C-30 Fighting Falcon	THK 152 Filo/10 TÜK, Incirlik	
87-0021	TUSAS (GD) F-16C-30 Fighting Falcon	THK 132 Filo/3 AJEÜ, Konya	
88-0013	TUSAS (GD) F-16D-30 Fighting Falcon	THK 152 Filo/10 TÜK, Incirlik	
88-0014	TUSAS (GD) F-16D-40 Fighting Falcon	THK 193 Filo/9 AJÜ, Balikesir	
88-0015	TUSAS (GD) F-16D-40 Fighting Falcon	THK 192 Filo/9 AJÜ, Balikesir	
88-0019	TUSAS (GD) F-16C-30 Fighting Falcon	THK 113 Filo/1 AJÜ, Eskisehir	
88-0020	TUSAS (GD) F-16C-30 Fighting Falcon	THK 132 Filo/3 AJEÜ, Konya	
88-0021	TUSAS (GD) F-16C-30 Fighting Falcon$	THK 132 Filo/3 AJEÜ, Konya	
88-0024	TUSAS (GD) F-16C-30 Fighting Falcon	THK 152 Filo/10 TÜK, Incirlik	
88-0025	TUSAS (GD) F-16C-30 Fighting Falcon	THK 132 Filo/3 AJEÜ, Konya	
88-0026	TUSAS (GD) F-16C-30 Fighting Falcon $	THK 152 Filo/10 TÜK, Incirlik	
88-0027	TUSAS (GD) F-16C-30 Fighting Falcon	THK 152 Filo/10 TÜK, Incirlik	
88-0028	TUSAS (GD) F-16C-30 Fighting Falcon	THK 192 Filo/9 AJÜ, Balikesir	
88-0029	TUSAS (GD) F-16C-30 Fighting Falcon $	THK 132 Filo/3 AJEÜ, Konya	
88-0030	TUSAS (GD) F-16C-30 Fighting Falcon	THK 152 Filo/10 TÜK, Incirlik	
88-0031	TUSAS (GD) F-16C-30 Fighting Falcon	THK 401 Filo/1 AJÜ, Eskisehir	
88-0032	TUSAS (GD) F-16C-30 Fighting Falcon $	THK 132 Filo/3 AJEÜ, Konya	
88-0033	TUSAS (GD) F-16C-40 Fighting Falcon	THK 152 Filo/10 TÜK, Incirlik	
88-0034	TUSAS (GD) F-16C-40 Fighting Falcon	THK 192 Filo/9 AJÜ, Balikesir	
88-0035	TUSAS (GD) F-16C-40 Fighting Falcon	THK 152 Filo/10 TÜK, Incirlik	
88-0036	TUSAS (GD) F-16C-40 Fighting Falcon	THK 192 Filo/9 AJÜ, Balikesir	
88-0037	TUSAS (GD) F-16C-40 Fighting Falcon	THK 132 Filo/3 AJEÜ, Konya	
89-0022	TUSAS (GD) F-16C-40 Fighting Falcon	THK	
89-0023	TUSAS (GD) F-16C-40 Fighting Falcon	THK 192 Filo/9 AJÜ, Balikesir	
89-0025	TUSAS (GD) F-16C-40 Fighting Falcon	THK 192 Filo/9 AJÜ, Balikesir	
89-0026	TUSAS (GD) F-16C-40 Fighting Falcon	THK	
89-0027	TUSAS (GD) F-16C-40 Fighting Falcon	THK	
89-0028	TUSAS (GD) F-16C-40 Fighting Falcon	THK 132 Filo/3 AJEÜ, Konya	
89-0030	TUSAS (GD) F-16C-40 Fighting Falcon	THK	
89-0034	TUSAS (GD) F-16C-40 Fighting Falcon	THK 161 Filo/6 AJÜ, Bandirma	
89-0035	TUSAS (GD) F-16C-40 Fighting Falcon	THK 152 Filo/10 TÜK, Incirlik	
89-0036	TUSAS (GD) F-16C-40 Fighting Falcon	THK 161 Filo/6 AJÜ, Bandirma	
89-0037	TUSAS (GD) F-16C-40 Fighting Falcon	THK 161 Filo/6 AJÜ, Bandirma	
89-0038	TUSAS (GD) F-16C-40 Fighting Falcon	THK 161 Filo/6 AJÜ, Bandirma	
89-0039	TUSAS (GD) F-16C-40 Fighting Falcon	THK 152 Filo/10 TÜK, Incirlik	
89-0040	TUSAS (GD) F-16C-40 Fighting Falcon	THK 113 Filo/1 AJÜ, Eskisehir	
89-0041	TUSAS (GD) F-16C-40 Fighting Falcon	THK 152 Filo/10 TÜK, Incirlik	
89-0042	TUSAS (GD) F-16D-40 Fighting Falcon	THK 113 Filo/1 AJÜ, Eskisehir	
89-0043	TUSAS (GD) F-16D-40 Fighting Falcon	THK 151 Filo/5 AJÜ, Merzifon	
89-0044	TUSAS (GD) F-16D-40 Fighting Falcon	THK 132 Filo/3 AJEÜ, Konya	
89-0045	TUSAS (GD) F-16D-40 Fighting Falcon	THK 161 Filo/6 AJÜ, Bandirma	
90-0004	TUSAS (GD) F-16C-40 Fighting Falcon	THK 152 Filo/10 TÜK, Incirlik	
90-0005	TUSAS (GD) F-16C-40 Fighting Falcon	THK 161 Filo/6 AJÜ, Bandirma	
90-0006	TUSAS (GD) F-16C-40 Fighting Falcon	THK 182 Filo/8 AJÜ, Diyarbakir	
90-0007	TUSAS (GD) F-16C-40 Fighting Falcon	THK 132 Filo/3 AJEÜ, Konya	
90-0008	TUSAS (GD) F-16C-40 Fighting Falcon	THK 161 Filo/6 AJÜ, Bandirma	
90-0009	TUSAS (GD) F-16C-40 Fighting Falcon	THK 152 Filo/10 TÜK, Incirlik	
90-0010	TUSAS (GD) F-16C-40 Fighting Falcon	THK 132 Filo/3 AJEÜ, Konya	

Notes	Serial	Type (code/other identity)	Owner/operator, location or fate
	90-0011	TUSAS (GD) F-16C-40 Fighting Falcon $	THK
	90-0012	TUSAS (GD) F-16C-40 Fighting Falcon	THK 192 Filo/9 AJÜ, Balikesir
	90-0013	TUSAS (GD) F-16C-40 Fighting Falcon	THK 182 Filo/8 AJÜ, Diyarbakir
	90-0014	TUSAS (GD) F-16C-40 Fighting Falcon	THK 161 Filo/6 AJÜ, Bandirma
	90-0016	TUSAS (GD) F-16C-40 Fighting Falcon	THK 182 Filo/8 AJÜ, Diyarbakir
	90-0017	TUSAS (GD) F-16C-40 Fighting Falcon	THK 192 Filo/9 AJÜ, Balikesir
	90-0018	TUSAS (GD) F-16C-40 Fighting Falcon	THK 161 Filo/6 AJÜ, Bandirma
	90-0019	TUSAS (GD) F-16C-40 Fighting Falcon	THK 161 Filo/6 AJÜ, Bandirma
	90-0020	TUSAS (GD) F-16C-40 Fighting Falcon	THK 161 Filo/6 AJÜ, Bandirma
	90-0021	TUSAS (GD) F-16C-40 Fighting Falcon	THK 401 Filo/1 AJÜ, Eskisehir
	90-0022	TUSAS (GD) F-16D-40 Fighting Falcon	THK 182 Filo/8 AJÜ, Diyarbakir
	90-0023	TUSAS (GD) F-16D-40 Fighting Falcon	THK 152 Filo/10 TÜK, Incirlik
	90-0024	TUSAS (GD) F-16D-40 Fighting Falcon	THK 182 Filo/8 AJÜ, Diyarbakir
	91-003	Grumman G.1159C Gulfstream IV	THK 212 Filo/11 HUAÜK, Ankara/Etimesgut
	91-0001	TUSAS (GD) F-16C-40 Fighting Falcon	THK 162 Filo/6 AJÜ, Bandirma
	91-0002	TUSAS (GD) F-16C-40 Fighting Falcon	THK 401 Filo/1 AJÜ, Eskisehir
	91-0003	TUSAS (GD) F-16C-40 Fighting Falcon	THK 161 Filo/6 AJÜ, Bandirma
	91-0004	TUSAS (GD) F-16C-40 Fighting Falcon	THK 161 Filo/6 AJÜ, Bandirma
	91-0005	TUSAS (GD) F-16C-40 Fighting Falcon	THK 182 Filo/8 AJÜ, Diyarbakir
	91-0006	TUSAS (GD) F-16C-40 Fighting Falcon	THK 161 Filo/6 AJÜ, Bandirma
	91-0007	TUSAS (GD) F-16C-40 Fighting Falcon	THK 161 Filo/6 AJÜ, Bandirma
	91-0008	TUSAS (GD) F-16C-40 Fighting Falcon	THK 161 Filo/6 AJÜ, Bandirma
	91-0010	TUSAS (GD) F-16C-40 Fighting Falcon	THK 162 Filo/6 AJÜ, Bandirma
	91-0011	TUSAS (GD) F-16C-40 Fighting Falcon $	THK 132 Filo/3 AJEÜ, Konya
	91-0012	TUSAS (GD) F-16C-40 Fighting Falcon	THK 182 Filo/8 AJÜ, Diyarbakir
	91-0014	TUSAS (GD) F-16C-40 Fighting Falcon	THK
	91-0015	TUSAS (GD) F-16C-40 Fighting Falcon	THK 401 Filo/1 AJÜ, Eskisehir
	91-0016	TUSAS (GD) F-16C-40 Fighting Falcon	THK 182 Filo/8 AJÜ, Diyarbakir
	91-0017	TUSAS (GD) F-16C-40 Fighting Falcon	THK 113 Filo/1 AJÜ, Eskisehir
	91-0018	TUSAS (GD) F-16C-40 Fighting Falcon	THK 192 Filo/9 AJÜ, Balikesir
	91-0020	TUSAS (GD) F-16C-40 Fighting Falcon	THK 161 Filo/6 AJÜ, Bandirma
	91-0022	TUSAS (GD) F-16D-40 Fighting Falcon	THK 192 Filo/9 AJÜ, Balikesir
	91-0024	TUSAS (GD) F-16D-40 Fighting Falcon	THK 132 Filo/3 AJEÜ, Konya
	92-0001	TUSAS (GD) F-16C-40 Fighting Falcon	THK 132 Filo/3 AJEÜ, Konya
	92-0002	TUSAS (GD) F-16C-40 Fighting Falcon	THK 182 Filo/8 AJÜ, Diyarbakir
	92-0003	TUSAS (GD) F-16C-40 Fighting Falcon	THK 192 Filo/9 AJÜ, Balikesir
	92-0004	TUSAS (GD) F-16C-40 Fighting Falcon	THK 161 Filo/6 AJÜ, Bandirma
	92-0005	TUSAS (GD) F-16C-40 Fighting Falcon	THK 192 Filo/9 AJÜ, Balikesir
	92-0006	TUSAS (GD) F-16C-40 Fighting Falcon	THK 182 Filo/8 AJÜ, Diyarbakir
	92-0007	TUSAS (GD) F-16C-40 Fighting Falcon	THK 192 Filo/9 AJÜ, Balikesir
	92-0008	TUSAS (GD) F-16C-40 Fighting Falcon	THK 152 Filo/10 TÜK, Incirlik
	92-0010	TUSAS (GD) F-16C-40 Fighting Falcon	THK 192 Filo/9 AJÜ, Balikesir
	92-0011	TUSAS (GD) F-16C-40 Fighting Falcon	THK 182 Filo/8 AJÜ, Diyarbakir
	92-0012	TUSAS (GD) F-16C-40 Fighting Falcon	THK 182 Filo/8 AJÜ, Diyarbakir
	92-0013	TUSAS (GD) F-16C-40 Fighting Falcon	THK 132 Filo/3 AJEÜ, Konya
	92-0014	TUSAS (GD) F-16C-40 Fighting Falcon $	THK 192 Filo/9 AJÜ, Balikesir
	92-0015	TUSAS (GD) F-16C-40 Fighting Falcon	THK 161 Filo/6 AJÜ, Bandirma
	92-0016	TUSAS (GD) F-16C-40 Fighting Falcon	THK 161 Filo/6 AJÜ, Bandirma
	92-0017	TUSAS (GD) F-16C-40 Fighting Falcon	THK 151 Filo/5 AJÜ, Merzifon
	92-0018	TUSAS (GD) F-16C-40 Fighting Falcon	THK 151 Filo/5 AJÜ, Merzifon
	92-0019	TUSAS (GD) F-16C-40 Fighting Falcon	THK 181 Filo/8 AJÜ, Diyarbakir
	92-0020	TUSAS (GD) F-16C-40 Fighting Falcon	THK 181 Filo/8 AJÜ, Diyarbakir
	92-0021	TUSAS (GD) F-16C-40 Fighting Falcon	THK 192 Filo/9 AJÜ, Balikesir
	92-0022	TUSAS (GD) F-16D-40 Fighting Falcon	THK 161 Filo/6 AJÜ, Bandirma
	92-0023	TUSAS (GD) F-16D-40 Fighting Falcon	THK 132 Filo/3 AJEÜ, Konya
	92-0024	TUSAS (GD) F-16D-40 Fighting Falcon	THK 191 Filo/9 AJÜ, Balikesir
	93-005	Cessna 650 Citation VII	THK 212 Filo/11 HUAÜK, Ankara/Etimesgut
	93-0001	TUSAS (GD) F-16C-40 Fighting Falcon	THK 401 Filo/1 AJÜ, Eskisehir
	93-0003	TUSAS (GD) F-16C-40 Fighting Falcon	THK 151 Filo/5 AJÜ, Merzifon
	93-0004	TUSAS (GD) F-16C-40 Fighting Falcon	THK 181 Filo/8 AJÜ, Diyarbakir
	93-0005	TUSAS (GD) F-16C-40 Fighting Falcon	THK 182 Filo/8 AJÜ, Diyarbakir
	93-0006	TUSAS (GD) F-16C-40 Fighting Falcon	THK 181 Filo/8 AJÜ, Diyarbakir

Serial	Type (code/other identity)	Owner/operator, location or fate	Notes
93-0007	TUSAS (GD) F-16C-40 Fighting Falcon	THK 182 Filo/8 AJÜ, Diyarbakir	
93-0008	TUSAS (GD) F-16C-40 Fighting Falcon	THK 132 Filo/3 AJEÜ, Konya	
93-0009	TUSAS (GD) F-16C-40 Fighting Falcon	THK 182 Filo/8 AJÜ, Diyarbakir	
93-0011	TUSAS (GD) F-16C-40 Fighting Falcon	THK 181 Filo/8 AJÜ, Diyarbakir	
93-0012	TUSAS (GD) F-16C-40 Fighting Falcon	THK 181 Filo/8 AJÜ, Diyarbakir	
93-0013	TUSAS (GD) F-16C-40 Fighting Falcon	THK 181 Filo/8 AJÜ, Diyarbakir	
93-0658	TUSAS (GD) F-16C-50 Fighting Falcon	THK 132 Filo/3 AJEÜ, Konya	
93-0659	TUSAS (GD) F-16C-50 Fighting Falcon	THK 192 Filo/9 AJÜ, Balikesir	
93-0660	TUSAS (GD) F-16C-50 Fighting Falcon	THK 152 Filo/10 TÜK, Incirlik	
93-0661	TUSAS (GD) F-16C-50 Fighting Falcon	THK 132 Filo/3 AJEÜ, Konya	
93-0663	TUSAS (GD) F-16C-50 Fighting Falcon	THK 132 Filo/3 AJEÜ, Konya	
93-0664	TUSAS (GD) F-16C-50 Fighting Falcon	THK 132 Filo/3 AJEÜ, Konya	
93-0665	TUSAS (GD) F-16C-50 Fighting Falcon	THK 193 Filo/9 AJÜ, Balikesir	
93-0667	TUSAS (GD) F-16C-50 Fighting Falcon	THK 151 Filo/5 AJÜ, Merzifon	
93-0668	TUSAS (GD) F-16C-50 Fighting Falcon	THK 151 Filo/5 AJÜ, Merzifon	
93-0669	TUSAS (GD) F-16C-50 Fighting Falcon	THK 151 Filo/5 AJÜ, Merzifon	
93-0670	TUSAS (GD) F-16C-50 Fighting Falcon	THK 193 Filo/9 AJÜ, Balikesir	
93-0671	TUSAS (GD) F-16C-50 Fighting Falcon	THK 151 Filo/5 AJÜ, Merzifon	
93-0672	TUSAS (GD) F-16C-50 Fighting Falcon	THK 132 Filo/3 AJEÜ, Konya	
93-0673	TUSAS (GD) F-16C-50 Fighting Falcon	THK 132 Filo/3 AJEÜ, Konya	
93-0674	TUSAS (GD) F-16C-50 Fighting Falcon	THK 132 Filo/3 AJEÜ, Konya	
93-0675	TUSAS (GD) F-16C-50 Fighting Falcon	THK 192 Filo/9 AJÜ, Balikesir	
93-0676	TUSAS (GD) F-16C-50 Fighting Falcon	THK 192 Filo/9 AJÜ, Balikesir	
93-0677	TUSAS (GD) F-16C-50 Fighting Falcon	THK	
93-0678	TUSAS (GD) F-16C-50 Fighting Falcon	THK 191 Filo/9 AJÜ, Balikesir	
93-0679	TUSAS (GD) F-16C-50 Fighting Falcon	THK 191 Filo/9 AJÜ, Balikesir	
93-0680	TUSAS (GD) F-16C-50 Fighting Falcon	THK 193 Filo/9 AJÜ, Balikesir	
93-0681	TUSAS (GD) F-16C-50 Fighting Falcon	THK 193 Filo/9 AJÜ, Balikesir	
93-0682	TUSAS (GD) F-16C-50 Fighting Falcon $	THK 193 Filo/9 AJÜ, Balikesir	
93-0683	TUSAS (GD) F-16C-50 Fighting Falcon	THK 193 Filo/9 AJÜ, Balikesir	
93-0684	TUSAS (GD) F-16C-50 Fighting Falcon	THK	
93-0685	TUSAS (GD) F-16C-50 Fighting Falcon	THK	
93-0687	TUSAS (GD) F-16C-50 Fighting Falcon	THK 132 Filo/3 AJEÜ, Konya	
93-0689	TUSAS (GD) F-16C-50 Fighting Falcon	THK 192 Filo/9 AJÜ, Balikesir	
93-0690	TUSAS (GD) F-16C-50 Fighting Falcon	THK	
93-0691	TUSAS (GD) F-16D-50 Fighting Falcon $	THK 192 Filo/9 AJÜ, Balikesir	
93-0692	TUSAS (GD) F-16D-50 Fighting Falcon	THK 193 Filo/9 AJÜ, Balikesir	
93-0693	TUSAS (GD) F-16D-50 Fighting Falcon	THK 152 Filo/10 TÜK, Incirlik	
93-0694	TUSAS (GD) F-16D-50 Fighting Falcon	THK 151 Filo/5 AJÜ, Merzifon	
93-0695	TUSAS (GD) F-16D-50 Fighting Falcon	THK 193 Filo/9 AJÜ, Balikesir	
93-0696	TUSAS (GD) F-16D-50 Fighting Falcon	THK 151 Filo/5 AJÜ, Merzifon	
94-0071	TUSAS (GD) F-16C-50 Fighting Falcon	THK 193 Filo/9 AJÜ, Balikesir	
94-0072	TUSAS (GD) F-16C-50 Fighting Falcon	THK 151 Filo/5 AJÜ, Merzifon	
94-0073	TUSAS (GD) F-16C-50 Fighting Falcon	THK 151 Filo/5 AJÜ, Merzifon	
94-0074	TUSAS (GD) F-16C-50 Fighting Falcon	THK 193 Filo/9 AJÜ, Balikesir	
94-0075	TUSAS (GD) F-16C-50 Fighting Falcon	THK 151 Filo/5 AJÜ, Merzifon	
94-0076	TUSAS (GD) F-16C-50 Fighting Falcon	THK 151 Filo/5 AJÜ, Merzifon	
94-0077	TUSAS (GD) F-16C-50 Fighting Falcon	THK 193 Filo/9 AJÜ, Balikesir	
94-0078	TUSAS (GD) F-16C-50 Fighting Falcon	THK 113 Filo/1 AJÜ, Eskisehir	
94-0080	TUSAS (GD) F-16C-50 Fighting Falcon	THK 193 Filo/9 AJÜ, Balikesir	
94-0082	TUSAS (GD) F-16C-50 Fighting Falcon	THK 151 Filo/5 AJÜ, Merzifon	
94-0083	TUSAS (GD) F-16C-50 Fighting Falcon	THK 193 Filo/9 AJÜ, Balikesir	
94-0084	TUSAS (GD) F-16C-50 Fighting Falcon	THK	
94-0085	TUSAS (GD) F-16C-50 Fighting Falcon	THK 192 Filo/9 AJÜ, Balikesir	
94-0086	TUSAS (GD) F-16C-50 Fighting Falcon	THK 193 Filo/9 AJÜ, Balikesir	
94-0088	TUSAS (GD) F-16C-50 Fighting Falcon	THK 151 Filo/5 AJÜ, Merzifon	
94-0089	TUSAS (GD) F-16C-50 Fighting Falcon	THK 151 Filo/5 AJÜ, Merzifon	
94-0090	TUSAS (GD) F-16C-50 Fighting Falcon $	THK 192 Filo/9 AJÜ, Balikesir	
94-0091	TUSAS (GD) F-16C-50 Fighting Falcon	THK 132 Filo/3 AJEÜ, Konya	
94-0092	TUSAS (GD) F-16C-50 Fighting Falcon	THK 132 Filo/3 AJEÜ, Konya	
94-0093	TUSAS (GD) F-16C-50 Fighting Falcon	THK 113 Filo/1 AJÜ, Eskisehir	
94-0094	TUSAS (GD) F-16C-50 Fighting Falcon	THK	

Notes	Serial	Type (code/other identity)	Owner/operator, location or fate
	94-0095	TUSAS (GD) F-16C-50 Fighting Falcon	THK 192 Filo/9 AJÜ, Balikesir
	94-0096	TUSAS (GD) F-16C-50 Fighting Falcon	THK 193 Filo/9 AJÜ, Balikesir
	94-0105	TUSAS (GD) F-16D-50 Fighting Falcon	THK
	94-0106	TUSAS (GD) F-16D-50 Fighting Falcon	THK 401 Filo/1 AJÜ, Eskisehir
	94-0108	TUSAS (GD) F-16D-50 Fighting Falcon	THK 192 Filo/9 AJÜ, Balikesir
	94-0109	TUSAS (GD) F-16D-50 Fighting Falcon	THK 193 Filo/9 AJÜ, Balikesir
	94-0110	TUSAS (GD) F-16D-50 Fighting Falcon	THK 191 Filo/9 AJÜ, Balikesir
	94-1557	TUSAS (GD) F-16D-50 Fighting Falcon	THK 192 Filo/9 AJÜ, Balikesir
	94-1558	TUSAS (GD) F-16D-50 Fighting Falcon	THK 132 Filo/3 AJEÜ, Konya
	94-1559	TUSAS (GD) F-16D-50 Fighting Falcon	THK 152 Filo/10 TÜK, Incirlik
	94-1560	TUSAS (GD) F-16D-50 Fighting Falcon	THK 113 Filo/1 AJÜ, Eskisehir
	94-1561	TUSAS (GD) F-16D-50 Fighting Falcon	THK 193 Filo/9 AJÜ, Balikesir
	94-1562	TUSAS (GD) F-16D-50 Fighting Falcon	THK 193 Filo/9 AJÜ, Balikesir
	94-1563	TUSAS (GD) F-16D-50 Fighting Falcon	THK 193 Filo/9 AJÜ, Balikesir
	94-1564	TUSAS (GD) F-16D-50 Fighting Falcon	THK 193 Filo/9 AJÜ, Balikesir
	07-1001	TUSAS (GD) F-16C-50 Fighting Falcon	THK 161 Filo/6 AJÜ, Bandirma
	07-1002	TUSAS (GD) F-16C-50 Fighting Falcon	THK 181 Filo/8 AJÜ, Diyarbakir
	07-1003	TUSAS (GD) F-16C-50 Fighting Falcon	THK 181 Filo/8 AJÜ, Diyarbakir
	07-1004	TUSAS (GD) F-16C-50 Fighting Falcon	THK 161 Filo/6 AJÜ, Bandirma
	07-1005	TUSAS (GD) F-16C-50 Fighting Falcon	THK 181 Filo/8 AJÜ, Diyarbakir
	07-1006	TUSAS (GD) F-16C-50 Fighting Falcon	THK 161 Filo/6 AJÜ, Bandirma
	07-1007	TUSAS (GD) F-16C-50 Fighting Falcon	THK 161 Filo/6 AJÜ, Bandirma
	07-1008	TUSAS (GD) F-16C-50 Fighting Falcon	THK
	07-1009	TUSAS (GD) F-16C-50 Fighting Falcon	THK 152 Filo/10 TÜK, Incirlik
	07-1010	TUSAS (GD) F-16C-50 Fighting Falcon	THK 152 Filo/10 TÜK, Incirlik
	07-1011	TUSAS (GD) F-16C-50 Fighting Falcon	THK 181 Filo/8 AJÜ, Diyarbakir
	07-1012	TUSAS (GD) F-16C-50 Fighting Falcon	THK 161 Filo/6 AJÜ, Bandirma
	07-1013	TUSAS (GD) F-16C-50 Fighting Falcon	THK 181 Filo/8 AJÜ, Diyarbakir
	07-1014	TUSAS (GD) F-16C-50 Fighting Falcon	THK 161 Filo/6 AJÜ, Bandirma
	07-1015	TUSAS (GD) F-16D-50 Fighting Falcon	THK 161 Filo/6 AJÜ, Bandirma
	07-1016	TUSAS (GD) F-16D-50 Fighting Falcon	THK 181 Filo/8 AJÜ, Diyarbakir
	07-1017	TUSAS (GD) F-16D-50 Fighting Falcon	THK 181 Filo/8 AJÜ, Diyarbakir
	07-1018	TUSAS (GD) F-16D-50 Fighting Falcon	THK 161 Filo/6 AJÜ, Bandirma
	07-1019	TUSAS (GD) F-16D-50 Fighting Falcon	THK 161 Filo/6 AJÜ, Bandirma
	07-1020	TUSAS (GD) F-16D-50 Fighting Falcon	THK 181 Filo/8 AJÜ, Diyarbakir
	07-1021	TUSAS (GD) F-16D-50 Fighting Falcon	THK 181 Filo/8 AJÜ, Diyarbakir
	07-1022	TUSAS (GD) F-16D-50 Fighting Falcon	THK 161 Filo/6 AJÜ, Bandirma
	07-1023	TUSAS (GD) F-16D-50 Fighting Falcon	THK 161 Filo/6 AJÜ, Bandirma
	07-1024	TUSAS (GD) F-16D-50 Fighting Falcon	THK 181 Filo/8 AJÜ, Diyarbakir
	07-1025	TUSAS (GD) F-16D-50 Fighting Falcon	THK 181 Filo/8 AJÜ, Diyarbakir
	07-1026	TUSAS (GD) F-16D-50 Fighting Falcon	THK 181 Filo/8 AJÜ, Diyarbakir
	07-1027	TUSAS (GD) F-16D-50 Fighting Falcon	THK 161 Filo/6 AJÜ, Bandirma
	07-1028	TUSAS (GD) F-16D-50 Fighting Falcon	THK 161 Filo/6 AJÜ, Bandirma
	07-1029	TUSAS (GD) F-16D-50 Fighting Falcon	THK 161 Filo/6 AJÜ, Bandirma
	07-1030	TUSAS (GD) F-16D-50 Fighting Falcon	THK 181 Filo/8 AJÜ, Diyarbakir
	09-001	Gulfstream Aerospace G.550	THK 212 Filo/11 HUAÜK, Ankara/Etimesgut
	13-001	Boeing 737-7FS AEW&C (E-7T)	THK 131 Filo/3 AJEÜ, Konya
	13-002	Boeing 737-7FS AEW&C (E-7T)	THK 131 Filo/3 AJEÜ, Konya
	13-003	Boeing 737-7FS AEW&C (E-7T)	THK 131 Filo/3 AJEÜ, Konya
	13-0009	Airbus Military A.400M	THK 221 Filo/12 HUAÜ, Erkilet
	13-004	Boeing 737-7FS AEW&C (E-7T)	THK 131 Filo/3 AJEÜ, Konya
	14-0013	Airbus Military A.400M	THK 221 Filo/12 HUAÜ, Erkilet
	14-0028	Airbus Military A.400M	THK 221 Filo/12 HUAÜ, Erkilet
	15-0051	Airbus Military A.400M	THK 221 Filo/12 HUAÜ, Erkilet
	16-0055	Airbus Military A.400M	THK 221 Filo/12 HUAÜ, Erkilet
	17-0078	Airbus Military A.400M	THK 221 Filo/12 HUAÜ, Erkilet
	17-0080	Airbus Military A.400M	THK 221 Filo/12 HUAÜ, Erkilet
	18-0093	Airbus Military A.400M (17-0095)	THK 221 Filo/12 HUAÜ, Erkilet
	18-0094	Airbus Military A.400M (17-0096)	THK 221 Filo/12 HUAÜ, Erkilet
	21-0118	Airbus Military A.400M	THK 221 Filo/12 HUAÜ, Erkilet
	......	Bombardier Global 6000 (TC-SJA)	TAI, Akinci (ELINT conversion for THK)
	......	Bombardier Global 6000 (TC-SJB)	TAI, Akinci (ELINT conversion for THK)

Serial	Type (code/other identity)	Owner/operator, location or fate	Notes
......	Bombardier Global 6000 (TC-SJC)	TAI, Akinci (ELINT conversion for THK)	
......	Bombardier Global 6000 (TC-SJD)	TAI, Akinci (ELINT conversion for THK)	
TC-ANK	Airbus A.318-112 (VQ-BDD)	Turkish Government, Istanbul/Sabiha Gokcen	
TC-ATA	Gulfstream Aerospace G.550	Turkish Government, Ankara	
TC-CAN	Airbus A.340-541 (TC-TRK)	Turkish Government, Istanbul/ Sabiha Gokcen	
TC-CBK	Gulfstream Aerospace G.550	THK 212 Filo/11 HUAÜK, Ankara/Etimesgut	
TC-DAP	Gulfstream Aerospace G.550	Turkish Government, Ankara	
TC-GVA	Grumman G.1159C Gulfstream IV (TC-ATA/91-002)	*Sold to civil, 2022*	
TC-GVB	Gulfstream Aerospace G.450 (TC-GAP)	*Sold to civil, 2022*	
TC-IST	Airbus A.319CJ-133	Turkish Government, Istanbul/Sabiha Gokcen	
TC-TRK	Boeing 747-8ZV (VQ-BSK)	Turkish Government, Istanbul/Sabiha Gokcen	
TC-TUR	Airbus A.330-243	Turkish Government, Istanbul/Sabiha Gokcen	

TURKMENISTAN

Serial	Type (code/other identity)	Owner/operator, location or fate	Notes
EZ-A007	Boeing 737-7GL (N1786B)	Government of Turkmenistan, Ashgabat	
EZ-A700	Boeing 737-700 (BBJ) (N6065Y)	Government of Turkmenistan, Ashgabat	
EZ-A777	Boeing 777-22KLR	Government of Turkmenistan, Ashgabat	
EZ-B021	BAe 1000B	Government of Turkmenistan, Ashgabat	
EZ-B022	Canadair Challenger 605	Government of Turkmenistan, Ashgabat	
EZ-B023	Canadair Challenger 605	Government of Turkmenistan, Ashgabat	
EZ-B024	Canadair Challenger 870CS	Government of Turkmenistan, Ashgabat	

UGANDA

Serial	Type (code/other identity)	Owner/operator, location or fate	Notes
5X-UGF	Gulfstream Aerospace G.550	Government of Uganda, Entebbe	

UKRAINE
Ukrainian Air Force
NOTE: Due to the ongoing conflict in Ukraine, it is not currently possible to verify the continued status of the Air Force aircraft, so these have been omitted until the picture becomes clearer.
Government of Ukraine

Serial	Type (code/other identity)	Owner/operator, location or fate	Notes
UR-ABA	Airbus A.319CJ-115X	Government of Ukraine, Katowice, Poland	

UNITED ARAB EMIRATES
United Arab Emirates Air Force (UAEAF)

Serial	Type (code/other identity)	Owner/operator, location or fate	Notes
311	Lockheed L.100-30 Hercules (A6-QFY)	UAEAF 4 Sqn/Transport Wing, Abu Dhabi	
312	Lockheed C-130H-30 Hercules	UAEAF 4 Sqn/Transport Wing, Abu Dhabi	
430	Aermacchi MB339NAT	UAEAF *Al Fursan*, Dubai/Minhad	
431	Aermacchi MB339NAT	UAEAF *Al Fursan*, Dubai/Minhad	
432	Aermacchi MB339NAT	UAEAF *Al Fursan*, Dubai/Minhad	
433	Aermacchi MB339NAT	UAEAF *Al Fursan*, Dubai/Minhad	
434	Aermacchi MB339NAT	UAEAF *Al Fursan*, Dubai/Minhad	
435	Aermacchi MB339NAT	UAEAF *Al Fursan*, Dubai/Minhad	
436	Aermacchi MB339NAT	UAEAF *Al Fursan*, Dubai/Minhad	
437	Aermacchi MB339NAT	UAEAF *Al Fursan*, Dubai/Minhad	
438	Aermacchi MB339NAT	UAEAF *Al Fursan*, Dubai/Minhad	
439	Aermacchi MB339NAT	UAEAF *Al Fursan*, Dubai/Minhad	
440	Aermacchi MB339NAT	UAEAF *Al Fursan*, Dubai/Minhad	
441	Aermacchi MB339NAT	UAEAF *Al Fursan*, Dubai/Minhad	
442	Aermacchi MB339NAT	UAEAF *Al Fursan*, Dubai/Minhad	
1211	Lockheed C-130H Hercules	UAEAF 4 Sqn/Transport Wing, Abu Dhabi	
1213	Lockheed C-130H Hercules	UAEAF 4 Sqn/Transport Wing, Abu Dhabi	
1214	Lockheed C-130H Hercules	UAEAF 4 Sqn/Transport Wing, Abu Dhabi	
1215	Lockheed L.100-30 Hercules	UAEAF 4 Sqn/Transport Wing, Abu Dhabi	
1216	Lockheed L.100-30 Hercules	UAEAF 4 Sqn/Transport Wing, Abu Dhabi	
1217	Lockheed L.100-30 Hercules	UAEAF 4 Sqn/Transport Wing, Abu Dhabi	
1223	Boeing C-17A Globemaster III (10-0401)	UAEAF Heavy Transport Sqn, Abu Dhabi	
1224	Boeing C-17A Globemaster III (10-0402)	UAEAF Heavy Transport Sqn, Abu Dhabi	
1225	Boeing C-17A Globemaster III (10-0403)	UAEAF Heavy Transport Sqn, Abu Dhabi	
1226	Boeing C-17A Globemaster III (10-0404)	UAEAF Heavy Transport Sqn, Abu Dhabi	
1227	Boeing C-17A Globemaster III (10-0405)	UAEAF Heavy Transport Sqn, Abu Dhabi	
1228	Boeing C-17A Globemaster III (10-0406)	UAEAF Heavy Transport Sqn, Abu Dhabi	
1229	Boeing C-17A Globemaster III (14-0007)	UAEAF Heavy Transport Sqn, Abu Dhabi	

Notes	Serial	Type (code/other identity)	Owner/operator, location or fate
	1230	Boeing C-17A Globemaster III (14-0008)	UAEAF Heavy Transport Sqn, Abu Dhabi
	1300	Airbus A.330-243 MRTT (EC-339)	UAEAF MRTT Sqn, Al Ain
	1301	Airbus A.330-243 MRTT (EC-334)	UAEAF MRTT Sqn, Al Ain
	1302	Airbus A.330-243 MRTT (EC-332)	UAEAF MRTT Sqn, Al Ain
	1303	Airbus A.330-243 MRTT (EC-345)	UAEAF (on order)
	1304	Airbus A.330-243 MRTT	UAEAF (on order)
	1305	Airbus A.330-243 MRTT	UAEAF (on order)
	1325	Bombardier Global 6000	UAEAF, Dubai/Minhad
	1326	Bombardier Global 6000	UAEAF, Dubai/Minhad
	1340	Bombardier Global 6000	UAEAF, Dubai/Minhad
	1341	Bombardier Global 6000	UAEAF, Dubai/Minhad
	1342	Bombardier Global 6000	UAEAF, Dubai/Minhad
	13..	Bombardier Global 6500	UAEAF (on order)
	1350	Bombardier Challenger 650 (T7-AQL)	UAEAF
	1351	Bombardier Challenger 650 (T7-AQA)	UAEAF
	2012	AgustaWestland AW.139	UAEAF, Stansted, UK (Summer)
	2013	AgustaWestland AW.139	UAEAF, Stansted, UK (Summer)
UAE Government			
	A6-ALN	Boeing 777-2ANER	Amiri Flight, Abu Dhabi
	A6-AUH	Boeing 737-8EX	Amiri Flight, Abu Dhabi
	A6-COM	Boeing 747-433	Dubai Air Wing
	A6-DAW	Boeing 747-48E	*Sold to Air Atlanta, 2022*
	A6-DFR	Boeing 737-7BC	*Sold to Royal Jet, 2022*
	A6-DLM	Airbus A.320-232	Amiri Flight, Abu Dhabi
	A6-ESH	Airbus A.319-113X	*Sold to USA, 2022*
	A6-FZZ	Boeing 737-8KN	Dubai Air Wing
	A6-GGP	Boeing 747-412F	Dubai Air Wing
	A6-HEH	Boeing 737-8AJ	Dubai Air Wing
	A6-HHH	Grumman G.1159C Gulfstream IV	Stored Stuttgart, Germany
	A6-HMM	Gulfstream Aerospace G.650ER (A6-HHH)	Dubai Air Wing
	A6-HMS	Airbus A.320-232	Dubai Air Wing
	A6-HRM	Boeing 747-422	Dubai Air Wing
	A6-HRS	Boeing 737-7F0	Dubai Air Wing
	A6-MMM	Boeing 747-422	Dubai Air Wing
	A6-MRM	Boeing 737-8EC	Dubai Air Wing
	A6-MRS	Boeing 737-8EO	Dubai Air Wing
	A6-PFC	Boeing 787-8	Amiri Flight, Abu Dhabi
	A6-PFE	Boeing 787-9	Amiri Flight, Abu Dhabi
	A6-PFG	Boeing 787-9	Amiri Flight, Abu Dhabi
	A6-PFH	Boeing 787-9	Amiri Flight, Abu Dhabi
	A6-RJ1	BAE RJ.85	*Sold to Iran, 2021*
	A6-RJ2	BAE RJ.85	*Sold to Iran, 2021*
	A6-SHJ	Airbus A.320-232X	Ruler of Sharjah Air Wing
	A6-SIL	Boeing 777-35RER	Amiri Flight, Abu Dhabi
	A6-YST	Boeing 737-8SA	Dubai Air Wing
	P4-HHH	Boeing 777-29MLR	Dubai Air Wing
UZBEKISTAN			
	UK-001	Boeing 787-8	Government of Uzbekistan, Tashkent

This section lists the codes worn by some overseas air forces and, alongside, the serial of the aircraft currently wearing this code. This list will be updated occasionally and those with Internet access can download the latest version via the 'Military Aircraft Markings' Web Site, www.militaryaircraftmarkings.co.uk and via the Military Aircraft Markings Group, MilitaryAircraftMarkings@Groups.io.

FRANCE
FRENCH AIR FORCE

Code	Serial	Code	Serial	Code	Serial	Code	Serial
D-BD Alpha Jet		705-AO	E112	3-IG	668	115-KD	123
0 [PDF]	E73	705-RB	E163	3-IH	631	115-KN	121
1 [PDF]	E48	705-RH	E94	3-IJ	638	115-LC	108
2 [PDF]	E20	705-RR	E114	3-IL	622	115-LJ	105
3 [PDF]	E119	705-RW	E166	3-IN	640	115-OA	524
4 [PDF]	E45	705-RY	E170	3-IO	647	115-OC	529
5 [PDF]	E129	705-RZ	E171	3-IP	604	115-OR	527
6 [PDF]	E35	705-TB	E67	3-IQ	666	115-YC	83
7 [PDF]	E105	705-TM	E128	3-IR	674	115-YD	107
8 [PDF]	E87	F-TELC	E87	3-IS	617	115-YE	122
9 [PDF]	E81	F-TELP	E129	3-IT	624	115-YG	118
8-AF	E108	F-TEMF	E98	3-IU	620	115-YH	109
8-AG	E109	F-TEMH	E48	3-IV	683	115-YO	113
8-AK	E144	F-TEMS	E20	3-JC	606	115-YT	124
8-AL	E154	F-TENE	E73	3-JD	643	133-IW	664
8-FD	E151	F-TETD	E113	3-JF	660	133-JE	634
8-FJ	E33	F-TETF	E45	3-JG	601	133-LF	605
8-FN	E116	F-UGFC	E139	3-JH	686	133-XX	610
8-FP	E168	F-UGFE	E119	3-JI	675	188-ED	62
8-LH	E38	F-UGFM	E105	3-JJ	639	188-EE	71
8-LL	E88	F-UGFO	E81	3-JL	628	188-EL	58
8-LM	E102	F-UHRE	E44	3-JM	657	188-ET	57
8-LN	E118	F-UHRT	E152	3-JN	658	188-EW	48
8-LO	E142	F-UHRX	E169	3-JO	627	188-EZ	54
8-LS	E22			3-JP	611	188-MK	74
8-LT	E147	**Dassault Mirage 2000**		3-JR	682		
8-LU	E148	2-AX	77	3-JT	677	**Dassault Rafale**	
8-LW	E82	2-EA	49	3-JU	614	4-EA	303
8-MA	E173	2-EC	78	3-JV	636	4-FF	339
8-MB	E176	2-ED	62	3-JW	641	4-FG	340
8-MO	E68	2-EF	45	3-JX	679	4-FH	341
8-MR	E115	2-EG	56	3-JY	615	4-FI	342
8-NA	E79	2-EH	52	3-KJ	523	4-FJ	343
8-NF	E141	2-EI	38	3-KS	528	4-FK	344
8-RF	E46	2-EL	58	3-LH	655	4-FL	345
8-RI	E117	2-EM	63	3-MO	613	4-FM	346
8-RJ	E162	2-EN	46	3-MQ	646	4-FN	347
8-RM	E123	2-EO	66	3-OL	530	4-FP	349
8-RN	E124	2-EP	47	3-XA	662	4-FQ	350
8-RO	E131	2-EQ	44	3-XC	618	4-FR	351
8-RP	E130	2-ET	57	3-XD	630	4-FS	352
8-RQ	E138	2-EU	55	3-XE	632	4-FT	353
8-RV	E164	2-EV	59	3-XF	670	4-FU	354
8-TA	E42	2-EX	40	3-XG	625	4-FV	355
8-TH	E90	2-EY	42	3-XI	661	4-FW	356
8-TJ	E25	2-FZ	41	3-XJ	602	4-FX	357
8-TM	E128	2-ME	61	3-XK	671	4-FY	358
8-TX	E93	2-MG	65	3-XL	603	4-GO	136
8-TZ	E83	2-MH	67	3-XM	680	4-GR	139
8-UB	E11	3-AG	681	3-XN	652	4-GS	140
8-UC	E157	3-AM	525	3-XO	629	4-GZ	147
8-UD	E107	3-AS	635	3-XP	645	4-HA	308
8-UH	E160	3-AU	653	3-XR	659	4-HC	310
102-FI	E32	3-IA	650	3-XT	648	4-HD	311
102-LI	E53	3-IC	626	3-XV	672	4-HF	312
102-NB	E29	3-ID	654	3-XY	649	4-HI	313
		3-IE	642	3-XZ	685	4-HK	315
		3-IF	609	115-KC	120	4-HM	318

Code	No.		Code	No.		Code	No.		Code	No.		Code	No.
4-HN	319		113-HJ	107		DBJ	1510		GBW	4142
4-HO	317					DBK	1512		GBX	4144
4-HP	314		**Pilatus PC-21**			DBL	1519		GBY	4145
4-HQ	321		(NB: These codes do not have			DBM	1617		GCC	4160
4-HT	323		hyphens)			DBN	1632		GCD	4161
4-HU	322		709 FC	01		DBO	1634		GCE	4162
4-HV	320		709 FD	02		DBP	1654		GCF	4164
4-HX	325		709 FE	03		DBQ	1663		GCG	4168
4-HY	326		709 FF	04		DBR	5682		GCI	4175
4-HZ	327		709 FG	05		DCE	1071		GCJ	4179
4-IA	307		709 FH	06		DCF	1073		GCK	4180
4-IC	328		709 FI	07		DDD	1198		GCL	4181
4-IE	330		709 FJ	08		DDG	1222		GCM	4186
4-IF	331		709 FK	09		DDK	1231		GCN	4189
4-IG	332		709 FL	10		DDM	1236		GCO	4191
4-IH	333		709 FM	11		DDP	1252		GCP	4195
4-II	334		709 FN	12		DDT	1269		GCQ	4198
4-IJ	335		709 FO	13		DDW	1447		GEA	4205
4-IK	336		709 FP	14		DDX	1662		GEB	4206
4-IL	337		709 FQ	15					GEC	4207
4-IO	338		709 FR	16		**SA.342 Gazelle**			GED	4208
7-GI	130		709 FS	17		GAA	3459		GEF	4210
7-GK	132		709-GA	18		GAC	3512		GEG	4211
7-GP	137		709-GB	19		GAD	3530		GEI	4214
7-GQ	138		709-GC	20		GAF	3664		GEJ	4215
7-VA	148		709-GD	21		GAG	3848		GEK	4216
30-EB	304		709-GE	22		GAH	3849		GEL	4217
30-EF	102		709-GF	23		GAI	3850		GEM	4218
30-GA	122		709-GG	24 (on order)		GAJ	3856		GEN	4219
30-GC	124		709-GH	25 (on order)		GAK	3859		GEO	4220
30-GD	125		709-GI	26 (on order)		GAL	3862		GEP	4221
30-GE	126					GAM	3863		GEQ	4222
30-GF	127		**FRENCH ARMY**			GAN	3865		GER	4223
30-GG	128		**SA.330 Puma**			GAO	3868		GES	4224
30-GH	129		DAA	1006		GAP	3911		GET	4225
30-GJ	131		DAC	1036		GAQ	3921		GEU	4226
30-GL	133		DAD	1037		GAR	3938		GEV	4227
30-GM	134		DAE	1049		GAS	3947		GEW	4228
30-GN	135		DAF	1055		GAT	3948		GEX	4229
30-GT	141		DAG	1069		GAU	3957		GEY	4230
30-GU	142		DAH	1078		GAV	3964		GFA	4232
30-GV	143		DAI	1092		GAW	3996		GFB	4233
30-GW	144		DAJ	1100		GAX	4018		GJC	3511
30-GX	145		DAK	1102		GBA	4026		GMA	3567
30-GY	146		DAL	1107		GBB	4034		GMB	4042
30-HB	309		DAM	1109		GBC	4039		GMC	4079
30-HE	105		DAN	1128		GBE	4053		GND	3617
30-HG	106		DAO	1143		GBF	4059		GNS	4071
30-HH	104		DAP	1149		GBG	4061			
30-HS	108		DAQ	1156		GBH	4066		**AS.532UL/EC.725AP Cougar**	
30-HW	324		DAR	1173		GBI	4072		CAA	2611
30-ID	329		DAS	1176		GBJ	4084		CAB	2628
30-IM	109		DAW	1211		GBL	4095		CAC	2630
30-IN	110		DAX	1214		GBN	4109		CAD	2631
30-IR	113		DAY	1217		GBO	4114		CAE	2633
30-IS	114		DAZ	1219		GBP	4115		CAF	2638
30-IT	115		DBA	1232		GBQ	4119		CAG	2640
30-IU	116		DBB	1243		GBR	4120		CAH	2642
30-IV	117		DBF	1417		GBS	4124		CGA	2252
30-IX	119		DBG	1438		GBT	4136		CGB	2266
30-IY	120		DBH	1451		GBU	4140		CGC	2267
30-IZ	121		DBI	1507		GBV	4141		CGD	2271

CGF	2273
CGG	2282
CGH	2285
CGI	2290
CGJ	2292
CGK	2299
CGL	2300
CGM	2301
CGN	2303
CGO	2316
CGQ	2323
CGR	2324
CGS	2325
CGT	2327
CGU	2331
CGW	2443
CGX	2446
CHA	2342
CHB	2369
CHC	2375

EC.665 Tigre

BHA	2010
BHB	2009
BHC	2013
BHD	2015
BHE	2018
BHF	2019
BHG	2022
BHH	2001
BHI	2002
BHJ	2003
BHK	2004
BHL	2006
BHM	2011
BHN	2021
BHO	2024
BHP	2023
BHQ	2025
BHR	2026
BHS	2027
BHT	2012
BHV	2029
BHW	2030
BHX	2031
BHZ	2033
BIA	2016
BIB	2034
BIC	2035
BIE	2037
BIF	2038
BIG	2039
BIH	2040
BII	2041
BIJ	2042
BIK	2043
BIL	2044
BIM	2045
BIN	2046
BIO	2047
BJA	6001
BJB	6002

BJC	6003
BJD	6004
BJE	6005
BJF	6006
BJG	6007
BJH	6008
BJI	6009
BJJ	6010
BJK	6011
BJL	6012
BJM	6013
BJN	6014
BJO	6015
BJP	6016
BJR	6018
BJS	6019
BJT	6020
BJU	6021
BJV	6022
BJW	6023
BJX	6024
BJY	6025
BJZ	6026
BKA	6027
BKB	6028
BKC	6029
BKD	6030
BKE	6031

NH.90-TTH

EAA	1239
EAB	1256
EAC	1271
EAD	1273
EAE	1290
EAF	1291
EAG	1292
EAH	1293
EAI	1294
EAJ	1295
EAK	1306
EAL	1307
EAM	1308
EAN	1309
EAO	1310
EAP	1311
EAQ	1312
EAR	1313
EAS	1332
EAT	1333
EAU	1334
EAV	1335
EAW	1336
EAX	1337
EAY	1338
EAZ	1386
EBA	1390
EBB	1391
EBC	1387
EBD	1392
EBE	1401
EBF	1402

EBG	1403
EBH	1404
EBI	1405
EBJ	1432
EBK	1427
EBL	1428
EBM	1429
EBN	1433
EBO	1430
EBP	1431
EBQ	1442
EBR	1441
EBS	1443
EBT	1454
EBU	1455
EBV	1456
EBW	1457
EBX	1458
EBY	1479
EBZ	1480
ECA	1481 (on order)
ECB	1482 (on order)
ECC	1483 (on order)
ECD	1484 (on order)
ECF	1496 (on order)

ITALY

Aeritalia-EMB AMX

32-10	MM7160
32-15	MM7129
32-16	MM7165
32-51	MM55036
32-53	MM55047
32-56	MM55042
32-60	MM55046
51-26	MM7149
51-27	MM7114
51-30	MM7170
51-31	MM7161
51-32	MM7166
51-33	MM7162
51-34	MM7191
51-35	MM7196
51-36	MM7185
51-40	MM7164
51-41	MM7183
51-42	MM7177
51-43	MM7178
51-44	MM7198
51-45	MM7175
51-46	MM7197
51-47	MM7176
51-50	MM7186
51-52	MM7171
51-53	MM7180
51-55	MM7168
51-56	MM7167
51-57	MM7190
51-60	MM7174
51-61	MM7126
51-62	MM7182
51-65	MM7184

51-66	MM7169
51-67	MM7172
51-70	MM7192
51-71	MM7189
51-72	MM7163
51-80	MM55037
51-81	MM55043
51-82	MM55044
51-83	MM55049
51-84	MM55051
RS-20	MM55034

Aermacchi MB339

0 [FT]	MM54510
1 [FT]	MM55053
2 [FT]	MM55058
3 [FT]	MM54518
4 [FT]	MM54534
5 [FT]	MM55059
6 [FT]	MM55052
7 [FT]	MM54538
8 [FT]	MM54482
9 [FT]	MM54551
10 [FT]	MM54510
32-161	MM55089
36-06	MM55074
61-10	MM54456
61-11	MM54457
61-32	MM54488
61-36	MM54492
61-37	MM54493
61-42	MM54496
61-45	MM54499
61-52	MM54504
61-55	MM54507
61-57	MM54509
61-60	MM54510
61-61	MM54511
61-62	MM54512
61-65	MM54515
61-66	MM54516
61-72	MM54533
61-74	MM54535
61-106	MM54548
61-107	MM54549
61-116	MM54465
61-121	MM54458
61-126	MM55062
61-127	MM55063
61-130	MM55064
61-132	MM55066
61-133	MM55067
61-135	MM55069
61-136	MM55070
61-140	MM55072
61-141	MM55073
61-143	MM55075
61-145	MM55077
61-146	MM55078
61-147	MM55079
61-150	MM55080
61-151	MM55081

61-152	MM55082	4-25	MM55092	51-01	MM7298	6-41	MM7067
61-154	MM55084	4-30	MM55096	51-02	MM7320	6-42	MM55010
61-155	MM55085	4-31	MM55093	51-04	MM7319	6-43	MM7066
61-156	MM55086	4-32	MM55129	51-05	MM7290	6-44	MM55009
61-157	MM55087	4-33	MM55130	51-06	MM7356	6-45	MM55008
61-160	MM55088	4-34	MM55131	51-11	MM7307	6-50	MM7024
61-161	MM55089	4-41	MM7299	51-12	MM7339	6-52	MM55002
61-162	MM55090	4-42	MM7316	51-14	MM7311	6-53	MM55004
61-241	MM54468	4-43	MM7317	51-15	MM7295	6-55	MM7004
RS-32	MM55091	4-44	MM7300	51-22	MM55132	6-56	MM55007
RS-33	MM55068	4-46	MM7326	RS-22	MM7350	6-57	MM7081
		4-50	MM7306			6-60	MM7086
Aermacchi T-345A		4-52	MM7294	**Lockheed Martin F-35A/**		6-61	MM7047
61-202	MM55234	4-56	MM7330	**F-35B Lightning II**		6-62	MM7082
61-203	MM55235	4-57	MM7238	4-01	MM7451	6-63	MM7023
61-204	MM55236	4-58	MM7329	4-02	MM7452	6-64	MM7052
61-205	MM55237	4-60	MM7338	4-03	MM7454	6-65	MM7055
		4-61	MM7353	4-04	MM7456	6-66	MM7059
Aermacchi T-346A Master		4-62	MM7344	6-01	MM7366	6-67	MM7068
61-01	MM55154	4-64	MM7340	32-01	MM7332	6-71	MM7070
61-02	MM55144	4-66	MM7355	32-02	MM7333	6-72	MM7051
61-03	MM55145	4-67	MM7341	32-03	MM7334	6-73	MM7030
61-04	MM55155	4-68	MM7342	32-04	MM7335	6-74	MM7062
61-05	MM55153	36-03	MM7281	32-05	MM7336	6-75	MM7013
61-06	MM55213	36-05	MM7276	32-06	MM7363	6-76	MM7044
61-07	MM55214	36-07	MM7279	32-07	MM7357	6-77	MM7020
61-10	MM55215	36-10	MM7302	32-08	MM7358	6-100	MM7054
61-11	MM55152	36-14	MM7277	32-09	MM7359	6-101	MM7053
61-12	MM55216	36-15	MM7284	32-10	MM7360	36-50	CSX7085
61-13	MM55217	36-22	MM7296	32-11	MM7361	50-50	MM7034
61-14	MM55218	36-23	MM7297	32-12	MM7362	50-53	MM7008
61-15	MM55221	36-30	MM7280	32-13	MM7337	RS-01	CSX7079
61-16	MM55220	36-31	MM7308	32-14	MM7453	RS-05	CSX7047
61-20	MM55219	36-32	MM7310	32-15	MM7364		
61-21	MM55222	36-34	MM7312	32-16	MM7365	**SPAIN**	
61-22	MM55223	36-40	MM7322			**Airtech CN.235**	
61-23	MM55224	36-41	MM7324	**Panavia Tornado**		37-02	D.4-02
61-24	MM55229	36-42	MM7288	6-01	MM7007	37-03	D.4-03
61-25	MM55230	36-43	MM7321	6-02	MM7019	37-06	D.4-06
61-26	MM55231	36-44	MM7325	6-03	MM7084	37-08	D.4-08
61-27	MM55232	36-46	MM7315	6-04	MM7057	74-13	T.19B-13
61-30	MM55239	36-50	MM7343	6-05	MM7025	74-18	T.19B-18
61-31	MM55240	36-53	MM7347	6-06	MM7036	403-01	T.19A-01
61-32	MM55241	36-54	MM7349	6-07	MM7075	403-02	T.19A-02
61-33	MM55242	36-55	MM7352	6-10	MM7088	744-07	T.19B-07
		36-60	MM55094	6-11	MM7058	744-11	T.19B-11
Eurofighter Typhoon		36-64	MM55128	6-12	MM7071	744-16	T.19B-16
4-1	MM7286	37-03	MM7309	6-13	MM7014	744-17	T.19B-17
4-2	MM7303	37-04	MM7304	6-15	MM55006	744-19	T.19B-19
4-3	MM7287	37-05	MM7313	6-20	MM7021	744-20	T.19B-20
4-4	MM7274	37-21	MM7292	6-21	MM7040		
4-5	MM7289	37-22	MM7293	6-22	MM7029	**CASA 101EB Aviojet**	
4-8	MM7282	37-23	MM7323	6-25	MM7043	54-20	E.25-33
4-9	MM7351	37-24	MM7348	6-26	MM7063	54-21	E.25-55
4-10	MM7273	37-27	MM7327	6-27	MM7035	54-22	E.25-61
4-11	MM7291	37-33	MM7314	6-30	MM7072	74-02	E.25-33
4-13	MM7235	37-34	MM55168	6-31	MM7006	74-07	E.25-51
4-15	MM7271	37-35	MM7318	6-32	MM7015	74-09	E.25-53
4-18	MM7272	37-37	MM7346	6-33	MM7039	74-11	E.25-56
4-19	MM7275	37-45	MM7345	6-34	MM7073	74-13	E.25-59
4-23	MM55095	37-47	MM7331	6-35	MM7026	74-17	E.25-63
4-24	MM55097	37-54	MM7354	6-37	MM7038	74-20	E.25-66

74-21	E.25-67	35-03	T.21-03	14-45	C.16-45	15-17	C.15-30
74-25	E.25-71	35-05	T.21-05	14-47	C.16-47	15-18	C.15-31
74-26	E.25-72	35-06	T.21-06	14-48	C.16-48	15-19	C.15-32
74-28	E.25-73	35-07	T.21-07	14-49	C.16-49	15-20	C.15-33
74-30	E.25-76	35-08	T.21-08	14-58	C.16-58	15-22	C.15-35
74-35	E.25-83	35-09	T.21-09	14-60	C.16-60	15-23	C.15-36
74-39	E.25-88	35-11	T.21-11	14-61	C.16-61	15-24	C.15-37
74-40	E.25-17	35-12	T.21-12	14-62	C.16-62	15-25	C.15-38
74-42	E.25-18	35-13	T.21-13	14-64	C.16-64	15-26	C.15-39
74-43	E.25-43	35-42	T.21-04	14-66	C.16-66	15-27	C.15-40
74-44	E.25-34			14-67	C.16-67	15-28	C.15-41
79-02	E.25-78	**Eurofighter Tifón**		14-68	C.16-68	15-30	C.15-43
79-03	E.25-80	11-01	CE.16-01	14-71	C.16-71	15-31	C.15-47
79-04	E.25-84	11-02	C.16-22* &	14-72	C.16-72	15-33	C.15-67
79-05	E.25-05	CE.16-02 [* to be 11-22]		14-74	C.16-74	15-34	C.15-64
79-06	E.25-06	11-04	C.16-24* &	14-75	C.16-75	15-70	CE.15-01
79-08	E.25-08	CE.16-04 [* to be 11-24]		14-77	C.16-77	15-71	CE.15-02
79-11	E.25-11	11-05	CE.16-05	14-78	C.16-78	15-72	CE.15-03
79-12	E.25-12	11-07	CE.16-07			15-73	CE.15-04
79-13	E.25-13	11-09	CE.16-09	**McDonnell-Douglas**		15-74	CE.15-05
79-14	E.25-14	11-10	CE.16-10	**F/A-18A+/EF-18M Hornet**		15-75	CE.15-06
79-15	E.25-15	11-13	CE.16-13	12-01	C.15-13	15-76	CE.15-07
79-17	E.25-62	11-14	CE.16-14	12-02	C.15-44	15-77	CE.15-09
79-21	E.25-21	11-21	C.16-21	12-03	C.15-45	46-01	C.15-73
79-24	E.25-24	11-23	C.16-23	12-04	C.15-46	46-03	C.15-75
79-25	E.25-25	11-25	C.16-25	12-06	C.15-48	46-05	C.15-77
79-26	E.25-26	11-26	C.16-26	12-07	C.15-49	46-07	C.15-79
79-27	E.25-27	11-27	C.16-27	12-08	C.15-50	46-08	C.15-80
79-28	E.25-28	11-28	C.16-28	12-09	C.15-51	46-09	C.15-81
79-29	E.25-87	11-29	C.16-29	12-11	C.15-53	46-10	C.15-82
79-31	E.25-31	11-30	C.16-30	12-12	C.15-54	46-11	C.15-83
79-32	E.25-86	11-32	C.16-32	12-13	C.15-55	46-12	C.15-84
79-35	E.25-54	11-33	C.16-33	12-14	C.15-56	46-13	C.15-85
79-37	E.25-37	11-35	C.16-35	12-15	C.15-57	46-14	C.15-86
79-38	E.25-38	11-38	C.16-38	12-17	C.15-59	46-15	C.15-87
79-39	E.25-79	11-40	C.16-40	12-18	C.15-60	46-16	C.15-88
79-44	E.25-44	11-41	C.16-41	12-19	C.15-61	46-17	C.15-89
79-97	E.25-69	11-42	C.16-42	12-20	C.15-62	46-18	C.15-90
79-98	E.25-73	11-43	C.16-43	12-23	C.15-65	46-20	C.15-92
741-68	E.25-68	11-46	C.16-46	12-24	C.15-66	46-21	C.15-93
793-57	E.25-57	11-51	C.16-51	12-26	C.15-68	46-22	C.15-94
793-81	E.25-81	11-52	C.16-52	12-27	C.15-69	46-23	C.15-95
794-40	E.25-40	11-53	C.16-53	12-28	C.15-70	46-24	C.15-96
794-50	E.25-52	11-54	C.16-54	12-30	C.15-72		
		11-55	C.16-55	12-50	C.15-34	**Pilatus PC-21**	
CASA 212 Aviocar		11-56	C.16-56	12-71	CE.15-08	792-01	E.27-01
47-14	T.12D-75	11-57	C.16-57	12-73	CE.15-10	792-02	E.27-02
54-11	T.12D-74	11-63	C.16-63	12-74	CE.15-11	792-03	E.27-03
72-11	T.12B-65	11-72	CE.16-03	12-75	CE.15-12	792-04	E.27-04
72-12	T.12B-67	11-75	CE.16-06	15-01	C.15-14	792-05	E.27-05
72-13	T.12B-13	11-91	C.16-20	15-02	C.15-15	792-06	E.27-06
72-49	T.12B-49	14-01	C.16-31	15-03	C.15-16	792-07	E.27-07
72-62	T.12B-62	14-03	C.16-36	15-05	C.15-18	792-08	E.27-08
72-63	T.12B-63	14-09	C.16-44	15-08	C.15-21	792-09	E.27-09
72-66	T.12B-66	14-11	CE.16-11	15-09	C.15-22	792-10	E.27-10
72-69	T.12B-69	14-12	CE.16-12	15-10	C.15-23	792-11	E.27-11
72-70	T.12B-70	14-14	C.16-50	15-11	C.15-24	792-12	E.27-12
72-71	T.12B-71	14-28	C.16-70	15-12	C.15-25	792-13	E.27-13
		14-31	C.16-73	15-13	C.15-26	792-14	E.27-14
		14-34	C.16-76	15-14	C.15-27	792-15	E.27-15
CASA C-295M		14-37	C.16-37	15-15	C.15-28	792-16	E.27-16
35-01	T.21-01	14-39	C.16-39	15-16	C.15-29	792-17	E.27-17
35-02	T.21-02						

| 792-18 | E.27-18 | 792-20 | E.27-20 | 792-22 | E.27-22 | 792-24 | E.27-24 |
| 792-19 | E.27-19 | 792-21 | E.27-21 | 792-23 | E.27-23 | | |

France's Rafale is well-established with both the Air Force and the Navy. Navy example 28 is seen here catching the last of the evening sun at RNAS Yeovilton. *SRS*

After much political wrangling, the end of the Tornado IDS in German Air Force service is finally in sight. The NATO B-61 nuclear delivery role will be taken over by the recently ordered F-35As, having previously looked to F-18E/Fs for this task, until that order was recently cancelled. 43+48 is seen recovering into Cambrai Air Base in France after a Tiger Meet mission. *SRS*

All USAF and US Army aircraft have been allocated a fiscal year (FY) number since 1921. Individual aircraft are given a serial according to the fiscal year in which they are ordered. The numbers commence at 0001 and are prefixed with the year of allocation. For example, F-15E Eagle 91-0301 was the 301st aircraft ordered in 1991. The fiscal year (FY) serial is carried on the technical data block which is usually stencilled on the left-hand side of the aircraft just below the cockpit. The number displayed on the fin is a corruption of the FY serial. Most tactical aircraft carry the fiscal year in small figures followed by the last three or four digits of the serial in large figures. Large transport and tanker aircraft such as C-130s and KC-135s sometimes display a five-figure number commencing with the last digit of the appropriate fiscal year and four figures of the production number. An example of this is Boeing KC-135R Stratotanker 58-0128 which displays 80128 on its fin.

US Army serials have been allocated in a similar way to USAF serials although in recent years an additional zero has been added so that all US Army serials now have the two-figure fiscal year part followed by five digits.

USN and USMC serials follow a straightforward numerical sequence which commenced, for the present series, with the allocation of 00001 to an SB2C Helldiver by the Bureau of Aeronautics in 1940. Numbers in the 170000 series are presently being issued. They are usually carried in full on the rear fuselage of the aircraft.

US Coast Guard serials began with the allocation of the serial 1 to a Loening OL-5 in 1927.

UK-BASED USAF AIRCRAFT

The following aircraft are normally based in the UK. They are listed in numerical order of type with individual aircraft in serial number order, as depicted on the aircraft. Where it is possible to identify the allocation of aircraft to individual squadrons by means of colours carried on fin or cockpit edge, this is also provided. Deliveries of F-35As continued apace throughout 2022 and early 2023, with the 495th FS almost at full complement of 24 aircraft now. 2022 also saw the final F-15C and -D retirements from Lakenheath, heralding the end of another era.

Serial	Type (code/other identity)	Owner/operator, location or fate	Notes
McDonnell Douglas F-15E Strike Eagle			
91-0301	McD F-15E Strike Eagle [LN] *bl/w*	USAF 492nd FS/48th FW, RAF Lakenheath	
91-0302	McD F-15E Strike Eagle [LN] *bl/w*	USAF 492nd FS/48th FW, RAF Lakenheath	
91-0303	McD F-15E Strike Eagle [LN] *bl/w*	USAF 492nd FS/48th FW, RAF Lakenheath	
91-0306	McD F-15E Strike Eagle [LN] *bl/w*	USAF 492nd FS/48th FW, RAF Lakenheath	
91-0307	McD F-15E Strike Eagle [LN] *bl/w*	USAF 492nd FS/48th FW, RAF Lakenheath	
91-0308	McD F-15E Strike Eagle [LN] *bl/w*	USAF 492nd FS/48th FW, RAF Lakenheath	
91-0309	McD F-15E Strike Eagle [LN] *r/w*	USAF 494th FS/48th FW, RAF Lakenheath	
91-0310	McD F-15E Strike Eagle [LN] *r/w*	USAF 494th FS/48th FW, RAF Lakenheath	
91-0311	McD F-15E Strike Eagle [LN] *r/w*	USAF 494th FS/48th FW, RAF Lakenheath	
91-0312	McD F-15E Strike Eagle [LN] *bl/w* [48 OG]	USAF 492nd FS/48th FW, RAF Lakenheath	
91-0313	McD F-15E Strike Eagle [LN] *r/w*	USAF 494th FS/48th FW, RAF Lakenheath	
91-0314	McD F-15E Strike Eagle [LN] *r/w* [494 FS]	USAF 494th FS/48th FW, RAF Lakenheath	
91-0315	McD F-15E Strike Eagle [LN] *bl/w*	USAF 492nd FS/48th FW, RAF Lakenheath	
91-0316	McD F-15E Strike Eagle [LN] *bl/w*	USAF 492nd FS/48th FW, RAF Lakenheath	
91-0317	McD F-15E Strike Eagle [LN] *bl/w*	USAF 492nd FS/48th FW, RAF Lakenheath	
91-0318	McD F-15E Strike Eagle [LN] *bl/w*	USAF 492nd FS/48th FW, RAF Lakenheath	
91-0320	McD F-15E Strike Eagle [LN] *r/w*	USAF 494th FS/48th FW, RAF Lakenheath	
91-0321	McD F-15E Strike Eagle [LN] *bl/w*	USAF 492nd FS/48th FW, RAF Lakenheath	
91-0324	McD F-15E Strike Eagle [LN] *r/w*	USAF 494th FS/48th FW, RAF Lakenheath	
91-0326	McD F-15E Strike Eagle [LN] *r/w*	USAF 494th FS/48th FW, RAF Lakenheath	
91-0327	McD F-15E Strike Eagle [LN] *bl/w*	USAF 492nd FS/48th FW, RAF Lakenheath	
91-0329	McD F-15E Strike Eagle [LN] *r/w*	USAF 494th FS/48th FW, RAF Lakenheath	
91-0331	McD F-15E Strike Eagle [LN] *bl/w*	USAF 492nd FS/48th FW, RAF Lakenheath	
91-0332	McD F-15E Strike Eagle [LN] *bl/w*	USAF 492nd FS/48th FW, RAF Lakenheath	
91-0334	McD F-15E Strike Eagle [LN] *r/w*	USAF 494th FS/48th FW, RAF Lakenheath	
91-0335	McD F-15E Strike Eagle [LN] *r/w*	USAF 494th FS/48th FW, RAF Lakenheath	
91-0602	McD F-15E Strike Eagle [LN] *r/w*	USAF 494th FS/48th FW, RAF Lakenheath	
91-0603	McD F-15E Strike Eagle [LN] *r/w*	USAF 494th FS/48th FW, RAF Lakenheath	
91-0604	McD F-15E Strike Eagle [LN] *r/w*	USAF 494th FS/48th FW, RAF Lakenheath	
91-0605	McD F-15E Strike Eagle [LN] *bl/w*	USAF 492nd FS/48th FW, RAF Lakenheath	
92-0364	McD F-15E Strike Eagle [LN] *r/w*	USAF 494th FS/48th FW, RAF Lakenheath	
96-0201	McD F-15E Strike Eagle [LN] *m* [48 FW]	USAF 494th FS/48th FW, RAF Lakenheath	
96-0202	McD F-15E Strike Eagle [LN] *bl/w*	USAF 492nd FS/48th FW, RAF Lakenheath	
96-0204	McD F-15E Strike Eagle [LN] *r/w*	USAF 494th FS/48th FW, RAF Lakenheath	
96-0205	McD F-15E Strike Eagle [LN] *bl/w*	USAF 492nd FS/48th FW, RAF Lakenheath	

Notes	Serial	Type (code/other identity)	Owner/operator, location or fate
	97-0218	McD F-15E Strike Eagle [LN] *bl/w*	USAF 492nd FS/48th FW, RAF Lakenheath
	97-0219	McD F-15E Strike Eagle [LN] *bl/w*	USAF 492nd FS/48th FW, RAF Lakenheath
	97-0220	McD F-15E Strike Eagle [LN] *bl/w*	USAF 492nd FS/48th FW, RAF Lakenheath
	97-0221	McD F-15E Strike Eagle [LN] *bl/w* [492 FS]	USAF 492nd FS/48th FW, RAF Lakenheath
	97-0222	McD F-15E Strike Eagle [LN] *bl/w*	USAF 492nd FS/48th FW, RAF Lakenheath
	98-0131	McD F-15E Strike Eagle [LN] *bl/w*	USAF 492nd FS/48th FW, RAF Lakenheath
	98-0133	McD F-15E Strike Eagle [LN] *bl/w*	USAF 492nd FS/48th FW, RAF Lakenheath
	98-0134	McD F-15E Strike Eagle [LN] *bl/w*	USAF 492nd FS/48th FW, RAF Lakenheath
	98-0135	McD F-15E Strike Eagle [LN] *bl/w*	USAF 492nd FS/48th FW, RAF Lakenheath
	00-3000	McD F-15E Strike Eagle [LN] *r/w*	USAF 494th FS/48th FW, RAF Lakenheath
	00-3001	McD F-15E Strike Eagle [LN] *r/w*	USAF 494th FS/48th FW, RAF Lakenheath
	00-3002	McD F-15E Strike Eagle [LN] *r/w*	USAF 494th FS/48th FW, RAF Lakenheath
	00-3003	McD F-15E Strike Eagle [LN] *r/w*	USAF 494th FS/48th FW, RAF Lakenheath
	00-3004	McD F-15E Strike Eagle [LN] *r/w*	USAF 494th FS/48th FW, RAF Lakenheath
	01-2000	McD F-15E Strike Eagle [LN] *r/w*	USAF 494th FS/48th FW, RAF Lakenheath
	01-2001	McD F-15E Strike Eagle [LN] *r/w*	USAF 494th FS/48th FW, RAF Lakenheath
	01-2002	McD F-15E Strike Eagle [LN] *r/w*	USAF 494th FS/48th FW, RAF Lakenheath
	01-2003	McD F-15E Strike Eagle [LN] *r/w*	USAF 494th FS/48th FW, RAF Lakenheath
	01-2004	McD F-15E Strike Eagle [LN] *m* [48 FW]	USAF 494th FS/48th FW, RAF Lakenheath
		Bell-Boeing CV-22B Osprey	
	08-0047	Bell-Boeing CV-22B Osprey	*Returned to USA, 2022*
	08-0048	Bell-Boeing CV-22B Osprey	USAF 7th SOS/352nd SOW, RAF Mildenhall
	08-0049	Bell-Boeing CV-22B Osprey	USAF 7th SOS/352nd SOW, RAF Mildenhall
	08-0050	Bell-Boeing CV-22B Osprey $	USAF 7th SOS/352nd SOW, RAF Mildenhall
	09-0042	Bell-Boeing CV-22B Osprey	USAF 7th SOS/352nd SOW, RAF Mildenhall
	10-0052	Bell-Boeing CV-22B Osprey	*Returned to USA, 2022*
	10-0053	Bell-Boeing CV-22B Osprey	USAF 7th SOS/352nd SOW, RAF Mildenhall
	10-0057	Bell-Boeing CV-22B Osprey	USAF 7th SOS/352nd SOW, RAF Mildenhall
	11-0058	Bell-Boeing CV-22B Osprey	USAF 7th SOS/352nd SOW, RAF Mildenhall
	11-0059	Bell-Boeing CV-22B Osprey	*Returned to USA, 2022*
	11-0060	Bell-Boeing CV-22B Osprey	*Returned to USA, 2022*
	11-0061	Bell-Boeing CV-22B Osprey	USAF 7th SOS/352nd SOW, RAF Mildenhall
	12-0063	Bell-Boeing CV-22B Osprey	USAF 7th SOS/352nd SOW, RAF Mildenhall
	16-0076	Bell-Boeing CV-22B Osprey	USAF 7th SOS/352nd SOW, RAF Mildenhall
		Lockheed Martin F-35A Lightning II	
	19-5473	Lockheed Martin F-35A Lightning II [LN]	USAF 495th FS/48th FW, RAF Lakenheath
	19-5474	Lockheed Martin F-35A Lightning II [LN]	USAF 495th FS/48th FW, RAF Lakenheath
	19-5475	Lockheed Martin F-35A Lightning II [LN]	USAF 495th FS/48th FW, RAF Lakenheath
	19-5476	Lockheed Martin F-35A Lightning II [LN]	USAF 495th FS/48th FW, RAF Lakenheath
	19-5484	Lockheed Martin F-35A Lightning II [LN] [48 FW]	USAF 495th FS/48th FW, RAF Lakenheath
	19-5485	Lockheed Martin F-35A Lightning II [LN] {48 OG]	USAF 495th FS/48th FW, RAF Lakenheath
	19-5486	Lockheed Martin F-35A Lightning II [LN]	USAF 495th FS/48th FW, RAF Lakenheath
	19-5493	Lockheed Martin F-35A Lightning II [LN] [493 FS]	USAF 495th FS/48th FW, RAF Lakenheath
	19-5495	Lockheed Martin F-35A Lightning II [LN] [495 FS]	USAF 495th FS/48th FW, RAF Lakenheath
	20-5570	Lockheed Martin F-35A Lightning II [LN]	USAF 495th FS/48th FW, RAF Lakenheath
	20-5571	Lockheed Martin F-35A Lightning II [LN]	USAF 495th FS/48th FW, RAF Lakenheath
	20-5572	Lockheed Martin F-35A Lightning II [LN]	USAF 495th FS/48th FW, RAF Lakenheath
	20-5573	Lockheed Martin F-35A Lightning II [LN]	USAF 495th FS/48th FW, RAF Lakenheath
	20-5574	Lockheed Martin F-35A Lightning II [LN]	USAF 495th FS/48th FW, RAF Lakenheath
	20-5580	Lockheed Martin F-35A Lightning II [LN]	USAF 495th FS/48th FW, RAF Lakenheath
	20-5581	Lockheed Martin F-35A Lightning II [LN]	USAF 495th FS/48th FW, RAF Lakenheath
	20-5582	Lockheed Martin F-35A Lightning II [LN]	USAF 495th FS/48th FW, RAF Lakenheath
	20-5583	Lockheed Martin F-35A Lightning II [LN]	USAF 495th FS/48th FW, RAF Lakenheath
	20-5588	Lockheed Martin F-35A Lightning II [LN]	USAF 495th FS/48th FW, RAF Lakenheath
	20-5589	Lockheed Martin F-35A Lightning II [LN]	USAF 495th FS/48th FW, RAF Lakenheath
	20-5590	Lockheed Martin F-35A Lightning II [LN]	USAF 495th FS/48th FW, RAF Lakenheath
	20-5594	Lockheed Martin F-35A Lightning II [LN]	USAF 48th FW (on order)
	20-5595	Lockheed Martin F-35A Lightning II [LN]	USAF 48th FW (on order)
	20-5596	Lockheed Martin F-35A Lightning II [LN]	USAF 48th FW (on order)
	20-5598	Lockheed Martin F-35A Lightning II [LN]	USAF 48th FW (on order)

Serial	Type (code/other identity)	Owner/operator, location or fate	Notes
..-....	Lockheed Martin F-35A Lightning II [LN]	USAF 48th FW (on order)	
..-....	Lockheed Martin F-35A Lightning II [LN]	USAF 48th FW (on order)	
..-....	Lockheed Martin F-35A Lightning II [LN]	USAF 48th FW (on order)	
..-....	Lockheed Martin F-35A Lightning II [LN]	USAF 48th FW (on order)	

Lockheed MC-130J Commando II

08-6205	Lockheed MC-130J Commando II	*Returned to the USA, August 2022*	
09-5713	Lockheed MC-130J Commando II	USAF 67th SOS/352nd SOW, RAF Mildenhall	
09-6207	Lockheed MC-130J Commando II	*Returned to the USA, November 2022*	
12-5759	Lockheed MC-130J Commando II	USAF 67th SOS/352nd SOW, RAF Mildenhall	
13-5776	Lockheed MC-130J Commando II	USAF 67th SOS/352nd SOW, RAF Mildenhall	
13-5778	Lockheed MC-130J Commando II	*Returned to the USA, August 2022*	
14-5805	Lockheed MC-130J Commando II	USAF 67th SOS/352nd SOW, RAF Mildenhall	
20-5941	Lockheed MC-130J Commando II	USAF 67th SOS/352nd SOW, RAF Mildenhall	

Boeing KC-135R Stratotanker/Boeing KC-135T Stratotanker

57-2605	Boeing KC-135R Stratotanker [D] *r/w/bl*	USAF 351st ARS/100th ARW, RAF Mildenhall	
58-0089	Boeing KC-135T Stratotanker [D] *r/w/bl*	*Returned to the USA, 2022*	
58-0095	Boeing KC-135R Stratotanker [D] *r/w/bl*	USAF 351st ARS/100th ARW, RAF Mildenhall	
58-0100	Boeing KC-135R Stratotanker [D] *r/w/bl*	USAF 351st ARS/100th ARW, RAF Mildenhall	
58-0125	Boeing KC-135T Stratotanker [D] *r/w/bl*	USAF 351st ARS/100th ARW, RAF Mildenhall	
59-1464	Boeing KC-135T Stratotanker [D] *r/w/bl*	USAF 351st ARS/100th ARW, RAF Mildenhall	
59-1470	Boeing KC-135T Stratotanker [D] *r/w/bl*	USAF 351st ARS/100th ARW, RAF Mildenhall	
59-1475	Boeing KC-135T Stratotanker [D] r/w/bl *(01475)*	USAF 351st ARS/100th ARW, RAF Mildenhall	
59-1511	Boeing KC-135R Stratotanker [D] *r/w/bl*	USAF 351st ARS/100th ARW, RAF Mildenhall	
60-0324	Boeing KC-135R Stratotanker [D] *r/w/bl*	USAF 351st ARS/100th ARW, RAF Mildenhall	
60-0333	Boeing KC-135R Stratotanker [D] *r/w/bl*	USAF 351st ARS/100th ARW, RAF Mildenhall	
60-0335	Boeing KC-135R Stratotanker [D] *r/w/bl*	USAF 351st ARS/100th ARW, RAF Mildenhall	
60-0353	Boeing KC-135T Stratotanker [D] *r/w/bl*	*To Tinker ALC for rework, December 2022*	
60-0355	Boeing KC-135R Stratotanker [D] *r/w/bl*	USAF 351st ARS/100th ARW, RAF Mildenhall	
61-0315	Boeing KC-135R Stratotanker [D] *r/w/bl*	USAF 351st ARS/100th ARW, RAF Mildenhall	
62-3540	Boeing KC-135R Stratotanker [D] *r/w/bl*	USAF 351st ARS/100th ARW, RAF Mildenhall	
62-3551	Boeing KC-135R Stratotanker [D] *r/w/bl*	*Returned to the USA, 2022*	
63-7999	Boeing KC-135R Stratotanker [D] *r/w/bl*	*To 309th AMARG, November 2022*	
63-8008	Boeing KC-135R Stratotanker [D] *r/w/bl*	USAF 351st ARS/100th ARW, RAF Mildenhall	
63-8878	Boeing KC-135R Stratotanker [D] *r/w/bl*	USAF 351st ARS/100th ARW, RAF Mildenhall	
63-8887	Boeing KC-135R Stratotanker [D] *r/w/bl*	*Returned to the USA, 2022*	

These aircraft are normally based in Western Europe with the USAFE. They are shown in numerical order of type designation, with individual aircraft in serial number order as carried on the aircraft. Fiscal year (FY) details are also provided if necessary. The unit allocation and operating bases are given for most aircraft.

Notes	Serial	Type (code/other identity)	Owner/operator, location or fate
	Beech C-12 Huron		
	73-1217	Beech C-12C Huron	USAF US Embassy Flight, Taszár, Hungary
	83-0499	Beech C-12D Huron	USAF US Embassy Flight, Taszár, Hungary
	Lockheed (GD) F-16CM/F-16DM Fighting Falcon		
	87-0350	Lockheed (GD) F-16CM-40 Fighting Falcon [AV] *gn/y*	USAF 555th FS/31st FW, Aviano, Italy
	87-0351	Lockheed (GD) F-16CM-40 Fighting Falcon [AV] *gn/y*	USAF 555th FS/31st FW, Aviano, Italy
	87-0355	Lockheed (GD) F-16CM-40 Fighting Falcon [AV] *pr/w*	USAF 510th FS/31st FW, Aviano, Italy
	87-0359	Lockheed (GD) F-16CM-40 Fighting Falcon [AV] *gn/y*	USAF 555th FS/31st FW, Aviano, Italy
	88-0413	Lockheed (GD) F-16CM-40 Fighting Falcon [AV] *pr/w*	USAF 510th FS/31st FW, Aviano, Italy
	88-0425	Lockheed (GD) F-16CM-40 Fighting Falcon [AV] $	USAF 555th FS/31st FW, Aviano, Italy
	88-0435	Lockheed (GD) F-16CM-40 Fighting Falcon [AV] *gn/y*	USAF 555th FS/31st FW, Aviano, Italy
	88-0443	Lockheed (GD) F-16CM-40 Fighting Falcon [AV] *pr/w*	USAF 510th FS/31st FW, Aviano, Italy
	88-0444	Lockheed (GD) F-16CM-40 Fighting Falcon [AV] *pr/w*	USAF 510th FS/31st FW, Aviano, Italy
	88-0446	Lockheed (GD) F-16CM-40 Fighting Falcon [AV] *gn/y*	USAF 555th FS/31st FW, Aviano, Italy
	88-0460	Lockheed (GD) F-16CM-40 Fighting Falcon [AV] *gn/y*	USAF 555th FS/31st FW, Aviano, Italy
	88-0462	Lockheed (GD) F-16CM-40 Fighting Falcon [AV] *pr/w*	USAF 510th FS/31st FW, Aviano, Italy
	88-0491	Lockheed (GD) F-16CM-40 Fighting Falcon [AV] *pr/w*	USAF 510th FS/31st FW, Aviano, Italy
	88-0516	Lockheed (GD) F-16CM-40 Fighting Falcon [AV] *pr/w*	USAF 510th FS/31st FW, Aviano, Italy
	88-0521	Lockheed (GD) F-16CM-40 Fighting Falcon [AV] *pr/w*	USAF 510th FS/31st FW, Aviano, Italy
	88-0525	Lockheed (GD) F-16CM-40 Fighting Falcon [AV] *pr/w*	USAF 510th FS/31st FW, Aviano, Italy
	88-0526	Lockheed (GD) F-16CM-40 Fighting Falcon [AV] *gn/y*	USAF 555th FS/31st FW, Aviano, Italy
	88-0532	Lockheed (GD) F-16CM-40 Fighting Falcon [AV] *gn/y*	USAF 555th FS/31st FW, Aviano, Italy
	88-0535	Lockheed (GD) F-16CM-40 Fighting Falcon [AV] $	USAF 555th FS/31st FW, Aviano, Italy
	88-0541	Lockheed (GD) F-16CM-40 Fighting Falcon [AV] *pr/w*	USAF 510th FS/31st FW, Aviano, Italy
	89-2001	Lockheed (GD) F-16CM-40 Fighting Falcon [AV] *gn/y*	USAF 555th FS/31st FW, Aviano, Italy
	89-2008	Lockheed (GD) F-16CM-40 Fighting Falcon [AV] *pr/w*	USAF 510th FS/31st FW, Aviano, Italy
	89-2009	Lockheed (GD) F-16CM-40 Fighting Falcon [AV] *pr/gn* [31 FW]	31st FW, Aviano, Italy
	89-2011	Lockheed (GD) F-16CM-40 Fighting Falcon [AV] *pr/w*	USAF 510th FS/31st FW, Aviano, Italy
	89-2016	Lockheed (GD) F-16CM-40 Fighting Falcon [AV] *gn/y*	USAF 555th FS/31st FW, Aviano, Italy
	89-2018	Lockheed (GD) F-16CM-40 Fighting Falcon [AV] *pr/w*	USAF 510th FS/31st FW, Aviano, Italy
	89-2023	Lockheed (GD) F-16CM-40 Fighting Falcon [AV] *gn/y*	USAF 555th FS/31st FW, Aviano, Italy
	89-2024	Lockheed (GD) F-16CM-40 Fighting Falcon [AV] *gn/y*	USAF 555th FS/31st FW, Aviano, Italy
	89-2026	Lockheed (GD) F-16CM-40 Fighting Falcon [AV] *pr/w*	USAF 510th FS/31st FW, Aviano, Italy
	89-2029	Lockheed (GD) F-16CM-40 Fighting Falcon [AV] *pr/w*	USAF 510th FS/31st FW, Aviano, Italy
	89-2030	Lockheed (GD) F-16CM-40 Fighting Falcon [AV] *pr/w* [510 FS]	USAF 510th FS/31st FW, Aviano, Italy
	89-2035	Lockheed (GD) F-16CM-40 Fighting Falcon [AV] *gn/y*	USAF 555th FS/31st FW, Aviano, Italy
	89-2038	Lockheed (GD) F-16CM-40 Fighting Falcon [AV] *pr/w*	USAF 510th FS/31st FW, Aviano, Italy
	89-2039	Lockheed (GD) F-16CM-40 Fighting Falcon [AV] *gn/y*	USAF 555th FS/31st FW, Aviano, Italy
	89-2041	Lockheed (GD) F-16CM-40 Fighting Falcon [AV] *gn/y*	USAF 555th FS/31st FW, Aviano, Italy
	89-2044	Lockheed (GD) F-16CM-40 Fighting Falcon [AV] *gn/y*	USAF 555th FS/31st FW, Aviano, Italy
	89-2046	Lockheed (GD) F-16CM-40 Fighting Falcon [AV] $	USAF 510th FS/31st FW, Aviano, Italy
	89-2047	Lockheed (GD) F-16CM-40 Fighting Falcon [AV] *pr/w*	USAF 510th FS/31st FW, Aviano, Italy
	89-2049	Lockheed (GD) F-16CM-40 Fighting Falcon [AV] *pr/w*	USAF 510th FS/31st FW, Aviano, Italy
	89-2057	Lockheed (GD) F-16CM-40 Fighting Falcon [AV] *pr/w*	USAF 510th FS/31st FW, Aviano, Italy
	89-2068	Lockheed (GD) F-16CM-40 Fighting Falcon [AV] *gn/y*	USAF 555th FS/31st FW, Aviano, Italy
	89-2096	Lockheed (GD) F-16CM-40 Fighting Falcon [AV]	USAF 510th FS/31st FW, Aviano, Italy
	89-2102	Lockheed (GD) F-16CM-40 Fighting Falcon [AV] $	USAF 510th FS/31st FW, Aviano, Italy
	89-2118	Lockheed (GD) F-16CM-40 Fighting Falcon [AV] *gn/y*	USAF 555th FS/31st FW, Aviano, Italy
	89-2137	Lockheed (GD) F-16CM-40 Fighting Falcon [AV] *m* [31 OG]	31st FW, Aviano, Italy
	89-2152	Lockheed (GD) F-16CM-40 Fighting Falcon [AV] *gn/y*	USAF 555th FS/31st FW, Aviano, Italy
	89-2178	Lockheed (GD) F-16DM-40 Fighting Falcon [AV] *pr/w* $	USAF 510th FS/31st FW, Aviano, Italy
	90-0709	Lockheed (GD) F-16CM-40 Fighting Falcon [AV] $	USAF 510th FS/31st FW, Aviano, Italy
	90-0772	Lockheed (GD) F-16CM-40 Fighting Falcon [AV] *gn/y*	USAF 555th FS/31st FW, Aviano, Italy
	90-0773	Lockheed (GD) F-16CM-40 Fighting Falcon [AV] *gn/y*	USAF 555th FS/31st FW, Aviano, Italy

Serial	Type (code/other identity)	Owner/operator, location or fate	Notes
90-0777	Lockheed (GD) F-16DM-40 Fighting Falcon [AV] *pr/w*	USAF 510th FS/31st FW, Aviano, Italy	
90-0795	Lockheed (GD) F-16DM-40 Fighting Falcon [AV] *gn/y*	USAF 555th FS/31st FW, Aviano, Italy	
90-0796	Lockheed (GD) F-16DM-40 Fighting Falcon [AV] *gn/y*	USAF 555th FS/31st FW, Aviano, Italy	
90-0800	Lockheed (GD) F-16DM-40 Fighting Falcon [AV] *gn/y*	USAF 555th FS/31st FW, Aviano, Italy	
90-0813	Lockheed (GD) F-16CM-50 Fighting Falcon [SP] *r/w*	USAF 480th FS/52nd FW, Spangdahlem, Germany	
90-0818	Lockheed (GD) F-16CM-50 Fighting Falcon [SP] *r/w*	USAF 480th FS/52nd FW, Spangdahlem, Germany	
90-0827	Lockheed (GD) F-16CM-50 Fighting Falcon [SP] *r/w*	USAF 480th FS/52nd FW, Spangdahlem, Germany	
90-0828	Lockheed (GD) F-16CM-50 Fighting Falcon [SP] *r/w*	USAF 480th FS/52nd FW, Spangdahlem, Germany	
90-0829	Lockheed (GD) F-16CM-50 Fighting Falcon [SP] *r/w* [52 OG]	USAF 480th FS/52nd FW, Spangdahlem, Germany	
90-0833	Lockheed (GD) F-16CM-50 Fighting Falcon [SP] *r/w*	USAF 480th FS/52nd FW, Spangdahlem, Germany	
91-0338	Lockheed (GD) F-16CM-50 Fighting Falcon [SP] *r/w*	USAF 480th FS/52nd FW, Spangdahlem, Germany	
91-0342	Lockheed (GD) F-16CM-50 Fighting Falcon [SP] *r/w*	USAF 480th FS/52nd FW, Spangdahlem, Germany	
91-0343	Lockheed (GD) F-16CM-50 Fighting Falcon [SP] *r/w*	USAF 480th FS/52nd FW, Spangdahlem, Germany	
91-0344	Lockheed (GD) F-16CM-50 Fighting Falcon [SP] *r/w*	USAF 480th FS/52nd FW, Spangdahlem, Germany	
91-0351	Lockheed (GD) F-16CM-50 Fighting Falcon [SP] *r/w*	USAF 480th FS/52nd FW, Spangdahlem, Germany	
91-0352	Lockheed (GD) F-16CM-50 Fighting Falcon [SP] *m* [52 FW]	USAF 480th FS/52nd FW, Spangdahlem, Germany	
91-0358	Lockheed (GD) F-16CM-50 Fighting Falcon [SP] *r/w*	USAF 480th FS/52nd FW, Spangdahlem, Germany	
91-0360	Lockheed (GD) F-16CM-50 Fighting Falcon [SP] *r/w*	USAF 480th FS/52nd FW, Spangdahlem, Germany	
91-0361	Lockheed (GD) F-16CM-50 Fighting Falcon [SP] *r/w*	USAF 480th FS/52nd FW, Spangdahlem, Germany	
91-0402	Lockheed (GD) F-16CM-50 Fighting Falcon [SP] *r/w*	USAF 480th FS/52nd FW, Spangdahlem, Germany	
91-0403	Lockheed (GD) F-16CM-50 Fighting Falcon [SP] *r/w*	USAF 480th FS/52nd FW, Spangdahlem, Germany	
91-0407	Lockheed (GD) F-16CM-50 Fighting Falcon [SP] *r/w*	USAF 480th FS/52nd FW, Spangdahlem, Germany	
91-0412	Lockheed (GD) F-16CM-50 Fighting Falcon [SP] *r/w*	USAF 480th FS/52nd FW, Spangdahlem, Germany	
91-0416	Lockheed (GD) F-16CM-50 Fighting Falcon [SP] *r/w*	USAF 480th FS/52nd FW, Spangdahlem, Germany	
91-0417	Lockheed (GD) F-16CM-50 Fighting Falcon [SP] *r/w*	USAF 480th FS/52nd FW, Spangdahlem, Germany	
91-0418	Lockheed (GD) F-16CM-50 Fighting Falcon [SP] $	USAF 480th FS/52nd FW, Spangdahlem, Germany	
91-0472	Lockheed (GD) F-16DM-50 Fighting Falcon [SP] *r/w*	USAF 480th FS/52nd FW, Spangdahlem, Germany	
91-0481	Lockheed (GD) F-16DM-50 Fighting Falcon [SP] *r/w*	USAF 480th FS/52nd FW, Spangdahlem, Germany	
92-3918	Lockheed (GD) F-16CM-50 Fighting Falcon [SP] *r/w*	USAF 480th FS/52nd FW, Spangdahlem, Germany	
96-0080	Lockheed (GD) F-16CM-50 Fighting Falcon [SP] *r/w* $ [480 FS]	USAF 480th FS/52nd FW, Spangdahlem, Germany	
96-0083	Lockheed (GD) F-16CM-50 Fighting Falcon [SP] *r/w* $	USAF 480th FS/52nd FW, Spangdahlem, Germany	

Gates C-21A

84-0083	Gates C-21A Learjet	USAF 76th AS/86th AW, Ramstein, Germany	
84-0085	Gates C-21A Learjet	USAF 76th AS/86th AW, Ramstein, Germany	

Notes	Serial	Type (code/other identity)	Owner/operator, location or fate
	84-0087	Gates C-21A Learjet	USAF 76th AS/86th AW, Ramstein, Germany
	84-0096	Gates C-21A Learjet	USAF 76th AS/86th AW, Ramstein, Germany
	84-0126	Gates C-21A Learjet	USAF 76th AS/86th AW, Ramstein, Germany
	Gulfstream Aerospace C-37A Gulfstream V		
	01-0029	Gulfstream Aerospace C-37A Gulfstream V	USAF 309th AS/86th AW, Chièvres, Belgium
	01-0030	Gulfstream Aerospace C-37A Gulfstream V	USAF 76th AS/86th AW, Ramstein, Germany
	01-0076	Gulfstream Aerospace C-37A Gulfstream V	USAF 76th AS/86th AW, Ramstein, Germany
	Sikorsky HH-60G Pave Hawk		
	87-26007	Sikorsky HH-60G Pave Hawk [AV]	USAF 56th RQS/31st FW, Aviano, Italy
	88-26114	Sikorsky HH-60G Pave Hawk	USAF 56th RQS/31st FW, Aviano, Italy
	89-26205	Sikorsky HH-60G Pave Hawk [AV]	USAF 56th RQS/31st FW, Aviano, Italy
	89-26206	Sikorsky HH-60G Pave Hawk [AV]	USAF 56th RQS/31st FW, Aviano, Italy
	89-26208	Sikorsky HH-60G Pave Hawk [AV]	USAF 56th RQS/31st FW, Aviano, Italy
	92-26471	Sikorsky HH-60G Pave Hawk [AV]	USAF 56th RQS/31st FW, Aviano, Italy
	97-26774	Sikorsky HH-60G Pave Hawk [AV]	USAF 56th RQS/31st FW, Aviano, Italy
	Lockheed C-130J-30 Hercules II		
	04-3142	Lockheed C-130J-30 Hercules II [RS] *bl/w*	USAF 37th AS/86th AW, Ramstein, Germany
	06-4631	Lockheed C-130J-30 Hercules II [RS] *bl/w*	USAF 37th AS/86th AW, Ramstein, Germany
	06-8611	Lockheed C-130J-30 Hercules II [RS] *bl/w*	*Returned to USA, 2022*
	07-4635	Lockheed C-130J-30 Hercules II [RS] *bl/w*	USAF 37th AS/86th AW, Ramstein, Germany
	07-8608	Lockheed C-130J-30 Hercules II [RS] *bl/w* $	USAF 37th AS/86th AW, Ramstein, Germany
	07-8609	Lockheed C-130J-30 Hercules II [RS] *bl/w*	USAF 37th AS/86th AW, Ramstein, Germany
	07-8614	Lockheed C-130J-30 Hercules II [RS] *bl/w*	USAF 37th AS/86th AW, Ramstein, Germany
	08-3176	Lockheed C-130J-30 Hercules II [RS] *bl/w*	USAF 37th AS/86th AW, Ramstein, Germany
	08-5683	Lockheed C-130J-30 Hercules II [RS] *bl/w*	USAF 37th AS/86th AW, Ramstein, Germany
	08-8601	Lockheed C-130J-30 Hercules II [RS] *bl/w* [86 AW]	USAF 37th AS/86th AW, Ramstein, Germany
	08-8602	Lockheed C-130J-30 Hercules II [RS] *bl/w* [86 OG]	USAF 37th AS/86th AW, Ramstein, Germany
	08-8603	Lockheed C-130J-30 Hercules II [RS] *bl/w* [37 AS]	*Returned to the USA, January 2022*
	11-5736	Lockheed C-130J-30 Hercules II [RS] *bl/w*	Stored Ramstein AB (damaged)
	11-5738	Lockheed C-130J-30 Hercules II [RS] *bl/w*	USAF 37th AS/86th AW, Ramstein, Germany
	11-5740	Lockheed C-130J-30 Hercules II [RS] *bl/w* $	USAF 37th AS/86th AW, Ramstein, Germany
	15-5822	Lockheed C-130J-30 Hercules II [RS] *bl/w*	USAF 37th AS/86th AW, Ramstein, Germany
	15-5831	Lockheed C-130J-30 Hercules II [RS] *bl/w*	USAF 37th AS/86th AW, Ramstein, Germany
	16-5840	Lockheed C-130J-30 Hercules II [RS] *bl/w* $	USAF 37th AS/86th AW, Ramstein, Germany
	16-5856	Lockheed C-130J-30 Hercules II [RS] *bl/w*	USAF 37th AS/86th AW, Ramstein, Germany
	16-5883	Lockheed C-130J-30 Hercules II [RS] *bl/w*	USAF 37th AS/86th AW, Ramstein, Germany

EUROPEAN-BASED US NAVY AIRCRAFT

Notes	Serial	Type (code/other identity)	Owner/operator, location or fate
	Fairchild C-26D		
	900528	Fairchild C-26D	USN NAF Sigonella, Italy
	900530	Fairchild C-26D	USN NAF Sigonella, Italy
	900531	Fairchild C-26D	USN NAF Naples, Italy
	910502	Fairchild C-26D	USN NAF Naples, Italy

Serial	Type (code/other identity)	Owner/operator, location or fate	Notes
Beech C-12 Huron			
84-00156	Beech C-12U-3 Huron	US Army E/1-214th AVN, Wiesbaden, Germany	
84-00157	Beech C-12U-3 Huron	US Army E/1-214th AVN, Wiesbaden, Germany	
84-00162	Beech C-12U-3 Huron	US Army E/1-214th AVN, Wiesbaden, Germany	
84-00165	Beech C-12U-3 Huron	US Army E/1-214th AVN, Wiesbaden, Germany	
84-00173	Beech C-12U-3 Huron	US Army E/1-214th AVN, Wiesbaden, Germany	
Cessna UC-35A Citation V			
95-00123	Cessna UC-35A Citation V	US Army E/1-214th AVN, Wiesbaden, Germany	
96-00107	Cessna UC-35A Citation V	US Army E/1-214th AVN, Wiesbaden, Germany	
97-00102	Cessna UC-35A Citation V	US Army E/1-214th AVN, Wiesbaden, Germany	
97-00105	Cessna UC-35A Citation V	US Army E/1-214th AVN, Wiesbaden, Germany	
99-00102	Cessna UC-35A Citation V	US Army E/1-214th AVN, Wiesbaden, Germany	
Boeing-Vertol CH-47F Chinook			
13-08132	Boeing-Vertol CH-47F Chinook	US Army B/1-214th AVN, Ansbach, Germany	
13-08133	Boeing-Vertol CH-47F Chinook	US Army B/1-214th AVN, Ansbach, Germany	
13-08134	Boeing-Vertol CH-47F Chinook	US Army B/1-214th AVN, Ansbach, Germany	
13-08135	Boeing-Vertol CH-47F Chinook	US Army B/1-214th AVN, Ansbach, Germany	
13-08432	Boeing-Vertol CH-47F Chinook	US Army B/1-214th AVN, Ansbach, Germany	
13-08434	Boeing-Vertol CH-47F Chinook	US Army B/1-214th AVN, Ansbach, Germany	
13-08435	Boeing-Vertol CH-47F Chinook	US Army B/1-214th AVN, Ansbach, Germany	
13-08436	Boeing-Vertol CH-47F Chinook	US Army B/1-214th AVN, Ansbach, Germany	
13-08437	Boeing-Vertol CH-47F Chinook	US Army B/1-214th AVN, Ansbach, Germany	
14-08162	Boeing-Vertol CH-47F Chinook	US Army B/1-214th AVN, Ansbach, Germany	
15-08176	Boeing-Vertol CH-47F Chinook	US Army B/1-214th AVN, Ansbach, Germany	
15-08178	Boeing-Vertol CH-47F Chinook	US Army B/1-214th AVN, Ansbach, Germany	
Sikorsky H-60 Black Hawk			
10-20245	Sikorsky UH-60M Black Hawk	US Army A/1-214th AVN, Wiesbaden, Germany	
10-20272	Sikorsky UH-60M Black Hawk	US Army A/1-214th AVN, Wiesbaden, Germany	
10-20276	Sikorsky UH-60M Black Hawk	US Army A/1-214th AVN, Wiesbaden, Germany	
10-20311	Sikorsky UH-60M Black Hawk	US Army A/1-214th AVN, Wiesbaden, Germany	
15-20314	Sikorsky UH-60M Black Hawk	US Army A/1-214th AVN, Wiesbaden, Germany	
15-20741	Sikorsky UH-60M Black Hawk	US Army A/1-214th AVN, Wiesbaden, Germany	
15-20742	Sikorsky UH-60M Black Hawk	US Army A/1-214th AVN, Wiesbaden, Germany	
15-20743	Sikorsky UH-60M Black Hawk	US Army A/1-214th AVN, Wiesbaden, Germany	
15-20744	Sikorsky UH-60M Black Hawk	US Army A/1-214th AVN, Wiesbaden, Germany	
15-20745	Sikorsky UH-60M Black Hawk	US Army A/1-214th AVN, Wiesbaden, Germany	
15-20754	Sikorsky UH-60M Black Hawk	US Army A/1-214th AVN, Wiesbaden, Germany	
20-21128	Sikorsky HH-60M Black Hawk	US Army C/1-214th AVN, Grafenwöhr, Germany	
20-21129	Sikorsky HH-60M Black Hawk	US Army C/1-214th AVN, Grafenwöhr, Germany	
20-21130	Sikorsky HH-60M Black Hawk	US Army C/1-214th AVN, Grafenwöhr, Germany	
20-21131	Sikorsky HH-60M Black Hawk	US Army C/1-214th AVN, Grafenwöhr, Germany	
20-21132	Sikorsky HH-60M Black Hawk	US Army C/1-214th AVN, Grafenwöhr, Germany	
20-21133	Sikorsky HH-60M Black Hawk	US Army C/1-214th AVN, Grafenwöhr, Germany	
21-21200	Sikorsky HH-60M Black Hawk	US Army C/1-214th AVN, Grafenwöhr, Germany	
MDH AH-64D Apache			
10-05620	MDH AH-64D Apache	US Army 1-3rd AVN, Ansbach, Germany	
10-05623	MDH AH-64D Apache	US Army 1-3rd AVN, Ansbach, Germany	
10-05626	MDH AH-64D Apache	US Army 1-3rd AVN, Ansbach, Germany	
07-07038	MDH AH-64D Apache	US Army 1-3rd AVN, Ansbach, Germany	
07-07043	MDH AH-64D Apache	US Army 1-3rd AVN, Ansbach, Germany	
07-07045	MDH AH-64D Apache	US Army 1-3rd AVN, Ansbach, Germany	
07-07046	MDH AH-64D Apache	US Army 1-3rd AVN, Ansbach, Germany	
08-07048	MDH AH-64D Apache	US Army 1-3rd AVN, Ansbach, Germany	
08-07049	MDH AH-64D Apache	US Army 1-3rd AVN, Ansbach, Germany	
08-07051	MDH AH-64D Apache	US Army 1-3rd AVN, Ansbach, Germany	
09-05580	MDH AH-64D Apache	US Army 1-3rd AVN, Ansbach, Germany	
09-05581	MDH AH-64D Apache	US Army 1-3rd AVN, Ansbach, Germany	
09-05582	MDH AH-64D Apache	US Army 1-3rd AVN, Ansbach, Germany	

Notes	Serial	Type (code/other identity)	Owner/operator, location or fate
	09-05585	MDH AH-64D Apache	US Army 1-3rd AVN, Ansbach, Germany
	09-05587	MDH AH-64D Apache	US Army 1-3rd AVN, Ansbach, Germany
	09-05589	MDH AH-64D Apache	US Army 1-3rd AVN, Ansbach, Germany
	09-05591	MDH AH-64D Apache	US Army 1-3rd AVN, Ansbach, Germany
	09-05596	MDH AH-64D Apache	US Army 1-3rd AVN, Ansbach, Germany
	09-05597	MDH AH-64D Apache	US Army 1-3rd AVN, Ansbach, Germany
	09-05598	MDH AH-64D Apache	US Army 1-3rd AVN, Ansbach, Germany
	09-05601	MDH AH-64D Apache	US Army 1-3rd AVN, Ansbach, Germany
	09-05602	MDH AH-64D Apache	US Army 1-3rd AVN, Ansbach, Germany
	09-05604	MDH AH-64D Apache	US Army 1-3rd AVN, Ansbach, Germany
	09-05627	MDH AH-64D Apache	US Army 1-3rd AVN, Ansbach, Germany
	09-07060	MDH AH-64D Apache	US Army 1-3rd AVN, Ansbach, Germany
	Eurocopter UH-72A Lakota		
	09-72029	Eurocopter UH-72A Lakota	US Army JMRC, Hohenfels, Germany
	09-72097	Eurocopter UH-72A Lakota	US Army JMRC, Hohenfels, Germany
	09-72098	Eurocopter UH-72A Lakota	US Army JMRC, Hohenfels, Germany
	09-72100	Eurocopter UH-72A Lakota	US Army JMRC, Hohenfels, Germany
	09-72105	Eurocopter UH-72A Lakota	US Army JMRC, Hohenfels, Germany
	09-72106	Eurocopter UH-72A Lakota	US Army JMRC, Hohenfels, Germany
	09-72107	Eurocopter UH-72A Lakota	US Army JMRC, Hohenfels, Germany
	09-72108	Eurocopter UH-72A Lakota	US Army JMRC, Hohenfels, Germany

If you are a high-ranking officer in the US Army in Europe, you are likely to travel in style in one of a fleet of UC-35A Citations, such as 97-00105, seen here at RAF Fairford for RIAT. *SRS*

The following aircraft are normally based in the USA but are likely to be seen visiting the UK from time to time. The presentation is in numerical order of the type, commencing with the **B-1B** and concluding with the **C-146A**. The aircraft are listed in numerical progression by the serial allocated. Fiscal year information is provided, together with details of mark variations and in some cases operating units. Where base-code letter information is carried on the aircrafts' tails, this is detailed with the squadron/base data; for example the 7th Wing's B-1B 86-0105 carries the letters DY on its tail, thus identifying the Wing's home base as Dyess AFB, Texas.

Serial	Type (code/other identity)	Owner/operator, location or fate	Notes
Rockwell B-1B Lancer			
85-0059	Rockwell B-1B Lancer [DY] *bl/w*	USAF 28th BS/7th BW, Dyess AFB, TX	
85-0060	Rockwell B-1B Lancer [EL] *bk/r* $	USAF 34th BS/28th BW, Ellsworth AFB, SD	
85-0061	Rockwell B-1B Lancer [DY] *bl/w*	USAF 28th BS/7th BW, Dyess AFB, TX	
85-0064	Rockwell B-1B Lancer [DY]	USAF 7th BW, Dyess AFB, TX	
85-0068	Rockwell B-1B Lancer [ED] *bl/w*	USAF 419th FLTS/412th TW, Edwards AFB	
85-0069	Rockwell B-1B Lancer [EL] *bk/r*	USAF 34th BS/28th BW, Ellsworth AFB, SD	
85-0072	Rockwell B-1B Lancer [EL] *bk/r*	USAF 34th BS/28th BW, Ellsworth AFB, SD	
85-0073	Rockwell B-1B Lancer [DY] *bl/w* [7 OG]	USAF 28th BS/7th BW, Dyess AFB, TX	
85-0075	Rockwell B-1B Lancer [ED] *bl/w*	USAF 419th FLTS/412th TW, Edwards AFB	
85-0079	Rockwell B-1B Lancer [EL] *bk/r*	USAF 34th BS/28th BW, Ellsworth AFB, SD	
85-0084	Rockwell B-1B Lancer [EL] *bk/r*	USAF 34th BS/28th BW, Ellsworth AFB, SD	
85-0085	Rockwell B-1B Lancer [EL] *bk/y*	USAF 37th BS/28th BW, Ellsworth AFB, SD	
85-0088	Rockwell B-1B Lancer [DY] *bk/w*	USAF 9th BS/7th BW, Dyess AFB, TX	
85-0089	Rockwell B-1B Lancer [DY] *bk/w* [489 BS]	USAF 9th BS/7th BW, Dyess AFB, TX	
86-0094	Rockwell B-1B Lancer [EL] *bk/y* $	USAF 37th BS/28th BW, Ellsworth AFB, SD	
86-0095	Rockwell B-1B Lancer [EL] *bk/r*	USAF 34th BS/28th BW, Ellsworth AFB, SD	
86-0097	Rockwell B-1B Lancer [DY] *bk/w* [9 BS]	USAF 9th BS/7th BW, Dyess AFB, TX	
86-0098	Rockwell B-1B Lancer [DY] *bl/w*	USAF 28th BS/7th BW, Dyess AFB, TX	
86-0102	Rockwell B-1B Lancer [EL] *bk/y*	USAF 37th BS/28th BW, Ellsworth AFB, SD	
86-0103	Rockwell B-1B Lancer [DY] *bk/w*	USAF 9th BS/7th BW, Dyess AFB, TX	
86-0104	Rockwell B-1B Lancer [EL] *bk/y*	USAF 37th BS/28th BW, Ellsworth AFB, SD	
86-0105	Rockwell B-1B Lancer [DY] *bl/w*	USAF 28th BS/7th BW, Dyess AFB, TX	
86-0107	Rockwell B-1B Lancer [DY] *bl/w*	USAF 28th BS/7th BW, Dyess AFB, TX	
86-0108	Rockwell B-1B Lancer [EL] *bk/y*	USAF 37th BS/28th BW, Ellsworth AFB, SD	
86-0110	Rockwell B-1B Lancer [DY] *bl/w*	USAF 28th BS/7th BW, Dyess AFB, TX	
86-0111	Rockwell B-1B Lancer [EL] *bk/r*	USAF 34th BS/28th BW, Ellsworth AFB, SD	
86-0112	Rockwell B-1B Lancer [DY] *bl/w*	USAF 28th BS/7th BW, Dyess AFB, TX	
86-0113	Rockwell B-1B Lancer [EL] *bk/y*	USAF 37th BS/28th BW, Ellsworth AFB, SD	
86-0117	Rockwell B-1B Lancer [DY] [7 BW]	USAF 7th BW, Dyess AFB, TX	
86-0119	Rockwell B-1B Lancer [DY] *bl/w*	USAF 28th BS/7th BW, Dyess AFB, TX	
86-0120	Rockwell B-1B Lancer [EL] *bk/y*	USAF 37th BS/28th BW, Ellsworth AFB, SD	
86-0121	Rockwell B-1B Lancer [EL] *bk/y*	USAF 37th BS/28th BW, Ellsworth AFB, SD	
86-0122	Rockwell B-1B Lancer [DY] *bk/w*	USAF 9th BS/7th BW, Dyess AFB, TX	
86-0124	Rockwell B-1B Lancer [DY] *bk/w*	USAF 9th BS/7th BW, Dyess AFB, TX	
86-0125	Rockwell B-1B Lancer [DY] *bl/w*	USAF 28th BS/7th BW, Dyess AFB, TX	
86-0126	Rockwell B-1B Lancer [DY] *bl/w*	USAF 28th BS/7th BW, Dyess AFB, TX	
86-0127	Rockwell B-1B Lancer [DY] *bk/w*	USAF 9th BS/7th BW, Dyess AFB, TX	
86-0129	Rockwell B-1B Lancer [EL] *bk/r*	USAF 34th BS/28th BW, Ellsworth AFB, SD	
86-0134	Rockwell B-1B Lancer [EL] *bk/r* [34 BS]	USAF 34th BS/28th BW, Ellsworth AFB, SD	
86-0135	Rockwell B-1B Lancer [OT] *r/gy* [53 WG/337 CC]	USAF 337th TES/53rd Wg, Dyess AFB, TX	
86-0136	Rockwell B-1B Lancer [DY] *bl/w*	USAF 28th BS/7th BW, Dyess AFB, TX	
86-0137	Rockwell B-1B Lancer [EL] *bk/y* [37 BS]	USAF 37th BS/28th BW, Ellsworth AFB, SD	
86-0138	Rockwell B-1B Lancer [EL] *bk/y*	USAF 37th BS/28th BW, Ellsworth AFB, SD	
86-0139	Rockwell B-1B Lancer [EL] *bl/y* [34 BS]	USAF 34th BS/28th BW, Ellsworth AFB, SD	
86-0140	Rockwell B-1B Lancer [DY] *bk/r* [345 BS/CC]	USAF 28th BS/7th BW, Dyess AFB, TX	
Northrop B-2 Spirit			
(Names are given below. Each begins *Spirit of ...*)			
82-1066	Northrop B-2 Spirit [WM] *America*	USAF 509th BW, Whiteman AFB, MO	
82-1067	Northrop B-2 Spirit [WM] *Arizona*	USAF 509th BW, Whiteman AFB, MO	
82-1068	Northrop B-2 Spirit [WM] *New York*	USAF 509th BW, Whiteman AFB, MO (damaged)	
82-1069	Northrop B-2 Spirit [WM] *Indiana*	USAF 509th BW, Whiteman AFB, MO	
82-1070	Northrop B-2 Spirit [WM] *Ohio*	USAF 509th BW, Whiteman AFB, MO	
82-1071	Northrop B-2 Spirit [WM] *Mississippi*	USAF 509th BW, Whiteman AFB, MO	

Notes	Serial	Type (code/other identity)	Owner/operator, location or fate
	88-0328	Northrop B-2 Spirit [WM] *Texas*	USAF 509th BW, Whiteman AFB, MO
	88-0329	Northrop B-2 Spirit [WM] *Missouri*	USAF 509th BW, Whiteman AFB, MO
	88-0330	Northrop B-2 Spirit [WM] *California*	USAF 509th BW, Whiteman AFB, MO
	88-0331	Northrop B-2 Spirit [WM] *South Carolina*	USAF 509th BW, Whiteman AFB, MO
	88-0332	Northrop B-2 Spirit [WM] *Washington*	USAF 509th BW, Whiteman AFB, MO
	89-0128	Northrop B-2 Spirit [WM] *Nebraska*	USAF 509th BW, Whiteman AFB, MO
	89-0129	Northrop B-2 Spirit [WM] *Georgia*	USAF/LMTAS, Palmdale, CA (repairs)
	90-0040	Northrop B-2 Spirit [WM] *Alaska*	USAF 509th BW, Whiteman AFB, MO
	90-0041	Northrop B-2 Spirit [WM] *Hawaii*	USAF 509th BW, Whiteman AFB, MO
	92-0700	Northrop B-2 Spirit [WM] *Florida*	USAF 509th BW, Whiteman AFB, MO
	93-1085	Northrop B-2 Spirit [ED] *Oklahoma*	USAF 419th FLTS/412th TW, Edwards AFB,CA
	93-1086	Northrop B-2 Spirit [WM] *Kitty Hawk*	USAF 509th BW, Whiteman AFB, MO
	93-1087	Northrop B-2 Spirit [ED] *Pennsylvania*	USAF 419th FLTS/412th TW, Edwards AFB,CA
	93-1088	Northrop B-2 Spirit [WM] *Louisiana*	USAF 509th BW, Whiteman AFB, MO
	Lockheed U-2S		
	68-10329	Lockheed U-2S	USAF 99th ERS/9th RW, Fairford, UK
	68-10331	Lockheed U-2S [BB]	USAF 9th RW, Beale AFB, CA
	68-10336	Lockheed U-2S [BB]	USAF 9th RW, Beale AFB, CA
	68-10337	Lockheed U-2S	USAF 9th RW, Beale AFB, CA
	80-1064	Lockheed TU-2S [BB]	USAF 9th RW, Beale AFB, CA
	80-1065	Lockheed TU-2S [BB]	USAF 9th RW, Beale AFB, CA
	80-1066	Lockheed U-2S [BB]	USAF 9th RW, Beale AFB, CA
	80-1067	Lockheed U-2S [BB]	USAF 9th RW, Beale AFB, CA
	80-1069	Lockheed U-2S [BB]	USAF 99th ERS/9th RW, Fairford, UK
	80-1070	Lockheed U-2S [BB]	USAF 9th RW, Beale AFB, CA
	80-1071	Lockheed U-2S [BB]	USAF 9th RW, Beale AFB, CA
	80-1073	Lockheed U-2S [BB]	USAF 9th RW, Beale AFB, CA
	80-1074	Lockheed U-2S [BB]	USAF 9th RW, Beale AFB, CA
	80-1076	Lockheed U-2S [BB]	USAF 99th ERS/9th RW, Fairford, UK
	80-1077	Lockheed U-2S [BB]	USAF 9th RW, Beale AFB, CA
	80-1078	Lockheed TU-2S [BB]	USAF 9th RW, Beale AFB, CA
	80-1079	Lockheed U-2S [BB]	USAF 9th RW, Beale AFB, CA
	80-1080	Lockheed U-2S	USAF 9th RW, Beale AFB, CA
	80-1081	Lockheed U-2S [BB]	USAF 9th RW, Beale AFB, CA
	80-1082	Lockheed U-2S [BB]	USAF 9th RW, Beale AFB, CA
	80-1083	Lockheed U-2S [BB]	USAF 9th RW, Beale AFB, CA
	80-1084	Lockheed U-2S [BB]	USAF 9th RW, Beale AFB, CA
	80-1085	Lockheed U-2S [BB]	USAF 9th RW, Beale AFB, CA
	80-1086	Lockheed U-2S [BB]	USAF 9th RW, Beale AFB, CA
	80-1087	Lockheed U-2S [BB]	USAF 9th RW, Beale AFB, CA
	80-1089	Lockheed U-2S [BB]	*Damaged Al Dhafra, UAE, 2017*
	80-1090	Lockheed U-2S [BB]	USAF 9th RW, Beale AFB, CA
	80-1091	Lockheed TU-2S [BB]	USAF 9th RW, Beale AFB, CA
	80-1092	Lockheed U-2S [BB]	USAF 9th RW, Beale AFB, CA
	80-1093	Lockheed U-2S [BB]	USAF 9th RW, Beale AFB, CA
	80-1094	Lockheed U-2S [BB]	USAF 9th RW, Beale AFB, CA
	80-1096	Lockheed U-2S [BB]	USAF 9th RW, Beale AFB, CA
	80-1099	Lockheed U-2S [BB]	USAF/LMTAS, Palmdale, CA (rebuild)
	Boeing E-3 Sentry		
	71-1407	Boeing E-3B Sentry [OK] *w*	USAF 960th AACS/552nd ACW, Tinker AFB, OK
	71-1408	Boeing E-3B Sentry [AK] *gn*	USAF 962nd AACS/3rd Wg, Elmendorf, AK
	73-1675	Boeing E-3G Sentry [OK] *r*	USAF 964th AACS/552nd ACW, Tinker AFB, OK
	75-0556	Boeing E-3G Sentry [OK] *bl/bk*	USAF 552nd ACW, Tinker AFB, OK
	75-0557	Boeing E-3B Sentry [AK] *gn*	USAF 962nd AACS/3rd Wg, Elmendorf, AK
	75-0558	Boeing E-3G Sentry [OK] *r*	USAF 964th AACS/552nd ACW, Tinker AFB, OK
	75-0559	Boeing E-3G Sentry [OK] *w*	USAF 960th AACS/552nd ACW, Tinker AFB, OK
	75-0560	Boeing E-3G Sentry [ZZ] *or*	USAF 961st AACS/18th Wg, Kadena AB, Japan
	76-1604	Boeing E-3G Sentry [OK] *r*	USAF 964th AACS/552nd ACW, Tinker AFB, OK
	76-1605	Boeing E-3G Sentry [OK] *r*	USAF 964th AACS/552nd ACW, Tinker AFB, OK
	76-1606	Boeing E-3B Sentry [OK] *w*	USAF 960th AACS/552nd ACW, Tinker AFB, OK
	76-1607	Boeing E-3G Sentry [OK] *w*	USAF 960th AACS/552nd ACW, Tinker AFB, OK

Serial	Type (code/other identity)	Owner/operator, location or fate	Notes
77-0351	Boeing E-3G Sentry [OK] r	USAF 964th AACS/552nd ACW, Tinker AFB, OK	
77-0352	Boeing E-3B Sentry [ZZ] or	USAF 961st AACS/18th Wg, Kadena AB, Japan	
77-0353	Boeing E-3B Sentry [ZZ] or	USAF 961st AACS/18th Wg, Kadena AB, Japan	
77-0355	Boeing E-3B Sentry [OK] w	USAF 960th AACS/552nd ACW, Tinker AFB, OK	
77-0356	Boeing E-3G Sentry [OK] r	USAF 964th AACS/552nd ACW, Tinker AFB, OK	
78-0576	Boeing E-3G Sentry [OK] r	USAF 964th AACS/552nd ACW, Tinker AFB, OK	
78-0577	Boeing E-3G Sentry [OK] r	USAF 964th AACS/552nd ACW, Tinker AFB, OK	
78-0578	Boeing E-3G Sentry [OK] w/y/r	USAF 964th AACS/552nd ACW, Tinker AFB, OK	
79-0001	Boeing E-3G Sentry [OK] m [552 ACW]	USAF 552nd ACW, Tinker AFB, OK	
79-0002	Boeing E-3G Sentry [OK] r	USAF 964th AACS/552nd ACW, Tinker AFB, OK	
79-0003	Boeing E-3G Sentry [OK] m	USAF 964th AACS/552nd ACW, Tinker AFB, OK	
80-0137	Boeing E-3C Sentry [OK] w	USAF 960th AACS/552nd ACW, Tinker AFB, OK	
80-0138	Boeing E-3G Sentry [OK] r	USAF 964th AACS/552nd ACW, Tinker AFB, OK	
80-0139	Boeing E-3G Sentry [OK] r	USAF 964th AACS/552nd ACW, Tinker AFB, OK	
81-0004	Boeing E-3G Sentry [AK] gn	USAF 962nd AACS/3rd Wg, Elmendorf, AK	
81-0005	Boeing E-3G Sentry [OK] w	USAF 963rd ACCS/552nd ACW, Tinker AFB, OK	
82-0006	Boeing E-3G Sentry [OK] r	USAF 964th AACS/552nd ACW, Tinker AFB, OK	
82-0007	Boeing E-3G Sentry [ZZ] or	USAF 961st AACS/18th Wg, Kadena AB, Japan	
83-0009	Boeing E-3G Sentry [OK] w/bk/y	USAF 963rd ACCS/552nd ACW, Tinker AFB, OK	

Boeing E-4B

73-1676	Boeing E-4B	USAF 1st ACCS/595th CACG, Offutt AFB, NE	
73-1677	Boeing E-4B	USAF 1st ACCS/595th CACG, Offutt AFB, NE	
74-0787	Boeing E-4B	USAF 1st ACCS/595th CACG, Offutt AFB, NE	
75-0125	Boeing E-4B	USAF 1st ACCS/595th CACG, Offutt AFB, NE	

Lockheed C-5M Super Galaxy

68-0213	Lockheed C-5M Super Galaxy w/bk	USAF 22nd AS/60th AMW, Travis AFB, CA	
68-0216	Lockheed C-5M Super Galaxy w/bk	USAF 22nd AS/60th AMW, Travis AFB, CA	
69-0024	Lockheed C-5M Super Galaxy bl/y	USAF 9th AS/436th AW, Dover AFB, DE	
83-1285	Lockheed C-5M Super Galaxy bl/y	USAF 9th AS/436th AW, Dover AFB, DE	
84-0060	Lockheed C-5M Super Galaxy w/bk	USAF 22nd AS/60th AMW, Travis AFB, CA	
84-0061	Lockheed C-5M Super Galaxy bl/y	USAF 9th AS/436th AW, Dover AFB, DE	
84-0062	Lockheed C-5M Super Galaxy w/bk	USAF 22nd AS/60th AMW, Travis AFB, CA	
85-0001	Lockheed C-5M Super Galaxy bl/y	USAF 9th AS/436th AW, Dover AFB, DE	
85-0002	Lockheed C-5M Super Galaxy bl/y	USAF 9th AS/436th AW, Dover AFB, DE	
85-0003	Lockheed C-5M Super Galaxy bl/y	USAF 9th AS/436th AW, Dover AFB, DE	
85-0004	Lockheed C-5M Super Galaxy bl/y	USAF 9th AS/436th AW, Dover AFB, DE	
85-0005	Lockheed C-5M Super Galaxy bl/y	USAF 9th AS/436th AW, Dover AFB, DE	
85-0006	Lockheed C-5M Super Galaxy r/w/bl	USAF 68th AS/433rd AW AFRC, Kelly AFB, TX	
85-0007	Lockheed C-5M Super Galaxy bl/y	USAF 9th AS/436th AW, Dover AFB, DE	
85-0008	Lockheed C-5M Super Galaxy bl/y	USAF 9th AS/436th AW, Dover AFB, DE	
85-0009	Lockheed C-5M Super Galaxy r/w/bl	USAF 68th AS/433rd AW AFRC, Kelly AFB, TX	
85-0010	Lockheed C-5M Super Galaxy w/bk	USAF 22nd AS/60th AMW, Travis AFB, CA	
86-0011	Lockheed C-5M Super Galaxy w/bk	USAF 22nd AS/60th AMW, Travis AFB, CA	
86-0012	Lockheed C-5M Super Galaxy bl/r	USAF 337th AS/439th AW, Westover ARB, MA	
86-0013	Lockheed C-5M Super Galaxy r/w/bl	USAF 68th AS/433rd AW AFRC, Kelly AFB, TX	
86-0014	Lockheed C-5M Super Galaxy bl/r	USAF 337th AS/439th AW, Westover ARB, MA	
86-0015	Lockheed C-5M Super Galaxy r/w/bl	USAF 68th AS/433rd AW AFRC, Kelly AFB, TX	
86-0016	Lockheed C-5M Super Galaxy w/bk	USAF 22nd AS/60th AMW, Travis AFB, CA	
86-0017	Lockheed C-5M Super Galaxy bl/y	USAF 9th AS/436th AW, Dover AFB, DE	
86-0018	Lockheed C-5M Super Galaxy r/w/bl	USAF 356th AS/433rd AW AFRC, Kelly AFB, TX	
86-0019	Lockheed C-5M Super Galaxy r/w/bl	USAF 68th AS/433rd AW AFRC, Kelly AFB, TX	
86-0020	Lockheed C-5M Super Galaxy bl/y	USAF 9th AS/436th AW, Dover AFB, DE	
86-0021	Lockheed C-5M Super Galaxy r/w/bl	USAF 68th AS/433rd AW AFRC, Kelly AFB, TX	
86-0022	Lockheed C-5M Super Galaxy w/bk	USAF 22nd AS/60th AMW, Travis AFB, CA	
86-0023	Lockheed C-5M Super Galaxy w/bk	USAF 22nd AS/60th AMW, Travis AFB, CA	
86-0024	Lockheed C-5M Super Galaxy w/bk	USAF 22nd AS/60th AMW, Travis AFB, CA	
86-0025	Lockheed C-5M Super Galaxy bl/y	USAF 9th AS/436th AW, Dover AFB, DE	
86-0026	Lockheed C-5M Super Galaxy w/bk	USAF 22nd AS/60th AMW, Travis AFB, CA	
87-0027	Lockheed C-5M Super Galaxy r/w/bl	USAF 68th AS/433rd AW AFRC, Kelly AFB, TX	
87-0028	Lockheed C-5M Super Galaxy w/bk	USAF 22nd AS/60th AMW, Travis AFB, CA	

Notes	Serial	Type (code/other identity)	Owner/operator, location or fate
	87-0029	Lockheed C-5M Super Galaxy *w/bk*	USAF 22nd AS/60th AMW, Travis AFB, CA
	87-0030	Lockheed C-5M Super Galaxy *w/bk*	USAF 22nd AS/60th AMW, Travis AFB, CA
	87-0031	Lockheed C-5M Super Galaxy *bl/r*	USAF 337th AS/439th AW, Westover ARB, MA
	87-0032	Lockheed C-5M Super Galaxy *w/bk*	USAF 22nd AS/60th AMW, Travis AFB, CA
	87-0033	Lockheed C-5M Super Galaxy *r/w/bl*	USAF 68th AS/433rd AW AFRC, Kelly AFB, TX
	87-0034	Lockheed C-5M Super Galaxy *w/bk*	USAF 22nd AS/60th AMW, Travis AFB, CA
	87-0035	Lockheed C-5M Super Galaxy *bl/y*	USAF 9th AS/436th AW, Dover AFB, DE
	87-0036	Lockheed C-5M Super Galaxy *bl/y*	USAF 9th AS/436th AW, Dover AFB, DE
	87-0037	Lockheed C-5M Super Galaxy *bl/r*	USAF 337th AS/439th AW, Westover ARB, MA
	87-0038	Lockheed C-5M Super Galaxy *r/w/bl*	USAF 68th AS/433rd AW AFRC, Kelly AFB, TX
	87-0039	Lockheed C-5M Super Galaxy *bl/r*	USAF 337th AS/439th AW, Westover ARB, MA
	87-0040	Lockheed C-5M Super Galaxy *bl/y*	USAF 9th AS/436th AW, Dover AFB, DE
	87-0041	Lockheed C-5M Super Galaxy *bl/r*	USAF 337th AS/439th AW, Westover ARB, MA
	87-0042	Lockheed C-5M Super Galaxy *w/bk*	USAF 22nd AS/60th AMW, Travis AFB, CA
	87-0043	Lockheed C-5M Super Galaxy *bl/r*	USAF 337th AS/439th AW, Westover ARB, MA
	87-0044	Lockheed C-5M Super Galaxy *w/bk*	USAF 22nd AS/60th AMW, Travis AFB, CA
	87-0045	Lockheed C-5M Super Galaxy *bl/y*	USAF 9th AS/436th AW, Dover AFB, DE

Boeing E-8C J-STARS

Notes	Serial	Type (code/other identity)	Owner/operator, location or fate
	86-0416	Boeing TE-8C J-STARS [GA] *r/bk*	USAF 116th ACW GA ANG, Warner Robins AFB
	92-3289	Boeing E-8C J-STARS [GA] *r/bk*	*To 309th AMARG, February 2022*
	92-3290	Boeing E-8C J-STARS [GA] *r/bk*	USAF 116th ACW GA ANG, Warner Robins AFB
	93-1097	Boeing E-8C J-STARS [GA] *r/bk*	USAF 116th ACW GA ANG, Warner Robins AFB
	94-0284	Boeing E-8C J-STARS [GA] *r/bk*	USAF 116th ACW GA ANG, Warner Robins AFB
	94-0285	Boeing E-8C J-STARS [GA] *r/bk*	USAF 116th ACW GA ANG, Warner Robins AFB
	95-0121	Boeing E-8C J-STARS [GA] *r/bk*	USAF 116th ACW GA ANG, Warner Robins AFB
	95-0122	Boeing E-8C J-STARS [GA] *r/bk*	USAF 116th ACW GA ANG, Warner Robins AFB
	96-0042	Boeing E-8C J-STARS [GA] *r/bk*	USAF 116th ACW GA ANG, Warner Robins AFB
	96-0043	Boeing E-8C J-STARS [GA] *r/bk*	*To 309th AMARG, July 2022*
	97-0100	Boeing E-8C J-STARS [GA] *r/bk*	*To 309th AMARG, September 2022*
	97-0200	Boeing E-8C J-STARS [GA] *r/bk*	USAF 116th ACW GA ANG, Warner Robins AFB
	97-0201	Boeing E-8C J-STARS [GA] *r/bk*	*To 309th AMARG, November 2022*
	99-0006	Boeing E-8C J-STARS [GA] *r/bk*	USAF 116th ACW GA ANG, Warner Robins AFB
	00-2000	Boeing E-8C J-STARS [GA] *r/bk*	USAF 116th ACW GA ANG, Warner Robins AFB
	01-2005	Boeing E-8C J-STARS [GA] *r/bk*	*To 309th AMARG, March 2022*
	02-9111	Boeing E-8C J-STARS [GA] *r/bk*	USAF 116th ACW GA ANG, Warner Robins AFB

McDonnell Douglas KC-10A Extender

Notes	Serial	Type (code/other identity)	Owner/operator, location or fate
	79-0433	McDonnell Douglas KC-10A Extender *bl*	*Preserved at Dover AFB, DE, 2022*
	79-0434	McDonnell Douglas KC-10A Extender *bl*	*To 309th AMARG, June 2021*
	79-1710	McDonnell Douglas KC-10A Extender *bl*	*To 309th AMARG, May 2022*
	79-1711	McDonnell Douglas KC-10A Extender *bl*	USAF 305th AMW, McGuire AFB, NJ
	79-1712	McDonnell Douglas KC-10A Extender *bl*	*To 309th AMARG, September 2022*
	79-1946	McDonnell Douglas KC-10A Extender *w/bk*	USAF 60th AMW, Travis AFB, CA
	79-1947	McDonnell Douglas KC-10A Extender *bl*	*To 309th AMARG, October 2022*
	79-1948	McDonnell Douglas KC-10A Extender *w/bk*	USAF 60th AMW, Travis AFB, CA
	79-1950	McDonnell Douglas KC-10A Extender *w/bk*	USAF 60th AMW, Travis AFB, CA
	79-1951	McDonnell Douglas KC-10A Extender *w/bk*	USAF 60th AMW, Travis AFB, CA
	82-0191	McDonnell Douglas KC-10A Extender *w/bk*	USAF 60th AMW, Travis AFB, CA
	82-0192	McDonnell Douglas KC-10A Extender *w/bk*	*To 309th AMARG, September 2022*
	82-0193	McDonnell Douglas KC-10A Extender *w/bk*	USAF 60th AMW, Travis AFB, CA
	83-0075	McDonnell Douglas KC-10A Extender *w/bk*	USAF 60th AMW, Travis AFB, CA
	83-0076	McDonnell Douglas KC-10A Extender *w/bk*	USAF 60th AMW, Travis AFB, CA
	83-0078	McDonnell Douglas KC-10A Extender *w/bk*	USAF 60th AMW, Travis AFB, CA
	83-0079	McDonnell Douglas KC-10A Extender *bl*	*To 309th AMARG, April 2022*
	83-0080	McDonnell Douglas KC-10A Extender *w/bk*	USAF 60th AMW, Travis AFB, CA
	83-0082	McDonnell Douglas KC-10A Extender *bl*	*To 309th AMARG, June 2022*
	84-0185	McDonnell Douglas KC-10A Extender *w/bk*	USAF 60th AMW, Travis AFB, CA
	84-0186	McDonnell Douglas KC-10A Extender *bl*	USAF 305th AMW, McGuire AFB, NJ
	84-0187	McDonnell Douglas KC-10A Extender *w/bk*	*To 309th AMARG, June 2022*
	84-0188	McDonnell Douglas KC-10A Extender *bl*	USAF 305th AMW, McGuire AFB, NJ
	84-0189	McDonnell Douglas KC-10A Extender *bl*	USAF 305th AMW, McGuire AFB, NJ

Serial	Type (code/other identity)	Owner/operator, location or fate	Notes
84-0191	McDonnell Douglas KC-10A Extender *w/bk*	USAF 60th AMW, Travis AFB, CA	
84-0192	McDonnell Douglas KC-10A Extender *bl*	*To 309th AMARG, April 2022*	
85-0027	McDonnell Douglas KC-10A Extender *bl*	*To 309th AMARG, August 2022*	
85-0028	McDonnell Douglas KC-10A Extender *bl*	*To 309th AMARG, July 2022*	
85-0029	McDonnell Douglas KC-10A Extender *w/bk*	USAF 60th AMW, Travis AFB, CA	
85-0030	McDonnell Douglas KC-10A Extender *bl*	USAF 305th AMW, McGuire AFB, NJ	
85-0031	McDonnell Douglas KC-10A Extender *bl*	USAF 305th AMW, McGuire AFB, NJ	
85-0032	McDonnell Douglas KC-10A Extender *bl*	USAF 305th AMW, McGuire AFB, NJ	
85-0033	McDonnell Douglas KC-10A Extender *w/bk*	USAF 60th AMW, Travis AFB, CA	
85-0034	McDonnell Douglas KC-10A Extender *bl*	USAF 305th AMW, McGuire AFB, NJ	
86-0027	McDonnell Douglas KC-10A Extender *bl*	USAF 305th AMW, McGuire AFB, NJ	
86-0028	McDonnell Douglas KC-10A Extender *bl*	USAF 305th AMW, McGuire AFB, NJ	
86-0029	McDonnell Douglas KC-10A Extender *w/bk*	USAF 60th AMW, Travis AFB, CA	
86-0030	McDonnell Douglas KC-10A Extender *w/bk*	USAF 60th AMW, Travis AFB, CA	
86-0031	McDonnell Douglas KC-10A Extender *w/bk*	USAF 60th AMW, Travis AFB, CA	
86-0032	McDonnell Douglas KC-10A Extender *bl*	USAF 305th AMW, McGuire AFB, NJ	
86-0033	McDonnell Douglas KC-10A Extender *w/bk*	USAF 60th AMW, Travis AFB, CA	
86-0035	McDonnell Douglas KC-10A Extender *bl*	USAF 305th AMW, McGuire AFB, NJ	
86-0037	McDonnell Douglas KC-10A Extender *w/bk*	USAF 60th AMW, Travis AFB, CA	
86-0038	McDonnell Douglas KC-10A Extender *w/bk*	USAF 60th AMW, Travis AFB, CA	
87-0117	McDonnell Douglas KC-10A Extender *w/bk*	USAF 60th AMW, Travis AFB, CA	
87-0118	McDonnell Douglas KC-10A Extender *bl*	*To 309th AMARG, April 2022*	
87-0119	McDonnell Douglas KC-10A Extender *w/bk*	USAF 60th AMW, Travis AFB, CA	
87-0121	McDonnell Douglas KC-10A Extender *bl*	*To 309th AMARG, May 2022*	
87-0123	McDonnell Douglas KC-10A Extender *w/bk*	*To 309th AMARG, November 2022*	

Bombardier E-11A Global Express

Serial	Type (code/other identity)	Owner/operator, location or fate	Notes
11-9001	Bombardier E-11A Global Express	USAF 430th EECS/653rd ELSG, Hanscom MA	
11-9355	Bombardier E-11A Global Express	USAF 430th EECS/653rd ELSG, Hanscom MA	
12-9506	Bombardier E-11A Global Express	USAF 430th EECS/653rd ELSG, Hanscom MA	
21-9045	Bombardier E-11A Global Express	USAF 430th EECS/653rd ELSG, Hanscom MA	
21-9056	Bombardier E-11A Global Express	USAF (on order)	

McDonnell Douglas F-15E Strike Eagle

Serial	Type (code/other identity)	Owner/operator, location or fate	Notes
86-0184	McD F-15E Strike Eagle [ET] *bk/wh*	USAF 40th FLTS/96th TW, Eglin AFB, FL	
86-0185	McD F-15E Strike Eagle [ET] *bk/wh*	USAF 40th FLTS/96th TW, Eglin AFB, FL	
86-0186	McD F-15E Strike Eagle [SJ] *bl*	USAF 334th FS/4th FW, Seymour-Johnson AFB, SC	
86-0187	McD F-15E Strike Eagle [SJ] *y*	USAF 336th FS/4th FW, Seymour-Johnson AFB, SC	
86-0188	McD F-15E Strike Eagle [ET] *bk/wh*	USAF 40th FLTS/96th TW, Eglin AFB, FL	
86-0189	McD F-15E Strike Eagle [SJ] *gn*	USAF 335th FS/4th FW, Seymour-Johnson AFB, SC	
86-0190	McD F-15E Strike Eagle [SJ] *r*	USAF 333rd FS/4th FW, Seymour-Johnson AFB, SC	
87-0169	McD F-15E Strike Eagle [MO] *r/y*	USAF 389th FS/366th FW, Mountain Home AFB, ID	
87-0170	McD F-15E Strike Eagle [MO] *r/y*	USAF 389th FS/366th FW, Mountain Home AFB, ID	
87-0171	McD F-15E Strike Eagle [SJ] *gn*	USAF 335th FS/4th FW, Seymour-Johnson AFB, SC	
87-0173	McD F-15E Strike Eagle [MO] *r/y*	USAF 389th FS/366th FW, Mountain Home AFB, ID	
87-0174	McD F-15E Strike Eagle [SJ] *gn*	USAF 335th FS/4th FW, Seymour-Johnson AFB, SC	
87-0175	McD F-15E Strike Eagle [SJ] *gn*	USAF 335th FS/4th FW, Seymour-Johnson AFB, SC	
87-0176	McD F-15E Strike Eagle [SJ] *y*	USAF 336th FS/4th FW, Seymour-Johnson AFB, SC	
87-0177	McD F-15E Strike Eagle [SJ] *y*	USAF 336th FS/4th FW, Seymour-Johnson AFB, SC	

Notes	Serial	Type (code/other identity)	Owner/operator, location or fate
	87-0178	McD F-15E Strike Eagle [SJ] *bl*	USAF 334th FS/4th FW, Seymour-Johnson AFB, SC
	87-0179	McD F-15E Strike Eagle [SJ] *r*	USAF 333rd FS/4th FW, Seymour-Johnson AFB, SC
	87-0180	McD F-15E Strike Eagle [ET] *bk/wh*	USAF 40th FLTS/96th TW, Eglin AFB, FL
	87-0181	McD F-15E Strike Eagle [SJ] *y*	USAF 336th FS/4th FW, Seymour-Johnson AFB, SC
	87-0182	McD F-15E Strike Eagle [MO] *r/y*	USAF 389th FS/366th FW, Mountain Home AFB, ID
	87-0183	McD F-15E Strike Eagle [MO] *r/y*	USAF 389th FS/366th FW, Mountain Home AFB, ID
	87-0184	McD F-15E Strike Eagle [SJ] *bl*	USAF 334th FS/4th FW, Seymour-Johnson AFB, SC
	87-0185	McD F-15E Strike Eagle [SJ] *r*	USAF 333rd FS/4th FW, Seymour-Johnson AFB, SC
	87-0187	McD F-15E Strike Eagle [SJ] *y*	USAF 336th FS/4th FW, Seymour-Johnson AFB, SC
	87-0188	McD F-15E Strike Eagle [SJ] *r*	USAF 333rd FS/4th FW, Seymour-Johnson AFB, SC
	87-0189	McD F-15E Strike Eagle [SJ] *r*	USAF 333rd FS/4th FW, Seymour-Johnson AFB, SC
	87-0190	McD F-15E Strike Eagle [SJ] *r*	USAF 333rd FS/4th FW, Seymour-Johnson AFB, SC
	87-0191	McD F-15E Strike Eagle [SJ] *r*	USAF 333rd FS/4th FW, Seymour-Johnson AFB, SC
	87-0192	McD F-15E Strike Eagle [SJ] *gn*	USAF 335th FS/4th FW, Seymour-Johnson AFB, SC
	87-0193	McD F-15E Strike Eagle [SJ] *gn*	USAF 335th FS/4th FW, Seymour-Johnson AFB, SC
	87-0194	McD F-15E Strike Eagle [SJ]	USAF 4th FW, Seymour-Johnson AFB, SC
	87-0195	McD F-15E Strike Eagle [SJ] *r*	USAF 333rd FS/4th FW, Seymour-Johnson AFB, SC
	87-0196	McD F-15E Strike Eagle [SJ] *gn*	USAF 335th FS/4th FW, Seymour-Johnson AFB, SC
	87-0197	McD F-15E Strike Eagle [SJ] *bl*	USAF 334th FS/4th FW, Seymour-Johnson AFB, SC
	87-0198	McD F-15E Strike Eagle [MO] *r/y*	USAF 389th FS/366th FW, Mountain Home AFB, ID
	87-0199	McD F-15E Strike Eagle [SJ] *r*	USAF 333rd FS/4th FW, Seymour-Johnson AFB, SC
	87-0200	McD F-15E Strike Eagle [SJ] *bl*	USAF 334th FS/4th FW, Seymour-Johnson AFB, SC
	87-0201	McD F-15E Strike Eagle [MO] *r/y*	USAF 389th FS/366th FW, Mountain Home AFB, ID
	87-0202	McD F-15E Strike Eagle [MO] *r/y*	USAF 389th FS/366th FW, Mountain Home AFB, ID
	87-0204	McD F-15E Strike Eagle [MO] *r/y*	USAF 389th FS/366th FW, Mountain Home AFB, ID
	87-0205	McD F-15E Strike Eagle [SJ] *bl*	USAF 334th FS/4th FW, Seymour-Johnson AFB, SC
	87-0206	McD F-15E Strike Eagle [SJ] *y*	USAF 336th FS/4th FW, Seymour-Johnson AFB, SC
	87-0207	McD F-15E Strike Eagle [MO] *r/y*	USAF 389th FS/366th FW, Mountain Home AFB, ID
	87-0208	McD F-15E Strike Eagle [MO] *r/y*	USAF 389th FS/366th FW, Mountain Home AFB, ID
	87-0209	McD F-15E Strike Eagle [MO] *r/y*	USAF 389th FS/366th FW, Mountain Home AFB, ID
	87-0210	McD F-15E Strike Eagle [MO] *r/y*	USAF 389th FS/366th FW, Mountain Home AFB, ID
	88-1667	McD F-15E Strike Eagle [MO] *r/y*	USAF 389th FS/366th FW, Mountain Home AFB, ID

Serial	Type (code/other identity)	Owner/operator, location or fate	Notes
88-1668	McD F-15E Strike Eagle [SJ] *bl*	USAF 334th FS/4th FW, Seymour-Johnson AFB, SC	
88-1669	McD F-15E Strike Eagle [SJ] *y*	USAF 336th FS/4th FW, Seymour-Johnson AFB, SC	
88-1670	McD F-15E Strike Eagle [SJ] *gn*	USAF 335th FS/4th FW, Seymour-Johnson AFB, SC	
88-1671	McD F-15E Strike Eagle [SJ] *y*	USAF 336th FS/4th FW, Seymour-Johnson AFB, SC	
88-1672	McD F-15E Strike Eagle [SJ] *bl*	USAF 334th FS/4th FW, Seymour-Johnson AFB, SC	
88-1673	McD F-15E Strike Eagle [SJ] *y*	USAF 336th FS/4th FW, Seymour-Johnson AFB, SC	
88-1674	McD F-15E Strike Eagle [SJ] *r*	USAF 333rd FS/4th FW, Seymour-Johnson AFB, SC	
88-1675	McD F-15E Strike Eagle [SJ] *y*	USAF 336th FS/4th FW, Seymour-Johnson AFB, SC	
88-1676	McD F-15E Strike Eagle [SJ] *gn*	USAF 335th FS/4th FW, Seymour-Johnson AFB, SC	
88-1677	McD F-15E Strike Eagle [SJ] *bl*	USAF 334th FS/4th FW, Seymour-Johnson AFB, SC	
88-1678	McD F-15E Strike Eagle [MO] *r/y*	USAF 389th FS/366th FW, Mountain Home AFB, ID	
88-1679	McD F-15E Strike Eagle [SJ] *bl*	USAF 334th FS/4th FW, Seymour-Johnson AFB, SC	
88-1680	McD F-15E Strike Eagle [SJ] [4 TS] *r/bl*	USAF 333rd FS/4th FW, Seymour-Johnson AFB, SC	
88-1681	McD F-15E Strike Eagle [OT] *bk/wh*	USAF 85th TES/53rd Wg, Eglin AFB, FL	
88-1682	McD F-15E Strike Eagle [SJ] *gn*	USAF 335th FS/4th FW, Seymour-Johnson AFB, SC	
88-1683	McD F-15E Strike Eagle [SJ] *r*	USAF 333rd FS/4th FW, Seymour-Johnson AFB, SC	
88-1684	McD F-15E Strike Eagle [SJ]	USAF 4th FW, Seymour-Johnson AFB, SC	
88-1685	McD F-15E Strike Eagle [SJ] *r*	USAF 333rd FS/4th FW, Seymour-Johnson AFB, SC	
88-1686	McD F-15E Strike Eagle [SJ] *bl*	USAF 334th FS/4th FW, Seymour-Johnson AFB, SC	
88-1687	McD F-15E Strike Eagle [SJ] *r*	USAF 333rd FS/4th FW, Seymour-Johnson AFB, SC	
88-1688	McD F-15E Strike Eagle [SJ] *y*	USAF 336th FS/4th FW, Seymour-Johnson AFB, SC	
88-1690	McD F-15E Strike Eagle [SJ] *bl*	USAF 334th FS/4th FW, Seymour-Johnson AFB, SC	
88-1691	McD F-15E Strike Eagle [SJ] *bl*	USAF 334th FS/4th FW, Seymour-Johnson AFB, SC	
88-1693	McD F-15E Strike Eagle [SJ] *r*	USAF 333rd FS/4th FW, Seymour-Johnson AFB, SC	
88-1695	McD F-15E Strike Eagle [SJ] *gn*	USAF 335th FS/4th FW, Seymour-Johnson AFB, SC	
88-1696	McD F-15E Strike Eagle [SJ] *r*	USAF 333rd FS/4th FW, Seymour-Johnson AFB, SC	
88-1697	McD F-15E Strike Eagle [MO] *r/y*	USAF 389th FS/366th FW, Mountain Home AFB, ID	
88-1698	McD F-15E Strike Eagle [SJ] *bl*	USAF 334th FS/4th FW, Seymour-Johnson AFB, SC	
88-1699	McD F-15E Strike Eagle [MO] *r/y*	USAF 389th FS/366th FW, Mountain Home AFB, ID	
88-1700	McD F-15E Strike Eagle [SJ] *y*	USAF 336th FS/4th FW, Seymour-Johnson AFB, SC	
88-1702	McD F-15E Strike Eagle [SJ] [4 FW]	USAF 4th FW, Seymour-Johnson AFB, SC	
88-1703	McD F-15E Strike Eagle [SJ] *gn*	USAF 335th FS/4th FW, Seymour-Johnson AFB, SC	

Notes	Serial	Type (code/other identity)	Owner/operator, location or fate
	88-1704	McD F-15E Strike Eagle [SJ] *bl* [334 FS]	USAF 334th FS/4th FW, Seymour-Johnson AFB, SC
	88-1705	McD F-15E Strike Eagle [MO] *r/y* [389 FS]	USAF 389th FS/366th FW, Mountain Home AFB, ID
	88-1706	McD F-15E Strike Eagle [SJ] *gn*	USAF 335th FS/4th FW, Seymour-Johnson AFB, SC
	88-1707	McD F-15E Strike Eagle [MO] *r/y*	USAF 389th FS/366th FW, Mountain Home AFB, ID
	88-1708	McD F-15E Strike Eagle [SJ] *gn*	USAF 335th FS/4th FW, Seymour-Johnson AFB, SC
	89-0471	McD F-15E Strike Eagle [SJ] *y*	USAF 336th FS/4th FW, Seymour-Johnson AFB, SC
	89-0472	McD F-15E Strike Eagle [SJ] *r*	USAF 333rd FS/4th FW, Seymour-Johnson AFB, SC
	89-0473	McD F-15E Strike Eagle [SJ] *r*	USAF 333rd FS/4th FW, Seymour-Johnson AFB, SC
	89-0474	McD F-15E Strike Eagle [SJ] *gn*	USAF 335th FS/4th FW, Seymour-Johnson AFB, SC
	89-0475	McD F-15E Strike Eagle [SJ] *bl*	USAF 334th FS/4th FW, Seymour-Johnson AFB, SC
	89-0476	McD F-15E Strike Eagle [SJ] *gn*	USAF 335th FS/4th FW, Seymour-Johnson AFB, SC
	89-0477	McD F-15E Strike Eagle [SJ] *gn*	USAF 335th FS/4th FW, Seymour-Johnson AFB, SC
	89-0478	McD F-15E Strike Eagle [SJ] *gn*	USAF 335th FS/4th FW, Seymour-Johnson AFB, SC
	89-0480	McD F-15E Strike Eagle [SJ] *r*	USAF 333rd FS/4th FW, Seymour-Johnson AFB, SC
	89-0481	McD F-15E Strike Eagle [SJ] *bl*	USAF 334th FS/4th FW, Seymour-Johnson AFB, SC
	89-0482	McD F-15E Strike Eagle [SJ] *r*	USAF 333rd FS/4th FW, Seymour-Johnson AFB, SC
	89-0483	McD F-15E Strike Eagle [SJ]	USAF 4th FW, Seymour-Johnson AFB, SC
	89-0484	McD F-15E Strike Eagle [SJ] *r*	USAF 333rd FS/4th FW, Seymour-Johnson AFB, SC
	89-0485	McD F-15E Strike Eagle [SJ] *gn*	USAF 335th FS/4th FW, Seymour-Johnson AFB, SC
	89-0486	McD F-15E Strike Eagle [SJ] *gn*	USAF 335th FS/4th FW, Seymour-Johnson AFB, SC
	89-0487	McD F-15E Strike Eagle [SJ] *gn*	USAF 335th FS/4th FW, Seymour-Johnson AFB, SC
	89-0488	McD F-15E Strike Eagle [SJ] *y*	USAF 336th FS/4th FW, Seymour-Johnson AFB, SC
	89-0489	McD F-15E Strike Eagle [SJ] *y*	USAF 336th FS/4th FW, Seymour-Johnson AFB, SC
	89-0490	McD F-15E Strike Eagle [SJ]	USAF 4th FW, Seymour-Johnson AFB, SC
	89-0492	McD F-15E Strike Eagle [SJ] *y* [4 OG]	USAF 336th FS/4th FW, Seymour-Johnson AFB, SC
	89-0493	McD F-15E Strike Eagle [SJ]	USAF 4th FW, Seymour-Johnson AFB, SC
	89-0494	McD F-15E Strike Eagle [SJ] *y*	USAF 336th FS/4th FW, Seymour-Johnson AFB, SC
	89-0495	McD F-15E Strike Eagle [SJ] *y*	USAF 336th FS/4th FW, Seymour-Johnson AFB, SC
	89-0496	McD F-15E Strike Eagle [SJ] *bl*	USAF 334th FS/4th FW, Seymour-Johnson AFB, SC
	89-0498	McD F-15E Strike Eagle [SJ] *gn*	USAF 335th FS/4th FW, Seymour-Johnson AFB, SC
	89-0499	McD F-15E Strike Eagle [SJ] *bl*	USAF 334th FS/4th FW, Seymour-Johnson AFB, SC
	89-0500	McD F-15E Strike Eagle [SJ] *bl*	USAF 334th FS/4th FW, Seymour-Johnson AFB, SC

Serial	Type (code/other identity)	Owner/operator, location or fate	Notes
89-0501	McD F-15E Strike Eagle [SJ] y	USAF 336th FS/4th FW, Seymour-Johnson AFB, SC	
89-0502	McD F-15E Strike Eagle [SJ] gn	USAF 335th FS/4th FW, Seymour-Johnson AFB, SC	
89-0503	McD F-15E Strike Eagle [SJ]	USAF 4th FW, Seymour-Johnson AFB, SC	
89-0505	McD F-15E Strike Eagle [SJ] y	USAF 336th FS/4th FW, Seymour-Johnson AFB, SC	
89-0506	McD F-15E Strike Eagle [MO] r/y	USAF 389th FS/366th FW, Mountain Home AFB, ID	
90-0227	McD F-15E Strike Eagle [MO] r/y	USAF 389th FS/366th FW, Mountain Home AFB, ID	
90-0228	McD F-15E Strike Eagle [SJ] r	USAF 333rd FS/4th FW, Seymour-Johnson AFB, SC	
90-0229	McD F-15E Strike Eagle [SJ] r	USAF 333rd FS/4th FW, Seymour-Johnson AFB, SC	
90-0230	McD F-15E Strike Eagle [SJ] y	USAF 336th FS/4th FW, Seymour-Johnson AFB, SC	
90-0232	McD F-15E Strike Eagle [SJ] gn	USAF 335th FS/4th FW, Seymour-Johnson AFB, SC	
90-0233	McD F-15E Strike Eagle [MO] tig	USAF 391st FS/366th Wg, Mountain Home AFB, ID	
90-0234	McD F-15E Strike Eagle [MO] tig	USAF 391st FS/366th Wg, Mountain Home AFB, ID	
90-0236	McD F-15E Strike Eagle [MO] tig	USAF 391st FS/366th Wg, Mountain Home AFB, ID	
90-0237	McD F-15E Strike Eagle [MO] tig	USAF 391st FS/366th Wg, Mountain Home AFB, ID	
90-0238	McD F-15E Strike Eagle [MO] tig	USAF 391st FS/366th Wg, Mountain Home AFB, ID	
90-0239	McD F-15E Strike Eagle [WA] bk/y	USAF 17th WPS/57th Wg, Nellis AFB, NV	
90-0240	McD F-15E Strike Eagle [MO] tig	USAF 391st FS/366th Wg, Mountain Home AFB, ID	
90-0241	McD F-15E Strike Eagle [MO] tig	USAF 391st FS/366th Wg, Mountain Home AFB, ID	
90-0242	McD F-15E Strike Eagle [MO] tig	USAF 391st FS/366th Wg, Mountain Home AFB, ID	
90-0243	McD F-15E Strike Eagle [MO] tig	USAF 391st FS/366th Wg, Mountain Home AFB, ID	
90-0244	McD F-15E Strike Eagle [MO] tig	USAF 391st FS/366th Wg, Mountain Home AFB, ID	
90-0245	McD F-15E Strike Eagle [MO] tig	USAF 391st FS/366th Wg, Mountain Home AFB, ID	
90-0246	McD F-15E Strike Eagle [MO] tig	USAF 391st FS/366th Wg, Mountain Home AFB, ID	
90-0247	McD F-15E Strike Eagle [MO] tig	USAF 391st FS/366th Wg, Mountain Home AFB, ID	
90-0248	McD F-15E Strike Eagle [MO] tig	USAF 391st FS/366th Wg, Mountain Home AFB, ID	
90-0249	McD F-15E Strike Eagle [MO] tig	USAF 391st FS/366th Wg, Mountain Home AFB, ID	
90-0250	McD F-15E Strike Eagle [MO] tig	USAF 391st FS/366th Wg, Mountain Home AFB, ID	
90-0251	McD F-15E Strike Eagle [WA] bk/y	USAF 17th WPS/57th Wg, Nellis AFB, NV	
90-0252	McD F-15E Strike Eagle [ET] bk/wh	USAF 40th FLTS/96th TW, Eglin AFB, FL	
90-0253	McD F-15E Strike Eagle [MO] tig	USAF 391st FS/366th Wg, Mountain Home AFB, ID	
90-0255	McD F-15E Strike Eagle [MO] tig	USAF 391st FS/366th Wg, Mountain Home AFB, ID	
90-0256	McD F-15E Strike Eagle [ET] bk/wh	USAF 40th FLTS/96th TW, Eglin AFB, FL	
90-0257	McD F-15E Strike Eagle [WA] bk/y [57 WPSS]	USAF 17th WPS/57th Wg, Nellis AFB, NV	
90-0258	McD F-15E Strike Eagle [OT] bk/gn	USAF 422nd TES/53rd Wg, Nellis AFB, NV	

Notes	Serial	Type (code/other identity)	Owner/operator, location or fate
	90-0259	McD F-15E Strike Eagle [MO] *tig*	USAF 391st FS/366th Wg, Mountain Home AFB, ID
	90-0260	McD F-15E Strike Eagle [WA] *bk/y*	USAF 17th WPS/57th Wg, Nellis AFB, NV
	90-0261	McD F-15E Strike Eagle [WA] *bk/y*	USAF 17th WPS/57th Wg, Nellis AFB, NV
	90-0262	McD F-15E Strike Eagle [WA] *bk/y*	USAF 17th WPS/57th Wg, Nellis AFB, NV
	91-0300	McD F-15E Strike Eagle [MO] *tig*	USAF 391st FS/366th Wg, Mountain Home AFB, ID
	91-0305	McD F-15E Strike Eagle [WA] *bk/y*	USAF 17th WPS/57th Wg, Nellis AFB, NV
	91-0319	McD F-15E Strike Eagle [MO] *tig*	USAF 391st FS/366th Wg, Mountain Home AFB, ID
	91-0322	McD F-15E Strike Eagle [OT] *bk/gn*	USAF 422nd TES/53rd Wg, Nellis AFB, NV
	91-0323	McD F-15E Strike Eagle [MO] *tig*	USAF 391st FS/366th Wg, Mountain Home AFB, ID
	91-0325	McD F-15E Strike Eagle [OT] *bk/gn*	USAF 422nd TES/53rd Wg, Nellis AFB, NV
	91-0328	McD F-15E Strike Eagle [WA] *bk/y*	USAF 17th WPS/57th Wg, Nellis AFB, NV
	91-0330	McD F-15E Strike Eagle [MO] *tig*	USAF 391st FS/366th Wg, Mountain Home AFB, ID
	91-0333	McD F-15E Strike Eagle [MO] *tig*	USAF 391st FS/366th Wg, Mountain Home AFB, ID
	91-0600	McD F-15E Strike Eagle [MO] *tig*	USAF 391st FS/366th Wg, Mountain Home AFB, ID
	91-0601	McD F-15E Strike Eagle [OT] *bk/gn*	USAF 422nd TES/53rd Wg, Nellis AFB, NV
	92-0365	McD F-15E Strike Eagle [OT] *bk/gn*	USAF 422nd TES/53rd Wg, Nellis AFB, NV
	92-0366	McD F-15E Strike Eagle [MO] *tig*	USAF 391st FS/366th Wg, Mountain Home AFB, ID
	96-0200	McD F-15E Strike Eagle [OT] *bk/gn*	USAF 422nd TES/53rd Wg, Nellis AFB, NV
	97-0217	McD F-15E Strike Eagle [OT] *bk/gn*	USAF 422nd TES/53rd Wg, Nellis AFB, NV
	98-0132	McD F-15E Strike Eagle [ET] *bk/wh*	USAF 40th FLTS/96th TW, Eglin AFB, FL
	Boeing C-17A Globemaster III		
	88-0265	Boeing C-17A Globemaster III *gn*	USAF 62nd AW, McChord AFB, WA
	88-0266	Boeing C-17A Globemaster III *y/bl*	USAF 437th AW, Charleston AFB, SC
	89-1189	Boeing C-17A Globemaster III *bk/y*	USAF 758th AS/911th AW AFRC, Greater Pittsburgh, PA
	89-1190	Boeing C-17A Globemaster III *r/w*	USAF 167th AS/167th AW, Martinsburg, WV ANG
	89-1191	Boeing C-17A Globemaster III *bl*	USAF 137th AS/105th AW, Stewart AFB, NY ANG
	89-1192	Boeing C-17A Globemaster III *y/bl*	USAF 437th AW, Charleston AFB, SC
	90-0532	Boeing C-17A Globemaster III *bk*	USAF 156th AS/145th AW, Charlotte-Douglas, NC ANG
	90-0533	Boeing C-17A Globemaster III [HH] *r/y*	USAF 535th AS/15th Wg, Hickam AFB, HI
	90-0534	Boeing C-17A Globemaster III *y/bl*	USAF 437th AW, Charleston AFB, SC
	90-0535	Boeing C-17A Globemaster III *r/w*	USAF 89th AS/445th AW AFRC, Wright-Patterson AFB, OH
	92-3291	Boeing C-17A Globemaster III *r/w*	USAF 155th AS/164th AW, Memphis, TN ANG
	92-3292	Boeing C-17A Globemaster III *bk/y*	USAF 758th AS/911th AW AFRC, Greater Pittsburgh, PA
	92-3293	Boeing C-17A Globemaster III *bk*	USAF 156th AS/145th AW, Charlotte-Douglas, NC ANG
	92-3294	Boeing C-17A Globemaster III *bk*	USAF 156th AS/145th AW, Charlotte-Douglas, NC ANG
	93-0599	Boeing C-17A Globemaster III[AK] *bl/y*	USAF 144th AS/176th Wg, Elmendorf AFB, AK ANG
	93-0600	Boeing C-17A Globemaster III *r/w*	USAF 155th AS/164th AW, Memphis, TN ANG
	93-0601	Boeing C-17A Globemaster III *bk/y*	USAF 758th AS/911th AW AFRC, Greater Pittsburgh, PA
	93-0602	Boeing C-17A Globemaster III *bk* $	USAF 156th AS/145th AW, Charlotte-Douglas, NC ANG
	93-0603	Boeing C-17A Globemaster III *r/w*	USAF 89th AS/445th AW AFRC, Wright-Patterson AFB, OH

Serial	Type (code/other identity)	Owner/operator, location or fate	Notes
93-0604	Boeing C-17A Globemaster III r/w	USAF 89th AS/445th AW AFRC, Wright-Patterson AFB, OH	
94-0065	Boeing C-17A Globemaster III r/w	USAF 155th AS/164th AW, Memphis, TN ANG	
94-0066	Boeing C-17A Globemaster III gn	USAF 62nd AW, McChord AFB, WA	
94-0067	Boeing C-17A Globemaster III bl	USAF 137th AS/105th AW, Stewart AFB, NY ANG	
94-0068	Boeing C-17A Globemaster III or/y	USAF 729th AS/452nd AMW AFRC, March ARB, CA	
94-0069	Boeing C-17A Globemaster III r/w	USAF 167th AS/167th AW, Martinsburg, WV ANG	
94-0070	Boeing C-17A Globemaster III r/w	USAF 167th AS/167th AW, Martinsburg, WV ANG	
95-0102	Boeing C-17A Globemaster III y/bl	USAF 437th AW, Charleston AFB, SC	
95-0103	Boeing C-17A Globemaster III gn	USAF 62nd AW, McChord AFB, WA	
95-0104	Boeing C-17A Globemaster III gn	USAF 62nd AW, McChord AFB, WA	
95-0105	Boeing C-17A Globemaster III bl	USAF 137th AS/105th AW, Stewart AFB, NY ANG	
95-0106	Boeing C-17A Globemaster III gn	USAF 62nd AW, McChord AFB, WA	
95-0107	Boeing C-17A Globemaster III y/bl	USAF 437th AW, Charleston AFB, SC	
96-0001	Boeing C-17A Globemaster III bk/y	USAF 758th AS/911th AW AFRC, Greater Pittsburgh, PA	
96-0002	Boeing C-17A Globemaster III y/bl	USAF 437th AW, Charleston AFB, SC	
96-0003	Boeing C-17A Globemaster III gn	USAF 62nd AW, McChord AFB, WA	
96-0004	Boeing C-17A Globemaster III gn	USAF 62nd AW, McChord AFB, WA	
96-0005	Boeing C-17A Globemaster III bl	USAF 137th AS/105th AW, Stewart AFB, NY ANG	
96-0006	Boeing C-17A Globemaster III r/w	USAF 167th AS/167th AW, Martinsburg, WV ANG	
96-0007	Boeing C-17A Globemaster III bl/gd	USAF 183rd AS/172nd AW, Jackson Int'l Airport, MS ANG	
96-0008	Boeing C-17A Globemaster III r/y	USAF 58th AS/97th AMW, Altus AFB, OK	
97-0041	Boeing C-17A Globemaster III y/bl	USAF 437th AW, Charleston AFB, SC	
97-0042	Boeing C-17A Globemaster III r/w	USAF 155th AS/164th AW, Memphis, TN ANG	
97-0043	Boeing C-17A Globemaster III or/y	USAF 729th AS/452nd AMW AFRC, March ARB, CA	
97-0044	Boeing C-17A Globemaster III r/w	USAF 89th AS/445th AW AFRC, Wright-Patterson AFB, OH	
97-0045	Boeing C-17A Globemaster III bl	USAF 137th AS/105th AW, Stewart AFB, NY ANG	
97-0046	Boeing C-17A Globemaster III y/bl	USAF 437th AW, Charleston AFB, SC	
97-0047	Boeing C-17A Globemaster III y/bl	USAF 437th AW, Charleston AFB, SC	
97-0048	Boeing C-17A Globemaster III r/w	USAF 89th AS/445th AW AFRC, Wright-Patterson AFB, OH	
98-0049	Boeing C-17A Globemaster III r/y	USAF 58th AS/97th AMW, Altus AFB, OK	
98-0050	Boeing C-17A Globemaster III r/y	USAF 58th AS/97th AMW, Altus AFB, OK	
98-0051	Boeing C-17A Globemaster III [AK] bl/y [517 AS]	USAF 144th AS/176th Wg, Elmendorf AFB, AK ANG	
98-0052	Boeing C-17A Globemaster III gn	USAF 62nd AW, McChord AFB, WA	
98-0053	Boeing C-17A Globemaster III gn	USAF 62nd AW, McChord AFB, WA	
98-0054	Boeing C-17A Globemaster III y/bl	USAF 437th AW, Charleston AFB, SC	
98-0055	Boeing C-17A Globemaster III r/y [58 AS]	USAF 58th AS/97th AMW, Altus AFB, OK	
98-0056	Boeing C-17A Globemaster III [AK] bl/y	USAF 144th AS/176th Wg, Elmendorf AFB, AK ANG	
98-0057	Boeing C-17A Globemaster III bl	USAF 137th AS/105th AW, Stewart AFB, NY ANG	
99-0058	Boeing C-17A Globemaster III gn	USAF 62nd AW, McChord AFB, WA	
99-0059	Boeing C-17A Globemaster III gn	USAF 62nd AW, McChord AFB, WA	
99-0060	Boeing C-17A Globemaster III gn	USAF 62nd AW, McChord AFB, WA	
99-0061	Boeing C-17A Globemaster III r/y	USAF 58th AS/97th AMW, Altus AFB, OK	
99-0062	Boeing C-17A Globemaster III y/bl	USAF 437th AW, Charleston AFB, SC	
99-0063	Boeing C-17A Globemaster III r/y	USAF 58th AS/97th AMW, Altus AFB, OK	
99-0064	Boeing C-17A Globemaster III r/y	USAF 58th AS/97th AMW, Altus AFB, OK	

Notes	Serial	Type (code/other identity)	Owner/operator, location or fate
	99-0165	Boeing C-17A Globemaster III r/w	USAF 89th AS/445th AW AFRC, Wright-Patterson AFB, OH
	99-0166	Boeing C-17A Globemaster III gn	USAF 62nd AW, McChord AFB, WA
	99-0167	Boeing C-17A Globemaster III [AK] bl/y	USAF 144th AS/176th Wg, Elmendorf AFB, AK ANG
	99-0168	Boeing C-17A Globemaster III [AK] bl/y	USAF 144th AS/176th Wg, Elmendorf AFB, AK ANG
	99-0169	Boeing C-17A Globemaster III y/bl	USAF 437th AW, Charleston AFB, SC
	99-0170	Boeing C-17A Globemaster III r/y	USAF 58th AS/97th AMW, Altus AFB, OK
	00-0171	Boeing C-17A Globemaster III [AK] bl/y	USAF 144th AS/176th Wg, Elmendorf AFB, AK ANG
	00-0172	Boeing C-17A Globemaster III bk	USAF 156th AS/145th AW, Charlotte-Douglas, NC ANG
	00-0174	Boeing C-17A Globemaster III [AK] bl/y	USAF 144th AS/176th Wg, Elmendorf AFB, AK ANG
	00-0175	Boeing C-17A Globemaster III bl	USAF 6th AS/305th AMW, McGuire AFB, NJ
	00-0176	Boeing C-17A Globemaster III r/w	USAF 155th AS/164th AW, Memphis, TN ANG
	00-0177	Boeing C-17A Globemaster III bl	USAF 137th AS/105th AW, Stewart AFB, NY ANG
	00-0178	Boeing C-17A Globemaster III r/w	USAF 89th AS/445th AW AFRC, Wright-Patterson AFB, OH
	00-0179	Boeing C-17A Globemaster III r/y	USAF 58th AS/97th AMW, Altus AFB, OK
	00-0180	Boeing C-17A Globemaster III bk/y	USAF 758th AS/911th AW AFRC, Greater Pittsburgh, PA
	00-0181	Boeing C-17A Globemaster III r/w	USAF 167th AS/167th AW, Martinsburg, WV ANG
	00-0182	Boeing C-17A Globemaster III r/w	USAF 167th AS/167th AW, Martinsburg, WV ANG
	00-0183	Boeing C-17A Globemaster III bk	USAF 156th AS/145th AW, Charlotte-Douglas, NC ANG
	00-0184	Boeing C-17A Globemaster III bk/y	USAF 758th AS/911th AW AFRC, Greater Pittsburgh, PA
	00-0185	Boeing C-17A Globemaster III [AK] bl/y	USAF 144th AS/176th Wg, Elmendorf AFB, AK ANG
	01-0186	Boeing C-17A Globemaster III bl/y	USAF 3rd AS/436th AW, Dover AFB, DE
	01-0187	Boeing C-17A Globemaster III gn	USAF 62nd AW, McChord AFB, WA
	01-0188	Boeing C-17A Globemaster III bl	USAF 137th AS/105th AW, Stewart AFB, NY ANG
	01-0189	Boeing C-17A Globemaster III r/w	USAF 155th AS/164th AW, Memphis, TN ANG
	01-0190	Boeing C-17A Globemaster III r/y	USAF 58th AS/97th AMW, Altus AFB, OK
	01-0191	Boeing C-17A Globemaster III bl/y	USAF 3rd AS/436th AW, Dover AFB, DE
	01-0192	Boeing C-17A Globemaster III bl	USAF 137th AS/105th AW, Stewart AFB, NY ANG
	01-0193	Boeing C-17A Globemaster III y/bl	USAF 437th AW, Charleston AFB, SC
	01-0194	Boeing C-17A Globemaster III r/w	USAF 89th AS/445th AW AFRC, Wright-Patterson AFB, OH
	01-0195	Boeing C-17A Globemaster III r/y	USAF 58th AS/97th AMW, Altus AFB, OK
	01-0196	Boeing C-17A Globemaster III r/w	USAF 167th AS/167th AW, Martinsburg, WV ANG
	01-0197	Boeing C-17A Globemaster III bk	USAF 156th AS/145th AW, Charlotte-Douglas, NC ANG
	02-1098	Boeing C-17A Globemaster III bl	USAF 6th AS/305th AMW, McGuire AFB, NJ
	02-1099	Boeing C-17A Globemaster III bk/y	USAF 758th AS/911th AW AFRC, Greater Pittsburgh, PA
	02-1100	Boeing C-17A Globemaster III r/w	USAF 155th AS/164th AW, Memphis, TN ANG
	02-1101	Boeing C-17A Globemaster III bk/y	USAF 758th AS/911th AW AFRC, Greater Pittsburgh, PA
	02-1102	Boeing C-17A Globemaster III r/y	USAF 58th AS/97th AMW, Altus AFB, OK
	02-1103	Boeing C-17A Globemaster III r/y	USAF 58th AS/97th AMW, Altus AFB, OK
	02-1104	Boeing C-17A Globemaster III r/y [97 OG]	USAF 58th AS/97th AMW, Altus AFB, OK
	02-1105	Boeing C-17A Globemaster III gn	USAF 62nd AW, McChord AFB, WA
	02-1106	Boeing C-17A Globemaster III gn	USAF 62nd AW, McChord AFB, WA
	02-1107	Boeing C-17A Globemaster III bk	USAF 156th AS/145th AW, Charlotte-Douglas, NC ANG

Serial	Type (code/other identity)	Owner/operator, location or fate	Notes
02-1108	Boeing C-17A Globemaster III *gn*	USAF 62nd AW, McChord AFB, WA	
02-1109	Boeing C-17A Globemaster III *gn*	USAF 62nd AW, McChord AFB, WA	
02-1110	Boeing C-17A Globemaster III *gn*	USAF 62nd AW, McChord AFB, WA	
02-1111	Boeing C-17A Globemaster III *gn*	USAF 62nd AW, McChord AFB, WA	
02-1112	Boeing C-17A Globemaster III *bl/gd*	USAF 183rd AS/172nd AW, Jackson Int'l Airport, MS ANG	
03-3113	Boeing C-17A Globemaster III *bl/gd*	USAF 183rd AS/172nd AW, Jackson Int'l Airport, MS ANG	
03-3114	Boeing C-17A Globemaster III *bl/gd*	USAF 183rd AS/172nd AW, Jackson Int'l Airport, MS ANG	
03-3115	Boeing C-17A Globemaster III *bl/gd*	USAF 183rd AS/172nd AW, Jackson Int'l Airport, MS ANG	
03-3116	Boeing C-17A Globemaster III *bl/gd*	USAF 183rd AS/172nd AW, Jackson Int'l Airport, MS ANG	
03-3117	Boeing C-17A Globemaster III *bl/gd*	USAF 183rd AS/172nd AW, Jackson Int'l Airport, MS ANG	
03-3118	Boeing C-17A Globemaster III *bl/gd*	USAF 183rd AS/172nd AW, Jackson Int'l Airport, MS ANG	
03-3119	Boeing C-17A Globemaster III *bl/gd*	USAF 183rd AS/172nd AW, Jackson Int'l Airport, MS ANG	
03-3120	Boeing C-17A Globemaster III *gn*	USAF 62nd AW, McChord AFB, WA	
03-3121	Boeing C-17A Globemaster III [ED]	USAF 418th FLTS/412th TW, Edwards AFB, CA	
03-3122	Boeing C-17A Globemaster III *y/bl*	USAF 437th AW, Charleston AFB, SC	
03-3123	Boeing C-17A Globemaster III *r/w*	USAF 167th AS/167th AW, Martinsburg, WV ANG	
03-3124	Boeing C-17A Globemaster III *y/bl*	USAF 437th AW, Charleston AFB, SC	
03-3125	Boeing C-17A Globemaster III *bl*	USAF 6th AS/305th AMW, McGuire AFB, NJ	
03-3126	Boeing C-17A Globemaster III *bl*	USAF 6th AS/305th AMW, McGuire AFB, NJ	
03-3127	Boeing C-17A Globemaster III *gn*	USAF 62nd AW, McChord AFB, WA	
04-4128	Boeing C-17A Globemaster III *bl*	USAF 6th AS/305th AMW, McGuire AFB, NJ	
04-4129	Boeing C-17A Globemaster III *r/y* [97 AMW]	USAF 58th AS/97th AMW, Altus AFB, OK	
04-4130	Boeing C-17A Globemaster III *bl*	USAF 6th AS/305th AMW, McGuire AFB, NJ	
04-4131	Boeing C-17A Globemaster III *bl*	USAF 6th AS/305th AMW, McGuire AFB, NJ	
04-4132	Boeing C-17A Globemaster III *bl*	USAF 6th AS/305th AMW, McGuire AFB, NJ	
04-4133	Boeing C-17A Globemaster III *bl*	USAF 6th AS/305th AMW, McGuire AFB, NJ	
04-4134	Boeing C-17A Globemaster III *bl*	USAF 6th AS/305th AMW, McGuire AFB, NJ	
04-4135	Boeing C-17A Globemaster III *r/y*	USAF 58th AS/97th AMW, Altus AFB, OK	
04-4136	Boeing C-17A Globemaster III *bl*	USAF 6th AS/305th AMW, McGuire AFB, NJ	
04-4137	Boeing C-17A Globemaster III *bl*	USAF 6th AS/305th AMW, McGuire AFB, NJ	
04-4138	Boeing C-17A Globemaster III *or/y*	USAF 729th AS/452nd AMW AFRC, March ARB, CA	
05-5139	Boeing C-17A Globemaster III *or/y*	USAF 729th AS/452nd AMW AFRC, March ARB, CA	
05-5140	Boeing C-17A Globemaster III *or/y*	USAF 729th AS/452nd AMW AFRC, March ARB, CA	
05-5141	Boeing C-17A Globemaster III *or/y*	USAF 729th AS/452nd AMW AFRC, March ARB, CA	
05-5142	Boeing C-17A Globemaster III *or/y*	USAF 729th AS/452nd AMW AFRC, March ARB, CA	
05-5143	Boeing C-17A Globemaster III *r/w*	USAF 89th AS/445th AW AFRC, Wright-Patterson AFB, OH	
05-5144	Boeing C-17A Globemaster III *or/y*	USAF 729th AS/452nd AMW AFRC, March ARB, CA	
05-5145	Boeing C-17A Globemaster III *or/y*	USAF 729th AS/452nd AMW AFRC, March ARB, CA	
05-5146	Boeing C-17A Globemaster III [HH] *r/y*	USAF 535th AS/15th Wg, Hickam AFB, HI	
05-5147	Boeing C-17A Globemaster III [HH] *r/y*	USAF 535th AS/15th Wg, Hickam AFB, HI	
05-5148	Boeing C-17A Globemaster III [HH] *r/y*	USAF 535th AS/15th Wg, Hickam AFB, HI	
05-5149	Boeing C-17A Globemaster III [HH] *r/y*	USAF 535th AS/15th Wg, Hickam AFB, HI	
05-5150	Boeing C-17A Globemaster III [HH] *r/y*	USAF 535th AS/15th Wg, Hickam AFB, HI	
05-5151	Boeing C-17A Globemaster III [HH] *r/y*	USAF 535th AS/15th Wg, Hickam AFB, HI	
05-5152	Boeing C-17A Globemaster III [HH] *r/y*	USAF 535th AS/15th Wg, Hickam AFB, HI	

Notes	Serial	Type (code/other identity)	Owner/operator, location or fate
	05-5153	Boeing C-17A Globemaster III [HH] *r/y*	USAF 535th AS/15th Wg, Hickam AFB, HI
	06-6154	Boeing C-17A Globemaster III *w/bk*	USAF 21st AS/60th AMW, Travis AFB, CA
	06-6155	Boeing C-17A Globemaster III *w/bk*	USAF 21st AS/60th AMW, Travis AFB, CA
	06-6156	Boeing C-17A Globemaster III *w/bk*	USAF 21st AS/60th AMW, Travis AFB, CA
	06-6157	Boeing C-17A Globemaster III *w/bk*	USAF 21st AS/60th AMW, Travis AFB, CA
	06-6158	Boeing C-17A Globemaster III *w/bk*	USAF 21st AS/60th AMW, Travis AFB, CA
	06-6159	Boeing C-17A Globemaster III *w/bk*	USAF 21st AS/60th AMW, Travis AFB, CA
	06-6160	Boeing C-17A Globemaster III *w/bk*	USAF 21st AS/60th AMW, Travis AFB, CA
	06-6161	Boeing C-17A Globemaster III *w/bk*	USAF 21st AS/60th AMW, Travis AFB, CA
	06-6162	Boeing C-17A Globemaster III *w/bk*	USAF 21st AS/60th AMW, Travis AFB, CA
	06-6163	Boeing C-17A Globemaster III *w/bk*	USAF 21st AS/60th AMW, Travis AFB, CA
	06-6164	Boeing C-17A Globemaster III *w/bk*	USAF 21st AS/60th AMW, Travis AFB, CA
	06-6165	Boeing C-17A Globemaster III *bl/y*	USAF 3rd AS/436th AW, Dover AFB, DE
	06-6166	Boeing C-17A Globemaster III *bl/y*	USAF 3rd AS/436th AW, Dover AFB, DE
	06-6167	Boeing C-17A Globemaster III *bl/y*	USAF 3rd AS/436th AW, Dover AFB, DE
	06-6168	Boeing C-17A Globemaster III *bl/y*	USAF 3rd AS/436th AW, Dover AFB, DE
	07-7169	Boeing C-17A Globemaster III *bl/y*	USAF 3rd AS/436th AW, Dover AFB, DE
	07-7170	Boeing C-17A Globemaster III *bl/y*	USAF 3rd AS/436th AW, Dover AFB, DE
	07-7171	Boeing C-17A Globemaster III *bl*	USAF 6th AS/305th AMW, McGuire AFB, NJ
	07-7172	Boeing C-17A Globemaster III *w/bk*	USAF 21st AS/60th AMW, Travis AFB, CA
	07-7173	Boeing C-17A Globemaster III *bl/y*	USAF 3rd AS/436th AW, Dover AFB, DE
	07-7174	Boeing C-17A Globemaster III *bl/y*	USAF 3rd AS/436th AW, Dover AFB, DE
	07-7175	Boeing C-17A Globemaster III *bl/y*	USAF 3rd AS/436th AW, Dover AFB, DE
	07-7176	Boeing C-17A Globemaster III *bl/y*	USAF 3rd AS/436th AW, Dover AFB, DE
	07-7177	Boeing C-17A Globemaster III *bl/y*	USAF 3rd AS/436th AW, Dover AFB, DE
	07-7178	Boeing C-17A Globemaster III *y/bl*	USAF 437th AW, Charleston AFB, SC
	07-7179	Boeing C-17A Globemaster III *w/bk*	USAF 21st AS/60th AMW, Travis AFB, CA
	07-7180	Boeing C-17A Globemaster III *y/bl*	USAF 437th AW, Charleston AFB, SC
	07-7181	Boeing C-17A Globemaster III *y/bl*	USAF 437th AW, Charleston AFB, SC
	07-7182	Boeing C-17A Globemaster III *y/bl*	USAF 437th AW, Charleston AFB, SC
	07-7183	Boeing C-17A Globemaster III *y/bl*	USAF 437th AW, Charleston AFB, SC
	07-7184	Boeing C-17A Globemaster III *y/bl*	USAF 437th AW, Charleston AFB, SC
	07-7185	Boeing C-17A Globemaster III *y/bl*	USAF 437th AW, Charleston AFB, SC
	07-7186	Boeing C-17A Globemaster III *y/bl*	USAF 437th AW, Charleston AFB, SC
	07-7187	Boeing C-17A Globemaster III *y/bl*	USAF 437th AW, Charleston AFB, SC
	07-7188	Boeing C-17A Globemaster III *y/bl*	USAF 535th AW, Charleston AFB, SC
	07-7189	Boeing C-17A Globemaster III *y/bl*	USAF 437th AW, Charleston AFB, SC
	08-8190	Boeing C-17A Globemaster III *y/bl*	USAF 437th AW, Charleston AFB, SC
	08-8191	Boeing C-17A Globemaster III *y/bl*	USAF 437th AW, Charleston AFB, SC
	08-8192	Boeing C-17A Globemaster III *gn*	USAF 62nd AW, McChord AFB, WA
	08-8193	Boeing C-17A Globemaster III *gn*	USAF 62nd AW, McChord AFB, WA
	08-8194	Boeing C-17A Globemaster III *gn*	USAF 62nd AW, McChord AFB, WA
	08-8195	Boeing C-17A Globemaster III *gn*	USAF 62nd AW, McChord AFB, WA
	08-8196	Boeing C-17A Globemaster III *gn*	USAF 62nd AW, McChord AFB, WA
	08-8197	Boeing C-17A Globemaster III *gn*	USAF 62nd AW, McChord AFB, WA
	08-8198	Boeing C-17A Globemaster III *y/bl*	USAF 437th AW, Charleston AFB, SC
	08-8199	Boeing C-17A Globemaster III *gn*	USAF 62nd AW, McChord AFB, WA
	08-8200	Boeing C-17A Globemaster III *gn*	USAF 62nd AW, McChord AFB, WA
	08-8201	Boeing C-17A Globemaster III *gn*	USAF 62nd AW, McChord AFB, WA
	08-8202	Boeing C-17A Globemaster III *gn*	USAF 62nd AW, McChord AFB, WA
	08-8203	Boeing C-17A Globemaster III *gn*	USAF 62nd AW, McChord AFB, WA
	08-8204	Boeing C-17A Globemaster III *y/bl*	USAF 437th AW, Charleston AFB, SC
	09-9205	Boeing C-17A Globemaster III *y/bl*	USAF 437th AW, Charleston AFB, SC
	09-9206	Boeing C-17A Globemaster III *y/bl*	USAF 437th AW, Charleston AFB, SC
	09-9207	Boeing C-17A Globemaster III *y/bl*	USAF 437th AW, Charleston AFB, SC
	09-9208	Boeing C-17A Globemaster III *y/bl*	USAF 437th AW, Charleston AFB, SC
	09-9209	Boeing C-17A Globemaster III *gn*	USAF 62nd AW, McChord AFB, WA
	09-9210	Boeing C-17A Globemaster III *gn*	USAF 62nd AW, McChord AFB, WA
	09-9211	Boeing C-17A Globemaster III *gn*	USAF 62nd AW, McChord AFB, WA
	09-9212	Boeing C-17A Globemaster III *y/bl*	USAF 437th AW, Charleston AFB, SC
	10-0213	Boeing C-17A Globemaster III *y/bl*	USAF 437th AW, Charleston AFB, SC
	10-0214	Boeing C-17A Globemaster III *y/bl*	USAF 437th AW, Charleston AFB, SC

Serial	Type (code/other identity)	Owner/operator, location or fate	Notes
10-0215	Boeing C-17A Globemaster III *y/bl*	USAF 437th AW, Charleston AFB, SC	
10-0216	Boeing C-17A Globemaster III *gn*	USAF 62nd AW, McChord AFB, WA	
10-0217	Boeing C-17A Globemaster III *gn*	USAF 62nd AW, McChord AFB, WA	
10-0218	Boeing C-17A Globemaster III *gn*	USAF 62nd AW, McChord AFB, WA	
10-0219	Boeing C-17A Globemaster III *gn*	USAF 62nd AW, McChord AFB, WA	
10-0220	Boeing C-17A Globemaster III *gn*	USAF 62nd AW, McChord AFB, WA	
10-0221	Boeing C-17A Globemaster III *y/bl*	USAF 437th AW, Charleston AFB, SC	
10-0222	Boeing C-17A Globemaster III *y/bl*	USAF 437th AW, Charleston AFB, SC	
10-0223	Boeing C-17A Globemaster III *y/bl*	USAF 437th AW, Charleston AFB, SC (damaged)	

Lockheed Martin F-22A Raptor

Serial	Type (code/other identity)	Owner/operator, location or fate	Notes
91-4004	Lockheed Martin F-22A Raptor [ED]	USAF 411th FLTS/412th TW, Edwards AFB, CA	
91-4006	Lockheed Martin F-22A Raptor [ED]	USAF 411th FLTS/412th TW, Edwards AFB, CA	
91-4007	Lockheed Martin F-22A Raptor [ED]	USAF 411th FLTS/412th TW, Edwards AFB, CA	
91-4009	Lockheed Martin F-22A Raptor [ED]	USAF 411th FLTS/412th TW, Edwards AFB, CA	
99-4010	Lockheed Martin F-22A Raptor [OT] [422 TES]	USAF 422nd TES/53rd Wg, Nellis AFB, NV	
99-4011	Lockheed Martin F-22A Raptor [WA]	USAF 433rd WPS/57th Wg, Nellis AFB, NV	
00-4012	Lockheed Martin F-22A Raptor [TY]	USAF 43rd FS/325th FW, Eglin AFB, FL	
00-4015	Lockheed Martin F-22A Raptor [TY]	USAF 43rd FS/325th FW, Eglin AFB, FL	
00-4016	Lockheed Martin F-22A Raptor [TY] [325 FW]	USAF 43rd FS/325th FW, Eglin AFB, FL	
00-4017	Lockheed Martin F-22A Raptor [TY]	USAF 43rd FS/325th FW, Eglin AFB, FL	
01-4018	Lockheed Martin F-22A Raptor [TY]	USAF 43rd FS/325th FW, Eglin AFB, FL	
01-4019	Lockheed Martin F-22A Raptor [TY]	USAF 43rd FS/325th FW, Eglin AFB, FL	
01-4020	Lockheed Martin F-22A Raptor [TY]	USAF 43rd FS/325th FW, Eglin AFB, FL	
01-4021	Lockheed Martin F-22A Raptor [TY]	USAF 43rd FS/325th FW, Eglin AFB, FL	
01-4023	Lockheed Martin F-22A Raptor [TY]	USAF 43rd FS/325th FW, Eglin AFB, FL	
01-4024	Lockheed Martin F-22A Raptor [TY]	USAF 43rd FS/325th FW, Eglin AFB, FL	
01-4025	Lockheed Martin F-22A Raptor [TY]	USAF 43rd FS/325th FW, Eglin AFB, FL	
01-4026	Lockheed Martin F-22A Raptor [TY]	USAF 43rd FS/325th FW, Eglin AFB, FL	
01-4027	Lockheed Martin F-22A Raptor [TY]	USAF 43rd FS/325th FW, Eglin AFB, FL	
02-4028	Lockheed Martin F-22A Raptor [TY]	USAF 43rd FS/325th FW, Eglin AFB, FL	
02-4029	Lockheed Martin F-22A Raptor [TY]	USAF 43rd FS/325th FW, Eglin AFB, FL	
02-4030	Lockheed Martin F-22A Raptor [TY]	USAF 43rd FS/325th FW, Eglin AFB, FL	
02-4031	Lockheed Martin F-22A Raptor [TY]	USAF 43rd FS/325th FW, Eglin AFB, FL	
02-4032	Lockheed Martin F-22A Raptor [TY]	USAF 43rd FS/325th FW, Eglin AFB, FL	
02-4033	Lockheed Martin F-22A Raptor [TY]	USAF 43rd FS/325th FW, Eglin AFB, FL	
02-4034	Lockheed Martin F-22A Raptor [TY]	USAF 43rd FS/325th FW, Eglin AFB, FL	
02-4035	Lockheed Martin F-22A Raptor [TY] [325 OG]	USAF 43rd FS/325th FW, Eglin AFB, FL	
02-4036	Lockheed Martin F-22A Raptor [TY]	USAF 43rd FS/325th FW, Eglin AFB, FL	
02-4037	Lockheed Martin F-22A Raptor [TY]	USAF 43rd FS/325th FW, Eglin AFB, FL	
02-4038	Lockheed Martin F-22A Raptor [TY]	USAF 43rd FS/325th FW, Eglin AFB, FL	
02-4039	Lockheed Martin F-22A Raptor [TY]	USAF 43rd FS/325th FW, Eglin AFB, FL	
02-4040	Lockheed Martin F-22A Raptor [TY]	USAF 43rd FS/325th FW, Eglin AFB, FL	
03-4041	Lockheed Martin F-22A Raptor [TY]	USAF 43rd FS/325th FW, Eglin AFB, FL	
03-4042	Lockheed Martin F-22A Raptor [TY]	USAF 43rd FS/325th FW, Eglin AFB, FL	
03-4043	Lockheed Martin F-22A Raptor [TY] [43 FS]	USAF 43rd FS/325th FW, Eglin AFB, FL	
03-4044	Lockheed Martin F-22A Raptor [TY]	USAF 43rd FS/325th FW, Eglin AFB, FL	
03-4045	Lockheed Martin F-22A Raptor [HH]	USAF 199th FS/154th Wg, Hickam AFB, HI ANG	
03-4046	Lockheed Martin F-22A Raptor [HH] [199 FS]	USAF 199th FS/154th Wg, Hickam AFB, HI ANG	
03-4047	Lockheed Martin F-22A Raptor [HH]	USAF 199th FS/154th Wg, Hickam AFB, HI ANG	
03-4048	Lockheed Martin F-22A Raptor [HH]	USAF 199th FS/154th Wg, Hickam AFB, HI ANG	
03-4049	Lockheed Martin F-22A Raptor [HH]	USAF 199th FS/154th Wg, Hickam AFB, HI ANG	
03-4050	Lockheed Martin F-22A Raptor [HH]	USAF 199th FS/154th Wg, Hickam AFB, HI ANG	
03-4051	Lockheed Martin F-22A Raptor [HH]	USAF 199th FS/154th Wg, Hickam AFB, HI ANG	
03-4052	Lockheed Martin F-22A Raptor [HH]	USAF 199th FS/154th Wg, Hickam AFB, HI ANG	
03-4053	Lockheed Martin F-22A Raptor [HH]	USAF 199th FS/154th Wg, Hickam AFB, HI ANG	
03-4054	Lockheed Martin F-22A Raptor [HH] [154 Wg]	USAF 199th FS/154th Wg, Hickam AFB, HI ANG	
03-4055	Lockheed Martin F-22A Raptor [HH]	USAF 199th FS/154th Wg, Hickam AFB, HI ANG	
03-4056	Lockheed Martin F-22A Raptor [HH]	USAF 199th FS/154th Wg, Hickam AFB, HI ANG	
03-4057	Lockheed Martin F-22A Raptor [HH]	USAF 199th FS/154th Wg, Hickam AFB, HI ANG	
03-4058	Lockheed Martin F-22A Raptor [HH]	USAF 199th FS/154th Wg, Hickam AFB, HI ANG	

Notes	Serial	Type (code/other identity)	Owner/operator, location or fate
	03-4059	Lockheed Martin F-22A Raptor [HH]	USAF 199th FS/154th Wg, Hickam AFB, HI ANG
	03-4060	Lockheed Martin F-22A Raptor [HH]	USAF 199th FS/154th Wg, Hickam AFB, HI ANG
	03-4061	Lockheed Martin F-22A Raptor [HH]	USAF 199th FS/154th Wg, Hickam AFB, HI ANG
	04-4062	Lockheed Martin F-22A Raptor [HH]	USAF 199th FS/154th Wg, Hickam AFB, HI ANG
	04-4063	Lockheed Martin F-22A Raptor [HH]	USAF 199th FS/154th Wg, Hickam AFB, HI ANG
	04-4064	Lockheed Martin F-22A Raptor [HH]	USAF 199th FS/154th Wg, Hickam AFB, HI ANG
	04-4065	Lockheed Martin F-22A Raptor [OT]	USAF 422nd TES/53rd Wg, Nellis AFB, NV
	04-4066	Lockheed Martin F-22A Raptor [OT]	USAF 422nd TES/53rd Wg, Nellis AFB, NV
	04-4067	Lockheed Martin F-22A Raptor [FF]	USAF 94th FS/1st FW, Langley AFB, VA
	04-4068	Lockheed Martin F-22A Raptor [OT]	USAF 422nd TES/53rd Wg, Nellis AFB, NV
	04-4069	Lockheed Martin F-22A Raptor [OT]	USAF 422nd TES/53rd Wg, Nellis AFB, NV
	04-4070	Lockheed Martin F-22A Raptor	USAF 433rd WPS/57th Wg, Nellis AFB, NV
	04-4071	Lockheed Martin F-22A Raptor [WA]	USAF 433rd WPS/57th Wg, Nellis AFB, NV
	04-4072	Lockheed Martin F-22A Raptor [OT]	USAF 422nd TES/53rd Wg, Nellis AFB, NV
	04-4073	Lockheed Martin F-22A Raptor [OT]	USAF 422nd TES/53rd Wg, Nellis AFB, NV
	04-4074	Lockheed Martin F-22A Raptor [AK]	USAF 90th FS/3rd Wg, Elmendorf AFB, AK
	04-4075	Lockheed Martin F-22A Raptor [AK]	USAF 90th FS/3rd Wg, Elmendorf AFB, AK
	04-4076	Lockheed Martin F-22A Raptor [FF]	USAF 27th FS/1st FW, Langley AFB, VA
	04-4077	Lockheed Martin F-22A Raptor [AK]	USAF 525th FS/3rd Wg, Elmendorf AFB, AK
	04-4078	Lockheed Martin F-22A Raptor [FF]	USAF 27th FS/1st FW, Langley AFB, VA
	04-4079	Lockheed Martin F-22A Raptor [HH]	USAF 199th FS/154th Wg, Hickam AFB, HI ANG
	04-4080	Lockheed Martin F-22A Raptor [HH]	USAF 199th FS/154th Wg, Hickam AFB, HI ANG
	04-4082	Lockheed Martin F-22A Raptor [FF] [149 FS]	USAF 149th FS/192nd FW/1st FW, Langley AFB, VA ANG
	04-4083	Lockheed Martin F-22A Raptor [TY] [301 FS]	USAF 301st FS/44th FG AFRES/325th FW, Eglin AFB, FL
05-4081	Lockheed Martin F-22A Raptor (04-4081) [HH]	USAF 199th FS/154th Wg, Hickam AFB, HI ANG
	05-4084	Lockheed Martin F-22A Raptor [HH]	USAF 199th FS/154th Wg, Hickam AFB, HI ANG
	05-4085	Lockheed Martin F-22A Raptor [FF]	USAF 94th FS/1st FW, Langley AFB, VA
	05-4086	Lockheed Martin F-22A Raptor [AK]	USAF 90th FS/3rd Wg, Elmendorf AFB, AK
	05-4087	Lockheed Martin F-22A Raptor [AK]	USAF 90th FS/3rd Wg, Elmendorf AFB, AK
	05-4088	Lockheed Martin F-22A Raptor [AK]	USAF 90th FS/3rd Wg, Elmendorf AFB, AK
	05-4089	Lockheed Martin F-22A Raptor [FF]	USAF 149th FS/192nd Wg/1st FW, Langley AFB, VA ANG
	05-4090	Lockheed Martin F-22A Raptor [AK] [90 FS]	USAF 90th FS/3rd Wg, Elmendorf AFB, AK
	05-4091	Lockheed Martin F-22A Raptor [FF]	USAF 27th FS/1st FW, Langley AFB, VA
	05-4092	Lockheed Martin F-22A Raptor [AK]	USAF 525th FS/3rd Wg, Elmendorf AFB, AK
	05-4093	Lockheed Martin F-22A Raptor [HH]	USAF 199th FS/154th Wg, Hickam AFB, HI ANG
	05-4094	Lockheed Martin F-22A Raptor [AK]	USAF 525th FS/3rd Wg, Elmendorf AFB, AK
	05-4095	Lockheed Martin F-22A Raptor [FF]	USAF 27th FS/1st FW, Langley AFB, VA
	05-4096	Lockheed Martin F-22A Raptor [WA]	USAF 433rd WPS/57th Wg, Nellis AFB, NV
	05-4097	Lockheed Martin F-22A Raptor [FF]	USAF 94th FS/1st FW, Langley AFB, VA
	05-4098	Lockheed Martin F-22A Raptor [HH]	USAF 199th FS/154th Wg, Hickam AFB, HI ANG
	05-4099	Lockheed Martin F-22A Raptor [FF]	USAF 94th FS/1st FW, Langley AFB, VA
	05-4100	Lockheed Martin F-22A Raptor [FF]	USAF 27th FS/1st FW, Langley AFB, VA
	05-4101	Lockheed Martin F-22A Raptor [AK]	USAF 3rd Wg, Elmendorf AFB, AK
	05-4102	Lockheed Martin F-22A Raptor [AK] [302 FS]	USAF 302nd FS/477th FG AFRES/3rd Wg, Elmendorf AFB, AK
	05-4103	Lockheed Martin F-22A Raptor [AK] [3 Wg]	USAF 90th FS/3rd Wg, Elmendorf AFB, AK
	05-4104	Lockheed Martin F-22A Raptor [FF]	USAF 27th FS/1st FW, Langley AFB, VA
	05-4105	Lockheed Martin F-22A Raptor [HH]	USAF 199th FS/154th Wg, Hickam AFB, HI ANG
	05-4106	Lockheed Martin F-22A Raptor [AK]	USAF 525th FS/3rd Wg, Elmendorf AFB, AK
	05-4107	Lockheed Martin F-22A Raptor [FF]	USAF 95th FS/1st FW, Langley AFB, VA
	06-4108	Lockheed Martin F-22A Raptor [AK]	USAF 525th FS/3rd Wg, Elmendorf AFB, AK
	06-4109	Lockheed Martin F-22A Raptor [WA]	USAF 433rd WPS/57th Wg, Nellis AFB, NV
	06-4110	Lockheed Martin F-22A Raptor [AK] [11 AF]	USAF 525th FS/3rd Wg, Elmendorf AFB, AK
	06-4111	Lockheed Martin F-22A Raptor [OT]	USAF 422nd TES/53rd Wg, Nellis AFB, NV
	06-4112	Lockheed Martin F-22A Raptor [AK]	USAF 525th FS/3rd Wg, Elmendorf AFB, AK
	06-4113	Lockheed Martin F-22A Raptor [AK] [3 OG]	USAF 525th FS/3rd Wg, Elmendorf AFB, AK
	06-4114	Lockheed Martin F-22A Raptor [AK]	USAF 525th FS/3rd Wg, Elmendorf AFB, AK
	06-4115	Lockheed Martin F-22A Raptor [AK] [525 FS]	USAF 525th FS/3rd Wg, Elmendorf AFB, AK
	06-4116	Lockheed Martin F-22A Raptor [WA] [433 WPS]	USAF 433rd WPS/57th Wg, Nellis AFB, NV

Serial	Type (code/other identity)	Owner/operator, location or fate	Notes
06-4117	Lockheed Martin F-22A Raptor [AK]	USAF 525th FS/3rd Wg, Elmendorf AFB, AK	
06-4118	Lockheed Martin F-22A Raptor [AK]	USAF 525th FS/3rd Wg, Elmendorf AFB, AK	
06-4119	Lockheed Martin F-22A Raptor [AK]	USAF 525th FS/3rd Wg, Elmendorf AFB, AK	
06-4120	Lockheed Martin F-22A Raptor [OT]	USAF 422nd TES/53rd Wg, Nellis AFB, NV	
06-4121	Lockheed Martin F-22A Raptor [AK]	USAF 525th FS/3rd Wg, Elmendorf AFB, AK	
06-4122	Lockheed Martin F-22A Raptor [AK]	USAF 525th FS/3rd Wg, Elmendorf AFB, AK	
06-4123	Lockheed Martin F-22A Raptor [AK]	USAF 525th FS/3rd Wg, Elmendorf AFB, AK	
06-4124	Lockheed Martin F-22A Raptor [OT]	USAF 422nd TES/53rd Wg, Nellis AFB, NV	
06-4126	Lockheed Martin F-22A Raptor [AK]	USAF 525th FS/3rd Wg, Elmendorf AFB, AK	
06-4127	Lockheed Martin F-22A Raptor [AK]	USAF 525th FS/3rd Wg, Elmendorf AFB, AK	
06-4128	Lockheed Martin F-22A Raptor [OT]	USAF 422nd TES/53rd Wg, Nellis AFB, NV	
06-4129	Lockheed Martin F-22A Raptor [AK]	USAF 525th FS/3rd Wg, Elmendorf AFB, AK	
06-4130	Lockheed Martin F-22A Raptor [AK]	USAF 525th FS/3rd Wg, Elmendorf AFB, AK	
07-4131	Lockheed Martin F-22A Raptor [AK]	USAF 525th FS/3rd Wg, Elmendorf AFB, AK	
07-4132	Lockheed Martin F-22A Raptor [ED] [411 FLTS]	USAF 411th FLTS/412th TW, Edwards AFB, CA	
07-4133	Lockheed Martin F-22A Raptor [AK]	USAF 525th FS/3rd Wg, Elmendorf AFB, AK	
07-4134	Lockheed Martin F-22A Raptor [AK]	USAF 525th FS/3rd Wg, Elmendorf AFB, AK	
07-4135	Lockheed Martin F-22A Raptor [AK]	USAF 90th FS/3rd Wg, Elmendorf AFB, AK	
07-4136	Lockheed Martin F-22A Raptor [AK]	USAF 90th FS/3rd Wg, Elmendorf AFB, AK	
07-4137	Lockheed Martin F-22A Raptor [AK]	USAF 90th FS/3rd Wg, Elmendorf AFB, AK	
07-4138	Lockheed Martin F-22A Raptor [AK]	USAF 90th FS/3rd Wg, Elmendorf AFB, AK	
07-4139	Lockheed Martin F-22A Raptor [AK]	USAF 90th FS/3rd Wg, Elmendorf AFB, AK	
07-4140	Lockheed Martin F-22A Raptor [AK]	USAF 90th FS/3rd Wg, Elmendorf AFB, AK	
07-4141	Lockheed Martin F-22A Raptor [AK]	USAF 90th FS/3rd Wg, Elmendorf AFB, AK	
07-4142	Lockheed Martin F-22A Raptor [AK]	USAF 90th FS/3rd Wg, Elmendorf AFB, AK	
07-4143	Lockheed Martin F-22A Raptor [AK]	USAF 90th FS/3rd Wg, Elmendorf AFB, AK	
07-4144	Lockheed Martin F-22A Raptor [AK]	USAF 90th FS/3rd Wg, Elmendorf AFB, AK	
07-4145	Lockheed Martin F-22A Raptor [AK]	USAF 90th FS/3rd Wg, Elmendorf AFB, AK	
07-4146	Lockheed Martin F-22A Raptor [AK]	USAF 90th FS/3rd Wg, Elmendorf AFB, AK	
07-4147	Lockheed Martin F-22A Raptor [AK] [477 FG]	USAF 90th FS/3rd Wg, Elmendorf AFB, AK	
07-4148	Lockheed Martin F-22A Raptor [AK]	USAF 90th FS/3rd Wg, Elmendorf AFB, AK	
07-4149	Lockheed Martin F-22A Raptor [AK]	USAF 90th FS/3rd Wg, Elmendorf AFB, AK	
07-4150	Lockheed Martin F-22A Raptor [AK]	USAF 90th FS/3rd Wg, Elmendorf AFB, AK	
07-4151	Lockheed Martin F-22A Raptor [AK]	USAF 90th FS/3rd Wg, Elmendorf AFB, AK	
08-4152	Lockheed Martin F-22A Raptor [FF]	USAF 94th FS/1st FW, Langley AFB, VA	
08-4153	Lockheed Martin F-22A Raptor [FF]	USAF 27th FS/1st FW, Langley AFB, VA	
08-4154	Lockheed Martin F-22A Raptor [FF]	USAF 27th FS/1st FW, Langley AFB, VA	
08-4155	Lockheed Martin F-22A Raptor [FF]	USAF 149th FS/192nd Wg/1st FW, Langley AFB, VA ANG	
08-4156	Lockheed Martin F-22A Raptor [FF]	USAF 94th FS/1st FW, Langley AFB, VA	
08-4157	Lockheed Martin F-22A Raptor [FF]	USAF 27th FS/1st FW, Langley AFB, VA	
08-4158	Lockheed Martin F-22A Raptor [FF]	USAF 27th FS/1st FW, Langley AFB, VA	
08-4159	Lockheed Martin F-22A Raptor [FF]	USAF 27th FS/1st FW, Langley AFB, VA	
08-4160	Lockheed Martin F-22A Raptor [FF]	USAF 94th FS/1st FW, Langley AFB, VA	
08-4161	Lockheed Martin F-22A Raptor [FF]	USAF 27th FS/1st FW, Langley AFB, VA	
08-4162	Lockheed Martin F-22A Raptor [FF] [1 FW]	USAF 94th FS/1st FW, Langley AFB, VA	
08-4163	Lockheed Martin F-22A Raptor [FF]	USAF 27th FS/1st FW, Langley AFB, VA	
08-4164	Lockheed Martin F-22A Raptor [FF]	USAF 94th FS/1st FW, Langley AFB, VA	
08-4165	Lockheed Martin F-22A Raptor [FF]	USAF 27th FS/1st FW, Langley AFB, VA	
08-4166	Lockheed Martin F-22A Raptor [FF]	USAF 94th FS/1st FW, Langley AFB, VA	
08-4167	Lockheed Martin F-22A Raptor [FF]	USAF 149th FS/192nd Wg/1st FW, Langley AFB, VA ANG	
08-4168	Lockheed Martin F-22A Raptor [FF]	USAF 94th FS/1st FW, Langley AFB, VA	
08-4169	Lockheed Martin F-22A Raptor [FF]	USAF 27th FS/1st FW, Langley AFB, VA	
08-4170	Lockheed Martin F-22A Raptor [FF]	USAF 27th FS/1st FW, Langley AFB, VA	
08-4171	Lockheed Martin F-22A Raptor [FF]	USAF 94th FS/1st FW, Langley AFB, VA	
09-4172	Lockheed Martin F-22A Raptor [FF] [27 FS]	USAF 27th FS/1st FW, Langley AFB, VA	
09-4173	Lockheed Martin F-22A Raptor [OT]	USAF 422nd TES/53rd Wg, Nellis AFB, NV	
09-4174	Lockheed Martin F-22A Raptor [FF]	USAF 27th FS/1st FW, Langley AFB, VA	
09-4175	Lockheed Martin F-22A Raptor [FF]	USAF 94th FS/1st FW, Langley AFB, VA	
09-4176	Lockheed Martin F-22A Raptor [FF]	USAF 27th FS/1st FW, Langley AFB, VA	

Notes	Serial	Type (code/other identity)	Owner/operator, location or fate
	09-4177	Lockheed Martin F-22A Raptor [FF]	USAF 149th FS/192nd Wg/1st FW, Langley AFB, VA ANG
	09-4178	Lockheed Martin F-22A Raptor [FF]	USAF 27th FS/1st FW, Langley AFB, VA
	09-4179	Lockheed Martin F-22A Raptor [FF]	USAF 149th FS/192nd Wg/1st FW, Langley AFB, VA ANG
	09-4180	Lockheed Martin F-22A Raptor [FF]	USAF 27th FS/1st FW, Langley AFB, VA
	09-4181	Lockheed Martin F-22A Raptor [FF]	USAF 94th FS/1st FW, Langley AFB, VA
	09-4182	Lockheed Martin F-22A Raptor [FF]	USAF 27th FS/1st FW, Langley AFB, VA
	09-4183	Lockheed Martin F-22A Raptor [FF]	USAF 94th FS/1st FW, Langley AFB, VA
	09-4184	Lockheed Martin F-22A Raptor [FF]	USAF 27th FS/1st FW, Langley AFB, VA
	09-4185	Lockheed Martin F-22A Raptor [FF] [1 OG]	USAF 27th FS/1st FW, Langley AFB, VA
	09-4186	Lockheed Martin F-22A Raptor [FF]	USAF 27th FS/1st FW, Langley AFB, VA
	09-4187	Lockheed Martin F-22A Raptor [FF]	USAF 94th FS/1st FW, Langley AFB, VA
	09-4188	Lockheed Martin F-22A Raptor [OT]	USAF 422nd TES/53rd Wg, Nellis AFB, NV
	09-4189	Lockheed Martin F-22A Raptor [FF]	USAF 27th FS/1st FW, Langley AFB, VA
	09-4190	Lockheed Martin F-22A Raptor [AK] [90 FS]	USAF 90th FS/3rd Wg, Elmendorf AFB, AK
	09-4191	Lockheed Martin F-22A Raptor [FF]	USAF 149th FS/192nd Wg/1st FW, Langley AFB, VA ANG
	10-4192	Lockheed Martin F-22A Raptor [FF] [192 FW]	USAF 149th FS/192nd Wg/1st FW, Langley AFB, VA ANG
	10-4193	Lockheed Martin F-22A Raptor [AK] [3 Wg]	USAF 90th FS/3rd Wg, Elmendorf AFB, AK
	10-4194	Lockheed Martin F-22A Raptor [FF] [94 FS]	USAF 94th FS/1st FW, Langley AFB, VA
	10-4195	Lockheed Martin F-22A Raptor [AK] [525 FS]	USAF 525th FS/3rd Wg, Elmendorf AFB, AK

Boeing VC-25A/VC-25B

	82-8000	Boeing VC-25A	USAF PAS/89th AW, Andrews AFB, MD
	92-9000	Boeing VC-25A	USAF PAS/89th AW, Andrews AFB, MD
	N894BA	Boeing VC-25B	USAF (on order)
	N895BA	Boeing VC-25B	USAF (on order)

Pilatus U-28A Draco

	01-0415	Pilatus U-28A Draco (N415PB)	USAF 318th SOS/27th SOW, Cannon AFB, NM
	04-0688	Pilatus U-28A Draco (N707KH)	USAF 318th SOS/27th SOW, Cannon AFB, NM
	05-0409	Pilatus U-28A Draco (N922RG)	USAF 319th SOS/1st SOW, Hurlburt Field, FL
	05-0419	Pilatus U-28A Draco (N419WA)	USAF 319th SOS/1st SOW, Hurlburt Field, FL
	05-0424	Pilatus U-28A Draco (N424PB)	USAF 318th SOS/27th SOW, Cannon AFB, NM
	05-0446	Pilatus U-28A Draco (N131JN)	USAF 318th SOS/27th SOW, Cannon AFB, NM
	05-0447	Pilatus U-28A Draco (N447PC)	USAF 319th SOS/1st SOW, Hurlburt Field, FL
	05-0482	Pilatus U-28A Draco (N482WA)	USAF 319th SOS/1st SOW, Hurlburt Field, FL
	05-0556	Pilatus U-28A Draco (N556HL)	USAF 318th SOS/27th SOW, Cannon AFB, NM
	05-0573	Pilatus U-28A Draco (N666GT)	USAF 319th SOS/1st SOW, Hurlburt Field, FL
	05-0597	Pilatus U-28A Draco (N597CH)	USAF 318th SOS/27th SOW, Cannon AFB, NM
	06-0692	Pilatus U-28A Draco (N692BC)	USAF 318th SOS/27th SOW, Cannon AFB, NM
	06-0740	Pilatus U-28A Draco (N740AF)	USAF 318th SOS/27th SOW, Cannon AFB, NM
	07-0488	Pilatus U-28A Draco (N56EZ)	USAF 319th SOS/1st SOW, Hurlburt Field, FL
	07-0691	Pilatus U-28A Draco (N691PC)	USAF 318th SOS/27th SOW, Cannon AFB, NM
	07-0711	Pilatus U-28A Draco (N711PN)	USAF 319th SOS/1st SOW, Hurlburt Field, FL
	07-0712	Pilatus U-28A Draco (N609TW)	USAF 319th SOS/1st SOW, Hurlburt Field, FL
	07-0777	Pilatus U-28A Draco (N72DZ)	USAF 318th SOS/27th SOW, Cannon AFB, NM
	07-0779	Pilatus U-28A Draco (N779PC)	USAF 319th SOS/1st SOW, Hurlburt Field, FL
	07-0793	Pilatus U-28A Draco (N96MV)	USAF 319th SOS/1st SOW, Hurlburt Field, FL
	07-0808	Pilatus U-28A Draco (N531MP)	USAF 318th SOS/27th SOW, Cannon AFB, NM
	07-0821	Pilatus U-28A Draco (N821PE)	USAF 319th SOS/1st SOW, Hurlburt Field, FL
	07-0829	Pilatus U-28A Draco (N829PE)	USAF 319th SOS/1st SOW, Hurlburt Field, FL
	07-0838	Pilatus U-28A Draco (N838PE)	USAF 319th SOS/1st SOW, Hurlburt Field, FL
	07-0840	Pilatus U-28A Draco (N840PE)	USAF 319th SOS/1st SOW, Hurlburt Field, FL
	08-0519	Pilatus U-28A Draco (N519PC)	USAF 319th SOS/1st SOW, Hurlburt Field, FL
	08-0581	Pilatus U-28A Draco (N581PC)	USAF 34th SOS/1st SOW, Hurlburt Field, FL
	08-0646	Pilatus U-28A Draco (N875RJ)	USAF 319th SOS/1st SOW, Hurlburt Field, FL
	08-0700	Pilatus U-28A Draco (N600KP)	USAF 319th SOS/1st SOW, Hurlburt Field, FL
	08-0718	Pilatus U-28A Draco (N824BK)	USAF 319th SOS/1st SOW, Hurlburt Field, FL
	08-0790	Pilatus U-28A Draco (N757ED)	USAF 319th SOS/1st SOW, Hurlburt Field, FL

Serial	Type (code/other identity)	Owner/operator, location or fate	Notes
08-0809	Pilatus U-28A Draco (N36EG)	USAF 319th SOS/1st SOW, Hurlburt Field, FL	
08-0822	Pilatus U-28A Draco (N822BM)	USAF 319th SOS/1st SOW, Hurlburt Field, FL	
08-0835	Pilatus U-28A Draco (N100MS)	USAF 318th SOS/27th SOW, Cannon AFB, NM	
08-0850	Pilatus U-28A Draco (N850CB)	USAF 319th SOS/1st SOW, Hurlburt Field, FL	

Boeing C-32

* Please note that there is evidence to suggest that the serials 25001 and 96143 have been used by more than one airframe. In recent times 25001 has been used by N610G and 96143 by N226G.

98-0001	Boeing C-32A	USAF 1st AS/89th AW, Andrews AFB, MD	
98-0002	Boeing C-32A	USAF 1st AS/89th AW, Andrews AFB, MD	
99-0003	Boeing C-32A	USAF 1st AS/89th AW, Andrews AFB, MD	
99-0004	Boeing C-32A	USAF 1st AS/89th AW, Andrews AFB, MD	
99-6143	Boeing C-32B	USAF 486th FLTS/46th TW, Eglin AFB, FL	
00-9001	Boeing C-32B	USAF 150th SOS/108th Wg, McGuire AFB, NJ	
02-4452	Boeing C-32B	USAF 150th SOS/108th Wg, McGuire AFB, NJ	
02-5001	Boeing C-32B	USAF 486th FLTS/46th TW, Eglin AFB, FL	
09-0015	Boeing C-32A	USAF 1st AS/89th AW, Andrews AFB, MD	
09-0016	Boeing C-32A	USAF 1st AS/89th AW, Andrews AFB, MD	
09-0017	Boeing C-32A	USAF 1st AS/89th AW, Andrews AFB, MD	
19-0018	Boeing C-32A	USAF 1st AS/89th AW, Andrews AFB, MD	

Gulfstream Aerospace C-37 Gulfstream V

97-0400	Gulfstream Aerospace C-37A Gulfstream V	USAF 99th AS/89th AW, Andrews AFB, MD	
97-0401	Gulfstream Aerospace C-37A Gulfstream V	USAF 99th AS/89th AW, Andrews AFB, MD	
97-1944	Gulfstream Aerospace C-37A Gulfstream V	US Army OSAC/PAT, Andrews AFB, MD	
99-0402	Gulfstream Aerospace C-37A Gulfstream V	USAF 99th AS/89th AW, Andrews AFB, MD	
99-0404	Gulfstream Aerospace C-37A Gulfstream V	USAF 99th AS/89th AW, Andrews AFB, MD	
01-0028	Gulfstream Aerospace C-37A Gulfstream V	USAF 99th AS/89th AW, Andrews AFB, MD	
01-0065	Gulfstream Aerospace C-37A Gulfstream V	USAF 65th AS/15th Wg, Hickam AFB, HI	
02-01863	Gulfstream Aerospace C-37A Gulfstream V [1863]	US Army OSAC/PAT, Andrews AFB, MD	
04-01778	Gulfstream Aerospace C-37A Gulfstream V [1778]	US Army OSAC/PAT, Andrews AFB, MD	
06-0500	Gulfstream Aerospace C-37B Gulfstream V	USAF 99th AS/89th AW, Andrews AFB, MD	
09-0525	Gulfstream Aerospace C-37B Gulfstream V	USAF 99th AS/89th AW, Andrews AFB, MD	
11-0550	Gulfstream Aerospace C-37B Gulfstream V	USAF 99th AS/89th AW, Andrews AFB, MD	
18-1942	Gulfstream Aerospace C-37B Gulfstream V [1942]	USAF 99th AS/89th AW, Andrews AFB, MD	
18-1947	Gulfstream Aerospace C-37B Gulfstream V [1947]	USAF 99th AS/89th AW, Andrews AFB, MD	
20-1941	Gulfstream Aerospace C-37B Gulfstream V	USAF 99th AS/89th AW, Andrews AFB, MD	
20-1949	Gulfstream Aerospace C-37B Gulfstream V	USAF 99th AS/89th AW, Andrews AFB, MD	
..-....	Gulfstream Aerospace EC-37B Compass Call (N967GA)	USAF (on order)	
..-....	Gulfstream Aerospace EC-37B Compass Call (N591GA)	USAF (on order)	
..-....	Gulfstream Aerospace EC-37B Compass Call	USAF (on order)	
..-....	Gulfstream Aerospace EC-37B Compass Call	USAF (on order)	
..-....	Gulfstream Aerospace EC-37B Compass Call	USAF (on order)	
..-....	Gulfstream Aerospace EC-37B Compass Call	USAF (on order)	
..-....	Gulfstream Aerospace EC-37B Compass Call	USAF (on order)	
..-....	Gulfstream Aerospace EC-37B Compass Call	USAF (on order)	
..-....	Gulfstream Aerospace EC-37B Compass Call	USAF (on order)	
..-....	Gulfstream Aerospace EC-37B Compass Call	USAF (on order)	

Boeing C-40

01-0015	Boeing C-40B (N378BJ)	USAF 65th AS/15th Wg, Hickam AFB, HI	
01-0040	Boeing C-40B (N371BJ)	USAF 1st AS/89th AW, Andrews AFB, MD	
01-0041	Boeing C-40B (N374BC)	USAF 1st AS/89th AW, Andrews AFB, MD	
02-0042	Boeing C-40B (N237BA)	USAF 1st AS/89th AW, Andrews AFB, MD	
02-0201	Boeing C-40C (N752BC)	USAF 201st AS/113th FW DC ANG, Andrews AFB, MD	
02-0202	Boeing C-40C (N754BC)	USAF 201st AS/113th FW DC ANG, Andrews AFB, MD	
02-0203	Boeing C-40C (N236BA)	USAF 201st AS/113th FW DC ANG, Andrews AFB, MD	
05-0730	Boeing C-40C (N365BJ)	USAF 73rd AS/932nd AW AFRC, Scott AFB, IL	

Notes	Serial	Type (code/other identity)	Owner/operator, location or fate
	05-0932	Boeing C-40C (N366BJ)	USAF 73rd AS/932nd AW AFRC, Scott AFB, IL
	05-4613	Boeing C-40C (N368BJ)	USAF 73rd AS/932nd AW AFRC, Scott AFB, IL
	09-0540	Boeing C-40C (N736JS)	USAF 73rd AS/932nd AW AFRC, Scott AFB, IL
	Boeing 767-2C/KC-46A Pegasus		
	11-46001	Boeing 767-2LKC (N461FT)	Boeing, Everett, for USAF
	11-46002	Boeing KC-46A Pegasus (N462KC)	Boeing, Seattle, for USAF
	11-46003	Boeing 767-2LKC (N463FT)	Boeing, Everett, for USAF
	11-46004	Boeing KC-46A Pegasus (N464KC)	Boeing, Seattle, for USAF
	15-46005	Boeing KC-46A Pegasus (N842BA)	Boeing, Everett, for USAF
	15-46006	Boeing 767-2LKC (N884BA)	Boeing, Everett, for USAF
	15-46008	Boeing KC-46A Pegasus	Boeing, Everett, for USAF (stored)
	15-46009	Boeing KC-46A Pegasus (N50217)	USAF 22nd ARW, McConnell AFB, KS
	15-46010	Boeing KC-46A Pegasus	Boeing, Everett, for USAF
	15-46011	Boeing KC-46A Pegasus (N6009F)	USAF 77th ARS/916th ARW AFRC, Seymour Johnson AFB, NC
	15-46066	Boeing KC-46A Pegasus (N2014H/19-46066)	USAF 77th ARS/916th ARW AFRC, Seymour Johnson AFB, NC
	15-46067	Boeing KC-46A Pegasus (N1785B/19-46067)	USAF 22nd ARW, McConnell AFB, KS
	15-46068	Boeing KC-46A Pegasus (N1794B/19-46068)	USAF 77th ARS/916th ARW AFRC, Seymour Johnson AFB, NC
	15-46069	Boeing KC-46A Pegasus (N5014K/19-46069)	USAF 305th AMW, McGuire AFB, NJ
	15-46070	Boeing KC-46A Pegasus (N5020K/19-46070)	USAF 305th AMW, McGuire AFB, NJ
	16-46012	Boeing KC-46A Pegasus (N1785B)	USAF 56th ARS/97th AMW, Altus AFB, OK
	16-46013	Boeing KC-46A Pegasus	USAF 133rd ARS/157th ARW, Pease ANGB, NH ANG
	16-46014	Boeing KC-46A Pegasus (N5573S)	USAF 77th ARS/916th ARW AFRC, Seymour Johnson AFB, NC
	16-46015	Boeing KC-46A Pegasus (N6009F) *bl/w*	USAF 133rd ARS/157th ARW, Pease ANGB, NH ANG
	16-46016	Boeing KC-46A Pegasus (N6018N)	USAF 22nd ARW, McConnell AFB, KS
	16-46017	Boeing KC-46A Pegasus (N5573S)	USAF 22nd ARW, McConnell AFB, KS
	16-46018	Boeing KC-46A Pegasus (N5514J)	USAF 133rd ARS/157th ARW, Pease ANGB, NH ANG
	16-46019	Boeing KC-46A Pegasus (N5514K)	USAF 133rd ARS/157th ARW, Pease ANGB, NH ANG
	16-46020	Boeing KC-46A Pegasus (N5514V)	USAF 133rd ARS/157th ARW, Pease ANGB, NH ANG
	16-46021	Boeing KC-46A Pegasus (N5514X)	USAF 305th AMW, McGuire AFB, NJ
	16-46022	Boeing KC-46A Pegasus (N5573S)	USAF 22nd ARW, McConnell AFB, KS
	16-46023	Boeing KC-46A Pegasus (N6018N)	USAF 22nd ARW, McConnell AFB, KS
	17-46024	Boeing KC-46A Pegasus (N5514J)	USAF 77th ARS/916th ARW AFRC, Seymour Johnson AFB, NC
	17-46025	Boeing KC-46A Pegasus (N5017V)	USAF 22nd ARW, McConnell AFB, KS
	17-46026	Boeing KC-46A Pegasus (N6018N)	USAF 22nd ARW, McConnell AFB, KS
	17-46027	Boeing KC-46A Pegasus (N5014K)	USAF 22nd ARW, McConnell AFB, KS
	17-46028	Boeing KC-46A Pegasus (N55141)	USAF 56th ARS/97th AMW, Altus AFB, OK
	17-46029	Boeing KC-46A Pegasus (N55141)	USAF 133rd ARS/157th ARW, Pease ANGB, NH ANG
	17-46030	Boeing KC-46A Pegasus (N6009F)	USAF 22nd ARW, McConnell AFB, KS
	17-46031	Boeing KC-46A Pegasus (N5513X)	USAF 22nd ARW, McConnell AFB, KS
	17-46032	Boeing KC-46A Pegasus (N5016R)	USAF 22nd ARW, McConnell AFB, KS
	17-46033	Boeing KC-46A Pegasus (N5016R)	USAF 22nd ARW, McConnell AFB, KS
	17-46034	Boeing KC-46A Pegasus (N5017Q)	USAF 133rd ARS/157th ARW, Pease ANGB, NH ANG
	17-46035	Boeing KC-46A Pegasus (N5017V)	USAF 22nd ARW, McConnell AFB, KS
	17-46036	Boeing KC-46A Pegasus (N5017V)	USAF 22nd ARW, McConnell AFB, KS
	17-46037	Boeing KC-46A Pegasus (N5511Y)	USAF 22nd ARW, McConnell AFB, KS
	17-46038	Boeing KC-46A Pegasus (N5020K)	USAF 56th ARS/97th AMW, Altus AFB, OK
	18-46039	Boeing KC-46A Pegasus (N1785B)	USAF 56th ARS/97th AMW, Altus AFB, OK
	18-46040	Boeing KC-46A Pegasus (N6018N)	USAF 56th ARS/97th AMW, Altus AFB, OK
	18-46041	Boeing KC-46A Pegasus (N50217)	USAF 418th FLTS/412th TW, Edwards AFB, CA

Serial	Type (code/other identity)	Owner/operator, location or fate	Notes
18-46042	Boeing KC-46A Pegasus (N5512A)	USAF 22nd ARW, McConnell AFB, KS	
18-46043	Boeing KC-46A Pegasus (N1785B)	USAF 56th ARS/97th AMW, Altus AFB, OK	
18-46044	Boeing KC-46A Pegasus (N5511V)	USAF 22nd ARW, McConnell AFB, KS	
18-46045	Boeing KC-46A Pegasus (N1794B)	USAF 56th ARS/97th AMW, Altus AFB, OK	
18-46046	Boeing KC-46A Pegasus (N55077)	USAF 418th FLTS/412th TW, Edwards AFB, CA	
18-46047	Boeing KC-46A Pegasus (N5016R)	USAF 133rd ARS/157th ARW, Pease ANGB, NH ANG	
18-46048	Boeing KC-46A Pegasus (N1794B)	USAF 56th ARS/97th AMW, Altus AFB, OK	
18-46049	Boeing KC-46A Pegasus (N5510E) r/y $	USAF 56th ARS/97th AMW, Altus AFB, OK	
18-46050	Boeing KC-46A Pegasus (N5511Z)	USAF 133rd ARS/157th ARW, Pease ANGB, NH ANG	
18-46051	Boeing KC-46A Pegasus (N6018N)	USAF 133rd ARS/157th ARW, Pease ANGB, NH ANG	
18-46052	Boeing KC-46A Pegasus (N55077)	USAF 77th ARS/916th ARW AFRC, Seymour Johnson AFB, NC	
18-46053	Boeing KC-46A Pegasus (N1785B)	USAF 133rd ARS/157th ARW, Pease ANGB, NH ANG	
18-46054	Boeing KC-46A Pegasus (N50254)	USAF 133rd ARS/157th ARW, Pease ANGB, NH ANG	
18-46055	Boeing KC-46A Pegasus (N50281)	USAF 77th ARS/916th ARW AFRC, Seymour Johnson AFB, NC	
18-46056	Boeing KC-46A Pegasus (N5514K)	USAF 22nd ARW, McConnell AFB, KS	
19-46007	Boeing KC-46A Pegasus (N2015U/15-46007)	Boeing, for USAF, stored Paine Field	
19-46061	Boeing KC-46A Pegasus (N20144)	USAF 305th AMW, McGuire AFB, NJ	
19-46062	Boeing KC-46A Pegasus (N2011A)	USAF 77th ARS/916th ARW AFRC, Seymour Johnson AFB, NC	
19-46063	Boeing KC-46A Pegasus (N2011E)	Boeing, Seattle, for USAF	
19-46064	Boeing KC-46A Pegasus (N20129)	USAF 305th AMW, McGuire AFB, NJ	
19-46065	Boeing KC-46A Pegasus (N20140)	USAF 77th ARS/916th ARW AFRC, Seymour Johnson AFB, NC	
19-46071	Boeing KC-46A Pegasus (N461FT)	USAF (on order)	
20-46072	Boeing KC-46A Pegasus	USAF 305th AMW, McGuire AFB, NJ	
20-46073	Boeing KC-46A Pegasus	USAF 305th AMW, McGuire AFB, NJ	
20-46074	Boeing KC-46A Pegasus	USAF (on order)	
20-46075	Boeing KC-46A Pegasus	USAF 22nd ARW, McConnell AFB, KS	
20-46076	Boeing KC-46A Pegasus	USAF (on order)	
20-46077	Boeing KC-46A Pegasus	USAF (on order)	
20-46078	Boeing KC-46A Pegasus	USAF (on order)	
20-46079	Boeing KC-46A Pegasus	USAF (on order)	
20-46080	Boeing KC-46A Pegasus	USAF (on order)	
20-46081	Boeing KC-46A Pegasus	USAF (on order)	
20-46082	Boeing KC-46A Pegasus	USAF (on order)	
20-46083	Boeing KC-46A Pegasus	USAF (on order)	
21-46057	Boeing KC-46A Pegasus (N2013S/19-46057)	USAF 305th AMW, McGuire AFB, NJ	
21-46058	Boeing KC-46A Pegasus (N5107Q/19-46058)	USAF 77th ARS/916th ARW AFRC, Seymour Johnson AFB, NC	
21-46059	Boeing KC-46A Pegasus (N5020K/19-46059)	USAF 56th ARS/97th AMW, Altus AFB, OK	
21-46060	Boeing KC-46A Pegasus (N2013Z/19-46060)	USAF 305th AMW, McGuire AFB, NJ	

Boeing B-52H Stratofortress

Serial	Type (code/other identity)	Owner/operator, location or fate	Notes
60-0001	Boeing B-52H Stratofortress [LA] gn	USAF 96th BS/2nd BW, Barksdale AFB, LA	
60-0002	Boeing B-52H Stratofortress [LA] gn [2 BW]	USAF 96th BS/2nd BW, Barksdale AFB, LA	
60-0003	Boeing B-52H Stratofortress [BD] or/bl	USAF 93rd BS/307th BW AFRC, Barksdale AFB, LA	
60-0004	Boeing B-52H Stratofortress [MT] r/y	USAF 23rd BS/5th BW, Minot AFB, ND	
60-0005	Boeing B-52H Stratofortress [MT] m [5 BW]	USAF 23rd BS/5th BW, Minot AFB, ND	
60-0007	Boeing B-52H Stratofortress [MT] r/y	USAF 23rd BS/5th BW, Minot AFB, ND	
60-0008	Boeing B-52H Stratofortress [LA] bl [8th AF]	USAF 20th BS/2nd BW, Barksdale AFB, LA	

Notes	Serial	Type (code/other identity)	Owner/operator, location or fate
	60-0009	Boeing B-52H Stratofortress [MT] y/bk [69 BS]	USAF 69th BS/5th BW, Minot AFB, ND
	60-0011	Boeing B-52H Stratofortress [BD] or/bl [11 BS]	USAF 93rd BS/307th BW AFRC, Barksdale AFB, LA
	60-0012	Boeing B-52H Stratofortress [MT] y/bk	USAF 69th BS/5th BW, Minot AFB, ND
	60-0013	Boeing B-52H Stratofortress [LA] bl	USAF 20th BS/2nd BW, Barksdale AFB, LA
	60-0015	Boeing B-52H Stratofortress [BD] or/bl	USAF 93rd BS/307th BW AFRC, Barksdale AFB, LA
	60-0017	Boeing B-52H Stratofortress [MT] y/bk	USAF 69th BS/5th BW, Minot AFB, ND
	60-0018	Boeing B-52H Stratofortress [MT] y/bk	USAF 69th BS/5th BW, Minot AFB, ND
	60-0021	Boeing B-52H Stratofortress [LA] r	USAF 96th BS/2nd BW, Barksdale AFB, LA
	60-0022	Boeing B-52H Stratofortress [LA] r	USAF 96th BS/2nd BW, Barksdale AFB, LA
	60-0023	Boeing B-52H Stratofortress [MT] y/bk	USAF 69th BS/5th BW, Minot AFB, ND
	60-0024	Boeing B-52H Stratofortress [LA] bl	USAF 20th BS/2nd BW, Barksdale AFB, LA
	60-0025	Boeing B-52H Stratofortress [LA] bl	USAF 20th BS/2nd BW, Barksdale AFB, LA
	60-0026	Boeing B-52H Stratofortress [MT] r/y	USAF 23rd BS/5th BW, Minot AFB, ND
	60-0028	Boeing B-52H Stratofortress [LA] r	USAF 96th BS/2nd BW, Barksdale AFB, LA
	60-0029	Boeing B-52H Stratofortress [MT] r/y	USAF 23rd BS/5th BW, Minot AFB, ND
	60-0031	Boeing B-52H Stratofortress [OT] or/w	USAF 49th TES/53rd TEG, Barksdale AFB, LA
	60-0032	Boeing B-52H Stratofortress [LA] r	USAF 96th BS/2nd BW, Barksdale AFB, LA
	60-0033	Boeing B-52H Stratofortress [MT] y/bk	USAF 69th BS/5th BW, Minot AFB, ND
	60-0034	Boeing B-52H Stratofortress [MT] r/y	USAF 23rd BS/5th BW, Minot AFB, ND
	60-0035	Boeing B-52H Stratofortress [BD] or/bl	USAF 93rd BS/307th BW AFRC, Barksdale AFB, LA
	60-0036	Boeing B-52H Stratofortress [ED]	USAF 419th FLTS/412th TW, Edwards AFB, CA
	60-0037	Boeing B-52H Stratofortress [MT] y/bk	USAF 69th BS/5th BW, Minot AFB, ND
	60-0038	Boeing B-52H Stratofortress [BD] or/bl	USAF 93rd BS/307th BW AFRC, Barksdale AFB, LA
	60-0041	Boeing B-52H Stratofortress [BD] or/bl	USAF 93rd BS/307th BW AFRC, Barksdale AFB, LA
	60-0042	Boeing B-52H Stratofortress [BD] or/bl	USAF 93rd BS/307th BW AFRC, Barksdale AFB, LA
	60-0044	Boeing B-52H Stratofortress [MT] r/y	USAF 23rd BS/5th BW, Minot AFB, ND
	60-0045	Boeing B-52H Stratofortress [BD] or/bl [307 OG]	USAF 93rd BS/307th BW AFRC, Barksdale AFB, LA
	60-0048	Boeing B-52H Stratofortress [LA] r	USAF 96th BS/2nd BW, Barksdale AFB, LA
	60-0050	Boeing B-52H Stratofortress [ED]	USAF 419th FLTS/412th TW, Edwards AFB, CA
	60-0051	Boeing B-52H Stratofortress [BD] or/bl	USAF 93rd BS/307th BW AFRC, Barksdale AFB, LA
	60-0052	Boeing B-52H Stratofortress [LA] r	USAF 96th BS/2nd BW, Barksdale AFB, LA
	60-0054	Boeing B-52H Stratofortress [LA] bl	USAF 20th BS/2nd BW, Barksdale AFB, LA
	60-0055	Boeing B-52H Stratofortress [MT] r/y [5 OG]	USAF 23rd BS/5th BW, Minot AFB, ND
	60-0056	Boeing B-52H Stratofortress [MT] r/y	USAF 23rd BS/5th BW, Minot AFB, ND
	60-0057	Boeing B-52H Stratofortress [BD] or/bl [340 WPS]	USAF 93rd BS/307th BW AFRC, Barksdale AFB, LA
	60-0058	Boeing B-52H Stratofortress [LA] bl	USAF 20th BS/2nd BW, Barksdale AFB, LA
	60-0059	Boeing B-52H Stratofortress [LA] r [96 BS]	USAF 96th BS/2nd BW, Barksdale AFB, LA (damaged)
	60-0060	Boeing B-52H Stratofortress [MT] r/y	USAF 23rd BS/5th BW, Minot AFB, ND
	60-0061	Boeing B-52H Stratofortress [BD] or/bl [307 BW]	USAF 93rd BS/307th BW AFRC, Barksdale AFB, LA
	60-0062	Boeing B-52H Stratofortress [LA] r	USAF 96th BS/2nd BW, Barksdale AFB, LA
	61-0001	Boeing B-52H Stratofortress [MT] y/bk	USAF 69th BS/5th BW, Minot AFB, ND
	61-0002	Boeing B-52H Stratofortress [LA] bl [2 OG]	USAF 20th BS/2nd BW, Barksdale AFB, LA
	61-0003	Boeing B-52H Stratofortress [MT] y/bk	USAF 69th BS/5th BW, Minot AFB, ND
	61-0004	Boeing B-52H Stratofortress [LA] bl	USAF 20th BS/2nd BW, Barksdale AFB, LA
	61-0005	Boeing B-52H Stratofortress [MT] y/bk	USAF 69th BS/5th BW, Minot AFB, ND
	61-0006	Boeing B-52H Stratofortress [LA] r	USAF 96th BS/2nd BW, Barksdale AFB, LA
	61-0007	Boeing B-52H Stratofortress [MT] y/bk	USAF 69th BS/5th BW, Minot AFB, ND

Serial	Type (code/other identity)	Owner/operator, location or fate	Notes
61-0008	Boeing B-52H Stratofortress [BD] or/bl	USAF 93rd BS/307th BW AFRC, Barksdale AFB, LA	
61-0010	Boeing B-52H Stratofortress [LA] or/bl [343 BS]	USAF 93rd BS/307th BW AFRC, Barksdale AFB, LA	
61-0011	Boeing B-52H Stratofortress [BD] or/bl	USAF 93rd BS/307th BW AFRC, Barksdale AFB, LA	
61-0012	Boeing B-52H Stratofortress [LA] r	USAF 96th BS/2nd BW, Barksdale AFB, LA	
61-0013	Boeing B-52H Stratofortress [LA] bl	USAF 20th BS/2nd BW, Barksdale AFB, LA	
61-0014	Boeing B-52H Stratofortress [ED]	USAF 419th FLTS/412th TW, Edwards AFB, CA	
61-0015	Boeing B-52H Stratofortress [LA] r	USAF 96th BS/2nd BW, Barksdale AFB, LA	
61-0016	Boeing B-52H Stratofortress [LA] bl	USAF 20th BS/2nd BW, Barksdale AFB, LA	
61-0017	Boeing B-52H Stratofortress [BD] or/bl	USAF 93rd BS/307th BW AFRC, Barksdale AFB, LA	
61-0018	Boeing B-52H Stratofortress [MT] y/bk	USAF 69th BS/5th BW, Minot AFB, ND	
61-0019	Boeing B-52H Stratofortress [LA] bl	USAF 20th BS/2nd BW, Barksdale AFB, LA	
61-0020	Boeing B-52H Stratofortress [LA] bl [20 BS]	USAF 20th BS/2nd BW, Barksdale AFB, LA	
61-0021	Boeing B-52H Stratofortress [LA] [343 BS]	USAF 93rd BS/307th BW AFRC, Barksdale AFB, LA	
61-0028	Boeing B-52H Stratofortress [OT] w/or [49 TES]	USAF 49th TES/53rd TEG, Barksdale AFB, LA	
61-0029	Boeing B-52H Stratofortress [BD] or/bl [93 BS]	USAF 93rd BS/307th BW AFRC, Barksdale AFB, LA	
61-0031	Boeing B-52H Stratofortress [BD] or/bl	USAF 93rd BS/307th BW AFRC, Barksdale AFB, LA	
61-0032	Boeing B-52H Stratofortress [MT] r/y	USAF 23rd BS/5th BW, Minot AFB, ND	
61-0034	Boeing B-52H Stratofortress [MT] r/y	USAF 23rd BS/5th BW, Minot AFB, ND	
61-0035	Boeing B-52H Stratofortress [MT] r/y	USAF 23rd BS/5th BW, Minot AFB, ND	
61-0036	Boeing B-52H Stratofortress [LA] r	USAF 96th BS/2nd BW, Barksdale AFB, LA	
61-0038	Boeing B-52H Stratofortress [BD] or/bl	USAF 93rd BS/307th BW AFRC, Barksdale AFB, LA	
61-0039	Boeing B-52H Stratofortress [MT] y/bk	USAF 69th BS/5th BW, Minot AFB, ND	
61-0040	Boeing B-52H Stratofortress [MT] r/y	USAF 23rd BS/5th BW, Minot AFB, ND	
Lockheed C-130			
65-0967	Lockheed EC-130H Compass Call [DM]	USAF 43rd ECS/55th ECG, Davis-Monthan AFB, AZ	
65-0974	Lockheed HC-130P Combat King	USAF 102nd RQS/106th RQW, Suffolk Field, NY ANG	
65-0978	Lockheed HC-130P Combat King	To Fort Bragg, NC for G.I.	
69-5829	Lockheed HC-130N Combat King	Instructional airframe, Kirtland AFB, NM	
73-1581	Lockheed EC-130H Compass Call [DM] $	USAF 43rd ECS/55th ECG, Davis-Monthan AFB, AZ	
73-1583	Lockheed EC-130H Compass Call [DM] r	USAF 43rd ECS/55th ECG, Davis-Monthan AFB, AZ	
73-1584	Lockheed EC-130H Compass Call [DM]	USAF 43rd ECS/55th ECG, Davis-Monthan AFB, AZ	
73-1586	Lockheed EC-130H Compass Call [DM]	To 309th AMARG, 2022	
73-1588	Lockheed EC-130H Compass Call [DM]	To 309th AMARG, March 2022	
73-1590	Lockheed EC-130H Compass Call [DM]	USAF 43rd ECS/55th ECG, Davis-Monthan AFB, AZ	
73-1594	Lockheed EC-130H Compass Call [DM]	USAF 43rd ECS/55th ECG, Davis-Monthan AFB, AZ	
73-1595	Lockheed EC-130H Compass Call [DM]	USAF 43rd ECS/55th ECG, Davis-Monthan AFB, AZ	
73-3300	Lockheed LC-130H Hercules	USAF 139th AS/109th AW, Schenectady, NY ANG	
74-1685	Lockheed C-130H Hercules y/bk	USAF 118th AS/103rd AW, Bradley ANGB, CT ANG	
74-1687	Lockheed C-130H Hercules y/bk	Instructional airframe, Laguna AAF, AZ	
74-1692	Lockheed C-130H Hercules r/bk	USAF 164th AS/179th AW, Mansfield, OH ANG	
74-2061	Lockheed C-130H Hercules r/bk	Withdrawn from use, Mansfield, OH	

Notes	Serial	Type (code/other identity)	Owner/operator, location or fate
	74-2069	Lockheed C-130H Hercules *y/bk*	USAF 118th AS/103rd AW, Bradley ANGB, CT ANG
	76-3301	Lockheed LC-130H Hercules	USAF 139th AS/109th AW, Schenectady, NY ANG
	76-3302	Lockheed LC-130H Hercules	USAF 139th AS/109th AW, Schenectady, NY ANG
	80-0322	Lockheed C-130H-2 Hercules *y/bk*	USAF 118th AS/103rd AW, Bradley ANGB, CT ANG
	80-0324	Lockheed C-130H-2 Hercules	USAF 186th AS/120th AW, Great Falls, MT ANG
	80-0326	Lockheed C-130H-2 Hercules *y/bk*	*Instructional Airframe Niagara Falls, NY*
	81-0629	Lockheed C-130H-2 Hercules *r/w* $	USAF 154th TS/189th AW, Little Rock, AR ANG
	83-0489	Lockheed C-130H-2 Hercules	USAF 139th AS/109th AW, Schenectady, NY ANG
	83-0490	Lockheed LC-130H Hercules	USAF 139th AS/109th AW, Schenectady, NY ANG
	83-0491	Lockheed LC-130H Hercules	USAF 139th AS/109th AW, Schenectady, NY ANG
	83-0492	Lockheed LC-130H Hercules	USAF 139th AS/109th AW, Schenectady, NY ANG
	83-0493	Lockheed LC-130H Hercules	USAF 139th AS/109th AW, Schenectady, NY ANG
	84-0206	Lockheed C-130H-2 Hercules *bl/bk*	USAF 142nd AS/166th AW, New Castle County, DE ANG
	84-0207	Lockheed C-130H-2 Hercules *r/bk*	USAF 187th AS/153rd AW, Cheyenne, WY ANG
	84-0208	Lockheed C-130H-2 Hercules	USAF 139th AS/109th AW, Schenectady, NY ANG
	84-0209	Lockheed C-130H-2 Hercules	USAF 139th AS/109th AW, Schenectady, NY ANG
	84-0210	Lockheed C-130H-2 Hercules *bl/bk*	USAF 142nd AS/166th AW, New Castle County, DE ANG
	84-0212	Lockheed C-130H-2 Hercules *bl/bk*	USAF 142nd AS/166th AW, New Castle County, DE ANG
	84-0213	Lockheed C-130H-2 Hercules *bl/bk*	USAF 142nd AS/166th AW, New Castle County, DE ANG
	85-0011	Lockheed MC-130H Combat Talon II	USAF 15th SOS/1st SOW, Hurlburt Field, FL
	85-1363	Lockheed C-130H-2 Hercules (85-1363) *r/w*	USAF 154th TS/189th AW, Little Rock, AR ANG
	85-1364	Lockheed C-130H-2 Hercules (85-1364)	USAF
	85-1365	Lockheed C-130H-2 Hercules (85-1365) *r/w*	USAF 154th TS/189th AW, Little Rock, AR ANG
	85-1366	Lockheed C-130H-2 Hercules	USAF
	85-1367	Lockheed C-130H-2 Hercules *r/w*	USAF 154th TS/189th AW, Little Rock, AR ANG
	86-0419	Lockheed C-130H-2 Hercules *r/bk*	USAF 164th AS/179th AW, Mansfield, OH ANG
	86-1699	Lockheed MC-130H Combat Talon II	USAF 15th SOS/1st SOW, Hurlburt Field, FL
	87-0023	Lockheed MC-130H Combat Talon II	USAF 15th SOS/1st SOW, Hurlburt Field, FL
	87-0125	Lockheed MC-130H Combat Talon II	USAF 15th SOS/1st SOW, Hurlburt Field, FL
	87-0126	Lockheed MC-130H Combat Talon II	*Eradicated from AMARG inventory by Nov 2022*
	87-9281	Lockheed C-130H-2 Hercules *r/bk*	USAF 164th AS/179th AW, Mansfield, OH ANG
	87-9283	Lockheed C-130H-2 Hercules *r/bk*	USAF 164th AS/179th AW, Mansfield, OH ANG
	87-9285	Lockheed C-130H-2 Hercules *r/bk*	USAF 164th AS/179th AW, Mansfield, OH ANG
	87-9286	Lockheed AC-130W Stinger II	USAF 16th SOS/27th SOW, Cannon AFB, NM
	87-9287	Lockheed C-130H-2 Hercules *r/bk*	*Eradicated from AMARG inventory by Nov 2022*
	87-9288	Lockheed AC-130W Stinger II	USAF 16th SOS/27th SOW, Cannon AFB, NM
	88-0191	Lockheed MC-130H Combat Talon II	USAF 15th SOS/1st SOW, Hurlburt Field, FL
	88-0264	Lockheed MC-130H Combat Talon II	USAF 15th SOS/1st SOW, Hurlburt Field, FL
	88-1301	Lockheed AC-130W Stinger II	*To 309th AMARG, May 2022*
	88-1302	Lockheed AC-130W Stinger II	*To 309th AMARG, April 2022*
	88-1304	Lockheed AC-130W Stinger II	USAF 16th SOS/27th SOW, Cannon AFB, NM
	88-1306	Lockheed MC-130H Combat Talon II	*To 309th AMARG, July 2022*
	88-1307	Lockheed AC-130W Stinger II	*To 309th AMARG, June 2022*
	88-1308	Lockheed AC-130W Stinger II	USAF 16th SOS/27th SOW, Cannon AFB, NM
	88-4401	Lockheed C-130H-2 Hercules *r/bk*	*Preserved Akron-Canton, OH, Jan 2022*
	88-4405	Lockheed C-130H-2 Hercules *r/bk*	USAF 164th AS/179th AW, Mansfield, OH ANG

Serial	Type (code/other identity)	Owner/operator, location or fate	Notes
88-4406	Lockheed C-130H-2 Hercules *bl/w*	USAF 357th AS/908th AW AFRC, Maxwell AFB, AL	
89-0280	Lockheed MC-130H Combat Talon II	USAF 15th SOS/1st SOW, Hurlburt Field, FL	
89-0283	Lockheed MC-130H Combat Talon II	USAF 15th SOS/1st SOW, Hurlburt Field, FL	
89-1051	Lockheed AC-130W Stinger II	*To 309th AMARG, June 2022*	
89-1055	Lockheed C-130H-2 Hercules *bl/w*	USAF 357th AS/908th AW AFRC, Maxwell AFB, AL	
89-1181	Lockheed C-130H-2 Hercules *r/w*	USAF 154th TS/189th AW, Little Rock, AR ANG	
89-1182	Lockheed C-130H-2 Hercules *r/w*	USAF 154th TS/189th AW, Little Rock, AR ANG	
89-1183	Lockheed C-130H-2 Hercules *r/w*	USAF 154th TS/189th AW, Little Rock, AR ANG	
89-1184	Lockheed C-130H-2 Hercules *r/w* $	USAF 154th TS/189th AW, Little Rock, AR ANG	
89-1185	Lockheed C-130H-2 Hercules *r/w*	USAF 154th TS/189th AW, Little Rock, AR ANG	
89-1186	Lockheed C-130H-2 Hercules *r/w*	USAF 154th TS/189th AW, Little Rock, AR ANG	
89-1187	Lockheed C-130H-2 Hercules *bl/w*	USAF 357th AS/908th AW AFRC, Maxwell AFB, AL	
89-1188	Lockheed C-130H-2 Hercules *bl/w*	USAF 357th AS/908th AW AFRC, Maxwell AFB, AL	
89-9102	Lockheed C-130H-2 Hercules *r/w*	USAF 154th TS/189th AW, Little Rock, AR ANG	
89-9103	Lockheed C-130H-2 Hercules *bl/w*	USAF 357th AS/908th AW AFRC, Maxwell AFB, AL	
89-9104	Lockheed C-130H-2 Hercules *bl/r*	USAF 757th AS/910th AW AFRC, Youngstown ARS, OH	
89-9105	Lockheed C-130H-2 Hercules *bl/r*	USAF 757th AS/910th AW AFRC, Youngstown ARS, OH	
89-9106	Lockheed C-130H-2 Hercules *bl/r*	USAF 757th AS/910th AW AFRC, Youngstown ARS, OH	
90-0162	Lockheed MC-130H Combat Talon II	*To 309th AMARG, April 2022*	
90-1057	Lockheed C-130H-2 Hercules	USAF 142nd AS/166th AW, New Castle County, DE ANG	
90-1058	Lockheed AC-130W Stinger II	*To 309th AMARG, July 2022*	
90-1791	Lockheed C-130H-2 Hercules	USAF 180th AS/139th AW, Rosencrans Memorial, MO ANG	
90-1792	Lockheed C-130H-2 Hercules	USAF 180th AS/139th AW, Rosencrans Memorial, MO ANG	
90-1793	Lockheed C-130H-2 Hercules	USAF 180th AS/139th AW, Rosencrans Memorial, MO ANG	
90-1794	Lockheed C-130H-2 Hercules	USAF 180th AS/139th AW, Rosencrans Memorial, MO ANG	
90-1795	Lockheed C-130H-2 Hercules	USAF 180th AS/139th AW, Rosencrans Memorial, MO ANG	
90-1796	Lockheed C-130H-2 Hercules	USAF 180th AS/139th AW, Rosencrans Memorial, MO ANG	
90-1797	Lockheed C-130H-2 Hercules	USAF 180th AS/139th AW, Rosencrans Memorial, MO ANG	
90-1798	Lockheed C-130H-2 Hercules	USAF 180th AS/139th AW, Rosencrans Memorial, MO ANG	
90-9107	Lockheed C-130H-2 Hercules *bl/r*	USAF 757th AS/910th AW AFRC, Youngstown ARS, OH	
90-9108	Lockheed C-130H-2 Hercules *bl/r*	USAF 757th AS/910th AW AFRC, Youngstown ARS, OH	
91-1231	Lockheed C-130H-2 Hercules *bl/bk*	USAF 142nd AS/166th AW, New Castle County, DE ANG	
91-1232	Lockheed C-130H-2 Hercules *bl/bk*	USAF 142nd AS/166th AW, New Castle County, DE ANG	
91-1233	Lockheed C-130H-2 Hercules *bl/bk*	USAF 142nd AS/166th AW, New Castle County, DE ANG	
91-1234	Lockheed C-130H-2 Hercules *bl/bk*	USAF 142nd AS/166th AW, New Castle County, DE ANG	
91-1235	Lockheed C-130H-2 Hercules *bl/bk*	USAF 142nd AS/166th AW, New Castle County, DE ANG	

Notes	Serial	Type (code/other identity)	Owner/operator, location or fate
	91-1236	Lockheed C-130H-2 Hercules *bl/bk*	USAF 142nd AS/166th AW, New Castle County, DE ANG
	91-1237	Lockheed C-130H-2 Hercules *bl/bk*	USAF 142nd AS/166th AW, New Castle County, DE ANG
	91-1238	Lockheed C-130H-2 Hercules *bl/bk*	USAF 142nd AS/166th AW, New Castle County, DE ANG
	91-1652	Lockheed C-130H-2 Hercules	USAF 180th AS/139th AW, Rosencrans Memorial, MO ANG
	91-1653	Lockheed C-130H-2 Hercules	USAF 180th AS/139th AW, Rosencrans Memorial, MO ANG
	91-9141	Lockheed C-130H-2 Hercules *bl/w*	USAF 357th AS/908th AW AFRC, Maxwell AFB, AL
	91-9142	Lockheed C-130H-2 Hercules *bl/w*	USAF 357th AS/908th AW AFRC, Maxwell AFB, AL
	91-9143	Lockheed C-130H-2 Hercules *bl/w*	USAF 357th AS/908th AW AFRC, Maxwell AFB, AL
	91-9144	Lockheed C-130H-2 Hercules *bl/w*	USAF 357th AS/908th AW AFRC, Maxwell AFB, AL
	92-0547	Lockheed C-130H-2 Hercules *bl/w*	USAF 192nd AS/152nd AW, Reno, NV ANG
	92-0548	Lockheed C-130H-2 Hercules *bl/w*	USAF 192nd AS/152nd AW, Reno, NV ANG
	92-0549	Lockheed C-130H-2 Hercules *bl/w*	USAF 192nd AS/152nd AW, Reno, NV ANG
	92-0550	Lockheed C-130H-2 Hercules *bl/bk*	USAF 700th AS/94th AW AFRC, Dobbins ARB, GA
	92-0551	Lockheed C-130H-2 Hercules *bl/bk*	USAF 700th AS/94th AW AFRC, Dobbins ARB, GA
	92-0552	Lockheed C-130H-2 Hercules *bl/bk*	USAF 700th AS/94th AW AFRC, Dobbins ARB, GA
	92-0553	Lockheed C-130H-2 Hercules *bl/w*	USAF 192nd AS/152nd AW, Reno, NV ANG
	92-0554	Lockheed C-130H-2 Hercules *bl/w*	USAF 192nd AS/152nd AW, Reno, NV ANG
	92-1094	Lockheed LC-130H Hercules	USAF 139th AS/109th AW, Schenectady, NY ANG
	92-1095	Lockheed LC-130H Hercules	USAF 139th AS/109th AW, Schenectady, NY ANG
	92-1451	Lockheed C-130H-3 Hercules *or/bk*	USAF 169th AS/182nd AW, Peoria, IL ANG
	92-1452	Lockheed C-130H-3 Hercules *or/bk*	USAF 169th AS/182nd AW, Peoria, IL ANG
	92-1453	Lockheed C-130H-3 Hercules	USAF 118th AS/103rd AW, Bradley ANGB, CT ANG
	92-1454	Lockheed C-130H-3 Hercules	USAF 186th AS/120th AW, Great Falls, MT ANG
	92-1531	Lockheed C-130H-3 Hercules *y/bk*	USAF 187th AS/153rd AW, Cheyenne, WY ANG
	92-1532	Lockheed C-130H-3 Hercules *y/bk*	USAF 187th AS/153rd AW, Cheyenne, WY ANG
	92-1533	Lockheed C-130H-3 Hercules *y/bk*	USAF 187th AS/153rd AW, Cheyenne, WY ANG
	92-1534	Lockheed C-130H-3 Hercules *y/bk*	USAF 187th AS/153rd AW, Cheyenne, WY ANG
	92-1535	Lockheed C-130H-3 Hercules *y/bk*	USAF 187th AS/153rd AW, Cheyenne, WY ANG
	92-1536	Lockheed C-130H-3 Hercules *y/bk*	USAF 187th AS/153rd AW, Cheyenne, WY ANG
	92-1537	Lockheed C-130H-3 Hercules *y/bk*	USAF 187th AS/153rd AW, Cheyenne, WY ANG
	92-1538	Lockheed C-130H-3 Hercules *y/bk*	USAF 187th AS/153rd AW, Cheyenne, WY ANG
	92-3021	Lockheed C-130H-2 Hercules *bl/r*	USAF 757th AS/910th AW AFRC, Youngstown ARS, OH
	92-3022	Lockheed C-130H-2 Hercules *bl/r*	USAF 757th AS/910th AW AFRC, Youngstown ARS, OH
	92-3023	Lockheed C-130H-2 Hercules *bl/r*	USAF 757th AS/910th AW AFRC, Youngstown ARS, OH
	92-3024	Lockheed C-130H-2 Hercules *bl/r*	USAF 757th AS/910th AW AFRC, Youngstown ARS, OH
	92-3281	Lockheed C-130H-3 Hercules *pr/w*	USAF 96th AS/934th AW AFRC, Minneapolis/ St Paul, MN
	92-3282	Lockheed C-130H-3 Hercules *pr/w*	USAF 96th AS/934th AW AFRC, Minneapolis/ St Paul, MN
	92-3283	Lockheed C-130H-3 Hercules *pr/w*	USAF 96th AS/934th AW AFRC, Minneapolis/ St Paul, MN
	92-3284	Lockheed C-130H-3 Hercules *pr/w* $	USAF 96th AS/934th AW AFRC, Minneapolis/ St Paul, MN

Serial	Type (code/other identity)	Owner/operator, location or fate	Notes
92-3285	Lockheed C-130H-3 Hercules *pr/w*	USAF 96th AS/934th AW AFRC, Minneapolis/ St Paul, MN	
92-3286	Lockheed C-130H-3 Hercules *pr/w*	USAF 96th AS/934th AW AFRC, Minneapolis/ St Paul, MN	
92-3287	Lockheed C-130H-3 Hercules *pr/w*	USAF 96th AS/934th AW AFRC, Minneapolis/ St Paul, MN	
92-3288	Lockheed C-130H-3 Hercules *pr/w*	USAF 96th AS/934th AW AFRC, Minneapolis/ St Paul, MN	
93-1036	Lockheed C-130H-3 Hercules *bl/bk*	USAF 700th AS/94th AW AFRC, Dobbins ARB, GA	
93-1037	Lockheed C-130H-3 Hercules *bl/bk*	USAF 700th AS/94th AW AFRC, Dobbins ARB, GA	
93-1038	Lockheed C-130H-3 Hercules *bl/bk*	USAF 700th AS/94th AW AFRC, Dobbins ARB, GA	
93-1039	Lockheed C-130H-3 Hercules *bl/bk*	USAF 700th AS/94th AW AFRC, Dobbins ARB, GA	
93-1040	Lockheed C-130H-3 Hercules *bl/bk*	USAF 700th AS/94th AW AFRC, Dobbins ARB, GA	
93-1041	Lockheed C-130H-3 Hercules *pr/w*	USAF 731st AS/302nd AW AFRC, Peterson AFB, CO	
93-1096	Lockheed LC-130H Hercules	USAF 139th AS/109th AW, Schenectady, NY ANG	
93-1455	Lockheed C-130H-3 Hercules	USAF 186th AS/120th AW, Great Falls, MT ANG	
93-1456	Lockheed C-130H-3 Hercules $	USAF 118th AS/103 rd AW, Bradley ANGB, CT ANG	
93-1457	Lockheed C-130H-3 Hercules *y/bk*	USAF 118th AS/103rd AW, Bradley ANGB, CT ANG	
93-1459	Lockheed C-130H-3 Hercules *y/bk*	USAF 118th AS/103rd AW, Bradley ANGB, CT ANG	
93-1561	Lockheed C-130H-3 Hercules *r/bk*	USAF 158th AS/165th AW, Savannah, GA ANG	
93-1562	Lockheed C-130H-3 Hercules *r/bk*	USAF 158th AS/165th AW, Savannah, GA ANG	
93-1563	Lockheed C-130H-3 Hercules *r/bk*	USAF 158th AS/165th AW, Savannah, GA ANG	
93-2041	Lockheed C-130H-3 Hercules *or/bk*	USAF 169th AS/182nd AW, Peoria, IL ANG	
93-2042	Lockheed C-130H-3 Hercules *or/bk*	USAF 169th AS/182nd AW, Peoria, IL ANG	
93-7311	Lockheed C-130H-3 Hercules *bl/w*	USAF 192nd AS/152nd AW, Reno, NV ANG	
93-7312	Lockheed C-130H-3 Hercules *or/bk*	USAF 169th AS/182nd AW, Peoria, IL ANG	
93-7313	Lockheed C-130H-3 Hercules *bl/w*	USAF 192nd AS/152nd AW, Reno, NV ANG	
93-7314	Lockheed C-130H-3 Hercules *bl/w*	USAF 192nd AS/152nd AW, Reno, NV ANG	
94-6701	Lockheed C-130H-3 Hercules *or/bk*	USAF 169th AS/182nd AW, Peoria, IL ANG	
94-6702	Lockheed C-130H-3 Hercules *or/bk*	USAF 169th AS/182nd AW, Peoria, IL ANG	
94-6703	Lockheed C-130H-3 Hercules *or/bk*	USAF 169th AS/182nd AW, Peoria, IL ANG	
94-6705	Lockheed C-130H-3 Hercules *r/bk*	USAF 158th AS/165th AW, Savannah, GA ANG	
94-6707	Lockheed C-130H-3 Hercules *r/bk*	USAF 158th AS/165th AW, Savannah, GA ANG	
94-6708	Lockheed C-130H-3 Hercules *r/bk*	USAF 158th AS/165th AW, Savannah, GA ANG	
94-7310	Lockheed C-130H-3 Hercules *pr/w*	USAF 731st AS/302nd AW AFRC, Peterson AFB, CO	
94-7315	Lockheed C-130H-3 Hercules *pr/w*	USAF 731st AS/302nd AW AFRC, Peterson AFB, CO	
94-7316	Lockheed C-130H-3 Hercules *pr/w*	USAF 731st AS/302nd AW AFRC, Peterson AFB, CO	
94-7317	Lockheed C-130H-3 Hercules *pr/w*	USAF 731st AS/302nd AW AFRC, Peterson AFB, CO	
94-7318	Lockheed C-130H-3 Hercules *pr/w*	USAF 731st AS/302nd AW AFRC, Peterson AFB, CO	
94-7319	Lockheed C-130H-3 Hercules *pr/w*	USAF 731st AS/302nd AW AFRC, Peterson AFB, CO	
94-7320	Lockheed C-130H-3 Hercules *pr/w*	USAF 731st AS/302nd AW AFRC, Peterson AFB, CO	
94-7321	Lockheed C-130H-3 Hercules *r/bk*	USAF 158th AS/165th AW, Savannah, GA ANG	
94-8151	Lockheed C-130J Hercules II *bl/bk*	USAF 62nd AS/314th AW, Little Rock AFB, AR	
94-8152	Lockheed C-130J Hercules II *r/bk*	USAF 815th AS/403rd AW AFRC, Keesler AFB, MO	

Notes	Serial	Type (code/other identity)	Owner/operator, location or fate
	95-1001	Lockheed C-130H-3 Hercules *pr/bk*	USAF 109th AS/133rd AW, Minneapolis, MN ANG
	95-1002	Lockheed C-130H-3 Hercules *pr/bk*	USAF 109th AS/133rd AW, Minneapolis, MN ANG
	95-6709	Lockheed C-130H-3 Hercules	USAF 186th AS/120th AW, Great Falls, MT ANG
	95-6710	Lockheed C-130H-3 Hercules *y/bk*	USAF 118th AS/103rd AW, Bradley ANGB, CT ANG
	95-6711	Lockheed C-130H-3 Hercules	USAF 186th AS/120th AW, Great Falls, MT ANG
	95-6712	Lockheed C-130H-3 Hercules *y/bk*	USAF 118th AS/103rd AW, Bradley ANGB, CT ANG
	96-1003	Lockheed C-130H-3 Hercules *pr/bk*	USAF 109th AS/133rd AW, Minneapolis, MN ANG
	96-1004	Lockheed C-130H-3 Hercules *pr/bk*	USAF 109th AS/133rd AW, Minneapolis, MN ANG
	96-1005	Lockheed C-130H-3 Hercules *pr/bk*	USAF 109th AS/133rd AW, Minneapolis, MN ANG
	96-1006	Lockheed C-130H-3 Hercules *pr/bk*	USAF 109th AS/133rd AW, Minneapolis, MN ANG
	96-1007	Lockheed C-130H-3 Hercules *pr/bk*	USAF 109th AS/133rd AW, Minneapolis, MN ANG
	96-1008	Lockheed C-130H-3 Hercules *pr/bk*	USAF 109th AS/133rd AW, Minneapolis, MN ANG
	96-5300	Lockheed WC-130J Hercules II	USAF 53rd WRS/403rd AW AFRC, Keesler AFB, MO
	96-5301	Lockheed WC-130J Hercules II	USAF 53rd WRS/403rd AW AFRC, Keesler AFB, MO
	96-5302	Lockheed WC-130J Hercules II	USAF 53rd WRS/403rd AW AFRC, Keesler AFB, MO
	96-7322	Lockheed C-130H-3 Hercules *y/bk*	USAF 118th AS/103rd AW, Bradley ANGB, CT ANG
	96-7323	Lockheed C-130H-3 Hercules	USAF 186th AS/120th AW, Great Falls, MT ANG
	96-7324	Lockheed C-130H-3 Hercules	USAF 186th AS/120th AW, Great Falls, MT ANG
	96-7325	Lockheed C-130H-3 Hercules	USAF 186th AS/120th AW, Great Falls, MT ANG
	96-8153	Lockheed EC-130J Commando Solo III	USAF 193rd SOS/193rd SOW, Harrisburg, PA ANG
	96-8154	Lockheed EC-130J Commando Solo III	USAF 193rd SOS/193rd SOW, Harrisburg, PA ANG
	97-1351	Lockheed C-130J Hercules II	USAF 48th AS/314th AW, Little Rock AFB, AR
	97-1352	Lockheed C-130J Hercules II	USAF 48th AS/314th AW, Little Rock AFB, AR
	97-1353	Lockheed C-130J Hercules II *r/bk*	USAF 815th AS/403rd AW AFRC, Keesler AFB, MO
	97-1354	Lockheed C-130J Hercules II	USAF 48th AS/314th AW, Little Rock AFB, AR
	97-1931	Lockheed EC-130J Commando Solo III	USAF 193rd SOS/193rd SOW, Harrisburg, PA ANG
	97-5303	Lockheed WC-130J Hercules II	USAF 53rd WRS/403rd AW AFRC, Keesler AFB, MO
	97-5304	Lockheed WC-130J Hercules II	USAF 53rd WRS/403rd AW AFRC, Keesler AFB, MO
	97-5305	Lockheed WC-130J Hercules II	USAF 53rd WRS/403rd AW AFRC, Keesler AFB, MO
	97-5306	Lockheed WC-130J Hercules II	USAF 53rd WRS/403rd AW AFRC, Keesler AFB, MO
	98-1355	Lockheed C-130J Hercules II *bl/bk*	USAF 62nd AS/314th AW, Little Rock AFB, AR
	98-1356	Lockheed C-130J Hercules II *bl/bk*	USAF 62nd AS/314th AW, Little Rock AFB, AR
	98-1357	Lockheed C-130J Hercules II *bl/bk*	USAF 62nd AS/314th AW, Little Rock AFB, AR
	98-1358	Lockheed C-130J Hercules II *bl/bk*	USAF 62nd AS/314th AW, Little Rock AFB, AR
	88-1803	Lockheed MC-130H Combat Talon II	USAF 15th SOS/1st SOW, Hurlburt Field, FL
	98-1932	Lockheed EC-130J Commando Solo III	USAF 193rd SOS/193rd SOW, Harrisburg, PA ANG

Serial	Type (code/other identity)	Owner/operator, location or fate	Notes
98-5307	Lockheed WC-130J Hercules II	USAF 53rd WRS/403rd AW AFRC, Keesler AFB, MO	
98-5308	Lockheed WC-130J Hercules II	USAF 53rd WRS/403rd AW AFRC, Keesler AFB, MO	
99-1431	Lockheed C-130J-30 Hercules II *r/bk*	USAF 143rd AS/143rd AW, Quonset, RI ANG	
99-1432	Lockheed C-130J-30 Hercules II *r/bk*	USAF 143rd AS/143rd AW, Quonset, RI ANG	
99-1433	Lockheed C-130J-30 Hercules II *r/bk*	USAF 143rd AS/143rd AW, Quonset, RI ANG	
99-1933	Lockheed EC-130J Commando Solo III	USAF 193rd SOS/193rd SOW, Harrisburg, PA ANG	
99-5309	Lockheed WC-130J Hercules II	USAF 53rd WRS/403rd AW AFRC, Keesler AFB, MO	
00-1934	Lockheed EC-130J Commando Solo III	USAF 193rd SOS/193rd SOW, Harrisburg, PA ANG	
01-1461	Lockheed C-130J-30 Hercules II *gn/bk*	USAF 115th AS/146th AW, Channel Island ANGS, CA ANG	
01-1462	Lockheed C-130J-30 Hercules II *gn/bk* [4]	USAF 115th AS/146th AW, Channel Island ANGS, CA ANG	
01-1935	Lockheed EC-130J Commando Solo III	USAF 193rd SOS/193rd SOW, Harrisburg, PA ANG	
02-0314	Lockheed C-130J-30 Hercules II *si/bk*	USAF 41st AS/19th AW Little Rock AFB, AR	
02-1434	Lockheed C-130J-30 Hercules II *r/bk*	USAF 143rd AS/143rd AW, Quonset, RI ANG	
02-1463	Lockheed C-130J Hercules II *gn/bk*	USAF 115th AS/146th AW, Channel Island ANGS, CA ANG	
02-1464	Lockheed C-130J Hercules II *gn/bk*	USAF 115th AS/146th AW, Channel Island ANGS, CA ANG	
02-8155	Lockheed C-130J-30 Hercules II *r/bk*	USAF 815th AS/403rd AW AFRC, Keesler AFB, MO	
03-8154	Lockheed C-130J-30 Hercules II *r/bk*	USAF 815th AS/403rd AW AFRC, Keesler AFB, MO	
04-3143	Lockheed C-130J-30 Hercules II	USAF 39th AS/317th AW, Dyess AFB, TX	
04-8153	Lockheed C-130J-30 Hercules II *r/bk*	USAF 815th AS/403rd AW AFRC, Keesler AFB, MO	
05-1435	Lockheed C-130J-30 Hercules II *r/bk*	USAF 143rd AS/143rd AW, Quonset, RI ANG	
05-1436	Lockheed C-130J-30 Hercules II *r/bk*	USAF 143rd AS/143rd AW, Quonset, RI ANG	
05-1465	Lockheed C-130J-30 Hercules II *gn/bk*	USAF 115th AS/146th AW, Channel Island-ANGS, CA ANG	
05-1466	Lockheed C-130J-30 Hercules II *gn/bk*	USAF 115th AS/146th AW, Channel Island-ANGS, CA ANG	
05-3145	Lockheed C-130J-30 Hercules II *si/bk*	USAF 41st AS/19th AW Little Rock AFB, AR	
05-3146	Lockheed C-130J-30 Hercules II *gn/bk*	USAF 61st AS/19th AW Little Rock AFB, AR	
05-3147	Lockheed C-130J-30 Hercules II *gn/bk*	USAF 61st AS/19th AW Little Rock AFB, AR	
05-8152	Lockheed C-130J-30 Hercules II *r/bk*	USAF 815th AS/403rd AW AFRC, Keesler AFB, MO	
05-8156	Lockheed C-130J-30 Hercules II *r/bk*	USAF 815th AS/403rd AW AFRC, Keesler AFB, MO	
05-8157	Lockheed C-130J-30 Hercules II *r/bk*	USAF 815th AS/403rd AW AFRC, Keesler AFB, MO	
05-8158	Lockheed C-130J-30 Hercules II *r/bk*	USAF 815th AS/403rd AW AFRC, Keesler AFB, MO	
06-1437	Lockheed C-130J-30 Hercules II *r/bk*	USAF 143rd AS/143rd AW, Quonset, RI ANG	
06-1438	Lockheed C-130J-30 Hercules II *r/bk*	USAF 143rd AS/143rd AW, Quonset, RI ANG	
06-1467	Lockheed C-130J-30 Hercules II *gn/bk*	USAF 115th AS/146th AW, Channel Island ANGS, CA ANG	
06-3171	Lockheed C-130J-30 Hercules II *bl*	USAF 40th AS/317th AW, Dyess AFB, TX	
06-4632	Lockheed C-130J-30 Hercules II *si/bk*	USAF 41st AS/19th AW Little Rock AFB, AR	
06-4633	Lockheed C-130J-30 Hercules II [YJ] *r*	USAF 36th AS/374th AW, Yokota AB, Japan	
06-4634	Lockheed C-130J-30 Hercules II *si/bk*	USAF 41st AS/19th AW Little Rock AFB, AR	
06-8159	Lockheed C-130J Hercules II *r/bk*	USAF 815th AS/403rd AW AFRC, Keesler AFB, MO	
06-8610	Lockheed C-130J-30 Hercules II [YJ] *r*	USAF 36th AS/374th AW, Yokota AB, Japan	
06-8612	Lockheed C-130J-30 Hercules II *gn/bk*	USAF 61st AS/19th AW Little Rock AFB, AR	

Notes	Serial	Type (code/other identity)	Owner/operator, location or fate
	07-1468	Lockheed C-130J-30 Hercules II *gn/bk*	USAF 115th AS/146th AW, Channel Island ANGS, CA ANG
	07-3170	Lockheed C-130J-30 Hercules II *bl*	USAF 40th AS/317th AW, Dyess AFB, TX
	07-4636	Lockheed C-130J-30 Hercules II *si/bk*	USAF 41st AS/19th AW Little Rock AFB, AR
	07-4637	Lockheed C-130J-30 Hercules II *si/bk*	USAF 41st AS/19th AW Little Rock AFB, AR
	07-4638	Lockheed C-130J-30 Hercules II	USAF 317th AW, Dyess AFB, TX
	07-4639	Lockheed C-130J-30 Hercules II *si/bk*	USAF
	07-8613	Lockheed C-130J-30 Hercules II *si/bk*	USAF 41st AS/19th AW Little Rock AFB, AR
	07-46310	Lockheed C-130J-30 Hercules II *si/bk*	USAF 41st AS/19th AW Little Rock AFB, AR
	07-46311	Lockheed C-130J-30 Hercules II *si/bk*	USAF 41st AS/19th AW Little Rock AFB, AR
	07-46312	Lockheed C-130J-30 Hercules II *gn/bk*	USAF 61st AS/19th AW Little Rock AFB, AR
	08-3172	Lockheed C-130J-30 Hercules II *bl*	USAF 40th AS/317th AW, Dyess AFB, TX
	08-3173	Lockheed C-130J-30 Hercules II *bl*	USAF 40th AS/317th AW, Dyess AFB, TX
	08-3175	Lockheed C-130J-30 Hercules II *bl*	USAF 40th AS/317th AW, Dyess AFB, TX
	08-3177	Lockheed C-130J-30 Hercules II [YJ] *r*	USAF 36th AS/374th AW, Yokota AB, Japan
	08-3178	Lockheed C-130J-30 Hercules II	USAF 317th AW, Dyess AFB, TX
	08-3179	Lockheed C-130J-30 Hercules II	USAF 39th AS/317th AW, Dyess AFB, TX
	08-5675	Lockheed C-130J-30 Hercules II	USAF 317th AW, Dyess AFB, TX
	08-5678	Lockheed C-130J-30 Hercules II	USAF 317th AW, Dyess AFB, TX
	08-5679	Lockheed C-130J-30 Hercules II *bl/bk*	USAF 62nd AS/314th AW, Little Rock AFB, AR
	08-5684	Lockheed C-130J-30 Hercules II *si/bk*	USAF 41st AS/19th AW Little Rock AFB, AR
	08-5685	Lockheed C-130J-30 Hercules II	USAF 314th AW, Little Rock AFB, AR
	08-5686	Lockheed C-130J-30 Hercules II	USAF 317th AW, Dyess AFB, TX
	08-5691	Lockheed C-130J-30 Hercules II	USAF 39th AS/317th AW, Dyess AFB, TX
	08-5692	Lockheed C-130J-30 Hercules II [YJ] *r*	USAF 36th AS/374th AW, Yokota AB, Japan
	08-5693	Lockheed C-130J-30 Hercules II *si/bk*	USAF 41st AS/19th AW Little Rock AFB, AR
	08-5697	Lockheed MC-130J Commando II	USAF 19th SOS/492nd SOW, Hurlburt Field, FL
	08-5705	Lockheed C-130J-30 Hercules II $	USAF 19th AW Little Rock AFB, AR
	08-5708	Lockheed HC-130J Combat King II [FT]	USAF 71st RQS/347th RQG, Moody AFB, GA
	08-5712	Lockheed C-130J-30 Hercules II	USAF 39th AS/317th AW, Dyess AFB, TX
	08-5715	Lockheed C-130J-30 Hercules II	USAF 317th AW, Dyess AFB, TX
	08-5724	Lockheed C-130J-30 Hercules II	USAF 39th AS/317th AW, Dyess AFB, TX
	08-5726	Lockheed C-130J-30 Hercules II	USAF 317th AW, Dyess AFB, TX
	08-6201	Lockheed MC-130J Commando II	USAF 9th SOS/27th SOW, Cannon AFB, NM
	08-6202	Lockheed MC-130J Commando II	USAF 1st SOS/353rd SOG, Kadena AB, Japan
	08-6203	Lockheed MC-130J Commando II	USAF 415th SOS/58th SOW, Kirtland AFB, NM
	08-6204	Lockheed MC-130J Commando II	USAF 9th SOS/27th SOW, Cannon AFB, NM
	08-6206	Lockheed MC-130J Commando II	USAF 193rd SOS/193rd SOW, Harrisburg, PA ANG
	08-8604	Lockheed C-130J-30 Hercules II [YJ] *r*	USAF 36th AS/374th AW, Yokota AB, Japan
	08-8605	Lockheed C-130J-30 Hercules II [YJ] *r*	USAF 36th AS/374th AW, Yokota AB, Japan
	08-8606	Lockheed C-130J-30 Hercules II $	USAF 19th AW Little Rock AFB, AR
	08-8607	Lockheed C-130J-30 Hercules II	USAF 39th AS/317th AW, Dyess AFB, TX
	09-0108	Lockheed HC-130J Combat King II [OT]	USAF 418th TES/412nd TW, Davis-Monthan AFB, AZ
	09-0109	Lockheed HC-130J Combat King II [FT]	USAF 79th RQS/355th Wg, Davis-Monthan AFB, AZ
	09-5706	Lockheed HC-130J Combat King II	USAF 415th SOS/58th SOW, Kirtland AFB, NM
	09-5707	Lockheed HC-130J Combat King II [DM]	USAF 79th RQS/355th Wg, Davis-Monthan AFB, AZ
	09-5709	Lockheed HC-130J Combat King II [DM]	USAF 79th RQS/355th Wg, Davis-Monthan AFB, AZ
	09-5711	Lockheed MC-130J Commando II	USAF 9th SOS/27th SOW, Cannon AFB, NM
	09-6208	Lockheed MC-130J Commando II	USAF 415th SOS/58th SOW, Kirtland AFB, NM
	09-6209	Lockheed MC-130J Commando II	USAF 9th SOS/27th SOW, Cannon AFB, NM
	09-6210	Lockheed MC-130J Commando II	USAF
	10-5700	Lockheed C-130J-30 Hercules II *gn/bk*	USAF 61st AS/19th AW Little Rock AFB, AR
	10-5701	Lockheed C-130J-30 Hercules II [317 AG]	USAF 39th AS/317th AW, Dyess AFB, TX
	10-5714	Lockheed MC-130J Commando II	USAF 1st SOS/353rd SOG, Kadena AB, Japan
	10-5716	Lockheed HC-130J Combat King II [DM]	USAF 79th RQS/355th Wg, Davis-Monthan AFB, AZ
	10-5717	Lockheed HC-130J Combat King II [FT]	USAF 71st RQS/347th RQG, Moody AFB, GA
	10-5728	Lockheed C-130J-30 Hercules II *bl/bk*	USAF 62nd AS/314th AW, Little Rock AFB, AR

Serial	Type (code/other identity)	Owner/operator, location or fate	Notes
10-5771	Lockheed C-130J-30 Hercules II gn/bk	USAF 61st AS/19th AW Little Rock AFB, AR	
11-5719	Lockheed HC-130J Combat King II [DM]	USAF 79th RQS/355th Wg, Davis-Monthan AFB AFB, AZ	
11-5725	Lockheed HC-130J Combat King II [FT]	USAF 71st RQS/347th RQG, Moody AFB, GA	
11-5727	Lockheed HC-130J Combat King II [FT]	USAF 71st RQS/347th RQG, Moody AFB, GA	
11-5729	Lockheed MC-130J Commando II	USAF 9th SOS/27th SOW, Cannon AFB, NM	
11-5731	Lockheed MC-130J Commando II	USAF 9th SOS/27th SOW, Cannon AFB, NM	
11-5732	Lockheed C-130J-30 Hercules II	USAF 317th AW, Dyess AFB, TX	
11-5733	Lockheed MC-130J Commando II	USAF 9th SOS/27th SOW, Cannon AFB, NM	
11-5734	Lockheed C-130J-30 Hercules II gn/bk	USAF 61st AS/19th AW Little Rock AFB, AR	
11-5735	Lockheed AC-130J Ghostrider	USAF 4th SOS/1st SOW, Hurlburt Field, FL	
11-5737	Lockheed MC-130J Commando II	USAF 1st SOS/353rd SOG, Kadena AB, Japan	
11-5745	Lockheed C-130J-30 Hercules II si/bk	USAF 41st AS/19th AW Little Rock AFB, AR	
11-5748	Lockheed C-130J-30 Hercules II	USAF 317th AW, Dyess AFB, TX	
11-5752	Lockheed C-130J-30 Hercules II gn/bk	USAF 61st AS/19th AW Little Rock AFB, AR	
11-5765	Lockheed HC-130J Combat King II [FT]	USAF 71st RQS/347th RQG, Moody AFB, GA	
12-5753	Lockheed AC-130J Ghostrider	USAF 73rd SOS/1st SOW, Hurlburt Field, FL	
12-5755	Lockheed HC-130J Combat King II	USAF 415th SOS/58th SOW, Kirtland AFB, NM	
12-5756	Lockheed C-130J-30 Hercules II gn/bk	USAF 61st AS/19th AW Little Rock AFB, AR	
12-5757	Lockheed MC-130J Commando II	USAF	
12-5760	Lockheed MC-130J Commando II	USAF	
12-5761	Lockheed MC-130J Commando II	USAF 1st SOS/353rd SOG, Kadena AB, Japan	
12-5762	Lockheed MC-130J Commando II	USAF 1st SOS/353rd SOG, Kadena AB, Japan	
12-5763	Lockheed MC-130J Commando II	USAF 1st SOS/353rd SOG, Kadena AB, Japan	
12-5768	Lockheed HC-130J Combat King II [FT]	USAF 71st RQS/347th RQG, Moody AFB, GA	
12-5769	Lockheed HC-130J Combat King II [DM]	USAF 79th RQS/355th Wg, Davis-Monthan AFB, AZ	
12-5772	Lockheed AC-130J Ghostrider	USAF 73rd SOS/1st SOW, Hurlburt Field, FL	
12-5773	Lockheed HC-130J Combat King II [FT]	USAF 71st RQS/347th RQG, Moody AFB, GA	
13-5770	Lockheed MC-130J Commando II	USAF 9th SOS/27th SOW, Cannon AFB, NM	
13-5775	Lockheed MC-130J Commando II	USAF 9th SOS/27th SOW, Cannon AFB, NM	
13-5777	Lockheed MC-130J Commando II	USAF 9th SOS/27th SOW, Cannon AFB, NM	
13-5782	Lockheed HC-130J Combat King II [DM]	USAF 79th RQS/355th Wg, Davis-Monthan AFB, AZ	
13-5783	Lockheed AC-130J Ghostrider	USAF 73rd SOS/1st SOW, Hurlburt Field, FL	
13-5784	Lockheed C-130J-30 Hercules II gn/bk	USAF 61st AS/19th AW Little Rock AFB, AR	
13-5785	Lockheed HC-130J Combat King II [FT]	USAF 71st RQS/347th RQG, Moody AFB, GA	
13-5786	Lockheed MC-130J Commando II	USAF 1st SOS/353rd SOG, Kadena AB, Japan	
13-5790	Lockheed HC-130J Combat King II [FT]	USAF 71st RQS/347th RQG, Moody AFB, GA	
14-5787	Lockheed AC-130J Ghostrider	USAF 73rd SOS/1st SOW, Hurlburt Field, FL	
14-5788	Lockheed C-130J-30 Hercules II si/bk	USAF 41st AS/19th AW Little Rock AFB, AR	
14-5789	Lockheed AC-130J Ghostrider	USAF 73rd SOS/1st SOW, Hurlburt Field, FL	
14-5791	Lockheed C-130J-30 Hercules II y/bk	USAF 41st AS/19th AW Little Rock AFB, AR	
14-5793	Lockheed MC-130J Commando II	USAF 1st SOS/353rd SOG, Kadena AB, Japan	
14-5795	Lockheed MC-130J Commando II	USAF 9th SOS/27th SOW, Cannon AFB, NM	
14-5796	Lockheed C-130J-30 Hercules II gn/bk	USAF 61st AS/19th AW Little Rock AFB, AR	
14-5797	Lockheed AC-130J Ghostrider	USAF 4th SOS/1st SOW, Hurlburt Field, FL	
14-5800	Lockheed MC-130J Commando II	USAF	
14-5802	Lockheed C-130J-30 Hercules II bl/bk $	USAF 62nd AS/314th AW, Little Rock AFB, AR	
14-5803	Lockheed AC-130J Ghostrider	USAF 73rd SOS/1st SOW, Hurlburt Field, FL	
14-5804	Lockheed C-130J-30 Hercules II y	USAF 48th AS/314th AW, Little Rock AFB, AR	
14-5807	Lockheed C-130J-30 Hercules II [YJ] r [374 AW]	USAF 36th AS/374th AW, Yokota AB, Japan	
14-5809	Lockheed AC-130J Ghostrider	USAF 73rd SOS/1st SOW, Hurlburt Field, FL	
14-5815	Lockheed HC-130J Combat King II [AK]	USAF 211th RQS/176th Wg, Elmendorf AFB, AK ANG	
14-5864	Lockheed HC-130J Combat King II [CA]	USAF 130th RQS/129th RQW, Moffett Field CA ANG	
15-5810	Lockheed C-130J-30 Hercules II [YJ] r [374 OG]	USAF 36th AS/374th AW, Yokota AB, Japan	
15-5811	Lockheed AC-130J Ghostrider	USAF 73rd SOS/1st SOW, Hurlburt Field, FL	

US-BASED USAF AIRCRAFT

Notes	Serial	Type (code/other identity)	Owner/operator, location or fate
	15-5813	Lockheed C-130J-30 Hercules II [YJ] *r* [36 AS]	USAF 36th AS/374th AW, Yokota AB, Japan
	15-5817	Lockheed C-130J-30 Hercules II [YJ] *r*	USAF 36th AS/374th AW, Yokota AB, Japan
	15-5825	Lockheed AC-130J Ghostrider	USAF 73rd SOS/1st SOW, Hurlburt Field, FL
	15-5826	Lockheed C-130J-30 Hercules II	USAF 40th AS/317th AW, Dyess AFB, TX
	15-5827	Lockheed HC-130J Combat King II [AK]	USAF 211th RQS/176th Wg, Elmendorf AFB, AK ANG
	15-5828	Lockheed C-130J-30 Hercules II *gn/bk*	USAF 61st AS/19th AW Little Rock AFB, AR
	15-5829	Lockheed HC-130J Combat King II [AK]	USAF 211th RQS/176th Wg, Elmendorf AFB, AK ANG
	15-5832	Lockheed HC-130J Combat King II [AK]	USAF 211th RQS/176th Wg, Elmendorf AFB, AK ANG
	15-5842	Lockheed HC-130J Combat King II [CA]	USAF 130th RQS/129th RQW, Moffett Field CA ANG
	15-5893	Lockheed C-130J-30 Hercules II *si/bk*	USAF 41st AS/19th AW Little Rock AFB, AR
	16-5833	Lockheed C-130J-30 Hercules II [YJ] *r* [5 AF]	USAF 36th AS/374th AW, Yokota AB, Japan
	16-5834	Lockheed C-130J-30 Hercules II	USAF 40th AS/317th AW, Dyess AFB, TX
	16-5835	Lockheed AC-130J Ghostrider	USAF 73rd SOS/1st SOW, Hurlburt Field, FL
	16-5837	Lockheed AC-130J Ghostrider	USAF 4th SOS/1st SOW, Hurlburt Field, FL
	16-5638	Lockheed C-130J-30 Hercules II [YJ] *r*	USAF 36th AS/374th AW, Yokota AB, Japan
	16-5839	Lockheed MC-130J Commando II	USAF 415th SOS/58th SOW, Kirtland AFB, NM
	16-5641	Lockheed C-130J-30 Hercules II [YJ] *r*	USAF 36th AS/374th AW, Yokota AB, Japan
	16-5843	Lockheed C-130J-30 Hercules II [YJ] *r*	USAF 36th AS/374th AW, Yokota AB, Japan
	16-5844	Lockheed AC-130J Ghostrider	USAF 4th SOS/1st SOW, Hurlburt Field, FL
	16-5846	Lockheed AC-130J Ghostrider	USAF 4th SOS/1st SOW, Hurlburt Field, FL
	16-5849	Lockheed C-130J-30 Hercules II *gn/bk*	USAF 61st AS/19th AW Little Rock AFB, AR
	16-5850	Lockheed MC-130J Commando II	USAF 9th SOS/27th SOW, Cannon AFB, NM
	16-5851	Lockheed C-130J-30 Hercules II *bl/bk*	USAF 181st AS/136th AW, NAS Dallas, TX ANG
	16-5852	Lockheed AC-130J Ghostrider	USAF 4th SOS/1st SOW, Hurlburt Field, FL
	16-5853	Lockheed C-130J-30 Hercules II	USAF 40th AS/317th AW, Dyess AFB, TX
	16-5855	Lockheed C-130J-30 Hercules II *si/bk*	USAF 41st AS/19th AW Little Rock AFB, AR
	16-5857	Lockheed HC-130J Combat King II [CA]	USAF 130th RQS/129th RQW, Moffett Field CA ANG
	16-5858	Lockheed HC-130J Combat King II [CA]	USAF 130th RQS/129th RQW, Moffett Field CA ANG
	16-5859	Lockheed C-130J-30 Hercules II (16-5859)*wh/bk*	USAF 165th AS/123rd AW, Standiford Field, KY ANG
	16-5861	Lockheed AC-130J Ghostrider	USAF 4th SOS/1st SOW, Hurlburt Field, FL
	16-5862	Lockheed MC-130J Commando II	USAF 9th SOS/27th SOW, Cannon AFB, NM
	16-5863	Lockheed HC-130J Combat King II [LI]	USAF 102nd RQS/106th RQW, Suffolk Field, NY ANG
	16-5873	Lockheed HC-130J Combat King II [LI]	USAF 102nd RQS/106th RQW, Suffolk Field, NY ANG
	16-5880	Lockheed C-130J-30 Hercules II *bl*	USAF 40th AS/317th AW, Dyess AFB, TX
	16-5895	Lockheed HC-130J Combat King II [FL]	USAF 39th RQS/920th RQW AFRC, Patrick SFB, FL
	17-5865	Lockheed C-130J-30 Hercules II *gn/bk*	USAF 61st AS/19th AW Little Rock AFB, AR
	17-5867	Lockheed C-130J-30 Hercules II *bl/bk*	USAF 181st AS/136th AW, NAS Dallas, TX ANG
	17-5869	Lockheed AC-130J Ghostrider	USAF 4th SOS/1st SOW, Hurlburt Field, FL
	17-5870	Lockheed HC-130J Combat King II [LI]	USAF 102nd RQS/106th RQW, Suffolk Field, NY ANG
	17-5872	Lockheed AC-130J Ghostrider	USAF 4th SOS/1st SOW, Hurlburt Field, FL
	17-5875	Lockheed MC-130J Commando II	USAF 415th SOS/58th SOW, Kirtland AFB, NM
	17-5876	Lockheed MC-130J Commando II	USAF 415th SOS/58th SOW, Kirtland AFB, NM
	17-5877	Lockheed AC-130J Ghostrider	USAF 4th SOS/1st SOW, Hurlburt Field, FL
	17-5878	Lockheed HC-130J Combat King II [LI]	USAF 102nd RQS/106th RQW, Suffolk Field, NY ANG
	17-5892	Lockheed HC-130J Combat King II [FL]	USAF 39th RQS/920th RQW AFRC, Patrick SFB, FL
	17-5897	Lockheed C-130J-30 Hercules II (17-5897) *pr/y*	USAF 130th AS/130th AW, Yeager Int'l, Charleston, WV ANG

Serial	Type (code/other identity)	Owner/operator, location or fate	Notes
17-5898	Lockheed HC-130J Combat King II [FL]	USAF 39th RQS/920th RQW AFRC, Patrick SFB, FL	
17-5900	Lockheed C-130J-30 Hercules II bl/bk	USAF 181st AS/136th AW, NAS Dallas, TX ANG	
17-5901	Lockheed HC-130J Combat King II [FL]	USAF 39th RQS/920th RQW AFRC, Patrick SFB, FL	
17-5902	Lockheed HC-130J Combat King II [FL]	USAF 39th RQS/920th RQW AFRC, Patrick SFB, FL	
17-5903	Lockheed MC-130J Commando II	USAF 9th SOS/27th SOW, Cannon AFB, NM	
17-5904	Lockheed C-130J-30 Hercules II bl/bk	USAF 181st AS/136th AW, NAS Dallas, TX ANG	
18-5879	Lockheed HC-130J Combat King II [LI]	USAF 102nd RQS/106th RQW, Suffolk Field, NY ANG	
18-5882	Lockheed AC-130J Ghostrider	USAF 4th SOS/1st SOW, Hurlburt Field, FL	
18-5884	Lockheed MC-130J Commando II	USAF 9th SOS/27th SOW, Cannon AFB, NM	
18-5886	Lockheed AC-130J Ghostrider	USAF 4th SOS/1st SOW, Hurlburt Field, FL	
18-5888	Lockheed AC-130J Ghostrider	USAF 17th SOS/27th SOW, Cannon AFB, NM	
18-5891	Lockheed AC-130J Ghostrider (18-5891)	LMTAS, Crestview, FL	
18-5905	Lockheed AC-130J Ghostrider	USAF 17th SOS/27th SOW, Cannon AFB, NM	
18-5906	Lockheed HC-130J Combat King II [FL]	USAF 39th RQS/920th RQW AFRC, Patrick SFB, FL	
18-5908	Lockheed C-130J-30 Hercules II pr/y	USAF 130th AS/130th AW, Yeager Int'l, Charleston, WV ANG	
18-5910	Lockheed MC-130J Commando II	USAF 9th SOS/27th SOW, Cannon AFB, NM	
18-5911	Lockheed C-130J-30 Hercules II bl/bk	USAF 181st AS/136th AW, NAS Dallas, TX ANG	
18-5913	Lockheed AC-130J Ghostrider	LMTAS, Crestview, FL	
18-5914	Lockheed C-130J-30 Hercules II pr/y	USAF 130th AS/130th AW, Yeager Int'l, Charleston, WV ANG	
18-5916	Lockheed AC-130J Ghostrider	USAF 15th SOS/1st SOW, Hurlburt Field, FL	
18-5917	Lockheed C-130J-30 Hercules II pr/y	USAF 130th AS/130th AW, Yeager Int'l, Charleston, WV ANG	
18-5919	Lockheed C-130J-30 Hercules II w/bk	USAF 165th AS/123rd AW, Standiford Field, KY ANG	
18-5920	Lockheed AC-130J Ghostrider	USAF 4th SOS/1st SOW, Hurlburt Field, FL	
18-5921	Lockheed C-130J-30 Hercules II w/bk	USAF 165th AS/123rd AW, Standiford Field, KY ANG	
19-5922	Lockheed AC-130J Ghostrider	USAF 4th SOS/1st SOW, Hurlburt Field, FL	
19-5924	Lockheed MC-130J Commando II	USAF 19th SOS/492nd SOW, Hurlburt Field, FL	
19-5926	Lockheed AC-130J Ghostrider	USAF 17th SOS/27th SOW, Cannon AFB, NM	
19-5927	Lockheed C-130J-30 Hercules II bl/bk	USAF 181st AS/136th AW, NAS Dallas, TX ANG	
19-5928	Lockheed C-130J-30 Hercules II pr/y	USAF 130th AS/130th AW, Yeager Int'l, Charleston, WV ANG	
19-5932	Lockheed C-130J-30 Hercules II w/bk	USAF 165th AS/123rd AW, Standiford Field, KY ANG	
19-5934	Lockheed C-130J-30 Hercules II pr/y	USAF 130th AS/130th AW, Yeager Int'l, Charleston, WV ANG	
19-5936	Lockheed C-130J-30 Hercules II bl/bk	USAF 181st AS/136th AW, NAS Dallas, TX ANG	
19-5940	Lockheed C-130J-30 Hercules II pr/y	USAF 130th AS/130th AW, Yeager Int'l, Charleston, WV ANG	
19-5942	Lockheed C-130J-30 Hercules II	USAF/LMTAS, Marietta, GA (on order)	
19-5947	Lockheed HC-130J Combat King II [DM]	USAF 79th RQS/355th Wg, Davis-Monthan AFB, AZ	
19-5948	Lockheed HC-130J Combat King II [FT]	USAF 71st RQS/347th RQG, Moody AFB, GA	
19-5953	Lockheed MC-130J Commando II	USAF 9th SOS/27th SOW, Cannon AFB, NM	
20-5931	Lockheed MC-130J Commando II	USAF 415th SOS/58th SOW, Kirtland AFB, NM	
20-5933	Lockheed MC-130J Commando II	USAF 9th SOS/27th SOW, Cannon AFB, NM	
20-5935	Lockheed MC-130J Commando II	LMTAS, Marietta, GA	
20-5937	Lockheed MC-130J Commando II	LMTAS, Marietta, GA	
20-5939	Lockheed MC-130J Commando II	LMTAS, Marietta, GA	
20-5943	Lockheed MC-130J Commando II	LMTAS, Marietta, GA	
20-5945	Lockheed C-130J-30 Hercules II w/bk	USAF 165th AS/123rd AW, Standiford Field, KY ANG	
20-5946	Lockheed C-130J-30 Hercules II	LMTAS, Marietta, GA	

Notes	Serial	Type (code/other identity)	Owner/operator, location or fate
	Boeing C-135		
	57-1419	Boeing KC-135R Stratotanker	USAF 197th ARS/161st ARW, Phoenix, AZ ANG
	57-1427	Boeing KC-135R Stratotanker bl/y	USAF 117th ARS/190th ARW, Forbes Field, KS ANG
	57-1428	Boeing KC-135R Stratotanker w/or	USAF 151st ARS/134th ARW, Knoxville, TN ANG
	57-1430	Boeing KC-135R Stratotanker [ZZ] or/bk	USAF 909th ARS/18th Wg, Kadena AB, Japan
	57-1432	Boeing KC-135R Stratotanker bl/bk	USAF 191st ARS/151st ARW, Salt Lake City, UT ANG
	57-1435	Boeing KC-135R Stratotanker bl/bk	USAF 191st ARS/151st ARW, Salt Lake City, UT ANG
	57-1436	Boeing KC-135R Stratotanker w/or	USAF 151st ARS/134th ARW, Knoxville, TN ANG
	57-1437	Boeing KC-135R Stratotanker	USAF 412th FLTS/412th TW, Edwards, CA
	57-1438	Boeing KC-135R Stratotanker or/y	*To 309th AMARG, 18th November 2022*
	57-1439	Boeing KC-135R Stratotanker	USAF 92nd ARW, Fairchild AFB, WA
	57-1440	Boeing KC-135R Stratotanker	USAF 92nd ARW, Fairchild AFB, WA
	57-1441	Boeing KC-135R Stratotanker y/bk	USAF 174th ARS/185th ARW, Sioux City, IA ANG
	57-1451	Boeing KC-135R Stratotanker w/or	USAF 151st ARS/134th ARW, Knoxville, TN ANG
	57-1453	Boeing KC-135R Stratotanker w/r	USAF 106th ARS/117th ARW, Birmingham, AL ANG
	57-1454	Boeing KC-135R Stratotanker	USAF 92nd ARW, Fairchild AFB, WA
	57-1456	Boeing KC-135R Stratotanker y/bk	USAF 756th ARS/459th ARW AFRC, Andrews AFB, MD
	57-1459	Boeing KC-135R Stratotanker or/y	USAF 336th ARS/452nd AMW AFRC, March ARB, CA
	57-1461	Boeing KC-135R Stratotanker r/w	USAF 173rd ARS/155th ARW, Lincoln, NE ANG
	57-1462	Boeing KC-135R Stratotanker	USAF 153rd ARS/186th ARW, Meridian, MS ANG
	57-1468	Boeing KC-135R Stratotanker or/y	USAF 336th ARS/452nd AMW AFRC, March ARB, CA
	57-1469	Boeing KC-135R Stratotanker $	USAF 197th ARS/161st ARW, Phoenix, AZ ANG
	57-1472	Boeing KC-135R Stratotanker bl	USAF 72nd ARS/434th ARW AFRC, Grissom AFB, IN
	57-1473	Boeing KC-135R Stratotanker w/r	USAF 106th ARS/117th ARW, Birmingham, AL ANG
	57-1474	Boeing KC-135R Stratotanker y/bl	USAF 6th ARW, MacDill AFB, FL
	57-1479	Boeing KC-135R Stratotanker y/bk	USAF 756th ARS/459th ARW AFRC, Andrews AFB, MD
	57-1483	Boeing KC-135R Stratotanker	USAF 92nd ARW, Fairchild AFB, WA
	57-1486	Boeing KC-135R Stratotanker	USAF 153rd ARS/186th ARW, Meridian, MS ANG
	57-1487	Boeing KC-135R Stratotanker y/bk	USAF 756th ARS/459th ARW AFRC, Andrews AFB, MD
	57-1488	Boeing KC-135R Stratotanker	USAF 92nd ARW, Fairchild AFB, WA
	57-1493	Boeing KC-135R Stratotanker y/bl	USAF 6th ARW, MacDill AFB, FL
	57-1499	Boeing KC-135R Stratotanker bl/bk	USAF 191st ARS/151st ARW, Salt Lake City, UT ANG
	57-1502	Boeing KC-135R Stratotanker	USAF 116th ARS/141st ARW, Fairchild AFB, WA ANG
	57-1506	Boeing KC-135R Stratotanker	USAF 22nd ARW, McConnell AFB, KS
	57-1508	Boeing KC-135R Stratotanker	USAF 314th ARS/940th ARW, Beale AFB, CA
	57-1512	Boeing KC-135R Stratotanker y/bk	USAF 756th ARS/459th ARW AFRC, Andrews AFB, MD
	57-1514	Boeing KC-135R Stratotanker w/bl	USAF 126th ARS/128th ARW, Mitchell Field, WI ANG
	57-2597	Boeing KC-135R Stratotanker w/or	USAF 151st ARS/134th ARW, Knoxville, TN ANG
	57-2598	Boeing KC-135R Stratotanker or/y	USAF 336th ARS/452nd AMW AFRC, March ARB, CA
	57-2599	Boeing KC-135R Stratotanker	USAF 314th ARS/940th ARW, Beale AFB, CA
	57-2603	Boeing KC-135R Stratotanker or/y	USAF 336th ARS/452nd AMW AFRC, March ARB, CA
	58-0001	Boeing KC-135R Stratotanker	USAF 6th ARW, MacDill AFB, FL

Serial	Type (code/other identity)	Owner/operator, location or fate	Notes
58-0004	Boeing KC-135R Stratotanker w/r	USAF 106th ARS/117th ARW, Birmingham, AL ANG	
58-0009	Boeing KC-135R Stratotanker w/bl	To 309th AMARG, 15th November 2022	
58-0010	Boeing KC-135R Stratotanker r	USAF 141st ARS/108th Wg, McGuire AFB, NJ ANG	
58-0011	Boeing KC-135R(RT) Stratotanker	USAF Ogden ALC, UT	
58-0015	Boeing KC-135R Stratotanker bl/y	USAF 465th ARS/507th ARW AFRC, Tinker AFB, OK	
58-0016	Boeing KC-135R Stratotanker	USAF 92nd ARW, Fairchild AFB, WA	
58-0018	Boeing KC-135R(RT) Stratotanker	USAF 22nd ARW, McConnell AFB, KS	
58-0021	Boeing KC-135R Stratotanker w/gn	USAF 132nd ARS/101st ARW, Bangor, MN ANG	
58-0023	Boeing KC-135R Stratotanker y/bl	USAF 6th ARW, MacDill AFB, FL	
58-0027	Boeing KC-135R Stratotanker bl/bk	USAF 191st ARS/151st ARW, Salt Lake City, UT ANG	
58-0030	Boeing KC-135R Stratotanker w/gn	USAF 132nd ARS/101st ARW, Bangor, MN ANG	
58-0034	Boeing KC-135R Stratotanker y/r	USAF 54th ARS/97th AMW, Altus AFB, OK	
58-0035	Boeing KC-135R Stratotanker	USAF 92nd ARW, Fairchild AFB, WA	
58-0036	Boeing KC-135R Stratotanker	USAF 92nd ARW, Fairchild AFB, WA	
58-0038	Boeing KC-135R Stratotanker	USAF 328th ARS/914th ARW AFRC, Niagara Falls NY	
58-0042	Boeing KC-135T Stratotanker	USAF 22nd ARW, McConnell AFB, KS	
58-0045	Boeing KC-135T Stratotanker	USAF 171st ARW, Greater Pittsburgh, PA ANG	
58-0046	Boeing KC-135T Stratotanker y/r	USAF 54th ARS/97th AMW, Altus AFB, OK	
58-0047	Boeing KC-135T Stratotanker	USAF 22nd ARW, McConnell AFB, KS	
58-0049	Boeing KC-135T Stratotanker bk/y	USAF 171st ARS/127th Wg, Selfridge ANGB, MI ANG	
58-0050	Boeing KC-135T Stratotanker	USAF 92nd ARW, Fairchild AFB, WA	
58-0051	Boeing KC-135R Stratotanker bl/y	USAF 465th ARS/507th ARW AFRC, Tinker AFB, OK	
58-0052	Boeing KC-135R Stratotanker or/y	USAF 336th ARS/452nd AMW AFRC, March ARB, CA	
58-0054	Boeing KC-135R Stratotanker or/y	USAF 336th ARS/452nd AMW AFRC, March ARB, CA	
58-0055	Boeing KC-135T Stratotanker [ZZ] or/bk	USAF 909th ARS/18th Wg, Kadena AB, Japan	
58-0056	Boeing KC-135R Stratotanker [HH] y/bk	USAF 203rd ARS/15th Wg, Hickam AFB, HI ANG	
58-0057	Boeing KC-135R Stratotanker y/bk	USAF 174th ARS/185th ARW, Sioux City, IA ANG	
58-0058	Boeing KC-135R Stratotanker bl/y	To 309th AMARG, 16th December 2022	
58-0059	Boeing KC-135R Stratotanker bl/y	USAF 117th ARS/190th ARW, Forbes Field, KS ANG	
58-0060	Boeing KC-135T Stratotanker y/bk	USAF 171st ARW, Greater Pittsburgh, PA ANG	
58-0061	Boeing KC-135T Stratotanker	USAF 22nd ARW, McConnell AFB, KS	
58-0062	Boeing KC-135T Stratotanker bk/y	USAF 171st ARS/127th Wg, Selfridge ANGB, MI ANG	
58-0063	Boeing KC-135R Stratotanker	USAF 328th ARS/914th ARW AFRC, Niagara Falls NY	
58-0065	Boeing KC-135T Stratotanker	USAF 22nd ARW, McConnell AFB, KS	
58-0066	Boeing KC-135R Stratotanker w/r	USAF 6th ARW, MacDill AFB, FL	
58-0067	Boeing KC-135R Stratotanker y/bk	USAF 174th ARS/185th ARW, Sioux City, IA ANG	
58-0069	Boeing KC-135T Stratotanker y/bl	USAF 6th ARW, MacDill AFB, FL	
58-0071	Boeing KC-135T Stratotanker y/bl	USAF 6th ARW, MacDill AFB, FL	
58-0072	Boeing KC-135T Stratotanker y/bk	USAF 171st ARW, Greater Pittsburgh, PA ANG	
58-0073	Boeing KC-135R Stratotanker w/r	USAF 106th ARS/117th ARW, Birmingham, AL ANG	
58-0074	Boeing KC-135T Stratotanker y/bk	USAF 171st ARW, Greater Pittsburgh, PA ANG	
58-0075	Boeing KC-135R Stratotanker y/bk	USAF 756th ARS/459th ARW AFRC, Andrews AFB, MD	
58-0076	Boeing KC-135R Stratotanker r/w	USAF 74th ARS/434th ARW AFRC, Grissom AFB, IN	
58-0077	Boeing KC-135T Stratotanker y/bk	USAF 171st ARW, Greater Pittsburgh, PA ANG	

Notes	Serial	Type (code/other identity)	Owner/operator, location or fate
	58-0079	Boeing KC-135R Stratotanker	USAF 153rd ARS/186th ARW, Meridian, MS ANG
	58-0083	Boeing KC-135R Stratotanker r/w	USAF 166th ARS/121st ARW, Rickenbacker ANGB, OH ANG
	58-0084	Boeing KC-135T Stratotanker y/bk	USAF 171st ARW, Greater Pittsburgh, PA ANG
	58-0085	Boeing KC-135R Stratotanker or/y	USAF 336th ARS/452nd AMW AFRC, March ARB, CA
	58-0086	Boeing KC-135T Stratotanker [ZZ] or/bk	USAF 909th ARS/18th Wg, Kadena AB, Japan
	58-0088	Boeing KC-135T Stratotanker bk/y	USAF 171st ARS/127th Wg, Selfridge ANGB, MI ANG
	58-0089	Boeing KC-135T Stratotanker y/bl	USAF 6th ARW, MacDill AFB, FL
	58-0092	Boeing KC-135R Stratotanker	USAF 92nd ARW, Fairchild AFB, WA
	58-0093	Boeing KC-135R Stratotanker [ZZ] or/bk	USAF 909th ARS/18th Wg, Kadena AB, Japan
	58-0094	Boeing KC-135T Stratotanker y/bl	USAF 6th ARW, MacDill AFB, FL
	58-0098	Boeing KC-135R Stratotanker w/gn	USAF 132nd ARS/101st ARW, Bangor, MN ANG
	58-0099	Boeing KC-135T Stratotanker y/bk	USAF 171st ARW, Greater Pittsburgh, PA ANG
	58-0102	Boeing KC-135R Stratotanker bl/y	USAF 465th ARS/507th ARW AFRC, Tinker AFB, OK
	58-0103	Boeing KC-135T Stratotanker	USAF 6th ARW, MacDill AFB, FL
	58-0104	Boeing KC-135R Stratotanker w/bl	USAF 108th ARS/126th ARW, Scott AFB, IL ANG
	58-0106	Boeing KC-135R Stratotanker w/r	USAF 106th ARS/117th ARW, Birmingham, AL ANG
	58-0107	Boeing KC-135R Stratotanker w/gn	USAF 132nd ARS/101st ARW, Bangor, MN ANG
	58-0109	Boeing KC-135R Stratotanker y/bk	USAF 174th ARS/185th ARW, Sioux City, IA ANG
	58-0112	Boeing KC-135T Stratotanker y/bk	USAF 171st ARW, Greater Pittsburgh, PA ANG
	58-0113	Boeing KC-135R Stratotanker	USAF 92nd ARW, Fairchild AFB, WA
	58-0117	Boeing KC-135T Stratotanker y/bk	USAF 171st ARW, Greater Pittsburgh, PA ANG
	58-0118	Boeing KC-135R Stratotanker	USAF 92nd ARW, Fairchild AFB, WA
	58-0119	Boeing KC-135R Stratotanker w/or	USAF 151st ARS/134th ARW, Knoxville, TN ANG
	58-0120	Boeing KC-135R Stratotanker	USAF 153rd ARS/186th ARW, Meridian, MS ANG
	58-0121	Boeing KC-135R Stratotanker bl/y	USAF 465th ARS/507th ARW AFRC, Tinker AFB, OK
	58-0122	Boeing KC-135R Stratotanker bl/y	USAF 117th ARS/190th ARW, Forbes Field, KS ANG
	58-0123	Boeing KC-135R Stratotanker y/r	USAF 54th ARS/97th AMW, Altus AFB, OK
	58-0124	Boeing KC-135R(RT) Stratotanker	USAF 22nd ARW, McConnell AFB, KS
	58-0126	Boeing KC-135R(RT) Stratotanker	USAF 22nd ARW, McConnell AFB, KS
	58-0128	Boeing KC-135R Stratotanker	USAF 92nd ARW, Fairchild AFB, WA
	58-0129	Boeing KC-135T Stratotanker bk/y	USAF 171st ARS/127th Wg, Selfridge ANGB, MI ANG
	59-1444	Boeing KC-135R Stratotanker	USAF 92nd ARW, Fairchild AFB, WA
	59-1446	Boeing KC-135R Stratotanker w/gn	USAF 132nd ARS/101st ARW, Bangor, MN ANG
	59-1448	Boeing KC-135R Stratotanker	USAF 153rd ARS/186th ARW, Meridian, MS ANG
	59-1450	Boeing KC-135R Stratotanker	USAF 197th ARS/161st ARW, Phoenix, AZ ANG
	59-1453	Boeing KC-135R Stratotanker	USAF 153rd ARS/186th ARW, Meridian, MS ANG
	59-1455	Boeing KC-135R Stratotanker [HH] y/bk	USAF 203rd ARS/15th Wg, Hickam AFB, HI ANG
	59-1458	Boeing KC-135R Stratotanker r/w	USAF 166th ARS/121st ARW, Rickenbacker ANGB, OH ANG
	59-1459	Boeing KC-135R Stratotanker y/bk	USAF 756th ARS/459th ARW AFRC, Andrews AFB, MD
	59-1460	Boeing KC-135T Stratotanker y/bk	USAF 171st ARW, Greater Pittsburgh, PA ANG
	59-1461	Boeing KC-135R Stratotanker w/bl	USAF 126th ARS/128th ARW, Mitchell Field, WI ANG
	59-1462	Boeing KC-135T Stratotanker	USAF 92nd ARW, Fairchild AFB, WA
	59-1463	Boeing KC-135R Stratotanker r/w	USAF 173rd ARS/155th ARW, Lincoln, NE ANG
	59-1466	Boeing KC-135R Stratotanker w/bl	USAF 108th ARS/126th ARW, Scott AFB, IL ANG
	59-1467	Boeing KC-135T Stratotanker y/bk	USAF 171st ARW, Greater Pittsburgh, PA ANG

Serial	Type (code/other identity)	Owner/operator, location or fate	Notes
59-1468	Boeing KC-135T Stratotanker *y/bk*	USAF 171st ARW, Greater Pittsburgh, PA ANG	
59-1469	Boeing KC-135R Stratotanker *y/bk*	USAF 756th ARS/459th ARW AFRC, Andrews AFB, MD	
59-1471	Boeing KC-135T Stratotanker	USAF 92nd ARW, Fairchild AFB, WA	
59-1472	Boeing KC-135R Stratotanker	USAF 314th ARS/940th ARW, Beale AFB, CA	
59-1474	Boeing KC-135T Stratotanker *bk/y*	USAF 171st ARS/127th Wg, Selfridge ANGB, MI ANG	
59-1476	Boeing KC-135R Stratotanker	USAF 92nd ARW, Fairchild AFB, WA	
59-1478	Boeing KC-135R Stratotanker *w/or*	USAF 151st ARS/134th ARW, Knoxville, TN ANG	
59-1480	Boeing KC-135T Stratotanker	USAF 92nd ARW, Fairchild AFB, WA	
59-1482	Boeing KC-135R Stratotanker	USAF 328th ARS/914th ARW AFRC, Niagara Falls NY	
59-1483	Boeing KC-135R Stratotanker *r/w*	USAF 166th ARS/121st ARW, Rickenbacker ANGB, OH ANG	
59-1486	Boeing KC-135R Stratotanker	USAF 92nd ARW, Fairchild AFB, WA	
59-1488	Boeing KC-135R Stratotanker *w/gn*	USAF 132nd ARS/101st ARW, Bangor, MN ANG	
59-1490	Boeing KC-135T Stratotanker *y/bk*	*To 309th AMARG, 20th April 2022*	
59-1492	Boeing KC-135R Stratotanker	USAF 92nd ARW, Fairchild AFB, WA	
59-1495	Boeing KC-135R Stratotanker *r/w*	USAF 173rd ARS/155th ARW, Lincoln, NE ANG	
59-1498	Boeing KC-135R Stratotanker *w/gn*	USAF 132nd ARS/101st ARW, Bangor, MN ANG	
59-1499	Boeing KC-135R Stratotanker [HH] *y/bk*	USAF 203rd ARS/15th Wg, Hickam AFB, HI ANG	
59-1500	Boeing KC-135R Stratotanker *w/bl*	USAF 108th ARS/126th ARW, Scott AFB, IL ANG	
59-1501	Boeing KC-135R Stratotanker *y/r*	USAF 54th ARS/97th AMW, Altus AFB, OK	
59-1502	Boeing KC-135R Stratotanker	USAF 22nd ARW, McConnell AFB, KS	
59-1504	Boeing KC-135T Stratotanker *y/bk*	USAF 171st ARW, Greater Pittsburgh, PA ANG	
59-1505	Boeing KC-135R Stratotanker *w/or*	USAF 151st ARS/134th ARW, Knoxville, TN ANG	
59-1506	Boeing KC-135R Stratotanker *y/bk*	USAF 174th ARS/185th ARW, Sioux City, IA ANG	
59-1507	Boeing KC-135R Stratotanker *bl/y*	USAF 117th ARS/190th ARW, Forbes Field, KS ANG	
59-1508	Boeing KC-135R Stratotanker	USAF 92nd ARW, Fairchild AFB, WA	
59-1509	Boeing KC-135R Stratotanker *w/or*	USAF 151st ARS/134th ARW, Knoxville, TN ANG	
59-1510	Boeing KC-135T Stratotanker [ZZ] *or/bk*	USAF 909th ARS/18th Wg, Kadena AB, Japan	
59-1512	Boeing KC-135T Stratotanker *bk/y*	USAF 171st ARS/127th Wg, Selfridge ANGB, MI ANG	
59-1513	Boeing KC-135T Stratotanker	USAF	
59-1515	Boeing KC-135R Stratotanker	USAF 92nd ARW, Fairchild AFB, WA	
59-1516	Boeing KC-135R Stratotanker *w/bl*	USAF 126th ARS/128th ARW, Mitchell Field, WI ANG	
59-1517	Boeing KC-135R Stratotanker *w/or*	USAF 151st ARS/134th ARW, Knoxville, TN ANG	
59-1519	Boeing KC-135R Stratotanker *y/bk*	USAF 174th ARS/185th ARW, Sioux City, IA ANG	
59-1520	Boeing KC-135T Stratotanker	USAF 92nd ARW, Fairchild AFB, WA	
59-1521	Boeing KC-135R Stratotanker [AK] *bl/y*	USAF 168th ARS/168th ARW, Eielson AFB, AK ANG	
59-1522	Boeing KC-135R Stratotanker *w/bl*	USAF 108th ARS/126th ARW, Scott AFB, IL ANG	
59-1523	Boeing KC-135T Stratotanker *y/bk*	USAF 171st ARW, Greater Pittsburgh, PA ANG	
60-0313	Boeing KC-135R Stratotanker	USAF 22nd ARW, McConnell AFB, KS	
60-0314	Boeing KC-135R Stratotanker *r/w*	USAF 74th ARS/434th ARW AFRC, Grissom AFB, IN	
60-0315	Boeing KC-135R Stratotanker *w/bl*	USAF 126th ARS/128th ARW, Mitchell Field, WI ANG	
60-0316	Boeing KC-135R Stratotanker *bl/bk*	USAF 191st ARS/151st ARW, Salt Lake City, UT ANG	
60-0318	Boeing KC-135R Stratotanker	USAF 314th ARS/940th ARW, Beale AFB, CA	
60-0320	Boeing KC-135R Stratotanker	USAF 92nd ARW, Fairchild AFB, WA	
60-0322	Boeing KC-135R Stratotanker *bl*	USAF 72nd ARS/434th ARW AFRC, Grissom AFB, IN	
60-0323	Boeing KC-135R Stratotanker	USAF 314th ARS/940th ARW, Beale AFB, CA	
60-0328	Boeing KC-135R Stratotanker	USAF 92nd ARW, Fairchild AFB, WA	

Notes	Serial	Type (code/other identity)	Owner/operator, location or fate
	60-0329	Boeing KC-135R Stratotanker [HH] *y/bk*	*Preserved at Wright-Patterson AFB, April 2022*
	60-0331	Boeing KC-135R Stratotanker	USAF 6th ARW, MacDill AFB, FL
	60-0332	Boeing KC-135R Stratotanker [AK] *bl/y*	USAF 168th ARS/168th ARW, Eielson AFB, AK ANG
	60-0334	Boeing KC-135R Stratotanker [AK] *bl/y*	USAF 168th ARS/168th ARW, Eielson AFB, AK ANG
	60-0336	Boeing KC-135T Stratotanker *y/bl*	USAF 6th ARW, MacDill AFB, FL
	60-0337	Boeing KC-135T Stratotanker *y/bl*	USAF 6th ARW, MacDill AFB, FL
	60-0339	Boeing KC-135T Stratotanker [ZZ] *or/bk*	USAF 909th ARS/18th Wg, Kadena AB, Japan
	60-0341	Boeing KC-135R Stratotanker	USAF 153rd ARS/186th ARW, Meridian, MS ANG
	60-0342	Boeing KC-135T Stratotanker	USAF 92nd ARW, Fairchild AFB, WA
	60-0343	Boeing KC-135T Stratotanker	USAF 22nd ARW, McConnell AFB, KS
	60-0344	Boeing KC-135T Stratotanker	*To 309th AMARG, December 2022*
	60-0345	Boeing KC-135T Stratotanker *bk/y* $	USAF 171st ARS/127th Wg, Selfridge ANGB, MI ANG
	60-0346	Boeing KC-135T Stratotanker *bk/y*	USAF 171st ARS/127th Wg, Selfridge ANGB, MI ANG
	60-0347	Boeing KC-135R Stratotanker *r/w*	USAF 166th ARS/121st ARW, Rickenbacker ANGB, OH ANG
	60-0348	Boeing KC-135R Stratotanker *y/r*	USAF 54th ARS/97th AMW, Altus AFB, OK
	60-0349	Boeing KC-135R Stratotanker *bl/y*	USAF 465th ARS/507th ARW AFRC, Tinker AFB, OK
	60-0350	Boeing KC-135R Stratotanker *y/r*	USAF 54th ARS/97th AMW, Altus AFB, OK
	60-0351	Boeing KC-135R Stratotanker *y/r* [97 OG]	USAF 54th ARS/97th AMW, Altus AFB, OK
	60-0353	Boeing KC-135R Stratotanker *y/bl*	USAF, OK-ALC
	60-0355	Boeing KC-135R Stratotanker	USAF 92nd ARW, Fairchild AFB, WA
	60-0356	Boeing KC-135R(RT) Stratotanker	USAF 22nd ARW, McConnell AFB, KS
	60-0357	Boeing KC-135R(RT) Stratotanker	USAF 22nd ARW, McConnell AFB, KS
	60-0358	Boeing KC-135R Stratotanker *w/bl*	USAF 108th ARS/126th ARW, Scott AFB, IL ANG
	60-0359	Boeing KC-135R Stratotanker *r/w*	USAF 74th ARS/434th ARW AFRC, Grissom AFB, IN
	60-0360	Boeing KC-135R Stratotanker *y/bl*	USAF 6th ARW, MacDill AFB, FL
	60-0362	Boeing KC-135R(RT) Stratotanker	USAF 22nd ARW, McConnell AFB, KS
	60-0363	Boeing KC-135R Stratotanker *bl*	USAF 72nd ARS/434th ARW AFRC, Grissom AFB, IN
	60-0364	Boeing KC-135R Stratotanker *r/w*	USAF 74th ARS/434th ARW AFRC, Grissom AFB, IN
	60-0365	Boeing KC-135R Stratotanker *bl/y*	USAF 117th ARS/190th ARW, Forbes Field, KS ANG
	60-0366	Boeing KC-135R Stratotanker *r*	USAF 141st ARS/108th Wg, McGuire AFB, NJ ANG
	60-0367	Boeing KC-135R Stratotanker *r/w*	USAF 166th ARS/121st ARW, Rickenbacker ANGB, OH ANG
	61-0264	Boeing KC-135R Stratotanker *r/w*	USAF 166th ARS/121st ARW, Rickenbacker ANGB, OH ANG
	61-0266	Boeing KC-135R Stratotanker *bl/y*	USAF 117th ARS/190th ARW, Forbes Field, KS ANG
	61-0267	Boeing KC-135R Stratotanker	USAF 92nd ARW, Fairchild AFB, WA
	61-0272	Boeing KC-135R Stratotanker *r/w*	USAF 74th ARS/434th ARW AFRC, Grissom AFB, IN
	61-0275	Boeing KC-135R Stratotanker *bl/bk*	USAF 191st ARS/151st ARW, Salt Lake City, UT ANG
	61-0276	Boeing KC-135R Stratotanker *r/w*	USAF 173rd ARS/155th ARW, Lincoln, NE ANG
	61-0277	Boeing KC-135R Stratotanker *bl/y*	USAF 117th ARS/190th ARW, Forbes Field, KS ANG
	61-0280	Boeing KC-135R Stratotanker *or/y*	USAF 336th ARS/452nd AMW AFRC, March ARB, CA
	61-0284	Boeing KC-135R Stratotanker	USAF 197th ARS/161st ARW, Phoenix, AZ ANG
	61-0288	Boeing KC-135R Stratotanker [AK] *bl/y*	USAF 168th ARS/168th ARW, Eielson AFB, AK ANG

Serial	Type (code/other identity)	Owner/operator, location or fate	Notes
61-0290	Boeing KC-135R Stratotanker [HH] y/bk	USAF 203rd ARS/15th Wg, Hickam AFB, HI ANG	
61-0292	Boeing KC-135R Stratotanker bl/y	USAF 117th ARS/190th ARW, Forbes Field, KS ANG	
61-0293	Boeing KC-135R(RT) Stratotanker	USAF 22nd ARW, McConnell AFB, KS	
61-0294	Boeing KC-135R Stratotanker	USAF 328th ARS/914th ARW AFRC, Niagara Falls NY	
61-0295	Boeing KC-135R Stratotanker y/r	USAF 54th ARS/97th AMW, Altus AFB, OK	
61-0298	Boeing KC-135R Stratotanker w/bl	USAF 126th ARS/128th ARW, Mitchell Field, WI ANG	
61-0299	Boeing KC-135R Stratotanker or/y	USAF 336th ARS/452nd AMW AFRC, March ARB, CA	
61-0300	Boeing KC-135R Stratotanker w/bl	USAF 108th ARS/126th ARW, Scott AFB, IL ANG	
61-0305	Boeing KC-135R Stratotanker y/r	USAF 54th ARS/97th AMW, Altus AFB, OK	
61-0307	Boeing KC-135R Stratotanker y/bk	USAF 756th ARS/459th ARW AFRC, Andrews AFB, MD	
61-0308	Boeing KC-135R Stratotanker y/bl	USAF 6th ARW, MacDill AFB, FL	
61-0309	Boeing KC-135R Stratotanker w/bl	USAF 126th ARS/128th ARW, Mitchell Field, WI ANG	
61-0310	Boeing KC-135R Stratotanker w/bl	USAF 126th ARS/128th ARW, Mitchell Field, WI ANG	
61-0311	Boeing KC-135R Stratotanker	USAF 92nd ARW, Fairchild AFB, WA	
61-0313	Boeing KC-135R Stratotanker [ZZ] or/bk	USAF 909th ARS/18th Wg, Kadena AB, Japan	
61-0314	Boeing KC-135R Stratotanker y/bl	USAF 6th ARW, MacDill AFB, FL	
61-0317	Boeing KC-135R Stratotanker	USAF 197th ARS/161st ARW, Phoenix, AZ ANG	
61-0318	Boeing KC-135R Stratotanker w/r	USAF 106th ARS/117th ARW, Birmingham, AL ANG	
61-0320	Boeing KC-135NK Stratotanker [ED]	USAF 418th FLTS/412th TW, Edwards AFB, CA	
61-0321	Boeing KC-135R Stratotanker y/bl	USAF 6th ARW, MacDill AFB, FL	
61-0323	Boeing KC-135R Stratotanker y/bl	USAF 6th ARW, MacDill AFB, FL	
61-0324	Boeing KC-135R Stratotanker or/y	USAF 336th ARS/452nd AMW AFRC, March ARB, CA	
61-2662	Boeing RC-135S Cobra Ball [OF] bk	USAF 45th RS/55th Wg, Offutt AFB, NE	
61-2663	Boeing RC-135S Cobra Ball [OF] bk	USAF 45th RS/55th Wg, Offutt AFB, NE	
61-2666	Boeing NC-135W	USAF 645th Materiel Sqn, Greenville, TX	
61-2667	Boeing WC-135W Constant Phoenix [OF] bk	To 309th AMARG, 19th September 2022	
62-3498	Boeing KC-135R Stratotanker y/bl	USAF 6th ARW, MacDill AFB, FL	
62-3499	Boeing KC-135R Stratotanker	USAF 92nd ARW, Fairchild AFB, WA	
62-3500	Boeing KC-135R Stratotanker	USAF 197th ARS/161st ARW, Phoenix, AZ ANG	
62-3502	Boeing KC-135R Stratotanker	USAF 92nd ARW, Fairchild AFB, WA	
62-3503	Boeing KC-135R Stratotanker bl/y	USAF 108th ARS/126th ARW, Scott AFB, IL ANG	
62-3505	Boeing KC-135R Stratotanker y/r	USAF 54th ARS/97th AMW, Altus AFB, OK	
62-3506	Boeing KC-135R Stratotanker bl/y	USAF 117th ARS/190th ARW, Forbes Field, KS ANG	
62-3507	Boeing KC-135R Stratotanker or/y	USAF 336th ARS/452nd AMW AFRC, March ARB, CA	
62-3508	Boeing KC-135R Stratotanker r $	USAF 141st ARS/108th Wg, McGuire AFB, NJ ANG	
62-3509	Boeing KC-135R Stratotanker bl/y	USAF 465th ARS/507th ARW AFRC, Tinker AFB, OK	
62-3510	Boeing KC-135R Stratotanker r/w	USAF 74th ARS/434th ARW AFRC, Grissom AFB, IN	
62-3511	Boeing KC-135R Stratotanker r/w	USAF 166th ARS/121st ARW, Rickenbacker ANGB, OH ANG	
62-3512	Boeing KC-135R Stratotanker w/bl	USAF 126th ARS/128th ARW, Mitchell Field, WI ANG	
62-3513	Boeing KC-135R Stratotanker w/gn	USAF 132nd ARS/101st ARW, Bangor, MN ANG	
62-3514	Boeing KC-135R Stratotanker r	USAF 141st ARS/108th Wg, McGuire AFB, NJ ANG	
62-3515	Boeing KC-135R Stratotanker w/bl	USAF 108th ARS/126th ARW, Scott AFB, IL ANG	
62-3516	Boeing KC-135R Stratotanker $	USAF 197th ARS/161st ARW, Phoenix, AZ ANG	
62-3517	Boeing KC-135R Stratotanker y/bl	USAF 6th ARW, MacDill AFB, FL	

Notes	Serial	Type (code/other identity)	Owner/operator, location or fate
	62-3518	Boeing KC-135R Stratotanker *bl*	USAF 72nd ARS/434th ARW AFRC, Grissom AFB, IN
	62-3519	Boeing KC-135R Stratotanker	USAF 92nd ARW, Fairchild AFB, WA
	62-3521	Boeing KC-135R Stratotanker *bl*	USAF 72nd ARS/434th ARW AFRC, Grissom AFB, IN
	62-3523	Boeing KC-135R Stratotanker	USAF 22nd ARW, McConnell AFB, KS
	62-3524	Boeing KC-135R Stratotanker [AK] *bl/y*	USAF 168th ARS/168th ARW, Eielson AFB, AK ANG
	62-3526	Boeing KC-135R Stratotanker *r/w*	USAF 173rd ARS/155th ARW, Lincoln, NE ANG
	62-3528	Boeing KC-135R Stratotanker	USAF 92nd ARW, Fairchild AFB, WA
	62-3529	Boeing KC-135R Stratotanker	USAF 314th ARS/940th ARW, Beale AFB, CA
	62-3530	Boeing KC-135R Stratotanker *bl*	USAF 72nd ARS/434th ARW AFRC, Grissom AFB, IN
	62-3531	Boeing KC-135R Stratotanker *r/w*	USAF 166th ARS/121st ARW, Rickenbacker ANGB, OH ANG
	62-3533	Boeing KC-135R Stratotanker	USAF 328th ARS/914th ARW AFRC, Niagara Falls NY
	62-3534	Boeing KC-135R Stratotanker	USAF 22nd ARW, McConnell AFB, KS
	62-3537	Boeing KC-135R Stratotanker	USAF 92nd ARW, Fairchild AFB, WA
	62-3538	Boeing KC-135R Stratotanker *y/r*	USAF 54th ARS/97th AMW, Altus AFB, OK
	62-3541	Boeing KC-135R Stratotanker	USAF 92nd ARW, Fairchild AFB, WA
	62-3542	Boeing KC-135R Stratotanker	USAF 314th ARS/940th ARW, Beale AFB, CA
	62-3543	Boeing KC-135R Stratotanker *y/bk*	USAF 756th ARS/459th ARW AFRC, Andrews AFB, MD
	62-3544	Boeing KC-135R Stratotanker *r* $	USAF 141st ARS/108th Wg, McGuire AFB, NJ ANG
	62-3545	Boeing KC-135R Stratotanker	USAF 22nd ARW, McConnell AFB, KS
	62-3547	Boeing KC-135R Stratotanker *bl/y*	USAF 117th ARS/190th ARW, Forbes Field, KS ANG
	62-3549	Boeing KC-135R Stratotanker *y/bk*	USAF 174th ARS/185th ARW, Sioux City, IA ANG
	62-3550	Boeing KC-135R Stratotanker	USAF 197th ARS/161st ARW, Phoenix, AZ ANG
	62-3551	Boeing KC-135R Stratotanker	USAF 92nd ARW, Fairchild AFB, WA
	62-3552	Boeing KC-135R Stratotanker	USAF 6th ARW, MacDill AFB, FL
	62-3553	Boeing KC-135R Stratotanker	USAF 92nd ARW, Fairchild AFB, WA
	62-3554	Boeing KC-135R Stratotanker	USAF 22nd ARW, McConnell AFB, KS
	62-3556	Boeing KC-135R Stratotanker *y/bk*	USAF 756th ARS/459th ARW AFRC, Andrews AFB, MD
	62-3557	Boeing KC-135R Stratotanker	USAF 328th ARS/914th ARW AFRC, Niagara Falls NY
	62-3558	Boeing KC-135R Stratotanker *or/y*	USAF 336th ARS/452nd AMW AFRC, March ARB, CA
	62-3559	Boeing KC-135R Stratotanker	USAF 92nd ARW, Fairchild AFB, WA
	62-3561	Boeing KC-135R Stratotanker [ZZ] *or/bk*	USAF 909th ARS/18th Wg, Kadena AB, Japan
	62-3562	Boeing KC-135R Stratotanker	USAF 92nd ARW, Fairchild AFB, WA
	62-3564	Boeing KC-135R Stratotanker	USAF 92nd ARW, Fairchild AFB, WA
	62-3565	Boeing KC-135R Stratotanker [ZZ] *or/bk*	USAF 909th ARS/18th Wg, Kadena AB, Japan
	62-3566	Boeing KC-135R Stratotanker *y/bk*	USAF 174th ARS/185th ARW, Sioux City, IA ANG
	62-3568	Boeing KC-135R Stratotanker	USAF 116th ARS/141st ARW, Fairchild AFB, WA ANG
	62-3569	Boeing KC-135R Stratotanker	USAF 22nd ARW, McConnell AFB, KS
	62-3571	Boeing KC-135R Stratotanker [AK] *bl/y*	USAF 168th ARS/168th ARW, Eielson AFB, AK ANG
	62-3572	Boeing KC-135R Stratotanker *bl/y*	*To 309th AMARG, 12th May 2022*
	62-3573	Boeing KC-135R Stratotanker	USAF 92nd ARW, Fairchild AFB, WA
	62-3575	Boeing KC-135R Stratotanker	USAF 92nd ARW, Fairchild AFB, WA
	62-3576	Boeing KC-135R Stratotanker *w/bl*	USAF 108th ARS/126th ARW, Scott AFB, IL ANG
	62-3577	Boeing KC-135R Stratotanker	USAF 92nd ARW, Fairchild AFB, WA
	62-3578	Boeing KC-135R Stratotanker *r*	USAF 141st ARS/108th Wg, McGuire AFB, NJ ANG

Serial	Type (code/other identity)	Owner/operator, location or fate	Notes
62-3580	Boeing KC-135R Stratotanker	USAF 328th ARS/914th ARW AFRC, Niagara Falls NY	
62-4125	Boeing RC-135W Rivet Joint [OF] bl	USAF 38th RS/55th Wg, Offutt AFB, NE	
62-4126	Boeing RC-135W Rivet Joint [OF] bl	USAF 38th RS/55th Wg, Offutt AFB, NE	
62-4127	Boeing TC-135W [OF] bl	USAF 38th RS/55th Wg, Offutt AFB, NE	
62-4128	Boeing RC-135S Cobra Ball [OF] bk	USAF 45th RS/55th Wg, Offutt AFB, NE	
62-4129	Boeing TC-135W [OF] bl	USAF 343rd RS/55th Wg, Offutt AFB, NE	
62-4130	Boeing RC-135W Rivet Joint [OF] bl	USAF 38th RS/55th Wg, Offutt AFB, NE	
62-4131	Boeing RC-135W Rivet Joint [OF] bl	USAF 38th RS/55th Wg, Offutt AFB, NE	
62-4132	Boeing RC-135W Rivet Joint [OF] bl	USAF 38th RS/55th Wg, Offutt AFB, NE	
62-4133	Boeing TC-135W [OF] bk	USAF 45th RS/55th Wg, Offutt AFB, NE	
62-4134	Boeing RC-135W Rivet Joint [OF] bl	USAF 38th RS/55th Wg, Offutt AFB, NE	
62-4135	Boeing RC-135W Rivet Joint [OF] bl	USAF 38th RS/55th Wg, Offutt AFB, NE	
62-4138	Boeing RC-135W Rivet Joint [OF] bl	USAF 38th RS/55th Wg, Offutt AFB, NE	
62-4139	Boeing RC-135W Rivet Joint [OF] bl	USAF 38th RS/55th Wg, Offutt AFB, NE	
63-7976	Boeing KC-135R Stratotanker y/bl	USAF 6th ARW, MacDill AFB, FL	
63-7977	Boeing KC-135R Stratotanker y/r	USAF 54th ARS/97th AMW, Altus AFB, OK	
63-7978	Boeing KC-135R Stratotanker r/w	USAF 54th ARS/97th AMW, Altus AFB, OK	
63-7979	Boeing KC-135R Stratotanker y/bl	USAF 6th ARW, MacDill AFB, FL	
63-7981	Boeing KC-135R Stratotanker w/bl	USAF 108th ARS/126th ARW, Scott AFB, IL ANG	
63-7982	Boeing KC-135R Stratotanker [ZZ] or/bk	USAF 909th ARS/18th Wg, Kadena AB, Japan	
63-7984	Boeing KC-135R Stratotanker w/r	USAF 106th ARS/117th ARW, Birmingham, AL ANG	
63-7985	Boeing KC-135R Stratotanker bl/y	USAF 465th ARS/507th ARW AFRC, Tinker AFB, OK	
63-7987	Boeing KC-135R Stratotanker y/r	USAF 54th ARS/97th AMW, Altus AFB, OK	
63-7988	Boeing KC-135R Stratotanker r/w	USAF 173rd ARS/155th ARW, Lincoln, NE ANG	
63-7991	Boeing KC-135R Stratotanker r/w	USAF 173rd ARS/155th ARW, Lincoln, NE ANG	
63-7992	Boeing KC-135R Stratotanker	USAF 153rd ARS/186th ARW, Meridian, MS ANG	
63-7993	Boeing KC-135R Stratotanker m	USAF 166th ARS/121st ARW, Rickenbacker ANGB, OH ANG	
63-7995	Boeing KC-135R Stratotanker	USAF 22nd ARW, McConnell AFB, KS	
63-7996	Boeing KC-135R Stratotanker	USAF 72nd ARS/434th ARW AFRC, Grissom AFB, IN	
63-7997	Boeing KC-135R Stratotanker y/r	USAF 54th ARS/97th AMW, Altus AFB, OK	
63-8000	Boeing KC-135R Stratotanker y/bl	USAF 6th ARW, MacDill AFB, FL	
63-8002	Boeing KC-135R Stratotanker	USAF 22nd ARW, McConnell AFB, KS	
63-8003	Boeing KC-135R Stratotanker or/bk $	USAF 141st ARS/108th Wg, McGuire AFB, NJ ANG	
63-8004	Boeing KC-135R Stratotanker bl/y	USAF 117th ARS/190th ARW, Forbes Field, KS ANG	
63-8006	Boeing KC-135R Stratotanker r/w	USAF 54th ARS/97th AMW, Altus AFB, OK	
63-8007	Boeing KC-135R Stratotanker w/r	USAF 106th ARS/117th ARW, Birmingham, AL ANG	
63-8011	Boeing KC-135R Stratotanker y/r [54 ARS]	USAF 54th ARS/97th AMW, Altus AFB, OK	
63-8012	Boeing KC-135R Stratotanker or/y	USAF 336th ARS/452nd AMW AFRC, March ARB, CA	
63-8013	Boeing KC-135R Stratotanker r/w	USAF 166th ARS/121st ARW, Rickenbacker ANGB, OH ANG	
63-8014	Boeing KC-135R Stratotanker	USAF 92nd ARW, Fairchild AFB, WA	
63-8015	Boeing KC-135R Stratotanker [AK] bl/y	USAF 168th ARS/168th ARW, Eielson AFB, AK ANG	
63-8017	Boeing KC-135R Stratotanker	USAF 328th ARS/914th ARW AFRC, Niagara Falls NY	
63-8018	Boeing KC-135R Stratotanker r/w	USAF 173rd ARS/155th ARW, Lincoln, NE ANG	
63-8019	Boeing KC-135R Stratotanker	USAF 92nd ARW, Fairchild AFB, WA	
63-8020	Boeing KC-135R Stratotanker	USAF 22nd ARW, McConnell AFB, KS	
63-8021	Boeing KC-135R Stratotanker	USAF 92nd ARW, Fairchild AFB, WA	
63-8022	Boeing KC-135W Stratotanker [ZZ] or/bk	USAF 909th ARS/18th Wg, Kadena AB, Japan	
63-8023	Boeing KC-135R Stratotanker w/bl	USAF 126th ARS/128th ARW, Mitchell Field, WI ANG	

US-BASED USAF AIRCRAFT

Notes	Serial	Type (code/other identity)	Owner/operator, location or fate
	63-8024	Boeing KC-135R Stratotanker *or/y*	USAF 336th ARS/452nd AMW AFRC, March ARB, CA
	63-8025	Boeing KC-135R Stratotanker	USAF 92nd ARW, Fairchild AFB, WA
	63-8026	Boeing KC-135R Stratotanker *bl/bk*	USAF 191st ARS/151st ARW, Salt Lake City, UT ANG
	63-8027	Boeing KC-135R Stratotanker *y/r*	USAF 54th ARS/97th AMW, Altus AFB, OK
	63-8028	Boeing KC-135R Stratotanker [AK] *bl/y*	USAF 168th ARS/168th ARW, Eielson AFB, AK ANG
	63-8029	Boeing KC-135R Stratotanker *r* $	USAF 141st ARS/108th Wg, McGuire AFB, NJ ANG
	63-8030	Boeing KC-135R Stratotanker [HH] *y/bk*	USAF 203rd ARS/15th Wg, Hickam AFB, HI ANG
	63-8031	Boeing KC-135R Stratotanker	USAF 92nd ARW, Fairchild AFB, WA
	63-8032	Boeing KC-135R Stratotanker *bl*	USAF 72nd ARS/434th ARW AFRC, Grissom AFB, IN
	63-8033	Boeing KC-135R Stratotanker *y/r*	USAF 54th ARS/97th AMW, Altus AFB, OK
	63-8034	Boeing KC-135R Stratotanker	USAF 6th ARW, MacDill AFB, FL
	63-8035	Boeing KC-135R Stratotanker *w/r*	USAF 106th ARS/117th ARW, Birmingham, AL ANG
	63-8036	Boeing KC-135R Stratotanker	USAF 197th ARS/161st ARW, Phoenix, AZ ANG
	63-8038	Boeing KC-135R Stratotanker [HH] *y/bk*	USAF 203rd ARS/15th Wg, Hickam AFB, HI ANG
	63-8039	Boeing KC-135R Stratotanker *bl/y*	USAF 465th ARS/507th ARW AFRC, Tinker AFB, OK
	63-8040	Boeing KC-135R Stratotanker *r*	USAF 141st ARS/108th Wg, McGuire AFB, NJ ANG
	63-8041	Boeing KC-135R Stratotanker *bl*	USAF 72nd ARS/434th ARW AFRC, Grissom AFB, IN
	63-8043	Boeing KC-135R Stratotanker [AK] *bl/y*	USAF 168th ARS/168th ARW, Eielson AFB, AK ANG
	63-8044	Boeing KC-135R Stratotanker	USAF 328th ARS/914th ARW AFRC, Niagara Falls NY
	63-8045	Boeing KC-135R Stratotanker	USAF 92nd ARW, Fairchild AFB, WA
	63-8871	Boeing KC-135R Stratotanker	USAF 92nd ARW, Fairchild AFB, WA
	63-8872	Boeing KC-135R Stratotanker *w/gn*	USAF 132nd ARS/101st ARW, Bangor, MN ANG
	63-8873	Boeing KC-135R Stratotanker *w/gn*	USAF 132nd ARS/101st ARW, Bangor, MN ANG
	63-8874	Boeing KC-135R Stratotanker	USAF 92nd ARW, Fairchild AFB, WA
	63-8875	Boeing KC-135R Stratotanker *bl/y*	USAF 117th ARS/190th ARW, Forbes Field, KS ANG
	63-8876	Boeing KC-135R Stratotanker [AK] *bl/y*	USAF 168th ARS/168th ARW, Eielson AFB, AK ANG
	63-8879	Boeing KC-135R Stratotanker	USAF 6th ARW, MacDill AFB, FL
	63-8880	Boeing KC-135R Stratotanker [HH] *y/bk*	USAF 203rd ARS/15th Wg, Hickam AFB, HI ANG
	63-8881	Boeing KC-135R Stratotanker *bl/bk*	USAF 191st ARS/151st ARW, Salt Lake City, UT ANG
	63-8883	Boeing KC-135R Stratotanker *y/bl*	USAF 6th ARW, MacDill AFB, FL
	63-8884	Boeing KC-135R Stratotanker *y/bl*	USAF 6th ARW, MacDill AFB, FL
	63-8885	Boeing KC-135R Stratotanker *y/bl*	USAF 6th ARW, MacDill AFB, FL
	63-8888	Boeing KC-135R Stratotanker	USAF 6th ARW, MacDill AFB, FL
	63-9792	Boeing RC-135V Rivet Joint [OF] *bl*	USAF 38th RS/55th Wg, Offutt AFB, NE
	64-14828	Boeing KC-135R Stratotanker *bl/bk*	USAF 191st ARS/151st ARW, Salt Lake City, UT ANG
	64-14829	Boeing KC-135R Stratotanker	USAF, *Greenville Majors, TX – For conversion to a WC-135R Constant Phoenix*
	64-14831	Boeing KC-135R Stratotanker	USAF, *Greenville Majors, TX – For conversion to a WC-135R Constant Phoenix*
	64-14832	Boeing KC-135R Stratotanker *w/or*	USAF 151st ARS/134th ARW, Knoxville, TN ANG
	64-14834	Boeing KC-135R Stratotanker *r/w*	USAF 74th ARS/434th ARW AFRC, Grissom AFB, IN
	64-14835	Boeing KC-135R Stratotanker *or/y*	USAF 336th ARS/452nd AMW AFRC, March ARB, CA
	64-14836	Boeing WC-135W Constant Phoenix	USAF 38th RS/55th Wg, Offutt AFB, NE
	64-14837	Boeing KC-135R Stratotanker	USAF 92nd ARW, Fairchild AFB, WA
	64-14839	Boeing KC-135R Stratotanker *w/bl*	USAF 108th ARS/126th ARW, Scott AFB, IL ANG

Serial	Type (code/other identity)	Owner/operator, location or fate	Notes
64-14840	Boeing KC-135R Stratotanker *r/w*	USAF 166th ARS/121st ARW, Rickenbacker ANGB, OH ANG	
64-14841	Boeing RC-135V Rivet Joint [OF] *bl*	USAF 38th RS/55th Wg, Offutt AFB, NE	
64-14842	Boeing RC-135V Rivet Joint [OF] *r*	USAF 38th RS/55th Wg, Offutt AFB, NE	
64-14843	Boeing RC-135V Rivet Joint [OF] *bl*	USAF 38th RS/55th Wg, Offutt AFB, NE	
64-14844	Boeing RC-135V Rivet Joint [OF] *r*	USAF 38th RS/55th Wg, Offutt AFB, NE	
64-14845	Boeing RC-135V Rivet Joint [OF] *m* $ [55 Wg]	USAF 38th RS/55th Wg, Offutt AFB, NE	
64-14846	Boeing RC-135V Rivet Joint [OF] *r*	USAF 38th RS/55th Wg, Offutt AFB, NE	
64-14847	Boeing RC-135U Combat Sent [OF] *bk*	USAF 45th RS/55th Wg, Offutt AFB, NE	
64-14848	Boeing RC-135V Rivet Joint [OF] *r*	USAF 38th RS/55th Wg, Offutt AFB, NE	
64-14849	Boeing RC-135U Combat Sent [OF] *bk*	USAF 45th RS/55th Wg, Offutt AFB, NE	

PZL-Mielec C-145A Combat Coyote

Serial	Type (code/other identity)	Owner/operator, location or fate	Notes
12-0331	PZL-Mielec C-145A Combat Coyote (N331MF)	Withdrawn from use, Duke Field, FL (for sale)	
12-0335	PZL-Mielec C-145A Combat Coyote (N335RH)	Withdrawn from use, Duke Field, FL (for sale)	
12-0336	PZL-Mielec C-145A Combat Coyote (N336MJ)	Withdrawn from use, Duke Field, FL (for sale)	
12-0337	PZL-Mielec C-145A Combat Coyote (N337GU)	Withdrawn from use, Duke Field, FL (for sale)	
12-0338	PZL-Mielec C-145A Combat Coyote (N338CH)	Withdrawn from use, Duke Field, FL (for sale)	

Dornier C-146A Wolfhound

NOTE: There have also been reports that 3058, 3091, 3093 and 3106 MAY be FY05, 07 and 09 respectively

Serial	Type (code/other identity)	Owner/operator, location or fate	Notes
95-3058	Dornier C-146A Wolfhound (N570EF)	USAF 524th SOS/492nd SOW, Duke Field, FL	
97-3091	Dornier C-146A Wolfhound (N391EF)	USAF 524th SOS/492nd SOW, Duke Field, FL	
97-3093	Dornier C-146A Wolfhound (N545EF)	USAF 859th SOS/919th SOW, Duke Field, FL	
99-3106	Dornier C-146A Wolfhound (N525EF)	USAF 859th SOS/919th SOW, Duke Field, FL	
10-3026	Dornier C-146A Wolfhound (N929EF)	USAF 524th SOS/492nd SOW, Duke Field, FL	
10-3068	Dornier C-146A Wolfhound (N565EF)	USAF 524th SOS/492nd SOW, Duke Field, FL	
10-3077	Dornier C-146A Wolfhound (N577EF)	USAF 524th SOS/492nd SOW, Duke Field, FL	
11-3013	Dornier C-146A Wolfhound (N645HM)	USAF 524th SOS/492nd SOW, Duke Field, FL	
11-3016	Dornier C-146A Wolfhound (N941EF)	USAF 524th SOS/492nd SOW, Duke Field, FL	
11-3031	Dornier C-146A Wolfhound (N975EF)	USAF 524th SOS/492nd SOW, Duke Field, FL	
11-3075	Dornier C-146A Wolfhound (N953EF)	USAF 524th SOS/492nd SOW, Duke Field, FL	
11-3097	Dornier C-146A Wolfhound (N307EF)	USAF 524th SOS/492nd SOW, Duke Field, FL	
11-3104	Dornier C-146A Wolfhound (N907EF)	USAF 524th SOS/492nd SOW, Duke Field, FL	
12-3040	Dornier C-146A Wolfhound (N340LS)	USAF 524th SOS/492nd SOW, Duke Field, FL	
12-3047	Dornier C-146A Wolfhound (N347EF)	USAF 524th SOS/492nd SOW, Duke Field, FL	
12-3050	Dornier C-146A Wolfhound (N355EF)	USAF 524th SOS/492nd SOW, Duke Field, FL	
12-3060	Dornier C-146A Wolfhound (N360EF)	USAF 524th SOS/492nd SOW, Duke Field, FL	
12-3085	Dornier C-146A Wolfhound (N385EF)	USAF 524th SOS/492nd SOW, Duke Field, FL	
15-3086	Dornier C-146A Wolfhound (N328ST)	USAF 524th SOS/492nd SOW, Duke Field, FL	
16-3020	Dornier C-146A Wolfhound (N524AW)	USAF 524th SOS/492nd SOW, Duke Field, FL	
16-3025	Dornier C-146A Wolfhound (N250BG)	USAF 859th SOS/919th SOW, Duke Field, FL	

Notes	Serial	Type (code/other identity)	Owner/operator, location or fate
	150521	Lockheed NP-3D Orion [341]	USN VX-30, NAS Point Mugu, CA
	156511	Lockheed EP-3E ARIES II [511]	USN VQ-1, NAS Whidbey Island, WA
	156517	Lockheed EP-3E ARIES II [517]	USN VQ-1, NAS Whidbey Island, WA
	156528	Lockheed EP-3E ARIES II [528]	USN VQ-1, NAS Whidbey Island, WA
	156529	Lockheed EP-3E ARIES II [529]	USN VQ-1, NAS Whidbey Island, WA
	157316	Lockheed EP-3E ARIES II [316]	USN VQ-1, NAS Whidbey Island, WA
	157318	Lockheed EP-3E ARIES II [318]	USN VQ-1, NAS Whidbey Island, WA
	157325	Lockheed EP-3E ARIES II [325]	USN VQ-1, NAS Whidbey Island, WA
	157326	Lockheed EP-3E ARIES II [326]	USN VQ-1, NAS Whidbey Island, WA
	158570	Lockheed P-3C-IIIR Orion [RL-570]	USN VXS-1, Patuxent River, MD
	158912	Lockheed NP-3C Orion [RL-912]	USN VXS-1, Patuxent River, MD
	158934	Lockheed P-3C AIP+ Orion [302]	USN VX-30, NAS Point Mugu, CA
	159887	Lockheed EP-3E ARIES II [887]	USN VQ-1, NAS Whidbey Island, WA
	159893	Lockheed EP-3E ARIES II [893]	USN VQ-1, NAS Whidbey Island, WA
	160293	Lockheed P-3C BMUP Orion [LL-293]	USN VP-30, NAS Jacksonville, FL
	160610	Lockheed P-3C AIP+ Orion [610]	USN VQ-1, NAS Whidbey Island, WA
	160627	Lockheed KC-130R Hercules	*To Chile as 999*
	160764	Lockheed EP-3E ARIES II [764]	USN VQ-1, NAS Whidbey Island, WA
	161337	Lockheed P-3C-II½ Orion [RL-337]	USN VXS-1, Patuxent River, MD
	161339	Lockheed P-3C BMUP Orion [339]	*To 309th AMARG, 14th October 2022*
	161404	Lockheed P-3C BMUP+ Orion [LL-404]	USN VP-30, NAS Jacksonville, FL
	161405	Lockheed P-3C BMUP+ Orion [405]	USN VP-69, NAS Whidbey Island, WA
	161410	Lockheed EP-3E ARIES II [410]	USN VQ-1, NAS Whidbey Island, WA
	161414	Lockheed P-3C BMUP+ Orion [414]	USN VQ-1, NAS Whidbey Island, WA
	161415	Lockheed P-3C BMUP+ Orion [415]	USN VP-69, NAS Whidbey Island, WA
	161586	Lockheed P-3C BMUP+ Orion [586]	*To 309th AMARG, 10th June 2022*
	161587	Lockheed P-3C BMUP+ Orion [LT-587]	*To 309th AMARG, 12th June 2022*
	161588	Lockheed P-3C BMUP+ Orion [588]	USN VQ-1, NAS Whidbey Island, WA
	161589	Lockheed P-3C BMUP+ Orion [589]	*To 309th AMARG, 23rd January 2023*
	161590	Lockheed P-3C BMUP+ Orion [LL-590]	USN VP-30, NAS Jacksonville, FL
	162308	Lockheed KC-130T Hercules [WB-407]	USN VX-30, NAS Point Mugu, CA
	162309	Lockheed KC-130T Hercules [309]	USN VX-20, Patuxent River, MD
	162310	Lockheed KC-130T Hercules [310]	USN VX-20, Patuxent River, MD
	162311	Lockheed KC-130T Hercules [405]	USN VX-30, NAS Point Mugu, CA
	162318	Lockheed P-3C AIP+ Orion [318]	USN VP-30, NAS Jacksonville, FL
	162777	Lockheed P-3C AIP+ Orion [777]	USN VQ-1, NAS Whidbey Island, WA
	162782	Boeing E-6B Mercury	USN VQ-3/SCW-1, Tinker AFB, OK
	162783	Boeing E-6B Mercury	USN VQ-3/SCW-1, Tinker AFB, OK
	162784	Boeing E-6B Mercury	USN VQ-4/SCW-1, Tinker AFB, OK
·	162999	Lockheed P-3C AIP+ Orion [300]	USN VX-30, NAS Point Mugu, CA
	163001	Lockheed P-3C AIP+ Orion [001]	USN VQ-1, NAS Whidbey Island, WA
	163259	Sikorsky VH-60N White Hawk	USMC HMX-1, Quantico, VA
	163260	Sikorsky VH-60N White Hawk	USMC HMX-1, Quantico, VA
	163261	Sikorsky VH-60N White Hawk	USMC HMX-1, Quantico, VA
	163262	Sikorsky VH-60N White Hawk	USMC HMX-1, Quantico, VA
	163263	Sikorsky VH-60N White Hawk	USMC HMX-1, Quantico, VA
	163264	Sikorsky VH-60N White Hawk	USMC HMX-1, Quantico, VA
	163265	Sikorsky VH-60N White Hawk	USMC HMX-1, Quantico, VA
	163266	Sikorsky VH-60N White Hawk	USMC HMX-1, Quantico, VA
	163290	Lockheed P-3C AIP+ Orion [LL-290]	*To 309th AMARG, 21st September 2022*
	163291	Lockheed P-3C AIP+ Orion [291]	USN VX-30, NAS Point Mugu, CA
	163294	Lockheed P-3C AIP+ Orion [303]	USN VX-30, NAS Point Mugu, CA
	163295	Lockheed P-3C AIP+ Orion [295]	USN VP-30, NAS Jacksonville, FL
	163310	Lockheed KC-130T Hercules [WB-310]	USN VX-20, Patuxent River, MD
	163311	Lockheed KC-130T Hercules [RU-311]	USN VR-55, NAS Point Mugu, CA
	163591	Lockheed KC-130T Hercules [RU-591]	USN VR-55, NAS Point Mugu, CA
	163918	Boeing E-6B Mercury	USN VQ-4/SCW-1, Tinker AFB, OK
	163919	Boeing E-6B Mercury	USN VQ-3/SCW-1, Tinker AFB, OK
	163920	Boeing E-6B Mercury	USN VQ-3/SCW-1, Tinker AFB, OK
	164105	Lockheed KC-130T Hercules [NY-105]	USN VR-55, NAS Point Mugu, CA
	164106	Lockheed KC-130T Hercules [RU-106]	USN VR-55, NAS Point Mugu, CA
	164180	Lockheed KC-130T Hercules [JW-180]	USN VR-62, NAS Jacksonville, FL

Serial	Type (code/other identity)	Owner/operator, location or fate	Notes
164386	Boeing E-6B Mercury	USN VQ-4/SCW-1, Tinker AFB, OK	
164387	Boeing E-6B Mercury	USN VQ-3/SCW-1, Tinker AFB, OK	
164388	Boeing E-6B Mercury	USN VQ-4/SCW-1, Tinker AFB, OK	
164404	Boeing E-6B Mercury	USN VQ-4/SCW-1, Tinker AFB, OK	
164405	Boeing E-6B Mercury	USN VQ-4/SCW-1, Tinker AFB, OK	
164406	Boeing E-6B Mercury	USN VQ-3/SCW-1, Tinker AFB, OK	
164407	Boeing E-6B Mercury	USN VQ-4/SCW-1, Tinker AFB, OK	
164408	Boeing E-6B Mercury	USN VX-20, Patuxent River, MD	
164409	Boeing E-6B Mercury	USN VQ-3/SCW-1, Tinker AFB, OK	
164410	Boeing E-6B Mercury	USN VQ-4/SCW-1, Tinker AFB, OK	
164441	Lockheed KC-130T Hercules [JW-441]	USN, stored NAS Jacksonville, FL	
164597	Lockheed KC-130T-30 Hercules [AX-597]	USN VR-53, NAF Washington, MD	
164598	Lockheed C-130T-30 Hercules [AX-598]	USN VR-53, NAF Washington, MD	
164762	Lockheed C-130T Hercules [JW-762]	USN VR-62, NAS Jacksonville, FL	
164993	Lockheed C-130T Hercules [BD-993]	USN VR-64, NAS Willow Grove, PA	
164994	Lockheed C-130T Hercules [CW-994]	USN VR-54, NAS New Orleans, LA	
164995	Lockheed C-130T Hercules [AX-995]	USN VR-53, NAF Washington, MD	
164996	Lockheed C-130T Hercules [RU-996]	USN VR-55, NAS Point Mugu, CA	
164997	Lockheed C-130T Hercules [AX-997]	USN VR-53, NAF Washington, MD	
164998	Lockheed C-130T Hercules [BD-998]	USN VR 64, NAS Willow Grove, PA	
165094	Grumman C-20G Gulfstream IV	USN VX-30, NAS Point Mugu, CA	
165151	Grumman C-20G Gulfstream IV	*To NASA as N522NA*	
165152	Grumman C-20G Gulfstream IV	USMC VMR-Det, MCBH Kaneohe Bay, HI	
165153	Grumman C-20G Gulfstream IV	USMC VMR-Det, MCBH Kaneohe Bay, HI	
165158	Lockheed C-130T Hercules [CW-158]	USN VR-54, NAS New Orleans, LA	
165159	Lockheed C-130T Hercules [CW-159]	USN VR-54, NAS New Orleans, LA	
165160	Lockheed C-130T Hercules [CW-160]	USN VR-54, NAS New Orleans, LA	
165161	Lockheed C-130T Hercules [BD-161]	USN VR-64, NAS Willow Grove, PA	
165313	Lockheed C-130T Hercules [AX-313]	USN VR-53, NAF Washington, MD	
165314	Lockheed C-130T Hercules [AX-314]	USN VR-53, NAF Washington, MD	
165315	Lockheed KC-130T Hercules [AX-315]	USN VR-53, NAF Washington, MD	
165316	Lockheed KC-130T Hercules [BD-316]	USN VR-64, NAS Willow Grove, PA	
165348	Lockheed C-130T Hercules [AX-348]	USN VR-53, NAF Washington, MD	
165349	Lockheed C-130T Hercules [AX-349]	USN VR-53, NAF Washington, MD	
165350	Lockheed C-130T Hercules [350]	USN VX-20, Patuxent River, MD	
165351	Lockheed C-130T Hercules [AX-351]	USN VR-53, NAF Washington, MD	
165352	Lockheed KC-130T Hercules [352]	USN VR-64, NAS Willow Grove, PA	
165378	Lockheed C-130T Hercules [JW-378]	USN VR-62, NAS Jacksonville, FL	
165379	Lockheed C-130T Hercules [BD-379]	USN VR-64, NAS Willow Grove, PA	
165735	Lockheed KC-130J Hercules II [QB-735]	USMC VMGR-352, Miramar MCAS, CA	
165736	Lockheed KC-130J Hercules II [QB-736]	USMC VMGR-352, Miramar MCAS, CA	
165737	Lockheed KC-130J Hercules II [BH-737]	USMC VMGR-252, Cherry Point MCAS, NC	
165738	Lockheed KC-130J Hercules II [BH-738]	USMC VMGR-252, Cherry Point MCAS, NC	
165739	Lockheed KC-130J Hercules II [QB-739]	USMC VMGR-352, Miramar MCAS, CA	
163266	Sikorsky VH-60N White Hawk	USMC HMX-1, Quantico, VA	
165809	Lockheed KC-130J Hercules II [BH-809]	USMC VMGR-252, Cherry Point MCAS, NC	
165810	Lockheed KC-130J Hercules II [BH-810]	USMC VMGR-252, Cherry Point MCAS, NC	
165829	Boeing C-40A Clipper (N1003N) [829]	USN VR-58, NAS Jacksonville, FL	
165830	Boeing C-40A Clipper (N1003M) [830]	USN VR-59, Fort Worth JRB, TX	
165831	Boeing C-40A Clipper (N1786B) [831]	USN VR-59, Fort Worth JRB, TX	
165832	Boeing C-40A Clipper (N1787B) [832]	USN VR-58, NAS Jacksonville, FL	
165833	Boeing C-40A Clipper [833]	USN VR-59, Fort Worth JRB, TX	
165834	Boeing C-40A Clipper [834]	USN VR-61, Fort Worth JRB, TX	
165835	Boeing C-40A Clipper (N543BA) [835]	USN VR-57, NAS North Island, CA	
165836	Boeing C-40A Clipper [836]	USN VR-61, Fort Worth JRB, TX	
165939	Cessna UC-35D Citation V	USMC H&HS Miramar, Miramar MCAS, CA	
165957	Lockheed KC-130J Hercules II [QD-957] $	USMC VMGR-152, Iwakuni MCAS, Japan	
166374	Cessna UC-35D Citation V	USMC H&HS Andrews, NAF Washington, MD	
166375	Gulfstream Aerospace C-37A Gulfstream V [365]	USN CFLSW Det, MCBH Kaneohe Bay, HI	
166376	Gulfstream Aerospace C-37B Gulfstream V [376]	USN VR-1, NAF Washington, MD	
166377	Gulfstream Aerospace C-37B Gulfstream V [377]	USN VR-1, NAF Washington, MD	
166378	Gulfstream Aerospace C-37B Gulfstream V [378]	USN VR-1, NAF Washington, MD	

Notes	Serial	Type (code/other identity)	Owner/operator, location or fate
	166379	Gulfstream Aerospace NC-37B Gulfstream V [BH-100]	USN VX-30, NAS Point Mugu, CA
	166380	Lockheed KC-130J Hercules II [QD-380]	USMC VMGR-152, Iwakuni MCAS, Japan
	166381	Lockheed KC-130J Hercules II [BH-381]	USMC VMGR-252, Cherry Point MCAS, NC
	166382	Lockheed KC-130J Hercules II [QB-382]	USMC VMGR-352, Miramar MCAS, CA
	166472	Lockheed KC-130J Hercules II [BH-472]	USMC VMGR-252, Cherry Point MCAS, NC
	166473	Lockheed KC-130J Hercules II [QH-473]	USMC VMGR-234, Fort Worth JRB, TX
	166474	Cessna UC-35D Citation V	USMC H&HS Cherry Point, Fort Worth JRB, TX
	166500	Cessna UC-35D Citation V	USMC H&HS Miramar, Miramar MCAS, CA
	166511	Lockheed KC-130J Hercules II [BH-511]	USN VX-20, Patuxent River, MD
	166512	Lockheed KC-130J Hercules II [QB-512]	USMC VMGR-352, Miramar MCAS, CA
	166513	Lockheed KC-130J Hercules II [BH-513]	USMC VMGR-252, Cherry Point MCAS, NC
	166514	Lockheed KC-130J Hercules II [BH-514]	USMC VMGR-252, Cherry Point MCAS, NC
	166693	Boeing C-40A Clipper [693]	USN VR-51, MCBH Kaneohe Bay, Hawaii
	166694	Boeing C-40A Clipper [694]	USN VR-56, NAS Oceana, VA
	166695	Boeing C-40A Clipper (N1787B) [695]	USN VR-61, Fort Worth JRB, TX
	166696	Boeing C-40A Clipper [696]	USN VR-59, Fort Worth JRB, TX
	166712	Cessna UC-35D Citation V	H&HS Cherry Point, Fort Worth JRB, TX
	166713	Cessna UC-35D Citation V	USMC H&HS Futenma, Futenma MCAS, Japan
	166714	Cessna UC-35D Citation V	USMC H&HS Andrews, NAF Washington, MD
	166715	Cessna UC-35D Citation V	USMC H&HS Cherry Point, Fort Worth JRB, TX
	166762	Lockheed KC-130J Hercules II [BH-762]	USMC VMGR-252, Cherry Point MCAS, NC
	166763	Lockheed KC-130J Hercules II [NY-763]	USMC VMGR-452, Stewart Field, NY
	166764	Lockheed KC-130J Hercules II [QH-764]	USMC VMGR-234, Fort Worth JRB, TX
	166766	Cessna UC-35D Citation V	USMC H&HS Futenma, Futenma MCAS, Japan
	166767	Cessna UC-35D Citation V [VM]	USMC H&HS Miramar, Miramar MCAS, CA
	167108	Lockheed KC-130J Hercules II [QB-108]	USMC VMGR-352, Miramar MCAS, CA
	167109	Lockheed KC-130J Hercules II [QD-109]	USMC VMGR-152, Iwakuni MCAS, Japan
	167110	Lockheed KC-130J Hercules II [QB-110]	USMC VMGR-352, Miramar MCAS, CA
	167111	Lockheed KC-130J Hercules II [NY-111]	USMC VMGR-452, Stewart Field, NY
	167112	Lockheed KC-130J Hercules II [BH-112]	USMC VMGR-252, Cherry Point MCAS, NC
	167923	Lockheed KC-130J Hercules II [QD-923]	USMC VMGR-152, Iwakuni MCAS, Japan
	167924	Lockheed KC-130J Hercules II [QB-924]	USMC VMGR-352, Miramar MCAS, CA
	167925	Lockheed KC-130J Hercules II [QH-925]	USMC VMGR-234, Fort Worth JRB, TX
	167926	Lockheed KC-130J Hercules II [QD-926]	USMC VMGR-152, Iwakuni MCAS, Japan
	167927	Lockheed KC-130J Hercules II [QD-927]	USMC VMGR-152, Iwakuni MCAS, Japan
	167951	Boeing P-8A Poseidon (N541BA) [951]	USN VX-20, Patuxent River, MD
	167952	Boeing P-8A Poseidon (N398DS) [952]	USN BUPERS SDC, Dallas/Love Field, TX
	167953	Boeing P-8A Poseidon (N441BA) [953]	USN VX-20, Patuxent River, MD
	167954	Boeing P-8A Poseidon (N397DS)	USN VX-20, Patuxent River, MD
	167955	Boeing P-8A Poseidon (N328DS) [955]	USN VX-1, NAS Patuxent River, MD
	167956	Boeing P-8A Poseidon (N391DS) [JA-956]	USN VX-1, NAS Patuxent River, MD
	167982	Lockheed KC-130J Hercules II [QD-982]	USMC VMGR-152, Iwakuni MCAS, Japan
	167983	Lockheed KC-130J Hercules II [QD-983]	USMC VMGR-152, Iwakuni MCAS, Japan
	167984	Lockheed KC-130J Hercules II [QB-984]	USMC VMGR-352, Miramar MCAS, CA
	167985	Lockheed KC-130J Hercules II [QB-985]	USMC VMGR-352, Miramar MCAS, CA
	168065	Lockheed KC-130J Hercules II [QD-065]	USMC VMGR-152, Iwakuni MCAS, Japan
	168066	Lockheed KC-130J Hercules II [QD-066]	USMC VMGR-152, Iwakuni MCAS, Japan
	168067	Lockheed KC-130J Hercules II [QB-067]	USMC VMGR-352, Miramar MCAS, CA
	168068	Lockheed KC-130J Hercules II [QH-068]	USMC VMGR-234, Fort Worth JRB, TX
	168069	Lockheed KC-130J Hercules II [BH-069]	USMC VMGR-252, Cherry Point MCAS, NC
	168070	Lockheed KC-130J Hercules II [BH-070]	USMC VMGR-252, Cherry Point MCAS, NC
	168071	Lockheed KC-130J Hercules II [BH-071]	USMC VMGR-252, Cherry Point MCAS, NC
	168072	Lockheed KC-130J Hercules II [QB-072]	USMC VMGR-352, Miramar MCAS, CA
	168073	Lockheed KC-130J Hercules II [QH-073]	USMC VMGR-234, Fort Worth JRB, TX
	168074	Lockheed KC-130J Hercules II [QD-074]	USMC VMGR-152, Iwakuni MCAS, Japan
	168075	Lockheed KC-130J Hercules II [QD-075]	USMC VMGR-152, Iwakuni MCAS, Japan
	168280	Bell/Boeing MV-22B Osprey [01]	USMC HMX-1, Quantico, VA
	168284	Bell/Boeing MV-22B Osprey [02]	USMC HMX-1, Quantico, VA
	168289	Bell/Boeing MV-22B Osprey [03]	USMC HMX-1, Quantico, VA
	168292	Bell/Boeing MV-22B Osprey [04]	USMC HMX-1, Quantico, VA
	168297	Bell/Boeing MV-22B Osprey [05]	USMC HMX-1, Quantico, VA
	168302	Bell/Boeing MV-22B Osprey [06]	USMC HMX-1, Quantico, VA

Serial	Type (code/other identity)	Owner/operator, location or fate	Notes
168306	Bell/Boeing MV-22B Osprey [07]	USMC HMX-1, Quantico, VA	
168324	Bell/Boeing MV-22B Osprey [08]	USMC HMX-1, Quantico, VA	
168327	Bell/Boeing MV-22B Osprey [09]	USMC HMX-1, Quantico, VA	
168332	Bell/Boeing MV-22B Osprey [10]	USMC HMX-1, Quantico, VA	
168335	Bell/Boeing MV-22B Osprey [11]	USMC HMX-1, Quantico, VA	
168339	Bell/Boeing MV-22B Osprey [12]	USMC HMX-1, Quantico, VA	
168428	Boeing P-8A Poseidon (N392DS) [LL-428]	USN VP-30, NAS Jacksonville, FL	
168429	Boeing P-8A Poseidon (N397DS) [LN-429]	USN VP-45, NAS Jacksonville, FL	
168430	Boeing P-8A Poseidon (N398DS) [LD-430]	USN VP-10, NAS Jacksonville, FL	
168431	Boeing P-8A Poseidon (N507DS) [YB-431]	USN VP-1, NAS Whidbey Island, WA	
168432	Boeing P-8A Poseidon (N516DS) [LL-432]	USN VP-30, NAS Jacksonville, FL	
168433	Boeing P-8A Poseidon (N530DS) [LK-433]	USN VP-26, NAS Jacksonville, FL	
168434	Boeing P-8A Poseidon (N532DS) [LL-434]	USN VP-30, NAS Jacksonville, FL	
168435	Boeing P-8A Poseidon (N533DS) [LL-435]	USN VP-30, NAS Jacksonville, FL	
168436	Boeing P-8A Poseidon (N536DS) [LL-436]	USN VP-30, NAS Jacksonville, FL	
168437	Boeing P-8A Poseidon (N537DS) [LL-437]	USN VP-30, NAS Jacksonville, FL	
168438	Boeing P-8A Poseidon (N327DS) [438]	USN VPU-2, NAS Whidbey Island, WA	
168439	Boeing P-8A Poseidon (N539DS) [QE-439]	USN VP-40, NAS Whidbey Island, WA	
168440	Boeing P-8A Poseidon (N708DS) [LD-440]	USN VP-10, NAS Jacksonville, FL	
168689	Bell/Boeing MV-22B Osprey [00]	USMC HMX-1, Quantico, VA	
168754	Boeing P-8A Poseidon (N736DS) [LN-754]	USN VP-45, NAS Jacksonville, FL	
168755	Boeing P-8A Poseidon (N740DS) [YD-755]	USN VP-4, NAS Whidbey Island, WA	
168756	Boeing P-8A Poseidon (N753DS) [LF-756]	USN VP-16, NAS Jacksonville, FL	
168757	Boeing P-8A Poseidon (N755DS) [YB-757]	USN VP-1, NAS Whidbey Island, WA	
168758	Boeing P-8A Poseidon (N758DS) [RD-758]	USN VP-47, NAS Whidbey Island, WA	
168759	Boeing P-8A Poseidon (N762DS) [LF-759]	USN VP-16, NAS Jacksonville, FL	
168760	Boeing P-8A Poseidon (N768DS) [RD-760]	USN VP-47, NAS Whidbey Island, WA	
168761	Boeing P-8A Poseidon (N771DS) [LF-761]	USN VP-16, NAS Jacksonville, FL	
168762	Boeing P-8A Poseidon (N780DS) [LF-762]	USN VP-16, NAS Jacksonville, FL	
168763	Boeing P-8A Poseidon (N781DS) [LK-763]	USN VP-26, NAS Jacksonville, FL	
168764	Boeing P-8A Poseidon (N783DS) [LL-764]	USN VP-30, NAS Jacksonville, FL	
168848	Boeing P-8A Poseidon (N784DS) [LN-848]	USN VP-45, NAS Jacksonville, FL	
168849	Boeing P-8A Poseidon (N785DS) [RC-849]	USN VP-46, NAS Whidbey Island, WA	
168850	Boeing P-8A Poseidon (N789DS) [850]	USN VP-9, NAS Whidbey Island, WA	
168851	Boeing P-8A Poseidon (N790DS) [YD-851]	USN VP-4, NAS Whidbey Island, WA	
168852	Boeing P-8A Poseidon (N715DS) [PD-852]	USN VP-9, NAS Whidbey Island, WA	
168853	Boeing P-8A Poseidon (N717DS) [PD-853]	USN VP-9, NAS Whidbey Island, WA	
168854	Boeing P-8A Poseidon (N722DS) [441] (as 168441)	USN VPU-2, NAS Whidbey Island, WA	
168855	Boeing P-8A Poseidon (N729DS) [LF-855]	USN VP-16, NAS Jacksonville, FL	
168856	Boeing P-8A Poseidon (N805DS) [LL-856]	USN VP-30, NAS Jacksonville, FL	
168857	Boeing P-8A Poseidon (N590DS) [857]	USN	
168858	Boeing P-8A Poseidon (N591DS) [LD-858]	USN VP-10, NAS Jacksonville, FL	
168859	Boeing P-8A Poseidon (N592DS) [LD-859]	USN VP-10, NAS Jacksonville, FL	
168860	Boeing P-8A Poseidon (N593DS) [LL-860]	USN VP-30, NAS Jacksonville, FL	
168980	Boeing C-40A Clipper (N513NV) [980]	USN VR-58, NAS Jacksonville, FL	
168981	Boeing C-40A Clipper (N514NV) [981]	USN VR-61, Fort Worth JRB, TX	
168996	Boeing P-8A Poseidon (N595DS) [996]	USN BUPERS SDC, Dallas/Love Field, TX	
168997	Boeing P-8A Poseidon (N597DS) [YB-997]	USN VP-1, NAS Whidbey Island, WA	
168998	Boeing P-8A Poseidon (N598DS) [LD-998]	USN VP-10, NAS Jacksonville, FL	
168999	Boeing P-8A Poseidon (N910DS) [012] (as 169012)	USN VPU-2, NAS Whidbey Island, WA	
169000	Boeing P-8A Poseidon (N914DS) [LF-000]	USN VP-16, NAS Jacksonville, FL	
169001	Boeing P-8A Poseidon (N931DS) [001]	USN	
169002	Boeing P-8A Poseidon (N934DS) [RD-002]	USN VP-47, NAS Whidbey Island, WA	
169003	Boeing P-8A Poseidon (N935DS) [003]	USN VP-45, NAS Jacksonville, FL	
169004	Boeing P-8A Poseidon (N936DS) [004]	USN VP-1, NAS Whidbey Island, WA	
169005	Boeing P-8A Poseidon (N941DS) [005]	USN VP-9, NAS Whidbey Island, WA	
169006	Boeing P-8A Poseidon (N942DS) [RC-006]	USN VP-46, NAS Whidbey Island, WA	
169007	Boeing P-8A Poseidon (N943DS) [007]	USN BUPERS SDC, Dallas/Love Field, TX	
169008	Boeing P-8A Poseidon (N944DS) [RC-008]	USN VP-46, NAS Whidbey Island, WA	
169009	Boeing P-8A Poseidon (N949DS) [YD-009]	USN VP-4, NAS Whidbey Island, WA	
169010	Boeing P-8A Poseidon (N957DS) [010]	USN BUPERS SDC, Dallas/Love Field, TX	
169011	Boeing P-8A Poseidon (N958DS) [011]	USN VPU-2, NAS Whidbey Island, WA	

Notes	Serial	Type (code/other identity)	Owner/operator, location or fate
	169018	Lockheed KC-130J Hercules II [QH-018]	USMC VMGR-234, Fort Worth JRB, TX
	169036	Boeing C-40A Clipper (N515NV) [036]	USN VR-61, Fort Worth JRB, TX
	169225	Lockheed KC-130J Hercules II [QH-225]	USMC VMGR-234, Fort Worth JRB, TX
	169226	Lockheed KC-130J Hercules II [QB-226]	USMC VMGR-352, Miramar MCAS, CA
	169227	Lockheed KC-130J Hercules II [QD-227]	USMC VMGR-152, Iwakuni MCAS, Japan
	169228	Lockheed KC-130J Hercules II [QH-228]	USMC VMGR-234, Fort Worth JRB, TX
	169229	Lockheed KC-130J Hercules II [QH-229]	USMC VMGR-234, Fort Worth JRB, TX
	169230	Lockheed KC-130J Hercules II [QB-230]	USMC VMGR-352, Miramar MCAS, CA
	169324	Boeing P-8A Poseidon (N960DS) [LF-324]	USN VP-16, NAS Jacksonville, FL
	169325	Boeing P-8A Poseidon (N962DS) [YD-325]	USN VP-4, NAS Whidbey Island, WA
	169326	Boeing P-8A Poseidon (N969DS) [LL-326]	USN VP-30, NAS Jacksonville, FL
	169327	Boeing P-8A Poseidon (N963DS) [384]	USN VPU-2, NAS Whidbey Island, WA
	169328	Boeing P-8A Poseidon (N964DS) [RD-328]	USN VP-47, NAS Whidbey Island, WA
	169329	Boeing P-8A Poseidon (N968DS) [YB-329]	USN VP-1, NAS Whidbey Island, WA
	169330	Boeing P-8A Poseidon (N843DS) [LL-330]	USN VP-30, NAS Jacksonville, FL
	169331	Boeing P-8A Poseidon (N852DS) [RD-331]	USN VP-47, NAS Whidbey Island, WA
	169332	Boeing P-8A Poseidon (N848DS) [RC-332]	USN VP-46, NAS Whidbey Island, WA
	169333	Boeing P-8A Poseidon (N838DS) [333]	USN VX-1, NAS Patuxent River, MD
	169334	Boeing P-8A Poseidon (N839DS) [RD-334]	USN VP-47, NAS Whidbey Island, WA
	169335	Boeing P-8A Poseidon (N854DS) [335]	USN BUPERS SDC, Dallas/Love Field, TX
	169336	Boeing P-8A Poseidon (N857DS) [LC-336]	USN VP-8, NAS Jacksonville, FL
	169337	Boeing P-8A Poseidon (N858DS) [YB-337]	USN VP-1, NAS Whidbey Island, WA
	169338	Boeing P-8A Poseidon (N860DS) [323] *(as 169323)*	USN VPU-2, NAS Whidbey Island, WA
	169339	Boeing P-8A Poseidon (N863DS) [RC-339]	USN VP-46, NAS Whidbey Island, WA
	169340	Boeing P-8A Poseidon (N864DS) [LA-340]	USN VP-5, NAS Jacksonville, FL
	169341	Boeing P-8A Poseidon (N869DS) [341]	USN BUPERS SDC, Dallas/Love Field, TX
	169342	Boeing P-8A Poseidon (N874DS) [LL-342]	USN VP-30, NAS Jacksonville, FL
	169343	Boeing P-8A Poseidon (N873DS) [YB-343]	USN VP-1, NAS Whidbey Island, WA
	169344	Boeing P-8A Poseidon (N304DS) [RC-344]	USN VP-46, NAS Whidbey Island, WA
	169345	Boeing P-8A Poseidon (N308DS) [345]	USN VP-40, NAS Whidbey Island, WA
	169346	Boeing P-8A Poseidon (N318DS) [RC-346]	USN VP-46, NAS Whidbey Island, WA
	169347	Boeing P-8A Poseidon (N322DS) [YB-347]	USN VP-1, NAS Whidbey Island, WA
	169348	Boeing P-8A Poseidon (N323DS) [348]	USN VP-40, NAS Whidbey Island, WA
	169349	Boeing P-8A Poseidon (N328DS) [RC-349]	USN VP-46, NAS Whidbey Island, WA
	169426	Boeing P-8A Poseidon (N332DS) [426]	USN BUPERS SDC, Dallas/Love Field, TX
	169532	Lockheed KC-130J Hercules II [QD-532]	USMC VMGR-152, Iwakuni MCAS, Japan
	169533	Lockheed KC-130J Hercules II [QB-533]	USMC VMGR-352, Miramar MCAS, CA
	169534	Lockheed KC-130J Hercules II [BH-534]	USMC VMGR-252, Cherry Point MCAS, NC
	169535	Lockheed KC-130J Hercules II [QD-535]	USMC VMGR-152, Iwakuni MCAS, Japan
	169536	Lockheed KC-130J Hercules II [QB-536]	USMC VMGR-352, Miramar MCAS, CA
	169542	Boeing P-8A Poseidon (N348DS) [YD-542]	USN VP-4, NAS Whidbey Island, WA
	169543	Boeing P-8A Poseidon (N347DS) [543]	USN VP-47, NAS Whidbey Island, WA
	169544	Boeing P-8A Poseidon (N360DS) [PD-544]	USN VP-9, NAS Whidbey Island, WA
	169545	Boeing P-8A Poseidon (N364DS) [LK-545]	USN VP-26, NAS Jacksonville, FL
	169546	Boeing P-8A Poseidon (N368DS) [546]	USN VP-9, NAS Whidbey Island, WA
	169547	Boeing P-8A Poseidon (N374DS) [PD-547]	USN VP-9, NAS Whidbey Island, WA
	169548	Boeing P-8A Poseidon (N383DS) [548]	USN VP-9, NAS Whidbey Island, WA
	169549	Boeing P-8A Poseidon (N392DS) [549]	USN VP-10, NAS Jacksonville, FL
	169550	Boeing P-8A Poseidon (N410DS) [LC-550]	USN VP-8, NAS Jacksonville, FL
	169551	Boeing P-8A Poseidon (N438DS) [LA-551]	USN VP-5, NAS Jacksonville, FL
	169552	Boeing P-8A Poseidon (N459DS) [LC-552]	USN VP-8, NAS Jacksonville, FL
	169553	Boeing P-8A Poseidon (N486DS) [LC-553]	USN VP-8, NAS Jacksonville, FL
	169554	Boeing P-8A Poseidon (N489DS) [LL-554]	USN VP-30, NAS Jacksonville, FL
	169555	Boeing P-8A Poseidon (N508DS) [LL-555]	USN VP-30, NAS Jacksonville, FL
	169556	Boeing P-8A Poseidon (N512DS) [LC-556]	USN VP-8, NAS Jacksonville, FL
	169557	Boeing P-8A Poseidon (N480DS) [YD-557]	USN VP-4, NAS Whidbey Island, WA
	169558	Boeing P-8A Poseidon (N516DS) [YD-558]	USN VP-4, NAS Whidbey Island, WA
	169559	Boeing P-8A Poseidon (N532DS) [LN-559]	USN VP-45, NAS Jacksonville, FL
	169560	Boeing P-8A Poseidon (N530DS) [LD-560]	USN VP-10, NAS Jacksonville, FL
	169561	Boeing P-8A Poseidon (N487DS) [YD-561]	USN VP-4, NAS Whidbey Island, WA
	169562	Boeing P-8A Poseidon (N483DS) [QE-562]	USN VP-40, NAS Whidbey Island, WA
	169563	Boeing P-8A Poseidon (N533DS) [LD-563]	USN VP-16, NAS Jacksonville, FL

Serial	Type (code/other identity)	Owner/operator, location or fate	Notes
169564	Boeing P-8A Poseidon (N533DS) [LL-564]	USN VP-30, NAS Jacksonville, FL	
169565	Boeing P-8A Poseidon (N601DS) [LD-565]	USN VP-16, NAS Jacksonville, FL	
169566	Boeing P-8A Poseidon (N602DS) [LL-566]	USN VP-30, NAS Jacksonville, FL	
169567	Boeing P-8A Poseidon (N603DS) [567]	USN BUPERS SDC, Dallas/Love Field, TX	
169568	Boeing P-8A Poseidon (N604DS) [568]	USN VP-30, NAS Jacksonville, FL	
169569	Boeing P-8A Poseidon (N610DS) [LA-569]	USN VP-5, NAS Jacksonville, FL	
169570	Boeing P-8A Poseidon (N612DS) [LC-570]	USN VP-8, NAS Jacksonville, FL	
169571	Boeing P-8A Poseidon (N619DS) [571]	USN	
169572	Boeing P-8A Poseidon (N631DS) [LC-572]	USN VP-8, NAS Jacksonville, FL	
169792	Boeing C-40A Clipper (N1799B) [792]	USN VR-51, MCBH Kaneohe Bay, Hawaii	
169793	Boeing C-40A Clipper (N517NV) [793]	USN VR-57, NAS North Island, CA	
170000	Lockheed C-130J Hercules II (N41030/ZH885)	USN Blue Angels, Pensacola, FL	
170013	Boeing P-8A Poseidon (N689DS) [013]	USN VX-1, NAS Patuxent River, MD	
170014	Boeing P-8A Poseidon (N780DS) [014]	USN BUPERS SDC, Dallas/Love Field, TX	
170015	Boeing P-8A Poseidon (N781DS) [LL-015]	USN VP-30, NAS Jacksonville, FL	
170016	Boeing P-8A Poseidon (N782DS) [016]	USN VP-30, NAS Jacksonville, FL	
170017	Boeing P-8A Poseidon (N783DS) [017]	USN VP-5, NAS Jacksonville, FL	
170018	Boeing P-8A Poseidon (N785DS)	USN (on order)	
170...	Boeing P-8A Poseidon	USN (on order)	
170...	Boeing P-8A Poseidon	USN (on order)	
170...	Boeing P-8A Poseidon	USN (on order)	
170...	Boeing P-8A Poseidon	USN (on order)	
170...	Boeing P-8A Poseidon	USN (on order)	
170...	Boeing P-8A Poseidon	USN (on order)	
170...	Boeing P-8A Poseidon	USN (on order)	
170...	Boeing P-8A Poseidon	USN (on order)	
170...	Boeing P-8A Poseidon	USN (on order)	
170...	Boeing P-8A Poseidon	USN (on order)	
170037	Lockheed KC-130J Hercules II [BH-037]	USMC VMGR-252, Cherry Point MCAS, NC	
170038	Lockheed KC-130J Hercules II [BH-038]	USMC VMGR-252, Cherry Point MCAS, NC	
170039	Lockheed KC-130J Hercules II [BH-039]	USMC VMGR-252, Cherry Point MCAS, NC	
170040	Lockheed KC-130J Hercules II [BH-040]	USMC VMGR-252, Cherry Point MCAS, NC	
170041	Boeing C-40A Clipper (N743A)	USMC VMR-1, Fort Worth JRB, TX	
170042	Boeing C-40A Clipper (N745A)	USMC VMR-1, Fort Worth JRB, TX	
170271	Lockheed KC-130J Hercules II [BH-271]	USMC VMGR-252, Cherry Point MCAS, NC	
170272	Lockheed KC-130J Hercules II [KB-272]	USMC VMGR-153, MCBH Kaneohe Bay, Hawaii	
170273	Lockheed KC-130J Hercules II [KB-273]	USMC VMGR-153, MCBH Kaneohe Bay, Hawaii	
170274	Lockheed KC-130J Hercules II [BH-274]	USMC VMGR-252, Cherry Point MCAS, NC	
170275	Lockheed KC-130J Hercules II [QB-275]	LMTAS, Marietta, GA (on order)	
170276	Lockheed KC-130J Hercules II [BH-276]	LMTAS, Marietta, GA (on order)	
170277	Lockheed KC-130J Hercules II [..-277]	LMTAS, Marietta, GA (on order)	

Additionally, the following false markings have been noted on VPU-2 P-8A Poseidons: 168384, 168441, 169012, 169323 and 169564.

Notes	Serial	Type (code/other identity)	Owner/operator, location or fate
	01	Gulfstream Aerospace C-37A Gulfstream V (N527GA)	USCG, Commandants Flt, Washington DC
	02	Gulfstream Aerospace C-37B Gulfstream V (N517GA)	USCG, Commandants Flt, Washington DC
	03	Gulfstream Aerospace C-37B Gulfstream V	USCG (on order)
	1701	Lockheed HC-130H Hercules	USCG, USCGS Elizabeth City, NC
	1702	Lockheed HC-130H Hercules	USCG, USCGS Clearwater, FL
	1703	Lockheed HC-130H Hercules	USCG, USCGS Barbers Point, HI
	1704	Lockheed HC-130H Hercules	USCG, USCGS Clearwater, FL
	1706	Lockheed HC-130H Hercules	*To US Forestry Service, October 2022*
	1707	Lockheed HC-130H Hercules	USCG, USCGS Elizabeth City, NC
	1709	Lockheed HC-130H Hercules	*To US Forestry Service*
	1711	Lockheed HC-130H Hercules	USCG, USCGS Barbers Point, HI
	1712	Lockheed HC-130H Hercules	USCG, USCGS Clearwater, FL
	1713	Lockheed HC-130H Hercules	*To US Forestry Service*
	1714	Lockheed HC-130H Hercules	*To US Forestry Service*
	1715	Lockheed HC-130H Hercules	USCG, USCGS Clearwater, FL
	1716	Lockheed HC-130H Hercules	USCG, USCGS Clearwater, FL
	1718	Lockheed HC-130H Hercules	USCG, USCGS Clearwater, FL
	1720	Lockheed HC-130H Hercules	USCG, USCGS Clearwater, FL
	2001	Lockheed HC-130J Hercules II	USCG, USCGS Elizabeth City, NC
	2002	Lockheed HC-130J Hercules II	USCG, USCGS Elizabeth City, NC
	2003	Lockheed HC-130J Hercules II	USCG, USCGS Elizabeth City, NC
	2004	Lockheed HC-130J Hercules II	USCG, USCGS Elizabeth City, NC
	2005	Lockheed HC-130J Hercules II	USCG, USCGS Elizabeth City, NC
	2006	Lockheed HC-130J Hercules II	USCG, USCGS Kodiak, AK
	2007	Lockheed HC-130J Hercules II	USCG, USCGS Barbers Point, HI
	2008	Lockheed HC-130J Hercules II	USCG, USCGS Barbers Point, HI
	2009	Lockheed HC-130J Hercules II	USCG, USCGS Kodiak, AK
	2010	Lockheed HC-130J Hercules II	USCG, USCGS Kodiak, AK
	2011	Lockheed HC-130J Hercules II	USCG, USCGS Kodiak, AK
	2012	Lockheed HC-130J Hercules II	USCG, USCGS Elizabeth City, NC
	2013	Lockheed HC-130J Hercules II	USCG, USCGS Elizabeth City, NC
	2014	Lockheed HC-130J Hercules II	USCG, USCGS Barbers Point, HI
	2015	Lockheed HC-130J Hercules II	USCG, USCGS Elizabeth City, NC
	2016	Lockheed HC-130J Hercules II	USCG (on order)
	2017	Lockheed HC-130J Hercules II	USCG (on order)

Aircraft in US Government or Military Service with Civil Registrations

Notes	Serial	Type (code/other identity)	Owner/operator, location or fate
	N85	Canadair CL.601 Challenger	Federal Aviation Administration, Oklahoma City, OK
	N86	Canadair CL.601 Challenger	Federal Aviation Administration, Oklahoma City, OK
	N87	Canadair CL.601 Challenger	Federal Aviation Administration, Oklahoma City, OK
	N88	Canadair CL.604 Challenger	Federal Aviation Administration, Oklahoma City, OK
	N89	Canadair CL.605 Challenger	Federal Aviation Administration, Oklahoma City, OK
	N90	Canadair CL.605 Challenger	Federal Aviation Administration, Oklahoma City, OK

MILITARY AVIATION SITES ON THE INTERNET

The list below is not intended to be a complete list of military aviation sites on the Internet. The sites listed cover Museums, Locations, Air Forces, Companies and Organisations that are mentioned elsewhere in 'Military Aircraft Markings'. Sites listed are in English or contain sufficient English to be reasonably easily understood. Each site address was correct at the time of going to press. Additions are welcome, via the usual address found at the front of the book, or via e-mail to admin@aviation-links.co.uk. An up to date copy of this list is to be found at The 'Military Aircraft Markings' Web Site, http://www.militaryaircraftmarkings.co.uk/.

Name of Site	Web Address All prefixed 'http://')
MILITARY SITES-UK	
No 1 Sqn	www.raf.mod.uk/our-organisation/squadrons/1-f-squadron/
No 2 Sqn	www.raf.mod.uk/our-organisation/squadrons/ii-ac-squadron/
No 3 Sqn	www.raf.mod.uk/our-organisation/squadrons/3-f-squadron/
No 4 Sqn	www.raf.mod.uk/our-organisation/squadrons/iv-squadron/
No 6 Sqn	www.raf.mod.uk/our-organisation/squadrons/6-squadron/
No 7 Sqn	www.raf.mod.uk/our-organisation/squadrons/7-squadron/
No 8 Sqn	www.raf.mod.uk/our-organisation/squadrons/8-squadron/
No 9 Sqn	www.raf.mod.uk/our-organisation/squadrons/ix-b-squadron/
No 10 Sqn	www.raf.mod.uk/our-organisation/squadrons/10-squadron/
No 11 Sqn	www.raf.mod.uk/our-organisation/squadrons/xi-f-squadron/
No 12 Sqn	www.raf.mod.uk/our-organisation/squadrons/12-squadron/
No 13 Sqn	www.raf.mod.uk/our-organisation/squadrons/13-squadron/
No 14 Sqn	www.raf.mod.uk/our-organisation/squadrons/14-squadron/
No 16 Sqn	www.raf.mod.uk/our-organisation/squadrons/16-squadron/
No 17 Sqn	www.raf.mod.uk/our-organisation/squadrons/17-squadron/
No 18 Sqn	www.raf.mod.uk/our-organisation/squadrons/18-squadron/
No 22 Sqn	www.raf.mod.uk/our-organisation/squadrons/22-squadron/
No 24 Sqn	www.raf.mod.uk/our-organisation/squadrons/xxiv-squadron/
No 25 Sqn	www.raf.mod.uk/our-organisation/squadrons/xxv-f-squadron/
No 27 Sqn	www.raf.mod.uk/our-organisation/squadrons/27-squadron/
No 28 Sqn	www.raf.mod.uk/our-organisation/squadrons/28-squadron/
No 29 Sqn	www.raf.mod.uk/our-organisation/squadrons/29-squadron/
No 32(The Royal) Sqn	www.raf.mod.uk/our-organisation/squadrons/32-squadron/
No 33 Sqn	www.raf.mod.uk/our-organisation/squadrons/33-squadron/
No 39 Sqn	www.raf.mod.uk/our-organisation/squadrons/39-squadron/
No 41 Sqn	www.raf.mod.uk/our-organisation/squadrons/41-squadron/
No 45 Sqn	www.raf.mod.uk/our-organisation/squadrons/45-squadron/
No 47 Sqn	www.raf.mod.uk/our-organisation/squadrons/47-squadron/
No 51 Sqn	www.raf.mod.uk/our-organisation/squadrons/51-squadron/
No 54 Sqn	www.raf.mod.uk/our-organisation/squadrons/54-squadron/
No 56 Sqn	www.raf.mod.uk/our-organisation/squadrons/56-squadron/
No 57 Sqn	www.raf.mod.uk/our-organisation/squadrons/lvii-squadron/
No 60 Sqn	www.raf.mod.uk/our-organisation/squadrons/60-squadron/
No 70 Sqn	www.raf.mod.uk/our-organisation/squadrons/lxx-squadron/
No 72 Sqn	www.raf.mod.uk/our-organisation/squadrons/72-squadron/
No 84 Sqn	www.raf.mod.uk/our-organisation/squadrons/84-squadron/
No 92 Sqn	www.raf.mod.uk/our-organisation/squadrons/92-squadron/
No 99 Sqn	www.raf.mod.uk/our-organisation/squadrons/99-squadron/
No 100 Sqn	www.raf.mod.uk/our-organisation/squadrons/100-squadron/
No 101 Sqn	www.raf.mod.uk/our-organisation/squadrons/101-squadron/
No 115 Sqn	www.raf.mod.uk/our-organisation/squadrons/115-squadron/
No 120 Sqn	www.raf.mod.uk/our-organisation/squadrons/120-squadron/
No 202 Sqn	www.raf.mod.uk/our-organisation/squadrons/202-squadron/
No 206 Sqn	www.raf.mod.uk/our-organisation/squadrons/206-squadron/
No 230 Sqn	www.raf.mod.uk/our-organisation/squadrons/230-squadron/
No 617 Sqn	www.raf.mod.uk/our-organisation/squadrons/617-squadron/
No 700X NAS	www.royalnavy.mod.uk/our-organisation/the-fighting-arms/fleet-air-arm/support-and-training/700x-naval-air-squadron
No 703 NAS	www.royalnavy.mod.uk/our-organisation/the-fighting-arms/fleet-air-arm/support-and-training/703-naval-air-squadron
No 705 NAS	www.royalnavy.mod.uk/our-organisation/the-fighting-arms/fleet-air-arm/support-and-training/705-naval-air-squadron
No 727 NAS	www.royalnavy.mod.uk/our-organisation/the-fighting-arms/fleet-air-arm/support-and-training/727-naval-air-squadron

Name of Site	Web Address All prefixed 'http://')
No 736 NAS	www.royalnavy.mod.uk/our-organisation/the-fighting-arms/fleet-air-arm/hawk-jets/736-naval-air-squadron
No 750 NAS	www.royalnavy.mod.uk/our-organisation/the-fighting-arms/fleet-air-arm/support-and-training/750-naval-air-squadron
No 809 NAS	www.royalnavy.mod.uk/our-organisation/the-fighting-arms/fleet-air-arm/future-aircraft/809-naval-air-squadron
No 814 NAS	www.royalnavy.mod.uk/our-organisation/the-fighting-arms/fleet-air-arm/helicopter-squadrons/merlin-mk2/814-naval-air-squadron
No 815 NAS	www.royalnavy.mod.uk/our-organisation/the-fighting-arms/fleet-air-arm/helicopter-squadrons/wildcat/815-naval-air-squadron
No 820 NAS	www.royalnavy.mod.uk/our-organisation/the-fighting-arms/fleet-air-arm/helicopter-squadrons/merlin-mk2/820-naval-air-squadron
No 824 NAS	www.royalnavy.mod.uk/our-organisation/the-fighting-arms/fleet-air-arm/helicopter-squadrons/merlin-mk2/824-naval-air-squadron
No 825 NAS	www.royalnavy.mod.uk/our-organisation/the-fighting-arms/fleet-air-arm/helicopter-squadrons/wildcat/825-naval-air-squadron
No 845 NAS	www.royalnavy.mod.uk/our-organisation/the-fighting-arms/fleet-air-arm/helicopter-squadrons/merlin-mk-4/845-naval-air-squadron
No 846 NAS	www.royalnavy.mod.uk/our-organisation/the-fighting-arms/fleet-air-arm/helicopter-squadrons/merlin-mk-4/846-naval-air-squadron
No 847 NAS	www.royalnavy.mod.uk/our-organisation/the-fighting-arms/fleet-air-arm/helicopter-squadrons/wildcat/847-naval-air-squadron
The Army Air Corps	www.army.mod.uk/who-we-are/corps-regiments-and-units/army-air-corps/
Fleet Air Arm	www.royalnavy.mod.uk/our-organisation/the-fighting-arms/fleet-air-arm
Ministry of Defence	www.gov.uk/government/organisations/ministry-of-defence
QinetiQ	www.qinetiq.com/
RAF Akrotiri	www.raf.mod.uk/our-organisation/stations/raf-akrotiri/
RAF Benson	www.raf.mod.uk/our-organisation/stations/raf-benson/
RAF Brize Norton	www.raf.mod.uk/our-organisation/stations/raf-brize-norton/
RAF College Cranwell	www.raf.mod.uk/our-organisation/stations/raf-college-cranwell/
RAF Coningsby	www.raf.mod.uk/our-organisation/stations/raf-coningsby/
Coningsby Aviation Site (unofficial)	milky01.co.uk/
RAF Cosford	www.raf.mod.uk/our-organisation/stations/raf-cosford/
RAF Leeming	www.raf.mod.uk/our-organisation/stations/raf-leeming/
RAF Lossiemouth	www.raf.mod.uk/our-organisation/stations/raf-lossiemouth/
RAF Marham	www.raf.mod.uk/our-organisation/stations/raf-marham/
RAF Mount Pleasant	www.raf.mod.uk/our-organisation/stations/raf-mount-pleasant/
RAF Northolt	www.raf.mod.uk/our-organisation/stations/raf-northolt/
RAF Odiham	www.raf.mod.uk/our-organisation/stations/raf-odiham/
RAF Scampton	www.raf.mod.uk/our-organisation/stations/raf-scampton/
RAF Shawbury	www.raf.mod.uk/our-organisation/stations/raf-shawbury/
RAF Syerston	www.raf.mod.uk/our-organisation/stations/raf-syerston/
RAF Valley	www.raf.mod.uk/our-organisation/stations/raf-valley/
RAF Waddington	www.raf.mod.uk/our-organisation/stations/raf-waddington/
RAF Wittering	www.raf.mod.uk/our-organisation/stations/raf-wittering/
RAF Woodvale	www.raf.mod.uk/our-organisation/stations/raf-woodvale/
RAF Wyton	www.raf.mod.uk/our-organisation/stations/raf-wyton/
Red Arrows	www.raf.mod.uk/display-teams/red-arrows/
Royal Air Force	www.raf.mod.uk/
University Air Squadrons	www.raf.mod.uk/our-organisation/university-air-squadrons/

MILITARY SITES-US

Air Combat Command	www.acc.af.mil/
Air Force Reserve Command	www.afrc.af.mil/
Air National Guard	www.ang.af.mil/
Aviano Air Base	www.aviano.af.mil/
Liberty Wing Home Page (48th FW)	www.lakenheath.af.mil/
NASA	www.nasa.gov/
Mildenhall	www.mildenhall.af.mil/
Ramstein Air Base	www.ramstein.af.mil/
Spangdahlem Air Base	www.spangdahlem.af.mil/
USAF	www.af.mil/

Name of Site	Web Address All prefixed 'http://')
USAF Europe	www.usafe.af.mil/
USAF World Wide Web Sites	www.af.mil/AF-Sites/
US Army	www.army.mil/
US Marine Corps	www.marines.mil/
US Navy	www.navy.mil/
US Navy Patrol Squadrons (unofficial)	www.vpnavy.com/
MILITARY SITES-ELSEWHERE	
Armée de l'Air et de l'Espace	www.defense.gouv.fr/air/
Aeronautica Militare	www.aeronautica.difesa.it
Austrian Armed Forces (in German)	www.bundesheer.at/
Finnish Defence Force	puolustusvoimat.fi/en/frontpage
Força Aérea Portuguesa	www.emfa.pt/
German Marine	www.bundeswehr.de/en/organization/ navy/organization/naval-aviation-command
Hellenic Air Force	www.haf.gr/en/
Irish Air Corps	www.military.ie/en/who-we-are/air-corps/
Luftforsvaret	forsvaret.no/en/
Luftwaffe	www.luftwaffe.de
NATO	www.nato.int/
Royal Australian Air Force	www.airforce.gov.au/
Royal Canadian Air Force	www.airforce.forces.gc.ca/
Royal Danish Air Force	forsvaret.dk/en/organisation/airforce/
Royal Netherlands AF	www.defensie.nl/organisatie/luchtmacht
Royal New Zealand AF	www.nzdf.mil.nz/air-force/
Singapore Air Force	www.mindef.gov.sg/web/portal/rsaf/home/
South African AF Site (unofficial)	www.saairforce.co.za/
Swedish Air Force	www.forsvarsmakten.se/sv/var-verksamhet/verksamhetsomraden/flygvapnet/
Turkish Air Force	www.hvkk.tsk.tr/Portal/Page/HvkkEN
AIRCRAFT & AERO ENGINE MANUFACTURERS	
Airbus Defence & Security	www.airbus.com/defence.html
BAE Systems	www.baesystems.com/
Beechcraft	beechcraft.txtav.com/
Bell	www.bellflight.com/
Boeing	www.boeing.com/
Bombardier	www.bombardier.com/
Britten-Norman	www.britten-norman.com/
Dassault	www.dassault-aviation.com/
Embraer	www.embraer.com/
General Electric	www.ge.com/
Grob Aircraft AG	grob-aircraft.com/en/
Gulfstream Aerospace	www.gulfstream.com/
Kaman Aerospace	www.kaman.com/
Leonardo	www.leonardocompany.com/
Lockheed Martin	www.lockheedmartin.com/
Rolls-Royce	www.rolls-royce.com/
Sikorsky	www.lockheedmartin.com/en-us/capabilities/sikorsky.html
UK AVIATION MUSEUMS	
Army Flying Museum	www.armyflying.com/
Boscombe Down Aviation Collection, Old Sarum	www.boscombedownaviationcollection.co.uk/
Bournemouth Aviation Museum	www.bamhurn.org/
Brooklands Museum	www.brooklandsmuseum.com/
City of Norwich Aviation Museum	www.cnam.org.uk/
Cornwall Aviation Heritage Centre	cornwallaviationhc.co.uk/
de Havilland Aircraft Museum	www.dehavillandmuseum.co.uk/
Dumfries & Galloway Aviation Museum	www.dumfriesaviationmuseum.com/
Fleet Air Arm Museum	www.fleetairarm.com/
Gatwick Aviation Museum	www.gamc.org.uk/
IWM, Duxford	www.iwm.org.uk/visits/iwm-duxford
Imperial War Museum, Duxford (unofficial)	abetheaviator.wixsite.com/website/about

Name of Site	Web Address All prefixed 'http://'
The Jet Age Museum	jetagemuseum.org/
Lincs Aviation Heritage Centre	www.lincsaviation.co.uk/
Midland Air Museum	www.midlandairmuseum.co.uk/
Museum of Berkshire Aviation	www.museumofberkshireaviation.co.uk/
Museum of Science & Industry, Manchester	www.scienceandindustrymuseum.org.uk/
National Museum of Flight, East Fortune	www.nms.ac.uk/national-museum-of-flight
Newark Air Museum	www.newarkairmuseum.org/
North East Land, Sea & Air Museums	www.nelsam.org.uk/
RAF Museum, Cosford & Hendon	www.rafmuseum.org.uk/
Science Museum, South Kensington	www.sciencemuseum.org.uk/
South Wales Aviation Museum	www.swam.online/
South Yorkshire Aircraft Museum	www.southyorkshireaircraftmuseum.org.uk/
Wattisham Station Heritage Museum	www.wattishamstationheritage.org/
Yorkshire Air Museum, Elvington	www.yorkshireairmuseum.org/

AVIATION SOCIETIES

Air Britain	www.air-britain.com/
Air Yorkshire	www.airyorkshire.org.uk/
Aviation Heritage UK (was BAPC)	aviationheritageuk.org/
LAAS International	www.laasdata.com/
Military Aviation Review	militaryaviationreview.com/
Royal Aeronautical Society	www.aerosociety.com/
Scramble (Dutch Aviation Society)	www.scramble.nl/
Solent Aviation Society	www.solent-aviation-society.co.uk/
Spitfire Society	www.spitfiresociety.org/
The Aviation Society Manchester	www.tasmanchester.com/
Ulster Aviation Society	www.ulsteraviationsociety.org/
Wolverhampton Aviation Group	www.wolverhamptonaviationgroup.co.uk/

OPERATORS OF HISTORIC AIRCRAFT

The Aircraft Restoration Company	www.aircraftrestorationcompany.com/
B-17 Preservation Ltd.	www.sallyb.org.uk/
Battle of Britain Memorial Flight	www.raf.mod.uk/display-teams/battle-of-britain-memorial-flight/
The Catalina Society	www.catalina.org.uk/
Hangar 11 Collection	www.hangar11.co.uk/
Historic Helicopters	www.historichelicopters.com/
Navy Wings	www.navywings.org.uk/
The Fighter Collection	www.fighter-collection.com/
The Real Aeroplane Company	www.realaero.com/
The Shuttleworth Collection	www.shuttleworth.org/

SITES RELATING TO SPECIFIC TYPES OF MILITARY AIRCRAFT

The 655 Maintenance & Preservation Society	www.xm655.com/
B-24 Liberator	www.b24bestweb.com/
C-130 Hercules	www.c-130hercules.net/
EE Canberra	www.bywat.co.uk/
The Eurofighter site	www.eurofighter.com/
The ex FRADU Canberra Site	www.fradu-canberras.co.uk/
The ex FRADU Hunter Site	www.fradu-hunters.co.uk/
F-4 Phantom II Society	www.f4phantom.com/
F-16: The Complete Reference	www.f-16.net/
F-35 Lightning II	www.f35.com/
The Gripen	www.saab.com/products/air/fighter-systems
Jet Provost Heaven	www.jetprovosts.com
K5083 - Home Page (Hawker Hurricane)	www.k5083.mistral.co.uk/
Lockheed SR-71 Blackbird	www.wvi.com/~lelandh/sr-71~1.htm
The MiG-21 Page	www.topedge.com/panels/aircraft/sites/kraft/mig.htm
P-3 Orion Research Group	www.p3orion.nl/
Thunder & Lightnings (Postwar British Aircraft)	www.thunder-and-lightnings.co.uk/
UK Apache Resource Centre	ukapache.com/

Name of Site	Web Address All prefixed 'http://')
MISCELLANEOUS	
Aerodata Software Ltd.	www.aerodata.org/
AeroResource	www.aeroresource.co.uk/
The AirNet Web Site	www.aviation-links.co.uk/
ALAT.FR	www.alat.fr/
Aviation Databases	www.aviationdatabases.com/
Delta Reflex	www.deltareflex.com/forum
Demobbed - Out of Service British Military Aircraft	demobbed.org.uk/
Euro Demobbed	www.eurodemobbed.org.uk/
Fighter Control	fightercontrol.co.uk/
Freebird Aviation Database	www.freebirddb.com/
Iconic Aircraft	www.iconicaircraft.co.uk/
Joseph F. Baugher's US Military Serials Site	www.joebaugher.com/
The 'Military Aircraft Markings' Web Site	www.militaryaircraftmarkings.co.uk/
Pacific Aviation Database	www.gfiapac.org/
PlaneBaseNG	www.planebase.biz/
Thunder & Lightnings: Airfield Viewing Guides	www.thunder-and-lightnings.co.uk/spotting/
UK Airshow Review	www.airshows.co.uk/
UK Military Aircraft Serials Resource Centre	www.ukserials.com/

The Indian Air Force upgraded its transport capability a number of years ago, buying both C-17As and C-130Js. Here a C-17A is seen landing at RAF Coningsby supporting a deployment of SU-30MKI Flankers. *SRS*

Mainstay of the Swiss Air Force fighter fleet for almost 30 years, here we see F/A-18C Hornet J-5014 is seen here taking part in a NATO Tiger Meet, and is about to recover to Cambrai Air Base in Northern France. *SRS*

Serial	Type (other identity) [code]	Owner/operator, location or fate

US-BASED USAF AIRCRAFT

Boeing 767-2C/KC-46A Pegasus

11-46057	Boeing KC-46A Pegasus (N2103S/19-46057)	USAF 305th AMW, McGuire AFB, NJ
11-46058	Boeing KC-46A Pegasus (N5107Q/19-46058)	USAF 77th ARS/916th ARW AFRC, Seymour Johnson AFB, NC
11-46059	Boeing KC-46A Pegasus (N5020K/19-46059)	USAF 56th ARS/97th AMW, Altus AFB, OK
11-46060	Boeing KC-46A Pegasus (N2013Z/19-46060)	USAF 305th AMW, McGuire AFB, NJ

OVERSEAS MILITARY AIRCRAFT MARKINGS

GREECE

Elliniki Polemiki Aeroporía/Hellenic Air Force (HAF)

441	Dassault Rafale DG	HAF 332 MAPK/114 PM, Tanagra

PORTUGAL

Força Aérea Portuguesa (FAP)/Marinha

...	Dassault Falcon 900B (CS-DTP)	FAP Esq 504, Lisbon/Montijo